The United States Government Manual 2000/2001

Office of the Federal Register
National Archives and Records Administration

Revised June 1, 2000

Raymond A. Mosley,
Director of the Federal Register.

John W. Carlin,
Archivist of the United States.

On the cover: The Washington Monument and the Lincoln Memorial during the restoration of the monument (from the holdings of the National Park Service).

In preparation for the bicentennial of the Nation's Capital and the new millennium, the National Park Service embarked on a mission to repair the external damage to the monument caused by weather and time and renovate various systems of the interior of the monument. The monument, which opened to the public in 1888, was erected in honor of the Nation's first President, George Washington, and is the tallest freestanding masonry structure in the world. The restoration project includes repairing the stonework, cleaning the facade, modernizing the heating and cooling systems, improving the elevator, and updating the facilities and refurbishing the exhibits on the observation level. To beautify the monument during its restoration while creating a safe workplace for restoration workers, National Park Service constructors erected scaffolding that, in the words of designer Michael Graves, "echoes the obelisk's beauty even while covering its exterior." For more information on the Washington Monument and its restoration, scheduled for completion in 2000, visit the National Park Service Internet site at www.nps.gov/wamo.

Special thanks to Terry J. Adams, Office of Public Affairs, National Park Service for his cooperation and permission to use the photograph of the monument for the cover of the *Manual*.

For sale by the U.S. Government Printing Office
Superintendent of Documents, Congressional Sales Office, Washington, DC 20402

ISBN 0-16-050292-6

Preface

As the official handbook of the Federal Government, *The United States Government Manual* provides comprehensive information on the agencies of the legislative, judicial, and executive branches. The *Manual* also includes information on quasi-official agencies; international organizations in which the United States participates; and boards, commissions, and committees.

A typical agency description includes a list of principal officials, a summary statement of the agency's purpose and role in the Federal Government, a brief history of the agency, including its legislative or executive authority, a description of its programs and activities, and a "Sources of Information" section. This last section provides information on consumer activities, contracts and grants, employment, publications, and many other areas of public interest.

The 2000/2001 *Manual* was prepared by the Presidential and Legislative Publications Unit, Office of the Federal Register. Maxine L. Hill was Lead Editor, Karen L. Ashlin was Managing Editor, and Anna Glover was Chief Editor, assisted by Brad Brooks and Karen Thornton.

The Federal Register and Its Special Editions

The *Manual* is published as a special edition of the *Federal Register* (*see* 1 CFR 9.1). Its focus is on programs and activities. Persons interested in detailed organizational structure, the regulatory documents of an agency, or Presidential documents should refer to the *Federal Register* or one of its other special editions, described below.

Issued each Federal working day, the *Federal Register* provides a uniform system for publishing Presidential documents, regulatory documents with general applicability and legal effect, proposed rules, notices, and documents required to be published by statute.

The *Code of Federal Regulations* is an annual codification of the general and permanent rules published in the *Federal Register.* The *Code* is divided into 50 titles that represent broad areas subject to Federal regulation. The *Code* is kept up to date by the individual issues of the *Federal Register.*

The *Weekly Compilation of Presidential Documents* serves as a timely, up-to-date reference source for the public policies and activities of the President. It contains remarks, news conferences, messages, statements, and other Presidential material of a public nature issued by the White House during the week reported.

A companion publication to the *Weekly Compilation* is the *Public Papers of the Presidents,* which contains public Presidential documents and speeches in convenient book form. Volumes of the *Public Papers* have been published for every President since Herbert Hoover, with the exception of Franklin D. Roosevelt, whose papers were published privately.

Other Office of the Federal Register Publications

The Office of the Federal Register publishes slip laws, which are pamphlet prints of each public and private law enacted by Congress. Slip laws are compiled annually as the *United States Statutes at Large*. The *Statutes* volumes contain all public and private laws and concurrent resolutions enacted during a session of Congress;

recommendations for executive, legislative, and judicial salaries; reorganization plans; proposed and ratified amendments to the Constitution; and Presidential proclamations. Included with many of these documents are sidenotes, U.S. Code and statutes citations, and a summary of their legislative histories.

Publication Availability

The publications of the Office of the Federal Register are available for sale by writing to the following address:

Superintendent of Documents
P.O. Box 371954
Pittsburgh, PA 15250–7954.

Publications are also available for sale through the Government Printing Office online bookstore, at www.access.gpo.gov/su_docs/sale.html, and from Government Printing Office bookstores located in several major cities. Telephone inquiries should be directed to 202–512–1800.

Electronic Services

The Office of the Federal Register maintains an Internet site for public law numbers, the Federal Register's public inspection list, and information on the Office and its activities at www.nara.gov/fedreg. This site also contains links to the texts of *The United States Government Manual,* Public Laws, the *Weekly Compilation of Presidential Documents,* the *Federal Register,* and the *Code of Federal Regulations* in electronic format through *GPO Access.* For more information about these online publications, contact the Electronic Information Dissemination Services, U.S. Government Printing Office. Phone, 202–512–1530, or 888–293–6498 (toll-free). Internet, www.access.gpo.gov/su_docs. E-mail, gpoaccess@gpo.gov.

Further Information

Information on *The United States Government Manual* and other publications of the Office of the Federal Register may be obtained by writing to the following address:

Office of the Federal Register
National Archives and Records Administration
Washington, DC 20408

Inquiries should be directed by phone to 202–523–5227, faxed to 202–523–6866, or E-mailed to info@fedreg.nara.gov.

Contents

The Declaration of Independence

IN CONGRESS, JULY 4, 1776.

THE UNANIMOUS DECLARATION of the thirteen united STATES OF AMERICA,

WHEN in the Course of human events, it becomes necessary for one people to dissolve the political bands which have connected them with another, and to assume among the powers of the earth, the separate and equal station to which the Laws of Nature and of Nature's God entitle them, a decent respect to the opinions of mankind requires that they should declare the causes which impel them to the separation.—We hold these truths to be self-evident, that all men are created equal, that they are endowed by their Creator with certain unalienable Rights, that among these are Life, Liberty and the pursuit of Happiness.—That to secure these rights, Governments are instituted among Men, deriving their just powers from the consent of the governed,—That whenever any Form of Government becomes destructive of these ends, it is the Right of the People to alter or to abolish it, and to institute new Government, laying its foundation on such principles and organizing its powers in such form, as to them shall seem most likely to effect their Safety and Happiness. Prudence, indeed, will dictate that Governments long established should not be changed for light and transient causes; and accordingly all experience hath shown, that mankind are more disposed to suffer, while evils are sufferable, than to right themselves by abolishing the forms to which they are accustomed. But when a long train of abuses and usurpations, pursuing invariably the same Object evinces a design to reduce them under absolute Despotism, it is their right, it is their duty, to throw off such Government, and to provide new Guards for their future security.—Such has been the patient sufferance of these Colonies; and such is now the necessity which constrains them to alter their former Systems of Government. The history of the present King of Great Britain is a history of repeated injuries and usurpations, all having in direct object the establishment of an absolute Tyranny over these States. To prove this, let Facts be submitted to a candid world.—He has refused his Assent to Laws, the most wholesome and necessary for the public good.—He has forbidden his Governors to pass Laws of immediate and pressing importance, unless suspended in their operation till his Assent should be obtained; and when so suspended, he has utterly neglected to attend to them.—He has refused to pass other Laws for the accommodation of large districts of people, unless those people would relinquish the right of Representation in the Legislature, a right inestimable to them and formidable to tyrants only.—He has called together legislative bodies at places unusual, uncomfortable, and distant from the depository of their public Records, for the sole purpose of fatiguing them into compliance with his measures.—He has dissolved Representative Houses repeatedly, for opposing with manly firmness his invasions on the rights of the people.—He has refused for a long time, after such dissolutions, to cause others to be elected; whereby the Legislative powers, incapable of Annihilation, have returned to the People at large for their exercise; the State remaining in the mean time exposed to all the dangers of invasion from without, and convulsions within.—He has endeavored to prevent the population of these States; for that purpose obstructing the Laws for Naturalization of Foreigners; refusing to pass others to encourage their migration hither, and raising the conditions of new Appropriations of Lands.—He has obstructed the Administration of Justice, by refusing his Assent to Laws for establishing Judiciary powers.—He has made Judges dependent on his Will alone, for the tenure of their offices, and the amount and payment of their salaries.—He has erected a multitude of New Offices, and sent hither swarms of Officers to harrass our people, and eat out their substance.—He has kept among us, in times of peace, Standing Armies, without the Consent of our legislatures.—He has affected to render the Military independent of and superior to the Civil power.—He has combined with others to subject us to a jurisdiction foreign to our constitution, and unacknowledged by our laws; giving his Assent to their Acts of pretended Legislation:—For quartering large bodies of armed troops among us:—For protecting them, by a mock Trial, from punishment for any Murders which they should commit on the Inhabitants of these States:—For cutting off our Trade with all parts of the world:—For imposing Taxes on us without our Consent:—For depriving us in many cases, of the benefits of Trial by Jury:—For transporting us beyond Seas to be tried for pretended offences:—For abolishing the free System of English Laws in a neighbouring Province, establishing therein an Arbitrary government, and enlarging its Boundaries so as to render it at once an example and fit instrument for introducing the same absolute rule into these Colonies:—For taking away our Charters, abolishing our most valuable Laws, and altering fundamentally the Forms of our Governments:—For suspending our own Legislatures, and declaring themselves invested with power to legislate for us in all cases whatsoever.—He has abdicated Government here, by declaring us out of his Protection and waging War against us.—He has plundered our seas, ravaged our Coasts, burnt our towns, and destroyed the lives of our people.—He is at this time transporting large Armies of foreign Mercenaries to compleat the works of death, desolation and tyranny, already begun with circumstances of Cruelty & perfidy scarcely paralleled in the most barbarous ages, and totally unworthy the Head of a civilized nation.—He has constrained our fellow Citizens taken Captive on the high Seas to bear Arms against their Country, to become the executioners of their friends and Brethren, or to fall themselves by their Hands.—He has excited domestic insurrections amongst us, and has endeavoured to bring on the inhabitants of our frontiers, the merciless Indian Savages, whose known rule of warfare, is an undistinguished destruction of all ages, sexes and conditions. In every stage of these Oppressions We have Petitioned for Redress in the most humble terms: Our repeated Petitions have been answered only by repeated injury. A Prince, whose character is thus marked by every act which may define a Tyrant, is unfit to be the ruler of a free people. Nor have We been wanting in attentions to our Brittish brethren. We have warned them from time to time of attempts by their legislature to extend an unwarrantable jurisdiction over us. We have reminded them of the circumstances of our emigration and settlement here. We have appealed to their native justice and magnanimity, and we have conjured them by the ties of our common kindred to disavow these usurpations, which, would inevitably interrupt our connections and correspondence. They too have been deaf to the voice of justice and of consanguinity. We must, therefore, acquiesce in the necessity, which denounces our Separation, and hold them, as we hold the rest of mankind, Enemies in War, in Peace Friends.—

We, therefore, the Representatives of the United States of America, in General Congress, Assembled, appealing to the Supreme Judge of the world for the rectitude of our intentions, do, in the Name, and by Authority of the good People of these Colonies, solemnly publish and declare, That these United Colonies are, and of Right ought to be **Free and Independent States;** that they are Absolved from all Allegiance to the British Crown, and that all political connection between them and the State of Great Britain, is and ought to be totally disolved; and that as Free and

Independent States, they have full Power to levy War, conclude Peace, contract Alliances, establish Commerce, and to do all other Acts and Things which Independent States may of right do.—And for the support of this Declaration, with a firm reliance on the protection of Divine Providence, we mutually pledge to each other our Lives, our Fortunes and our sacred Honor.

John Hancock
Button Gwinnett
Lyman Hall
Geo. Walton
Wm. Hooper
Joseph Hewes
John Penn
Edward Rutledge
Thos. Heyward, Jr.
Thomas Lynch, Jr.
Arthur Middleton
Samuel Chase
Wm. Paca
Thos. Stone
Charles Carroll of Carrollton
George Wythe
Richard Henry Lee
Th. Jefferson

Benj. Harrison
Thos. Nelson, Jr.
Francis Lightfoot Lee
Carter Braxton
Robt. Morris
Benjamin Rush
Benj. Franklin
John Morton
Geo. Clymer
Jas. Smith
Geo. Taylor
James Wilson
Geo. Ross
Caesar Rodney
Geo. Read
Tho. M: Kean
Wm. Floyd
Phil. Livingston
Frans. Lewis

Lewis Morris
Richd. Stockton
Jno. Witherspoon
Fras. Hopkinson
John Hart
Abra. Clark
Josiah Bartlett
Wm. Whipple
Saml. Adams
John Adams
Robt. Treat Paine
Elbridge Gerry
Step. Hopkins
William Ellery
Roger Sherman
Sam. Huntington
Wm. Williams
Oliver Wolcott
Matthew Thornton

The Constitution of the United States

We the People of the United States, in Order to form a more perfect Union, establish Justice, insure domestic Tranquility, provide for the common defence, promote the general Welfare, and secure the Blessings of Liberty to ourselves and our Posterity, do ordain and establish this Constitution for the United States of America.

Article I

Section 1. All legislative Powers herein granted shall be vested in a Congress of the United States, which shall consist of a Senate and House of Representatives.

Section 2. The House of Representatives shall be composed of Members chosen every second Year by the People of the several States, and the Electors in each State shall have the Qualifications requisite for Electors of the most numerous Branch of the State Legislature.

No Person shall be a Representative who shall not have attained to the Age of twenty five Years, and been seven Years a Citizen of the United States, and who shall not, when elected, be an Inhabitant of that State in which he shall be chosen.

Representatives and direct Taxes shall be apportioned among the several States which may be included within this Union, according to their respective Numbers, which shall be determined by adding to the whole Number of free Persons, including those bound to Service for a Term of Years, and excluding Indians not taxed, three fifths of all other Persons. The actual Enumeration shall be made within three Years after the first Meeting of the Congress of the United States, and within every subsequent Term of ten Years, in such Manner as they shall by Law direct. The Number of Representatives shall not exceed one for every thirty Thousand, but each State shall have at Least one Representative; and until such enumerations shall be made, the State of New Hampshire shall be entitled to chuse three, Massachusetts eight, Rhode-Island and Providence Plantations one, Connecticut five, New-York six, New Jersey four, Pennsylvania eight, Delaware one, Maryland six, Virginia ten, North Carolina five, South Carolina five, and Georgia three.

When vacancies happen in the Representation from any State, the Executive Authority thereof shall issue Writs of Election to fill such Vacancies.

The House of Representatives shall chuse their speaker and other Officers; and shall have the sole Power of Impeachment.

Section 3. The Senate of the United States shall be composed of two Senators from each State, chosen by the Legislature thereof, for six Years; and each Senator shall have one Vote.

Immediately after they shall be assembled in Consequence of the first Election, they shall be divided as equally as may be into three Classes. The Seats of the

Senators of the first Class shall be vacated at the Expiration of the second Year, of the second Class at the Expiration of the fourth Year, and of the third Class at the Expiration of the sixth Year, so that one third may be chosen every second Year; and if Vacancies happen by Resignation, or otherwise, during the Recess of the Legislature of any State, the Executive thereof may make temporary Appointments until the next Meeting of the Legislature, which shall then fill such Vacancies.

No Person shall be a Senator who shall not have attained to the Age of thirty Years, and been nine Years a Citizen of the United States, and who shall not, when elected, be an Inhabitant of that State for which he shall be chosen.

The Vice President of the United States shall be President of the Senate, but shall have no Vote, unless they be equally divided.

The Senate shall chuse their other Officers, and also a President pro tempore, in the Absence of the Vice President, or when he shall exercise the Office of President of the United States.

The Senate shall have the sole Power to try all Impeachments. When sitting for that Purpose, they shall be on Oath or Affirmation. When the President of the United States is tried, the Chief Justice shall preside: And no Person shall be convicted without the concurrence of two thirds of the Members present. Judgment in Cases of Impeachment shall not extend further than to removal from Office, and disqualification to hold and enjoy any Office of honor, Trust or Profit under the United States: but the Party convicted shall nevertheless be liable and subject to Indictment, Trial, Judgment and Punishment, according to law.

Section 4. The Times, Places and Manner of holding Elections for Senators and Representatives, shall be prescribed in each State by the Legislature thereof; but the Congress may at any time by Law make or alter such Regulations, except as to the Places of chusing Senators.

The Congress shall assemble at least once in every Year, and such Meeting shall be on the first Monday in December, unless they shall by Law appoint a different Day.

Section 5. Each House shall be the Judge of the Elections, Returns and Qualifications of its own Members, and a Majority of each shall constitute a Quorum to do business; but a smaller Number may adjourn from day to day, and may be authorized to compel the Attendance of absent Members, in such Manner, and under such Penalties as each House may provide.

Each House may determine the Rules of its Proceedings, punish its Members for disorderly Behaviour, and, with the Concurrence of two thirds, expel a Member.

Each House shall keep a Journal of its Proceedings, and from time to time publish the same, excepting such Parts as may in their Judgment require Secrecy; and the yeas and Nays of the Members of either House on any question shall, at the Desire of one fifth of those Present, be entered on the Journal.

Neither House, during the Session of Congress, shall, without the Consent of the other, adjourn for more than three days, nor to any other place than that in which the two Houses shall be sitting.

Section 6. The Senators and Representatives shall receive a Compensation for their Services, to be ascertained by Law, and paid out of the Treasury of the United States. They shall in all Cases, except Treason, Felony and Breach of the Peace, be privileged from Arrest during their Attendance at the Session of their respective Houses, and in going to and returning from the same; and for any Speech or Debate in either House, they shall not be questioned in any other Place.

No Senator or Representative shall, during the Time for which he was elected, be appointed to any civil Office under the Authority of the United States, which shall have been created, or the Emoluments whereof shall have been encreased during such time; and no Person holding any Office under the United States, shall be a Member of either House during his Continuance in Office.

Section 7. All Bills for raising Revenue shall originate in the House of Representatives; but the Senate may propose or concur with Amendments as on other Bills.

Every Bill which shall have passed the House of Representatives and the Senate, shall, before it become a Law, be presented to the President of the United States; If he approve he shall sign it, but if not he shall return it, with his Objections to that House in which it shall have originated, who shall enter the Objections at large on their Journal, and proceed to reconsider it. If after such Reconsideration two thirds of that House shall agree to pass the Bill, it shall be sent, together with the Objections, to the other House, by which it shall likewise be reconsidered, and if approved by two thirds of that House, it shall become a Law. But in all such Cases the Votes of both Houses shall be determined by yeas and Nays, and the Names of the Persons voting for and against the Bill shall be entered on the Journal of each House respectively. If any Bill shall not be returned by the President within ten Days (Sundays excepted) after it shall have been presented to him, the Same shall be a Law, in like Manner as if he had signed it, unless the Congress by their Adjournment prevent its Return, in which Case it shall not be a Law.

Every Order, Resolution, or Vote to which the Concurrence of the Senate and House of Representatives may be necessary (except on a question of Adjournment) shall be presented to the President of the United States; and before the Same shall take Effect, shall be approved by him, or being disapproved by him, shall be repassed by two thirds of the Senate and House of Representatives, according to the Rules and Limitations prescribed in the Case of a Bill.

Section 8. The Congress shall have Power To lay and collect Taxes, Duties, Imposts and Excises, to pay the Debts and provide for the common Defence and general Welfare of the United States; but all duties, Imposts and Excises shall be uniform throughout the United States;

To borrow Money on the Credit of the United States;

To regulate Commerce with foreign Nations, and among the several States, and with the Indian Tribes;

To establish an uniform Rule of Naturalization, and uniform Laws on the subject of Bankruptcies throughout the United States;

To coin Money, regulate the Value thereof, and of foreign Coin, and fix the Standard of Weights and Measures;

To provide for the Punishment of counterfeiting the Securities and current Coin of the United States;

To establish Post Offices and post Roads;

To promote the Progress of Science and useful Arts, by securing for limited Times to Authors and Inventors exclusive Right to their respective Writings and Discoveries;

To constitute Tribunals inferior to the supreme Court;

To define and punish Piracies and Felonies committed on the high Seas, and Offences against the Law of Nations;

To declare War, grant Letters of Marque and Reprisal, and make rules concerning Captures on Land and Water;

To raise and support Armies, but no Appropriation of Money to that Use shall be for a longer Term than two Years;

To provide and maintain a Navy;

To make rules for the Government and Regulation of the land and naval Forces;

To provide for calling forth the Militia to execute the Laws of the Union, suppress Insurrections and repel Invasions;

To provide for organizing, arming, and disciplining, the Militia, and for governing such Part of them as may be employed in the Service of the United States, reserving to the States respectively, the Appointment of the Officers, and the Authority of training the Militia according to the discipline prescribed by Congress;

To exercise exclusive Legislation in all Cases whatsoever, over such District (not exceeding ten Miles square), as may, by Cession of particular States, and the Acceptance of Congress, become the Seat of the Government of the United States, and to exercise like Authority over all Places purchased by the Consent of the Legislature of the State in which the Same shall be for the Erection of Forts, Magazines, Arsenals, dock-Yards, and other needful Buildings;—And

To make all Laws which shall be necessary and proper for carrying into Execution the foregoing Powers, and all other Powers vested by this Constitution in the Government of the United States, or in any Department or Officer thereof.

Section 9. The Migration or Importation of such Persons as any of the States now existing shall think proper to admit, shall not be prohibited by the Congress prior to the Year one thousand eight hundred and eight, but a Tax or duty may be imposed on such Importation, not exceeding ten dollars for each Person.

The Privilege of the Writ of Habeas Corpus shall not be suspended, unless when in Cases of Rebellion or Invasion the public Safety may require it.

No Bill of Attainder or ex post facto Law shall be passed.

No Capitation, or other direct, Tax shall be laid, unless in Proportion to the Census or Enumeration herein before directed to be taken.

No Tax or Duty shall be laid on Articles exported from any State.

No Preference shall be given by any Regulation of Commerce or Revenue to the Ports of one State over those of another: nor shall Vessels bound to, or from, one State, be obliged to enter, clear, or pay Duties in another.

No money shall be drawn from the Treasury, but in Consequence of Appropriations made by Law; and a regular Statement and Account of the Receipts and Expenditures of all public Money shall be published from time to time.

No Title of Nobility shall be granted by the United States: And no Person holding any Office of Profit or Trust under them, shall, without the Consent of the Congress, accept of any present, Emolument, Office, or Title, of any kind whatever, from any King, Prince, or foreign State.

Section 10. No State shall enter into any Treaty, Alliance, or Confederation; grant Letters of Marque and Reprisal; coin Money; emit Bills of Credit; make any Thing but gold and silver Coin a Tender in Payment of Debts; pass any Bill of Attainder, ex post facto Law, or Law impairing the Obligation of Contracts, or grant any Title of Nobility.

No State shall, without the Consent of the Congress, lay any Imposts or Duties on Imports or Exports, except what may be absolutely necessary for executing it's inspection Laws: and the net Produce of all Duties and Imposts, laid by any State on Imports or Exports, shall be for the Use of the Treasury of the United States; and all such Laws shall be subject to the Revision and Controul of the Congress.

No State shall, without the Consent of Congress, lay any Duty of Tonnage, keep Troops, or Ships of War in time of Peace, enter into any Agreement or Compact with another State, or with a foreign Power, or engage in War, unless actually invaded, or in such imminent Danger as will not admit of delay.

Article II

Section 1. The executive Power shall be vested in a President of the United States of America. He shall hold his Office during the Term of four Years, and, together with the Vice President, chosen for the same Term, be elected, as follows

Each State shall appoint, in such Manner as the Legislature thereof may direct, a Number of Electors, equal to the whole Number of Senators and Representatives to which the State may be entitled in the Congress: but no Senator or Representative, or Person holding an Office of Trust or Profit under the United States, shall be appointed an Elector.

The Electors shall meet in their respective States, and vote by Ballot for two Persons, of whom one at least shall not be an Inhabitant of the same State with themselves. And they shall make a List of all the Persons voted for, and of the Number of Votes for each; which List they shall sign and certify, and transmit sealed to the Seat of the Government of the United States, directed to the President of the Senate. The President of the Senate shall, in the Presence of the Senate and House of Representatives, open all the Certificates, and the Votes shall then be counted. The Person having the greatest Number of Votes shall be the President, if such Number be a Majority of the whole Number of Electors appointed; and if there be more than one who have such Majority, and have an equal Number of Votes, then the House of Representatives shall immediately chuse by Ballot one of them for President: and if no Person have a Majority, then from the five highest on the List the said House shall in like Manner chuse the President. But in chusing the President, the Votes shall be taken by States, the Representation from each State having one Vote; A quorum for this Purpose shall consist of a Member or Members from two thirds of the States, and a Majority of all the States shall be necessary to a Choice. In every Case, after the Choice of the President, the Person having the greatest Number of Votes of the Electors shall be the Vice President. But if there should remain two or more who have equal Votes, the Senate shall chuse from them by Ballot the Vice President.

The Congress may determine the Time of chusing the Electors, and the Day on which they shall give their Votes; which Day shall be the same throughout the United States.

No Person except a natural born Citizen, or a Citizen of the United States, at the time of the Adoption of this Constitution, shall be eligible to the Office of President; neither shall any Person be eligible to that Office who shall not have attained to the Age of thirty five Years, and been fourteen Years a Resident within the United States.

In Case of the Removal of the President from Office, or of his Death, Resignation, or Inability to discharge the Powers and Duties of the said Office, the Same shall devolve on the Vice President, and the Congress may by Law provide for the Case of Removal, Death, Resignation or Inability, both of the President and Vice President, declaring what Officer shall then act as President, and such Officer shall act accordingly, until the Disability be removed, or a President shall be elected.

The President shall, at stated Times, receive for his Services, a Compensation, which shall neither be encreased nor diminished during the Period for which he shall have been elected, and he shall not receive within that Period any other Emolument from the United States, or any of them.

Before he enter on the Execution of his Office, he shall take the following Oath or Affirmation:—"I do solemnly swear (or affirm) that I will faithfully execute the Office of President of the United States, and will to the best of my Ability, preserve, protect and defend the Constitution of the United States."

Section 2. The President shall be Commander in Chief of the Army and Navy of the United States, and of the Militia of the several States, when called into the actual

Service of the United States; he may require the Opinion, in writing, of the principal Officer in each of the executive Departments, upon any Subject relating to the Duties of their respective Offices, and he shall have Power to grant Reprieves and Pardons for Offences against the United States, except in Cases of Impeachment.

He shall have Power, by and with the Advice and Consent of the Senate, to make Treaties, provided two thirds of the Senators present concur; and he shall nominate, and by and with the Advice and Consent of the Senate, shall appoint Ambassadors, other public Ministers and Consuls, Judges of the supreme Court, and all other Officers of the United States, whose Appointments are not herein otherwise provided for, and which shall be established by Law: but the Congress may by Law vest the Appointment of such inferior Officers, as they think proper, in the President alone, in the Courts of Law, or in the Heads of Departments.

The President shall have Power to fill up all Vacancies that may happen during the Recess of the Senate, by granting Commissions which shall expire at the End of their next Session.

Section 3. He shall from time to time give to the Congress Information of the State of the Union, and recommend to their Consideration such Measures as he shall judge necessary and expedient; he may, on extraordinary Occasions, convene both Houses, or either of them, and in Case of Disagreement between them, with Respect to the Time of Adjournment, he may adjourn them to such Time as he shall think proper; he shall receive Ambassadors and other public Ministers; he shall take Care that the Laws be faithfully executed, and shall Commission all the Officers of the United States.

Section 4. The President, Vice President and all civil Officers of the United States, shall be removed from Office on Impeachment for, and Conviction of, Treason, Bribery, or other High Crimes and Misdemeanors.

Article III

Section 1. The judicial Power of the United States, shall be vested in one supreme Court, and in such inferior Courts as the Congress may from time to time ordain and establish. The Judges, both of the supreme and inferior Courts, shall hold their Offices during good Behaviour, and shall, at stated Times, receive for their Services, a Compensation, which shall not be diminished during their Continuance in Office.

Section 2. The judicial Power shall extend to all Cases, in Law and Equity, arising under this Constitution, the Laws of the United States, and Treaties made, or which shall be made, under their Authority;—to all Cases affecting Ambassadors, other public Ministers and Consuls;—to all Cases of admiralty and maritime Jurisdiction;—to Controversies to which the United States shall be a Party;—to Controversies between two or more States; between a State and Citizens of another State;—between Citizens of different States;—between Citizens of the same State claiming Lands under Grants of different States, and between a State, or the Citizens thereof, and foreign States, Citizens or Subjects.

In all Cases affecting Ambassadors, other public Ministers and Consuls, and those in which a State shall be Party, the supreme Court shall have original Jurisdiction. In all the other Cases before mentioned, the supreme Court shall have appellate Jurisdiction, both as to Law and Fact, with such Exceptions, and under such Regulations as the Congress shall make.

The Trial of all Crimes, except in Cases of Impeachment, shall be by Jury; and such Trial shall be held in the State where the said Crimes shall have been committed; but when not committed within any State, the Trial shall be at such Place or Places as the Congress may by Law have directed.

Section 3. Treason against the United States, shall consist only in levying War against them, or in adhering to their Enemies, giving them Aid and Comfort. No Person shall be convicted of Treason unless on the Testimony of two Witnesses to the same overt Act, or on Confession in open Court.

The Congress shall have Power to declare the Punishment of Treason, but no Attainder of Treason shall work Corruption of Blood, or Forfeiture except during the Life of the Person attainted.

Article IV

Section 1. Full Faith and Credit shall be given in each State to the public Acts, Records, and judicial Proceedings of every other State. And the Congress may by general Laws prescribe the Manner in which such Acts, Records and Proceedings shall be proved, and the Effect thereof.

Section 2. The Citizens of each State shall be entitled to all Privileges and Immunities of Citizens in the several States.

A Person charged in any State with Treason, Felony, or other Crime, who shall flee from Justice, and be found in another State, shall on Demand of the executive Authority of the State from which he fled, be delivered up, to be removed to the State having Jurisdiction of the Crime.

No person held to Service or Labour in one State, under the Laws thereof, escaping into another, shall, in Consequence of any Law or Regulation therein, be discharged from such Service or Labour, but shall be delivered up on Claim of the Party to whom such Service or Labour may be due.

Section 3. New States may be admitted by the Congress into this Union; but no new State shall be formed or erected within the Jurisdiction of any other State; nor any State be formed by the Junction of two or more States, or Parts of States, without the Consent of the Legislatures of the States concerned as well as of the Congress.

The Congress shall have Power to dispose of and make all needful Rules and Regulations respecting the Territory or other Property belonging to the United States; and nothing in this Constitution shall be so construed as to Prejudice any Claims of the United States, or of any particular State.

Section 4. The United States shall guarantee to every State in this Union a Republican Form of Government, and shall protect each of them against Invasion; and on Application of the Legislature, or of the Executive (when the Legislature cannot be convened) against domestic Violence.

Article V

The Congress, whenever two thirds of both Houses shall deem it necessary, shall propose Amendments to this Constitution, or, on the Application of the Legislatures of two thirds of the several States, shall call a Convention for proposing Amendments, which, in either Case, shall be valid to all Intents and Purposes, as Part of this Constitution, when ratified by the Legislatures of three fourths of the several States, or by Conventions in three fourths thereof, as the one or the other Mode of Ratification may be proposed by the Congress; Provided that no Amendment which may be made prior to the Year One thousand eight hundred and eight shall in any Manner affect the first and fourth Clauses in the Ninth Section of the first Article; and that no State, without its Consent, shall be deprived of its equal Suffrage in the Senate.

Article VI

All Debts contracted and Engagements entered into, before the Adoption of this Constitution, shall be as valid against the United States under this Constitution, as under the Confederation.

This Constitution, and the Laws of the United States which shall be made in Pursuance thereof; and all Treaties made, or which shall be made, under the Authority of the United States, shall be the supreme Law of the Land; and the Judges in every State shall be bound thereby, any Thing in the Constitution or Laws of any State to the Contrary notwithstanding.

The Senators and Representatives before mentioned, and the Members of the several State Legislatures, and all executive and judicial Officers, both of the United States and of the several States, shall be bound by Oath or Affirmation, to support this Constitution; but no religious Test shall ever be required as a Qualification to any Office or public Trust under the United States.

Article VII

The Ratification of the Conventions of nine States, shall be sufficient for the Establishment of this Constitution between the States so ratifying the Same.

done in Convention by the Unanimous Consent of the States present the Seventeenth Day of September in the Year of our Lord one thousand seven hundred and Eighty seven and of the Independence of the United States of America the Twelfth *In witness whereof We have hereunto subscribed our Names,*

G^o^ Washington—Presid^t^
and deputy from Virginia

New Hampshire	John Langdon Nicholas Gilman
Massachusetts	Nathaniel Gorham Rufus King
Connecticut	Wm Saml Johnson Roger Sherman
New York	Alexander Hamilton
New Jersey	Wil: Livingston David Brearley. Wm Paterson. Jona: Dayton
Pennsylvania [1]	B Franklin Thomas Mifflin Robt Morris Geo. Clymer Thos FitzSimons Jared Ingersoll

[1] Spelled with one "n" on the original document.

James Wilson
Gouv Morris

Delaware
Geo: Read
Gunning Bedford jun
John Dickinson
Richard Bassett
Jaco: Broom

Maryland
James McHenry
Dan of St Thos Jenifer
Danl Carroll

Virginia
John Blair—
James Madison Jr.

North Carolina
Wm Blount
Richd Dobbs Spaight.
Hu Williamson

South Carolina
J. Rutledge
Charles Cotesworth Pinckney
Charles Pinckney
Pierce Butler.

Georgia
William Few
Abr Baldwin

Amendments

(*The first 10 Amendments were ratified December 15, 1791, and form what is known as the Bill of Rights*)

Amendment 1

Congress shall make no law respecting an establishment of religion, or prohibiting the free exercise thereof; or abridging the freedom of speech, or of the press; or the right of the people peaceably to assemble, and to petition the Government for a redress of grievances.

Amendment 2

A well regulated Militia, being necessary to the security of a free State, the right of the people to keep and bear Arms, shall not be infringed.

Amendment 3

No Soldier shall, in time of peace be quartered in any house, without the consent of the Owner, nor in time of war, but in a manner to be prescribed by law.

Amendment 4

The right of the people to be secure in their persons, houses, papers, and effects, against unreasonable searches and seizures, shall not be violated, and no Warrants shall issue, but upon probable cause, supported by Oath or affirmation, and particularly describing the place to be searched, and the persons or things to be seized.

Amendment 5

No person shall be held to answer for a capital, or otherwise infamous crime, unless on a presentment or indictment of a Grand Jury, except in cases arising in the land or naval forces, or in the Militia, when in actual service in time of War or public danger; nor shall any person be subject for the same offence to be twice put in jeopardy of life or limb; nor shall be compelled in any criminal case to be a witness against himself, nor be deprived of life, liberty, or property, without due process of law; nor shall private property be taken for public use, without just compensation.

Amendment 6

In all criminal prosecutions, the accused shall enjoy the right to a speedy and public trial, by an impartial jury of the State and district wherein the crime shall have been committed, which district shall have been previously ascertained by law, and to be informed of the nature and cause of the accusation; to be confronted with the witnesses against him; to have compulsory process for obtaining witnesses in his favor, and to have the Assistance of Counsel for his defence.

Amendment 7

In Suits at common law, where the value in controversy shall exceed twenty dollars, the right of trial by jury shall be preserved, and no fact tried by a jury, shall be otherwise re-examined in any Court of the United States, than according to the rules of the common law.

Amendment 8

Excessive bail shall not be required, nor excessive fines imposed, nor cruel and unusual punishments inflicted.

Amendment 9

The enumeration in the Constitution, of certain rights, shall not be construed to deny or disparage others retained by the people.

Amendment 10

The powers not delegated to the United States by the Constitution, nor prohibited by it to the States, are reserved to the States respectively, or to the people.

Amendment 11

(*Ratified February 7, 1795*)

The Judicial power of the United States shall not be construed to extend to any suit in law or equity, commenced or prosecuted against one of the United States by Citizens of another State, or by Citizens or Subjects of any Foreign State.

Amendment 12

(*Ratified July 27, 1804*)

The Electors shall meet in their respective states, and vote by ballot for President and Vice-President, one of whom, at least, shall not be an inhabitant of the same state with themselves; they shall name in their ballots the person voted for as President, and in distinct ballots the person voted for as Vice-President, and they shall make distinct lists of all persons voted for as President, and of all persons voted for as Vice-President, and of the number of votes for each, which lists they shall sign and certify, and transmit sealed to the seat of the government of the United States, directed to the President of the Senate;—The President of the Senate shall, in the presence of the Senate and House of Representatives, open all the certificates and the votes shall then be counted;—The person having the greatest number of votes for President, shall be the President, if such number be a majority of the whole number of Electors appointed; and if no person have such majority, then from the persons having the highest numbers not exceeding three on the list of those voted for as President, the House of Representatives shall choose immediately, by ballot, the President. But in choosing the President, the votes shall be taken by states, the representation from each state having one vote; a quorum for this purpose shall consist of a member or members from two-thirds of the states, and a majority of all the states shall be necessary to a choice. And if the House of Representatives shall not choose a President whenever the right of choice shall devolve upon them, before the fourth day of March next following, then the Vice-President shall act as President, as in the case of the death or other constitutional disability of the President.—The person having the greatest number of votes as Vice-President, shall be the Vice-President, if such number be a majority of the whole number of Electors appointed, and if no person have a majority, then from the two highest numbers on the list, the Senate shall choose the Vice-President; a quorum for the purpose shall consist of two-thirds of the whole number of Senators, and a majority of the whole number shall be necessary to a choice. But no person constitutionally ineligible to the office of President shall be eligible to that of Vice-President of the United States.

Amendment 13

(*Ratified December 6, 1865*)

Section 1. Neither slavery nor involuntary servitude, except as a punishment for crime whereof the party shall have been duly convicted, shall exist within the United States, or any place subject to their jurisdiction.

Section 2. Congress shall have power to enforce this article by appropriate legislation.

Amendment 14

(*Ratified July 9, 1868*)

Section 1. All persons born or naturalized in the United States, and subject to the jurisdiction thereof, are citizens of the United States and of the State wherein they reside. No State shall make or enforce any law which shall abridge the privileges or immunities of citizens of the United States; nor shall any State deprive any person of life, liberty, or property, without due process of law; nor deny to any person within its jurisdiction the equal protection of the laws.

Section 2. Representatives shall be apportioned among the several States according to their respective numbers, counting the whole number of persons in each State, excluding Indians not taxed. But when the right to vote at any election for the choice of electors for President and Vice President of the United States, Representatives in Congress, the Executive and Judicial officers of a State, or the members of the Legislature thereof, is denied to any of the male inhabitants of such State, being twenty-one years of age, and citizens of the United States, or in any way abridged, except for participation in rebellion, or other crime, the basis of representation therein shall be reduced in the proportion which the number of such male citizens shall bear to the whole number of male citizens twenty-one years of age in such State.

Section 3. No person shall be a Senator or Representative in Congress, or elector of President and Vice President, or hold any office, civil or military, under the United States, or under any State, who, having previously taken an oath, as a member of Congress, or as an officer of the United States, or as a member of any State legislature, or as an executive or judicial officer of any State, to support the Constitution of the United States, shall have engaged in insurrection or rebellion against the same, or given aid or comfort to the enemies thereof. But Congress may by a vote of two-thirds of each House, remove such disability.

Section 4. The validity of the public debt of the United States, authorized by law, including debts incurred for payment of pensions and bounties for services in suppressing insurrection or rebellion, shall not be questioned. But neither the United States nor any State shall assume or pay any debt or obligation incurred in aid of insurrection or rebellion against the United States, or any claim for the loss or emancipation of any slave; but all such debts, obligations and claims shall be held illegal and void.

Section 5. The Congress shall have power to enforce, by appropriate legislation, the provisions of this article.

Amendment 15

(*Ratified February 3, 1870*)

Section 1. The right of citizens of the United States to vote shall not be denied or abridged by the United States or by any State on account of race, color, or previous condition of servitude.

Section 2. The Congress shall have power to enforce this article by appropriate legislation.

Amendment 16

(*Ratified February 3, 1913*)

The Congress shall have power to lay and collect taxes on incomes, from whatever source derived, without apportionment among the several States, and without regard to any census or enumeration.

Amendment 17

(*Ratified April 8, 1913*)

The Senate of the United States shall be composed of two Senators from each State, elected by the people thereof for six years; and each Senator shall have one vote. The electors in each State shall have the qualifications requisite for electors of the most numerous branch of the State legislatures.

When vacancies happen in the representation of any State in the Senate, the executive authority of such State shall issue writs of election to fill such vacancies: *Provided,* That the legislature of any State may empower the executive thereof to make temporary appointments until the people fill the vacancies by election as the legislature may direct.

This amendment shall not be so construed as to affect the election or term of any Senator chosen before it becomes valid as part of the Constitution.

Amendment 18

(*Ratified January 16, 1919. Repealed December 5, 1933 by Amendment 21*)

Section 1. After one year from the ratification of this article the manufacture, sale, or transportation of intoxicating liquors within, the importation thereof into, or the exportation thereof from the United States and all territory subject to the jurisdiction thereof for beverage purposes is hereby prohibited.

Section 2. The Congress and the several States shall have concurrent power to enforce this article by appropriate legislation.

Section 3. This article shall be inoperative unless it shall have been ratified as an amendment to the Constitution by the legislatures of the several States as provided in the Constitution, within seven years from the date of the submission hereof to the States by the Congress.

Amendment 19

(*Ratified August 18, 1920*)

The right of citizens of the United States to vote shall not be denied or abridged by the United States or by any State on account of sex.

Congress shall have power to enforce this article by appropriate legislation.

Amendment 20

(*Ratified January 23, 1933*)

Section 1. The terms of the President and Vice President shall end at noon on the 20th day of January, and the terms of Senators and Representatives at noon on the 3d day of January, of the years in which such terms would have ended if this article had not been ratified; and the terms of their successors shall then begin.

Section 2. The Congress shall assemble at least once in every year, and such meeting shall begin at noon on the 3d day of January, unless they shall by law appoint a different day.

Section 3. If, at the time fixed for the beginning of the term of the President, the President elect shall have died, the Vice President elect shall become President. If a President shall not have been chosen before the time fixed for the beginning of his term, or if the President elect shall have failed to qualify, then the Vice President elect shall act as President until a President shall have qualified; and the Congress may by law provide for the case wherein neither a President elect nor a Vice President elect shall have qualified, declaring who shall then act as President, or the manner in which one who is to act shall be selected, and such person shall act accordingly until a President or Vice President shall have qualified.

Section 4. The Congress may by law provide for the case of the death of any of the persons from whom the House of Representatives may choose a President whenever the right of choice shall have devolved upon them, and for the case of the death of any of the persons from whom the Senate may choose a Vice President whenever the right of choice shall have devolved upon them.

Section 5. Sections 1 and 2 shall take effect on the 15th day of October following the ratification of this article.

Section 6. This article shall be inoperative unless it shall have been ratified as an amendment to the Constitution by the legislatures of three-fourths of the several States within seven years from the date of its submission.

Amendment 21

(*Ratified December 5, 1933*)

Section 1. The eighteenth article of amendment to the Constitution of the United States is hereby repealed.

Section 2. The transportation or importation into any State, Territory, or possession of the United States for delivery or use therein of intoxicating liquors, in violation of the laws thereof, is hereby prohibited.

Section 3. This article shall be inoperative unless it shall have been ratified as an amendment to the Constitution by conventions in the several States, as provided in the Constitution, within seven years from the date of the submission hereof to the States by the Congress.

Amendment 22

(*Ratified February 27, 1951*)

Section 1. No person shall be elected to the office of the President more than twice, and no person who has held the office of President, or acted as President, for more than two years of a term to which some other person was elected President shall be elected to the office of the President more than once. But this Article shall not apply to any person holding the office of President when this Article was proposed by the Congress, and shall not prevent any person who may be holding the office of President, or acting as President, during the term within which this Article becomes operative from holding the office of President or acting as President during the remainder of such term.

Section 2. This article shall be inoperative unless it shall have been ratified as an amendment to the Constitution by the legislatures of three-fourths of the several States within seven years from the date of its submission to the States by the Congress.

Amendment 23

(*Ratified March 29, 1961*)

Section 1. The District constituting the seat of Government of the United States shall appoint in such manner as the Congress may direct:

A number of electors of President and Vice President equal to the whole number of Senators and Representatives in Congress to which the District would be entitled if it were a State, but in no event more than the least populous State; they shall be in addition to those appointed by the States, but they shall be considered, for the purposes of the election of President and Vice President, to be electors appointed by a State; and they shall meet in the District and perform such duties as provided by the twelfth article of amendment.

Section 2. The Congress shall have power to enforce this article by appropriate legislation.

Amendment 24

(*Ratified January 23, 1964*)

Section 1. The right of citizens of the United States to vote in any primary or other election for President or Vice President, for electors for President or Vice President, or for Senator or Representative in Congress, shall not be denied or abridged by the United States or any State by reason of failure to pay any poll tax or other tax.

Section 2. The Congress shall have power to enforce this article by appropriate legislation.

Amendment 25

(*Ratified February 10, 1967*)

Section 1. In case of the removal of the President from office or of his death or resignation, the Vice President shall become President.

Section 2. Whenever there is a vacancy in the office of the Vice President, the President shall nominate a Vice President who shall take office upon confirmation by a majority vote of both Houses of Congress.

Section 3. Whenever the President transmits to the President pro tempore of the Senate and the Speaker of the House of Representatives his written declaration that he is unable to discharge the powers and duties of his office, and until he transmits to them a written declaration to the contrary, such powers and duties shall be discharged by the Vice President as Acting President.

Section 4. Whenever the Vice President and a majority of either the principal officers of the executive departments or of such other body as Congress may by law provide, transmit to the President pro tempore of the Senate and the Speaker of the House of Representatives their written declaration that the President is unable to discharge the powers and duties of his office, the Vice President shall immediately assume the powers and duties of the office as Acting President.

Thereafter, when the President transmits to the President pro tempore of the Senate and the Speaker of the House of Representatives his written declaration that no inability exists, he shall resume the powers and duties of his office unless the Vice President and a majority of either the principal officers of the executive department or of such other body as Congress may by law provide, transmit within four days to the President pro tempore of the Senate and the Speaker of the House of Representatives their written declaration that the President is unable to discharge the powers and duties of his office. Thereupon Congress shall decide the issue, assembling within forty-eight hours for that purpose if not in session. If the Congress, within twenty-one days after receipt of the latter written declaration, or, if Congress is not in session, within twenty-one days after Congress is required to assemble, determines by two-thirds vote of both Houses that the President is unable to discharge the powers and duties of his office, the Vice President shall continue to discharge the same as Acting President; otherwise, the President shall resume the powers and duties of his office.

Amendment 26

(*Ratified July 1, 1971*)

Section 1. The right of citizens of the United States, who are eighteen years of age or older, to vote shall not be denied or abridged by the United States or by any State on account of age.

Section 2. The Congress shall have the power to enforce this article by appropriate legislation.

Amendment 27

(*Ratified May 7, 1992*)

No law, varying the compensation for the services of the Senators and Representatives, shall take effect, until an election of Representatives shall have intervened.

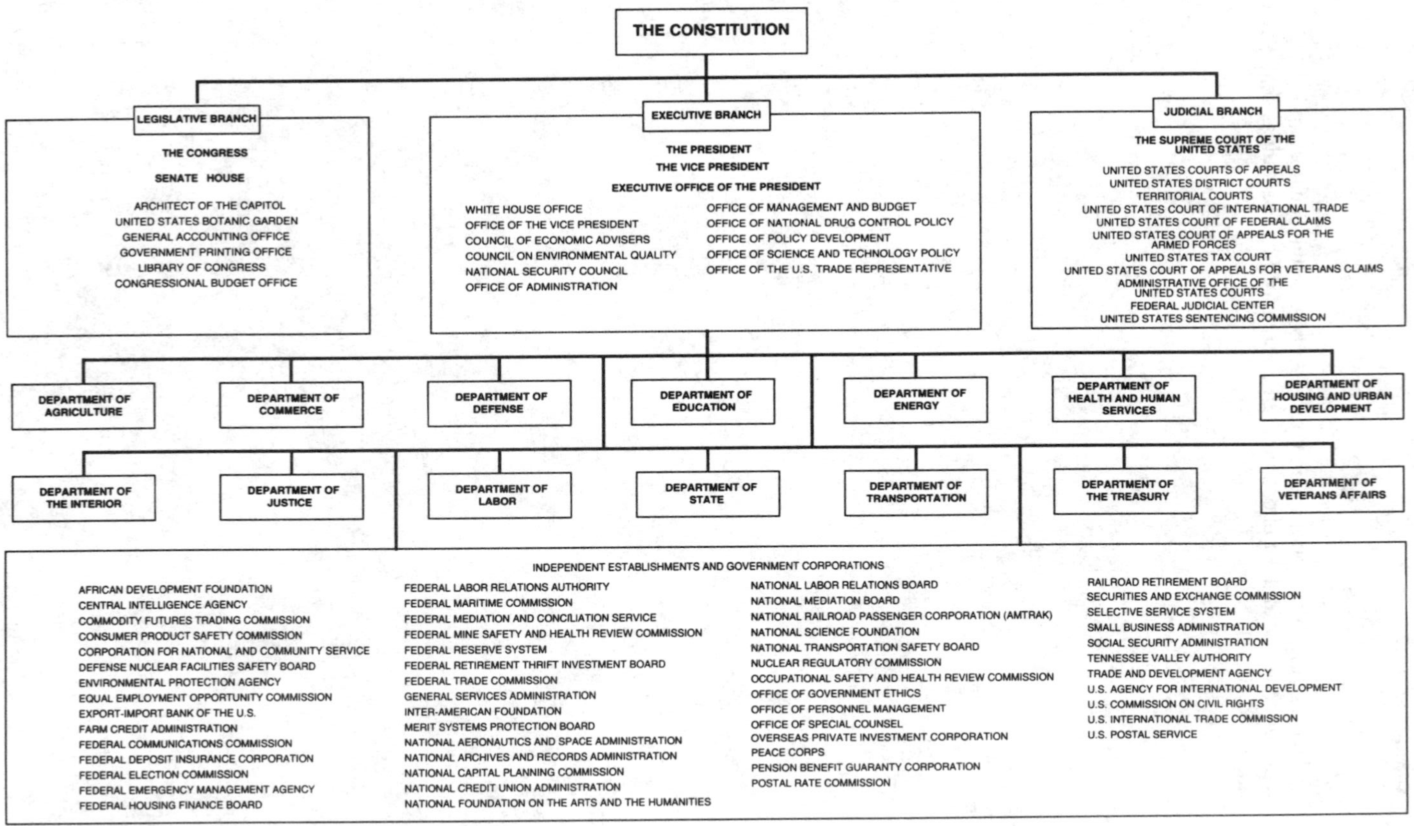
THE GOVERNMENT OF THE UNITED STATES
THE CONSTITUTION
LEGISLATIVE BRANCH
THE CONGRESS
SENATE HOUSE
ARCHITECT OF THE CAPITOL
UNITED STATES BOTANIC GARDEN
GENERAL ACCOUNTING OFFICE
GOVERNMENT PRINTING OFFICE
LIBRARY OF CONGRESS
CONGRESSIONAL BUDGET OFFICE
EXECUTIVE BRANCH
THE PRESIDENT
THE VICE PRESIDENT
EXECUTIVE OFFICE OF THE PRESIDENT
WHITE HOUSE OFFICE
OFFICE OF THE VICE PRESIDENT
COUNCIL OF ECONOMIC ADVISERS
COUNCIL ON ENVIRONMENTAL QUALITY
NATIONAL SECURITY COUNCIL
OFFICE OF ADMINISTRATION
OFFICE OF MANAGEMENT AND BUDGET
OFFICE OF NATIONAL DRUG CONTROL POLICY
OFFICE OF POLICY DEVELOPMENT
OFFICE OF SCIENCE AND TECHNOLOGY POLICY
OFFICE OF THE U.S. TRADE REPRESENTATIVE
JUDICIAL BRANCH
THE SUPREME COURT OF THE UNITED STATES
UNITED STATES COURTS OF APPEALS
UNITED STATES DISTRICT COURTS
TERRITORIAL COURTS
UNITED STATES COURT OF INTERNATIONAL TRADE
UNITED STATES COURT OF FEDERAL CLAIMS
UNITED STATES COURT OF APPEALS FOR THE ARMED FORCES
UNITED STATES TAX COURT
UNITED STATES COURT OF APPEALS FOR VETERANS CLAIMS
ADMINISTRATIVE OFFICE OF THE UNITED STATES COURTS
FEDERAL JUDICIAL CENTER
UNITED STATES SENTENCING COMMISSION
DEPARTMENT OF AGRICULTURE
DEPARTMENT OF COMMERCE
DEPARTMENT OF DEFENSE
DEPARTMENT OF EDUCATION
DEPARTMENT OF ENERGY
DEPARTMENT OF HEALTH AND HUMAN SERVICES
DEPARTMENT OF HOUSING AND URBAN DEVELOPMENT
DEPARTMENT OF THE INTERIOR
DEPARTMENT OF JUSTICE
DEPARTMENT OF LABOR
DEPARTMENT OF STATE
DEPARTMENT OF TRANSPORTATION
DEPARTMENT OF THE TREASURY
DEPARTMENT OF VETERANS AFFAIRS
INDEPENDENT ESTABLISHMENTS AND GOVERNMENT CORPORATIONS
AFRICAN DEVELOPMENT FOUNDATION
CENTRAL INTELLIGENCE AGENCY
COMMODITY FUTURES TRADING COMMISSION
CONSUMER PRODUCT SAFETY COMMISSION
CORPORATION FOR NATIONAL AND COMMUNITY SERVICE
DEFENSE NUCLEAR FACILITIES SAFETY BOARD
ENVIRONMENTAL PROTECTION AGENCY
EQUAL EMPLOYMENT OPPORTUNITY COMMISSION
EXPORT-IMPORT BANK OF THE U.S.
FARM CREDIT ADMINISTRATION
FEDERAL COMMUNICATIONS COMMISSION
FEDERAL DEPOSIT INSURANCE CORPORATION
FEDERAL ELECTION COMMISSION
FEDERAL EMERGENCY MANAGEMENT AGENCY
FEDERAL HOUSING FINANCE BOARD
FEDERAL LABOR RELATIONS AUTHORITY
FEDERAL MARITIME COMMISSION
FEDERAL MEDIATION AND CONCILIATION SERVICE
FEDERAL MINE SAFETY AND HEALTH REVIEW COMMISSION
FEDERAL RESERVE SYSTEM
FEDERAL RETIREMENT THRIFT INVESTMENT BOARD
FEDERAL TRADE COMMISSION
GENERAL SERVICES ADMINISTRATION
INTER-AMERICAN FOUNDATION
MERIT SYSTEMS PROTECTION BOARD
NATIONAL AERONAUTICS AND SPACE ADMINISTRATION
NATIONAL ARCHIVES AND RECORDS ADMINISTRATION
NATIONAL CAPITAL PLANNING COMMISSION
NATIONAL CREDIT UNION ADMINISTRATION
NATIONAL FOUNDATION ON THE ARTS AND THE HUMANITIES
NATIONAL LABOR RELATIONS BOARD
NATIONAL MEDIATION BOARD
NATIONAL RAILROAD PASSENGER CORPORATION (AMTRAK)
NATIONAL SCIENCE FOUNDATION
NATIONAL TRANSPORTATION SAFETY BOARD
NUCLEAR REGULATORY COMMISSION
OCCUPATIONAL SAFETY AND HEALTH REVIEW COMMISSION
OFFICE OF GOVERNMENT ETHICS
OFFICE OF PERSONNEL MANAGEMENT
OFFICE OF SPECIAL COUNSEL
OVERSEAS PRIVATE INVESTMENT CORPORATION
PEACE CORPS
PENSION BENEFIT GUARANTY CORPORATION
POSTAL RATE COMMISSION
RAILROAD RETIREMENT BOARD
SECURITIES AND EXCHANGE COMMISSION
SELECTIVE SERVICE SYSTEM
SMALL BUSINESS ADMINISTRATION
SOCIAL SECURITY ADMINISTRATION
TENNESSEE VALLEY AUTHORITY
TRADE AND DEVELOPMENT AGENCY
U.S. AGENCY FOR INTERNATIONAL DEVELOPMENT
U.S. COMMISSION ON CIVIL RIGHTS
U.S. INTERNATIONAL TRADE COMMISSION
U.S. POSTAL SERVICE

Legislative Branch

LEGISLATIVE BRANCH

CONGRESS

One Hundred and Sixth Congress, First Session

The Senate

The Capitol, Washington, DC 20510
Phone, 202–224–3121. Internet, www.senate.gov.

President of the Senate (Vice President of the United States)	AL GORE
President pro tempore	STROM THURMOND
Majority Leader	TRENT LOTT
Minority Leader	THOMAS A. DASCHLE
Secretary of the Senate	GARY SISCO
Sergeant at Arms	JAMES W. ZIGLAR
Secretary for the Majority	ELIZABETH B. LETCHWORTH
Secretary for the Minority	MARTIN P. PAONE
Chaplain	LLOYD J. OGILVIE

The House of Representatives

The Capitol, Washington, DC 20515
Phone, 202–225–3121. Internet, www.house.gov.

The Speaker	J. DENNIS HASTERT
Clerk	JEFF TRANDAHL
Sergeant at Arms	WILSON L. LIVINGOOD
Chief Administrative Officer	JAMES M. EAGEN III
Chaplain	REV. DANIEL P. COUGHLIN

The Congress of the United States was created by Article I, section 1, of the Constitution, adopted by the Constitutional Convention on September 17, 1787, providing that "All legislative Powers herein granted shall be vested in a Congress of the United States, which shall consist of a Senate and House of Representatives."

The first Congress under the Constitution met on March 4, 1789, in the Federal Hall in New York City. The membership then consisted of 20[1] *Senators and 59 Representatives.*

[1]New York ratified the Constitution on July 26, 1788, but did not elect its Senators until July 15 and 16, 1789. North Carolina did not ratify the Constitution until November 21, 1789; Rhode Island ratified it on May 29, 1790.

186-873 D-00--2

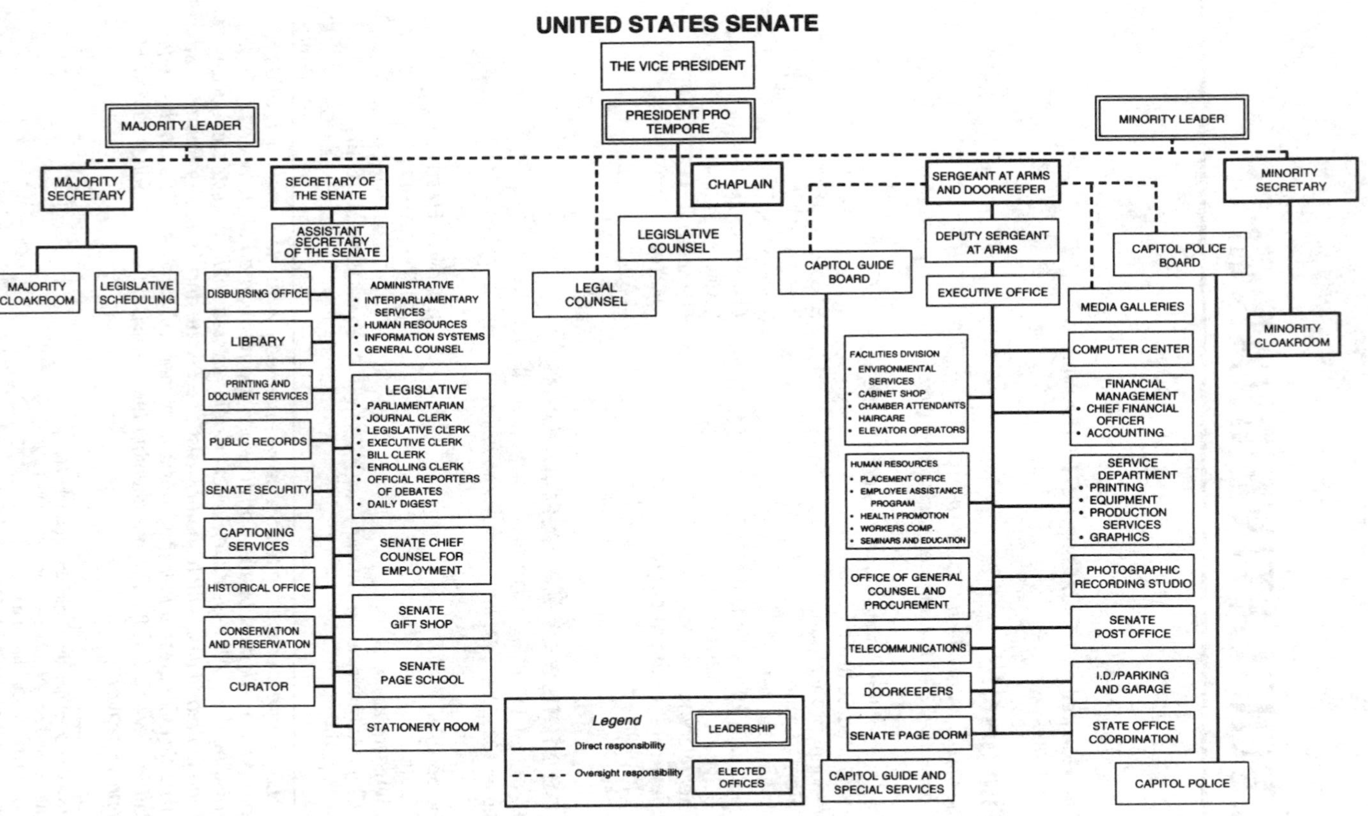
UNITED STATES SENATE
THE VICE PRESIDENT
PRESIDENT PRO TEMPORE
MAJORITY LEADER
MINORITY LEADER
MAJORITY SECRETARY
SECRETARY OF THE SENATE
CHAPLAIN
SERGEANT AT ARMS AND DOORKEEPER
MINORITY SECRETARY
ASSISTANT SECRETARY OF THE SENATE
LEGISLATIVE COUNSEL
LEGAL COUNSEL
DEPUTY SERGEANT AT ARMS
CAPITOL GUIDE BOARD
CAPITOL POLICE BOARD
MAJORITY CLOAKROOM
LEGISLATIVE SCHEDULING
DISBURSING OFFICE
ADMINISTRATIVE
• INTERPARLIAMENTARY SERVICES
• HUMAN RESOURCES
• INFORMATION SYSTEMS
• GENERAL COUNSEL
EXECUTIVE OFFICE
MEDIA GALLERIES
MINORITY CLOAKROOM
LIBRARY
COMPUTER CENTER
FACILITIES DIVISION
• ENVIRONMENTAL SERVICES
• CABINET SHOP
• CHAMBER ATTENDANTS
• HAIRCARE
• ELEVATOR OPERATORS
PRINTING AND DOCUMENT SERVICES
LEGISLATIVE
• PARLIAMENTARIAN
• JOURNAL CLERK
• LEGISLATIVE CLERK
• EXECUTIVE CLERK
• BILL CLERK
• ENROLLING CLERK
• OFFICIAL REPORTERS OF DEBATES
• DAILY DIGEST
FINANCIAL MANAGEMENT
• CHIEF FINANCIAL OFFICER
• ACCOUNTING
PUBLIC RECORDS
HUMAN RESOURCES
• PLACEMENT OFFICE
• EMPLOYEE ASSISTANCE PROGRAM
• HEALTH PROMOTION
• WORKERS COMP.
• SEMINARS AND EDUCATION
SERVICE DEPARTMENT
• PRINTING
• EQUIPMENT
• PRODUCTION SERVICES
• GRAPHICS
SENATE SECURITY
CAPTIONING SERVICES
SENATE CHIEF COUNSEL FOR EMPLOYMENT
HISTORICAL OFFICE
OFFICE OF GENERAL COUNSEL AND PROCUREMENT
PHOTOGRAPHIC RECORDING STUDIO
SENATE GIFT SHOP
SENATE POST OFFICE
CONSERVATION AND PRESERVATION
TELECOMMUNICATIONS
SENATE PAGE SCHOOL
CURATOR
DOORKEEPERS
I.D./PARKING AND GARAGE
STATIONERY ROOM
SENATE PAGE DORM
STATE OFFICE COORDINATION
Legend
Direct responsibility
Oversight responsibility
LEADERSHIP
ELECTED OFFICES
CAPITOL GUIDE AND SPECIAL SERVICES
CAPITOL POLICE

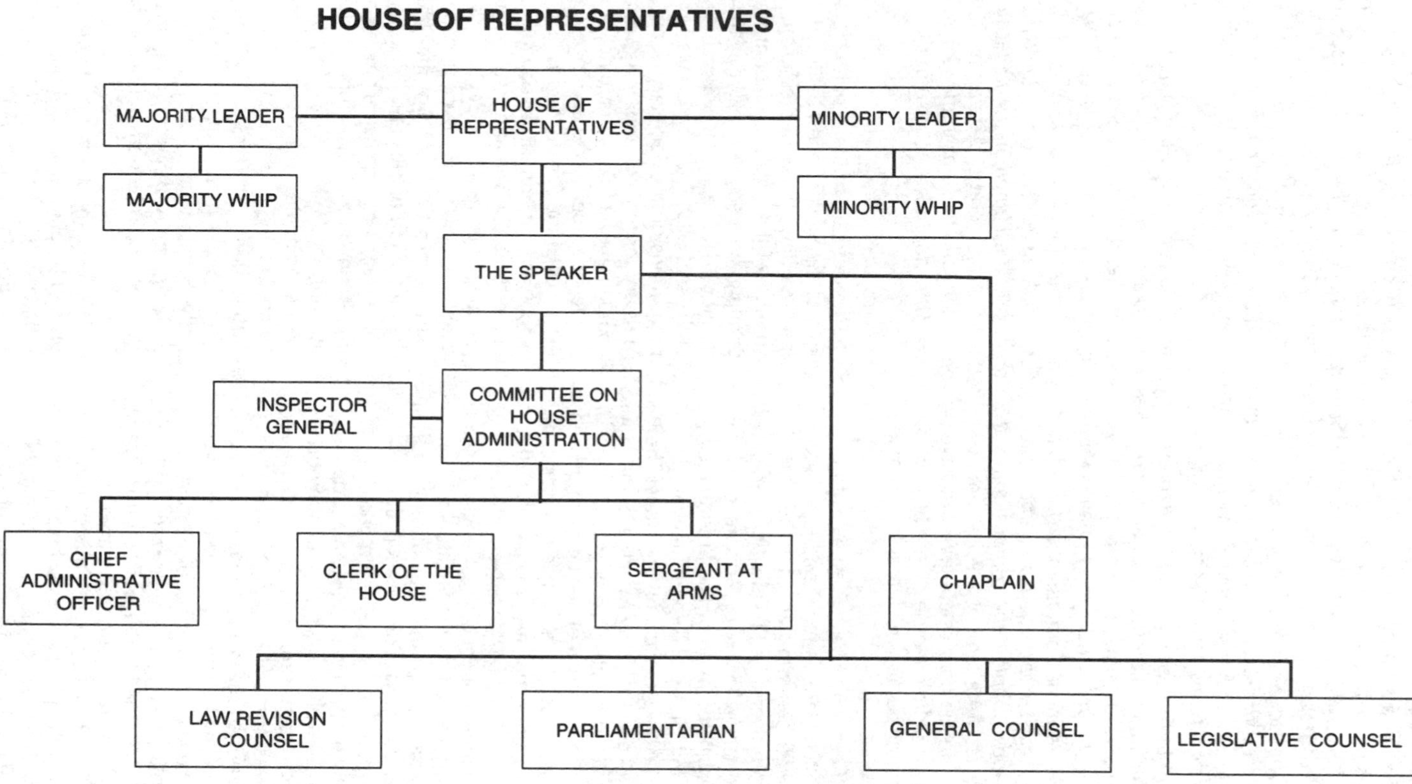
HOUSE OF REPRESENTATIVES
MAJORITY LEADER
HOUSE OF REPRESENTATIVES
MINORITY LEADER
MAJORITY WHIP
MINORITY WHIP
THE SPEAKER
INSPECTOR GENERAL
COMMITTEE ON HOUSE ADMINISTRATION
CHIEF ADMINISTRATIVE OFFICER
CLERK OF THE HOUSE
SERGEANT AT ARMS
CHAPLAIN
LAW REVISION COUNSEL
PARLIAMENTARIAN
GENERAL COUNSEL
LEGISLATIVE COUNSEL

The Senate is composed of 100 Members, 2 from each State, who are elected to serve for a term of 6 years. Senators were originally chosen by the State legislatures. This procedure was changed by the 17th amendment to the Constitution, adopted in 1913, which made the election of Senators a function of the people. There are three classes of Senators, and a new class is elected every 2 years.

The House of Representatives comprises 435 Representatives. The number representing each State is determined by population, but every State is entitled to at least one Representative. Members are elected by the people for 2-year terms, all terms running for the same period.

Both the Senators and the Representatives must be residents of the State from which they are chosen. In addition, a Senator must be at least 30 years of age and must have been a citizen of the United States for at least 9 years; a Representative must be at least 25 years of age and must have been a citizen for at least 7 years.

A Resident Commissioner from Puerto Rico (elected for a 4-year term) and Delegates from American Samoa, the District of Columbia, Guam, and the Virgin Islands complete the composition of the Congress of the United States. Delegates are elected for a term of 2 years. The Resident Commissioner and Delegates may take part in the floor discussions but have no vote in the full House or in the Committee of the Whole House on the State of the Union. They do, however, vote in the committees to which they are assigned.

Officers The Vice President of the United States is the Presiding Officer of the Senate; in his absence the duties are taken over by a President pro tempore, elected by that body, or someone designated by him. The Presiding Officer of the House of Representatives, the Speaker, is elected by the House; he may designate any Member of the House to act in his absence.

The positions of Senate majority and minority leader have been in existence only since the early years of the 20th century. Leaders are elected at the beginning of each new Congress by a majority vote of the Senators in their political party. In cooperation with their party organizations, leaders are responsible for the design and achievement of a legislative program. This involves managing the flow of legislation, expediting noncontroversial measures, and keeping Members informed regarding proposed action on pending business. Each leader serves as an *ex officio* member of his party's policymaking and organizational bodies and is aided by an assistant floor leader (whip) and a party secretary.

The House leadership is structured essentially the same as the Senate, with the Members in the political parties responsible for the election of their respective leader and whips.

The Secretary of the Senate, elected by vote of the Senate, performs the duties of the Presiding Officer of the Senate in the absence of the Vice President and pending the election of a President pro tempore. The Secretary is the custodian of the seal of the Senate, draws requisitions on the Secretary of the Treasury for moneys appropriated for the compensation of Senators, officers, and employees, and for the contingent expenses of the Senate, and is empowered to administer oaths to any officer of the Senate and to any witness produced before it. The Secretary's executive duties include certification of extracts from the Journal of the Senate; the attestation of bills and joint, concurrent, and Senate resolutions; in impeachment trials, issuance, under the authority of the Presiding Officer, of all orders, mandates, writs, and precepts authorized by the Senate; and certification to the President of the United States of the advice and consent of the Senate to ratification of treaties and the names of persons confirmed or rejected upon the nomination of the President.

The Sergeant at Arms of the Senate is elected by and serves as the Executive Officer of that body. He directs and supervises the various departments and facilities under his jurisdiction. He is also the Law Enforcement and Protocol Officer. As Law Enforcement Officer, he has statutory power to make arrests; to locate absentee Senators for a quorum; to enforce Senate rules and regulations as they pertain to the Senate Chamber, the Senate wing of the Capitol, and the Senate Office Buildings. He serves as a member of the Capitol Police Board and as its chairman each odd year; and, subject to the Presiding Officer, maintains order in the Senate Chamber. As Protocol Officer, he is responsible for many aspects of ceremonial functions, including the inauguration of the President of the United States; arranging funerals of Senators who die in office; escorting the President when he addresses a Joint Session of Congress or attends any function in the Senate; and escorting heads of state when they visit the Senate.

The elected officers of the House of Representatives include the Clerk, the Sergeant at Arms, the Chief Administrative Officer, and the Chaplain.

The Clerk is custodian of the seal of the House and administers the primary legislative activities of the House. These duties include: accepting the credentials of the Members-elect and calling the Members to order at the commencement of the first session of each Congress; keeping the Journal; taking all votes and certifying the passage of bills; and processing all legislation. Through various departments, the Clerk is also responsible for floor and committee reporting services; legislative information and reference services; the administration of House reports pursuant to House rules and certain legislation including the Ethics in Government Act and the Lobbying Disclosure Act of 1995; the distribution of House documents; and administration of the House Page Program. The Clerk is also charged with supervision of the offices vacated by Members due to death, resignation, or expulsion.

The Sergeant at Arms maintains the order of the House under the direction of the Speaker and is the keeper of the Mace. As a member of the U.S. Capitol Police Board, the Sergeant at Arms is the chief law enforcement officer for the House and serves as Board Chairman each even year. The ceremonial and protocol duties parallel those of the Senate Sergeant at Arms and include arranging the inauguration of the President of the United States, Joint Sessions of Congress, visits to the House of heads of state, and funerals of Members of Congress. The Sergeant at Arms enforces the rules relating to the privileges of the Hall of the House, including admission to the galleries, oversees garage and parking security of the House, and distributes all House staff identification cards.

Committees The work of preparing and considering legislation is done largely by committees of both Houses of Congress. There are 16 standing committees in the Senate and 19 in the House of Representatives. The standing committees of the Senate and the House of Representatives are shown in the list below. In addition, there are select committees in each House (one in the House of Representatives), and various congressional commissions and joint committees composed of Members of both Houses. Each House may also appoint special investigating committees. The membership of the standing committees of each House is chosen by a vote of the entire body; members of other committees are appointed under the provisions of the measure establishing them.

Each bill and resolution is usually referred to the appropriate committee, which may report a bill out in its original form, favorably or unfavorably, recommend amendments, report original measures, or allow the proposed legislation to die in committee without action.

Standing Committees of the Congress

House Committee	Room [1]	Senate Committee	Room [2]
Agriculture	1301	Agriculture, Nutrition, and Forestry	SR–328A
Appropriations	H218	Appropriations	S–128

Standing Committees of the Congress—Continued

House Committee	Room[1]	Senate Committee	Room[2]
Banking and Financial Services	2129	Armed Services	SR–228
Budget	309	Banking, Housing, and Urban Affairs	SD–534
Commerce	2125	Budget	SD–621
Education and the Workforce	2181	Commerce, Science, and Transportation	SD–508
Government Reform	2157	Energy and Natural Resources	SD–364
House Administration	1309	Environment and Public Works	SD–410
Franking Commission:			
Majority	1309		
Minority	1216		
International Relations	2170	Finance	SD–219
Judiciary	2138	Foreign Relations	SD–450
Publications	B29		
Armed Services	2120	Governmental Affairs	SD–340
Resources	1324	Health, Education, Labor and Pensions	SD–428
Rules	H312	Judiciary	SD–224
Minority	234		
Science	2320	Rules and Administration	SR–305
Small Business	2361	Small Business	SR–428A
Standards of Official Conduct	HT2	Veterans' Affairs	SR–412
Office of Advice and Education	HT2		
Transportation and Infrastructure	2165		
Veterans' Affairs	335		
Ways and Means	1102		

[1] Room numbers with three digits are in the Cannon House Office Building, four digits beginning with 1 are in the Longworth House Office Building, and four digits beginning with 2 are in the Rayburn House Office Building. Room numbers preceded by H or HT are in the House wing of the Capitol Building.

[2] Room numbers preceded by S are in the Senate wing of the Capitol Building; those preceded by SD are in the Dirksen Office Building; and those preceded by SR are in the Russell Office Building.

Congressional Record Proceedings of Congress are published in the *Congressional Record,* which is issued each day when Congress is in session. Publication of the *Record* began March 4, 1873; it was the first record of debate officially reported, printed, and published directly by the Federal Government. The Daily Digest of the *Congressional Record,* printed in the back of each issue of the *Record,* summarizes the proceedings of that day in each House, and each of their committees and subcommittees, respectively. The Digest also presents the legislative program for each day and, at the end of the week, gives the program for the following week. Its publication was begun March 17, 1947.

Sessions Section 4 of Article I of the Constitution makes it mandatory that "The Congress shall assemble at least once in every Year. . . ." Under this provision, also, the date for convening Congress was designated originally as the first Monday in December, "unless they shall by Law appoint a different Day." Eighteen acts were passed, up to 1820, providing for the meeting of Congress on other days of the year. From 1820 to 1934, however, Congress met regularly on the first Monday in December. In 1934 the Twentieth Amendment changed the convening of Congress to January 3, unless Congress "shall by law appoint a different day." In addition, the President, according to Article II, section 3, of the Constitution "may, on extraordinary Occasions, convene both Houses, or either of them, and in Case of Disagreement between them, with Respect to the Time of Adjournment, he may adjourn them to such Time as he shall think proper. . . ."

Powers of Congress Article I, section 8, of the Constitution defines the powers of Congress. Included are the powers to assess and collect taxes—called the chief power; to regulate commerce, both interstate and foreign; to coin money; to establish post offices and post roads; to establish courts inferior to the Supreme Court; to declare war; and to raise and maintain an army and navy. Congress is further empowered "To provide for calling forth the Militia to execute the Laws of the Union, suppress Insurrections and repel Invasions;" and "To make all Laws which shall be necessary and proper for carrying into Execution the foregoing Powers, and all other Powers vested by this Constitution in the Government of the United States, or in any Department or Officer thereof."

Amendments to the Constitution Another power vested in the Congress is the right to propose amendments to the Constitution, whenever two-thirds of both Houses shall deem it necessary. Should two-thirds of the State legislatures demand changes in the Constitution, it is the duty of Congress to call a constitutional convention. Proposed amendments shall be valid as part of the Constitution when ratified by the legislatures or by conventions of three-fourths of the States, as one or the other mode of ratification may be proposed by Congress.

Special Powers of the Senate Under the Constitution, the Senate is granted certain powers not accorded to the House of Representatives. The Senate approves or disapproves certain Presidential appointments by majority vote, and treaties must be concurred in by a two-thirds vote.

Special Powers of the House of Representatives The House of Representatives is granted the power of originating all bills for the raising of revenue. Both Houses of Congress act in impeachment proceedings, which, according to the Constitution, may be instituted against the President, Vice President, and all civil officers of the United States. The House of Representatives has the sole power of impeachment, and the Senate has the sole power to try impeachments.

Prohibitions Upon Congress Section 9 of Article I of the Constitution also imposes prohibitions upon Congress. "The Privilege of the Writ of Habeas Corpus shall not be suspended, unless when in Cases of Rebellion or Invasion the public Safety may require it." A bill of attainder or an ex post facto law cannot be passed. No export duty can be imposed. Ports of one State cannot be given preference over those of another State. "No money shall be drawn from the Treasury, but in Consequence of Appropriations made by Law. . . ." No title of nobility may be granted.

Rights of Members According to section 6 of Article I, Members of Congress are granted certain privileges. In no case, except in treason, felony, and breach of the peace, can Members be arrested while attending sessions of Congress "and in going to and returning from the same. . . ." Furthermore, the Members cannot be questioned in any other place for remarks made in Congress. Each House may expel a Member of its body by a two-thirds vote.

Enactment of Laws All bills and joint resolutions must pass both the House of Representatives and the Senate and must be signed by the President, except those proposing a constitutional amendment, in order to become law, or be passed over the President's veto by a two-thirds vote of both Houses of Congress. Section 7 of Article I states: "If any Bill shall not be returned by the President within ten Days (Sundays excepted) after it shall have been presented to him, the Same shall be a Law, in like Manner as if he had signed it, unless the Congress by their Adjournment prevent its Return, in which Case it shall not be a Law."

When a bill or joint resolution is introduced in the House, the usual procedure for its enactment into law is as follows:

—assignment to House committee having jurisdiction;

—if favorably considered, it is reported to the House either in its original form or with recommended amendments;

—if the bill or resolution is passed by the House, it is messaged to the Senate and referred to the committee having jurisdiction;

—in the Senate committee the bill, if favorably considered, may be reported in the form as received from the House, or with recommended amendments;

—the approved bill or resolution is reported to the Senate, and if passed by that body, is returned to the House;

—if one body does not accept the amendments to a bill by the other body, a conference committee comprised of Members of both bodies is usually appointed to effect a compromise;

—when the bill or joint resolution is finally approved by both Houses, it is signed by the Speaker (or Speaker pro tempore) and the Vice President (or President pro tempore or acting President pro tempore) and is presented to the President; and

—once the President's signature is affixed, the measure becomes a law. If the President vetoes the bill, it cannot become a law unless it is re-passed by a two-thirds vote of both Houses.

Electronic Access Specific information and legislation can be found on the Internet, at thomas.loc.gov.

Publications The *Congressional Directory,* the *Senate Manual,* telephone directories for the U.S. Senate and the House of Representatives, and the *House Rules* and *Manual* may be obtained from the Superintendent of Documents, Government Printing Office, Washington, DC 20402.

Senators

[Republicans in roman (54); Democrats in italic (46); total, 100]

Room numbers preceded by SR are in the Russell Office Building (Delaware and Constitution Avenues); those preceded by SD are in the Dirksen Office Building (First Street and Constitution Avenue); and those preceded by SH are in the Hart Office Building (Second and C Streets). Members' offices may be reached by phone at 202–224–3121.

Name	State	Room
Abraham, Spencer	Michigan	SD329
Akaka, Daniel K	Hawaii	SH720
Allard, Wayne	Colorado	SH513
Ashcroft, John	Missouri	SH316
Baucus, Max	Montana	SH511
Bayh, Evan	Indiana	SH717
Bennett, Robert F	Utah	SD431
Biden, Joseph R., Jr	Delaware	SR221
Bingaman, Jeff	New Mexico	SH703
Bond, Christopher S	Missouri	SR274
Boxer, Barbara	California	SH112
Breaux, John B	Louisiana	SH503
Brownback, Sam	Kansas	SH303
Bryan, Richard H	Nevada	SR269
Bunning, Jim	Kentucky	SH502
Burns, Conrad R	Montana	SD187
Byrd, Robert C	West Virginia	SH311
Campbell, Ben Nighthorse	Colorado	SR380
Chafee, Lincoln D	Rhode Island	SD505
Cleland, Max	Georgia	SD461
Cochran, Thad	Mississippi	SR326
Collins, Susan M	Maine	SR172
Conrad, Kent	North Dakota	SH530
Craig, Larry E	Idaho	SH520
Crapo, Mike	Idaho	SR111
Daschle, Tom	South Dakota	SH509
DeWine, Mike	Ohio	SR140
Dodd, Christopher J	Connecticut	SR448
Domenici, Pete V	New Mexico	SH328
Dorgan, Byron L	North Dakota	SH713
Durbin, Richard J	Illinois	SR364
Edwards, John	North Carolina	SD225
Enzi, Mike	Wyoming	SR290
Feingold, Russell D	Wisconsin	SH716
Feinstein, Dianne	California	SH331
Fitzgerald, Peter G	Illinois	SD555
Frist, Bill	Tennessee	SR416
Gorton, Slade	Washington	SH730
Graham, Bob	Florida	SH524
Gramm, Phil	Texas	SR370

Senators—Continued

[Republicans in roman (54); Democrats in italic (46); total, 100]

Room numbers preceded by SR are in the Russell Office Building (Delaware and Constitution Avenues); those preceded by SD are in the Dirksen Office Building (First Street and Constitution Avenue); and those preceded by SH are in the Hart Office Building (Second and C Streets). Members' offices may be reached by phone at 202–224–3121.

Name	State	Room
Grams, Rod	Minnesota	SD257
Grassley, Charles E	Iowa	SH135
Gregg, Judd	New Hampshire	SR393
Hagel, Chuck	Nebraska	SR346
Harkin, Tom	Iowa	SH731
Hatch, Orrin G	Utah	SR131
Helms, Jesse	North Carolina	SD403
Hollings, Ernest F	South Carolina	SR125
Hutchinson, Y. Tim	Arkansas	SD239
Hutchison, Kay Bailey	Texas	SR284
Inhofe, James M	Oklahoma	SR453
Inouye, Daniel K	Hawaii	SH722
Jeffords, James M	Vermont	SH728
Johnson, Tim	South Dakota	SH324
Kennedy, Edward M	Massachusetts	SR315
Kerrey, J. Robert	Nebraska	SH141
Kerry, John F	Massachusetts	SR304
Kohl, Herb	Wisconsin	SH330
Kyl, Jon	Arizona	SH724
Landrieu, Mary L	Louisiana	SH702
Lautenberg, Frank R	New Jersey	SH506
Leahy, Patrick J	Vermont	SR433
Levin, Carl	Michigan	SR459
Lieberman, Joseph I	Connecticut	SH706
Lincoln, Blanche L	Arkansas	SD359
Lott, Trent	Mississippi	SR487
Lugar, Richard G	Indiana	SH306
Mack, Connie	Florida	SH517
McCain, John	Arizona	SR241
McConnell, Mitch	Kentucky	SR361A
Mikulski, Barbara A	Maryland	SH709
Miller, Zell	Georgia	SR200
Moynihan, Daniel Patrick	New York	SR464
Murkowski, Frank H	Alaska	SH322
Murray, Patty	Washington	SR173
Nickles, Don	Oklahoma	SH133
Reed, Jack	Rhode Island	SH320
Reid, Harry	Nevada	SH528
Robb, Charles S	Virginia	SR154
Roberts, Pat	Kansas	SH302
Rockefeller, John D., IV	West Virginia	SH531
Roth, William V., Jr	Delaware	SH104
Santorum, Rick	Pennsylvania	SR120
Sarbanes, Paul S	Maryland	SH309
Schumer, Charles E	New York	SH313
Sessions, Jeff	Alabama	SR493
Shelby, Richard C	Alabama	SH110
Smith, Bob	New Hampshire	SD307
Smith, Gordon	Oregon	SR404
Snowe, Olympia J	Maine	SR250
Specter, Arlen	Pennsylvania	SH711
Stevens, Ted	Alaska	SH522
Thomas, Craig	Wyoming	SH109

Senators—Continued

[Republicans in roman (54); Democrats in italic (46); total, 100]

Room numbers preceded by SR are in the Russell Office Building (Delaware and Constitution Avenues); those preceded by SD are in the Dirksen Office Building (First Street and Constitution Avenue); and those preceded by SH are in the Hart Office Building (Second and C Streets). Members' offices may be reached by phone at 202–224–3121.

Name	State	Room
Thompson, Fred	Tennessee	SD521
Thurmond, Strom	South Carolina	SR217
Torricelli, Robert G	New Jersey	SD113
Voinovich, George V	Ohio	SH317
Warner, John W	Virginia	SR225
Wellstone, Paul	Minnesota	SH136
Wyden, Ron	Oregon	SH516

Representatives

[Republicans in roman (221); Democrats in italic (211); Independents in bold (2); total, 435]

Room numbers with three digits are in the Cannon House Office Building (New Jersey and Independence Avenues), four digits beginning with 1 are in the Longworth House Office Building (between South Capitol Street and New Jersey Avenue on Independence Avenue), and four digits beginning with 2 are in the Rayburn House Office Building (between First and South Capitol Streets on Independence Avenue). Members' offices may be reached by phone at 202–225–3121. The most current listing of House Members can be found on the Internet, at clerkweb.house.gov.

Name	State (District)	Room
Abercrombie, Neil	Hawaii (1)	1502
Ackerman, Gary L	New York (5)	2243
Aderholt, Robert B	Alabama (4)	1007
Allen, Thomas H	Maine (1)	1717
Andrews, Robert E	New Jersey (1)	2439
Archer, Bill	Texas (7)	1236
Armey, Richard K	Texas (26)	301
Baca, Joe	California (42)	2300
Bachus, Spencer	Alabama (6)	442
Baird, Brian	Washington (3)	1721
Baker, Richard H	Louisiana (6)	434
Baldacci, John Elias	Maine (2)	1740
Baldwin, Tammy	Wisconsin (2)	1020
Ballenger, Cass	North Carolina (10)	2182
Barcia, James A	Michigan (5)	2419
Barr, Bob	Georgia (7)	1207
Barrett, Bill	Nebraska (3)	2458
Barrett, Thomas M	Wisconsin (5)	1214
Bartlett, Roscoe G	Maryland (6)	2412
Barton, Joe	Texas (6)	2264
Bass, Charles F	New Hampshire (2)	218
Bateman, Herbert H	Virginia (1)	2211
Becerra, Xavier	California (30)	1119
Bentsen, Ken	Texas (25)	326
Bereuter, Doug	Nebraska (1)	2184
Berkley, Shelley	Nevada (1)	1505
Berman, Howard L	California (26)	2330
Berry, Marion	Arkansas (1)	1113
Biggert, Judy	Illinois (13)	508
Bilbray, Brian P	California (49)	1530
Bilirakis, Michael	Florida (9)	2369
Bishop, Sanford D., Jr	Georgia (2)	1433
Blagojevich, Rod R	Illinois (5)	331
Bliley, Tom	Virginia (7)	2409

Representatives—Continued

[Republicans in roman (221); Democrats in italic (211); Independents in bold (2); total, 435]

Room numbers with three digits are in the Cannon House Office Building (New Jersey and Independence Avenues), four digits beginning with 1 are in the Longworth House Office Building (between South Capitol Street and New Jersey Avenue on Independence Avenue), and four digits beginning with 2 are in the Rayburn House Office Building (between First and South Capitol Streets on Independence Avenue). Members' offices may be reached by phone at 202–225–3121. The most current listing of House Members can be found on the Internet, at clerkweb.house.gov.

Name	State (District)	Room
Blumenauer, Earl	Oregon (3)	1406
Blunt, Roy	Missouri (7)	217
Boehlert, Sherwood L	New York (23)	2246
Boehner, John A	Ohio (8)	1011
Bonilla, Henry	Texas (23)	1427
Bonior, David E	Michigan (10)	2207
Bono, Mary	California (44)	516
Borski, Robert A	Pennsylvania (3)	2267
Boswell, Leonard L	Iowa (3)	1029
Boucher, Rick	Virginia (9)	2329
Boyd, Allen	Florida (2)	107
Brady, Kevin	Texas (8)	1531
Brady, Robert A	Pennsylvania (1)	216
Brown, Corrine	Florida (3)	2444
Brown, Sherrod	Ohio (13)	201
Bryant, Ed	Tennessee (7)	408
Burr, Richard	North Carolina (5)	1513
Burton, Dan	Indiana (6)	2185
Buyer, Steve	Indiana (5)	227
Callahan, Sonny	Alabama (1)	2466
Calvert, Ken	California (43)	2201
Camp, Dave	Michigan (4)	137
Campbell, Tom	California (15)	2442
Canady, Charles T	Florida (12)	2432
Cannon, Chris	Utah (3)	118
Capps, Lois	California (22)	1118
Capuano, Michael E	Massachusetts (8)	1232
Cardin, Benjamin L	Maryland (3)	104
Carson, Julia	Indiana (10)	1541
Castle, Michael N	Delaware (At Large)	1227
Chabot, Steve	Ohio (1)	129
Chambliss, Saxby	Georgia (8)	1019
Chenoweth-Hage, Helen	Idaho (1)	1727
Clay, William (Bill)	Missouri (1)	2306
Clayton, Eva M	North Carolina (1)	2440
Clement, Bob	Tennessee (5)	2229
Clyburn, James E	South Carolina (6)	319
Coble, Howard	North Carolina (6)	2468
Coburn, Tom A	Oklahoma (2)	429
Collins, Mac	Georgia (3)	1131
Combest, Larry	Texas (19)	1026
Condit, Gary A	California (18)	2234
Conyers, John, Jr	Michigan (14)	2426
Cook, Merrill	Utah (2)	1431
Cooksey, John	Louisiana (5)	317
Costello, Jerry F	Illinois (12)	2454
Cox, Christopher	California (47)	2402
Coyne, William J	Pennsylvania (14)	2455
Cramer, Robert E. (Bud), Jr	Alabama (5)	2350
Crane, Philip M	Illinois (8)	233
Crowley, Joseph	New York (7)	1517

Representatives—Continued

[Republicans in roman (221); Democrats in italic (211); Independents in bold (2); total, 435]

Room numbers with three digits are in the Cannon House Office Building (New Jersey and Independence Avenues), four digits beginning with 1 are in the Longworth House Office Building (between South Capitol Street and New Jersey Avenue on Independence Avenue), and four digits beginning with 2 are in the Rayburn House Office Building (between First and South Capitol Streets on Independence Avenue). Members' offices may be reached by phone at 202–225–3121. The most current listing of House Members can be found on the Internet, at clerkweb.house.gov.

Name	State (District)	Room
Cubin, Barbara	Wyoming (At Large)	1114
Cummings, Elijah E	Maryland (7)	1632
Cunningham, Randy (Duke)	California (51)	2238
Danner, Pat	Missouri (6)	2262
Davis, Danny K	Illinois (7)	1222
Davis, Jim	Florida (11)	418
Davis, Thomas M	Virginia (11)	224
Deal, Nathan	Georgia (9)	2437
DeFazio, Peter A	Oregon (4)	2134
DeGette, Diana	Colorado (1)	1339
Delahunt, William D	Massachusetts (10)	1317
DeLauro, Rosa L	Connecticut (3)	436
DeLay, Tom	Texas (22)	341
DeMint, Jim	South Carolina (4)	507
Deutsch, Peter	Florida (20)	204
Diaz-Balart, Lincoln	Florida (21)	404
Dickey, Jay	Arkansas (4)	2453
Dicks, Norman D	Washington (6)	2467
Dingell, John D	Michigan (16)	2328
Dixon, Julian C	California (32)	2252
Doggett, Lloyd	Texas (10)	328
Dooley, Calvin M	California (20)	1201
Doolittle, John T	California (4)	1526
Doyle, Michael F	Pennsylvania (18)	133
Dreier, David	California (28)	237
Duncan, John J., Jr	Tennessee (2)	2400
Dunn, Jennifer	Washington (8)	432
Edwards, Chet	Texas (11)	2459
Ehlers, Vernon J	Michigan (3)	1714
Ehrlich, Robert L., Jr	Maryland (2)	315
Emerson, Jo Ann	Missouri (8)	132
Engel, Eliot L	New York (17)	2303
English, Phil	Pennsylvania (21)	1410
Eshoo, Anna G	California (14)	205
Etheridge, Bob	North Carolina (2)	1641
Evans, Lane	Illinois (17)	2335
Everett, Terry	Alabama (2)	2312
Ewing, Thomas W	Illinois (15)	2417
Farr, Sam	California (17)	1221
Fattah, Chaka	Pennsylvania (2)	1205
Filner, Bob	California (50)	2463
Fletcher, Ernie	Kentucky (6)	1117
Foley, Mark	Florida (16)	113
Forbes, Michael P	New York (1)	125
Ford, Harold E., Jr	Tennessee (9)	325
Fossella, Vito	New York (13)	431
Fowler, Tillie K	Florida (4)	106
Frank, Barney	Massachusetts (4)	2210
Franks, Bob	New Jersey (7)	225
Frelinghuysen, Rodney P	New Jersey (11)	228
Frost, Martin	Texas (24)	2256

Representatives—Continued

[Republicans in roman (221); Democrats in italic (211); Independents in bold (2); total, 435]

Room numbers with three digits are in the Cannon House Office Building (New Jersey and Independence Avenues), four digits beginning with 1 are in the Longworth House Office Building (between South Capitol Street and New Jersey Avenue on Independence Avenue), and four digits beginning with 2 are in the Rayburn House Office Building (between First and South Capitol Streets on Independence Avenue). Members' offices may be reached by phone at 202–225–3121. The most current listing of House Members can be found on the Internet, at clerkweb.house.gov.

Name	State (District)	Room
Gallegly, Elton	California (23)	2427
Ganske, Greg	Iowa (4)	1108
Gejdenson, Sam	Connecticut (2)	2304
Gekas, George W	Pennsylvania (17)	2410
Gephardt, Richard A	Missouri (3)	1226
Gibbons, Jim	Nevada (2)	100
Gilchrest, Wayne T	Maryland (1)	2245
Gillmor, Paul E	Ohio (5)	1203
Gilman, Benjamin A	New York (20)	2449
Gonzalez, Charles A	Texas (20)	327
Goode, Virgil H., Jr	Virginia (5)	1520
Goodlatte, Bob	Virginia (6)	2240
Goodling, William F	Pennsylvania (19)	2107
Gordon, Bart	Tennessee (6)	2368
Goss, Porter J	Florida (14)	108
Graham, Lindsey O	South Carolina (3)	1429
Granger, Kay	Texas (12)	435
Green, Gene	Texas (29)	2429
Green, Mark	Wisconsin (8)	1218
Greenwood, James C	Pennsylvania (8)	2436
Gutierrez, Luis V	Illinois (4)	2438
Gutknecht, Gil	Minnesota (1)	425
Hall, Ralph M	Texas (4)	2221
Hall, Tony P	Ohio (3)	1432
Hansen, James V	Utah (1)	242
Hastert, J. Dennis	Illinois (14)	2263
Hastings, Alcee L	Florida (23)	2235
Hastings, Doc	Washington (4)	1323
Hayes, Robin	North Carolina (8)	130
Hayworth, J. D	Arizona (6)	1023
Hefley, Joel	Colorado (5)	2230
Herger, Wally	California (2)	2433
Hill, Baron P	Indiana (9)	1208
Hill, Rick	Montana (At Large)	1609
Hilleary, Van	Tennessee (4)	114
Hilliard, Earl F	Alabama (7)	1314
Hinchey, Maurice D	New York (26)	2431
Hinojosa, Rubén	Texas (15)	1032
Hobson, David L	Ohio (7)	1514
Hoeffel, Joseph M	Pennsylvania (13)	1229
Hoekstra, Peter	Michigan (2)	1124
Holden, Tim	Pennsylvania (6)	1421
Holt, Rush D	New Jersey (12)	1630
Hooley, Darlene	Oregon (5)	1130
Horn, Stephen	California (38)	2331
Hostettler, John N	Indiana (8)	1507
Houghton, Amo	New York (31)	1110
Hoyer, Steny H	Maryland (5)	1705
Hulshof, Kenny C	Missouri (9)	412
Hunter, Duncan	California (52)	2265
Hutchinson, Asa	Arkansas (3)	1535

Representatives—Continued

[Republicans in roman (221); Democrats in italic (211); Independents in bold (2); total, 435]

Room numbers with three digits are in the Cannon House Office Building (New Jersey and Independence Avenues), four digits beginning with 1 are in the Longworth House Office Building (between South Capitol Street and New Jersey Avenue on Independence Avenue), and four digits beginning with 2 are in the Rayburn House Office Building (between First and South Capitol Streets on Independence Avenue). Members' offices may be reached by phone at 202–225–3121. The most current listing of House Members can be found on the Internet, at clerkweb.house.gov.

Name	State (District)	Room
Hyde, Henry J	Illinois (6)	2110
Inslee, Jay	Washington (1)	308
Isakson, Johnny	Georgia (6)	2428
Istook, Ernest J., Jr	Oklahoma (5)	2404
Jackson, Jesse L., Jr	Illinois (2)	313
Jackson Lee, Sheila	Texas (18)	410
Jefferson, William J	Louisiana (2)	240
Jenkins, William L	Tennessee (1)	1708
John, Christopher	Louisiana (7)	1504
Johnson, Eddie Bernice	Texas (30)	1511
Johnson, Nancy L	Connecticut (6)	2113
Johnson, Sam	Texas (3)	1030
Jones, Stephanie Tubbs	Ohio (11)	1516
Jones, Walter B	North Carolina (3)	422
Kanjorski, Paul E	Pennsylvania (11)	2353
Kaptur, Marcy	Ohio (9)	2366
Kasich, John R	Ohio (12)	1111
Kelly, Sue W	New York (19)	1122
Kennedy, Patrick J	Rhode Island (1)	312
Kildee, Dale E	Michigan (9)	2187
Kilpatrick, Carolyn C	Michigan (15)	503
Kind, Ron	Wisconsin (3)	1713
King, Peter T	New York (3)	403
Kingston, Jack	Georgia (1)	1034
Kleczka, Gerald D	Wisconsin (4)	2301
Klink, Ron	Pennsylvania (4)	2448
Knollenberg, Joe	Michigan (11)	2349
Kolbe, Jim	Arizona (5)	2266
Kucinich, Dennis J	Ohio (10)	1730
Kuykendall, Steven T	California (36)	512
LaFalce, John J	New York (29)	2310
LaHood, Ray	Illinois (18)	329
Lampson, Nick	Texas (9)	417
Lantos, Tom	California (12)	2217
Largent, Steve	Oklahoma (1)	426
Larson, John B	Connecticut (1)	1419
Latham, Tom	Iowa (5)	324
LaTourette, Steven C	Ohio (19)	1224
Lazio, Rick	New York (2)	2244
Leach, James A	Iowa (1)	2186
Lee, Barbara	California (9)	414
Levin, Sander M	Michigan (12)	2268
Lewis, Jerry	California (40)	2112
Lewis, John	Georgia (5)	343
Lewis, Ron	Kentucky (2)	223
Linder, John	Georgia (11)	2447
Lipinski, William O	Illinois (3)	1501
LoBiondo, Frank A	New Jersey (2)	222
Lofgren, Zoe	California (16)	318
Lowey, Nita M	New York (18)	2421
Lucas, Frank D	Oklahoma (6)	438

Representatives—Continued

[Republicans in roman (221); Democrats in italic (211); Independents in bold (2); total, 435]

Room numbers with three digits are in the Cannon House Office Building (New Jersey and Independence Avenues), four digits beginning with 1 are in the Longworth House Office Building (between South Capitol Street and New Jersey Avenue on Independence Avenue), and four digits beginning with 2 are in the Rayburn House Office Building (between First and South Capitol Streets on Independence Avenue). Members' offices may be reached by phone at 202–225–3121. The most current listing of House Members can be found on the Internet, at clerkweb.house.gov.

Name	State (District)	Room
Lucas, Ken	Kentucky (4)	1237
Luther, Bill	Minnesota (6)	117
McCarthy, Carolyn	New York (4)	1725
McCarthy, Karen	Missouri (5)	1330
McCollum, Bill	Florida (8)	2109
McCrery, Jim	Louisiana (4)	2104
McDermott, Jim	Washington (7)	1035
McGovern, James P	Massachusetts (3)	416
McHugh, John M	New York (24)	2441
McInnis, Scott	Colorado (3)	320
McIntosh, David M	Indiana (2)	1610
McIntyre, Mike	North Carolina (7)	1605
McKeon, Howard P. (Buck)	California (25)	2242
McKinney, Cynthia A	Georgia (4)	124
McNulty, Michael R	New York (21)	2161
Maloney, Carolyn B	New York (14)	2430
Maloney, James H	Connecticut (5)	1213
Manzullo, Donald A	Illinois (16)	409
Markey, Edward J	Massachusetts (7)	2108
Martinez, Matthew G	California (31)	2269
Mascara, Frank	Pennsylvania (20)	314
Matsui, Robert T	California (5)	2308
Meehan, Martin T	Massachusetts (5)	2434
Meek, Carrie P	Florida (17)	401
Meeks, Gregory W	New York (6)	1710
Menendez, Robert	New Jersey (13)	405
Metcalf, Jack	Washington (2)	1510
Mica, John L	Florida (7)	2445
Millender-McDonald, Juanita	California (37)	419
Miller, Dan	Florida (13)	102
Miller, Gary G	California (41)	1037
Miller, George	California (7)	2205
Minge, David	Minnesota (2)	1415
Mink, Patsy T	Hawaii (2)	2135
Moakley, John Joseph	Massachusetts (9)	235
Mollohan, Alan B	West Virginia (1)	2346
Moore, Dennis	Kansas (3)	506
Moran, James P	Virginia (8)	2239
Moran, Jerry	Kansas (1)	1519
Morella, Constance A	Maryland (8)	2228
Murtha, John P	Pennsylvania (12)	2423
Myrick, Sue Wilkins	North Carolina (9)	230
Nadler, Jerrold	New York (8)	2334
Napolitano, Grace F	California (34)	1407
Neal, Richard E	Massachusetts (2)	2236
Nethercutt, George R., Jr	Washington (5)	1527
Ney, Robert W	Ohio (18)	1024
Northup, Anne M	Kentucky (3)	1004
Norwood, Charlie	Georgia (10)	1707
Nussle, Jim	Iowa (2)	303
Oberstar, James L	Minnesota (8)	2365

Representatives—Continued

[Republicans in roman (221); Democrats in italic (211); Independents in bold (2); total, 435]

Room numbers with three digits are in the Cannon House Office Building (New Jersey and Independence Avenues), four digits beginning with 1 are in the Longworth House Office Building (between South Capitol Street and New Jersey Avenue on Independence Avenue), and four digits beginning with 2 are in the Rayburn House Office Building (between First and South Capitol Streets on Independence Avenue). Members' offices may be reached by phone at 202–225–3121. The most current listing of House Members can be found on the Internet, at clerkweb.house.gov.

Name	State (District)	Room
Obey, David R	Wisconsin (7)	2314
Olver, John W	Massachusetts (1)	1027
Ortiz, Solomon P	Texas (27)	2136
Ose, Doug	California (3)	1508
Owens, Major R	New York (11)	2305
Oxley, Michael G	Ohio (4)	2233
Packard, Ron	California (48)	2372
Pallone, Frank, Jr	New Jersey (6)	420
Pascrell, Bill, Jr	New Jersey (8)	1722
Pastor, Ed	Arizona (2)	2465
Paul, Ron	Texas (14)	203
Payne, Donald M	New Jersey (10)	2209
Pease, Edward A	Indiana (7)	119
Pelosi, Nancy	California (8)	2457
Peterson, Collin C	Minnesota (7)	2159
Peterson, John E	Pennsylvania (5)	307
Petri, Thomas E	Wisconsin (6)	2462
Phelps, David D	Illinois (19)	1523
Pickering, Charles W. (Chip)	Mississippi (3)	427
Pickett, Owen B	Virginia (2)	2133
Pitts, Joseph R	Pennsylvania (16)	504
Pombo, Richard W	California (11)	2411
Pomeroy, Earl	North Dakota (At Large)	1533
Porter, John Edward	Illinois (10)	2373
Portman, Rob	Ohio (2)	238
Price, David E	North Carolina (4)	2162
Pryce, Deborah	Ohio (15)	221
Quinn, Jack	New York (30)	229
Radanovich, George	California (19)	123
Rahall, Nick J., II	West Virginia (3)	2307
Ramstad, Jim	Minnesota (3)	103
Rangel, Charles B	New York (15)	2354
Regula, Ralph	Ohio (16)	2309
Reyes, Silvestre	Texas (16)	514
Reynolds, Thomas M	New York (27)	413
Riley, Bob	Alabama (3)	322
Rivers, Lynn N	Michigan (13)	1724
Rodriguez, Ciro D	Texas (28)	323
Roemer, Tim	Indiana (3)	2352
Rogan, James E	California (27)	126
Rogers, Harold	Kentucky (5)	2470
Rohrabacher, Dana	California (45)	2338
Ros-Lehtinen, Ileana	Florida (18)	2160
Rothman, Steven R	New Jersey (9)	1607
Roukema, Marge	New Jersey (5)	2469
Roybal-Allard, Lucille	California (33)	2435
Royce, Edward R	California (39)	1133
Rush, Bobby L	Illinois (1)	2416
Ryan, Paul	Wisconsin (1)	1217
Ryun, Jim	Kansas (2)	330
Sabo, Martin Olav	Minnesota (5)	2336

Representatives—Continued

[Republicans in roman (221); Democrats in italic (211); Independents in bold (2); total, 435]

Room numbers with three digits are in the Cannon House Office Building (New Jersey and Independence Avenues), four digits beginning with 1 are in the Longworth House Office Building (between South Capitol Street and New Jersey Avenue on Independence Avenue), and four digits beginning with 2 are in the Rayburn House Office Building (between First and South Capitol Streets on Independence Avenue). Members' offices may be reached by phone at 202–225–3121. The most current listing of House Members can be found on the Internet, at clerkweb.house.gov.

Name	State (District)	Room
Salmon, Matt	Arizona (1)	115
Sanchez, Loretta	California (46)	1529
Sanders, Bernard	Vermont (At Large)	2202
Sandlin, Max	Texas (1)	214
Sanford, Marshall (Mark)	South Carolina (1)	1233
Sawyer, Tom	Ohio (14)	1414
Saxton, Jim	New Jersey (3)	339
Scarborough, Joe	Florida (1)	127
Schaffer, Bob	Colorado (4)	212
Schakowsky, Janice D	Illinois (9)	515
Scott, Robert C	Virginia (3)	2464
Sensenbrenner, F. James, Jr	Wisconsin (9)	2332
Serrano, José E	New York (16)	2342
Sessions, Pete	Texas (5)	1318
Shadegg, John B	Arizona (4)	430
Shaw, E. Clay, Jr	Florida (22)	2408
Shays, Christopher	Connecticut (4)	1126
Sherman, Brad	California (24)	1524
Sherwood, Don	Pennsylvania (10)	1223
Shimkus, John	Illinois (20)	513
Shows, Ronnie	Mississippi (4)	509
Shuster, Bud	Pennsylvania (9)	2188
Simpson, Michael K	Idaho (2)	1440
Sisisky, Norman	Virginia (4)	2371
Skeen, Joe	New Mexico (2)	2302
Skelton, Ike	Missouri (4)	2206
Slaughter, Louise McIntosh	New York (28)	2347
Smith, Adam	Washington (9)	116
Smith, Christopher H	New Jersey (4)	2370
Smith, Lamar S	Texas (21)	2231
Smith, Nick	Michigan (7)	306
Snyder, Vic	Arkansas (2)	1319
Souder, Mark E	Indiana (4)	109
Spence, Floyd	South Carolina (2)	2405
Spratt, John M., Jr	South Carolina (5)	1536
Stabenow, Debbie	Michigan (8)	1039
Stark, Fortney Pete	California (13)	239
Stearns, Cliff	Florida (6)	2227
Stenholm, Charles W	Texas (17)	1211
Strickland, Ted	Ohio (6)	336
Stump, Bob	Arizona (3)	211
Stupak, Bart	Michigan (1)	2348
Sununu, John E	New Hampshire (1)	316
Sweeney, John E	New York (22)	437
Talent, James M	Missouri (2)	1022
Tancredo, Thomas G	Colorado (6)	1123
Tanner, John S	Tennessee (8)	1127
Tauscher, Ellen O	California (10)	1239
Tauzin, W. J. (Billy)	Louisiana (3)	2183
Taylor, Charles H	North Carolina (11)	231
Taylor, Gene	Mississippi (5)	2311

Representatives—Continued

[Republicans in roman (221); Democrats in italic (211); Independents in bold (2); total, 435]

Room numbers with three digits are in the Cannon House Office Building (New Jersey and Independence Avenues), four digits beginning with 1 are in the Longworth House Office Building (between South Capitol Street and New Jersey Avenue on Independence Avenue), and four digits beginning with 2 are in the Rayburn House Office Building (between First and South Capitol Streets on Independence Avenue). Members' offices may be reached by phone at 202–225–3121. The most current listing of House Members can be found on the Internet, at clerkweb.house.gov.

Name	State (District)	Room
Terry, Lee	Nebraska (2)	1728
Thomas, William M	California (21)	2208
Thompson, Bennie G	Mississippi (2)	1408
Thompson, Mike	California (1)	415
Thornberry, Mac	Texas (13)	131
Thune, John R	South Dakota (At Large)	1005
Thurman, Karen L	Florida (5)	440
Tiahrt, Todd	Kansas (4)	428
Tierney, John F	Massachusetts (6)	120
Toomey, Patrick J	Pennsylvania (15)	511
Towns, Edolphus	New York (10)	2232
Traficant, James A., Jr	Ohio (17)	2446
Turner, Jim	Texas (2)	208
Udall, Mark	Colorado (2)	128
Udall, Tom	New Mexico (3)	502
Upton, Fred	Michigan (6)	2333
Velázquez, Nydia M	New York (12)	2241
Vento, Bruce F	Minnesota (4)	2413
Visclosky, Peter J	Indiana (1)	2313
Vitter, David	Louisiana (1)	2406
Walden, Greg	Oregon (2)	1404
Walsh, James T	New York (25)	2351
Wamp, Zach	Tennessee (3)	423
Waters, Maxine	California (35)	2344
Watkins, Wes	Oklahoma (3)	1401
Watt, Melvin L	North Carolina (12)	1230
Watts, J. C., Jr	Oklahoma (4)	1210
Waxman, Henry A	California (29)	2204
Weiner, Anthony D	New York (9)	501
Weldon, Curt	Pennsylvania (7)	2452
Weldon, Dave	Florida (15)	332
Weller, Jerry	Illinois (11)	424
Wexler, Robert	Florida (19)	213
Weygand, Robert A	Rhode Island (2)	215
Whitfield, Ed	Kentucky (1)	236
Wicker, Roger F	Mississippi (1)	206
Wilson, Heather	New Mexico (1)	226
Wise, Robert E., Jr	West Virginia (2)	2367
Wolf, Frank R	Virginia (10)	241
Woolsey, Lynn C	California (6)	439
Wu, David	Oregon (1)	510
Wynn, Albert Russell	Maryland (4)	407
Young, C. W. Bill	Florida (10)	2407
Young, Don	Alaska (At Large)	2111
	Delegates	
Christensen, Donna M.C	Virgin Islands	1711
Faleomavaega, Eni F.H	American Samoa	2422
Norton, Eleanor Holmes	District of Columbia	1424
Underwood, Robert A	Guam	2418

Representatives—Continued

[Republicans in roman (221); Democrats in italic (211); Independents in bold (2); total, 435]

Room numbers with three digits are in the Cannon House Office Building (New Jersey and Independence Avenues), four digits beginning with 1 are in the Longworth House Office Building (between South Capitol Street and New Jersey Avenue on Independence Avenue), and four digits beginning with 2 are in the Rayburn House Office Building (between First and South Capitol Streets on Independence Avenue). Members' offices may be reached by phone at 202–225–3121. The most current listing of House Members can be found on the Internet, at clerkweb.house.gov.

Name	State (District)	Room
Resident Commissioner		
Romero-Barceló, Carlos A	Puerto Rico	2443

For further information concerning the United States Senate, contact the Secretary of the Senate, The Capitol, Washington, DC 20510. Phone, 202–224–2115. Internet, www.senate.gov. For further information concerning the House of Representatives, contact the Clerk, The Capitol, Washington, DC 20515. Phone, 202–225–7000. Internet, www.house.gov.

ARCHITECT OF THE CAPITOL

U.S. Capitol Building, Washington, DC 20515
Phone, 202–228–1793. Internet, www.aoc.gov.

Architect of the Capitol	Alan M. Hantman
Assistant Architect of the Capitol	Michael G. Turnbull
Head, Architecture Division	Bruce Arthur
Special Assistant	James E. Ellison
Superintendent of Construction	William B. Holmes
Director of Engineering	Dan E. Hanlon
Assistant Director of Engineering	Scott Birkhead
Administrative Assistant	Herbert M. Franklin
Director, Human Resources Management Division	Hector E. Suarez
Director, Equal Employment Opportunity	Kathleen Gause
Director, Information Resources Management	Rick Kashurba
Employment Counsel	Kevin Mulshine
Curator	Barbara Wolanin
Inspector General	Arthur L. McIntye
Executive Officer	Lynne M. Theiss
Director, Life Safety Programs Division	Phil Tapper
Head, Procurement Division	Richard N. Mueller
Safety Officer, Occupational Health, Environmental, and Safety Office	Charles Bowman
Budget Officer/Director of Financial Services	W. Stuart Pregnall III
Assistant Budget Officer	John T. Bortlein, Jr.
Accounting Officer	Elliott Burnham
General Counsel	Charles K. Tyler
Senior Labor-Management Counsel	Margaret Cox
Senior Landscape Architect	Matthew Evans
Superintendent, House Office Buildings	Robert Miley
Superintendent, Senate Office Buildings	Lawrence R. Stoffel
Supervising Engineer, Library of Congress	(vacancy)
Supervising Engineer of the U.S. Capitol	Amita N. Poole

The Architect of the Capitol is responsible for the care and maintenance of the U.S. Capitol and nearby buildings and grounds and for implementing construction, renovation, conservation, and landscape improvement projects as authorized by the Congress.

The Architect of the Capitol is charged with operating and maintaining the buildings of the Capitol complex committed to his care by Congress. Permanent authority for the care and maintenance of the Capitol was established by the act of August 15, 1876 (40 U.S.C. 162, 163). The Architect's duties include the mechanical and structural maintenance of the Capitol, the conservation and care of works of art in the building under the Architect's jurisdiction, the upkeep and improvement of the Capitol grounds, and the arrangement of inaugural and other ceremonies held in the building or on the grounds. Legislation has been enacted from time to time to provide for additional buildings and grounds placed under the jurisdiction of the Architect of the Capitol.

In addition to the Capitol, the Architect is responsible for the upkeep of all of the congressional office buildings, the Library of Congress buildings, the U.S. Supreme Court building, the Thurgood Marshall Federal Judiciary Building, the Capitol Power Plant, the Capitol Police headquarters, and the Robert A. Taft Memorial. The Architect performs his duties in connection with the Senate side of the Capitol, the Senate office buildings, and the operation of the Senate restaurants subject to the approval of the Senate Committee on Rules and Administration. In matters of general policy in connection with the House office buildings and the Capitol Power Plant, his activities are subject to the approval and direction of the House Office Building Commission. The Architect is under the direction of the Speaker in matters concerning the House side of the Capitol. He is subject to the oversight of the Committee on House Administration with respect to many administrative matters affecting operations on the House side of the Capitol complex. In addition, the Architect of the Capitol serves as the Acting Director of the U.S. Botanic Garden under the Joint Committee on the Library.

The position of Architect of the Capitol was historically filled by Presidential appointment for an indefinite term. Legislation enacted in 1989 provides that the Architect is to be appointed for a term of 10 years by the President, with the advice and consent of the Senate, from a list of 3 candidates recommended by a congressional commission. Upon confirmation by the Senate, the Architect becomes an official of the legislative branch as an officer and agent of Congress; he is eligible for reappointment after completion of his term. The present Architect, Alan M. Hantman, is the 10th to hold this position since the office was established in 1793 and the first to be appointed in accordance with the new procedure.

Recent and ongoing projects carried out by the Architect of the Capitol include the rehabilitation of the Capitol dome; conservation of murals and decorative paintings in the first-floor Senate corridors in the Capitol; repair of the Capitol terraces; conversion of the Capitol courtyards into meeting rooms; replacement of worn Minton tile in the Senate corridors of the Capitol; conservation of the Statue of Freedom atop the Capitol dome; completion of the murals in the first-floor House corridors; improvement of speech-reinforcement, electrical, and fire-protection systems in the Capitol and congressional office buildings; removal of architectural barriers throughout the Capitol complex; preparation and publication of a new book on the artist Constantino Brumidi, whose paintings decorate much of the Capitol; installation of an improved Senate subway system; preparation of a telecommunications plan for the legislative branch agencies; work on security improvements within the Capitol complex; construction of new House and Senate child care facilities; construction of a new Senate Page school; renovation, restoration, and modification of the interiors and exteriors of the Thomas Jefferson and John Adams Buildings of the Library of Congress and provision of off-site book storage facilities for the Library; management oversight of the Thurgood Marshall Federal Judiciary Building; design and construction of the National Garden adjacent to the U.S. Botanic Garden Conservatory; restoration of the U.S.Botanic Garden Conservatory; and planning for a proposed Capitol Visitor Center.

For further information, contact the Office of the Architect of the Capitol, U.S. Capitol Building, Washington, DC 20515. Phone, 202–228–1793. Internet, www.aoc.gov.

UNITED STATES BOTANIC GARDEN

Office of Executive Director, 245 First Street SW., Washington, DC 20024
Phone, 202–225–8333. Internet, www.aoc.gov.

Conservatory, Maryland Avenue, First to Second Streets SW., Washington, DC 20024
Phone, 202–225–6647

Production Facility, 4700 Shepherd Parkway SW., Washington, DC 20032
Phone, 202–563–2220

Director (Architect of the Capitol)	ALAN M. HANTMAN
Executive Director	(VACANCY)

The United States Botanic Garden informs visitors about the aesthetic, cultural, economic, therapeutic, and ecological importance of plants to the well-being of humankind.

The U.S. Botanic Garden carries out its mission by presenting artistic displays of plants, exhibits, and a program of educational activities; promoting botanical knowledge through the cultivation of an ordered collection of plants; fostering plant conservation by acting as a repository for endangered species; and growing plants for the beautification of the Capitol complex. Uniquely situated at the heart of the U.S. Government, the Botanic Garden seeks to promote the exchange of ideas and information relevant to this mission among national and international visitors and policymakers.

Collections of the U.S. Botanic Garden include orchids, epiphytes, bromeliads, carnivorous plants, ferns, cycads, cacti, succulents, medicinal plants, rare and endangered plants, and plants valued as sources of food, beverages, fibers, and other industrial products.

The U.S. Botanic Garden is currently undergoing a significant expansion and transformation. The Conservatory, one of the largest structures of its kind in this country, closed to the public on September 2, 1997, for a complete renovation. In addition to upgraded amenities for visitors, it will feature 12 new exhibit and plant display areas interpreting plants in their relationship to humankind and to the environment. The Conservatory is expected to reopen in the year 2001. Construction for the National Garden, a 3-acre site just west of the Conservatory, is scheduled for 2001. This new public facility will feature a First Ladies water garden, a formal rose garden, a showcase garden displaying the outstanding native plants of the Mid-Atlantic region in naturalistic settings, and the Senator John Heinz Environmental Learning Center.

Outdoor plantings are showcased in Bartholdi Park, a home landscape demonstration area. Each of the displays is sized and scaled for suitability in an urban or suburban house site. The gardens display ornamental plants that perform well in this region arrayed in a variety of styles and themes. Also located in this park is Bartholdi Fountain, created by Frederic-Auguste Bartholdi (1834–1904), sculptor of the Statue of Liberty.

The Botanic Garden makes available many rare and interesting botanical specimens for study to students, botanists, and floriculturists . In addition to educational programs and special exhibits, a horticultural hotline is available to answer questions from the public.

The U.S. Botanic Garden was founded in 1820 under the auspices of the Columbian Institute for the Promotion of Arts and Sciences, an organization that was the outgrowth of an association known as the Metropolitan Society and that received its charter from Congress on April 20, 1818. The Garden continued under the direction of this Institute until 1837, when the Institute ceased to exist as an active organization.

The Botanic Garden remained abandoned until 1842, when it became necessary for the Government to provide accommodations for the botanical collections brought to Washington, DC, from the South Seas by the U.S. Exploring Expedition of 1838–42, under the leadership of Capt. Charles Wilkes. The collections were placed temporarily on exhibition at the Patent Office upon return of the expedition in June 1842. The first greenhouse for this purpose was constructed in 1842 on a lot behind the Patent Office Building under the direction and control of the Joint Committee of Congress on the Library, from funds appropriated by Congress.

The act of May 15, 1850 (9 Stat. 427), provided for the relocation of the Botanic Garden under the direction of the Joint Committee on the Library. The site selected was on The Mall at the west end of the Capitol Grounds, practically the same site the Garden occupied during the period it functioned under the Columbia Institute. This site was later enlarged, and the main area continued to serve as the principal Botanic Garden site from 1850 to 1933, when the Garden was relocated to its present site.

Although the Botanic Garden began functioning as a Government-owned institution in 1842, the records indicate that it was not until 1856 that the maintenance of the Garden was specifically placed under the direction of the Joint Committee on the Library and a regular, annual appropriation was provided by Congress (11 Stat. 104).

At the present time the Joint Committee exercises its supervision through the Architect of the Capitol, who has been serving as Acting Director since 1934.

For further information concerning the United States Botanic Garden, contact the Office of the Architect of the Capitol, U.S. Capitol Building, Washington, DC 20515. Phone, 202–228–1793. Horticulture Hotline, 202–563–1222. Internet, www.aoc.gov.

GENERAL ACCOUNTING OFFICE

441 G Street NW., Washington, DC 20548
Phone, 202–512–3000. Internet, www.gao.gov.

Comptroller General of the United States	David M. Walker
Deputy Comptroller General of the United States	(vacancy)
Principal Assistant Comptroller General	Gene L. Dodaro

Assistant Comptroller General, Accounting and Information Management Division	JEFFREY C. STEINHOFF, *Acting*
Assistant Comptroller General for Field Offices	THOMAS J. BREW
Assistant Comptroller General for Quality and Risk Management	RICHARD L. HEMBRA
Assistant Comptroller General, General Government Division	NANCY KINGSBURY, *Acting*
Assistant Comptroller General, Health, Education, and Human Services Division	VICTOR S. REZENDES
Assistant Comptroller General, National Security and International Affairs Division	HENRY L. HINTON, JR.
Assistant Comptroller General, Resources, Community, and Economic Development Division	KEITH O. FULTZ
Assistant Comptroller General for Special Investigations	ROBERT H. HAST, *Acting*
Chief Mission Support Officer	SALLYANNE HARPER
Assistant Comptroller General, Office of Information Management and Communications	ANTHONY CICCO, *Acting*
Director, Administration and Resources Management for Mission Support Units	CHERYL GIDEON
Director, Personnel	PATRICIA M. RODGERS
Chief Accountant	PHILIP CALDER
Support Functions:	
Chair, Personnel Appeals Board	MICHAEL WOLF
Chief Economist	LOREN YAGER, *Acting*
Director, Civil Rights Office	ALLEN ELLIOTT, *Acting*
Director, Office of Congressional Relations	HELEN H. HSING
Director, Office of Counseling and Career Development	CHRISTINE SMITH, *Acting*
Director, Office of International Liaison	LINDA L. WEEKS
Director, Office of Public Affairs	SUSAN L. BECKER, *Acting*
Director, Office of Recruitment	PAUL JONES
Director, Training Institute	ANNE K. KLEIN
General Counsel	ROBERT P. MURPHY
Inspector General	FRANCES GARCIA

The General Accounting Office is the investigative arm of the Congress and is charged with examining all matters relating to the receipt and disbursement of public funds.

The General Accounting Office (GAO) was established by the Budget and Accounting Act of 1921 (31 U.S.C. 702), to independently audit Government agencies. Over the years, the Congress has expanded GAO's audit authority, added new responsibilities and duties, and strengthened GAO's ability to perform independently.

The Office is under the control and direction of the Comptroller General of the United States, who is appointed by the President with the advice and consent of the Senate for a term of 15 years.

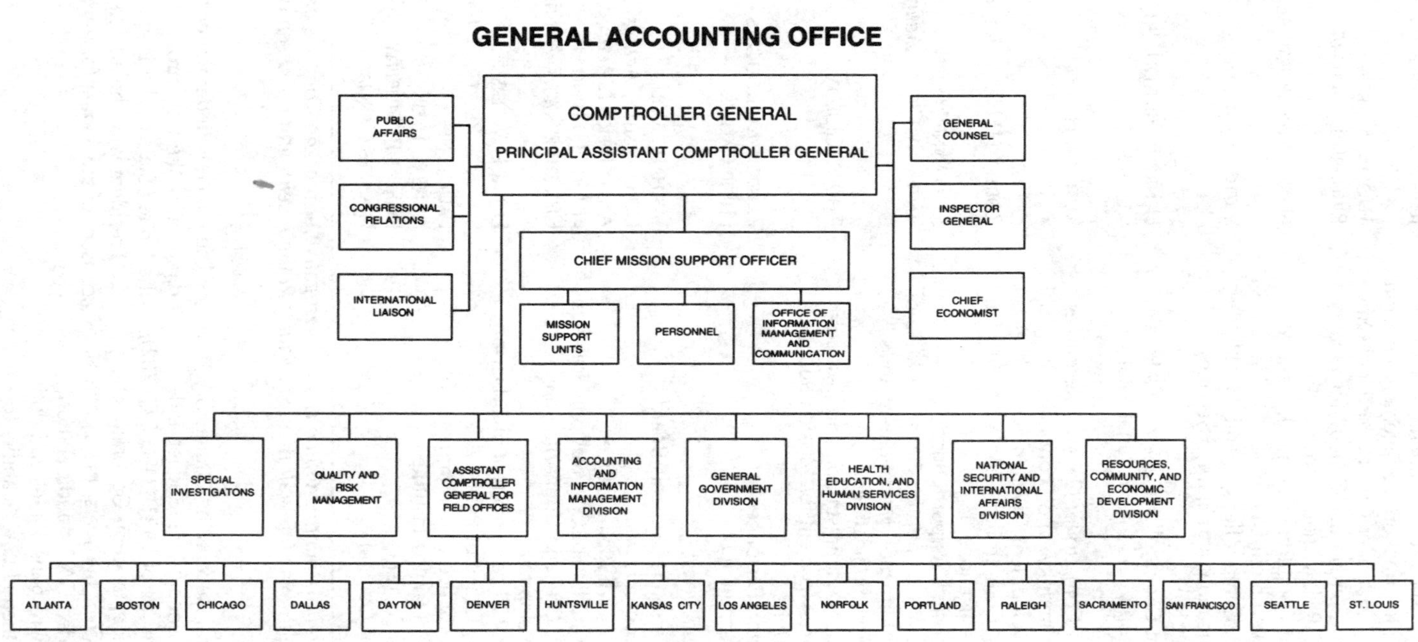
GENERAL ACCOUNTING OFFICE
COMPTROLLER GENERAL
PRINCIPAL ASSISTANT COMPTROLLER GENERAL
PUBLIC AFFAIRS
CONGRESSIONAL RELATIONS
INTERNATIONAL LIAISON
GENERAL COUNSEL
INSPECTOR GENERAL
CHIEF ECONOMIST
CHIEF MISSION SUPPORT OFFICER
MISSION SUPPORT UNITS
PERSONNEL
OFFICE OF INFORMATION MANAGEMENT AND COMMUNICATION
SPECIAL INVESTIGATONS
QUALITY AND RISK MANAGEMENT
ASSISTANT COMPTROLLER GENERAL FOR FIELD OFFICES
ACCOUNTING AND INFORMATION MANAGEMENT DIVISION
GENERAL GOVERNMENT DIVISION
HEALTH EDUCATION, AND HUMAN SERVICES DIVISION
NATIONAL SECURITY AND INTERNATIONAL AFFAIRS DIVISION
RESOURCES, COMMUNITY, AND ECONOMIC DEVELOPMENT DIVISION
ATLANTA
BOSTON
CHICAGO
DALLAS
DAYTON
DENVER
HUNTSVILLE
KANSAS CITY
LOS ANGELES
NORFOLK
PORTLAND
RALEIGH
SACRAMENTO
SAN FRANCISCO
SEATTLE
ST. LOUIS

Activities

Audits and Evaluations Supporting the Congress is GAO's fundamental responsibility. In meeting this objective, GAO performs a variety of services, the most prominent of which are audits and evaluations of Government programs and activities. The majority of these reviews are made in response to specific congressional requests. The Office is required to perform work requested by committee chairpersons and, as a matter of policy, assigns equal status to requests from Ranking Minority Members. The Office also responds to individual Member requests, as possible. Other assignments are initiated pursuant to standing commitments to congressional committees, and some reviews are specifically required by law. Finally, some assignments are independently undertaken in accordance with GAO's basic legislative responsibilities.

The ability to review practically any Government function requires a multidisciplined staff able to conduct assignments wherever needed. The Office's staff has expertise in a variety of disciplines, including accounting, law, public and business administration, economics, the social and physical sciences, and others.

The Office is organized so that staff members concentrate on specific subject areas, enabling them to develop a detailed level of knowledge. When an assignment requires specialized experience not available within GAO, outside experts assist the permanent staff. Staff members go wherever necessary on assignments, working onsite to gather data and observe firsthand how Government programs and activities are carried out.

Legal Services The Office provides various legal services to the Congress. In response to inquiries from committees and Members, the Comptroller General provides advice on legal issues involving Government programs and activities. The Office is also available to assist in drafting legislation and reviewing legislative proposals before the Congress. In addition, it reviews and reports to the Congress on proposed rescissions and deferrals of Government funds.

Other legal services include resolving bid protests that challenge Government contract awards and assisting Government agencies in interpreting the laws governing the expenditure of public funds.

Investigations GAO's staff of professional investigators conducts special investigations and assists auditors and evaluators when they encounter possible criminal and civil misconduct. When warranted, GAO refers the results of its investigations to the Department of Justice and other law enforcement authorities.

Auditing and Accounting Policy GAO issues *Government Auditing Standards* for audits of Government organizations, programs, activities, and functions. These standards pertain to auditors' professional qualifications, the quality of audit effort, and the characteristics of professional and meaningful audit reports.

The Comptroller General, along with the Secretary of the Treasury and the Director of the Office of Management and Budget, serves as a principal on the Federal Accounting Standards Advisory Board. The Board considers and recommends issuance of accounting standards and principles and provides interpretations of existing ones.

Reporting GAO offers a range of products to communicate the results of its work. The type of product depends on the assignment's objectives and the needs of the intended user. Product types include testimony, oral briefings, and written reports. Virtually all of GAO's reports are available to the public.

A list of GAO reports issued or released during the previous month is furnished monthly to the Congress, its Members, and committees. Copies of GAO reports are also furnished to interested congressional parties; Federal, State, local, and foreign governments; members of the press; college faculty, students, and libraries; and nonprofit organizations.

Copies of unclassified reports are available from the U.S. General

Accounting Office, P.O. Box 37050, Washington, DC 20013. Phone, 202–512–6000. The first copy of each report and testimony is free; additional copies are $2 each. There is a 25-percent discount on orders of 100 or more copies mailed to a single address. Orders should be sent with a check or money order payable to the Superintendent of Documents. VISA and MasterCard are also accepted.

Electronic Access Reports, Comptroller General decisions, and GAO special publications may be obtained on the Internet, at www.gao.gov. Information about the reorganization of GAO, taking place in 2000, is also available on the Internet.

For further information, contact the Office of Public Affairs, General Accounting Office, 441 G Street NW., Washington, DC 20548. Phone, 202–512–4800. Internet, www.gao.gov.

GOVERNMENT PRINTING OFFICE

732 North Capitol Street NW., Washington, DC 20401
Phone, 202–512–0000. Internet, www.access.gpo.gov.

Public Printer	MICHAEL F. DIMARIO
Deputy Public Printer	ROBERT T. MANSKER
Superintendent of Documents	FRANCIS J. BUCKLEY, JR.
Director, Documents Sales Service	(VACANCY)
Director, Electronic Information Dissemination	(VACANCY)
Director, Library Programs Service	ERNEST G. (GIL) BALDWIN
Chief, Technical Support Group	(VACANCY)
Director, Customer Services	JAMES C. BRADLEY
Superintendent, Congressional Printing Management Division	CHARLES C. COOK, SR.
Superintendent, Departmental Accounts Representative Division	GEORGE S. O'DONNOGHUE
Superintendent, Typography and Design Division	JOHN W. SAPP
Director, Institute for Federal Printing and Electronic Publishing	LOIS SCHUTTE
Manager, Printing Procurement Department	MEREDITH L. (BO) ARNESON
Manager, Production Department	DONALD L. LADD
Manager, Quality Control and Technical Department	ROBERT H. THOMAS
Comptroller	ROBERT B. (BRUCE) HOLSTEIN
Director, Congressional, Legislative, and Public Affairs	ANDREW M. SHERMAN
Director, Engineering Service	JOSEPH A. PALANK
Director, Materials Management Service	JAMES K. MEHAN
Director, Occupational Health and Environmental Services	WILLIAM T. HARRIS
Director, Office of Administrative Support	RAYMOND J. GARVEY
Director, Office of Budget	WILLIAM M. GUY
Director, Office of Equal Employment Opportunity	NADINE L. ELZY
Director, Office of Information Resources Management	PATRICIA G. GARDNER

Director, Office of Labor and Employee Relations	Neal H. Fine
Director, Office of Personnel	Edward A. Blatt
Director, Office of Planning	Thomas J. Muldoon
Director, Policy Coordination Staff	Vincent F. Arendes
Administrative Law Judge	Kerry L. Miller
General Counsel	Anthony J. Zagami
Inspector General	Robert G. Andary

The mission of the Government Printing Office is to inform the Nation by producing, procuring, and disseminating printed and electronic publications of the Congress as well as the executive departments and establishments of the Federal Government.

The Government Printing Office (GPO) began operations on June 23, 1860. The activities of GPO are defined in the public printing and documents chapters of title 44 of the U.S. Code.

The Public Printer, who serves as the head of GPO, is appointed by the President with the advice and consent of the Senate.

Activities

The Government Printing Office produces and procures printed and electronic publications for Congress and the departments and establishments of the Federal Government. It furnishes printing supplies to all governmental activities on order. It catalogs, distributes, and sells Government publications in printed and electronic formats.

Printing processes used are electronic prepress, including networked on-demand printing systems; offset presswork, featuring computer-to-plate technology; and bookbinding. Electronic databases prepared for printing are premastered for CD–ROM replication and are used to provide online access.

GPO invites bids from commercial suppliers on a wide variety of printing and reproduction services, awards and administers contracts, and maintains liaison between ordering agencies and contractors.

GPO sells approximately 10,000 different printed and electronic publications that originate in various Government agencies. It administers the depository library program through which a comprehensive range of Government publications are made available for the free use of the public in approximately 1,300 libraries throughout the country. GPO also provides online access to more than 170,000 Federal Government publications, including the *Congressional Record* and the *Federal Register*. GPO's online information service, GPO Access, may be reached at www.access.gpo.gov/su_docs.

Sources of Information

Congressional, Legislative, and Public Affairs General inquiries about GPO should be directed to the Office of Congressional, Legislative, and Public Affairs. Phone, 202–512–1991. Fax, 202–512–1293. E-mail, gpoinfo@gpo.gov.

Contracts Commercial printers interested in Government printing contract opportunities should direct inquiries to the Manager, Printing Procurement Department, Government Printing Office, Washington, DC 20401. Phone, 202–512–0327. Internet, www.access.gpo.gov/procurement/index.html. Information is also available from the GPO Regional Printing Procurement Offices listed below.

Regional Printing and Procurement Offices—Government Printing Office

(R: Regional Printing Procurement Office; S: Satellite Printing Procurement Office)

Office	Address	Telephone
ATLANTA, GA (R)	Suite 110, 1888 Emery St., 30318–2542	404–605–9160

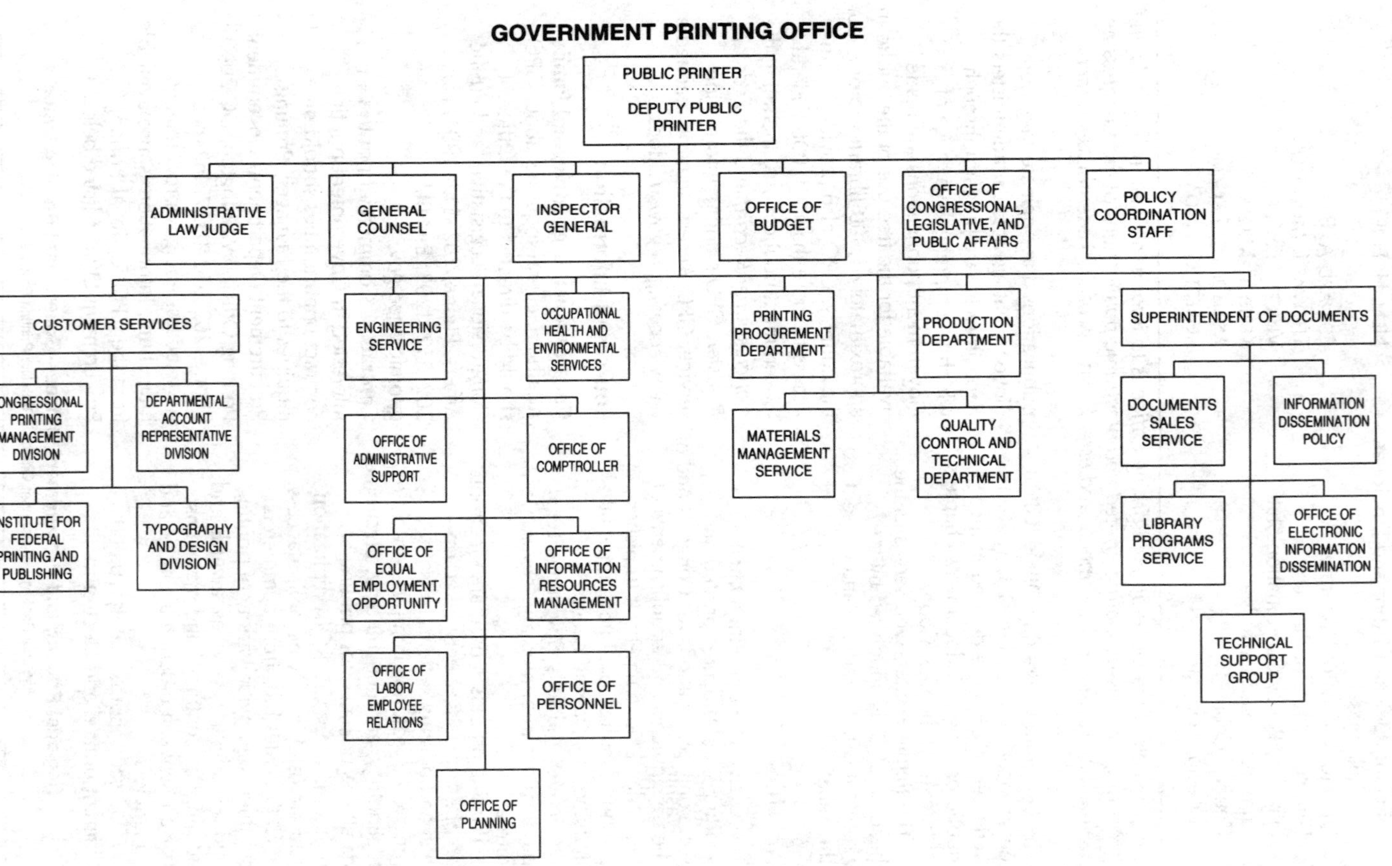
GOVERNMENT PRINTING OFFICE
PUBLIC PRINTER
DEPUTY PUBLIC PRINTER
ADMINISTRATIVE LAW JUDGE
GENERAL COUNSEL
INSPECTOR GENERAL
OFFICE OF BUDGET
OFFICE OF CONGRESSIONAL, LEGISLATIVE, AND PUBLIC AFFAIRS
POLICY COORDINATION STAFF
CUSTOMER SERVICES
CONGRESSIONAL PRINTING MANAGEMENT DIVISION
DEPARTMENTAL ACCOUNT REPRESENTATIVE DIVISION
INSTITUTE FOR FEDERAL PRINTING AND PUBLISHING
TYPOGRAPHY AND DESIGN DIVISION
ENGINEERING SERVICE
OCCUPATIONAL HEALTH AND ENVIRONMENTAL SERVICES
OFFICE OF ADMINISTRATIVE SUPPORT
OFFICE OF COMPTROLLER
OFFICE OF EQUAL EMPLOYMENT OPPORTUNITY
OFFICE OF INFORMATION RESOURCES MANAGEMENT
OFFICE OF LABOR/ EMPLOYEE RELATIONS
OFFICE OF PERSONNEL
OFFICE OF PLANNING
PRINTING PROCUREMENT DEPARTMENT
PRODUCTION DEPARTMENT
MATERIALS MANAGEMENT SERVICE
QUALITY CONTROL AND TECHNICAL DEPARTMENT
SUPERINTENDENT OF DOCUMENTS
DOCUMENTS SALES SERVICE
INFORMATION DISSEMINATION POLICY
LIBRARY PROGRAMS SERVICE
OFFICE OF ELECTRONIC INFORMATION DISSEMINATION
TECHNICAL SUPPORT GROUP

Regional Printing and Procurement Offices—Government Printing Office

(R: Regional Printing Procurement Office; S: Satellite Printing Procurement Office)

Office	Address	Telephone
Charleston, SC (S)	2825 Ave. D N., 29405–1819	843–743–2036
BOSTON, MA (R)	28 Court Square, 02108–2504	617–720–3680
CHICAGO, IL (R)	Suite 810, 200 N. LaSalle St., 60601–1055	312–353–3916
COLUMBUS, OH (R)	Suite 112–B, 1335 Dublin Rd., 43215–7034	614–488–4616
DALLAS, TX (R)	Rm. 7B7, 1100 Commerce St., 75242–0395	214–767–0451
New Orleans, LA (S)	Rm. 310, 423 Canal St., 70130–2352	504–589–2538
Oklahoma City, OK (S)	Suite 100, 3420 D Ave., Tinker AFB, OK 73145–9188	405–610–4146
San Antonio, TX (S)	Bldg. 1552, Door 2, Kelly AFB, TX 78241–5000	210–924–4245
DENVER, CO (R)	Rm. D–1010, Bldg. 53, Denver Federal Center, 80225–0347	303–236–5292
HAMPTON, VA (R)	Suite 400, 11836 Canon Blvd., Newport News, VA 23606–2555	757–873–2800
LOS ANGELES, CA (R)	Suite 110, 12501 E. Imperial Hwy., Norwalk, CA 90650–3136	562–863–1708
San Diego, CA (S)	Suite 109, 2221 Camino Del Rio S., 92108–3609	619–497–6050
NEW YORK, NY (R)	Rm. 709, 201 Varick St., 10014–4879	212–620–3321
PHILADELPHIA, PA (R)	Suite A–190, 928 Jaymore Rd., Southampton, PA 18966–3820	215–364–6465
Pittsburgh, PA (S)	Rm. 501, 1000 Liberty Ave., 15222–4000	412–395–4858
RAPID RESPONSE CENTER	Bldg. 136, Washington Navy Yard, First and N Sts. SE., Washington, DC 20403.	202–755–2110
ST. LOUIS, MO (R)	Rm. 328, 815 Olive St., 63101–1597	314–241–0349
SAN FRANCISCO, CA (R)	Suite I, 536 Stone Rd., Benicia, CA 94510–1170	707–748–1970
SEATTLE, WA (R)	4735 E. Marginal Way S., Federal Center South, 98134–2397	206–764–3726

Suppliers of paper products and printing equipment and supplies; purchasers of surplus printing equipment, waste, and salvage materials; and freight carriers should contact the Director of Materials Management, Government Printing Office, Washington, DC 20401. Phone, 202–512–0935. Internet, www.access.gpo.gov/procurement/mm_contents.html.

The booklet *How To Do Business With the Government Printing Office, A Guide for Contractors* is available upon request from the GPO Central Office or any GPO Regional Printing Procurement Office.

Employment Office of Personnel Management registers are used in filling administrative, technical, crafts, and clerical positions. Inquiries should be directed to the Chief, Employment Branch, Government Printing Office, Washington, DC 20401. Phone, 202–512–1124. Internet, www.access.gpo.gov/employment/index.html.

Government Publications Orders and inquiries concerning publications and subscriptions for sale by GPO should be directed to the Superintendent of Documents, Government Printing Office, Washington, DC 20402. Phone, 202–512–1800. Fax, 202–512–2250. Internet, www.access.gpo.gov/su_docs/sale.html.

The *GPO Sales Product Catalog* provides access to Government publications available for sale through the Superintendent of Documents and is searcheable online, at www.access.gpo.gov/su_docs/sale.html.

The *Monthly Catalog of U.S. Government Publications* is the most comprehensive listing of Government publications issued by Federal departments and agencies.

There also are two free catalogs of new or popular publications available: *U.S. Government Information,* which lists new and best-selling titles; and *New Products,* a bimonthly list of all Government publications placed on sale in the preceding 2 months. These publications can be obtained by calling the Superintendent of Documents at 202–512–1800.

Remittance for all publications ordered from the Superintendent of Documents must be received in advance of shipment by check, money order, charge cards, or a GPO deposit account.

Depository Libraries GPO distributes printed and electronic publications to approximately 1,300 depository libraries nationwide where they may be used by the public free of charge. A list of depository libraries is available from the Superintendent of Documents. Phone, 202–512–1119. It may also be accessed online at www.access.gpo.gov/su_docs/libpro.html.

Electronic Access GPO Access provides online access to key Government publications through the Internet at www.access.gpo.gov/su_docs. For information about this service, contact the GPO Access support team. Phone, 202–512–1530. E-mail, gpoaccess@gpo.gov.

Bookstores Popular Government publications may be purchased at the GPO bookstores listed below.

Bookstores—Government Printing Office

City	Address	Telephone
Washington, DC, area:		
Main Bookstore	710 N. Capitol St. NW.	202–512–0132
McPherson Square	1510 H St. NW.	202–653–5075
Retail Sales Outlet	8660 Cherry Ln., Laurel, MD	301–953–7974
Atlanta, GA	Suite 120, 999 Peachtree St. NE.	404–347–1900
Birmingham, AL	2021 3d Ave. N.	205–731–1056
Boston, MA	Rm. 169, 10 Causeway St.	617–720–4180
Chicago, IL	Rm. 124, 401 S. State St.	312–353–5133
Cleveland, OH	Rm. 1653, 1240 E. 9th St.	216–522–4922
Columbus, OH	Rm. 207, 200 N. High St.	614–469–6956
Dallas, TX	Rm. 1C42, 1100 Commerce St.	214–767–0076
Denver, CO	Suite 130, 1660 Wyncoop St.	303–844–3964
Detroit, MI	Suite 160, 477 Michigan Ave.	313–226–7816
Houston, TX	801 Travis St.	713–228–1187
Jacksonville, FL	Rm. 100, 100 W. Bay St.	904–353–0569
Kansas City, MO	120 Bannister Mall, 5600 E. Bannister Rd.	816–767–8225
Los Angeles, CA	C–Level, 505 S. Flower St.	213–239–9844
Milwaukee, WI	Rm. 150, 310 W. Wisconsin Ave.	414–297–1304
New York, NY	Rm. 2–120, 26 Federal Plz.	212–264–3825
Philadelphia, PA	100 N. 17th St.	215–636–1900
Pittsburgh, PA	Rm. 118, 1000 Liberty Ave.	412–395–5021
Portland, OR	1305 SW. 1st St.	503–221–6217
Pueblo, CO	201 W. 8th St.	719–544–3142
San Francisco, CA	Rm. 141–S, 303 2d St.	415–512–2770
Seattle, WA	Rm. 194, 915 2d Ave.	206–553–4270

For further information, contact the Office of Congressional, Legislative, and Public Affairs, Government Printing Office, 732 North Capitol Street NW., Washington, DC 20401. Phone, 202–512–1991. Fax, 202–512–1293. Internet, www.access.gpo.gov/public-affairs/index.html. E-mail, gpoinfo@gpo.gov.

LIBRARY OF CONGRESS

101 Independence Avenue SE., Washington, DC 20540
Phone, 202–707–5000. Internet, lcweb.loc.gov.

Librarian of Congress	JAMES H. BILLINGTON
Deputy Librarian of Congress	DONALD L. SCOTT
Chief of Staff	JOANN JENKINS
Associate Librarian for Library Services	WINSTON TABB
Associate Librarian for Human Resources Services	TERESA SMITH
Director, Congressional Research Service	DANIEL MULHOLLAN
Register of Copyrights and Associate Librarian for Copyright Services	MARYBETH PETERS
Law Librarian	RUBENS MEDINA
General Counsel	ELIZABETH PUGH
Inspector General	DALE C. WILLIAMS
Chief, Loan Division	L. CHRISTOPHER WRIGHT
Library of Congress Trust Fund Board	
Chairman (Librarian of Congress)	JAMES H. BILLINGTON
(Fiscal Assistant Secretary of the Treasury)	DONALD V. HAMMOND

(U.S. Senator from Alaska and Chairman, Joint Committee on the Library)	TED STEVENS
Appointive Members	WAYNE L. BERMAN, EDWIN L. COX, PATRICIA DUFF, JULIE FINLEY, ADELE HALL, JOHN HENRY, DONALD G. JONES, JOHN KLUGE, CEIL PULITZER, BERNARD RAPOPORT

The Library of Congress is the national library of the United States, offering diverse materials for research including the world's most extensive collections in many areas such as American history, music, and law.

The Library of Congress was established by act of April 24, 1800 (2 Stat. 56), appropriating $5,000 "for the purchase of such books as may be necessary for the use of Congress . . . ." The Library's scope of responsibility has been widened by subsequent legislation (2 U.S.C. 131–168d). The Librarian, appointed by the President with the advice and consent of the Senate, directs the Library.

The Library's first responsibility is service to Congress. As the Library has developed, its range of service has come to include the entire governmental establishment and the public at large, making it a national library for the United States.

Activities

Collections The Library's extensive collections are universal in scope. They include books, serials, and pamphlets on every subject and in a multitude of languages, and research materials in many formats, including maps, photographs, manuscripts, motion pictures, and sound recordings. Among them are the most comprehensive collections of Chinese, Japanese, and Russian language books outside Asia and the former Soviet Union; volumes relating to science and legal materials outstanding for American and foreign law; the world's largest collection of published aeronautical literature; and the most extensive collection in the Western Hemisphere of books printed before 1501 A.D.

The manuscript collections relate to manifold aspects of American history and civilization, and include the personal papers of most of the Presidents from George Washington through Calvin Coolidge. The music collections contain volumes and pieces—manuscript and published—from classic works to the newest popular compositions. Other materials available for research include maps and views; photographic records from the daguerreotype to the latest news photo; recordings, including folksongs and other music, speeches, and poetry readings; prints, drawings, and posters; government documents, newspapers, and periodicals from all over the world; and motion pictures, microforms, and audio and video tapes.

Reference Resources Admission to the various research facilities of the Library is free. No introduction or credentials are required for persons over high school age. Readers must register by presenting valid photo identification with a current address and, for certain collections there are additional requirements. As demands for service to Congress and Federal Government agencies increase, reference service available through correspondence has become limited. The Library must decline some requests and refer correspondents to a library within their area that can provide satisfactory assistance. While priority is given to inquiries pertaining to its holdings of special materials or to subjects in which its resources are unique, the Library does attempt to provide helpful responses to all inquirers.

Copyrights With the enactment of the second general revision of the U.S. copyright law by Act of July 8, 1870 (16 Stat. 212–217), all activities relating to copyright, including deposit and

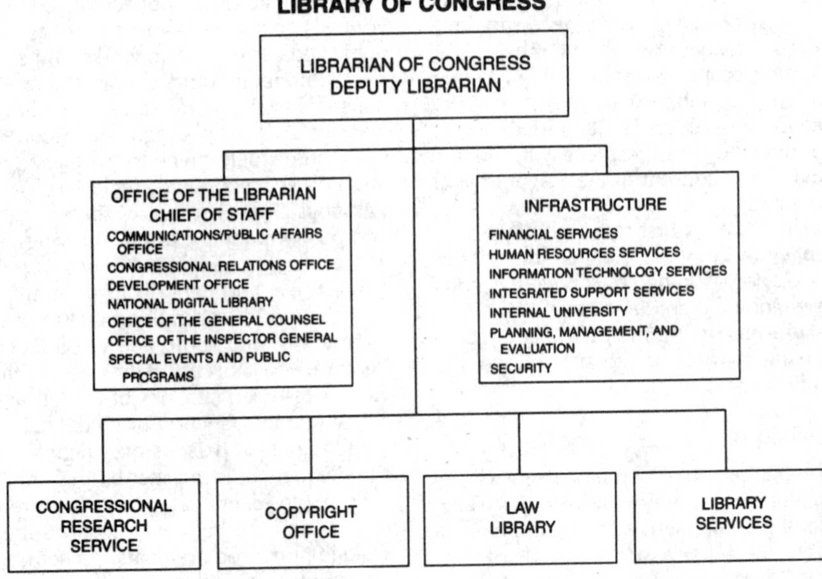
LIBRARY OF CONGRESS
LIBRARIAN OF CONGRESS
DEPUTY LIBRARIAN
OFFICE OF THE LIBRARIAN
CHIEF OF STAFF
COMMUNICATIONS/PUBLIC AFFAIRS OFFICE
CONGRESSIONAL RELATIONS OFFICE
DEVELOPMENT OFFICE
NATIONAL DIGITAL LIBRARY
OFFICE OF THE GENERAL COUNSEL
OFFICE OF THE INSPECTOR GENERAL
SPECIAL EVENTS AND PUBLIC PROGRAMS
INFRASTRUCTURE
FINANCIAL SERVICES
HUMAN RESOURCES SERVICES
INFORMATION TECHNOLOGY SERVICES
INTEGRATED SUPPORT SERVICES
INTERNAL UNIVERSITY
PLANNING, MANAGEMENT, AND EVALUATION
SECURITY
CONGRESSIONAL RESEARCH SERVICE
COPYRIGHT OFFICE
LAW LIBRARY
LIBRARY SERVICES

registration, were centralized in the Library of Congress. The Copyright Act of 1976 (90 Stat. 2541) brought all forms of copyrightable authorship, both published and unpublished, under a single statutory system which gives authors protection immediately upon creation of their works. Exclusive rights granted to authors under the statute include the right to reproduce and prepare derivative works, distribute copies or phonorecords, perform and display the work publicly, and in the case of sound recordings, to perform the work publicly by means of a digital audio transmission. Works eligible for copyright include literary works (books and periodicals), musical works, dramatic works, pantomimes and choreographic works, pictorial, graphic, and sculptural works, motion pictures, sound recordings, vessel hull designs, mask works, and architectural works. Serving in its capacity as a national registry for creative works, the Copyright Office registers nearly 620,000 claims to copyright annually (representing more than 800,000 works) and is a major source of acquisitions for the universal collections of the Library of Congress. Most of the information available on paper is also accessible online, at www.loc.gov/copyright.

Extension of Service The Library extends its service through:

—an interlibrary loan system;

—the photoduplication, at reasonable cost, of books, manuscripts, maps, newspapers, and prints in its collections;

—the sale of sound recordings, which are released by its Recording Laboratory;

—the exchange of duplicates with other institutions;

—the sale of CD–ROM cataloging tools and magnetic tapes and the publication in book format or microform of cumulative catalogs, which make available the results of the expert bibliographical and cataloging work of its technical personnel;

—a centralized cataloging program whereby the Library of Congress acquires material published all over the world, catalogs it promptly, and distributes cataloging information in machine-readable form as well as by printed cards and other means to the Nation's libraries;

—a cooperative cataloging program whereby the cataloging of data, by name authority and bibliographic records, prepared by other libraries becomes part of the Library of Congress database and is distributed through the MARC Distribution Service;

—a cataloging-in-publication program in cooperation with American publishers for printing cataloging information in current books;

—the National Serials Data Program, a national center that maintains a record of serial titles to which International Standard Serial Numbers have been assigned and serves, with this file, as the United States Register; and

—the development of general schemes of classification (Library of Congress and Dewey Decimal), subject headings, and cataloging, embracing the entire field of printed matter.

Furthermore, the Library provides for:

—the preparation of bibliographical lists responsive to the needs of Government and research;

—the maintenance and the publication of cooperative publications;

—the publication of catalogs, bibliographical guides, and lists, and of texts of original manuscripts and rare books in the Library of Congress;

—the circulation in traveling exhibitions of items from the Library's collections;

—the provision of books in braille, electronic access to braille books on the Internet, "talking book" records, and books on tape for the blind and the physically handicapped through 143 cooperating libraries throughout the Nation;

—the distribution of its electronic materials via the Internet; and

—the provision of research and analytical services on a fee-for-service basis to agencies in the executive and judicial branches.

Congressional Research Service The mission of the Congressional Research Service (CRS) is to provide to the Congress, throughout the legislative process, comprehensive and reliable legislative research, analysis, and

186-873 D-00--3

information services that are timely, objective, nonpartisan, and confidential, thereby contributing to an informed national legislature. In the past several years, CRS has responded to more than 500,000 requests for services from the Congress annually. CRS evolved from the Legislative Reference Service, established in 1914 by an act of Congress.

CRS provides multidisciplinary assistance to the Congress at every stage of the legislative process concerning subject areas relevant to policy issues before the Congress. Research at CRS ranges in the arears of American law; domestic social policy; foreign affairs, defense, and trade; government and finance; information research; and resources, science, and industry. In addition to responding to individual requests for information and analysis, CRS prepares products and services in anticipation of topics that likely will be on the legislative agenda, and develops and presents seminars that provide a forum for discussion among Members of Congress and their staffs, CRS specialists, and nationally recognized experts on important legislative issues.

For further information, call 202–707–5700.

American Folklife Center The Center, which was established in the Library of Congress by Act of January 2, 1976 (20 U.S.C. 2102 *et seq.*). The Center supports, preserves, and presents American folklife by receiving and maintaining folklife collections, scholarly research, field projects, performances, exhibitions, festivals, workshops, publications, and audiovisual presentations. The Center has conducted projects in many locations across the country, such as the ethnic communities of Chicago, IL; southern Georgia; a ranching community in northern Nevada; the Blue Ridge Parkway in southern Virginia and northern North Carolina; and the States of New Jersey, Rhode Island, and Montana. The projects have provided large collections of recordings and photographs for the Archive of Folk Culture. The Center administers the Federal Cylinder Project, which is charged with preserving and disseminating music and oral traditions recorded on wax cylinders dating from the late 1800's to the early 1940's. A cultural conservation study was developed at the Center, in cooperation with the Department of the Interior, pursuant to a congressional mandate. Various conferences, workshops, and symposia are given throughout the year.

The *Folklife Center News,* a quarterly newsletter, and other informational publications are available upon request. Many Center publications and a number of collections are available online through the Internet, at lcweb.loc.gov/folklife.

The American Folklife Center maintains and administers the Archive of Folk Culture, an extensive collection of ethnographic materials from this country and around the world. It is the national repository for folk-related recordings, manuscripts, and other unpublished materials. The Center's reading room contains over 3,500 books and periodicals; a sizable collection of magazines, newsletters, unpublished theses, and dissertations; field notes; and many textual and some musical transcriptions and recordings.

For further information, call 202–707–5510.

Center for the Book The Center was established in the Library of Congress by an act of October 13, 1977 (2 U.S.C. 171 *et seq.*), to stimulate public interest in books, reading, and libraries, and to encourage the study of books and print culture. The Center is a catalyst for promoting and exploring the vital role of books, reading, and libraries—nationally and internationally. As a partnership between the Government and the private sector, the Center for the Book depends on tax-deductible contributions from individuals and corporations to support its programs.

The Center's activities are directed toward the general public and scholars. The overall program includes reading promotion projects with television and radio networks, symposia, lectures, exhibitions, special events, and publications. More than 50 national educational and civic organizations participate in the Center's annual reading promotion campaign.

Since 1984, 39 States and the District of Columbia have established statewide book centers that are affiliated with the Center for the Book in the Library of Congress. State centers plan and fund their own projects, involving members of the State's "community of the book," including authors, readers, prominent citizens, and public officials who serve as honorary advisers.

For further information, contact the Center for the Book. Phone, 202–707–5221. Fax, 202–707–0269. E-mail, cfbook@loc.gov.

National Film Preservation Board The National Film Preservation Board, presently authorized by the National Film Preservation Act of 1996 (2 U.S.C. 179), serves as a public advisory group to the Librarian of Congress. The Board works to ensure the survival, conservation, and increased public availability of America's film heritage, including advising the Librarian on the annual selection of films to the National Film Registry and counseling the Librarian on development and implementation of the national film preservation plan. Key publications are *Film Preservation 1993: A Study of the Current State of American Film Preservation, Redefining Film Preservation: A National Plan,* and *Television and Video Preservation 1997: A Study of the Current State of American Television and Video Preservation.*

For further information, call 202–707–5912.

Preservation The Library provides technical information related to the preservation of library and archival material. A series of handouts on various preservation and conservation topics has been prepared by the Preservation Office. Information and publications are available from the Office of the Director for Preservation, Library of Congress, Washington, DC 20540–4500. Phone, 202–707–1840.

Sources of Information

Books for the Blind and Physically Handicapped Talking and braille books and magazines are distributed through 142 regional and subregional libraries to blind and physically handicapped residents of the United States and its territories. Information is available at public libraries throughout the United States and from the headquarters office, National Library Service for the Blind and Physically Handicapped, Library of Congress, 1291 Taylor Street NW., Washington, DC 20542–4960. Phone, 202–707–5100.

Cataloging Data Distribution Cataloging and bibliographic information in the form of microfiche catalogs, book catalogs, magnetic tapes, CD–ROM cataloging tools, bibliographies, and other technical publications is distributed to libraries and other institutions. Information about ordering materials is available from the Cataloging Distribution Service, Library of Congress, Washington, DC 20541–4910. Phone, 202–707–6100. TDD, 202–707–0012. Fax, 202–707–1334. E-mail, cdsinfo@mail.loc.gov.

Library of Congress card numbers for new publications are assigned by the Cataloging in Publication Division. Direct inquiries to CIP Division, Library of Congress, Washington, DC 20540–4320. Phone, 202–707–6372.

Contracts Persons seeking to do business with the Library of Congress should contact the Contracts and Logistics Services, Library of Congress, Landover Center Annex, 1701 Brightseat Road, Landover, MD 20785. Phone, 202–707–8717.

Copyright Services Information about the copyright law (title 17 of the U.S. Code), the method of securing copyright, and copyright registration procedures may be obtained by writing to the Copyright Office, Library of Congress, 101 Independence Avenue SE., Washington, DC 20559–6000. Phone, 202–707–3000. Copyright information is also available through the Internet, at lcweb.loc.gov. Registration application forms may be ordered by calling the forms hotline at 202–707–9100. Copyright records may be researched and reported by the Copyright Office for a fee; for an estimate, call 202–707–6850. Members of the public may, however, use the copyright card catalog in the Copyright Office without charge. The database of Copyright Office records cataloged from January 1, 1978, to the present is available through the Internet, at lcweb.loc.gov/copyright/rb.html. The Copyright Information Office is located in Room LM–401, James Madison Memorial Building, 101 Independence Avenue SE., Washington, DC 20559–6000, and is open to the public Monday through Friday, 8:30 a.m. to 5 p.m. eastern time, except Federal holidays.

Employment Employment inquiries should be directed to the Directorate of Personnel, Library of Congress, 101 Independence Avenue SE., Washington, DC 20540–2200. Vacancy announcements and applications are also available from the Employment Office, Room LM–107, 101 Independence Avenue SE. Phone, 202–707–4315. Internet, lcweb.loc.gov.

Photoduplication Service Copies of manuscripts, prints, photographs, maps, and book material not subject to copyright and other restrictions are available for a fee. Order forms for photoreproduction and price schedules are available from the Photoduplication Service, Library of Congress, 101 Independence Avenue SE., Washington, DC 20540–4570. Phone, 202–707–5640.

Publications A list of Library of Congress publications, many of which are of interest to the general public, is available through the Internet, at lcweb.loc.gov. A monthly *Calendar of Events,* listing programs and exhibitions at the Library of Congress, can be mailed regularly to persons within 100 miles of Washington, DC. Make requests to the Office Systems Services, Mail and Distribution Management Section, Library of Congress, 101 Independence Avenue SE., Washington, DC 20540–9441.

Reference and Bibliographic Services Guidance is offered to readers in the identification and use of the material in the Library's collections, and reference service in answer to inquiries is offered to those who have exhausted local, State, and regional resources. Persons requiring services that cannot be performed by the Library staff can be supplied with names of private researchers who work on a fee basis. Requests for information should be directed to the Reference Referral Service, Library of Congress, 101 Independence Avenue SE., Washington, DC 20540–4720. Phone, 202–707–5522. Fax, 202–707–1389.

Research and Reference Services in Science and Technology Reference specialists in the Science, Technology, and Business Division answer without charge brief technical inquiries entailing a bibliographic response. Requests for reference services should be directed to the Science, Technology, and Business Division, Library of Congress, Science Reference Section, 101 Independence Avenue SE., Washington, DC 20540–4750. Phone, 202–707–5639. Internet, lcweb2.loc.gov/sctb.

Research Services in General Topics Federal Government agencies can procure directed research and analytical products on foreign and domestic topics using the collections of the Library of Congress through the Federal Research Division. Science, technology, humanities, and social science topics of research are conducted by staff specialists exclusively on behalf of Federal agencies on a fee-for-service basis. Requests for service should be directed to Federal Research Division, Marketing Office, Library of Congress, Washington, DC 20540–4840. Phone, 202–707–3909. Fax, 202–245–3920.

For further information, contact the Public Affairs Office, Library of Congress, 101 Independence Avenue SE., Washington, DC 20540–8610. Phone, 202–707–2905. Fax, 202–707–9199. Internet, www.loc.gov.

CONGRESSIONAL BUDGET OFFICE

Second and D Streets SW., Washington, DC 20515
Phone, 202–226–2600. Internet, www.cbo.gov.

Director	DAN L. CRIPPEN
Deputy Director	BARRY B. ANDERSON
Executive Associate Director	STEVEN M. LIEBERMAN
General Counsel	JENNIFER SMITH, *Acting*
Associate Director for Business, Management, and Information Services	WILLIAM J. GAINER
Associate Director for Communications	SUSAN TANAKA
Associate Director for Research and Reports	ARLENE HOLEN
Assistant Director for Budget Analysis	ROBERT A. SUNSHINE
Assistant Director for Health and Human Resources	JOSEPH R. ANTOS
Assistant Director for Long-Term Modeling	STEVEN M. LIEBERMAN, *Acting*
Assistant Director for Macroeconomic Analysis	ROBERT A. DENNIS
Assistant Director for Microeconomic and Financial Studies	ROGER E. HITCHNER
Assistant Director for National Security	CHRISTOPHER JEHN
Assistant Director for Tax Analysis	G. THOMAS WOODWARD

The Congressional Budget Office provides the Congress with assessments of the economic impact of the Federal budget.

The Congressional Budget Office (CBO) was established by the Congressional Budget Act of 1974 (2 U.S.C. 601), which also created a procedure by which the United States Congress considers and acts upon the annual Federal budget. This process enables the Congress to have an overview of the Federal budget and to make overall decisions regarding spending and taxing levels and the deficit or surplus these levels incur.

The Office provides Congress with basic budget data and with analyses of alternative fiscal, budgetary, and programmatic policy issues.

Activities

Economic Forecasting and Fiscal Policy Analysis The Federal budget affects and is affected by the national economy. The Congressional Budget Office provides Congress with biannual forecasts of the economy and analyses of economic trends and alternative fiscal policies.

Scorekeeping Under the budget process the Congress establishes, by concurrent resolution, targets for overall expenditures, budget authority and budget outlays, and broad functional categories. The Congress also establishes targets for the levels of revenues, the deficit, and the public debt. The Office "keeps score" for the Congress by monitoring the results of congressional action on individual authorization, appropriation, and revenue bills against the targets specified in the concurrent resolution.

Cost Projections The Office prepares multiyear cost estimates for carrying out any public bill or resolution reported by congressional committees. As soon as practicable after the beginning of each fiscal year, CBO also provides multiyear projections on the costs of continuing current Federal spending and taxation policies.

Annual Report on the Budget The Office is responsible for submitting to the House and Senate Budget Committees each year a report with respect to fiscal policy that includes alternative spending and revenue levels and 5-year baseline projections of the Federal budget.

Federal Mandates To better assess the impact of laws on State, local, and tribal

CONGRESSIONAL BUDGET OFFICE

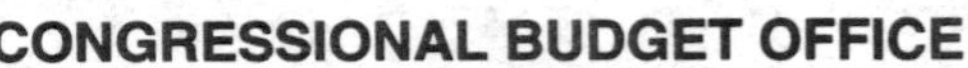

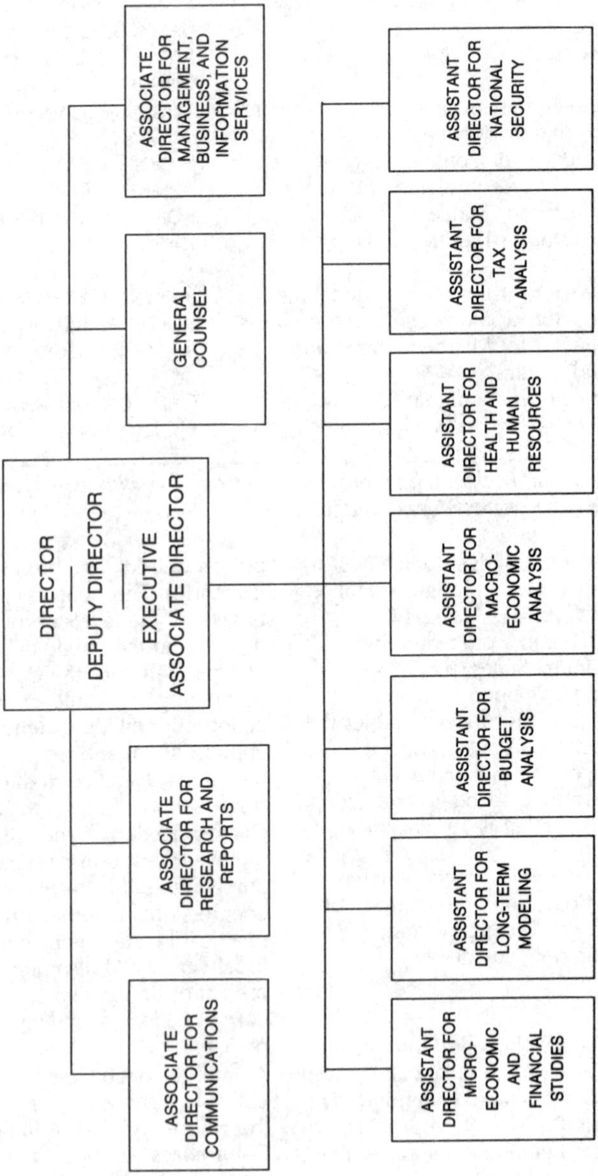
DIRECTOR
DEPUTY DIRECTOR
EXECUTIVE ASSOCIATE DIRECTOR
ASSOCIATE DIRECTOR FOR COMMUNICATIONS
ASSOCIATE DIRECTOR FOR RESEARCH AND REPORTS
GENERAL COUNSEL
ASSOCIATE DIRECTOR FOR MANAGEMENT, BUSINESS, AND INFORMATION SERVICES
ASSISTANT DIRECTOR FOR MICRO-ECONOMIC AND FINANCIAL STUDIES
ASSISTANT DIRECTOR FOR LONG-TERM MODELING
ASSISTANT DIRECTOR FOR BUDGET ANALYSIS
ASSISTANT DIRECTOR FOR MACRO-ECONOMIC ANALYSIS
ASSISTANT DIRECTOR FOR HEALTH AND HUMAN RESOURCES
ASSISTANT DIRECTOR FOR TAX ANALYSIS
ASSISTANT DIRECTOR FOR NATIONAL SECURITY

governments and the private sector, the Congress passed the Unfunded Mandates Reform Act of 1995. The act amends the Congressional Budget Act to require CBO to give authorizing committees a statement about whether reported bills contain Federal mandates. If the 5-year direct costs of an intergovernmental or private-sector mandate exceed specified thresholds, CBO must provide an estimate of those costs (if feasible) and the basis of the estimate.

Budget-Related Studies The Office undertakes studies requested by the Congress on budget-related areas. This service is provided in the following order of priority to: the House and Senate Budget Committees; the House and Senate Appropriations Committees, the Senate Finance Committee, and the House Ways and Means Committee; and all other congressional committees.

Sequestration Reports The Office prepares advisory reports mandated by the Balanced Budget and Emergency Deficit Control Act of 1985, as amended (2 U.S.C. 901), to estimate whether legislation enacted will breach categorical spending limits or result in a negative balance under the pay-as-you-go system. If so, CBO must then estimate the amount and percentage of budgetary resources that should be sequestered to eliminate any excesses.

Pay-As-You-Go The Balanced Budget and Emergency Deficit Control Act of 1985, as amended (2 U.S.C. 901), requires CBO to provide the Office of Management and Budget with an estimate of the amount of change in outlays or receipts for each fiscal year for any direct spending or receipts legislation as soon as practicable after Congress completes action on that legislation.

For further information, contact the Management, Business, and Information Services Division, Congressional Budget Office, Second and D Streets SW., Washington, DC 20515. Phone, 202–226–2600. Fax, 202–226–2714. Internet, www.cbo.gov.

Judicial Branch

JUDICIAL BRANCH

THE SUPREME COURT OF THE UNITED STATES

United States Supreme Court Building
One First Street NE., Washington, DC 20543
Phone, 202–479–3000

Members:

Chief Justice of the United States	WILLIAM H. REHNQUIST
Associate Justices	JOHN PAUL STEVENS, SANDRA DAY O'CONNOR, ANTONIN SCALIA, ANTHONY M. KENNEDY, DAVID H. SOUTER, CLARENCE THOMAS, RUTH BADER GINSBURG, STEPHEN G. BREYER

Officers:

Administrative Assistant to the Chief Justice	JAMES C. DUFF
Clerk	WILLIAM K. SUTER
Court Counsel	JANE E. PETKOFSKY
Curator	GAIL GALLOWAY
Director of Budget and Personnel	CYRIL A. DONNELLY
Director of Data Systems	DONNA CLEMENT
Librarian	SHELLEY L. DOWLING
Marshal	DALE E. BOSLEY
Public Information Officer	KATHLEEN L. ARBERG
Reporter of Decisions	FRANK D. WAGNER

Article III, section 1, of the Constitution of the United States provides that "[t]he judicial Power of the United States, shall be vested in one supreme Court, and in such inferior Courts as the Congress may from time to time ordain and establish."

The Supreme Court of the United States was created in accordance with this provision and by authority of the Judiciary Act of September 24, 1789 (1 Stat. 73). It was organized on February 2, 1790. Article III, section 2 of the Constitution defines the jurisdiction of the Supreme Court.

The Supreme Court is comprised of the Chief Justice of the United States and such number of Associate Justices as may be fixed by Congress, which is currently fixed at eight (28 U.S.C. 1). The President nominates the Justices with the advice and consent of the Senate. Article III, section 1, of the Constitution further provides that "[t]he Judges, both of the supreme and inferior Courts, shall hold their Offices during good Behaviour, and shall, at stated Times, receive for their Services, a Compensation, which shall not be diminished during their Continuance in Office."

Court officers assist the Court in the performance of its functions. They include the Administrative Assistant to the Chief Justice, the Clerk, the Reporter of Decisions, the Librarian, the Marshal, the Director of Budget and Personnel, the Court Counsel, the Curator, the Director of Data Systems, and the Public Information Officer.

Appellate Jurisdiction Appellate jurisdiction has been conferred upon the Supreme Court by various statutes under the authority given Congress by the Constitution. The basic statute effective at this time in conferring and controlling jurisdiction of the Supreme Court may be found in 28 U.S.C. 1251, 1253, 1254, 1257–1259, and various special statutes. Congress has no authority to change the original jurisdiction of this Court.

Rulemaking Power Congress has from time to time conferred upon the Supreme Court power to prescribe rules of procedure to be followed by the lower courts of the United States.

Court Term The term of the Court begins on the first Monday in October and lasts until the first Monday in October of the next year. Approximately 7,000 cases are filed with the Court in the course of a term, and some 1,200 applications of various kinds are filed each year that can be acted upon by a single Justice.

Access to Facilities The Supreme Court is open to the public from 9 a.m. to 4:30 p.m., Monday through Friday, except on Federal legal holidays. Unless the Court or Chief Justice orders otherwise, the Clerk's office is open from 9 a.m. to 5 p.m., Monday through Friday, except on Federal legal holidays. The library is open to members of the bar of the Court, attorneys for the various Federal departments and agencies, and Members of Congress.

For further information concerning the Supreme Court, contact the Public Information Office, United States Supreme Court Building, One First Street NE., Washington, DC 20543. Phone, 202–479–3211.

Lower Courts

Article III of the Constitution declares, in section 1, that the judicial power of the United States shall be invested in one Supreme Court and in "such inferior Courts as the Congress may from time to time ordain and establish." The Supreme Court has held that these constitutional courts ". . . share in the exercise of the judicial power defined in that section, can be invested with no other jurisdiction, and have judges who hold office during good behavior, with no power in Congress to provide otherwise."

United States Courts of Appeals The courts of appeals are intermediate appellate courts created by act of March 3, 1891 (28 U.S.C. ch. 3), to relieve the Supreme Court of considering all appeals in cases originally decided by the Federal trial courts. They are empowered to review all final decisions and certain interlocutory decisions (18 U.S.C. 3731; 28 U.S.C. 1291, 1292) of district courts. They also are empowered to review and enforce orders of many Federal administrative bodies. The decisions of the courts of appeals are final except as they are subject to review on writ of certiorari by the Supreme Court.

The United States is divided geographically into 12 judicial circuits, including the District of Columbia. Each circuit has a court of appeals (28 U.S.C. 41, 1294). Each of the 50 States is assigned to one of the circuits, and the Territories are assigned variously to the first, third, and ninth circuits. There is also a Court of Appeals for the Federal Circuit, which has nationwide jurisdiction defined by subject matter. At present each court of appeals has from 6 to 28 permanent circuit judgeships (179 in all), depending upon the amount of judicial work in the circuit. Circuit judges hold their offices during good behavior as provided by Article III, section 1, of the Constitution. The judge senior in commission who is under 70 years of age (65 at inception of term), has been in office at least 1 year, and has not previously been chief judge, serves as the chief judge of the circuit for a 7-year term. One of the justices of the Supreme Court is assigned as circuit justice for each of the 13 judicial circuits. Each court of appeals normally hears cases in panels consisting of three judges but may sit *en banc* with all judges present.

The judges of each circuit (except the Federal Circuit) by vote determine the size of the judicial council for the circuit, which consists of the chief judge and an equal number of circuit and district judges. The council considers the state of Federal judicial business in the circuit and may "make all necessary and appropriate orders for [its] effective and expeditious administration . . ." (28 U.S.C. 332). The chief judge of each circuit may summon periodically a judicial conference of all judges of the circuit, including members of the bar, to discuss the business of the Federal courts of the circuit (28 U.S.C. 333). The chief judge of each circuit and a district judge elected from each of the 12 geographical circuits, together with the chief judge of the Court of International Trade, serve as members of the Judicial Conference of the United States, over which the Chief Justice of the United States presides. This is the governing body for the administration of the Federal judicial system as a whole (28 U.S.C. 331).

United States Court of Appeals for the Federal Circuit This court was established under Article III of the Constitution pursuant to the Federal Courts Improvement Act of 1982 (28 U.S.C. 41, 44, 48), as successor to the former United States Court of Customs and Patent Appeals and the United States Court of Claims. The jurisdiction of the court is nationwide (as provided by 28 U.S.C. 1295) and includes appeals from the district courts in patent cases; appeals from the district courts in contract, and certain other civil actions in which the United States is a defendant; and appeals from final decisions of the U.S. Court of International Trade, the U.S. Court of Federal Claims, and the U.S. Court of Appeals for Veterans Claims. The jurisdiction of the court also includes the review of administrative rulings by the Patent and Trademark Office, U.S. International Trade Commission, Secretary of Commerce, agency boards of contract appeals, and the Merit Systems Protection Board, as well as rulemaking of the Department of Veterans Affairs; review of decisions of the U.S. Senate Select Committee on Ethics concerning discrimination claims of Senate employees; and review of a final order of an entity to be designated by the President concerning discrimination claims of Presidential appointees.

The court consists of 12 circuit judges. It sits in panels of three or more on each case and may also hear or rehear a case *en banc*. The court sits principally in Washington, DC, and may hold court wherever any court of appeals sits (28 U.S.C. 48).

Judicial Circuits—United States Courts of Appeals

Circuit	Judges	Official Station
	District of Columbia Circuit	
(*Clerk*: Mark J. Langer; *Circuit Executive*: Jill C. Sayenga; Washington, DC)	*Circuit Justice*	
	Chief Justice William H. Rehnquist	
	Circuit Judges	
	Harry T. Edwards, *Chief Judge*	Washington, DC
	Laurence H. Silberman	Washington, DC
	Stephen F. Williams	Washington, DC
	Douglas H. Ginsburg	Washington, DC
	David Bryan Sentelle	Washington, DC
	Karen LeCraft Henderson	Washington, DC
	A. Raymond Randolph	Washington, DC
	Judith W. Rogers	Washington, DC
	David S. Tatel	Washington, DC
	Merrick B. Garland	Washington, DC

Judicial Circuits—United States Courts of Appeals—Continued

Circuit	Judges	Official Station
	(2 vacancies)	
	First Circuit	
Districts of Maine, New Hampshire, Massachusetts, Rhode Island, and Puerto Rico (*Clerk*: Phoebe Morse; *Circuit Executive*: Vincent F. Flanagan; Boston, MA)	*Circuit Justice*	
	Justice David H. Souter	
	Circuit Judges	
	Juan R. Torruella, *Chief Judge*	Hato Rey, PR
	Bruce M. Selya	Providence, RI
	Michael Boudin	Boston, MA
	Norman H. Stahl	Concord, NH
	Sandra L. Lynch	Boston, MA
	Kermit V. Lipez	Portland, ME
	Second Circuit	
Districts of Vermont, Connecticut, northern New York, southern New York, eastern New York, and western New York (*Clerk*: Roseann B. MacKechnie; *Circuit Executive*: Karen Milton; New York, NY)	*Circuit Justice*	
	Justice Ruth Bader Ginsburg	
	Circuit Judges	
	Ralph K. Winter, Jr., *Chief Judge*	New Haven, CT
	Amalya Lyle Kearse	New York, NY
	John M. Walker, Jr.	New Haven, CT
	Dennis G. Jacobs	New York, NY
	Pierre N. Leval	New York, NY
	Guido Calabresi	New Haven, CT
	Jose A. Cabranes	New Haven, CT
	Fred I. Parker	Burlington, VT
	Rosemary S. Pooler	Syracuse, NY
	Robert D. Sack	New York, NY
	Sonia Sotomayor	New York, NY
	Chester J. Straub	New York, NY
	Robert A. Katzmann	New York, NY
	Third Circuit	
Districts of New Jersey, eastern Pennsylvania, middle Pennsylvania, western Pennsylvania, Delaware, and the Virgin Islands (*Clerk*: (vacancy); *Circuit Executive*: Toby D. Slawsky; Philadelphia, PA)	*Circuit Justice*	
	Justice David H. Souter	
	Circuit Judges	
	Edward R. Becker, *Chief Judge*	Philadelphia, PA
	Dolores Korman Sloviter	Philadelphia, PA
	Carol Los Mansmann	Pittsburgh, PA
	Morton I. Greenberg	Trenton, NJ
	Anthony J. Scirica	Philadelphia, PA
	Richard Lowell Nygaard	Erie, PA
	Samuel A. Alito, Jr.	Newark, NJ
	Jane R. Roth	Wilmington, DE
	Thomas L. Ambro	Philadelphia, PA
	Theodore A. McKee	Philadelphia, PA
	Marjorie O. Rendell	Philadelphia, PA
	(3 vacancies)	
	Fourth Circuit	
Districts of Maryland, northern West Virginia, southern West Virginia, eastern Virginia, western Virginia, eastern North Carolina, middle North Carolina, western North Carolina, and South Carolina (*Clerk*: Patricia S. Connor; *Circuit Executive*: Samuel W. Phillips; Richmond, VA)	*Circuit Justice*	
	Chief Justice William H. Rehnquist	
	Circuit Judges	
	James Harvie Wilkinson III, *Chief Judge*	Charlottesville, VA
	H. Emory Widener, Jr.	Abingdon, VA
	Francis D. Murnaghan, Jr.	Baltimore, MD
	William W. Wilkins, Jr.	Greenville, SC
	Paul V. Niemeyer	Baltimore, MD
	J. Michael Luttig	Alexandria, VA
	Karen J. Williams	Orangeburg, SC
	M. Blane Michael	Charleston, WV
	Diana Gribbon Motz	Baltimore, MD
	Robert B. King	Charleston, WV
	William B. Traxler, Jr.	Greenville, SC
	(4 vacancies)	

Judicial Circuits—United States Courts of Appeals—Continued

Circuit	Judges	Official Station
Fifth Circuit		
Districts of northern Mississippi, southern Mississippi, eastern Louisiana, middle Louisiana, western Louisiana, northern Texas, southern Texas, eastern Texas, and western Texas (*Clerk*: Charles R. Fulbruge III; *Circuit Executive*: Gregory A. Nussel; New Orleans, LA)	*Circuit Justice*	
	Justice Antonin Scalia	
	Circuit Judges	
	Carolyn Dineen King, *Chief Judge*	Houston, TX
	E. Grady Jolly	Jackson, MS
	Patrick E. Higginbotham	Dallas, TX
	W. Eugene Davis	Lafayette, LA
	Edith H. Jones	Houston, TX
	Jerry Edwin Smith	Houston, TX
	Rhesa H. Barksdale	Jackson, MS
	Jacques L. Wiener, Jr.	New Orleans, LA
	Emilio M. Garza	San Antonio, TX
	Harold R. Demoss, Jr.	Houston, TX
	Fortunado P. Benavides	Austin, TX
	Carl E. Stewart	Shreveport, LA
	Robert M. Parker	Tyler, TX
	James L. Dennis	New Orleans, LA
	(3 vacancies)	
Sixth Circuit		
Districts of northern Ohio, southern Ohio, eastern Michigan, western Michigan, eastern Kentucky, western Kentucky, eastern Tennessee, middle Tennessee, and western Tennessee (*Clerk*: Leonard Green; *Circuit Executive*: James A. Higgins; Cincinnati, OH)	*Circuit Justice*	
	Justice John Paul Stevens	
	Circuit Judges	
	Boyce F. Martin, Jr., *Chief Judge*	Louisville, KY
	Gilbert S. Merritt	Nashville, TN
	Danny J. Boggs	Louisville, KY
	Alan E. Norris	Columbus, OH
	Richard F. Suhrheinrich	Lansing, MI
	Eugene E. Siler, Jr.	London, KY
	Alice M. Batchelder	Medina, OH
	Martha Craig Daughtrey	Nashville, TN
	Karen Nelson Moore	Cleveland, OH
	Ransey Guy Cole, Jr.	Columbus, OH
	Eric L. Clay	Detroit, MI
	Ronald Lee Gilman	Memphis, TN
	(4 vacancies)	
Seventh Circuit		
Districts of northern Indiana, southern Indiana, northern Illinois, central Illinois, southern Illinois, eastern Wisconsin, and western Wisconsin (*Clerk*: Gino J. Agnello; *Circuit Executive*: Collins T. Fitzpatrick; Chicago, IL)	*Circuit Justice*	
	Justice John Paul Stevens	
	Circuit Judges	
	Richard A. Posner, *Chief Judge*	Chicago, IL
	John L. Coffey	Milwaukee, WI
	Joel M. Flaum	Chicago, IL
	Frank H. Easterbrook	Chicago, IL
	Kenneth F. Ripple	South Bend, IN
	Daniel A. Manion	South Bend, IN
	Michael S. Kanne	Lafayette, IN
	Ilana Diamond Rovner	Chicago, IL
	Diane P. Wood	Chicago, IL
	Terence T. Evans	Milwaukee, WI
	(Vacancy)	
Eighth Circuit		
Districts of Minnesota, northern Iowa, southern Iowa, eastern Missouri, western Missouri, eastern Arkansas, western Arkansas, Nebraska, North Dakota, and South Dakota (*Clerk*: Michael Ellis Gans; *Circuit Executive*: Millie B. Adams; St. Louis, MO)	*Circuit Justice*	
	Justice Clarence Thomas	
	Circuit Judges	
	Roger L. Wollman, *Chief Judge*	Sioux Falls, SD
	Richard S. Arnold	Little Rock, AR
	Theodore McMillian	St. Louis, MO
	Pasco M. Bowman II	Kansas City, MO
	Clarence Arlen Beam	Lincoln, NE
	James B. Loken	Minneapolis, MN
	David R. Hansen	Cedar Rapids, IA

Judicial Circuits—United States Courts of Appeals—Continued

Circuit	Judges	Official Station
	Morris S. Arnold	Little Rock, AR
	Diana E. Murphy	Minneapolis, MN
	(2 vacancies)	
	Ninth Circuit	
Districts of northern California, eastern California, central California, southern California, Oregon, Nevada, Montana, eastern Washington, western Washington, Idaho, Arizona, Alaska, Hawaii, Territory of Guam, and District Court for the Northern Mariana Islands (*Clerk*: Cathy A. Catterson; *Circuit Executive*: Gregory B. Walters; San Francisco, CA)	*Circuit Justice*	
	Justice Sandra Day O'Connor	
	Circuit Judges	
	Procter Hug, Jr., *Chief Judge*	Reno, NV
	James R. Browning	San Francisco, CA
	Mary M. Schroeder	Phoenix, AZ
	Harry Pregerson	Woodland Hills, CA
	Stephan Reinhardt	Los Angeles, CA
	Alex Kozinski	Pasadena, CA
	Diarmuid F. O'Scannlain	Portland, OR
	Stephen S. Trott	Boise, ID
	Ferdinand F. Fernandez	Pasadena, CA
	Pamela A. Rymer	Pasadena, CA
	Thomas G. Nelson	Boise, ID
	Andrew J. Kleinfeld	Fairbanks, AK
	Michael D. Hawkins	Phoenix, AZ
	A. Wallace Tashima	Pasadena, CA
	Sidney R. Thomas	Billings, MT
	Barry G. Silverman	Phoenix, AZ
	William A. Fletcher	San Francisco, CA
	Susan P. Graber	Portland, OR
	M. Margaret McKeown	Seattle, WA
	Ronald M. Gould	Seattle, WA
	Kim M. Wardlaw	Pasadena, CA
	Raymond C. Fisher	Pasadena, CA
	Richard A. Paez	Los Angeles, CA
	Marsha L. Berzon	San Francisco, CA
	Richard C. Tallman	Seattle, WA
	(3 vacancies)	
	Tenth Circuit	
Districts of Colorado, Wyoming, Utah, Kansas, eastern Oklahoma, western Oklahoma, northern Oklahoma, and New Mexico (*Clerk*: Patrick J. Fisher; *Circuit Executive*: Robert L. Hoecker; Denver, CO)	*Circuit Justice*	
	Justice Stephen G. Breyer	
	Circuit Judges	
	Stephanie K. Seymour, *Chief Judge*	Tulsa, OK
	Deanell Reece Tacha	Lawrence, KS
	Bobby R. Baldock	Roswell, NM
	Wade Brorby	Cheyenne, WY
	David M. Ebel	Denver, CO
	Paul J. Kelly, Jr.	Santa Fe, NM
	Robert H. Henry	Oklahoma City, OK
	Mary Beck Briscoe	Lawrence, KS
	Carlos F. Lucero	Denver, CO
	Michael R. Murphy	Salt Lake City, UT
	(2 vacancies)	
	Eleventh Circuit	
Districts of northern Georgia, middle Georgia, southern Georgia, northern Florida, middle Florida, southern Florida, northern Alabama, middle Alabama, southern Alabama (*Clerk*: Thomas Kahn; *Circuit Executive*: Norman E. Zoller; Atlanta, GA)	*Circuit Justice*	
	Justice Anthony M. Kennedy	
	Circuit Judges	
	R. Lanier Anderson III, *Chief Judge*	Macon, GA
	Gerald B. Tjoflat	Jacksonville, FL
	J.L. Edmondson	Atlanta, GA
	Emmett Ripley Cox	Mobile, AL
	Stanley F. Birch, Jr.	Atlanta, GA
	Joel F. Dubina	Montgomery, AL
	Susan H. Black	Jacksonville, FL
	Edward E. Carnes	Montgomery, AL
	Rosemary Barkett	Miami, FL
	Frank Mays Hull	Atlanta, GA
	Stanley Marcus	Miami, FL
	Charles R. Wilson	Tampa, FL

Federal Circuit—Washington, DC

Circuit Justice
Chief Justice William H. Rehnquist

Chief Judge
Haldane Robert Mayer

Judges
Pauline Newman
Paul R. Michel
S. Jay Plager
Alan D. Lourie
Raymond C. Clevenger III
Randall R. Rader
Alvin A. Schall
William C. Bryson
Arthur J. Gajarsa
Richard Linn
Timothy B. Dyk

Clerk: Jan Horbaly
Administrative Services Officer: Ruth A. Butler

United States District Courts The district courts are the trial courts of general Federal jurisdiction. Each State has at least one district court, while the larger States have as many as four. Altogether there are 89 district courts in the 50 States, plus the one in the District of Columbia. In addition, the Commonwealth of Puerto Rico has a district court with jurisdiction corresponding to that of district courts in the various States.

At present, each district court has from 2 to 28 Federal district judgeships, depending upon the amount of judicial work within its territory. Only one judge is usually required to hear and decide a case in a district court, but in some limited cases it is required that three judges be called together to comprise the court (28 U.S.C. 2284). The judge senior in commission who is under 70 years of age (65 at inception of term), has been in office for at least 1 year, and has not previously been chief judge, serves as chief judge for a 7-year term. There are altogether 619 permanent district judgeships in the 50 States and 15 in the District of Columbia. There are 7 district judgeships in Puerto Rico. District judges hold their offices during good behavior as provided by Article III, section 1, of the Constitution. However, Congress may create temporary judgeships for a court with the provision that when a vacancy occurs in that district, such vacancy shall not be filled. Each district court has one or more United States magistrate judges and bankruptcy judges, a clerk, a United States attorney, a United States marshal, probation officers, court reporters, and their staffs. The jurisdiction of the district courts is set forth in title 28, chapter 85, of the United States Code and at 18 U.S.C. 3231.

Cases from the district courts are reviewable on appeal by the applicable court of appeals.

Territorial Courts Pursuant to its authority to govern the Territories (art. IV, sec. 3, clause 2, of the Constitution), Congress has established district courts in the territories of Guam and the Virgin Islands. The District Court of the Canal Zone was abolished on April 1, 1982, pursuant to the Panama Canal Act of 1979 (22 U.S.C. 3601 note). Congress has also established a district court in the Northern Mariana Islands, which presently is administered by the United States under a trusteeship agreement with the United Nations. These Territorial courts have jurisdiction not only over the subjects described in the judicial article of the Constitution but also over many local matters that, within the States, are decided in State courts. The district court of Puerto Rico, by contrast, is established under Article III, is classified like other "district courts," and is called a "court of the United States" (28 U.S.C. 451). There is one judge each in Guam and the Northern Mariana Islands, and two in the Virgin Islands. The judges in these courts are appointed for terms of 10 years.

For further information concerning the lower courts, contact the Administrative Office of the United States Courts, Thurgood Marshall Federal Judiciary Building, One Columbus Circle NE., Washington, DC 20544. Phone, 202–273–0107.

United States Court of International Trade This court was originally established as the Board of United States General Appraisers by act of June 10, 1890, which conferred upon it jurisdiction theretofore held by the district and circuit courts in actions arising under the tariff acts (19 U.S.C. ch. 4). The act of May 28, 1926 (19 U.S.C. 405a), created the United States Customs Court to supersede the Board; by acts of August 7, 1939, and June 25, 1948 (28 U.S.C. 1582, 1583), the court was integrated into the United States court structure, organization, and procedure. The act of July 14, 1956 (28 U.S.C. 251), established the court as a court of record of the United States under Article III of the Constitution. The Customs Court Act of 1980 (28 U.S.C. 251) constituted the court as the United States Court of International Trade.

The Court of International Trade has jurisdiction over any civil action against the United States arising from Federal laws governing import transactions. This includes classification and valuation cases, as well as authority to review certain agency determinations under the Trade Agreements Act of 1979 (19 U.S.C. 2501) involving antidumping and countervailing duty matters. In addition, it has exclusive jurisdiction of civil actions to review determinations as to the eligibility of workers, firms, and communities for adjustment assistance under the Trade Act of 1974 (19 U.S.C. 2101). Civil actions commenced by the United States to recover customs duties, to recover on a customs bond, or for certain civil penalties alleging fraud or negligence are also within the exclusive jurisdiction of the court.

The court is composed of a chief judge and eight judges, not more than five of whom may belong to any one political party. Any of its judges may be temporarily designated and assigned by the Chief Justice of the United States to sit as a court of appeals or district court judge in any circuit or district. The court has a clerk and deputy clerks, a librarian, court reporters, and other supporting personnel. Cases before the court may be tried before a jury. Under the Federal Courts Improvement Act of 1982 (28 U.S.C. 1295), appeals are taken to the U.S. Court of Appeals for the Federal Circuit, and ultimately review may be sought in appropriate cases in the Supreme Court of the United States.

The principal offices are located in New York, NY, but the court is empowered to hear and determine cases arising at any port or place within the jurisdiction of the United States.

For further information, contact the Clerk, United States Court of International Trade, One Federal Plaza, New York, NY 10007. Phone, 212–264–2814.

Judicial Panel on Multidistrict Litigation The Panel, created by act of April 29, 1968 (28 U.S.C. 1407), and consisting of seven Federal judges designated by the Chief Justice from the courts of appeals and district courts, is authorized to temporarily transfer to a single district, for coordinated or consolidated pretrial proceedings, civil actions pending in different districts that involve one or more common questions of fact.

For further information, contact the Clerk, Judicial Panel on Multidistrict Litigation, Room G–255, Thurgood Marshall Federal Judiciary Building, One Columbus Circle NE., Washington, DC 20002. Phone, 202–502–2800.

Special Courts

The Supreme Court has held that ". . . Article III [of the Constitution] does not express the full authority of Congress to create courts, and that other Articles invest Congress with powers in the exertion of which it may create inferior courts and clothe them with functions deemed essential or helpful in carrying those powers into execution." Such courts, known as legislative courts, have functions which ". . . are directed to the execution of one or more of such powers and are prescribed by Congress independently of section 2 of Article III; and their judges hold office for such term as Congress prescribes, whether it be a fixed period of years or during good behavior." Appeals from the decisions of these courts, with the exception of the U.S. Tax Court and the U.S. Court of Appeals for the Armed Forces, may be taken to the U.S. Court of Appeals for the Federal Circuit. Appeals from the decisions of the Tax Court may be taken to the court of appeals in which judicial circuit the case was initially heard.

Certain decisions of the U.S. Court of Appeals for the Armed Forces are reviewable by writ of certiorari in the Supreme Court.

United States Court of Federal Claims The Claims Court was established on October 1, 1982, as an Article I court (28 U.S.C. 171, Article I, U.S. Constitution). The Claims Court succeeds to the original trial jurisdiction of the former Court of Claims, as provided for in 28 U.S.C. 1491 *et seq.* Its name was changed to the United States Court of Federal Claims by the Federal Courts Administration Act of 1992 (28 U.S.C. 1 note, 106 Stat. 4516). The court is composed of 16 judges, one of whom is designated by the President as chief judge. All judges are appointed for 15-year terms by the President with the advice and consent of the Senate.

The court has jurisdiction over claims seeking money judgments against the United States. A claim must be founded upon either: the United States Constitution; an act of Congress; the regulation of an executive department; an express or implied-in-fact contract with the United States; or damages, liquidated or unliquidated, in cases not sounding in tort.

If a bidder files a claim with the court either before or after the award of a Government contract, it has jurisdiction to grant declaratory judgments and equitable relief. Under the Contract Disputes Act (41 U.S.C. 601 *et seq.*), the court may render judgments upon a claim by or against a contractor, or any dispute between a contractor and the United States Government arising under the act.

The Congress, from time to time, also grants the court jurisdiction over specific types of claims against the United States. The National Vaccine Injury Compensation Program, established by 42 U.S.C. 300aa-10 (the Vaccine Act), is an example of such special jurisdiction.

The court also reports to Congress on bills referred by either the House of Representatives or the Senate.

Judgments of the court are final and conclusive on both the claimant and the United States. All judgments are subject to appeal to the U.S. Court of Appeals for the Federal Circuit. Collateral to any judgment, the court may issue orders directing the restoration to office or status of any claimant or the correction of applicable records.

The court's jurisdiction is nationwide. Trials are conducted before individual judges at locations most convenient and least expensive to citizens.

For further information, contact the Clerk, United States Court of Federal Claims, 717 Madison Place NW., Washington, DC 20005. Phone, 202–219–9657.

United States Court of Appeals for the Armed Forces This court was established under Article I of the Constitution of the United States pursuant to act of May 5, 1950, as amended (10 U.S.C. 867). Subject only to certiorari review by the Supreme Court of the United States in a limited number of cases, the court serves as the final appellate tribunal to review court-martial convictions of all the Armed Forces. It is exclusively an appellate criminal court, consisting of five civilian judges who are appointed for 15-year terms by the President with the advice and consent of the Senate. The court is called upon to exercise jurisdiction to review the record in all cases:

—extending to death;

—certified to the court by a Judge Advocate General of an armed force or by the General Counsel of the Department of Transportation, acting for the Coast Guard; or

—petitioned by accused who have received a sentence of confinement for 1 year or more, and/or a punitive discharge.

The court also exercises authority under the All Writs Act (28 U.S.C. 1651 (a)).

In addition, the judges of the court are required by law to work jointly with the senior uniformed lawyer from each armed force, the Chief Counsel of the Coast Guard, and two members of the public appointed by the Secretary of Defense, to make an annual comprehensive survey and to report annually to the Congress on the operation and progress of the military justice system under the Uniform Code of Military Justice, and to recommend improvements wherever necessary.

For further information, contact the Clerk, United States Court of Appeals for the Armed Forces, 450 E Street NW., Washington, DC 20442–0001. Phone, 202–761–1448. Fax, 202–761–4672.

United States Tax Court This is a court of record under Article I of the Constitution of the United States (26 U.S.C. 7441). Currently an independent judicial body in the legislative branch, the court was originally created as the United States Board of Tax Appeals, an independent agency in the executive branch, by the Revenue Act of 1924 (43 Stat. 336) and continued by the Revenue Act of 1926 (44 Stat. 105), the Internal Revenue Codes of 1939, 1954, and 1986. The name was changed to the Tax Court of the United States by the Revenue Act of 1942 (56 Stat. 957), and the Article I status and change in name to United States Tax Court were effected by the Tax Reform Act of 1969 (83 Stat. 730).

The court is composed of 19 judges. Its strength is augmented by senior judges who may be recalled by the chief judge to perform further judicial duties and by special trial judges who are appointed by the chief judge and serve at the pleasure of the court. The chief judge is elected biennially from among the 19 judges of the court.

The matters over which the Court has jurisdiction are set forth in the various sections of title 26 of the U.S. Code.

At the option of the individual taxpayer, simplified procedures may be utilized for the trials of small tax cases, provided that in a case conducted under these procedures the decision of the court would be final and not subject to review by any court. The jurisdictional maximum for such cases is $50,000 for any disputed year.

All decisions, other than small tax case decisions, are subject to review by the courts of appeals and thereafter by the Supreme Court of the United States upon the granting of a writ of certiorari.

The office of the court and all of its judges are located in Washington, DC, with the exception of a field office located in Los Angeles, CA. The court conducts trial sessions at various locations within the United States as reasonably convenient to taxpayers as practicable. Each trial session is conducted by a single judge or a special trial judge. All proceedings are public and are conducted judicially in accordance with the court's Rules of Practice and the rules of evidence applicable in trials without a jury in the U.S. District Court for the District of Columbia. A fee of $60 is prescribed for the filing of a petition. Practice before the court is limited to practitioners admitted under the court's Rules.

For further information, contact the Administrative Office, United States Tax Court, 400 Second Street NW., Washington, DC 20217. Phone, 202–606–8751.

United States Court of Appeals for Veterans Claims The United States Court of Veterans Appeals was established on November 18, 1988 (102 Stat. 4105, 38 U.S.C. 7251) pursuant to Article I of the Constitution, and given exclusive jurisdiction to review decisions of the Board of Veterans Appeals. The court was renamed the United States Court of Appeals for Veterans Claims by the Veterans Programs Enhancement Act of 1998 (38 U.S.C. 7251 note). The court may not review the schedule of ratings for disabilities or actions of the Secretary in adopting or revising that schedule. Decisions of the Court of Appeals for Veterans Claims may be appealed to the United States Court of Appeals for the Federal Circuit.

The court consists of seven judges appointed by the President, with the advice and consent of the Senate, for 15-year terms. One of the judges serves as chief judge.

The court's principal office is in the District of Columbia, but the court can also act at any place within the United States.

For further information, contact the Clerk, United States Court of Appeals for Veterans Claims, Suite 900, 625 Indiana Avenue NW., Washington, DC 20004–2950. Phone, 202–501–5970. Internet, www.vetapp.uscourts.gov.

Other Courts There have also been created two courts of local jurisdiction for the District of Columbia: the District of Columbia Court of Appeals and the Superior Court.

Business of the Federal Courts

The business of all the Federal courts described here, except the Court of Appeals for the Armed Forces, the Tax Court, the Court Appeals for Veterans Claims, and the District of Columbia courts, is discussed in detail in the text and tables of the *Annual Report of the Director of the Administrative Office of the United States Courts (1940–99).*

ADMINISTRATIVE OFFICE OF THE UNITED STATES COURTS

One Columbus Circle NE., Washington, DC 20544
Phone, 202–502–2600

Director	LEONIDAS RALPH MECHAM
Deputy Director	(VACANCY)
Associate Director, Management and Operations	CLARENCE A. (PETE) LEE, JR.
Audit Officer	DAVID L. GELLMAN
Management Coordination and Planning Officer	CATHY A. MCCARTHY
Program Assessment Officer	DUANE REX LEE
Associate Director and General Counsel	WILLIAM R. BURCHILL, JR.
Deputy General Counsel	ROBERT K. LOESCHE
Assistant Director, Office of Judicial Conference Executive Secretariat	KAREN K. SIEGEL
Deputy Assistant Director	WENDY JENNIS
Assistant Director, Office of Legislative Affairs	MICHAEL W. BLOMMER
Deputy Assistant Director	ARTHUR E. WHITE
Assistant Director, Office of Public Affairs	CHARLES D. CONNOR
Deputy Assistant Director	DAVID A. SELLERS
Assistant Director, Office of Court Programs	NOEL J. AUGUSTYN
Deputy Assistant Director for Court Administration	GLEN K. PALMAN
Chief, Appellate Court and Circuit Administration Division	JOHN P. HEHMAN
Chief, Bankruptcy Court Administration Division	GLEN K. PALMAN
Chief, Court Administration Policy Staff	ABEL J. MATTOS
Chief, Defender Services Division	THEODORE J. LIDZ
Chief, District Court Administration Division	ROBERT LOWNEY
Chief, Federal Corrections and Supervision Division	JOHN M. HUGHES
Assistant Director, Office of Facilities and Security	ROSS EISENMAN
Deputy Assistant Director	WILLIAM J. LEHMAN
Chief, Court Security Office	DENNIS P. CHAPAS
Chief, Policy and Resource Management Staff	SARA K. WALTERS
Chief, Space and Facilities Division	RODGERS A. STEWART
Assistant Director, Office of Finance and Budget	GEORGE H. SCHAFER

Deputy Assistant Director	Gregory D. Cummings
Chief, Accounting and Financial Systems Division	Philip L. McKinney
Chief, Budget Division	Bruce Johnson
Chief, Economy Subcommittee Support Office	Diane V. James
Financial Liaison Officer	Penny Jacobs Fleming
Assistant Director, Office of Human Resources and Statistics	Alton C. Ressler
Deputy Assistant Director	R. Townsend Robinson
Chief, Employee Relations Office	Trudi M. Morrison
Chief, Human Resources Division	Charlotte G. Peddicord
Chief, Judiciary Benefits Program Office	Lee Horvath
Chief, Program and Workforce Development Division	Maurice E. White
Chief, Statistics Division	Steven R. Schlesinger
Chief, Work Measurement Staff	Beverly J. Bone
Assistant Director, Office of Information Technology	Melvin J. Bryson, *Acting*
Chief, Applications Management and Development Division	Nicholas B. DiSabatino, *Acting*
Chief, Computer Security and Independent Testing Office	Robert N. Sinsheimer, *Acting*
Chief, Information Management and Resources Office	Joyce A. Lagana, *Acting*
Chief, Technology Enhancement Office	John R. Brinkema, *Acting*
Chief, Networks and Systems Integration Division	Richard D. Fennell, *Acting*
Chief, Technology Training and Support Division	Howard J. Grandier
Assistant Director, Office of Internal Services	Laura C. Minor
Deputy Assistant Director	Nancy Lee Bradshaw
Chief, Administrative Services Division	Doreen G.B. Bydume
Chief, Information Management Services Division	Frank S. Dozier, *Acting*
Chief, Personnel Division	Nancy Lee Bradshaw
Chief, Procurement Management Division	L. Henry Weeks, *Acting*
Assistant Director, Office of Judges Programs	Peter G. McCabe
Deputy Assistant Director for Policy Development	Jeffrey A. Hennemuth
Chief, Analytical Services Office	David L. Cook
Chief, Rules Committee Support Office	John K. Rabiej
Chief, Article III Judges Division	Michael W. Dolan
Chief, Bankruptcy Judges Division	Francis F. Szczebak
Chief, Magistrate Judges Division	Thomas C. Hnatowski

The Administrative Office of the United States Courts is charged with the nonjudicial, administrative business of the United States Courts, including the maintenance of workload statistics and the disbursement of funds appropriated for the maintenance of the U.S. judicial system.

The Administrative Office of the United States Courts was created by act of August 7, 1939 (28 U.S.C. 601). The Office was established November 6, 1939. Its Director and Deputy Director are appointed by the Chief Justice of the United States after consultation with the Judicial Conference.

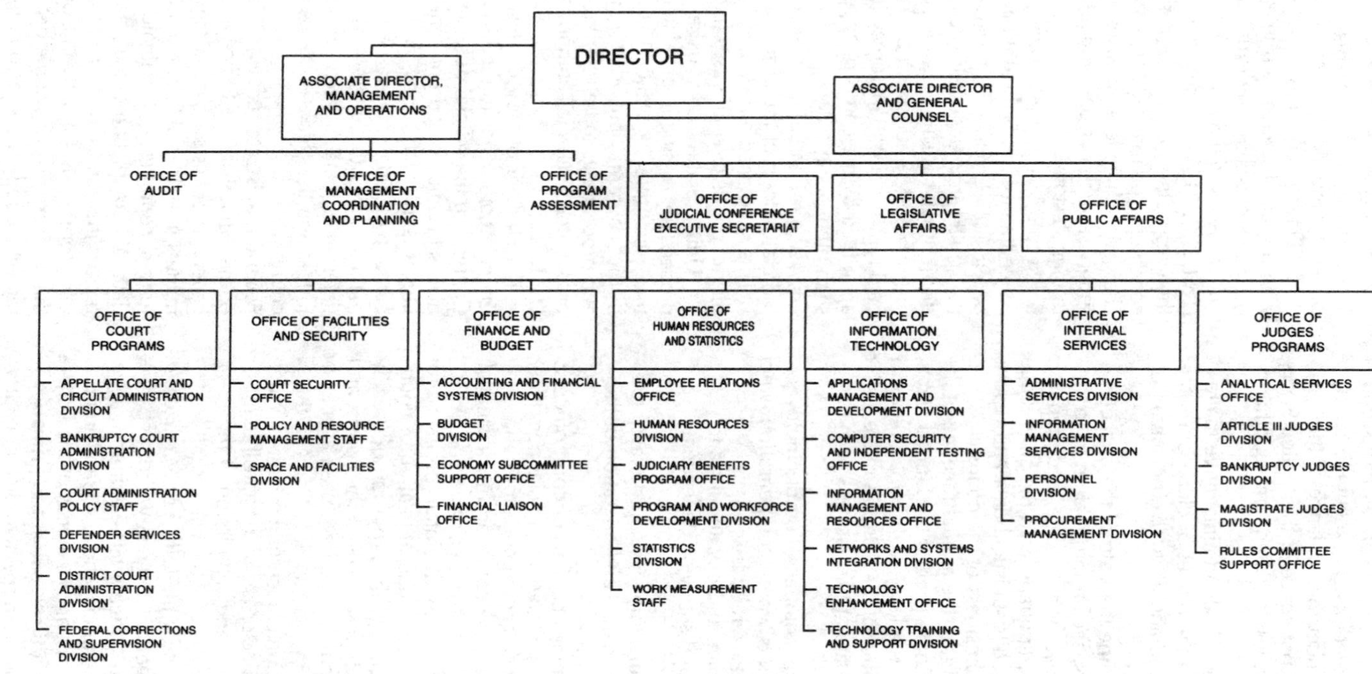
ADMINISTRATIVE OFFICE OF THE UNITED STATES COURTS
DIRECTOR
ASSOCIATE DIRECTOR, MANAGEMENT AND OPERATIONS
ASSOCIATE DIRECTOR AND GENERAL COUNSEL
OFFICE OF AUDIT
OFFICE OF MANAGEMENT COORDINATION AND PLANNING
OFFICE OF PROGRAM ASSESSMENT
OFFICE OF JUDICIAL CONFERENCE EXECUTIVE SECRETARIAT
OFFICE OF LEGISLATIVE AFFAIRS
OFFICE OF PUBLIC AFFAIRS
OFFICE OF COURT PROGRAMS
APPELLATE COURT AND CIRCUIT ADMINISTRATION DIVISION
BANKRUPTCY COURT ADMINISTRATION DIVISION
COURT ADMINISTRATION POLICY STAFF
DEFENDER SERVICES DIVISION
DISTRICT COURT ADMINISTRATION DIVISION
FEDERAL CORRECTIONS AND SUPERVISION DIVISION
OFFICE OF FACILITIES AND SECURITY
COURT SECURITY OFFICE
POLICY AND RESOURCE MANAGEMENT STAFF
SPACE AND FACILITIES DIVISION
OFFICE OF FINANCE AND BUDGET
ACCOUNTING AND FINANCIAL SYSTEMS DIVISION
BUDGET DIVISION
ECONOMY SUBCOMMITTEE SUPPORT OFFICE
FINANCIAL LIAISON OFFICE
OFFICE OF HUMAN RESOURCES AND STATISTICS
EMPLOYEE RELATIONS OFFICE
HUMAN RESOURCES DIVISION
JUDICIARY BENEFITS PROGRAM OFFICE
PROGRAM AND WORKFORCE DEVELOPMENT DIVISION
STATISTICS DIVISION
WORK MEASUREMENT STAFF
OFFICE OF INFORMATION TECHNOLOGY
APPLICATIONS MANAGEMENT AND DEVELOPMENT DIVISION
COMPUTER SECURITY AND INDEPENDENT TESTING OFFICE
INFORMATION MANAGEMENT AND RESOURCES OFFICE
NETWORKS AND SYSTEMS INTEGRATION DIVISION
TECHNOLOGY ENHANCEMENT OFFICE
TECHNOLOGY TRAINING AND SUPPORT DIVISION
OFFICE OF INTERNAL SERVICES
ADMINISTRATIVE SERVICES DIVISION
INFORMATION MANAGEMENT SERVICES DIVISION
PERSONNEL DIVISION
PROCUREMENT MANAGEMENT DIVISION
OFFICE OF JUDGES PROGRAMS
ANALYTICAL SERVICES OFFICE
ARTICLE III JUDGES DIVISION
BANKRUPTCY JUDGES DIVISION
MAGISTRATE JUDGES DIVISION
RULES COMMITTEE SUPPORT OFFICE

Administering the Courts The Director is the administrative officer of the courts of the United States (except the Supreme Court). Under the guidance of the Judicial Conference of the United States the Director is required, among other things, to:

—supervise all administrative matters relating to the offices of clerks and other clerical and administrative personnel of the courts;

—examine the state of the dockets of the courts, secure information as to the courts' need of assistance, and prepare and transmit quarterly to the chief judges of the circuits statistical data and reports as to the business of the courts;

—submit to the annual meeting of the Judicial Conference of the United States, at least 2 weeks prior thereto, a report of the activities of the Administrative Office and the state of the business of the courts;

—fix the compensation of employees of the courts whose compensation is not otherwise fixed by law;

—regulate and pay annuities to widows and surviving dependent children of judges;

—disburse moneys appropriated for the maintenance and operation of the courts;

—examine accounts of court officers;

—regulate travel of judicial personnel;

—provide accommodations and supplies for the courts and their clerical and administrative personnel;

—establish and maintain programs for the certification and utilization of court interpreters and the provision of special interpretation services in the courts; and

—perform such other duties as may be assigned by the Supreme Court or the Judicial Conference of the United States.

The Director is also responsible for the preparation and submission of the budget of the courts, which shall be transmitted by the Office of Management and Budget to Congress without change.

Probation Officers The Administrative Office exercises general supervision of the accounts and practices of the Federal probation offices, subject to primary control by the respective district courts that they serve. The Office publishes quarterly, in cooperation with the Bureau of Prisons of the Department of Justice, a magazine entitled *Federal Probation,* which is a journal "of correctional philosophy and practice."

The Director also has responsibility with respect to the establishment of pretrial services in the district courts under the Pretrial Services Act of 1982 (18 U.S.C. 3152). These offices report to their respective courts information concerning pretrial release of persons charged with Federal offenses and supervise such persons who are released to their custody.

Bankruptcy The Bankruptcy Amendments and Federal Judgeship Act of 1984 (28 U.S.C. 151) provided that the bankruptcy judges for each judicial district shall constitute a unit of the district court to be known as the bankruptcy court. Bankruptcy judges are appointed by the courts of appeals in such numbers as authorized by Congress and serve for a term of 14 years as judicial officers of the district courts.

This act placed jurisdiction in the district courts over all cases under title 11, United States Code, and all proceedings arising in or related to cases under that title (28 U.S.C. 1334). The district court may provide for such cases and proceedings to be referred to its bankruptcy judges (as authorized by 28 U.S.C. 157).

The Director of the Administrative Office recommends to the Judicial Conference the official duty stations and places of holding court of bankruptcy judges, surveys the need for additional bankruptcy judgeships to be recommended to Congress, and determines the staff needs of bankruptcy judges and the clerks of the bankruptcy courts.

Federal Magistrate Judges The Director of the Administrative Office exercises general supervision over administrative matters in offices of U.S. magistrate judges, compiles and evaluates statistical data relating to such offices, and submits reports thereon to the Conference. The Director reports annually to Congress on the business that has come before U.S. magistrate judges and also prepares legal and administrative manuals for the use of the magistrate judges. The act provides for surveys to be conducted by the Administrative Office of the conditions in the judicial districts in order to make recommendations as to the number, location, and salaries of magistrate judges, which are determined by the Conference subject to the availability of appropriated funds.

Federal Defenders The Criminal Justice Act (18 U.S.C. 3006A) establishes the procedure for the appointment of counsel in Federal criminal cases for individuals who are unable to afford adequate representation under plans adopted by each district court. The act also permits the establishment of Federal public defender or Federal community defender organizations by the district courts in districts where at least 200 persons annually require the appointment of counsel. Two adjacent districts may be combined to reach this total.

Each defender organization submits to the Director of the Administrative Office an annual report of its activities along with a proposed budget or, in the case of community defender organizations, a proposed grant for the coming year. The Director is responsible for the submission of the proposed budgets and grants to the Judicial Conference for approval. The Director also makes payments to the defender organizations out of appropriations in accordance with the approved budgets and grants, as well as compensating private counsel appointed to defend criminal cases in the United States courts.

Sources of Information

Information may be obtained from the following offices:

Bankruptcy Judges Division. Phone, 202–502–1900.

Budget Division. Phone, 202–502–2100.

Defender Services Division. Phone, 202–502–1670.

Federal Corrections and Supervision Division. Phone, 202–502–1610.

General Counsel. Phone, 202–502–1100.

Human Resources Division. Phone, 202–502–3100.

Judicial Conference Executive Secretariat. Phone, 202–502–2400.

Legislative Affairs Office. Phone, 202–502–1700.

Magistrate Judges Division. Phone, 202–502–1830.

Public Affairs Office. Phone, 202–502–2600.

Statistics Division. Phone, 202–502–1440.

For further information, contact one of the offices listed above, Administrative Office of the United States Courts, Thurgood Marshall Federal Judiciary Building, One Columbus Circle NE., Washington, DC 20544.

FEDERAL JUDICIAL CENTER

Thurgood Marshall Federal Judiciary Building, One Columbus Circle NE., Washington, DC 20002–8003
Phone, 202–502–4000. Internet, www.fjc.gov.

Director	FERN M. SMITH
Deputy Director	RUSSELL R. WHEELER
Director of Research	JAMES B. EAGLIN
Director of Judicial Education	JOHN S. COOKE
Director of Court Education	EMILY Z. HUEBNER
Director of Communications Policy and Design	SYLVAN A. SOBEL

The Federal Judicial Center is the judicial branch's agency for policy research and continuing education.

The Federal Judicial Center was created by act of December 20, 1967 (28 U.S.C. 620), to further the development and adoption of improved judicial administration in the courts of the United States.

The Center's basic policies and activities are determined by its Board, which is composed of the Chief Justice of the United States, who is permanent Chairman of the Board by statute, and two judges of the U.S. courts of appeals, three judges of the U.S. district courts, one bankruptcy judge, and one magistrate judge, all of whom are elected for 4-year terms by the Judicial Conference of the United States. The Director of the Administrative Office of the United States Courts is also a permanent member of the Board.

Pursuant to statute the Center:

—develops and administers orientation and continuing education programs for Federal judges, Federal defenders, and nonjudicial court personnel, including probation officers, pretrial services officers, and clerks' office employees;

—conducts empirical and exploratory research and evaluation on Federal judicial processes, court management, and sentencing and its consequences, usually for the committees of the Judicial Conference or the courts themselves;

—produces research reports, training manuals, satellite broadcasts, video programs, and periodicals about the Federal courts;

—provides guidance and advice and maintains data and records to assist those interested in documenting and conserving the history of the Federal courts; and

—cooperates with and assists other agencies and organizations in providing advice to improve the administration of justice in the courts of foreign countries.

Sources of Information

Information may be obtained from the following offices:

Director and Deputy Director's Office. Phone, 202–502–4162, or 202–502–4164. Fax, 202–502–4099.

Research Division. Phone, 202–502–4071. Fax, 202–502–4199.

Judicial Education Division. Phone, 202–502–4060. Fax, 202–502–4299.

Court Education Division. Phone, 202–502–4110. Fax, 202–502–4088.

Communications Policy and Design Division. Phone 202–502–4250. Fax, 202–502–4077.

Federal Judicial History Office. Phone, 202–502–4181. Fax, 202–502–4077.

Information Services Office. Phone, 202–502–4153. Fax, 202–502–4077.

Interjudicial Affairs Office. Phone, 202–502–4161. Fax, 202–502–4099.

Personnel Office. Phone, 202–502–4165. Fax, 202–502–4099.

Systems Innovations and Development Office. Phone, 202–502–4223. Fax, 202–502–4288.

Electronic Access Selected Federal Judicial Center publications are available in electronic form through the Internet, at www.fjc.gov.

Publications Single copies of most Federal Judicial Center publications are available free of charge. Phone, 202–502–4153. Fax, 202–502–4077.

For further information, contact the Federal Judicial Center, Thurgood Marshall Federal Judiciary Building, One Columbus Circle NE., Washington, DC 20002–8003. Phone, 202–502–4000. Internet, www.fjc.gov.

UNITED STATES SENTENCING COMMISSION

Suite 2–500, South Lobby, One Columbus Circle NE., Washington, DC 20002–8002
Phone, 202–502–4500. Internet, www.ussc.gov.

Chair	Diana E. Murphy
Vice Chairs	Ruben Castillo, William K. Sessions III, John R. Steer
Commissioners	Sterling Johnson, Jr., Joe Kendall, Michael O'Neill

Commissioners (*ex officio*)	MICHAEL J. GAINES, LAIRD C. KIRKPATRICK
Staff Director	TIMOTHY B. MCGRATH, *Acting*
General Counsel	DONALD A. PURDY, JR., *Acting*
Public Affairs Officer	MICHAEL COURLANDER
Director of Administration and Planning	SUSAN L. WINARSKY
Director of Education and Sentencing Practice	SHARON O. HENEGAN
Director of Legislative and Governmental Affairs	KENNETH P. COHEN
Director of Monitoring	RICHARD J. MCNEIL
Director of Policy Analysis	LOUIS W. REEDT, *Acting*
Special Counsel	JUDITH W. SHEON

The United States Sentencing Commission develops sentencing policies and practices for the Federal criminal justice system.

The United States Sentencing Commission was established as an independent agency in the judicial branch of the Federal Government by the Sentencing Reform Act of 1984 (28 U.S.C. 991 *et seq.* and 18 U.S.C. 3551 *et seq.*). The Commission establishes sentencing policies and practices for the Federal courts, including guidelines prescribing the appropriate form and severity of punishment for offenders convicted of Federal crimes.

The Commission is composed of seven voting members appointed by the President with the advice and consent of the Senate for 6-year terms, and two nonvoting members. One of the voting members is appointed Chairperson.

The Commission evaluates the effects of the sentencing guidelines on the criminal justice system, advises Congress regarding the modification or enactment of statutes relating to criminal law and sentencing matters, establishes a research and development program on sentencing issues, and performs other related duties.

In executing its duties, the Commission promulgates and distributes to Federal courts and to the U.S. probation system guidelines to be used in determining sentences to be imposed in criminal cases, general policy statements regarding the application of guidelines, and policy statements on the appropriate use of probation and supervised release revocation provisions. These sentencing guidelines and policy statements are designed to further the purposes of just punishment, deterrence, incapacitation, and rehabilitation; provide fairness in meeting the purposes of sentencing; avoid unwarranted disparity; and reflect advancement in the knowledge of human behavior as it relates to the criminal justice process.

In addition, the Commission provides training, conducts research on sentencing-related issues, and serves as an information resource for Congress, criminal justice practitioners, and the public.

Sources of Information

Electronic Access Commission information and materials may be obtained through the Internet, at www.ussc.gov.

Guideline Application Assistance Helpline Phone, 202–502–4545.

Public Information Information concerning Commission activities is available from the Office of Publishing and Public Affairs. Phone, 202–502–4590.

For further information, contact the Office of Publishing and Public Affairs, United States Sentencing Commission, Suite 2–500, South Lobby, One Columbus Circle NE., Washington, DC 20002–8002. Phone, 202–502–4590. Internet, www.ussc.gov.

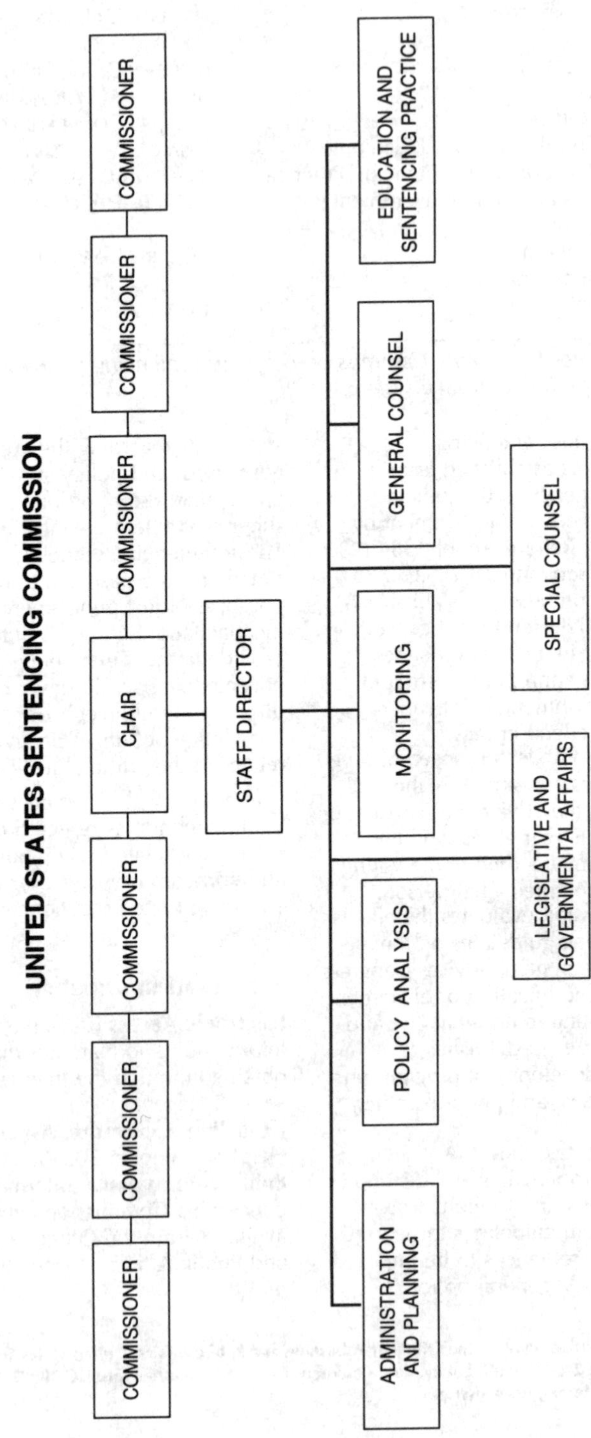
UNITED STATES SENTENCING COMMISSION
COMMISSIONER
COMMISSIONER
COMMISSIONER
CHAIR
COMMISSIONER
COMMISSIONER
COMMISSIONER
STAFF DIRECTOR
EDUCATION AND SENTENCING PRACTICE
GENERAL COUNSEL
SPECIAL COUNSEL
MONITORING
LEGISLATIVE AND GOVERNMENTAL AFFAIRS
POLICY ANALYSIS
ADMINISTRATION AND PLANNING

Executive Branch

EXECUTIVE BRANCH

THE PRESIDENT OF THE UNITED STATES

THE PRESIDENT OF THE UNITED STATES WILLIAM J. CLINTON

Article II, section 1, of the Constitution provides that "[t]he executive Power shall be vested in a President of the United States of America. He shall hold his Office during the Term of four Years, . . . together with the Vice President, chosen for the same Term . . . ." In addition to the powers set forth in the Constitution, the statutes have conferred upon the President specific authority and responsibility covering a wide range of matters (United States Code Index).

The President is the administrative head of the executive branch of the Government, which includes numerous agencies, both temporary and permanent, as well as the 14 executive departments.

The Cabinet

The Cabinet, a creation of custom and tradition dating back to George Washington's administration, functions at the pleasure of the President. Its purpose is to advise the President upon any subject, relating to the duties of the respective offices, on which he requests information (pursuant to Article II, section 2, of the Constitution).

The Cabinet is composed of the heads of the 14 executive departments—the Secretaries of Agriculture, Commerce, Defense, Education, Energy, Health and Human Services, Housing and Urban Development, Interior, Labor, State, Transportation, Treasury, and Veterans Affairs, and the Attorney General. Additionally, in the Clinton administration, Cabinet-level rank has been accorded to: the Chief of Staff to the President; the Director of Central Intelligence; the Chairman, Council of Economic Advisers; the Counselor to the President; the Administrator, Environmental Protection Agency; the Director, Federal Emergency Management Agency; the Director, Office of Management and Budget; the Director, Office of National Drug Control Policy; the Administrator, Small Business Administration; the U.S. Representative to the United Nations; and the U.S. Trade Representative. The Vice President also participates in Cabinet meetings, and from time to time, other individuals are invited to participate in discussions of particular subjects. A Secretary to the Cabinet is designated to provide for the orderly handling and followup of matters brought before the Cabinet.

THE VICE PRESIDENT OF THE UNITED STATES

THE VICE PRESIDENT	AL GORE

Article II, section I, of the Constitution provides that the President "shall hold his Office during the Term of four Years . . . together with the Vice President . . . ." In addition to his role as President of the Senate, the Vice President is empowered to succeed to the Presidency, pursuant to Article II and the 20th and 25th amendments to the Constitution.

The executive functions of the Vice President include participation in Cabinet meetings and, by statute, membership on the National Security Council and the Board of Regents of the Smithsonian Institution.

EXECUTIVE OFFICE OF THE PRESIDENT

Under authority of the Reorganization Act of 1939 (5 U.S.C. 133–133r, 133t note), various agencies were transferred to the Executive Office of the President by the President's Reorganization Plans I and II of 1939 (5 U.S.C. app.), effective July 1, 1939. Executive Order 8248 of September 8, 1939, established the divisions of the Executive Office and defined their functions. Subsequently, Presidents have used Executive orders, reorganization plans, and legislative initiatives to reorganize the Executive Office to make its composition compatible with the goals of their administrations.

The White House Office

1600 Pennsylvania Avenue NW., Washington, DC 20500
Phone, 202–456–1414. Internet, www.whitehouse.gov.

Chief of Staff to the President	JOHN D. PODESTA
Assistant to the President	SIDNEY BLUMENTHAL
Assistant to the President and Cabinet Secretary	THURGOOD MARSHALL, JR.
Assistant to the President and Chief of Staff to the First Lady	MELANNE VERVEER
Assistant to the President and Counselor to the Chief of Staff	KAREN TRAMONTANO
Assistant to the President and Deputy Counsel to the President	BRUCE LINDSEY
Assistant to the President and Director of Advance	DAN K. ROSENTHAL
Assistant to the President and Director of Communications	LORETTA UCELLI
Assistant to the President and Director of Intergovernmental Affairs	MICKEY IBARRA
Assistant to the President and Director of Legislative Affairs	CHARLES M. BRAIN
Assistant to the President and Director of Political Affairs	MINYON MOORE
Assistant to the President and Director of Presidential Personnel	BOB NASH

Assistant to the President and Director of Public Liaison	MARY ELIZABETH CAHILL
Assistant to the President and Director of Scheduling	STEPHANIE STREETT
Assistant to the President and Director of Speechwriting	J. TERRY EDMONDS
Assistant to the President and Director of the President's Initiative for One America	ROBERT B. JOHNSON
Assistant to the President and Press Secretary	JOSEPH LOCKHART
Assistant to the President and Special Envoy to the Americas	KENNETH H. MACKAY
Assistant to the President and Staff Secretary	SEAN P. MALONEY
Assistant to the President for Domestic Policy and Director of the Domestic Policy Council	BRUCE N. REED
Assistant to the President for Economic Policy and Director of the National Economic Council	GENE SPERLING
Assistant to the President for Management and Administration	MARK F. LINDSAY
Assistant to the President for National Security Affairs	SAMUEL R. BERGER
Assistants to the President and Deputy Chiefs of Staff	MARIA ECHAVESTE, STEPHEN J. RICCHETTI
Associate Counsels to the President	DAVID APOL, MEREDITH CABE, DAWN CHIRWA, DIMITRI NIONAKIS, MICHAEL E. O'CONNOR, J. PAUL OETKEN, MICHELLE PETERSON, KARL RACINE, PETER F. RUNDLET
Counsel to the President	BETH NOLAN
Counselor to the President	ANN F. LEWIS
Deputy Assistant to the President and Advisor to the First Lady for the Millennium Program	ELLEN LOVELL
Deputy Assistant to the President and Deputy Cabinet Secretary	KRIS M. BALDERSTON
Deputy Assistant to the President and Deputy Chief of Staff to the First Lady	SHIRLEY SAGAWA
Deputy Assistant to the President and Deputy Counsel to the President	WILLIAM MARSHALL
Deputy Assistant to the President and Deputy Director of Advance	DOUGLAS J. BAND
Deputy Assistant to the President and Deputy Director of Communication	STEPHANIE CUTTER
Deputy Assistant to the President and Deputy Director of Intergovernmental Affairs	RAY MARTINEZ III
Deputy Assistant to the President and Deputy Director of Legislative Affairs	KAY CASSTEVENS
Deputy Assistant to the President and Deputy Director of Political Affairs	LINDA L. MOORE
Deputy Assistant to the President and Deputy Director of Public Liaison	LAURA EFURD
Deputy Assistant to the President and Deputy Director of Speechwriting	JEFFREY SHESOL

186-873 D-00--4

Deputy Assistant to the President and Deputy Staff Secretary	LISEL LOY
Deputy Assistant to the President and Director of Communications for the First Lady	ALLISON MUSCATINE
Deputy Assistant to the President and Director of Correspondence and Presidential Messages	DANIEL BURKHARDT
Deputy Assistant to the President and Director of Oval Office Operations	NANCY HERNREICH
Deputy Assistant to the President and Director of Scheduling for the First Lady	PATRICIA SOLIS DOYLE
Deputy Assistant to the President and Trip Director	KELLY CRAIGHEAD
Deputy Assistant to the President and Director of the White House Military Office	JOSEPH J. SIMMONS IV
Deputy Assistant to the President and Director, Women's Initiatives and Outreach	LAUREN SUPINA
Deputy Assistant to the President and Senior Advisor to the Chief of Staff for Indian Affairs and Special Projects	LYNN CUTLER
Deputy Assistant to the President and Senior Legislative Counsel	MARTHA FOLEY
Deputy Assistant to the President and Social Secretary	CAPRICIA MARSHALL
Deputy Assistant to the President for Domestic Policy	ERIC LIU
Deputy Assistant to the President for Environmental Initiatives	ROGER BALLENTINE
Deputy Assistant to the President for Health Policy	CHRISTOPHER C. JENNINGS
Deputy Assistant to the President for Legislative Affairs (House)	BRODERICK JOHNSON
Deputy Assistant to the President for Legislative Affairs and Senate Liaison	KAREN ROBB
Deputy Assistant to the President for Management and Administration	BRADLEY J. KILEY
Deputy Assistant to the President for National Security Affairs	MARA RUDMAN
Deputy Assistant to the President for National Security Affairs and Deputy National Security Advisor	JAMES B. STEINBERG
Deputy Assistants to the President and Deputy Directors of Presidential Personnel	MARIA L. HALEY, MARSHA SCOTT
Deputy Assistants to the President and Deputy Press Secretaries	JAMES KENNEDY, JENNIFER PALMIERI, RICHARD SIEWERT, JR.
Senior Adviser to the President for Policy and Communications	JOEL P. JOHNSON
Senior Adviser to the President for Policy and Strategy	THOMAS FREEDMAN
Senior Associate Counsel to the President	STEVEN REICH
Special Assistant to the President and Assistant Press Secretary	NANDA CHITRE
Special Assistant to the President and Associate Director of Advance	ROBERT ROSEN

Special Assistant to the President and Chief of Staff for Political Affairs	CYNTHIA JASSO-ROTUNNO
Special Assistant to the President and Chief of Staff for Public Liaison	CHRISTINE STANEK
Special Assistant to the President and Chief of Staff to the Special Envoy to the Americas	FRANCISCO SANCHEZ
Special Assistant to the President and Deputy Director of Presidential Scheduling	LAURA GRAHAM
Special Assistant to the President and Deputy Director of Communications	THOMAS D. JANENDA
Special Assistant to the President and Deputy Director, President's Initiative for One America	KATHLEEN AHN
Special Assistant to the President and Director of Media Operations	DORINDA SALCIDO
Special Assistant to the President and Director of Personal Correspondence	ANN MCCOY
Special Assistant to the President and Director of Press Advance	ANNE M. EDWARDS
Special Assistant to the President and Director of Television News	JULIA PAYNE
Special Assistant to the President and Director of the White House Travel Office	SUSAN L. HAZARD
Special Assistant to the President and Director, First Lady's Correspondence	ALICE PUSHKAR
Special Assistant to the President and Director, Visitors Office	MELINDA BATES
Special Assistant to the President and Senior Presidential Speechwriter	PAUL GLASTRIS
Special Assistant to the President and Special Adviser for Presidential History	JANIS F. KEARNEY
Special Assistant to the President and Special Counselor to the Chief of Staff	MICHELE BALLANTYNE
Special Assistant to the President and Trip Director	KIRK HANLIN
Special Assistants to the President and Associate Directors of Presidential Personnel	LEE ANN BRACKETT, VERONICA DE LA GARZA, CHERYL TATES-MACIAS
Special Assistants to the President and Associate Directors of Public Liaison	MAUREEN SHEA, BARBARA WOOLLEY
Special Assistants to the President and Deputy Directors of Presidential Advance	BRIAN ALCORN, MARISA LUZZATTO
Special Assistants to the President and Deputy Directors of Presidential Scheduling	HEATHER DAVIS, JULIE EDDY, STEPHEN LAMB
Special Assistants to the President and Presidential Speechwriters	SAMIR AFRIDI, HEATHER HURLBURT, LOWELL WEISS
Special Assistants to the President and Senior Speechwriters	LAURA SCHILLER, JUNE SHIH
Special Assistants to the President for Domestic Policy	IRENE BUENO, ANN O'LEARY
Special Assistants to the President for Intergovernmental Affairs	MATTHEW BENNETT, ZINA PIERRE
Special Assistants to the President for Legislative Affairs (House)	LISA KOUNTOUPES, MARK MAGANA

Special Assistants to the President for Legislative Affairs (Senate)	JULIE M. ANDERSON, JOANNA SLANEY, JOEL WIGINTON
Special Counsel to the President for Nominations	SARAH WILSON

The White House Office serves the President in the performance of the many detailed activities incident to his immediate office.

The staff of the President facilitates and maintains communication with the Congress, the individual Members of the Congress, the heads of executive agencies, the press and other information media, and the general public.

The various Assistants to the President assist the President in such matters as he may direct.

Office of the Vice President of the United States

Eisenhower Executive Office Building, Washington, DC 20501
Phone, 202–456–2326

Assistant to the President and Chief of Staff and Counselor to the Vice President	CHARLES BURSON
Deputy Chief of Staff	MONICA MAPLES DIXON
Chief Domestic Policy Adviser for the Vice President	DAVID BEIER
Chief of Staff to Mrs. Gore	AUDREY HAYNES
Counsel to the Vice President	ELIZABETH BROWN
Director of Correspondence for the Vice President	ERIC ANDERSON
Director of Legislative Affairs for the Vice President	RONNA FREIBERG
Director of Scheduling and Advance for the Vice President	LISA BERG
Executive Assistant to the Vice President	PATRICIA MCHUGH
National Security Adviser for the Vice President	LEON S. FUERTH
Political Director	MAURICE DANIEL
Senior Adviser to the Vice President	MICHAEL FELDMAN
Senior Adviser to the Vice President for Policy	WILLIAM SAMUEL
Senior Policy Adviser for the Vice President	MORLEY WINOGRAD

The Office of the Vice President serves the Vice President in the performance of the many detailed activities incident to his immediate office.

Council of Economic Advisers

Old Executive Office Building, Washington, DC 20502
Phone, 202–395–5084. Internet, www.whitehouse.gov/WH/EOP/CEA/html/CEA.html.

Chairman	MARTIN N. BAILY

Members	ROBERT Z. LAWRENCE, KATHRYN L. SHAW
Chief of Staff	ADUREY CHOI

The Council of Economic Advisers primarily performs an analysis and appraisal of the national economy for the purpose of providing policy recommendations to the President.

The Council of Economic Advisers (CEA) was established in the Executive Office of the President by the Employment Act of 1946 (15 U.S.C. 1023). It now functions under that statute and Reorganization Plan No. 9 of 1953 (5 U.S.C. app.), effective August 1, 1953.

The Council consists of three members appointed by the President with the advice and consent of the Senate. One of the members is designated by the President as Chairman.

The Council analyzes the national economy and its various segments; advises the President on economic developments; appraises the economic programs and policies of the Federal Government; recommends to the President policies for economic growth and stability; assists in the preparation of the economic reports of the President to the Congress; and prepares the Annual Report of the Council of Economic Advisers.

For further information, contact the Council of Economic Advisers, Old Executive Office Building, Washington, DC 20502. Phone, 202–395–5084. Internet, www.whitehouse.gov/WH/EOP/CEA/html/CEA.html.

Council on Environmental Quality

Room 360, Eisenhower Executive Office Building, Washington, DC 20501
Phone, 202–456–6224. Internet, www.whitehouse.gov/ceq.
722 Jackson Place NW., Washington, DC 20503
Phone, 202–395–5750

Chair	GEORGE T. FRAMPTON, *Acting*
Chief of Staff	DANIEL SAKURA
Associate Director for Congressional Relations	JUDY JABLOW
Associate Director for Fisheries and Coastal Issues	SARAH LASKIN
Associate Director for International Affairs	IAN BOWLES
Associate Director for Natural Resources	WILLIAM LEARY
Associate Director for NEPA Oversight	HORST GRECZMIEL
Associate Director for Transportation, Energy, and Land Management	LINDA LANCE
Associate Director for Sustainable Development	KEITH LAUGHLIN
Associate Director for Toxins and Environmental Protection	GABRIELLE TENZER
Director for Outreach	SUSAN KASLOW
Director of Communications	ELLIOT DIRINGER
General Counsel	DINAH BEAR

The Council on Environmental Quality formulates and recommends national policies to promote the improvement of the quality of the environment.

The Council on Environmental Quality (CEQ) was established within the Executive Office of the President by the National Environmental Policy Act of 1969 (NEPA) (42 U.S.C. 4321 *et seq.*). The Environmental Quality Improvement Act of 1970 (42 U.S.C. 4371 *et seq.*) established the Office of Environmental Quality (OEQ) to provide professional and administrative support for the Council. The Council and OEQ are collectively referred to as the Council on Environmental Quality, and the CEQ Chair, who is appointed by the President, serves as the Director of OEQ.

The Council develops policies which bring into productive harmony the Nation's social, economic, and environmental priorities, with the goal of improving the quality of Federal decisionmaking. As required by NEPA, CEQ evaluates, coordinates, and mediates Federal activities; advises and assists the President on both national and international environmental policy matters; and prepares the President's annual environmental quality report to Congress. In addition, it oversees Federal agency and department implementation of NEPA.

For further information, contact the Information Office, Council on Environmental Quality, 722 Jackson Place NW., Washington, DC 20503. Phone, 202–395–5750. Fax, 202–456–6546. Internet, www.whitehouse.gov/ceq.

National Security Council

Eisenhower Executive Office Building, Washington, DC 20506
Phone, 202–456–1414

Members:	
The President	WILLIAM J. CLINTON
The Vice President	AL GORE
The Secretary of State	MADELEINE K. ALBRIGHT
The Secretary of Defense	WILLIAM S. COHEN
Statutory Advisers:	
Director of Central Intelligence	GEORGE J. TENET
Chairman, Joint Chiefs of Staff	GEN. HENRY H. SHELTON, USA
Standing Participants:	
The Secretary of the Treasury	LAWRENCE H. SUMMERS
U.S. Representative to the United Nations	PETER BURLEIGH, *Acting*
Chief of Staff to the President	JOHN PODESTA
Assistant to the President for National Security Affairs	SAMUEL R. BERGER
Assistant to the President for Economic Policy	GENE SPERLING
Officials:	
Assistant to the President for National Security Affairs	SAMUEL R. BERGER
Deputy Assistants to the President for National Security Affairs	MARA RUDMAN, JAMES B. STEINBERG
Executive Secretary	ROBERT BRADTKE

The National Security Council was established by the National Security Act of 1947, as amended (50 U.S.C. 402). The Council was placed in the Executive

Office of the President by Reorganization Plan No. 4 of 1949 (5 U.S.C. app.).

The National Security Council is chaired by the President. Its statutory members, in addition to the President, are the Vice President and the Secretaries of State and Defense. The Chairman of the Joint Chiefs of Staff is the statutory military adviser to the Council, and the Director of Central Intelligence is its intelligence adviser. The Secretary of the Treasury, the U.S. Representative to the United Nations, the Assistant to the President for National Security Affairs, the Assistant to the President for Economic Policy, and the Chief of Staff to the President are invited to all meetings of the Council. The Attorney General and the Director of National Drug Control Policy are invited to attend meetings pertaining to their jurisdictions; other officials are invited, as appropriate.

The Council advises and assists the President in integrating all aspects of national security policy as it affects the United States—domestic, foreign, military, intelligence, and economic—in conjunction with the National Economic Council.

For further information, contact the National Security Council, Old Executive Office Building, Washington, DC 20506. Phone, 202–456–1414.

Office of Administration

Eisenhower Executive Office Building
725 Seventeenth Street NW., Washington, DC 20503
Phone, 202–395–6963

Director	MICHAEL J. LYLE
General Counsel	JOHN H. YOUNG
Associate Director for Equal Employment Opportunity	SHARON L. SOLOMON
Associate Director for Facilities Management	LARRY E. HANDELAND
Associate Director for Financial Management	ELIZABETH GELFER, *Acting*
Associate Director for General Services	KENNETH K. HEMBREE, *Acting*
Associate Director for Human Resources	MARY COUTTS BECK
Associate Director for Information Systems and Technology	LEANNA F. TERRELL
Associate Director for Library and Research Services	MARY ANN NOWELL
Associate Director for Operations and Legislative Liaison	JOYCE A. LARKIN
Associate Director for Security	CHARLES C. EASLEY

The Office of Administration was established within the Executive Office of the President by Reorganization Plan No. 1 of 1977 (5 U.S.C. app.). The Office was activated, effective December 4, 1977, by Executive Order 12028 of December 12, 1977.

The Office of Administration provides administrative support services to all units within the Executive Office of the President. The services provided include information, personnel, and financial management; data processing; library services; records maintenance; and general office operations, such as mail, messenger, printing, procurement, and supply services.

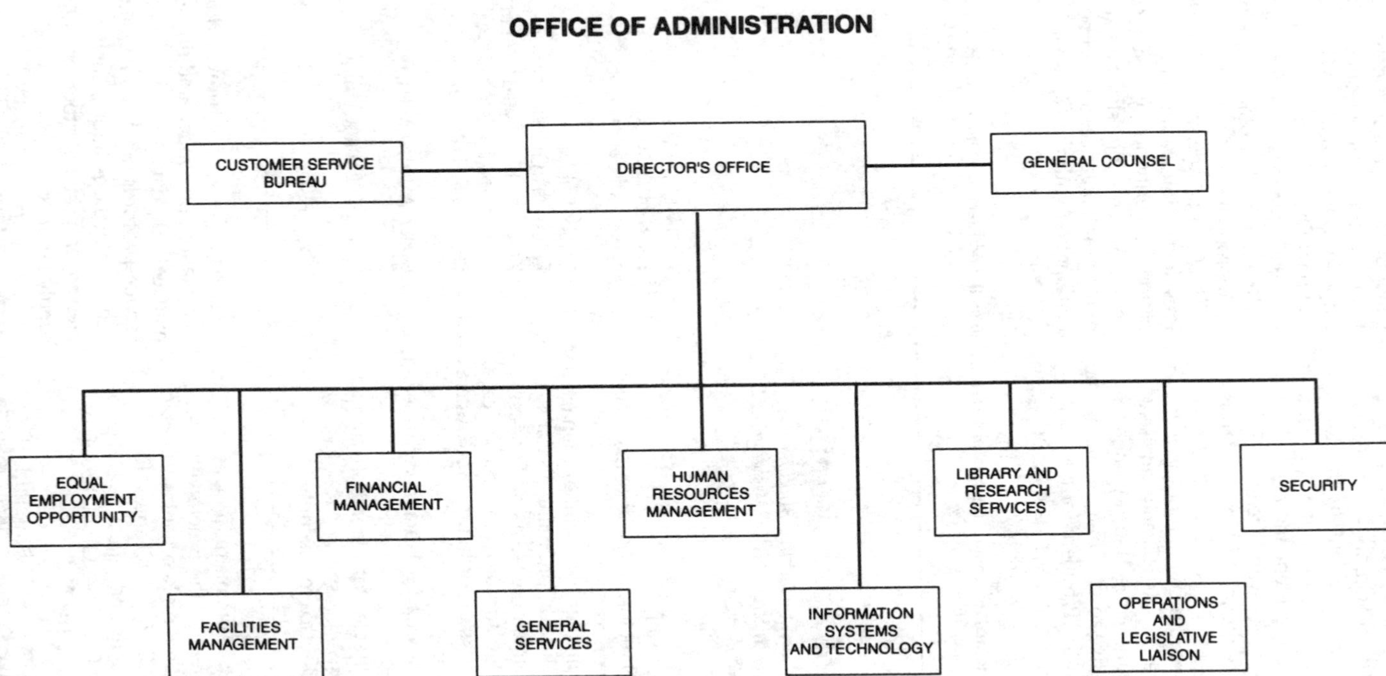
OFFICE OF ADMINISTRATION
CUSTOMER SERVICE BUREAU
DIRECTOR'S OFFICE
GENERAL COUNSEL
EQUAL EMPLOYMENT OPPORTUNITY
FACILITIES MANAGEMENT
FINANCIAL MANAGEMENT
GENERAL SERVICES
HUMAN RESOURCES MANAGEMENT
INFORMATION SYSTEMS AND TECHNOLOGY
LIBRARY AND RESEARCH SERVICES
OPERATIONS AND LEGISLATIVE LIAISON
SECURITY

For further information, contact the Office of the Director, Office of Administration, Washington, DC 20503. Phone, 202–456–2861.

Office of Management and Budget

Executive Office Building, Washington, DC 20503
Phone, 202–395–3080. Internet, www.whitehouse.gov/omb.

Director	JACOB J. LEW
Deputy Director	SYLVIA MATHEWS
Deputy Director for Management	(VACANCY)
Executive Secretary and Associate Director for Administration	ROBERT L. NABORS II
Administrator, Office of Federal Procurement Policy	DEIDRE LEE
Administrator, Office of Information and Regulatory Affairs	JOHN SPOTILA
Assistant Director for Budget	DICK EMERY
Assistant Director for Legislative Reference	JAMES J. JUKES
Associate Director for Communications	LINDA RICCA
Associate Director for Economic Policy	JOSEPH MINARIK
Associate Director for Education, Income Maintenance, and Labor	BARBARA CHOW
Associate Director for Health and Personnel	JEANNE LAMBREW
Associate Director for General Government and Finance	MICHAEL DEICH
Associate Director for Legislative Affairs	CHARLES KIEFFER, *Acting*
Associate Director for National Security and International Affairs	BOB KYLE
Associate Director for Natural Resources, Energy, and Science	WESLEY WARREN
Controller and Executive Associate Director, Office of Federal Financial Management	JOSHUA GOTBAUM
General Counsel	ROBERT DAMUS

The Office of Management and Budget evaluates, formulates, and coordinates management procedures and program objectives within and among Federal departments and agencies. It also controls the administration of the Federal budget, while routinely providing the President with recommendations regarding budget proposals and relevant legislative enactments.

The Office of Management and Budget (OMB), formerly the Bureau of the Budget, was established in the Executive Office of the President pursuant to Reorganization Plan No. 1 of 1939 (5 U.S.C. app.).

The Office's primary functions are:

—to assist the President in developing and maintaining effective government by reviewing the organizational structure and management procedures of the executive branch to ensure that the intended results are achieved;

—to assist in developing efficient coordinating mechanisms to implement Government activities and to expand interagency cooperation;

—to assist the President in preparing the budget and in formulating the Government's fiscal program;

—to supervise and control the administration of the budget;

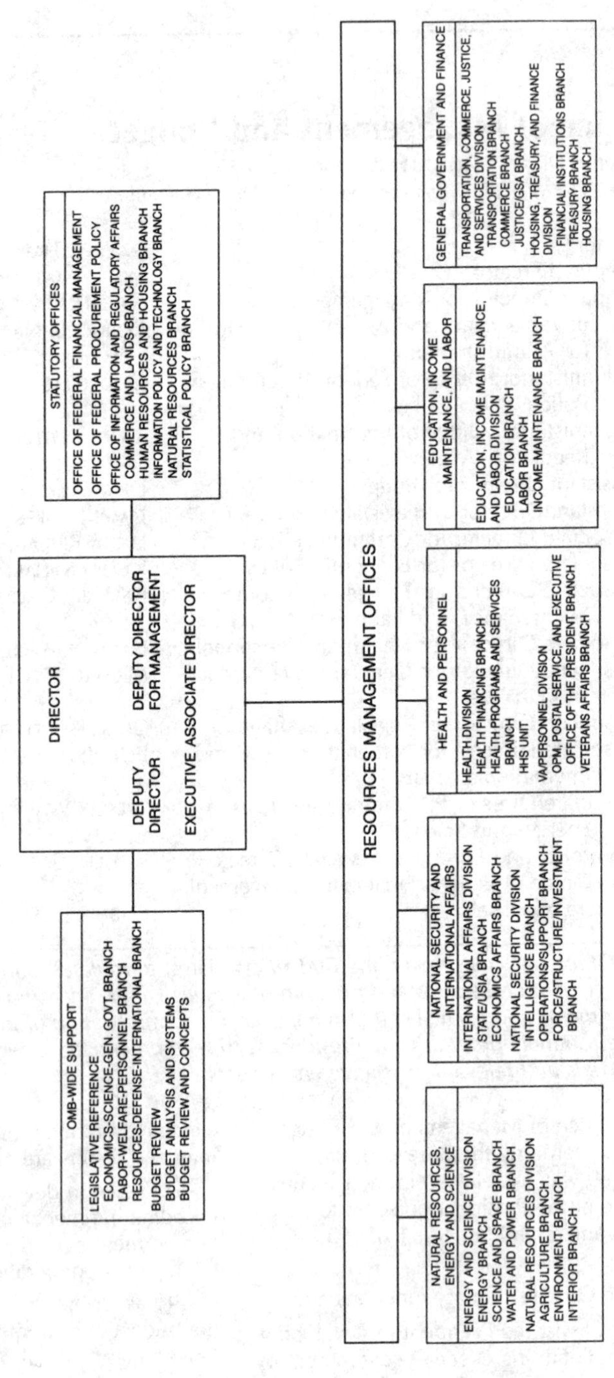
OFFICE OF MANAGEMENT AND BUDGET
OMB-WIDE SUPPORT
LEGISLATIVE REFERENCE
ECONOMICS-SCIENCE-GEN. GOVT. BRANCH
LABOR-WELFARE-PERSONNEL BRANCH
RESOURCES-DEFENSE-INTERNATIONAL BRANCH
BUDGET REVIEW
BUDGET ANALYSIS AND SYSTEMS
BUDGET REVIEW AND CONCEPTS
DIRECTOR
DEPUTY DIRECTOR
DEPUTY DIRECTOR FOR MANAGEMENT
EXECUTIVE ASSOCIATE DIRECTOR
STATUTORY OFFICES
OFFICE OF FEDERAL FINANCIAL MANAGEMENT
OFFICE OF FEDERAL PROCUREMENT POLICY
OFFICE OF INFORMATION AND REGULATORY AFFAIRS
COMMERCE AND LANDS BRANCH
HUMAN RESOURCES AND HOUSING BRANCH
INFORMATION POLICY AND TECHNOLOGY BRANCH
NATURAL RESOURCES BRANCH
STATISTICAL POLICY BRANCH
RESOURCES MANAGEMENT OFFICES
NATURAL RESOURCES, ENERGY AND SCIENCE
ENERGY AND SCIENCE DIVISION
ENERGY BRANCH
SCIENCE AND SPACE BRANCH
WATER AND POWER BRANCH
NATURAL RESOURCES DIVISION
AGRICULTURE BRANCH
ENVIRONMENT BRANCH
INTERIOR BRANCH
NATIONAL SECURITY AND INTERNATIONAL AFFAIRS
INTERNATIONAL AFFAIRS DIVISION
STATE/USIA BRANCH
ECONOMICS AFFAIRS BRANCH
NATIONAL SECURITY DIVISION
INTELLIGENCE BRANCH
OPERATIONS/SUPPORT BRANCH
FORCE/STRUCTURE/INVESTMENT BRANCH
HEALTH AND PERSONNEL
HEALTH DIVISION
HEALTH FINANCING BRANCH
HEALTH PROGRAMS AND SERVICES BRANCH
HHS UNIT
VA/PERSONNEL DIVISION
OPM, POSTAL SERVICE, AND EXECUTIVE OFFICE OF THE PRESIDENT BRANCH
VETERANS AFFAIRS BRANCH
EDUCATION, INCOME MAINTENANCE, AND LABOR
EDUCATION, INCOME MAINTENANCE, AND LABOR DIVISION
EDUCATION BRANCH
LABOR BRANCH
INCOME MAINTENANCE BRANCH
GENERAL GOVERNMENT AND FINANCE
TRANSPORTATION, COMMERCE, JUSTICE, AND SERVICES DIVISION
TRANSPORTATION BRANCH
COMMERCE BRANCH
JUSTICE/GSA BRANCH
HOUSING, TREASURY, AND FINANCE DIVISION
FINANCIAL INSTITUTIONS BRANCH
TREASURY BRANCH
HOUSING BRANCH

—to assist the President by clearing and coordinating departmental advice on proposed legislation and by making recommendations effecting Presidential action on legislative enactments, in accordance with past practice;

—to assist in developing regulatory reform proposals and programs for paperwork reduction, especially reporting burdens of the public;

—to assist in considering, clearing, and, where necessary, preparing proposed Executive orders and proclamations;

—to plan and develop information systems that provide the President with program performance data;

—to plan, conduct, and promote evaluation efforts that assist the President in assessing program objectives, performance, and efficiency;

—to keep the President informed of the progress of activities by Government agencies with respect to work proposed, initiated, and completed, together with the relative timing of work between the several agencies of the Government, all to the end that the work programs of the several agencies of the executive branch of the Government may be coordinated and that the moneys appropriated by the Congress may be expended in the most economical manner, barring overlapping and duplication of effort; and

—to improve the economy, efficiency, and effectiveness of the procurement processes by providing overall direction of procurement policies, regulations, procedures, and forms.

Sources of Information

Employment Various civil service examinations and registers are used for filling positions, such as economist, budget examiner, and management analyst. Inquiries on employment should be directed to the Human Resources Division, Office of Administration, Washington, DC 20500. Phone, 202–395–1088.

Inquiries Contact the Office of Administration, Office of Management and Budget, New Executive Office Building, Washington, DC 20503. Phone, 202–395–3080. Fax, 202–395–3504. Internet, www.whitehouse.gov/omb.

Publications *The Budget of the U.S. Government* and *The Budget System and Concepts* are available for sale by the Superintendent of Documents, Government Printing Office, Washington, DC 20402.

For further information, contact the Office of Management and Budget, Executive Office Building, Washington, DC 20503. Phone, 202–395–3080. Internet, www.whitehouse.gov/omb.

Office of National Drug Control Policy

Executive Office of the President, Washington, DC 20503
Phone, 202–395–6700. Internet, www.whitehousedrugpolicy.gov.

Director	BARRY R. MCCAFFREY
Deputy Director	DONALD VEREEN
Chief of Staff	JANET L. CRIST
Deputy Director for Demand Reduction	(VACANCY)
Deputy Director for State and Local Affairs	(VACANCY)
Deputy Director for Supply Reduction	(VACANCY)
Director, Counter-Drug Technology Assessment Center	ALBERT BRANDENSTEIN
Director for Legislative Affairs	MICHELE MANATT
Director for Public Affairs	(VACANCY)
Director of Administration	TILMAN DEAN
Director of Financial Management	MICHELE MARX

Director of Programs, Budget, Research, and Evaluation	ROSS DECK, *Acting*
Director of Strategic Planning	FRACIS X. KINNEY
General Counsel	EDWARD JURITH

The Office of National Drug Control Policy coordinates Federal, State, and local efforts to control illegal drug abuse and devises national strategies to effectively carry out antidrug activities.

The Office of National Drug Control Policy was established by the National Narcotics Leadership Act of 1988 (21 U.S.C. 1501 *et seq.*), effective January 29, 1989, as amended by the Violent Crime Control and Law Enforcement Act of 1994 (21 U.S.C. 1502, 1506, 1508).

The Director of National Drug Control Policy is appointed by the President with the advice and consent of the Senate. The Director is assisted by a Deputy Director, a Deputy Director for Demand Reduction, a Deputy Director for Supply Reduction, and a Deputy Director for State and Local Affairs.

The Director of National Drug Control Policy is responsible for establishing policies, objectives, priorities, and performance measurement for the national drug control program, and for annually promulgating a national drug control strategy and supporting annual reports to be submitted to the Congress by the President. The Director advises the President regarding necessary changes in the organization, management, budgeting, and personnel allocation of Federal agencies involved in drug enforcement activities and is also responsible for notifying Federal agencies if their policies are not in compliance with their responsibilities under the national drug control strategy.

Sources of Information

Employment Inquiries regarding employment should be directed to the Personnel Section, Office of National Drug Control Policy (phone, 202–395–6695) or the Office of the Chief of Staff (phone, 202–395–6732).

Publications To receive publications about drugs and crime, to get specific drug-related data, to obtain customized bibliographic searches, and to find out about data availability and other information resources that may meet your needs, contact the Drugs and Crime Clearinghouse. Phone, 800–666–3332. Fax, 301–251–5212. E-mail, askncjrs@aspensys.com. Internet, www.whitehousedrugpolicy.gov.

For further information, contact the Office of National Drug Control Policy, Executive Office of the President, Washington, DC 20503. Phone, 202–395–6700. Internet, www.whitehousedrugpolicy.gov.

Office of Policy Development

Domestic Policy Council

Room 216, Eisenhower Executive Office Building, Washington, DC 20502
Phone, 202–456–2216

Assistant to the President for Domestic Policy and Director of the Domestic Policy Council	BRUCE N. REED
Deputy Assistant to the President for Domestic Policy	ERIC LIU

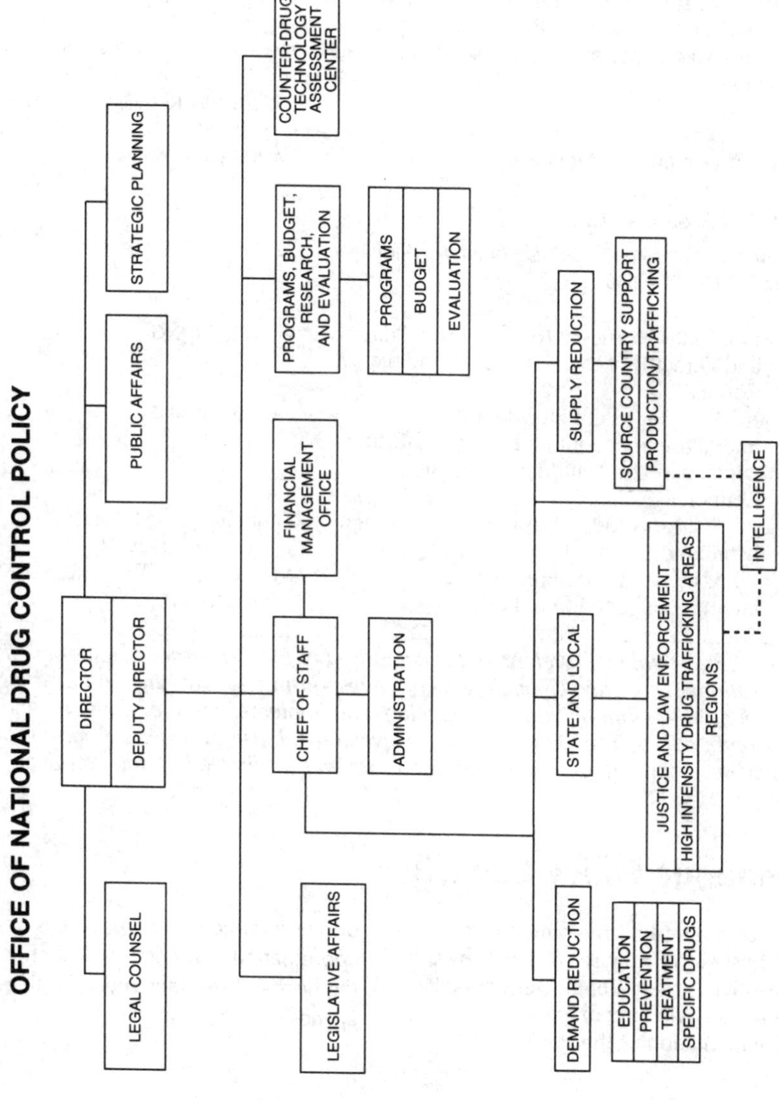
OFFICE OF NATIONAL DRUG CONTROL POLICY
DIRECTOR
DEPUTY DIRECTOR
LEGAL COUNSEL
PUBLIC AFFAIRS
STRATEGIC PLANNING
LEGISLATIVE AFFAIRS
CHIEF OF STAFF
ADMINISTRATION
FINANCIAL MANAGEMENT OFFICE
PROGRAMS, BUDGET, RESEARCH, AND EVALUATION
PROGRAMS
BUDGET
EVALUATION
COUNTER-DRUG TECHNOLOGY ASSESSMENT CENTER
DEMAND REDUCTION
EDUCATION
PREVENTION
TREATMENT
SPECIFIC DRUGS
STATE AND LOCAL
JUSTICE AND LAW ENFORCEMENT
HIGH INTENSITY DRUG TRAFFICKING AREAS
REGIONS
SUPPLY REDUCTION
SOURCE COUNTRY SUPPORT
PRODUCTION/TRAFFICKING
INTELLIGENCE

Deputy Assistant to the President for Health Policy	CHRISTOPHER C. JENNINGS
Special Assistant to the President and Chief of Staff to the Domestic Policy Council	PAUL WEINSTEIN, JR.
Special Assistants to the President for Domestic Policy	IRENE BUENO, ANDREA KANE, ANN O'LEARY, NICOLE RABNER, ANDREW ROTHERHAM, LEANNE SHIMABUKURO
Director of National AIDS Policy	SANDRA THURMAN

National Economic Council

Room 235, Old Executive Office Building, Washington, DC 20502
Phone, 202–456–6630

Assistant to the President for Economic Policy and Director of the National Economic Council	GENE SPERLING
Deputy Assistant to the President for International Economic Policy and Deputy Director of the National Economic Council	LAEL BRAINARD
Special Assistants to the President for Economic Policy	GIGI GEORGES, THOMAS KALIL, DOROTHY ROBYN
Special Assistants to the President for International Economic Policy	MALCOLM LEE, RICHARD SAMANS, ROBERT WESCOTT

The Office of Policy Development is comprised of the Domestic Policy Council and the National Economic Council, which are responsible for advising and assisting the President in the formulation, coordination, and implementation of domestic and economic policy. The Office of Policy Development also provides support for other policy development and implementation activities as directed by the President.

Domestic Policy Council

The Domestic Policy Council was established on August 16, 1993, by Executive Order 12859. The Council oversees development and implementation of the President's domestic policy agenda and ensures coordination and communication among the heads of relevant Federal offices and agencies.

National Economic Council

The National Economic Council was created on January 25, 1993, by Executive Order 12835, to coordinate the economic policymaking process and provide economic policy advice to the President. The Council also ensures that economic policy decisions and programs are consistent with the President's stated goals, and monitors the implementation of the President's economic goals.

Office of Science and Technology Policy

Eisenhower Executive Office Building, Washington, DC 20502
Phone, 202–395–7347. Fax, 202–456–6022. Internet, www.whitehouse.gov/ostp.html.

Assistant to the President for Science and Technology, and Director	NEAL LANE
Associate Director for Environment	ROSINA BIERBAUM
Associate Director for National Security and International Affairs	(VACANCY)
Associate Director for Science	ARTHUR BIENENSTOCK
Associate Director for Technology	DUNCAN MOORE
Executive Secretary for the National Science and Technology Council and the President's Committee of Advisors on Science and Technology	RUSSELL MOY

The Office of Science and Technology Policy was established within the Executive Office of the President by the National Science and Technology Policy, Organization, and Priorities Act of 1976 (42 U.S.C. 6611).

The Office serves as a source of scientific, engineering, and technological analysis and judgment for the President with respect to major policies, plans, and programs of the Federal Government. In carrying out this mission, the Office advises the President of scientific and technological considerations involved in areas of national concern, including the economy, national security, health, foreign relations, and the environment; evaluates the scale, quality, and effectiveness of the Federal effort in science and technology; provides advice and assistance to the President, the Office of Management and Budget, and Federal agencies throughout the Federal budget development process; and assists the President in providing leadership and coordination for the research and development programs of the Federal Government.

For further information, contact the Office of Science and Technology Policy, Old Executive Office Building, Washington, DC 20502. Phone, 202–395–7347. Fax, 202–456–6022. Internet, www.whitehouse.gov/ostp.html.

Office of the United States Trade Representative

600 Seventeenth Street NW., Washington, DC 20508
Phone, 202–395–3230

United States Trade Representative	CHARLENE BARSHEFSKY
Deputy U.S. Trade Representatives (Washington)	SUSAN ESSERMAN, RICHARD FISHER
Deputy U.S. Trade Representative (Geneva)	RITA HAYES
Chief of Staff	NANCY LEAMOND
Chief Textile Negotiator	C. DONALD JOHNSON
Counselor to the U.S. Trade Representative	JANET HALL

General Counsel	Robert Novick
Special Trade Negotiator	Greg Frazier
Assistant U.S. Trade Representative for Administration	John Hopkins
Assistant U.S. Trade Representative for Agricultural Affairs	James Murphy
Assistant U.S. Trade Representative for Asia and the Pacific	Joseph Damond, *Acting*
Assistant U.S. Trade Representative for China	Donald Phillips
Assistant U.S. Trade Representative for Congressional Affairs	Emily Beizer
Assistant U.S. Trade Representative for Economic Affairs	David Walters
Assistant U.S. Trade Representative for Environment and Natural Resources	Jennifer Haverkamp
Assistant U.S. Trade Representative for Europe and the Mediterranean	Cathy Novelli
Assistant U.S. Trade Representative for Industry	Gordana Earp, *Acting*
Assistant U.S. Trade Representative for Intergovernmental Affairs and Public Liaison	J. Pate Felts
Assistant U.S. Trade Representative for Japan	Wendy Cutler
Assistant U.S. Trade Representative for Monitoring and Enforcement	Jane Bradley
Assistant U.S. Trade Representative for North American Affairs	(vacancy)
Assistant U.S. Trade Representative for Policy Coordination	Carmen Suro-Bredie, *Acting*
Assistant U.S. Trade Representative for Public/Media Affairs	Brendan Daly
Assistant U.S. Trade Representative for Trade and Development	Jon Rosenbaum
Assistant U.S. Trade Representative for World Trade Organization (WTO) and Multilateral Affairs	Dorothy Dwoskin
Associate U.S. Trade Representative for Western Hemisphere	Peter Allgeier

The United States Trade Representative is responsible for directing all trade negotiations of and formulating trade policy for the United States.

The Office of the United States Trade Representative was created as the Office of the Special Representative for Trade Negotiations by Executive Order 11075 of January 15, 1963. The Trade Act of 1974 (19 U.S.C. 2171) established the Office as an agency of the Executive Office of the President charged with administering the trade agreements program.

The Office is responsible for setting and administering overall trade policy. It also provides that the United States Trade Representative shall be chief representative of the United States for:

—all activities concerning the General Agreement on Tariffs and Trade;

—discussions, meetings, and negotiations in the Organization for Economic Cooperation and Development when such activities deal primarily with trade and commodity issues;

—negotiations in the U.N. Conference on Trade and Development and other multilateral institutions when such negotiations deal primarily with trade and commodity issues;

—other bilateral and multilateral negotiations when trade, including East-West trade, or commodities is the primary issue;

—negotiations under sections 704 and 734 of the Tariff Act of 1930 (19 U.S.C. 1671c and 1673c); and

—negotiations concerning direct investment incentives and disincentives and bilateral investment issues concerning barriers to investment.

The Omnibus Trade and Competitiveness Act of 1988 codified these prior authorities and added additional authority, including the implementation of section 301 actions (regarding enforcement of U.S. rights under international trade agreements).

The Office is headed by the United States Trade Representative, a Cabinet-level official with the rank of Ambassador, who is directly responsible to the President. There are three Deputy United States Trade Representatives, who also hold the rank of Ambassador, two located in Washington and one in Geneva. The Chief Textile Negotiator also holds the rank of Ambassador.

The United States Trade Representative serves as an *ex officio* member of the Boards of Directors of the Export-Import Bank and the Overseas Private Investment Corporation, and serves on the National Advisory Council for International Monetary and Financial Policy.

For further information, contact the Office of Public Affairs, Office of the United States Trade Representative, 600 Seventeenth Street NW., Washington, DC 20506. Phone, 202–395–3230.

Departments

DEPARTMENT OF AGRICULTURE

Fourteenth Street and Independence Avenue SW., Washington, DC 20250
Phone, 202–720–2791. Internet, www.usda.gov.

SECRETARY OF AGRICULTURE	DAN GLICKMAN
Deputy Secretary	RICHARD ROMINGER
Under Secretary for Farm and Foreign Agricultural Services	AUGUST SCHUMACHER
Deputy Under Secretaries	THOMAS L. GRAU, JAMES SCHROEDER
Administrator, Farm Service Agency	KEITH KELLY
Administrator, Foreign Agricultural Service	TIM GALVIN
Administrator, Risk Management Agency	KEN ACKERMAN
Under Secretary for Food, Nutrition, and Consumer Services	SHIRLEY WATKINS
Deputy Under Secretary	JULIE PARADIS
Administrator, Food and Nutrition Service	SAMUEL CHAMBERS, JR.
Executive Director, Center for Nutrition Policy and Promotion	RAJEN S. ANAND
Under Secretary for Food Safety	CATHERINE WOTEKI
Administrator, Food Safety and Inspection Service	THOMAS BILLY
Under Secretary for Natural Resources and Environment	JAMES LYONS
Deputy Under Secretary for Forestry	ANNE KEYS KENNEDY
Deputy Under Secretary for Conservation	GLENDA HUMISTON
Chief, Forest Service	MIKE DOMBECK
Chief, Natural Resources Conservation Service	PEARLIE S. REED
Under Secretary for Research, Education, and Economics	MILEY GONZALEZ
Deputy Under Secretary	EILEEN KENNEDY
Administrator, Agricultural Research Service	FLOYD HORN
Administrator, Cooperative State Research, Education, and Extension Service	CHARLES LAUGHLIN
Administrator, Economic Research Service	SUSAN E. OFFUTT
Administrator, National Agricultural Statistics Service	RON BOSECKER
Under Secretary for Rural Development	JILL LONG-THOMPSON
Deputy Under Secretaries	ARTHUR C. CAMPBELL, INGA SMULKSTYS
Administrator, Rural Business-Cooperative Service	DAYTON WATKINS

Administrator, Rural Housing Service	Eileen Fitzgerald, *Acting*
Administrator, Rural Utilities Service	Chris McLean, *Acting*
Assistant Secretary for Congressional Relations	Andrew Fish
Deputy Assistant Secretary	Jay Johnson, *Acting*
Under Secretary for Marketing and Regulatory Programs	Michael V. Dunn
Deputy Under Secretary	Enrique Figueroa
Administrator, Agricultural Marketing Service	Kathleen Merrigan
Administrator, Animal and Plant Health Inspection Service	Craig A. Reed
Administrator, Grain Inspection, Packers, and Stockyards Administration	James R. Baker
Assistant Secretary for Administration	Paul Feddick
Deputy Assistant Secretary	Debbie Matz
Chairman, Board of Contract Appeals	Edward Houry
Judicial Officer	William G. Jenson
Chief Judge, Administrative Law Judges	Edward Bernstein
Director, Office of Civil Rights	Rosalind Gray
Director, Office of Ethics	John Surina
Director, Office of Human Resources Management	Donna D. Beecher
Director, Office of Operations	Priscilla Carey
Director, Office of Outreach	Sharron Harris, *Acting*
Director, Office of Procurement, Property, and Emergency Preparedness	W.R. Ashworth
Director, Office of Small and Disadvantaged Business Utilization	Sharron Harris
Chief Information Officer	Joseph Leo
Deputy Chief Information Officer	Ira L. Hobbs
Chief Financial Officer	Sally Thompson
Deputy Chief Financial Officer	Patricia Healy
General Counsel	Charles Rawls
Deputy General Counsel	Frank Stenger-Castro
Inspector General	Roger C. Viadero
Deputy Inspector General	Joyce N. Fleischman
Director, Office of Communications	Sedelta Verble
Chief Economist	Keith Collins
Director, Office of Risk Assessment and Cost-Benefit Analysis	Alwynelle S. Ahl
Chairman, World Agricultural Outlook Board	Gerald Bange
Director, Global Change Program Office	Margot Anderson
Director, Office of Energy Policy and New Uses	Roger Conway
Director, National Appeals Division	Norman Cooper
Director, Office of Budget and Program Analysis	Stephen B. Dewhurst
Director, Office of the Executive Secretariat	Lynne Finnerty
Director, Sustainable Development and Small Farms	Adela Backiel

[For the Department of Agriculture statement of organization, see the *Code of Federal Regulations,* Title 7, Part 2]

The Department of Agriculture works to improve and maintain farm income and to develop and expand markets abroad for agricultural products. The Department helps to curb and to cure poverty, hunger, and malnutrition. It works to enhance the environment and to maintain production capacity by helping landowners protect the soil, water, forests, and other natural resources. Rural development, credit, and conservation programs are key resources for carrying out national growth policies. Department research findings directly or indirectly benefit all Americans. The Department, through inspection and grading services, safeguards and ensures standards of quality in the daily food supply.

The Department of Agriculture (USDA) was created by act of May 15, 1862 (7 U.S.C. 2201).

In carrying out its work in the program mission areas, USDA relies on the support of departmental administration staff, as well as the Office of the Chief Financial Officer, Office of Communications, Office of Congressional and Intergovernmental Relations, Office of the Inspector General, and the Office of the General Counsel.

Rural Development

The rural development mission of USDA is to assist rural Americans in using their abilities to improve their quality of life. To accomplish this, USDA works to foster new cooperative relationships among Government, industry, and communities. The mission is carried out by the Rural Housing Service, which includes rural housing and rural community facility loan and grant programs; the Rural Business-Cooperative Service, which includes business and cooperative development programs; and the Rural Utilities Service, which includes telephone, electric, water, and sewer programs. Approximately 850 rural development field offices provide frontline delivery of all rural development loan and grant programs at the local level.

Rural Business-Cooperative Service

The mission of the Rural Business-Cooperative Service (RBS) is to enhance the quality of life for all rural Americans by providing leadership in building competitive businesses and sustainable cooperatives that can prosper in the global marketplace. To meet business credit needs in under-served areas, RBS business programs are usually leveraged with commercial, cooperative, or other private sector lenders. RBS business programs include:

Business and Industry Direct Loans This program provides loans to public entities and private parties who cannot obtain credit from other sources. Loans to private parties can be made for improving, developing, or financing business and industry, creating jobs, and improving the economic and environmental climate in rural communities, including pollution abatement.

Business and Industry Guaranteed Loans This program helps create jobs and stimulates rural economies by providing financial backing for rural businesses. Loan proceeds may be used for working capital, machinery and equipment, buildings and real estate, and certain types of debt refinancing.

Business Enterprise These grants help public bodies, nonprofit corporations, and federally recognized Indian tribal groups finance and facilitate development of small and emerging private business enterprises located in rural areas. Grant funds can pay for the acquisition and development of land and the construction of buildings, plants, equipment, access streets and roads, parking areas, utility and service extensions, refinancing, and fees for professional services, as well as technical assistance and related training, startup costs and working capital, financial assistance to a third party,

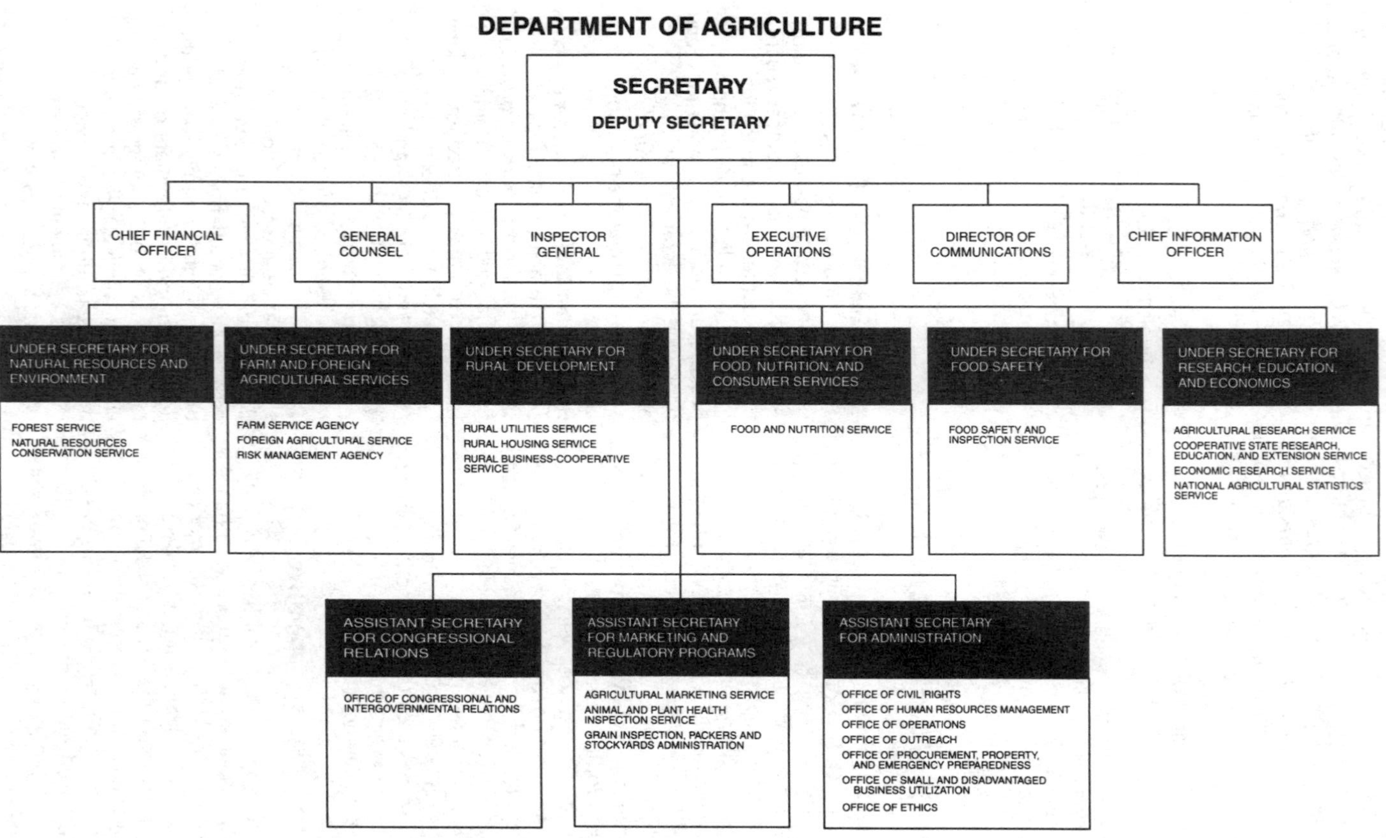
DEPARTMENT OF AGRICULTURE
SECRETARY
DEPUTY SECRETARY
CHIEF FINANCIAL OFFICER
GENERAL COUNSEL
INSPECTOR GENERAL
EXECUTIVE OPERATIONS
DIRECTOR OF COMMUNICATIONS
CHIEF INFORMATION OFFICER
UNDER SECRETARY FOR NATURAL RESOURCES AND ENVIRONMENT
FOREST SERVICE
NATURAL RESOURCES CONSERVATION SERVICE
UNDER SECRETARY FOR FARM AND FOREIGN AGRICULTURAL SERVICES
FARM SERVICE AGENCY
FOREIGN AGRICULTURAL SERVICE
RISK MANAGEMENT AGENCY
UNDER SECRETARY FOR RURAL DEVELOPMENT
RURAL UTILITIES SERVICE
RURAL HOUSING SERVICE
RURAL BUSINESS-COOPERATIVE SERVICE
UNDER SECRETARY FOR FOOD NUTRITION, AND CONSUMER SERVICES
FOOD AND NUTRITION SERVICE
UNDER SECRETARY FOR FOOD SAFETY
FOOD SAFETY AND INSPECTION SERVICE
UNDER SECRETARY FOR RESEARCH, EDUCATION, AND ECONOMICS
AGRICULTURAL RESEARCH SERVICE
COOPERATIVE STATE RESEARCH, EDUCATION, AND EXTENSION SERVICE
ECONOMIC RESEARCH SERVICE
NATIONAL AGRICULTURAL STATISTICS SERVICE
ASSISTANT SECRETARY FOR CONGRESSIONAL RELATIONS
OFFICE OF CONGRESSIONAL AND INTERGOVERNMENTAL RELATIONS
ASSISTANT SECRETARY FOR MARKETING AND REGULATORY PROGRAMS
AGRICULTURAL MARKETING SERVICE
ANIMAL AND PLANT HEALTH INSPECTION SERVICE
GRAIN INSPECTION, PACKERS AND STOCKYARDS ADMINISTRATION
ASSISTANT SECRETARY FOR ADMINISTRATION
OFFICE OF CIVIL RIGHTS
OFFICE OF HUMAN RESOURCES MANAGEMENT
OFFICE OF OPERATIONS
OFFICE OF OUTREACH
OFFICE OF PROCUREMENT, PROPERTY, AND EMERGENCY PREPAREDNESS
OFFICE OF SMALL AND DISADVANTAGED BUSINESS UTILIZATION
OFFICE OF ETHICS

production of television programs targeted to rural residents, and rural distance learning networks.

Business Opportunities This program promotes sustainable economic development in rural communities with exceptional needs. Funds are provided for technical assistance, training, and planning activities that improve economic conditions. Applicants must be located in rural areas.

Cooperative Development These grants finance the establishment and operation of centers for cooperative development. The primary purpose of this program is to enhance the economic condition of rural areas through the development of new cooperatives and improving operations of existing cooperatives.

Cooperative Opportunities and Problems Research This program encourages research, funded through cooperative agreements, on critical issues vital to the development and sustainability of agricultural and other rural cooperatives as a means of improving the quality of life in America's rural communities.

Cooperative Services This program helps farmers and rural communities become self-reliant through the use of cooperative organizations. Studies are conducted to support cooperatives that market farm products, purchase production supplies, and perform related business services. These studies concentrate on the financial, organizational, legal, social, and economic aspects of cooperative activity. Technical assistance and research is provided to improve cooperative performance in organizing new cooperatives, merging existing cooperatives, changing business structures, and developing strategies for growth. Applied research is conducted to give farmers and rural communities expert assistance pertaining to their cooperatives. The program also collects and publishes statistics regarding the role and scope of cooperative activity in U.S. agriculture. The Service's bimonthly magazine, *Rural Cooperatives*, reports current developments and research for cooperative management leadership.

Economic Development These loans and grants finance economic development and job creation projects based on sound economic plans in rural areas. Loans and grants are available to any eligible Rural Utilities Service electric or telecommunications borrower to assist in developing rural areas from an economic standpoint, to create new job opportunities, and to help retain existing employment. Loans at zero interest are made primarily to finance business startup ventures and business expansion projects. Grants are made to eligible telephone and electric utilities to establish revolving loan programs operated at the local level. The revolving loan program provides capital to nonprofit entities and municipal organizations to finance business or community facilities which promote job creation in rural areas, for facilities which extend or improve medical care to rural residents, and for facilities which promote education and training to enhance marketable job skills for rural residents.

Intermediary Relending These loans finance business facilities and community development projects in rural areas. The Service lends these funds to intermediaries, which in turn provide loans to recipients who are developing business facilities or community development projects.

Sheep Industry The National Sheep Industry Improvement Center promotes strategic development activities to strengthen and enhance the production and marketing of sheep and goat products in the United States. It works to improve infrastructure development, business development, and market and environmental research and designs unique responses to the needs of the industries for their long-term sustainable development. The Center's board of directors oversees its activities and operates a revolving fund for loans and grants.

Technology Transfer This program provides information to farmers and other rural users on a variety of sustainable agricultural practices that include both cropping and livestock operations. It offers reliable, practical information on production techniques and practices that reduce costs and that are environmentally friendly. Farmers can request such information by telephone at 800–346–9140 (toll-free).

Venture Capital To demonstrate the usefulness of guarantees to attract increased investment in private business enterprises in rural areas, this program designates up to 10 community development venture capital organizations to establish a rural business private investment pool to make equity investments in rural private business enterprises. The program is available in rural areas. Authority for this program, unless extended, expires after the end of fiscal year 2002.

For further information, contact Rural Development, Legislative and Public Affairs Staff, Stop 0705, Department of Agriculture, 1400 Independence Avenue SW., Washington, DC 20250–0320. Phone, 202–720–6903.

Rural Housing Service

The Rural Housing Service (RHS) provides affordable rental housing, homeownership opportunities, and essential community facilities to rural Americans through a broad array of direct loan, guarantee, and grant programs. Rural residents and communities may inquire about any of these programs through local and State rural development offices. The Service provides financial and management assistance through the following services:

—guaranteed single-family housing (SFH) loans which guarantee loans made by commercial lenders to moderate-income rural residents with sufficient income and acceptable credit, who may lack the downpayment to secure a loan without assistance;

—direct single-family housing loans made available to people with incomes less than 80 percent of area median to build, purchase, and repair rural homes;

—home improvement and repair loans and grants are available to owner-occupants to remove health and safety hazards from a home;

—mutual self-help housing technical assistance grants for nonprofit organizations and public bodies to help groups of six to eight very-low and low income families to build their own homes by providing "sweat equity" which reduces the families' mortgage;

—rural housing site loans for private or public nonprofit organizations to purchase sites for the development of housing for very-low and low income families;

—direct and guaranteed multi-family housing loans for private nonprofit corporations, consumer cooperatives, State or local public agencies, and individuals or organizations operating on a nonprofit or limited profit basis to provide rental or cooperative housing in rural areas for persons of very-low, low, and moderate income;

—farm labor housing loans and grants enabling farmers, public or private nonprofit organizations, or units of local government to build, buy, or rehabilitate farm labor housing;

—housing preservation grants made to a public body or public/private nonprofit organization to provide assistance to homeowners and landlords to repair and rehabilitate housing for very-low and low income families in rural areas;

—housing for the homeless, SFH real-estate-owned (REO) property to nonprofit organizations or public bodies for transitional housing for the homeless and to the Federal Emergency Management Agency to house families affected by natural disasters; and

—community program loans, direct and guaranteed loans and grants for public and quasi-public bodies, nonprofit associations, and Indian tribes for essential community facilities such as health care centers, public safety buildings and vehicles, and child care centers.

For further information, contact Rural Development, Legislative and Public Affairs Staff, Stop 0705, Department of Agriculture, 1400 Independence Avenue SW., Washington, DC 20250–0320. Phone, 202–720–6903.

Rural Utilities Service

The Rural Utilities Service (RUS) is a credit agency that assists rural electric and telecommunications utilities in obtaining financing and administers a nationwide water and waste loan and grant program to improve the quality of life and promote economic development in rural America. A total of 890 rural electric and 800 rural telecommunications utilities in 47 States, Puerto Rico, the Virgin Islands, Guam, the Republic of the Marshall Islands, the Northern Mariana Islands, and the Federated States of Micronesia have received financial assistance. Approximately 7,200 rural communities are currently served through financial assistance received from water and waste loans and grants. RUS provides assistance by use of the following programs:

—The electric program provides loans for improving electric service to persons in rural areas, including construction of electric generating plants and transmission and distribution lines to provide reliable electric service.

—The telecommunications program provides telephone service in rural areas.

—The water and waste direct and guaranteed loan program provides assistance to develop water and wastewater systems, including solid waste disposal and storm drainage, in rural areas, cities, and towns.

—Water and waste disposal grants assist in reducing water and waste disposal costs to a reasonable level for users of the system.

—Emergency community water assistance grants provide assistance to rural communities experiencing a significant decline in quantity or quality of drinking water.

—Technical assistance and training grants are available to nonprofit organizations to provide rural water and waste system officials with technical assistance and training on a wide range of issues relating to the delivery of water and waste service to rural residents.

—Solid waste management grants are available for nonprofit organizations and public bodies to provide technical assistance and training to rural areas and towns to reduce or eliminate pollution of water resources and improve planning and management of solid waste facilities.

—The rural water circuit rider technical assistance program provides, through the National Rural Water Association, technical assistance to rural water systems to solve operational, financial, and management problems.

—The distance learning and telemedicine program provides assistance to help rural schools and health care providers invest in telecommunications facilities and equipment to bring to rural areas educational and medical resources that otherwise might be unavailable.

—The Service also guarantees loans from the Department of the Treasury's Federal Financing Bank (FFB), which it lends to borrowers, primarily for large-scale electric and telecommunication facilities. RUS may also guarantee electric and telecommunications loans from private sources.

For further information, contact the Rural Utilities Service, Department of Agriculture, Room 4051–S, 1400 Independence Avenue SW., Washington, DC 20250–0320. Phone, 202–720–1255.

Alternative Agricultural Research and Commercialization Corporation

As an independent entity within USDA, the Alternative Agricultural Research and Commercialization Corporation (AARCC) provides and monitors financial assistance for the development and commercialization of new nonfood and nonfeed products made from agricultural/forestry commodities. AARCC is administered by an 11-member board comprising representatives for processing, financial, producer, and scientific interests.

The Corporation's mission is to assist the private sector in closing the gap between research results and commercialization of industrial nonfood and nonfeed products made from farm and forestry materials. It also seeks to expand market opportunities through development of value-added industrial products and promotion of environmentally friendly products. Any private individual or firm may apply for assistance. While most of the Corporation's clients are small firms, nonprofit organizations and large businesses have also been successful applicants. Universities and similar institutions may participate as well.

The Corporation can supply financial assistance at the precommercialization stage of a project, that point in a project when the costs are the greatest and the ability to obtain lending from traditional sources is the most difficult. Financial assistance is in the form of a repayable cooperative agreement and includes a repayment portion that recognizes the investment risk taken by AARCC. Applicants are expected to provide at least a 1:1 match when seeking funding from AARCC. The Corporation receives an annual appropriation from Congress and operates under a revolving fund. As Corporation-funded projects become profitable and reimburse AARCC, the money will be returned to the fund to help finance future projects.

For further information, contact the Alternative Agricultural Research and Commercialization Corporation, Room 0156, 1400 Independence Avenue SW., Washington, DC 20250–0401. Phone, 202–690–1633.

Marketing and Regulatory Programs

This mission area includes marketing and regulatory programs other than those concerned with food safety.

Agricultural Marketing Service

The Agricultural Marketing Service (AMS) was established by the Secretary of Agriculture on April 2, 1972, under the authority of Reorganization Plan No. 2 of 1953 (5 U.S.C. app.) and other authorities. The Service administers standardization, grading, certification, market news, marketing orders, research and promotion, and regulatory programs.

Market News The Service provides current, unbiased information to producers, processors, distributors, and others to assist them in the orderly marketing and distribution of farm commodities. Information is collected on supplies, demand, prices, movement, location, quality, condition, and other market data on farm products in specific markets and marketing areas. The data is disseminated nationally via a modern satellite system and is shared with several countries. The Service also assists countries in developing their own marketing information systems.

Standardization, Grading, and Classing Grade standards have been established for about 230 agricultural commodities to help buyers and sellers trade on agreed-upon quality levels. Standards are developed with the benefit of views from those in the industries directly affected and others interested. The Service also participates in developing international standards to facilitate trade.

Grading and classing services are provided to certify the grade and quality of products. These grading services are provided to buyers and sellers of live cattle, swine, sheep, meat, poultry, eggs, rabbits, fruits, vegetables, tree nuts, peanuts, dairy products, and tobacco. Classing services are provided to buyers and sellers of cotton and cotton products. These services are mainly voluntary and are provided upon request and for a fee. The Service also is responsible for the certification of turpentine and other naval stores products, and the testing of seed.

Laboratory Testing The Service provides scientific and laboratory support to its commodity programs relating to testing of microbiological and chemical factors in food products through grading, certification, acceptance, and regulatory programs; testing of peanuts for aflatoxin; testing of imported flue-cured and burley tobacco for pesticide residues; and testing seeds for germination and purity. The agency also carries out quality assurance and safety oversight activities with respect to the Service's commodity division laboratory and testing activities relating to milk market administrators, resident grading programs, and State and private laboratory programs.

The Service also administers the Pesticide Data Program which, in cooperation with States, samples and analyzes 33 agricultural commodities for pesticide residues. It shares residue test results with the Environmental Protection Agency and other public agencies.

Food Quality Assurance Under a governmentwide quality assurance program, AMS is responsible for the development and revision of specifications used by Federal agencies in procuring food for military and civilian uses. The Service coordinates and approves certification programs designed to ensure that purchased products conform to the specification requirements.

Regulatory Programs The Service administers several regulatory programs designed collectively to protect producers, handlers, and consumers of agricultural commodities from financial loss or personal injury resulting from careless, deceptive, or fraudulent marketing practices. Such regulatory programs encourage fair trading practices in the marketing of fruits and vegetables, require truth in seed labeling and in advertising. The Service provides voluntary laboratory analyses of egg products, and monitors the disposition of restricted shell eggs—eggs that are a potential health hazard.

Marketing Agreements and Orders These programs help to establish and maintain orderly marketing conditions for certain commodities. Milk marketing orders establish minimum prices that handlers or distributors are required to pay producers. Programs for fruits, vegetables, and related specialty crops like nuts and spearmint oil help stabilize supplies and market prices. In some cases, they also authorize research and market development activities, including advertising supported by assessments that handlers pay. Through orderly marketing, adjusting the supply to demand, and avoiding unreasonable fluctuations during the marketing season, the income of producers is increased by normal market forces, and consumer interests are protected through quality and quantity control.

Plant Variety Protection Program The Service administers a program that provides for the issuance of certificates of plant variety protection. These certificates afford developers of novel varieties of sexually reproduced plants exclusive rights to sell, reproduce, import, or export such varieties, or use them in the production of hybrids or different varieties for a period of 20 years for non-woody plants and 25 years for woody plants.

Research and Promotion Programs The Service monitors certain industry-sponsored research, promotion, and information programs authorized by Federal laws. These programs provide farmers with a means to finance and operate various research, promotion, and information activities for cotton, potatoes, eggs, milk and dairy products, beef, pork, honey, watermelon, mushrooms, soybeans, and popcorn.

Transportation Programs The Service is also responsible for the development of an efficient transportation system for rural America that begins at the farm gate and moves agricultural and other rural products through the Nation's highways, railroads, airports, and waterways, and into the domestic and international marketplace. To accomplish this, AMS conducts economic studies and analyses of these systems, and represents agricultural and rural transportation interests in policy and regulatory forums. To provide direct assistance to the transportation community, AMS supplies research and technical information to producers, producer groups, shippers, exporters, rural communities, carriers, governmental agencies, and universities.

Organic Standards The Service, with the assistance of the National Organic Standards Board, develops national organic standards.

Other Programs Other marketing service activities include financial grants to States for marketing improvement projects. The agency also has responsibility for the conduct of studies of the facilities and methods used in the physical distribution of food and other farm products; for research designed to improve the handling of all agricultural products as they move from farm to consumers; and for increasing marketing efficiency by developing improved operating methods, facilities, and equipment for processing, handling, and distributing dairy, poultry, and meat products.

The Agricultural Marketing Service manages the Pesticide Recordkeeping Program in coordination with the National Agricultural Statistics Service and the Environmental Protection Agency. The Service has developed educational programs and assists State agencies in inspecting applicator records.

For further information, contact the Information Staff, Agricultural Marketing Service, Department of Agriculture, P.O. Box 96456, Washington, DC 20250. Phone, 202–720–8999.

Animal and Plant Health Inspection Service

[For the Animal and Plant Health Inspection Service statement of organization, see the *Code of Federal Regulations,* Title 7, Part 371]

The Animal and Plant Health Inspection Service (APHIS) was reestablished by the Secretary of Agriculture on March 14, 1977, pursuant to authority contained in 5 U.S.C. 301 and Reorganization Plan No. 2 of 1953 (5 U.S.C. app.).

The Service was established to conduct regulatory and control programs to protect and improve animal and plant health for the benefit of man and the environment. In cooperation with State governments, the agency administers Federal laws and regulations pertaining to animal and plant health and quarantine, humane treatment of animals, and the control and eradication of pests and diseases. Regulations to prevent the introduction or interstate spread of certain animal or plant pests or diseases are also enforced by the Service. It also carries out research and operational activities to reduce crop and livestock depredations caused by birds, rodents, and predators.

Plant Protection and Quarantine Plant protection officials are responsible for programs to control or eradicate plant pests and diseases. These programs are carried out in cooperation with the States involved, other Federal agencies, farmers, and private organizations. Pest control programs use a single tool or a combination of pest control techniques, both chemical and nonchemical, which are both effective and safe.

Agricultural quarantine inspection officials administer Federal regulations that prohibit or restrict the entry of foreign pests and plants, plant products, animal products and byproducts, and other materials that may harbor pests or diseases. Inspection service is maintained at all major sea, air, border, and interior ports of entry in the continental United States and in Hawaii, Alaska, Puerto Rico, U.S. Virgin Islands, Bahamas, and Bermuda. Services also are provided on a regular or on-call basis at some 500 outlying ports and military installations throughout the country.

Veterinary Services Animal health officials are responsible for programs to protect and improve the health, quality, and marketability of U.S. animals and animal products. The programs are carried out through cooperative links with States, foreign governments, livestock producers, and other Federal Agencies.

Service officials exclude, control, and eradicate animal pests and diseases by carrying out eradication and control programs for certain diseases, providing diagnostic services, and gathering and disseminating information regarding animal health in the United States through land, air, and ocean ports. They also certify as to the health status of animals and animal products being exported to other countries and respond to animal disease incursions or epidemics which threaten the health status of U.S. livestock and poultry.

The Service also administers a Federal law intended to ensure that all veterinary biological products, whether developed by conventional or new biotechnological procedures, used in the diagnosis, prevention, and treatment of animal disease are safe, pure, potent, and effective. The Service regulates firms that manufacture veterinary biological products subject to the act, including licensing the manufacturing establishment and its products, inspecting production facilities and production methods, and testing products under a surveillance program.

Animal Care The Service administers Federal laws concerned with the humane care and handling of all warm-blooded animals bought, sold, and transported in commerce and used or intended for use as pets at the wholesale level, or used or intended for use in exhibitions or for research purposes. The agency also enforces the Horse Protection Act of 1970, which prohibits the soring of horses at shows and sales.

International Services Service activities in the international arena include conducting cooperative plant and animal pest and disease control, eradication, and surveillance programs in foreign countries. These programs provide a first line of defense for the United States against threats such as screwworm, medfly, foot-and-mouth disease, and other exotic diseases and pests. The Service also provides international representation concerning sanitary and phytosanitary technical trade issues, and manages programs for overseas preclearance of commodities, passengers, and U.S. military activities.

Wildlife Services Wildlife services officials cooperate with States, counties, local communities, and agricultural producer groups to reduce crop and livestock depredations caused by birds, rodents, and predators. Using methods and techniques that are biologically sound, environmentally acceptable, and economically feasible, they participate in efforts to educate and advise farmers and ranchers on proper uses of control methods and techniques; they suppress serious nuisances and threats to public health and safety caused by birds, rodents, and other wildlife in urban and rural communities; and they work with airport managers to reduce risks of bird strikes. In addition, they conduct research into predator-prey relationships, new control methods, and more efficient and safe uses of present methods such as toxicants, repellants and attractants, biological controls, scare devices, and habitat alteration.

For further information, contact Legislative and Public Affairs, Animal and Plant Health Inspection Service, Department of Agriculture, Washington, DC 20250. Phone, 202–720–2511.

Grain Inspection, Packers, and Stockyards Administration

The Grain Inspection, Packers, and Stockyards Administration (GIPSA) was established in 1994 to facilitate the marketing of livestock, poultry, meat, cereals, oilseeds, and related agricultural products and promote fair and competitive trading practices for the overall benefit of consumers and Americal agriculture. The agency's mission is carried out in two different segments of American agriculture: the Federal Grain Inspection Service provides the U.S. grain market with Federal quality standards and a uniform system for applying them, and the Packers and Stockyards Programs ensures open and competitive markets for livestock, meat, and poultry. GIPSA also certifies State central filing systems for notification of liens against farm products. GIPSA is responsible for establishing official U.S. standards for grain and other assigned commodities, and for administrating a nationwide official inspection and weighing system.

Inspection The United States Grain Standards Act requires that, with some exceptions, all U.S. export grain be officially inspected. At export port locations, inspection is performed by GIPSA or by State agencies that have been delegated export inspection authority by the Administrator. For domestic grain, marketed at inland locations, the Administrator designates private and State agencies to provide official inspection services upon request. Both export and domestic services are provided on a fee basis.

Weighing Official weighing of U.S. export grain is performed at port locations by GIPSA or by State agencies that have been delegated export weighing authority by the Administrator. For domestic grain marketed at inland locations, the weighing services may be provided by GIPSA or by designated private or State agencies. Weighing services are provided on a fee basis, upon request.

Standardization The Administration is responsible for establishing, maintaining, and revising official U.S. standards. Such standards exist for corn, wheat, rye, oats, barley, flaxseed, sorghum, soybeans, triticale, sunflower seed, canola, and mixed grain. It is authorized to perform applied research to develop methods of improving accuracy and uniformity in grading grain. It is also responsible for standardization and inspection activities for rice, dry beans, peas, lentils, hay, straw, hops, and related processed grain commodities. Although standards no longer exist for hay, straw, and hops, GIPSA maintains inspection procedures for and retains authority to inspect these commodities.

Methods Development The Administration's methods development activities include applied research or tests that produce new or improved techniques for measuring grain quality. Examples include new knowledge gained through study of how to establish the framework for real-time grain inspection and develop reference methods to maintain consistency and standardization in the grain inspection system, and the comparison of different techniques for evaluation of end use quality in wheat. Included in this program area are also the development of a new wheat classification system, evaluation of prototype wheat hardness meters, and adapting measurement techniques for pesticides, mycotoxins, heavy metals, vitamins, and grain odor for use in the official grain inspection system.

Packers and Stockyards Activities The Packers and Stockyards Act is an antitrust, trade practice, and financial protection law. Its principal purpose is to maintain effective competition and fair trade practices in the marketing of livestock, meat, and poultry for the protection of livestock and poultry producers. Members of the livestock, poultry, and meat industries are also protected against unfair or monopolistic practices of competitors. The act also protects consumers against unfair business practices in the marketing of meats and poultry and against restrictions of competition that could unduly affect meat and poultry prices.

For further information, contact the Grain Inspection, Packers, and Stockyards Administration, Department of Agriculture, Washington, DC 20250. Phone, 202–720–0219.

Food Safety

Food Safety and Inspection Service

The Food Safety and Inspection Service (FSIS) was established by the Secretary of Agriculture on June 17, 1981, pursuant to authority contained in 5 U.S.C. 301 and Reorganization Plan No. 2 of 1953 (5 U.S.C. app.).

Meat, Poultry, and Egg Products Inspection Federal meat and poultry inspection is mandatory for cattle, calves, swine, goats, sheep, lambs, horses (and other equines), chickens, turkeys, ducks, geese, and guineas used for human food. The work includes inspection of each animal or bird at slaughter, and inspection of processed products during various stages of production. The Service conducts mandatory, continuous inspection of the production of liquid, dried, and frozen egg products, to ensure that egg products are safe, wholesome, unadulterated, and accurately labeled. The Service tests samples of egg products, and meat and poultry products for microbial and chemical contaminants to monitor trends for enforcement purposes.

Each product label must be approved by the agency before products can be sold. The agency monitors meat and poultry products in storage, distribution, and retail channels; and takes necessary compliance actions to protect the public, including detention of products, voluntary product recalls, court-ordered seizures of products, administrative withdrawal of inspection, and referral for criminal prosecution. The Service also conducts State programs for the inspection of meat and poultry products sold in intrastate commerce.

The Service monitors livestock upon arrival at federally inspected facilities; conducts voluntary reimbursed inspection for rabbits, other domestic food animals, bison, other exotic food animals, ratites, and certain egg products not covered by the inspection law; and ensures that inedible egg products and inedible products from meat or poultry, such as offal rendered for animal feed, are properly identified and isolated from edible products.

The Service maintains a toll-free meat and poultry hotline (800–535–4555; in the Washington metropolitan area, 202–720–5604) to answer questions about labeling and safe handling of meat and poultry, meat and poultry products, and egg products. The hotline is also accessible (on the same extension) by TDD.

For further information, contact the Director, Food Safety Education and Communications Staff, Food Safety and Inspection Service, Department of Agriculture, Washington, DC 20250. Phone, 202–720–7943. Fax, 202–720–1843. Internet, www.usda.gov/agency/fsis/homepage.htm.

Food, Nutrition, and Consumer Services

The mission of the Food, Nutrition, and Consumer Services is to reduce hunger and food insecurity, in partnership with cooperating organizations, by providing access to food, a healthful diet, and nutrition education to children and needy people in a manner that supports American agriculture.

Food and Nutrition Service

The Food and Nutrition Service (FNS) administers the USDA food assistance programs. These programs, which serve one in six Americans, represent our Nation's commitment to the principle that no one in this country should fear hunger or experience want. They provide a Federal safety net to people in need. The goals of the programs are to provide needy persons with access to a more nutritions diet, to improve the eating habits of the Nation's children, and to help America's farmers by providing an outlet for distributing foods purchased under farmer assistance authorities.

The Service works in partnership with the States in all its programs. State and local agencies determine most administrative details regarding distribution of food benefits and eligibility of participants, and FNS provides commodities and funding for additional food and to cover administrative costs. FNS administers the following food assistance programs:

—The Food Stamp Program provides food benefits through State and local welfare agencies to needy persons to increase their food purchasing power. The benefits are used by program participants to buy food in retail stores approved by the Food and Nutrition Service to accept and redeem the benefits.

—The Special Supplemental Nutrition Program for Women, Infants, and Children (WIC) improves the health of low-income pregnant, breastfeeding, and nonbreastfeeding postpartum women, and infants and children up to 5 years of age by providing them with specific nutritious food supplements, nutrition education, and health care referrals.

—The WIC Farmers' Market Nutrition Program provides WIC participants with increased access to fresh produce. WIC participants receive coupons to purchase fresh fruits and vegetables from authorized farmers.

—The Commodity Supplemental Food Program provides a package of foods monthly to low-income pregnant, postpartum, and breastfeeding women, their infants and children under age 6, and the elderly. Nutrition education is also provided through this program.

—The National School Lunch Program supports nonprofit food services in elementary and secondary schools and in residential child-care institutions. More than half of the meals served through these institutions are free or at reduced cost.

—The School Breakfast Program supplements the National School Lunch Program by supporting schools in providing needy children with free or low cost breakfasts that meet established nutritional standards.

—The Special Milk Program for Children provides milk for children in those schools, summer camps, and child-care institutions that have no federally supported meal programs.

—The Child and Adult Care Food Program provides cash and commodities for meals for preschool and school-aged children in child-care facilities and for functionally impaired adults in facilities that provide nonresidential care for such individuals.

—The Summer Food Service Program for Children helps various organizations get nutritious meals to needy preschool and school-aged children during the summer months and during school vacations.

—The Emergency Food Assistance Program provides State agencies with commodities for distribution to food banks, food pantries, soup kitchens, and other charitable institutions throughout the country, with administrative funds to assist in distribution.

—The Food Distribution Program on Indian Reservations and the Trust Territories provides an extensive package of commodities monthly to low-income households on or near Indian reservations in lieu of food stamps. This program is administered at the local level by Indian tribal organizations or State agencies.

—The Nutrition Program for the Elderly provides cash and commodities to States for meals for senior citizens. The food is delivered through senior citizen centers or meals-on-wheels programs.

—The Nutrition Assistance Programs for Puerto Rico and the Northern Marianas are block grant programs that replace the Food Stamp Programs in these two territories and provide cash and coupons to resident participants.

—The Nutrition Education and Training Program grants funds to States for the development and dissemination of nutrition information and materials to children and for training of food service and teaching personnel.

For further information, contact the Public Information Officer, Food and Nutrition Service, Department of Agriculture, Alexandria, VA 22302. Phone, 703–305–2286. Internet, www.usda.gov/fns.htm.

Center for Nutrition Policy and Promotion

The Center coordinates nutrition policy in USDA and provides overall leadership in nutrition education for the American public. It also coordinates with the Department of Health and Human Services in the review, revision, and dissemination of the *Dietary Guidelines for Americans,* the Federal Government's statement of nutrition policy formed by a consensus of scientific and medical professionals.

For further information, contact the Office of Public Information, Center for Nutrition Policy and Promotion, Suite 200, 1120 20th Street NW., Washington, DC 20036–3406. Phone, 202–418–2312. Internet, www.usda.gov/fns/cnpp.htm.

Farm and Foreign Agricultural Services

Farm Service Agency

The Farm Service Agency (FSA) administers farm commodity, crop insurance, and resource conservation programs for farmers and ranchers, and makes and guarantees farm emergency, ownership, and operating loans through a network of State and county offices.

Farm Commodity Programs The Agency manages programs for conservation efforts through commodity programs such as production flexibility contracts, commodity and livestock disaster programs, marketing assistance loan programs, noninsured crop disaster assistance programs, and tobacco and peanut programs. It administers commodity loan programs for wheat, rice, corn, grain sorghum, barley, oats, oilseeds, tobacco, peanuts, upland and extra-long-staple cotton, and sugar. FSA provides operating personnel for the Commodity Credit Corporation (CCC), A Government owned and operated organization providing short-term loans using the commodity as collateral, providing farmers with interim financing and orderly distribution of farm commodities throughout the year and in times of surplus and scarcity.

Farm Loan Programs FSA makes and guarantees loans to family farmers and ranchers to purchase farmland and finance agricultural production. These programs help farmers who are temporarily unable to obtain private commercial credit. These may be beginning farmers who have insufficient net worth to qualify for commercial credit, who have suffered financial setbacks from natural disasters, or who have limited resources with which to establish and maintain profitable farming operations.

Noninsured Crop Disaster Assistance Program (NAP) For crops for which Federal crop insurance is not available, NAP provides crop loss protection. Crops that are eligible include commercial crops grown for food and fiber, floriculure, ornamental nursery products, Christmas tree crops, turfgrass sod, seed crops, aquaculture (including ornamental fish such as goldfish), and industrial crops. Losses resulting from natural disasters not covered by the crop insurance policy may also be eligible for NAP assistance. NAP does not include trees grown for wood, paper, or pulp products.

Other Emergency Assistance In the aftermath of a natural disaster, FSA makes available a variety of emergency assistance programs to farmers in counties that have been designated or declared disaster areas, including cost-share assistance to producers who do not have enough feed to maintain livestock because of a loss of a substantial amount of their normal feed production.

Conservation Programs Conservation programs of FSA include preservation of farmland, wildlife habitat, and water and air quality. The Conservation Reserve Program is the Federal Government's single largest environmental improvement program on private lands. It safeguards millions of acres of topsoil from erosion improving air quality, increasing wildlife habitat, and protecting ground and surface water by reducing water runoff and sedimentation. In return for planting a protective cover of grass or trees on vulnerable property, the owner receives a rental payment each year of a multi-year contract. Cost-share payments are also available to help establish permanent areas of grass, legumes, trees, windbreaks, or plants that improve water quality and give shelter and food to wildlife.

Commodity Operations Under the dairy price support program, CCC buys surplus butter, cheese, and nonfat dry milk from processors at announced prices to support the price of milk. These purchases help maintain market prices at the legislated support level, and the commodities are used for hunger relief both domestically and internationally. Commodity operations personnel also aid in the storage, management, and disposition of food security commodity reserve grain and food products used to

186-873 D-00--5

meet humanitarian needs abroad and the disaster reserve used to meet emergency livestock feed needs domestically. CCC commodities are also used to supply the national school lunch and domestic and international food aid programs to help fight hunger worldwide.

For further information, contact the Public Affairs Branch, Farm Service Agency, Department of Agriculture, Stop 0506, 1400 Independence Avenue SW., Washington, DC 20250. Phone, 202–720–5237. Internet, www.fsa.usda.gov.

Commodity Credit Corporation

The Commodity Credit Corporation was organized in 1933, and was managed and operated in close affiliation with the Reconstruction Finance Corporation until 1939, when it was transferred to the Department of Agriculture. CCC stabilizes, supports, and protects farm income and prices, assists in maintaining balanced and adequate supplies of agricultural commodities and their products, and facilitates the orderly distribution of commodities.

Foreign Assistance The Corporation carries out assigned foreign assistance activities, such as guaranteeing the credit sale of U.S. agricultural commodities abroad. Major emphasis is also being directed toward meeting the needs of developing nations. Agricultural commodities are supplied and exported to combat hunger and malnutrition and to encourage economic development in developing countries. In addition, under the Food for Progress Program, the Corporation supplies commodities to provide assistance to developing democracies.

For further information, contact the Information Division, Foreign Agricultural Service, Department of Agriculture, Stop 1004, 1400 Independence Avenue SW., Washington, DC 20250. Phone, 202–720–7115. Fax, 202–720–1727.

Risk Management Agency

The Risk Management Agency (RMA) helps to stabilize the agricultural economy by providing a sound system of crop insurance. RMA administers the programs of the Federal Crop Insurance Corporation (FCIC) and has oversight for other programs related to the risk management of U.S. crops and commodities. Generally, multiple peril crop insurance (MPCI) policies insure farmers and ranchers against unexpected production losses from natural causes, including drought, excessive moisture, hail, wind, flooding, hurricanes, tornadoes, and lightning. Policies do not cover losses resulting from neglect, poor farming practices, or theft.

RMA also reinsures several revenue based plans of insurance. Generally, revenue insurance provides protection against loss of income due to low yields, prices, or both. One plan, crop revenue coverage, is widely available on corn, grain sorghum, cotton, soybeans, and wheat. Producers must purchase crop insurance by the sales closing date established for the crop they wish to insure. Policies are sold and serviced by private crop insurance agents and companies.

For information about Federal crop insurance programs, contact the Research and Development Division, 9435 Holmes Road, Kansas City, MO 64131. Phone, 816–926–7394. Internet, act.fcic.usda.gov. For information about the Risk Management Education outreach initiative, contact the Risk Management Education Division, Risk Management Agency, Department of Agriculture, 1400 Independence Avenue SW., Washington, DC 20250. Phone, 202–690–2957.

For further information, contact the Office of the Administrator, Risk Management Agency, Department of Agriculture, 1400 Independence Avenue SW., Washington, DC 20250. Phone, 202–690–2803. Internet, www.usda.gov/rma.

Foreign Agricultural Service

The Foreign Agricultural Service (FAS) has primary responsibility for USDA's overseas market information, access, and development programs. It also administers USDA's export assistance and foreign food assistance programs. The Service carries out its tasks through its network of agricultural counselors, attachés, and trade officers stationed overseas and its U.S.-based team of analysts, marketing specialists, negotiators, and other professionals.

The Foreign Agricultural Service maintains a worldwide agricultural intelligence and reporting system through its attaché service with staff posted in more than 75 countries around the world. They represent the Department of Agriculture and provide information and data on foreign government agricultural policies, analyses of supply and demand conditions, commercial trade relationships, and market opportunities. They report on more than 100 farm commodities, weather, economic factors, and related subjects that affect agriculture and agricultural trade.

At the Foreign Agricultural Service in Washington, DC, agricultural economists and marketing specialists analyze these and other reports. These analyses are supplemented by accumulated background information and by the crop condition assessment system, which analyzes Landsat satellite weather and other data.

To improve access for U.S. farm products abroad, FAS international trade policy specialists coordinate and direct USDA's responsibilities in international trade agreement programs and negotiations. They maintain an ongoing effort to reduce foreign trade barriers and practices that discourage the export of U.S. farm products.

To follow foreign governmental actions that affect the market for U.S. agricultural commodities, FAS relies on its agricultural counselors and attachés. In Washington, a staff of international trade specialists analyzes the trade policies and practices of foreign governments to ensure conduct in conformance with international treaty obligations. During international negotiations, FAS provides staff and support for U.S. agricultural representation.

The Service has a continuing market development program to create, maintain, and expand commercial export markets for U.S. agricultural products. It carries out programs with nonprofit commodity groups, trade associations, and State agriculture departments and their regional associations. It manages market opportunity referral services and organizes trade fairs and sales teams.

The Export Credit Guarantee Program (GSM–102) and the Intermediate Export Credit Guarantee Program (GSM–103) provide guarantees on private financing of U.S. exports to foreign buyers purchasing on credit terms.

The Supplier Credit Guarantee Program guarantees a portion of a payment due for purchase of U.S. agricultural products for import, for which the exporter has directly extended short-term financing.

The Facility Guarantee Program facilitates the financing of U.S. manufactured goods and services exported to emerging markets.

The Emerging Markets Program promotes agricultural exports to emerging markets through sharing U.S. agricultural expertise by technical assistance.

The Export Enhancement Program and the Dairy Export Incentive Program are export assistance programs designed to counter or offset the adverse effects from competitors' unfair trade practices on U.S. agriculture.

The Market Access Program provides cost-share assistance to trade promotion organizations, cooperatives, and small businesses to help fund their market development activities overseas.

The Service helps other USDA agencies, U.S. universities, and others enhance America's agricultural competitiveness globally; and increases income and food availability in developing nations by mobilizing expertise for agriculturally led economic growth.

The Service also manages programs to exchange visits, germplasm, and technologies between U.S. and international scientists; supports collaborative research projects of mutual interest to the United States and other nations; taps the U.S. agricultural community to provide technical assistance and professional development and training programs to assist economic development in lower income nations; serves as U.S. liaison with international organizations; and organizes overseas trade and investment missions.

For further information, contact the Information Division, Foreign Agricultural Service, Stop 1004, 1400 Independence Avenue SW., Department of Agriculture, Washington, DC 20250–1004. Phone, 202–720–7115. Fax, 202–720–1727. Internet, www.fas.usda.gov.

Research, Education, and Economics

This mission area's main focus is to create, apply, and transfer knowledge and technology to provide affordable food and fiber, ensure food safety and nutrition, and support rural development and natural resource needs of people by conducting integrated national and international research, information, education, and statistical programs and services that are in the national interest.

Agricultural Research Service

The Agricultural Research Service conducts research to develop and transfer solutions to agricultural problems of high national priority. It provides information access and dissemination to ensure high-quality, safe food and other agricultural products; assess the nutritional needs of Americans; sustain a competitive agricultural economy; enhance the natural resource base and the environment; and provide economic opportunities for rural citizens, communities, and society as a whole.

Research activities are carried out at 103 domestic locations (including Puerto Rico) and 3 overseas locations. Much of this research is conducted in cooperation with partners in State universities and experiment stations, other Federal agencies, and private organizations. A national program staff, headquartered in Beltsville, MD, is the focal point in the overall planning and coordination of ARS' research programs. Day-to-day management of the respective programs for specific field locations is assigned to eight area offices.

Area Offices—Agricultural Research Service

Office	Address
Beltsville Area—Beltsville Agricultural Research Center, National Arboretum, Washington, DC	Bldg. 003, Beltsville Agricultural Research Ctr. W., Beltsville, MD 20705
Midsouth Area—AL, KY, LA, MS, TN	P.O. Box 225, Stoneville, MS 38776
Midwest Area—IA, IL, IN, MI, MN, MO, OH, WI	1815 N. University St., Peoria, IL 61604
Northern Plains Area—CO, KS, MT, ND, NE, SD, UT, WY	Suite 150, 1201 Oakridge Rd., Fort Collins, CO 80525–5562
North Atlantic Area—CT, DE, MA, MD, ME, NH, NJ, NY, PA, RI, VT, WV	600 E. Mermaid Ln., Philadelphia, PA 19038
Pacific West Area—AK, AZ, CA, HI, ID, NV, OR, WA	800 Buchanan St., Albany, CA 94710
South Atlantic Area—FL, GA, NC, PR, SC, VI, VA	P.O. Box 5677, Athens, GA 30604–5677
Southern Plains Area—AR, NM, OK, TX	Suite 230, 7607 Eastmark Dr., College Station, TX 77840

The National Agricultural Library (NAL) provides information services over a broad range of agricultural interests to a wide cross-section of users, from research scientists to the general public. The Library assists its users through a variety of specialized information centers. Its staff uses advanced information technologies to generate new information products, creating an electronic library as it improves access to the knowledge stored in its multimedia collection of more than 2 million items.

Information is made available through loans, photocopies, reference services, and literature searches. A subject profiling system for selective searches of agricultural databases is available for USDA scientists. Citations to the agricultural literature are stored in the agricultural online access (AGRICOLA) database, available through online computer systems and on compact disc (CD's). The Library also distributes in the United States the AGRIS database of citations to the agricultural literature prepared by centers in various parts of the world and coordinated by the Food and Agriculture Organization of the United Nations.

For further information, contact the Information Staff, Agricultural Research Service, Department of Agriculture, Room 1–2250, 5601 Sunnyside Avenue, Beltsville, MD 20705–5128. Phone, 301–504–1638. Fax, 301–504–1648.

Cooperative State Research, Education, and Extension Service

The Cooperative State Research, Education, and Extension Service (CSREES) expands the research and higher education functions of the former Cooperative State Research Service and the education and outreach functions of the former Extension Service. The result is better customer service and an enhanced ability to respond to national priorities.

The Service links the research and education resources and activities of USDA and works with academic and land-grant institutions throughout the Nation. In cooperation with its partners and customers, CSREES provides the focus to advance a global system of research, extension, and higher education in the food and agricultural sciences and related environmental and human sciences to benefit people, communities, and the Nation.

The Service's mission emphasizes partnerships with the public and private sectors to maximize the effectiveness of limited resources. Its programs increase and provide access to scientific knowledge; strengthen the capabilities of land-grant and other institutions in research, extension, and higher education; increase access to and use of improved communication and network systems; and promote informed decisionmaking by producers, families, and social conditions in the United States and globally. These conditions include improved agricultural and other economic enterprises; safer, cleaner water, food, and air; enhanced stewardship and management of natural resources; healthier, more responsible and more productive individuals, families, and communities; and a stable, secure, diverse, and affordable national food supply.

The Service provides research, extension, and education leadership through programs in plant and animal systems; natural resources and environment; economic and community systems; families, 4–H, and nutrition; partnerships; competitive research grants and awards management; science and education resources development; and communications, technology, distance education, and special activities.

The Service's partnership with the land-grant universities and their representatives is critical to the effective shared planning, delivery, and accountability for research, higher education, and extension programs.

As a recognized leader in the design, organization, and application of advanced communication technologies and in meeting the growing demand for enhanced distance education capabilities, CSREES provides essential community access to research and education knowledge and connects the private citizen to other Federal Government information.

For further information, contact the Communications, Technology, and Distance Education Office, Cooperative State Research, Education, and Extension Service, Department of Agriculture, Washington, DC 20250–0906. Phone, 202–720–4651. Fax, 202–690–0289. TDD, 202–690–1899. E-mail, CSREES@reeusda.gov. Internet, www.reeusda.gov.

Economic Research Service

The mission of the Economic Research Service is to provide economic and other social science information and analysis for public and private decisions on agriculture, food, natural resources, and rural America. The Service produces such information for use by the general public and to help the executive and legislative branches develop, administer, and evaluate agricultural and rural policies and programs.

The Service produces economic information through a program of research and analysis on domestic and international agricultural developments; statistical indicators of food and consumer issues and concerns, including nutrition education and food assistance, food safety regulation, determinants of consumer demand for quality and safety, and food marketing trends and developments; agricultural resource and environmental issues; and the effect of public and private actions and policies on national rural and agricultural conditions, including the transformation of the rural economy, the financial performance of the farm sector, and the implications of changing farm credit and financial market structures.

For further information, contact the Information Services Division, Economics Research Service, Department of Agriculture, Washington, DC 20036–5831. Phone, 202–694–5100. Fax, 202–694–5641.

National Agricultural Statistics Service

The National Agricultural Statistics Service (NASS) prepares estimates and reports on production, supply, price, chemical use, and other items necessary for the orderly operation of the U.S. agricultural economy.

The reports include statistics on field crops, fruits and vegetables, dairy, cattle, hogs, sheep, poultry, aquaculture, and related commodities or processed products. Other estimates concern farm numbers, farm production expenditures, agricultural chemical use, prices received by farmers for products sold, prices paid for commodities and services, indexes of prices received and paid, parity prices, farm employment, and farm wage rates.

The Service prepares these estimates through a complex system of sample surveys of producers, processors, buyers, and others associated with agriculture. Information is gathered by mail, telephone, personal interviews, and field visits.

NASS is responsible for conducting the census of agriculture, formerly conducted by the Bureau of the Census. The census of agriculture is taken every 5 years and provides comprehensive data on the agricultural economy down to the county level. Periodic reports are also issued on irrigation and horticultural specialities.

The Service performs reimbursable survey work and statistical consulting services for other Federal and State agencies and provides technical assistance for developing agricultural data systems in other countries.

For further information, contact the Executive Assistant to the Administrator, National Agricultural Statistics Service, Department of Agriculture, Washington, DC 20250–2000. Phone, 202–720–2707. Fax, 202–720–9013.

Natural Resources and Environment

This mission area is responsible for fostering sound stewardship of 75 percent of the Nation's total land area. Ecosystems are the underpinning for the Department's operating philosophy in this area, in order to maximize stewardship of our natural resources. This approach ensures that products, values, services, and uses desired by people are produced in ways that sustain healthy, productive ecosystems.

Forest Service

[For the Forest Service statement of organization, see the *Code of Federal Regulations,* Title 36, Part 200.1]

The Forest Service was created by the Transfer Act of February 1, 1905 (16 U.S.C. 472), which transferred the Federal forest reserves and the responsibility for their management from the Department of the Interior to the Department of Agriculture. The mission of the Forest Service is to achieve quality land management under the sustainable, multiple-use management concept to meet the diverse needs of people. It's objectives include:

—advocating a conservation ethic in promoting the health, productivity, diversity, and beauty of forests and associated lands;

—listening to people and responding to their diverse needs in making decisions;

—protecting and managing the national forests and grasslands to best demonstrate the sustainable, multiple-use management concept;

—providing technical and financial assistance to State and private forest landowners, encouraging them toward active stewardship and quality land management in meeting their specific objectives;

—providing technical and financial assistance to cities and communities to improve their natural environment by planting trees and caring for their forests;

—providing international technical assistance and scientific exchanges to sustain and enhance global resources and to encourage quality land management;

—assisting States and communities in using the forests wisely to promote rural economic development and a quality rural environment;

—developing and providing scientific and technical knowledge, improving our capability to protect, manage, and use forests and rangelands; and

—providing work, training, and education to the unemployed, underemployed, elderly, youth, and the disadvantaged.

National Forest System The Service manages 155 national forests, 20 national grasslands, and 8 land utilization projects on over 191 million acres in 44 States, the Virgin Islands, and Puerto Rico under the principles of multiple-use and sustained yield. The Nation's tremendous need for wood and paper products is balanced with the other vital, renewable resources or benefits that the national forests and grasslands provide: recreation and natural beauty, wildlife habitat, livestock forage, and water supplies. The guiding principle is the greatest good to the greatest number in the long run.

These lands are protected as much as possible from wildfire, epidemics of disease and insect pests, erosion, floods, and water and air pollution. Burned areas get emergency seeding treatment to prevent massive erosion and stream siltation. Roads and trails are built where needed to allow for closely regulated timber harvesting and to give the public access to outdoor recreation areas and provide scenic drives and hikes. Picnic, camping, water-sport, skiing, and other areas are provided with facilities for public convenience and enjoyment. Timber harvesting methods are used that will protect the land and streams, assure rapid renewal of the forest, provide food and cover for wildlife and fish, and have minimum impact on scenic and recreation values. Local communities benefit from the logging and milling activities. These lands also provide needed oil, gas, and minerals. Rangelands are improved for millions of livestock and game animals. The national forests provide a refuge for many species of endangered birds, animals, and fish. Some 34.6 million acres are set aside as wilderness and 175,000 acres as primitive areas where timber will not be harvested.

Forest Research The Service performs basic and applied research to develop the scientific information and technology needed to protect, manage, use, and sustain the natural resources of the Nation's forests and rangelands. The Service's forest research strategy focuses on three major program components: understanding the structure and functions of forest and range ecosystems; understanding how people perceive and value the protection, management, and use of natural resources; and determining which protection, management, and utilization practices are most suitable for sustainable production and use of the world's natural resources.

Manpower Programs The Service operates the Youth Conservation Corps and the Volunteers in the National Forests programs and participates with the Department of Labor on several human resource programs that involve the Nation's citizens, both young and old, in forestry-related activities. Included in these programs are the Job Corps and the Senior Community Service Employment Program. These programs annually accomplish millions of dollars worth of conservation work, while providing participants with such benefits as training, paid employment, and meaningful outdoor experience.

For further information, contact the Office of Communications, Forest Service, Department of Agriculture, P.O. Box 96090, Washington, DC 20090–6090. Phone, 202–205–8333.

Field Offices—Forest Service

Region/Station/Area	Address
	National Forest System Regions—Regional Forester
1. Northern	Federal Bldg. (P.O. Box 7669), Missoula, MT 59807
2. Rocky Mountain	740 Simms St., P.O. Box 25127, Lakewood, CO 80225
3. Southwestern	517 Gold Ave. SW., Albuquerque, NM 87102
4. Intermountain	324 25th St., Ogden, UT 84401
5. Pacific Southwest	630 Sansome St., San Francisco, CA 94111
6. Pacific Northwest	333 SW. 1st Ave., P.O. Box 3623, Portland, OR 97208
8. Southern	1720 Peachtree Rd. NW., Atlanta, GA 30367
9. Eastern	310 W. Wisconsin Ave., Milwaukee, WI 53203
10. Alaska	Federal Office Bldg. (P.O. Box 21628), Juneau, AK 99802
	Research Stations—Director
Forest Products Laboratory	1 Gifford Pinchot Dr., Madison, WI 53705
North Central	1992 Folwell Ave., St. Paul, MN 55108
Northeastern	Suite 200, 100 Matson Ford Rd., P.O. Box 6775, Radnor, PA 19087–4585
Pacific Northwest	333 SW. 1st Ave., P.O. Box 3890, Portland, OR 97208
Pacific Southwest	800 Buchanan St., P.O. Box 245, Albany, CA 94710
Rocky Mountain	240 W. Prospect Ave., Fort Collins, CO 80526
Southern	200 Weaver Blvd., P.O. Box 2860, Asheville, NC 28802
	State and Private Forestry Areas—Director
Northeastern	Suite 200, 100 Matson Ford Rd., P.O. Box 6775, Radnor, PA 19087–4585
International Institute of Tropical Forestry	UPR Experimental Station Grounds, Botanical Garden, Call Box 25000, Rio Piedras, PR 00928

Natural Resources Conservation Service

[For the Natural Resources Conservation Service statement of organization, see the *Code of Federal Regulations,* Title 7, Parts 600 and 601]

The Natural Resources Conservation Service (NRCS), formerly the Soil Conservation Service, has national responsibility for helping America's farmers, ranchers, and other private landowners develop and carry out voluntary efforts to conserve and protect our natural resources. The Service is USDA's technical delivery arm for conservation.

Colorado River Basin Salinity Control Program This voluntary incentive program supports the Nation's commitment to water quality in the Colorado River, which provides water to more than 18 million people in parts of seven Western States and Mexico. The Service provides financial and technical assistance to control salt loading to the Colorado River from both natural and human-caused sources. Among the remedies used are management practices to prevent irrigation-induced erosion.

Conservation Farm Option This pilot program for producers of wheat, feed grains, cotton, and rice is open to owners or operators of farms that have a production flexibility contract. Under the program, producers may receive one consolidated USDA program payment in lieu of a list of specified payments. The producers must implement a conservation plan that addresses soil, water, and related resources; water quality; wetlands; and wildlife habitat. Participation is voluntary and is based on a 10-year contract.

Conservation Technical Assistance This is the foundation program of NRCS. Under this program, NRCS provides technical assistance to land users and units of government for the purpose of sustaining agricultural productivity and protecting and enhancing the natural resource base. This assistance is based on the voluntary cooperation of private landowners and involves comprehensive approaches to reduce soil erosion, improve soil and water quantity and quality, improve and conserve wetlands, enhance fish and wildlife habitat, improve air quality, improve pasture and range condition, reduce upstream flooding, and improve woodlands.

Emergency Watershed Protection Program This program provides emergency assistance to safeguard lives and property in jeopardy due to sudden watershed impairment by natural disasters. Emergency work includes quickly establishing a protective plant cover on denuded land and stream banks; opening dangerously restricted channels; and repairing diversions and levees. An emergency area need not be declared a national disaster area to be eligible for help under this program.

Environmental Quality Incentive Program This program assists producers with environmental and natural resource conservation improvements on their agricultural lands. One-half of the available funds are for conservation activities related to livestock production. Technical assistance, cost-share payments, incentive payments, and education focus on priority areas and natural resource concerns identified in cooperation with State technical committees.

Farmland Protection Program (FPP) This program protects soil by encouraging landowners to limit conversion of their farmland to nonagricultural uses. States, Indian tribes, or local governments administer all aspects of acquiring lands that are in FPP except when it is more effective and efficient for the Federal Government to do so.

Farms-for-the-Future Program This program guarantees USDA loans and subsidizes interest on State loans to purchase agricultural land or development rights to preserve vital farmland resources for future generations. The money also can be reinvested by the States to generate earnings for future farmland protection efforts.

Flood Prevention Program This program applies to 11 specific flood prevention projects covering about 35 million acres in 11 States. It provides help in flood prevention, water management, and reduction of erosion sedimentation. It also can help in developing recreational facilities and improving fish and wildlife habitat.

Forestry Incentives Program This program helps to increase the Nation's supply of products from nonindustrial private forest lands. This also ensures more effective use of existing forest lands and, over time, helps to prevent shortages and price increases for forest products. The program shares the cost incurred by landowners for tree planting and timberstand improvement.

Great Plains Conservation Program This program (GPCP) helps bring about long-term solutions to natural resource problems in the 10 Great Plains States. It is aimed at total conservation treatment of entire farms or ranches. Participation in GPCP is voluntary and provides technical assistance and a long-term cost-share contract between the participant and NRCS. In addition to providing significant erosion and sediment reduction benefits, it addresses problems related to water quality, wildlife habitat protection, and other environmental concerns.

National Cooperative Soil Survey The National Cooperative Soil Survey provides the public with local information on the uses and capabilities of their soils. The published soil survey for a county or other designated area includes maps and interpretations that are the foundation for farm planning and other private land use decisions as well as for resource planning and policy by Federal, State, and local governments. The surveys are conducted cooperatively with other Federal, State, and local agencies and land grant universities. The Service is the national and world leader in soil classification and soil mapping, and is now expanding its work in soil quality.

Plant Materials Program At 26 plant materials centers across the country, NRCS tests, selects, and ensures the commercial availability of new and improved conservation plants for erosion reduction, wetland restoration, water quality improvement, streambank and riparian area protection, coastal dune stabilization, biomass production, carbon sequestration, and other needs. The Plant Materials Program is a cooperative effort with conservation districts, other Federal and State agencies, commercial businesses, and seed and nursery associations.

Resource Conservation and Development Program This program (RC&D) is a locally driven program—an opportunity for civic-oriented groups to work together sharing knowledge and resources in solving common problems facing their region. The program offers aid in balancing the environmental, economic, and social needs of an area. A USDA coordinator helps each designated RC&D council plan, develop, and carry out programs for resource conservation, water management, community development, and environmental enhancement.

River Basin Surveys and Investigations This program involves NRCS with Federal, State, and local agencies in river basin surveys and investigations, flood hazard analysis, and floodplain management assistance. It addresses a variety of natural resource concerns: water quality, water conservation, wetlands protection, agricultural drought, rural development, municipal and industrial water needs, and fish and wildlife habitat.

Rural Abandoned Mine Program This program helps protect people and the environment from the adverse effects of past coal-mining practices and promotes the development of soil and water resources on unreclaimed mine land. It provides technical and financial assistance to land users who voluntarily enter into 5- to 10-year contracts for the reclamation of eligible land and water.

Small Watersheds Program The program helps local sponsoring groups to voluntarily plan and install watershed protection projects on private lands. These projects include flood prevention, water quality improvement, soil erosion and sediment reduction, rural and municipal water supply, irrigation water management, fish and wildlife habitat enhancement, and wetlands restoration. The Service helps local community groups, government entities, and private landowners working together using an integrated, comprehensive watershed approach to natural resource planning.

Snow Survey and Water Supply Forecasting Program This program collects snowpack moisture data and forecasts seasonal water supplies for streams that derive most of their water from snowmelt. It helps farm operators, rural communities, and municipalities manage water resources through water supply forecasts. It also provides hydrometeorological data for regulating reservoir storage and managing streamflow. The Snow Supply Program is conducted in 11 Western States and Alaska.

Water Bank Program The Service helps landowners protect, improve, or restore wetlands by identifying eligible lands, helping owners develop conservation plans, and implementing necessary land treatments. Through 10-year rental agreements between USDA and landowners, the Water Bank Program protects important nesting, breeding, and feeding areas for migratory waterfowl. Other benefits of the program include water conservation, erosion control, flood control, and landscape beautification.

Wetlands Reserve Program Under this program, USDA purchases easements from agricultural land owners who voluntarily agree to restore and protect wetlands. Service employees help these owners develop plans to retire critical wetland habitat from crop production. The primary objectives are to preserve and restore wetlands, improve wildlife habitat, and protect migratory waterfowl.

For further information, contact the Management Services Division, Natural Resources Conservation Service, Department of Agriculture, P.O. Box 2890, Washington, DC 20013. Phone, 202–690–4811.

Graduate School, U.S. Department of Agriculture

Fourteenth Street and Independence Avenue SW., Washington, DC 20250
Phone, 202–314–3300

Director	PHILIP H. HUDSON
Deputy Director	LYNN EDWARDS
Associate Director	ROBERT BROWN

The Graduate School was established by act of May 15, 1862 (7 U.S.C. 2201). It is a continuing education school offering career-related training to adults. Courses are planned with the assistance of Government professionals and specialists. The Graduate School's objective is to improve Government services by providing needed continuing education and training opportunities for Government employees and agencies.

The faculty is mostly part-time and is drawn from throughout Government and the community at large. They are selected because of their professional and specialized knowledge and experience and thus bring a practicality and experience to their classrooms.

The school does not grant degrees but does provide planned sequences of courses leading to certificates of accomplishment in a number of occupational and career fields important to government. Training areas include management, auditing, computer science, communications, foreign language, procurement, financial management, and others.

For further information, contact the Communications Office, Graduate School, U.S. Department of Agriculture, Room 160, 600 Maryland Avenue SW., Washington, DC 20024. Phone, 202–401–9129.

Sources of Information

Consumer Activities Educational, organizational, and financial assistance is offered to consumers and their families in such fields as rural housing and farm operating programs, improved nutrition, family living and recreation, food stamp, school lunch, donated foods, and other food programs. Contact the Office of Public Affairs, Department of Agriculture, Washington, DC 20250. Phone, 202–720–2791.

Contracts and Small Business Activities To obtain information about contracting or subcontracting opportunities, attending small business outreach activities, or how to do business with USDA, contact the Office of Small and Disadvantaged Business Utilization. Phone, 202–720–7117. Internet, www.usda.gov/da/smallbus.html.

Employment Most jobs in the Department are in the competitive service and are filled by applicants who have established eligibility under an appropriate examination administered by the Office of Personnel Management or Department Special Examining Units. General employment inquiries should be directed to the agencies.

Persons interested in employment in the Food and Consumer Service should contact the regional offices located in Atlanta, Boston, Chicago, Dallas, Denver, San Francisco, and Robbinsville, NJ, or the national headquarters in Alexandria, VA. Phone, 703–305–2351.

Persons interested in employment in the Office of the Inspector General should contact the USDA Office of Personnel, Room 31–W, Jamie L. Whitten Building, Washington, DC 20250. Phone, 202–720–5781.

In addition, all Forest Service field offices (addresses indicated in the preceding text) accept employment applications.

Environment Educational, organizational, technical, and financial assistance is offered to local citizens, organizations, and communities in such fields as watershed protection, flood prevention, soil and water conservation practices to reduce erosion and sedimentation, community water and waste disposal systems, safe use of pesticides, and the development of pesticide alternatives.

Contact the nearest county extension agent or USDA office, or write to the Office of Communications, Department of Agriculture, Washington, DC 20250. Phone, 202–720–2791.

Films Motion pictures on a variety of agricultural subjects are available for loan through various State Extension Service film libraries. Contact the Video, Teleconference, and Radio Center, Office of Communications, Department of Agriculture, Washington, DC 20250, for a listing of cooperating film libraries. Phone, 202–720–6072.

Color filmstrips and slide sets on a variety of subjects are available for purchase. For a listing of titles and prices, contact the Photography Center, Office of Communications, Department of Agriculture, Washington, DC 20250. Phone, 202–720–6633.

Whistleblower Hotline Persons wishing to register complaints of alleged improprieties concerning the Department should contact one of the regional offices or the Inspector General's whistleblower hotline. Phone, 800–424–9121 (toll-free, outside Washington, DC); 202–690–1622 (within the Washington, DC, metropolitan area); or 202–690–1202 (TDD). Fax, 202–690–2474.

Reading Rooms Located at each USDA agency at addresses indicated in the preceding text.

Speakers Contact the nearest Department of Agriculture office or county Extension agent. In the District of Columbia, contact the Office of Public Liaison, Office of Communications, Department of Agriculture, Washington, DC 20250. Phone, 202–720–2798.

For further information concerning the Department of Agriculture, contact the Office of Communications, Department of Agriculture, Washington, DC 20250. Phone, 202–720–2791. Internet, www.usda.gov.

DEPARTMENT OF COMMERCE

Fourteenth Street and Constitution Avenue NW., Washington, DC 20230
Phone, 202–482–2000. Internet, www.doc.gov.

SECRETARY OF COMMERCE	WILLIAM M. DALEY
Deputy Secretary of Commerce	ROBERT L. MALLETT
Chief of Staff	DAVID J. LANE
Assistant to the Secretary and Director, Office of Policy and Strategic Planning	DAVID FESTA, *Acting*
Director, Office of White House Liaison	PARNICE GREEN
Director, Office of Small and Disadvantaged Business Utilization	T.J. GARCIA
Assistant Secretary for Communications and Information	GREGORY L. ROHDE
Deputy Assistant Secretary	BERNADETTE A. MCGUIRE-RIVERA, *Acting*
Assistant Secretary for Economic Development	CHESTER J. STRAUB, JR., *Acting*
Deputy Assistant Secretary	(VACANCY)
Assistant Secretary for Legislative and Intergovernmental Affairs	DEBORAH K. KILMER
Deputy Assistant Secretary for Legislative and Intergovernmental Affairs	TODD MENOTH, *Acting*
Deputy Assistant Secretary for Intergovernmental Affairs	EDWARD PREWITT
Chief Financial Officer and Assistant Secretary for Administration	LINDA J. BILMES
Deputy Assistant Secretary for Administration	RAUL PEREA-HENZE
Chief Information Officer	ROGER W. BAKER
Deputy Chief Information Officer	JEFFREY R. NEAL
Director, Minority Business Development Agency	COURTLAND V. COX
Deputy Director	RUTH E. SANDOVAL
Director, Office of Business Liaison	JOHN GRAY
Director, Office of Public Affairs and Press Secretary	MAURICE F. GOODMAN
General Counsel	ANDREW J. PINCUS
Deputy General Counsel	(VACANCY)
Assistant General Counsel for Administration	BARBARA S. FREDERICKS
Assistant General Counsel for Legislation and Regulation	MICHAEL A. LEVITT
Assistant General Counsel for Finance and Litigation	ALDEN F. ABBOTT
Inspector General	JOHNNIE E. FRAZIER
Deputy Inspector General	EDWARD L. BLANSITT
Assistant Inspector General for Auditing	MARY CASEY, *Acting*

Assistant Inspector General for Investigations	STEPHEN E. GARMON
Assistant Inspector General for Systems Evaluation	JUDITH J. GORDON
Assistant Inspector General for Inspections and Program Evaluations	JILL A. GROSS
Assistant Inspector General for Compliance and Administration	(VACANCY)
Deputy Assistant Secretary for Security	K. DAVID HOLMES, JR.

ECONOMICS AND STATISTICS ADMINISTRATION

Department of Commerce, Washington, DC 20230
Phone, 800–782–8872

Under Secretary for Economic Affairs	ROBERT J. SHAPIRO
Deputy Under Secretary	(VACANCY)
Associate Under Secretary	MARTINA A. HONE
Chief Economist	LEE PRICE
Director, Bureau of the Census	KENNETH PREWITT
Director, Bureau of Economic Analysis	J. STEVEN LANDEFELD

BUREAU OF EXPORT ADMINISTRATION

Fourteenth Street and Constitution Avenue NW., Washington, DC 20230
Phone, 202–482–2721

Under Secretary for Export Administration	WILLIAM A. REINSCH
Deputy Under Secretary	THOMAS S. BUNTON
Assistant Secretary for Export Administration	ROGER R. MAJAK
Assistant Secretary for Export Enforcement	AMANDA F. DEBUSK

INTERNATIONAL TRADE ADMINISTRATION

Department of Commerce, Washington, DC 20230
Phone, 202–482–3809

Under Secretary for International Trade	(VACANCY)
Deputy Under Secretary	TIMOTHY J. HAUSER
Deputy Under Secretary for Trade Policy Development	ERIC R. BIEL
Assistant Secretary for Import Administration	ROBERT S. LARUSSA
Assistant Secretary for Market Access and Compliance	PATRICK A. MULLOY
Assistant Secretary for Trade Development	MICHAEL J. COPPS
Assistant Secretary and Director General of the U.S. and Foreign Commercial Service	MARJORY SEARING, *Acting*

NATIONAL OCEANIC AND ATMOSPHERIC ADMINISTRATION

Department of Commerce, Washington, DC 20230
Phone, 202–482–2985. Internet, www.noaa.gov.

Under Secretary for Oceans and Atmosphere	D. JAMES BAKER
Assistant Secretary for Oceans and Atmosphere and Deputy Administrator	(VACANCY)
Deputy Under Secretary for Oceans and Atmosphere	SCOTT B. GUDES
Chief Scientist	(VACANCY)

U.S. PATENT AND TRADEMARK OFFICE

2121 Crystal Drive, Arlington, VA 22202
Phone, 703–305–8341. Internet, www.uspto.gov.

Under Secretary for Intellectual Property	Q. TODD DICKINSON
Deputy Under Secretary and Deputy Commissioner	(VACANCY)
Assistant Commissioner for Patents	NICHOLAS P. GODICI
Assistant Commissioner for Trademarks	ANNE H. CHASSER

TECHNOLOGY ADMINISTRATION

Department of Commerce, Washington, DC 20230
Phone, 202–482–1575

Under Secretary for Technology	CHERYL SHAVERS
Deputy Under Secretary	GARY R. BACHULA
Assistant Secretary for Technology Policy	KELLY H. CARNES
Director, National Institute of Standards and Technology	RAYMOND G. KAMMER, JR.
Director, National Technical Information Service	RONALD E. LAWSON

The Department of Commerce encourages, serves, and promotes the Nation's international trade, economic growth, and technological advancement. The Department provides a wide variety of programs through the competitive free enterprise system. It offers assistance and information to increase America's competitiveness in the world economy; administers programs to prevent unfair foreign trade competition; provides social and economic statistics and analyses for business and government planners; provides research and support for the increased use of scientific, engineering, and technological development; works to improve our understanding and benefits of the Earth's physical environment and oceanic resources; grants patents and registers trademarks; develops policies and conducts research on telecommunications; provides assistance to promote domestic economic development; and assists in the growth of minority businesses.

The Department was designated as such by act of March 4, 1913 (15 U.S.C. 1501), which reorganized the Department of Commerce and Labor, created by act of February 14, 1903 (15 U.S.C. 1501), by transferring all labor activities into a new, separate Department of Labor.

Office of the Secretary

Secretary The Secretary is responsible for the administration of all functions and authorities assigned to the Department of Commerce and for advising the President on Federal policy and programs affecting the industrial and commercial segments of the national economy. The Secretary is served by the offices of Deputy Secretary, Inspector General, General Counsel, and the Assistant Secretaries of Administration, Legislative and Intergovernmental Affairs, and Public Affairs. Other offices whose public purposes are widely administered are detailed below.

Business Liaison This office develops and promotes a cooperative working relationship and ensures effective communication between the Department of Commerce and the business community. It also promotes business involvement in departmental policymaking and program development, and provides technical assistance to businesses that desire help in dealing with the Government.

For further information, call 202–482–1360.

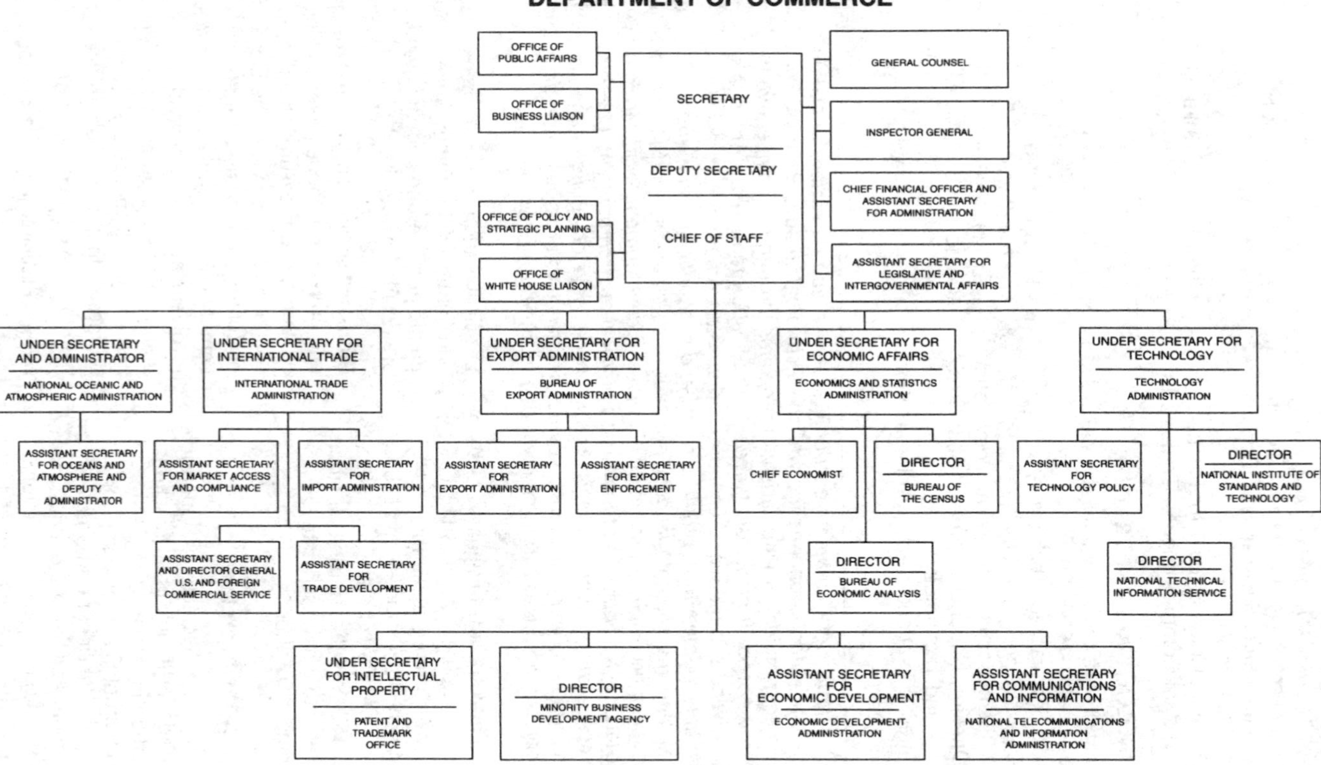
DEPARTMENT OF COMMERCE
OFFICE OF PUBLIC AFFAIRS
OFFICE OF BUSINESS LIAISON
SECRETARY
DEPUTY SECRETARY
CHIEF OF STAFF
GENERAL COUNSEL
INSPECTOR GENERAL
CHIEF FINANCIAL OFFICER AND ASSISTANT SECRETARY FOR ADMINISTRATION
OFFICE OF POLICY AND STRATEGIC PLANNING
OFFICE OF WHITE HOUSE LIAISON
ASSISTANT SECRETARY FOR LEGISLATIVE AND INTERGOVERNMENTAL AFFAIRS
UNDER SECRETARY AND ADMINISTRATOR
NATIONAL OCEANIC AND ATMOSPHERIC ADMINISTRATION
UNDER SECRETARY FOR INTERNATIONAL TRADE
INTERNATIONAL TRADE ADMINISTRATION
UNDER SECRETARY FOR EXPORT ADMINISTRATION
BUREAU OF EXPORT ADMINISTRATION
UNDER SECRETARY FOR ECONOMIC AFFAIRS
ECONOMICS AND STATISTICS ADMINISTRATION
UNDER SECRETARY FOR TECHNOLOGY
TECHNOLOGY ADMINISTRATION
ASSISTANT SECRETARY FOR OCEANS AND ATMOSPHERE AND DEPUTY ADMINISTRATOR
ASSISTANT SECRETARY FOR MARKET ACCESS AND COMPLIANCE
ASSISTANT SECRETARY FOR IMPORT ADMINISTRATION
ASSISTANT SECRETARY FOR EXPORT ADMINISTRATION
ASSISTANT SECRETARY FOR EXPORT ENFORCEMENT
CHIEF ECONOMIST
DIRECTOR
BUREAU OF THE CENSUS
ASSISTANT SECRETARY FOR TECHNOLOGY POLICY
DIRECTOR
NATIONAL INSTITUTE OF STANDARDS AND TECHNOLOGY
ASSISTANT SECRETARY AND DIRECTOR GENERAL U.S. AND FOREIGN COMMERCIAL SERVICE
ASSISTANT SECRETARY FOR TRADE DEVELOPMENT
DIRECTOR
BUREAU OF ECONOMIC ANALYSIS
DIRECTOR
NATIONAL TECHNICAL INFORMATION SERVICE
UNDER SECRETARY FOR INTELLECTUAL PROPERTY
PATENT AND TRADEMARK OFFICE
DIRECTOR
MINORITY BUSINESS DEVELOPMENT AGENCY
ASSISTANT SECRETARY FOR ECONOMIC DEVELOPMENT
ECONOMIC DEVELOPMENT ADMINISTRATION
ASSISTANT SECRETARY FOR COMMUNICATIONS AND INFORMATION
NATIONAL TELECOMMUNICATIONS AND INFORMATION ADMINISTRATION

Economics and Statistics Administration

The Under Secretary for Economic Affairs advises the Secretary and other Government officials on matters relating to economic developments and forecasts and on the development of macroeconomic and microeconomic policy. The Under Secretary, as Administrator of the Economics and Statistics Administration, exercises general supervision over the Bureau of the Census and the Bureau of Economic Analysis.

Current economic data are available to the public through the STAT–USA website (Internet, www.stat-usa.gov), the National Trade Data Bank, and the Economic Bulletin Board.

Bureau of the Census

[For the Bureau of the Census statement of organization, see the *Federal Register* of Sept. 16, 1975, 40 FR 42765]

The Bureau of the Census was established as a permanent office by act of March 6, 1902 (32 Stat. 51). The major functions of the Bureau are authorized by the Constitution, which provides that a census of population shall be taken every 10 years, and by laws codified as title 13 of the United States Code. The law also provides that the information collected by the Bureau from individual persons, households, or establishments be kept strictly confidential and be used only for statistical purposes. The Bureau is responsible for:

—the decennial censuses of population and housing;

—the quinquennial censuses of State and local governments, manufacturers, mineral industries, distributive trades, construction industries, and transportation;

—current surveys that provide information on many of the subjects covered in the censuses at monthly, quarterly, annual, or other intervals;

—compilation of current statistics on U.S. foreign trade, including data on imports, exports, and shipping;

—special censuses at the request and expense of States and local government units;

—publication of estimates and projections of the population;

—publication of current data on population and housing characteristics; and

—current reports on manufacturing, retail and wholesale trade, services, construction, imports and exports, State and local government finances and employment, and other subjects.

The Bureau makes available statistical results of its censuses, surveys, and other programs to the public through printed reports, computer tape, CD–ROM's, the Internet, and other media and prepares special tabulations sponsored and paid for by data users. It also produces statistical compendia, catalogs, guides, and directories that are useful in locating information on specific subjects. Upon request, the Bureau makes searches of decennial census records and furnishes certificates to individuals for use as evidence of age, relationship, or place of birth. A fee is charged for searches.

For further information, contact the Human Resources Division, Bureau of the Census, Department of Commerce, Washington, DC 20233. Phone, 301–457–8353. Fax, 301–457–1906.

Field Organization—Bureau of the Census

Regional Office (Areas Served)	Address
Atlanta, GA (AL, FL, GA)	Suite 3200, 101 Marietta St. NW., 30303–2700
Boston, MA (CT, MA, ME, NH, NY (all counties not listed under the New York Regional Office), PR, RI, VI, and VT)	Suite 301, 2 Copley Pl., 02117–9108
Charlotte, NC (KY, NC, SC, TN, VA)	Suite 106, 901 Ctr. Park Dr., 28217–2935
Chicago, IL (IL, IN, WI)	Suite 5501, 2255 Enterprise Dr., Westchester, IL 60154–5800
Dallas, TX (LA, MS, TX)	Suite 210, 6303 Harry Hines Blvd., 75235–5269

Field Organization—Bureau of the Census—Continued

Regional Office (Areas Served)	Address
Denver, CO (AZ, CO, MT, NE, ND, NM, NV, SD, UT, and WY)	Suite 100, 6900 W. Jefferson Ave., 80235–2032
Detroit, MI (MI, OH, WV)	P.O. Box 33405, 1395 Brewery Park Blvd., 48207
Kansas City, KS (AR, IA, KS, MN, MO, OK)	Suite 600, 400 State Ave., 66101–2410
Los Angeles, CA (CA (counties of Fresno, Imperial, Inyo, Kern, Kings, Los Angeles, Madera, Mariposa, Merced, Monterey, Orange, Riverside, San Benito, San Bernadino, San Diego, San Luis Obispo, Santa Barbara, Tulare, and Ventura), HI)	Suite 300, 15350 Sherman Way, Van Nuys, CA 91406–4224
New York, NY (NJ (counties of Bergen, Essex, Hudson, Middlesex, Morris, Passaic, Somerset, Sussex, Union, and Warren), NY (counties of Bronx, Kings, Nassau, New York, Queens, Richmond, Rockland, Suffolk, and Westchester))	Rm. 37–100, 26 Federal Plz., 10278–0044
Philadelphia, PA (DC, DE, MD, NJ (all counties not listed under the New York Regional Office), PA)	21st Fl., 1601 Market St., 19103–2395
Seattle, WA (AK, CA (all counties not listed under the Los Angeles Regional Office), ID, OR, WA)	Rm. 5100, 700 5th Ave., 98104–5018

Bureau of Economic Analysis

[For the Bureau of Economic Analysis statement of organization, see the *Federal Register* of Dec. 29, 1980, 45 FR 85496]

The Bureau of Economic Analysis (BEA) is the Nation's economic accountant, integrating and interpreting a variety of source data to draw a complete and consistent picture of the U.S. economy. Its economic accounts provide information on such key issues as economic growth, regional development, and the Nation's position in the world economy.

The national income and product accounts, featuring the gross domestic product, provide a quantitative view of the production, distribution, and use of the Nation's output. The Bureau also prepares estimates of the Nation's tangible wealth and input-output tables that show how industries interact.

The regional economic accounts provide estimates of personal income, population, and employment for regions, States, and metropolitan areas. The Bureau also prepares estimates of gross State product.

The international economic accounts encompass U.S. international transactions (balance of payments) with foreign countries and the international investment position of the United States. The Bureau provides survey-based data on foreign direct investment in the U.S. and U.S. direct investment abroad.

For further information, contact the Public Information Office, Bureau of Economic Analysis, Department of Commerce, Washington, DC 20230. Phone, 202–606–9900. Fax, 202–606–5310.

For further information, contact the Economics and Statistics Administration, Department of Commerce, Washington, DC 20230. Phone, 800–782–8872.

Bureau of Export Administration

[For the Bureau of Export Administration statement of organization, see the *Federal Register* of June 7, 1988, 53 FR 20881]

The Bureau of Export Administration was established as a separate agency within the Department of Commerce on October 1, 1987, to separate the functions of export promotion and export control as mandated by the Export Administration Act (50 U.S.C. app. 2401 *et seq.*).

The Bureau directs the Nation's dual-use export control policy. Major functions include processing license applications and enforcing export control laws. These activities are central not only to fighting proliferation, but also to pursuing other national security, short supply, and foreign policy goals.

Export Administration The Office of Export Administration is responsible for export control policy and licensing activities relating to dual-use goods and technologies. The Office implements commercial encryption policy and is responsible for supporting defense industrial- and technology-based issues to ensure that the United States remains competitive in those sectors and subsectors critical to national security. The Office has the major role of overseeing U.S. industry compliance with the Chemical Weapons Convension.

Export Enforcement The Office investigates suspected violations of U.S. export control laws, enforces the antiboycott regulations, and develops and implements preventive enforcement measures. Enforcement agents work with the export industry to detect and prevent illegal shipments, and they work with other U.S. Government agencies and foreign governments on export enforcement issues.

Nonproliferation and Export Control The Nonproliferation and Export Control International Cooperation Team participates in the Government initiative to help other countries strengthen national export control systems and to help reduce the threat of proliferation of weapons of mass destruction.

Critical Infrastructure Assurance The Office was created by a presidential directive to coordinate actions both within the Federal Government and with the private sector to protect critical infrastructure. The national plan for information systems protection for the year 2000 was the first attempt by any national government to protect electric systems, communications, and transportation networks, all of which are computer controlled, from deliberate attack and sabotage.

Field Offices—Bureau of Export Administration

Field Area	Address
Export Enforcement	
Boston, MA	Rm. 350, 10 Causeway St., 02222
Dallas, TX	Rm. 622, 525 S. Griffin St., 75202
Des Plaines, IL	Suite 300, 2400 E. Devon Ave., 60018
El Segundo, CA	Suite 720, 222 N. Sepulveda Blvd., 90245
Fort Lauderdale, FL	Suite 2060, 200 E. Lasolas Blvd., 33301
Herndon, VA	Suite 1125, 381 Elden St., 20170
Irvine, CA	Suite 310, 2601 Main St., 92714
Jamaica, NY	Rm. 204A, Halnar Cargo Bldg. 75, JFK Airport, 11430
San Jose, CA	Suite 250, 96 N. 3d St., 95112–5519
Staten Island, NY	Suite 104, 1200 South Ave., 10314
Export Administration	
Newport Beach, CA	Suite 345, 3300 N. Irvine Ave., 95113
San Jose, CA	Suite 1001, 101 Park Ctr. Plz., 95113

For further information, contact the Bureau of Export Administration, Office of Public Affairs, Room 3897, Fourteenth Street and Constitution Avenue NW., Washington, DC 20230. Phone, 202–482–2721.

Economic Development Administration

The Economic Development Administration (EDA) was created in 1965 under the Public Works and Economic Development Act (42 U.S.C. 3121) as part of an effort to target Federal resources to economically distressed areas and to help develop local economies in the United States. It was mandated to assist rural and urban communities that were outside the mainstream economy and that lagged in economic development, industrial growth, and personal income.

The Administration provides grants for public works and development facilities, planning and coordination, economic adjustment, and other financial assistance to reduce substantial and persistent unemployment in economically distressed areas.

Public works and development facilities grants support infrastructure projects that foster the establishment or expansion of industrial and commercial businesses, supporting the retention and creation of jobs.

Planning grants support the design and implementation of effective economic development policies and programs, by local development organizations, in States and communities. EDA funds a network of over 300 planning districts throughout the country.

Technical assistance rovide for local feasibility and industry studies, management and operational assistance, natural resource development, and export promotion. In addition, EDA funds a network of university centers that provides technical assistance.

Research, evaluation, and demonstration funds are used to support studies about the causes of economic distress and to seek solutions to counteract and prevent such problems.

Economic adjustment grants help communities adjust to a gradual erosion or sudden dislocation of their local economic structure.

Defense conversion grants assist communities adversely affected by Department of Defense base closures and defense contract cutbacks, as well as Department of Energy realignments, by providing development tools that can be effectively and easily implemented.

Regional Offices—Economic Development Administration

Region (Areas Served)	Address
Atlanta, GA (AL, FL, GA, MS, TN)	Suite 1820, 401 W. Peachtree St. NW., 30308–3610
Kentucky	Suite 200, 771 Corporate Dr., Lexington, 40503–5477
North Carolina and South Carolina	P.O. Box 1707, Lugoff, SC 29078
Austin, TX (NM, OK, TX)	Suite 200, 327 Congress Ave., 78701–4037
Arkansas	Rm. 2509, 700 W. Capital St., Little Rock, 72201
Louisiana	Rm. 1025, 501 Magazine St., New Orleans, 70130
Chicago, IL	Suite 855, 111 N. Canal, 60606–7204
Illinois and Minnesota	Rm. 104, 515 W. 1st St., Duluth, MN 55802
Indiana and Ohio	Rm. 740, 200 N. High St., Columbus, OH 43215
Michigan and Wisconsin	P.O. Box 517, Acme, MI 49610–0517
Denver, CO (CO, KS, UT)	Rm. 670, 1244 Speer Blvd., 80204
Iowa and Nebraska	Rm. 823, 210 Walnut St., Des Moines, IA 50309
Missouri	Rm. B–2, 608 E. Cherry St., Columbia, 65201
Montana and Wyoming	Rm. 196, 301 S. Park Ave., Helena, MT 59626
North Dakota and South Dakota	Rm. 216, 102 4th Ave., Aberdeen, SD 57401
Philadelphia, PA (DC, DE, NJ)	Suite 140 S., Independence Sq. W., 19106
Connecticut, Maine, and Rhode Island	48 Highland Ave., Bangor, ME 04401–4656
Maryland and Virginia	Rm. 474, 400 N. 8th St., Richmond, VA 23240–1001
Massachusetts and New Hampshire	Suite 209, 143 N. Main St., Concord, NH 03301–5089
New York and Vermont	Suite 104, 620 Erie Blvd. W., Syracuse, NY 13204–2442
Pennsylvania	525 N. Broad St., W. Hazelton, 18201–1107
Puerto Rico and Virgin Islands	Suite 602, 654 Munoz Rivera Ave., Hato Rey, PR 00918–1738
West Virginia	Rm. 411, 405 Capital St., Charleston, 25301–1727
Seattle, WA (AZ, WA)	Rm. 1856, 915 2d Ave., 98174
Alaska	Suite 1780, 550 W. 7th Ave., Anchorage, 99501–7594
California and Oregon	Suite 244, 121 SW. Salmon St., Portland, OR 97204
Hawaii, Guam, American Samoa, Marshall Islands, Micronesia, Northern Marianas and Republic of Palau.	Rm. 5180, 300 Ala Moana Blvd., Honolulu, HI 96850
Idaho and Nevada	Rm. 441, 304 N. 8th St., Boise, ID 83702

For further information, contact the Economic Development Administration, Department of Commerce, Washington, DC 20230. Phone, 202–482–2309. Fax, 202–482–0995.

International Trade Administration

[For the International Trade Administration statement of organization, see the *Federal Register* of Jan. 25, 1980, 45 FR 6148]

The International Trade Administration was established on January 2, 1980, by the Secretary of Commerce to promote world trade and to strengthen the international trade and investment position of the United States.

The Administration is headed by the Under Secretary for International Trade, who coordinates all issues concerning trade promotion, international commercial policy, market access, and trade law enforcement. The Administration is responsible for nonagricultural trade operations of the U.S. Government and supports the trade policy negotiation efforts of the U.S. Trade Representative.

Imports The Office of the Assistant Secretary for Import Administration defends American industry against injurious and unfair trade practices by administering efficiently, fairly, and in a manner consistent with U.S. international trade obligations the antidumping and countervailing duty laws of the United States. The Office ensures the proper administration of foreign trade zones and advises the Secretary on establishment of new zones; and administers programs governing watch assemblies, and other statutory import programs.

Market Access and Compliance The Office of the Assistant Secretary for Market Access and Compliance advises on the analysis, formulation, and implementation of U.S. international economic policies and carries out programs to promote international trade, improve access by U.S. companies to overseas markets, and strengthen the international trade and investment position of the United States. The Office analyzes and develops recommendations for region- and country-specific international economic, trade, and investment policy strategies and objectives. In addition, the Office is responsible for implementing, monitoring, and enforcing foreign compliance with bilateral and multilateral trade agreements.

Trade Development The Office of the Assistant Secretary for Trade Development advises on international trade and investment policies pertaining to U.S. industrial sectors, carries out programs to strengthen domestic export competitiveness, and promotes U.S. industry participation in international markets. The Office manages an integrated trade development program that includes industry analysis, project advocacy support, and trade assistance organized by industry sectors.

U.S. and Foreign Commercial Service The U.S. and Foreign Commercial Service develops, produces, markets, and manages an effective line of high-quality products and services geared to the marketing information needs of the U.S. exporting and international business community. The Service delivers programs through 100 U.S. export assistance centers located in the United States, and 140 posts located in 78 countries throughout the world. It supports overseas trade promotion events; manages a variety of export promotion services and products; promotes U.S. products and services throughout the world market; conducts conferences and seminars in the United States; and assists State and private-sector organizations on export financing.

Export Assistance Centers—International Trade Administration

Address	Director/Manager	Telephone	Fax
Alabama (Rm. 707, 950 22d St. N., Birmingham, 35203)	George Norton	205–731–1331	205–731–0076
Alaska (Suite 700, 3601 C St., Anchorage, 99503)	Chuck Becker	907–271–6237	907–271–6242
Arizona (Suite 970, 2901 N. Central Ave., Phoenix, 85012)	Frank Woods	602–640–2513	602–640–2518
(166 W. Alameda, Tucson, 85726)	Eric Nielsen	520–670–5540	520–791–5413
Arkansas (Suite 700, 425 W. Capitol Ave., Little Rock, 72201).	Lon J. Hardin	501–324–5794	501–324–7380
California (390–B Fir Ave., Clovis, 93611)	Eduardo Torres	209–325–1619	209–325–1647
(Suite 1670, 1 World Trade Ctr., Long Beach, 90831)	Mary Boscia	562–980–4550	562–980–4561
(Suite 172, 350 S. Figueroa St., Los Angeles, 90071)	Richard Swanson	213–894–8784	213–894–8789
(Suite 200, 411 Pacific St., Monterey, 93940)	Mark Weaver	408–641–9850	408–641–9849
(Suite 305, 3300 Irvine Ave., Newport Beach, 92660)	Paul Tambakis	714–660–1688	714–660–8039
(Suite 102, 330 Ignacio Blvd., Novato, 94949)	Elizabeth Krauth	415–883–1966	415–883–2711
(Suite 740, 530 Water St., Oakland, 94607)	Raj Shea	510–273–7350	510–251–7352
(Suite 121, 2940 Inland Empire Blvd., Ontario, 91764)	Fred Latuperissa	909–466–4134	909–466–4140
(Suite 2090, 300 Esplanade Dr., Oxnard, 93030)	Gerald Vaughn	805–981–8150	805–981–1855
(2d Fl., 917 7th St., Sacramento, 95814)	Dale Wright	916–498–5155	916–498–5923

Export Assistance Centers—International Trade Administration—Continued

Address	Director/Manager	Telephone	Fax
(Suite 230, 6363 Greenwich Dr., San Diego, 92122)	Matt Andersen	619–557–5395	619–557–6176
(14th Fl., 250 Montgomery St., San Francisco, 94104)	Stephan Crawford	415–705–2300	415–705–2297
(Suite 1001, 101 Park Center Plz., San Jose, 95113)	(Vacancy)	408–271–7300	408–271–7307
(Rm. 456, 5201 Great America Pkwy., Santa Clara, 95054).	R.J. Donovan	408–970–4610	408–970–4618
(Suite 310, 5700 Ralston St., Ventura, 93003)	Gerald Vaughn	805–676–1573	805–676–1892
(Suite 975, 11150 Olympic Blvd., West Los Angeles, 90064).	Julie Anne Hennesey	310–235–7104	310–235–7220
Colorado (Suite 680, 1625 Broadway, Denver, 80202)	Nancy Charles-Parker	303–844–6622	303–844–5651
Connecticut (Suite 903, 213 Court St., Middletown, 06457–3346).	Carl Jacobsen	860–638–6950	860–638–6970
Florida (1130 Cleveland St., Clearwater, 34615)	George Martinez	727–441–1742	727–449–2889
(Suite 1600, 200 E. Las Olas Blvd., Ft. Lauderdale 33301	John McCartney	954–356–6640	954–356–6644
(Suite 617, 5600 NW. 36th St., Miami, 33166)	John McCartney	305–526–7425	305–526–7434
(Suite 1270, 200 E. Robinson St., Orlando, 32801)	Philip A. Ouzts	407–648–6235	407–648–6756
(Suite 2001, The Capitol, Tallahassee, 32399–0001)	Michael Higgins	850–488–6469	850–487–3014
Georgia (Suite 200, 285 Peachtree Ctr. Ave. NE., Atlanta, 30303–1229).	Samuel P. Troy	404–657–1900	404–657–1970
(Suite 100, 6001 Chatham Ctr. Dr., Savannah, 31405)	Barbara Myrick	912–652–4204	912–652–4241
Hawaii (Suite 1140, 1001 Bishop St., Honolulu, 96813)	Greg Wong	808–522–8040	808–522–8045
Idaho (2d Fl., 700 W. State St., Boise, 83720)	James Hellwig	208–334–3857	208–334–2783
Illinois (Suite 2440, 55 W. Monroe St., Chicago, 60603)	Mary N. Joyce	312–353–8045	312–353–8120
(Suite 150, 610 Central Ave., Highland Park, 60035)	Robin F. Mugford	847–681–8010	847–681–8012
(Rm. 141, 922 N. Glenwood Ave., Peoria, 61606)	John Hall	815–997–8123	815–963–7943
(515 N. Court St., Rockford, 61110)	James Mied	815–987–8123	815–963–7943
Indiana (Suite 106, 11405 N. Pennsylvania St., Carmel, 46032).	Dan Swart	317–582–2300	317–582–2301
Iowa (Suite 100, 601 Locust St., Des Moines, 50309–3739)	Allen Patch	515–288–8614	515–288–1437
Kansas (151 N. Volutsia, Wichita, 67214)	George D. Lavid	316–269–6160	316–683–7326
Kentucky (Rm. 634B, 601 W. Broadway, Louisville, 40202)	John Autin	502–582–5066	502–582–6573
(Suite 320, 2292 S. Hwy. 27, Somerset, 42501)	Sara Melton	606–677–6160	606–677–6161
Louisiana (Suite 2150, 365 Canal St., New Orleans, 70130)	(Vacancy)	504–589–6546	504–589–2337
(7100 W. Park Dr., Shreveport, 71129)	Patricia Holt	318–676–3064	318–676–3063
Maine (511 Congress St., Portland, 04101)	Jeffrey Porter	207–541–7400	207–541–7420
Maryland (Suite 2432, 401 E. Pratt St., Baltimore, 21202)	Tom Cox	410–962–4539	410–962–4529
Massachusetts (Suite 307, 164 Northern Ave., Boston, 02210).	Frank J. O'Connor	617–424–5990	617–424–5992
Michigan (Suite 103, 425 S. Main St., Ann Arbor, 48104)	Paul E. Litton	313–741–2430	313–741–2432
(Suite 2220, 211 W. Fort St., Detroit, 48226)	Neil Hesse	313–226–3650	313–226–3657
(Suite 718–S, 301 W. Fulton St., Grand Rapids, 49504)	Thomas Maguire	616–458–3564	616–458–3872
(250 Elizabeth Lake Rd., Pontiac, 48341)	Richard Corson	248–975–9600	248–975–9606
Minnesota (Suite 2240, 45 S. 7th St., Minneapolis, 55402)	Ronald E. Kramer	612–348–1638	612–348–1650
Mississippi (704 E. Main St., Raymond, 39154)	Harrison Ford	601–857–0128	601–857–0026
Missouri (Suite 650, 2345 Grand, Kansas City, 64108)	Thomas A. Strauss	816–410–9201	816–410–9208
(Suite 303, 8182 Maryland Ave., St. Louis, 63105)	Randall J. LaBounty	314–425–3302	314–425–3381
Montana (Suite 257, Gallagher Business Bldg., MT World Trade Ctr., Missoula, 59812).	Mark Peters	406–243–2098	406–243–5259
Nebraska (11135 O St., Omaha, 68137)	Meredith Bond	402–221–3664	402–221–3668
Nevada (Suite 152, 1755 E. Plumb Lane, Reno, 89502)	Jere Dabbs	702–784–5203	702–784–5343
New Hampshire (17 New Hampshire Ave., Portsmouth, 03801–2838).	Susan Berry	603–334–6074	603–334–6110
New Jersey (9th Fl., 1 Gateway Ctr., Newark, 07102)	William Spitler	201–645–4682	201–645–4783
(Suite 100, 3131 Princeton Pk., Trenton, 08648)	Rod Stuart	609–989–2100	609–989–2395
New Mexico (1100 St. Francis Dr., Santa Fe, 87503)	Sandra Necessary	505–827–0350	505–827–0263
New York (Rm. 1304, 111 W. Huron St., Buffalo, 14202)	James Mariano	716–551–4191	716–551–5290
(Rm. 207, 1550 Franklin Ave., Mineola, 11501)	George Soteros	516–739–1765	516–739–3310
(Suite 904, 163 W. 125th St., New York, 10027)	K.L. Fredericks	212–860–6200	212–860–6203
(Rm. 635, 6 World Trade Ctr., New York, 10048)	John Lavelle, *Acting*	212–466–5222	212–264–1356
(Suite 209, 707 Westchester Ave., White Plains, 10604)	Joan Kanlian	914–682–6712	914–682–6698
North Carolina (Suite 435, 521 E. Morehead St., Charlotte, 28202).	Roger Fortner	704–333–4886	704–332–2681
(Suite 400, 400 W. Market St., Greensboro, 27401)	(Vacancy)	910–333–5345	910–333–5158
(Suite 1150, 333 Fayetteville Street Mall, Raleigh, 27601)	(Vacancy)	919–715–7373	919–715–7777
Ohio (Suite 2650, 36 E. 7th St., Cincinnati, 45202)	Cheryl Waldon, *Acting*	513–684–2944	513–684–3227
(Suite 700, 600 Superior Ave. E., Cleveland, 44114)	Michael Miller	216–522–4750	216–522–2235
(Suite 1400, 2 Nationwide Plz., Columbus, 43215)	Mary Beth Double	614–365–9510	614–365–9598
(300 Madison Ave., Toledo, 43604)	Robert Abrahams	419–241–0683	419–241–0684
Oklahoma (Suite 330, 301 NW. 63d St., Oklahoma City, 73116).	Ronald L. Wilson	405–231–5302	405–231–4211
(Suite 1400, 700 N. Greenwood Ave., Tulsa, 74106)	(Vacancy)	918–581–7650	918–594–8413
Oregon (Suite 13, 1445 Willamette St., Eugene, 97401–4003).	(Vacancy)	541–465–6575	541–465–6704
(Suite 242, 121 SW. Salmon St., Portland, 97204)	Scott Goddin	503–326–3001	503–326–6351
Pennsylvania (Rm. 850, 228 Walnut St., Harrisburg, 17108–1698).	Deborah Doherty	717–221–4510	717–221–4505

Export Assistance Centers—International Trade Administration—Continued

Address	Director/Manager	Telephone	Fax
(Suite B, 1 Montage Mt. Rd., Moosic, 18507)	(Vacancy)	717–969–2530	717–969–2539
(Suite 1501, 615 Chestnut St., Philadelphia, 19106)	Edward Burton	215–597–6101	215–597–6123
(2002 Federal Bldg, 1000 Liberty Ave., Pittsburgh, 15222)	Ted Amn	412–395–5050	412–395–4875
Puerto Rico (Rm. G–55, Chardon Ave., Hato Rey, 00918)	(Vacancy)	787–766–5555	787–766–5692
Rhode Island (1 W. Exchange St., Providence, 02903)	Keith Yatsuhashi	401–528–5104	401–528–5067
South Carolina (81 Mary St., Charleston, 29403)	(Vacancy)	803–727–4051	803–727–4052
(Suite 172, 1835 Assembly St., Columbia, 29201)	Ann Watts	803–765–5345	803–253–3614
(Suite 109, 555 N. Pleasantburg Dr., Greenville, 29607)	Denis Csizmadia	864–271–1976	864–271–4171
South Dakota (Rm. SS–29A, 2001 S. Summit Ave., Sioux Falls, 57197).	Cinnamon King	605–330–4264	605–330–4266
Tennessee (Suite 301, 600 W. Summit Hill, Knoxville, 37902–2011).	George Frank	423–545–4637	423–545–4435
(Suite 348, 650 E. Pkwy. S., Memphis, 38104)	Ree Russell	901–323–1543	901–320–9128
(Suite 114, 404 James Robertson Pkwy., Nashville, 37219).	Michael Speck	615–736–5161	615–736–2454
Texas (2d Fl., 1700 Congress, Austin, 78701)	Karen Parker	512–916–5939	512–916–5940
(Suite 170, 2050 N. Stemmons Fwy., Dallas, 75207)	Loree Silloway	214–767–0542	214–767–8240
(711 Houston St., Fort Worth, 76102)	Vavie Sellschopp	817–212–2673	817–978–0178
(Suite 1160, 500 Dallas, Houston, 77002)	James D. Cook	713–718–3062	713–718–3060
(3d Fl., 203 S. 3d St., San Antonio, 78205)	Daniel G. Rodriquez	210–228–9878	210–228–9874
Utah (Suite 221, 324 S. State St., Salt Lake City, 84111)	Stanley Rees	801–524–5116	801–524–5886
Vermont (Drawer 20, National Life Bldg., Montpelier, 05620–0501).	Susan Murray	802–828–4508	802–828–3258
Virginia (Suite 1300, 1616 N. Fort Myer Dr., Arlington, 22209).	Sylvia Burns	703–524–2885	703–524–2649
(Rm. 540, 400 N. 8th St., Richmond, 23240–0026)	Helen D. Lee-Hwang	804–771–2246	804–771–2390
Washington (Suite 650, 2001 6th Ave., Seattle, 98121)	David Spann	206–553–5615	206–553–7253
(Suite 400, 801 W. Riverside Ave., Spokane, 99201)	(Vacancy)	509–353–2625	509–353–2449
(Suite 410, 950 Pacific Ave., Tacoma, 98401)	William Marshak	253–593–6736	253–383–4676
West Virginia (Suite 807, 405 Capitol St., Charleston, 25301)	Harvey Timberlake	304–347–5123	304–347–5408
(316 Washington Ave., Wheeling, 26003)	David Koller	304–243–5493	304–243–5494
Wisconsin (Rm. 596, 517 E. Wisconsin Ave., Milwaukee, 53202).	Paul D. Churchill	414–297–3473	414–297–3470
Wyoming (Suite 680, 1625 Broadway, Denver, CO 80202)	Nancy Charles-Parker	303–844–6622	303–844–5651

Regional Offices—International Trade Administration

Region (Address)	Director/Manager	Telephone	Fax
Eastern Region, (Suite 2450, 401 E. Pratt St., Baltimore, MD 21202).	Thomas McGinty	410–962–2805	410–962–2799
Mid-Eastern Region, (Suite 2025, 36 E. 7th St., Cincinnati, OH 45202).	James Kennedy	513–684–2947	513–684–3200
Mid-Western Region, (Suite 1011, 8182 Maryland Ave., St. Louis, MO 63105).	Sandra Gerley	314–425–3300	314–425–3375
Western Region, (14th Fl., 250 Montgomery St., San Francisco, CA 94104).	Mary Delmage, *Acting*	415–705–2310	415–705–2299

For further information, contact the International Trade Administration, Department of Commerce, Washington, DC 20230. Phone, 202–482–3809.

Minority Business Development Agency

[For the Minority Business Development Agency statement of organization, see the *Federal Register* of Mar. 17, 1972, 37 FR 5650, as amended]

The Minority Business Development Agency, formerly the Office of Minority Business Enterprise, was established by the Secretary of Commerce on November 1, 1979, and operates under the authority of Executive Order 11625 of October 13, 1971. The Agency develops and coordinates a national program for minority business enterprise.

The Agency was created to assist minority businesses in achieving effective and equitable participation in the American free enterprise system and in overcoming social and economic disadvantages that have limited their participation in the past. The Agency provides national policies and leadership in forming and strengthening a partnership of business, industry, and government with the Nation's minority businesses.

Business development services are provided to the minority business community through three vehicles: the minority business opportunity committees which disseminate information on business opportunities; the minority business development centers that provide management and technical assistance and other business development services; and electronic commerce which includes a webpage on the Internet that will show how to start a business and use the service to electronically match business with contract opportunities.

The Agency promotes and coordinates the efforts of other Federal agencies in assisting or providing market opportunities for minority business. It coordinates opportunities for minority firms in the private sector. Through such public and private cooperative activities, the Agency promotes the participation of Federal, State, and local governments, and business and industry in directing resources for the development of strong minority businesses.

Regional Offices—Minority Business Development Agency

Region	Address	Director	Telephone
Atlanta, GA	Suite 1715, 401 W. Peachtree St. NW., 30308–3516	Robert Henderson	404–730–3300
Chicago, IL	Suite 1406, 55 E. Monroe St., 60603	David Vega	312–353–0182
Dallas, TX	Suite 7B23, 1100 Commerce St., 75242	John Iglehart	214–767–8001
New York, NY	Suite 3720, 26 Federal Plz., 10278	Heyward Davenport	212–264–3262
San Francisco, CA	Rm. 1280, 221 Main St., 94105	Melda Cabrera	415–744–3001

District Offices—Minority Business Development Agency

District	Address	Officer	Telephone
Boston, MA	Rm. 418, 10 Causeway St., 02222–1041	Rochelle K. Schwartz	617–565–6850
El Monte, CA	Suite 455, 9660 Flair Dr., 91713	Rodolfo Guerra	818–453–8636
Miami, FL	Rm. 1314, 51 SW. 1st Ave., 33130	Rodolfo Suarez	305–536–5054
Philadelphia, PA	Rm. 10128, 600 Arch St., 19106	Alfonso C. Jackson	215–597–9236

For further information, contact the Office of the Director, Minority Business Development Agency, Department of Commerce, Washington, DC 20230. Phone, 202–482–5061. Internet, www.mbda.gov.

National Oceanic and Atmospheric Administration

Department of Commerce, Washington, DC 20230
Phone, 202–482–2985. Internet, www.noaa.gov.

[For the National Oceanic and Atmospheric Administration statement of organization, see the *Federal Register* of Feb. 13, 1978, 43 FR 6128]

The National Oceanic and Atmospheric Administration (NOAA) was formed on October 3, 1970, by Reorganization Plan No. 4 of 1970 (5 U.S.C. app.).

NOAA's mission entails environmental assessment, prediction, and stewardship. It is dedicated to monitoring and assessing the state of the environment in order to make accurate and timely forecasts to protect life, property, and natural resources, as well as to promote the economic well-being of the United States and to enhance its environmental security. NOAA is committed to protecting America's ocean, coastal, and living marine resources while promoting sustainable economic development.

National Weather Service

The National Weather Service (NWS) provides daily forecasts and warnings for severe weather events such as hurricanes, tornadoes, winter storms, flooding, and tsunamis. With its modernization program, NWS will be able to maximize its use of advanced computer technology to capture, integrate, and analyze Doppler radar imagery and data from satellites and automated surface instruments, and to speed up the dissemination of its forecasts and warnings. This will allow NWS to provide the public with more localized, timely, and accurate forecasts, increasing the lead time it has to prepare for severe weather events. NWS also provides services in support of aviation and marine activities, agriculture, forestry, and urban air quality control.

For further information, contact the National Weather Service, 1325 East-West Highway, Silver Spring, MD 20910–3283. Phone, 301–713–0689. Fax, 301–713–0610. Internet, www.nws.noaa.gov.

National Environmental Satellite, Data, and Information Service

The National Environmental Satellite, Data, and Information Service (NESDIS) operates the Nation's civilian geostationary and polar-orbiting environmental satellites. It also manages the largest collection of atmospheric, geophysical, and oceanographic data in the world. From these sources, NESDIS develops and provides, through various media, environmental data for forecasts, national security, and weather warnings to protect life and property. This data is also used to assist in energy distribution, the development of global food supplies, the management of natural resources, and in the recovery of downed pilots and mariners in distress.

For further information, contact the National Environmental Satellite, Data, and Information Service, Room 2069, 4401 Suitland Road, Suitland, MD 20233. Phone, 301–457–5115. Fax, 301–457–5276. Internet, www.noaa.gov/nesdis/nesdis.html.

National Marine Fisheries Service

The National Marine Fisheries Service (NMFS) supports the management, conservation, and sustainable development of domestic and international living marine resources. NMFS is involved in the stock assessment of the Nation's multi-billion dollar marine fisheries, protecting marine mammals and threatened species, habitat conservation operations, trade and industry assistance, and fishery enforcement activities.

For further information, contact the National Marine Fisheries Service, 1315 East-West Highway, Silver Spring, MD 20910. Phone, 301–713–2239. Fax, 301–713–2258. Internet, kingfish.ssp.nmfs.gov.

National Ocean Service

The National Ocean Service (NOS), works to balance the Nation's use of coastal resources through research, management, and policy. NOS monitors the health of U.S. coasts by examining how human use and natural events impact coastal ecosystems. Coastal communities rely on NOS for information about natural hazards so they can more effectively reduce or eliminate the destructive effects of coastal hazards. NOS assesses the damage caused by hazardous material spills and works to restore or replace the affected coastal resources. Through varied programs, NOS protects wetlands, water quality, beaches, and wildlife. In addition, NOS provides a wide range of navigational products and data that help vessels move safely through U.S. waters and provides the basic set of information that establishes the latitude, longitude, and elevation framework necessary for the Nation's surveying, navigation, positioning, and mapping activities.

For further information, contact the National Ocean Service, Room 13231, SSMC 4, 1305 East-West Highway, Silver Spring, MD 20910. Phone, 301–713–3070. Fax, 301–713–4307. Internet, www.nos.noaa.gov.

Office of Oceanic and Atmospheric Research

The Office of Oceanic and Atmospheric Research (OAR) carries out research into such phenomena as El Niño, global warming, ozone depletion, solar storms that can disrupt telecommunications and electrical power systems, and coastal and Great Lakes ecosystems. OAR conducts and directs its research programs in coastal, marine, atmospheric, and space sciences through its own laboratories and offices, as well as through networks of university-based programs across the country.

For further information, contact the Office of Oceanic and Atmospheric Research, Room 11627, 1315 East-West Highway, Silver Spring, MD 20910. Phone, 301–713–2458. Fax, 301–713–0163. Internet, www.oar.noaa.gov.

Office of NOAA Corps Operations

NOAA also maintains a fleet of ships and aircraft under the auspices of its Office of NOAA Corps Operations. These are used for scientific, engineering, and technical services, as well as to serve as research platforms for gathering critical marine and atmospheric data in support of a number of NOAA's research programs. This includes flying "hurricane hunter" aircraft into nature's most turbulent storms to collect data critical to hurricane research.

For further information, contact the Office of NOAA Corps Operations, Room 12857, 1315 East-West Highway, Silver Spring, MD 20910–3282. Phone, 301–713–1045.

Field Organization—National Oceanic and Atmospheric Administration

Organization	Address/Telephone	Director
National Weather Service		
Headquarters	1325 East-West Hwy., Silver Spring, MD 20910–3283. Phone, 301–713–0689. Fax, 301–713–0610.	John J. Kelly, Jr.
Office of Meteorology	1325 East-West Hwy., Silver Spring, MD 20910–3283. Phone, 301–713–0700. Fax, 301–713–1598.	Gregory A. Mandt, *Acting*
Office of Hydrology	1325 East-West Hwy., Silver Spring, MD 20910–3283. Phone, 301–713–1658. Fax, 301–713–0963.	Danny L. Fread
National Centers for Environmental Prediction.	5200 Auth Rd., Camp Springs, MD 20746–4304. Phone, 301–763–8016. Fax, 301–763–8434.	Louis W. Uccellini
Office of Systems Development	1325 East-West Hwy., Silver Spring, MD 20910–3283. Phone, 301–713–0745. Fax, 301–713–0003.	Harry Glahn
Office of Systems Operations	1325 East-West Hwy., Silver Spring, MD 20910–3283. Phone, 301–713–0165. Fax, 301–713–0657.	Walter Telesetsky
National Data Buoy Center	Rm. 344, Bldg. 1100, Stennis Space Center, MS 39529–6000. Phone, 601–688–2800. Fax, 601–688–3153.	Jerry C. McCall
Eastern region	630 Johnson Ave., Bohemia, NY 11716–2626. Phone, 516–244–0100. Fax, 516–244–0109.	John T. Forsing
Southern region	Rm. 10A26, 819 Taylor St., Fort Worth, TX 76102–6171. Phone, 817–978–2651. Fax, 817–334–4187.	X. William Proenza
Central region	Rm. 1836, 601 E. 12th St., Kansas City, MO 64106–2897. Phone, 816–426–5400. Fax, 816–426–3270.	Richard P. Augulis
Training center	Rm. 116, 617 Hardesty St., Kansas City, MO 64124–3097. Phone, 816–374–6238. Fax, 816–374–6726.	John L. Vogel
Western region	Rm. 1210, 125 S. State St., Salt Lake City, UT 84138–1102. Phone, 801–524–6295. Fax, 801–524–5270.	Vicki L. Nadolski
Alaska region	Rm. 517, 222 W. 7th Ave., Anchorage, AK 99513–7575. Phone, 907–271–5136. Fax, 907–271–3711.	Richard J. Hutcheon
Pacific region	Suite 2200, 737 Bishop St., Honolulu, HI 96813. Phone, 808–532–6416. Fax, 808–532–5569.	Richard H. Hagemeyer
Office of the Federal Coordinator for Meteorological Services and Supporting Research.	1500 Ctr., 8455 Colesville Rd., Silver Spring, MD 20910–3315. Phone, 301–427–2002.	Samuel Williamson
National Marine Fisheries Service		
Headquarters	1315 East-West Hwy., Silver Spring, MD 20910. Phone, 301–713–2239. Fax, 301–713–2258.	Rolland A. Schmitten
Alaska region	P.O. Box 21668, Juneau, AK 99802–1668. Phone, 907–586–7221. Fax, 907–586–7249.	Steven Pennoyer
Alaska Fisheries Science Center	Bin C15700, Bldg. 4, 7600 Sand Point Way NE., Seattle, WA 98115. Phone, 206–526–4000. Fax, 206–526–4004.	James W. Balsiger
Northwest region	Bin C15700, Bldg. 1, 7600 Sand Point Way NE., Seattle, WA 98115–0070. Phone, 206–526–6150. Fax, 206–526–6426.	William W. Stelle, Jr.

Field Organization—National Oceanic and Atmospheric Administration—Continued

Organization	Address/Telephone	Director
Northwest Fisheries Science Center	2725 Montlake Blvd. E., Seattle, WA 98112. Phone, 206–860–3200. Fax, 206–860–3217.	Usha Varanasi
Northeast region	1 Blackburn Dr., Gloucester, MA 01930. Phone, 978–281–9250. Fax, 978–281–9371.	Jon Rittgers, *Acting*
Northeast Fisheries Science Center	166 Water St., Woods Hole, MA 02543. Phone, 508–548–5123. Fax, 508–495–2232.	Michael Sissenwine
Southeast region	9721 Executive Ctr. Dr. N., St. Petersburg, FL 33702. Phone, 813–570–5301. Fax, 813–570–5300.	Andrew J. Kammerer
Southeast Fisheries Science Center	75 Virginia Beach Dr., Miami, FL 33149. Phone, 305–361–5761. Fax, 305–361–4219.	Brad Brown
Southwest region	Suite 4200, 501 W. Ocean Blvd., Long Beach, CA 90802. Phone, 562–980–4001. Fax, 562–980–4018.	William T. Hogarth
Southwest Fisheries Science Center	P.O. Box 271, 8604 La Jolla Shores Dr., La Jolla, CA 92038. Phone, 619–546–7067. Fax, 619–546–5655.	Michael Tillman
National Environmental Satellite, Data, and Information Service		
Headquarters	Rm. 2069, 5200 Auth Rd., Suitland, MD 20746. Phone, 301–457–5115. Fax, 301–457–5276.	Robert S. Winokur
Satellite operations	Rm. 0135, 5200 Auth Rd., Suitland, MD 20746. Phone, 301–457–5130. Fax, 301–457–5175.	Gary K. Davis
Satellite data processing and distribution.	Rm. 1069, 5200 Auth Rd., Suitland, MD 20746. Phone, 301–457–5120. Fax, 301–457–5184.	Helen M. Wood
Research and applications	NOAA Science Center, 5200 Auth Rd., Camp Springs, MD 20233. Phone, 301–763–8127. Fax, 301–763–8108.	James Purdom
Systems development	Rm. 3301C, 5200 Auth Rd., Suitland, MD 20746. Phone, 301–457–5277. Fax, 301–457–5722.	Gary K. Davis, *Acting*
National Climatic Data Center	151 Patton Ave., Asheville, NC 28801–5001. Phone, 704–271–4476. Fax, 704–271–4246.	Tom Karl
National Geophysical Data Center	RL–3, 325 Broadway, Boulder, CO 80303–3328. Phone, 303–497–6215. Fax, 303–497–6513.	Michael S. Loughridge
National Oceanographic Data Center	1315 East-West Hwy., Silver Spring, MD 20910. Phone, 301–713–3303. Fax, 301–713–3300.	Henry Frey
National Ocean Service		
Headquarters	Rm. 13632, 1305 East-West Hwy., Silver Spring, MD 20910. Phone, 301–713–3074. Fax, 301–713–4269.	Nancy Foster
International Programs	Rm. 13442, 1305 East-West Hwy., Silver Spring, MD 20910. Phone, 301–713–3078. Fax, 301–713–4263.	Charles N. Ehler
NOAA Coastal Services Center	2234 S. Hobson Ave., Charleston, SC 29405–2409. Phone, 843–740–1200. Fax 843–740–1224.	Margaret Davidson
Center for Operational Oceanographic Products and Services.	Rm. 6633, 1305 East-West Hwy., Silver Spring, MD 20910. Phone, 301–713–2981. Fax, 301–713–4392.	Richard Barazato
National Centers for Coastal Ocean Science.	Rm. 13508, 1305 East-West Hwy., Silver Spring, MD 20910. Phone, 301–713–3060. Fax, 301–713–4270.	Don Scavia
Coast survey	Rm. 6147, 1315 East-West Hwy., Silver Spring, MD 20910. Phone, 301–713–2770. Fax, 301–713–4019.	David B. McFarland
Aeronautical charting	Rm. 3426, 1305 East-West Hwy., Silver Spring, MD 20910. Phone, 301–713–2619. Fax, 301–713–4587.	Terry M. Laydom
National Geodetic Survey	Rm. 8657, 1315 East-West Hwy., Silver Spring, MD 20910. Phone, 301–713–3222. Fax, 301–713–4175.	Charles W. Challstrom
Office of Response and Restoration	Rm. 6633, 1305 East-West Hwy., Silver Spring, MD 20910. Phone, 301–713–2989. Fax, 301–713–4387.	David M. Kennedy
Ocean and coastal resource management.	Rm. 11523, 1305 East-West Hwy., Silver Spring, MD 20910. Phone, 301–713–3155. Fax, 301–713–4012.	Jeffrey R. Benoit
Office of Oceanic and Atmospheric Research		
Headquarters	Rm. 11627, 1315 East-West Hwy., Silver Spring, MD 20910. Phone, 301–713–2458. Fax, 301–713–0163.	David L. Evans
Environmental Research Laboratories	Rm. 11618, 1315 East-West Hwy., Silver Spring, MD 20910. Phone, 301–713–2458. Fax, 301–713–0163.	(Vacancy)

Field Organization—National Oceanic and Atmospheric Administration—Continued

Organization	Address/Telephone	Director
Aeronomy Laboratory	Rm. 2204, Bldg. 24, 325 Broadway, Boulder, CO 80303. Phone, 303–497–3134. Fax, 303–497–5340.	Daniel L. Albritton
Air Resources Laboratory	Rm. 3151, 1315 East-West Hwy., Silver Spring, MD 20910. Phone, 301–713–0684, ext. 100. Fax, 301–713–0295.	Bruce Hicks
Atlantic Oceanographic and Meteorological Laboratory.	4301 Rickenbacker Causeway, Miami, FL 33149. Phone, 305–361–4300. Fax, 305–361–4449.	Kristina Katsaros
Climate Diagnostics Center	Rm. 247, RL3, 325 Broadway, Boulder, CO 80303. Phone, 303–497–6878. Fax, 303–497–7013.	Randall Dole
Climate Monitoring and Diagnostics Laboratory.	Rm. A336, RL3, 325 Broadway, Boulder, CO 80303. Phone, 303–497–6074. Fax, 303–497–6975.	David Hofmann
Environmental Technology Laboratory	Rm. A450, RL3, 325 Broadway, Boulder, CO 80303. Phone, 303–497–6291. Fax, 303–497–6020.	Steven Clifford
Forecast Systems Laboratory	Rm. 615, RL3, 325 Broadway, Boulder, CO 80303. Phone, 303–497–6818. Fax, 303–497–6821.	Sandy MacDonald
Geophysical Fluid Dynamics Laboratory.	P.O. Box 308, Princeton University Forrestral Campus, Princeton, NJ 08452. Phone, 609–452–6503. Fax, 609–987–5070.	Jerry Mahlman
Great Lakes Environmental Research Laboratory.	2205 Commonwealth Blvd., Ann Arbor, MI 48105. Phone, 734–741–2244. Fax, 734–741–2003.	Stephen Brandt
National Severe Storms Laboratory	1313 Halley Circle, Norman, OK 73069. Phone, 405–366–0426. Fax, 405–366–0472.	James Kimpel
Pacific Marine Environmental Laboratory.	Bin C 15700, Bldg. 3, 7600 Sand Point Way NE., Seattle, WA 98115. Phone, 206–526–6800. Fax, 206–526–6815.	Eddie N. Bernard
Space Environment Center	Rm. 3050, Bldg. 1, 325 Broadway, Boulder, CO 80303. Phone, 303–497–3314. Fax, 303–497–3645.	Ernest G. Hildner
National Undersea Research Program	Rm. 11350, 1315 East-West Hwy., Silver Spring, MD 20910. Phone, 301–713–2427. Fax, 301–713–1967.	Barbara S.P. Moore
National Sea Grant College Program	Rm. 11716, 1315 East-West Hwy., Silver Spring, MD 20910. Phone, 301–713–2448. Fax, 301–713–0799.	Ronald Baird
Office of Research and Technology Applications.	Rm. 11464, 1315 East-West Hwy., Silver Spring, MD 20910. Phone, 301–713–3565. Fax, 301–713–4100.	Joe Bishop
Office of Finance and Administration		
Headquarters	Rm. 6811, 14th St. and Constitution Ave. NW., Washington, DC 20230. Phone, 202–482–2291.	Sonya G. Stewart
Chief Financial Officer/Chief Administrative Officer.	Rm. 6811, 14th St. and Constitution Ave. NW., Washington, DC 20230. Phone, 202–482–2291. Fax, 202–482–4823.	Sonya G. Stewart
Office of Civil Rights	Rm. 13356, 1315 East-West Hwy., Silver Spring, MD 20910. Phone, 301–713–0500.	Al Corea
Diversity Program Office	Rm. 12122, 1305 East-West Hwy., Silver Spring, MD 20910. Phone, 301–713–1966.	Barbara Marshall-Bailey
Audit and Internal Control Branch	Rm. 8419, 1305 East-West Hwy., Silver Spring, MD 20910. Phone, 301–713–1150.	Barbara Martin
Management and Budget	Rm. 6863, 14th St. and Constitution Ave. NW., Washington, DC 20230. Phone, 202–482–6226.	Tyra D. Smith
Budget Office	Rm. 6114, 14th St. and Constitution Ave. NW., Washington, DC 20230. Phone, 202–482–4600.	(Vacancy)
Finance Office	Rm. 3110, Century 21 Bldg., Germantown, MD 20874–1143. Phone, 301–413–8795.	R.J. Dominic
Environmental Compliance Staff	Rm. 10148, 1305 East-West Hwy., Silver Spring, MD 20910. Phone, 301–713–0845.	Susan A. Kennedy
Human Resources Management Office	Rm. 12434, 1305 East-West Hwy., Silver Spring, MD 20910. Phone, 301–713–0530.	Gloria Harris, *Acting*
Information Systems Office	Rm. 724, 6100 Executive Blvd., Rockville, MD 20852–3809. Phone, 301–763–6300.	Robert Swisher, *Acting*
Acquisition, Grants, and Facilities Services Office.	Rm. 4131, 1305 East-West Hwy., Silver Spring, MD 20910. Phone, 301–713–0820.	Claire B. Mansberg, *Acting*
Mountain Administrative Support Center.	325 Broadway, Boulder, CO 80303–3228. Phone, 303–497–6431.	Dennis R. Connors

Field Organization—National Oceanic and Atmospheric Administration—Continued

Organization	Address/Telephone	Director
Eastern Administrative Support Center	Suite 201, 200 World Trade Ctr., Norfolk, VA 23510–1624. Phone, 757–441–6864.	Hugh L. Brennan
Western Administrative Support Center.	Bldg. 1, 7600 Sand Point Way NE., Seattle, WA 98115–0070. Phone, 206–526–6026. Fax, 206–526–6660.	Kelly C. Sandy
Central Administrative Support Center	Rm. 1736, 601 E. 12th St., Kansas City, MO 64106–2897. Phone, 816–426–2050. Fax, 816–426–7459.	Martha R. Lumpkin
NOAA Corps Operations		
Headquarters	Rm. 12857, 1315 East-West Hwy., Silver Spring, MD 20910–3282. Phone, 301–713–1045.	Rear Adm. John C. Albright, USN, *Acting*
Atlantic Marine Center	439 W. York St., Norfolk, VA 23510–1114. Phone, 757–441–6776.	Rear Adm. John C. Albright, USN
Commissioned Personnel Center	1315 East-West Hwy., Silver Spring, MD 20910. Phone, 301–713–3475.	Capt. Evelyn Fields, USN
Pacific Marine Center	1801 Fairview Ave. E., Seattle, WA 98102–3767. Phone, 206–553–7656.	Rear Adm. John C. Albright, USN
Aircraft Operations Center	7917 Hangar Loop Dr., MacDill AFB, FL 33621–5401. Phone, 813–828–3310.	Capt. George C. Player III, USN

For further information, contact the Office of Public Affairs, National Oceanic and Atmospheric Administration, Department of Commerce, Washington, DC 20230. Phone, 202–482–4190.

National Telecommunications and Information Administration

[For the National Telecommunications and Information Administration statement of organization, see the *Federal Register* of June 5, 1978, 43 FR 24348]

The National Telecommunications and Information Administration (NTIA) was established in 1978 by Reorganization Plan No. 1 of 1977 (5 U.S.C. app.) and Executive Order 12046 of March 27, 1978 (3 CFR, 1978 Comp., p. 158), by combining the Office of Telecommunications Policy of the Executive Office of the President and the Office of Telecommunications of the Department of Commerce to form a new agency reporting to the Secretary of Commerce.

The Administration's principal responsibilities and functions include:

—serving as the principal executive branch adviser to the President on telecommunications and information policy;

—developing and presenting U.S. plans and policies at international communications conferences and related meetings;

—prescribing policies for and managing Federal use of the radio frequency spectrum;

—serving as the principal Federal telecommunications research and engineering laboratory, through NTIA's Institute for Telecommunication Sciences (ITS), headquartered in Boulder, CO;

—providing grants through the Technology Opportunities Program for planning and demonstration projects to promote the goals of the development and widespread availability of advanced telecommunications technologies, to enhance the delivery of social services and generally serve the public interest, to promote access to government information and increase civic participation, and to support the development of an advanced nationwide telecommunications and information infrastructure;

—providing grants through the Public Telecommunications Facilities Program to extend delivery of public telecommunications services to U.S. citizens, to increase ownership and management by women and minorities, and to strengthen the capabilities of existing public broadcasting stations to provide telecommunications services; and

—monitoring grants awarded through the National Endowment for Children's Educational Television to enhance the creation and production of educational television programming for children to develop fundamental intellectual skills.

For further information, contact the National Telecommunications and Information Administration, Department of Commerce, Washington, DC 20230. Phone, 202–482–1551.

Patent and Trademark Office

[For the Patent and Trademark Office statement of organization, see the *Federal Register* of Apr. 14, 1975, 40 FR 16707]

The patent system was established by Congress ". . . to promote the progress of . . . the useful arts. . ." The registration of trademarks is based on the commerce clause of the U.S. Constitution.

The Office examines applications for patents to determine if the applicants are entitled to patents and grants the patents when they are so entitled. The patent law provides for the granting of patents in three major categories: utility patents, design patents, and plant patents. The term of a design patent is 14 years from the date of grant. It also issues statutory invention registrations, which have the defensive but not the enforceable attributes of a patent. It also processes international applications for patents.

PTO registers and renews trademarks. A trademark includes any distinctive word, name, symbol, device, or any combination thereof adopted and used or intended to be used by a manufacturer or merchant to identify his goods or services and distinguish them from those manufactured or sold by others. Trademarks are examined by the Office for compliance with various statutory requirements to prevent unfair competition and consumer deception.

In addition to the examination of patent and trademark applications, issuance of patents, and registration of trademarks, the Patent and Trademark Office:

—sells printed copies of issued patents and trademark registrations;

—records and indexes documents transferring ownership;

—maintains a scientific library and search files containing over 30 million documents, including U.S. and foreign patents and U.S. trademarks;

—provides research facilities for the public;

—hears and decides appeals from prospective inventors and trademark applicants;

—participates in legal proceedings involving the issue of patents or registration of trademarks;

—advocates strengthening intellectual property protection worldwide;

—compiles the *Official Gazettes*, a weekly notice of patents issued and trademarks registered by the Office, including other information; and

—maintains a roster of patent agents and attorneys qualified and recognized to practice before the Office.

Patents and trademarks may be reviewed and searched at PTO in over 80 patent and trademark depository libraries throughout the country and online. The patent system fosters innovation, investment in developing and marketing inventions, and prompt disclosure of technological information.

For further information, contact the Office of Public Affairs, Patent and Trademark Office, Washington, DC 20231. Phone, 703–305–8341. Internet, www.uspto.gov. The Office's operations are located at 2121 Crystal Drive, Arlington, VA 22202.

Technology Administration

The Technology Administration was established by Congress in 1988 (15 U.S.C. 3704). It is headed by the Under Secretary for Technology, who serves as a principal adviser to the Secretary of Commerce and as the Department's spokesperson for science and technology issues.

The Technology Administration serves as the premier technology agency working with U.S. industry in addressing competitiveness and in exercising leadership both within the Department of Commerce and governmentwide. It advocates coherent policies for maximizing the impact of technology on economic growth; carries out technology programs with U.S. industry; and disseminates technology information.

Office of Technology Policy

The primary role of the Office of Technology Policy is to offer assistance to private sector and communities in advocating and pursuing policies that maximize the impact of technology on economic growth, and by exercising leadership to define the role of government in supporting U.S. industrial competitiveness in the post-cold war environment. The Office serves as a liaison to the private sector, identifying barriers to the rapid commercialization of technology, eliciting support for Administration civilian technology policies, and ensuring that industry's interests are reflected in standards and technology agreements and civilian technology policy. It also assists Federal, State, and local officials, industry, and academic institutions in promoting the technological growth and competitiveness of the U.S. economy.

For further information, call 202–482–5687.

National Institute of Standards and Technology

The National Institute of Standards and Technology (NIST) assists industry in developing technology to improve product quality, modernize manufacturing processes, ensure product reliability, and facilitate rapid commercialization of products based on new scientific discoveries.

The Institute's primary mission is to strengthen the U.S. economy and improve the quality of life by working with industry to develop and apply technology, measurements, and standards. It carries out this mission through four major programs:

—measurement and standards laboratories that perform research in the areas of electronics, electrical engineering, manufacturing engineering, chemical science and technology, physics, materials science and engineering, building and fire research, and information technology;

—a rigorously competitive advanced technology program that provides cost-shared awards to industry to develop high-risk enabling technologies with broad economic potential;

—a manufacturing extension partnership offering technical and business assistance to smaller manufacturers in adopting new technologies and business practices; and

—a highly visible quality outreach program associated with the Malcolm Baldrige National Quality Award that recognizes continuous improvements in quality management by U.S. manufacturers, service companies, education institutions, and health care organizations.

For further information, call 301–975–NIST (301–975–6478). Fax, 301–926–1630. E-mail, inquiries@nist.gov. Internet, www.nist.gov.

National Technical Information Service

The National Technical Information Service (NTIS) is the Nation's largest central clearinghouse and governmentwide resource for scientific, technical, engineering, and other business-related information. It acquires information from U.S. Government agencies and their contractors and grantees, as well as from foreign sources, primarily governments.

The NTIS collection of more than 3 million works covers a broad array of subjects and includes reports on the results of research and development and scientific studies on manufacturing processes, current events, and foreign and domestic trade; business and management studies; social, economic, and trade statistics; computer software and databases; health care reports, manuals, and data; environmental handbooks, regulations, economic studies, and applied technologies; directories to Federal laboratory and technical resources; and global competitive intelligence. The collection also includes audiovisual training materials in such areas as foreign languages, workplace safety and health, law enforcement, and fire services.

Information products in the NTIS collection are cataloged in the *NTIS Bibliographic Database,* which is available online through commercial vendors, on CD–ROM from NTIS, and for recently acquired materials, via FedWorld, NTIS' online information network (Internet, www.ntis.gov).

For further information, contact the National Technical Information Service, 5285 Port Royal Road, Springfield, VA 22161. Phone, 800–553–NTIS. Internet, www.ntis.gov.

For further information about the Technology Administration, contact the Office of Technology Policy, U.S. Department of Commerce, Room 4814C HCHB, Washington, DC 20230. Phone, 202–482–1575. Internet, www.ta.doc.gov.

Sources of Information

Age and Citizenship Age search and citizenship information is available from the Personal Census Search Unit, Bureau of the Census, National Processing Center, P.O. Box 1545, Jeffersonville, IN 47131. Phone, 812–218–3046.

Consumer Affairs Information is available to businesses and consumers regarding good business practices and resolving consumer complaints. Tip sheets, in English and Spanish, on how to resolve complaints and consumer bulletins, describing programs in the Department of Commerce, are available. Many publications are available on the Internet at www.doc.gov. For further information, contact the Office of Consumer Affairs, U.S. Department of Commerce, Room H5718, Washington, DC 20230. Phone, 202–482–5001. Consumer response line, 202–482–8021. Fax, 202–482–6007. Internet, www.doc.gov/oca. E-mail, caffairs@doc.gov.

Economic Development Information Clearinghouse The EDA will host on its website the Economic Development Information Clearinghouse, an online depository of information on economic development (Internet, www.doc.gov/eda).

Employment Information is available electronically through the Internet, at www.doc.gov/ohrm. Phone, 202–482–5138.

The National Oceanic and Atmospheric Administration has field employment offices at the Western Administrative Support Center, Bin C15700, 7600 Sand Point Way NE., Seattle, WA 98115 (phone, 206–526–6294); the Mountain Administrative Support Center, 325 Broadway, Boulder, CO 80303 (phone, 303–497–6332); the Central Administrative Support Center, 601 East Twelfth Street, Kansas City, MO 64106 (phone, 816–426–2056); and the Eastern Administrative Support Center, 200 World Trade Center, Norfolk, VA 23510–1624 (phone, 757–441–6516).

Environment The National Oceanic and Atmospheric Administration conducts research and gathers data about the oceans, atmosphere, space, and Sun, and applies this knowledge to science and service in ways that touch the lives of all Americans, including warning of dangerous weather, charting seas and skies, guiding our use and protection of ocean and coastal resources, and improving our understanding and stewardship of the environment which sustains us all. For further information, contact the Office of Public and Constituent Affairs, National Oceanic and Atmospheric Administration, Room 6013, Fourteenth Street and Constitution Avenue NW., Washington, DC 20230. Phone, 202–482–6090. Fax, 202–482–3154. Internet, www.noaa.gov.

The Patent and Trademark Office has priority programs for advancement of examination of certain patent applications where the invention could materially enhance the quality of the environment of mankind. For further information, contact the Assistant Commissioner for Patents, Office of Petitions, Washington, DC 20231. Phone, 703–305–9282.

Inspector General Hotline The Office of Inspector General works to promote economy, efficiency, and effectiveness and to prevent and detect fraud, waste, abuse, and mismanagement in departmental programs and operations. Contact the Hotline, Inspector General, P.O. Box 612, Ben Franklin Station, Washington, DC 20044. Phone, 202–482–2495, or 800–424–5197 (toll free). TTD, 202–482–5923, or 800–854–8407 (toll free). Fax, 202–789–0522. Internet, www.oig.doc.gov. E-mail, oighotline@doc.gov.

Publications The titles of selected publications are printed below with the operating units responsible for their issuance. These and other publications dealing with a wide range of business, economic, environmental, scientific, and technical matters are announced in the weekly *Business Service Checklist,* which may be purchased from the Superintendent of Documents, Government Printing Office, Washington, DC 20402. Phone, 202–512–1800.

The Secretary's *Annual Report to Congress* and *Serving the Nation,* two publications which describe the missions, functions, and accomplishments of Commerce agencies and offices, are available by writing the Department of Commerce, Office of Public Affairs, Pennsylvania Avenue and Fourteenth Street NW., Room 5610, Washington, DC, or by calling 202–219–3605 for the *Annual Report* and 202–482–4901 for *Serving the Nation.*

Further information on Commerce publications is available at any of the Department's International Trade Administration export assistance centers.

Lists of Other Documents Individuals with access to fax machines can dial 202–501–1191 *(Flash Facts)* to obtain lists of other publication contacts, Secretarial speeches and biographies, press releases, audiovisuals, Commerce bureau public affairs contacts, and Department programs by subject.

Bureau of the Census Numerous publications presenting statistical information on a wide variety of subjects are available from the Government Printing Office, including the following: *Statistical Abstract of the U.S.; Historical Statistics of the United States, Colonial Times to 1970; County and City Data Book, 1994;* and *State and Metropolitan Area Data Book, 1997–1998.*

Employment opportunities, data highlights, large data files, access tools, and other material are available on the World Wide Web. Internet, www.census.gov. E-mail, webmaster@census.gov.

Bureau of Economic Analysis Publications available from the Government Printing Office include the following: *Fixed Reproducible Tangible Wealth in the United States, 1925–94; Foreign Direct Investment in the United States: Preliminary Results from the 1997 Benchmark Survey;* and *State Personal Income, 1929–97.* Current and historical estimates, general information, and employment opportunities are available through the Internet, at www.bea.doc.gov. BEA data products are described in the *Catalog of Products,* which is available on the BEA website (Internet, www.bea.doc.gov) or by request from the BEA Order Desk (phone, 800–704–0415). For more information, contact the Public Information Office. Phone, 202–606–9900. E-mail, webmaster@bea.doc.gov.

186-873 D-00--6

Bureau of Export Administration The Bureau's website (Internet, www.bxa.doc.gov) provides guidance on topics of interest to exporters and companies in defense-related industries. Publications available on the site include the Bureau's annual report, foreign policy report, and international diversification and defense market assessment guides. The Government Printing Office, in conjunction with the Bureau, has created a website that contains an up-to-date database of the entire export administration regulations, including the commerce control list, the commerce country chart, and the denied persons list (Internet, www.access.gpo.gov/bxa/ear/ear_data.html). The Exporter Counseling Division has offices in Washington, DC (phone, 202–482–4811; fax, 202–482–3617) and on the West Coast (phone 949–660–0144, or 408–998–7402; fax, 949–660–9347, or 408–998–7470). For enforcement-related questions, contact the partnership-in-security hotline (phone, 800–424–2980).

International Trade Administration The Administration maintains a website, (Internet, www.ita.doc.gov), which offers the single best place for individuals or firms seeking reports, documents, import case/regulations, texts of international agreements like NAFTA and GATT, market research, and points of contact for assistance in exporting, obtaining remedies from unfair trading practices, or receiving help with market access problems. Customers are able to review comprehensive information on how to export, search for trade information by either industry or by country, learn how to petition against unfairly priced imports, and obtain information on a number of useful international trade related products like overseas trade leads and agent distributor reports. The website also features E-mail addresses and locations for trade contacts in Washington, overseas, in major exporting centers in the U.S., and in other parts of the Federal Government.

Minority Business Development Agency Copies of *Minority Business Today, BDC Directory,* and the *MBDA Annual Business Assistance Report (ABAR)* may be obtained by contacting the Office of Program Support Services. Phone, 202–482–6022. Comprehensive information about programs, policy, centers, and access the job matching database, is available through the Internet, at www.mbda.gov).

National Institute of Standards and Technology *Journal of Research; Publications of the Advanced Technology Program and Manufacturing Extension Partnership Program; Handbook of Mathematical Functions; Experimental Statistics; International System of Units (SI); Standard Reference Materials Catalog; Specifications, Tolerances, and Other Technical Requirements for Weighing and Measuring Devices Handbook;* and *Uniform Laws and Regulations Handbook* are available from the Government Printing Office.

National Technical Information Service To place an order, request the *Catalog of NTIS Products and Services,* or other general inquiries, contact the NTIS Sales Desk from 8 a.m. to 8 p.m. (eastern time) (phone, 800–553–NTIS; fax, 703–321–8547; TDD, 703–605–6043; Internet, www.ntis.gov).

To inquire about NTIS information services for other Federal agencies, call 703–605–6540.

National Oceanic and Atmospheric Administration The Administration provides technical memoranda, technical reports, monographs, nautical and aeronautical charts, coastal zone maps, data tapes, and a wide variety of raw and processed environmental data. Information on NOAA products is available through the Internet, at www.noaa.gov. Contact the Office of Public and Constituent Affairs, Fourteenth Street and Constitution Avenue NW., Washington, DC 20230. Phone, 202–482–6090. Fax, 202–482–3154.

National Telecommunications and Information Administration Several hundred Technical Reports, Technical Memoranda, Special Publications, Contractor Reports, and other information products have been published by NTIA or its predecessor agency since 1970. The publications are available from the National Telecommunications and Information Administration, Department of Commerce, Washington, DC 20230 (phone, 202–482–1551); or the National Telecommunications and Information Administration, Institute for Telecommunication Sciences, Department of Commerce, Boulder, CO 80302 (phone, 303–497–3572). Electronic information can be obtained from the NTIA homepage (Internet, www.ntia.doc.gov).

Patent and Trademark Office *General Information Concerning Patents, Basic Facts About Trademarks, Official Gazette of the United States Patent and Trademark Office,* and *Attorneys and Agents Registered To Practice Before the U.S. Patent and Trademark Office* are available from the Government Printing Office. Publications can be accessed through the Internet, at www.uspto.gov. File transfer protocol, ftp.uspto.gov. Electronic bulletin board (by modem), 703–305–8950. Phone, 703–308–HELP, or 800–PTO–9199.

Small Business and Minority Business Activities Contact the Office of Small and Disadvantaged Business Utilization. Phone, 202–482–1472. E-mail, tjgarcia@doc.gov.

Telephone Directory The Department of Commerce telephone directory is available for sale by the Superintendent of Documents, Government Printing Office, Washington, DC 20402. Phone, 202–512–1800.

For further information concerning the Department of Commerce, contact the Office of Public Affairs, Department of Commerce, Fourteenth Street and Constitution Avenue NW., Washington, DC 20230. Phone, 202–219–3605. Internet, www.doc.gov.

DEPARTMENT OF DEFENSE

Office of the Secretary, The Pentagon, Washington, DC 20301–1155
Phone, 703–545–6700. Internet, www.defenselink.mil.

SECRETARY OF DEFENSE	WILLIAM S. COHEN
Deputy Secretary of Defense	RUDY F. DE LEON
Chief of Staff	ROBERT S. TYRER
The Special Assistant to the Secretary and Deputy Secretary of Defense	PHEBE NOVAKOVIC
Special Assistant to the Secretary of Defense for White House Liaison	LIZ BAILEY
Special Assistant to the Deputy Secretary of Defense for Gulf War Illnesses	BERNARD D. ROSTKER
Director, Defense Reform Initiative	STAN Z. SOLOWAY
Executive Secretary	COL. MARIA I. CRIBBS, USAF
Under Secretary of Defense for Acquisition, Technology, and Logistics	JACQUES S. GANSLER
Principal Deputy Under Secretary of Defense for Acquisition, Technology, and Logistics	DAVID R. OLIVER, JR.
Assistant to the Secretary of Defense for Nuclear and Chemical and Biological (NCB) Defense Programs	(VACANCY)
Deputy Under Secretary of Defense (Acquisition and Technology)	DAVID R. OLIVER, JR.
Deputy Under Secretary of Defense (Acquisition Reform)	STAN Z. SOLOWAY
Deputy Under Secretary of Defense (Advanced Systems and Concepts)	JOSEPH J. EASH III
Deputy Under Secretary of Defense (Environmental Security)	SHERRI W. GOODMAN
Deputy Under Secretary of Defense (Industrial Affairs)	JEFFREY P. BIALOS
Deputy Under Secretary of Defense (Installations)	RANDALL A. YIM
Deputy Under Secretary of Defense (Logistics and Materiel Readiness)	(VACANCY)
Deputy Under Secretary of Defense (Science and Technology)	(VACANCY)
Director, Defense Research and Engineering	HANS MARK
Director, Small and Disadvantaged Business Utilization	ROBERT L. NEAL, JR.
Under Secretary of Defense for Policy	WALTER B. SLOCOMBE
Principal Deputy Under Secretary of Defense for Policy	JAMES M. BODNER
Assistant Secretary of Defense (International Security Affairs)	FRANKLIN D. KRAMER
Assistant Secretary of Defense (Special Operations and Low-Intensity Conflict)	BRIAN E. SHERIDAN

Assistant Secretary of Defense (Strategy and Threat Reduction)	EDWARD L. WARNER III
Deputy Under Secretary of Defense (Policy Support)	PETER F. VERGA
Deputy Under Secretary of Defense (Technology Security Policy)	DAVID TARBELL
Under Secretary of Defense for Personnel and Readiness	BERNARD D. ROSTKER
Assistant Secretary of Defense (Force Management Policy)	ALPHONSO MALDON, JR.
Assistant Secretary of Defense (Health Affairs)	(VACANCY)
Deputy Under Secretary of Defense (Planning)	(VACANCY)
Deputy Under Secretary of Defense (Program Integration)	JEANNE FITES
Assistant Secretary of Defense (Reserve Affairs)	(VACANCY)
Deputy Under Secretary of Defense (Readiness)	THOMAS LONGSTRETH
Under Secretary of Defense (Comptroller)/Chief Financial Officer	WILLIAM J. LYNN III
Principal Deputy Under Secretary (Comptroller)	ALICE C. MARONI
Director, Program Analysis and Evaluation	ROBERT R. SOULE
Assistant Secretary of Defense (Command, Control, Communications, and Intelligence)	ARTHUR L. MONEY
Assistant Secretary of Defense (Legislative Affairs)	JOHN VERONEAU
Assistant Secretary of Defense (Public Affairs)	KENNETH H. BACON
General Counsel	(VACANCY)
Director, Operational Test and Evaluation	PHILIP E. COYLE III
Inspector General	(VACANCY)
Assistant to the Secretary of Defense (Intelligence Oversight)	GEORGE B. LOTZ II
Director of Administration and Management	D.O. COOKE

Joint Chiefs of Staff

Chairman	GEN. HENRY H. SHELTON, USA
Vice Chairman	GEN. RICHARD B. MYERS, USAF
Chief of Staff, Army	GEN. ERIC K. SHINSEKI, USA
Chief of Naval Operations	ADM. JAY L. JOHNSON, USN
Chief of Staff, Air Force	GEN. MICHAEL E. RYAN, USAF
Commandant, Marine Corps	GEN. JAMES L. JONES, USMC

Joint Staff

Director	LT. GEN. CARLTON W. FULFORD, JR., USMC
Vice Director	MAJ. GEN. GARRY R. TREXLER, USAF
Director for Manpower and Personnel—J–1	BRIG. GEN. ROBERT L. SMOLEN, USAF
Director, Intelligence—J–2	REAR ADM. LOWELL E. JACOBY, USN
Director for Operations—J–3	VICE ADM. SCOTT A. FRY, USN

Director for Logistics—J–4	LT. GEN. JOHN M. MCDUFFIE, USA
Director for Strategic Plans and Policy—J–5	LT. GEN. EDWARD G. ANDERSON III, USA
Director for Command, Control, Communications, and Computer Systems—J–6	LT. GEN. JOHN L. WOODWARD, JR., USAF
Director for Operational Plans and Interoperability—J–7	MAJ. GEN. HENRY P. OSMAN, USMC
Director for Force Structure, Resources, and Assessment—J–8	LT. GEN. BRUCE A. CARLSON, USAF

[For the Department of Defense statement of organization, see the *Code of Federal Regulations,* Title 32, Chapter I, Subchapter R]

The Department of Defense is responsible for providing the military forces needed to deter war and protect the security of our country.

The major elements of these forces are the Army, Navy, Marine Corps, and Air Force, consisting of about 1.4 million men and women on active duty. They are backed, in case of emergency, by the 1 million members of the Reserve and National Guard. In addition, there are about 700,000 civilian employees in the Defense Department.

Under the President, who is also Commander in Chief, the Secretary of Defense exercises authority, direction, and control over the Department, which includes the separately organized military departments of Army, Navy, and Air Force, the Joint Chiefs of Staff providing military advice, the unified combatant commands, and various defense agencies established for specific purposes.

The National Security Act Amendments of 1949 redesignated the National Military Establishment as the Department of Defense and established it as an executive department (10 U.S.C. 111), with the Secretary of Defense as its head.

Structure

The Department of Defense is composed of the Office of the Secretary of Defense; the military departments and the military services within those departments; the Chairman of the Joint Chiefs of Staff and the Joint Staff; the unified combatant commands; the defense agencies; DOD field activities; and such other offices, agencies, activities, and commands as may be established or designated by law, or by the President or the Secretary of Defense.

Each military department is separately organized under its own Secretary and functions under the authority, direction, and control of the Secretary of Defense. The Secretary of each military department is responsible to the Secretary of Defense for the operation and efficiency of his department. Orders to the military departments are issued through the Secretaries of these departments or their designees, by the Secretary of Defense, or under authority specifically delegated in writing by the Secretary of Defense or provided by law.

The commanders of the unified combatant commands are responsible to the President and the Secretary of Defense for accomplishing the military missions assigned to them and exercising command authority over forces assigned to them. The operational chain of command runs from the President to the Secretary of Defense to the commanders of the unified combatant commands. The Chairman of the Joint Chiefs of Staff functions within the chain of command by transmitting the orders of the President or the Secretary of Defense to the commanders of the unified combatant commands.

Secretary of Defense The Secretary of Defense is the principal defense policy adviser to the President and is responsible for the formulation of general defense policy and policy related to DOD, and for the execution of

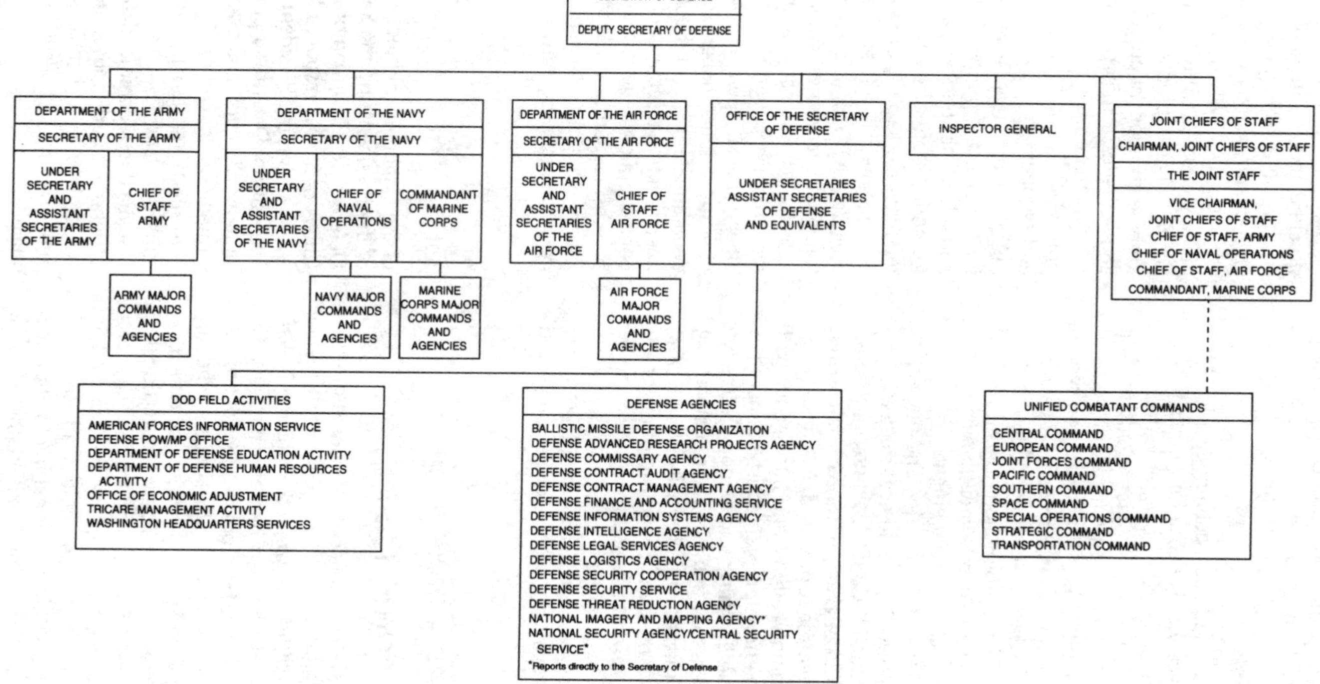
DEPARTMENT OF DEFENSE
SECRETARY OF DEFENSE
DEPUTY SECRETARY OF DEFENSE
DEPARTMENT OF THE ARMY
SECRETARY OF THE ARMY
UNDER SECRETARY AND ASSISTANT SECRETARIES OF THE ARMY
CHIEF OF STAFF ARMY
ARMY MAJOR COMMANDS AND AGENCIES
DEPARTMENT OF THE NAVY
SECRETARY OF THE NAVY
UNDER SECRETARY AND ASSISTANT SECRETARIES OF THE NAVY
CHIEF OF NAVAL OPERATIONS
COMMANDANT OF MARINE CORPS
NAVY MAJOR COMMANDS AND AGENCIES
MARINE CORPS MAJOR COMMANDS AND AGENCIES
DEPARTMENT OF THE AIR FORCE
SECRETARY OF THE AIR FORCE
UNDER SECRETARY AND ASSISTANT SECRETARIES OF THE AIR FORCE
CHIEF OF STAFF AIR FORCE
AIR FORCE MAJOR COMMANDS AND AGENCIES
OFFICE OF THE SECRETARY OF DEFENSE
UNDER SECRETARIES ASSISTANT SECRETARIES OF DEFENSE AND EQUIVALENTS
INSPECTOR GENERAL
JOINT CHIEFS OF STAFF
CHAIRMAN, JOINT CHIEFS OF STAFF
THE JOINT STAFF
VICE CHAIRMAN, JOINT CHIEFS OF STAFF
CHIEF OF STAFF, ARMY
CHIEF OF NAVAL OPERATIONS
CHIEF OF STAFF, AIR FORCE
COMMANDANT, MARINE CORPS
DOD FIELD ACTIVITIES
AMERICAN FORCES INFORMATION SERVICE
DEFENSE POW/MP OFFICE
DEPARTMENT OF DEFENSE EDUCATION ACTIVITY
DEPARTMENT OF DEFENSE HUMAN RESOURCES ACTIVITY
OFFICE OF ECONOMIC ADJUSTMENT
TRICARE MANAGEMENT ACTIVITY
WASHINGTON HEADQUARTERS SERVICES
DEFENSE AGENCIES
BALLISTIC MISSILE DEFENSE ORGANIZATION
DEFENSE ADVANCED RESEARCH PROJECTS AGENCY
DEFENSE COMMISSARY AGENCY
DEFENSE CONTRACT AUDIT AGENCY
DEFENSE CONTRACT MANAGEMENT AGENCY
DEFENSE FINANCE AND ACCOUNTING SERVICE
DEFENSE INFORMATION SYSTEMS AGENCY
DEFENSE INTELLIGENCE AGENCY
DEFENSE LEGAL SERVICES AGENCY
DEFENSE LOGISTICS AGENCY
DEFENSE SECURITY COOPERATION AGENCY
DEFENSE SECURITY SERVICE
DEFENSE THREAT REDUCTION AGENCY
NATIONAL IMAGERY AND MAPPING AGENCY*
NATIONAL SECURITY AGENCY/CENTRAL SECURITY SERVICE*
*Reports directly to the Secretary of Defense
UNIFIED COMBATANT COMMANDS
CENTRAL COMMAND
EUROPEAN COMMAND
JOINT FORCES COMMAND
PACIFIC COMMAND
SOUTHERN COMMAND
SPACE COMMAND
SPECIAL OPERATIONS COMMAND
STRATEGIC COMMAND
TRANSPORTATION COMMAND

approved policy. Under the direction of the President, the Secretary exercises authority, direction, and control over the Department of Defense.

Activties

Acquisition and Technology The Under Secretary of Defense for Acquisition, Technology, and Logistics is the principal staff assistant and adviser to the Secretary of Defense for all matters relating to the DOD acquisition system, research and development, advanced technology, developmental test and evaluation, production, logistics, installation management, military construction, procurement, environmental security, and nuclear, chemical, and biological matters.

Command, Control, Communications, and Intelligence The Assistant Secretary of Defense (Command, Control, Communications, and Intelligence (C^3I)) is the principal staff assistant and adviser to the Secretary and Deputy Secretary of Defense for achieving and maintaining information superiority in support of DOD missions, while exploiting or denying an adversary's ability to do the same.

Personnel and Readiness The Under Secretary of Defense for Personnel and Readiness is the principal staff assistant and adviser to the Secretary of Defense for policy matters relating to the structure and readiness of the total force. Functional areas include: readiness; civilian and military personnel policies, programs, and systems; civilian and military equal opportunity programs; health policies, programs, and activities; Reserve component programs, policies, and activities; family policy, dependent's education, and personnel support programs; and mobilization planning and requirements.

Policy The Under Secretary of Defense for Policy is the principal staff assistant and adviser to the Secretary of Defense for policy matters relating to overall international security policy and political-military affairs. Functional areas include NATO affairs; net assessments; foreign military sales; arms limitation agreements; international trade and technology security; regional security affairs; special operations and low-intensity conflict; integration of departmental plans and policies with overall national security objectives; drug control policy, requirements, priorities, systems, resources, and programs; and issuance of policy guidance affecting departmental programs.

Joint Chiefs of Staff

Joint Chiefs of Staff

The Joint Chiefs of Staff consist of the Chairman; the Vice Chairman; the Chief of Staff of the Army; the Chief of Naval Operations; the Chief of Staff of the Air Force; and the Commandant of the Marine Corps. The Chairman of the Joint Chiefs of Staff is the principal military adviser to the President, the National Security Council, and the Secretary of Defense. The other members of the Joint Chiefs of Staff are military advisers who may provide additional information upon request from the President, the National Security Council, or the Secretary of Defense. They may also submit their advice when it does not agree with that of the Chairman. Subject to the authority of the President and the Secretary of Defense, the Chairman of the Joint Chiefs of Staff is responsible for:

—assisting the President and the Secretary of Defense in providing for the strategic direction and planning of the Armed Forces;

—allocating resources to fulfill strategic plans;

—making recommendations for the assignment of responsibilities within the Armed Forces in accordance with and in support of those logistic and mobility plans;

—comparing the capabilities of American and allied Armed Forces with those of potential adversaries;

—preparing and reviewing contingency plans that conform to policy guidance from the President and the Secretary of Defense;

—preparing joint logistic and mobility plans to support contingency plans; and

—recommending assignment of logistic and mobility responsibilities to the Armed Forces to fulfill logistic and mobility plans.

The Chairman, while so serving, holds the grade of general or admiral and outranks all other officers of the Armed Forces.

The Vice Chairman of the Joint Chiefs performs duties assigned by the Chairman, with the approval of the Secretary of Defense. The Vice Chairman acts as Chairman when there is a vacancy in the office of the Chairman, or in the absence or disability of the Chairman. The Vice Chairman, while so serving, holds the grade of general or admiral and outranks all other officers of the Armed Forces except the Chairman of the Joint Chiefs of Staff.

Joint Staff

The Joint Staff, under the Chairman of the Joint Chiefs of Staff, assists the Chairman and the other members of the Joint Chiefs of Staff in carrying out their responsibilities.

The Joint Staff is headed by a Director who is selected by the Chairman in consultation with the other members of the Joint Chiefs of Staff and with the approval of the Secretary of Defense. Officers assigned to serve on the Joint Staff are selected by the Chairman in approximate equal numbers from the Army, Navy, Marine Corps, and Air Force.

Unified Combatant Commands

The unified combatant commands are military commands with broad continuing missions maintaining the security and defense of the United States against attack; supporting and advancing the national policies and interests of the United States and discharging U.S. military responsibilities in their area of responsibility; and preparing plans, conducting operations, and coordinating activities of the forces assigned to them in accordance with the directives of higher authority. The Chairman of the Joint Chiefs of Staff serves as the spokesman for the commanders of the unified combatant commands, especially on the operational requirements of their commands.

Unified Combatant Commands

Command	Address	Commander
Central	USCENTCOM, 7115 S. Boundary Blvd., MacDill AFB, FL 35621–5101.	Gen. Anthony C. Zinni, USMC
European	USEUCOM, CMR 450, Box 7100, APO AE 09705	Gen. Joseph W. Ralston, USAF
Joint Forces	USJFCOM, Suite 200, 1562 Mitscher Ave., Norfolk, VA 23511–2488.	Adm. Harold W. Gehman, Jr., USN
Pacific	USPACCOM, Box 64028, Camp H.M. Smith, HI 96861–4028.	Adm. Dennis C. Blair, USN
Southern	USSOUTHCOM, 3511 NW. 91st Ave., Miami, FL 33172	Gen. Charles E. Wilhelm, USMC
Space	USSPACECOM, Suite 116, 250 S. Peterson Blvd., Peterson AFB, CO 80914–3010.	Gen. Ralph E. Eberhart, USAF
Special Operations	USSOCOM, 7701 Tampa Point Blvd., MacDill AFB, FL 33621–5323.	Gen. Peter J. Schoomaker, USA
Strategic	USSTRATCOM, Suite 2A1, 901 SAC Blvd., Offutt AFB, NE 68113–6000.	Adm. Richard W. Mies, USN
Transportation	USTRANSCOM, Rm. 310, 508 Scott Dr., Scott AFB, IL 62225–5357.	Gen. Charles T. Robertson, Jr., USAF

Field Activities

American Forces Information Service The American Forces Information Service (AFIS) was established in 1977. AFIS provides internal information to U.S. forces worldwide in order to promote and sustain military unit and individual readiness, quality of life, and morale; trains public affairs, broadcast, and visual information professionals for DOD; and provides communications services to military commanders and combat forces. AFIS provides news, features, photography, videography, news clippings, and other internal command information products and services to DOD. It provides policy guidance and oversight for departmental periodicals and pamphlets, military command newspapers, the broadcast elements of the military departments, DOD audiovisual matters, and public affairs and visual information training.

For further information, contact the American Forces Information Service, Department of Defense, Suite 311, 601 North Fairfax Street, Alexandria, VA 22314–2007. Phone, 703–428–1200. Internet, www.defenselink.mil/afis.

Education The Department of Defense Education Activity (DODEA) was established in 1992. It consists of two subordinate organizational entities: the Department of Defense Dependents Schools (DODDS) and the Department of Defense Domestic Dependent Elementary and Secondary Schools (DOD DDESS). DODEA formulates, develops, and implements policies, technical guidance, and standards for the effective management of Defense dependents education activities and programs. It also plans, directs, coordinates, and manages the education programs for eligible dependents of U.S. military and civilian personnel stationed overseas and stateside; evaluates the programmatic and operational policies and procedures for DODDS and DOD DDESS; and provides education activity representation at meetings and deliberations of educational panels and advisory groups.

For further information, contact the Department of Defense Education Activity, 4040 North Fairfax Drive, Arlington, VA 22203–1635. Phone, 703–696–4236. Internet, www.odedodea.edu.

Human Resources and Manpower The Department of Defense Human Resources Activity (DODHRA) is chartered to support departmental and congressionally mandated programs in the benefits, readiness, and force protection areas. DODHRA collects, maintains, and analyzes manpower, personnel, training, and financial data; establishes and maintains data and systems used to determine entitlements to DOD benefits; and manages civilian personnel administrative services for the Department. It plans and executes changes to existing permanent and reserve duty travel policies and processes and performs long-term programmatic research and analysis to improve DOD personnel and industrial security systems.

For further information, contact the Department of Defense Human Resources Activity-Headquarters, Suite 200, 4040 Fairfax Drive, Arlington, VA 22203–1613. Phone, 703–696–1036. Internet, www.dhra.osd.mil.

Health Care The TRICARE Management Activity (TMA) was formed in 1998 from the consolidation of the TRICARE Support Office (formerly Civilian Health and Medical Program of the Uniformed Services (CHAMPUS) headquarters), the Defense Medical Programs Activity, and the integration of health management program functions formerly located in the Office of the Assistant Secretary of Defense for Health Affairs. The mission of TMA is to manage TRICARE; manage the Defense Health Program appropriation; provide operational direction and support to the Uniformed Services in the management and administration of the TRICARE program; and administer CHAMPUS.

For further information, contact the TRICARE Management Activity, Suite 810, Skyline 5, 5111 Leesburg Pike, Falls Church, VA 22041–3206. Phone, 703–681–1730. Fax, 703–681–3665. Internet, www.tricare.osd.mil.

Prisoners of War and Missing Personnel The Defense Prisoner of War/Missing Personnel Office (DPMO) was established in 1993 and provides centralized management of prisoner of war/missing personnel affairs within the Department of Defense, including leadership and policy oversight for all efforts to reach an accounting for Americans still unaccounted for as a result of U.S. involvement in past conflicts since World War II and the recovery and accounting of those Americans isolated in harm's way in future conflicts. The Office assembles and maintains databases on U.S. military and civilian personnel who are or were prisoners of war or missing as a result of a hostile action; declassifies DOD documents for disclosure and release; and maintains channels of communication on prisoner of war/missing personnel matters between DOD and the Congress, prisoner of war/missing personnel families, and the American public through periodic consultations and other appropriate measures.

For further information, contact the Defense Prisoner of War/Missing Personnel Office, Department of Defense, OASD/ISA, The Pentagon, Washington, DC 20301–2400. Phone, 703–602–2102. Fax, 703–602–1890. Internet, www.dtic.mil/dpmo.

Sources of Information

Audiovisual Products Certain Department of Defense productions on film and videotapes, CD–ROM's, and other audiovisual products such as stock footage and still photographs are available to the public. An up-to-date, full-text searchable listing of the Department's inventory of film, videotape, and interactive multimedia titles is available on the Internet. For information and obtaining productions, contact the following sources:

—For newer productions, contact the National Technical Information Service, 5285 Port Royal Road, Springfield, VA 22161 (phone, 703–605–6000), or the defense visual information site (Internet, dodimagery.afis.osd.mil, and select "Search DAVIS/DITIS").

—For older productions, contact the Motion Picture, Sound, and Video Branch (NWDNM), National Archives and Records Administration, 8601 Adelphi Road, College Park, MD 20740–6001. Phone, 301–713–7050.

—For CD–ROM's, stock footage, and still photographs, contact the Defense Visual Information Center, 1363 Z Street, Building 2730, March Air Reserve Base, CA 92518–2073. Phone, 909–413–2515.

There is usually a fee charged for the Department's audiovisual and multimedia products.

Contracts and Small Business Activities Contact the Director, Small and Disadvantaged Business Utilization, Office of the Secretary of Defense, 3061 Defense Pentagon, Washington, DC 20301–3061. Phone, 703–588–8620.

DOD Directives and Instructions Contact the Correspondence and Directives Directorate, Washington Headquarters Services, Room 2A286, 1155 Defense Pentagon, Washington, DC 20301–1155. Phone, 703–697–4111.

Electronic Access Information about the following offices is available as listed below:

Office of the Secretary of Defense: www.defenselink.mil.

Joint Chiefs of Staff: www.dtic.mil/jcs.

Unified combatant commands: www.defenselink.mil/pubs/almanac/unified.html.

Central Command: www.centcom.mil.

European Command: www.eucom.mil.

Joint Forces Command: www.jfcom.mil.

Pacific Command: www.pacom.mil.

Southern Command: www.southcom.mil.

Space Command: www.spacecom.af.mil.

Special Operations Command: www.socom.mil.
Strategic Command: www.stratcom.mil.
Transportation Command: www.transcom.mil.

Employment Almost all positions are in the competitive service and are filled from civil service registers. College recruiting requirements are limited primarily to management intern positions at the B.S. and M.S. levels. For additional information, inquiries should be addressed to the Human Resource Services Center, Washington Headquarters Services, Room 2E22, AMC Building, Alexandria, VA 22233–0001. Phone, 703–617–7211. Internet, www.hrsc.osd.mil.

Pentagon Tours Guided tours of the Pentagon are available Monday through Friday, from 9 a.m. through 3 p.m., excluding Federal holidays. The 75-minute tour starts on the hour at the Metro entrance to the Pentagon and is approximately one mile long. Groups of more than 100 should schedule the tour 2 weeks in advance. For further information or reservations, write to Pentagon Tours, Director for Programs and Community Relations, 1400 Defense Pentagon, Room 1E776, Washington, DC 20301–1400. Phone, 703–695–1776.

Speakers Civilian and military representatives of the Department of Defense are available to speak on a variety of defense subjects in response to invitations, usually at no cost to the local sponsor. Written requests for speakers should be addressed to the Director for Programs and Community Relations, Office of the Assistant Secretary of Defense for Public Affairs, 1400 Defense Pentagon, Washington, DC 20301–1400 (phone, 703–695–3845); or to the public affairs officer of the nearest military installation.

Telephone Directory The Department of Defense telephone directory is available for sale by the Superintendent of Documents, Government Printing Office, Washington, DC 20402. Phone, 202–512–1800.

For further information concerning the Department of Defense, contact the Director, Directorate for Public Communication, Office of the Assistant Secretary of Defense for Public Affairs, 1400 Defense Pentagon, Washington, DC 20301–1400. Phone, 703–697–5737. Internet, www.defenselink.mil.

DEPARTMENT OF THE AIR FORCE

1670 Air Force Pentagon, Washington, DC 20330–1670
Phone, 703–697–6061. Internet, www.af.mil.

SECRETARY OF THE AIR FORCE	F. WHITTEN PETERS, *Acting*
Under Secretary of the Air Force	CAROL A. DIBATTISTE
Deputy Under Secretary (International Affairs)	WILLARD H. MITCHELL
Principal Assistant Deputy Under Secretary (International Affairs)	MAJ. GEN. TOME H. WALTERS, JR.
Assistant Deputy Under Secretaries (International Affairs)	BRIG. GEN. HOWARD G. DEWOLF, BRIG. GEN. JEFFREY B. KOHLER
Director, Small and Disadvantaged Business Utilization	ANTHONY J. DELUCA
Assistant Secretary (Manpower, Reserve Affairs, Installations, and Environment)	RUBY B. DEMESME
Executive Director, Air Force Board for Correction of Military Records	MACK M. BURTON
Director, Air Force Personnel Council	COL. KENNETH M. PARSONS
Director, Air Force Civilian Appellate Review Office	SOPHIE A. CLARK
Principal Deputy Assistant Secretary (Manpower, Reserve Affairs, Installations, and Environment)	PHILLIP P. UPSCHULTE
Deputy Assistant Secretary (Force Management and Personnel)	MARY L. KEENER
Deputy Assistant Secretary (Reserve Affairs)	BRYAN E. SHARRATT
Deputy Assistant Secretary (Installations)	JIMMY G. DISHNER
Deputy Assistant Secretary (Environment, Safety, and Occupational Health)	THOMAS W.L. MCCALL, JR.
Deputy Assistant Secretary (Equal Opportunity)	(VACANCY)
Assistant Secretary (Financial Management and Comptroller of the Air Force)	ROBERT F. HALE
Principal Deputy Assistant Secretary (Financial Management)	JAMES R. SPEER
Deputy Assistant Secretary (Budget)	MAJ. GEN. LARRY W. NORTHINGTON
Deputy Assistant Secretary (Cost and Economics)	JOSEPH T. KAMMERER
Deputy Assistant Secretary (Management Systems)	A. ERNEST FITZGERALD
Deputy Assistant Secretary (Financial Operations)	JOHN J. NETHERY
Assistant Secretary (Acquisition)	LAWERENCE S. DELANEY
Principal Deputy Assistant Secretary (Acquisition)	LT. GEN. GREGORY S. MARTIN
Principal Deputy Assistant Secretary (Acquisition and Management)	DARLENE A. DRUYUN
Deputy Assistant Secretary (Contracting)	(VACANCY)

Deputy Assistant Secretary (Management Policy and Program Integration)	Blaise J. Durante
Deputy Assistant Secretary (Science, Technology, and Engineering)	Donald Daniel
Director, Joint Strike Fighter Technology Program	Brig. Gen. Leslie F. Kenne
Assistant Secretary (Space)	Keith R. Hall
Principal Deputy Assistant Secretary (Space)	David A. Kier
Deputy Assistant Secretary (Space Plans and Policy)	Richard M. McCormick
General Counsel	Jeh C. Johnson
Inspector General of the Air Force	Lt. Gen. Nicholas B. Kehoe III
Administrative Assistant to the Secretary	William A. Davidson
Chief, Civilian Personnel Division	Craig Arigo
Chief, Military Personnel Division	Maj. Al Bruner
Director, Plans, Programs, and Budget	Carolyn Lunsford
Director, Security and Special Programs Oversight	Gene Boesch
Auditor General of the Air Force	Jackie R. Crawford
Director, Legislative Liaison	Maj. Gen. Michael T. Moseley
Chief, Congressional Inquiry Division	Col. Walter Washabaugh
Director, Public Affairs	Col. R.T. Rand

Air Staff

Chief of Staff	Gen. Michael E. Ryan
Vice Chief of Staff	Gen. Lester L. Lyles
Assistant Vice Chief of Staff	Lt. Gen. David L. Vesely
Deputy Chief of Staff (Plans and Programs)	Lt. Gen. Roger G. DeKok
Deputy Chief of Staff (Personnel)	Lt. Gen. Donald L Peterson
Deputy Chief of Staff (Air and Space Operations)	Lt. Gen. Marvin R. Esmond
Deputy Chief of Staff (Installations and Logistics)	Lt. Gen. John W. Handy
Director of Communications and Information	Lt. Gen. William J. Donahue
Chief Master Sergeant of the Air Force	Ch. M. Sgt. Jim Finch
Chief, Safety/Director, Air Force Safety Center	Maj. Gen. Francis C. Gideon, Jr.
Director of Security Forces	Brig. Gen. Richard A. Coleman, Jr.
Chairs, Scientific Advisory Board	William F. Ballhaus, Jr., Natalie W. Crawford
Director, Test and Evaluation	John Manclark
Air Force Historian	Richard P. Hallion
Chief Scientist of the Air Force	Louis S. Metzger
Chief, Air Force Reserve	Maj. Gen. James E. Sherrard III
Chief, National Guard Bureau	Lt. Gen. Russell C. Davis
Surgeon General of the Air Force	Lt. Gen. Paul K. Carlton, Jr.
Chief of the Chaplain Service	Maj. Gen. William J. Dendinger
Judge Advocate General	Maj. Gen. William A. Moorman

Named Activities

Commander, Air Force Office of Colonel Matters	Col. Paul M. Hankins
Commander, Air Force General Officer Matters Office	Col. Richard S. Hassan

Director, Air Force Office of Senior Executive Matters	GREGORY W. DEN HERDER

The Department of the Air Force is responsible for defending the United States through control and exploitation of air and space.

The Department of the Air Force (USAF) was established as part of the National Military Establishment by the National Security Act of 1947 (61 Stat. 502) and came into being on September 18, 1947. The National Security Act Amendments of 1949 redesignated the National Military Establishment as the Department of Defense, established it as an executive department, and made the Department of the Air Force a military department within the Department of Defense (63 Stat. 578). The Department of the Air Force is separately organized under the Secretary of the Air Force. It operates under the authority, direction, and control of the Secretary of Defense (10 U.S.C. 8010). The Department consists of the Office of the Secretary of the Air Force, the Air Staff, and field organizations.

Secretary The Secretary is responsible for matters pertaining to organization, training, logistical support, maintenance, welfare of personnel, administrative, recruiting, research and development, and other activities prescribed by the President or the Secretary of Defense.

Air Staff The mission of the Air Staff is to furnish professional assistance to the Secretary, the Under Secretary, the Assistant Secretaries, and the Chief of Staff in executing their responsibilities.

Field Organizations The major commands, field operating agencies, and direct reporting units together represent the field organizations of the Air Force. These are organized primarily on a functional basis in the United States and on an area basis overseas. These commands are responsible for accomplishing certain phases of the worldwide activities of the Air Force. They also are responsible for organizing, administering, equipping, and training their subordinate elements for the accomplishment of assigned missions.

Major Commands

The Continental U.S. Commands

Air Combat Command This Command operates Air Force bombers and CONUS-based, combat-coded fighter and attack aircraft. It organizes, trains, equips, and maintains combat-ready forces for rapid deployment and employment while ensuring strategic air defense forces are ready to meet the challenges of peacetime air sovereignty and wartime air defense.

Air Force Materiel Command This Command advances, integrates, and uses technology to develop, test, acquire, and sustain weapons systems. It also performs single-manager continuous product and process improvement throughout a product's life cycle.

Air Mobility Command This Command provides airlift, air refueling, special air mission, and aeromedical evacuation for U.S. forces. It also supplies forces to theater commands to support wartime tasking.

Air Force Reserve Command This Command supports the Air Force mission of defending the Nation through control and exploitation of air and space. It plays an integral role in the day-to-day Air Force mission and is not a force held in reserve for possible war or contingency operations.

Air Force Space Command This Command operates space and ballistic missile systems, including ballistic missile warning, space control, spacelift, and satellite operations.

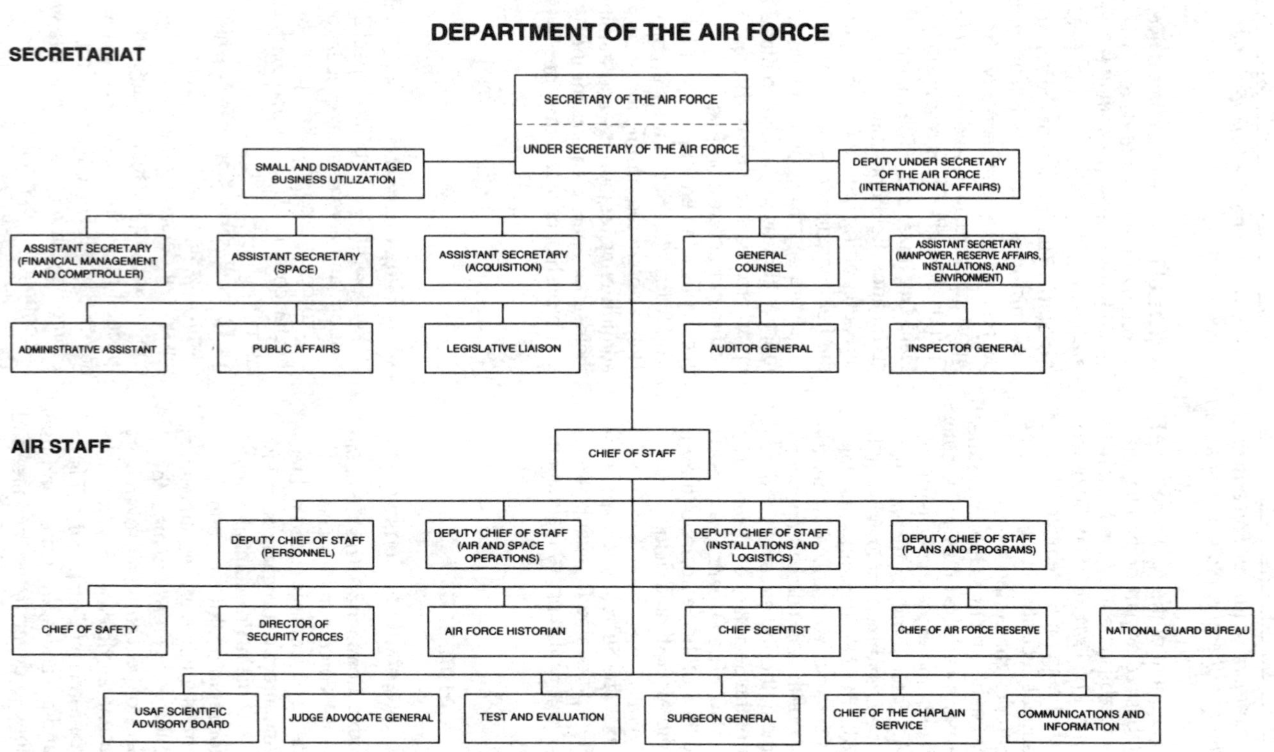
DEPARTMENT OF THE AIR FORCE
SECRETARIAT
SECRETARY OF THE AIR FORCE
UNDER SECRETARY OF THE AIR FORCE
SMALL AND DISADVANTAGED BUSINESS UTILIZATION
DEPUTY UNDER SECRETARY OF THE AIR FORCE (INTERNATIONAL AFFAIRS)
ASSISTANT SECRETARY (FINANCIAL MANAGEMENT AND COMPTROLLER)
ASSISTANT SECRETARY (SPACE)
ASSISTANT SECRETARY (ACQUISITION)
GENERAL COUNSEL
ASSISTANT SECRETARY (MANPOWER, RESERVE AFFAIRS, INSTALLATIONS, AND ENVIRONMENT)
ADMINISTRATIVE ASSISTANT
PUBLIC AFFAIRS
LEGISLATIVE LIAISON
AUDITOR GENERAL
INSPECTOR GENERAL
AIR STAFF
CHIEF OF STAFF
DEPUTY CHIEF OF STAFF (PERSONNEL)
DEPUTY CHIEF OF STAFF (AIR AND SPACE OPERATIONS)
DEPUTY CHIEF OF STAFF (INSTALLATIONS AND LOGISTICS)
DEPUTY CHIEF OF STAFF (PLANS AND PROGRAMS)
CHIEF OF SAFETY
DIRECTOR OF SECURITY FORCES
AIR FORCE HISTORIAN
CHIEF SCIENTIST
CHIEF OF AIR FORCE RESERVE
NATIONAL GUARD BUREAU
USAF SCIENTIFIC ADVISORY BOARD
JUDGE ADVOCATE GENERAL
TEST AND EVALUATION
SURGEON GENERAL
CHIEF OF THE CHAPLAIN SERVICE
COMMUNICATIONS AND INFORMATION

Air Force Special Operations Command This Command provides the air component of U.S. Special Operations Command, deploying specialized air power and delivering special operations combat power.

Air Education and Training Command This Command recruits, accesses, commissions, educates, and trains Air Force enlisted and officer personnel. It provides basic military training, initial and advanced technical training, flying training, and professional military and degree-granting professional education. The Command also conducts joint, medical service, readiness, and Air Force security assistance training.

Major Commands

Command	Address	Commander
Air Combat Command	Langley AFB, VA 23665–2788	Gen. Richard E. Hawley
Air Education and Training Command	Randolph AFB, TX 78150–4324	Gen. Lloyd W. Newton
Air Force Materiel Command	Wright-Patterson AFB, OH 45433–5001	Gen. George T. Babbitt, Jr.
Air Force Reserve Command	Robins AFB, GA 31098–1635	Maj. Gen. James E. Sherrard III
Air Force Space Command	Peterson AFB, CO 80914–4020	Gen. Richard B. Myers
Air Force Special Operations Command	Hurlburt Field, FL 32544–5273	Maj. Gen. Charles R. Holland
Air Mobility Command	Scott AFB, IL 62225–5310	Gen. Charles T. Robertson, Jr.

Overseas Commands

Pacific Air Forces The Command is responsible for planning, conducting, and coordinating offensive and defensive air operations in the Pacific and Asian theaters.

United States Air Forces in Europe The Command plans, conducts, controls, coordinates, and supports air and space operations to achieve United States national and NATO objectives.

Overseas Commands

Command	Address	Commander
Pacific Air Forces	Hickam AFB, HI 96853–5420	Gen. Patrick K. Gamble
U.S. Air Forces in Europe	APO AE 09094–0501	Gen. John P. Jumper

Field Activities

Air National Guard The Center performs the operational and technical tasks associated with manning, equipping, and training Air National Guard units to required readiness levels.

Base Closures The Agency serves as the Federal real property disposal agent and provides integrated executive management for Air Force bases in the United States as they are closed under the delegated authorities of the Base Closure and Realignment Act of 1988 and the Defense Base Closure and Realignment Act of 1990.

Communications The Agency ensures that command, control, communications, and computer systems used by USAF warfighters are integrated and interoperable. It develops and validates C^4 architectures, technical standards, technical reference codes, policies, processes and procedures, and technical solutions, supporting information superiority through technical excellence.

Emergency Preparedness The Office is responsible for Air Force-related national security emergency preparedness functions, including military support to civil authorities, civil defense, and law enforcement agencies and planning for continuity of operations during emergencies.

Engineering The Agency maximizes Air Force civil engineers' capabilities in base and contingency operations by providing tools, practices, and professional support for readiness, training, technical support, management practices, automation support, vehicles and equipment, and research, development, and acquisition consultation.

Environmental Quality The Center provides the Air Force with services in environmental remediation, compliance, planning, and pollution prevention, as well as construction management and facilities design.

Flight Standards The Agency performs worldwide inspection of airfields, navigation systems, and instrument approaches. It provides flight standards to develop Air Force instrument requirements, and certifies procedures and directives for cockpit display and navigation systems. It also provides air traffic control and airlift procedures and evaluates air traffic control systems and airspace management procedures.

Historic Publications The Office researches, writes, and publishes books and other studies on Air Force history and provides historical support to Air Force headquarters.

Historical Research The Agency serves as a repository for Air Force historical records and provides research facilities for scholars and the general public.

Intelligence The Agency provides intelligence services to support Air Force operations through flexible collection, tailored air and space intelligence, weapons monitoring, and information warfare products and services.

Medical Operations The Agency assists the USAF Surgeon General in developing plans, programs, and policies for the medical service, aerospace medicine, clinical investigations, quality assurance, health promotion, family advocacy, bioenvironmental engineering, military public health, and radioactive material management.

Modeling and Simulation The Agency implements policies and standards and supports field operations in the areas of modeling and simulation.

News The Agency gathers information and packages and disseminates electronic and printed news and information products. It manages and operationally controls Air Force Internal Information, the Army and Air Force Hometown News Service, the Air Force Broadcasting Service, and the Air Force Armed Forces Radio and Television outlets worldwide; operates the Air Force hotline; and provides electronic information through the Air Force bulletin board and the Internet.

Nuclear Weapons Monitoring The Air Force Technical Applications Center monitors compliance with various nuclear treaties. It provides real-time reporting of nuclear weapons tests and operates a global network of sensors and analytical laboratories to monitor foreign nuclear activity. It conducts research and development of proliferation detection technologies for all weapons of mass destruction.

Real Estate The Agency acquires, manages, and disposes of land for the Air Force worldwide and maintains a complete land and facilities inventory.

Weather Services The Service provides centralized weather services to the Air Force, Army joint staff, designated unified commands, and other agencies, ensuring standardization of procedures and interoperability within the USAF weather system and assessing its technical performance and effectiveness.

Field Operating Agencies

Agency	Address	Commander/Director
Air Force Agency for Modeling and Simulation	Orlando, FL 32826–3276	Col. Jimmy H. Wilson
Air Force Audit Agency	Washington, DC 20330–1125	Jackie Crawford
Air Force Base Conversion Agency	Arlington, VA 22209–2808	(Vacancy)
Air Force Center for Environmental Excellence	Brooks AFB, TX 78235–5318	Gary M. Erickson
Air Force Center for Quality and Management Innovation	Randolph AFB, TX 78150–4451	(Vacancy)
Air Force Civil Engineer Support Agency	Tyndall AFB, FL 32403–5319	Col. Donald J. Thomas
Air Force Cost Analysis Agency	Arlington, VA 22202–4306	Robert F. Hale
Air Force Flight Standards Agency	Washington, DC 20330–1480	(Vacancy)
Air Force Historical Research Agency	Maxwell AFB, AL 36112–6424	Col. Richard Rauschkolb
Air Force History Support Office	Bolling AFB, Washington, DC 20332–4113	Jacob Neufeld
Air Force Inspection Agency	Kirtland AFB, NM 87117–5670	(Vacancy)

Field Operating Agencies—Continued

Agency	Address	Commander/Director
Air Force Legal Services Agency	Bolling AFB, Washington, DC 20332	Col. Richard F. Rohenberg
Air Force Logistics Management Agency	Maxwell AFB, AL 36114–3236	Col. Russell G. Stafford
Air Force Medical Operations Agency	Bolling AFB, Washington, DC 20332–7050	Maj. Gen. Earl W. Mabry II
Air Force Medical Support Agency	Brooks AFB, TX 78235–5121	Col. Richard Rushmore
Air Force National Security Emergency Preparedness Office	Washington, DC 20330–1480	Col. Bob Manning
Air Force News Agency	Kelly AFB, TX 78241–5601	Col. Teddy G. Tilma
Air Force Office of Special Investigations	Bolling AFB, Washington, DC 20332–6000	Brig. Gen. Francis X. Taylor
Air Force Operations Group	Washington, DC 20330–1480	Col. James Shechan
Air Force Pentagon Communications Agency	Washington, DC 20330–1600	Col. Richard Hange
Air Force Personnel Center	Randolph AFB, TX 78150–4703	Maj. Gen. Donald A. Lamontagne
Air Force Personnel Operations Agency	Washington, DC 20330–1040	Brig. Gen. John F. Regni
Air Force Program Executive Office	Washington, DC 20330–1060	(Vacancy)
Air Force Real Estate Agency	Bolling AFB, Washington, DC 20332–5107	William E. Edwards
Air Force Review Boards Agency	Washington, DC 20330–1661	Joe G. Lineberger
Air Force Safety Center	Kirtland AFB, NM 87117	Maj. Gen. Francis C. Gideon, Jr.
Air Force Services Agency	Randolph AFB, TX 78150–4755	Col. David F. Honeycutt
Air Force Studies and Analyses Agency	Washington, DC 20330–1570	Col. Thomas A. Cardwell III
Air Force Technical Applications Center	Patrick AFB, FL 32925–3002	(Vacancy)
Air Intelligence Agency	San Antonio, TX 78243–7009	Brig. Gen. John R. Baker
Air National Guard Readiness Center	Andrews AFB, MD 20331–5157	(Vacancy)
Air Weather Service	Scott AFB, IL 62225–5206	Col. Charles French
Joint Services Survival, Evasion, Resistance, and Escape Agency	Fort Belvoir, VA 22060–5788	Col. Robert C. Bonn, Jr.

Direct Reporting Units

Air Force Communication and Information Center The Center applies information technology to improve operations processes and manages all Air Force information technology systems.

Air Force Doctrine Center The Center develops and publishes basic and operational level doctrine for the USAF. It provides USAF input into joint and multinational doctrine development, ensures that Air Force doctrine is consistent with policy and joint doctrine, and serves as the Air Force's primary source of expertise for military operations other than war doctrine and strategy development as well as training, education, exercises, and simulations.

Air Force Operational Test and Evaluation Center The Center plans and conducts test and evaluation procedures to determine operational effectiveness and suitability of new or modified USAF systems and their capacity to meet mission needs.

Air Force Security Forces Center The Center ensures quick and effective security responses to protect U.S. personnel around the globe.

Eleventh Wing The Wing provides support for Headquarters Air Force and other Air Force units in the National Capital Region, including day-to-day operations of Bolling Air Force Base. The Wing plans and directs the Air Force Band and the Air Force Honor Guard support to ceremony activities of the Air Force Chief of Staff, the Air Force Secretary, the White House, and Arlington National Cemetery.

U.S. Air Force Academy The Academy provides academic and military instruction and experience to prepare future USAF career officers. Graduates receive Bachelor of Science degrees in one of 26 academic majors and commissions as second lieutenants.

Direct Reporting Units

Unit	Address	Commander
11th Wing	Bolling AFB, Washington, DC 20332–0101	Col. Duane W. Deal
Air Force Communications and Information Center	Washington, DC 20330–1250	Lt. Gen. William J. Donahue
Air Force Doctrine Center	Maxwell AFB, AL 36112–6335	Maj. Gen. Timothy A. Kinnan
Air Force Operational Test and Evaluation Center	Kirtland AFB, NM 87117–5558	Maj. Gen. Jeffrey G. Cliver
Air Force Security Forces Center	Lackland AFB, TX 78236–5226	Brig. Gen. Richard A. Coleman, Jr.

Direct Reporting Units—Continued

Unit	Address	Commander
U.S. Air Force Academy	CO 80840–5001	Lt. Gen. Tad J. Oelstrom

For further information concerning the Department of the Air Force, contact the Office of the Director of Public Affairs, Department of the Air Force, 1670 Air Force Pentagon, Washington, DC 20330–1670. Phone, 703–697–6061. Internet, www.af.mil.

DEPARTMENT OF THE ARMY

The Pentagon, Washington, DC 20310
Phone, 703–695–2442. Internet, www.army.mil.

SECRETARY OF THE ARMY	LOUIS CALDERA
Under Secretary of the Army	GREGORY ROBERT DAHLBERG
Assistant Secretary of the Army (Acquisition, Logistics, and Technology)	PAUL J. HOEPER
Assistant Secretary of the Army (Civil Works)	JOSEPH W. WESTPHAL
Assistant Secretary of the Army (Financial Management and Comptroller)	HELEN T. MCCOY
Assistant Secretary of the Army (Installations and Environment)	MAHLON APGAR IV
Assistant Secretary of the Army (Manpower and Reserve Affairs)	P.T. HENRY
General Counsel	CHARLES A. BLANCHARD
Administrative Assistant to the Secretary of the Army	JOEL B. HUDSON
Director, Information Systems for Command, Control, Communications, and Computers	LT. GEN. WILLIAM H. CAMPBELL
Inspector General	LT. GEN. MICHAEL W. ACKERMAN
Auditor General	FRANCIS E. REARDON
Deputy Under Secretary of the Army (International Affairs)	GAYDEN E. THOMPSON
Deputy Under Secretary of the Army (Operations Research)	WALTER W. HOLLIS
Chief of Legislative Liaison	WILLIAM J. LENNOX, JR.
Chief of Public Affairs	MAJ. GEN. JOHN G. MEYER, JR.
Director, Small and Disadvantaged Business Utilization	TRACEY L. PINSON
Office of the Chief of Staff:	
Chief of Staff, United States Army	GEN. ERIC K. SHINSEKI
Vice Chief of Staff	GEN. JOHN M. KEANE
Assistant Vice Chief of Staff	LT. GEN. KEVIN BYRNES
Director of the Army Staff	LT. GEN. JOHN M. PICKLER
Army Staff:	
Assistant Chief of Staff for Installation Management	MAJ. GEN. R.L. VAN ANTWERP
Deputy Chief of Staff for Intelligence	LT. GEN. CLAUDIA J. KENNEDY
Deputy Chief of Staff for Logistics	MAJ. GEN. CHARLES C. CUNNON, JR.
Deputy Chief of Staff for Operations and Plans	LT. GEN. LARRY R. ELLIS
Deputy Chief of Staff for Personnel	LT. GEN. DAVID H. OHLE
Chief of Engineers	LT. GEN. JOE N. BALLARD
The Surgeon General	LT. GEN. RONALD R. BLANCK
Chief, Army Reserve	MAJ. GEN. THOMAS J. PLEWES
Chief, National Guard Bureau	LT. GEN. RUSSELL C. DAVIS
Judge Advocate General	MAJ. GEN. WALTER B. HUFFMAN

Chief of Chaplains	MAJ. GEN. GAYLORD T. GUNHUS
Major Army Commands:	
Commanding General, U.S. Army Materiel Command	GEN. JOHN G. COBURN
Commanding General, U.S. Army Corps of Engineers	LT. GEN. JOE N. BALLARD
Commanding General, U.S. Army Criminal Investigation Command	BRIG. GEN. DAVID W. FOLEY
Commanding General, U.S. Army Forces Command	GEN. JOHN W. HENDRIX
Commanding General, U.S. Army Intelligence and Security Command	MAJ. GEN. ROBERT W. NOONAN, JR.
Commanding General, U.S. Army Medical Command	LT. GEN. RONALD R. BLANCK
Commanding General, U.S. Army Military District of Washington	MAJ. GEN. ROBERT R. IVANY
Commanding General, U.S. Army Military Traffic Management Command	MAJ. GEN. KENNETH L. PRIVRATSKY
Commanding General, U.S. Army Space and Missile Defense Command	LT. GEN. JOHN COSTELLO
Commanding General, U.S. Army Special Operations Command	LT. GEN. WILLIAM P. TANGNEY
Commanding General, U.S. Army Training and Doctrine Command	GEN. JOHN N. ABRAMS
Commanding General, 8th U.S. Army	LT. GEN. DANIEL J. PETROSKY
Commanding General, U.S. Army South	MAJ. GEN. PHILIP R. KENSINGER, JR.
Commanding General, U.S. Army Pacific	LT. GEN. EDWIN P. SMITH
Commanding General, U.S. Army Europe and 7th Army	GEN. MONTGOMERY C. MEIGS

The mission of the Department of the Army is to organize, train, and equip active duty and reserve forces for the preservation of peace, security, and the defense of our Nation. As part of our national military team, the Army focuses on land operations; its soldiers must be trained with modern arms and equipment and be ready to respond quickly. The Army also administers programs aimed at protecting the environment, improving waterway navigation, flood and beach erosion control, and water resource development. It provides military assistance to Federal, State, and local government agencies, including natural disaster relief assistance.

The American Continental Army, now called the United States Army, was established by the Continental Congress on June 14, 1775, more than a year before the Declaration of Independence. The Department of War was established as an executive department at the seat of government by act approved August 7, 1789 (1 Stat. 49). The Secretary of War was established as its head. The National Security Act of 1947 (50 U.S.C. 401) created the National Military Establishment, and the Department of War was designated the Department of the Army. The title of its Secretary became Secretary of the Army (5 U.S.C. 171). The National Security Act Amendments of 1949 (63 Stat. 578) provided that the Department of the Army be a military department within the Department of Defense.

Secretary The Secretary of the Army is the head of the Department of the Army. Subject to the direction, authority, and control of the President as Commander in Chief and of the Secretary of Defense, the Secretary of the Army is responsible for and has the authority to conduct all affairs of the Department of the Army, including its organization,

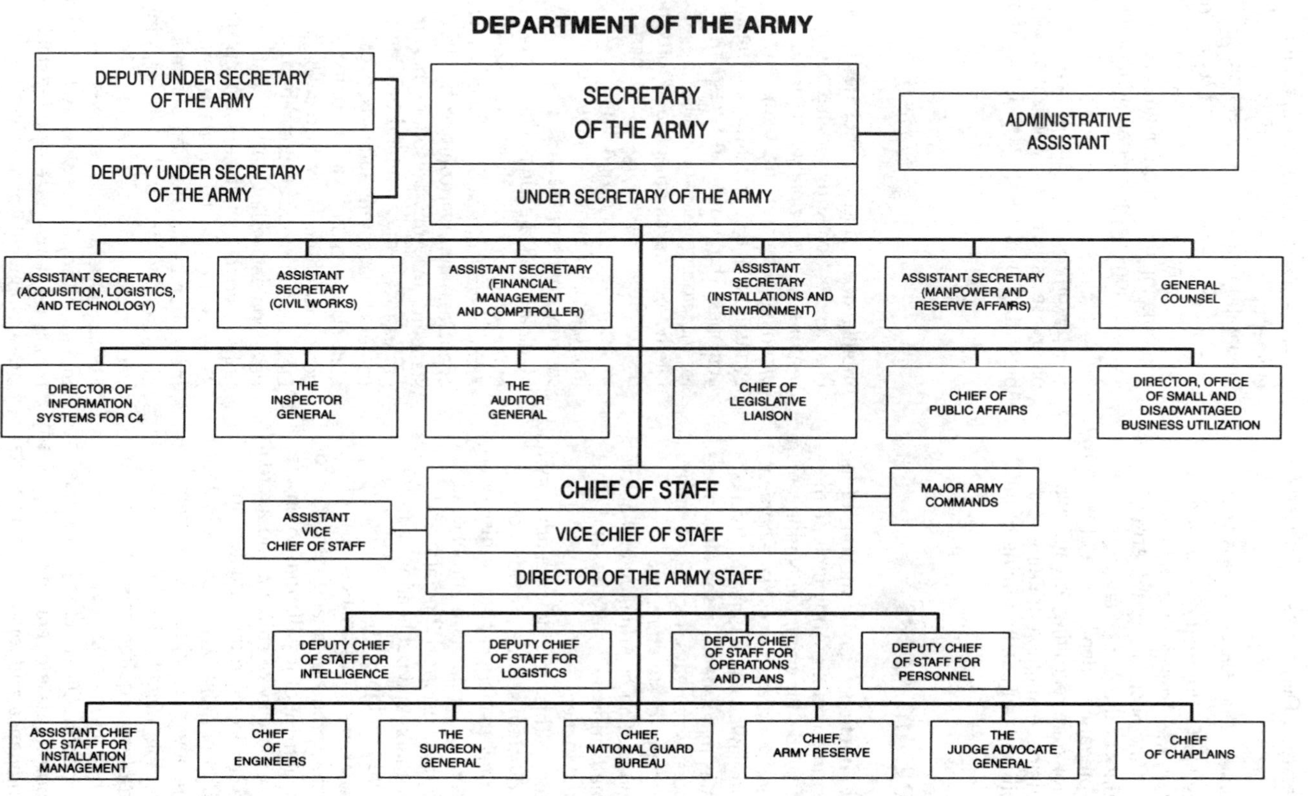
DEPARTMENT OF THE ARMY
DEPUTY UNDER SECRETARY OF THE ARMY
DEPUTY UNDER SECRETARY OF THE ARMY
SECRETARY OF THE ARMY
UNDER SECRETARY OF THE ARMY
ADMINISTRATIVE ASSISTANT
ASSISTANT SECRETARY (ACQUISITION, LOGISTICS, AND TECHNOLOGY)
ASSISTANT SECRETARY (CIVIL WORKS)
ASSISTANT SECRETARY (FINANCIAL MANAGEMENT AND COMPTROLLER)
ASSISTANT SECRETARY (INSTALLATIONS AND ENVIRONMENT)
ASSISTANT SECRETARY (MANPOWER AND RESERVE AFFAIRS)
GENERAL COUNSEL
DIRECTOR OF INFORMATION SYSTEMS FOR C4
THE INSPECTOR GENERAL
THE AUDITOR GENERAL
CHIEF OF LEGISLATIVE LIAISON
CHIEF OF PUBLIC AFFAIRS
DIRECTOR, OFFICE OF SMALL AND DISADVANTAGED BUSINESS UTILIZATION
CHIEF OF STAFF
VICE CHIEF OF STAFF
DIRECTOR OF THE ARMY STAFF
ASSISTANT VICE CHIEF OF STAFF
MAJOR ARMY COMMANDS
DEPUTY CHIEF OF STAFF FOR INTELLIGENCE
DEPUTY CHIEF OF STAFF FOR LOGISTICS
DEPUTY CHIEF OF STAFF FOR OPERATIONS AND PLANS
DEPUTY CHIEF OF STAFF FOR PERSONNEL
ASSISTANT CHIEF OF STAFF FOR INSTALLATION MANAGEMENT
CHIEF OF ENGINEERS
THE SURGEON GENERAL
CHIEF, NATIONAL GUARD BUREAU
CHIEF, ARMY RESERVE
THE JUDGE ADVOCATE GENERAL
CHIEF OF CHAPLAINS

administration, operation, efficiency, and such other activities as may be prescribed by the President or the Secretary of Defense as authorized by law.

For further information, call 703–695–7922.

Army Staff Presided over by the Chief of Staff, the Army Staff is the military staff of the Secretary of the Army. It is the duty of the Army Staff to:

—prepare for deployment of the Army and for such recruiting, organizing, supplying, equipping, training, mobilizing, and demobilizing of the Army as will assist the execution of any power, duty, or function of the Secretary or the Chief of Staff;

—investigate and report upon the efficiency of the Army and its preparation for military operations;

—act as the agent of the Secretary of the Army and the Chief of Staff in coordinating the action of all organizations of the Department of the Army; and

—perform such other duties not otherwise assigned by law as may be prescribed by the Secretary of the Army.

Program Areas

Civil Functions Civil functions of the Department of the Army include the Civil Works Program, the Nation's major Federal water resources development activity involving engineering works such as major dams, reservoirs, levees, harbors, waterways, locks, and many other types of structures; the administration of Arlington and Soldiers' Home National Cemeteries; and other related matters.

History This area includes advisory and coordination service provided on historical matters, including historical properties; formulation and execution of the Army Historical Program; and preparation and publication of histories required by the Army.

Installations This area consists of policies, procedures, and resources for management of installations to ensure the availability of efficient and affordable base services and infrastructure in support of military missions. It includes the review of facilities requirements and stationing, identification and validation of resource requirements, and program and budget development and justification. Other activities include support for base operations; real property maintenance and repair; environmental programs; military construction; family housing; base realignment and closure; and competitive sourcing.

Intelligence This area includes management of Army intelligence with responsibility for policy formulation, planning, programming, budgeting, evaluation, and oversight of intelligence activities. The Army staff is responsible for monitoring relevant foreign intelligence developments and foreign disclosure; imagery, signals, human, measurements, and signatures intelligence; counterintelligence; and security countermeasures.

Medical This area includes management of health services for the Army and, as directed for other services, agencies, and organizations; health standards for Army personnel; health professional education and training; career management authority over commissioned and warrant officer personnel of the Army Medical Department; medical research, materiel development, testing and evaluation; policies concerning health aspects of Army environmental programs and prevention of disease; and planning, programming, and budgeting for Army-wide health services.

Military Operations and Plans This includes Army forces strategy formation; mid-range, long-range, and regional strategy application; arms control, negotiation, and disarmament; national security affairs; joint service matters; net assessment; politico-military affairs; force mobilization and demobilization; force planning, programming structuring, development, analysis, and management; operational readiness; overall roles and missions; collective security; individual and unit training; psychological operations; information operations; unconventional warfare; counterterrorism; operations security; signal security; military aspects of space and sea; special plans; table of equipment development and approval; electronic warfare; nuclear and chemical matters; civil affairs; military support of civil defense; civil disturbance; domestic actions; audiovisual activities; command and control; automation and communications programs and activities; management of the program for law enforcement, correction, and crime prevention for military members of the Army; and physical security.

Reserve Components This area includes management of individual and unit readiness and mobilization for Reserve components, comprised of the Army National Guard and the U.S. Army Reserve.

Religious This area includes management of religious and moral leadership and chaplain support activities throughout the Department; religious ministrations, religious education, pastoral care, and counseling for Army military personnel; liaison with the ecclesiastical agencies; chapel construction requirements and design approval; and career management of clergymen serving in the Chaplains Branch.

Major Army Commands

Eighth U.S. Army Eighth U.S. Army provides forces to the commander in chief of United Nations Command and the Republic of Korea/U.S. Combined Forces Command.

For further information, contact Eighth U.S. Army. Phone, 011–82–279–13–8431. Internet, www.korea.army.mil/usfk/eusa/eusa.htm.

U.S. Army Corps of Engineers The U.S. Army Corps of Engineers (USACE) provides engineering, construction management, and environmental services in peace and war. The civil works program includes navigation, flood damage reduction, recreation, hydropower, environmental regulation, and other missions. The military program includes construction of Army and Air Force facilities, base realignment and closure activities, installation support, military contingency support, environmental restoration, strategic mobility, and international activities. USACE provides real estate acquisition, management, and disposal for the Army and Air Force, and researches and develops advanced technology for mobility/countermobility, force protection, and sustainment engineering. It also supports several Federal agencies and responds to natural disasters and other emergencies as the Nation's primary engineering agency.

For further information, contact USACE. Phone, 202–761–0000. Internet, www.usace.army.mil.

U.S. Army Criminal Investigation Command The U.S. Army Criminal Investigation Command (CID) investigates felony violations of the Uniform Code of Military Justice and other criminal provisions of the United States Code in which the Army has an interest. CID also provides protective services for senior Defense Department and Army leaders and supports field commanders and communities to solve major and violent crimes.

For further information, contact CID. Phone, 703–806–0400. Internet, www.belvoir.army.mil/cidc/index.htm.

U.S. Army Europe As U.S. European Command's primary land component, U.S. Army Europe (USAREUR) monitors armed conflicts and potential flashpoints throughout a 98-nation area. The U.S. Army's largest forward-deployed command, USAREUR supports NATO and U.S. bilateral, multinational, and unilateral objectives. It supports U.S. Army forces in the European Command area; receives and assists in the reception, staging, and onward movement and integration of U.S. forces; establishes, operates, and expands operational lines of communication; and supports U.S. combat commanders and joint and combined commanders.

For further information, contact USAREUR. Phone, 011–49–6221–39–4100. Internet, www.hqusareur.army.mil.

U.S. Army Forces Command The U.S. Army Forces Command (FORSCOM) trains, mobilizes, deploys, and sustains combat-ready forces capable of responding rapidly to crises worldwide. FORSCOM is the Army component of U.S. Atlantic Command. Consequently, the FORSCOM commander functions as commander of the Army forces of this unified command and plans for and provides military support to civil authorities, including response to natural disasters and civil emergencies.

For further information, contact FORSCOM. Phone, 404–464–5054. Internet, www.forscom.army.mil.

U.S. Army Intelligence and Security Command The U.S. Army Intelligence and Security Command (INSCOM) plans and conducts intelligence, security, and information operations for military commanders and national decisionmakers.

For further information, contact INSCOM. Phone, 703–706–1603. Internet, www.vulcan.belvoir.army.mil.

U.S. Army Materiel Command The U.S. Army Materiel Command (AMC) is the Army's principal materiel developer. AMC's missions include the development of weapon systems, advanced research on future technologies, and maintenance and distribution of spare parts and equipment. AMC works closely with industry, academia, the other military services, and other Government agencies to develop, test, and acquire every piece of equipment that soldiers and units need to accomplish their missions.

For further information, contact AMC. Phone, 703–617–9625. Internet, www.amc.army.mil.

U.S. Army Medical Command The U.S. Army Medical Command (MEDCOM) provides direction and planning for the Army Medical Department in conjunction with the Office of the Surgeon General. It develops and integrates doctrine, training, leader development, organization, and materiel for Army health services. MEDCOM also allocates resources and evaluates delivery of services.

For further information, contact MEDCOM. Phone, 703–681–3000. Internet, www.armymedicine.army.mil.

U.S. Army Military District of Washington The U.S. Army Military District of Washington conducts security and disaster-relief operations in the National Capital Region (NCR), provides base operations support to Army and other Defense Department organizations in the NCR, and conducts official and public events on behalf of the Nation's civilian and military leadership.

For further information, contact the U.S. Army Military District. Phone, 202–685–2807. Internet, www.mdw.army.mil.

U.S. Army Military Traffic Management Command The U.S. Army Military Traffic Management Command (MTMC) manages, for the Department of Defense, the worldwide transportation of troops, equipment, and personal property during peace and war. This entails single-port management, transportation, and traffic-management services, deployment planning and engineering, and development of new technologies. MTMC is also the link between DOD shippers and the commercial surface transportation industry, and maintains a presence in 22 ports worldwide as DOD's port manager.

For further information, contact MTMC. Phone, 703–681–6724. Internet, mtmc.army.mil.

U.S. Army Pacific The U.S. Army Pacific (USARPAC) provides trained and ready forces in support of military operations and peacetime engagements in the Asia-Pacific area of operations. USARPAC carries out a cooperative engagement strategy known as the Expanded Relations Program with the 41 Asian and Pacific nations within or bordering its area of responsibility. These countries include The Philippines, Thailand, Vietnam, Japan, Mongolia, Russia, China, South Korea, India, Bangladesh, Australia, New Zealand, Marshall Islands, and Papua New Guinea.

For further information, contact USARPAC. Phone, 808–438–2206. Internet, www.usarpac.army.mil.

U.S. Army South The U.S. Army South (USARSO) acts as the primary land component for United States Southern Command and provides support to U.S. Embassies and military groups throughout Central and South America and the Caribbean. USARSO is a major hub for deploying U.S. Army Reserve and National Guard forces to participate in humanitarian and civic assistance exercises in underdeveloped portions of countries in Latin America. It frequently supports missions to conduct search and rescue missions and render disaster assistance requested by host governments through U.S. Embassies.

For further information, contact USARSO. Phone, 011–507–288–3003. Internet, www.army.mil/USARSO.

U.S. Army Special Operations Command The U.S. Army Special Operations Command (USASOC) trains, equips, deploys, and sustains Army special operations forces for worldwide special operations supporting regional combatant commanders and country ambassadors. USASOC soldiers deploy to numerous countries conducting missions such as peacekeeping, humanitarian assistance, demining, and foreign internal defense. USASOC includes special forces, rangers, civil affairs, psychological operations, special operations aviation, and signal and support.

For further information, contact USASOC. Phone, 910–432–3000. Internet, www.usasoc.soc.mil.

U.S. Army Space and Missile Defense Command The U.S. Army Space and Missile Defense Command (SMDC) is the proponent for space and national missile defense, a materiel developer, and the Army's integrator for theater missile defense. SMDC ensures missile defense to protect the Nation and deployed forces, and facilitates Army access to space assets and products.

For further information, contact SMDC. Phone, 703–607–1873. Internet, www.smdc.army.mil.

U.S. Army Training and Doctrine Command The U.S. Army Training and Doctrine Command (TRADOC) serves as the architect for the 21st century Army, while ensuring that the Army is prepared to fight and win wars today. It does this through training, doctrine, and combat developments. To assist in these efforts, TRADOC integrates the activities of battlefield laboratories that develop and experiment with concepts in battlefield dynamics.

For further information, contact TRADOC. Phone, 757–727–3514. Internet, www.tradoc.army.mil.

United States Military Academy

West Point, NY 10996

Superintendent	LT. GEN. DANIEL W. CHRISTMAN
Commandant of Cadets	BRIG. GEN. ERIC T. OLSON
Dean of the Academic Board	BRIG. GEN. FLETCHER M. LAMKIN

The United States Military Academy is located at West Point, NY. The course is of 4 years' duration, during which the cadets receive, besides a general education, theoretical and practical training as junior officers. Cadets who complete the course satisfactorily receive the degree of Bachelor of Science and a commission as second lieutenant in the Army.

For further information, contact the Public Affairs Office, United States Military Academy, West Point, NY 10996. Phone, 914–938–4261. For information about Military Academy admission criteria and policies, contact the Office of the Registrar, United States Military Academy, West Point, NY 10996.

Sources of Information

Arlington and Soldiers' and Airmen's Home National Cemeteries For information write to the Superintendent, Arlington National Cemetery, Arlington, VA 22211–5003. Phone, 703–695–3175.

Army Historical Program For information concerning the Army Historical Program, write to the U.S. Army Center of Military History, HQDA (DAMH), CSA, 103 Third Avenue, Fort Lesley J. McNair, Washington, DC 20319–5058. Phone, 202–685–2714. Fax, 202–685–4564. Internet, www.army.mil/cmh-pg.

Information on historic buildings preservation and reuse is available through the Office of Historic Properties. Phone, 703–692–9892.

Civilian Employment For information, visit the Army civilian personnel website (Internet, www.cpol.army.mil) or contact the civilian personnel advisory center at the desired Army installation.

Contracts Contract procurement policies and procedures are the responsibility of the Deputy for Procurement, Office of the Assistant Secretary of the Army (Research, Development, and Acquisition), Room 2E661, The Pentagon, Washington, DC 20310–0103. Phone, 703–695–4101.

Environment Contact the Public Affairs Office, Office of the Chief of Public Affairs Headquarters, Department of the Army, Washington, DC 20314–1000 (phone, 202–761–0010); the Army Environmental Center (Internet, aec.army.mil); or the Army Environmental Policy Institute (Internet, www.aepi.army.mil).

Films, Videotapes, and Videodiscs Requests for loan of Army-produced films, videotapes, and videodiscs should be addressed to the Visual Information Support Centers of Army installations. Army productions are available for sale from the National Audiovisual Center (NAC), Washington, DC 20409–3701. Department of the Army pamphlet 25–90, *Visual Information Products Catalog,* lists the products that have been cleared for public release.

Freedom of Information and Privacy Act Requests Requests should be addressed to the Information Management Officer of the Army installation or activity responsible for the requested information.

Military Traffic Management Command Information concerning military transportation news and issues is available electronically through the Internet, at mtmc.army.mil.

Public Affairs and Community Relations For official Army information and community relations, contact the Office of the Chief of Public Affairs, Department of the Army, Washington, DC 20310–1508. Phone, 703–697–5081. During nonoffice hours, call 703–697–4200.

Publications Requests should be addressed to the Information Management Officer of the Army activity that publishes the requested publication. Official publications published by Headquarters, Department of the Army, are available from the National Technical Information Service, Department of Commerce, Attn: Order Preprocessing Section, 5285 Port Royal Road, Springfield, VA 22161–2171. Phone, 703–487–4600. If it is uncertain which Army activity published the publication, requests should be addressed to the Publishing Division, U.S. Army Publications and Printing Command, Room 1050, 2461 Eisenhower Avenue, Alexandria, VA 22331–0301. Phone, 202–325–6292.

Research Industry may obtain information on long-range research and development plans concerning future materiel requirements and objectives from the Commander, U.S. Army Materiel Command, Attn: AMCPA, 5001 Eisenhower Avenue, Alexandria, VA 22333–0001.

Small Business Activities Aids to assist small businesses in obtaining defense procurement contracts are available through the Office of Small and Disadvantaged Business Utilization, Office of the Secretary of the Army, Room 2A712, The Pentagon, Washington, DC 20310–0106. Phone, 703–697–2868.

Speakers Civilian organizations desiring an Army speaker may contact a nearby Army installation or write or call the Community Relations Division, Office of the Chief of Public Affairs, Department of the Army, Washington, DC 20310–1508. Phone, 703–697–5081. Requests for Army Reserve speakers may be addressed to HQDA (DAAR–PA), Washington, DC 20310–2423, or the local Army Reserve Center. Organizations in the Washington, DC, area desiring chaplain speakers may contact the Chief of Chaplains, Department of the Army, Washington, DC 20310–2700. Phone, 703–601–1140. Information on speakers may be obtained by contacting the Public Affairs Office, Office of the Chief of Engineers, Washington, DC 20314, or the nearest Corps of Engineer Division or District Office.

Military Career and Training Opportunities Information on all phases of Army enlistments and specialized training is available by writing to the U.S. Army Recruiting Command, Fort Sheridan, IL 60037 (phone, 312–926–3322). For information about career and training opportunities, contact the appropriate office listed below:

Army health professions: HQDA (SGPS–PD), Skyline No. 5, 5100 Leesburg Pike, Falls Church, VA 22041–3258. Phone, 703–681–8022.

Army reserves training opportunities for enlisted personnel: U.S. Army Recruiting Command, Public Affairs Office, 1307 Third Avenue, Fort Knox, KY 40121. Phone, 502–626–0167 or 800–223–3735, extension 6–0167. Internet, www.goarmy.com/job/usar/usar.htm.

Army reserves training opportunities for officers: Army Reserve Personnel Command, Public Affairs Office, One Reserve Way, St. Louis, MO 63132–5200. Phone, 314–592–0726, or 800–318–5298, extension 0726. Internet, www.goarmy.com/job/usar/usar.htm.

Army Reserve Officers' Training Corps: Professor of Military Science at the nearest college or university offering the program, or Army ROTC Regional Headquarters in your area.

Army National Guard training opportunities: Army National Guard, ARO–OAC–ME, Edgewood, MD 21010–5420. Phone, 301–671–4789.

Chaplains Corps: Office of the Chief of Chaplains, HQDA (DACH–PER), Washington, DC 20310–2700. Phone, 703–601–1172.

Judge Advocate General's Corps: Personnel, Plans, and Training Office, Office of the Judge Advocate General, Department of the Army, HQDA (DAJA–PT), Washington, DC 20310–2200. Phone, 703–588–6799.

U.S. Military Academy: Director of Admissions, United States Military Academy, West Point, NY 10996. Phone, 914–938–4041.

For further information concerning the Department of the Army, contact the Office of the Chief of Public Affairs, Headquarters, Department of the Army, Washington, DC 20310–1508. Phone, 703–697–5081. Internet, www.army.mil.

DEPARTMENT OF THE NAVY

The Pentagon, Washington, DC 20350
Phone, 703–545–6700. Internet, www.navy.mil.

SECRETARY OF THE NAVY	RICHARD DANZIG
Director, Office of Program Appraisal	REAR ADM. K.J. COSGRIFF, USN
Under Secretary of the Navy	JERRY M. HULTIN
Director, Small and Disadvantaged Business Utilization	J. HORVATH, *Acting*
Auditor General of the Navy	RICHARD A. LEACH, *Acting*
Director, Naval Criminal Investigative Service	DAVID L. BRANT
Chief of Information	REAR ADM. T.J. JURKOWSKY, USN
Chief of Legislative Affairs	REAR ADM. J.C. DAWSON, JR., USN
General Counsel	STEPHEN W. PRESTON
Principal Deputy General Counsel	J.E. SPARKS
Deputy General Counsel	EUGENE P. ANGRIST
Naval Inspector General	VICE ADM. L.F. GUNN, USN
Judge Advocate General of the Navy	REAR ADM. JOHN D. HUTSON, JAGC, USN
Deputy Judge Advocate General	REAR ADM. D.J. GUTER, JAGC, USN
Assistant Secretary of the Navy (Financial Management and Comptroller)	(VACANCY)
Principal Deputy	GLADYS J. COMMONS
Director, Office of Budget	REAR ADM. A.T. CHURCH, USN
Director, Office of Financial Operations	A. ANTHONY TISONE
Assistant Secretary of the Navy (Manpower and Reserve Affairs)	CAROLYN H. BECRAFT
Principal Deputy Assistant Secretary (Manpower)	KAREN S. HEATH
Deputy Assistant Secretary (Reserve Affairs)	MARK H. DAVIDSON
Deputy Assistant Secretary (Personnel Programs)	CHARLES L. TOMPKINS
Deputy Assistant Secretary (Civilian Personnel/Equal Employment Opportunity)	BETTY S. WELCH
Director, Naval Council of Personnel Boards	COL. R.S. MELTON, USMC
Executive Director, Board for Correction of Naval Records	W. DEAN PFEIFFER
Assistant Secretary of the Navy (Installations and Environment)	ROBERT B. PIRIE, JR.
Principal Deputy	DIANA H. JOSEPHSON
Deputy Assistant Secretary (Environment and Safety)	ELSIE L. MUNSELL
Deputy Assistant Secretary (Installation and Facilities)	DUNCAN HOLADAY
Deputy Assistant Secretary (Shore Resources)	RICHARD O. THOMAS

Deputy Assistant Secretary (Conversion and Redevelopment)	WILLIAM J. CASSIDY, JR.
Assistant Secretary of the Navy (Research, Development, and Acquisition)	H. LEE BUCHANAN
Principal Deputy	P. SCHNEIDER
Deputy Assistant Secretary (Air Programs)	WILLIAM A. STUSSIE
Deputy Assistant Secretary (Command, Control, Communications, Computers, and Intelligence)	D. UHLER
Deputy Assistant Secretary (Expeditionary Forces Programs)	BRIG. GEN. E.R. LANGSTON, USMC
Deputy Assistant Secretary (Mines and Undersea Warfare Programs)	D.F. GERRY
Deputy Assistant Secretary (Planning, Programming, and Resources)	WILLIAM J. SCHAEFER, JR.
Deputy Assistant Secretary (Ships)	MICHAEL C. HAMMES
Deputy for Acquisition and Business Management/Competition Advocate General	REAR ADM. G. JENKINS, JR., USN
Director, Acquisition Career Management	W.H. HAUENSTEIN
Acquisition Reform Executive	EILEEN ROBERSON
Chief of Naval Research	REAR ADM. PAUL G. GAFFNEY II, USN
Program Executive Officers/Direct Reporting Program Managers	REAR ADM. J. CHENEVEY, USN; REAR ADM. B. COBB, USN; REAR ADM. J. COOK, USN; REAR ADM. B. CROSS, USN; REAR ADM. J. DAVIS, USN; TIM DOUGLASS; BILL EATON; REAR ADM. J.B. GODWIN III, USN; REAR ADM. C.A. KEMP, USN; MAJ. GEN. L. KENNE, USMC; REAR ADM. D.G. MORRAL, USN; REAR ADM. L. NEWSOME, USN; COL. B. ROBERTSON, USMC; REAR ADM. J. SHIPWAY, USN

U.S. Navy

Chief of Naval Operations	ADM. J.L. JOHNSON, USN
Vice Chief of Naval Operations	ADM. D.L. PILLING, USN
Deputy Chief, Manpower and Personnel	VICE ADM. N.R. RYAN, JR., USN
Director of Naval Intelligence	REAR ADM. L.E. JACOBY, USN
Deputy Chief, Logistics	VICE ADM. J.F. AMERAULT, USN
Deputy Chief, Plans, Policy and Operations	VICE ADM. R.J. NATTER, USN
Director of Space and Information Warfare	REAR ADM. R.W. MAYO, USN
Director of Naval Training	VICE ADM. J.W. CRAINE, JR., USN
Deputy Chief, Resources, Warfare Requirements and Assessments	VICE ADM. C.C. LAUTENBACHER, JR., USN
Director of Navy Staff	REAR ADM. G.L. TALBOT, USN
Director of Naval Nuclear Propulsion Program	ADM. F.L. BOWMAN, USN
Director of Test and Evaluation and Technology Requirements	REAR ADM. P.G. GAFFNEY, USN
Surgeon General of the Navy	VICE ADM. R.A. NELSON, MC, USN
Director of Naval Reserve	REAR ADM. J.B. TOTUSHEK, USN

Oceanographer of the Navy	REAR ADM. R.D. WEST, USN
Chief of Chaplains of the Navy/Director of Religious Ministries	REAR ADM. A.B. HOLDERBY, JR., CHC, USN
Major Shore Commands:	
Commander, Naval Air Systems Command	VICE ADM. J.A. LOCKARD, USN
Commander, Naval Computer and Telecommunications Command	CAPT. G. ALLISON, USN
Commander, Naval Facilities Engineering Command	REAR ADM. L.M. SMITH, CEC, USN
Commander, Naval Legal Service Command	REAR ADM. D.J. GUTER, JAGC, USN
Commander, Naval Meteorology and Oceanography Command	REAR ADM. K.E. BARBOR, USN
Commander, Naval Sea Systems Command	VICE ADM. G.P. NANOS, JR., USN
Commander, Naval Security Group Command	REAR ADM. H.W. WHITON, USN
Commander, Naval Space Command	REAR ADM. T.E. ZELIBOR, USN
Commander, Naval Supply Systems Command	REAR ADM. K.W. LIPPERT, SC, USN
Commander, Space and Naval Warfare Systems Command	REAR ADM. J.A. GAUSS, USN
Commander, Naval Warfare Development Command	REAR ADM. B.J. SMITH, USN
Chief, Bureau of Medicine and Surgery	VICE ADM. R.A. NELSON, MC, USN
Chief of Naval Education and Training	VICE ADM. J.W. CRAINE, JR., USN
Chief of Naval Personnel	VICE ADM. N.R. RYAN, JR., USN
Director, Office of Naval Intelligence	REAR ADM. P.M. RATLIFF, USN
Director, Strategic Systems Program	REAR ADM. J.F. SHIPWAY, USN
Major Fleet Commands:	
Commander in Chief, U.S. Atlantic Fleet	ADM. V.E. CLARK, USN
Commander in Chief, U.S. Pacific Fleet	ADM. T.B. FARGO, USN
Commander in Chief, U.S. Naval Forces Europe	ADM. J.O. ELLIS, JR., USN
Commander, Military Sealift Command	REAR ADM. G.S. HOLDER, USN
Commander, Naval Forces Central Command	VICE ADM. C.W. MOORE, JR., USN
Commander, Naval Reserve Force	REAR ADM. J.B. TOTUSHEK, USN
Commander, Naval Special Warfare Command	REAR ADM. ERIC T. OLSON, USN
Commander, Operational Test and Evaluation Force	REAR ADM. R.E. BESAL, USN

U.S. Marine Corps

Commandant of the Marine Corps	GEN. J.L. JONES, USMC
Assistant Commandant of the Marine Corps	GEN. T.R. DAKE, USMC
Sergeant Major of the Marine Corps	SGT. MAJ. A.L. MCMICHAEL, USMC
Director, Marine Corps Staff	MAJ. GEN. A. FIELDS, USMC
Assistant Chief of Staff for Command, Control, Communications, Computers, and Intelligence	BRIG. GEN. R.M. SHEA, USMC
Deputy Chief of Staff for Aviation	LT. GEN. F. MCCORKLE, USMC
Deputy Chief of Staff for Installations and Logistics	LT. GEN. G.S. MCKISSOCK, USMC
Deputy Chief of Staff for Manpower and Reserve Affairs	LT. GEN. J.W. KLIMP, USMC
Deputy Chief of Staff for Plans, Policies, and Operations	LT. GEN. R.P. AYRES, JR., USMC
Deputy Chief of Staff for Programs and Resources	LT. GEN. M.J. WILLIAMS, USMC

Counsel for the Commandant	PETER M. MURPHY
Director of Administration and Resource Management	L.J. KELLY
Director of Intelligence	(VACANCY)
Director of Marine Corps History and Museums	COL. M.F. MONIGAN, USMC
Director of Public Affairs	BRIG. GEN. W.A. WHITLOW, USMC
Director, Special Projects Directorate	COL. T.W. GRIFFIN, USMC
Legislative Assistant to the Commandant	BRIG. GEN. T.L. CORWIN, USMC
Marine Corps Chaplain	CAPT. J.R. LAMONDE, USN
Marine Corps Dental Officer	CAPT. G. KVASKA, USN
Marine Corps Medical Officer	REAR ADM. J. JOHNSON, USN
President, Permanent Marine Corps Uniform Board	BRIG. GEN. J.T. CONWAY, USMC
Commanding General, Marine Corps Recruiting Command	MAJ. GEN. G.L. PARKS, USMC
Commanding General, Marine Corps Combat Development Command	LT. GEN. J.E. RHODES, USMC
Commander, Marine Corps Systems Command	BRIG. GEN. J.M. FEIGLEY, USMC
Commanding General, Marine Corps Base, Quantico	BRIG. GEN. L.H. HENDRICKSON, USMC

[For the Department of the Navy statement of organization, see the *Code of Federal Regulations*, Title 32, Part 700]

The primary mission of the Department of the Navy is to protect the United States, as directed by the President or the Secretary of Defense, by the effective prosecution of war at sea including, with its Marine Corps component, the seizure or defense of advanced naval bases; to support, as required, the forces of all military departments of the United States; and to maintain freedom of the seas.

The United States Navy was founded on October 13, 1775, when Congress enacted the first legislation creating the Continental Navy of the American Revolution. The Department of the Navy and the Office of Secretary of the Navy were established by act of April 30, 1798 (10 U.S.C. 5011, 5031). For 9 years prior to that date, by act of August 7, 1789 (1 Stat. 49), the conduct of naval affairs was under the Secretary of War.

The National Security Act Amendments of 1949 provided that the Department of the Navy be a military department within the Department of Defense (63 Stat. 578).

The Secretary of the Navy is appointed by the President as the head of the Department of the Navy and is responsible to the Secretary of Defense for the operation and efficiency of the Navy (10 U.S.C. 5031). The Department of the Navy includes the U.S. Coast Guard when it is operating as a Service in the Navy.

Secretary The Secretary of the Navy is the head of the Department of the Navy, responsible for the policies and control of the Department of the Navy, including its organization, administration, functioning, and efficiency. The members of the Secretary's executive administration assist in the discharge of the responsibilities of the Secretary of the Navy.

Advocacy The Office of the Judge Advocate General provides all legal advice and related services throughout the Department of the Navy, except for the advice and services provided by the General Counsel. It also provides legal and policy advice to the Secretary of the Navy on military justice, ethics, administrative law, claims, environmental law, operational and international law and treaty interpretation, and litigation involving

186-873 D-00--7

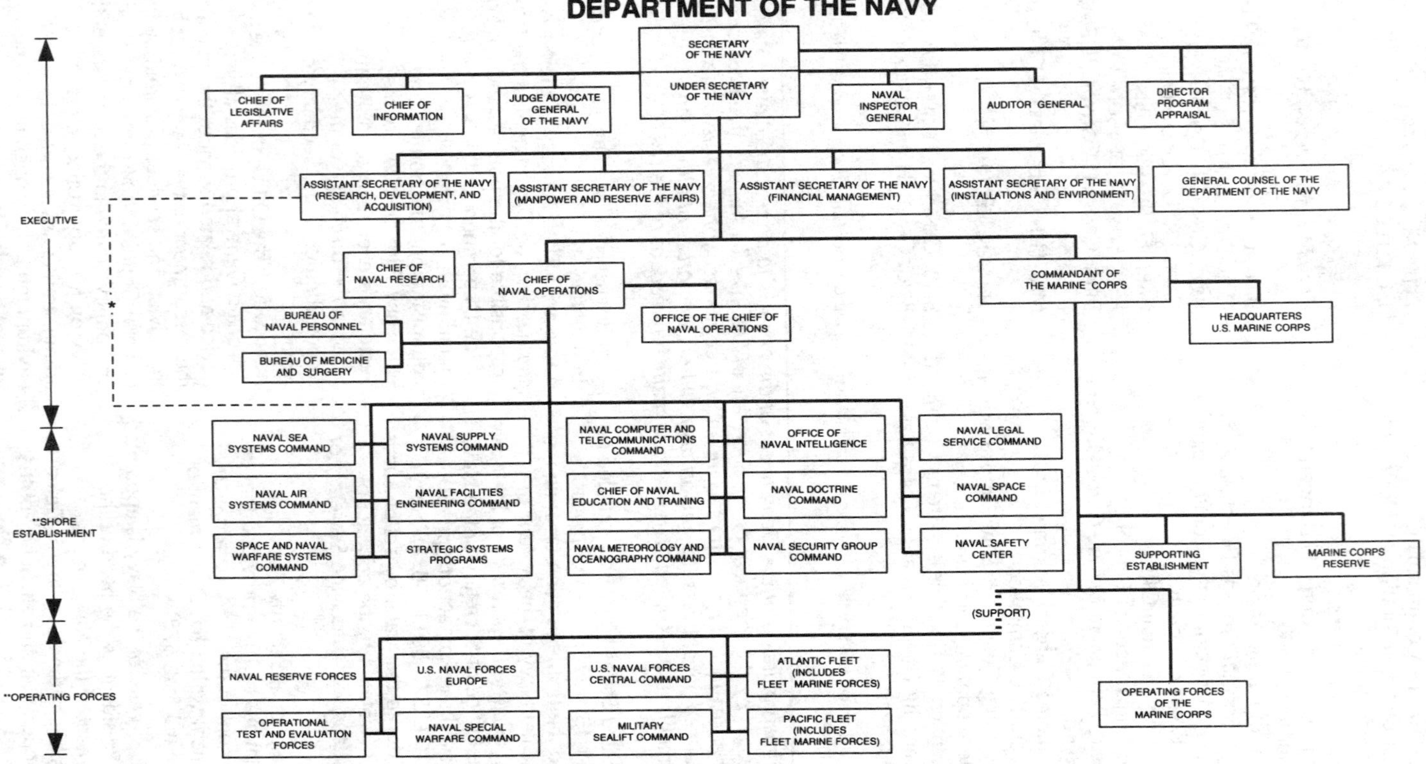

*Systems commands and SSP report to ASN (RDA) for acquisition matters only.
**Also includes other Echelon 2 commands and subordinate activities under the command or supervision of the designated organizations.

these issues. The Judge Advocate General provides technical supervision for the Naval Justice School at Newport, RI.

For further information, contact the Public Affairs Officer, Office of the Judge Advocate General, Department of the Navy, Washington Navy Yard, Suite 3000, 1322 Patterson Avenue SE., Washington, DC 20374–5066. Phone, 202–685–5193.

Criminal Investigations The Naval Criminal Investigative Service provide criminal investigative, counterintelligence, law enforcement and physical security, and information and personnel security support to Navy and Marine Corps organizations and personnel worldwide, both ashore and afloat. The Naval Criminal Investigative Service is comprised of law enforcement professionals who are investigators, crime laboratory technicians, technical investigative specialists, security specialists, and administrative support personnel.

For further information, contact the Director, Naval Criminal Investigative Service, Department of the Navy, Washington, DC 20388–5000 (phone, 202–433–8800) or the Operations Control Center/ Headquarters Duty Officer (phone, 202–433–9323).

Research The Office of Naval Research encourages, promotes, plans, initiates, and coordinates naval research; coordinates naval research and development conducted by other agencies and offices of the Department of the Navy; and supervises, manages, and controls activities within or for the Department of the Navy relating to patents, inventions, trademarks, copyrights, and royalty payments.

For further information, contact the Public Affairs Office, Office of Naval Research, Ballston Tower One, 800 North Quincy Street, Arlington, VA 22217–5660. Phone, 703–696–5031. Fax, 703–696–5940.

Operating Forces The operating forces of the Navy are responsible for naval operations necessary to carry out the Department of the Navy's role in upholding and advancing the national policies and interests of the United States. The operating forces of the Navy include the several fleets, seagoing forces, fleet marine forces and other assigned Marine Corps forces, the Military Sealift Command, Naval Reserve forces, and other forces and activities as may be assigned by the President or the Secretary of the Navy. The Chief of Naval Operations is responsible for the command and administration of the operating forces of the Navy.

The Atlantic Fleet is composed of ships, submarines, and aircraft that operate throughout the Atlantic Ocean and Mediterranean Sea.

The Naval Forces, Europe, includes forces assigned by the Chief of Naval Operations or made available from either the Pacific or Atlantic Fleet to operate in the European theater.

The Pacific Fleet is composed of ships, submarines, and aircraft operating throughout the Pacific and Indian Oceans.

The Military Sealift Command provides ocean transportation for personnel and cargo of all components of the Department of Defense and, as authorized, for other Federal agencies; operates and maintains underway replenishment ships and other vessels providing mobile logistic support to elements of the combatant fleets; and operates ships in support of scientific projects and other programs for Federal agencies.

Other major commands of the operating forces of the Navy are the Naval Forces Central Command, Operational Test and Evaluation Force, Naval Special Warfare Command, and Naval Reserve Force.

Activities

Air Systems The Naval Air Systems Command provides material support to the Navy and Marine Corps for aircraft, airborne weapon systems, avionics, related photographic and support equipment, ranges, and targets.

For further information, contact the Commander, Naval Air Systems Command, Naval Air Warfare Center, Patuxent River, MD 20570. Phone, 301–342–3282.

Coast Guard The Commandant of the Coast Guard reports to the Secretary of the Navy and the Chief of Naval Operations when the Coast Guard is operating as a service in the Navy, and represents the Coast Guard before the Joint Chiefs of Staff. During such service, Coast Guard operations are integrated and uniform with Department of the Navy operations to the maximum extent possible. The Commandant of the Coast Guard organizes, trains, prepares, and maintains the readiness of the Coast Guard for the performance of national defense missions, as directed. The Commandant also maintains a security capability; enforces Federal laws and regulations on and under the high seas and waters subject to the jurisdiction of the United States; and develops, establishes, maintains, and operates aids to maritime navigation and ice breaking and rescue facilities, with due regard to the requirements of national defense.

Computers and Telecommunications The Naval Computer and Telecommunications Command performs functions to provide, operate, and maintain all Navy ashore communications resources and all non-tactical information and resources for command, control, and administration of the Navy and those elements of the Defense Communications System assigned to the Navy.

For further information, contact the Commander, Naval Computer and Telecommunications Command, 4401 Massachusetts Avenue NW., Washington, DC 20390–5290. Phone, 202–685–1085.

Cryptology The Naval Security Group Command performs cryptologic functions; provides, operates, and maintains an adequate naval security group; approves requirements for the use of existing naval security group capabilities and resources; and coordinates the execution of approved cryptologic programs.

For further information, contact the Commander, Naval Security Group Command, 9800 Savage Road, Fort Meade, MD 20755. Phone, 240–373–3000.

Education and Training The Office of Naval Education and Training provides shore-based education and training for Navy, certain Marine Corps, and other personnel; develops specifically designated education and training afloat programs for the fleet; Provides voluntary and dependents education; and participates with research and development activities in the development and implementation of the most effective teaching and training systems and devices for optimal education and training.

For further information, contact the Chief of Naval Education and Training, Naval Air Station, Department of the Navy, Pensacola, FL 32508–5100. Phone, 904–452–4858.

Facilities The Naval Facilities Engineering Command provides material and technical support to the Navy and Marine Corps for shore facilities, real property and utilities, fixed ocean systems and structures, transportation and construction equipment, energy, environmental and natural resources management, and support of the naval construction forces.

For further information, contact the Commander, Naval Facilities Engineering Command, Washington Navy Yard, Suite 1000, 1322 Patterson Avenue SE., Washington, DC 20374. Phone, 202–685–9000.

Intelligence The Office of Naval Intelligence ensures the fulfillment of the intelligence requirements and responsibilities of the Department of the Navy.

For further information, contact the Director, Office of Naval Intelligence, Department of the Navy, 4600 Silver Hill Road, Washington, DC 20389–5000. Phone, 202–763–3552; or 301–763–3557 (hotline).

Manpower The Office of Naval Personnel directs the procurement, distribution, administration, and career motivation of the military personnel of the regular and reserve components of the U.S. Navy to meet the quantitative and qualitative manpower requirements determined by the Chief of Naval Operations. It also directs the management and administration of the Navy civilian personnel/equal employment opportunity programs and develops servicewide programs for improved human resources management.

For further information, contact the Naval Personnel Command, Department of the Navy, Federal Office Building 2, Washington, DC 20370–5000. Phone, 703–614–1271.

Medicine The Bureau of Medicine and Surgery directs the provision of medical and dental services for Navy and Marine Corps personnel and their dependants; administers the execution and implementation of contingency support plans and programs to provide effective medical and dental readiness capability; provides professional and technical medical and dental service to the fleet, fleet marine force, and shore activities of the Navy; and ensures cooperation with civil authorities in matters pertaining to public health disasters and other emergencies.

For further information, contact the Bureau of Medicine and Surgery, Department of the Navy, Twenty-third and E Streets NW., Washington, DC 20372–5120. Phone, 202–762–3701.

Oceanography The Naval Meteorology and Oceanography Command and the Naval Observatory are responsible for the science, technology, and engineering operations which are essential to explore the ocean and the atmosphere and to provide astronomical data and time for naval and related national objectives. To that end, the naval oceanographic program studies astrometry, hydrography, meteorology, oceanography, and precise time.

For further information, contact the following offices: Oceanographer of the Navy, U.S. Naval Observatory, Washington, DC 20392–1800. Phone, 202–762–1026. Commander, Naval Meteorology and Oceanography Command, Stennis Space Center, MS 39529–5005. Phone, 601–688–4726. Superintendent, Naval Observatory, Washington, DC 20392–5100. Phone, 202–653–1541.

Sea Systems The Naval Sea Systems Command provides material support to the Navy and Marine Corps and to the Departments of Defense and Transportation for ships, submarines, and other sea platforms, shipboard combat systems and components, other surface and undersea warfare and weapons systems, and ordnance expendables not specifically assigned to other system commands.

For further information, contact the Commander, Naval Sea Systems Command, Washington, DC 20362–5101. Phone, 703–602–3328.

Space and Naval Warfare The Space and Naval Warfare Systems Command provides technical and material support to the Department of the Navy for space systems; command, control, communications, and intelligence systems; and electronic warfare and undersea surveillance.

For further information, contact the Commander, Space and Naval Warfare Systems Command, 4301 Pacific Highway, San Diego, CA 92110. Phone, 619–524–7059.

Strategic Systems The Office of Strategic Systems Programs provides development, production, and material support to the Navy for fleet ballistic missile and strategic weapon systems, security, training of personnel, and the installation and direction of necessary supporting facilities.

For further information, contact the Director, Strategic Systems Programs, Department of the Navy, 1931 Jefferson Davis Highway, Arlington, VA 22202–3518. Phone, 703–607–2715.

Supply Systems The Naval Supply Systems Command provides supply management policies and methods and administers related support service systems for the Navy and Marine Corps.

For further information, contact the Commander, Naval Supply Systems Command, 5450 Carlisle Pike, Mechanicsburg, PA 17055–0791. Phone, 717–790–6906.

Warfare Development The Navy Warfare Development Command plans and coordinates experiments employing emerging operational concepts; represents the Department of the Navy in joint and other service laboratories and facilities and tactical development commands; and publishes and disseminates naval doctrine.

For further information, contact the Commander, Navy Warfare Development Command, 686 Chushing Road, Newport, RI 02841. Phone, 401–841–4262.

United States Marine Corps

Commandant of the Marine Corps,
Headquarters, U.S. Marine Corps, Washington, DC 20380–0001
Phone, 703–614–2344. Internet, www.usmc.mil.

The United States Marine Corps was established on November 10, 1775, by resolution of the Continental Congress. Marine Corps composition and functions are detailed in 10 U.S.C. 5063.

The Marine Corps, which is part of the Department of the Navy, is the smallest of the Nation's combat forces and is the only service specifically tasked by Congress to be able to fight in the air, on land, and at sea. Although marines fight in each of these dimensions, they are primarily a maritime force, inextricably linked with the Navy to move from the sea to fight on land.

The Marine Corps conducts entry-level training for its enlisted marines at two bases, Marine Corps Recruit Depot, Parris Island, SC, and Marine Corps Recruit Depot, San Diego, CA. Officer candidates are evaluated at Officer Candidate School at Marine Corps Combat Development Command, Quantico, VA. Marines train to be first on the scene to respond to attacks on the United States or its interests, acts of political violence against Americans abroad, disaster relief, humanitarian assistance, or evacuation of Americans from foreign countries.

Marine Corps Districts

District	Address
1st	605 Stewart Ave., Garden City, NY 11530–4761
4th	Bldg. 54, Suite 3, New Cumberland, PA 17072–0806
6th	Marine Corps Recruit Depot, P.O. Box 19201, Parris Island, SC 29905–9201
8th	Bldg. 10, Naval Support Activity, New Orleans, LA 70142
9th	3805 E. 155th St., Kansas City, MO 64147–1309
12th	3704 Hochmuth Ave., San Diego, CA 92140–5191

For further information, contact the Division of Public Affairs, Headquarters, U.S. Marine Corps, 2 Navy Annex, Washington, DC 20380–1775. Phone, 703–614–1034. Internet, www.usmc.mil.

United States Naval Academy

Annapolis, MD 21402–5018
Phone, 800–638–9156. Internet, www.nadn.navy.mil.

The United States Naval Academy is the undergraduate college of the naval service. Through its comprehensive 4-year program, which stresses excellence in academics, physical education, professional training, conduct, and honor, the Academy prepares young men and women morally, mentally, and physically to be professional officers in the Navy and Marine Corps. All graduates receive a bachelor of science degree in 1 of 18 majors.

For further information concerning the United States Naval Academy, contact the Superintendent, United States Naval Academy, Annapolis, MD 21402–5018.

Sources of Information

Civilian Employment Information about civilian employment opportunities within the Department of the Navy in the Washington, DC, metropolitan area can be obtained from the Human Resources Service Center, Capital Region, Suite 40102, 321 Cryptologic Court NW., Washington, DC 20393–5442; or the Commandant of the Marine Corps (ARCA), Headquarters, U.S. Marine

Corps, Washington, DC 20380 (phone, 703–697–7474).

Consumer Activities Research programs of the Office of Naval Research cover a broad spectrum of scientific fields, primarily for the needs of the Navy, but much information is of interest to the public. Inquiries on specific research programs should be directed to the Office of Naval Research (Code 10), 800 North Quincy Street, Arlington, VA 22217–5660. Phone, 703–696–5031. Inquiries on specific technology programs should be directed to the Director, Office of Naval Technology (Code 20), 800 North Quincy Street, Arlington, VA 22217–5000. Phone, 703–696–5115.

Contracts and Small Business Activities Information in these areas can be obtained from the Assistant Secretary of the Navy (Research, Engineering, and Systems), Department of the Navy, 2211 Jefferson Davis Highway, Arlington, VA 22244–5120 (phone, 703–602–2700). Information about small businesses, minority-owned businesses, and labor surplus activities with the Marine Corps can be obtained from the Marine Corps Small Business Specialist (LS), Installations and Logistics Department, Headquarters, U.S. Marine Corps, Washington, DC 20380. Phone, 703–696–1022.

Environment For information on environmental protection and natural resources management programs of the Navy and Marine Corps, contact the Assistant Secretary of the Navy (Installations and Environment), Environment and Safety, 1000 Navy Pentagon, Room 4A686, Washington, DC, 20350–1000. Phone, 703–614–1304.

General Inquiries Navy and Marine Corps recruiting offices, installation commanders, and Commanding Officers of Marine Corps Districts (see listing in the preceding text) can answer general inquiries concerning the Navy and Marine Corps and their community and public information programs.

The Office of Information provides accurate and timely information about the Navy so that the general public, the press, and Congress may understand and assess the Navy's programs, operations, and needs. The Office also coordinates Navy participation in community events and supervises the Navy's internal information programs. Phone, 703–697–5342.

Speakers and Films Information can be obtained on the following: speakers (phone, 703–697–8711); films (phone, 703–697–5342); and the Naval Recruiting Exhibit Center (phone, 904–452–5348). For information on Navy speakers, contact the Office of Information, Department of the Navy, Washington, DC 20350. Phone, 202–695–0965. For information on Marine Corps speakers, contact the Director of Public Affairs, Headquarters, U.S. Marine Corps, Washington, DC 20380–0001; or contact the Director of any Marine Corps District (see listing in the preceding text).

Tours To broaden the understanding of the mission, functions, and programs of the Naval Observatory, regular night tours and special group day tours are conducted. The night tours are open to the general public and are given every Monday night, except on Federal holidays. Information concerning activities of the observatory and public tours may be obtained by writing to the Superintendent, Naval Observatory, Washington, DC 20392–5100. Phone, 202–762–1538.

Marine Corps Military Career and Training Opportunities The Marine Corps conducts enlisted personnel and officer training programs; provides specialized skill training; participates in the Naval Reserve Officers Training Corps Program for commissioning officers in the Marine Corps; provides the Platoon Leaders Class program for commissioning officers in the Marine Corps Reserve to college freshmen, sophomores, or juniors and the Officer Candidate Class program for college graduates or seniors.

Information about these programs is available at most civilian educational institutions and Navy and Marine Corps recruiting stations. Interested persons also may write directly to the Commandant of the Marine Corps

(M&RA), Washington, DC 20380–0001. Phone, 703–614–2914. Information about Marine Corps Reserve opportunities can be obtained from local Marine Corps recruiting stations or Marine Corps Reserve Drill Centers. Interested persons may also write directly to the Commandant of the Marine Corps (M&RA, RA), Washington, DC 20380–0001.

For further information concerning the Navy, contact the Office of Information, Department of the Navy, Washington, DC 20350. Phone, 703–697–7391. Internet, www.navy.mil. For further information regarding the Marine Corps, contact the Legislative Assistant to the Commandant and Director of Public Affairs, Headquarters, U.S. Marine Corps, Washington, DC 20380. Phone, 703–614–1492.

DEFENSE AGENCIES

Ballistic Missile Defense Organization

The Pentagon, Washington, DC 20301–7100
Phone, 703–697–4040. Internet, www.acq.osd.mil/bmdo/html/bmdolink.html.

Director	LT. GEN. RONALD KADISH, USAF
Deputy Director	MAJ. GEN. PETER FRANKLIN, USA
Executive Director	ROBERT SNYDER
Chief of Staff	CHARLES RANDOW

[For the Ballistic Missile Defense Organization statement of organization, see the *Code of Federal Regulations,* Title 32, Part 388]

The Ballistic Missile Defense Organization (BMDO) (formerly the Strategic Defense Initiative Organization) was established to develop ballistic and cruise missile defense systems that are capable of providing a limited defense of the United States and a flexible, interoperable family of theater missile defense systems that may be forward deployed to protect elements of the U.S. Armed Forces and allies of the United States. BMDO is under the authority, direction, and control of the Under Secretary of Defense for Acquisition, Technology, and Logistics.

BMDO's mission is to manage and direct DOD's ballistic missile defense acquisition programs, which include theater missile defense, and to develop and deploy, if directed, a national missile defense program designed to protect the United States from a long-range missile threat posed by rogue nations. It is responsible for the continuing research and development of technologies that are relevant for long-term ballistic missile defense.

For further information, contact the Financial Management Directorate, Ballistic Missile Defense Organization, Washington, DC 20301–7100. Phone, 703–604–3993. Internet, www.acq.osd.mil/bmdo/html/bmdolink.html.

Defense Advanced Research Projects Agency

3701 North Fairfax Drive, Arlington, VA 22203–1714
Phone, 703–526–6624. Internet, www.darpa.mil.

Director	F.L. FERNANDEZ
Deputy Director	JANE ALEXANDER

The Defense Advanced Research Projects Agency is a separately organized agency within DOD and is under the authority, direction, and control of the Director of Defense Research and Engineering. The Agency engages in research and development projects essential to DOD and conducts prototype projects that embody technology that may be incorporated into joint programs, programs in support of deployed U.S. forces, selected military department programs, or dual-use programs and, on request, assists the military departments in their research and development efforts. To this end, the Agency arranges, manages, and directs the performance of work connected with assigned advanced projects by the military departments, other Government agencies, individuals, private business entities, and educational or research institutions, as appropriate.

For further information, contact the Defense Advanced Research Projects Agency, 3701 North Fairfax Drive, Arlington, VA 22203–1714. Phone, 703–526–6624. Internet, www.darpa.mil.

Defense Commissary Agency

1300 ''E'' Avenue, Fort Lee, VA 23801–1800
Phone, 804–734–8721. Internet, www.commissaries.com.

Director	MAJ. GEN. ROBERT J. COURTER, JR., USAF
Chief Executive Officer	JOHN F. MCGOWAN
Executive Director for Support	CROSBY H. JOHNSON

The Defense Commissary Agency was established in 1990 and is under the authority, direction, and control of the Under Secretary of Defense for Personnel and Readiness. The Agency is responsible for providing an efficient and effective worldwide system of commissaries for selling groceries and household supplies at low, practical prices to members of the military services, their families, and other authorized patrons, while maintaining high standards of quality, facilities, products, and service.

Sources of Information

Employment General employment inquiries should be addressed to the Human Resources Business Unit, Defense Commissary Agency, 5001 Eisenhower Avenue, Alexandria, VA 22333–0000. Phone, 703–274–0183 or 703–274–0184.

Procurement and Small Business Activities For information, contact the Director, Small and Disadvantaged Business Utilization, Defense Commissary Agency, 1300 ''E'' Avenue, Fort Lee, VA 23801–1800. Phone, 804–734–8740.

Publication *A Business Guide for Marketing to the Defense Commissary Agency* is available free of charge from the Director, Small and Disadvantaged Business Utilization, Defense Commissary Agency, 1300 ''E'' Avenue, Fort Lee, VA 23801–1800. Phone, 804–734–8740.

For further information, contact the Chief, Safety, Security, and Administration, 1300 ''E'' Avenue, Fort Lee, VA 23801–1800. Phone, 804–734–8808. Internet, www.commissaries.com.

Defense Contract Audit Agency

Suite 2135, 8725 John J. Kingman Road, Fort Belvoir, VA 22060–6219
Phone, 703–767–3200. Internet, www.dcaa.mil.

Director	WILLIAM H. REED
Deputy Director	MICHAEL J. THIBAULT

The Defense Contract Audit Agency was established in 1965 and is under the authority, direction, and control of the Under Secretary of Defense (Comptroller)/Chief Financial Officer. The Agency performs all necessary contract audit functions for DOD and provides accounting and financial advisory services to all Defense components responsible for procurement and contract administration. These services are provided in connection with the negotiation, administration, and settlement of contracts and subcontracts. They include evaluating the acceptability of costs claimed or proposed by contractors and reviewing the efficiency and economy of contractor operations. Other Government agencies may request the Agency's services under appropriate arrangements.

The Agency manages its operations through 5 regional offices responsible for approximately 81 field audit offices throughout the United States and overseas. Each region is responsible for the contract auditing function in its assigned area.

Regional Offices—Defense Contract Audit Agency

Region	Address	Director	Telephone
CENTRAL	6321 E. Campus Circle, Irving, TX 75063–2742	Francis P. Summers, Jr.	972–753–2513
EASTERN	Suite 300, 2400 Lake Park Dr., Smyrna, GA 30080–7644.	Richard R. Buhre	770–319–4400
MID–ATLANTIC	Suite 1000, 615 Chestnut St., Philadelphia, PA 19106–4498.	Barbara C. Reilly	215–597–7451
NORTHEASTERN	Suite 300, 59 Composite Way, Lowell, MA 01851–5150	Dave Dzivak	978–551–9715
WESTERN	Suite 300, 16700 Valley View Ave., La Mirada, CA 90638–5830.	Robert W. Matter	714–228–7001

For further information, contact the Executive Officer, Defense Contract Audit Agency, Suite 2135, 8725 John J. Kingman Road, Fort Belvoir, VA 22060–6219. Phone, 703–767–3265. Internet, www.dcaa.mil.

Defense Contract Management Agency

John J. Kingman Road, Fort Belvoir, VA 22060
Phone, 703–767–2454. Internet, www.dcmc.hq.dla.mil.

Director	MAJ. GEN. TIMOTHY P. MALISHENKO, USAF
Deputy Director	THOMAS E. BRUNK

The Defense Contract Management Agency was established by the Deputy Secretary of Defense on March 27, 2000, and is under the authority, direction, and control of the Under Secretary of Defense (Acquisition, Technology, and Logistics). It is responsible for DOD contract management in support of the military departments, other DOD components, the National Aeronautics and Space Administration, other designated Federal and State agencies, foreign governments, and international organizations, as appropriate.

For further information, contact the Public Affairs Office, Defense Contract Management Agency, John J. Kingman Road, Fort Belvoir, VA 22060. Phone, 703–767–2454. Internet, www.dcmc.hq.dla.mil.

Defense Finance and Accounting Service

Room 425, Crystal Mall 3, Arlington, VA 22240–5291
Phone, 703–607–2616. Internet, www.dfas.mil.

Director	THOMAS R. BLOOM
Deputy Director	BRUCE M. CARNES

The Defense Finance and Accounting Service was established in 1990 and is under the authority, direction, and control of the Under Secretary of Defense (Comptroller)/Chief Financial Officer. The Service is responsible for making all payments, including payroll and contracts, and for maintaining all finance and accounting records for DOD. It is responsible for preparing annual financial statements for DOD and for the consolidation, standardization, upgrading, and integration of finance and accounting requirements, functions, processes, operations, and systems in the Department.

For further information, contact the Public Affairs Office, Room 228, Crystal Mall 3, Arlington, VA 22240–5291. Phone, 703–607–2716. Internet, www.dfas.mil.

Defense Information Systems Agency

701 South Courthouse Road, Arlington, VA 22204–2199
Phone, 703–607–6900. Internet, www.disa.mil/disahomejs.html.

Director	LT. GEN. DAVID J. KELLEY, USA
Vice Director	MAJ. GEN. JOHN H. CAMPBELL, USAF
Chief of Staff	CAPT. PAUL T. HAUSER, USN

The Defense Information Systems Agency (DISA), originally established as the Defense Communications Agency, is is under the authority, direction, and control of the Assistant Secretary of Defense (Command, Control, Communications, and Intelligence). The Agency is responsible for planning, developing, and supporting command, control, communications, and information systems that serve the needs of the national command authorities under all conditions of peace and war. It manages the defense information infrastructure and ensures the interoperability of the infrastructure with theater and tactical command and control systems, NATO and/or allied C^3 systems, and those national and/or international commercial systems that affect the DISA mission. It is responsible for the DOD telecommunications and information processing facilities; supports national security emergency preparedness telecommunications functions of the National Communications System.

For further information, contact the Public Affairs Office, Defense Information Systems Agency, 701 South Courthouse Road, Arlington, VA 22204–2199. Phone, 703–607–6900. Internet, www.disa.mil/disahomejs.html.

Defense Intelligence Agency

The Pentagon, Washington, DC 20301–7400
Phone, 703–695–0071. Internet, www.dia.mil.

Director	VICE ADM. THOMAS R. WILSON, USN
Deputy Director	JEREMY C. CLARK
Chief of Staff	BARBARA A. DUCKWORTH

The Defense Intelligence Agency (DIA) was established in 1961 and is under the authority, direction, and control of the Assistant Secretary of Defense (Command, Control, Communications, and Intelligence). DIA provides timely, objective, and cogent military intelligence to soldiers, sailors, airmen, and marines and to the decisionmakers and policymakers of DOD and the Federal Government. To accomplish its assigned mission, DIA produces foreign military intelligence for national foreign intelligence and counterintelligence products; coordinates all DOD intelligence collection requirements; operates the Central Measurement and Signature Intelligence Organization; manages the Defense Human Intelligence Service and the Defense Attaché System; operates the Joint Military Intelligence College; provides key foreign weapons systems intelligence to U.S. weapons planners and the weapons acquisition community; and overseas the defense intelligence community, under the auspices of the Military Intelligence Board, on major intelligence issues involving support to deployed forces, assessments, policy, and resources.

For further information, contact the Public Affairs Office, Defense Intelligence Agency, Washington, DC 20301. Phone, 703–695–0071. Internet, www.dia.mil.

Defense Legal Services Agency

The Pentagon, Washington, DC 20301–1600
Phone, 703–695–3341. Internet, www.defenselink.mil/dodgc.

Director (General Counsel, Department of Defense)	(VACANCY)
Principal Deputy Director (Principal Deputy General Counsel)	DOUGLAS A. DWORKIN

The Defense Legal Services Agency was established in 1981 and is under the authority, direction, and control of the General Counsel of the Department of Defense, who also serves as its Director.

The Agency provides legal advice and services for defense agencies and DOD field activities. It also provides technical support and assistance for development of the Department's legislative program; coordinates positions on legislation and Presidential Executive orders; provides a centralized legislative and congressional document reference and distribution point for the Department; and maintains the Department's historical legislative files.

For further information, contact the Administrative Officer, Defense Legal Services Agency, The Pentagon, Washington, DC 20301–1600. Phone, 703–697–8343. Internet, www.defenselink.mil/dodgc.

Defense Logistics Agency

Suite 2533, 8725 John J. Kingman Road, Fort Belvoir, VA 22060–6221
Phone, 703–767–6666. Internet, www.dla.mil.

Director	LT. GEN. H.T. GLISSON, USA
Principal Deputy Director	REAR ADM. RAYMOND A. ARCHER III, SC, USN

The Defense Logistics Agency (DLA) is under the authority, direction, and control of the Under Secretary of Defense for Acquisition, Technology, and Logistics. It supports both the logistics requirements of the military services and their acquisition of weapons and other materiel. The Agency provides logistics support and technical services to all branches of the military and to a number of Federal agencies. Agency supply centers consolidate the requirements of the military services and procure the supplies in sufficient quantities to meet their projected needs. The Agency manages supplies in eight commodity areas: fuel, food, clothing, construction material, electronic supplies, general supplies, industrial supplies, and medical supplies. The Defense National Stockpile of strategic and critical materials is maintained to reduce the Nation's dependence upon foreign sources of supply for such materials in times of national emergency.

Primary Level Field Activities—Defense Logistics Agency

Activity	Commander
Defense Distribution Center	Brig. Gen. B. Doomick, USA
Defense Energy Support Center	Jeff Jones
Defense Industrial Supply Center	N. Ranalli
Defense Logistics Information Service	Col. R.L. Songer, USMC
Defense National Stockpile Center	R.H. Connelly
Defense Reutilization and Marketing Service	Capt. Richard H. Feirabend, SC, USN
Defense Supply Centers:	
Columbus	Brig. Gen. M.L. Saunders, USAF
Philadelphia	Brig. Gen. D.G. Mongeon, USA
Richmond	Rear Adm. Mark A. Young, SC, USN

Sources of Information

DOD Surplus Sales Program Questions concerning this program or placement on the Department of Defense bidders list should be addressed to DOD Surplus Sales, International Sales Office, 74 Washington Avenue North, Battle Creek, MI 49017–3092. Phone, 800–468–8289.

Employment For the Washington, DC, metropolitan area, inquiries and applications should be addressed to Defense Logistics Agency, Attn: DASC–R, 8725 John J. Kingman Road, Fort Belvoir, VA 22060–6221. Phone, 703–767–7100.

Schools interested in participating in the Agency's job recruitment program should direct inquiries to the Defense Logistics Agency, Attn: CAHS, 8725 John J. Kingman Road, Fort Belvoir, VA 22060–6221.

Environment For information concerning the Agency's program, contact the Defense Logistics Agency, Attn: CAAE, 8725 John J. Kingman Road, Fort Belvoir, VA 22060–6221. Phone, 703–767–6303.

Procurement and Small Business Activities For information, contact the Director, Small and Disadvantaged Business Utilization, Defense Logistics Agency, Attn: DDAS, 8725 John J. Kingman Road, Fort Belvoir, VA 22060–6221. Phone, 703–767–1650.

For further information, contact the Defense Logistics Agency, Suite 2533, 8725 John J. Kingman Road, Fort Belvoir, VA 22060–6221. Phone, 703–767–6666. Internet, www.dla.mil.

Defense Security Cooperation Agency

2800 Defense Pentagon, Washington, DC 20301–2800
Phone, 703–604–6604. Internet, www.dsca.osd.mil.

Director	LT. GEN. MICHAEL S. DAVISON, JR., USA
Deputy Director	ROBERT KELTZ

The Defense Security Cooperation Agency (formerly the Defense Security Assistance Agency) was established in 1998 and is under the authority, direction, and control of the Assistant Secretary of Defense for International Security Affairs. Under its new and expanded mission, the Agency executes the traditional security assistance functions such as military assistance, international military education and training, and foreign military sales, as well as program management responsibilities for humanitarian assistance and demining.

For further information, contact the Defense Security Cooperation Agency, 2800 Defense Pentagon, Washington, DC 20301–2800. Phone, 703–604–6604. Internet, www.dsca.osd.mil.

Defense Security Service

1340 Braddock Place, Alexandria, VA 22314–1651
Phone, 703–325–9471. Internet, www.dss.mil.

Director	LT. GEN. CHARLES J. CUNNINGHAM, JR., USAF (RET.)
Deputy Director	MICHAEL G. NEWMAN
Deputy Director for Acquisition and Augmentation	DELORES I. MOELLER

Deputy Director for Standards and Quality	(VACANCY)
Chief of Staff	JUDITH M. HUGHES

The Defense Security Service (formerly the Defense Investigative Service) was established in 1972 and is under the authority, direction, and control of the Assistant Secretary of Defense for Command, Control, Communications, and Intelligence. DSS administers programs to investigate requests for security clearances; to ensure the safeguard of classified information used by contractors; to protect conventional arms, munitions, and explosives in custody of contractors; to secure the Department's critical infrastructure; and to provide security education, training, and awareness. DSS also has a counterintelligence office to support the national counterintelligence strategy.

Operating Locations and Centers—Defense Security Service

Region/Center	Director
Regional Headquarters	
Central (No. 110A, 5800 E. Campus Cir., Irving, TX 75063	James S. Rogner
Northeast (1340 Braddock Pl., Alexandria, VA 22314–1651	Johnnie R. St. Clair
Southeast (Suite 250, 2300 Lake Park Dr., Smyrna, GA 30080–7606	Patricia F. Dodson
West (Suite 622, 1 World Trade Ctr., Long Beach, CA 09831–0622)	David P. Hopkins
Defense Industrial Security Clearance Office (P.O. Box 2499, Columbus, OH 43216–5006	John W. Faulkner
Personnel Investigations Center (881 Elkridge Landing Rd., Linthicum, MD 21090	Linda J. Howes

For further information, contact the Office of Congressional and Public Affairs, Defense Security Service, 1340 Braddock Place, Alexandria, VA 22314–1651. Phone, 703–325–9471 or 888–282–7682. Internet, www.dss.mil.

Defense Threat Reduction Agency

45045 Aviation Drive, Dulles, VA 20166–7517
Phone, 703–325–2102. Internet, www.dtra.mil.

Director	JAY C. DAVIS
Deputy Director	MAJ. GEN. ROBERT P. BONGIOVI, USAF

The Defense Threat Reduction Agency (DTRA) was established in 1998 by the consolidation of selected elements of the Office of the Secretary of Defense, the Defense Special Weapons Agency, the On-Site Inspection Agency, and the Defense Technology Security Administration. DTRA is under the authority, direction, and control of the Under Secretary of Defense for Acquisition, Technology, and Logistics. It is responsible for threat reduction to the United States and its allies from weapons of mass destruction and prevention of future threats. Through the execution of technology security activities, cooperative threat reduction programs, arms control treaty monitoring and on-site inspection, force protection, and counterproliferation, DTRA supports nuclear stockpile stewardship and technical support for nuclear weapons in DOD custody. DTRA reviews licenses for the export of U.S. technologies that could be used in the production of delivery of weapons of mass destruction or conventional weapons in order to ensure that the transfers are consistent with U.S. national security interests. It also implements the Cooperative Threat Reduction Program, which assists former Soviet Union countries in reducing their weapons of mass destruction infrastructure.

For further information, contact the Office of Public Affairs, Defense Threat Reduction Agency, 45045 Aviation Drive, Dulles, VA 20166–7517. Phone, 703–810–4326. Internet, www.dtra.mil.

National Imagery and Mapping Agency

4600 Sangamore Road, Bethesda, MD 20816–5003
Phone, 301–227–7400. Internet, www.nima.mil.

Director	LT. GEN. JAMES C. KING, USA
Deputy Director	JOHN L. HELGERSON
Chief of Staff	COL. MICHAEL THOMPSON, USA

The National Imagery and Mapping Agency (NIMA) was established in 1996 and operates under the authority, direction, and control of the Assistant Secretary of Defense (Command, Control, Communications, and Intelligence). The Agency is responsible for providing timely, relevant, and accurate imagery, imagery intelligence, and geospatial information in support of the national security objectives. NIMA provides analyses on data relating to diplomatic and regional security policy, arms control and treaty monitoring activities, counterterrorism, nonproliferation, chemical and biological warfare, and information operations activities; provides geospatial information including natural and cultural feature data, elevation data, controlled imagery, international boundaries, and place names necessary to understanding the context of intelligence information; and provides accurate and current geospatial information required by the unified combatant commands to plan, operate, and if necessary, fight and win.

For further information, contact the National Imagery and Mapping Agency, 4600 Sangamore Road, Bethesda, MD 20816–5003. Phone, 800–826–0342, or 301–227–7386. Fax, 301–227–7638. Internet, www.nima.mil.

National Security Agency/Central Security Service

Fort George G. Meade, MD 20755–6000
Phone, 301–688–6524. Internet, www.nsa.gov.

Director	MAJ. GEN. MICHAEL V. HAYDEN, USAF
Deputy Director	BARBARA A. MCNAMARA

The National Security Agency (NSA)was established in 1952, and the Central Security Service (CSS) was established in 1972. As the Nation's cryptologic organization, the Agency employs the Nation's premier codemakers and codebreakers. It ensures an informed, alert, and secure environment for U.S.

warfighters and policymakers. The cryptologic resources of NSA/CSS unite to provide U.S. policymakers with intelligence information derived from America's adversaries while protecting U.S. signals and information systems from exploitation by those same adversaries.

For further information, contact the Public Affairs Office, National Security Agency/Central Security Service, Fort Meade, MD 20755–6248. Phone, 301–688–6524. Internet, www.nsa.gov.

JOINT SERVICE SCHOOLS

Defense Acquisition University

2001 North Beauregard Street, Alexandria, VA 22311–1772
Phone, 703–845–6772. Internet, www.acq.osd.mil/dau.

President	THOMAS M. CREAN

The Defense Acquisition University (DAU), established pursuant to the Defense Acquisition Workforce Improvement Act of 1990 (10 U.S.C. 1701 note), serves as the DOD center for acquisition education, training, research, and publication. The University is a unified structure with four campuses, three education and training centers, and six regional sites. DAU centrally plans and manages the acquisition education and training activities of Army, Navy, Air Force, and DOD component schools. The University's mission is to educate and train military and civilian professionals for effective service in defense acquisition, to manage resources for course development delivery, research, and publications.

Defense Systems Management College

Fort Belvoir, VA 22060–5565
Phone, 703–805–3363; 800–845–7606 (toll-free). Internet, www.dsmc.dsm.mil.

Commandant	BRIG. GEN. FRANK ANDERSON, JR., USAF
Provost	RICHARD H. REED

The Defense Systems Management College (DSMC), established July 1, 1971, is a joint service educational institution and is the largest school in the Defense Acquisition University. The mission of the College is to promote and support the adoption and practice of sound systems management principles by the acquisition work force through education, research, consulting, and information dissemination.

In addition to a 14-week advanced program management course, DSMC's academic program consists of over 30 other courses created to educate DOD acquisition professionals in a broad spectrum of management activities. Many of these courses are mandatory for certification in various career fields. Individuals from the defense industry and other Federal agencies may attend DSMC courses on a space-available basis.

For further information, contact the Office of the Registrar, Defense Systems Management College, Fort Belvoir, VA 22060. Phone, 703–805–3003, or 888–284–4906 (toll-free). Internet, www.dsmc.dsm.mil.

For further information, contact the Director for University Operations, Defense Acquisition University, 2001 North Beauregard Street, Alexandria, VA 22311–1772. Phone, 703–845–6763. Internet, www.acq.osd.mil/dau.

Joint Military Intelligence College

Defense Intelligence Analysis Center, Washington, DC 20340–5100
Phone, 202–231–4545. Internet, www.dia.mil/jmic.html.

President	A. DENIS CLIFT
Deputy to the President	COL. DAVID F. TODD, USAF
Provost	RONALD D. GARST

The Joint Military Intelligence College (previously the Defense Intelligence College) was established in 1962. It is a joint service educational institution serving the intelligence community and operates under the authority of the Director, Defense Intelligence Agency. Its mission is to educate military and civilian intelligence professionals and conduct and disseminate relevant intelligence research. The College is authorized by Congress to award the Bachelor of Science in Intelligence (BSI) and Master of Science of Strategic Intelligence (MSSI) degrees and also offers two diploma intelligence programs, at the undergraduate and postgraduate level. Evening and weekend programs are available as well, one of which is specifically for military reservists and is taught by reserve faculty.

For further information, contact the Admissions Office, MCA–2, Joint Military Intelligence College, Defense Intelligence Analysis Center, Washington, DC 20340–5100. Phone, 202–231–5624. Internet, www.dia.mil/jmic.html.

National Defense University

Building 62, 300 Fifth Avenue, Fort McNair, Washington, DC 20319–5066
Phone, 202–685–3922. Internet, www.ndu.edu.

President	LT. GEN. RICHARD A. CHILCOAT, USA
Vice President	DANIEL H. SIMPSON
Chief of Staff	COL. CLYDE M. NEWMAN, USA

The National Defense University was established in 1976 and it incorporates the following colleges and programs: the Industrial College of the Armed Forces, the National War College, the Armed Forces Staff College; the Information Resources Management College, the Institute for National Strategic Studies, the Center for Hemispheric Defense Studies, the Defense Leadership and Management Program, the National Security Education Program, the Office of Net Assessment, the Near East and South Asia Center, and the Center for the Study of Chinese Affairs.

The mission of the National Defense University is to educate military and civilian leaders through teaching, research, and outreach in national security, military, and national resource strategy; joint and multinational operations; information strategies, operations, and resource management; acquisition; and hemispheric defense studies.

The National War College

Building 61, 300 D Street, Fort McNair, Washington, DC 20319–5078
Phone, 202–685–3715. Fax, 202–685–6461. Internet, www.ndu.edu/ndu/nwc/nwchp.html.

Commandant	REAR ADM. DANIEL R. BOWLER, USN
Dean of Students/Executive Officer	COL. JOHN ODELL, USA
Dean of Faculty and Academic Programs	COL. DAVE MCINTYRE, USA

The National War College provides education in national security policy to selected military officers and career civil service employees of Federal departments and agencies concerned with national security. It is the only senior service college with the primary mission of offering a course of study that emphasizes national security policy formulation and the planning and implementation of national strategy. Its 10-month academic program is an issue-centered study in U.S. national security. The elective program is designed to permit each student to tailor his academic experience to meet individual professional development needs.

For further information, contact the Department of Administration, The National War College, Building 61, 300 D Street, Fort McNair, Washington, DC 20319–5078. Phone, 202–685–3715. Internet, www.ndu.edu/ndu/nwc/nwchp.html.

Industrial College of the Armed Forces

Building 59, 408 Fourth Avenue, Fort McNair, Washington, DC 20319–5062
Phone, 202–685–4337. Internet, www.ndu.edu/ndu/icaf.

Commandant	MAJ. GEN. RICHARD L. ENGEL, USAF

The Industrial College of the Armed Forces provides education in the study of the resources component of national power and its integration into national security strategy. The College prepares selected military and civilian personnel for senior leadership positions by conducting postgraduate executive-level courses of study and associated research with emphasis on materiel acquisition and joint logistics and their integration into national security strategy for peace and war.

For further information, contact the Director of Administration, Industrial College of the Armed Forces, Building 59, 408 Fourth Avenue, Fort McNair, Washington, DC 20319–5062. Phone, 202–685–4333. Internet, www.ndu.edu/ndu/icaf.

Armed Forces Staff College

Norfolk, VA 23511–1702
Phone, 757–443–6202. Internet, www.afsc.edu.

Commandant	BRIG. GEN. FRANKLIN J. BLAISDELL, USAF

The Armed Forces Staff College (AFSC) is an intermediate- and senior-level joint college in the professional military education system dedicated to the study of the principles, perspectives, and techniques of joint operational-level planning and warfare. The mission of AFSC is to educate staff officers and other leaders in joint operational-level planning and warfare in order to instill a primary commitment to joint, multinational, and interagency teamwork, attitudes, and perspectives. The College accomplishes this mission through three schools: the Joint and Combined Warfighting School, the Joint and Combined Staff Officer School, and the Joint Command, Control, and Information Warfare School.

For further information, contact the Directorate of Academic Affairs, Armed Forces Staff College, 7800 Hampton Boulevard, Norfolk, VA 23511–1702. Phone, 757–443–6185. Fax, 757–443–6034. Internet, www.afsc.edu.

Information Resources Management College

Building 62, 300 Fifth Avenue, Fort McNair, Washington, DC 20319–5066
Phone, 202–685–3892. Internet, www.ndu.edu/irmc.

Director	ROBERT D. CHILDS

The Information Resources Management College provides graduate-level courses in information resources management (IRM). The College prepares senior DOD officials for joint management of the information resources component of national power and its integration with and support to national strategy. The College's curriculum is designed to provide a forum where senior defense professionals gain knowledge, qualifications, and competencies for defense IRM leadership and contribute to the growth and excellence of the field itself.

For further information, contact the Registrar, Information Resources Management College, Building 62, 300 Fifth Avenue, Fort McNair, Washington, DC 20319–5066. Phone, 202–685–3892. Internet, www.ndu.edu/irmc.

For further information, contact the Personnel, Administration, and Security Office, National Defense University, Building 62, 300 Fifth Avenue, Fort McNair, Washington, DC 20319–5066. Phone, 202–685–2169. Internet, www.ndu.edu.

Uniformed Services University of the Health Sciences

4301 Jones Bridge Road, Bethesda, MD 20814–4799
Phone, 301–295–3030. Internet, www.usuhs.mil.

President	JAMES A. ZIMBLE

Dean, School of Medicine	VAL G. HEMMING
Dean, Graduate School of Nursing	FAYE G. ABDELLAH

Authorized by act of September 21, 1972 (10 U.S.C. 2112), the Uniformed Services University of the Health Sciences was established to educate career-oriented medical officers for the Military Departments and the Public Health Service. The University currently incorporates the F. Edward Hebert School of Medicine (including graduate and continuing education programs) and the Graduate School of Nursing.

Students are selected by procedures recommended by the Board of Regents and prescribed by the Secretary of Defense. The actual selection is carried out by a faculty committee on admissions and is based upon motivation and dedication to a career in the uniformed services and an overall appraisal of the personal and intellectual characteristics of the candidates without regard to sex, race, religion, or national origin. Applicants must be U.S. citizens.

Medical school matriculants will be commissioned officers in one of the uniformed services. They must meet the physical and personal qualifications for such a commission and must give evidence of a strong commitment to serving as a uniformed medical officer. The graduating medical student is required to serve a period of obligation of not less than 7 years, excluding graduate medical education.

Students of the Graduate School of Nursing must be commissioned officers of the Army, Navy, Air Force, or Public Health Service prior to application. Graduate nursing students must serve a commitment determined by their respective service.

For further information, contact the President, Uniformed Services University of the Health Sciences, 4301 Jones Bridge Road, Bethesda, MD 20814–4799. Phone, 301–295–3030. Internet, www.usuhs.mil.

DEPARTMENT OF EDUCATION

400 Maryland Avenue SW., Washington, DC 20202
Phone, 800–USA–LEARN (toll-free). Internet, www.ed.gov.

SECRETARY OF EDUCATION	RICHARD W. RILEY
Chief of Staff	DIANE ROSSI
Director, Office of Public Affairs	ALEX WOHL, *Acting*
General Counsel	JUDITH A. WINSTON
Inspector General	LORRAINE LEWIS
Deputy Secretary	FRANK S. HOLLEMAN III
Assistant Secretary for Legislation and Congressional Affairs	SCOTT FLEMING
Assistant Secretary for Intergovernmental and Interagency Affairs	GILBERTO MARIO MORENO
Chief Financial Officer	THOMAS SKELLY, *Acting*
Chief Information Officer	CRAIG LUIGART
Director for Management	WILLIE GILMORE
Under Secretary	JUDITH A. WINSTON, *Acting*
Assistant Secretary for Civil Rights	NORMA V. CANTÚ
Assistant Secretary for Educational Research and Improvement	C. KENT MCGUIRE
Assistant Secretary for Elementary and Secondary Education	MICHAEL COHEN
Assistant Secretary for Postsecondary Education	LEE FRITSCHLER
Assistant Secretary for Special Education and Rehabilitative Services	JUDITH E. HEUMANN
Assistant Secretary for Vocational and Adult Education	PATRICIA W. MCNEIL
Chief Operating Officer for Student Financial Assistance	GREG WOODS
Director, Office of Bilingual Education and Minority Languages Affairs	ARTHUR LOVE, *Acting*

The Department of Education establishes policy for, administers, and coordinates most Federal assistance to education. Its mission is to ensure equal access to education and to promote educational excellence throughout the Nation.

The Department of Education was created by the Department of Education Organization Act (20 U.S.C. 3411) and is administered under the supervision and direction of the Secretary of Education.

Secretary The Secretary of Education advises the President on education plans, policies, and programs of the Federal Government and serves as the chief executive officer of the Department, coordinating and overseeing all Department activities, providing support and encouragement to States and localities on matters related to education, and focusing the resources of the Department and the attention of the country on ensuring equal access to education and promoting educational excellence throughout the Nation.

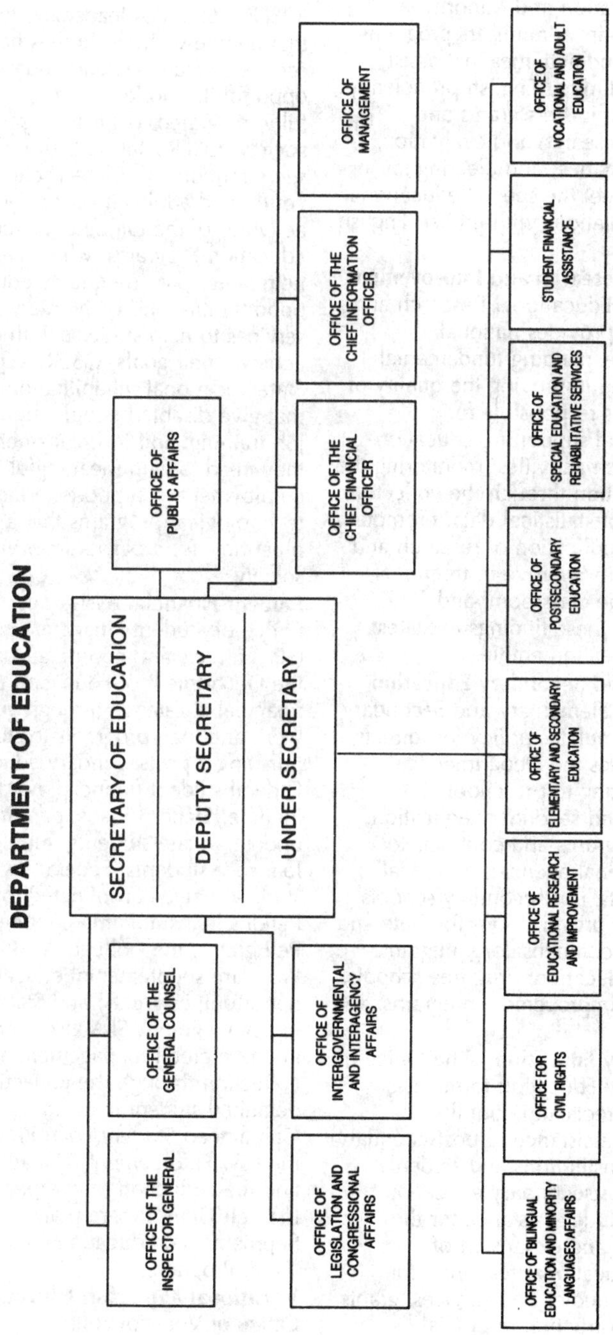
DEPARTMENT OF EDUCATION
SECRETARY OF EDUCATION
DEPUTY SECRETARY
UNDER SECRETARY
OFFICE OF THE INSPECTOR GENERAL
OFFICE OF THE GENERAL COUNSEL
OFFICE OF PUBLIC AFFAIRS
OFFICE OF LEGISLATION AND CONGRESSIONAL AFFAIRS
OFFICE OF INTERGOVERNMENTAL AND INTERAGENCY AFFAIRS
OFFICE OF THE CHIEF FINANCIAL OFFICER
OFFICE OF THE CHIEF INFORMATION OFFICER
OFFICE OF MANAGEMENT
OFFICE OF BILINGUAL EDUCATION AND MINORITY LANGUAGES AFFAIRS
OFFICE FOR CIVIL RIGHTS
OFFICE OF EDUCATIONAL RESEARCH AND IMPROVEMENT
OFFICE OF ELEMENTARY AND SECONDARY EDUCATION
OFFICE OF POSTSECONDARY EDUCATION
OFFICE OF SPECIAL EDUCATION AND REHABILITATIVE SERVICES
STUDENT FINANCIAL ASSISTANCE
OFFICE OF VOCATIONAL AND ADULT EDUCATION

Activities

Bilingual Education The Office of Bilingual Education and Minority Languages Affairs administers programs designed to fund activities that assist students with limited English proficiency. The Office administers grants and contracts for research and evaluation, technical assistance, and clearinghouse activities to meet the special educational needs of populations with limited English proficiency.

Educational Research and Improvement The Office of Educational Research and Improvement provides national leadership in expanding fundamental knowledge and improving the quality of education. It is responsible for conducting and supporting education-related research activities; monitoring the state of education through the collection and analysis of statistical data; promoting the use and application of research and development to improve instructional practices in the classroom; and disseminating these findings to States and local education entities.

Elementary and Secondary Education The Office of Elementary and Secondary Education formulates policy for, directs, and coordinates the Department's activities relating to preschool, elementary, and secondary education. Included are grants and contracts to State educational agencies and local school districts, postsecondary schools, and nonprofit organizations for State and local reform, compensatory, migrant, and Indian education; drug-free schools; other school improvement programs; and impact aid.

Postsecondary Education The Office of Postsecondary Education formulates policy and directs and coordinates programs for assistance to postsecondary educational institutions and students pursuing a postsecondary education. Programs include assistance for the improvement and expansion of American educational resources for international studies and services, grants to improve instruction in crucial academic subjects, and construction assistance for academic facilities.

Special Education and Rehabilitative Services The Office of Special Education and Rehabilitative Services (OSERS) provides leadership to ensure that people with disabilities have services, resources, and equal opportunities to learn, work, and live as fully integrated, contributing members of society. OSERS supports programs that serve millions of disabled children, youth, and adults. It coordinates the activities of the Office of Special Education Programs, which works to help States provide quality educational opportunities and early-intervention services to help students with disabilities achieve their goals. OSERS supports State vocational rehabilitation programs that give disabled people the education, job training, and job placement services they need to gain meaningful employment. It supports research and technological programs that are crafting blueprints for a barrier-free, inclusive society.

Student Financial Assistance The Office of Student Financial Assistance (SFA) directs and coordinates activities of the Department of Education to provide financial assistance through grants and work and loan programs to students pursuing a postsecondary education. The Federal student financial aid programs include: Stafford loans; parent loans for undergraduate students; supplemental loans for students; Federal insured student loans; consolidated loans; Perkins loans; income contingent loans; Pell grants; the College Work-Study Program; supplemental educational opportunities grants; and State student incentive grants. SFA also works to improve credit management and debt collection through the collection of defaulted student loans under the Guaranteed Student Loan Program and the Law Enforcement Education Program, and the collection of overpayments in the Pell Grant Program and Supplemental Educational Opportunities Grant Program.

Vocational and Adult Education The Office of Vocational and Adult Education administers grant, contract, and technical assistance programs for vocational-technical education and for adult education and literacy.

Regional Offices Each regional office serves as a center for the dissemination of information and provides technical assistance to State and local educational agencies and other institutions and individuals interested in Federal education activities. Offices are located in Atlanta, GA; Boston, MA; Chicago, IL; Dallas, TX; Denver, CO; Kansas City, MO; New York, NY; Philadelphia, PA; San Francisco, CA; and Seattle, WA.

Federally Aided Corporations

American Printing House for the Blind

P.O. Box 6085, Louisville, KY 40206
Phone, 502–895–2405

President	TUCK TINSLEY
Chairman of the Board	JOHN BARR III

The American Printing House for the Blind was incorporated by the Kentucky Legislature in 1858 to assist in the education of the blind by distributing Braille books, talking books, and educational aids without cost to educational institutions educating blind children.

For further information, contact the American Printing House for the Blind, P.O. Box 6085, Louisville, KY 40206. Phone, 502–895–2405.

Gallaudet University

800 Florida Avenue NE., Washington, DC 20002
Phone, 202–651–5000. Internet, www.gallaudet.edu.

Chairman, Board of Trustees	GLENN B. ANDERSON
President, Gallaudet University	I. KING JORDAN

The Columbia Institution for the Instruction of the Deaf and Dumb, and the Blind was incorporated by act of February 16, 1857 (11 Stat. 161). The name of the institution was changed in 1865, 1911, 1954, and eventually in 1986 to Gallaudet University. The University was established to provide a liberal higher education for deaf persons who need special facilities to compensate for their loss of hearing. The primary purpose of the university is to afford its students the intellectual and spiritual development that can be acquired through a study of the liberal arts and sciences.

In addition to its undergraduate program, the University operates a graduate program at the master's level to prepare teachers and other professional personnel to work with persons who are deaf, a research program focusing on problems related to deafness, and continuing education for deaf adults.

Accreditation The University is accredited by the Middle States Association of Colleges and Secondary Schools, the National Council for Accreditation of Teacher Education, and the Council on Social Work Education.

Model Secondary School for the Deaf The school was established by act of October 15, 1966 (20 U.S.C. 693), to provide maximum flexibility in curricula and to encourage the originality, imagination, and innovation needed to satisfy deaf students' high aspirations. The school provides day and residential facilities for deaf youth of high school age, in order to prepare them for college or for postsecondary opportunities other than college; prepares all students to the maximum extent possible to be independent, contributing members of society; and stimulates the development of similar programs throughout the Nation.

Kendall Demonstration Elementary School The School became the Nation's first demonstration elementary school for the deaf by act of December 24, 1970 (20 U.S.C. 695), which authorized Gallaudet College to operate and maintain it as a model that will experiment in techniques and materials and to disseminate information from these and future projects to educational facilities for deaf children throughout the country.

For further information, contact the Public Relations Office, Gallaudet University, 800 Florida Avenue NE., Washington, DC 20002. Phone, 202–651–5505. Internet, www.gallaudet.edu.

Howard University

2400 Sixth Street NW., Washington, DC 20059
Phone, 202–806–6100. Internet, www.howard.edu.

President	H. PATRICK SWYGERT

Howard University was established by act of March 2, 1867 (14 Stat. 438). It offers instruction in 12 schools and colleges: the colleges of arts and sciences; dentistry; engineering, architecture, and computer sciences; medicine; and pharmacy, nursing, and allied health sciences; the graduate school of arts and sciences; the schools of business; communications; divinity; education; law; and social work; and a summer school. In addition, Howard University has research institutes, centers, and special programs in the following areas: disability and socioeconomic policy studies; terrestrial and extraterrestrial atmospheric studies; aerospace science and technology; materials science research; the New York African burial ground project; speech and hearing; vitiligo; drug abuse and addiction; science, space, and technology; African-American resources; cancer; child development; computational science and engineering; international affairs; sickle cell disease; and small business development.

For further information, contact the Office of University Communications, Howard University, 2400 Sixth Street NW., Washington, DC 20059. Phone, 202–806–0970. Internet, www.howard.edu.

National Institute for Literacy

Suite 730, 1775 I Street NW., Washington, DC 20006
Phone, 202–632–1500

Director	ANDREW HARTMAN

The National Institute for Literacy leads the national effort towards a fully literate America. By building and strengthening national, regional, and State literacy infrastructures, the Institute fosters collaboration and innovation. Its goal is to ensure that all Americans with literacy needs receive the high-quality education and basic skills services necessary to achieve success in the workplace, family, and community.

National Technical Institute for the Deaf

Rochester Institute of Technology

52 Lomb Memorial Drive, Rochester, NY 14623
Phone, 716–475–6853 (voice/TDD)

President, Rochester Institute of Technology	ALBERT J. SIMONE
Dean, National Technical Institute for the Deaf	T. ALAN HURWITZ

The National Technical Institute for the Deaf (NTID) was established by act of June 8, 1965 (20 U.S.C. 681). It is an integral part of a larger institution known as the Rochester Institute of Technology (RIT). The presence of NTID at RIT is the first effort to educate large numbers of deaf students within a college campus planned primarily for hearing students. It provides educational opportunities for qualified students from every State in the Nation and, through educational outreach, publications, and related services, serves deaf persons throughout the world. In addition, NTID conducts research to better understand the role of deafness in education and employment, and to develop innovative teaching techniques. It develops training activities for its faculty and staff, as well as for other professionals working with deaf persons across the country.

Both Institutes are accredited by the Middle States Association of Colleges and Secondary Schools. Rochester Institute of Technology also has been accredited by the Engineers' Council for Professional Development, National Association of Schools of Art, Committee on Professional Training of American Chemical Society, Council on Social Work Education, and the National Accrediting Agency for Clinical Laboratory Sciences.

For further information, contact the Rochester Institute of Technology, National Technical Institute for the Deaf, Department of Recruitment and Admissions, Lyndon Baines Johnson Building, 52 Lomb Memorial Drive, Rochester, NY 14623–5604. Phone, 716–475–6700.

Sources of Information

Inquiries on the following information may be directed to the specified office, Department of Education, 400 Maryland Avenue SW., Washington, DC 20202.

Contracts and Small Business Activities Call or write the Office of Small and Disadvantaged Business Utilization. Phone, 202–708–9820.

Employment Inquiries and applications for employment, and inquiries regarding the college recruitment program, should be directed to the Human Resources Group. Phone, 202–401–0553.

Organization Contact the Executive Office, Office of Management. Phone, 202–401–0690. TDD, 202–260–8956.

For further information, contact the Information Resources Center, Department of Education, Room 5E248 (FB–6), 400 Maryland Avenue SW., Washington, DC 20202. Phone, 800–USA–LEARN. Internet, www.ed.gov.

DEPARTMENT OF ENERGY

1000 Independence Avenue SW., Washington, DC 20585
Phone, 202–586–5000. Internet, www.doe.gov.

SECRETARY OF ENERGY	BILL RICHARDSON
Deputy Secretary	T.J. GLAUTHIER
Under Secretary for Energy, Science, and Environment	ERNEST MONIZ
Assistant Secretary, Fossil Energy	ROBERT W. GEE
Assistant Secretary, Energy Efficiency and Renewable Energy	DAN W. REICHER
Director of Nuclear Energy, Science, and Technology	WILLIAM D. MAGWOOD IV
Administrator, Energy Information Administration	JAY E. HAKES
Director of Science	JAMES F. DECKER, *Acting*
Assistant Secretary, Environmental Management	CAROLYN L. HUNTOON
Director of Civilian Radioactive Waste Management	IVAN ITKIN
Under Secretary for Nuclear Security and Administrator for Nuclear Security	(VACANCY)
Deputy Administrator for Defense Programs	BRIG. GEN. THOMAS F. GIACONDA, USAF, *Acting*
Deputy Administrator for Defense Nuclear Nonproliferation	ROSE E. GOTTEMOELLER
Deputy Administrator for Naval Reactors	ADM. F.L. BOWMAN, USN
Chief Financial Officer	MICHAEL L. TELSON
Chief Information Officer	JOHN M. GILLIGAN
Director, Security and Emergency Operations	EUGENE E. HABIGER
General Counsel	MARY ANNE SULLIVAN
Inspector General	GREGORY H. FRIEDMAN
Assistant Secretary, Congressional and Intergovernmental Affairs	JOHN C. ANGELL
Assistant Secretary, Environment, Safety, and Health	DAVID M. MICHAELS
Assistant Secretary, International Affairs	DAVID L. GOLDWYN
Director, Contract Reform and Privatization Project Office	WALTER S. HOWES
Director, Independent Oversight and Performance Assurance	GLENN S. PODONSKY
Director, Public Affairs	(VACANCY)
Director of Counterintelligence	EDWARD J. CURRAN
Director of Economic Impact and Diversity	JAMES B. LEWIS
Director of Hearings and Appeals	GEORGE B. BREZNAY
Director of Intelligence	LAWRENCE H. SANCHEZ
Director of Management and Administration	DAVID M. KLAUS
Director of Policy	MARK J. MAZUR

Director, Worker and Community Transition	GARY K. KING
Executive Director, Secretary of Energy Advisory Board	BETSY MULLINS
Defense Nuclear Facilities Safety Board Liaison	MARK B. WHITTAKER

FEDERAL ENERGY REGULATORY COMMISSION

888 First Street NE., Washington, DC 20426
Phone, 202–208–0055. Internet, www.ferc.fed.us.

Chair	JAMES J. HOECKER

The Department of Energy, in partnership with its customers, is entrusted to contribute to the welfare of the Nation by providing the technical information and the scientific and educational foundation for the technology, policy, and institutional leadership necessary to achieve efficiency in energy use, diversity in energy sources, a more productive and competitive economy, improved environmental quality, and a secure national defense.

The Department of Energy (DOE) was established by the Department of Energy Organization Act (42 U.S.C. 7131), effective October 1, 1977, pursuant to Executive Order 12009 of September 13, 1977. The act consolidated the major Federal energy functions into one Cabinet-level Department.

Secretary The Secretary decides major energy policy and planning issues; acts as the principal spokesperson for the Department; and ensures the effective communication and working relationships with Federal, State, local, and tribal governments and the public. The Secretary is the principal adviser to the President on energy policies, plans, and programs.

Counterintelligence The Office of Counterintelligence develops and implements an effective counterintelligence program to identify, neutralize, and deter foreign government or industrial intelligence activities directed at or involving Department programs, personnel, facilities, technologies, classified information, and sensitive information. The Office approves, conducts, and coordinates all policy and investigative matters with the Federal Bureau of Investigation.

For further information, contact the Office of Counterintelligence. Phone, 202–586–5901.

Defense Nuclear Facilities Safety Board Liaison The Office of the Departmental Representative to the Defense Nuclear Facilities Safety Board (DNFSB) manages the Department's interaction with DNFSB as mandated by law, including achievement of the mutual goal of ensuring protection of public and employee health and safety and the environment by appropriate and timely resolution of DNFSB recommendations and concerns.

For further information, contact the Departmental Representative to the Defense Nuclear Facilities Safety Board. Phone, 202–586–3887.

Intelligence The Office of Intelligence ensures that departmental intelligence information requirements are met and that the Department's technical, analytical, and research expertise is made available to support U.S. intelligence efforts. The Office ensures effective use of the U.S. Government's intelligence apparatus in support of the Department of Energy's needs for information on global nuclear weapons development, nonproliferation, and foreign hydrocarbon, nuclear, and other energy production and consumption.

For further information, contact the Office of Intelligence. Phone, 202–586–2610.

Security and Emergency Operations The Office of Security and Emergency Operations develops and promulgates all safeguards and security policy and is responsible for cybersecurity and

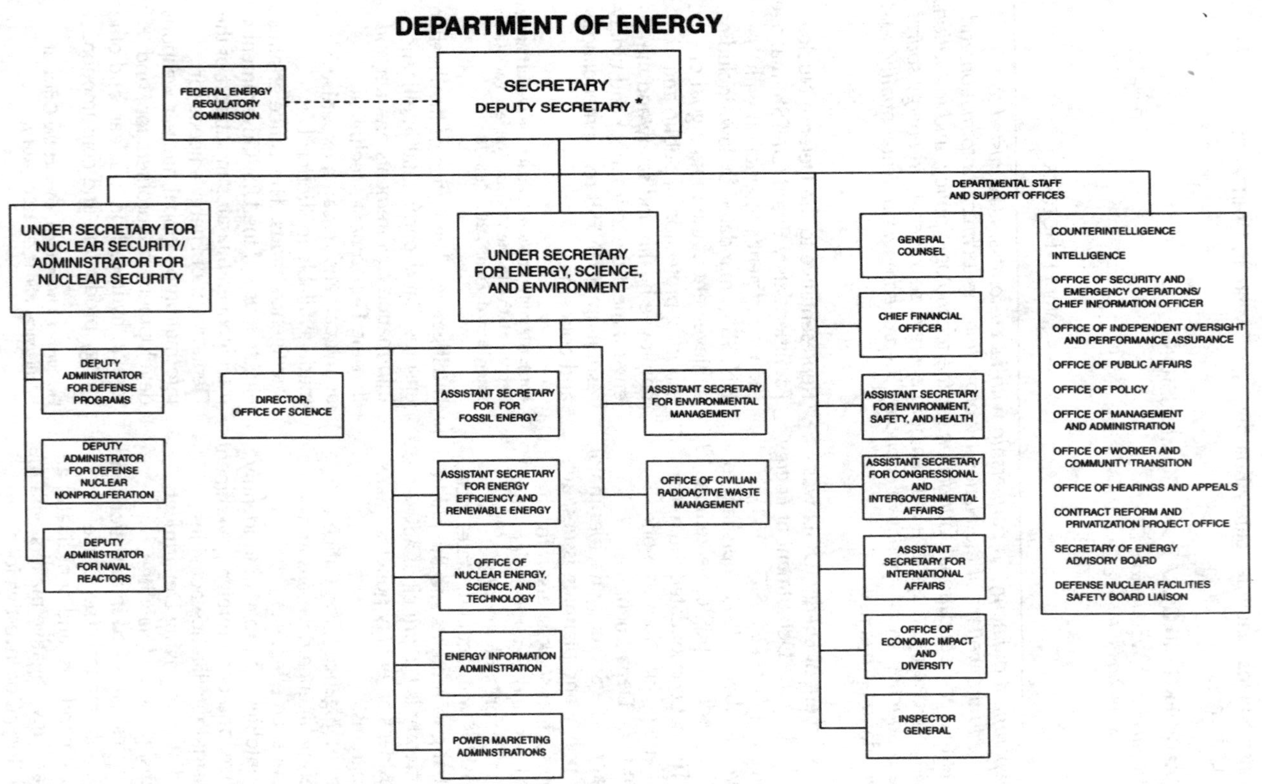

* The Deputy Secretary also serves as the Chief Operating Officer

emergency operations throughout the Department.

For more information, contact the Director of Resource Management. Phone 202–586–6378.

Energy Programs

Energy Efficiency and Renewable Energy The Office of the Assistant Secretary for Energy Efficiency and Renewable Energy is responsible for formulating and directing programs designed to increase the production and utilization of renewable energy (solar, biomass, wind, geothermal, alcohol fuels, etc.) and improving the energy efficiency of the transportation, buildings, industrial, and utility sectors through support of long-term, high-risk research and development and technology transfer activities. It also has responsibility for administering programs that provide financial assistance for State energy planning; weatherization of housing owned by the poor and disadvantaged; the implementation of energy conservation measures by schools and hospitals, local units of government, and public care institutions; and the promotion of energy efficient construction and renovation of Federal facilities.

For further information, contact the Director of Management and Operations. Phone, 202–586–6768.

Fossil Energy The Office of the Assistant Secretary for Fossil Energy is responsible for research and development of programs involving fossil fuels. The fossil energy program involves applied research, exploratory development, and limited proof-of-concept testing targeted to high-risk and high-payoff endeavors. The objective of the program is to provide the general technology and knowledge base that the private sector can use to complete development and initiate commercialization of advanced processes and energy systems. The program is principally executed through the National Energy Technology Laboratory. The Office also manages the clean coal technology program, the strategic petroleum reserve, and the naval petroleum and oil shale reserves.

For further information, contact the Office of Communications. Phone, 202–586–6503.

Nuclear Energy, Science, and Technology The Office of Nuclear Energy, Science, and Technology manages the Department's research and development programs associated with fission and fusion energy. This includes programs relating to naval and civilian nuclear reactor development, nuclear fuel cycle, and space nuclear applications. The Office manages a program to provide radioactive and stable isotope products to various domestic and international markets for medical research, health care, and industrial research. The Office also conducts technical analyses concerning nonproliferation; assesses alternative nuclear systems and new reactor and fuel cycle concepts; manages depleted uranium hexafluoride activities, highly enriched uranium downblend, natural uranium sales, and uranium enrichment legacy activities; and evaluates proposed advanced nuclear fission energy concepts and technical improvements for possible application to nuclear powerplant systems.

For further information, contact the Director of Management, Planning and Analysis. Phone, 301–903–3796.

Energy Information The Energy Information Administration is responsible for collecting, processing, publishing, and distributing data in the areas of energy resource reserves, energy production, demand, consumption, distribution, and technology. It performs analyses of energy data to assist government and nongovernment users in understanding energy trends.

For further information, contact the Director, National Energy Information Center. Phone, 202–586–6537.

Nuclear Security Programs

Defense Activities The Office of the Deputy Administrator for Defense Programs directs the Nation's nuclear weapons research, development, testing,

186-873 D-00--8

production, and surveillance program. It is also responsible for the production of the special nuclear materials used by the weapons program within the Department and the management of defense nuclear waste and byproducts. The Office ensures the technology base for the surety, reliability, military effectiveness, and credibility of the nuclear weapon stockpile. It also manages research in inertial confinement fusion.

For further information, contact the Assistant Deputy Administrator for Program Support. Phone, 301–903–4016.

Naval Reactors The Office of the Deputy Administrator for Naval Reactors manages and performs research, development, design, acquisition, specification, construction, inspection, installation, certification, testing overhaul, refueling, operations procedures, maintenance, supply support, and ultimate disposition of naval nuclear propulsion plants.

For further information, contact the Deputy Administrator for Naval Reactors. Phone, 703–603–5502.

Nuclear Nonproliferation The Office of the Deputy Administrator for Defense Nuclear Nonproliferation directs the development of the Department's policy, plans, procedures, and research and development activities relating to arms control, nonproliferation, export controls, international nuclear safety and safeguard, and surplus fissile materials inventories elimination activities.

For further information, contact the Assistant Deputy Administrator for Resource Management. Phone, 202–586–4544.

Environmental Quality Programs

Civilian Radioactive Waste Management The Office of Civilian Radioactive Waste Management has responsibility for the nuclear waste fund and for the management of Federal programs for recommending, constructing, and operating repositories for disposal of high-level radioactive waste and spent nuclear fuel; interim storage of spent nuclear fuel; monitored retrievable storage; and research, development, and demonstration of disposal of high-level radioactive waste and spent nuclear fuel.

For further information, contact the Director for Human Resources. Phone, 202–586–5975.

Environmental Management The Office of the Assistant Secretary for Environmental Management manages the assessment and cleanup of inactive waste sites and facilities, directs a program in safe and effective waste management operations, and develops and implements an aggressive applied waste research and development program to provide innovative environmental technologies that yield permanent disposal solutions at reduced costs.

For further information, contact the Director of Resource Management. Phone, 202–586–2661.

Science Program

The Office of Science manages the Department's program of basic and applied physical and energy research and development and provides financial assistance and budgetary priorities for these activities. The Office monitors Department research and development programs for deficiencies or duplications and monitors the international exchange of scientific and technical personnel.

For further information, contact the Associate Director of Resource Management. Phone, 301–903–4944.

Federal Energy Regulatory Commission

An independent five-member commission within the Department of Energy, the Federal Energy Regulatory Commission sets interstate commerce rates for the transportation and sale for resale of natural gas, and for the transmission and sale at wholesale of electricity. It also licenses hydroelectric power projects. In addition, the Commission establishes rates for the interstate transportation of oil by pipeline.

For further information, contact the Office of External Affairs, Federal Energy Regulatory Commission, 888 First Street NE, Washington, DC 20426. Phone, 202–208–0055. Internet, www.ferc.fed.us.

Operations and Field Offices

The vast majority of the Department's energy and physical research and development, nuclear weapons research and development, testing and production, environmental restoration, and waste management activities are carried out by contractors who operate Government-owned facilities. Management and administration of Government-owned, contractor-operated facility contracts are the major responsibility of the Department's eight operations offices and two special purpose field offices.

Department operations offices provide a formal link between Department headquarters and the field laboratories and other operating facilities. They also manage programs and projects as assigned from lead headquarters program offices. Routine management guidance, coordination, and oversight of the operations and field offices is provided by the Office of Field Integration. Daily specific program direction for the operations offices is provided by the cognizant Assistant Secretary, Office Director, or program officer.

Operations and Field Offices—Department of Energy

Office/Address	Telephone
Operations Offices	
Albuquerque, NM (P.O. Box 5400, 87185–5400)	505–845–6050
Chicago, IL (9800 S. Cass Ave., Argonne, IL 60439–4802)	630–252–2110
Idaho Falls, ID (850 Energy Dr., 83401–1563)	208–526–5665
Las Vegas, NV (P.O. Box 98518, 89193–8518)	702–295–3211
Oak Ridge, TN (P.O. Box 2001, 37831–8763)	423–576–4444
Oakland, CA (Rm. 700N, 1301 Clay St., 94612–5208)	510–637–1800
Richland, WA (P.O. Box 550, 825 Jadwin Ave., 99352–0550)	509–376–7395
Savannah River, SC (P.O. Box A, Aiken, SC 29802–0900)	803–725–2405
Field Offices	
Miamisburg, OH (P.O. Box 3020, 45343–3020)	937–865–3977
Rocky Flats, CO (P.O. Box 928, Golden, CO 80402–0928)	303–966–2025

Power Administrations

The marketing and transmission of electric power produced at Federal hydroelectric projects and reservoirs is carried out by the Department's four Power Administrations. Management oversight of the Power Administrations is the responsibility of the Deputy Secretary.

Bonneville Power Administration The Administration markets power produced by the Federal Columbia River Power System at the lowest rates, consistent with sound business practices, and gives preference to public entities.

In addition, the Administration is responsible for energy conservation, renewable resource development, and fish and wildlife enhancement under the provisions of the Pacific Northwest Electric Power Planning and Conservation Act of 1980 (16 U.S.C. 839 note).

For further information, contact the Bonneville Power Administration, 905 NE. Eleventh Avenue, Portland, OR 97232–4169. Phone, 503–230–5101.

Southeastern Power Administration The Administration is responsible for the transmission and disposition of surplus electric power and energy generated at reservoir projects in the States of West Virginia, Virginia, North Carolina, South Carolina, Georgia, Florida, Alabama, Mississippi, Tennessee, and Kentucky.

The Administration sets the lowest possible rates to consumers, consistent with sound business principles, and gives preference in the sale of such power and energy to public bodies and cooperatives.

For further information, contact the Southeastern Power Administration, Samuel Elbert Building, 2 Public Square, Elberton, GA 30635–1850. Phone, 706–213–3805.

Southwestern Power Administration The Administration is responsible for the sale and disposition of electric power and energy in the States of Arkansas, Kansas, Louisiana, Missouri, Oklahoma, and Texas.

The Southwestern Power Administration transmits and disposes of the electric power and energy generated at Federal reservoir projects, supplemented by power purchased from public and private utilities, in such a manner as to encourage the most widespread and economical use. The Administration sets the lowest possible rates to consumers, consistent with sound business principles, and gives preference in the sale of power and energy to public bodies and cooperatives.

The Administration also conducts and participates in the comprehensive planning of water resource development in the Southwest.

For further information, contact the Southwestern Power Administration, Suite 1600, Williams Center Tower One, One West Third Street, Tulsa, OK 74103–3532. Phone, 918–595–6601.

Western Area Power Administration The Administration is responsible for the Federal electric power-marketing and transmission functions in 15 central and western States, encompassing a geographic area of 1.3 million square miles. The Administration sells power to cooperatives, municipalities, public utility districts, private utilities, Federal and State agencies, and irrigation districts. The wholesale power customers, in turn, provide service to millions of retail consumers in the States of Arizona, California, Colorado, Iowa, Kansas, Minnesota, Montana, Nebraska, Nevada, New Mexico, North Dakota, South Dakota, Texas, Utah, and Wyoming.

The Administration is responsible for the operation and maintenance of transmission lines, substations, and various auxiliary power facilities in the aforementioned geographic area and also for planning, construction, and operation and maintenance of additional Federal transmission facilities that may be authorized in the future.

For further information, contact the Western Area Power Administration, 12155 West Alameda Parkway, Lakewood, CO 80228–2802. Phone 702–962–7707.

Sources of Information

Consumer Information For information on the consumer impact of Department policies and operations and for other DOE consumer information, call 202–586–1908.

Contracts and Small and Disadvantaged Business Utilization Activities Information on business opportunities with the Department and its contractors is available electronically through the Internet, at www.pr.doe.gov/prbus.html. For assistance, call 202–634–4511. For information on existing DOE awards, call 202–586–9051.

Electronic Access Information concerning the Department is available through the Internet, at www.doe.gov.

Employment Most jobs in the Department are in the competitive service. Positions are filled through hiring individuals with Federal civil service status, but may also be filled using lists of competitive eligibles from the Office of Personnel Management or the Department's special examining units. Contact the Office of Personnel. Phone, 202–586–1234.

Freedom of Information Act To obtain administrative and technical support in matters involving the Freedom of Information, Privacy, and Computer Matching Acts, call 202–586–5955.

Inspector General Hotline Persons who wish to raise issues of concern regarding departmental operations, processes, or practices or who may be aware of or suspect illegal acts or noncriminal violations should contact the hotline. Phone, 202–586–4073.

Public Information Issuances, Press Releases, and Publications For media contacts, call 202–586–5575.

Public Reading Room For information materials on DOE and public access to DOE records, call 202–586–3142.

Scientific and Technical Information The Office manages a system for the centralized collection, announcement, and dissemination of and historical reference to the Department's scientific and technical information and worldwide energy information. Contact the Office of Scientific and Technical Information, 175 Oak Ridge Turnpike, Oak Ridge, TN 37830–7255. Phone, 423–576–1188.

Whistleblower Assistance Federal or DOE contractor employees wishing to make complaints of alleged wrongdoing against the Department or its contractors should call 202–586–8289.

For further information concerning the Department of Energy, contact the Office of Public Affairs, Department of Energy, 1000 Independence Avenue SW., Washington, DC 20585. Phone, 202–586–4940. Internet, www.doe.gov.

DEPARTMENT OF HEALTH AND HUMAN SERVICES

200 Independence Avenue SW., Washington, DC 20201
Phone, 202–619–0257. Internet, www.dhhs.gov.

SECRETARY OF HEALTH AND HUMAN SERVICES	DONNA E. SHALALA
Deputy Secretary	KEVIN THURM
Chief of Staff	MARY BETH DONAHUE
Chair, Departmental Appeals Board	CECILIA SPARKS FORD
Director, Intergovernmental Affairs	ANDREW HYMAN
Executive Officer	MIKE BLANK
Assistant Secretary for Health and Surgeon General	DAVID SATCHER
Principal Deputy Assistant Secretary	NICOLE LURIE
Deputy Assistant Secretary for Health	BEVERLY MALONE
Deputy Assistant Secretary, Disease Prevention and Health Promotion	RANDOLPH F. WYKOFF
Deputy Assistant Secretary, Minority Health	NATHAN STINSON
Deputy Assistant Secretary, Population Affairs	DENESE SHERVINGTON
Deputy Assistant Secretary, Women's Health	WANDA JONES
Director, Office of Emergency Preparedness	ROBERT KNOUSS
Director, Office of HIV/AIDS Policy	ERIC GOOSBY
Director, Office of International and Refugee Health	GREGORY PAPPAS, *Acting*
Director, Office of Research Integrity	THOMAS NOVOTNY
Executive Director, President's Council on Physical Fitness and Sports	SANDRA PERLMUTTER
Assistant Secretary for Legislation	RICHARD J. TARPLIN
Principal Deputy Assistant Secretary	(VACANCY)
Deputy Assistant Secretary (Congressional Liaison)	M. HELEN MATHIS
Deputy Assistant Secretary (Health)	JANE C. HORVATH
Deputy Assistant Secretary (Human Services)	MARY M. BOURDETTE
Assistant Secretary for Management and Budget	JOHN J. CALLAHAN
Principal Deputy Assistant Secretary	(VACANCY)
Deputy Assistant Secretary, Policy Initiatives	ELIZABETH D'JAMOOS
Deputy Assistant Secretary, Budget	DENNIS P. WILLIAMS
Deputy Assistant Secretary, Finance	GEORGE H. STRADER
Deputy Assistant Secretary, Grants and Acquisition Management	TERRENCE J. TYCHAN
Deputy Assistant Secretary, Human Resources	EVELYN WHITE

Deputy Assistant Secretary, Information Resources Management	BRIAN BURNS
Assistant Secretary for Planning and Evaluation	MARGARET A. HAMBURG
Deputy Assistant Secretary, Policy Initiatives	ANN SEGAL
Deputy Assistant Secretary, Disability, Aging, and Long-Term Care Policy	ROBERT WILLIAMS
Deputy Assistant Secretary, Health Policy	GARY CLAXTON
Deputy Assistant Secretary, Human Services Policy	PATRICIA RUGGLES
Deputy Assistant Secretary, Program Systems	DELORES L. PARRON
Deputy Assistant Secretary, Science Policy	WILLIAM RAUB
Assistant Secretary for Public Affairs	MELISSA SKOLFIELD
Deputy Assistant Secretary, Policy and Communications	LYNNETTE WILLIAMS
Deputy Assistant Secretary, Media	(VACANCY)
General Counsel	HARRIET S. RABB
Deputy General Counsels	DAVID S. CADE, ANNA D. KRAUS
Associate General Counsel, Business and Administrative Law Division	TIMOTHY M. WHITE
Associate General Counsel, Children, Families, and Aging Division	ROBERT E. KEITH
Associate General Counsel, Civil Rights Division	GEORGE C. LYON
Associate General Counsel, Ethics Division	EDGAR M. SWINDELL, *Acting*
Associate General Counsel, Food and Drug Division	MARGARET J. PORTER
Associate General Counsel, Health Care Financing Division	SHEREE KANNER
Associate General Counsel, Legislation Division	SONDRA S. WALLACE
Associate General Counsel, Public Health	RICHARD RISEBERG
Inspector General	JUNE GIBBS BROWN
Principal Deputy Inspector General	MICHAEL F. MANGANO
Deputy Inspector General, Audit Services	THOMAS D. ROSLEWICZ
Deputy Inspector General, Evaluation and Inspections	GEORGE F. GROB
Deputy Inspector General, Investigations	JOHN E. HARTWIG
Deputy Inspector General, Management and Policy	DENNIS J. DUQUETTE

ADMINISTRATION ON AGING

330 Independence Avenue SW., Washington, DC 20201
Phone, 202–401–4541. Internet, www.aoa.dhhs.gov.

Assistant Secretary	JEANETTE C. TAKAMURA
Principal Deputy Assistant Secretary	DIANE E. JUSTICE
Deputy Assistant Secretary for Governmental Affairs and Elder Rights	(VACANCY)
Director, Office of American Indian, Alaskan Native, and Native Hawaiian Programs	M. YVONNE JACKSON
Director, Office of Management	JOHN F. MCCARTHY

Director, Office of Program Operations and Development	EDWIN L. WALKER
Director, Office of Program Development	JUDITH R. SATINE
Director, Office of State and Community Programs	CAROL M. CRECY

ADMINISTRATION FOR CHILDREN AND FAMILIES

370 L'Enfant Promenade SW., Washington, DC 20447
Phone, 202–401–9200. Internet, www.acf.gov.

Assistant Secretary	OLIVIA A. GOLDEN
Principal Deputy Assistant Secretary	CARMEN NAZARIO
Deputy Assistant Secretary, Administration	ELIZABETH M. JAMES-DUKE
Deputy Assistant Secretary, Policy and External Affairs	EMIL PARKER
Commissioner, Children, Youth, and Families	PAT MONTOYA
Commissioner, Developmental Disabilities	SUE SWENSON
Commissioner, Native Americans	GARY N. KIMBLE
Commissioner, Child Support Enforcement	DAVID G. ROSS
Director, Legislative Affairs and Budget	MADELINE MOCKO
Director, Planning, Research, and Evaluation	HOWARD ROLSTON
Director, Public Affairs	MICHAEL KHARFEN
Director, Regional Operations	DIANN DAWSON

AGENCY FOR HEALTHCARE RESEARCH AND QUALITY

2101 East Jefferson Street, Rockville, MD 20852
Phone, 301–594–6662. Internet, www.ahrq.gov. E-mail, info@ahrq.gov.

Director	JOHN M. EISENBERG
Deputy Director	LISA SIMPSON
Director, Practice and Technology Assessment	DOUGLAS B. KAMEROW
Director, Management	WILLIARD B. EVANS
Director, Research Review, Education and Policy	FRANCIS CHESLEY
Director, Cost and Financing Studies	ROSS H. ARNETT III
Director, Health Care Information	CHRISTINE G. WILLIAMS
Director, Organization and Delivery Studies	IRENE FRASER
Director, Outcomes and Effectiveness Research	CAROLYN M. CLANCY
Director, Primary Care Research	HELEN BURSTIN
Director, Quality Measurement and Improvement	GREGG MEYER

AGENCY FOR TOXIC SUBSTANCES AND DISEASE REGISTRY

1600 Clifton Road NE., Atlanta, GA 30333
Phone, 404–639–0700. Internet, www.atsdr.cdc.gov.

Administrator	JEFFREY KOPLAN
Deputy Administrator	LYNN S. WILCOX, *Acting*
Assistant Administrator	HENRY FALK

CENTERS FOR DISEASE CONTROL AND PREVENTION

1600 Clifton Road NE., Atlanta, GA 30333
Phone, 404–639–3311. Internet, www.cdc.gov.

Director	JEFFREY P. KOPLAN
Deputy Director for Science and Public Health	LYNN S. WILCOX, *Acting*
Deputy Director for Policy and Legislation	MARTHA F. KATZ
Deputy Director for Program Management	VIRGINIA S. BALES

FOOD AND DRUG ADMINISTRATION

5600 Fishers Lane, Rockville, MD 20857
Phone, 301–443–1544. Internet, www.fda.gov.

Commissioner	JANE E. HENNEY
Deputy Commissioner/Senior Adviser	(VACANCY)
Lead Deputy Commissioner for Operations	MICHAEL A. FRIEDMAN
Deputy Commissioner, External Affairs	SHARON SMITH HOLSTON
Deputy Commissioner, Management and Systems	ROBERT J. BYRD
Deputy Commissioner, Policy	WILLIAM K. HUBBARD, *Acting*

HEALTH CARE FINANCING ADMINISTRATION

200 Independence Avenue SW., Washington, DC 20201
Phone, 202–690–6726. Internet, www.hcfa.gov.

Administrator	NANCY-ANN MIN DEPARLE
Deputy Administrator	MICHAEL HASH
Executive Associate Administrator	KATHLEEN KING
Chief Actuary	RICHARD FOSTER
Administrator, Northeastern Consortium	JUDY BEREK
Administrator, Southern Consortium	ROSE CRUM-JOHNSON
Administrator, Midwestern Consortium	JOE TILGHMAN
Administrator, Western Consortium	(VACANCY)

HEALTH RESOURCES AND SERVICES ADMINISTRATION

5600 Fishers Lane, Rockville, MD 20857
Phone, 301–443–2086. Internet, www.hrsa.gov.

Administrator	CLAUDE EARL FOX
Deputy Administrator	THOMAS G. MORFORD
Associate Administrator, Bureau of Health Professions	VINCENT C. RODGERS
Associate Administrator, Bureau of Primary Health Care	MARILYN HUGHES GASTON
Associate Administrator, HIV/AIDS Bureau	JOSEPH F. O'NEILL
Associate Administrator, Maternal and Child Health Bureau	PETER C. VAN DYCK
Associate Administrator, Field Operations	SAM SHEKAR
Associate Administrator, Operations, Management and Program Support	JAMES J. CORRIGAN

INDIAN HEALTH SERVICE

5600 Fishers Lane, Rockville, MD 20857
Phone, 301–443–1083. Internet, www.ihs.gov.

Director	MICHAEL H. TRUJILLO
Deputy Director	MICHEL E. LINCOLN

Director, Office of Tribal Self-Governance	PAULA WILLIAMS
Director, Office of Tribal Programs	DOUGLAS BLACK
Director, Urban Indian Health Program Staff	JAMES CUSSEN

NATIONAL INSTITUTES OF HEALTH

9000 Rockville Pike, Bethesda, MD 20892
Phone, 301–496–4000. Internet, www.nih.gov.

Director	RUTH L. KIRSCHSTEIN, *Acting*
Deputy Director	YVONNE MADDOX, *Acting*
Deputy Director, Extramural Research	WENDY BALDWIN
Deputy Director, Intramural Research	MICHAEL M. GOTTESMAN
Deputy Director, Management	ANTHONY L. ITTEILAG
Associate Director, Administration	LEAMON M. LEE
Associate Director, AIDS Research	NEAL NATHANSON
Associate Director, Behavioral and Social Sciences Research	PETER G. KAUFMANN, *Acting*
Associate Director, Budget	SUSAN QUANTIUM
Associate Director, Clinical Research	JOHN I. GALLIN
Associate Director, Communications	R. ANNE THOMAS
Associate Director, Disease Prevention	WILLIAM R. HARLAN
Associate Director, International Health	GERALD T. KEUSCH
Associate Director, Legislative Policy and Analysis	MARC SMOLONSKY
Associate Director, Research on Minority Health	JOHN RUFFIN
Associate Director, Research on Women's Health	VIVIAN W. PINN
Associate Director, Research Services	STEPHEN A. FICCA
Associate Director, Science Policy	LANA R. SKIRBOLL

PROGRAM SUPPORT CENTER

5600 Fishers Lane, Rockville, MD 20857
Phone, 301–443–3921. Internet, www.psc.gov.

Director	LYNNDA M. REGAN
Director, Office of Budget and Management	JERRILYN ANDERSON
Director, Office of Marketing	HARLAN K. ZINN
Director, Administrative Operations Service	WAYNE C. RICHEY, JR.
Director, Financial Management Service	JOHN C. WEST
Director, Human Resources Service	JOSEPH V. COLANTUONI

SUBSTANCE ABUSE AND MENTAL HEALTH SERVICES ADMINISTRATION

5600 Fishers Lane, Rockville, MD 20857
Phone, 301–443–4797. Internet, www.samhsa.gov.

Administrator	NELBA CHAVEZ
Deputy Administrator	JOSEPH H. AUTRY III
Associate Administrator, Communications	MARK WEBER
Associate Administrator, Managed Care	ERIC GOPLERUD
Associate Administrator, Minority Health	DELORIS L-JAMES HUNTER
Associate Administrator, Policy and Program Coordination	ERIC GOPLERUD, *Acting*

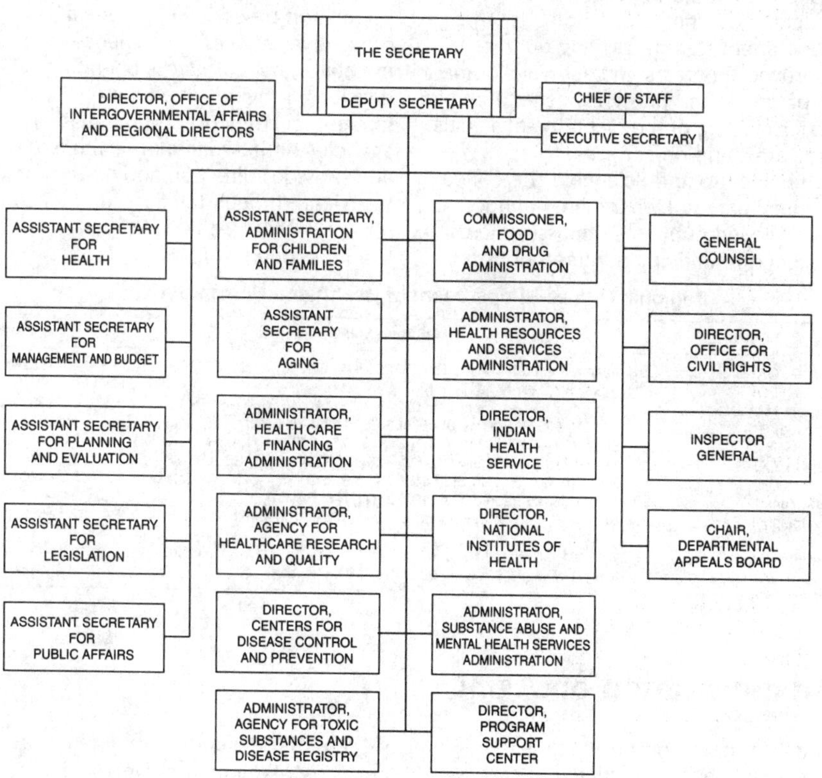
DEPARTMENT OF HEALTH AND HUMAN SERVICES
THE SECRETARY
DEPUTY SECRETARY
DIRECTOR, OFFICE OF INTERGOVERNMENTAL AFFAIRS AND REGIONAL DIRECTORS
CHIEF OF STAFF
EXECUTIVE SECRETARY
ASSISTANT SECRETARY FOR HEALTH
ASSISTANT SECRETARY FOR MANAGEMENT AND BUDGET
ASSISTANT SECRETARY FOR PLANNING AND EVALUATION
ASSISTANT SECRETARY FOR LEGISLATION
ASSISTANT SECRETARY FOR PUBLIC AFFAIRS
ASSISTANT SECRETARY, ADMINISTRATION FOR CHILDREN AND FAMILIES
ASSISTANT SECRETARY FOR AGING
ADMINISTRATOR, HEALTH CARE FINANCING ADMINISTRATION
ADMINISTRATOR, AGENCY FOR HEALTHCARE RESEARCH AND QUALITY
DIRECTOR, CENTERS FOR DISEASE CONTROL AND PREVENTION
ADMINISTRATOR, AGENCY FOR TOXIC SUBSTANCES AND DISEASE REGISTRY
COMMISSIONER, FOOD AND DRUG ADMINISTRATION
ADMINISTRATOR, HEALTH RESOURCES AND SERVICES ADMINISTRATION
DIRECTOR, INDIAN HEALTH SERVICE
DIRECTOR, NATIONAL INSTITUTES OF HEALTH
ADMINISTRATOR, SUBSTANCE ABUSE AND MENTAL HEALTH SERVICES ADMINISTRATION
DIRECTOR, PROGRAM SUPPORT CENTER
GENERAL COUNSEL
DIRECTOR, OFFICE FOR CIVIL RIGHTS
INSPECTOR GENERAL
CHAIR, DEPARTMENTAL APPEALS BOARD

The Department of Health and Human Services is the Cabinet-level department of the Federal executive branch most involved with the Nation's human concerns. In one way or another, it touches the lives of more Americans than any other Federal agency. It is literally a department of people serving people, from newborn infants to persons requiring health services to our most elderly citizens.

The Department of Health and Human Services (HHS) was created as the Department of Health, Education, and Welfare on April 11, 1953 (5 U.S.C. app.).

Secretary The Secretary of Health and Human Services advises the President on health, welfare, and income security plans, policies, and programs of the Federal Government; and directs Department staff in carrying out the approved programs and activities of the Department and promotes general public understanding of the Department's goals, programs, and objectives.

Public Health and Science The Office ensures that the Department conducts broad-based public health assessments designed to anticipate future public health issues and problems and devises and implements appropriate interventions and evaluations to maintain, sustain, and improve the health of the Nation; provides assistance in managing the implementation and coordination of Secretarial decisions for Public Health Service (PHS) operating divisions and coordination of population-based health, clinical preventive services, and science initiatives that cut across operating divisions; provides presentations to foreign governments and multilateral agencies on international health issues; and provides direction and policy oversight, through the Surgeon General, for the Public Health Service Commissioned Corps.

Regional Offices—Department of Health and Human Services

Area	Address/Areas Served	Telephone
Atlanta, GA	Atlanta Federal Center, Rm. 5B95, 61 Forsyth St., 20202–8909 (AL, FL, GA, KY, MS, NC, SC, TN).	404–562–7888
Boston, MA	Rm. 2100, Government Ctr., 02203 (CT, MA, ME, NH, RI, VT)	617–565–1500
Chicago, IL	23d Fl., 105 W. Adams St., 60603 (IL, IN, MI, OH, WI)	312–353–5160
Dallas, TX	Suite 1124–ORD, 1301 Young St., 75202–4348 (AR, LA, NM, OK, TX)	214–767–3301
Denver, CO	Rm. 1076, 1961 Stout St., 80294–3538 (CO, MT, ND, SD, UT, WY)	303–844–3372
Kansas City, MO	Rm. 210, 601 E. 12th St., 64106 (IA, KS, MO, NE)	816–426–2821
New York, NY	Rm. 3835, 26 Federal Plz., 10278 (NJ, NY, PR, VI)	212–264–4600
Philadelphia, PA	Suite 436, 150 S. Independence Mall W., 19106–3499 (DC, DE, MD, PA, VA, WV).	215–596–6492
San Francisco, CA	Rm. 431, 50 United Nations Plz., 94102 (AS, AZ, CA, GU, HI, NV)	415–437–8500
Seattle, WA	Rm. 911F, 2201 6th Ave., 98121 (AK, ID, OR, WA)	206–615–2010

Administration on Aging

The Administration on Aging is the principal agency designated to carry out the provisions of the Older Americans Act of 1965. It is responsible for all issues involving the elderly. The Administration develops policies, plans, and programs designed to promote the welfare of the elderly; promotes their needs by planning programs and developing policy; provides policy, procedural direction, and technical assistance to States and Native American tribal governments.

For further information, contact the Administration on Aging, 330 Independence Avenue SW., Washington, DC 20201. Phone, 202–401–4634. Internet, www.aoa.dhhs.gov.

Administration for Children and Families

The Administration for Children and Families (ACF) was created on April 15, 1991, to provide advice to the Secretary on issues pertaining to children and families, including Native Americans, people with developmental disabilities, refugees, and legalized aliens.

Child Support Enforcement The Office provides direction, guidance, and oversight to State activities to develop programs which locate absent parents, establish paternity, and obtain and enforce child support orders; assists States in establishing adequate reporting procedures and records maintenance; operates the Federal parent locator service; assists the States with automation of their child support enforcement programs; and reviews State applications for U.S. courts to enforce child support orders.

For further information, contact the Public Inquiries and Information Branch. Phone, 202–401–9373. Internet, www.acf.gov/programs/cse.

Children, Youth, and Families The Administration manages State grant and child care programs including programs to increase child abuse prevention and treatment activities and to develop family preservation and family support services; the Head Start Program; programs which provide services for runaway and homeless youth and their families; child welfare training programs; and child abuse and neglect research and demonstration programs.

For further information, call 202–205–8347 or 202–401–2337. Internet, www.acf.gov/programs/acyf.

Community Services The Office is responsible for administering the community services block grant, the social services block grant, and the Low-Income Home Energy Assistance Program. It also oversees a variety of discretionary grant programs which foster family stability, economic security, responsibility, and self-support, as well as the programs and services for homeless, low-income, and needy individuals, leading to the development of new and innovative approaches to reduce welfare dependency.

For further information, call 202–401–9333. Internet, www.acf.gov/programs/ocs.

Developmental Disabilities The Administration supports and encourages provision of quality services to persons with developmental disabilities; assists States in increasing the independence, productivity, and community inclusion of all persons with developmental disabilities, through the design and implementation of a comprehensive and continuing State plan; administers the State developmental disabilities councils, the Protection and Advocacy Grant Program, and the discretionary grant programs.

For further information, call 202–690–6590. Internet, www.acf.gov/programs/add.

Family Assistance The Office is responsible for administering the public assistance and economic self-sufficiency programs and for providing leadership, direction, and technical guidance in the administration of the Temporary Assistance for Needy Families Program and the Aid to the Aged, Blind, and Disabled Program in Guam, Puerto Rico, and the Virgin Islands.

For further information, call 202–401–9275. Internet, www.acf.gov/programs/ofa.

Native Americans The Administration represents and promotes the goal of developmental, social, economic, and lasting self-sufficiency of American Indians, Alaskan Natives, and Pacific Natives.

For further information, call 202–690–7776. Internet, www.acf.gov/programs/ana.

Refugee Resettlement The Office is responsible for the policies and programs regarding refugee and entrant resettlement and the U.S. Repatriate Program. It is responsible for planning, developing, and directing the implementation of a comprehensive program for domestic refugee and entrant resettlement assistance.

For further information, call 202–401–9246. Internet, www.acf.gov/programs/orr.

For further information, contact the Administration for Children and Families, 370 L'Enfant Promenade SW., Washington, DC 20447. Phone, 202–401–4634. Internet, www.acf.gov.

Agency for Healthcare Research and Quality

The Agency for Healthcare Research and Quality was established in 1989 as the Agency for Health Care Policy and Research, which was then established as an operating division within the Public Health Service. The Agency was renamed by act of November 1999 and charged with research designed to improve the quality of health care, reduce its cost, and broaden access to essential services.

For further information, contact the Agency for Healthcare Research and Quality, 2101 East Jefferson Street, Rockville, MD 20852. Phone, 301–594–1364. Internet, www.ahrq.gov. E-mail, info@ahrq.gov.

Agency for Toxic Substances and Disease Registry

A departmental reorganization order of October 31, 1995, established the Agency for Toxic Substances and Disease Registry (ATSDR) as an operating division within the Public Health Service. The Agency's mission is to prevent exposure and adverse health effects and diminished quality of life associated with exposure to hazardous substances from waste sites, unplanned releases, and other sources of pollution present in the environment. ATSDR evaluates information on hazardous substance releases to assess the impact on public health; establishes and maintains registries of human exposure for long-term follow-up and complete listings of areas restricted or closed to the public due to contamination; makes available data on the health effects of hazardous substances; conducts or sponsors research on the effects of hazardous substances released from waste sites or during transportation accidents on human health; and provides health-related support for first responders to ensure adequate response to public health emergencies.

For further information, contact the Office of Policy and External Affairs, Agency for Toxic Substances and Disease Registry, MS E–60, 1600 Clifton Road NE., Atlanta, GA 30333. Phone, 404–639–0501. Internet, www.atsdr.cdc.gov.

Centers for Disease Control and Prevention

A departmental reorganization order of October 31, 1999, established the Centers for Disease Control and Prevention (CDC) as an operating division within the Public Health Service. CDC is charged with protecting the public health of the Nation by providing leadership and direction in the prevention and control of diseases and other preventable conditions and responding to public health emergencies.

For further information, contact the Centers for Disease Control and Prevention, 1600 Clifton Road NE., Atlanta, GA, 30333. Phone, 404–639–3286, Internet, www.cdc.gov.

Food and Drug Administration

A departmental reorganization order of October 31, 1995, established the Food and Drug Administration (FDA) as an operating division of the Public Health Service. FDA's mission is to ensure that food is safe, pure, and wholesome; human and animal drugs, biological products, and medical devices are safe and effective; and electronic products that emit radiation are safe.

Biologics Evaluation and Research The Center regulates biological products, plans and conducts research on both new and old biological products, inspects manufacturers' facilities for compliance with standards, tests products submitted for release, establishes written and physical standards, and approves licensing of manufacturers to produce biological products. It plans and conducts research on the preparation, preservation, and safety of blood and blood products; the methods of testing safety, purity, potency, and efficacy of such products for therapeutic use; and the immunological problems concerned with products, testing, and use of diagnostic reagents employed in grouping and typing blood.

For further information, call 301–827–2000.

Devices and Radiological Health The Center develops and carries out a national program designed to control unnecessary exposure of humans to potentially hazardous ionizing and nonionizing radiation and ensure its safe use. It develops policy and priorities regarding FDA programs relating to the safety, effectiveness, and labeling of medical devices for human use; conducts an electronic product radiation control program, including the development and administration of performance standards; develops regulations, standards, and criteria and recommends changes in FDA legislative authority necessary to protect the public health; and provides scientific and technical support to other components within FDA and other agencies on matters relating to radiological health and medical devices.

For further information, call 800–638–2041.

Drug Evaluation and Research The Center develops administrative policy with regard to the safety, effectiveness, and labeling of all drug products for human use; reviews and evaluates new drug applications and investigates new drug applications; develops and implements standards for the safety and effectiveness of all over-the-counter drugs; and monitors the quality of marketed drug products through product testing, surveillance, and compliance programs.

For further information, call 301–827–4573.

Food Safety and Applied Nutrition The Center conducts research and develops standards on the composition, quality, nutrition, and safety of food, food additives, colors, and cosmetics, and maintains a nutritional databank. It conducts research designed to improve the detection, prevention, and control of contamination that may be responsible for illness or injury conveyed by foods, colors, and cosmetics; and it coordinates and evaluates FDA's surveillance and compliance programs relating to foods, colors, and cosmetics.

For further information, call 800–332–4010.

Toxicological Research The Center conducts peer-reviewed scientific research which supports and anticipates FDA current and future regulatory needs. This involves fundamental and applied research specifically designed to define mechanisms of action underlying the toxicity of products regulated by FDA. The research is aimed at understanding critical biological events in the expression of toxicity and at development methods to improve assessment of human exposure, susceptibility, and risk.

For further information, contact the National Center for Toxicological Research, 3900 NCTR Road, Jefferson, AR 70279. Phone, 501–543–7000. Internet, www.fda.gov/nctr.

Veterinary Medicine The Center develops and conducts programs with respect to the safety and efficacy of veterinary preparations and devices, evaluates proposed use of veterinary preparations for animal safety, and evaluates the FDA's surveillance and compliance programs relating to veterinary drugs and other veterinary medical matters.

For further information, call 301–594–1755.

For further information, contact the Food and Drug Administration, 5600 Fishers Lane, Rockville, MD 20857. Phone, 301–443–1544. Internet, www.fda.gov.

Health Care Financing Administration

[For the Health Care Financing Administration statement of organization, see the *Federal Register* of May 2, 1997, 62 FR 24120]

The Health Care Financing Administration (HCFA) was created in 1977 to combine under one administration the oversight of the Medicare program, the Federal portion of the Medicaid program, and related quality assurance activities.

Medicare provides health insurance coverage for people age 65 and over, younger people who are receiving social security disability benefits, and persons who need dialysis or kidney transplants for treatment of end-stage renal disease.

Medicaid is a medical assistance program jointly financed by State and Federal governments for eligible low-income individuals. It covers health care expenses for all recipients of Aid to Families With Dependent Children, and most States also cover the needy elderly, blind, and disabled receiving cash assistance under the Supplemental Security Income Program. Coverage also is extended to certain infants and low-income pregnant women and, at the option of the State, other low-income individuals with medical bills that qualify them as categorically or medically needy.

The Medicare/Medicaid programs include a quality assurance focal point to carry out the quality assurance provisions of the Medicare and Medicaid programs; the development and implementation of health and safety standards of care providers in Federal health programs; and the implementation of the end-stage renal disease and the peer review provisions.

For further information, contact the Health Care Financing Administration, Department of Health and Human Services, 200 Independence Avenue SW., Washington, DC 20201. Phone, 202–690–6726.

Health Resources and Services Administration

A departmental reorganization order of October 31, 1995, established the Health Resources and Services Administration (HRSA) as an operating division within the Public Health Service. The Administration is the principal primary health care service agency of the Federal Government making essential primary care services accessible to the poor, uninsured, and geographically isolated. Programs administered by HRSA include a broad array of grants; the National Health Service Corps; the national practitioner databank; the healthcare integrity and protection databank; the Vaccine Injury Compensation Program; the Ricky Ray Hemophilia Relief Fund; and HIV/AIDS assistance programs. HRSA encourages the donation of organs, tissue, and bone marrow for transplantation and ensures their equitable distribution; provides health care to people with Hansen's disease; and attends to the special health care needs of people with chronic health needs, minorities, and those living along the U.S. border with Mexico.

Health Professions The Bureau provides national leadership in coordinating, evaluating, and supporting the development and utilization of the Nation's health personnel, providing for financial aid to health professions students and support for health professions data analysis and research. It also provides leadership for promoting equity in access to health services and health careers for the disadvantaged, and provides technical assistance activities for international projects relevant to domestic health personnel problems.

For further information, contact the Information Officer. Phone, 301–443–1590. Fax, 301–443–7904. Internet, www.hrsa.gov/bhpr.

HIV/AIDS The Bureau administers the Ryan White Comprehensive AIDS Resources Emergency (CARE) Act and conducts a wide range of programs which provide primary care and support services to low-income, uninsured, and underinsured individuals and families affected by HIV/AIDS. It also provides HIV emergency relief grants to eligible metropolitan areas, and HIV care grants to States and U.S. territories; funds the AIDS Drug Assistance Program for all States and eligible territories; and supports projects examining economic changes and managed care effects on the Nation's network of HIV/AIDS care delivery.

For further information, contact the Communications Office. Phone, 301–443–6652. Fax, 301–443–0791. Internet, www.hrsa.gov/hab.

Maternal and Child Health The Bureau provides national leadership in supporting, identifying, and interpreting national trends and issues relating to the health needs of mothers, infants, children, and adolescents, including those with special health care needs. It administers the Maternal and Child Health Services Block Grant to States, the Emergency Medical Services for Children Program, the healthy start initiative, the Traumatic Brain Injury Demonstration Grant Program, and the Abstinence Education Program.

For further information, contact the Communications Office. Phone, 301–443–0205.

Primary Health Care The Bureau provides national leadership for efforts to increase access to comprehensive preventive and primary health care for underserved and vulnerable populations; provides grants to community, migrant, and school-based health centers, health care for the homeless programs, and public housing primary care programs; and administers the Federal occupational health program and the PHS drug pricing program.

For further information, contact the Information Dissemination and Communications Office. Phone, 301–594–4100. Fax, 301–594–5008. Internet, www.hrsa.gov/bphc.

For further information, contact the Office of Communications, Health Resources and Services Administration, 5600 Fishers Lane, Rockville, MD 20857. Phone, 301–443–2086. Internet, www.hrsa.gov.

Indian Health Service

A departmental reorganization order of October 31, 1995, established the Indian Health Service (IHS) as an operating division within the Public Health Service. IHS provides a comprehensive health services delivery system for American Indians and Alaska Natives, with opportunity for maximum tribal involvement in developing and managing programs to meet their health needs. It assists Native American tribes in developing their health programs; facilitates and assists tribes in coordinating health planning, obtaining and utilizing health resources available through Federal, State, and local programs, operating comprehensive health programs, and evaluating health programs; and provides comprehensive health care services including hospital and ambulatory medical care, preventive and rehabilitative services, and development of community sanitation facilities.

For further information, contact the Communications Office, Indian Health Service, 5600 Fishers Lane, Rockville, MD 20857. Phone, 301–443–3593. Internet, www.ihs.gov.

National Institutes of Health

A departmental reorganization order of October 31, 1995, established the National Institutes of Health (NIH) as an operating division within the Public Health Service. NIH supports biomedical and behavioral research domestically and abroad, conducts research in its own laboratories and clinics, trains promising young researchers, and promotes acquisition and distribution of medical knowledge. Research activities conducted or supported by NIH will determine the scope and direction of medical treatment and disease prevention in the future.

Aging The Institute conducts and supports biomedical and behavioral research to increase knowledge of the aging process and the physical, psychological, and social factors associated with aging. Alzheimer's disease, health and retirement, menopause, and frailty are among the areas of special concern.

For further information, contact the National Institute on Aging. Phone, 301–496–1752. Internet, www.nih.gov/nia.

Alcohol Abuse and Alcoholism The Institute conducts and supports biomedical and behavioral research, in order to provide science-based approaches to the prevention and treatment of alcohol abuse and alcoholism. It provides a national focus for the Federal effort to increase knowledge and disseminate research findings to the scientific community, health care system, and the public.

For further information, contact the National Institute of Alcohol Abuse and Alcoholism. Phone, 301–443–3885, or 301–443–3860. Internet, www.niaaa.nih.gov.

Allergy and Infectious Diseases The Institute conducts and supports research, research training, and clinical evaluations on the causes, treatment, and prevention of a wide variety of infectious, allergic, and immunologic diseases. Areas of special emphasis include AIDS; asthma and allergic diseases; immunologic diseases; transplantation; emerging and reemerging infectious diseases; sexually transmitted diseases; enteric diseases such as hepatitis; food-borne diseases; influenza and other respiratory infections; malaria and other parasitic diseases; and tuberculosis.

For further information, contact the National Institute of Allergy and Infectious Diseases. Phone, 301–496–5717. Internet, www.niaid.nih.gov.

Arthritis and Musculoskeletal and Skin Diseases The Institute supports research into the causes, treatment, and prevention of arthritis and musculoskeletal and skin diseases; the training of basic and clinical scientists to carry out this research; and the dissemination of information on research progress in these diseases.

For further information, contact the National Institute of Arthritis and Musculoskeletal and Skin Diseases. Phone, 301–496–4353. Internet, www.nih.gov/niams.

Cancer The National Institute of Cancer developed a national cancer program to expand existing scientific knowledge on cancer cause and prevention as well as on the diagnosis, treatment, and rehabilitation of cancer patients. Research activities cover a broad spectrum encompassing basic biological, clinical, prevention, and behavioral research.

For further information, contact the Cancer Information Service. Phone, 800–422–6237 or 301–435–3848. Internet, www.cancer.gov.

Child Health and Human Development The Institute conducts and supports biomedical and behavioral research on child and maternal health; sudden infant dealth syndrome (SIDS); pediatric, maternal, and adolescent AIDS; the reproductive process; problems of human development; mental retardation and developmental disabilities; family structure; and the dynamics of human population.

For further information, contact the National Institute of Child Health and Human Development. Phone, 301–496–5133. Internet, www.nichd.nih.gov.

Clinical Center The Center is designed to bring scientists working in Institute laboratories into proximity with clinicians caring for patients, so that they may collaborate on problems of mutual concern. The research institutes select patients, referred to NIH by themselves or by physicians throughout the United States and overseas, for clinical studies of specific diseases and disorders.

For further information, contact the Clinical Center. Phone, 301–496–3227. Internet, www.cc.nih.gov.

Complementary and Alternative Medicine. The Center works to prevent and alleviate human suffering by stimulating, developing, conducting, and supporting research on complementary and alternative medicine. Research training programs develop skilled investigators necessary to conduct rigorous and relevant research to determine which complementary and alternative medicine practices work, which do not, and why.

For further information, call 301–435–5042. Internet, nccam.nih.gov.

Deafness and Other Communication Disorders The Institute conducts and supports biomedical and behavioral research and research training on normal mechanisms as well as diseases and disorders of hearing, balance, smell, taste, voice, speech, and language through a diversity of research performed in its own laboratories, and a program of research grants, individual and institutional research training awards, career development awards, center grants, and contracts to public and private research institutions and organizations.

For further information, contact the National Institute on Deafness and Other Communication Disorders. Phone, 301–496–7243. Internet, www.nidcd.nih.gov.

Dental and Craniofacial Diseases The Institute conducts and supports research and research training into the causes, prevention, diagnosis, and treatment of craniofacial, oral, and dental diseases and disorders. Areas of special emphasis include inherited diseases and disorders; infectious diseases and immunity; oral, pharyngeal, and esophageal cancers; chronic and disabling diseases, including pain research; biomaterials, biomimetics, and tissue engineering; and behavior, health promotion, and environment.

For further information, contact the National Institute of Dental and Craniofacial Research. Phone, 301–496–4261. Internet, www.nidr.nih.gov.

Diabetes, Digestive, and Kidney Diseases The Institute conducts, fosters, and supports basic and clinical research into the causes, prevention, diagnosis, and treatment of diabetes, endocrine, and metabolic diseases, digestive diseases and nutrition, kidney and urologic diseases, and blood diseases. It provides research grants and individual and institutional research training awards, and conducts and supports epidemiological and clinical studies on selected populations in the United States.

For further information, contact the National Institute of Diabetes, Digestive, and Kidney Diseases. Phone, 301–496–3583. Internet, www.niddk.nih.gov.

Drug Abuse The Institute's primary mission is to lead the Nation in bringing the power of science to bear on drug abuse and addiction through the strategic support and conduct of research across a broad range of disciplines and the rapid and effective dissemination and use of the results of that research to significantly improve drug abuse and addiction prevention, treatment, and policy.

For further information, contact the National Institute on Drug Abuse. Phone, 301–443–6480. Internet, www.nida.nih.gov.

Environmental Health Sciences The Institute seeks to reduce the burden of human illness and dysfunction by understanding the elements of environmental exposures, human susceptibility, and time and how these elements interrelate. This mission is achieved through multidisciplinary biomedical research programs, prevention and intervention efforts, and communication strategies that encompass training, education, technology transfer, and community outreach.

For further information, contact the National Institute of Environmental Health Sciences. Phone, 919–541–3211. Internet, www.niehs.nih.gov.

Fogarty International Center The Center is dedicated to advancing the health of people through international scientific cooperation. The Center fosters biomedical research partnership between U.S. scientists and foreign counterparts through grants, fellowships, and international agreements, and provides leadership in international science policy and research strategies.

For further information, contact the Fogarty International Center. Phone, 301–496–2075. Internet, www.nih.gov/fic.

General Medical Sciences The Institute supports programs for research and research training emphasizing basic biomedical science with activities ranging from cell biology, chemistry, and biophysics to genetics, pharmacology, and systemic response to trauma.

For further information, contact the National Institute of General Medical Sciences. Phone, 301–496–7301. Internet, www.nih.gov/nigms.

Heart, Lung, and Blood Diseases The Institute provides leadership for a national program in diseases of the heart, blood vessels, lung, and blood; sleep disorders; and blood resources. It conducts, fosters, and supports an integrated and coordinated program of basic research, clinical investigations and trials, and observational studies.

For further information, contact the National Heart, Lung, and Blood Institute. Phone, 301–496–2411. Internet, www.nhlbi.nih.gov.

Human Genome Research The Institute formulates research goals and long-range plans to accomplish the mission of the human genome project, including the study of ethical, legal, and social implications of human genome research; supports and administers research and research training programs in human genome research including chromosome mapping, DNA sequencing, database development, and technology development for genome research; provides coordination of genome research and with industry and academia; and conducts research on human genetic disease.

For further information, contact the National Human Genome Research Institute. Phone, 301–496–0844. Internet, www.nhgri.nih.gov.

Medical Library The Library is the Nation's primary medical information source and is authorized to provide medical library services and online bibliographic search capabilities to public and private agencies, organizations, institutions, and individuals. It sponsors and conducts research and development in biomedical communications, in such areas as telemedicine, expert systems, and advanced medical imaging projects.

For further information, contact the National Library of Medicine. Phone, 301–496–6308. Internet, www.nlm.nih.gov.

Mental Health The Institute (NIMH) supports and conducts fundamental research in neuroscience, genetics, molecular biology, and behavior as the foundation of an extensive clinical research portfolio which seeks to expand and refine treatments available for illnesses such as schizophrenia; depressive disorders; severe anxiety; childhood mental disorders, including autism and attention-deficit/hyperactivity disorder; and other mental disorders. It supports research on treatment outcomes in actual practice settings, including primary care settings; and seeks to establish a sound scientific basis for the prevention of mental illness.

For further information, contact the National Institute of Mental Health. Phone, 301–443–3673. Internet, www.nimh.nih.gov.

Neurological Disorders and Stroke The Institute conducts and supports fundamental and applied research on human neurological disorders such as Parkinson's disease, epilepsy, multiple sclerosis, muscular dystrophy, head and spinal cord injuries, and stroke. The Institute also conducts and supports research on the development and function of the normal brain and nervous system in order to better understand normal processes relating to disease states.

For further information, contact the National Institute of Neurological Disorders and Stroke. Phone, 301–496–5751. Internet, www.ninds.nih.gov.

Nursing Research The Institute provides leadership for nursing research, supports and conducts research and training, and disseminates information to build a scientific base for nursing practice and patient care and to promote health and ameliorate the effects of illness on the American people.

For further information, contact the National Institute of Nursing Research. Phone, 301–496–0207. Internet, www.nih.gov.ninr.

Ophthalmological Diseases The Institute conducts, fosters, and supports research on the causes, natural history, prevention, diagnosis, and treatment of disorders of the eye and visual system, directs the National Eye Health Education Program, provides research grants and individual and institutional research training awards, works in cooperation and collaboration with voluntary organizations and other institutions engaged in research and training in the special health problems of the blind, and collects and disseminates information on research and findings.

For further information, contact the National Eye Institute. Phone, 301–496–4583, or 301–496–5248. Internet, www.nei.nih.gov.

Research Resources The Center supports the development of technologies to enable sophisticated research; creates and supports a broad range of sophisticated multi-disciplinary research facilities for basic, clinical, and animal research; and supports institutions development for minority-serving institutions which doctoral degrees in health-related sciences. Programs include supporting biorepositories with companion web-based databases for a wide range of organisms.

For further information, contact the National Center for Research Resources. Phone, 301–435–0888. Internet, www.ncrr.nih.gov.

Scientific Review The Center receives and assigns applications for peer reviews to scientific review groups whose members hold advanced degrees and are established investigators in the extramural community. After review, applications are referred to funding components for potential award. The Center develops and implements innovative, flexible ways to conduct referral and review for all aspects of science.

For further information, contact the Center for Scientific Review. Phone 303–435–1111. Internet, www.csr.nih.gov.

For further information, contact the National Institutes of Health, 9000 Rockville Pike, Bethesda, MD 20892. Phone, 301–496–4000. Internet, www.nih.gov.

Program Support Center

[For the Program Support Center statement of organization, see the *Federal Register* of November 15, 1995, 60 FR 57452]

The Program Support Center provides support services to HHS components and other Federal agencies. The Center was created as a business enterprise to provide services on a competitive service-for-fee basis to customers who wish to purchase services in the areas of human resources, financial management, and administrative operations.

For further information, contact the Director of Marketing, Program Support Center, Department of Health and Human Services, Room 17A–18, 5600 Fishers Lane, Rockville, MD 20857. Phone, 301–443–1494.

Substance Abuse and Mental Health Services Administration

A departmental reorganization order of October 31, 1995, established the Substance Abuse and Mental Health Services Administration (SAMHSA) as an operating division within the Public Health Service. The Administration provides national leadership to ensure that knowledge acquired is effectively used for the prevention and treatment of addictive and mental disorders. It strives to improve access and reduce barriers to high quality, effective programs and services for individuals who suffer from or are at risk for these disorders, as well as for their families and communities.

Mental Health Services The Center provides national leadership to promote improved state of mental health and the rehabilitation of people with mental disorders and others affected. The Center administers grants, contracts, and cooperative agreements which support the development and application of new knowledge in the mental health field; supports activities to improve management of mental health care; collects data on the various forms of mental illnesses; cooperates with other Federal components to coordinate disaster assistance, community response, and other mental health emergency services as a consequence of national disasters; and collaborates with the alcohol, drug abuse, and mental heath institutes of NIH on services research issues.

For further information, call 301–443–0001.

Substance Abuse Prevention The Center provides a national focus for the Federal effort to demonstrate and promote effective strategies to prevent the abuse of alcohol and other drugs; reviews and approves or disapproves State prevention plans developed under the Substance Abuse Prevention and Treatment Block Grant Program authority; implements the tobacco regulations and other appropriate regulations; administers grants, contracts, and cooperative agreements which support the development and application of new knowledge in the substance abuse prevention field; fosters interagency and State prevention networks; supports a clearinghouse to disseminate literature on substance abuse prevention; and provides a focus for addressing the substance abuse prevention needs of individuals with multiple, co-occurring drug, alcohol, mental, and physical problems.

For further information, call 301–443–0365.

Substance Abuse Treatment The Center provides leadership for the Federal effort to enhance approaches and provide resources to ensure provision of programs providing services for the treatment of substance abuse and co-occurring physical and/or psychiatric conditions; addresses the treatment needs of individuals with multiple, co-occurring drug, alcohol, mental, and physical problems; administers grants, contracts, and cooperative agreements which support the development and application of new knowledge in the substance abuse treatment field; collaborates with States and the National Institute on Drug Abuse to promote the development, dissemination, and application of treatment outcome standards; administers programs for training health care providers; manages the Substance Abuse Prevention and Treatment Block Grant Program; conducts managed care activities; and collaborates with the alcohol, drug abuse, and mental health institutes of NIH on services research issues.

For further information, call 301–443–5700.

For further information, contact the Substance Abuse and Mental Health Services Administration, 5600 Fishers Lane, Rockville, MD 20857. Phone, 301–443–4795. Internet, www.samhsa.gov.

Sources of Information

Office of the Secretary

Unless otherwise indicated, inquiries on the following subjects may be directed to the specified office, Department of Health and Human Services, Hubert H. Humphrey Building, 200 Independence Avenue SW., Washington, DC 20201.

Civil Rights For information on enforcement of civil rights laws, contact the Office for Civil Rights, Room 502E. Phone, 202–619–0671, or 800–368–1019 (toll-free). TDD, 800–537–7697 (toll-free). Internet, www.hhs.gov/progorg/ocr. E-mail, eocr@os.dhhs.gov.

Contracts and Small Business Activities For information concerning programs, contact the Director, Office of Small and Disadvantaged Business Utilization. Phone, 202–690–7300.

Electronic Access Information concerning the Department is available electronically through the Internet, at www.dhhs.gov.

Employment Inquiries regarding applications for employment and the college recruitment program should be directed to the SW Human Resources Service, Program Support Center, 330 C Street SW., Washington, DC 20201. Phone, 202–619–0146.

Inspector General General inquiries and requests for single copies of Office publications may be directed to the Office of Inspector General, Wilbur J. Cohen Building, 330 Independence Avenue SW., Washington, DC 20201. Phone, 202–619–1343. E-mail, esec@os.dhhs.gov. Internet, www.oig.hhs.gov.

Inspector General Hotline Individuals wishing to report fraud, waste, or abuse against Department programs should write to: Office of Inspector General, HHS–TIPS Hotline, P.O. Box 23489, L'Enfant Plaza Station, Washington, DC 20026–3489. Phone, 800–HHS–TIPS (800–447–8477) (toll-free). TTY, 800–377–4950. Fax, 800–223–8164. E-mail, htips@os.dhhs.gov.

Locator Inquiries about the location and telephone numbers of HHS offices should be directed to the Information Technology Service, HHS Locator, Room G–644, Wilbur J. Cohen Building, 330 Independence Avenue SW., Washington, DC 20201. Phone, 202–619–0257.

Public Health and Science Inquiries should be directed to the Assistant Secretary for Health, Room 716G. Phone, 202–690–7694. Internet, www.surgeongeneral.gov.

Administration on Aging

Inquiries on the following subjects may be directed to the specified office, Department of Health and Human Services, Wilbur J. Cohen Building, 330 Independence Avenue SW., Washington, DC 20201.

Aging Individuals seeking biographic data; practical material for planners/practitioners; reports on the demographic, health, social, and economic status of older Americans; specialized technical reports on current aging issues; and analytical reports on aging statistics should contact the National Aging Information Center, Room 4656. Phone, 202–619–7501. TDD, 202–401–7575. Fax, 202–401–7620. E-mail, naic@ageinfo.org.

Elder Care Services For information concerning services available to elderly persons in any given community in the Nation, contact the Elder Care Locator. Phone, 800–677–1116.

Employment Applications for employment and college recruitment

programs should be directed to the Director, Office of Management, Room 4644. Phone, 202–619–1557.
Locator For information about the location and telephone numbers of offices and programs, call 202–619–4541.
Public Inquiries/Publications Copies of publications are available free of charge by contacting the Office of the Executive Secretariat. Phone, 202–619–0724. TDD, 202–401–7575. Fax, 202–260–1012. Internet, www.aoa.dhhs.gov. E-mail, aoa_esec@ban-gate.aoa.dhhs.gov.

Administration for Children and Families

General inquiries may be directed to the Administration for Children and Families, DHHS, 370 L'Enfant Promenade SW., Washington, DC 20447. Phone, 202–401–9200. Inquiries on the following subjects may be directed to the specified office.
Contracts Contact the Division of Acquisition Management, Office of Administration. Phone, 202–401–5149.
Employment Contact the Program Support Center, Room 1100, 330 C Street SW., Washington, DC 20201.
Information Center Contact the Office of Public Affairs, Seventh Floor, 370 L'Enfant Promenade SW., Washington, DC 20744. Phone, 202–401–9215.
Mental Retardation For information on mental retardation programs, contact the President's Committee on Mental Retardation, Administration for Children and Families. Phone, 202–401–9316.

Agency for Healthcare Research and Quality

Inquiries on the following subjects may be directed to the appropriate office at the Agency for Healthcare Research and Quality, Department of Health and Human Services, 2101 East Jefferson Street, Rockville, MD 20852.
Contracts Contact the Division of Contracts Management. Phone, 301–594–1445.
Employment Inquiries should be addressed to the Division of Human Resources Management. Phone, 301–594–2408.
Grants Contact the Division of Grants Management. Phone, 301–594–1447.
Publications Single copies of most publications produced by the Agency are available free of charge from the AHRQ Publications Clearinghouse, P.O. Box 8547, Silver Spring, MD 20907. Phone, 800–358–9295 (toll-free).

Agency for Toxic Substances and Disease Registry

Information regarding programs and activities is available electronically through the Internet, at www.atsdr.cdc.gov.

Centers for Disease Control and Prevention

Inquiries on the following subjects may be directed to the office indicated at the Centers for Disease Control and Prevention, Department of Health and Human Services, 1600 Clifton Road NE., Atlanta, GA 30333.
Electronic Access Information regarding programs and activities is available electronically through the Internet, at www.cdc.gov.
Employment The majority of scientific and technical positions are filled through the Commissioned Corps of the Public Health Service, a uniformed service of the U.S. Government. Inquiries should be addressed to the Human Resources Management Office (phone, 770–488–1725) or the Division of Commissioned Personnel (Room 4A–15, 5600 Fishers Lane, Rockville, MD 20857).
Films Information concerning availability of audiovisual materials related to program activities may be obtained from the Office of Communications. Phone, 404–639–7290.
Publications Single copies of most publications are available, free of charge, from the Management Analysis and Services Office. Phone, 404–639–3534. Bulk quantities of publications may be purchased from the Superintendent of Documents, Government Printing Office, Washington, DC 20402.

Food and Drug Administration

Inquiries on the following subjects may be directed to the specified office, Food and Drug Administration, Department of Health and Human Services, 5600 Fishers Lane, Rockville, MD 20857.

Consumer Activities Recorded messages at FDA Public Affairs offices across the country provide information of interest to consumers. Contact the nearest Public Affairs Office (see table below) or call 301–443–5006.

Public Affairs Offices—Food and Drug Administration

Office	Address	Telephone
Alameda, CA	1431 Harbor Bay Pkwy., 94502–7070	510–337–6888
Atlanta, GA	60 8th St., NE., 30309	404–347–4001
Baltimore, MD	900 Madison Ave., 21201	410–962–3731
Boston, MA	1 Montvale Ave., Stoneham, 02180	617–279–1675
Brooklyn, NY	850 3d Ave., 11232	718–340–7000
Buffalo, NY	Suite 100, 300 Pearl St., 14202	716–551–4461
Chicago, IL	Suite 550–S, 300 S. Riverside Plz., 60606	312–353–5863
Cincinnati, OH	6751 Steger Dr., 45237–3097	513–679–2700
Cleveland, OH	P.O. Box 838, Brunswick, 44212	216–273–1038
Dallas, TX	3310 Live Oak St., 75204	214–655–5315
Denver, CO	Rm. B–1121, 6th Ave. & Kippling, 80225	303–236–3018
Detroit, MI	1560 E. Jefferson Ave., 48207	313–226–6158
Houston, TX	Suite 420, 1445 N. Loop W., 77008	713–802–9095
Indianapolis, IN	Suite 1300, 101 W. Ohio St., 46204	317–226–6500
Irvine, CA	Suite 300, 19900 MacArthur Blvd., 92715–2445	714–798–7607
Lenexa, KS	11630 W. 80th St., 66214	913–752–2141
Maitland, FL	Suite 200, 555 Winderley Pl., 32751	407–475–4704
Miami, FL	P.O. Box 59–2256, 33159–2256	305–526–2800
Milwaukee, WI	Suite 20, 2675 N. Mayfair Rd., 53226–1305	414–771–7167
Minneapolis, MN	240 Hennepin Ave., 55401	612–334–4100
Nashville, TN	297 Plus Park Blvd., 37217	615–781–5372
New Orleans, LA	4298 Elysian Fields Ave., 70122	504–589–2420
Omaha, NE	200 S. 16th St., 68102	402–331–8536
Orlando, FL	Suite 120, 7200 Lake Ellenor Dr., 32809	407–648–6922
Philadelphia, PA	Rm. 900, 2d & Chestnut Sts., 19106	215–597–4390
Phoenix, AZ	Suite 402, 4605 E. Elwood Street, 85040–1948	602–829–7396
Portland, OR	9780 SW. Nimbus Ave., 97008–7163	503–671–9322
San Antonio, TX	Rm. 119, 10127 Morocco, 78216	210–229–4531
San Juan, PR	466 Fernandez Juncos Ave., 00901–3223	787–729–6852
Seattle, WA	22201 23d Dr. SE., Bothell, WA 98201–4421	425–483–4953
St. Louis, MO	Suite 122, 12 Sunnen Dr., 63143	314–645–1167

Contracts Contact the Director, Office of Facilities, Acquisition, and Central Services (HFA–500). Phone, 301–827–6890.

Electronic Access Information on FDA is available electronically through the Internet, at www.fda.gov.

Employment FDA uses various civil service examinations and registers in its recruitment for positions such as consumer safety officers, pharmacologists, microbiologists, physiologists, chemists, mathematical statisticians, physicians, dentists, animal caretakers, etc. Inquiries for positions in the Washington, DC, metropolitan area should be directed to the Personnel Officer (HFA–400) (phone, 301–827–4120); inquiries for positions outside the Washington, DC, area should be directed to the appropriate local FDA office. Schools interested in the college recruitment program should contact the Personnel Officer (HFA–400) (phone, 301–827–4120).

Publications *FDA Consumer*, FDA's official magazine, is available from the Superintendent of Documents, Government Printing Office, Washington, DC 20402. Phone, 202–512–1800.

Reading Rooms Freedom of Information, Room 12A–30 (phone, 301–443–1813); Hearing Clerk and Documents Management Branch, Room 1061, 5630 Fishers Lane, Rockville, MD 20857 (phone, 301–827–6251); Press Office, Room 15A–07 or Room 3807, FB–8, 200 C Street SW., Washington, DC 20204 (phone, 202–205–4144).

Speakers Speakers are available for presentations to private organizations and community groups. Requests should be directed to the local FDA office.

Health Care Financing Administration

Inquiries on the following subjects may be directed to the Health Care Financing Administration, Department of Health and Human Services, 7500 Security Boulevard, Baltimore, MD 21244–1850.
Contracts and Small Business Activities Contact the Director, Division of Research Contracts and Grants. Phone, 410–786–5157.
Electronic Access Information on HCFA is available electronically through the Internet, at www.hcfa.gov.
Employment Inquiries should be directed to the Human Resources Management Group. Phone, 410–786–2032.
Publications Contact the Division of Publications Management Services. Phone, 410–786–7892.

Health Resources and Services Administration

Inquiries on the following subjects should be directed to the specified office, Health Resources and Services Administration, Department of Health and Human Services, 5600 Fishers Lane, Rockville, MD 20857. Internet, www.hrsa.gov.
Employment The majority of positions are in the Federal civil service. For positions in the Washington, DC, metropolitan area and field locations throughout the Nation, inquiries should be addressed to the Division of Personnel, Room 14A–46 (phone, 301–443–5460; TDD, 301–443–5278). For information on vacant positions, call 301–443–1230. Some health professional positions are filled through the Commissioned Corps of the Public Health Service, a uniformed service of the U.S. Government. Inquiries may be addressed to Division of Commissioned Personnel, Room 4A–15, 5600 Fishers Lane, Rockville, MD 20857.
Films Information concerning the availability of audiovisual materials related to program activities, including films for recruiting minorities into health professions and women into dentistry is available from the Office of Communications.
Publications Single copies of most publications are available free of charge from the HRSA Information Center (phone, 888–ASK–HRSA); the National Maternal and Child Health Clearinghouse (phone, 888–434–4MCH); or the National Clearinghouse for Primary Care Information, (phone, 703–821–8955; fax, 703–821–2098). Bulk quantities of publications may be purchased from the Superintendent of Documents, Government Printing Office, Washington, DC 20402.

Indian Health Service

Inquiries on the following subjects should be directed to the specified office, Indian Health Service, Department of Health and Human Services, 5600 Fishers Lane, Rockville, MD 20857.
Electronic Access Information on IHS is available electronically through the Internet, at www.ihs.gov.
Employment The majority of positions are in the Federal civil service. For positions in the Washington, DC, metropolitan area, employment inquiries may be addressed to the Division of Personnel Management, Office of Human Resources, Room 4B–44 (phone, 301–443–6520). Hiring in other parts of the country is decentralized to the 12 area offices. For specific area office addresses, see the U.S. Government listings in the commercial telephone directories for Aberdeen, SD; Albuquerque, NM; Anchorage, AK; Bemidji, MN; Billings, MT; Nashville, TN; Oklahoma City, OK; Phoenix, AZ; Portland, OR; Sacramento, CA; Tucson, AZ; and Window Rock, AZ. Some health professional positions are filled through the Commissioned Corps of the Public Health Service, a uniformed service of the U.S. Government. Inquiries may be addressed to the Division of Commissioned Personnel, Room 4A–15, 5600 Fishers Lane, Rockville, MD 20857. Phone, 301–443–3464.
Publications Single copies of publications describing the Indian Health Service and the health status of American Indians and Alaska Natives are available, free of charge, from the

Communications Office, Room 6–35. Phone, 301–443–3593.

National Institutes of Health

Inquiries on the following subjects may be directed to the office indicated at the National Institutes of Health, Bethesda, MD 20892, or at the address given.
Contracts For information on research and development contracts, contact the Office of Contracts Management. Phone, 301–496–4422. For all other contracts, contact the Office of Procurement Management. Phone, 301–496–7448.
Employment A wide range of civil service examinations and registers are used. Staff fellowships are available to recent doctorates in biomedical sciences. College recruitment is conducted as necessary to meet requirements. Contact the Office of Human Resource Management. Phone, 301–496–2404.
Environmental Research Research on the effects of environmental exposures to human health is conducted and supported by the National Institute of Environmental Health Sciences, Research Triangle Park, NC 22709. Phone, 919–541–3345.
Films Research and health-related films are available for loan from the National Library of Medicine, Collection Access Section, Bethesda, MD 20984.
Public Health Service Commissioned Officer Program For information on the Commissioned Officer programs at NIH and the program for early commissioning of senior medical students in the Reserve Corps of the Public Health Service, contact the Division of Senior Systems. Phone, 301–496–1443.
Publications Publications, brochures, and reports on health and disease problems, medical research, and biomedical communications, as well as single copies of *Journal of National Cancer Institute; Environmental Health Perspectives;* and *Scientific Directory and Annual Bibliography* are available through the Public Information Office, Office of Communications and Public Liaison, National Institutes of Health, Bethesda, MD 20892. Phone, 301–496–4461. Internet, www.nih.gov.

NIH Publications List, Index Medicus, Cumulated Index Medicus Annual, and *Research Grants Index* may be ordered from the Government Printing Office, Washington, DC 20402.

Program Support Center

General inquiries may be directed to the Program Support Center, Department of Health and Human Services, 5600 Fishers Lane, Rockville, MD 20857.
Electronic Access Information is available electronically through the Internet, www.psc.gov.
Employment Information is available electonically through the Internet, at www.psc.gov/spo/spo.html. Inquiries may be directed to the Division of Personnel Operations, Room 17–38, 5600 Fishers Lane, Rockville, MD 20857 (phone, 301–443–3201), or Room 1100, 300 C Street SW., Washington, DC 20201 (phone, 202–619–0146), or the Public Health Service Commissioned Corps, Room 4A–18, 5600 Fishers Lane, Rockville, MD 20857 (phone, 301–594–3360).

Substance Abuse and Mental Health Services Administration

Inquiries on the following subjects may be directed to the specified office, Substance Abuse and Mental Health Services Administration, Department of Health and Human Services, 5600 Fishers Lane, Rockville, MD 20857.
Contracts Contact the Director, Division of Contracts Management, Office of Program Services. Phone, 301–443–4980.
Electronic Access Information is available electronically through the Internet, at www.samhsa.gov, www.mentalhealth.org, or www.health.org.
Employment Inquiries should be addressed to the Director, Division of Human Resources Management, Office of Program Services. Phone, 301–443–3408.
Grants Contact the Director, Division of Grants Management, Office of Program Services. Phone, 301–443–8926.

Publications Contact the Associate Administrator for Communications. Phone, 301–443–8956.

For further information, contact the Information Center, Department of Health and Human Services, 200 Independence Avenue SW., Washington, DC 20201. Phone, 202–619–0257. Internet, www.dhhs.gov.

DEPARTMENT OF HOUSING AND URBAN DEVELOPMENT

451 Seventh Street SW., Washington, DC 20410
Phone, 202–708–1422. Internet, www.hud.gov.

SECRETARY OF HOUSING AND URBAN DEVELOPMENT	ANDREW M. CUOMO
Deputy Secretary	SAUL N. RAMIREZ, JR.
Assistant Deputy Secretary for Field Policy and Management	MARY E. MADDEN
Director, Office of Small and Disadvantaged Business Utilization	CASIMIR BONKOWSKI
Chair, HUD Board of Contract Appeals and Chief Administrative Judge	DAVID T. ANDERSON
Chief Administrative Law Judge	ALAN W. HEIFETZ
Assistant Secretary for Administration	JOSEPH F. SMITH
Assistant Secretary for Community Planning and Development	CARDELL COOPER
General Deputy Assistant Secretary for Office of General Counsel	GAIL W. LASTER
Assistant Secretary for Congressional and Intergovernmental Relations	HAL C. DECELL III
Assistant Secretary for Fair Housing and Equal Opportunity	EVA M. PLAZA
Assistant Secretary for Housing—Federal Housing Commissioner	WILLIAM APGAR
Assistant Secretary for Policy Development and Research	(VACANCY)
Assistant Secretary for Public Affairs	(VACANCY)
Assistant Secretary for Public and Indian Housing	HAROLD LUCAS
Director, Office of Departmental Equal Employment Opportunity	(VACANCY)
Chief Information Officer	GLORIA R. PARKER
Chief Financial Officer	(VACANCY)
Chief Procurement Officer	V. STEPHEN CARBERRY
Director, Departmental Enforcement Center	EDWARD KRAUS
Director, Departmental Real Estate Assessment Center	DAVID J. LAVOY
Director, Office of Departmental Operations and Coordination	FRANK L. DAVIS
Director, Office of Federal Housing Enterprise Oversight	(VACANCY)
Director, Office of Lead Hazard Control	DAVID E. JACOBS
Director, Office of Multifamily Housing Assistance Restructuring	IRA G. PEPPERCORN
Inspector General	SUSAN M. GAFFNEY
President, Government National Mortgage Association	GEORGE S. ANDERSON

The Department of Housing and Urban Development is the principal Federal agency responsible for programs concerned with the Nation's housing needs, fair housing opportunities, and improvement and development of the Nation's communities.

The Department of Housing and Urban Development (HUD) was established in the 1965 by the Department of Housing and Urban Development Act (42 U.S.C. 3532–3537). It was created to:

—administer the principal programs that provide assistance for housing and for the development of the Nation's communities;

—encourage the solution of housing and community development problems through States and localities; and

—encourage the maximum contributions that may be made by vigorous private homebuilding and mortgage lending industries, both primary and secondary, to housing, community development, and the national economy.

Although HUD administers many programs, its major functions may be grouped into six categories:

—insuring mortgages for single-family and multi-family dwellings, and extending loans for home improvement and for purchasing mobile homes;

—channeling funds from investors into the mortgage industry through the Government National Mortgage Association;

—making direct loans for construction or rehabilitation of housing projects for the elderly and the handicapped;

—providing Federal housing subsidies for low- and moderate-income families;

—providing grants to States and communities for community development activities; and

—promoting and enforcing fair housing and equal housing opportunity.

Secretary The Secretary formulates recommendations for basic policies in the fields of housing and community development; encourages private enterprise participation in housing and community development; promotes the growth of cities and States and the efficient and effective use of housing and community and economic development resources by stimulating private sector initiatives, public/private sector partnerships, and public entrepreneurship; ensures equal access to housing and affirmatively prevents discrimination in housing; and provides general oversight for the Federal National Mortgage Association.

Federal Housing Finance Board An independent agency in the executive branch, the Board oversees the Federal Home Loan Banks to ensure that they carry out their housing finance mission, remain adequately capitalized, and operate in a safe and sound manner.

Program Areas

Community Planning and Development The Office administers grant programs to help communities plan and finance their growth and development, increase their capacity to govern, and provide shelter and services for homeless people. The Office is responsible for implementing Community Development Block Grant (CDBG) programs for entitlement communities; State- and HUD-administered small cities programs; community development loan guarantees; special purpose grants for insular areas and historically black colleges and universities; Appalachian Regional Commission grants; Home Investment in Affordable Housing (HOME), which provides Federal assistance for housing rehabilitation, tenant-based assistance, assistance to first-time homebuyers, and new construction when a jurisdiction is determined to need new rental housing; the Department's programs to address

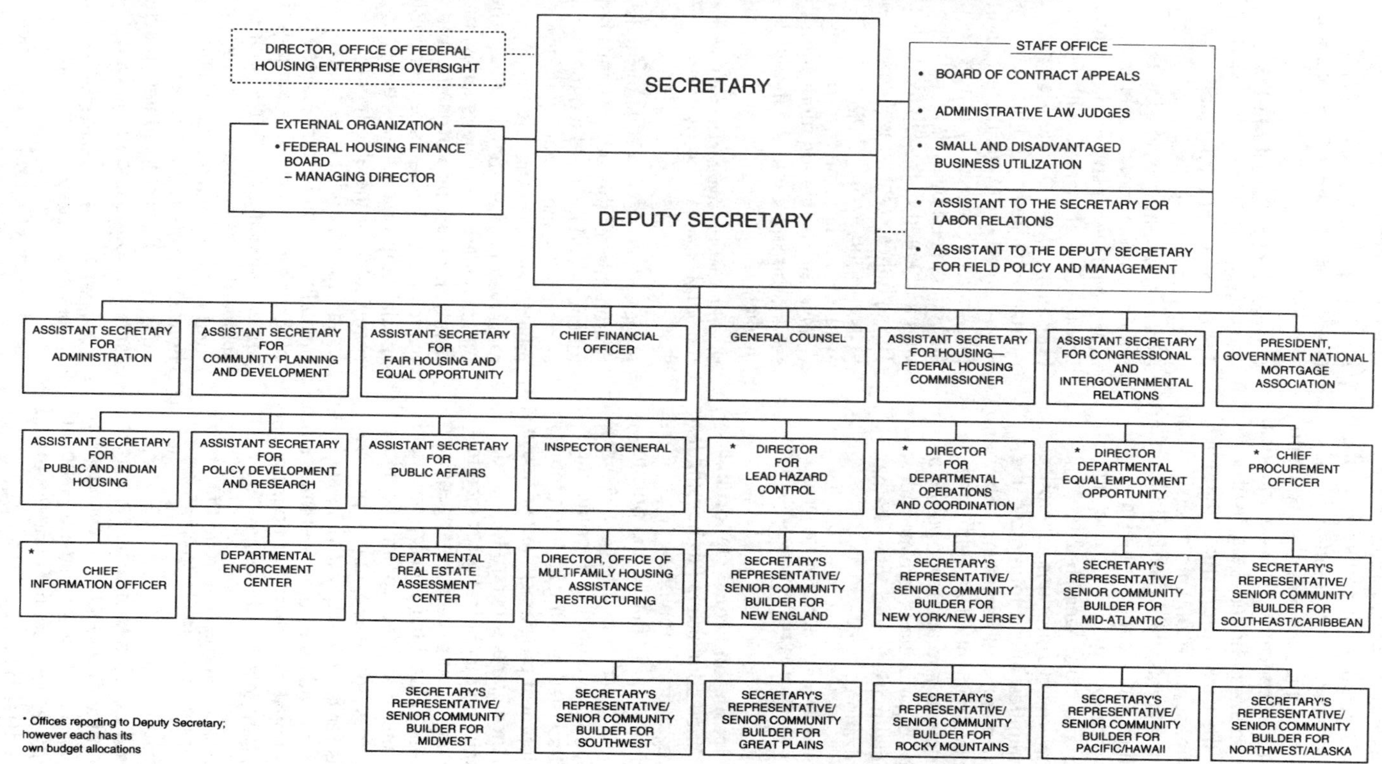
DEPARTMENT OF HOUSING AND URBAN DEVELOPMENT
DIRECTOR, OFFICE OF FEDERAL HOUSING ENTERPRISE OVERSIGHT
SECRETARY
DEPUTY SECRETARY
EXTERNAL ORGANIZATION
• FEDERAL HOUSING FINANCE BOARD – MANAGING DIRECTOR
STAFF OFFICE
• BOARD OF CONTRACT APPEALS
• ADMINISTRATIVE LAW JUDGES
• SMALL AND DISADVANTAGED BUSINESS UTILIZATION
• ASSISTANT TO THE SECRETARY FOR LABOR RELATIONS
• ASSISTANT TO THE DEPUTY SECRETARY FOR FIELD POLICY AND MANAGEMENT
ASSISTANT SECRETARY FOR ADMINISTRATION
ASSISTANT SECRETARY FOR COMMUNITY PLANNING AND DEVELOPMENT
ASSISTANT SECRETARY FOR FAIR HOUSING AND EQUAL OPPORTUNITY
CHIEF FINANCIAL OFFICER
GENERAL COUNSEL
ASSISTANT SECRETARY FOR HOUSING— FEDERAL HOUSING COMMISSIONER
ASSISTANT SECRETARY FOR CONGRESSIONAL AND INTERGOVERNMENTAL RELATIONS
PRESIDENT, GOVERNMENT NATIONAL MORTGAGE ASSOCIATION
ASSISTANT SECRETARY FOR PUBLIC AND INDIAN HOUSING
ASSISTANT SECRETARY FOR POLICY DEVELOPMENT AND RESEARCH
ASSISTANT SECRETARY FOR PUBLIC AFFAIRS
INSPECTOR GENERAL
* DIRECTOR FOR LEAD HAZARD CONTROL
* DIRECTOR FOR DEPARTMENTAL OPERATIONS AND COORDINATION
* DIRECTOR DEPARTMENTAL EQUAL EMPLOYMENT OPPORTUNITY
* CHIEF PROCUREMENT OFFICER
* CHIEF INFORMATION OFFICER
DEPARTMENTAL ENFORCEMENT CENTER
DEPARTMENTAL REAL ESTATE ASSESSMENT CENTER
DIRECTOR, OFFICE OF MULTIFAMILY HOUSING ASSISTANCE RESTRUCTURING
SECRETARY'S REPRESENTATIVE/ SENIOR COMMUNITY BUILDER FOR NEW ENGLAND
SECRETARY'S REPRESENTATIVE/ SENIOR COMMUNITY BUILDER FOR NEW YORK/NEW JERSEY
SECRETARY'S REPRESENTATIVE/ SENIOR COMMUNITY BUILDER FOR MID-ATLANTIC
SECRETARY'S REPRESENTATIVE/ SENIOR COMMUNITY BUILDER FOR SOUTHEAST/CARIBBEAN
SECRETARY'S REPRESENTATIVE/ SENIOR COMMUNITY BUILDER FOR MIDWEST
SECRETARY'S REPRESENTATIVE/ SENIOR COMMUNITY BUILDER FOR SOUTHWEST
SECRETARY'S REPRESENTATIVE/ SENIOR COMMUNITY BUILDER FOR GREAT PLAINS
SECRETARY'S REPRESENTATIVE/ SENIOR COMMUNITY BUILDER FOR ROCKY MOUNTAINS
SECRETARY'S REPRESENTATIVE/ SENIOR COMMUNITY BUILDER FOR PACIFIC/HAWAII
SECRETARY'S REPRESENTATIVE/ SENIOR COMMUNITY BUILDER FOR NORTHWEST/ALASKA
* Offices reporting to Deputy Secretary; however each has its own budget allocations

homelessness; the John Heinz Neighborhood Development Program; community outreach partnerships; the joint community development plan, assisting institutions of higher education working in concert with State and local governments to undertake activities under the CDBG program; community adjustment and economic diversification planning grants; the YouthBuild Program, which provides opportunities and assistance to very low income high school dropouts, ages 16–24; empowerment zones and enterprise communities; efforts to improve the environment; and community planning and development efforts with other departments and agencies, public and private organizations, private industry, financial markets, and international organizations.

For further information, contact the Office of Community Planning and Development. Phone, 202–708–2690.

Fair Housing and Equal Opportunity The Office administers fair housing laws and regulations prohibiting discrimination in public and private housing; equal opportunity laws and regulations prohibiting discrimination in HUD-assisted housing and community development programs; the fair housing assistance grants program to provide financial and technical assistance to State and local government agencies to implement local fair housing laws and ordinances; and the Community Housing Resources Boards program to provide grants for fair housing activities such as outreach and education, identification of institutional barriers to fair housing, and complaint telephone hotlines.

For further information, contact the Office of Fair Housing and Equal Opportunity. Phone, 202–708–4252.

Federal Housing Enterprise Oversight The Office oversees the financial safety and soundness of the Federal National Mortgage Association (Fannie Mae) and the Federal Home Loan Mortgage Corporation (Freddie Mac) to ensure that they are adequately capitalized and operating safely.

For further information, contact the Office of Federal Housing Enterprise Oversight. Phone, 202–414–3800.

Government National Mortgage Association (GNMA) The mission of this Government corporation, also known as Ginnie Mae, is to support expanded affordable housing by providing an efficient Government-guaranteed secondary market vehicle to link the capital markets with Federal housing markets. Ginnie Mae guarantees mortgage-backed securities composed of FHA-insured or VA-guaranteed mortgage loans that are issued by private lenders and guaranteed by GNMA with the full faith and credit of the United States. Through these programs, Ginnie Mae increases the overall supply of credit available for housing by providing a vehicle for channeling funds from the securities market into the mortgage market.

For further information, contact the Government National Mortgage Association. Phone, 202–708–0926.

Housing The Office of Housing is responsible for the Department's housing functions and oversees aid for construction and financing of new and rehabilitated housing and for preservation of existing housing. The Office underwrites single-family, multi-family, property improvement, and manufactured home loans; administers special purpose programs designed specifically for the elderly, the handicapped, and the chronically mentally ill; administers assisted housing programs for low-income families who are experiencing difficulties affording standard housing; administers grants to fund resident ownership of multi-family house properties; and protects consumers against fraudulent practices of land developers and promoters.

For further information, contact the Office of Housing. Phone, 202–708–3600.

Lead Hazard Control The Office is responsible for lead hazard control policy development, abatement, training, regulations, and research. Activities of the Office include increasing public and building industry awareness of the dangers of lead-based paint poisoning and the options for detection, risk reduction, and abatement; encouraging the development of safer, more effective, and less costly methods for detection, risk reduction, and abatement; and encouraging State and local governments to develop lead-based paint programs covering contractor certification, hazard reduction, financing, enforcement, and primary prevention, including public education.

For further information, contact the Office of Lead Hazard Control. Phone, 202–755–1785.

Public and Indian Housing The Office administers public and Indian housing programs; provides technical and financial assistance in planning, developing, and managing low-income projects; provides operating subsidies for public housing agencies (PHA's) and Indian housing authorities (IHA's), including procedures for reviewing the management of public housing agencies; administers the comprehensive improvement assistance and comprehensive grant programs for modernization of low-income housing projects to upgrade living conditions, correct physical deficiencies, and achieve operating efficiency and economy; administers program for resident participation, resident management, homeownership, economic development and supportive services, and drug-free neighborhood programs; protects tenants from the hazards of lead-based paint poisoning by requiring PHA's and IHA's to comply with HUD regulations for the testing and removal of lead-based paint from low-income housing units; implements and monitors program requirements related to program eligibility and admission of families to public and assisted housing, and tenant income and rent requirements pertaining to continued occupancy; administers the HOPE VI and vacancy reduction programs; administers voucher and certificate programs and the Moderate Rehabilitation Program; coordinates all departmental housing and community development programs for Indian and Alaskan Natives; and awards grants to PHA's and IHA's for the construction, acquisition, and operation of public and Indian housing projects, giving priority to projects for larger families and acquisition of existing units.

For further information, contact the Office of Public and Indian Housing. Phone, 202–708–0950.

Regional Offices—Department of Housing and Urban Development

Region	Address	Secretary's Representative	Telephone
New England	Rm. 375, 10 Causeway St., Boston, MA 02222–1092	Mary Lou K. Crane	617–565–5234
New York/New Jersey	26 Federal Plz., New York, NY 10278–0068	(Vacancy)	212–264–6500
Mid-Atlantic	100 Penn Sq. E., Philadelphia, PA 19107–3380	Karen A. Miller	215–656–0500
Southeast/Caribbean	75 Spring St. SW., Atlanta, GA 30303–3388	Davey L. Gibson	404–331–5136
Midwest	77 W. Jackson Blvd., Chicago, IL 60604–3507	(Vacancy)	312–353–5680
Southwest	P.O. Box 2905, Fort Worth, TX 76113–2905	Elizabeth Julian	817–885–5401
Great Plains	Rm. 200, 400 State Ave., Kansas City, KS 66106–2406	Michael L. Tramontina	913–551–5462
Rocky Mountains	1st Interstate Twr. N., 633 17th St., Denver, CO 80202–3607	Anthony J. Hernandez	303–672–5440
Pacific/Hawaii	P.O. Box 36003, 450 Golden Gate Ave., San Francisco, CA 94102–3448	Arthur C. Agnos	415–436–6532
Northwest/Alaska	Suite 200, 909 1st Ave., Seattle, WA 98104–1000	Robert N. Santos	206–220–5101

Sources of Information

Inquiries on the following subjects should be directed to the nearest regional office or to the specified headquarters office, Department of Housing and Urban Development, 451 Seventh Street SW., Washington, DC

186-873 D-00--9

20410. Phone, 202–708–1112. TDD, 202–708–1455.

Contracts Contact the Contracting Division. Phone, 202–708–1290.

Directory Locator Phone, 202–708–1112. TDD, 202–708–1455.

Employment Inquiries and applications should be directed to the headquarters Office of Personnel (phone, 202–708–0408); or the Personnel Division at the nearest HUD regional office.

Freedom of Information Act (FOIA) Requests Persons interested in inspecting documents or records under the Freedom of Information Act should contact the Freedom of Information Officer. Phone, 202–708–3054. Written requests should be directed to the Director, Executive Secretariat, Department of Housing and Urban Development, Room 10139, 451 Seventh Street SW., Washington, DC 20410.

HUD Hotline The Hotline is maintained by the Office of the Inspector General as a means for individuals to report activities involving fraud, waste, or mismanagement. Phone, 202–708–4200, or 800–347–3735 (toll-free). TDD, 202–708–2451.

Program Information Center The Center provides viewing facilities for information regarding departmental activities and functions and publications and other literature to headquarters visitors. Phone, 202–708–1420.

Property Disposition For single family properties, contact the Property Disposition Division (phone, 202–708–0740); or the Chief Property Officer at the nearest HUD regional office. For multifamily properties, contact the Property Disposition Division (phone, 202–708–3343); or the Regional Housing Director at the nearest HUD regional office.

For further information, contact the Office of Public Affairs, Department of Housing and Urban Development, 451 Seventh Street SW., Washington, DC 20410. Phone, 202–708–0980. Internet, www.hud.gov.

DEPARTMENT OF THE INTERIOR

1849 C Street NW., Washington, DC 20240
Phone, 202–208–3171. Internet, www.doi.gov.

SECRETARY OF THE INTERIOR	BRUCE BABBITT
Deputy Secretary	DAVID J. HAYES
Chief of Staff	ANNE H. SHIELDS
Deputy Chief of Staff	KENNETH L. SMITH
Special Trustee for American Indians	(VACANCY)
Chief Information Officer	DARYL W. WHITE
Director of Congressional and Legislative Affairs	LENNA M. AOKI
Counselors to the Secretary	ROBERT T. ANDERSON, MOLLIE S. MCUSIC
Special Assistant to the Secretary and White House Liaison	(VACANCY)
Science Adviser to the Secretary	WILLIAM BROWN
Director, Office of Communications	MICHAEL GAULDIN
Director of Intergovernmental Affairs	GRACE GARCIA
Special Assistant to the Secretary and Director, Executive Secretariat and Office of Regulatory Affairs	JULIETTE A. FALKNER
Special Assistant to the Secretary for Alaska	MARILYN HEIMAN
Solicitor	JOHN D. LESHY
Deputy Solicitor	EDWARD B. COHEN
Associate Solicitor (Administration)	ROBERT S. MORE
Associate Solicitor (Conservation and Wildlife)	RENEE STONE
Associate Solicitor (Land and Water Resources)	DALE PONTIUS
Associate Solicitor (General Law)	KAREN SPRECHER KEATING
Associate Solicitor (Indian Affairs)	DERRIL B. JORDAN
Associate Solicitor (Mineral Resources)	KATHRINE HENRY
Inspector General	EARL E. DEVANEY
Deputy Inspector General	MARY K. ADLER
Assistant Inspector General (Audits)	ROBERT J. WILLIAMS
Assistant Inspector General (Investigations)	DAVID A. MONTOYA
Assistant Inspector General (Management and Policy)	SHARON D. ELLER
General Counsel	ROBIN L. BREENWALD
Assistant Secretary—Water and Science	(VACANCY)
Deputy Assistant Secretary	MARK SCHAEFER
Director, U.S. Geological Survey	CHARLES G. GROAT
Commissioner, Bureau of Reclamation	ELUID L. MARTINEZ
Assistant Secretary—Fish and Wildlife and Parks	DONALD J. BARRY
Deputy Assistant Secretary	STEPHEN C. SAUNDERS
Director, U.S. Fish and Wildlife Service	JAMIE R. CLARK
Director, National Park Service	ROBERT G. STANTON

Assistant Secretary—Indian Affairs	KEVIN GOVER
Deputy Assistant Secretary	MICHAEL J. ANDERSON
Commissioner of Indian Affairs	(VACANCY)
Deputy Commissioner of Indian Affairs	HILDA MANUEL
Assistant Secretary—Land and Minerals Management	SYLVIA V. BACA
Principal Deputy Assistant Secretary	(VACANCY)
Director, Minerals Management Service	WALTER C. ROSENBUSCH
Director, Bureau of Land Management	THOMAS A. FRY III
Director, Office of Surface Mining Reclamation and Enforcement	KATHLEEN M. KARPAN
Assistant Secretary—Policy, Management, and Budget	M. JOHN BERRY
Director, Office of Hearings and Appeals	ROBERT L. BAUM
Director, Office of Small and Disadvantaged Business Utilization	ROBERT W. FAITHFUL
Director, Office of Information Resources Management	DARYL W. WHITE
Deputy Assistant Secretary—Human Resources	MARI R. BARR
Director, Office of Educational Partnerships	RICARDO DOW Y ANAYA
Director, Office of Personnel Policy	CAROLYN COHEN
Director, Ethics Staff	LINDA (TJ) SULLIVAN
Deputy Assistant Secretary—Workforce Diversity	MINNIJEAN BROWN-TRICKEY
Director, Office for Equal Opportunity	E. MELODEE STITH
Deputy Assistant Secretary—Policy and International Affairs	LISA A. GUIDE
Director, Office of Environmental Policy and Compliance	WILLIE R. TAYLOR
Director, Office of Policy Analysis	JAMES H. PIPKIN
Director, Office of Insular Affairs	FERDINAND G. ARANZA
Director, Office of Managing Risk and Public Safety	L. MICHAEL KAAS
Deputy Assistant Secretary—Budget and Finance	ROBERT J. LAMB
Director, Office of Planning and Performance Management	(VACANCY)
Director, Office of Budget	JOHN TREZISE
Director, Office of Financial Management	R. SCHUYLER LESHER
Director of Administration/Senior Procurement Executive	PAUL A. DENETT
Director, Interior Service Center	TIMOTHY G. VIGOTSKY
Director, Office of Aircraft Services	ELMER J. HURD
Director, Office of Acquisition and Property Management	DEBRA SONDERMAN

The mission of the Department of the Interior is to protect and provide access to our Nation's natural and cultural heritage and honor our trust responsibilities to tribes. The Department manages the Nation's public lands and minerals, national parks, national wildlife refuges, and western water resources and upholds Federal trust responsibilities to Indian tribes. It is responsible for migratory wildlife conservation; historic preservation; endangered species; surface-mined lands protection and restoration; mapping; and geological, hydrological, and biological science.

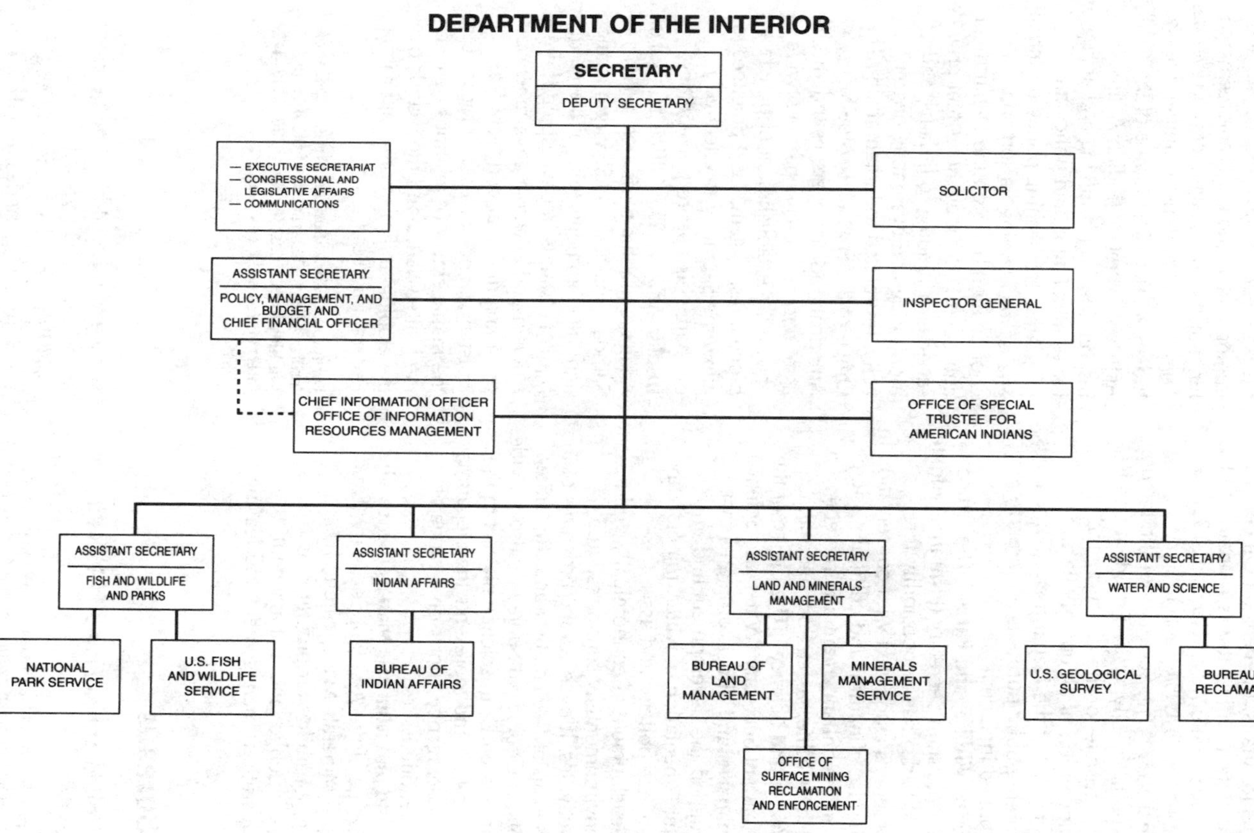
DEPARTMENT OF THE INTERIOR
SECRETARY
DEPUTY SECRETARY
— EXECUTIVE SECRETARIAT
— CONGRESSIONAL AND LEGISLATIVE AFFAIRS
— COMMUNICATIONS
SOLICITOR
ASSISTANT SECRETARY
POLICY, MANAGEMENT, AND BUDGET AND CHIEF FINANCIAL OFFICER
INSPECTOR GENERAL
CHIEF INFORMATION OFFICER OFFICE OF INFORMATION RESOURCES MANAGEMENT
OFFICE OF SPECIAL TRUSTEE FOR AMERICAN INDIANS
ASSISTANT SECRETARY
FISH AND WILDLIFE AND PARKS
NATIONAL PARK SERVICE
U.S. FISH AND WILDLIFE SERVICE
ASSISTANT SECRETARY
INDIAN AFFAIRS
BUREAU OF INDIAN AFFAIRS
ASSISTANT SECRETARY
LAND AND MINERALS MANAGEMENT
BUREAU OF LAND MANAGEMENT
MINERALS MANAGEMENT SERVICE
OFFICE OF SURFACE MINING RECLAMATION AND ENFORCEMENT
ASSISTANT SECRETARY
WATER AND SCIENCE
U.S. GEOLOGICAL SURVEY
BUREAU OF RECLAMATION

The Department of the Interior was created by act of March 3, 1849 (43 U.S.C. 1451), which transferred to it the General Land Office, the Office of Indian Affairs, the Pension Office, and the Patent Office. It was reorganized by Reorganization Plan No. 3 of 1950, as amended (5 U.S.C. app.).

Secretary The Secretary of the Interior reports directly to the President and is responsible for the direction and supervision of all operations and activities of the Department. Some areas where public purposes are broadly applied include:

Fish, Wildlife, and Parks The Office of the Assistant Secretary (Fish and Wildlife and Parks) has responsibility for programs associated with conservation in the use of natural and cultural resources, and the enhancement and protection of fish, wildlife, vegetation, and habitat.

Water and Science The Office of the Assistant Secretary (Water and Science) manages and directs programs that support the development and implementation of water, mineral, and science policies and assist the development of economically and environmentally sound resource activities. It oversees the programs of the Bureau of Reclamation and the United States Geological Survey. It also provides advice on Earth science matters to the Secretary and represents the Department in interagency efforts on a range of scientific issues.

Land and Minerals Management The Office of the Assistant Secretary (Land and Minerals Management) has responsibility for programs associated with public land management; operations management and leasing for minerals on public lands, including the Outer Continental Shelf to the outer limits of the United States economic jurisdiction; minerals operations management on Indian lands; surface mining reclamation and enforcement functions; and management of revenues from Federal and Indian mineral leases.

Indian Affairs The Office of the Assistant Secretary (Indian Affairs) is responsible for identifying and acting on issues affecting Indian policy and programs, establishing policy on Indian affairs, maintaining liaison and coordination between the Department and other Federal agencies that provide services or funding to Indians, and monitoring and evaluating ongoing activities related to Indian affairs. The Office of the Special Trustee for American Indians oversees Indian trust asset reform efforts departmentwide to ensure the establishment of policies, procedures, systems, and practices to allow the Secretary to effectively discharge his trust responsibilities.

Insular Affairs The Office of Insular Affairs assists the territories of American Samoa, Guam, the U.S. Virgin Islands, and the Commonwealth of the Northern Mariana Islands in developing more efficient and effective government by providing financial and technical assistance, and serves as a focal point for the management of relations between the United States and the islands by developing and promoting appropriate Federal policies.

For further information, contact the Office of Insular Affairs, Department of the Interior, Washington, DC 20240. Phone, 202–208–4736. Internet, www.doi.gov/oia.

Bureaus

United States Fish and Wildlife Service

[For the United States Fish and Wildlife Service statement of organization, see the *Code of Federal Regulations,* Title 50, Subchapter A, Part 2]

The United States Fish and Wildlife Service's national responsibility in the service of fish, wildlife, and people spans almost 130 years to the establishment of a predecessor agency, the Bureau of Fisheries, in 1871. First created as an independent agency, the Bureau of Fisheries was later placed in the Department of Commerce. A second predecessor agency, the Bureau of Biological Survey, was established in 1885 in the Department of Agriculture. In 1939, the two Bureaus and their functions were transferred to the Department of the Interior. They were consolidated into one agency and redesignated the Fish and Wildlife Service in 1940 by Reorganization Plan III (5 U.S.C. app.).

The Service manages more than 93 million acres of land and water consisting of more than 500 national wildlife refuges, thousands of small wetlands, and other special management areas. It also operates 66 national fish hatcheries, 64 fish and wildlife management assistance offices, 64 fishery resource offices, and 78 ecological services field stations. The Service is responsible for migratory birds, endangered species, certain marine mammals, and inland sport fisheries. Its mission is to conserve, protect, and enhance fish and wildlife and their habitats for the continuing benefit of the American people. Within this framework, the Service strives to foster an environmental stewardship ethic based on ecological principles and scientific knowledge of wildlife; works with the States to improve the conservation and management of the Nation's fish and wildlife resources; and administers a national program providing opportunities to the American public to understand, appreciate, and wisely use these resources.

In the area of resource management, the Service provides leadership for the protection and improvement of land and water environments (habitat preservation) which directly benefit the living natural resources and add quality to human life. Activities include:

—surveillance of pesticides, heavy metals, and other contaminants;

—studies of fish and wildlife populations;

—ecological studies;

—environmental impact assessment, including hydroelectric dams, nuclear power sites, stream channelization, and dredge-and-fill permits; and

—environmental impact statement review.

The Service is responsible for improving and maintaining fish and wildlife resources by proper management of wildlife and habitat. It also helps fulfill the public demand for recreational fishing while maintaining the Nation's fisheries at a level and in a condition that will ensure their continued survival. Specific wildlife and fishery resources programs include:

—migratory birds—wildlife refuge management for production, migration, and wintering; law enforcement; game; and bird population, production, and harvest surveys;

—mammals and nonmigratory birds—refuge management of resident species, law enforcement, protection of certain marine mammals, and technical assistance;

—coastal anadromous fish—hatchery production and stocking;

—Great Lakes fisheries—hatchery production of lake trout and fishery management in cooperation with Canada and the States; and

—other inland fisheries—hatchery production and stocking of Indian lands, and technical assistance.

The Service provides national and international leadership in identifying, protecting, and restoring endangered species of fish, wildlife, and plants. This program includes:

—developing the Federal Endangered and Threatened Species List, conducting status surveys, preparing recovery plans, and coordinating efforts nationally and internationally;

—operating national wildlife refuges;

—law enforcement;

—foreign importation enforcement; and

—consultation with foreign countries.

Public use and information programs include preparing leaflets and brochures; operating environmental study areas on Service lands; operating visitor centers, self-guided nature trails, observation towers, and display ponds; and providing recreational activities such as hunting, fishing, and wildlife photography.

The Service's Federal aid programs apportion funds generated by excise taxes on sporting arms and fishing equipment to the States and territories for projects designed to conserve and enhance the Nation's fish and wildlife resources.

Regional Offices—United States Fish and Wildlife Service

Region	Address	Telephone
ALBUQUERQUE—AZ, NM, OK, TX	P.O. Box 1306, Albuquerque, NM 87103–1306	505–248–6282
ANCHORAGE—AK	1011 E. Tudor Rd., Anchorage, AK 99503	907–786–3542
ATLANTA—AL, AR, FL, GA, KY, LA, MS, NC, PR, SC, TN, VI	1875 Century Blvd. NE., Atlanta, GA 30345	404–679–4000
HADLEY—CT, DE, MA, ME, MD, NH, NJ, NY, PA, RI, VT, VA, WV	300 Westgate Ctr. Dr., Hadley, MA 01035–9589	413–253–8300
DENVER—CO, KS, MT, NE, ND, SD, UT, WY	P.O. Box 25486, Denver Federal Center, Denver, CO 80225	303–236–7920
PORTLAND—CA, HI, ID, NV, OR, WA, Pacific Islands	911 NE. 11th Ave., Portland, OR 97232–4181	503–231–6118
TWIN CITIES—IL, IN, IA, MI, MN, MO, OH, WI	Federal Bldg., Fort Snelling, Twin Cities, MN 55111–4056	612–713–5301

For further information, contact the Office of Public Affairs, Fish and Wildlife Service, Department of the Interior, Washington, DC 20240. Phone, 202–208–5634. Internet, www.fws.gov.

National Park Service

The National Park Service was established in the Department of the Interior on August 25, 1916 (16 U.S.C. 1).

The National Park Service is dedicated to conserving unimpaired the natural and cultural resources and values of the National Park System for the enjoyment, education, and inspiration of this and future generations. There are more than 375 units in the National Park System, including national parks and monuments; scenic parkways, preserves, trails, riverways, seashores, lakeshores, and recreation areas; and historic sites associated with important movements, events, and personalities of the American past.

The National Park Service has a Service Center in Denver that provides planning, architectural, engineering, and other professional services. The Service is also responsible for managing a great variety of national and international programs designed to help extend the benefits of natural and cultural resource conservation and outdoor recreation throughout this country and the world.

Activities The National Park Service develops and implements park management plans and staffs the areas under its administration. It relates the natural values and historical significance of these areas to the public through talks, tours, films, exhibits, publications, and other interpretive media. It operates campgrounds and other visitor facilities and provides lodging, food, and transportation services in many areas.

The National Park Service also administers the following programs: the State portion of the Land and Water Conservation Fund, nationwide outdoor recreation coordination and information, State comprehensive outdoor recreation planning, planning and technical assistance for the national wild and scenic rivers system, the national trails system, natural area programs, the National Register of Historic Places, national historic landmarks, historic preservation, technical preservation services, the historic American buildings survey, the historic American engineering record, and interagency archeological services.

Regional Offices—National Park Service

Regions	Address	Telephone
ALASKA—AK	Rm. 107, 2525 Gambell St., Anchorage, AK 99503–2892	907–257–2687
INTERMOUNTAIN—AZ, CO, MT, NM, OK, TX, UT, WY	P.O. Box 25287, 12795 W. Alameda Pkwy., Denver, CO 80225–0287	303–969–2500

Regional Offices—National Park Service—Continued

Regions	Address	Telephone
MIDWEST—AR, IL, IN, IA, KS, MI, MN, MO, ND, NE, OH, SD, WI	1709 Jackson St., Omaha, NE 68102	402–221–3431
NATIONAL CAPITAL—Washington, DC, and nearby MD, VA, and WV	1100 Ohio Dr. SW., Washington, DC 20242	202–619–7000
NORTHEAST—CT, DE, ME, MA, MD, NH, NJ, NY, PA, RI, VT, VA, WV	5th Fl., 200 Chestnut St., Philadelphia, PA 19106	215–597–7013
PACIFIC WEST—CA, HI, ID, NV, OR, WA	Suite 600, 600 Harrison St., San Francisco, CA 94107–1372	415–427–1309
SOUTHEAST—AL, FL, GA, KY, LA, MS, NC, SC, TN	100 Alabama St. SW., Atlanta, GA 30303	404–562–3100

For further information, contact the Chief, Office of Communications, National Park Service, Department of the Interior, 1849 C Street NW., Washington, DC 20240. Phone, 202–208–6843. Internet, www.nps.gov.

United States Geological Survey

The United States Geological Survey (USGS) was established by the Organic Act of March 3, 1879 (43 U.S.C. 31). It is responsible for classifying the public lands and examining the geological structure, mineral resources, and products within and outside the national domain.

USGS provides relevant, objective scientific studies and information used to help address issues and solve problems dealing with natural resources, natural hazards, and the environmental effects on human and wildlife health. The major responsibilities of USGS are:

—investigating and assessing the Nation's land, water, energy, biological, and mineral resources;

—conducting research on global change;

—providing information to resource managers in the Department in a form that helps them to assess and manage the biological consequences of management practices;

—investigating natural hazards such as earthquakes, volcanoes, landslides, floods, and droughts;

—maintaining an archive of land-remote sensing data for historical, scientific, and technical purposes, including long-term global environmental monitoring;

—ensuring production and availability of basic biologic, cartographic, and geographic spatial data of the Nation;

—maintaining national geochemical, geophysical, mineral deposit, mineral commodity, and mine geology databases;

—collecting, interpreting, and disseminating a variety of information on world mineral commodities; and

—establishing and maintaining a national geologic mapping program.

To attain these objectives, USGS prepares maps and digital and cartographic data; collects and interprets data on energy and mineral resources; conducts nationwide assessments of the quality, quantity, and use of the Nation's water resources; performs fundamental and applied research in the sciences and techniques involved; and publishes the results of its investigations through new maps, technical reports and publications, and fact sheets.

For further information, contact the U.S. Geological Survey, Department of the Interior, 12201 Sunrise Valley Drive, Reston, VA 20192. Phone, 703–648–4000. Fax-on-demand, 703–648–4888. Internet, www.usgs.gov.

Office of Surface Mining Reclamation and Enforcement

The Office of Surface Mining Reclamation and Enforcement (OSM) was established in the Department of the Interior by the Surface Mining Control and Reclamation Act of 1977 (30 U.S.C. 1211).

The Office's primary goal is to assist States in operating a nationwide program that protects society and the environment from the adverse effects of coal mining, while ensuring that surface coal mining can be done without permanent damage to land and water resources. With most coal-mining States responsible for regulating coal mining and reclamation activities within their borders, OSM's main objectives are to oversee State mining regulatory and abandoned mine reclamation programs, assist States in meeting the objectives of the surface mining law, and regulate mining and reclamation activities on Federal and Indian lands, and in those States choosing not to assume primary responsibility.

Activities The Office establishes national policy for the surface mining control and reclamation program provided for in the surface mining law, reviews and approves amendments to previously approved State programs, and reviews and recommends approval of new State program submissions. Other activities include:

—managing the collection, disbursement, and accounting for abandoned mine land reclamation fees;

—administering civil penalties programs;

—establishing technical standards and regulatory policy for reclamation and enforcement efforts;

—providing guidance for environmental considerations, research, training, and technology transfer for State, tribal, and Federal regulatory and abandoned mine land reclamation programs;

—monitoring and evaluating State and tribal regulatory programs, cooperative agreements, and abandoned mine land reclamation programs; and

—coordinating the Appalachian clean streams initiative, a public-private joint effort, at the Federal, State, and local levels, to clean up streams and rivers polluted by acid mine drainage.

For further information, contact the Office of Communications, Office of Surface Mining Reclamation and Enforcement, Department of the Interior, Washington, DC 20240. Phone, 202–208–2719. TDD, 202–208–2737. Fax-on-demand, 202–219–1703. Internet, www.osmre.gov.

Bureau of Indian Affairs

The Bureau of Indian Affairs (BIA) was created as part of the War Department in 1824 and transferred to the Department of the Interior when the latter was established in 1849. The principal objectives of BIA are to encourage and assist Indian and Alaska Native people to manage their own affairs under the trust relationship to the Federal Government; to facilitate, with maximum involvement of Indian and Alaska Native people, full development of their human and natural resource potential; to mobilize all public and private aids to the advancement of Indian and Alaska Native people for use by them; and to promote self-determination by utilizing the skill and capabilities of Indian and Alaska Native people in the direction and management of programs for their benefit.

In carrying out these objectives, BIA works with Indian and Alaska Native people, tribal governments, Native American organizations, other Federal agencies, State and local governments, and other interested groups in the development and implementation of effective programs for their advancement.

Regional Offices—Bureau of Indian Affairs

Area	Address	Telephone
Alaska	P.O. Box 25520, Juneau, AK 99802–5520	907–586–7177
Eastern	Suite 260, 3701 N. Fairfax Dr., Arlington, VA 22203	703–235–2571
Eastern Oklahoma	101 N. 5th St., Muskogee, OK 74401–6202	918–687–2296
Great Plains	115 4th Ave. SE., Aberdeen, SD 57401–4382	605–226–7343
Midwest	Rm. 550, 1 Federal Dr., Ft. Snelling, MN 55111–4007	612–713–4400
Navajo	P.O. Box 1060, Gallup, NM 87305	505–863–8314
Northwest	911 NE. 11th Ave., Portland, OR 97232–4169	503–231–6702
Pacific	2800 Cottage Way, Sacramento, CA 95825	916–978–6000
Rocky Mountain	316 N. 26th St., Billings, MT 59101–1362	406–247–7943
Southern Plains	P.O. Box 368, Anadarko, OK 73005–0368	405–247–6673
Southwest	P.O. Box 26567, Albuquerque, NM 87125–6567	505–346–7590
Western	P.O. Box 10, Phoenix, AZ 85001	602–379–6600

For further information, contact the Public Affairs Office, Bureau of Indian Affairs, Department of the Interior, Washington, DC 20240. Phone, 202–208–3710. Internet, www.doi.gov/bureau-indian-affairs.html.

Minerals Management Service

The Minerals Management Service was established on January 19, 1982, by Secretarial order. The Service assesses the nature, extent, recoverability, and value of leasable minerals on the Outer Continental Shelf. It ensures the orderly and timely inventory and development and the efficient recovery of mineral resources; encourages utilization of the best available and safest technology; and safeguards against fraud, waste, and abuse.

Offshore Minerals Management The Service is responsible for resource evaluation, environmental review, leasing activities (including public liaison and planning functions), lease management, and inspection and enforcement programs for Outer Continental Shelf lands.

Five-year oil and gas leasing programs are developed for leasing on the Outer Continental Shelf in consultation with the Congress, the 23 coastal States, local governments, environmental groups, industry, and the public.

The Service conducts extensive environmental studies and consultations with State officials prior to issuing leases. Once leases have been issued, inspectors conduct frequent inspections of offshore operations, and environmental studies personnel collect more data to ensure that marine environments are kept free of pollutants.

Royalty Management The Service is responsible for the collection and distribution of all royalty payments, rentals, bonus payments, fines, penalties, assessments, and other revenues due the Federal Government and Indian lessors as monies or royalties-in-kind from the extraction of mineral resources from Federal and Indian lands onshore and from the leasing and extraction of mineral resources on the Outer Continental Shelf.

The basic organization of the Service consists of a headquarters in Washington, DC, with program components located in Herndon, VA, and Lakewood, CO; three Outer Continental Shelf regional offices; and two administrative service centers.

Field Offices—Minerals Management Service

Office	Address	Telephone
ROYALTY MANAGEMENT PROGRAM	P.O. Box 25165, Denver, CO 80225–0165	303–231–3162
	OCS Regional Offices	
ALASKA REGION	Rm. 308, 949 E. 36th Ave., Anchorage, AK 99508–4302	907–271–6010
GULF OF MEXICO REGION	1201 Elmwood Park Blvd., New Orleans, LA 70123–2394	504–736–2589
PACIFIC REGION	770 Paseo Camarillo, Camarillo, CA 93010–6064	805–389–7502
	Administrative Service Centers	
WESTERN SERVICE CENTER	P.O. Box 25165, Denver, CO 80225–0165	303–275–7300
SOUTHERN SERVICE CENTER	1201 Elmwood Park Blvd., New Orleans, LA 70123–2394	504–736–2616

For further information, contact the Office of Communications, Minerals Management Service, Department of the Interior, Room 4260, (MS 4230), 1849 C Street NW., Washington, DC 20240–7000. Phone, 202–208–3985. Internet, www.mms.gov.

Bureau of Land Management

The Bureau of Land Management (BLM) was established July 16, 1946, by the consolidation of the General Land Office (created in 1812) and the Grazing Service (formed in 1934).

The Bureau manages more land—264 million surface acres—than any other Federal Government agency. Most of this public land is located in 12 western States, including Alaska; there are also small, scattered parcels in States east of the Mississippi River. The Bureau also administers more than 560 million acres of subsurface mineral estate throughout the Nation. It preserves open space in the fast-growing, fast-changing West by managing the public lands for multiple uses and by conserving resources so that current and future generations may use and enjoy them.

Resources managed by the Bureau include timber, solid minerals, oil and gas, geothermal energy, wildlife habitat, endangered plant and animal species, rangeland vegetation, recreation and cultural values, wild and scenic rivers, designated conservation and wilderness areas, and open space. Bureau programs provide for the protection (including fire suppression), orderly development, and use of the public lands and resources under principles of multiple use and sustained yield. Land use plans are developed with public involvement to provide orderly use and development while maintaining and enhancing the quality of the environment. The Bureau also manages watersheds to protect soil and enhance water quality; develops recreational opportunities on public lands; administers programs to protect and manage wild horses and burros; and under certain conditions, makes land available for sale to individuals, organizations, local governments, and other Federal agencies when such transfer is in the public interest. Lands may be leased to State and local government agencies and to nonprofit organizations for certain purposes.

The Bureau oversees and manages the development of energy and mineral leases and ensures compliance with applicable regulations governing the extraction of these resources. It has responsibility to issue rights-of-way, leases, and permits.

The Bureau is also responsible for the survey of Federal lands and establishes and maintains public land records and mining claims records. It administers a program of payments in lieu of taxes based on the amount of federally owned lands in counties and other units of local government.

Field Offices—Bureau of Land Management

State Office	Address	Telephone
Alaska—AK	No. 13, 222 W. 7th Ave., Anchorage, 99513–7599	907–271–5080
Arizona—AZ	222 N. Central Ave., Phoenix, 85004–2203	602–417–9500
California—CA	2135 Butano Dr., Sacramento, 95825–0451	916–970–4600
Colorado—CO	2850 Youngfield St., Lakewood, 80215–7076	303–239–3700
Eastern States—All States bordering on and east of the Mississippi River.	7450 Boston Blvd., Springfield, VA 22153	703–440–1700
Idaho—ID	1387 S. Vinnell Way, Boise, 83709	208–373–4001
Montana—MT, ND, SD	P.O. Box 36800, 222 N. 32d St., Billings, MT 59107–6800	406–255–2904
Nevada—NV	P.O. Box 12000, 1340 Financial Blvd., Reno, 89520–0006	702–861–6590
New Mexico—KS, NM, OK, TX	P.O. Box 27115, 1474 Rodeo Rd., Santa Fe, NM 87502–0115.	505–438–7501
Oregon—OR, WA	P.O. Box 2965, 1515 SW. 5th Ave, Portland, OR 97208	503–952–6024
Utah—UT	P.O. Box 45155, 324 S. State St., Salt Lake City, 84145–0155.	801–539–4010
Wyoming—NE, WY	P.O. Box 1828, 5353 Yellowstone Rd., Cheyenne, WY 82003.	307–775–6001
	Service and Support Offices	
National Interagency Fire Center	3833 S. Development Ave., Boise, ID 83705–5354	208–387–5447
National Training Center	9828 N. 31st Ave., Phoenix, AZ 85051–2517	602–906–5500
National Business Center	Bldg. 50, BC–600, P.O. Box 25047, Denver, CO 80225–0047.	303–236–8857
National Human Resources Management Center.	Bldg. 50, HR–200, P.O. Box 25047, Denver, CO 80225–0047.	303–236–6503
National Applied Resource Sciences Center	Bldg. 50, RS–100, P.O. Box 25047, Denver, CO 80225–0047.	303–236–1142
National Information Resources Management Center.	Bldg. 40, NI–100, P.O. Box 25047, Denver, CO 80225–0047.	303–236–6965
Washington Office Headquarters Directorate	1849 C St. NW., Washington, DC 20240	202–452–7732
National Law Enforcement Office	1620 L St. NW., Washington, DC 20236	202–452–5118
Helium Operations	Suite 500, 801 S. Filmore, Amarillo, TX 79101–3545	806–324–2602

For further information, contact the Office of Public Affairs, Bureau of Land Management, Department of the Interior, LS–406, 1849 C Street NW., Washington, DC 20240. Phone, 202–452–5125. Internet, www.blm.gov.

Bureau of Reclamation

The Bureau of Reclamation was established pursuant to the Reclamation Act of 1902 (43 U.S.C. 371 *et seq.*). The mission of the Bureau of Reclamation is to manage, develop, and protect, for the public welfare, water and related resources in an environmentally and economically sound manner.

The reclamation program helped to settle and develop the West by providing for sustained economic growth, an improved environment, and an enhanced quality of life through the development of a water storage and delivery infrastructure, which provides safe and dependable water supplies and hydroelectric power for agricultural, municipal, and industrial users; protects and improves water quality; provides recreational and fish and wildlife benefits; enhances river regulations; and helps control damaging floods.

With this infrastructure largely in place, the reclamation program is now focusing greater emphasis on resource management and protection than on development. Following a balanced approach to the stewardship of the West's water and related land and energy resources, the Bureau:

—works in partnership with others to develop water conservation plans, provide for the efficient and effective use of water and related resources, and improve the management of existing water resources;

—designs and constructs water resources projects, as authorized by the Congress;

—helps to develop and supports or enhances recreational uses at Reclamation projects;

—conducts research and encourages technology transfer to improve resource management, development, and protection;

—ensures that the lands it manages are free from hazardous and toxic waste and assists other Federal and State agencies in protecting and restoring surface water and ground water resources from hazardous waste contamination;

—operates and maintains its facilities to ensure reliability, safety, and economic operation to protect the public, property, and the Nation's investment in the facilities, and to preserve and enhance environmental resources; and

—provides engineering and technical support to Federal and State agencies, to Native American tribes, and to other nations to help accomplish national, regional, and international resource management, development, and protection objectives.

Reclamation project facilities in operation include 355 storage reservoirs, 69,400 miles of canals and other water conveyances and distribution facilities, and 52 hydroelectric powerplants.

Major Offices—Bureau of Reclamation

Office/Region	Address	Telephone
Commissioner	Rm. 7654, Dept. of Interior, Washington, DC 20240–0001	202–208–4157
Reclamation Service Center	Bldg. 67, Box 25007, Denver, CO 80225	303–445–2692
Great Plains Region	Box 36900, 316 N. 26th St., Billings, MT 59107	406–247–7614
Lower Colorado Region	Box 61470, Nevada Hwy. & Park St., Boulder City, NV 89005.	702–293–8000
Mid-Pacific Region	2800 Cottage Way, Sacramento, CA 95825	916–978–5100
Pacific Northwest Region	1150 N. Curtis Rd., Boise, ID 83706	208–378–5012
Upper Colorado Region	Rm. 6107, 125 S. State St., Salt Lake City, UT 84147	801–524–3789

For further information, contact the Public Affairs Division, Bureau of Reclamation, Department of the Interior, Washington, DC 20240–0001. Phone, 202–208–4662. Internet, www.usbr.gov.

Sources of Information

Inquiries on the following subjects should be directed to the specified office, Department of the Interior, Washington, DC 20240.

Contracts Contact the Office of Acquisition and Property Management, Room 5512. Phone, 202–208–3668.

Electronic Access Information is available electronically from the Department of the Interior. Internet, www.doi.gov (or see listings for specific Department components).

Employment Direct general inquiries to the Personnel Liaison Staff, 202–208–6702, the personnel office of a specific bureau or office, or visit any of the field personnel offices.

Museum The Museum has exhibits on topics pertaining to the bureaus and a changing exhibits gallery with new displays every 3–4 months. It presents public programs related to departmental themes and provides tours to school and adult groups on the building's New Deal murals, the Museum, and American Indians. Contact the staff office, Room 1024, Main Interior Building. Phone, 202–208–4743.

Publications Most departmental publications are available from the Superintendent of Documents, Government Printing Office, Washington, DC 20402. Information regarding bibliographies on select subjects is available from the Natural Resources Library. Phone, 202–208–5815. All other inquiries regarding publications should be directed to the individual bureau or office's publications or public affairs office.

Reading Room Visit the Natural Resources Library, Main Interior Building. Phone, 202–208–5815.

Telephone Directory The Department of the Interior telephone directory is available for sale by the Superintendent of Documents, Government Printing Office, Washington, DC 20402.

Telephone Locator To locate an employee of the Department of the Interior, call 202–208–3100.

United States Fish and Wildlife Service

Inquiries on the following subjects should be directed to the specified office, U.S. Fish and Wildlife Service, Department of the Interior, Washington, DC 20240.

Congressional/Legislative Services Congressional staffers and persons seeking information about specific legislation should call the Congressional/Legislative Services office. Phone, 202–208–5403.

Contracts Contact the Washington, DC, headquarters Division of Contracting and General Services (phone, 703–358–1728) or any of the regional offices.

Electronic Access The Fish and Wildlife Service offers a range of information through the Internet, at www.fws.gov.

Employment For information regarding employment opportunities with the U.S. Fish and Wildlife Service, contact the Headquarters Personnel Office (phone, 703–358–1743) or the regional office within the area you are seeking employment.

Import/Export Permits To obtain CITES permits for importing and exporting wildlife, contact the Office of Management Authority. Phone, 800–358–2104 or 703–358–2104.

Law Enforcement To obtain information about the enforcement of wildlife laws or to report an infraction of those laws, contact the Division of Law Enforcement (phone, 703–358–1949) or the nearest regional law enforcement office.

National Wildlife Refuges For general information about the National Wildlife Refuge System, as well as information about specific refuges, contact the Division of Refuges (phone, 800–344–WILD or 703–358–2029) or the nearest national wildlife refuge or regional refuge office.

News Media Inquiries Specific information about the U.S. Fish and Wildlife Service and its activities is available from the Office of Media Services (phone, 202–208–5634) or the public affairs officer in each of the Service's regional offices.

Publications The U.S. Fish and Wildlife Service has publications available on subjects ranging from the National Wildlife Refuge System to endangered species. Some publications are only available as sales items from the Superintendent of Documents, Government Printing Office, Washington, DC 20402. Further information is available from the Publications Unit, U.S. Fish and Wildlife

Service, Mail Stop NCTC Washington, DC 20240. Phone, 304–876–7203.

National Park Service

Contracts Contact the nearest regional office; Administrative Services Division, National Park Service, 1849 C Street NW., Washington, DC 20240 (phone, 202–523–5133); or the Denver Service Center, P.O. Box 25287, 12795 West Alameda Parkway, Denver, CO 80225 (phone, 303–969–2110).
Employment Employment inquiries and applications may be sent to the Personnel Office, National Park Service, Department of the Interior, Washington, DC, and to the regional offices and individual parks. Applications for temporary employment should be sent to the Division of Personnel Management, National Park Service, 1849 C Street NW., Washington, DC 20240. Phone, 202–208–5074. Schools interested in the recruitment program should write to: Chief Personnel Officer, National Park Service, 1849 C Street NW., Washington, DC 20240. Phone, 202–208–5093.
Grants For information on grants authorized under the Land and Water Conservation Fund and the Urban Park and Recreation Recovery Program, contact the National Park Service, 1849 C Street NW., Washington, DC 20240. Phone, 202–565–1140. For information on grants authorized under the Historic Preservation Fund, contact the National Park Service, 800 North Capitol Street NW., Washington, DC 20001. Phone, 202–343–9564.
Publications Items related to the National Park Service are available from the Superintendent of Documents, Government Printing Office, Washington, DC 20402. Phone, 202–512–1800. Items available for sale include the *National Park System Map & Guide* (stock no. 024–005–01135–8); *The National Parks: Index 1999–2001* (stock no. 024–005–01199–4); and *National Parks: Lesser Known Areas* (stock no. 024–005–01152–8). Contact the Consumer Information Center, Pueblo, CO 81009, for other publications about the National Park Service available for sale. For general park and camping information, write to the National Park Service, Office of Public Inquiries, 1849 C Street NW., Washington, DC 20240.

United States Geological Survey

Contracts, Grants, and Cooperative Agreements Write to the Office of Program Support, Office of Acquisition and Federal Assistance, 205 National Center, 12201 Sunrise Valley Drive, Reston, VA 20192. Phone, 703–648–7373.
Employment Inquiries should be directed to one of the following Personnel Offices:

Recruitment and Placement, 601 National Center, 12201 Sunrise Valley Drive, Reston, VA 20192. Phone, 703–648–6131.

Personnel Office, United States Geological Survey, Suite 160, 3850 Holcomb Bridge Road, Norcross, GA 30092. Phone, 770–409–7750.

Personnel Office, United States Geological Survey, Box 25046, MS 603, Building 53, Denver, CO 80225. Phone, 303–236–5900 extension 361.

Personnel Office, United States Geological Survey, 345 Middlefield Road, MS 613, Menlo Park, CA 94025. Phone, 650–329–4104.

General Inquiries A network of eight Earth science information centers (ESIC's) responds to requests for natural science information that are made in person, by mail, by E-mail, or by telephone and assists in the selection and ordering of all U.S. Geological Survey products:

Rm. 101, 4230 University Drive, Anchorage, AK 99508–4664. Phone, 907–786–7011.

345 Middlefield Road, Menlo Park, CA 94025. Phone, 650–329–4309.

Box 25286, Building 810, Denver, CO 80225. Phone, 303–202–4200.

Room 2650, 1849 C Street NW., Washington, DC 20240. Phone, 202–208–4047.

MS 231, 1400 Independence Road, Rolla, MO 65401. Phone, 573–308–3500.

Rm. 1C402, 12201 Sunrise Valley Drive, Reston, VA 20192. Phone, 703–648–5953.

Room 135, 904 West Riverside Avenue, Spokane, WA 99201. Phone, 509–368–3130.

EROS Data Center, Sioux Falls, SD 57198. Phone, 605–594–6151.

Maps For maps sold by the branch of information services, contact the United States Geological Survey, Box 25286, Denver Federal Center, Denver, CO 80225 (phone, 303–202–4700).

Information about the status of U.S. Geological Survey mapping in any State and availability of maps by other Federal and State agencies can be obtained from the Earth Science Information Center, 507 National Center, 12201 Sunrise Valley Drive, Reston, VA 20192. Phone, 888–ASK–USGS.

External Affairs For news media and congressional inquiries, arranging interviews, and obtaining news releases and other informational products pertaining to Survey programs and activities, contact the Office of External Affairs, 119 National Center, 12201 Sunrise Valley Drive, Reston, VA 20192 (phone, 703–648–4460). Outreach and media affairs are also conducted on a regional basis at Menlo Park/San Francisco (phone, 650–329–4000); Denver (phone, 303–236–5900); and Reston, VA (phone, 703–648–4582).

Publications The U.S. Geological Survey publishes technical and scientific reports and maps and nontechnical general interest publications, described in the quarterly periodical *New Publications of the U.S. Geological Survey*, with yearly supplements; *Publications of the U.S. Geological Survey, 1879–1961; Publications of the Geological Survey, 1962–1970*. The catalog of new publications of the U.S. Geological Survey is available online monthly (Internet, pubs.usgs.gov/publications).

Book, map, and Digital Data Series (CD–ROM) publications are sold by the Information Services Branch, Denver Federal Center, Box 25286, Denver, CO 80225 (phone, 303–202–4700), and by the U.S. Geological Survey's Earth Science Information Centers (*see* General Inquiries).

Open-file reports, in the form of microfiche and/or black and white paper copies, diskettes, and CD–ROM's are sold by the United States Geological Survey, Open File Reports—ESIC, Denver Federal Center, Box 25286, Denver, CO 80225. Phone, 303–202–4700.

Single copies of a variety of nontechnical leaflets, technical reports, books, fact sheets, and special interest publications on natural science subjects and U.S. Geological Survey activities are available to the public at the Earth Science Information Centers or upon request from the U.S. Geological Survey, Information Services Branch, Denver Federal Center, Box 25286, Denver, CO 80225. Phone, 303–202–4700. Bulk quantities may be purchased from the Superintendent of Documents, Government Printing Office, Washington, DC 20402.

Reading Rooms Facilities for examination of reports, maps, publications of the U.S. Geological Survey, and a wide selection of general Earth science information resources and historical documents are located at the U.S. Geological Survey library system main branches (National Center, 12201 Sunrise Valley Drive, Reston, VA 20192; Denver Federal Center, Building 20, Box 25046, Denver, CO 80225; and 345 Middlefield Road, Menlo Park, CA 94025) and Earth Science Information Centers (*see* General Inquiries section). Maps, aerial photographs, geodetic control data or index material, and cartographic data in digital form may be examined at the following Earth Science Information Centers:

Room 1C402, 12201 Sunrise Valley Drive, Reston, VA 20192.

1400 Independence Road, Rolla, MO 65401.

Building 810, Box 25286, MS 504, Denver Federal Center, Denver, CO 80225.

345 Middlefield Road, Menlo Park, CA 94025.

4230 University Drive, Anchorage, AK 99508–4664.

Spacecraft and aircraft remote sensor data may be examined at the EROS Data Center, Sioux Falls, SD 57198. Phone, 605–594–6151.

Water Data Information on the availability of and access to water data acquired by the U.S. Geological Survey and other local, State, and Federal agencies can be obtained by contacting the U.S. Geological Survey, at 439–M National Center, Reston, VA 20192. Phone, 888–ASK–USGS. Internet, water.usgs.gov.

Office of Surface Mining Reclamation and Enforcement

Contracts Contact the Procurement Branch, Office of Surface Mining, Department of the Interior, 1951 Constitution Avenue NW., Washington, DC 20240. Phone, 202–208–2839. TDD, 202–208–2737.
Employment For information on employment opportunities throughout the United States, contact the Chief, Division of Personnel, Office of Surface Mining, Department of the Interior, 1951 Constitution Avenue NW., Washington, DC 20240. Phone, 202–208–2965. TDD, 202–208–2737.

Bureau of Indian Affairs

Inquiries regarding the Bureau of Indian Affairs may be obtained by calling the Office of Public Affairs at 202–208–3710, or writing to the Director, Office of Public Affairs, MS 4542 MIB, 1849 C Street, NW., Washington, DC 20240.

Minerals Management Service

Information about the Minerals Management Service and its activities is available from the Chief, Office of Communications, Room 4260, MS 4230, 1849 C Street NW., Washington, DC 20240. Phone, 202–208–3985.

Bureau of Land Management

Contracts Contracts for construction, nonprofessional services, architect/engineer services, supplies, and heavy equipment are awarded by the Construction and Nonprofessional Services Team (phone, 303–236–9433) and the Environmental and Professional Services Team (phone, 303–236–9439). Contracts for information technology are handled through the Acquisition Team (phone, 303–236–6498). Information about BLM contracts may also be obtained through the Internet, at ideasec.usgs.gov.
Employment Inquiries should be directed to the National Human Resources Management Center, any Bureau of Land Management State Office, or the Personnel Officer, Bureau of Land Management, Eastern States Office, Department of the Interior, Springfield, VA.
General Inquiries For information about parcels of land that the Bureau may on occasion sell, contact any of the State offices or the Bureau of Land Management, Office of Public Affairs, Department of the Interior, Washington, DC 20240. Phone, 202–452–5125. Fax, 202–452–5124.
Publications The annual publication *Public Land Statistics,* which relates to public lands, is available from the Superintendent of Documents, Government Printing Office, Washington, DC 20402.
Reading Rooms All State offices provide facilities for individuals who wish to examine status records, tract books, or other records relating to the public lands and their resources.
Small Business Activities The Bureau has four major buying offices that provide contacts for small business activities: the Headquarters Office in Washington, DC (phone, 202–452–5177); the national business center in Lakewood, CO (phone, 303–236–9447); the Oregon State office (phone, 503–952–6216); and the BLM Amarillo field office (phone, 806–324–2684). The acquisition plan and procurement office contacts are available through the Internet, at www.blm.gov/natacq.
Speakers Local Bureau offices will arrange for speakers to explain Bureau programs upon request from organizations within their areas of jurisdiction.

Bureau of Reclamation

Contracts Information is available to contractors, manufacturers, and suppliers from Acquisition and Assistance Management Services, Building 67, Denver Federal Center, Denver, CO 80225. Phone, 303–236–3750.
Employment Information on engineering and other positions is available from the Diversity and Human Resources Office, Denver, CO (phone, 303–445–2670) or from the nearest regional office.
Publications Publications for sale are available through the National Technical

Information Service. Phone, 800–553–6847.

Speakers and Films A volunteer speaker service provides engineers and scientists for schools and civic groups in the Denver area. Films are available on free loan. For speakers or films, contact the Reclamation Service Center in Denver, CO. Phone, 303–445–2692.

For further information, contact the U.S. Department of the Interior, 1849 C Street NW., Washington, DC 20240. Phone, 202–208–3171. Internet, www.doi.gov.

DEPARTMENT OF JUSTICE

950 Pennsylvania Avenue NW., Washington, DC 20530
Phone, 202–514–2000. Internet, www.usdoj.gov.

THE ATTORNEY GENERAL	JANET RENO
Chief of Staff	ANN M. HARKINS
Deputy Chief of Staff	WIFREDO FERRER
Deputy Attorney General	ERIC H. HOLDER, JR.
Principal Associate Deputy Attorney General	GARY G. GRINDLER
Associate Deputy Attorneys General	JAMES E. CASTELLO, BERNIE J. DELIA, NICHOLAS M. GESS, CRAIG S. ISCOE, BRIAN A. JACKSON, RONALD D. LEE, JOHN T. MORTON, ANTHONY S. MURRY, DEBORAH S. SMOLOVER, BEA WITZLEBEN
Director, Executive Office for National Security	RONALD D. LEE, *Acting*
Associate Attorney General	RAYMOND C. FISHER
Deputy Associate Attorneys General	KENNETH CHERNOF, IVAN FONG, MARY LOU LEARY, DOUGLAS LETTER, RICKI SEIDMAN
Assistant Associate Attorney General	ALEXANDRA VERVEER
Senior Counsel, Office of Alternative Dispute Resolution	PETER R. STEENLAND, JR.
Solicitor General	SETH P. WAXMAN
Inspector General	MICHAEL BROMWICH
Assistant Attorney General, Office of Legal Counsel	RANDOLPH MOSS, *Acting*
Assistant Attorney General, Office of Legislative Affairs	DENNIS K. BURKE, *Acting*
Assistant Attorney General, Office of Policy Development	ELEANOR D. ACHESON
Assistant Attorney General for Administration	STEPHEN R. COLGATE
Assistant Attorney General, Antitrust Division	JOEL I. KLEIN
Assistant Attorney General, Civil Division	DAVID O. OGDEN, *Acting*
Assistant Attorney General, Civil Rights Division	BILL LANN LEE, *Acting*
Assistant Attorney General, Criminal Division	JAMES K. ROBINSON
Assistant Attorney General, Environment and Natural Resources Division	LOIS J. SCHIFFER
Assistant Attorney General, Tax Division	LORETTA C. ARGRETT
Assistant Attorney General, Office of Justice Programs	LAURIE ROBINSON
Director, Office of Public Affairs	MYRON MARLIN
Directors, Office of Information and Privacy	RICHARD L. HUFF, DANIEL J. METCALFE

Director, Office of Intergovernmental Affairs	(VACANCY)
Director, Executive Office for U.S. Attorneys	DONNA BUCELLA
Director, Bureau of Prisons	KATHLEEN M. HAWK SAWYER
Director, Federal Bureau of Investigation	LOUIS J. FREEH
Director, United States Marshals Service	EDUARDO GONZALEZ
Director, Executive Office for Immigration Review	KEVIN ROONEY
Director, Executive Office for United States Trustees	JOSEPH PATCHAN
Director, Community Relations Service	ROSE OCHI
Director, Community Oriented Policing Services	JOSEPH BRANN
Administrator, Drug Enforcement Administration	DONNIE R. MARSHALL
Commissioner, Immigration and Naturalization Service	DORIS MEISSNER
Chairman, United States Parole Commission	MICHAEL J. GAINES
Chairman, Foreign Claims Settlement Commission	DAVID BRADLEY, *Acting*
Chief, INTERPOL–U.S. National Central Bureau	JOHN IMHOFF
Counsel, Office of Intelligence Policy and Review	FRANCES FRAGOS TOWNSEND
Counsel, Office of Professional Responsibility	MARSHALL JARRETT
Pardon Attorney	ROGER C. ADAMS

[For the Department of Justice statement of organization, see the *Code of Federal Regulations,* Title 28, Chapter I, Part 0]

As the largest law firm in the Nation, the Department of Justice serves as counsel for its citizens. It represents them in enforcing the law in the public interest. Through its thousands of lawyers, investigators, and agents, the Department plays the key role in protection against criminals and subversion, in ensuring healthy competition of business in our free enterprise system, in safeguarding the consumer, and in enforcing drug, immigration, and naturalization laws.

The Department of Justice was established by act of June 22, 1870 (28 U.S.C. 501, 503, 509 note), with the Attorney General as its head. The affairs and activities of the Department of Justice are generally directed by the Attorney General.

Attorney General The Attorney General represents the United States in legal matters generally and gives advice and opinions to the President and to the heads of the executive departments of the Government when so requested. The Attorney General appears in person to represent the Government before the U.S. Supreme Court in cases of exceptional gravity or importance.

Community Relations The Service offers assistance to communities in resolving disputes relating to race, color, or national origin and facilitates the development of viable agreements as alternatives to coercion, violence, or litigation. It also assists and supports communities in developing local mechanisms as proactive measures to prevent or reduce racial/ethnic tensions.

For further information, contact any regional office or the Director, Community Relations Service, Department of Justice, Suite 2000, 600 E Street NW., Washington, DC 20530. Phone, 202–305–2935.

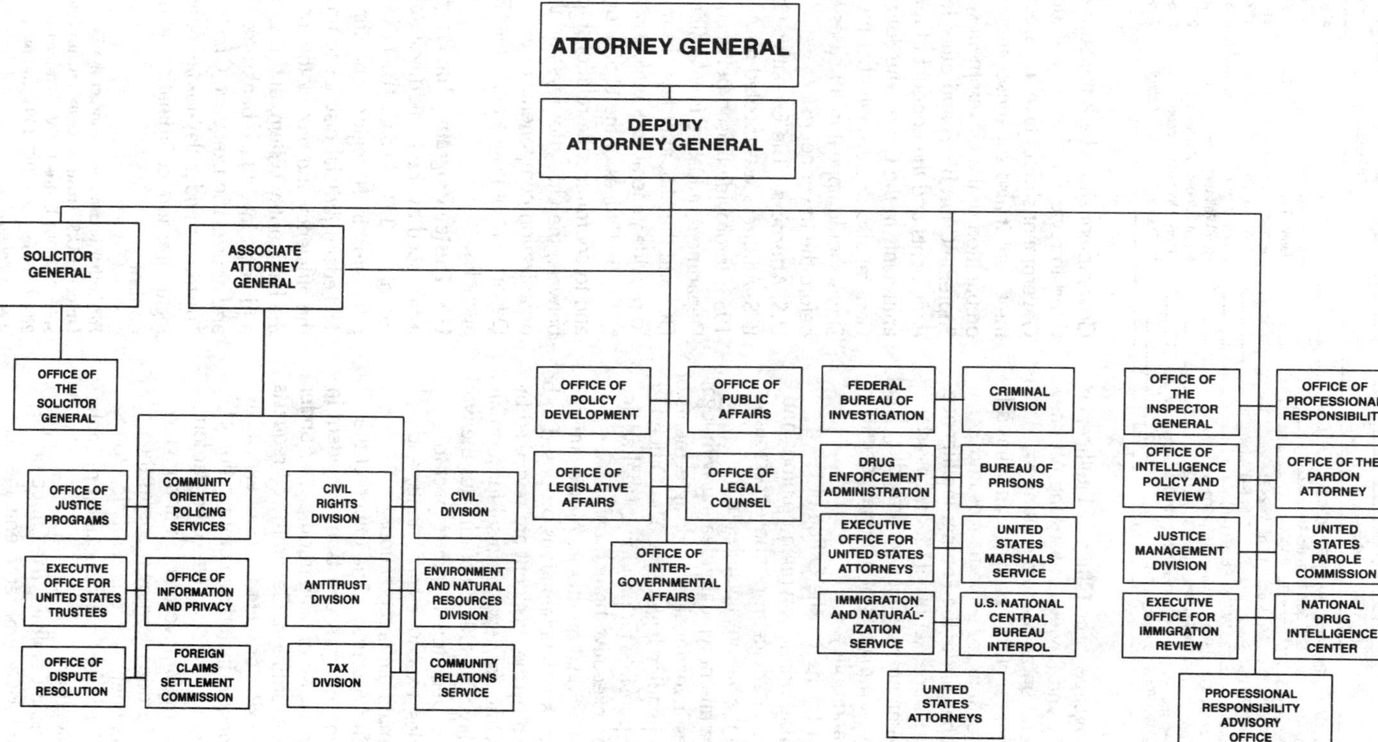
DEPARTMENT OF JUSTICE
ATTORNEY GENERAL
DEPUTY ATTORNEY GENERAL
SOLICITOR GENERAL
ASSOCIATE ATTORNEY GENERAL
OFFICE OF THE SOLICITOR GENERAL
OFFICE OF JUSTICE PROGRAMS
COMMUNITY ORIENTED POLICING SERVICES
EXECUTIVE OFFICE FOR UNITED STATES TRUSTEES
OFFICE OF INFORMATION AND PRIVACY
OFFICE OF DISPUTE RESOLUTION
FOREIGN CLAIMS SETTLEMENT COMMISSION
CIVIL RIGHTS DIVISION
CIVIL DIVISION
ANTITRUST DIVISION
ENVIRONMENT AND NATURAL RESOURCES DIVISION
TAX DIVISION
COMMUNITY RELATIONS SERVICE
OFFICE OF POLICY DEVELOPMENT
OFFICE OF PUBLIC AFFAIRS
OFFICE OF LEGISLATIVE AFFAIRS
OFFICE OF LEGAL COUNSEL
OFFICE OF INTER-GOVERNMENTAL AFFAIRS
FEDERAL BUREAU OF INVESTIGATION
CRIMINAL DIVISION
DRUG ENFORCEMENT ADMINISTRATION
BUREAU OF PRISONS
EXECUTIVE OFFICE FOR UNITED STATES ATTORNEYS
UNITED STATES MARSHALS SERVICE
IMMIGRATION AND NATURAL-IZATION SERVICE
U.S. NATIONAL CENTRAL BUREAU INTERPOL
UNITED STATES ATTORNEYS
OFFICE OF THE INSPECTOR GENERAL
OFFICE OF PROFESSIONAL RESPONSIBILITY
OFFICE OF INTELLIGENCE POLICY AND REVIEW
OFFICE OF THE PARDON ATTORNEY
JUSTICE MANAGEMENT DIVISION
UNITED STATES PAROLE COMMISSION
EXECUTIVE OFFICE FOR IMMIGRATION REVIEW
NATIONAL DRUG INTELLIGENCE CENTER
PROFESSIONAL RESPONSIBILITY ADVISORY OFFICE

Regional Offices—Community Relations Service

Address	Director	Phone/FTS
Atlanta, GA (75 Piedmont Ave. NE., 30303)	Ozell Sutton	404–331–6883
Boston, MA (Suite 222, 308 Atlantic Ave., 02201)	Martin A. Walsh	617–424–5715
Chicago, IL (55 W. Monroe St., 60603)	Jesse Taylor	312–353–4391
Dallas, TX (1420 W. Mockingbird Ln., 75247)	Richard Sombrano, *Acting*	214–655–8175
Denver, CO (1244 Speer Blvd., 80204–3584)	Philip Arreda	303–844–2973
Kansas City, MO (323 W. 8th St., 64105)	Atkins Warren	816–426–7434
Los Angeles, CA (888 S. Figuera St., 90017)	Ron Wakabayashi	213–894–2941
New York, NY (26 Federal Plz., 10278)	Moses Jones, *Acting*	212–264–0700
Philadelphia, PA (2d & Chestnut Sts., 19106)	Henry Mitchum, *Acting*	215–597–2344
Seattle, WA (915 2d Ave., 98101)	P. Diane Schneider, *Acting*	206–220–6700

Intelligence The Office of Intelligence Policy and Review advises the Attorney General on all matters relating to national security; prepares and files all applications for surveillances and searches under the Foreign Intelligence Surveillance Act of 1978; and assists Government agencies by providing legal advice on matters of national security law and policy.

Legal Counsel The Office of Legal Counsel provides written opinions and informal advice in response to requests from the various agencies of the Government typically dealing with legal issues involving agency disagreements or with pending legislation. The Office also is responsible for providing legal advice to the executive branch on all constitutional questions. All Executive orders and proclamations proposed to be issued by the President are reviewed by the Office of Legal Counsel for form and legality. The Office coordinates the work of the Department with respect to treaties, executive agreements, and international organizations.

Pardon Attorney The Office of the Pardon Attorney assists the President in the exercise of his pardon power under the Constitution. Generally, all requests for pardon or other forms of executive clemency, including commutation of sentence, are directed to the Pardon Attorney for investigation and review. The Pardon Attorney prepares the Department's recommendation to the President for final disposition of each application.

Solicitor General The Office of the Solicitor General represents the U.S. Government in cases before the Supreme Court. It decides what cases the Government should ask the Supreme Court to review and what position the Government should take in cases before the Court. It also supervises the preparation of the Government's Supreme Court briefs and other legal documents and the conduct of the oral arguments in the Court. The Solicitor General also decides whether the United States should appeal in all cases it loses before the lower courts.

U.S. Attorneys The Executive Office for U.S. Attorneys was created on April 6, 1953, to provide liaison between the Department of Justice in Washington, DC, and the U.S. attorneys. Its mission is to provide general executive assistance to the 94 Offices of the U.S. attorneys and to coordinate the relationship between the U.S. attorneys and the organization components of the Department of Justice and other Federal agencies.

U.S. Trustee Program The Program was established by the Bankruptcy Reform Act of 1978 (11 U.S.C. 101 *et seq.*) as a pilot effort in 10 regions encompassing 18 Federal judicial districts to promote the efficiency and protect the integrity of the bankruptcy system, and it identifies and helps investigate bankruptcy fraud and abuse. The Executive Office for U.S. Trustees provides day-to-day policy and legal direction, coordination, and control.

For further information, contact the Executive Office for U.S. Trustees, Department of Justice, Suite 700, 901 E Street NW., Washington, DC 20530. Phone, 202–307–1391. Internet, www.usdoj.gov/ust.

Divisions

Antitrust Division

The Assistant Attorney General in charge of the Antitrust Division is responsible for promoting and maintaining competitive markets by enforcing the Federal antitrust laws. This involves investigating possible antitrust violations, conducting grand jury proceedings, preparing and trying antitrust cases, prosecuting appeals, and negotiating and enforcing final judgments. The Division prosecutes serious and willful violations of antitrust laws by filing criminal suits that can lead to large fines and jail sentences. Where criminal prosecution is not appropriate, the Division seeks a court order forbidding future violations of the law and requiring steps by the defendant to remedy the anticompetitive effects of past violations.

The Division also is responsible for acting as an advocate of competition within the Federal Government. This involves formal appearances in Federal administrative agency proceedings, development of legislative initiatives to promote deregulation and eliminate unjustifiable exemptions from the antitrust laws, participation on executive branch policy task forces, and publication of reports on regulated industry performance. The Division provides formal advice to other agencies on the competitive implications of proposed transactions requiring Federal approval, such as construction of nuclear powerplants and mergers of financial institutions. It also consults with Federal agencies on a variety of other matters, including the issuance of Federal coal and oil drilling leases and the disposition of surplus Government property.

For further information, contact the FOIA Unit, Antitrust Division, Department of Justice, 325 Seventh Street NW., Washington, DC 20530. Phone, 202–514–2692.

Civil Division

The Civil Division represents the United States, its departments and agencies, Members of Congress, Cabinet officers, and other Federal employees. Its litigation reflects the diversity of Government activities, involving, for example, the defense of challenges to Presidential actions; national security issues; benefit programs; energy policies; commercial issues such as contract disputes, banking, insurance, patents, fraud, and debt collection; all manner of accident and liability claims; and violations of the immigration and consumer protection laws. The Division confronts significant policy issues, which often rise to constitutional dimensions, in defending and enforcing various Federal programs and actions.

The Division litigates cases in the following areas:

—Commercial litigation, litigation associated with the Government's diverse financial involvements including all monetary suits involving contracts, express or implied; actions to foreclose on Government mortgages and liens; bankruptcy and insolvency proceedings; suits against guarantors and sureties; patent cases and suits arising out of construction, procurement, service contracts, and claims associated with contract terminations; claims involving freight rate disputes arising out of the transportation of Government property; claims for just compensation under the fifth amendment; claims for salary or retirement by civilian and military personnel; and cases assigned by congressional reference or special legislation.

—Consumer litigation, including civil and criminal litigation and related matters arising under various consumer protection and public health statutes.

—Federal programs, including constitutional challenges to statutes, suits to overturn Government policies and programs, challenges to the legality of Government decisions, allegations that the President has violated the Constitution or Federal law, suits to enforce regulatory statutes and to remedy or prevent statutory or regulatory violations. The areas of litigation include: suits against the heads of Federal departments and agencies and other government officials to enjoin official actions, as well as suits for judicial review of administrative decisions, orders, and regulations; suits involving national security, including suits to protect sensitive intelligence sources and materials; suits to prevent interference with Government operations; litigation concerning the constitutionality of Federal laws; and suits raising employment discrimination claims and Government personnel issues.

—Immigration litigation, involving civil litigation under the Immigration and Nationality Act and related laws; district court litigation, removal order review proceedings, habeas corpus review and general advice, and immigration-related appellate matters; cases pertaining to the issuance of visas and passports; and litigation arising under the amnesty and employer sanctions provisions of immigration legislation.

—Torts, including the broad range of tort litigation arising from the operation of the Federal Government, aviation disasters, environmental and occupational disease, and radiation and toxic substance exposure. It also handles maritime litigation and suits that seek personal monetary judgements against individual officers or employees.

For further information, contact the Office of the Assistant Attorney General, Civil Division, Department of Justice, Tenth Street and Pennsylvania Avenue NW., Washington, DC 20530. Phone, 202–514–3301.

Civil Rights Division

The Civil Rights Division, headed by an Assistant Attorney General, was established in 1957 to secure effective Federal enforcement of civil rights. The Division is the primary institution within the Federal Government responsible for enforcing Federal statutes prohibiting discrimination on the basis of race, sex, disability, religion, and national origin. The Division has responsibilities in the following areas:

—Coordination and review of various civil rights statutes that prohibit discrimination on the basis of race, color, national origin, sex, and religion in programs and activities that receive Federal financial assistance by Federal agencies.

—Criminal cases involving conspiracies to interfere with federally protected rights; deprivation of rights under color of law; the use of force or threat of force to injure or intimidate someone in their enjoyment of specific rights (such as voting, housing, employment, education, public facilities, and accommodations); interference with the free exercise of religious beliefs or damage to religious property; the holding of a worker in a condition of slavery or involuntary servitude; and interference with persons seeking to obtain or provide reproductive services.

—Disability rights cases, involving violations of titles I, II, and III of the Americans with Disabilities Act of 1990 (ADA) and Department of Justice regulations implementing these provisions.

—Educational opportunities litigation, involving violations of title IV of the Civil Rights Act of 1964 and the Equal Educational Opportunities Act of 1974.

—Employment litigation, involving violations of Federal statutes prohibiting employment practices that discriminate on the grounds of race, sex, religion, and national origin, as they apply to State and local government employers.

—Housing and civil enforcement of statutes prohibiting discrimination in housing on the basis of race, color, religion, sex, national origin, disability, and familial status; discrimination in credit transactions; and discrimination in places of public accommodations, such as hotels, restaurants, and places of entertainment.

—Immigration-related unfair employment practices, with the responsibility to investigate and prosecute charges of national origin and citizenship status discrimination in hiring, firing, or recruitment.

—Special litigation protecting the constitutional and statutory rights of persons confined in certain institutions owned or operated by State or local governments, including facilities for individuals with mental and developmental disabilities, nursing homes, prisons, jails, and juvenile detention facilities where a pattern or practice of violations exist.

—Voting statutory provisions designed to safeguard the right to vote of racial and language minorities, illiterate persons, individuals with disabilities, overseas citizens, persons who change their residence shortly before a Presidential election, and persons 18 to 20 years of age.

For further information, contact the Executive Officer, Civil Rights Division, Department of Justice, P.O. Box 65310, Washington, DC 20035-5310. Phone, 202-514-4224. Internet, www.usdoj.gov/crt.

Criminal Division

The Criminal Division develops, enforces, and supervises the application of all Federal criminal laws, except those specifically assigned to other divisions. In addition to its direct litigation responsibilities, the Division formulates and implements criminal enforcement policy and provides advice and assistance. The Division approves or monitors sensitive areas of law enforcement such as participation in the Witness Security Program and the use of electronic surveillance; advises the Attorney General, Congress, the Office of Management and Budget, and the White House on matters of criminal law; provides legal advice and assistance to Federal prosecutors and investigative agencies; and provides leadership for coordinating international as well as Federal, State, and local law enforcement matters. Areas of responsibility include:

—Asset forfeiture and money laundering including developing regulatory and legislative initiatives; ensuring the uniform application of forfeiture and money laundering statutes; litigating complex, sensitive, and multidistrict cases; adjudicating petitions for remission or mitigation of forfeited assets; and distributing forfeited funds and properties to appropriates domestic and foreign law enforcement agencies and community groups within the United States.

—Child exploitation and obscenity, prosecuting violators of Federal criminal statutes relating to child support; sexual exploitation of minors; obscenity; possession, manufacture, and distribution of child pornography; selling, buying, or transporting women and children to engage in sexually explicit conduct; and international parental abduction.

—Computer crime and intellectual property, including cyberattacks on critical information systems, improving domestic and international infrastructure to pursue network criminals most effectively; and initiating and participating in international efforts to combat computer crime.

—Enforcement, overseeing the use of the most sophisticated investigative tools at the Department's disposal; reviewing all Federal electronic surveillance requests and requests to apply for court orders permitting the use of video surveillance; authorizing or denying the entry of applicants into the Federal Witness Security Program (WSP), coordinating and administering matters relating to all aspects of the WSP among all program components, and approving or denying requests by Federal agencies to utilize Federal prisoners for investigative purposes; and reviewing requests for witness immunity, transfer of prisoners to and from foreign countries to serve the remainder of their prison sentences, attorney and press subpoenas, applications for S-visa status, and disclosure of grand jury information.

—Fraud, including investigations and prosecutions of fraud and white-collar crime including business crimes such as financial institution fraud, Internet fraud, and insurance industry fraud; multi-district schemes that victimize consumers, such as telemarketing scams and fraudulent bankruptcy mills; and fraud involving Government programs and payments including health care, housing, and Government regulatory activity in the securities and commodities markets.

—Internal security including cases affecting national security, foreign relations, and the export of military and strategic commodities and technology.

—Narcotics and dangerous drugs, including statutes pertaining to controlled substances; developing and implementing domestic and international narcotics law enforcement policies and programs; developing and administering other cooperative drug enforcement strategies, initiatives, and projects conducted by the law enforcement and intelligence communities.

—Organized crime and racketeering efforts against traditional groups and emerging groups from Asia and Europe. such as Chinese triads, the Sicilian mafia, and Russian organized crime.

—Overseas prosecutorial development, assistance, and training for prosecutors and judicial personnel in other countries to develop and sustain democratic criminal justice institutions.

—Policy and legislation, developing legislative proposals, legal memoranda, and congressional testimony; preparing comments on pending legislation affecting the Federal criminal justice system; and working closely with the U.S. Sentencing Commission on a variety of sentencing-related issues.

—Public integrity efforts to combat corruption of elected and appointed public officials at all levels of Government.

—Special investigations of individuals who took part in Nazi-sponsored acts of persecution abroad before and during World War II and who subsequently entered or seek to enter the United States illegally and/or fradulently, and interagency investigation into assets looted from victims of Nazi persecution.

—Terrorism and violent crime, involving design, implementation, and support of law enforcement efforts, legislative initiatives, policies, and strategies relating to international and domestic terrorism; immigration enforcement efforts relating to alien terrorists; and prosecution of firearms and explosives violations.

For further information, contact the Office of the Assistant Attorney General, Criminal Division, Department of Justice, Tenth Street and Pennsylvania Avenue NW., Washington, DC 20530. Phone, 202–514–2601.

Environment and Natural Resources Division

The Environment and Natural Resources Division is the Nation's environmental lawyer. It is responsible for litigating cases ranging from protection of endangered species, to global climate change, to cleaning up the Nation's hazardous waste sites. A key responsibility is enforcing civil and criminal environmental laws in order to protect its citizens' health and environment. The Division defends environmental challenges to Government activities and programs and ensures that environmental laws are implemented in a fair and consistent manner nationwide. It also represents the United States in all matters concerning the protection, use, and development of the Nation's natural resources and public lands, wildlife protection, Indian rights and claims, and the acquisition of Federal property. To carry out this broad mission, the Division is responsible for litigation in the following areas:

—Environmental crimes, prosecuting individuals and corporate entities violating laws designed to protect the environment.

—Environmental defense, representing the United States in suits challenging the Government's administration of Federal environmental laws including claims by industries that regulations are too strict, claims by environmental groups that Federal standards are too lax, and claims by States and citizens alleging that Federal agencies are out of compliance with environmental standards.

—Environmental enforcement, responsible for most litigation on behalf of EPA; claims for damages to natural resources filed on behalf of the Departments of Interior, Commerce, and Agriculture; claims for contribution against private parties for contamination of public land; and recoupment of money spent to clean up certain oil spills on behalf of the U.S. Coast Guard.

—Wildlife and marine resources protection legislation focusing on smugglers and black-market dealers in protected wildlife.

—General litigation, primarily involving the use and protection of federally owned public lands and natural resources.

—Indian resources protection, including establishing water rights, establishing and protecting hunting and fishing rights, collecting damages for trespass on Indian lands, and establishing reservation boundaries and rights to land.

—Land acquisition for use by the Federal Government for purposes ranging from establishing public parks to creating missile sites.

For further information, contact the Office of the Assistant Attorney General, Environment and Natural Resources Division, Department of Justice, Tenth Street and Pennsylvania Avenue NW., Washington, DC 20530. Phone, 202–514–2701.

Tax Division

The primary mission of the Tax Division is to enforce the Nation's tax laws in Federal and State courts and thereby generate revenue for the Federal Government. The Division conducts enforcement activities to deter specific taxpayers, as well as the taxpaying public at large, from conduct that deprives the Federal Government of its tax-related revenue. It represents the United States and its officers in all civil and criminal litigation arising under the internal revenue laws, other than proceedings in the United States Tax Court. Other areas of civil litigation in which the Division is involved on behalf of the Federal Government include:

—suits brought by individuals to foreclose mortgages or to quiet title to property in which the United States is named as a party defendant because of the existence of a Federal tax lien on the property;

—suits brought by the United States to collect unpaid assessments, to foreclose Federal tax liens or determine the priority of such liens, to obtain judgments against delinquent taxpayers, to enforce summonses, and to establish tax claims in bankruptcy, receivership, or probate proceedings;

—proceedings involving mandamus, injunctions, and other specific writs arising in connection with internal revenue matters;

—suits against Internal Revenue Service employees for damages claimed because of alleged injuries caused in the performance of their official duties;

—suits against the Secretary of the Treasury, the Commissioner of Internal Revenue, or similar officials to test the validity of regulations or rulings not in the context of a specific refund action;

—suits brought by the United States to enjoin the promotion of abusive tax shelters and to enjoin activities relating to aiding and abetting the understatement of tax liabilities of others;

—suits brought by taxpayers for a judicial determination of the reasonableness of a jeopardy or termination assessment and the appropriateness of the amount;

—proceedings brought against the Tax Division and the Internal Revenue Service for disclosure of information under the Freedom of Information Act; and

—intergovernmental immunity suits in which the United States resists attempts to apply a State or local tax to some activity or property of the United States.

The Division also collects judgments in tax cases. To this end, the Division directs collection efforts and coordinates with, monitors the efforts of, and provides assistance to the various United States attorneys' offices in collecting outstanding judgments in tax cases.

For further information, contact the Office of the Assistant Attorney General, Tax Division, Department of Justice, Tenth Street and Pennsylvania Avenue NW., Washington, DC 20530. Phone, 202–514–2901. Internet, www.usdoj.gov/tax.

Bureaus

Federal Bureau of Investigation

935 Pennsylvania Avenue NW., Washington, DC 20535. Phone, 202–324–3000. Internet, www.fbi.gov.

The Federal Bureau of Investigation (FBI) is the principal investigative arm of the United States Department of Justice. It is charged with gathering and reporting facts, locating witnesses, and compiling evidence in cases involving Federal jurisdiction.

The Federal Bureau of Investigation was established in 1908 by the Attorney General, who directed that Department of Justice investigations be handled by its own staff. The Bureau is charged with investigating all violations of Federal law except those that have been assigned by legislative enactment or otherwise to another Federal agency. Its jurisdiction includes a wide range of responsibilities in the criminal, civil, and security fields. Priority has been assigned to the five areas that affect society the most: organized crime/drugs, counterterrorism, white-collar crime, foreign counterintelligence, and violent crime.

On January 28, 1982, the Attorney General assigned concurrent jurisdiction for the enforcement of the Controlled Substances Act (21 U.S.C. 801) to the Bureau and the Drug Enforcement Administration (DEA). The DEA Administrator reports to the Attorney General through the FBI Director.

The Bureau also offers cooperative services such as fingerprint identification, laboratory examination, police training, and the National Crime Information Center to duly authorized law enforcement agencies.

For further information, contact the Office of Public and Congressional Affairs, Federal Bureau of Investigation, J. Edgar Hoover FBI Building, 935 Pennsylvania Avenue NW., Washington, DC 20535. Phone, 202–324–2727.

Bureau of Prisons

320 First Street NW., Washington, DC 20534. Phone, 888–317–8455. Internet, www.bop.gov.

The mission of the Bureau of Prisons is to protect society by confining offenders in the controlled environments of prisons and community-based facilities that are safe, humane, and appropriately secure, and which provide work and other self-improvement opportunities to assist offenders in becoming law-abiding citizens.

The community corrections and detention division is responsible for program development and contracts relating to community-based and detention programs, as well as privatization and citizen participation.

The correctional programs division is responsible for managing the correctional services (security) operations in Bureau institutions and case and unit management, as well as religious and psychological services, drug treatment programs, programs for special needs offenders, and inmate systems.

UNICOR, the Federal Prison Industries, provides employment and training opportunities for inmates confined in Federal correctional facilities. Inmates manufacture a wide range of items from executive and systems furniture to electronics, textiles, and graphics/signage. Services performed by UNICOR's inmates include data entry, printing, and furniture refinishing. The corporation funds selected preindustrial, vocational, and experimental training programs.

The National Institute of Corrections provides technical assistance, information services, and training for State and local corrections agencies throughout the country. It also provides technical assistance for selected foreign governments.

For further information, contact the Public Information Officer, Bureau of Prisons, Department of Justice, Washington, DC 20534. Phone, 202–307–3198.

United States Marshals Service

600 Army Navy Drive, Arlington, VA 22202–4210. Phone, 202–307–9000

The United States Marshals Service is the Nation's oldest Federal law enforcement agency, having served as a vital link between the executive and judicial branches of the Government since 1789. The Marshals Service performs tasks that are essential to the operation of virtually every aspect of the Federal justice system. The Service is responsible for:

—providing support and protection for the Federal courts, including security for 800 judicial facilities and nearly 2,000 judges and magistrates, as well as countless other trial participants such as jurors and attorneys;

—apprehending the majority of all Federal fugitives;

—operating the Federal Witness Security Program, ensuring the safety of endangered government witnesses;

—maintaining custody of and transporting thousands of Federal prisoners annually;

—executing court orders and arrest warrants;

—managing and selling seized property forfeited to the Government by drug traffickers and other criminals, and assisting the Justice Department's asset forfeiture program;

—responding to emergency circumstances, including civil disturbances, terrorist incidents, and other crisis situations, through its Special Operations Group, and restoring order in riot and mob-violence situations; and

—operating the U.S. Marshals Service Training Academy.

For further information, contact the Office of Public Affairs, U.S. Marshals Service, Department of Justice, 600 Army Navy Drive, Arlington, VA 22202. Phone, 202–307–9065. Internet, www.usdoj.gov/marshals.

United States National Central Bureau–International Criminal Police Organization

Washington, DC 20530. Phone, 202–616–9000

The U.S. National Central Bureau (USNCB) represents the United States in INTERPOL, the International Criminal Police Organization. Also known as INTERPOL—Washington, USNCB provides an essential communications link between the U.S. police community and their counterparts in the foreign member countries.

INTERPOL is an association of 178 countries dedicated to promoting mutual assistance among law enforcement authorities in the prevention and suppression of international crime. With no police force of its own, INTERPOL has no powers of arrest or search and seizure. Instead, INTERPOL serves as a channel of communication among the police of the member countries, and provides a forum for discussions, working group meetings, and symposia to enable police to focus on specific areas of criminal activity affecting their countries.

Under the State and Local Law Enforcement Program, States establish an office within their own law enforcement community to serve as liaison to USNCB. International leads developed in criminal investigations being conducted by a State or local police entity can be pursued through their liaison office, and criminal investigative requests from abroad are funneled through the relevant State liaison office for action by the appropriate State or local agency. All 50 States and the District of Columbia now participate in the liaison program, which is currently coordinated by a representative from the Maryland State Police.

USNCB has three sub-bureaus which serve to more effectively address the law enforcement needs of U.S. territories. The sub-bureaus are located in Puerto Rico, American Samoa, and the U.S. Virgin Islands.

For further information, contact the U.S. National Central Bureau–INTERPOL, Washington, DC 20530. Phone, 202–616–9000.

Immigration and Naturalization Service

425 I Street NW., Washington, DC 20536. Phone, 202–514–4316, 4330, or 4354

[For the Immigration and Naturalization Service statement of organization, see the *Code of Federal Regulations,* Title 8, Aliens and Nationality]

The Immigration and Naturalization Service (INS) was created by act of March 3, 1891 (8 U.S.C. 1551 note). The Service carries out its mission through operational programs in adjudications and nationality, inspections, investigations, and detention and deportation, as well as the U.S. Border Patrol. These programs are divided into the following mission responsibilities:

—facilitating entry of those legally admissible as visitors or immigrants to the United States;

—granting benefits under the Immigration and Nationality Act, as amended, including providing assistance to those seeking asylum, temporary or permanent resident status, or naturalization;

—preventing improper entry and the granting of benefits to those not legally entitled to them;

—apprehending and removing those aliens who enter or remain illegally in the United States and/or whose stay is not in the public interest; and

—enforcing sanctions against those who act or conspire to subvert the requirements for selective and controlled entry, including sanctions against employers who knowingly hire aliens not authorized to work in the United States.

The Service also has a firm commitment to strengthen criminal investigations and seek the most effective deterrents to illegal immigration.

For further information, contact the Office of Information, Immigration and Naturalization Service, Department of Justice, 425 I Street NW., Washington, DC 20536. Phone, 202–514–4316, 4330, or 4354.

Drug Enforcement Administration

600–700 Army Navy Drive, Arlington, VA 22202. Phone, 202–307–1000. FTS, 367–1000

The Drug Enforcement Administration (DEA) is the lead Federal agency in enforcing narcotics and controlled substances laws and regulations. It was created in July 1973, by Reorganization Plan No. 2 of 1973 (5 U.S.C. app.).

The Administration enforces the provisions of the controlled substances and chemical diversion and trafficking laws and regulations of the United States, and operates on a worldwide basis. It presents cases to the criminal and civil justice systems of the United States—or any other competent jurisdiction—on those significant organizations and their members involved in cultivation, production, smuggling, distribution, or diversion of controlled substances appearing in or destined for illegal traffic in the United States. DEA immobilizes these organizations by arresting their members, confiscating their drugs, and seizing their assets; and creates, manages, and supports enforcement-related programs—domestically and internationally—aimed at reducing the availability of and demand for controlled substances.

The Administration's responsibilities include:

—investigation of major narcotic violators who operate at interstate and international levels;

—seizure and forfeiture of assets derived from, traceable to, or intended to be used for illicit drug trafficking;

—enforcement of regulations governing the legal manufacture, distribution, and dispensing of controlled substances;

—management of a national narcotics intelligence system;

—coordination with Federal, State, and local law enforcement authorities and cooperation with counterpart agencies abroad; and

—training, scientific research, and information exchange in support of drug traffic prevention and control.

The Administration maintains liaison with the United Nations, INTERPOL, and other organizations on matters relating to international narcotics control programs. It has offices throughout the United States and in 56 foreign countries.

For further information, contact the Public Affairs Section, Drug Enforcement Administration, Department of Justice, Washington, DC 20537. Phone, 202–307–7977.

Office of Justice Programs

810 Seventh Street NW., Washington, DC 20531. Phone, 202–307–0703

The Office of Justice Programs (OJP) was established by the Justice Assistance Act of 1984 and reauthorized in 1994 to provide Federal leadership, coordination, and assistance needed to make the Nation's justice system more efficient and effective in preventing and controlling crime. OJP is responsible for collecting statistical data and conducting analyses; identifying emerging criminal justice issues; developing and testing promising approaches to address these issues; evaluating program results, and disseminating these findings and other information to State and local governments. The Office is comprised of the following bureaus and offices:

The Bureau of Justice Assistance provides funding, training, and technical assistance to State and local governments to combat violent and drug-related crime and help improve the criminal justice system.

The Bureau of Justice Statistics is responsible for collecting and analyzing data on crime, criminal offenders, crime victims, and the operations of justice systems at all levels of government.

The National Institute of Justice sponsors research and development programs, conducts demonstrations of innovative approaches to improve criminal justice, and develops new criminal justice technologies.

The Office of Juvenile Justice and Delinquency Prevention provides grants and contracts to States to help them improve their juvenile justice systems and sponsors innovative research, demonstration, evaluation, statistics, replication, technical assistance, and training programs to help improve the Nation's understanding of and response to juvenile violence and delinquency.

The Office for Victims of Crime administers victim compensation and assistance grant programs and provides funding, training, and technical assistance to victim service organizations, criminal justice agencies, and other professionals to improve the Nation's response to crime victims.

The Violence Against Women Office coordinates legislative and other initiatives relating to violence against women and administers grant programs to help prevent, detect, and stop violence against women, including domestic violence, sexual assult, and stalking.

The Drug Court Program Office supports the development, implementation, and improvement of drug courts through technical assistance and training and grants to State, local, or tribal governments and courts.

The Corrections Program Office provides financial and technical assistance to State and local governments to implement corrections-related programs including correctional facility construction and corrections-based drug treatment programs.

The Executive Office for Weed and Seed helps communities build stronger, safer neighborhoods by implementing the weed and seed strategy, a community-based, multidisciplinary approach to combating crime.

The Office for State and Local Domestic Preparedness Support is responsible for enhancing the capacity of State and local jurisdictions to prepare for and respond to incidents of domestic terrorism involving chemical and biological agents, rediological and explosive devices, and other weapons of mass destruction.

The Office of the Police Corps and Law Enforcement Education provides college educational assistance to students who commit to public service in law enforcement and scholarships with no service commitment to dependents of law enforcement officers who died in the line of duty.

For further information, contact the Department of Justice Response Center. Phone, 800–421–6770. Internet, www.ojp.usdoj.gov. E-mail, askocpa@ojp.usdoj.gov.

Boards

Executive Office for Immigration Review

Falls Church, VA 22041. Phone, 703–305–0289. Internet, www.usdoj.gov/eoir.

The Executive Office for Immigration Review is charged with the administration and interpretation of various immigration statutes.

The Board of Immigration Appeals has nationwide jurisdiction to hear appeals of decisions made by immigration judges and by district and center directors of the Immigration and Naturalization Service. In addition, the Board is responsible for hearing appeals involving disciplinary actions against attorneys and representatives before the Service and the Board.

Decisions of the Board are binding on all Service officers and immigration judges unless modified or overruled by judicial review in the Federal courts. The majority of appeals reaching the Board involve orders of removal and application for relief from removal. Other cases before the Board include the removal of aliens applying for admission to the United States, petitions to classify the status of alien relatives for the issuance of preference immigrant visas, fines imposed upon carriers for the violation of the immigration laws, and motions for reopening and reconsideration of decisions previously rendered.

The Office of the Chief Immigration Judge provides overall direction for the 209 immigration judges located in approximately 52 immigration courts throughout the Nation. Immigration judges are responsible for conducting formal administrative proceedings and act independently in their decisionmaking capacity. Their decisions are administratively final, unless appealed or certified to the Board.

In removal proceedings, an immigration judge determines whether an individual from a foreign country should be admitted or allowed to stay in the United States or be removed. Judges are located throughout the United States, and each judge has jurisdiction to consider various forms of relief available under the law, including applications for asylum.

The Office of the Chief Administrative Hearing Officer is responsible for the general supervision of administrative law judges in the performance of their duties. Administrative law judge proceedings are mandated by the Immigration and Nationality Act and concern allegations of unlawful employment of aliens, unfair immigration-related employment practices, and immigration document fraud.

For further information, contact the Office of Public Affairs, Executive Office for Immigration Review, Department of Justice, Falls Church, VA 22041. Phone, 703–305–0289. Internet, www.usdoj.gov/eoir.

United States Parole Commission

5550 Friendship Boulevard, Chevy Chase, MD 20815. Phone, 301–492–5990

The Parole Commission has sole authority to grant, modify, or revoke paroles of eligible U.S. prisoners serving sentences of more than one year, including military prisoners and D.C. Code prisoners housed in Federal institutions. It is responsible for the supervision of parolees and prisoners released upon the expiration of their sentences with allowances for statutory good time, and the determination of supervisory conditions and terms. Probation officers supervise parolees and mandatory releases under the direction of the Commission.

The Commission determines whether or not persons convicted of certain crimes may serve as officials in the field of organized labor or in labor-oriented management positions; determines whether or not such persons may provide services to or be employed by employment benefit plans; and sets release dates for U.S. citizens who are returned to the United States to serve foreign criminal sentences.

For further information, contact the Office of the Chairman, United States Parole Commission, Department of Justice, 5550 Friendship Boulevard, Chevy Chase, MD 20815. Phone, 301–492–5990. Internet, www.usdoj.gov/uspc/parole.htm.

Office of Community Oriented Policing Services

The Office of Community Oriented Policing Services (COPS) was created to advance the philosophy of community policing as a national law enforcement strategy; to fund 100,000 new police officers in community policing roles; to reinforce partnerships that will sustain community policing; and to evaluate and demonstrate the effectiveness of community policing to improve the quality of life by reducing the levels of disorder, violence, and crime in our communities.

The primary activity of the COPS Office is awarding competitive discretionary grants directly to law enforcement agencies across the United States and its territories. The COPS Office includes the following program divisions:

The grants administration division, responsible for developing and designing new programs to provide resources for the hiring of new officers and to further the adoption and implementation of community policing, reviewing grant applications, and assisting grantees in the implementation of their grants.

The grants monitoring division, responsible for tracking grantees' compliance with the conditions of their grants. The Division conducts site visits and reviews grantee files to ensure that COPS funds are properly used to hire officers and implement community policing. The Division also provides onsite technical assistance to grantees and collects and disseminates examples of successful community policing strategies.

The training and technical assistance division is responsible for coordinating the provision of training and technical assistance to advance the adoption, implementation and sustaining of community policing in the thousands of communities served by the COPS Office.

For further information, contact the Office of Community Oriented Policing Services, Department of Justice, 1100 Vermont Avenue NW., Washington, DC 20530. Phone, 202–514–2058. Internet, www.usdoj.gov/cops.

Foreign Claims Settlement Commission of the United States

The Foreign Claims Settlement Commission of the United States is a quasi-judicial, independent agency within the Department of Justice which adjudicates claims of U.S. nationals against foreign governments, either under specific jurisdiction conferred by Congress or pursuant to international claims settlement agreements. The decisions of the Commission are final and are not reviewable under any standard by any court or other authority. Funds for payment of the Commission's awards are derived from congressional appropriations, international claims settlements, or the liquidation of foreign assets in the United States by the Departments of Justice and the Treasury.

The Commission also has authority to receive, determine the validity and amount, and provide for the payment of claims by members of the U.S. armed services and civilians held as prisoners of war or interned by a hostile force in Southeast Asia during the Vietnam conflict, or by the survivors of such service members and civilians.

The Commission is also responsible for maintaining records and responding to inquiries related to the various claims programs it has conducted against the Governments of Albania, Bulgaria, China, Cuba, Czechoslovakia, Egypt, Ethiopia, the German Democratic Republic, Hungary, Iran, Italy, Panama, Poland, Romania, the Soviet Union, Vietnam, and Yugoslavia, as well as those authorized under the War Claims Act of 1948 and other statutes.

For further information, contact the Office of the Chair, Foreign Claims Settlement Commission of the United States, Department of Justice, Suite 6002, 600 E Street NW., Washington, DC 20579. Phone, 202–616–6975. Fax, 202–616–6993.

186-873 D-00--10

Sources of Information

Controlled Substances Act Registration Information about registration under the Controlled Substances Act may be obtained from the Registration Section of the Drug Enforcement Administration, P.O. Box 28083, Central Station, Washington, DC 20038. Phone, 202–307–7255.

Disability-Related Matters Contact the Civil Rights Division's ADA Hotline. Phone, 800–514–0301. TDD, 800–514–0383. Internet, www.usdoj.gov/crt/ada/adahom1.htm.

Drugs and Crime Clearinghouse Phone, 800–666–3332 (toll-free).

Electronic Access Information concerning Department of Justice programs and activities is available electronically through the Internet, at www.usdoj.gov.

The NCJRS Electronic Bulletin Board may be accessed by calling 301–738–8895 (modem).

Employment The Department maintains an agencywide job line. Phone, 202–514–3397.

Attorneys' applications: Director, Office of Attorney Personnel Management, Department of Justice, Room 6150, Tenth Street and Constitution Avenue NW., Washington, DC 20530. Phone, 202–514–1432. Assistant U.S. attorney applicants should apply to individual U.S. attorneys.

United States Marshals Service: Field Staffing Branch, United States Marshals Service, Department of Justice, 600 Army Navy Drive, Arlington, VA 22202–4210.

Federal Bureau of Investigation: Director, Washington, DC 20535, or any of the field offices or resident agencies whose addresses are listed in the front of most local telephone directories.

Immigration and Naturalization Service: Central Office, 425 I Street NW., Washington, DC 20536 (phone, 202–514–2530); or any regional or district office.

Drug Enforcement Administration: regional offices, laboratories, or Washington Headquarters Office of Personnel.

Bureau of Prisons: Central Office, 320 First Street NW., Washington, DC 20534 (phone, 202–307–3082); or any regional or field office.

Office of Justice Programs: 633 Indiana Avenue NW., Washington, DC 20531. Phone, 202–307–0730.

United States Trustee Program, Room 770, 901 E Street NW., Washington, DC 20530. Phone, 202–616–1000.

Foreign Claims Settlement Commission: Attorneys: Office of the Chief Counsel, Suite 6002, 600 E Street NW., Washington, DC 20579 (phone, 202–616–6975); Other: Administrative Officer, same address and phone.

Housing Discrimination Matters Contact the Civil Rights Division's Housing and Civil Enforcement Section. Phone, 800–896–7743.

Immigration-Related Employment Matters The Civil Rights Division maintains a Worker Hotline. Phone, 800–255–7688. TDD, 800–237–2515. It also offers information for employers. Phone, 800–255–8155. TDD, 800–362–2735.

Publications and Films The *FBI Law Enforcement Bulletin* and *Uniform Crime Reports—Crime in the United States* are available from the Superintendent of Documents, Government Printing Office, Washington, DC 20402.

The Annual Report of the Attorney General of the United States is published each year by the Department of Justice, Washington, DC 20530.

Textbooks on citizenship consisting of teachers manuals and student textbooks at various reading levels are distributed free to public schools for applicants for citizenship and are on sale to all others from the Superintendent of Documents, Government Printing Office, Washington, DC 20402. Public schools or organizations under the supervision of public schools which are entitled to free textbooks should make their requests to the appropriate Immigration and Naturalization Service Regional Office. For general information, call 202–514–3946.

The Freedom of Information Act Guide and Privacy Act Overview and the *Freedom of Information Case List,* both published annually, are available from the Superintendent of Documents, Government Printing Office, Washington, DC 20530.

FOIA Update (Stock No. 727–002–00000–6), published quarterly, is available free of charge to FOIA offices and other interested offices Governmentwide. This publication is also available from the Superintendent of Documents, Government Printing Office, Washington, DC 20402.

Guidelines for Effective Human Relations Commissions, Annual Report of the Community Relations Service, Community Relations Service Brochure, CRS Hotline Brochure, Police Use of Deadly Force: A Conciliation Handbook for Citizens and Police, Principles of Good Policing: Avoiding Violence Between Police and Citizens, Resolving Racial Conflict: A Guide for Municipalities, and *Viewpoints and Guidelines on Court-Appointed Citizens Monitoring Commissions in School Desegregation* are available upon request from the Public Information Office, Community Relations Service, Department of Justice, Washington, DC 20530.

A limited number of drug educational films are available, free of charge, to civic, educational, private, and religious groups.

A limited selection of pamphlets and brochures is available. The most widely requested publication is *Drugs of Abuse,* an identification manual intended for professional use. Single copies are free.

Copies of the Foreign Claims Settlement Commission's semiannual (through December 1966) and annual (from January 1967) reports to the Congress concerning its activities are available at the Commission in limited quantities.

Copies of the *Program Plan* and other Office of Justice Programs publications and documents are available by calling the National Criminal Justice Reference Service (phone, 303–251–5500 or 800–851–3420 (toll free); Internet, www.ncjrs.org). Some documents are also available from the Office's website, (Internet, www.ojp.usdoj.gov).

Reading Rooms Located in Washington, DC, at the following locations:

Department of Justice, Room 6505, Tenth Street and Constitution Avenue NW., Washington, DC 20530. Phone, 202–514–3775.

Bureau of Prisons, 320 First Street NW., 20534. Phone, 202–307–3029.

Immigration and Naturalization Service, 425 I Street NW., 20536. Phone, 202–514–2837.

Foreign Claims Settlement Commission, 600 E Street NW., 20579. Phone, 202–616–6975.

U.S. Parole Commission, 5550 Friendship Boulevard, Chevy Chase, MD 20815. Phone, 301–492–5959.

Board of Immigration Appeals, Suite 2400, 5107 Leesburg Pike, Falls Church, VA 22041. Phone, 703–305–0168.

National Institute of Justice, 9th Floor, 633 Indiana Avenue NW., Washington, DC 20531 (phone, 202–307–5883).

Redress for Wartime Relocation/Internment Contact the Civil Rights Division's Office of Redress Administration. Helpline phone, 202–219–6900. TDD, 202–219–4710. Internet, www.usdoj.gov.

Small Business Activities Contract information for small businesses can be obtained from the Office of Small and Disadvantaged Business Utilization, Department of Justice, Tenth Street and Pennsylvania Avenue NW., Washington, DC 20530. Phone, 202–616–0521.

For further information concerning the Department of Justice, contact the Office of Public Affairs, Department of Justice, Tenth Street and Constitution Avenue NW., Washington, DC 20530. Phone, 202–514–2007. TDD, 202–786–5731. Internet, www.usdoj.gov.

DEPARTMENT OF LABOR

200 Constitution Avenue NW., Washington, DC 20210
Phone, 202–219–5000. Internet, www.dol.gov.

SECRETARY OF LABOR	ALEXIS M. HERMAN
Chief of Staff	LEE SATTERFIELD
Executive Secretary	MICHAEL GRANT
Deputy Secretary	EDWARD B. MONTGOMERY
Associate Deputy Secretary	JAMES MCMULLEN, *Acting*
Associate Deputy Secretary for Adjudication	NANCY S. DOLDER
Chief Administrative Law Judge	JOHN M. VITTONE
Chief Administrative Appeals Judge, Benefits Review Board	BETTY J. HALL
Chief Economist	WILLIAM M. RODGERS III
Chief Financial Officer	KEN BRESNAHAN
Chairman, Administrative Review Board	PAUL GREENBERG
Chairman, Employees Compensation Appeals Board	MICHAEL J. WALSH
Director, Office of Small Business Programs	JUNE M. ROBINSON
Director, Women's Bureau	IRASEMA GARZA
Assistant Secretary for Administration and Management	PATRICIA W. LATTIMORE
Assistant Secretary for Congressional and Intergovernmental Affairs	GERI D. PALAST
Assistant Secretary for Employment and Training	RAYMOND L. BRAMUCCI
Assistant Secretary for Employment Standards	BERNARD E. ANDERSON
Assistant Secretary for Mine Safety and Health	J. DAVITT MCATEER
Assistant Secretary for Occupational Safety and Health	CHARLES N. JEFFRESS
Assistant Secretary for Pension and Welfare Benefits	LESLIE B. KRAMERICH, *Acting*
Assistant Secretary for Policy	EDWARD B. MONTGOMERY
Assistant Secretary for Public Affairs	HOWARD WADDELL, *Acting*
Assistant Secretary for Veterans' Employment and Training	ESPIRIDION A. BORREGO
Commissioner of Labor Statistics	KATHARINE G. ABRAHAM
Deputy Under Secretary for International Labor Affairs	ANDREW J. SAMET
Inspector General	PATRICIA DALTON, *Acting*
Solicitor of Labor	HENRY L. SOLANO

The purpose of the Department of Labor is to foster, promote, and develop the welfare of the wage earners of the United States, to improve their working conditions, and to advance their opportunities for profitable employment. In carrying out this mission, the Department administers a variety of Federal labor laws guaranteeing workers' rights to safe and healthful working conditions, a minimum hourly wage and overtime pay, freedom from employment discrimination, unemployment insurance, and workers' compensation. The Department also protects workers' pension rights; provides for job training programs; helps workers find jobs; works to strengthen free collective bargaining; and keeps track of changes in employment, prices, and other national economic measurements. As the Department seeks to assist all Americans who need and want to work, special efforts are made to meet the unique job market problems of older workers, youths, minority group members, women, the handicapped, and other groups.

The Department of Labor (DOL) was created by act of March 4, 1913 (29 U.S.C. 551). A Bureau of Labor was first created by Congress in 1884 under the Interior Department. The Bureau of Labor later became independent as a Department of Labor without executive rank. It again returned to bureau status in the Department of Commerce and Labor, which was created by act of February 14, 1903 (15 U.S.C. 1501).

Secretary The Secretary is the principal adviser to the President on the development and execution of policies and the administration and enforcement of laws relating to wage earners, their working conditions, and their employment opportunities.

Women's Bureau The Women's Bureau is responsible for formulating standards and policies that promote the welfare of wage earning women, improve their working conditions, increase their efficiency, and advance their opportunities for profitable employment.

For further information, call 202–219–6611.

Regional Offices—Women's Bureau

Address (Areas Served)	Administrator
Atlanta, GA (Suite 7T95, 61 Forsyth St. SW., 30303) (AL, FL, GA, KY, MS, NC, SC, TN)	Delores L. Crockett
Boston, MA (Rm. E–270, JFK Federal Bldg., 02203) (CT, MA, ME, NH, RI, VT)	Jacqueline Cooke
Chicago, IL (230 S. Dearborn St., 60604) (IL, IN, MI, OH, WI)	Nancy Chen
Dallas, TX (525 Griffin St., 75202) (AR, LA, NM, OK, TX)	Beverly Lyle
Denver, CO (Suite 905, 1801 California St., 80202–2614) (CO, MT, ND, SD, UT, WY)	Frances Jefferson
Kansas City, MO (Suite 845, 1100 Main St., 64105) (IA, KS, MO, NE)	Rose A. Kemp
New York, NY (201 Varick St., 10014) (NJ, NY, PR, VI)	Mary Murphree
Philadelphia, PA (3535 Market St., 19104) (DC, DE, MD, PA, VA, WV)	Cornelia Moore
San Francisco, CA (71 Stevenson St., 94105) (AZ, CA, GU, HI, NV)	Jenny Erwin
Seattle, WA (1111 3d Ave., 98101) (AK, ID, OR, WA)	Karen Furia

International Affairs The Bureau of International Labor Affairs assists in formulating international economic, social, trade, and immigration policies affecting American workers, with a view to maximizing higher wage and higher value U.S. jobs derived from global economic integration; gathers and disseminates information on child labor practices worldwide; promotes respect for international labor standards to protect the economic and physical well-being of workers in the United States and around the world; gathers and disseminates information on foreign labor markets and programs so that U.S. employment policy formulation might benefit from international experiences; carries out overseas technical assistance projects; assists in the administration of U.S. labor attaché programs at embassies abroad; and conducts research on the labor market consequences of immigration proposals and legislation.

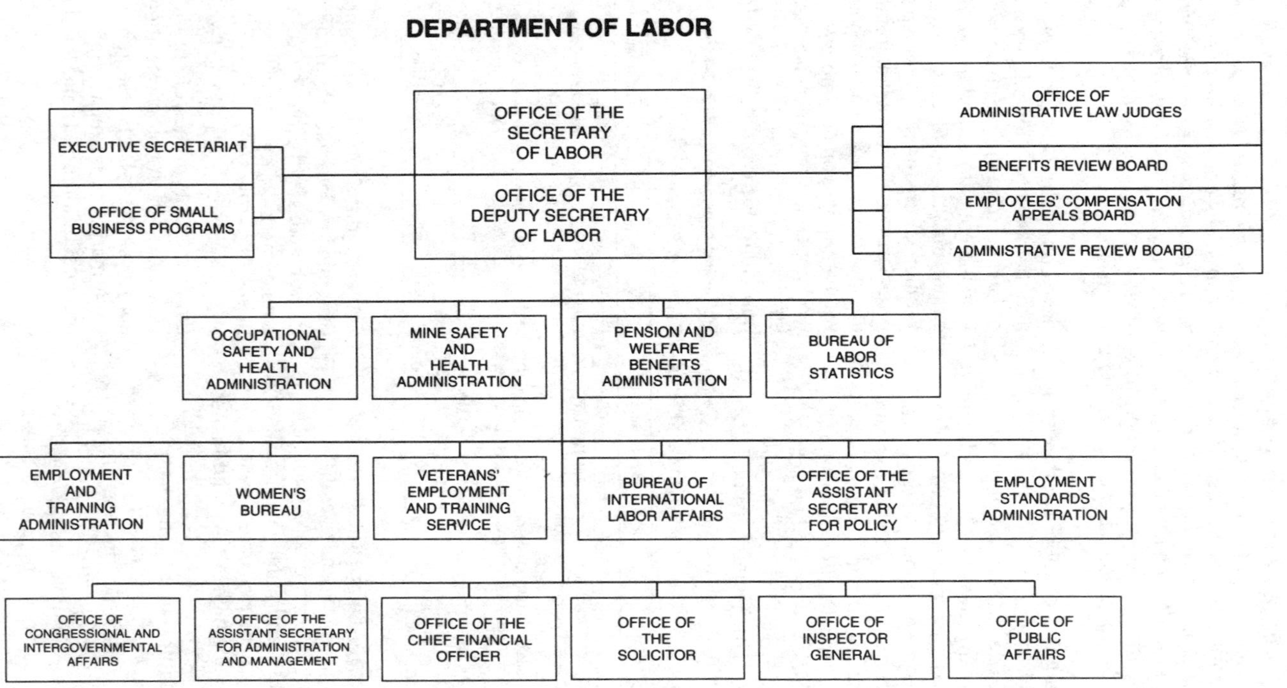
DEPARTMENT OF LABOR
EXECUTIVE SECRETARIAT
OFFICE OF SMALL BUSINESS PROGRAMS
OFFICE OF THE SECRETARY OF LABOR
OFFICE OF THE DEPUTY SECRETARY OF LABOR
OFFICE OF ADMINISTRATIVE LAW JUDGES
BENEFITS REVIEW BOARD
EMPLOYEES' COMPENSATION APPEALS BOARD
ADMINISTRATIVE REVIEW BOARD
OCCUPATIONAL SAFETY AND HEALTH ADMINISTRATION
MINE SAFETY AND HEALTH ADMINISTRATION
PENSION AND WELFARE BENEFITS ADMINISTRATION
BUREAU OF LABOR STATISTICS
EMPLOYMENT AND TRAINING ADMINISTRATION
WOMEN'S BUREAU
VETERANS' EMPLOYMENT AND TRAINING SERVICE
BUREAU OF INTERNATIONAL LABOR AFFAIRS
OFFICE OF THE ASSISTANT SECRETARY FOR POLICY
EMPLOYMENT STANDARDS ADMINISTRATION
OFFICE OF CONGRESSIONAL AND INTERGOVERNMENTAL AFFAIRS
OFFICE OF THE ASSISTANT SECRETARY FOR ADMINISTRATION AND MANAGEMENT
OFFICE OF THE CHIEF FINANCIAL OFFICER
OFFICE OF THE SOLICITOR
OFFICE OF INSPECTOR GENERAL
OFFICE OF PUBLIC AFFAIRS

Employment and Training Administration

The Employment and Training Administration fulfills responsibilities assigned to the Secretary of Labor that relate to employment services, job training, and unemployment insurance. Component offices and services administer a Federal/State employment security system; fund and oversee programs to provide work experience and training for groups having difficulty entering or returning to the work force; formulate and promote apprenticeship standards and programs; and conduct continuing programs of research, development, and evaluation.

Adult Services The Administration is responsible for planning and developing policies, legislative proposals, goals, strategies, budgets, and resource allocation for the operation of comprehensive services to adults in the work force investment system; designing, developing, and administering employment and training services for welfare recipients, Native Americans, migrant and seasonal farmworkers, older workers, individuals with disabilities, and individuals dislocated due to mass layoffs and emergencies; and providing direction for the investigation of worker petitions and the preparation of industry impact studies relating to trade adjustment assistance.

For more information, call 202–219–5339.

Apprenticeship Training and Employer and Labor Services The Administration is responsible for developing materials and conducting a program of public awareness to secure the adoption of training in skilled occupations and related training policies and practices used by employers, unions, and other organizations; developing policies and plans to enhance opportunities for minority and female participation in skilled training; and coordinating the effective use of Federal, labor, and employer resources to create a clear training-to-employment corridor for customers of the work force development system.

For more information, call 202–219–5921.

Work Force Security The Administration is responsible for interpreting Federal legislative requirements for State unemployment compensation and employment service programs and one-stop systems; guiding and assisting States in adopting laws, regulations, and policies that conform with and support Federal law; developing, negotiating, and monitoring reimbursable agreements with States to administer the Targeted Jobs Tax Credit Program; and overseeing the development and implementation of the Nation's labor market information system.

For more information, call 202–219–7831.

Youth Services The Administration is responsible for planning, developing, and recommending objectives, policies, and strategies for operations of a comprehensive youth employment and training system; and providing policy guidance and program performance oversight for youth employment and training services, youth services grant programs, and the school-to-work system.

For more information, call 202–219–6236.

The Administration has regional offices responsible for the oversight and grant administration of employment and training programs operated by State governments.

Regional Offices—Employment and Training Administration

Address (Areas Served)	Administrator	Telephone	Fax
Atlanta, GA (Rm. 6M12, 61 Forsyth St. SW., 30303) (AL, FL, GA, KY, MS, NC, SC, TN).	Toussaint L. Hayes ...	404–562–2092	404–562–2149
Boston, MA (Rm. E–350, JFK Federal Bldg., 02203) (CT, MA, ME, NH, RI, VT).	Robert J. Semler	617–565–3630	617–565–2229
Chicago, IL (Rm. 628, 230 S. Dearborn St., 60604) (IL, IN, MI, OH, WI).	Byron Zuidema	312–353–0313	312–353–4474

Regional Offices—Employment and Training Administration—Continued

Address (Areas Served)	Administrator	Telephone	Fax
Dallas, TX (Rm. 317, 525 Griffin St., 75202) (AR, LA, NM, OK, TX).	Joseph C. Juarez	214–767–8263	214–767–5113
Denver, CO (Suite 1780, 1999 Broadway St., 80202–5716) (CO, MT, ND, SD, UT, WY).	Thomas Dowd	303–844–1650	303–844–1685
Kansas City, MO (Suite 1050, 1100 Main St., 64105) (IA, KS, MO, NE).	Herman Wallace	816–426–3796	816–426–2729
New York, NY (Rm. 755, 201 Varick St., 10014) (NJ, NY, PR, VI)	Marilyn K. Shea	212–337–2139	212–337–2144
Philadelphia, PA (Rm. 13300, 3535 Market St., 19104) (DC, DE, MD, PA, VA, WV).	(Vacancy)	215–596–6336	215–596–0329
San Francisco, CA (Rm. 830, 71 Stevenson St., 94119–3767) (AZ, CA, HI, NV).	Armando Quiroz	415–975–4610	415–975–4612
Seattle, WA (Suite 900, 1111 3d Ave., 98101–3212) (AK, ID, OR, WA).	Michael Brauser	206–553–7700	206–553–0098

For further information, contact the Employment and Training Administration. Phone, 202–219–6050.

Pension and Welfare Benefits Administration

The Pension and Welfare Benefits Administration (PWBA) is responsible for promoting and protecting the pension, health, and other benefits of the over 150 million participants and beneficiaries in over 6 million private sector employee benefit plans. In administering its responsibilities, PWBA assists workers in understanding their rights and protecting their benefits; facilitates compliance by plan sponsors, plan officials, service providers, and other members of the regulated community; encourages the growth of employment-based benefits; and deters and corrects violations of the relevant statutes. ERISA is enforced through 15 PWBA field offices nationwide and the national office in Washington, DC.

Field Offices—Pension and Welfare Benefits Administration

Area/Address	Director
Atlanta, GA (Suite 7B54, 61 Forsyth St. SW., 30303)	Howard Marsh
Boston, MA (Rm. 575, John F. Kennedy Bldg., 02203)	James Benages
Chicago, IL (Suite 1600, 200 W. Adams St., 60606)	Kenneth Bazar
Cincinnati, OH (Suite 210, 1885 Dixie Hwy., Fort Wright, KY 41011)	Joseph Menez
Detroit, MI (Suite 1310, 211 W. Fort St., 48226–3211)	Robert Jogan
Dallas, TX (Rm. 707, 525 Griffin St., 75202)	Bruce Ruud
Kansas City, MO (Suite 1200, 1100 Main St., 64105–2112)	Gregory Egan
Los Angeles, CA (Suite 514, 790 E. Colorado Blvd., 91101)	Billy Beaver
New York, NY (Rm. 625, 6 World Trade Ctr., 10048)	Jonathan Kay, *Acting*
Philadelphia, PA (Rm. M300, 3535 Market St., 19104)	Mabel Capolongo
Plantation, FL (Suite 104, 8040 Peters Rd., 33324)	Jesse Day
St. Louis, MO (Rm. 338, 815 Olive St., 63101–1559)	Gary Newman
San Francisco, CA (Suite 915, 71 Stevenson St., 94119–0250)	Bette Briggs
Seattle, WA (Rm. 860, 1111 3d Ave., 98101–3212)	John Scanlon
Washington, DC (Suite 556, 1730 K St. NW., 20006)	Caroline Sullivan

For further information, contact the Pension and Welfare Benefits Administration. Phone, 202–219–8921. Internet, www.dol.gov/dol/pwba.

Employment Standards Administration

The Employment Standards Administration is responsible for managing and directing employment standards programs dealing with minimum wage and overtime standards; registration of farm labor contractors;

determining prevailing wage rates to be paid on Government contracts and subcontracts; nondiscrimination and affirmative action for minorities, women, veterans, and handicapped Government contract and subcontract workers; workers' compensation programs for Federal and certain private employers and employees; safeguarding the financial integrity and internal democracy of labor unions; and administering statutory programs to certify employee protection provisions for various federally sponsored transportation programs.

Contracts The Office of Federal Contract Compliance Programs (OFCCP) ensures that companies that do business with the Government promote affirmative action and equal employment opportunity on behalf of minorities, women, the disabled, and Vietnam veterans.

For further information, contact the Office of Federal Contract Compliance Programs Ombudsperson. Phone, 888–37–OFCCP (toll-free).

Regional Directors—Office of Federal Contract Compliance Programs

Address (Areas Served)	Director
Atlanta, GA (61 Forsyth St. SW., 30303) (AL, FL, GA, KY, MS, NC, SC, TN)	Carol A. Gaudin
Chicago, IL (230 S. Dearborn St., 60604) (IA, IL, IN, KS, MI, MN, MO, NE, OH, WI)	Halcolm Holliman
Dallas, TX (525 Griffin St., 75202) (AR, CO, LA, MT, ND, NM, OK, SD, TX, UT, WY)	Albert Padilla
New York, NY (201 Varick St., 10014) (CT, MA, ME, NH, NJ, NY, PR, RI, VI, VT)	James R. Turner
Philadelphia, PA (3535 Market St., 19104) (DC, DE, MD, PA, VA, WV)	Joseph J. Dubray, Jr.
San Francisco, CA (71 Stevenson St., 94105) (AK, AZ, CA, HI, ID, NV, OR, WA)	Helene Haase

Wages The Wage and Hour Division is responsible for planning, directing, and administering programs dealing with a variety of Federal labor legislation. These programs are designed to protect low-wage incomes; safeguard the health and welfare of workers by discouraging excessively long hours of work; safeguard the health and well-being of minors; prevent curtailment of employment and earnings for students, trainees, and handicapped workers; minimize losses of income and job rights caused by indebtedness; and direct a program of farm labor contractor registration designed to protect the health, safety, and welfare of migrant and seasonal agricultural workers.

For further information, contact the Office of the Administrator, Wage and Hour Division, Department of Labor, Room S–3502, 200 Constitution Avenue NW., Washington, DC 20210. Phone, 202–693–0051.

Regional Administrators—Wage and Hour Division

Address (Areas Served)	Regional Administrator
Atlanta, GA (Rm. 7M40, 61 Forsyth St. SW., 30303) (AL, GA, KY, MS, NC, SC, TN)	Alfred H. Perry
Boston, MA (Rm. 525, JFK Bldg., 02203) (CT, MA, ME, NH, RI, VT)	James E. Sykes, *Acting*
Chicago, IL (230 S. Dearborn St., 60604) (IL, IN, MI, OH, WI)	Alfred H. Perry, *Acting*
Dallas, TX (Rm. 800, 525 S. Griffin St., 75202) (AR, CO, LA, MT, ND, NM, OK, SD, TX, UT, WY).	Manuel J. Villareal
Kansas City, MO (Suite 700, 1100 Main St., 64105) (IA, KS, MO, NE)	Alfred H. Perry, *Acting*
New York, NY (Rm. 750, 201 Varick St., 10014) (NJ, NY)	James E. Sykes, *Acting*
Philadelphia, PA (Rm. 15210, 3535 Market St., 19104) (DC, DE, MD, PA, PR, VA, VI, WV).	James E. Sykes, *Acting*
San Francisco, CA (Suite 930, 71 Stevenson St., 94105) (AK, AZ, CA, HI, ID, NV, OR, WA).	George Friday, *Acting*

Labor-Management Standards The Office of Labor-Management Standars conducts criminal and civil investigations to safeguard the financial integrity of unions and to ensure union democracy, and conducts investigative audits of labor unions to uncover and remedy criminal and civil violations of the Labor-Management Reporting and Disclosure Act and related statutes.

For further information on union elections and reporting, call 202–693–0124. For general information, call 202–693–0123.

Regional Offices—Office of Labor-Management Standards

Region	Address	Director
Atlanta, GA	Suite 8B85, 61 Forsyth St. SW., 30303	Carol Carter
Chicago, IL	Suite 774, 230 S. Dearborn St., 60604	Ronald Lehman
Philadelphia, PA	Suite 415, 801 Arch St., 19107	Eric Feldman
San Francisco, CA	Suite 725, 71 Stevenson St., 94105	C. Russell Rock
Washington, DC	Suite 558, 1730 K St. NW., 20006	Robert L. Merriner

Workers' Compensation The Office of Workers' Compensation Programs is responsible for programs providing workers' compensation for Federal employees, benefits to employees in private enterprise while engaged in maritime employment on navigable waters in the United States, and benefits to coal miners who are totally disabled due to pneumoconiosis, a respiratory disease contracted after prolonged inhalation of coal mine dust, and to their survivors when the miner's death is due to pneumoconiosis.

For further information, contact the Office of the Director, Office of Workers' Compensation Programs, Department of Labor, Room S–3524, 200 Constitution Avenue NW., Washington, DC 20210. Phone, 202–219–7503.

Regional/District Offices—Office of Workers' Compensation Programs

Area	Address	Director
Regional Offices		
Chicago, IL (IL, IN, MI, OH, WI)	230 S. Dearborn St., 60604	Deborah Sanford
Dallas, TX (AR, LA, NM, OK, TX)	525 Griffin St., 75202	E. Martin Walker, *Acting*
Denver, CO (CO, MT, ND, SD, UT, WY)	1801 California St., 80294	Robert J. Mansanares
Jacksonville, FL (FL)	214 N. Hogan St., 32202	Nancy L. Ricker
Kansas City, MO (IA, KS, MO, NE)	1100 Main St., 64105	Charles O. Ketcham, Jr.
New York, NY (CT, MA, ME, NH, RI, NJ, NY, VT).	201 Varick St., 10014	Kenneth Hamlett
Philadelphia, PA (DC, DE, MD, PA, PR, VA, VI, WV).	3535 Market St., 19104	R. David Lotz
San Francisco, CA (AZ, CA, HI, NV)	71 Stevenson St., 94119	Donna Onodera
Seattle, WA (AK, ID, OR, WA)	1111 3d Ave., 98101	Donna Onodera, *Acting*
District Offices		
Federal Employee Compensation Act		
Boston, MA	Rm. E–260, JFK Federal Bldg., 02114	Michael Harvil
Chicago, IL	230 S. Dearborn St., 60604	Johnny Dawkins
Cleveland, OH	1240 E. 9th St., 44199	Robert M. Sullivan
Dallas, TX	525 Griffin St., 75202	E. Martin Walker
Denver, CO	1801 California St., 80202–2614	Shirley Bridge
Jacksonville, FL	214 N. Hogan St., 32202	William C. Franson
Kansas City, MO	Suite 750, 1100 Main St., 64105	Charles O. Ketcham, Jr.
New York, NY	201 Varick St., 10014	Jonathan G. Lawrence
Philadelphia, PA	3535 Market St., 19104	William Staarman
San Francisco, CA	71 Stevenson St., 94119	Sharon Tyler
Seattle, WA	1111 3d Ave., 98101–3212	Doris Carender
Washington, DC	800 N. Capitol St. NW., 20211	Michael A. Johnson
Division of Longshore and Harbor Workers' Compensation		
Baltimore, MD	Suite 240, 300 W. Pratt St., 21201	Basil Voultsides, *Acting*
Boston, MA	Rm. E–260, JFK Federal Bldg., 02114	Marcia Finn
Chicago, IL	230 S. Dearborn St., 60604	Thomas C. Hunter
Honolulu, HI	300 Ala Moana Blvd., 96850	(Vacancy)
Houston, TX	Suite 140, 8866 Gulf Freeway, 77014	Chris John Gleasman
Jacksonville, FL	214 N. Hogan St., 32202	Jeana La Rock
Long Beach, CA	401 E. Ocean Blvd., 90802	(Vacancy)
New Orleans, LA	701 Loyola St., 70113	Charles (Chuck) Lee
New York, NY	201 Varick St., 10014	Richard V. Robilotti
Norfolk, VA	200 Granby Mall, 23510	Basil E. Voultsides
Philadelphia, PA	3535 Market St., 19104	John McTaggart
San Francisco, CA	71 Stevenson St., 94119	Phil Williams
Seattle, WA	1111 3d Ave., 98101–3212	Karen Staats
Division of Coal Mine Workers' Compensation		
Charleston, WV	2 Hale St., 25301	Robert Hardesty
Columbus, OH	Suite 300, 1160 Dublin Rd., 43215	Don Dopps
Denver, CO	1801 California St., 80202–2614	John Martin
Greensburg, PA	1225 S. Main St., 15601	John Ciszek
Johnstown, PA	Rm. 201, 319 Washington St., 15901	Stuart Glassman
Pikeville, KY	334 Main St., 41501	Harry Skidmore

Regional/District Offices—Office of Workers' Compensation Programs—Continued

Area	Address	Director
Wilkes-Barre, PA	Suite 100, 105 N. Main St., 18701	Marybeth Girton

For further information, contact the Employment Standards Administration, Department of Labor, Room S–3524, 200 Constitution Avenue NW., Washington, DC 20210. Phone, 202–693–0001. Internet, www.dol.gov/dol/esa.

Occupational Safety and Health Administration

The Administration, headed by the Assistant Secretary for Occupational Safety and Health, sets and enforces workplace safety and health standards and assists employers in complying with those standards. The Occupational Safety and Health Administration (OSHA), created pursuant to the Occupational Safety and Health Act of 1970 (29 U.S.C. 651 et seq.), has established a four-fold focus: firm and fair enforcement of safety and health rules; partnership with States running their own OSHA-approved programs and with employers and employees interested in developing effective workplace safety and health programs; efficient promulgation of new rules that are clear and easy to understand and follow; and increased outreach and training to help employers and employees eliminate safety and health hazards.

Regional Offices—Occupational Safety and Health Administration

Address	Administrator	Telephone
Atlanta, GA (61 Forsyth St. SW., 30303) (AL, FL, GA, KY, MS, NC, SC, TN)	Cindy Coe	404–562–2300
Boston, MA (Rm. E–340, JFK Federal Bldg., 02203) (CT, MA, ME, NH, RI, VT)	Ruth McCully	617–565–9860
Chicago, IL (230 S. Dearborn St., 60604) (IL, IN, MI, OH, WI)	Michael Connors	312–353–2220
Dallas, TX (525 Griffin St., 75202) (AR, LA, NM, OK, TX)	John Miles	214–767–4731
Denver, CO (1999 Broadway, 80202) (CO, MT, ND, SD, UT, WY)	Gregory Baxter	303–844–1600
Kansas City, MO (1100 Main St., 64105) (IA, KS, MO, NE)	Charles Adkins	816–426–5861
New York, NY (201 Varick St., 10014) (NJ, NY)	Patricia Clark	212–337–2378
Philadelphia, PA (3535 Market St., 19104) (DC, DE, MD, PA, PR, VA, VI, WV)	Richard Soltan	215–596–1201
San Francisco, CA (71 Stevenson St., 94105) (AZ, CA, HI, NV)	Frank Strasheim	415–975–4310
Seattle, WA (1111 3d Ave., 98101) (AK, ID, OR, WA)	Richard Terrill	206–553–5930

For further information, contact the Occupational Safety and Health Administration, Department of Labor, 200 Constitution Avenue NW., Washington, DC 20210. Phone, 202–693–1999.

Mine Safety and Health Administration

The Mine Safety and Health Administration is responsible for safety and health in the Nation's mines. The Administration develops and promulgates mandatory safety and health standards, ensures compliance with such standards, assesses civil penalties for violations, and investigates accidents. It cooperates with and provides assistance to the States in the development of effective State mine safety and health programs; improves and expands training programs in cooperation with the States and the mining industry; and contributes to the improvement and expansion of mine safety and health research and development. All of these activities are aimed at preventing and reducing mine accidents and occupational diseases in the mining industry.

District Offices—Mine Safety and Health Administration

District/Address	Telephone
Coal Mine Safety and Health	
Barbourville, KY (HC 66, Box 1762, 40906)	606–546–5123
Birmingham, AL (Suite 213, 135 Gemini Cir., 35209–4896)	205–290–7300
Denver, CO (P.O. Box 25367, 80225–0367)	303–231–5458
Hunker, PA (RR 1, Box 736, 15639)	724–925–5150
Madisonville, KY (100 YMCA Dr., 42431–9019)	270–821–4180
Morgantown, WV (5012 Mountaineer Mall, 26501)	304–291–4277
Mount Hope, WV (100 Bluestone Rd., 25880)	304–877–3900
Norton, VA (P.O. Box 560, 24273)	540–679–0230
Pikeville, KY (4159 N. Mayo Trail, 41501)	606–432–0943
Vincennes, IN (Suite 200, 2300 Old Decker Rd., 47591)	812–882–7617
Wilkes-Barre, PA (Suite 034, 7 N. Wilkes-Barre Blvd., 18702)	717–826–6321
Metal/Nonmetal Mine Safety and Health	
Northeastern (230 Executive Dr., Cranberry Township, PA 16066–6415)	724–772–2333
Southeastern (Suite 212, 135 Gemini Cir., Birmingham, AL 35209–4896)	205–290–7294
North Central (515 W. 1st St., Duluth, MN 55802–1302)	218–720–5448
South Central (Rm. 4C50, 1100 Commerce St., Dallas, TX 75242–0499)	214–767–8401
Rocky Mountain (P.O. Box 25367, Denver, CO 80225–0367)	303–231–5465
Western (Suite 610, 2060 Peabody Rd., Vacaville, CA 95687)	707–447–9844

For further information, contact the Office of Information and Public Affairs, Mine Safety and Health Administration, Department of Labor, Room 601, 4015 Wilson Boulevard, Arlington, VA 22203. Phone, 703–235–1452.

Bureau of Labor Statistics

The Bureau of Labor Statistics (BLS) is the principal fact-finding agency of the Federal Government in the broad field of labor economics and statistics. The Bureau is an independent national statistical agency that collects, processes, analyzes, and disseminates essential statistical data to the American public, Congress, other Federal agencies, State and local governments, businesses, and labor. BLS also serves as a statistical resource to the Department of Labor. Data are available relating to employment, unemployment, and other characteristics of the labor force; consumer and producer prices, consumer expenditures, and import and export prices; wages and employee benefits; productivity and technological change; employment projections; occupational illness and injuries; and international comparisons of labor statistics. Most of the data are collected in surveys conducted by the Bureau, the Bureau of the Census (on a contract basis), or on a cooperative basis with State agencies.

The Bureau strives to have its data satisfy a number of criteria, including: relevance to current social and economic issues, timeliness in reflecting today's rapidly changing economic conditions, accuracy and consistently high statistical quality, and impartiality in both subject matter and presentation.

The basic data are issued in monthly, quarterly, and annual news releases; bulletins, reports, and special publications; and periodicals. Data are also made available through an electronic news service, magnetic tape, diskettes, and microfiche, as well as on Internet. Regional offices issue additional reports and releases usually presenting locality or regional detail.

Regional Offices—Bureau of Labor Statistics

Region	Address	Commissioner
Atlanta, GA (AL, FL, GA, KY, MS, NC, SC, TN)	61 Forsyth St. SW., 30303	Janet S. Rankin
Boston, MA (CT, ME, MA, NH, NY, PR, RI, VT)	JFK Federal Bldg., 02203	Denis S. Sweeney
Chicago, IL (IA, IL, IN, MI, MN, ND, NE, OH, SD, WI)	230 S. Dearborn St., 60604	Peter Hebein
Dallas, TX (AR, CO, KS, LA, MO, MT, NM, OK, TX, UT, WY).	525 Griffin Sq. Bldg., 75202	(Vacancy)

Regional Offices—Bureau of Labor Statistics—Continued

Region	Address	Commissioner
Philadelphia, PA (DE, DC, MD, NJ, PA, VA, WV)	3535 Market St., 19104	Alan M. Paisner
San Francisco, CA (AK, AS, AZ, CA, GU, HI, ID, NV, OR, Pacific Islands, WA).	71 Stevenson St., 94119–3766	Stanley P. Stephenson

For further information, contact the Associate Commissioner, Office of Publications, Bureau of Labor Statistics, Department of Labor, Room 4110, 2 Massachusetts Avenue NW., Washington, DC 20212. Phone, 202–606–5900.

Veterans' Employment and Training Service

The Veterans' Employment and Training Service is responsible for administering veterans' employment and training programs and activities to ensure that legislative and regulatory mandates are accomplished. The field staff works closely with and provides technical assistance to State employment security agencies and Job Training Partnership Act grant recipients to ensure that veterans are provided the priority services required by law. They also coordinate with employers, labor unions, veterans service organizations, and community organizations through planned public information and outreach activities. Federal contractors are provided management assistance in complying with their veterans affirmative action and reporting obligations. Staff also administer the veterans reemployment rights program. They provide assistance to help restore job, seniority, and pension rights to veterans following absences from work for active military service and to protect employment and retention rights of members of the Reserve or National Guard.

Regional Administrators/State Directors—Veterans' Employment and Training Service

(RA: Regional Administrator; D: Director)

Region/Address	Director	Telephone
Aberdeen, SD (420 S. Roosevelt St., 57402–4730)	Earl R. Schultz (D)	605–626–2325
Albany, NY (Rm. 518, Bldg. 12, Harriman State Campus, 12240)	James H. Hartman (D)	518–457–7465
Albuquerque, NM (401 Broadway NE., 87102)	Jacob Castillo (D)	505–766–2113
Atlanta, GA (Rm. 6–T85, 61 Forsyth St. SW., 30303)	William Bolls (RA)	404–562–2305
Atlanta, GA (Suite 504, 148 International Blvd. NE., 30303)	Hartwell H. Morris (D)	404–331–3893
Austin, TX (Suite 516–T, 1117 Trinity St., 78701)	John McKinny (D)	512–463–2207
Baltimore, MD (Rm. 210, 1100 N. Eutaw St., 21201)	Stanley Seidel (D)	410–767–2110
Baton Rouge, LA (Rm. 184, 1001 N. 23d St., 70802)	Lester Parmenter (D)	504–389–0440
Bismarck, ND (1000 E. Divide Ave., 58502–1632)	Richard Ryan (D)	701–250–4337
Boise, ID (Rm. 303, 317 Main St., 83735)	(Vacancy) (D)	208–334–6163
Boston, MA (2d Fl., 19 Staniford St., 02114–2502)	Paul Desmond (D)	617–626–6690
Boston, MA (Rm. E–315, JFK Federal Bldg., 02203)	David Houle (RA)	617–565–2080
Carson City, NV (Rm. 205, 1923 N. Carson St., 89702)	(Vacancy) (D)	702–687–4632
Casper, WY (100 W. Midwest Ave., 82602–2760)	David McNulty (D)	307–261–5454
Charleston, WV (Rm. 205, 112 California Ave., 25305–0112)	David L. Bush (D)	304–558–4001
Chicago, IL (Rm. 1064, 230 S. Dearborn St., 60604)	Ronald G. Bachman (RA)	312–353–0970
Chicago, IL (2 N., 401 S. State St., 60605)	Samuel Parks (D)	312–793–3433
Columbia, SC (Suite 140, 631 Hampton St., 29201)	William C. Plowden, Jr. (D)	803–765–5195
Columbus, OH (Rm. 523, 145 S. Front St., 43215)	Carl Price (D)	614–466–2768
Concord, NH (Rm. 208, 143 N. Main St., 03301)	Richard Ducey (D)	603–225–1424
Dallas, TX (Rm. 858, 525 Griffin St., 75202)	Lester L. Williams, Jr. (RA)	214–767–4987
Denver, CO (Suite 956, 1801 California St., 80202–2614)	Ronald G. Bachman (RA)	303–844–1175
Denver, CO (Suite 400, 1515 Arapahoe St., 80202–2117)	Mark A. McGinty (D)	303–844–2151
Des Moines, IA (150 Des Moines St., 50309–5563)	Leonard E. Shaw, Jr. (D)	515–281–9061
Detroit, MI (6th Fl., 7310 Woodward Ave., 48202)	Kim Fulton (D)	313–876–5613
Frankfort, KY (2d. Fl. W., 275 E. Main St., 40621–2339)	Charles R. Netherton (D)	502–564–7062
Harrisburg, PA (Rm. 1108, 7th & Forster Sts., 17121)	Larry Babbitts (D)	717–787–5834
Hato Rey, PR (No. 198, Calle Guayama, 00917)	Angel Mojica (D)	787–754–5391
Helena, MT (1215 8th Ave., 59601)	H. Polly LaTray-Holmes (D)	406–449–5431
Honolulu, HI (Rm. 315, 830 Punch Bowl St., 96813)	Gilbert Hough (D)	808–522–8216
Indianapolis, IN (Rm. SE–103, 10 N. Senate Ave., 46204)	Bruce Redman (D)	317–232–6804
Jackson, MS (1520 W. Capitol St., 39215–1699)	(Vacancy) (D)	601–965–4204

Regional Administrators/State Directors—Veterans' Employment and Training Service—Continued

(RA: Regional Administrator; D: Director)

Region/Address	Director	Telephone
Jefferson City, MO (421 E. Dunklin St., 65104–3138)	Mickey J. Jones (D)	573–751–3921
Juneau, AK (1111 W. 8th St., 99802–5509)	Daniel Travis (D)	907–465–2723
Kansas City, MO (Suite 850, 1100 Main St., 64105–2112)	Lester L. Williams, Jr. (RA)	816–426–7151
Lewiston, ME (522 Lisbon St., 04243)	Jon Guay (D)	207–783–5352
Lincoln, NE (550 S. 16th St., 68508)	Richard Nelson (D)	402–437–5289
Little Rock, AR (Rm. G–12, State Capitol Mall, 72201)	Billy R. Threlkeld (D)	501–682–3786
Madison, WI (Rm. 250, 201 E. Washington Ave., 53702)	James R. Gutowski (D)	608–266–3110
Montgomery, AL (Rm. 543, 649 Monroe St., 36131–6300)	Thomas M. Karrh (D)	334–223–7677
Montpelier, VT (Rm. 303, 87 State St., 05601)	Richard Gray (D)	802–828–4441
Nashville, TN (915 8th Ave. N., 37208)	Richard E. Ritchie (D)	615–736–7680
New York, NY (Rm. 766, 201 Varick St., 10014)	H. Miles Sisson (RA)	212–337–2211
Oklahoma City, OK (400 Will Rogers Memorial Office Bldg., 73105)	Darrell H. Hill (D)	405–557–7189
Olympia, WA (3d Fl., 605 Woodview Sq. Loop SE., 98503–1040)	Donald J. Hutt (D)	360–438–4600
Philadelphia, PA (Rm. 802, 2d & Chestnut Sts., 19106)	Joseph W. Hortiz, Jr. (RA)	215–597–1664
Phoenix, AZ (1400 W. Washington St., 85005)	Marco A. Valenzuela (D)	602–379–4961
Raleigh, NC (Bldg. M, 700 Wade Ave., 27605)	Steven Guess (D)	919–856–4792
Richmond, VA (Rm. 118, 703 E. Main St., 23219)	Roberto Pineda (D)	804–786–6599
Sacramento, CA (Rm. W1142, 800 Capitol Mall, 94280–0001)	Rosendo A. (Alex) Cuevas (D)	916–654–8178
St. Paul, MN (610 Piper Jaffray Plz., 444 Cedar St., 55101)	Michael D. Graham (D)	612–290–3028
Salem, OR (Rm. 108, 875 Union St. NE., 97311–0100)	Rex A. Newell (D)	503–947–1490
Salt Lake City, UT (Suite 209, 140 E. 300 South St., 84111–2333)	Dale Brockbank (D)	801–524–5703
San Francisco, CA (Suite 705, 71 Stevenson St., 94105)	Charles Martinez (RA)	415–975–4702
Seattle, WA (Suite 800, 1111 3d Ave., 98101–3212)	Charles Martinez (RA)	206–553–4831
Tallahassee, FL (Suite 205, 2574 Seagate Dr., 32399–0676)	Derek Taylor (D)	850–942–8800
Topeka, KS (401 Topeka Blvd., 66603–3182)	Gayle A. Gibson (D)	913–296–5032
Trenton, NJ (11th Fl., CN–058, Labor Bldg., 08625)	Alan E. Grohs (D)	609–292–2930
Washington, DC (Rm. 108, 500 C St. NW., 20001)	Stanley Williams (D)	202–724–7004
Westerly, RI (57 Spruce St., 02891–1921)	John Dunn (D)	401–528–5134
Wethersfield, CT (200 Follybrook Blvd., 06109)	William Mason (D)	860–263–6470
Wilmington, DE (Rm. 420, 4425 N. Market St., 19809–0828)	David White (D)	302–761–8138

For further information, contact the Assistant Secretary for Veterans' Employment and Training, Department of Labor, 200 Constitution Avenue NW., Washington, DC 20210. Phone, 202–693–4700.

Sources of Information

Contracts General inquiries may be directed to the Office of the Acquisition Advocate, OASAM, Room N–5425, 200 Constitution Avenue NW., Washington, DC 20210. Phone, 202–219–8904.

Inquiries on doing business with the job corps should be directed to the job corps regional director in the appropriate Employment and Training Administration regional office listed in the preceding text.

Electronic Access Information concerning Department of Labor agencies, programs, and activities is available electronically through the Internet, at www.dol.gov.

Employment Personnel offices use lists of eligibles from the clerical, scientific, technical, and general examinations of the Office of Personnel Management.

Inquiries and applications may be directed to any of the eight personnel offices at: Department of Labor, 200 Constitution Avenue NW., Washington, DC 20210, or the nearest regional office. Information on specific vacancies may be obtained by calling the Department's job opportunity bank system. Phone, 800–366–2753.

Publications The Office of Public Affairs distributes a brochure entitled *Department of Labor,* which describes the activities of the major agencies within the Department, and *Publications of the Department of Labor,* a subject listing of publications available from the Department.

The Employment and Training Administration issues periodicals such as *Area Trends in Employment and Unemployment* available by subscription through the Superintendent of Documents, Government Printing Office, Washington, DC 20402. Information about publications may be obtained from the Administration's Information Office. Phone, 202–219–6871.

The Office of Labor-Management Standards publishes the text of the Labor-Management Reporting and Disclosure Act and pamphlets that explain the reporting, election, bonding, and trusteeship provisions of the act. The pamphlets and reporting forms used by persons covered by the act are available free in limited quantities from the OLMS National Office at Room N–5616, 200 Constitution Avenue NW., Washington, DC 20210, and from OLMS field offices listed in the telephone directory under United States Government, Department of Labor.

The Pension and Welfare Benefits Administration distributes fact sheets, pamphlets, and booklets on employer obligations and employee rights under ERISA. A list of publications is available by writing to the Division of Public Information, Pension and Welfare Benefits Administration, Room N–5666, 200 Constitution Avenue NW., Washington, DC 20210. Phone, 202–219–8921.

The Bureau of Labor Statistics has an Information Office at 2 Massachusetts Avenue NE., Room 2850, Washington, DC 20212. Phone, 202–606–5886. Periodicals include the *Monthly Labor Review, Consumer Price Index, Producer Prices and Price Indexes, Employment and Earnings, Current Wage Developments, Occupational Outlook Handbook,* and *Occupational Outlook Quarterly.* Publications are both free and for sale, but for-sale items must be obtained from the Superintendent of Documents, Government Printing Office. Inquiries may be directed to the Washington Information Office or to the Bureau's regional offices.

Publications of the Employment Standards Administration, such as *Handy Reference Guide to the Fair Labor Standards Act,* and *OFCCP, Making Affirmative Action Work,* are available from the nearest area office. Single copies are free.

Reading Rooms Department of Labor Library, Room N2439, 200 Constitution Avenue NW., Washington, DC 20210. Phone, 202–219–6992.

The Office of Labor-Management Standards maintains a Public Disclosure Room at Room N–5616, 200 Constitution Avenue NW., Washington, DC 20210. Reports filed under the Labor-Management Reporting and Disclosure Act may be examined there and purchased for 15 cents per page. Reports also may be obtained by calling the Public Disclosure Room at 202–219–7393, or by contacting an Office field office listed in the telephone directory under United States Government, Department of Labor.

The Pension and Welfare Benefits Administration maintains a Public Disclosure Room at Room N–5507, 200 Constitution Avenue NW., Washington, DC 20210. Reports filed under the Employee Retirement Income Security Act may be examined there and purchased for 10 cents per page or by calling the Public Disclosure Room at 202–219–8771.

For further information concerning the Department of Labor, contact the Office of Public Affairs, Department of Labor, Room S–1032, 200 Constitution Avenue NW., Washington, DC 20210. Phone, 202–219–7316. Internet, www.dol.gov.

DEPARTMENT OF STATE

2201 C Street NW., Washington, DC 20520
Phone, 202–647–4000. Internet, www.state.gov.

SECRETARY OF STATE	MADELEINE K. ALBRIGHT
Assistant Secretary for Intelligence and Research	J. STAPLETON ROY
Assistant Secretary for Legislative Affairs	BARBARA LARKIN
Chairman, Foreign Service Grievance Board	EDWARD REIDY
Chief of Protocol	MARY MEL FRENCH
Chief of Staff	ELAINE K. SHOCAS
Civil Service Ombudsman	TED A. BOREK
Counselor of the Department of State	WENDY SHERMAN
Deputy Assistant Secretary for Equal Employment Opportunity and Civil Rights	DEIDRE A. DAVIS
Director, Policy Planning Staff	MORTON H. HALPERIN
Inspector General	JACQUELYN L. WILLIAMS-BRIDGERS
Legal Advisor	DAVID R. ANDREWS
Special Assistant to the Secretary and Executive Secretary of the Department	KRISTIE A. KENNEY
Deputy Secretary of State	STROBE TALBOTT
Under Secretary for Arms Control and International Security Affairs	JOHN D. HOLUM, *Acting*
Assistant Secretary for Arms Control	AVIS T. BOHLEN
Assistant Secretary for Nonproliferation	ROBERT J. EINHORN
Assistant Secretary for Political-Military Affairs	ERIC NEWSOM
Assistant Secretary for Verification and Compliance	(VACANCY)
Under Secretary for Economic, Business, and Agricultural Affairs	ALAN P. LARSON
Assistant Secretary for Economic and Business Affairs	EARL ANTHONY WAYNE
Under Secretary for Global Affairs	FRANK E. LOY
Assistant Secretary for Democracy, Human Rights, and Labor	HAROLD H. KOH
Assistant Secretary for International Narcotics and Law Enforcement Affairs	RAND BEERS
Assistant Secretary for Oceans and International Environmental and Scientific Affairs	DAVID B. SANDALOW
Assistant Secretary for Population, Refugee, and Migration Affairs	JULIA V. TAFT
Under Secretary for Management	BONNIE R. COHEN
Assistant Secretary for Administration	PATRICK F. KENNEDY
Assistant Secretary for Consular Affairs	MARY A. RYAN

Assistant Secretary for Diplomatic Security and Director of the Office of Foreign Missions	DAVID G. CARPENTER
Assistant Secretary for Information Resources Management and Chief Information Officer	FERNANDO BURBANO
Chief Financial Officer	BERT T. EDWARDS
Director General of the Foreign Service and Director of Personnel	EDWARD W. GNEHM, JR.
Director of the Foreign Service Institute	RUTH A. DAVIS
Under Secretary for Political Affairs	THOMAS R. PICKERING
Assistant Secretary for African Affairs	SUSAN E. RICE
Assistant Secretary for East Asian and Pacific Affairs	STANLEY O. ROTH
Assistant Secretary for European and Canadian Affairs	MARC GROSSMAN
Assistant Secretary for Western Hemisphere Affairs	ROBERT NOLAN
Assistant Secretary for Near East Affairs	EDWARD S. WALKER
Assistant Secretary for South Asian Affairs	KARL F. INDERFURTH
Assistant Secretary for International Organization Affairs	C. DAVID WELCH
Under Secretary for Public Diplomacy and Public Affairs	EVELYN S. LIEBERMAN
Assistant Secretary for Public Affairs and Spokesman for the Department of State	JAMES RUBIN
U.S. Coordinator, International Communications and Information Policy	RICHARD BEAIRD, *Acting*
Permanent Representative of the United States of America to the Organization of American States	VICTOR MARRERO

United States Mission to the United Nations[1]

799 United Nations Plaza, New York, NY 10017

United States Permanent Representative to the United Nations and Representative in the Security Council	RICHARD C. HOLBROOKE
Deputy United States Representative to the United Nations	JAMES CUNNINGHAM
United States Representative for Special Political Affairs in the United Nations	NANCY E. SODERBERG
United States Representative on the Economic and Social Council	BETTY E. KING
United States Representative for U.N. Management and Reform	DONALD S. HAYES

[For the Department of State statement of organization, see the *Code of Federal Regulations*, Title 22, Part 5]

The Department of State advises the President in the formulation and execution of foreign policy and promotes the long-range security and well-being of the United

[1] A description of the organization and functions of the United Nations can be found under *Selected Multilateral Organizations* in this book.

States. The Department determines and analyzes the facts relating to American overseas interests, makes recommendations on policy and future action, and takes the necessary steps to carry out established policy. In so doing, the Department engages in continuous consultations with the American public, the Congress, other U.S. departments and agencies, and foreign governments; negotiates treaties and agreements with foreign nations; speaks for the United States in the United Nations and other international organizations in which the United States participates; and represents the United States at international conferences.

The Department of State was established by act of July 27, 1789, as the Department of Foreign Affairs and was renamed Department of State by act of September 15, 1789 (22 U.S.C. 2651 note).

Secretary of State The Secretary of State is responsible for the overall direction, coordination, and supervision of U.S. foreign relations and for the interdepartmental activities of the U.S. Government abroad. The Secretary is the first-ranking member of the Cabinet, is a member of the National Security Council, and is in charge of the operations of the Department, including the Foreign Service.

Regional Bureaus Foreign affairs activities worldwide are handled by the geographic bureaus, which include the Bureaus of African Affairs, European Affairs, East Asian and Pacific Affairs, Near East Affairs, South Asian Affairs, and Western Hemisphere Affairs.

Arms Control The mission of the Arms Control Bureau is to strengthen national security by formulating, advocating, negotiating, and implementing effective arms control and disarmament policies, strategies, and agreements. The Bureau directs U.S. participation in multilateral arms control negotiations and the Organization for the Prohibition of Chemical Weapons and is also responsible for monitoring technology developments as they relate to arms control and weapons developments.

For further information, contact the Bureau of Arms Control at 202–647–8478. Fax, 202–736–4472.

Consular Affairs The Bureau of Consular Affairs is responsible for the protection and welfare of American citizens and interests abroad; the administration and enforcement of the provisions of the immigration and nationality laws insofar as they concern the Department and Foreign Service; and the issuance of passports and visas and related services. Approximately 7 million passports a year are issued by the Office of Passport Services of the Bureau at the processing centers in Portsmouth, NH, and Charleson, SC, and the regional agencies in Boston, MA; Chicago, IL; Honolulu, HI; Houston, TX; Los Angeles, CA; Miami, FL; New Orleans, LA; New York, NY; Philadelphia, PA; San Francisco, CA; Seattle, WA; Stamford, CT; and Washington, DC.

For further information, visit the Bureau of Consular Affairs website at travel.state.gov.

Democracy, Human Rights, and Labor The Bureau of Democracy, Human Rights, and Labor (DRL) is responsible for developing and implementing U.S. policy on democracy, human rights, labor, and religious freedom. The Bureau undertakes dialog with foreign governments and builds partnerships in multilateral organizations in order to build global consensus in support of democratic rule and universal human rights principles. It is responsible for preparing the annual *Country Reports on Human Rights Practices* which are regarded as the most comprehensive and objective assessment of human rights conditions around the world. Through the Human Rights and Democracy Fund, DRL provides comprehensive technical and financial support for democracy and human rights, which helps prosecute war criminals, promote religious freedom, monitor free and fair elections, support workers' rights, encourage the establishment of the rule of law, and facilitate the growth of civil society.

Diplomatic Security The Bureau of Diplomatic Security provides a secure environment for conducting American

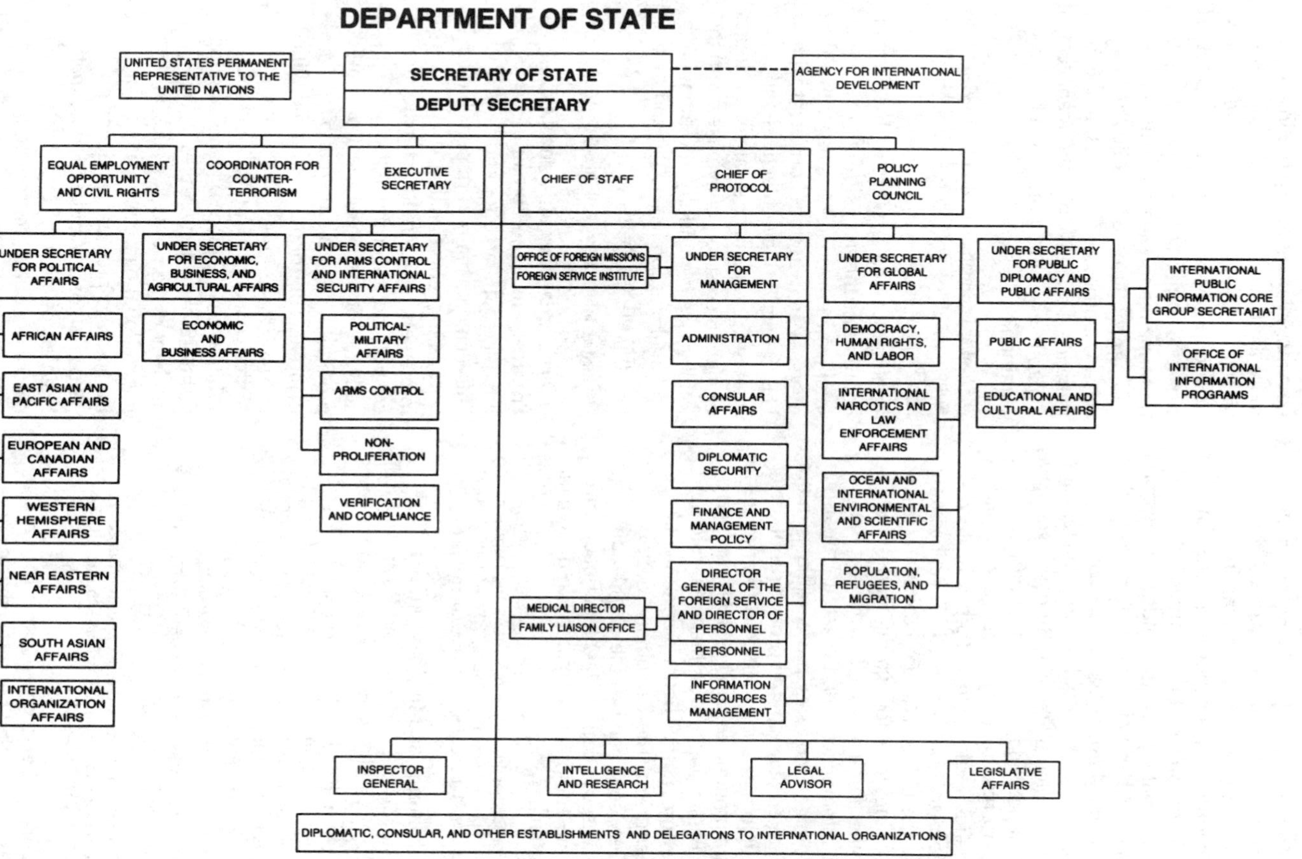
DEPARTMENT OF STATE
UNITED STATES PERMANENT REPRESENTATIVE TO THE UNITED NATIONS
SECRETARY OF STATE
DEPUTY SECRETARY
AGENCY FOR INTERNATIONAL DEVELOPMENT
EQUAL EMPLOYMENT OPPORTUNITY AND CIVIL RIGHTS
COORDINATOR FOR COUNTER-TERRORISM
EXECUTIVE SECRETARY
CHIEF OF STAFF
CHIEF OF PROTOCOL
POLICY PLANNING COUNCIL
UNDER SECRETARY FOR POLITICAL AFFAIRS
AFRICAN AFFAIRS
EAST ASIAN AND PACIFIC AFFAIRS
EUROPEAN AND CANADIAN AFFAIRS
WESTERN HEMISPHERE AFFAIRS
NEAR EASTERN AFFAIRS
SOUTH ASIAN AFFAIRS
INTERNATIONAL ORGANIZATION AFFAIRS
UNDER SECRETARY FOR ECONOMIC, BUSINESS, AND AGRICULTURAL AFFAIRS
ECONOMIC AND BUSINESS AFFAIRS
UNDER SECRETARY FOR ARMS CONTROL AND INTERNATIONAL SECURITY AFFAIRS
POLITICAL-MILITARY AFFAIRS
ARMS CONTROL
NON-PROLIFERATION
VERIFICATION AND COMPLIANCE
OFFICE OF FOREIGN MISSIONS
FOREIGN SERVICE INSTITUTE
UNDER SECRETARY FOR MANAGEMENT
ADMINISTRATION
CONSULAR AFFAIRS
DIPLOMATIC SECURITY
FINANCE AND MANAGEMENT POLICY
MEDICAL DIRECTOR
FAMILY LIAISON OFFICE
DIRECTOR GENERAL OF THE FOREIGN SERVICE AND DIRECTOR OF PERSONNEL
PERSONNEL
INFORMATION RESOURCES MANAGEMENT
UNDER SECRETARY FOR GLOBAL AFFAIRS
DEMOCRACY, HUMAN RIGHTS, AND LABOR
INTERNATIONAL NARCOTICS AND LAW ENFORCEMENT AFFAIRS
OCEAN AND INTERNATIONAL ENVIRONMENTAL AND SCIENTIFIC AFFAIRS
POPULATION, REFUGEES, AND MIGRATION
UNDER SECRETARY FOR PUBLIC DIPLOMACY AND PUBLIC AFFAIRS
PUBLIC AFFAIRS
EDUCATIONAL AND CULTURAL AFFAIRS
INTERNATIONAL PUBLIC INFORMATION CORE GROUP SECRETARIAT
OFFICE OF INTERNATIONAL INFORMATION PROGRAMS
INSPECTOR GENERAL
INTELLIGENCE AND RESEARCH
LEGAL ADVISOR
LEGISLATIVE AFFAIRS
DIPLOMATIC, CONSULAR, AND OTHER ESTABLISHMENTS AND DELEGATIONS TO INTERNATIONAL ORGANIZATIONS

diplomacy and promoting American interests worldwide. Overseas, the Bureau develops and maintains effective security programs for every U.S. Embassy and consulate abroad; protects U.S. diplomatic personnel and missions from physical and electronic attack as well as technical espionage; and advises U.S. Ambassadors on all security matters. In the United States, the Bureau investigates passport and visa fraud, conducts personnel security investigations, and issues security clearances. It protects the Secretary of State, the U.S. Ambassador to the United Nations, and many cabinet-level foreign dignitaries and other foreign officials who visit the United States. The Bureau also assists foreign Embassies and consulates in the United States in the protection of their diplomats and facilities, and arranges for training in the United States for foreign civilian police who then return to their own countries better able to fight terrorism. The Diplomatic Courier Service supervises the worldwide transportation of classified documents and equipment contained in diplomatic pouches.

For further information, contact the Bureau of Diplomatic Security. Phone, 202–663–0067. Fax, 202–663–0100. Internet, www.heroes.net.

Economic and Business Affairs The Bureau of Economic and Business Affairs has overall responsibility for formulating and implementing policy regarding foreign economic matters, including resource and food policy, international communications and information policy, international energy issues, trade, economic sanctions, international finance and development, and aviation and maritime affairs.

For further information, contact the Bureau of Economic and Business Affairs. Phone, 202–647–7971. Fax, 202–647–5713.

Foreign Service Institute The Foreign Service Institute of the Department of State is the Federal Government's primary training institution for officers and support personnel of the foreign affairs community. In addition to the Department of State, the Institute provides training for more than 40 other governmental agencies. The Institute's more than 350 courses, including 60 foreign language courses, range in length from one day to 2 years. The courses are designed to promote successful performance in each professional assignment, to ease the adjustment to other countries and cultures, and to enhance the leadership and management capabilities of the foreign affairs community.

For further information, contact the Foreign Service Institute. Phone, 703–302–6729. Fax, 703–302–7227.

Intelligence and Research The Bureau coordinates the activities of U.S. intelligence agencies to ensure that their overseas activities are consistent with U.S. foreign policy objectives and interests. It organizes seminars on topics of high interest to policymakers and the intelligence community and monitors and analyzes foreign public and media opinion on key issues.

For further information, call 202–647–1080.

International Narcotics and Law Enforcement The Bureau of International Narcotics and Law Enforcement Affairs is responsible for developing, coordinating, and implementing international narcotics control and anticrime assistance activities of the Department of State. It provides advice on international narcotics control matters for the Office of Management and Budget, the National Security Council, and the White House Office of National Drug Control Policy and ensures implementation of U.S. policy in international narcotics matters. The Bureau also provides guidance on narcotics control and anticrime matters to chiefs of missions and directs narcotics control coordinators at posts abroad. It communicates or authorizes communication, as appropriate, with foreign governments on drug control and anticrime matters including negotiating, concluding, and terminating agreements relating to international narcotics control and anticrime programs.

For further information, contact the Bureau of International Narcotics and Law Enforcement Affairs. Phone, 202–776–8750. Fax, 202–776–8775.

International Organizations The Bureau of International Organization Affairs provides guidance and support for U.S. participation in international organizations and conferences and formulates and implements U.S. policy toward international organizations, with particular emphasis on those organizations which make up the United Nations system. It provides direction in the development, coordination, and implementation of U.S. multilateral policy.

For further information, call 202–647–1663.

Medical Services The Office of Medical Services develops, manages, and staffs a worldwide primary health care system for U.S. citizen employees and their eligible dependents residing overseas. In support of its overseas operations, the Office approves and monitors the medical evacuation of patients, conducts pre-employment and in-service physical examinations, and provides clinical referral and advisory services. The Office also provides for emergency medical response in the event of a crisis at an overseas post.

For further information, call 202–663–1748.

Nonproliferation The Nonproliferation Bureau leads the U.S. Government's efforts to prevent the proliferation of weapons of mass destruction, their delivery systems, and advanced conventional arms. The Bureau is responsible for nuclear nonproliferation through support of the International Atomic Energy Agency, implementing the Nuclear Non-Proliferation Treaty, securing nuclear materials in the New Independent States of the former Soviet Union, disposing of stockpiles of fissile materials, advancing civil nuclear cooperation under safe and sound conditions, and promoting nuclear safety and effective protection, control, and accounting of nuclear material worldwide. The Bureau is also responsible for developing and implementing all policies to curb the proliferation of chemical and biological weapons and missiles, and promoting restraint in transfers of conventional arms. It also pursues regional and bilateral initiatives and negotiations designed to reduce proliferation pressures and destabilizing arms acquisitions, including negotiations with respect to Russia, China, South Asia, the Middle East, and the Korean peninsula.

For further information, contact the Bureau of Nonproliferation. Phone, 202–647–8699. Fax, 202–736–4863.

Oceans, Environment, and Science The Bureau of Oceans, Environment, and Science (OES) serves as the foreign policy focal point for international oceans, environmental, and scientific efforts. OES projects, protects, and promotes U.S. global interests in these areas by articulating U.S. foreign policy, encouraging international cooperation, and negotiating treaties and other instruments of international law. The Bureau serves as the principal adviser to the Secretary of State on international environment, science, and technology matters and takes the lead in coordinating and brokering diverse interests in the interagency process, where the development of international policies or the negotiation and implementation of relevant international agreements are concerned. The Bureau seeks to promote the peaceful exploitation of outer space, protect public health from reemerging infectious diseases, encourage government to government scientific cooperation, and prevent the destruction and degradation of the planet's natural resources and the global environment.

For further information, contact the Bureau of Oceans, Environment, and Science. Phone, 202–647–0978. Fax, 202–647–0217.

Political-Military Affairs The Political Military Affairs Bureau provides analytic support on defense-related policy issues, fosters bilateral and regional political-military relationships, manages security assistance funds, coordinates peacekeeping and other military operations, plans complex contingency operations, and is responsible for a variety of crisis management activities. The Bureau is responsible for arms transfers policy and defense trade controls, promoting political-military cooperation in critical infrastructure protection, and coordinating U.S. humanitarian demining activities worldwide.

For further information, contact the Bureau of Political-Military Affairs. Phone, 202–647–6968. Fax, 202–736–4434. Internet, www.state.gov/www/global/arms/bureaupm.html.

Population, Refugees, and Migration The Bureau of Population, Refugees, and Migration has primary responsibility for formulating U.S. policies on population, refugees, and migration and for administering U.S. refugee assistance and admissions programs. It administers and monitors U.S. contributions to multilateral organizations and nongovernmental organizations to provide assistance and protection to refugees abroad. The Bureau oversees the annual admissions of refugees to the United States for permanent resettlement, working closely with the Immigration and Naturalization Service, the Department of Health and Human Services, and various State and private voluntary agencies. It coordinates U.S. international population policy and promotes its goals through bilateral and multilateral cooperation. It works closely with the U.S. Agency for International Development, which administers U.S. international population programs. The Bureau also coordinates U.S. international migration policy within the U.S. Government and through bilateral and multilateral diplomacy.

For further information, contact the Bureau of Population, Refugees, and Migration. Phone, 202–663–1071. Fax, 202–663–1061. Internet, www.state.gov/www/global/prm/index.html.

Protocol The Chief of Protocol is the principal adviser to the U.S. Government, the President, the Vice President, and the Secretary of State on matters of diplomatic procedure governed by law or international custom and practice. The Office is responsible for:

—visits of foreign chiefs of state, heads of government, and other high officials to the United States;

—organizing credential presentations of newly arrived Ambassadors to the President and to the Secretary of State.

—operation of the President's guest house, Blair House;

—delegations representing the President at official ceremonies abroad;

—conducting official ceremonial functions and public events;

—official interpretation of the order of precedence;

—conducting an outreach program of cultural enrichment and substantive briefings of the Diplomatic Corps;

—accreditation of over 100,000 Embassy, consular, international organization, and other foreign Government personnel, members of their families, and domestics throughout the United States;

—determining entitlement to diplomatic or consular immunity;

—publication of diplomatic and consular lists;

—resolution of problems arising out of diplomatic or consular immunity such as legal and police matters; and

—approving the opening of Embassy and consular offices in conjunction with the Office of Foreign Missions.

For further information, contact the Office of the Chief of Protocol. Phone, 202–647–2663. Fax, 202–647–1560.

Foreign Service To a great extent the future of our country depends on the relations we have with other countries, and those relations are conducted principally by the U.S. Foreign Service. Trained representatives stationed worldwide provide the President and the Secretary of State with much of the raw material from which foreign policy is made and with the recommendations that help shape it.

Ambassadors are the personal representatives of the President and report to the President through the Secretary of State. Ambassadors have full responsibility for implementation of U.S. foreign policy by any and all U.S. Government personnel within their country of assignment, except those under military commands. Their responsibilities include negotiating agreements between the United States and the host country, explaining and disseminating official U.S. policy, and maintaining cordial relations with that country's government and people.

A listing of Foreign Service posts, together with addresses and telephone numbers and key personnel, appears in *Key Officers of Foreign Service Posts—Guide for Business Representatives,* which is for sale by the Superintendent of Documents, Government Printing Office, Washington, DC 20402.

United States Diplomatic Offices—Foreign Service

(C: Consular Office; N: No Embassy or Consular Office)

Country/Embassy	Ambassador
Albania/Tirana	Joseph Limprecht
Algeria/Algiers	Cameron R. Hume
Angola/Luanda	Joseph Sullivan
Antigua and Barbuda/St. John's (N).	Jeanette W. Hyde
Argentina/Buenos Aires	(Vacancy)
Armenia/Yerevan	Mike Lemmon
Australia/Canberra	Genta Hawkins Holmes
Austria/Vienna	Kathryn W. Hall
Azerbaijan/Baku	Stanley T. Escudero
Bahamas/Nassau	Sidney Williams
Bahrain/Manama	Johnny Young
Bangladesh/Dhaka	John C. Holzman
Barbados/Bridgetown	Jeanette W. Hyde
Belarus/Minsk	Daniel W. Speckhard
Belgium/Brussels	Paul Cejas
Belize/Belize City	Carolyn Curiel
Benin/Cotonou	Robert C. Felder
Bolivia/La Paz	Donna J. Hrinak
Bosnia and Herzegovina/Sarajevo.	Richard D. Kauzlarich
Botswana/Gaborone	John Lange
Brazil/Brasilia	Melvyn Levitsky
Brunei Darussalam/Bandar Seri Begawan.	Sylvia Stanfield
Bulgaria/Sofia	Richard Miles
Burkina Faso/Ouagadougou	Jimmy Kolker
Burma/Rangoon-CDIA	Priscilla Clapp
Burundi/Bujumbura	Mary Carlin Yates
Cambodia/Phnom Penh	Kent Wiedemann
Cameroon/Yaounde	John M. Yates
Canada/Ottawa	Gordon Giffen
Cape Verde/Prala	Michael Metelitis
Central African Republic/Bangui	Robert C. Perry
Chad/N'Djamena	Christopher Goldthwait
Chile/Santiago	Gabriel Guerra-Mondragon
China/Beijing	Joseph W. Prueher
Colombia/Bogota	Myles R.R. Frechette
Comoros/Moroni (N)	Mark Erwin
Congo, Democratic Republic of the (formerly Zaire)/Kinshasa.	William L. Swing
Congo, Republic of/Brazzaville	David Kaeuper
Costa Rica/San Jose	Thomas J. Dodd
Cote d'Ivoire/Abidjan	George Mu
Croatia/Zagreb	William D. Montgomery
Cuba/Havana (U.S. Interests Section).	Michael G. Kozak

United States Diplomatic Offices—Foreign Service—Continued

(C: Consular Office; N: No Embassy or Consular Office)

Country/Embassy	Ambassador
Cyprus/Nicosia	Kenneth C. Brill
Czech Republic/Prague	John Shattuck
Denmark/Copenhagen	Richard Swett
Djibouti, Republic of/Djibouti	Lange Schermerhorn
Dominica/Roseau (N)	Jeanette W. Hyde
Dominican Republic/Santo Domingo.	(Vacancy)
Ecuador/Quito	Leslie M. Alexander
Egypt/Cairo	Daniel C. Kurtzer
El Salvador/San Salvador	Anne W. Patterson
Equatorial Guinea/Malabo	John Yates
Eritrea/Asmara	William Clarke
Estonia/Tallinn	Melissa Wells
Ethiopia/Addis Ababa	Tibor Nagy
Fiji/Suva	Osman Siddique
Finland/Helsinki	Eric Edelman
France/Paris	Felix Rohatyn
Gabonese Republic/Libreville	James V. Ledesma
Gambia/Banjul	George Haley
Georgia/Tbilisi	Ken Yalowitz
Germany/Berlin	John C. Kornblum
Ghana/Accra	Katharyn D. Robinson
Greece/Athens	R. Nicholas Burns
Grenada/St. George (N)	Jeanette W. Hyde
Guatemala/Guatemala	Donald J. Planty
Guinea/Conakry	Joyce Leader
Guinea-Bissau/Bissau	Harriet Lee Elam
Guyana/Georgetown	James F. Mack
Haiti/Port-au-Prince	Timothy M. Carney
Holy See/Vatican City	Corinne Claiborne Boggs
Honduras/Tegucigalpa	James F. Creagan
Hong Kong/Hong Kong (C)	Michael Klosson
Hungary/Budapest	Peter F. Tufo
Iceland/Reykjavik	Barbara Griffiths
India/New Delhi	Richard F. Celeste
Indonesia/Jakarta	Robert S. Gelbard
Ireland/Dublin	Michael J. Sullivan
Israel/Tel Aviv	Martin S. Indyk
Italy/Rome	Thomas M. Foglietta
Jamaica/Kingston	Jerome G. Cooper
Japan/Tokyo	Thomas S. Foley
Jerusalem	John E. Herbst
Jordan/Amman	William J. Burns
Kazakstan/Almaty	Richard Jones
Kenya/Nairobi	Johnnie Carson
Kiribati/Tarawa (N)	Joan M. Plaisted
Korea/Seoul	Steven W. Bosworth
Kuwait/Kuwait	James A. Larocco
Kyrgyz Republic/Bishkek	Anne Marie Sigmund
Laos/Vientiane	(Vacancy)
Latvia/Riga	James Holmes
Lebanon/Beirut	David Satterfield
Lesotho/Maseru	Katharine Peterson
Liberia/Monrovia	Bismark Myrick
Lithuania/Vilnius	Keith C. Smith
Luxembourg/Luxembourg	James Hormel
Madagascar/Antananarivo	Shirley E. Barnes
Malawi/Lilongwe	Amelia E. Shippy
Malaysia/Kuala Lumpur	Lynn Pascoe
Maldives/Male (N)	Shaun E. Donnelly
Mali/Bamako	Michael Ranneberger
Malta/Valletta	Kathryn L. Haycock-Proffitt
Marshall Islands/Majuro	Joan M. Plaisted
Mauritania/Nouakchott	Timberlake Foster
Mauritius/Port Louis	Mark Erwin
Mexico/Mexico City	(Vacancy)
Micronesia/Kolonia	Diane Watson
Moldova/Chisinau	Rudolph Perina
Mongolia/Ulaanbaatar	Alphonse F. La Porta
Morocco/Rabat	Edward M. Gabriel

United States Diplomatic Offices—Foreign Service—Continued

(C: Consular Office; N: No Embassy or Consular Office)

Country/Embassy	Ambassador
Mozambique/Maputo	Brian D. Curran
Namibia/Windhoek	Jeffrey A. Bader
Nauru/Yaren (N)	(Vacancy)
Nepal/Kathmandu	Ralph Frank
Netherlands/The Hague	Cynthia Schneider
New Zealand/Wellington	Carol Mosely Braun
Nicaragua/Managua	Lino Gutierrez
Niger/Niamey	Barbara Owens-Kirkpatrick
Nigeria/Abuja	William H. Twaddell
Norway/Oslo	(Vacancy)
Oman/Muscat	John B. Craig
Pakistan/Islamabad	William B. Miland
Panama/Panama	William J. Hughes
Papua New Guinea/Port Moresby.	Arma Jane Karaer
Paraguay/Asuncion	Maura Harty
Peru/Lima	Dennis C. Jett
Philippines/Manila	Thomas Hubbard
Poland/Warsaw	Christopher Robert Hill
Portugal/Lisbon	Gerald S. McGowan
Qatar/Doha	Elizabeth McKune
Romania/Bucharest	James C. Rosapepe
Russian Federation/Moscow	James F. Collins
Rwanda/Kigali	George M. Staples
St. Kitts and Nevis (N)	Jeanette W. Hyde
St. Lucia/Castries (N)	Jeanette W. Hyde
St. Vincent and the Grenadines (N).	Jeanette W. Hyde
Sao Tome and Principe/Sao Tome (N).	James V. Ledesma
Saudi Arabia/Riyadh	Wyche Fowler, Jr.
Senegal/Dakar	Harriet Lee Elam
Seychelles/Victoria	Mark Erwin
Sierra Leone/Freetown	Joseph Melrose
Singapore/Singapore	Steven J. Green
Slovak Republic/Bratislava	(Vacancy)
Slovenia/Ljubljana	Nancy Eli-Raphel
Solomon Islands/Honiara	Arma Jane Karaer
South Africa/Pretoria	Delano Lewis
Spain/Madrid	Ed Romero
Sri Lanka/Colombo	Shaun E. Donnelly
Sudan/Khartoum	Donald Teitelbaum
Suriname/Paramaribo	Dennis K. Hays
Swaziland/Mbabane	Greg Johnson
Sweden/Stockholm	Lyndon L. Olson, Jr.
Switzerland/Bern	Richard Fredericks
Syrian Arab Republic/Damascus	Ryan C. Crocker
Tajikistan/Dushanbe	Robert Finn
Tanzania/Dar es Salaam	Charles R. Stith
Thailand/Bangkok	Richard Hecklinger
Togo/Lome	Brenda Schoonover
Tonga/Nuku'alofa (N)	(Vacancy)
Trinidad and Tobago/Port-of-Spain.	Edward E. Shumaker III
Tunisia/Tunis	Robin L. Raphel
Turkey/Ankara	Mark R. Parris
Turkmenistan/Ashgabat	Steven Mann
Tuvalu/Funafuti (N)	(Vacancy)
Uganda/Kampala	Martin Brennan
Ukraine/Kiev	Steven K. Pifer
United Arab Emirates/Abu Dhabi	Theodore H. Kattouf
United Kingdom/London	Philip Lader
Uruguay/Montevideo	Christopher C. Ashby
Uzbekistan/Tashkent	Joseph A. Presel
Vanuatu/Port Vila (N)	Arma Jane Karaer
Vietnam/Hanoi	Pete Peterson
Venezuela/Caracas	John F. Maisto
Western Samoa/Apia	Carol Mosely Braun
Yemen/Sanaa	Barbara K. Bodine
Zambia/Lusaka	David Dunn
Zimbabwe/Harare	Tom McDonald

United States Permanent Diplomatic Missions to International Organizations

Organization	Ambassador
European Union/Brussels	A. Vernon Weaver
International Civil Aviation Organization.	Edward Stimson
North Atlantic Treaty Organization/Brussels.	Alexander R. Vershbow
Organization of American States/ Washington, DC.	Victor Marrero
Organization for Economic Cooperation and Development/ Paris.	Amy L. Bondurant
United Nations/Geneva	George E. Moose
United Nations/New York	Richard C. Holbrooke
United Nations/Vienna	John B. Ritch III
U.S. Mission to United Nations Agencies for Food and Agriculture.	George S. McGovern

Sources of Information

Audiovisual Materials The Bureau of Consular Affairs has a 12-minute videotape on the safety of international travel. "Traveling Abroad More Safely" provides general practical advice to U.S. citizen travelers on avoiding the hazards of foreign travel. It includes steps to take prior to departure, ways to protect against theft and legal problems, and ways U.S. embassies and consulates can assist U.S. citizens who encounter difficulty abroad. The tape is available for $9 in VHS and $22 in 3/4-inch format, plus a $3 mailing and handling fee from Video Transfer, Inc., 5800 Arundel Avenue, Rockville, MD 20852. Phone, 301–881–0270. Fax, 301–770–9131.

Contracts General inquiries may be directed to the Office of Acquisitions Management (A/LM/AQM), Department of State, P.O. Box 9115, Arlington, VA 22219. Phone, 703–875–6060. Fax, 703–875–6085.

Diplomatic and Official Passports Inquiries regarding diplomatic and official passports should be directed to Passport Services, Special Issuance Agency. Phone, 202–955–0198.

Electronic Access The Department's Bureau of Public Affairs, Office of Public Communication, coordinates the dissemination of public electronic information for the Department. The main website (Internet, www.state.gov) and the Secretary's website (Internet, secretary.state.gov) provide comprehensive, up-to-date information on foreign policy, support for U.S. businesses, careers, the counterterrorism rewards program, and much more.

The Bureau of Consular Affairs website (Internet, travel.state.gov) provides travel warnings and other information designed to help Americans travel safely abroad, as well as information on U.S. passports and visas and downloadable applications. The Bureau of Intelligence and Research has established a geographic learning website (Internet, geography.state.gov/index.html), to assist in teaching geography and foreign affairs to students in grades K–12.

The State Department Electronic Reading Room at foia.state.gov uses new information technologies to enable access to unique historical records of international significance which have been made available to the public under the Freedom of Information Act or as a special collection.

Employment Inquiries about employment in the Foreign Service should be directed to PER/REE/REC, Room H–518, 2401 E Street NW, Washington, DC 20522. Phone, 703–875–7490. Inquiries about civil service positions in the Department of State should be directed to: PER/CSP/S, P.O. Box 58040, Washington, DC 20037–8040. Copies of civil service vacancy announcements can be accessed through the Internet, at www.usajobs.opm.gov. The Department's Civil Service Employment Information Office is located inside the D Street north lobby entrance of the Department of State building in Washington, DC. The Civil Service Personnel Office provides a 24-hour job information line. Phone, 202–647–7284.

Freedom of Information Act and Privacy Act Requests Requests from the public for Department of State records should be addressed to the Director, Office of IRM Programs and Services, Department of State, SA–2, 515 Twenty-second Street NW., Washington, DC 20522–6001. Phone, 202–261–8300. Individuals are requested to indicate on the outside of the envelope the statute under which they are requesting access: FOIA REQUEST or PRIVACY REQUEST.

A public reading room, where unclassified and declassified documents may be inspected, is located in the Department of State, SA–2, 515 Twenty-second Street NW., Washington, DC 20522–6001. Phone, 202–261–8484. Directions to the reading room may be obtained from receptionists at public entrances to the Department.

Additional information about the Department's FOIA program can be found on the FOIA electronic reading room (Internet, foia.state.gov).

Missing Persons, Emergencies, Deaths of Americans Abroad For information concerning missing persons, emergencies, travel warnings, overseas voting, judicial assistance, and arrests or deaths of Americans abroad, contact the Office of American Citizens Services and Crisis Management, Department of State. Phone, 202–647–5225. Fax, 202–647–3732. Internet, travel.state.gov. Correspondence should be directed to: Overseas Citizens Services, Bureau of Consular Affairs, Department of State, Washington, DC 20520.

Inquiries regarding international parental child abduction or adoption of foreign children by private U.S. citizens should be directed to the Office of Children's Issues, CA/OCS/CI, SA–1, Room H–120, Department of State, Washington, DC 20520. Phone, 202–736–7000. Fax, 202–647–2835. Internet, travel.state.gov.

Passports Passport information is available through the Internet, at travel.state.gov. For recorded general passport information, contact any of the Regional Passport Agencies at the telephone numbers listed in the following table. For passport assistance and information, you may call the National Passport Information Center (phone, 900–225–5674; TDD, 900–225–7778) and you will be charged 35 cents per minute to listen to automated messages and $1.05 per minute to speak with an operator. You may also call the National Passport Information Center using a major credit card at a flat rate of $4.95 (phone, 888–362–8668; TDD, 888–498–3648). These rates are subject to change. Correspondence should be directed to the appropriate Regional Agency or the Correspondence Branch, Passport Services, Room 510, 1111 Nineteenth Street NW., Washington, DC 20524.

Regional Passport Agencies

City	Address	Telephone
Boston, MA	10 Causeway St., 02222	617–565–6990
Charleston, SC	Bldg. 646A, 1969 Dyess Ave., 29405	843–308–5501
Chicago, IL	230 S. Dearborn St., 60604	312–341–6020
Honolulu, HI	1132 Bishop St., 96850	808–522–8283
Houston, TX	Suite 1400, 1919 Smith St., 77002	713–751–0294
Los Angeles, CA	Suite 1000, 11000 Wilshire Blvd., 90024–3615	310–575–5700
Miami, FL	3d Fl., 51 SW. 1st Ave., 33130	305–539–3600
New Orleans, LA	305 Canal St., 70130	504–412–2600
New York, NY	10th Fl., 376 Hudson St., 10014	212–206–3500
Philadelphia, PA	Rm. 103, 200 Chestnut St., 19106	215–418–5937
Portsmouth, NH	National Passport Center, 31 Rochester Ave., 03801–2900	603–334–0500
San Francisco, CA	5th Fl., 95 Hawthorne St., 94105–3901	415–538–2700
Seattle, WA	Suite 992, 915 2d Ave., 98174	206–808–5700
Stamford, CT	1 Landmark Sq., Broad & Atlantic Sts., 06901	203–969–9000
Washington, DC	1111 19th St. NW., 20524	202–647–0518

Public Affairs For information about the goals, development, and implementation of U.S. foreign policy, contact the Bureau of Public Affairs. Phone, 202–647–6575.

Publications Single copies of *U.S. Foreign Affairs on CD–ROM*—which provides a wealth of foreign policy information such as *Dispatch* magazine (the monthly foreign policy magazine issued by the Department of State), *Background Notes,* speeches and testimonies by senior State Department officials, reports to Congress, miscellaneous policy publications, and daily press briefings in a searchable format—are available from the Superintendent of Documents, U.S. Government Printing Office, P.O. Box 371954, Pittsburgh, PA 15250–7954. Phone, 202–512–1800. Fax, 202–512–2233.

Small Business Information Information about doing business with the Department of State is available from the Office of Small and Disadvantaged Business Utilization. Phone, 703–875–6822. Internet, www.statebuy.gov/home.htm.

Telephone Directory The Department's telephone directory is available for sale by the Superintendent of Documents, Government Printing Office, Washington, DC 20402.

Tips for U.S. Travelers Abroad The following pamphlets from the Bureau of Consular Affairs are posted on the Internet at travel.state.gov and are for sale for $1 (except where noted) by the Superintendent of Documents, U.S. Government Printing Office, Washington, DC 20402:

Travel Warning on Drugs Abroad contains important facts on the potential dangers of being arrested for illegal drugs abroad and the type of assistance that U.S. consular officers can and cannot provide. This booklet is free from the Department of State, Consular Affairs/Public Affairs Staff, Room 6831, Washington, DC 20520.

Travel Tips for Older Americans contains basic information on passports, currency, health, aid for serious problems, and other useful travel tips for senior citizens.

Your Trip Abroad ($1.25) contains basic information on passports, vaccinations, unusual travel requirements, dual nationality, drugs, modes of travel, customs, legal requirements, and many other topics for the American tourist, business representative, or student traveling overseas.

A Safe Trip Abroad contains helpful precautions to minimize one's chances of becoming a victim of terrorism and also provides other safety tips.

Tips for Americans Residing Abroad contains advice for almost 4 million Americans living in foreign countries.

Regional *Tips for Travelers* cover customs, currency regulations, dual nationality, and other local conditions. Currently available are: *Tips for Travelers to Canada; Tips for Travelers to the Caribbean; Tips for Travelers to Mexico; Tips for Travelers to the Middle East and North Africa* ($1.50); *Tips for Travelers to the People's Republic of China; Tips for Travelers to Russia and the Newly Independent States; Tips for Travelers to South Asia; Tips for Travelers to Central and South America;* and *Tips for Travelers to Sub-Saharan Africa* ($1.50).

Foreign Entry Requirements contains visa and other entry requirements of foreign countries. *Passports: Applying for Them the Easy Way* contains information on where, how, and when to apply for passports. Order these from the Consumer Information Center, Pueblo, CO 81009 (50 cents each).

Visas To obtain information on visas for foreigners wishing to enter the United States, call 202–663–1225. Internet, travel.state.gov.

For further information, contact the Office of Public Communication, Public Information Service, Bureau of Public Affairs, Department of State, Washington, DC 20520. Phone, 202–647–6575. Fax, 202–647–7120. Internet, www.state.gov.

DEPARTMENT OF TRANSPORTATION

400 Seventh Street SW., Washington, DC 20590
Phone, 202–366–4000. Internet, www.dot.gov.

SECRETARY OF TRANSPORTATION	RODNEY E. SLATER
Chief of Staff	JERRY MALONE
White House Liaison	RUTH EAGLIN
Deputy Secretary	MORTIMER L. DOWNEY
Assistant to the Secretary and Director of Public Affairs	(VACANCY)
Associate Deputy Secretary and Director, Office of Intermodalism	STEPHEN D. VAN BEEK
Chairman, Board of Contract Appeals	THADDEUS V. WARE
Chief Information Officer	GEORGE R. MOLASKI
Director, Executive Secretariat	JAMIE SHELL WILLIAMS
Director of Civil Rights	RONALD A. STROMAN
Director of Drug and Alcohol Policy and Compliance	MARY BERNSTEIN
Director of Small and Disadvantaged Business Utilization	LUZ A. HOPEWELL
Director of Intelligence and Security	REAR ADM. JAMES W. UNDERWOOD, USCG
Director, Transportation Administrative Service Center	GEORGE C. FIELDS
General Counsel	NANCY E. MCFADDEN
Inspector General	KENNETH M. MEAD
Assistant Secretary for Administration	MELISSA J. ALLEN
Assistant Secretary for Aviation and International Affairs	A. BRADLEY MIMS, *Acting*
Assistant Secretary for Budget and Programs and Chief Financial Officer	PETER J. BASSO
Assistant Secretary for Governmental Affairs	MICHAEL J. FRAZIER
Assistant Secretary for Transportation Policy	EUGENE A. CONTI, JR.

UNITED STATES COAST GUARD

2100 Second Street SE., Washington, DC 20593–0001
Phone, 202–267–2229. Internet, www.uscg.mil.

Commandant	ADM. JAMES M. LOY, USCG
Vice Commandant	VICE ADM. THOMAS H. COLLINS, USCG
Assistant Commandant for Governmental and Public Affairs	REAR ADM. PATRICK M. STILLMAN, USCG
Chairman, Marine Safety Council	REAR ADM. JAMES S. CARMICHAEL, USCG
Chaplain	CAPT. LEROY GILBERT, USN
Chief Administrative Law Judge	JOSEPH N. INGOLIA

Chief, Office of Civil Rights	WALTER R. SOMERVILLE
International Affairs Director/Foreign Policy Adviser	GERARD P. YOEST
Master Chief Petty Officer of the Coast Guard	VINCENT W. PATTON III, USCG
Medical Adviser to the Commandant and Director of Health and Safety	REAR ADM. JOYCE M. JOHNSON, USPHS
Chief of Staff	VICE ADM. TIMOTHY W. JOSIAH, USCG
Director of Resources	REAR ADM. DAVID R. NICHOLSON, USCG
Director of Finance and Procurement	WILLIAM H. CAMPBELL
Assistant Commandant for Acquisition	REAR ADM. ROY J. CASTO, USCG
Assistant Commandant for Human Resources	REAR ADM. FRED L. AMES, USCG
Assistant Commandant for Marine Safety	REAR ADM. ROBERT C. NORTH, USCG
Assistant Commandant for Operations	REAR ADM. TERRY M. CROSS, USCG
Assistant Commandant for Systems	REAR ADM. RONALD F. SILVA, USCG
Chief Counsel	REAR ADM. JAMES S. CARMICHAEL, USCG

FEDERAL AVIATION ADMINISTRATION

800 Independence Avenue SW., Washington, DC 20591
Phone, 202–366–4000. Internet, www.faa.gov.

Administrator	JANE F. GARVEY
Deputy Administrator	MONTE R. BELGER, *Acting*
Associate Administrator for Airports	WOODIE WOODWARD, *Acting*
Chief Counsel	NICHOLAS GARAUFIS
Chief Information Officer	DANIEL J. MEHAN
Associate Administrator for Civil Aviation Security	CATHAL L. FLYNN
Assistant Administrator for Civil Rights	FANNY RIVERA
Associate Administrator for Commercial Space Transportation	PATRICIA GRACE SMITH
Assistant Administrator for Government and Industry Affairs	SUZANNE SULLIVAN
Assistant Administrator for Financial Services	DONNA R. MCLEAN
Assistant Administrator for Human Resource Management	GLENDA TATE
Assistant Administrator for Policy, Planning, and International Aviation	DAVID B. TRAYNHAM
Assistant Administrator for Public Affairs	ELIOT B. BRENNER
Assistant Administrator for Region and Center Operations	RUTH A. LEVERENZ
Assistant Administrator for System Safety	CHRISTOPHER A. HART
Associate Administrator for Regulation and Certification	THOMAS E. MCSWEENEY
Associate Administrator for Air Traffic Services	STEVEN J. BROWN, *Acting*

Associate Administrator for Research and Acquisitions	STEVE ZAIDMAN

FEDERAL HIGHWAY ADMINISTRATION

400 Seventh Street SW., Washington, DC 20590
Phone, 202–366–0660

Administrator	KENNETH R. WYKLE
Deputy Administrator	WALTER L. SUTTON, JR., *Acting*
Executive Director	ANTHONY R. KANE
Chief Counsel	KAREN E. SKELTON
Director, National Highway Institute	MOGES AYELE
Director of Administration	MICHAEL J. VECCHIETTI
Director of Civil Rights	EDWARD W. MORRIS, JR.
Director of Corporate Management	FRED J. HEMPEL
Director of Policy	KING W. GEE, *Acting*
Director of Public Affairs	VIRGINIA MILLER, *Acting*
Director of Professional Development	JOSEPH S. TOOLE
Director of Research, Development, and Technology	DENNIS C. JUDYCKI
Program Manager, Federal Lands Highway	ARTHUR E. HAMILTON
Program Manager, Infrastructure	VINCENT F. SCHIMMOLLER
Program Manager, Operations	CHRISTINE M. JOHNSON
Program Manager, Planning and Environment	CYNTHIA J. BURBANK
Program Manager, Safety	FREDERICK G. (BUD) WRIGHT, JR.

FEDERAL RAILROAD ADMINISTRATION

1120 Vermont Avenue NW., Washington, DC 20590
Phone, 202–493–6000. Internet, www.fra.dot.gov.

Administrator	JOLENE M. MOLITORIS
Deputy Administrator	S. MARK LINDSEY, *Acting*
Associate Administrator for Administration and Finance	RAY ROGERS
Associate Administrator for Policy and Program Development	CHARLES H. WHITE, JR.
Associate Administrator for Railroad Development	ARRIGO MONGINI, *Acting*
Associate Administrator for Safety	GEORGE GAVALLA
Chief Counsel	S. MARK LINDSEY
Chief of Staff	T. MARKOS MULUGETA
Director, Office of Civil Rights	CARL-MARTIN RUIZ
Director, Office of Public Affairs	PAMELA BARRY

NATIONAL HIGHWAY TRAFFIC SAFETY ADMINISTRATION

400 Seventh Street SW., Washington, DC 20590
Phone, 202–366–9550

Administrator	ROSALYN G. MILLMAN, *Acting*
Deputy Administrator	ROSALYN G. MILLMAN
Executive Director	L. ROBERT SHELTON
Associate Administrator for Administration	HERMAN L. SIMMS

Associate Administrator for Plans and Policy	WILLIAM H. WALSH, JR.
Associate Administrator for Research and Development	RAYMOND P. OWINGS
Associate Administrator for Safety Assurance	KENNETH WEINSTEIN
Associate Administrator for Safety Performance Standards	STEPHEN R. KRATZKE, *Acting*
Associate Administrator for State and Community Services	ADELE DERBY
Associate Administrator for Traffic Safety Programs	ROSE A. MCMURRAY
Chief Counsel	FRANK SEALES, JR.
Director, Executive Correspondence	LINDA DIVELBISS
Director, Office of Civil Rights	GEORGE B. QUICK
Director, Office of Public and Consumer Affairs	RAE TYSON, *Acting*
Director, Office of Intergovernmental Affairs	CHARLOTTE HRNCIR

FEDERAL TRANSIT ADMINISTRATION

400 Seventh Street SW., Washington, DC 20590
Phone, 202–366–4043. Internet, www.fta.dot.gov.

Administrator	NURIA I. FERNANDEZ, *Acting*
Deputy Administrator	NURIA I. FERNANDEZ
Associate Administrator for Administration	DORRIE Y. ALDRICH
Associate Administrator for Budget and Policy	MICHAEL A. WINTER
Associate Administrator for Planning	CHARLOTTE M. ADAMS
Associate Administrator for Program Management	HIRAM J. WALKER
Associate Administrator for Research, Demonstration, and Innovation	EDWARD L. THOMAS
Chief Counsel	PATRICK W. REILLY
Director, Office of Civil Rights	ARTHUR A. LOPEZ
Director, Office of Public Affairs	BRUCE C. FRAME

MARITIME ADMINISTRATION

400 Seventh Street SW., Washington, DC 20590
Phone, 202–366–5807. Internet, www.marad.dot.gov.

Administrator	CLYDE J. HART, JR.
Deputy Administrator for Inland Waterways and Great Lakes	BONNIE M. GREEN
Deputy Administrator	JOHN E. GRAYKOWSKI
Associate Administrator for Administration	JOHN L. MANN, JR.
Associate Administrator for Policy and International Trade	BRUCE J. CARLTON
Associate Administrator for National Security	JAMES E. CAPONITI
Associate Administrator for Port, Intermodal, and Environmental Activities	MARGARET D. BLUM

Associate Administrator for Shipbuilding	(VACANCY)
Associate Administrator for Shipping Analysis and Cargo Preference	JAMES J. ZOK
Chief Counsel	ROBERT J. PATTON, JR., *Acting*
Director of Congressional and Public Affairs	WILLIAM G. NORTON, JR.
Director, Office of Maritime Labor, Training, and Safety	TAYLOR E. JONES II
Secretary, Maritime Administration/ Maritime Subsidy Board	JOEL C. RICHARD
Superintendent, United States Merchant Marine Academy	JOSEPH D. STEWART

SAINT LAWRENCE SEAWAY DEVELOPMENT CORPORATION

400 Seventh Street SW., Washington, DC 20590
Phone, 202–366–0091; 800–785–2779 (toll-free). Internet, www.dot.gov/slsdc.

180 Andrews Street, Massena, NY 13662
Phone, 315–764–3200

Administrator	ALBERT S. JACQUEZ
Deputy Administrator	CRAIG H. MIDDLEBROOK
Chief Counsel	MARC OWEN
Director of Trade Development	GINGER VUICH
Director of Budget and Logistics	KEVIN P. O'MALLEY
Director of Congressional and Public Affairs	(VACANCY)
Associate Administrator	ERMAN J. COCCI
Deputy Associate Administrator	SALVATORE L. PISANI
Director of Administration	MARY ANN HAZEL
Director of Engineering and Strategic Planning	STEPHEN C. HUNG
Director of Finance	EDWARD MARGOSIAN
Director of Lock Operations	CAROL A. FENTON
Director of Maintenance and Marine Services	PETER A. BASHAW

RESEARCH AND SPECIAL PROGRAMS ADMINISTRATION

400 Seventh Street SW., Washington, DC 20590
Phone, 202–366–4433

Administrator	KELLEY S. COYNER
Deputy Administrator	JOHN P. MURRAY, *Acting*
Chief Counsel	JUDITH S. KALETA
Director, Office of Civil Rights	HELEN HAGIN
Director, Office of Emergency Transportation	WILLIAM M. MEDIGOVICH
Director, Volpe National Transportation Systems Center	RICHARD R. JOHN
Associate Administrator for Policy and Program Support	JOHN P. MURRAY
Associate Administrator for Management and Administration	EDWARD BRIGHAM
Associate Administrator for Pipeline Safety	RICHARD B. FELDER

Associate Administrator for Hazardous Materials Safety	(VACANCY)
Associate Administrator for Innovation, Research, and Education	FENTON CAREY

BUREAU OF TRANSPORTATION STATISTICS

400 Seventh Street SW., Washington, DC 20590
Phone, 202–366–DATA. Internet, www.bts.gov.

Director	ASHISH K. SEN
Deputy Director	RICK KOWALEWSKI
Associate Director, Transportation Studies	ROLF R. SCHMITT
Associate Director, Statistical Programs and Services	SUSAN J. LAPHAM, *Acting*
Director, Office of Airline Information	TIMOTHY E. CARMODY

FEDERAL MOTOR CARRIER SAFETY ADMINISTRATION

400 Seventh Street, SW., Washington, DC 20590
Phone, 202–366–2519. Internet, www.fmcsa.dot.gov.

Administrator	(VACANCY)
Deputy Administrator	JULIE ANNA CIRILLO, *Acting*
Assistant Administrator (Chief Safety Officer)	JULIE ANNA CIRILLO, *Acting*
Associate Administrator for Administration	(VACANCY)
Associate Administrator for Enforcement and Program Delivery	(VACANCY)
Associate Administrator for Research, Technology, and Information Management	(VACANCY)
Associate Administrator for Policy and Program Development	(VACANCY)
Chief Counsel	(VACANCY)
Director, Office of Civil Rights	(VACANCY)
Director, Office of Public and Consumer Affairs	(VACANCY)

SURFACE TRANSPORTATION BOARD

1925 K Street NW., Washington, DC 20423–0001
Phone, 202–565–1674

Chairman	LINDA J. MORGAN
Vice Chairman	WAYNE O. BURKES
Commissioner	WILLIAM CLYBURN, JR.
Director, Office of Compliance and Enforcement	MELVIN F. CLEMENS, JR.
Director, Office of Congressional and Public Services	DAN G. KING
Director, Office of Economics, Environmental Analysis, and Administration	LELAND L. GARDNER
Director, Office of Proceedings	DAVID M. KONSCHNIK

186-873 D-00--11

General Counsel	Ellen D. Hanson
Secretary	Vernon A. Williams

[For the Department of Transportation statement of organization, see the *Code of Federal Regulations,* Title 49, Part 1, Subpart A]

The U.S. Department of Transportation establishes the Nation's overall transportation policy. Under its umbrella there are 10 administrations whose jurisdictions include highway planning, development, and construction; urban mass transit; railroads; aviation; and the safety of waterways, ports, highways, and oil and gas pipelines. Decisions made by the Department in conjunction with the appropriate State and local officials strongly affect other programs such as land planning, energy conservation, scarce resource utilization, and technological change.

The Department of Transportation (DOT) was established by act of October 15, 1966, as amended (49 U.S.C. 102 and 102 note), "to assure the coordinated, effective administration of the transportation programs of the Federal Government" and to develop "national transportation policies and programs conducive to the provision of fast, safe, efficient, and convenient transportation at the lowest cost consistent therewith." It became operational in April 1967 and was comprised of elements transferred from eight other major departments and agencies.

Secretary The Department of Transportation is administered by the Secretary of Transportation, who is the principal adviser to the President in all matters relating to Federal transportation programs.

Aviation and International Affairs The Office of the Assistant Secretary for Aviation and International Affairs has principal responsibility for the development, review, and coordination of policy for international transportation, and for development, coordination, and implementation of policy relating to economic regulation of the airline industry. The Office:

—licenses U.S. and foreign carriers to serve in international air transportation and conducts carrier fitness determinations;

—develops policies to support the Department in aviation and maritime multilateral and bilateral negotiations with foreign governments and participates on the U.S. negotiating delegations;

—develops policies on a wide range of international transportation and trade matters;

—arranges and coordinates cooperative agreements with foreign governments for the exchange of state-of-the-art scientific and technical information;

—processes and resolves complaints concerning unfair competitive practices in international fares and rates;

—establishes international and intra-Alaska mail rates;

—determines the disposition of requests for approval and immunization from the antitrust laws of international aviation agreements; and

—administers the essential air service program.

For further information, call 202–366–4551.

Drug and Alcohol Policy and Compliance The Office ensures that the national and international drug and alcohol policies and goals of the Secretary are developed and carried out in a consistent, efficient, and effective manner within the transportation industries. The Office provides expert advice, counsel, and recommendations to the Secretary regarding drugs and alcohol as it pertains to the Department of Transportation and testing within the transportation industry.

For further information, contact the Office of Drug and Alcohol Policy and Compliance. Phone, 202–366–3784.

Intelligence and Security The Office advises the Secretary on domestic and international intelligence and security matters; coordinates the development and implementation of long-term

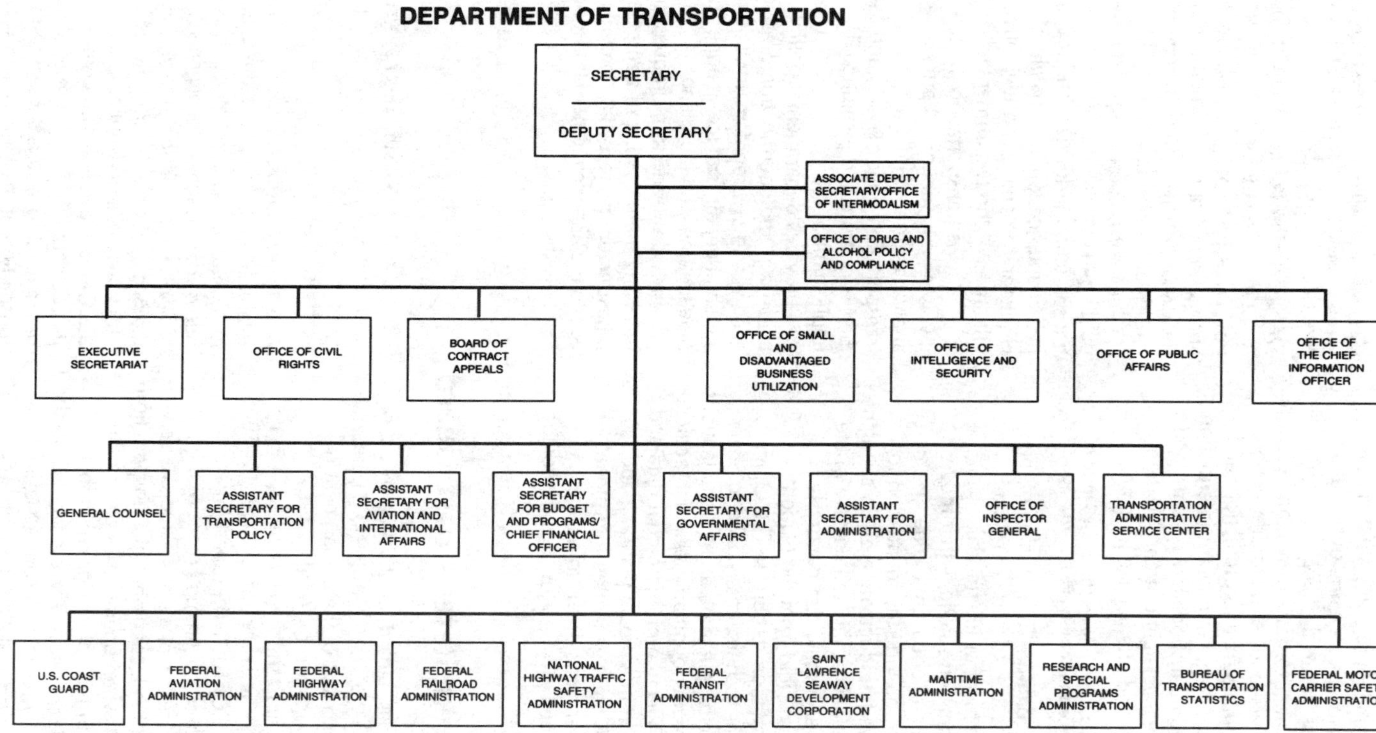
DEPARTMENT OF TRANSPORTATION
SECRETARY
DEPUTY SECRETARY
ASSOCIATE DEPUTY SECRETARY/OFFICE OF INTERMODALISM
OFFICE OF DRUG AND ALCOHOL POLICY AND COMPLIANCE
EXECUTIVE SECRETARIAT
OFFICE OF CIVIL RIGHTS
BOARD OF CONTRACT APPEALS
OFFICE OF SMALL AND DISADVANTAGED BUSINESS UTILIZATION
OFFICE OF INTELLIGENCE AND SECURITY
OFFICE OF PUBLIC AFFAIRS
OFFICE OF THE CHIEF INFORMATION OFFICER
GENERAL COUNSEL
ASSISTANT SECRETARY FOR TRANSPORTATION POLICY
ASSISTANT SECRETARY FOR AVIATION AND INTERNATIONAL AFFAIRS
ASSISTANT SECRETARY FOR BUDGET AND PROGRAMS/ CHIEF FINANCIAL OFFICER
ASSISTANT SECRETARY FOR GOVERNMENTAL AFFAIRS
ASSISTANT SECRETARY FOR ADMINISTRATION
OFFICE OF INSPECTOR GENERAL
TRANSPORTATION ADMINISTRATIVE SERVICE CENTER
U.S. COAST GUARD
FEDERAL AVIATION ADMINISTRATION
FEDERAL HIGHWAY ADMINISTRATION
FEDERAL RAILROAD ADMINISTRATION
NATIONAL HIGHWAY TRAFFIC SAFETY ADMINISTRATION
FEDERAL TRANSIT ADMINISTRATION
SAINT LAWRENCE SEAWAY DEVELOPMENT CORPORATION
MARITIME ADMINISTRATION
RESEARCH AND SPECIAL PROGRAMS ADMINISTRATION
BUREAU OF TRANSPORTATION STATISTICS
FEDERAL MOTOR CARRIER SAFETY ADMINISTRATION

strategic plans, information management systems, and integrated research and development programs affecting the security of the traveling public and cargo; serves as the focal point in the Department for intelligence and security policy, weapons of mass destruction, critical infrastructure protection, and drug and illegal immigrant interdiction effects on transportation systems; and provides oversight of transportation security and intelligence programs.

For further information, contact the Office of Intelligence and Security. Phone, 202–366–6525.

Intermodalism The mission of the Office is to lead and coordinate development of intermodal transportation solutions that move people and goods in an energy-efficient manner, provide the foundation for improved productivity growth, strengthen the Nation's ability to compete in the global economy, and obtain the optimum yield from the Nation's transportation resources. The Office provides technical assistance to States and metropolitan planning organizations in large metropolitan areas that facilitates their collection of intermodal data and assists in intermodal planning and reviews State-generated intermodal management systems to ensure continued progress towards improving and integrating modal transportation systems, where appropriate.

For further information, contact the Office of Intermodalism. Phone, 202–366–5781. Internet, www.dot.gov.

Transportation Policy The Office of the Assistant Secretary for Transportation Policy has principal responsibility for analysis, development, articulation, and review of policies and plans for all modes of transportation. The Office:

—develops, coordinates, and evaluates public policy related to the transportation industries, and maintains policy and economic oversight of regulatory programs and legislative initiatives of the Department;

—reviews transportation matters involving the public and private sectors, analyzes current and emerging transportation policy issues, and assesses their economic and institutional implications;

—provides departmental policy leadership and coordination on safety, energy, and environmental initiatives which affect air, surface, marine, and pipeline transportation; and

—provides leadership on questions involving the financing of transportation infrastructure projects, and provides economic analyses of new transportation technologies.

United States Coast Guard

The Coast Guard, established by act of January 28, 1915 (14 U.S.C. 1), became a component of the Department of Transportation on April 1, 1967, pursuant to the Department of Transportation Act of October 15, 1966 (49 U.S.C. 108). The Coast Guard is a branch of the Armed Forces of the United States at all times and is a service within the Department of Transportation except when operating as part of the Navy in time of war or when the President directs. The predecessor of the Coast Guard, the Revenue Marine, was established in 1790 as a Federal maritime law enforcement agency. Many other major responsibilities have since been added.

Activities

Aids to Navigation The Coast Guard establishes and maintains the U.S. aids to navigation system that includes lights, buoys, day beacons, fog signals, marine radiobeacons, and long-range radionavigation aids. Long-range radionavigation aids include loran-C and the Global Positioning System (GPS) and its augmentations. Aids are established in or adjacent to waters subject to the jurisdiction of the United States. These aids are intended to assist a navigator to determine a position or plot a safe course or to warn the navigator of dangers or obstructions to navigation. Other functions related to navigation aids include broadcasting marine information and publishing *Local Notices to Mariners* and *Light Lists*. Information regarding navigational aids is available electronically. Phone, 703–313–5900 (modem). Internet, www.navcen.uscg.mil.

For further information, call 202–267–0980.

Boating Safety The Coast Guard develops and directs a national boating safety program aimed at making the operation of small craft in U.S. waters both pleasurable and safe. This is accomplished by establishing uniform safety standards for recreational boats and associated equipment; encouraging State efforts through a grant-in-aid and liaison program; coordinating public education and information programs; administering the Coast Guard Auxiliary; and enforcing compliance with Federal laws and regulations relative to safe use and safety equipment requirements for small boats.

For further information, call 202–267–1077.

Bridge Administration The Coast Guard administers the statutes regulating the construction, maintenance, and operation of bridges and causeways across the navigable waters of the United States to provide for safe navigation through and under bridges.

For further information, call 202–267–0368.

Coast Guard Auxiliary The Auxiliary is a nonmilitary volunteer organization of private citizens who own small boats, aircraft, or radio stations. Auxiliary members assist the Coast Guard by conducting boating education programs, patrolling marine regattas, participating in search and rescue operations, and conducting courtesy marine examinations.

For further information, call 202–267–0982.

Deepwater Ports The Coast Guard administers a licensing and regulatory program governing the construction, ownership (international aspects), and operation of deepwater ports on the high seas to transfer oil from tankers to shore.

For further information, call 202–267–0495.

Ice Operations The Coast Guard operates the Nation's icebreaking vessels (icebreakers and ice-capable cutters), supported by aircraft, for ice reconnaissance, to facilitate maritime transportation in domestic waters. Additionally, icebreakers support logistics to U.S. polar installations and also support scientific research in Arctic and Antarctic waters.

For further information, call 202–267–1456.

Marine Environmental Response The Coast Guard is responsible for enforcing laws relating to the protection of the marine environment. Program objectives are to ensure that public health and welfare and the environment are protected when spills occur. Under these laws, U.S. and foreign vessels are prohibited from using U.S. waters unless they have insurance or other guarantees that potential pollution liability for cleanup and damages will be met.

Other functions include providing a national response center to receive reports of oil and hazardous substance spills, investigating spills, initiating subsequent civil penalty actions when warranted, encouraging and monitoring responsible party cleanups, and when necessary, coordinating federally funded spill response operations. The program also provides a national strike force to assist Federal on-scene coordinators in responding to pollution incidents.

For further information, call 202–267–0518.

Marine Inspection The Coast Guard is charged with formulating, administering, and enforcing various safety standards for the design, construction, equipment, and maintenance of commercial vessels of the United States and offshore structures on the Outer Continental Shelf. The program includes enforcement of safety standards on foreign vessels subject to U.S. jurisdiction.

Investigations are conducted of reported marine accidents, casualties, violations of law and regulations, misconduct, negligence, and incompetence occurring on commercial vessels subject to U.S. jurisdiction. Surveillance operations and boardings are conducted to detect violations of law and regulations. The program also functions to facilitate marine transportation by measuring and administering the vessel documentation laws.

For further information, call 202–267–1464.

Marine Licensing The Coast Guard administers a system for evaluating and licensing of U.S. merchant marine personnel. This program develops safe manning standards for commercial vessels. The Coast Guard also maintains oversight and approval authority for the numerous mariner training programs.

For further information, call 703–235–1951.

Maritime Law Enforcement The Coast Guard is the primary maritime law enforcement agency for the United States. It enforces or assists in the enforcement of applicable Federal laws and treaties and other international agreements to which the United States is party, on, over, and under the high seas and waters subject to the jurisdiction of the United States, and may conduct investigations into suspected violations of such laws and international agreements. The Coast Guard works with other Federal agencies in the enforcement of such laws as they pertain to the protection of living and nonliving marine resources and in the suppression of smuggling and illicit drug trafficking.

For further information, call 202–267–1890.

Military Readiness As required by law, the Coast Guard maintains a state of readiness to function as a specialized service in the Navy in time of war, or as directed by the President. Coastal and harbor defense, including port security and maritime interdiction operations, are the most important military tasks assigned to the Coast Guard in times of national crisis.

For further information, call 202–267–2025.

Port Safety and Security This program is administered by the Coast Guard Captains of the Port. The Coast Guard is authorized to enforce rules and regulations governing the safety and security of ports and anchorages, and the movement of vessels and prevention of pollution in U.S. waters. Port safety and security functions include supervising cargo transfer operations, both storage and stowage, conducting harbor patrols and waterfront facility inspections, establishing security zones as required, and the control of vessel movement.

For further information, call 202–267–0495.

Reserve Training The Coast Guard Reserve provides qualified individuals for active duty in time of war and other contingencies, as well as for day-to-day augmentation of Coast Guard cutters and shore units. The Coast Guard Reserve is unique among the Reserve components in that Coast Guard reservists may be involuntarily recalled for domestic emergencies.

For further information, call 202–267–1240.

Search and Rescue The Coast Guard maintains a system of rescue vessels, aircraft, and communications facilities to carry out its function of saving life and property in and over the high seas and the navigable waters of the United States. This function includes flood relief and removing hazards to navigation.

For further information, call 202–267–1943.

Waterways Management The Coast Guard has a significant role in the safe and orderly passage of cargo, people, and vessels on our nation's waterways. It has established vessel traffic services in six major ports to provide for the safe movement of vessels at all times, but particularly during hazardous conditions, restricted visibility, or bad weather. The program's goal is to ensure the safe, efficient flow of commerce. The Coast Guard also regulates the installation of equipment necessary for vessel safety.

For further information, call 202–267–0407.

District and Field Organizations—United States Coast Guard

Organization	Address	Commander	Telephone
Atlantic Area	431 Crawford St., Portsmouth, VA 23704–5004	Vice Adm. John E. Shkor, USCG	757–398–6287
Maintenance and Logistics Command-Atlantic	300 Main St. Twr., Norfolk, VA 23510	Rear Adm. James A. Kinghorn, Jr.	757–628–4275
1st District	408 Atlantic Ave., Boston, MA 02110–3350	Rear Adm. George N. Naccara	617–223–8480
5th District	431 Crawford St., Portsmouth, VA 23704–5004	Vice Adm. John E. Shkor	757–398–6287
7th District	Rm. 944, 909 SE. 1st Ave., Miami, FL 33131–3050	Rear Adm. Thad W. Allen	305–536–5654
8th District	501 Magazine St., New Orleans, LA 70130–3396	Rear Adm. Paul J. Pluta	504–589–6298
9th District	1240 E. 9th St., Cleveland, OH 44199–2060	Rear Adm. James D. Hull	216–902–6001
Pacific Area	Coast Guard Island, Alameda, CA 94501–5100	Vice Adm. Ernest R. Riutta	510–437–3196
Maintenance and Logistics Command-Pacific	Coast Guard Island, Alameda, CA 94501–5100	Rear Adm. John L. Parker	510–437–3939
11th District	Coast Guard Island, Alameda, CA 94501–5100	Vice Adm. Ernest R. Riutta	510–437–3196
13th District	915 2d Ave., Seattle, WA 98174–1067	Rear Adm. Erroll M. Brown	206–220–7090
14th District	9th Fl., 300 Ala Moana Blvd., Honolulu, HI 96850–4982	Rear Adm. Joseph J. McClelland	808–541–2051
17th District	P.O. Box 25517, Juneau, AK 99802–1217	Rear Adm. Thomas J. Barrett	907–463–2025
U.S. Coast Guard Academy	New London, CT 06320–4195	Rear Adm. Douglas H. Teeson	203–444–8285
National Pollution Funds Center	Suite 1000, 4200 Wilson Blvd., Arlington, VA 22203–1804	Jan Lane, *Acting*	703–235–4700
Coast Guard Personnel Command	2100 2d St. SW., Washington, DC 20593–0001	Capt. Steven E. Froehlich	202–267–2321

For further information, contact the Information Office, United States Coast Guard, Department of Transportation, 2100 Second Street SW., Washington, DC 20593. Phone, 202–267–2229. Internet, www.uscg.mil.

Federal Aviation Administration

The Federal Aviation Administration (FAA), formerly the Federal Aviation Agency, was established by the Federal Aviation Act of 1958. The agency became a component of the Department of Transportation in 1967 pursuant to the Department of Transportation Act (49 U.S.C. 106). The mission of the Federal Aviation Administration involves safety considerations and activities in the public interest, including:

—assigning, maintaining, and enhancing safety and security as the highest priorities in air commerce;

—regulating air commerce in a way that best promotes safety and fulfills national defense requirements;

—encouraging and developing civil aeronautics, including new aviation technology;

—controlling the use of the navigable airspace and regulating civil and military operations in that airspace in the interest of safety and efficiency of both of those operations;

—consolidating research and development for air navigation facilities and the installation and operation of those facilities;

—developing and operating a common system of air traffic control and navigation for military and civil aircraft;

—providing assistance to law enforcement agencies in the enforcement of laws related to regulation of controlled substances, to the extent consistent with aviation safety;

—developing and implementing a program to solve the aircraft noise and sonic boom problem; and

—regulating U.S. commercial space transportation.

Activities

Air Navigation Facilities The agency is responsible for the location, construction or installation, maintenance, operation, and quality assurance of Federal visual and electronic aids to air navigation. The agency operates and maintains voice/data communications equipment, radar facilities, computer systems, and visual display equipment at flight service stations, airport traffic control towers, and air route traffic control centers.

Airport Programs The agency maintains a national plan of airport requirements, administers a grant program for development of public use airports to assure and improve safety and to meet current and future airport capacity needs, evaluates the environmental impacts of airport development, and administers an airport noise compatibility program with the goal of reducing noncompatible uses around airports. It also develops standards and technical guidance on airport planning, design, safety, and operations and provides grants to assist public agencies in airport system and master planning and airport development and improvement.

Airspace and Air Traffic Management The safe and efficient utilization of the navigable airspace is a primary objective of the agency. To meet this objective, it operates a network of airport traffic control towers, air route traffic control centers, and flight service stations. It develops air traffic rules and regulations and allocates the use of the airspace. It also provides for the security control of air traffic to meet national defense requirements.

Civil Aviation Abroad Under the Federal Aviation Act of 1958 and the International Aviation Facilities Act (49 U.S.C. app. 1151), the agency encourages aviation safety and civil aviation abroad by exchanging aeronautical information with foreign aviation authorities; certifying foreign repair stations, airmen, and mechanics; negotiating bilateral airworthiness agreements to facilitate the import and export of aircraft and components; and providing technical assistance and training in all areas of the agency's expertise. It provides technical representation at international conferences, including participation in the International Civil Aviation Organization and other international organizations.

Commercial Space Transportation The agency regulates and encourages the U.S. commercial space transportation industry. It licenses the private sector launching of space payloads on expendable launch vehicles and commercial space launch facilities. It also sets insurance requirements for the protection of persons and property and ensures that space transportation activities comply with U.S. domestic and foreign policy.

Registration The agency provides a system for registering aircraft and recording documents affecting title or interest in the aircraft, aircraft engines, propellers, appliances, and spare parts.

Research, Engineering, and Development The research, engineering, and development activities of the agency are directed toward providing the systems, procedures, facilities, and devices needed for a safe and efficient system of air navigation and air traffic control to meet the needs of civil aviation and the air defense system. The agency also performs an aeromedical research function to apply knowledge gained from its research program and the work of others to the safety and promotion of civil aviation and the health, safety, and efficiency of agency employees. The agency also supports development and testing of improved aircraft, engines, propellers, and appliances.

Safety Regulation The Administration issues and enforces rules, regulations, and minimum standards relating to the manufacture, operation, and maintenance of aircraft, as well as the rating and certification (including medical) of airmen and the certification of airports serving air carriers. It performs flight inspection of air navigation facilities in the U.S. and, as required, abroad.

Test and Evaluation The agency conducts tests and evaluations of specified items such as aviation systems, subsystems, equipment, devices, materials, concepts, or procedures at any phase in the cycle of their development from conception to acceptance and implementation, as well as assigned independent testing at key decision points.

Other Programs The agency administers the aviation insurance program. It is an allotting agency under the defense materials system with respect to priorities and allocation for civil aircraft and civil aviation operations. The agency develops specifications for the preparation of aeronautical charts. It publishes current information on airways and airport service and issues technical publications for the improvement of safety in flight, airport planning and design, and other aeronautical activities. It serves as the executive administration for the operation and maintenance of the Department of Transportation automated payroll and personnel systems.

Major Field Organizations—Federal Aviation Administration

Region/Field Office	Address	Administrator/Director
Alaskan—AK	P.O. Box 14, 701 C St., Anchorage, AK 99513	Patrick N. Poe
Central—IA, KS, MO, NE	601 E. 12th St., Kansas City, MO 64106	John E. Turner
Eastern—DE, MD, NJ, NY, PA, VA, WV	1 Aviation Plz., Springfield Gardens, NY 11434	Arlene B. Feldman
Great Lakes—IL, IN, MI, MN, ND, OH, SD, WI	2300 E. Devon Ave., Des Plaines, IL 60018	Cecilia Hunziker
New England—CT, MA, ME, NH, RI, VT	12 New England Executive Park, Burlington, MA 01803	Robert S. Bartanowicz
Northwest Mountain—CO, ID, MT, OR, UT, WA, WY	1601 Lind Ave. SW., Renton, WA 98055	Larry Andriesen
Southern—AL, FL, GA, KY, MS, NC, PR, SC, TN	1701 Columbia Ave., College Park, GA 30337	Carolyn C. Blum
Southwest—AR, LA, NM, OK, TX	2601 Meacham Blvd., Fort Worth, TX 76137–4298	Ruth Leverenz, *Acting*
Western-Pacific—AZ, CA, HI, NV	15000 Aviation Blvd., Hawthorne, CA 90261	William C. Withycombe
Europe, Africa, and Middle East	15, Rue de la Loi B–1040, Brussels, Belgium	Lynne A. Osmus
Asia-Pacific	U.S. Embassy, FAA, Singapore	Eugene Ross Hamory
Latin America-Caribbean	8600 NW. 36th St., Miami, FL 33166	Joaquin Archilla
William J. Hughes Technical Center	Atlantic City, NJ 08405	Anne Harlan
Mike Monroney Aeronautical Center	6500 S. MacArthur, Oklahoma City, OK 73125	Lindy Ritz

For further information, contact the Office of Public Affairs, Federal Aviation Administration, Department of Transportation, 800 Independence Avenue SW., Washington, DC 20591. Phone, 202–267–8521. Fax, 202–267–5039.

Federal Highway Administration

The Federal Highway Administration (FHWA) was established as an agency of the Department of Transportation by the Department of Transportation Act (49 U.S.C. 104). It administers the Department's highway transportation programs. The Administration is responsible for:

—carrying out the Federal-aid highway program, in partnership with State transportation departments and metropolitan planning organizations, local governments, and the private sector;

—providing technical support grants to States for safety activities;

—working with other Federal agencies to design and build roads in national forests, parks, and Indian reservations; and

—cooperating with foreign governments through technology exchange and technical assistance.

FHWA administers programs to:

—plan, preserve, improve, and expand the surface transportation system and enhance its safety, operations, efficiency, and intermodal integration;

—provide innovative and effective research and development and develop means to market and implement this technology;

—provide oversight and accountability for public resources and ensure appropriate uniformity;

—provide for efficient and safe freight and passenger mobility to strengthen economic and social linkages;

—protect and enhance the environment; and

—improve highway-related aspects of surface transportation safety in coordination with the other DOT operating administrations.

Activities

Infrastructure The Administration manages the majority of the Federal-aid programs and engineering policies and standards, and provides technical expertise and assistance relating to the design, construction, and maintenance of the Nation's highways, pavement, bridges, tunnels, hydraulic/geotechnical structures, and other engineering activities. It also manages highway infrastructure assets.

Federal Lands Programs The Administration manages the Federal lands highway program, the emergency relief program for federally owned roads, and the defense access roads program. It also provides transportation services to Federal agencies, serves as an advocate for safe public access to Federal and Indian lands, and develops and disseminates technology relative to transportation access to Federal and Indian lands. In addition to the national program management of the above programs, the Administration manages the Indian reserve road category.

Field Operations FHWA's field structure is comprised of four resource centers that support the 52 State-level division offices. The offices provide Federal-aid program assistance to partners and customers in highway transportation and safety services including planning and research, preliminary engineering, technology transfer, right-of-way, bridges, highway safety, traffic operations, environment, civil rights, design, construction and maintenance, engineering coordination, highway beautification, and management.

Field Offices—Federal Highway Administration

Office	Address	Administrator	Telephone
	Resource Centers		
Eastern		Dale E. Wilken	
Baltimore, MD	Suite 4000, 10 S. Howard St., 21201		410–962–0077
Albany, NY	Rm. 719, Clinton Ave. & N. Pearl St., 12207		518–431–4224
Midwestern		A. George Ostensen	
Olympia Fields, IL	Suite 301, 19900 Governors Dr., 60461–1021		708–283–3510
Southern		Eugene Cleckley	
Atlanta, GA	Suite 17T26, 61 Forsyth St. SW., 30303–3104		404–562–3570
Ft. Worth, TX	Rm. 8A00, 819 Taylor St, 76102		817–978–3232
Western		Leon Whitman	
San Francisco, CA	Suite 2100, 201 Mission St., 94105		415–744–3102
Portland, OR	Gus J. Solomon Bldg., 620 SW. Main St., 97205		503–326–2053
	Metropolitan Offices		
Los Angeles, CA	Suite 1460, 201 N. Figueroa St., 90012	Pam Marston	213–202–3950
Chicago, IL	Rm. 2410, 200 W. Adams, 60606–5232	J.D. Stokes	312–886–1616
New York, NY	Rm. 428, 1 Bowling Green, 10004–1415	Arthur O'Connor	212–668–2206
Philadelphia	Suite 510, 1760 Market St., 19103	Carmine Fiscina	215–656–7070
	Federal Lands Highway Divisions		
Central	555 Zang St., Lakewood, CO 80228–1010	Larry C. Smith	303–716–2000
Eastern	Loudoun Tech. Ctr., 21400 Ridgetop Cir., Sterling, VA 20166–6511	Allen W. Burden	703–404–6201
Western	610 E. 5th St., Vancouver, WA 98661–3893	Ronald W. Carmichael	360–696–7710

For further information, contact the Office of Information and Management Services, Federal Highway Administration, Department of Transportation, 400 Seventh Street SW., Washington, DC 20590. Phone, 202–366–0534.

Federal Railroad Administration

The Federal Railroad Administration was created pursuant to section 3(e)(1) of the Department of Transportation Act of 1966 (49 U.S.C. 103). The purpose of the Administration is to promulgate and enforce rail safety regulations, administer railroad financial assistance programs, conduct research and development in support of improved railroad safety and national rail transportation policy, provide for the rehabilitation of Northeast Corridor rail passenger service, and consolidate government support of rail transportation activities.

Activities

Passenger and Freight Services The Administration oversees and provides financial assistance to Amtrak and administers financial assistance programs to demonstrate high-speed rail technology, to reduce grade crossing hazards in high-speed rail corridors, to provide for investments in small freight railroads and other rail projects, to plan for high-speed rail projects, and to plan and deploy magnetic levitation technology.

Railroad Safety The Administration administers and enforces the Federal laws and related regulations designed to promote safety on railroads; exercises jurisdiction over all areas of rail safety under the Rail Safety Act of 1970, such as track maintenance, inspection standards, equipment standards, and operating practices. Railroad and related industry equipment, facilities, and records are inspected and required reports reviewed. In addition, the administration educates the public about safety at highway-rail grade crossings and the danger of trespassing on rail property.

Research and Development The Administration's ground transportation research and development program seeks to advance all aspects of intercity ground transportation and railroad safety pertaining to the physical sciences and engineering, in order to improve railroad safety and ensure that railroads continue to be a viable national transportation resource.

Transportation Test Center FRA tests and evaluates conventional and advanced railroad systems and components at the Transportation Test Center near Pueblo, CO. Private sector companies and the Governments of the United States, Canada, and Japan use the facility to explore the operation of conventional and advanced systems under controlled conditions. It is used by Amtrack for the testing of new high-speed locomotives and trains and by the Federal Transit Administration for testing urban rapid transit vehicles.

For further information, contact the Transportation Technology Center, Pueblo, CO 81001. Phone, 719–584–0507.

Major Field Organizations—Federal Railroad Administration

Region	Address	Administrator	Telephone
Northeastern—CT, MA, ME, NH, NJ, NY, RI, VT	Rm. 1077, 55 Broadway, Cambridge, MA 02142	Mark H. McKeon	617–494–2302
Eastern—DC, DE, MA, OH, PA, VA, WV	Suite 550, Scott Plz. II, Philadelphia, PA 19113	David R. Myers	610–521–8200
Southern—AL, FL, GA, KY, MS, NC, SC, TN	Suite 16T20, 61 Forsyth St. SW., Atlanta, GA 30303–3104	L.F. Dennin II	404–562–3800
Central—IL, IN, MI, MN, WI	Suite 655, 111 N. Canal St., Chicago, IL 60606	Laurence A. Hasvold	312–353–6203
Southwestern—AR, LA, NM, OK, TX	Suite 425, 8701 Bedford Euless Rd., Hurst, TX 76053	John F. Megary	817–284–8142
Midwestern—CO, IA, KS, MO, NE	Suite 464, 901 Loost St., Kansas City, MO 64106	Darrell J. Tisor	816–392–3840
Western—AZ, CA, NV, UT	Suite 466, 801 I St., Sacramento, CA 95814	Alvin Settje	916–498–6540
Northwestern—AK, ID, MT, ND, OR, SD, WA, WY	Suite 650, 703 Broadway, Vancouver, WA 98660	Dick L. Clairmont	360–696–7536

For further information, contact the Office of Public Affairs, Federal Railroad Administration, Department of Transportation, 1120 Vermont Avenue NW., Washington, DC 20590. Phone, 202–493–6024. Internet, www.fra.dot.gov.

National Highway Traffic Safety Administration

[For the National Highway Traffic Safety Administration statement of organization, see the *Code of Federal Regulations,* Title 49, Part 501]

The National Highway Traffic Safety Administration (NHTSA) was established by the Highway Safety Act of 1970 (23 U.S.C. 401 note) to help reduce the mounting number of deaths, injuries, and economic losses resulting from motor vehicle crashes on the Nation's highway.

The Administration carries out programs relating to the safety performance of motor vehicles and related equipment; administers the Nation's State and community highway safety program (administered jointly with the Federal Highway Administration); carries out the National Driver Register (NDR) Program to facilitate the interstate exchange of State records on problem drivers; conducts studies and operates programs aimed at reducing economic losses in motor vehicle crashes and repairs through general motor vehicle programs; administers the Federal odometer law; and issues theft prevention standards for passenger and nonpassenger motor vehicles.

Activities

Research and Development The Administration provides a foundation for the development of motor vehicle and highway safety program standards by researching, developing, testing, and evaluating motor vehicles, motor vehicle equipment, and advanced technologies, and collecting and analyzing crash data. The research program covers numerous areas affecting safety problems and includes providing laboratory testing facilities to obtain necessary basic data. The objectives are to encourage industry to adopt advanced motor vehicle safety designs, stimulate public awareness of safety potentials, and provide a base for vehicle safety information.

The Administration maintains a collection of scientific and technical information related to motor vehicle safety, and operates the National Center for Statistics and Analysis, whose activities include the development and maintenance of highway crash data collection systems and related analysis efforts. These comprehensive motor vehicle safety information resources serve as documentary reference points for Federal, State, and local agencies, as well as industry, universities, and the public.

Safety Assurance The Office of Safety Assurance identifies and investigates problems with motor vehicles and motor vehicle equipment. If the Office determines that the vehicle or item of equipment contains a defect which is safety related or that it does not meet all applicable Federal motor vehicle safety standards, the Office will seek a recall in which owners are notified and the vehicles or equipment are remedied free of charge. The Office monitors recalls to ensure that owners are being notified, that the notifications are done in a timely manner, and that the scope of the recall and the remedy are adequate to correct the problem.

The Office operates the toll-free auto safety hotline to identify safety problems in motor vehicles and motor vehicle equipment. Consumers can call the hotline (phone, 800–424–9393) to report safety-related problems. These calls form the basis for investigations and ultimately recalls if safety-related defects are identified. The hotline also provides information and literature to consumers about vehicle and child-seat recalls, New Car Assessment Program test results, and a variety of other highway safety information.

Safety Performance Standards The Administration manages motor vehicle safety programs to reduce the occurrence of highway crashes and the severity of resulting injuries; reduce the economic losses in crashes; and provide consumer information in the areas of crash test results, proper usage of vehicle safety features, and tire grading for treadwear, temperature resistance, and traction.

The Administration issues Federal motor vehicle safety standards that prescribe safety features and levels of safety-related performance for vehicles and items of motor vehicle equipment. It conducts the New Car Assessment Program, under which high-speed crash tests are conducted on passenger cars, light trucks, and vans to assess their frontal and side impact safety performance. Results from these tests are provided to the public to assist them in selecting and purchasing safer motor vehicles. The Administration also informs consumers on how to properly use vehicle safety features. It manages a fuel economy program that establishes and revises fleet average fuel economy standards for passenger car and light truck manufacturers to ensure that maximum feasible fuel economy is attained. The Administration also carries out a theft program, issuing rules requiring the designation of likely high-theft vehicles that must comply with parts-marking requirements, and calculating and publishing annual motor vehicle theft rates.

Traffic Safety Programs The Administration leads the national traffic safety and emergency services efforts in order to save lives, reduce injuries, and lessen medical and other costs. In accomplishing these tasks, it utilizes behavioral research, demonstration, and evaluation, in addition to developing safety programs and strategies, for use by a variety of public and private agencies and organizations. The Administration maintains a national register of information on individuals whose licenses to operate a motor vehicle have been revoked, suspended, canceled, or denied; or who have been convicted of certain traffic-related violations such as driving while impaired by alcohol or other drugs. The information obtained from the register assists State driver licensing officials in determining whether or not to issue a license.

Regional Offices—National Highway Traffic Safety Administration

Region/Address	Administrator
Atlanta, GA (Suite 17T30, 61 Forsyth St. SW., 30303)	Troy Ayers
Baltimore, MD (Suite 4000, 10 S. Howard St., 21201)	Elizabeth A. Baker
Cambridge, MA (Kendall Sq., Code 903, 02142)	George A. Luciano
Denver, CO (4th Fl., 555 Zang St., 80228)	Louis R. De Carolis
Fort Worth, TX (819 Taylor St., 76102–6177)	Georgia Chakiris
Kansas City, MO (P.O. Box 412515, 64141)	Romell Cooks
Olympia Fields, IL (Suite 201, 19900 Governors Dr., 60461)	Donald J. McNamara
San Francisco, CA (201 Mission St., 94105)	Joseph M. Cindrich
Seattle, WA 98174 (915 2d Ave.)	David Manning
White Plains, NY (222 Mamaroneck Ave., 10605)	Tom Louizou

For further information, contact the Office of Public and Consumer Affairs, National Highway Traffic Safety Administration, Department of Transportation, 400 Seventh Street SW., Washington, DC 20590. Phone, 202–366–9550. Internet, www.nhtsa.dot.gov.

Federal Transit Administration

[For the Federal Transit Administration statement of organization, see the *Code of Federal Regulations,* Title 49, Part 601]

The Federal Transit Administration (FTA) (formerly the Urban Mass Transportation Administration) was established as a component of the Department of Transportation by section 1 of Reorganization Plan No. 2 of 1968 (5

U.S.C. app. 1), effective July 1, 1968. The missions of the Administration are:

—to assist in developing improved mass transportation equipment, facilities, techniques, and methods with the cooperation of public and private mass transportation companies;

—to encourage the planning and establishment of areawide mass transportation systems needed for economical and desirable development with the cooperation of public and private mass transportation companies;

—to assist States and local governments and their authorities in financing areawide mass transportation systems that are to be operated by public or private mass transportation companies as decided by local needs;

—to provide financial assistance to State and local governments and their authorities to help carry out national goals related to mobility for elderly individuals, individuals with disabilities, and economically disadvantaged individuals; and

—to establish a partnership that allows a community, with financial assistance from the Government, to satisfy its mass transportation requirements.

Programs

Capital Investment Grants are authorized to assist in financing the acquisition, construction, reconstruction, and improvement of facilities and equipment for use in mass transportation service in urban areas. There are three categories of funds available under the capital investment program: fixed guideway modernization, rolling stock renewal, safety-related improvements, and signal and power modernization; new starts funds for construction of new fixed guideway service; and bus funds for acquiring buses and rolling stock, ancillary equipment, and the construction of bus facilities.

For further information, call 202–366–2053.

Elderly and Persons With Disabilities The program provides financial assistance to private nonprofit agencies to meet the transportation needs of elderly persons and persons with disabilities where services provided by public operators are unavailable, insufficient, or inappropriate; to public bodies approved by the State to coordinate services for elderly persons or persons with disabilities; or to public bodies which certify to the Governor that no nonprofit corporation or association is readily available in an area to provide the service. Funds are allocated by formula to the States; local organizations apply for funding through a designated State agency.

For further information, call 202–366–2053.

Job Access and Reverse Commute Grants The program makes funding available to public agencies and nonprofit organizations to pay the capital and operating costs of delivering new or expanded job access or reverse commute services, and to promote the use of transit during non-traditional work hours, as well as encourage employer-based transportation strategies and use of transit pass programs. The program provides competitive grants for two kinds of projects:

—job access projects implementing new or expanded transportation services for transporting welfare recipients and low-income persons to and from jobs and needed employment support services such as child care; and

—reverse commute projects implementing new or expanded general-purpose public transportation services to transport residents of urban, rural, and suburban areas to suburban employment centers.

For further information, call 202–366–0176. Internet, www.fta.dot.gov/wtw.

Nonurbanized Area Assistance The Administration provides capital and operating assistance for public transportation in nonurbanized areas. Funds are allocated to the Governor and the program is administered at the State level by the designated transportation agency. Assistance is provided for planning, administrative and program development activities, coordination of public transportation programs, vehicle acquisition, and other capital investments in support of transit services, including services tailored to the needs of elderly and handicapped and other transit-dependent persons.

Planning The program provides financial assistance in meeting the transportation planning needs of metropolitan planning organizations, by allocating funds to States, which in turn, they allocate to the metropolitan planning organizations. Assistance is available for transportation planning, technical assistance studies, demonstrations, management training, and cooperative research.

For further information, call 202–366–1626.

Research and Technology The Administration provides funds for research, development, and demonstration projects in mass transportation for the purpose of increasing productivity and efficiency in urban and nonurban transportation systems, and works to expand private sector participation and cooperation in these efforts. It conducts research, development, and demonstration programs addressing equipment and infrastructure, fleet operations, human resources, information management, metropolitan and rural policy development, planning and project development, safety and security, and specialized customer services. Research is carried out in ways that maximize participation by State and local governments as well as private organizations, including colleges and universities. Special emphasis is placed on the following project areas:

—developing innovative transit technologies and more environmentally friendly vehicles;

—promoting and utilizing an educated, skilled work force with the ability to develop and utilize the latest technological advancements in mass transit transportation;

—encouraging participation by the private sector in providing transportation services through the use of joint public/private financing of transit capital investment;

—participating in exchange programs of transit ideas and resources with other countries;

—implementing a program of new model bus testing and testing facility improvements;

—creating new safety and security initiatives that cover passengers, transit agency personnel, vehicles, and facilities;

—promoting the delivery of safe and effective public transportation in rural and suburban areas and transportation between these areas and central city locations; and

—improving the mobility of low-income and elderly persons and persons with disabilities through more accessible and integrated services.

For further information, contact the nearest regional office.

Rural Transportation Assistance The Rural Transportation Assistance Program allocates funds annually to the States to provide assistance for transit research, technical assistance, training, and related support activities for transit providers serving nonurbanized areas. Additional funds are used at the national level for developing training materials, developing and maintaining a national clearinghouse on rural transit activities and information, and providing technical assistance through peer practitioners to promote exemplary techniques and practices.

For further information, call 202–366–2053.

Safety The Administration's safety program supports State and local agencies in fulfilling their responsibility for the safety and security of urban mass transportation facilities and services, through the encouragement and sponsorship of safety and security planning, training, information collection and analysis, drug control programs, system/safety assurance reviews, generic research, and other cooperative government/industry activities.

For further information, call 202–366–2896.

Training and Technical Assistance The National Transit Institute (NTI) was established by the Federal Transit Act

(49 U.S.C. 5315). NTI develops and conducts training and technical assistance activities in cooperation with the FTA and the transit industry. In addition, NTI provides technical support relating to training, a clearinghouse function which includes cataloging the curriculum offered at NTI and elsewhere, and referral services relating to the training and development needs of the transit industry.

For further information, call 202–366–0245.

Field Organization—Federal Transit Administration

Region/Address	Telephone
Atlanta, GA (Suite 17T50, 61 Forsyth St. SW., 30303)	404–562–3500
Cambridge, MA (Suite 920, 55 Broadway, 02142)	617–494–2055
Chicago, IL (Suite 2410, 200 W. Adams St., 60606)	312–353–2789
Denver, CO (Suite 650, 216 16th St., 80202)	303–844–3242
Fort Worth, TX (Suite 8A36, 819 Taylor St., 76102)	817–978–0550
Kansas City, MO (Suite 303, 6301 Rockhill Rd., 64131)	816–523–0204
New York, NY (Suite 429, 1 Bowling Green, 10004–1415)	212–668–2170
Philadelphia, PA (Suite 500, 1760 Market St., 19103)	215–656–7100
San Francisco, CA (Suite 2210, 201 Mission St., 94105)	415–744–3133
Seattle, WA (Suite 3142, 915 2d Ave., 98174)	206–220–7954

Metropolitan Offices—Federal Transit Administration

Office/Address	Telephone
Chicago, IL (24th Fl., 200 W. Adams St., 60606–5232)	312–886–1616
Los Angeles, CA (Suite 1460, 210 Figueroa, 90012)	213–202–3950
New York, NY (Suite 428, 1 Bowling Green, 10004–1415)	212–668–2201
Philadelphia, PA (Suite 500, 1760 Market St., 19103–4142)	215–656–7070

For further information, contact the Office of Public Affairs, Federal Transit Administration, Department of Transportation, 400 Seventh Street SW., Washington, DC 20590. Phone, 202–366–4043. Internet, www.fta.dot.gov.

Maritime Administration

The Maritime Administration was established by Reorganization Plan No. 21 of 1950 (5 U.S.C. app.). The Maritime Act of 1981 (46 U.S.C. 1601) transferred the Maritime Administration to the Department of Transportation. The Administration manages programs to aid in the development, promotion, and operation of the U.S. merchant marine. It is also charged with organizing and directing emergency merchant ship operations.

The Maritime Administration administers subsidy programs to pay the difference between certain costs of operating ships under the U.S. flag and foreign competitive flags on essential services, and the difference between the costs of constructing ships in U.S. and foreign shipyards. It provides financing guarantees for the construction, reconstruction, and reconditioning of ships; and enters into capital construction fund agreements that grant tax deferrals on moneys to be used for the acquisition, construction, or reconstruction of ships.

The Administration constructs or supervises the construction of merchant type ships for the Federal Government. It helps industry generate increased business for U.S. ships and conducts programs to develop ports, facilities, and intermodal transport, and to promote domestic shipping.

It conducts program and technical studies and administers a war risk insurance program that insures operators and seamen against losses caused by hostile action if domestic commercial insurance is not available.

Under emergency conditions the Maritime Administration charters Government-owned ships to U.S. operators, requisitions or procures ships owned by U.S. citizens, and allocates them to meet defense needs.

It maintains a national defense reserve fleet of Government-owned ships that it operates through ship managers and general agents when required in national defense interests. An element of this activity is the Ready Reserve force consisting of a number of ships available for quick-response activation.

The Administration regulates sales to aliens and transfers to foreign registry of ships that are fully or partially owned by U.S. citizens. It also disposes of Government-owned ships found nonessential for national defense.

The Administration operates the U.S. Merchant Marine Academy, Kings Point, NY, where young people are trained to become merchant marine officers, and conducts training in shipboard firefighting at Earle, NJ, and Toledo, OH. It also administers a Federal assistance program for the maritime academies operated by California, Maine, Massachusetts, Michigan, New York, and Texas.

Field Organization—Maritime Administration

Region	Address	Director	Telephone
Central	Rm. 1223, 501 Magazine St., New Orleans, LA 70130–3394	John W. Carnes	504–589–2000
Great Lakes	Suite 185, 2860 South River Rd., Des Plaines, IL 60018–2413.	Alpha H. Ames, Jr.	847–298–4535
North Atlantic	Rm. 418, 1 Bowling Green, New York, NY 10004–1415	Robert McKeon	212–668–3330
South Atlantic	Rm. 211, 7737 Hampton Blvd., Norfolk, VA 23505	Mayank Jain	757–441–6393
Western	Suite 2200, 201 Mission St., San Francisco, CA 94105–1905	Francis X. Johnston	415–744–3125
Merchant Marine Academy.	Kings Point, NY 11024–1699	Joseph D. Stewart	516–773–5000

For further information, contact the Office of Congressional and Public Affairs, Maritime Administration, Department of Transportation, 400 Seventh Street SW., Washington, DC 20590. Phone, 202–366–5807, or 800–996–2723 (toll-free). Internet, www.marad.dot.gov.

Saint Lawrence Seaway Development Corporation

The Saint Lawrence Seaway Development Corporation was established by the Saint Lawrence Seaway Act of May 13, 1954 (33 U.S.C. 981–990) and became an operating administration of the Department of Transportation in 1966.

The Corporation, working cooperatively with the Saint Lawrence Seaway Management Corporation (SLSMC) of Canada, is dedicated to operating and maintaining a safe, reliable, and efficient deep draft waterway between the Great Lakes and the Atlantic Ocean. It ensures the safe transit of commercial and noncommercial vessels through the two U.S. locks and the navigation channels of the Saint Lawrence Seaway System. The Corporation works jointly with SLSMC on all matters related to rules and regulations, overall operations, vessel inspections, traffic control, navigation aids, safety, operating dates, and trade development programs.

The Great Lakes/Saint Lawrence Seaway System extends from the Atlantic Ocean to the Lake Superior ports of Duluth/Superior, a distance of 2,342 miles. The Corporation's main customers are vessel owners and operators, Midwest States and Canadian provinces, Great Lakes port communities, shippers and receivers of domestic and international cargo, and the Lakes/Seaway maritime and related services industries. International and domestic commerce through the Seaway contributes to the economic prosperity of the entire Great Lakes region.

For further information, contact the Director of Congressional and Public Affairs, Saint Lawrence Seaway Development Corporation, Department of Transportation, P.O. Box 44090, Washington, DC 20026–4090. Phone, 202–366–0091. Fax, 202–366–7147. Internet, www.dot.gov/slsdc.

Research and Special Programs Administration

The Research and Special Programs Administration (RSPA) was established formally on September 23, 1977. It is responsible for hazardous materials transportation and pipeline safety, transportation emergency preparedness, safety training, and multimodal transportation research and development activities.

Hazardous Materials The Office of Hazardous Materials Safety develops and issues regulations for the safe transportation of hazardous materials by all modes, excluding bulk transportation by water. The regulations cover shipper and carrier operations, packaging and container specifications, and hazardous materials definitions. The Office is also responsible for the enforcement of regulations other than those applicable to a single mode of transportation. The Office manages a user-fee funded grant program to assist States in planning for hazardous materials emergencies and to assist States and Indian tribes with training for hazardous materials emergencies. Additionally, the Office executes a national safety program to safeguard food and certain other products from contamination during motor or rail transportation. The Office is the national focal point for coordination and control of the Department's multimodal hazardous materials regulatory program, ensuring uniformity of approach and action by all modal administrations.

For further information, contact the Office of Hazardous Materials Safety, 400 Seventh Street SW., Washington, DC 20590. Phone, 202–366–0656. Modem, 800–PLAN–FOR (752–6367).

Regional Offices—Office of Hazardous Materials Safety

Region	Address	Chief
Central—IA, IL, IN, KY, MI, MN, MO, ND, NE, OH, SD, WI	Suite 136, 2350 E. Devon Ave., Des Plaines, IL 60018	Kevin Boehne
Eastern—CT, DC, DE, MA, MD, ME, NH, NJ, NY, PA, RI, VA, VT, WV	Suite 306, 820 Bear Tavern Rd., W. Trenton, NJ 08628	Colleen Abbenhaus
Southern—AL, FL, GA, MS, NC, PR, SC, TN	Suite 520, 1701 Columbia Ave., College Park, GA 30337	John Heneghan
Southwest—AR, CO, KS, LA, NM, OK, TX	Suite 2118, 2320 LaBranch St., Houston, TX 77002	Jesse Hughes
Western—AK, AZ, CA, HI, ID, MT, NV, OR, UT, WA, WY	Suite 230, 3200 Inland Empire Blvd., Ontario, CA 91764	Anthony Smialek

Pipelines The Office of Pipeline Safety establishes and provides for compliance with standards that assure public safety and environmental protection in the transportation of gas and hazardous liquids by pipeline. The Office administers a program whereby a State agency can voluntarily assert safety regulatory jurisdiction over all or some intrastate pipeline facilities. The Federal Government is authorized to pay a State agency grant-in-aid funds of up to 50 percent of the actual cost for carrying out its pipeline safety program. The Office under the Oil Pollution Act of 1990 established regulations requiring petroleum pipeline operators to prepare and submit plans to respond to oil spills for Federal review and approval.

For further information, contact the Office of Pipeline Safety, 400 Seventh Street SW., Washington, DC 20590. Phone, 202–366–4595.

Regional Offices—Office of Pipeline Safety

Region	Address	Chief
Central—IA, IL, IN, KS, MI, MN, MO, ND, NE, OH, SD, WI	Rm. 1120, 1100 Main St., Kansas City, MO 64105	Ivan Huntoon
Eastern—CT, DC, DE, MA, MD, ME, NH, NJ, NY, PA, RI, VA, VT, WV	Rm. 2108, 400 7th St. SW., Washington, DC 20590	William Gute
Southern—AL, AR, FL, GA, KY, MS, NC, PR, SC, TN	Suite 6T15, 61 Forsyth St., Atlanta, GA 30303	Frederick Joyner
Southwest—AZ, LA, NM, OK, TX	Rm. 2116, 2320 LaBranch St., Houston, TX 77004	Rodrick M. Seeley
Western—AK, CA, CO, HI, ID, MT, NV, OR, UT, WA, WY	Suite A250, 12600 W. Colfax Ave., Lakewood, CO 80215	Edward Ondak

Research and Education The Office of Innovative Research and Education shapes and advances the Nation's transportation research and development agenda by leading departmental and national strategic planning efforts; conducting system-level assessments; facilitating national and international partnerships; stimulating university research and safety training; disseminating information on departmental, national, and international transportation R&D; and managing Department-wide strategic (intermodal/multimodal) transportation research, technology, and education.

For further information, contact the Office of Innovative Research and Education, 400 Seventh Street SW., Washington, DC 20590. Phone, 202–366–4434.

Transportation Safety The Transportation Safety Institute was established in 1971 by the Secretary of Transportation to support the Department's efforts to reduce the number and cost of transportation accidents by promoting safety and security management through education. The Institute is a primary source of transportation safety and security training and technical assistance on domestic and international levels for Department of Transportation elements, as well as other Federal, State, and local government agencies.

For further information, contact the Transportation Safety Institute, Department of Transportation, 6500 South McArthur Boulevard, Oklahoma City, OK 73125. Phone, 405–954–3153.

Emergency Transportation The Office of Emergency Transportation provides the staff to administer and execute the Secretary of Transportation's statutory and administrative responsibilities in the area of transportation civil emergency preparedness. It is the primary element of the Department engaged in the development, coordination, and review of policies, plans, and programs for attaining and maintaining a high state of Federal transportation emergency preparedness. This Office oversees the effective discharge of the Secretary's responsibilities in all emergencies affecting the national defense and in national or regional emergencies, including those caused by natural disasters and other crisis situations.

For further information, contact the Office of Emergency Transportation, 400 Seventh Street SW., Washington, DC 20590. Phone, 202–366–5270.

Volpe National Transportation Systems Center The Volpe National Transportation Systems Center (Volpe Center), as part of RSPA, provides research, analysis, and systems capability to the Department of Transportation (DOT) and other agencies requiring expertise in national transportation and logistics programs.

Integrated systems approaches are developed by Volpe Center to address Federal transportation issues of national importance. Volpe Center programs emphasize policy support and analysis, cost-effective Government procurement, environmental protection and remediation, transportation safety and security, and infrastructure modernization.

For further information, contact the Volpe National Transportation Systems Center, Kendall Square, Cambridge, MA 02142. Phone, 617–494–2224.

For further information, contact the Office of Program and Policy Support, Research and Special Programs Administration, Department of Transportation, 400 Seventh Street SW., Washington, DC 20590. Phone, 202–366–4831.

Bureau of Transportation Statistics

The Bureau of Transportation Statistics (BTS) was established by the Intermodal Surface Transportation Efficiency Act of 1991 (49 U.S.C. 111). The Bureau's mission is to establish and maintain a comprehensive information infrastructure for transportation statistics and analysis. These statistics support decisionmaking by all levels of government, transportation-related associations, private businesses, and consumers. The Bureau's programs cover all modes of transportation. The Bureau is mandated to:

—compile, analyze, and publish statistics;

—identify data needs and develop a long-term data collection program;

—make statistics accessible and understandable;

—develop guidelines to improve the credibility and effectiveness of the Department's statistics;

—develop and maintain an intermodal transportation database containing information on the volumes and patterns of movement of people and goods by relevant classifications, and a national accounting of expenditures and capital stocks;

—collect air carrier financial and traffic data (passenger and freight);

—develop and maintain online the National Transportation Library (Internet, www.ntl.bts.gov) to help improve the ability of the transportation community to share information; and

—develop and maintain geospatial databases that depict transportation networks, their use, and the social, economic, and environmental conditions that affect or are affected by the networks.

For further information, contact the Bureau of Transportation Statistics. Phone, 202–366–DATA. Fax, 202–366–3640. Internet, www.bts.gov. E-mail, infor@bts.gov.

Federal Motor Carrier Safety Administration

The Federal Motor Carrier Safety Administration was established within the Department of Transportation on January 1, 2000, pursuant to the Motor Carrier Safety Improvement Act of 1999 (49 U.S.C. 113).

Formerly a part of the Federal Highway Administration, the Federal Motor Carrier Safety Administration's primary mission is to prevent commercial motor vehicle-related fatalities and injuries. Activities of the Administration contribute to ensuring safety in motor carrier operations through strong enforcement of safety regulations, targeting high-risk carriers and commercial motor vehicle drivers; improving safety information systems and commercial motor vehicle technologies; strengthening commercial motor vehicle equipment and operating standards; and increasing safety awareness. To accomplish these activities, the Administration works with Federal, State, and local enforcement agencies, the motor carrier industry, labor safety interest groups, and others.

Activities

Commercial Driver's Licenses The Administration develops standards to test and license commercial motor vehicle drivers.

Data and Analysis The Administration collects and disseminates data on motor carrier safety and directs resources to improve motor carrier safety.

Regulatory Compliance and Enforcement The Administration operates a program to improve safety performance and remove high-risk carriers from the Nation's highways.

Research and Technology The Administration coordinates research and development to improve the safety of motor carrier operations and commercial motor vehicles and drivers.

Safety Assistance The Administration provides States with financial assistance for roadside inspections and other commercial motor vehicle safety programs. It promotes motor vehicle and motor carrier safety.

Other Activities The Administration supports the development of unified motor carrier safety requirements and procedures throughout North America. It participates in international technical organizations and committees to help share the best practices in motor carrier safety throughout North America and the rest of the world. It enforces regulations ensuring safe highway transportation of hazardous materials and has established a task force to identify and investigate those carriers of household goods which have exhibited a substantial pattern of consumer abuse.

Field Organization—Federal Motor Carrier Safety Administration Administration

Region	Address	Telephone
Eastern	Suite 4000, 10 S. Howard St., Baltimore, MD 21201–2819	410–962–0077
Southern	Suite 17T75, 61 Forsyth St., SW., Atlanta, GA 30303–3104	404–562–3600
Midwestern	Suite 210, 19900 Governors Dr., Olympia Fields, IL 60461–1021	708–283–3577
Western	Suite 2100, 201 Mission St., San Francisco, CA 94105	415–744–3088

For further information, contact the Federal Motor Carrier Safety Administration, 400 Seventh Street, SW., Washington, DC 20590. Phone, 202–366–2519. Internet, www.fmcsa.dot.gov.

Surface Transportation Board

The Surface Transportation Board was established in 1996 by the ICC Termination Act of 1995 (49 U.S.C. 10101 *et seq.*) as an independent adjudicatory body organizationally housed within the Department of Transportation with jurisdiction over certain surface transportation economic regulatory matters formerly under ICC jurisdiction. The Board consists of three members, appointed by the President with the advice and consent of the Senate for 5-year terms.

The Board adjudicates disputes and regulates interstate surface transportation through various laws pertaining to the different modes of surface transportation. The Board's general responsibilities include the oversight of firms engaged in transportation in interstate and foreign commerce to the extent that it takes place within the United States, or between or among points in the contiguous United States and points in Alaska, Hawaii, or U.S. territories or possessions. Surface transportation matters under the Board's jurisdiction in general include railroad rate and service issues, rail restructuring transactions (mergers, line sales, line construction, and line abandonments), and labor matters related thereto; certain trucking company, moving van, and noncontiguous ocean shipping company rate matters; certain intercity passenger bus company structure, financial, and operational matters; and certain pipeline matters not regulated by the Federal Energy Regulatory Commission.

In the performance of its functions, the Board is charged with promoting, where appropriate, substantive and procedural regulatory reform and providing an efficient and effective forum for the resolution of disputes. Through the granting of exemptions from regulations where warranted, the streamlining of its decisionmaking process and the regulations applicable thereto, and the consistent and fair application of legal and equitable principles, the Board seeks to provide an effective forum for efficient dispute resolution and facilitation of appropriate market-based business transactions. Through rulemakings and case disposition, it strives to develop new and better ways to analyze unique and complex problems, to reach fully justified decisions more quickly, to reduce the costs associated with regulatory oversight, and to encourage private sector negotiations and resolutions to problems, where appropriate.

For further information, contact the Office of Congressional and Public Affairs, Surface Transportation Board, Suite 840, 1925 K Street NW., Washington, DC 20423–0001. Phone, 202–565–1594.

Sources of Information

Inquiries for information on the following subjects should be directed to the specified office, Department of Transportation, Washington, DC 20590, or to the address indicated.

Civil Rights For information on equal employment opportunity, nondiscrimination in DOT employment and transportation services, or DOT's Disadvantaged Business Enterprise certification appeals program, contact the Director, Departmental Office of Civil Rights. Phone, 202–366–4648. Internet, www.dot.gov/ost/docr.

Coast Guard Career and Training Opportunities For information on the U.S. Coast Guard Academy, contact the Director of Admissions, U.S. Coast Guard Academy, New London, CT 06320. Phone, 860–444–8444. Internet, www.uscg.mil.

Information on the enlistment program and the Officer Candidate School may be obtained from the local recruiting offices or the U.S. Coast Guard Personnel Command (CGPC) Recruiting Center. Phone, 703–235–1169.

Persons interested in joining the Coast Guard Auxiliary may obtain information from the Commandant (G–OCX), U.S. Coast Guard, Washington, DC 20593. Phone, 202–267–0982.

Consumer Activities For information about air travelers' rights or for assistance in resolving consumer problems with providers of commercial air transportation services, contact the Consumer Affairs Division (phone, 202–366–2220); for consumer assistance, to report possible boat safety defects, and to obtain information on boats and associated equipment involved in safety defect (recall) campaigns, call the U.S. Coast Guard's Boating Safety Hotline. Residents of Washington, DC, call 267–0780. Other residents nationwide, call 800–368–5647 (toll-free).

To report vehicle safety problems, obtain information on motor vehicle and highway safety, or to request consumer information publications, call the National Highway Traffic Safety Administration's 24-hour auto safety hotline. Phone, 202–366–0123 (Washington, DC, area) or 800–424–9393 (toll-free except Alaska and Hawaii).

Contracts Contact the Office of the Senior Procurement Executive. Phone, 202–366–4263.

Employment The principal occupations in the Department are air traffic controller, aviation safety specialist, electronics maintenance technician, engineer (civil, aeronautical, automotive, electronic, highway, and general), administrative/management, and clerical. For further information, contact the Transportation Administrative Service Center (TASC) DOT Connection, Room PL–402, 400 Seventh Street SW., Washington, DC 20590. Phone, 202–366–9391 or 800–525–2878 (toll-free).

Environment Inquiries on environmental activities and programs should be directed to the Assistant Secretary for Transportation Policy, Office of Environment, Energy, and

Safety, Washington, DC 20590. Phone, 202–366–4366.

Films Many films on transportation subjects are available for use by educational institutions, community groups, private organizations, etc. Requests for specific films relating to a particular mode of transportation may be directed to the appropriate operating administration.

Fraud, Waste, and Abuse To report, contact the Office of Inspector General hotline, P.O. Box 23178, Washington, DC 20026–0178. Phone, 202–366–1461 or 800–424–9071 (toll-free).

Publications The Department and its operating agencies issue publications on a wide variety of subjects. Many of these publications are available from the issuing agency or for sale from the Government Printing Office and the National Technical Information Service, 5285 Port Royal Road, Springfield, VA 22151. Contact the Department or the specific agency at the addresses indicated in the text.

Reading Rooms Contact the Department of Transportation TASC Dockets, PL–401, 400 Seventh Street SW., Washington, DC 20590. Phone, 800–647–5527. Administrations and their regional offices maintain reading rooms for public use. Contact the specific administration at the address indicated in the text.

Other reading rooms include: TASC Department of Transportation Library, Room 2200, 400 Seventh Street SW., Washington, DC 20590 (phone, 202–366–0745); Department of Transportation/TASC Law Library, Room 2215, 400 Seventh Street SW., Washington, DC 20590 (phone, 202–366–0749); Department of Transportation/TASC Library, FB–10A Branch, Room 930, 800 Independence Avenue SW., Washington, DC 20591 (phone, 202–267–3115); and Department of Transportation/TASC Library, Transpoint Branch, B–726, 2100 Second Street SW., Washington, DC 20593 (phone, 202–267–2536).

Speakers The Department of Transportation and its operating administrations and regional offices make speakers available for civic, labor, and community groups. Contact the specific agency or the nearest regional office at the address indicated in the text.

Surface Transportation Board Proceedings and Public Records Requests for public assistance with pending or potential proceedings of the Board should be addressed to the Office of Public Services, Surface Transportation Board, Suite 840, 1925 K Street NW., Washington, DC 20423–0001. Phone, 202–565–1592.

Requests for access to the Board's public records should be made to the Office of the Secretary, Surface Transportation Board, Suite 700, 1925 K Street NW., Washington, DC 20423–0001. Phone, 202–565–1674.

Telephone Directory The Department of Transportation telephone directory is available for sale by the Superintendent of Documents, Government Printing Office, Washington, DC 20402.

For further information concerning the Department of Transportation, contact the Office of Public Affairs, Department of Transportation, 400 Seventh Street SW., Washington, DC 20590. Phone, 202–366–5580. Internet, www.dot.gov.

DEPARTMENT OF THE TREASURY

1500 Pennsylvania Avenue NW., Washington, DC 20220
Phone, 202–622–2000. Internet, www.treas.gov.

SECRETARY OF THE TREASURY	LAWRENCE H. SUMMERS
Chief of Staff	SHERYL SANDBERG
Executive Secretary	NEAL COMSTOCK
Deputy Secretary	STUART EISENSTAT
Inspector General	JEFFREY RUSH, JR.
Deputy Inspector General	RICHARD B. CALAHAN
General Counsel	NEAL WOLIN
Deputy General Counsel	JOAN A. DONOGHUE
Assistant Secretary (Economic Policy)	DAVID WILCOX
Deputy Assistant Secretary (Macroeconomics)	ROBERT E. CUMBY
Deputy Assistant Secretary for Policy Coordination	LYNDA DE LA VINA
Deputy Assistant Secretary (Microeconomic Analysis)	DOUGLAS ELMENDORF
Assistant Secretary (Legislative Affairs and Public Liaison)	MARTI THOMAS, *Acting*
Deputy Assistant Secretary (Appropriation and Management)	ARTHUR E. CAMERON
Deputy Assistant Secretary (Banking and Finance)	MARNE LEVINE
Deputy Assistant Secretary (International Affairs)	MARK JACKOWIAK
Deputy Assistant Secretary (Public Liaison)	LISA ANDREWS
Deputy Assistant Secretary (Tax and Budget)	MARTI THOMAS
Assistant Secretary for Management/Chief Financial Officer	LISA ROSS, *Acting*
Deputy Assistant Secretary (Administration)	SHELIA MCCANN
Deputy Assistant Secretary (Information Systems) and Chief Information Officer	JAMES J. FLYZIK
Deputy Assistant Secretary (Human Resources)	KAY FRANCES DOLAN
Deputy Assistant Secretary (Management Operations)	THEODORE CARTER
Deputy Assistant Secretary (Strategy and Finance)	LISA ROSS
Deputy Chief Financial Officer	STEVEN O. APP
Assistant Secretary (Public Affairs)	(VACANCY)
Deputy Assistant Secretary (Public Affairs)	MICHELLE A. SMITH
Assistant Secretary (Tax Policy)	JONATHAN TALISMAN, *Acting*
Deputy Assistant Secretary (International Tax Affairs)	(VACANCY)

Deputy Assistant Secretary (Tax Analysis)	LEONARD BURMAN
Deputy Assistant Secretary (Tax Policy)	JONATHAN TALISMAN
Treasurer of the United States	MARY ELLEN WITHROW
Under Secretary (Domestic Finance)	GARY GENSLER
Deputy Assistant Secretary for Development Policy	MICHAEL BARR
Director, Community Development Financial Institutions Fund	ELLEN W. LAZAR
Assistant Secretary (Financial Institutions)	GREGORY A. BAER
Deputy Assistant Secretary (Financial Institutions Policy)	GREGORY A. BAER
Assistant Secretary (Financial Markets)	LEE SACHS
Deputy Assistant Secretary (Federal Finance)	MICHAEL A. PAULUS
Deputy Assistant Secretary (Government Financial Policy)	HARRY HAIGOOD
Fiscal Assistant Secretary	DONALD V. HAMMOND
Deputy Assistant Secretary (Accounting Operations)	ROBERT N. REID
Deputy Assistant Secretary (Fiscal Operations and Policy)	DAVID LEBRYK
Under Secretary (Enforcement)	JAMES E. JOHNSON
Assistant Secretary (Enforcement)	ELISABETH A. BRESEE
Deputy Assistant Secretary (Enforcement Policy)	DAVID MEDINA
Deputy Assistant Secretary (Law Enforcement)	KAREN WEHNER
Deputy Assistant Secretary (Regulatory, Tariff, and Trade Enforcement)	JOHN P. SIMPSON
Director, Office of Financial Crimes Enforcement Network (FinCEN)	JAMES F. SLOAN
Under Secretary (International Affairs)	TIMOTHY F. GEITHNER
Assistant Secretary (International Affairs)	EDWIN TRUMAN
Deputy Assistant Secretary for International Monetary and Financial Policy	CAROLINE M. ATKINSON
Deputy Assistant Secretary for Asia, the Americas, and Africa	STEVEN RADELET
Deputy Assistant Secretary for International Development, Debt, and Environmental Policy	WILLIAM SCHUERCH
Deputy Assistant Secretary for Eurasia and Middle East	MARK MEDISH
Deputy Assistant Secretary for Technical Assistance Policy	JAMES H. FALL III
Deputy Assistant Secretary for Trade and Investment Policy	MARGRETHE LUNDSAGER

BUREAU OF ALCOHOL, TOBACCO, AND FIREARMS

650 Massachusetts Avenue NW., Washington, DC 20226
Phone, 202–927–8500. Fax, 202–927–8868. Internet, www.atf.treas.gov.

Director	BRADLEY A. BUCKLES
Deputy Director	(VACANCY)
Assistant Director (Alcohol and Tobacco)	ARTHUR J. LIBERTUCCI

Assistant Director (Field Operations)	Andy L. Vita
Assistant Director (Firearms, Explosives, and Arson)	John Malone
Assistant Director (Inspection)	Richard J. Hankinson
Assistant Director (Liaison and Public Information)	David Benton
Assistant Director (Management) and Chief Financial Officer	William T. Earle
Assistant Director (Science and Information Technology)/Chief Information Officer	Patrick R. Schambach
Assistant Director (Training and Professional Development)	Gale D. Rossides
Chief Counsel	John Manfreda
Chief, Strategic Planning Office	Wayne Miller
Executive Assistant (Equal Opportunity)	Toby Bishop
Executive Assistant (Legislative Affairs)	Lewis Raden
Ombudsman	Stanley Zimmerman

OFFICE OF THE COMPTROLLER OF THE CURRENCY

250 E Street SW., Washington, DC 20219
Phone, 202–874–5000

Comptroller	John D. Hawke, Jr.
Chief of Staff	Mark A. Nishan
Chief Information Officer	Steven M. Yohai
Deputy to the FDIC Director (Comptroller of the Currency)	Thomas E. Zemke
Ombudsman	Samuel P. Golden
First Senior Deputy Comptroller and Chief Counsel	Julie L. Williams
Senior Deputy Comptroller for Administration and Chief Financial Officer	Edward J. Hanley
Senior Deputy Comptroller for Bank Supervision Operations	Leann G. Britton
Senior Deputy Comptroller for Bank Supervision Policy	Emory Wayne Rushton
Senior Deputy Comptroller for Economic and Policy Analysis	Jonathan L. Fiechter
Senior Deputy Comptroller for International Affairs	Jonathan L. Fiechter
Senior Deputy Comptroller for Public Affairs	(vacancy)

UNITED STATES CUSTOMS SERVICE

1300 Pennsylvania Avenue NW., Washington, DC 20229
Phone, 202–927–6724

Commissioner of Customs	Raymond Kelly
Deputy Commissioner	Charles Winwood, *Acting*
Chief of Staff	David Cohen
Chief Counsel	Alfonso Robles
Assistant Commissioner (Congressional Affairs)	Seth Statler
Assistant Commissioner (Field Operations)	Bob McNamara, *Acting*

Assistant Commissioner (Finance)	WAYNE HAMILTON
Assistant Commissioner (Human Resources Management)	BOB SMITH, *Acting*
Assistant Commissioner (Information and Technology)	WOODY HALL
Assistant Commissioner (Internal Affairs)	WILLIAM KEEFER
Assistant Commissioner (International Affairs)	DOUGLAS BROWNING
Assistant Commissioner (Investigations)	BONNI TISCHLER
Assistant Commissioner (Regulations and Rulings)	STUART SEIDEL
Assistant Commissioner (Strategic Trade)	ROBERT TROTTER
Assistant Commissioner (Training and Development)	MARJORIE BUDD
Ombudsman	JOSEPH REES

BUREAU OF ENGRAVING AND PRINTING

Fourteenth and C Streets SW., Washington, DC 20228
Phone, 202–874–3019

Director	THOMAS A. FERGUSON
Deputy Director	THOMAS C. HARRIS
Associate Director (Chief Financial Officer)	GREGORY D. CARPER
Associate Director (Chief Operating Officer)	WILLIAM W. WILLS
Associate Director (Management)	JOEL C. TAUB
Associate Director (Technology)	CARLA F. KIDWELL
Chief Counsel	CARROL H. KINSEY

FEDERAL LAW ENFORCEMENT TRAINING CENTER

Glynco, GA 31524. Phone, 912–267–2224. Fax, 912–267–2495
Washington, DC. Phone, 202–927–8940. Fax, 202–927–8782
Artesia, NM, Operations. Phone, 505–748–8000. Fax, 505–748–8100

Director	W. RALPH BASHAM
Senior Associate Director (Washington Operations)	JOHN C. DOOHER
Assistant Director (Artesia, NM, Operations)	G. RAY HAVENS
Assistant Director (Federal Training)	KENNETH KEENE
Assistant Director (Office of State, Local, and International Training)	HOBART HENSON
Assistant Director (Training Support)	KENNETH HALL
Associate Director (Planning and Resources Directorate)	CONNIE PATRICK
Associate Director (Training Directorate)	PAUL HACKENBERRY

FINANCIAL MANAGEMENT SERVICE

401 Fourteenth Street SW., Washington, DC 20227
Phone, 202–874–6740. Internet, www.fms.treas.gov.

Commissioner	RICHARD L. GREGG
Deputy Commissioner	KENNETH R. PAPAJ
Director, Legislative and Public Affairs	ALVINA M. MCHALE
Director, Office of Quality and Diversity Management	SONDRA HUTCHINSON
Chief Counsel	DEBRA N. DIENER

Assistant Commissioner, Agency Services	KAROL A. FORSBERG
Assistant Commissioner, Debt Management Services	NANCY C. FLEETWOOD
Assistant Commissioner, Federal Finance	BETTSY H. LANE
Assistant Commissioner, Financial Operations	JUDITH R. TILLMAN
Assistant Commissioner, Governmentwide Accounting	LARRY D. STOUT
Assistant Commissioner, Information Resources	CONSTANCE E. CRAIG
Assistant Commissioner, Management (CFO)	SCOTT JOHNSON
Assistant Commissioner, Regional Operations	JOHN D. NEWELL

INTERNAL REVENUE SERVICE

1111 Constitution Avenue NW., Washington, DC 20224
Phone, 202–622–5000

Commissioner of Internal Revenue	CHARLES O. ROSSOTTI
Chief of Staff	JO ANN N. BLANK
Deputy Commissioner, Operations	BOB WENZEL
Deputy Commissioner, Modernization	JOHN D. LEFAVER
Executive Officer for Service Center Operations	JIMMY L. SMITH
National Taxpayer Advocate	W. VAL OVESON
Assistant Commissioner (Collection)	CHARLES W. PETERSON
Assistant Commissioner (Criminal Investigation)	TED F. BROWN
Assistant Commissioner (Customer Service)	MARILYN SOULSBURG
Assistant Commissioner (Electronic Tax Administration)	ROBERT E. BARR
Assistant Commissioner (Employee Plans/ Exempt Organizations)	STEVEN T. MILLER, *Acting*
Assistant Commissioner (Examination)	THOMAS W. WILSON
Assistant Commissioner (Forms and Submission Processing)	BRIEN T. DOWNING
Assistant Commissioner (Information Systems Field Operations)	DAVE GAUGLER
Assistant Commissioner (International)	JOHN T. LYONS
Assistant Commissioner (Procurement)	GREG ROTHWELL
Assistant Commissioner (Product Assurance)	RENEE SHAW
Assistant Commissioner (Program Management and Engineering Office)	AL MAZEI
Assistant Commissioner (Research and Statistics of Income)	WAYNE THOMAS
Assistant Commissioner (Service Center Operations)	TOM DEGA
Assistant Commissioner (Support Services)	JOHN E. BINNION II
Assistant Commissioner (Systems Development)	MARTIN BAER
Chief, Communications and Liaison	DAVID R. WILLIAMS
Chief, Headquarters Operations	BARRY PEINER
Chief, Management and Finance	DAVID MADER
Chief, Office of Executive Support	MARY O'BRIEN
Chief, Office of Management Operations	ED MARTIN
Chief Counsel	STUART BROWN
Chief Financial Officer	DONNA CUNNINGHAME
Chief Human Resources Officer	RONALD SANDERS

Chief Information Officer	Paul J. Cosgrave
Chief Operations Officer	John M. Dalrymple
National Director of Appeals	Daniel L. Black

UNITED STATES MINT

801 Ninth Street NW., Washington, DC 20220
Phone, 202–354–7200

Director	Jay Johnson
Deputy Director	John P. Mitchell
Chief Counsel	Kenneth B. Gubin
Associate Director, Chief Financial Officer	Jay Weinstein
Associate Director, Chief Information Officer	Jackie Fletcher
Associate Director, Circulating Strategic Business Unit	Bradford Cooper
Associate Director, Numismatic Strategic Business Unit	David Pickens
Associate Director, Protection Strategic Business Unit	William F. Daddio

BUREAU OF THE PUBLIC DEBT

999 E Street NW., Washington, DC 20239–0001
Phone, 202–219–3300. Internet, www.publicdebt.treas.gov.

Commissioner	Van Zeck
Deputy Commissioner	Anne Meister
Chief Counsel	Walter T. Eccard
Assistant Commissioner (Financing)	Carl M. Locken, Jr.
Assistant Commissioner (Information Technology)	Cynthia Z. Springer
Assistant Commissioner (Public Debt Accounting)	Debra Hines
Assistant Commissioner (Savings Bond Operations)	Arthur A. Klass
Assistant Commissioner (Securities and Accounting Services)	Jane O'Brien
Executive Director (Administration Resource Center)	Thomas W. Harrison
Executive Director (Government Securities Regulation Staff)	Lori Santamorena
Executive Director (Savings Bonds Marketing Office)	Dino DeConcini

UNITED STATES SECRET SERVICE

1800 G Street NW., Washington, DC 20373
Phone, 202–435–5708

Director	Brian L. Stafford
Deputy Director	Kevin T. Foley
Assistant Director (Administration)	Dana A. Brown
Assistant Director (Government Liaison and Public Affairs)	H. Terrence Samway
Assistant Director (Inspection)	Gordon S. Heddell
Assistant Director (Investigations)	James E. Bauer

Assistant Director (Protective Operations)	C. Danny Spriggs
Assistant Director (Protective Research)	Barbara S. Riggs
Assistant Director (Training)	Larry L. Cockell
Chief Counsel	John J. Kelleher

OFFICE OF THRIFT SUPERVISION

1700 G Street NW., Washington, DC 20552
Phone, 202–906–6000. Internet, www.ots.treas.gov.

Director	Ellen S. Seidman
Deputy Director	Richard M. Riccobono
Chief Counsel	Carolyn J. Buck
Chief Information Officer and Director, Office of Information Systems	Frank R. Digialleonardo
Executive Director, External Affairs	Darina McKelvie
Executive Director, Research and Analysis	(vacancy)
Managing Director, Compliance Policy and Specialty Examinations	Timothy R. Burniston
Managing Director, Supervision	Scott M. Albinson
Associate Director for FDIC	Walter B. Mason
Director, Congressional Affairs	Kevin Petrasic
Director, Press Relations	William E. Fulwider
Director, Office of Equality and Workplace Principles	Ruby Mae Thomas

---

The Department of the Treasury performs four basic functions: formulating and recommending economic, financial, tax, and fiscal policies; serving as financial agent for the U.S. Government; enforcing the law; and manufacturing coins and currency.

The Treasury Department was created by act of September 2, 1789 (31 U.S.C. 301 and 301 note). Many subsequent acts have figured in the development of the Department, delegating new duties to its charge and establishing the numerous bureaus and divisions that now comprise the Treasury.

Secretary As a major policy adviser to the President, the Secretary has primary responsibility for formulating and recommending domestic and international financial, economic, and tax policy; participating in the formulation of broad fiscal policies that have general significance for the economy; and managing the public debt. The Secretary also oversees the activities of the Department in carrying out its major law enforcement responsibility; in serving as the financial agent for the U.S. Government; and in manufacturing coins, currency, and other products for customer agencies. The Secretary also serves as the Government's chief financial officer.

Activities

Economic Policy The Office of the Assistant Secretary for Economic Policy assists policymakers in the determination of economic policies. The Office:

—reviews and analyzes domestic and international economic issues and developments in the financial markets;

—assists in the development of official economic projections; and

—works closely with Federal Government agencies to develop economic forecasts underlying the yearly budget process.

Enforcement The Office of the Assistant Secretary for Enforcement coordinates Treasury law enforcement matters, including the formulation of policies for Treasury enforcement activities, and cooperates on law enforcement matters with other Federal

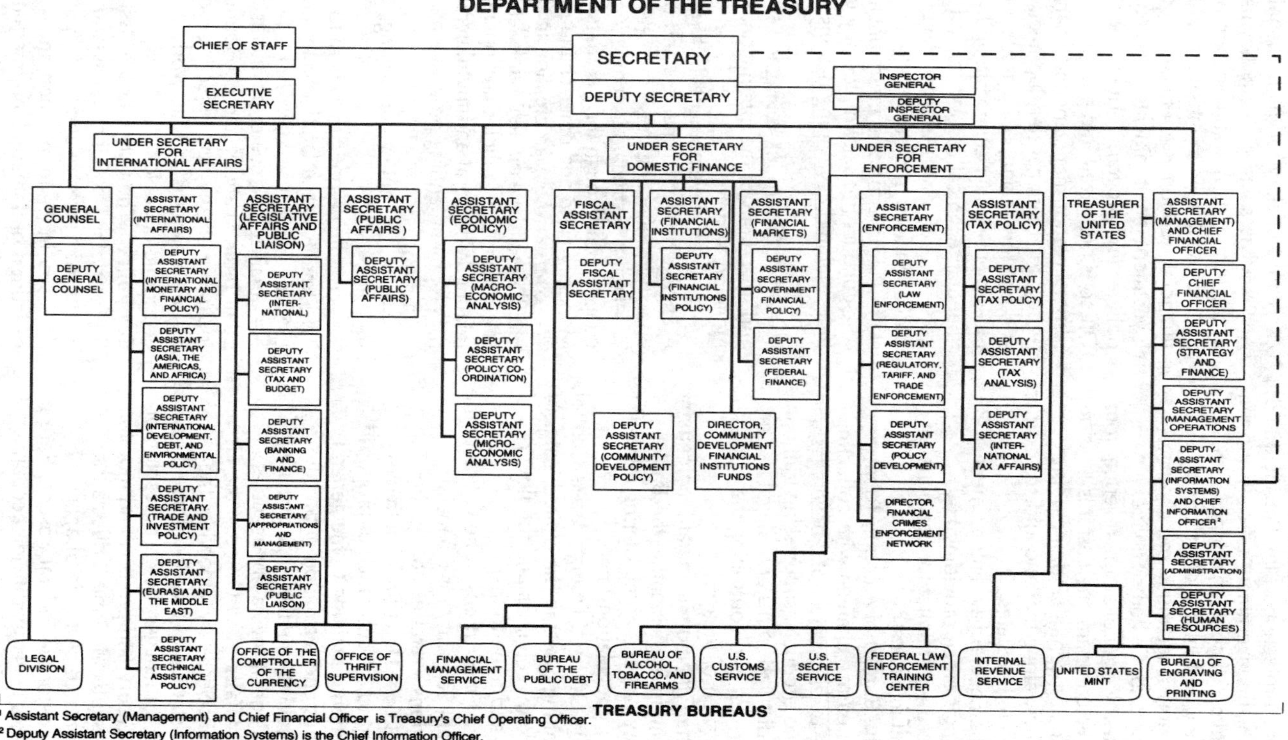

[1] Assistant Secretary (Management) and Chief Financial Officer is Treasury's Chief Operating Officer.
[2] Deputy Assistant Secretary (Information Systems) is the Chief Information Officer.

agencies. It oversees the following branches of the Department:

—the U.S. Secret Service, entrusted with the protection of the President and other high Government officials and the prevention of counterfeiting of U.S. currency and theft and forgery of Government securities and checks;

—the U.S. Customs Service, responsible for collecting revenue from imports; enforcing the customs laws; and interdicting contraband, including narcotics, along the land and sea borders of the United States;

—the Federal Law Enforcement Training Center, providing law enforcement training for personnel of Federal agencies;

—the Bureau of Alcohol, Tobacco, and Firearms, charged with collecting excise taxes on alcoholic beverages and tobacco products; suppressing traffic in illicit distilled spirits and illegal use of explosives; and controlling the sale and registration of firearms;

—the Office of Financial Enforcement, assisting in implementing the Bank Secrecy Act and administering related Treasury regulations; and

—the Office of Foreign Assets Control, controlling assets in the United States of "blocked" countries and the flow of funds and trade to them;

Financial Institutions The Office of the Assistant Secretary for Financial Institutions exercises policy direction and control over Department activities relating to the substance of proposed legislation pertaining to the general activities and regulation of private financial intermediaries and relating to other Federal regulatory agencies.

Fiscal Affairs The Office of the Fiscal Assistant Secretary supervises the administration of the Government's fiscal affairs. It manages the cash position of the Treasury and projects and monitors "debt subject-to-limit;" directs the performance of the fiscal agency functions of the Federal Reserve Banks; conducts governmentwide accounting and cash management activities; exercises supervision over depositories of the United States; and provides management overview of investment practices for Government trust and other accounts.

International Affairs The Office of the Assistant Secretary for International Affairs advises and assists policymakers in the formulation and execution of policies dealing with international financial, economic, monetary, trade, investment, environmental, and energy policies and programs. The work of the Office is organized into groups responsible for monetary and financial policy; international development, debt, and environmental policy; trade and investment policy; economic and financial technical assistance; and geographical areas (Asia, the Americas, Africa, Eurasia, and the Middle East). The staff offices performing these functions:

—conduct financial diplomacy with industrial and developing nations and regions;

—work toward improving the structure and operations of the international monetary system;

—monitor developments in foreign exchange and other markets and official operations affecting those markets;

—facilitate structural monetary cooperation through the International Monetary Fund and other channels;

—oversee U.S. participation in the multilateral development banks and coordinate U.S. policies and operations relating to bilateral and multilateral development lending programs and institutions;

—formulate policy concerning financing of trade;

—coordinate policies toward foreign investments in the United States and U.S. investments abroad; and

—analyze balance of payments and other basic financial and economic data, including energy data, affecting world payment patterns and the world economic outlook.

Tax Policy The Office of the Assistant Secretary for Tax Policy advises and assists the Secretary and the Deputy Secretary in the formulation and execution of domestic and international tax policies and programs. These functions include:

—analysis of proposed tax legislation and tax programs;

—projections of economic trends affecting tax bases;

—studies of effects of alternative tax measures;

—preparation of official estimates of Government receipts for the President's annual budget messages;

—legal advice and analysis on domestic and international tax matters;

—assistance in the development and review of tax legislation and domestic and international tax regulations and rulings; and

—participation in international tax treaty negotiations and in maintenance of relations with international organizations on tax matters.

Treasurer of the United States The Office of the Treasurer of the United States was established on September 6, 1777. The Treasurer was originally charged with the receipt and custody of Government funds, but many of these functions have been assumed by different bureaus of the Department of the Treasury. In 1981, the Treasurer was assigned responsibility for oversight of the Bureau of Engraving and Printing and the United States Mint. The Treasurer reports to the Secretary through the Assistant Secretary for Management/Chief Financial Officer.

For further information concerning the Departmental Offices, contact the Public Affairs Office, Department of the Treasury, 1500 Pennsylvania Avenue NW., Washington, DC 20220. Phone, 202–622–2960.

Bureau of Alcohol, Tobacco, and Firearms

The mission of the Bureau of Alcohol, Tobacco, and Firearms (ATF) is to reduce violent crime, collect revenue, and protect the public through criminal law enforcement, regulatory enforcement, and tax collection.

The Bureau was established by Department of Treasury Order No. 221, effective July 1, 1972, which transferred the functions, powers, and duties arising under laws relating to alcohol, tobacco, firearms, and explosives from the Internal Revenue Service to the Bureau. Responsibilities regarding enforcement of interstate trafficking laws in contraband cigarettes, combating commercial arson, and enforcement of laws pertaining to the transfer of handguns have also been assigned to ATF.

The Bureau is responsible for enforcing and administering firearms and explosives laws, as well as those covering the production, taxation, and distribution of alcohol and tobacco products. The Bureau's objectives are to maximize compliance with and investigate violations of these laws.

In collaborative partnerships with government agencies, industry, academia, and others, ATF works to reduce crime and violence by safeguarding the public from arson and explosives incidents, denying criminals access to firearms, removing violent offenders from communities, and preventing violence through community outreach; and to maintain a sound revenue management and regulatory system which reduces the burden on industry, collects revenues which are rightfully due, and uses electronic commerce. ATF also works to protect the public and prevent consumer deception by assuring the integrity of the products, people, and companies in the marketplace; ensuring compliance with laws and regulations through education, inspection, and investigations; and informing the public about ATF regulations and product safety using various media.

Field Operations Offices—Office of Enforcement

Field Division	Address	Special Agent in Charge	Telephone
Atlanta, GA	2600 Century Pkwy., 30345–3104	John C. Killorin	404–679–5170

186-873 D-00--12

Field Operations Offices—Office of Enforcement—Continued

Field Division	Address	Special Agent in Charge	Telephone
Baltimore, MD	6th Fl., 22 S. Howard St., 21201	Larry D. Stewart	410–962–0897
Boston, MA	Rm. 253, 10 Causeway St., 02222–1047	Steven J. Pirotte	617–565–7042
Brentwood, TN	Suite 215, 215 Centerview Dr., 37027	James M. Cavanaugh	615–781–5364
Charlotte, NC	Suite 400, 4530 Park Rd., 28209	Richard C. Fox	704–344–6125
Chicago, IL	Suite 350 S., 300 S. Riverdale Plz., 60606	Kathleen L. Kiernan	312–353–6935
Columbus, OH	Suite 200, 37 W. Broad St., 43215	Darrell C. Dyer	614–469–5303
Dallas, TX	Suite 2550, 1200 Main Twr. Bldg., 75250	Jimmy Wooten	214–767–2250
Detroit, MI	Suite 300, 1155 Brewery Park Blvd., 48207–2602	Michael W. Morrissey	313–393–6000
Houston, TX	Suite 210, 15355 Vantage Pkwy. W., 77032	Robert H. Valadez, Jr.	281–449–2073
Kansas City, MO	Suite 200, 2600 Grand Ave., 64108	James R. Switzer	816–421–3440
Los Angeles, CA	Suite 800, 350 S. Figueroa St., 90071	Donald R. Kincaid	213–894–4812
Louisville, KY	Suite 322, 600 Dr. Martin Luther King Jr. Pl., 40202	Karl Stankovic	502–582–5211
Metairie, LA	Suite 1050, 111 Veterans Blvd., 70005	Jerry W. Tate	504–589–2048
Miami, FL	Suite 300, 5225 NW. 87th Ave., 33178	Patricia L. Galupo	305–597–4800
New York, NY	Suite 600, 6 World Trade Ctr., 10048–0206	Edgar A. Domenech	212–466–5145
Philadelphia, PA	Rm. 607, 2d & Chestnut Sts., 19106	Lawrence L. Duchnowski	215–597–7266
Phoenix, AZ	Suite 1010, 3003 N. Central Ave., 85012	Christopher P. Sadowski	602–776–5400
San Francisco, CA	11th Fl., 221 Main St.,94105	(Vacancy)	415–744–7001
Seattle, WA	Rm. 806, 915 2d Ave., 98174	John C. Ross	206–220–6440
St. Paul, MN	1870 World Trade Ctr., 30 E. 7th St., 55101	Richard E. Chase	651–290–3092
Tampa, FL	Suite 700, 501 E. Polk St., 33602	Ralph Ostrowski	813–228–2021
Washington, DC	Suite 620, 607 14th St. NW., 20005	Patrick D. Hynes	202–927–8810

For further information, contact the Office of Liaison and Public Information, Bureau of Alcohol, Tobacco, and Firearms. Phone, 202–927–8500. Internet, www.atf.treas.gov.

Office of the Comptroller of the Currency

[For the Office of the Comptroller of the Currency statement of organization, see the *Code of Federal Regulations,* Title 12, Part 4]

The Office of the Comptroller of the Currency was created February 25, 1863 (12 Stat. 665), as a bureau of the Department of the Treasury. Its primary mission is to regulate national banks. The Office is headed by the Comptroller, who is appointed for a 5-year term by the President with the advice and consent of the Senate.

The Office regulates national banks by its power to examine banks; approve or deny applications for new bank charters, branches, or mergers; take enforcement action—such as bank closures—against banks that are not in compliance with laws and regulations; and issue rules, regulations, and interpretations on banking practices.

The Office supervises approximately 2,600 national banks, including their trust activities and overseas operations. Each bank is examined annually through a nationwide staff of approximately 1,900 bank examiners supervised in 6 district offices. The Office is independently funded through assessments of the assets of national banks.

For further information, contact the Communications Division, Office of the Comptroller of the Currency, Department of the Treasury, 250 E Street SW., Washington, DC 20219. Phone, 202–874–4700.

United States Customs Service

The fifth act of the first Congress, passed on July 31, 1789 (1 Stat. 29), established customs districts and authorized customs officers to collect duties on goods, wares, and merchandise imposed by the second act of the first Congress, dated July 4, 1789 (1 Stat. 24). The Bureau of Customs was established as a separate agency under the Treasury Department on March 3, 1927 (19 U.S.C. 2071) and was redesignated the U.S. Customs Service by Treasury Department Order 165–23 of April 4, 1973.

The Customs Service enforces customs and related laws and collects the revenue from imports. Some of the responsibilities the Customs Service is specifically charged with are:

—interdicting and seizing contraband, including narcotics and illegal drugs;

—assessing and collecting customs duties, excise taxes, fees, and penalties due on imported merchandise;

—processing persons, carriers, cargo, and mail into and out of the United States;

—administering certain navigation laws;

—detecting and apprehending persons engaged in fraudulent practices designed to circumvent customs and related laws; copyright, patent, and trademark provisions; quotas; and marking requirements for imported merchandise;

—enforces export control laws and intercepts illegal high-technology and weapons exports;

—enforces reporting requirements of the Bank Secrecy Act; and

—collects international trade statistics.

Also, the Customs Service enforces a wide range of requirements to protect the public, such as auto safety and emission control standards; radiation and radioactive material standards; counterfeit monetary instruments; flammable fabric restrictions; animal and plant quarantine requirements; and food, drug, and hazardous substance prohibitions.

Customs Management Centers—U.S. Customs Service

District Offices	Address	Director	Telephone
Mid-America	Suite 900, 610 S. Canal St., Chicago, IL 60607–4523.	Garnet Fee	312–983–9122
East Texas	Suite 1200, 2323 S. Shepard St., Houston, TX 77019.	John Babb	713–313–2841
Southern California	Suite 1200, 610 W. Ash St., San Diego, CA 92101.	Rudy Camacho	619–557–5455
North Pacific	Rm. 200, 8337 NE. Alderwood Rd., Portland, OR 97220.	Lois Fields	503–326–7625
Mid-Pacific	Rm. 1600, 33 New Montgomery Twr., San Francisco, CA 94105.	Paul Andrews	415–744–1530
Puerto Rico & Virgin Islands	Rm. D200, 1 La Puntilla St., San Juan, PR 00901.	Geneva Alexander	787–729–6950
West Great Lakes	Rm. 300, 613 Abbott St., Detroit, MI 48226	Kevin Weeks	313–226–2955
South Texas	P.O. Box 3130, Laredo, TX 78044–3130	Maria Reba	956–718–4161
Arizona	Suite 310, 4740 N. Oracle Rd., Tucson, AZ 85705.	Donna De La Torre	520–670–5900
South Atlantic	Suite 270, 1691 Phoenix Blvd., College Park, GA 30349.	Mamie Pollock	770–994–4101
Northwest Great Plains	Rm. 2200, 1000 2d Ave., Seattle, WA 98104–1049.	Thomas Hardy	206–553–8761
West Texas	Suite 104, 9400 Viscount Blvd., El Paso, TX 79925.	Gurdit Dhillon	915–633–7300
North Florida	Suite 301, 1624 E. 7th Avenue, Tampa, FL 33605.	Jeffrey Baldwin	813–228–2381
Mid-Atlantic	Suite 208, 103 S. Gay St., Baltimore, MD 21202.	Steven Knox	410–962–6200
New York	Rm. 716, 6 World Trade Ctr., New York, NY 10048.	John J. Martuge	212–637–7900
Gulf	Rm. 327, 423 Canal St., New Orleans, LA 70130–2341.	Patricia Duffy	504–670–2404
North Atlantic	Rm. 801, 10 Causeway St., Boston, MA 02222–1056.	Philip Spayd	617–565–6210
East Great Lakes	4455 Genessa St., Buffalo, NY 14225	Michael Dambrosio	716–626–0400
South Florida	Suite 980, 909 SE. 1st Ave., Miami, FL 33131	Thomas S. Winkowski, *Acting*.	305–810–5120
South Pacific	Rm. 705, 1 World Trade Ctr., Long Beach, CA 90831.	Audrey Adams	562–980–3100

For further information, contact the U.S. Customs Service, Department of the Treasury, 1300 Pennsylvania Avenue NW., Washington, DC 20229. Phone, 202–927–6724. Internet, www.customs.gov.

Bureau of Engraving and Printing

The Bureau of Engraving and Printing operates on basic authorities conferred by act of July 11, 1862 (31 U.S.C. 303) and additional authorities contained in past appropriations made to the Bureau that are still in force. The Bureau is headed by a Director, who is appointed by the Secretary of the Treasury and reports to the Treasurer of the United States.

The Bureau designs, prints, and finishes all of the Nation's paper currency (Federal Reserve notes), U.S. postage stamps, Treasury securities, certificates, and other security products, including White House invitations and military identification cards. It also is responsible for advising and assisting Federal agencies in the design and production of other Government documents that, because of their innate value or for other reasons, require security or counterfeit-deterrence characteristics.

The Bureau operates two facilities: the headquarters in Washington, DC, and a second currency manufacturing plant in Fort Worth, TX.

For further information, contact the Office of External Relations, Bureau of Engraving and Printing, Department of the Treasury, Room 533M, Fourteenth and C Streets SW., Washington, DC 20228. Phone, 202–874–3019.

Federal Law Enforcement Training Center

The Federal Law Enforcement Training Center was established by Treasury Department Order No. 217, effective March 2, 1970. The Center is headed by a Director, who is appointed by the Secretary of the Treasury. It conducts operations at its training facility located at Glynco, GA. The Center also maintains a Washington, DC, office at 650 Massachusetts Avenue NW., Washington, DC 20226 (phone, 202–927–8940). In addition, it has a satellite operation located at Artesia, NM 88210 (phone, 505–748–8000).

The Center is an interagency training facility serving over 70 Federal law enforcement organizations. The major training effort is in the area of basic programs to teach common areas of law enforcement skills to police and investigative personnel. The Center also conducts advanced programs in areas of common need, such as white-collar crime, the use of microcomputers as an investigative tool, advanced law enforcement photography, continuing legal education, marine law enforcement, and several instructor training courses. In addition to the basic and common advanced programs, the Center provides the facilities and support services for participating organizations to conduct advanced training for their own law enforcement personnel. The Center offers selective, highly specialized training programs to State and local officers as well as international law enforcement officers as an aid in deterring crime and furthering U.S. interests overseas. These programs include a variety of areas such as fraud and financial investigations, small-town and rural law enforcement, advanced medical fraud training, international banking/money laundering, and archeological resources protection training.

For further information, contact the Public Affairs Office, Federal Law Enforcement Training Center, Department of the Treasury, Glynco, GA 31524. Phone, 912–267–2447. Internet, www.ustreas.gov/fletc.

Financial Management Service

The mission of the Financial Management Service (FMS) is to develop and manage Federal financial systems to move the Government's cash flows efficiently, effectively, and securely. It supports other Federal agencies by serving as the Government's primary disbursing agent; collections agent; accountant and reporter of financial information; and collector of delinquent Federal debt.

Accounting and Reporting The Service maintains a central system that accounts for the monetary assets and liabilities of the Treasury and tracks Government collection and payment operations. Periodic reports are prepared to show budget results, the Government's overall financial status, and other financial operations.

Collections FMS is responsible for administering the world's largest collections system, gathering more than $2 trillion annually. The Service is working with all Federal agencies to improve the availability of collected funds and the reporting of collection information to Treasury. FMS also retains the services of private debt collection agencies and utilizes standard private sector techniques to collect delinquent debts on behalf of agencies.

Payments The Service issues nearly 880 non-Defense payments to a wide variety of recipients, pays all Treasury checks and reconciles them against the accounts of Government disbursing officers, receives and examines claims for checks that are cashed under forged endorsements or that are lost, stolen, or destroyed, and issues new checks on approved claims. The Service uses two electronic funds-transfer methods: automated clearinghouses and wire transfers. Additionally, FMS is testing new payment and collection technologies through its Electronic Money Program, including Internet and card technology, digital signatures, and biometrics.

Working Capital Management The Service is responsible for programs to improve cash management, credit management, debt collection, and financial management systems Governmentwide. To this end, it issues guidelines and regulations and assists other agencies in managing activities and programs. The Service is currently assisting agencies to develop programs to take advantage of new automation technology.

Regional Financial Centers—Financial Management Service

Center/Address	Director
Austin, TX (P.O. Box 149058, 78741)	Gordon Hickam
Birmingham, AL (P.O. Box 2451, 35201)	Andy Wilson
Chicago, IL (P.O. Box 8670, 60680)	Peter Bishop, *Acting*
Kansas City, MO (P.O. Box 12599, 64116)	Jack Adams
Philadelphia, PA (P.O. Box 8676, 19101)	Michael Colarusso
San Francisco, CA (P.O. Box 193858, 94119)	Philip Belisle

For further information, contact the Office of Legislative and Public Affairs, Financial Management Service, Department of the Treasury, Room 555, 401 Fourteenth Street SW., Washington, DC 20227. Phone, 202–874–6740. Internet, www.fms.treas.gov.

Internal Revenue Service

The Office of the Commissioner of Internal Revenue was established by act of July 1, 1862 (26 U.S.C. 7802). The Internal Revenue Service (IRS) is responsible for administering and enforcing the internal revenue laws and related statutes, except those relating to alcohol, tobacco, firearms, and explosives. Its mission is to collect the proper amount of tax revenue at the least cost to the public, and in a manner that warrants the highest degree of public confidence in the Service's integrity, efficiency, and fairness. To achieve that purpose, the Service:

—strives to achieve the highest possible degree of voluntary compliance in accordance with the tax laws and regulations;

—advises the public of their rights and responsibilities;

—determines the extent of compliance and the causes of noncompliance;

—properly administers and enforces the tax laws; and

—continually searches for and implements new, more efficient ways of accomplishing its mission.

Basic activities include:

—ensuring satisfactory resolution of taxpayer complaints, providing taxpayer service and education;

—determining, assessing, and collecting internal revenue taxes;

—determining pension plan qualifications and exempt organization status; and

—preparing and issuing rulings and regulations to supplement the provisions of the Internal Revenue Code.

The source of most revenues collected is the individual income tax and the social insurance and retirement taxes, with other major sources being the corporation income, excise, estate, and gift taxes. Congress first received authority to levy taxes on the income of individuals and corporations in 1913, pursuant to the 16th amendment of the Constitution.

Regional Offices—Internal Revenue Service

Region	Address	Commissioner
Mid-States—AR, IA, IL, KS, MN, MO, NE, ND, OK, SD, TX, WI	4050 Alpha Rd., Dallas, TX 75244–4203	Ladd Ellis, Jr.
Northeast—CT, MA, ME, MI, NH, NJ, NY, OH, PA, RI, VT	90 Church St., New York, NY 10007	Herma Hightower
Southeast—AL, DE, FL, GA, IN, KY, LA, MD, MS, NC, SC, TN, VA, WV	401 W. Peachtree St. NE., Atlanta, GA 30365	Robert T. Johnson
Western—AK, AZ, CA, CO, HI, ID, MT, NV, NM, OR, UT, WA, WY	1650 Mission St., San Francisco, CA 94103	Marilyn W. Day

District Offices—Internal Revenue Service

District	Address	Director
Alabama	600 S. Maestri Pl., New Orleans, LA 70130	Richard F. Moran
Alaska	915 2d Ave., Seattle, WA 98174	J. Paul Beene
Arizona	210 E. Earll Dr., Phoenix, 85012	James J. Walsh
Arkansas	55 N. Robinson St., Oklahoma City, OK 73102	Richard Auby
California:		
Laguna Niguel	24000 Avila Rd., 92677	Marilyn A. Soulsburg
Los Angeles	300 N. Los Angeles St., 90012	Steven A. Jensen
Sacramento/San Francisco	Suite 1600 S., 1301 Clay St., Oakland, 94612	Robert D. AhNee
San Jose	55 S. Market St., 95103	Billy J. Brown
Colorado	600 17th St., Denver, 80202–2490	Jack B. Cheskaty
Connecticut	135 High St., Hartford, 06103	Deborah Nolan
Delaware	31 Hopkins Plz., Baltimore, MD 21201	Paul M. Harrington
District of Columbia	31 Hopkins Plz., Baltimore, MD 21201	Paul M. Harrington
Florida:		
Fort Lauderdale	1 N. University Dr., Bldg. B, 33318	Bruce R. Thomas
Jacksonville	400 W. Bay St., 32202	Henry O. Lamar, Jr.
Georgia	401 W. Peachtree St. NW., Atlanta, 30385	James E. Donelson
Hawaii	915 2d Ave., Seattle, WA 98174	J. Paul Beene
Idaho	600 17th St., Denver, CO 80202–2490	Jack B. Cheskaty
Illinois	Suite 2890, 230 S. Dearborn St., Chicago, 60604	Robert E. Brazzil
Indiana	575 N. Pennsylvania St., Indianapolis, 46204	James E. Rogers, Jr.
Iowa	310 W. Wisconsin Ave., Milwaukee, WI 53203–2221	Glenda Papillion
Kansas	Suite 2300, 1222 Spruce St., St. Louis, MO 63103	David Palmer
Kentucky	801 Broadway, Nashville, TN 37202	Gayle Morin
Louisiana	600 S. Maestri Pl., New Orleans, 70130	Richard F. Moran
Maine	JFK Federal Bldg., Boston, MA 02203	Stephen L. Daige
Maryland	31 Hopkins Plz., Baltimore, 21201	Paul M. Harrington
Massachusetts	JFK Federal Bldg., Boston, 02203	Stephen L. Daige
Michigan	Suite 2483, 477 Michigan Ave., Detroit, 48226	Arlene G. Kay
Minnesota	316 N. Robert St., St. Paul, 55101	Thomas E. Palmer

District Offices—Internal Revenue Service—Continued

District	Address	Director
Mississippi	600 S. Maestri Pl., New Orleans, LA 70130	Richard F. Moran
Missouri	Suite 2300, 1222 Spruce St., St. Louis, MO 63103	David Palmer
Montana	600 17th St., Denver, CO 80202–2490	Jack B. Cheskaty
Nebraska	310 W. Wisconsin Ave., Milwaukee, WI 53203–2221	Glenda M. Papillion
Nevada	210 E. Earll Dr., Phoenix, AZ 85012	James J. Walsh
New Hampshire	JFK Federal Bldg., Boston, MA 02203	Stephen L. Daige
New Jersey	970 Broad St., Newark, 07102	Frank P. Nixon
New Mexico	210 E. Earll Dr., Phoenix, AZ 85012	James J. Walsh
New York:		
Albany/Buffalo	111 W. Huron St., Buffalo, 14202	Edward J. Weiler
Brooklyn	Suite 10, 625 Fulton St., 11201	Ellen Murphy
Manhattan	290 Broadway, New York, 10007	Charles R. Baugh
North Carolina	320 Federal Pl., Greensboro, 27401	Ray F. Howard
North Dakota	316 N. Robert St., St. Paul, MN 55101	Thomas E. Palmer
Ohio	Suite 5106, 550 Main St., Cincinnati, 45202	C. Ashley Bullard
Oklahoma	55 N. Robinson St., Oklahoma City, 73102	Richard Auby
Oregon	915 2d Ave., Seattle, WA 98174	J. Paul Beene
Pennsylvania	600 Arch St., Philadelphia, 19106	Deborah S. Reilly
Puerto Rico	Stop 27½, Ponce de Leon Ave., Hato Rey, 00917	Robert Keller
Rhode Island	135 High St., Hartford, CT 06103	Deborah Nolan
South Carolina	320 Federal Pl., Greensboro, NC, 27401	Ray F. Howard
South Dakota	316 N. Robert St., St. Paul, MN 55101	Thomas E. Palmer
Tennessee	801 Broadway, Nashville, 37203	Gayle Morin
Texas:		
Austin	300 E. 8th St., 78701	Pamela Bigelow
Dallas	1100 Commerce St., 75242	Glenn Henderson
Houston	1919 Smith St., 77002	Paul Cardova
Utah	600 17th St., Denver, CO 80202–2490	Jack B. Cheskaty
Vermont	JFK Federal Bldg., Boston, MA 02203	Stephen L. Daige
Virginia	400 N. 8th St., Richmond, 23240	Roger Burgess
Washington	915 2d Ave., Seattle, 98174	J. Paul Beene
West Virginia	400 N. 8th St., Richmond, VA 23240	Roger Burgess
Wisconsin	310 W. Wisconsin Ave., Milwaukee, 53203–2221	Glenda M. Papillion
Wyoming	600 17th St., Denver, CO 80202–2490	Jack B. Cheskaty

Overseas Taxpayers

Office	Address
Office of Taxpayer Service and Compliance	950 L'Enfant Plz. SW. (CP:IN), Washington, DC 20024

For further information, contact any District Office or the Internal Revenue Service Headquarters, Department of the Treasury, 1111 Constitution Avenue NW., Washington, DC 20224. Phone, 202–622–5000.

United States Mint

The establishment of a mint was authorized by act of April 2, 1792 (1 Stat. 246). The Bureau of the Mint was established by act of February 12, 1873 (17 Stat. 424) and recodified on September 13, 1982 (31 U.S.C. 304, 5131). The name was changed to United States Mint by Secretarial order dated January 9, 1984.

The primary mission of the Mint is to produce an adequate volume of circulating coinage for the Nation to conduct its trade and commerce. The Mint also produces and sells numismatic coins, American Eagle gold and silver bullion coins, and national medals. In addition, the Fort Knox Bullion Depository is the primary storage facility for the Nation's gold bullion.

The U.S. Mint maintains sales centers at the Philadelphia and Denver Mints, and at Union Station in Washington, DC. Public tours are conducted, with free admission, at the Philadelphia and Denver Mints.

Field Facilities

(PM: Plant Manager; O: Officer in Charge)

Facility/Address	Facility Head
Bullion Depository, Ft. Knox, KY 40121	James M. Curtis (O)
Denver, CO 80204	Jay Neal (PM)
Philadelphia, PA 19106	Steve Kunderewicz, *Acting* (PM)
San Francisco, CA 94102	Larry Eckerman (PM)
West Point, NY 10996	Ellen McCullom, *Acting* (PM)

For further information, contact the United States Mint, Department of the Treasury, Judiciary Square Building, 633 Third Street NW., Washington, DC 20220. Phone, 202–874–9696.

Bureau of the Public Debt

The Bureau of the Public Debt was established on June 30, 1940, pursuant to the Reorganization Act of 1939 (31 U.S.C. 306).

Its mission is to borrow the money needed to operate the Federal Government; account for the resulting public debt; and to issue Treasury securities to refund maturing debt and raise new money. The Bureau fulfills its mission through six programs: commercial book-entry securities, direct access securities, savings securities, Government securities, market regulation, and public debt accounting.

The Bureau auctions and issues Treasury bills, notes, and bonds and manages the U.S. Savings Bond Program. It issues, services, and redeems bonds through a nationwide network of issuing and paying agents. The Bureau also promotes the sale and retention of savings bonds through payroll savings plans and financial institutions and is supported by a network of volunteers. It provides daily and other periodic reports to account for the composition and size of the debt. In addition, the Bureau implements the regulations for the Government securities market. These regulations provide for investor protection while maintaining a fair and liquid market for Government securities.

For more information, contact the Public Affairs Officer, Office of the Commissioner, Bureau of the Public Debt, Washington, DC 20239–0001. Phone, 202–219–3302. Internet, www.publicdebt.treas.gov.

United States Secret Service

The Secret Service is responsible for:

—protecting the President, the Vice President, the President-elect, the Vice-President-elect, and members of their immediate families; major Presidential and Vice Presidential candidates; former Presidents and their spouses; minor children of a former President until the age of 16; visiting heads of foreign states or governments; other distinguished foreign visitors to the United States; and official representatives of the United States performing special missions abroad, as directed by the President;

—providing security at the White House complex and other Presidential offices, the temporary official residence of the Vice President in the District of Columbia, and foreign diplomatic missions in the Washington, DC, metropolitan area and throughout the United States, its territories and possessions;

—to detect and arrest any person committing any offense against the laws of the United States relating to currency, coins, obligations, and securities of the United States or of foreign governments;

—to suppress the forgery and fraudulent negotiation or redemption of Federal Government checks, bonds, and other obligations or securities of the United States;

—to conduct investigations relating to certain criminal violations of the Federal Deposit Insurance Act, the Federal Land Bank Act, and the Government Losses in Shipment Act; and

—to detect and arrest offenders of laws pertaining to electronic funds transfer frauds, credit and debit card frauds, false identification documents or devices, computer access fraud, and Department of Agriculture food coupons, including authority-to-participate cards.

District Offices—United States Secret Service

District	Address	Telephone
Akron, OH	Suite 403, 441 Wolf Ledges Pkwy., 44311–1054	330–761–0544
Albany, GA	Suite 221, 235 Roosevelt Ave., 31701–2374	912–430–8442
Albany, NY	2d Fl., 39 N. Pearl St., 12207	518–436–9600
Albuquerque, NM	Suite 1700, 505 Marquette St. NW., 87102	505–248–5290
Anchorage, AK	Rm. 529, 222 W. 7th Ave., 99513–7592	907–271–5148
Atlanta, GA	Suite 2906, 401 W. Peachtree St., 30308–3516	404–331–6111
Atlantic City, NJ	Suite 501, 6601 Ventnor Ave., Ventnor City, 08406	609–487–1300
Augusta, GA	P.O. Box 898, 30903	706–597–1027
Austin, TX	Suite 972, 300 E. 8th St., 78701	512–916–5103
Baltimore, MD	11th Fl., 100 S. Charles St., 21201	410–962–2200
Baton Rouge, LA	Rm. 1502, 1 American Pl., 70825	225–389–0763
Birmingham, AL	Suite 1125, 15 S. 20th St., 35233	205–731–1144
Boise, ID	Rm. 730, 550 W. Fort St., 83724–0001	208–334–1403
Boston, MA	Suite 791, 10 Causeway St., 02222–1080	617–565–5640
Buffalo, NY	Suite 300, 610 Main St., 14202	716–551–4401
Charleston, SC	Suite 500, 5900 Core Ave., 29406	843–747–7242
Charleston, WV	Suite 910, 1 Valley Sq., 25301	304–347–5188
Charlotte, NC	Suite 400, 6302 Fairview Rd., 28210	704–442–8370
Chattanooga, TN	Rm. 204, 900 Georgia Ave., 37402	423–752–5125
Cheyenne, WY	Suite 3026, 2120 Capitol Ave., 82001	307–772–2380
Chicago, IL	Suite 1200 N., 300 S. Riverside Plz., 60606	312–353–5431
Cincinnati, OH	Rm. 6118, 550 Main St., 45202	513–684–3585
Cleveland, OH	Rm. 440, 6100 Rockside Woods Blvd., 44131–2334	216–522–4365
Colorado Springs, CO	Rm. 204, 212 N. Wahsatch, 80903	719–632–3325
Columbia, SC	Suite 1425, 1835 Assembly St., 29201	803–765–5446
Columbus, OH	Suite 800, 500 S. Front St., 43215	614–469–7370
Concord, NH	Suite 250, 197 Loudon Rd., 03301	603–228–3428
Dallas, TX	Suite 300, 125 E. John W. Carpenter Fwy., Irving, 75062–2752	972–868–3200
Dayton, OH	Rm. 811, 200 W. 2d St., 45402	937–222–2013
Denver, CO	Suite 1430, 1660 Lincoln St., 80264	303–866–1010
Des Moines, IA	Suite 637, 210 Walnut St., 50309–2107	515–284–4565
Detroit, MI	Suite 1000, 477 Michigan Ave., 48226–2518	313–226–6400
El Paso, TX	Suite 210, 4849 N. Mesa, 79912	915–533–6950
Fresno, CA	Suite 207, 5200 N. Palm Ave., 93704	559–221–0980
Fort Myers, FL	Suite 804, 2000 Main St., 33901	941–334–0660
Grand Rapids, MI	Suite 302, 330 Ionia Ave. NW., 49503–2350	616–454–4671
Great Falls, MT	No. 11, 3d St. N., 59401	406–452–8515
Greensboro, NC	Suite 220, 4905 Koger Blvd., 27407	336–547–4180
Greenville, SC	Suite 508, 7 Laurens St., 29601	864–233–1490
Honolulu, HI	Rm. 6–210, 300 Ala Moana Blvd., 96850	808–541–1912
Houston, TX	Suite 500, 602 Sawyer St., 77007	713–868–2299
Indianapolis, IN	Suite 211, 575 N. Pennsylvania St., 46204	317–226–6444
Jackson, MS	Suite 840, 100 W. Capitol St., 39269	601–965–4436
Jacksonville, FL	Suite 500, 7820 Arlington Expy., 32211	904–724–6711
Jamaica, NY	Rm. 246, Bldg. 75, John F. Kennedy International Airport, 11430	718–553–0911
Kansas City, MO	Suite 510, 1150 Grand Ave., 64106	816–460–0600
Knoxville, TN	Rm. 517, 710 Locust St., 37902	423–545–4627
Las Vegas, NV	Suite 600, 600 Las Vegas Blvd. S., 89101	702–388–6446
Lexington, KY	Suite 201, 3141 Beaumont Centre Cir., 40513	606–233–2358
Little Rock, AR	Suite 1700, 111 Center St., 72201–4419	501–324–6241
Los Angeles, CA	17th Fl., 255 E. Temple St., 90012	213–894–4830
Louisville, KY	Rm. 377, 600 Dr. Martin Luther King, Jr., Pl., 40202	502–582–5171
Lubbock, TX	Rm. 813, 1205 Texas Ave., 79401	806–472–7347
Madison, WI	Suite 303, 131 W. Wilson St., 53703	608–264–5191
McAllen, TX	Suite 1107, 200 S. 10th St., 78501	956–630–5811
Melville, NY	Suite 216E, 35 Pinelawn Rd., 11747–3154	516–249–0984
Memphis, TN	Suite 204, 5350 Poplar Ave., 38119	901–544–0333
Miami, FL	Suite 100, 8375 NW. 53d St., 33166	305–591–3660
Milwaukee, WI	572 Federal Courthouse, 517 E. Wisconsin Ave., 53202	414–297–3587
Minneapolis, MN	Suite 750, 300 S. 4th St., 55415	612–348–1800
Mobile, AL	Suite 200, 182 St. Francis St., 36602–3501	334–441–5851

District Offices—United States Secret Service—Continued

District	Address	Telephone
Montgomery, AL	Suite 605, 1 Commerce St., 36104	334–223–7601
Nashville, TN	658 U.S. Courthouse, 801 Broadway St., 37203	615–736–5841
New Haven, CT	Suite 1201, 265 Church St., 06510	203–865–2449
New Orleans, LA	Rm. 807, 501 Magazine St., 70130	504–589–4041
New York, NY	9th Fl., 7 World Trade Ctr., 10048–1901	212–637–4500
Newark, NJ	Suite 700, W. Twr., Speedwell Ave., 07960–3990	973–984–5760
Norfolk, VA	Suite 640, 200 Granby St., 23510	757–441–3200
Oklahoma City, OK	Suite 650, 4013 NW. Expressway, 73102–9229	405–810–3000
Omaha, NE	Suite 301, 2707 N. 108th St., 68164	402–956–9670
Orlando, FL	Suite 670, 135 W. Central Blvd., 32801	407–648–6333
Philadelphia, PA	7236 Federal Bldg., 600 Arch St., 19106–1676	215–861–3300
Phoenix, AZ	Suite 1450, 3200 N. Central Ave., 85012	602–640–5580
Pittsburgh, PA	Rm. 835, 1000 Liberty Ave., 15222	412–395–6484
Portland, ME	2d Fl., W. Twr., 100 Middle St., 04104	207–780–3493
Portland, OR	Suite 1020, 1001 SW. 5th Ave., 97204	503–326–2162
Providence, RI	Suite 343, 380 Westminster St., 02903	401–331–6456
Raleigh, NC	Suite 210, 4407 Bland Rd., 27609–6296	919–790–2834
Reno, NV	Suite 850, 100 W. Liberty St., 89501	775–784–5354
Richmond, VA	Suite 1910, 600 E. Main St., 23219	804–771–2274
Riverside, CA	Suite 203, 4371 Latham St., 92501	909–276–6781
Roanoke, VA	Suite 2, 105 Franklin Rd. SW., 24011	540–345–4301
Rochester, NY	Rm. 606, 100 State St., 14614	716–263–6830
Sacramento, CA	Suite 9–500, 501 I St., 95814–2322	916–930–2130
Saginaw, MI	Suite 200, 301 E. Genesee Ave., 48607–1242	517–752–8076
St. Louis, MO	Rm. 924, 1114 Market St., 63101	314–539–2238
Salt Lake City, UT	Suite 450, 57 W. 200 S., 84101–1610	801–524–5910
San Antonio, TX	Rm. B410, 727 E. Durango Blvd., 78206–1265	210–472–6175
San Diego, CA	Suite 660, 550 W. C St., 92101–3531	619–557–5640
San Francisco, CA	Suite 530, 345 Spear St., 94105	415–744–9026
San Jose, CA	Suite 2050, 280 S. 1st St., 95113	408–535–5288
San Juan, PR	Suite 3–B, 1510 F.D. Roosevelt Ave., Guaynabo, 00968	787–277–1515
Santa Ana, CA	Suite 500, 200 W. Santa Ana Blvd., 92701–4164	714–246–8257
Savannah, GA	Suite 570, 33 Bull St., 31401–3334	912–652–4401
Scranton, PA	Suite 247, 235 N. Washington Ave., 18501	570–346–5781
Seattle, WA	Rm. 890, 915 2d Ave., 98174	206–220–6800
Shreveport, LA	Suite 525, 401 Edwards St., 71101	318–676–3500
Sioux Falls, SD	Suite 405, 230 S. Phillips Ave., 57104–6321	605–330–4565
Spokane, WA	Suite 1340, 601 W. Riverside Ave., 99201–0611	509–353–2532
Springfield, IL	Suite 301, 400 W. Monroe St., 62704	217–492–4033
Springfield, MO	Suite 306, 901 E. St. Louis St., 65806	417–864–8340
Syracuse, NY	Rm. 1371, 100 S. Clinton St., 13260	315–448–0304
Tallahassee, FL	Suite 120, Bldg. F, 325 John Knox Rd., 32303	850–942–9523
Tampa, FL	Rm. 1101, 501 E. Polk St., 33602	813–228–2636
Toledo, OH	Suite 702, 4 Seagate, 43604	419–259–6434
Trenton, NJ	Suite 3000, 402 E. State St., 08608	609–989–2174
Tucson, AZ	Rm 4–V, 300 W. Congress St., 85701	520–670–4730
Tulsa, OK	Suite 400, 125 W. 15 St., 74119–3824	918–581–7272
Tyler, TX	Suite 395, 6101 S. Broadway, 75703	903–534–2933
Ventura, CA	Suite 161, 5500 Telegraph Rd., 93003	805–339–9180
Washington, DC	Suite 6000, 1100 L St., NW., 20005	202–406–8800
West Palm Beach, FL	Suite 800, 505 S. Flagler Dr., 33401	561–659–0184
White Plains, NY	Suite 300, 140 Grand St., 10601	914–682–6300
Wichita, KS	Suite 275, 301 N. Main, 67202	316–267–1452
Wilmington, DE	Rm. 414, 920 King St., 19801	302–573–6188
Wilmington, NC	P.O. Box 120, 28402	910–815–4511

District Offices Overseas—United States Secret Service

District	Address	Telephone
Bangkok, Thailand	American Embassy, Box 64/Bangkok, APO AP 96546	011–66–2–205–4000
Berlin, Germany	PSC 120, Box 3000, APO AE 09265	011–49–30–8305–1450
Bogota, Colombia	U.S. Embassy, Unit 5146, APO AA 34038	011–57–1–315–0811
Bonn, Germany	American Embassy/Bonn, PSC 117, Box 300, APO AE 09080	011–49–228–339–2587
Hong Kong	25 Garden Rd., Central Hong Kong	011–852–2841–2524
London, England	American Embassy/USSS, PSC 801, Box 64, FPO AE 09498–4064	011–44–171–499–9000
Manila, Philippines	PSC 500, Box 12, FPO AP 96515	011–63–2–523–1167
Milan, Italy	Consulate General of the USA, Via Principe Amedeo 2/10 20121	011–39–02–290–35–477
Montreal, Quebec	U.S. Consulate-Montreal, P.O. Box 847, Champlain, NY	514–398–9488
Moscow, Russia	PSC 77, APO AE 09721	011–7–095–252–2451
Nicosia, Cyprus	U.S. Secret Service, American Embassy Nicosia, PSC 815, FPO AE 09836.	011–357–2–776–400–2549
Ottawa, Canada	U.S. Embassy, P.O. Box 5000, Ogdensburg, NY, 13669	613–688–5461

District Offices Overseas—United States Secret Service—Continued

District	Address	Telephone
Paris, France	PSC 116, Box D306 APO AE 09777–5000	011–33–1–4312–7100
Rome, Italy	PSC 59, Box 62, USSS, APO AE 09624	011–39–06–4674–1
Vancouver, Canada	P.O. Box 5002, Pt. Roberts, WA 98271–9602	604–689–3011

For further information, contact any District Office or the Office of Government Liaison and Public Affairs, United States Secret Service, Department of the Treasury, 1800 G Street NW., Washington, DC 20223. Phone, 202–435–5708.

Office of Thrift Supervision

The Office of Thrift Supervision (OTS) regulates Federal and State-chartered savings institutions. Created by the Financial Institutions Reform, Recovery, and Enforcement Act of 1989, its mission is to effectively and efficiently supervise thrift institutions in a manner that encourages a competitive industry to meet housing and other credit and financial services needs and ensure access to financial services for all Americans.

The Office is headed by a Director appointed by the President, with the advice and consent of the Senate, for a 5-year term. The Director is responsible for the overall direction and policy of the agency. OTS is responsible for:

—examining and supervising thrift institutions in the five OTS regions to ensure the safety and soundness of the industry;

—ensuring that thrifts comply with consumer protection laws and regulations;

—conducting a regional quality assurance program to ensure consistent applications of policies and procedures;

—developing national policy guidelines to enhance statutes and regulations and to establish programs to implement new policy and law;

—issuing various financial reports, including the quarterly report on the financial condition of the thrift industry;

—preparing regulations, bulletins, other policy documents, congressional testimony, and official correspondence on matters relating to the condition of the thrift industry, interest rate risk, financial derivatives, and economic issues; and

—prosecuting enforcement actions relating to thrift institutions.

For further information, contact the Dissemination Branch, Office of Thrift Supervision, 1700 G Street NW., Washington, DC 20552. Phone, 202–906–6000. Fax, 202–906–5900. Internet, www.ots.treas.gov.

Sources of Information

Departmental Offices

Comptroller of the Currency For Freedom of Information Act Requests, contact the disclosure officer, Communications Division, 250 E Street SW., Washington, DC 20219 (phone, 202–874–4700; fax, 202–874–5263). For information about contracts, contact the procurement officer at 250 E Street SW., Washington, DC 20219 (phone, 202–874–5040; fax, 202–874–5625). For information regarding national bank examiner employment opportunities (generally hired at the entry level through a college recruitment program) contact the Director for Human Resources, 250 E Street SW., Washington, DC 20219 (phone, 202–874–4490; fax, 202–874–5447). Publications are available from the Communications Division, 250 E Street SW., Washington, DC 20219 (phone, 202–874–4700; fax, 202–874–5263).

Contracts Write to the Director, Office of Procurement, Suite 400–W, 1310 G Street NW., Washington, DC 20220. Phone, 202–622–0203.
Environment Environmental statements prepared by the Department are available for review in the Departmental Library. Information on Treasury environmental matters may be obtained from the Office of the Assistant Secretary of the Treasury for Management and Chief Financial Officer, Treasury Department, Washington, DC 20220. Phone, 202–622–0043.
General Inquiries For general information about the Treasury Department, including copies of news releases and texts of speeches by high Treasury officials, write to the Office of the Assistant Secretary (Public Affairs and Public Liaison), Room 3430, Departmental Offices, Treasury Department, Washington, DC 20220. Phone, 202–622–2920.
Inspector General For general information, write to the Office of Inspector General, Room 4436, 1500 Pennsylvania Avenue NW., Washington, DC 20220. For information about employment, contact the Human Resources Division, Office of Inspector General, Suite 510, 740 15th Street NW., Washington, DC 20220 (phone, 202–927–5230). For Freedom of Information Act/Privacy Act Requests, write to Freedom of Information Act Request, Department of the Treasury, Room 1054, 1500 Pennsylvania Avenue NW., Washington, DC 20220. Semiannual reports to the Congress on the Office of Inspector General are available from the Office of Inspector General, Room 4436, 1500 Pennsylvania Avenue NW., Washington, DC 20220.
Reading Room The Reading Room is located in the Treasury Library, Room 1428, Main Treasury Building, 1500 Pennsylvania Avenue NW., Washington, DC 20220. Phone, 202–622–0990.
Small and Disadvantaged Business Activities Write to the Director, Office of Small and Disadvantaged Business Utilization, Suite 400–W, 1310 G Street NW., Washington, DC 20220. Phone, 202–622–0530.
Tax Legislation Information on tax legislation may be obtained from the Assistant Secretary (Tax Policy), Departmental Offices, Treasury Department, Washington, DC 20220. Phone, 202–622–0050.
Telephone Directory The Treasury Department telephone directory is available for sale by the Superintendent of Documents, Government Printing Office, Washington, DC 20402.

United States Customs Service

Address inquiries on the following subjects to the specified office, U.S. Customs Service, 1300 Pennsylvania Avenue NW., Washington, DC 20229. Phone, 202–927–6724.
Contracts Write to the Regional Procurement Center, 6026 Lakeside Boulevard, Indianapolis, IN 46278.
Employment The U.S. Customs Service recruits from the Treasury Enforcement Agent examination. Employment inquiries may be addressed to the Personnel Director, Office of Human Resources Management in Washington, DC.
Forms Forms are available from any port director's office. There is a nominal charge for large quantities of certain forms.
General Inquiries Contact the nearest port director's office for information regarding customs regulations and procedures for all persons entering the United States and the entry and clearance of imported merchandise.
Publications The U.S. Customs Service issues publications of interest to the general, importing, and traveling public that can be obtained from any of the port directors' offices or by writing to the Office of Public Affairs in Washington, DC. Single copies of many of these publications are available at no charge to the public.
Reading Rooms Reading rooms are located at the headquarters library and in some field offices.
Speakers Speakers are available for private organizations or community groups throughout the country. Contact any local customs officer or the Office of Public Affairs in Washington, DC.

Bureau of Engraving and Printing

Address inquiries on the following subjects to the specified office, Bureau of Engraving and Printing, Fourteenth and C Streets SW., Washington, DC 20228.

Contracts and Small Business Activities Information relating to contracts and small business activity may be obtained by contacting the Office of Procurement. Phone, 202–874–2534.

Employment Information regarding employment opportunities and required qualifications is available from the Staffing and Classification Division, Office of Human Resources. Phone, 202–874–3747.

Freedom of Information Act Requests Inquiries should be directed to the Bureau Disclosure Officer, Room 112M. Phone, 202–874–2769.

General Inquiries Requests for information about the Bureau, its products, or numismatic and philatelic interests should be addressed to the Office of External Relations, Room 533M, Fourteenth and C Streets SW., Washington, DC 20228. Phone, 202–874–3019.

Product Sales Uncut sheets of currency, engraved Presidential portraits, historical engravings of national landmarks, and other souvenirs and mementos are available for purchase in the Visitors Center or through the mail. The Visitors Center gift shop, located in the Fifteenth Street (Raoul Wallenberg Place) lobby of the main building, is open from 8:30 a.m. to 3:30 p.m. Monday through Friday, excluding Federal holidays and Christmas week. In June, July, and August, the gift shop reopens at 4:30 p.m. and closes at 8:30 p.m. Information and order forms for sales items by mail may be obtained by writing to the Office of External Relations and Customer Service, Room 533M, Fourteenth and C Streets SW., Washington, DC 20228, or by calling 800–456–3408.

Tours Tours of the Bureau's facility in Washington, DC are provided throughout the year according to the following schedule:

Peak season, April through September, 9 a.m. until 1:50 p.m. Tours begin every 20 minutes, with the last tour beginning at 1:50 p.m. The ticket booth is located on Raoul Wallenberg Place (formerly Fifteenth Street) and is open from 8 a.m. until 2 p.m. Tour tickets are free. Lines queue up on Raoul Wallenberg Place.

Evening tours, June through August, 5 p.m. until 7:30 p.m. Tours are offered every 20 minutes. The ticket booth for evening tour tickets is open from 3:30 until 7:30 p.m. Tour tickets are free. Lines queue up on Raoul Wallenberg Place.

Non-peak season, October through March, 9 a.m. until 2 p.m. No tickets are necessary for tours during this time. Lines queue up on Fourteenth Street.

No tours are given on weekends, Federal holidays, or between Christmas and New Year's Day.

Financial Management Service

Inquiries on the following subjects should be directed to the specified office, Financial Management Service, 401 Fourteenth Street SW., Washington, DC 20227. Fax, 202–874–7016.

Contracts Write to the Director, Acquisition Management Division, Room 428 LCB. Phone, 202–874–6910.

Employment Inquiries may be directed to the Personnel Management Division, Room 120 LCB. Phone, 202–874–7090.

Internal Revenue Service

Audiovisual Materials Films providing information on the American tax system, examination and appeal rights, and the tax responsibilities of running a small business are available. Some of the films are also available in Spanish. The films can be obtained by contacting any District Office.

Also available are audio and video cassette tapes that provide step-by-step instructions for preparing basic individual income tax forms. These tapes are available in many local libraries.

Contracts Write to the Internal Revenue Service, 1111 Constitution Avenue NW. (M:P:C), Washington, DC 20224 (phone, 202–283–1710); or the Director of Support Services, at any of the Internal Revenue regional offices.

Educational Programs The Service provides, free of charge, general tax information publications and booklets on specific tax topics. Taxpayer information materials also are distributed to major television networks and many radio and television stations, daily and weekly newspapers, magazines, and specialized publications. Special educational materials and films are provided for use in high schools and colleges. Individuals starting a new business are given specialized materials and information at small business workshops, and community colleges provide classes based on material provided by the Service. The community outreach tax assistance program provides assistance, through agency employees, to community groups.

Through the volunteer income tax assistance program and the tax counseling for the elderly program, the Service recruits, trains, and supports volunteers who offer free tax assistance to low-income, elderly, military, and non-English-speaking taxpayers.

Materials, films, and information on the educational programs can be obtained by contacting any district office.

Employment For information, write the the recruitment coordinator at any of the regional or district offices.

Publications The *Annual Report—Commissioner of Internal Revenue,* the *Internal Revenue Service Data Book,* and periodic reports of statistics of income are available from the Superintendent of Documents, Government Printing Office, Washington, DC 20402.

Audit of Returns, Appeal Rights, and Claims for Refund, Your Federal Income Tax, Farmers Tax Guide, Tax Guide for Small Business, and other publications are available at Internal Revenue Service offices free of charge.

Reading Rooms Public reading rooms are located in the national office and in each regional office or, in some cases, a district office located in a regional office building.

Speakers Arrangements for speakers on provisions of the tax law and operations of the Internal Revenue Service for professional and community groups may be made by writing to the District Directors or, for national organizations only, to the Communications Division at the IRS National Headquarters in Washington, DC.

Taxpayer Advocate Each district has a problem resolution staff which attempts to resolve taxpayer complaints not satisfied through regular channels.

Taxpayer Service The Internal Revenue Service provides year-round tax information and assistance to taxpayers, primarily through its toll-free telephone system, which also includes telephone assistance to deaf and hearing-impaired taxpayers who have access to a teletypewriter or television/phone. The toll-free numbers are listed in local telephone directories and in the annual tax form packages. Taxpayers may also visit agency offices for help with their tax problems. The Service provides return preparation assistance to taxpayers by guiding groups of individuals line by line on the preparation of their returns. Individual preparation is available for handicapped or other individuals unable to use the group preparation method. Foreign language tax assistance also is available at many locations.

United States Mint

Contracts and Employment Inquiries should be directed to the facility head of the appropriate field office or to the Director of the Mint.

Numismatic Services The United States Mint maintains public exhibit and sales areas at the Philadelphia and Denver Mints, and at Union Station in Washington, DC. Brochures and order forms for official coins, medals, and other numismatic items may also be obtained by writing to the United States Mint, 10003 Derekwood Lane, Lanham, MD 20706. Phone, 202–283–COIN.

Publications The *CFO Annual Financial Report* is available from the United States Mint, Department of the Treasury, Judiciary Square Building, 633 Third Street NW., Washington, DC 20220. Phone, 202–874–9696.

Bureau of the Public Debt

Electronic Access Information about the public debt, U.S. Savings Bonds, Treasury bills, notes, and bonds, and other Treasury securities is available through the Internet, at www.publicdebt.treas.gov. Forms and publications may be ordered electronically at the same address.

Employment General employment inquiries should be addressed to the Bureau of the Public Debt, Division of Personnel Management, Employment and Classification Branch, Parkersburg, WV 26106–1328. Phone, 304–480–6144.

Savings Bonds Savings bonds are continuously on sale at more than 40,000 financial institutions and their branches in virtually every locality in the United States. Information about bonds is provided by such issuing agents. Current rate information is available toll-free by calling 800–4US–BOND. Requests for information about all series of savings bonds, savings notes, and retirement plans or individual retirement bonds should be addressed to the Bureau of the Public Debt, Department of the Treasury, 200 Third Street, Parkersburg, WV 26106–1328. Phone, 304–480–6112.

Treasury Securities Information inquiries regarding the purchase of Treasury bills, bonds, and notes should be addressed to your local Federal Reserve Bank or branch, or to the Bureau of the Public Debt, Department F, Washington, DC 20239–1200. Phone, 202–874–4060.

United States Secret Service

Information about employment opportunities and publications and general public information may be obtained by contacting the nearest Secret Service field office or the Office of Government Liaison and Public Affairs, Suite 8400, 950 H Street NW., Washington, DC 20001. Phone, 202–406–5708.

Office of Thrift Supervision

Electronic Access Information about OTS and institutions regulated by OTS is available through the Internet, at www.ots.treas.gov.

Employment Inquiries about employment opportunities with the Office of Thrift Supervision should be directed to the Human Resources Office. Phone, 202–906–6061.

Freedom of Information Act/Privacy Act Requests For information not readily available from the Public Reference Room, the website, or the OTS order department, a request may be submitted to the Office of Thrift Supervision, Dissemination Branch, 1700 G Street NW., Washington, DC 20552. E-mail, publicinfo@ots.treas.gov. Fax, 202–906–7755.

General Information General information about OTS may be obtained by calling 202–906–6000. Information about the OTS public disclosure program may be obtained by calling 202–906–5900.

Public Reference Room The Public Reference Room makes available a wide variety of OTS records and information about federally insured savings associations. It is open Tuesdays and Thursdays from 1 to 4 p.m. and is located at 1700 G Street NW., Washington, DC 20552.

Publications Publications that provide information and guidance regarding the thrift industry are available for purchase. A complete publications list is available from the Public Reference Room and at the "Public Information" link on the website. Publications can be purchased by check or credit card through the OTS Order Department, P.O. Box 753, Waldorf, MD 20604. Phone, 301–645–6264.

For further information, ontact the Public Affairs Office, Department of the Treasury, 1500 Pennsylvania Avenue NW., Washington, DC 20220. Phone, 202–622–2960. Internet, www.treas.gov.

DEPARTMENT OF VETERANS AFFAIRS

810 Vermont Avenue NW., Washington, DC 20420
Phone, 202–273–4800. Internet, www.va.gov.

SECRETARY OF VETERANS AFFAIRS	TOGO D. WEST, JR.
Chief of Staff	JANICE F. JOYNER
Deputy Secretary	HERSHEL W. GOBER
Chairman, Board of Contract Appeals	GUY H. MCMICHAEL III
Chairman, Board of Veterans' Appeals	ELIGAH DANE CLARK
Vice Chairman, Board of Veterans' Appeals	RICHARD B. STANDEFER
Director, Office of Small and Disadvantaged Business Utilization	SCOTT F. DENNISTON
Director, Center for Minority Veterans	WILLIE L. HENSLEY
Director, Center for Women Veterans	JOAN A. FUREY
Director, Office of Employment Discrimination Complaint Adjudication	CHARLES R. DELOBE
General Counsel	LEIGH A. BRADLEY
Inspector General	RICHARD J. GRIFFIN
Veterans' Service Organizations Liaison	ALLEN (GUNNER) KENT
Under Secretary for Health, Veterans Health Administration	(VACANCY)
Deputy Under Secretary for Health	THOMAS GARTHWAITE
Under Secretary for Benefits, Veterans Benefits Administration	JOSEPH THOMPSON
Deputy Under Secretary for Operations	PATRICK NAPPI
Deputy Under Secretary for Management	NORA E. EGAN
Under Secretary for Memorial Affairs, National Cemetery Administration	ROGER R. RAPP, *Acting*
Assistant Secretary for Financial Management	EDWARD A. POWELL, JR.
Deputy Chief Financial Officer	W. TODD GRAMS
Deputy Assistant Secretary for Budget	D. MARK CATLETT
Deputy Assistant Secretary for Finance	FRANK W. SULLIVAN
Deputy Assistant Secretary for Acquisition and Materiel Management	GARY J. KRUMP
Assistant Secretary for Information and Technology	(VACANCY)
Principal Deputy Assistant Secretary for Information and Technology	HAROLD F. GRACEY, JR.
Deputy Assistant Secretary for Information Resources Management	(VACANCY)
Director, Austin Automation Center	LINDA VOGES, *Acting*
Assistant Secretary for Planning and Analysis	DENNIS DUFFY
Deputy Assistant Secretary for Program and Data Analysis	PATRICIA J. O'NEIL
Deputy Assistant Secretary for Planning and Evaluation	GARY A. STEINBERG
Assistant Secretary for Human Resources and Administration	EUGENE A. BRICKHOUSE
Deputy Assistant Secretary for Administration	ROBERT W. SCHULTZ

Deputy Assistant Secretary for Equal Opportunity	ELLIS JONES HODGES, *Acting*
Deputy Assistant Secretary for Human Resources Management	RONALD E. COWLES
Deputy Assistant Secretary for Security and Law Enforcement	JOHN H. BAFFA
Deputy Assistant Secretary for Resolution Management	VENTRIS C. GIBSON
Director, Shared Service Center	BRUCE C. CARRUTHERS
Assistant Secretary for Public and Intergovernmental Affairs	JOHN T. HANSON, *Acting*
Deputy Assistant Secretary for Public Affairs	JAMES H. HOLLEY
Deputy Assistant Secretary for Intergovernmental and International Affairs	MARIA FERNANDEZ GRECZMIEL
Assistant Secretary for Congressional Affairs	(VACANCY)
Principal Deputy Assistant Secretary for Congressional Affairs	(VACANCY)
Deputy Assistant Secretary for Congressional Operations	PHILIP RIGGIN

The Department of Veterans Affairs operates programs to benefit veterans and members of their families. Benefits include compensation payments for disabilities or death related to military service; pensions; education and rehabilitation; home loan guaranty; burial; and a medical care program incorporating nursing homes, clinics, and medical centers.

The Department of Veterans Affairs (VA) was established as an executive department by the Department of Veterans Affairs Act (38 U.S.C. 201 note). It. is comprised of three organizations that administer veterans programs: the Veterans Health Administration, the Veterans Benefits Administration, and the National Cemetery Administration. Each organization has field facilities and a central office component.

Activities

Cemeteries The National Cemetery Administration (NCA) provides services to veterans, active duty personnel, and reservists and National Guard members with 20 years' qualifying service and their families by operating national cemeteries; furnishing headstones and markers for the unmarked graves of U.S. veterans worldwide, service members, and reservists and National Guard members with 20 years' qualifying service; awarding grants to aid States in establishing, improving, and expanding veterans cemeteries; and serving as the operations element for the Presidential Memorial Certificate Program.

Center for Minority Veterans The Center for Minority Veterans was established under Public Law 103–446 (108 Stat. 4645) and is responsible for promoting the use of VA benefits, programs, and services by minority veterans and assessing the needs of minority group members. The work of the Center focuses on the unique and special needs of five distinct groups of veterans: African-Americans, Hispanics, Asian-Americans, Pacific Islanders, and Native Americans, which include American Indians, Native Hawaiians, and Alaskan Natives.

Center for Women Veterans The Center for Women Veterans acts as the Secretary's primary adviser on women veterans issues and evaluates VA programs, policies, and practices to ensure they are responsive and accessible to eligible women veterans.

Health Services The Veterans Health Administration, formerly the Veterans Health Services and Research

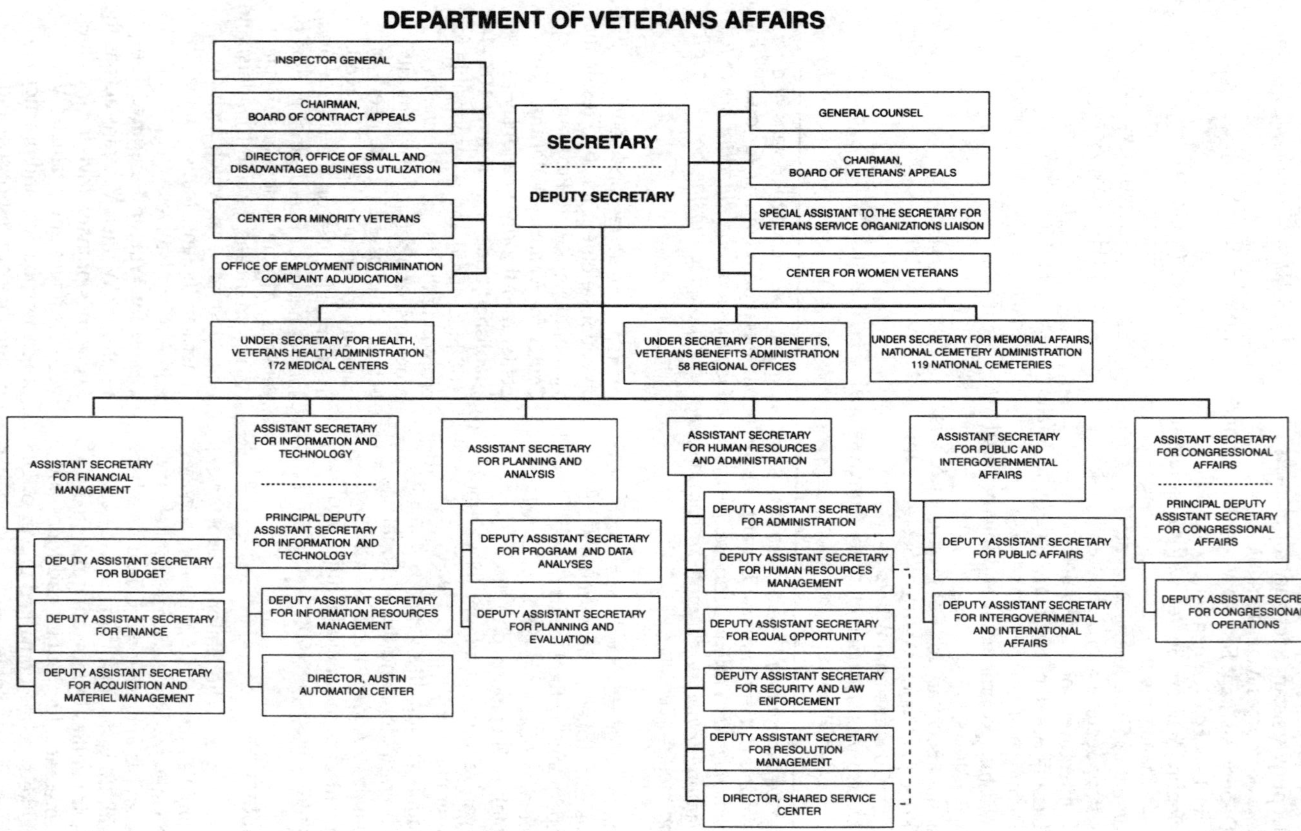
DEPARTMENT OF VETERANS AFFAIRS
INSPECTOR GENERAL
CHAIRMAN, BOARD OF CONTRACT APPEALS
DIRECTOR, OFFICE OF SMALL AND DISADVANTAGED BUSINESS UTILIZATION
CENTER FOR MINORITY VETERANS
OFFICE OF EMPLOYMENT DISCRIMINATION COMPLAINT ADJUDICATION
SECRETARY
DEPUTY SECRETARY
GENERAL COUNSEL
CHAIRMAN, BOARD OF VETERANS' APPEALS
SPECIAL ASSISTANT TO THE SECRETARY FOR VETERANS SERVICE ORGANIZATIONS LIAISON
CENTER FOR WOMEN VETERANS
UNDER SECRETARY FOR HEALTH, VETERANS HEALTH ADMINISTRATION 172 MEDICAL CENTERS
UNDER SECRETARY FOR BENEFITS, VETERANS BENEFITS ADMINISTRATION 58 REGIONAL OFFICES
UNDER SECRETARY FOR MEMORIAL AFFAIRS, NATIONAL CEMETERY ADMINISTRATION 119 NATIONAL CEMETERIES
ASSISTANT SECRETARY FOR FINANCIAL MANAGEMENT
DEPUTY ASSISTANT SECRETARY FOR BUDGET
DEPUTY ASSISTANT SECRETARY FOR FINANCE
DEPUTY ASSISTANT SECRETARY FOR ACQUISITION AND MATERIEL MANAGEMENT
ASSISTANT SECRETARY FOR INFORMATION AND TECHNOLOGY
PRINCIPAL DEPUTY ASSISTANT SECRETARY FOR INFORMATION AND TECHNOLOGY
DEPUTY ASSISTANT SECRETARY FOR INFORMATION RESOURCES MANAGEMENT
DIRECTOR, AUSTIN AUTOMATION CENTER
ASSISTANT SECRETARY FOR PLANNING AND ANALYSIS
DEPUTY ASSISTANT SECRETARY FOR PROGRAM AND DATA ANALYSES
DEPUTY ASSISTANT SECRETARY FOR PLANNING AND EVALUATION
ASSISTANT SECRETARY FOR HUMAN RESOURCES AND ADMINISTRATION
DEPUTY ASSISTANT SECRETARY FOR ADMINISTRATION
DEPUTY ASSISTANT SECRETARY FOR HUMAN RESOURCES MANAGEMENT
DEPUTY ASSISTANT SECRETARY FOR EQUAL OPPORTUNITY
DEPUTY ASSISTANT SECRETARY FOR SECURITY AND LAW ENFORCEMENT
DEPUTY ASSISTANT SECRETARY FOR RESOLUTION MANAGEMENT
DIRECTOR, SHARED SERVICE CENTER
ASSISTANT SECRETARY FOR PUBLIC AND INTERGOVERNMENTAL AFFAIRS
DEPUTY ASSISTANT SECRETARY FOR PUBLIC AFFAIRS
DEPUTY ASSISTANT SECRETARY FOR INTERGOVERNMENTAL AND INTERNATIONAL AFFAIRS
ASSISTANT SECRETARY FOR CONGRESSIONAL AFFAIRS
PRINCIPAL DEPUTY ASSISTANT SECRETARY FOR CONGRESSIONAL AFFAIRS
DEPUTY ASSISTANT SECRETARY FOR CONGRESSIONAL OPERATIONS

Administration, provides hospital, nursing home, and domiciliary care, and outpatient medical and dental care to eligible veterans of military service in the Armed Forces. It conducts both individual medical and health-care delivery research projects and multihospital research programs, and it assists in the education of physicians and dentists and with training of many other health care professionals through affiliations with educational institutions and organizations.

Veterans Benefits The Veterans Benefits Administration provides information, advice, and assistance to veterans, their dependents, beneficiaries, representatives, and others applying for VA benefits. It also cooperates with the Department of Labor and other Federal, State, and local agencies in developing employment opportunities for veterans and referral for assistance in resolving socioeconomic, housing, and other related problems.

The Compensation and Pension Service is responsible for claims for disability compensation and pension, specially adapted housing, accrued benefits, adjusted compensation in death cases, and reimbursement for headstone or marker; allowances for automobiles and special adaptive equipment; special clothing allowances; emergency officers' retirement pay; survivors' claims for death compensation, dependency and indemnity compensation, death pension, and burial and plot allowance claims; forfeiture determinations; and a benefits protection program for minors and incompetent adult beneficiaries.

The Education Service is responsible for the Montgomery GI Bill, assistance programs for dependents, post-Vietnam era veterans, and other pilot programs, school approvals, compliance surveys, and work study programs.

Life insurance operations for the benefit of service members, veterans, and their beneficiaries are available through the regional office and insurance center (phone, 800–669–8477) in Philadelphia, PA, which provides the full range of functional activities necessary for a national life insurance program. Activities include the complete maintenance of individual accounts, underwriting functions, life and death insurance claims awards, and any other insurance-related transactions. The agency also administers the Veterans Mortgage Life Insurance Program for those disabled veterans who receive a VA grant for specially adapted housing; the Servicemen's Group Life Insurance Program; and the Veterans Group Life Insurance Program.

Loan guaranty operations include appraising properties to establish their values; approving grants for specially adapted housing; supervising the construction of new residential properties; establishing the eligibility of veterans for the program; evaluating the ability of a veteran to repay a loan and the credit risk; making direct loans to Native American veterans to acquire a home on trust land; servicing and liquidating defaulted loans; and disposing of real estate acquired as the consequence of defaulted loans.

The Vocational Rehabilitation Service is responsible for outreach, motivation, evaluation, counseling, training, employment, and other rehabilitation services to disabled veterans; evaluation, counseling, and miscellaneous services to veterans and service persons and other VA education programs; evaluation, counseling, education, and miscellaneous services to sons, daughters, and spouses of totally and permanently disabled veterans and to surviving orphans, widows, or widowers of certain deceased veterans, including rehabilitation services to certain handicapped dependents; affirmative action activities; and vocational training and rehabilitation to children with spina bifida who are children of Vietnam veterans.

Veterans' Appeals The Board of Veterans' Appeals (BVA) is responsible for entering the final appellate decisions in claims of entitlement to veterans' benefits and for deciding matters concerning fees charged by attorneys and agents for representation of veterans before VA and requests for revision of prior BVA decisions on the basis of clear and unmistakable error. Final Board decisions are appealable to the U.S. Court of Appeals for Veterans Claims.

Field Facilities The Department's operations are handled through the following field facilities:

—cemeteries, the final resting places for burial of the remains of veterans, active duty personnel, and reservists and National Guard members with 20 years' qualifying service; their spouses; and certain eligible dependents;

—domiciliaries, providing the least intensive level of inpatient medical care including necessary ambulatory medical treatment, rehabilitation, and support services in a structured environment to veterans who are unable because of their disabilities to provide adequately for themselves in the community;

—medical centers, providing eligible beneficiaries with medical and other health care services equivalent to those provided by private-sector institutions, augmented in many instances by services to meet the special requirements of veterans;

—outpatient clinics to provide eligible beneficiaries with ambulatory care; and

—regional offices to grant benefits and services provided by law for veterans, their dependents, and beneficiaries within an assigned territory; furnish information regarding VA benefits and services; adjudicate claims and making awards for disability compensation and pension; supervise payment of VA benefits to incompetent beneficiaries; provide vocational rehabilitation and employment training; administer educational benefits; guarantee loans for purchase, construction, or alteration of homes; process grants for specially adapted housing; process death claims; and assist veterans in exercising rights to benefits and services.

National Facilities—Department of Veterans Affairs

Address	Type of facility	Director
ALABAMA:		
Birmingham (700 S. 19th St., 35233)	Medical Center	Y.C. Parris
Central Alabama Health Care System (215 Perry Hill Rd., Montgomery, 36109–3798).	Medical Center	Linda F. Watson
Mobile (1202 Virginia St., 36604) (Mail: Barrancas National Cemetery, FL).	National Cemetery	Sandra Beckley
Montgomery (345 Perry Hill Rd., 36109)	Regional Office	Montgomery Watson
Seale (Ft. Mitchell National Cemetery, 553 Hwy. 165, 36856).	National Cemetery	Sharon Bell-Goodrich
Tuscaloosa (35404)	Medical Center	W. Kenneth Ruyle
ALASKA:		
Anchorage (2925 Debarr Rd., 99508)	Outpatient Clinic and Regional Office.	Alex Spector
Ft. Richardson (P.O. Box 5–498, 99505)	National Cemetery	Virginia M. Walker
Sitka (803 Sawmill Creek Rd., 99835) (Mail: Ft. Richardson National Cemetery, AK).	National Cemetery	Virginia M. Walker
ARIZONA:		
Northern Arizona Health Care System (500 N. Hwy. 89, Prescott, 86313).	Medical Center (medical and domiciliary).	Patricia A. McKlem
Phoenix (7th St. & Indian School Rd., 85012)	Medical Center	John R. Fears
Phoenix (3225 N. Central Ave., 85012)	Regional Office	David M. Walls
Phoenix (23029 N. Cave Creek Rd., 85024) (National Memorial Cemetery of Arizona).	National Cemetery	Mark Maynard
Prescott (VA Medical Center, 500 Hwy. 89 N., 86301) (Mail: National Memorial Cemetery of Arizona).	National Cemetery	Mark Maynard
Southern Arizona Health Care System (3601 S. 6th Ave., Tucson, 85723).	Medical Center	Jonathan H. Gardner
ARKANSAS:		
Fayetteville (72701)	Medical Center	Michael Winn
Fayetteville (700 Government Ave., 72701)	National Cemetery	Darrell W. Lindsey
Ft. Smith (522 Garland Ave., 72901)	National Cemetery	John R. Smith
Little Rock (2523 Confederate Blvd., 72206)	National Cemetery	Ronald Zink
Little Rock (300 Roosevelt Rd., 72205) (John L. McClellan Memorial Veterans Hospital).	Medical Center	George Gray, Jr.
Little Rock Division		
North Little Rock Division (Mail: Little Rock)		
North Little Rock (P.O. Box 1280, Bldg. 65, Ft. Roots, 72115).	Regional Office	Fred King
CALIFORNIA:		
Central California Health Care System (2615 Clinton Ave., Fresno, 93703).	Medical Center	Alan S. Perry

National Facilities—Department of Veterans Affairs—Continued

Address	Type of facility	Director
Gustine (San Joaquin Valley National Cemetery, 32053 W. McCabe Rd., 95322).	National Cemetery	Carla Williams
Loma Linda (Jerry L. Pettis Memorial Veterans Hospital, 11201 Benton St., 92357).	Medical Center	Dean R. Stordahl
Long Beach (5901 E. 7th St., 90822)	Medical Center	Lawrence Stewart
Los Angeles (11301 Wilshire Blvd., Los Angeles, 90073)	Medical Center	Philip P. Thomas
Los Angeles (11000 Wilshire Blvd., 90024)	Regional Office	Stewart F. Liff
Los Angeles (950 S. Sepulveda Blvd., 90049)	National Cemetery	William L. Livingston
Northern California Health Care System (150 Muir Rd., Benicia, 94523).	Medical Center	Lucille Swanson
Oakland (Oakland Federal Bldg., 1301 Clay St., 94612–5209).	Regional Office	Donald E. Stout
Palo Alto Health Care System (3801 Miranda Ave., 94304).	Medical Center	James A. Goff
Riverside (22495 Van Buren Blvd., 92518)	National Cemetery	Steve Jorgensen
San Bruno (Golden Gate National Cemetery, 1300 Sneath Ln., 94066).	National Cemetery	(Vacancy)
San Diego (3350 La Jolla Village Dr., 92161)	Medical Center	Gary Rossio
San Diego (8810 Rio San Diego Dr., 92108)	Regional Office	Ray W. Hall
San Diego (Ft. Rosecrans National Cemetery, P.O. Box 6237, Point Loma, 92106).	National Cemetery	Cynthia Nunez
San Francisco (4150 Clement St., 94121)	Medical Center	Sheila Cullen, *Acting*
San Francisco (P.O. Box 29012, Presidio of San Francisco, 94129) (Mail: Golden Gate National Cemetery, San Bruno, CA).	National Cemetery	(Vacancy)
COLORADO:		
Denver (1055 Clermont St., 80220)	Medical Center	Edgar Thorsland, Jr.
Denver (80225)	Denver Distribution Center	Robert Shields
Denver (Ft. Logan National Cemetery, 3698 S. Sheridan Blvd., 80235).	National Cemetery	Leon Murphy
Ft. Lyon (VA Medical Center, 81038)	National Cemetery	Maintained by VAMC Engineering Service
Ft. Lyon (81038)	Medical Center	Stuart Collyer
Grand Junction (81501)	Medical Center	Kurt Schlegelmilch
Lakewood (P.O. Box 25126, 155 Van Gordon St., 80228).	Regional Office	Catherine L. Smith
CONNECTICUT:		
Connecticut Health Care System (950 Campbell Ave., West Haven, 06516).	Medical Center	Paul McCool
Hartford (450 Main St., 06103)	Regional Office	Jeffrey Alger
DELAWARE:		
Wilmington (1601 Kirkwood Hwy., 19805)	Medical and Regional Office Center	Dexter Dix
DISTRICT OF COLUMBIA:		
Washington (50 Irving St. NW., 20422)	Medical Center	Sanford M. Garfunkel
Washington (1120 Vermont Ave. NW., 20421)	Regional Office	Rowland Christian
FLORIDA:		
Bay Pines (1000 Bay Pines Blvd. N., 33504)	Medical Center (medical and domiciliary).	Thomas Weaver
Bay Pines (P.O. Box 477, 33504)	National Cemetery	Ronald R. Pemberton
Bushnell (Florida National Cemetery, 6502 SW. 102d Ave., 33513).	National Cemetery	Ronald R. Pemberton
Miami (1201 NW. 16th St., 33125)	Medical Center	Thomas C. Doherty
Northern Florida/Southern Georgia Health Care System (1601 SW. Archer Rd., Gainesville, 32608–1197).	Medical Center	Elwood J. Headley
Pensacola (Barrancas National Cemetery, Naval Air Station, 80 Hovey Rd. 32508–1054).	National Cemetery	Sandra Beckley
St. Augustine (104 Marine St., 32084) (Mail: Florida National Cemetery, Bushnell, FL).	National Cemetery	Ronald R. Pemberton
St. Petersburg (P.O. Box 1437, 33731)	Regional Office	William D. Stinger
Tampa (James A. Haley Veterans Hospital, 13000 Bruce B. Downs Blvd., 33612).	Medical Center	Richard A. Silver
West Palm Beach (7305 N. Military Trail, 33410–6400).	Medical Center	Edward H. Seiler
GEORGIA:		
Atlanta (1670 Clairmont Rd., 30033)	Medical Center	Robert Perreault
Atlanta (P.O. Box 100026, 1700 Clairmont Rd., Decatur, 30033).	Regional Office	Patrick Courtney
Augusta (2460 Wrightsboro Rd., 30904–6285) Forest Hills Division Lenwood Division	Medical Center	Ellen DeGeorge-Smith
Dublin (31021)	Medical Center (medical and domiciliary).	James Trusley
Marietta (500 Washington Ave., 30060)	National Cemetery	Sharon Bell-Goodrich

National Facilities—Department of Veterans Affairs—Continued

Address	Type of facility	Director
HAWAII:		
Honolulu (P.O. Box 50188, 96850)	Medical and Regional Office Center	H. David Burge
Honolulu (National Memorial Cemetery of the Pacific, 2177 Puowaina Dr., 96813–1729).	National Cemetery	Gene E. Castagnetti
IDAHO:		
Boise (805 W. Franklin St., 83702)	Regional Office	James Vance
Boise (5th & Ft. Sts., 83702–4598)	Medical Center	Wayne Tippets
ILLINOIS:		
Alton (600 Pearl St., 62003) (Mail: Jefferson Barracks National Cemetery, MO).	National Cemetery	Ralph E. Church
Chicago Health Care System (333 E. Huron St., 60611).	Medical Center	Richard S. Citron
Chicago (P.O. Box 8136, 536 S. Clark St., 60680)	Regional Office	Michael Olson
Danville (61832)	Medical Center	(Vacancy)
Danville (1900 E. Main St., 61832)	National Cemetery	(Vacancy)
Elwood (Abraham Lincoln National Cemetery, 27034 S. Diagonal Rd., 60421).	National Cemetery	Billy Murphy
Hines (Lock Box 66303, AMF O'Hare, 60666–0303)	Finance Center	James Burkett
Hines (Edward Hines, Jr., Hospital, 60141)	Medical Center	(Vacancy)
Hines (P.O. Box 76, 60141)	VA National Acquisition Center	George T. Patterson
Hines (P.O. Box 27, 60141)	Service and Distribution Center	David Garcia
Marion (2401 W. Main St., 62959)	Medical Center	Earl Falast
Moline (Rock Island National Cemetery, P.O. Box 737, Rock Island Arsenal, 61265).	National Cemetery	Larry Williams
Mound City (P.O. Box 128, Hwys. 37 & 51, 62963) (Mail: Jefferson Barracks National Cemetery, MO).	National Cemetery	Ralph E. Church
North Chicago (60064)	Medical Center	Alfred S. Pate
Quincy (36th & Maine Sts., 62301) (Mail: Rock Island National Cemetery, Rock Island, IL).	National Cemetery	Larry Williams
Springfield (Camp Butler National Cemetery, 5063 Camp Butler Rd., R No. 1, 62707).	National Cemetery	Dane Freeman
INDIANA:		
Indianapolis (1481 W. 10th St., 46202) Cold Spring Road Division Tenth Street Division	Medical Center	(Vacancy)
Indianapolis (575 N. Pennsylvania St., 46204)	Regional Office	(Vacancy)
Indianapolis (Crown Hill National Cemetery, 700 W. 38th St., 46208) (Mail: Marion National Cemetery, IN).	National Cemetery	Bobby A. Moton
Marion (1700 E. 38th St., 46952)	National Cemetery	Bobby A. Moton
New Albany (1943 Ekin Ave., 47150) (Mail: Zachary Taylor National Cemetery, KY).	National Cemetery	Gary D. Peak
Northern Indiana Health Care System (2121 Lake Ave., Ft. Wayne, 46805).	Medical Center	Michael W. Murphy
IOWA:		
Central Iowa Health Care System (30th and Euclid Ave., Des Moines, 50310–5774).	Medical Center	Donald Cooper
Des Moines (210 Walnut St., 50309)	Regional Office	(Vacancy)
Iowa City (Hwy. 6 W., 52246–5774)	Medical Center	Gary L. Wilkinson
Keokuk (1701 J St., 52632) (Mail: Rock Island National Cemetery, IL).	National Cemetery	Larry Williams
KANSAS:		
Eastern Kansas Health Care System (Leavenworth, 66048).	Medical Center (medical and domiciliary).	Edgar L. Tucker
Ft. Leavenworth (Mail: Leavenworth National Cemetery, KS).	National Cemetery	Jeffrey S. Barnes
Ft. Scott (P.O. Box 917, 66701)	National Cemetery	Jeffrey S. Barnes
Leavenworth (P.O. Box 1694, 66048)	National Cemetery	Jeffrey S. Barnes
Topeka (Bldg. 9, 3401 SW. 21st St., 66604)	Shared service center	Bruce C. Carruthers
Wichita (5500 E. Kellogg, 67218)	Medical Center	Kent Hill
Wichita (5500 E. Kellogg, 67218)	Regional Office	Kent Hill
KENTUCKY:		
Danville (277 N. 1st St., 40442) (Mail: Camp Nelson National Cemetery, KY).	National Cemetery	Patrick Lovett
Lebanon (20 Hwy. 208E, 40033) (Mail: Zachary Taylor National Cemetery, KY).	National Cemetery	Gary D. Peak
Lexington (40511) Cooper Drive Division Leestown Division	Medical Center	Helen K. Cornish
Lexington (833 W. Main St., 40508) (Mail: Camp Nelson National Cemetery, KY).	National Cemetery	Patrick Lovett
Louisville (545 S. 3d St., 40202)	Regional Office	Richard Kestevan
Louisville (800 Zorn Ave., 40202)	Medical Center	Larry J. Sander
Louisville (Cave Hill National Cemetery, 701 Baxter Ave., 40204) (Mail: Zachary Taylor National Cemetery, KY).	National Cemetery	Gary D. Peak

National Facilities—Department of Veterans Affairs—Continued

Address	Type of facility	Director
Louisville (Zachary Taylor National Cemetery, 4701 Brownsboro Rd., 40207).	National Cemetery	Gary D. Peak
Nancy (Mill Springs National Cemetery, 9044 W. Hwy. 80, 42544) (Mail: Camp Nelson National Cemetery, KY).	National Cemetery	Patrick Lovett
Nicholasville (Camp Nelson National Cemetery, 6980 Danville Rd., 40356).	National Cemetery	Patrick Lovett
LOUISIANA:		
Alexandria (71301)	Medical Center	(Vacancy)
Baton Rouge (220 N. 19th St., 70806) (Mail: Port Hudson National Cemetery, LA).	National Cemetery	Jorge Baltar
New Orleans (1601 Peridido St., 70146)	Medical Center	John D. Church, Jr.
New Orleans (701 Loyola Ave., 70113)	Regional Office	Gary Cole
Pineville (Alexandria National Cemetery, 209 E. Shamrock St., 71360) (Mail: Natchez, NC).	National Cemetery	Timothy Spain
Shreveport (510 E. Stoner Ave., 71101)	Medical Center	Billy Valentine
Zachary (20978 Port Hickey Rd., 70791) (Port Hudson National Cemetery).	National Cemetery	Jorge Baltar
MAINE:		
Togus (1 VA Ctr., 04330)	Medical and Regional Office Center	John H. Sims, Jr.
Togus (VA Medical and Regional Office Center, 04330) (Mail: Massachusetts National Cemetery, MA).	National Cemetery	Kurt Rotar
MARYLAND:		
Annapolis (800 West St., 21401) (Mail: Baltimore National Cemetery, MD).	National Cemetery	Robin Pohlman
Baltimore (31 Hopkins Plz., 21201)	Regional Office	Newell Quinton
Baltimore (5501 Frederick Ave., 21228)	National Cemetery	Robin Pohlman
Baltimore (Loudon Park National Cemetery, 3445 Frederick Ave., 21228) (Mail: Baltimore National Cemetery, MD).	National Cemetery	Robin Pohlman
Maryland Health Care System (10 N. Green St., Baltimore, 21201).	Medical Center	Dennis Smith
MASSACHUSETTS:		
Bedford (Edith Nourse Rogers Memorial Veterans Hospital, 200 Springs Rd., 01730).	Medical Center	William A. Conte
Boston Health Care Center (150 S. Huntington Ave., 02130).	Medical Center	Michael Lawson
Boston (John F. Kennedy Federal Bldg., 02203)	Regional Office	Fay Norred
Bourne (Massachusetts National Cemetery, Connery Ave., 02532).	National Cemetery	Kurt Rotar
Brockton (940 Belmont St., 02301)	Medical Center	Roland E. Moore
Northampton (01060)	Medical Center	Bruce A. Gordon
MICHIGAN:		
Ann Arbor (2215 Fuller Rd., 48105)	Medical Center	James Roseborough
Augusta (Ft. Custer National Cemetery, 15501 Dickman Rd., 49012).	National Cemetery	John Bacon
Battle Creek (49106)	Medical Center	Michael K. Wheeler
Detroit (48101–1932)	Medical Center	Carlos B. Lott, Jr.
Detroit (477 Michigan Ave., 48226)	Regional Office	Geraldine Johnson
Iron Mountain (49801)	Medical Center	(Vacancy)
Saginaw (1500 Weiss St., 48602)	Medical Center	Robert H. Sabin
MINNESOTA:		
Minneapolis (1 Veterans Dr., 55417)	Medical Center	(Vacancy)
Minneapolis (Ft. Snelling National Cemetery, 7601 34th Ave. S., 55450).	National Cemetery	Robert F. McCollum
St. Cloud (4801 8th St. N., 56303)	Medical Center	Barry I. Bahl
St. Paul (Bishop Henry Whipple Federal Bldg., Ft. Snelling, 55111) (Remittances: P.O. Box 1820, 55111).	Regional Office & Insurance Center	Ronald J. Henke
MISSISSIPPI:		
Biloxi (39531)	Medical Center (medical and domiciliary).	Julie Catellier
Biloxi Hospital and Domiciliary Division		
Gulfport Hospital Division		
Biloxi (P.O. Box 4968, 39535–4968)	National Cemetery	Douglas Miner
Corinth (1551 Horton St., 38834) (Mail: Memphis National Cemetery, TN).	Medical Center (medical and domiciliary).	Mark E. Maynard
Jackson (1500 E. Woodrow Wilson Dr., 39216)	Medical Center	(Vacancy)
Jackson (1600 E. Woodrow Wilson Ave., 39216)	Regional Office	(Vacancy)
Natchez (41 Cemetery Rd., 39120)	National Cemetery	Timothy Spain
MISSOURI:		
Columbia (Harry S. Truman Memorial Veterans Hospital, 800 Hospital Dr., 65201).	Medical Center	Gary Campbell

National Facilities—Department of Veterans Affairs—Continued

Address	Type of facility	Director
Jefferson City (1024 E. McCarthy, 65101) (Mail: Jefferson Barracks National Cemetery, MO).	National Cemetery	Ralph E. Church
Kansas City (4801 Linwood Blvd., 64128)	Medical Center	Hugh F. Doran
Poplar Bluff (63901)	Medical Center	Nancy Arnold
Springfield (1702 E. Seminole St., 65804)	National Cemetery	Gloria Mote
St. Louis (63125)	Medical Center	Linda Kurz
John J. Cochran Division, 63106		
St. Louis (P.O. Box 5020, Bldg. 104, 4300 Goodfellow Blvd., 63115).	Records Management Center	Brian Corley
St. Louis (400 S. 18th St., 63103–2271)	Regional Office	(Vacancy)
St. Louis (Jefferson Barracks National Cemetery, 2900 Sheridan Dr., 63125).	National Cemetery	Ralph E. Church
MONTANA:		
Montana Health Care System (Ft. Harrison, 59636)	Medical and Regional Office Center	Joseph M. Underkofler
NEBRASKA:		
Greater Nebraska Health Care System (600 S. 70th St., Lincoln, 68510).	Medical Center	(Vacancy)
Lincoln (5631 S. 48th St., 68516)	Regional Office	(Vacancy)
Maxwell (Ft. McPherson National Cemetery, 12004 S. Spur 56A, 69151–1031).	National Cemetery	Jim Schwartz
Omaha (4101 Woolworth Ave., 68105)	Medical Center	John J. Phillips
NEVADA:		
Las Vegas (102 Lake Mead Dr., 89106)	Outpatient Clinic	Ramon J. Reevey
Reno (1000 Locust St., 89520)	Medical Center	Gary R. Whitfield
Reno (1201 Terminal Way, 89520)	Regional Office	Eileen Straub
NEW HAMPSHIRE:		
Manchester (718 Smyth Rd., 02104)	Medical Center	(Vacancy)
Manchester (275 Chestnut St., 03101)	Regional Office	Edward J. Hubbard
NEW JERSEY:		
Beverly (R No. 1, Bridgeboro Rd., 08010)	National Cemetery	Delores T. Blake
Newark (20 Washington Pl., 07102)	Regional Office	William Nicholas
New Jersey Health Care System (East Orange, 07018).	Medical Center	Kenneth Mizrach
Salem (Finn's Point National Cemetery, R.F.D. 3, Ft. Mott Rd., Box 542, 08079) (Mail: Beverly National Cemetery, NJ).	National Cemetery	Delores T. Blake
Somerville (08876)	Asset Management Service	Sharon Dufour
NEW MEXICO:		
Albuquerque (2100 Ridgecrest Dr. SE., 87108–5138).	Medical Center	Norman E. Browne
Albuquerque (500 Gold Ave. SW., 87102)	Regional Office	Sandra D. Epps
Ft. Bayard (Ft. Bayard National Cemetery, P.O. Box 189, 88036) (Mail: Ft. Bliss National Cemetery, TX).	National Cemetery	Gerald T. Vitela
Santa Fe (P.O. Box 88, 501 N. Guadalupe St., 87501).	National Cemetery	Gilbert Gallo
NEW YORK:		
Albany (113 Holland Ave., 12208)	Medical Center	Clyde Parkis
Bath (14810)	Medical Center (medical and domiciliary).	(Vacancy)
Bath (VA Medical Center, 14810)	National Cemetery	Virgil Wertenberger
Bronx (130 W. Kingsbridge Rd., 10468)	Medical Center	MaryAnn Musumeci
Brooklyn Division		
St. Albans Division		
Brooklyn (Cypress Hills National Cemetery, 625 Jamaica Ave., 11208) (Mail: Long Island National Cemetery, NY).	National Cemetery	Art Smith
Buffalo (111 W. Huron St., 14202)	Regional Office	Gregory L. Mason
Calverton (210 Princeton Blvd., 11933)	National Cemetery	Patrick Hallinan
Canandaigua (14424)	Medical Center	W. David Smith
Elmira (Woodlawn National Cemetery, 1825 Davis St., 14901) (Mail: Bath National Cemetery, NY).	National Cemetery	Virgil Wertenberger
Farmingdale (Long Island National Cemetery, 2040 Wellwood Ave., 11735–1211).	National Cemetery	Art Smith
Hudson Valley Health Care System (Franklin Delano Roosevelt Hospital, Montrose, 10548).	Medical Center	Michael Sabo
New York (245 W. Houston Street, 10014)	Regional Office	Pat Amberg-Blyskal
New York Harbor Health Care System (Brooklyn, 11209).	Medical Center	John J. Donnellan, Jr.
Northport (Long Island, 11768)	Medical Center	Mary Dowling
Schuylerville (Saratoga National Cemetery, 200 Duell Rd., 12871–1721).	National Cemetery	Mary Ann Fisher
Syracuse (Irving Ave. & University Pl., 13210)	Medical Center	James Cody
Western New York Health Care System (3495 Bailey Ave., Buffalo, 14215).	Medical Center	William Feeley

National Facilities—Department of Veterans Affairs—Continued

Address	Type of facility	Director
NORTH CAROLINA:		
Asheville (28805)	Medical Center	James A. Christian
Durham (508 Fulton St. & Erwin Rd., 27705)	Medical Center	Michael Phaup
Fayetteville (2300 Ramsey St., 28301)	Medical Center	Richard Baltz
New Bern (1711 National Ave., 28560)	National Cemetery	Margaret S. Yaraborough
Raleigh (501 Rock Quarry Rd., 27610)	National Cemetery	Margaret S. Yaraborough
Salisbury (1601 Brenner Ave., 28144)	Medical Center	Timothy May
Salisbury (202 Government Rd., 28144)	National Cemetery	Margaret S. Yaraborough
Wilmington (2011 Market St., 28403) (Mail: New Bern National Cemetery, NC).	National Cemetery	Margaret S. Yaraborough
Winston-Salem (251 N. Main St., 27155)	Regional Office	John Montgomery
NORTH DAKOTA:		
Fargo (655 1st Ave., 58102)	Medical and Regional Office Center	Douglas M. Kenyon
OHIO:		
Chillicothe (45601)	Medical Center	Michael W. Walton
Cincinnati (3200 Vine St., 45220)	Medical Center	Gary N. Nugent
Cleveland (10701 East Blvd., 44106–3800)	Medical Center	William Montague
Brecksville Division		
Wade Park Division		
Cleveland (1240 E. 9th St., 44199)	Regional Office	Phillip J. Ross
Columbus (2090 Kenny Rd., 43221)	Outpatient Clinic	Lilian T. Thome
Dayton (VA Medical Center, 4100 W. 3d St., 45428)	Medical Center (medical and domiciliary).	Steve Cohen
Dayton (VA Medical Center, 4100 W. 3d St., 45428)	National Cemetery	Karen J. DuHart
Rittman (Ohio Western Reserve National Cemetery, P.O. Box 8, 44270).	National Cemetery	Jeffrey Teas
OKLAHOMA:		
Ft. Gibson (1423 Cemetery Rd., 74434)	National Cemetery	Kenny Rader
Muskogee (Memorial Station, Honor Heights Dr., 74401).	Medical Center	Allen J. Colston
Muskogee (125 S. Main St., 74401)	Regional Office	William D. Fillman, Jr.
Oklahoma City (921 NE. 13th St., 73104)	Medical Center	Steve J. Gentling
OREGON:		
Eagle Point (2763 Riley Rd., 97524)	National Cemetery	Darryl Ferrell
Portland (3710 SW. U.S. Veterans Hospital Rd., 97207).	Medical Center	James Tuchschmidt
Portland (1220 SW. 3d Ave., 97204)	Regional Office	Jerry McRae
Portland (Willamette National Cemetery, 11800 SE. Mt. Scott Blvd., P.O. Box 66147, 97266–6937).	National Cemetery	Gertrude Devenney
Roseburg (97470–6513)	Medical Center	George Marnell
Roseburg (VA Medical Center, 97470) (Mail: Willamette National Cemetery, OR).	National Cemetery	Darryl Ferrell
White City (97503)	Domiciliary	George H. Andries, Jr.
PENNSYLVANIA:		
Altoona (16602–4377)	Medical Center	Gerald L. Williams
Annville (Indiantown Gap National Cemetery, Rt. 2, Box 484, 17003–9618).	National Cemetery	Charlene R. Lewis
Butler (16001–2480)	Medical Center	Michael Moreland
Coatesville (19320)	Medical Center	Gary W. Devansky
Erie (135 E. 38th St. Blvd., 16504)	Medical Center	Stephen M. Lucas
Lebanon (17042)	Medical Center	Charlene Szabo
Philadelphia (5000 Wissahickon Ave., 19101) (Insurance remittances: P.O. Box 7787). (Mail: P.O. Box 42954).	Regional Office & Insurance Center	Thomas M. Lastowka
Philadelphia (University & Woodland Aves., 19104)	Medical Center	Michael Sullivan
Philadelphia (Haines St. & Limekiln Pike, 19138) (Mail: Beverly National Cemetery, NJ).	National Cemetery	Delores T. Blake
Pittsburgh (1000 Liberty Ave., 15222)	Regional Office	Barry S. Jackson
Pittsburgh Health Care System (University Dr. C, 15240).	Medical Center	(Vacancy)
Aspinwall Division		
Pittsburgh Division		
Wilkes-Barre (1111 E. End Blvd., 18711)	Medical Center	Reedes Hurt
PHILIPPINE REPUBLIC:		
Manila (1131 Roxas Blvd., FPO AP96515–1110)	Regional Office & Outpatient Clinic	Barry M. Barker
PUERTO RICO:		
Bayamon (Puerto Rico National Cemetery, Avenue Cementerio Nacional No. 50, 00960).	National Cemetery	William Trowler
Hato Rey (U.S. Courthouse & Federal Bldg., Carlos E. Chardon St., 00918).		
San Juan (Barrio Monacillos G.P.O., Box 364867, 00927–5800).	Medical Center	Jamie Palmer
San Juan (U.S. Courthouse & Federal Bldg., Carlos E. Chardon St., G.P.O. Box 364867, Hato Rey, 00936).	Regional Office	Mary F. Leyland

National Facilities—Department of Veterans Affairs—Continued

Address	Type of facility	Director
RHODE ISLAND:		
Providence (380 Westminster Mall, 02903)	Regional Office	Peter Wells
Providence (Davis Park, 02908)	Medical Center	(Vacancy)
SOUTH CAROLINA:		
Beaufort (1601 Boundary St., 29902)	National Cemetery	Walter A. Gray, Jr.
Charleston (109 Bee St., 29401–5799)	Medical Center	(Vacancy)
Columbia (William Jennings Bryan Dorn Veterans Hospital, 29209).	Medical Center	Brian Heckert
Columbia (1801 Assembly St., 29201)	Regional Office	Carl W. Hawkins
Florence (803 E. National Cemetery Rd., 29501)	National Cemetery	Kenneth LaFevor
SOUTH DAKOTA:		
Black Hills Health Care System (113 Comanche Rd., Ft. Meade, 57741).	Medical Center	Peter P. Henry
Hot Springs (VA Medical Center, 57747) (Mail: Black Hills National Cemetery, SD).	National Cemetery	Robert E. Poe
Sioux Falls (Royal C. Johnson Veterans Memorial Hospital, P.O. Box 5046, 25051 W. 22d St., 57117).	Medical Center and Regional Office	R. Vincent Crawford
Sturgis (P.O. Box 640, 57785) (Mail: Black Hills National Cemetery).		
Sturgis (Black Hills National Cemetery, P.O. Box 640, 57785).	National Cemetery	Robert E. Poe
TENNESSEE:		
Chattanooga (1200 Bailey Ave., 37404)	National Cemetery	Candice Underwood
Knoxville (939 Tyson St. NW., 37917) (Mail: Mountain Home National Cemetery).	National Cemetery	Candice Underwood
Madison (1420 Gallatin Rd. S., 37115–4619) (Nashville National Cemetery).	National Cemetery	Joe Nunnally
Memphis (1030 Jefferson Ave., 38104)	Medical Center	Kenneth L. Mulholland, Jr.
Memphis (3568 Townes Ave., 38122)	National Cemetery	Mary Dill
Mountain Home (Johnson City, 37684)	Medical Center (medical and domiciliary).	Carl J. Gerber
Mountain Home (P.O. Box 8, 37684)	National Cemetery	Rodney Dunn
Murfreesboro (37129–1236)	Medical Center	(Vacancy)
Nashville (1310 24th Ave. S., 37212–2637)	Medical Center	William Mountcastle
Nashville (110 9th Ave. S., 37203)	Regional Office	Thomas R. Jensen
TEXAS:		
Amarillo (6010 Amarillo Blvd. W., 79106)	Medical Center	Wallace M. Hopkins
Austin (1615 E. Woodward St., 78772)	Automation Center	Robert Evans
Austin (P.O. Box 149975, 78714–9575)	Financial Services Center	Debbie L. Clark
Big Spring (79720)	Medical Center	Cary Brown
Central Texas Health Care System (Olin E. Teague Veterans Center, Temple, 76504).	Medical Center (medical and domiciliary).	Dean Billik
Dallas (Dallas Ft. Worth National Cemetery, 2191 Mt. Creek Pkwy., 75211).	National Cemetery	Jimmy Adamson
El Paso Health Care System(5919 Brook Hollow Dr., 79925).	Medical Center	Byron K. Jaqua
Ft. Bliss (5200 Fred Wilson Rd., P.O. Box 6342, 79906).	National Cemetery	Gerald T. Vitela
Houston (2002 Holcombe Blvd., 77030)	Medical Center	David Whately
Houston (6900 Almeda Rd., 77030)	Regional Office	Thomas R. Wagner
Houston (10410 Veterans Memorial Dr., 77038)	National Cemetery	Jorge Lopez
Kerrville (VA Medical Center, 3600 Memorial Blvd., 78028) (Mail: Ft. Sam Houston, TX).	National Cemetery	Joe A. Ramos
North Texas Health Care System (4500 S. Lancaster Rd., 75216).	Medical Center	Alan Harper
San Antonio (517 Paso Hondo St., 78202) (Mail: Ft. Sam Houston National Cemetery).	National Cemetery	Joe A. Ramos
San Antonio (1520 Harry Wurzbach Rd., 78209) (Ft. Sam Houston National Cemetery).	National Cemetery	Joe A. Ramos
South Texas Veterans Health Care System (Audie L. Murphy Memorial Veterans Hospital, 7400 Merton Minter Blvd., San Antonio, 78284).	Medical Center	Jose R. Coronado
Waco (701 Clay Ave., 76799)	Regional Office	(Vacancy)
UTAH:		
Salt Lake City (125 S. State St., 84147)	Regional Office	Douglas B. Wadsworth
Salt Lake City (500 Foothill Blvd., 84148)	Medical Center	James Floyd
VERMONT:		
White River Junction (215 N. Main St., 05009)	Medical and Regional Office Center	Gary M. DeGasta
VIRGINIA:		
Alexandria (1450 Wilkes St., 22314) (Mail: Culpeper National Cemetery, VA).	National Cemetery	Patricia K. Novak
Culpeper (305 U.S. Ave., 22701)	National Cemetery	James Wallace
Danville (721 Lee St., 24541) (Mail: Salisbury National Cemetery, NC).	National Cemetery	Margaret S. Yarborough

National Facilities—Department of Veterans Affairs—Continued

Address	Type of facility	Director
Hampton (23667)	Medical Center (medical and domiciliary).	Bettye Story
Hampton (Cemetery Rd. at Marshall Ave., 23667)	National Cemetery	Homer D. Hardamon
Hampton (VA Medical Center, 23667) (Mail: Cemetery Rd. at Marshall Ave., VA).	National Cemetery	Homer D. Hardamon
Hopewell (10th Ave. & Davis St., 23860) (City Point National Cemetery) (Mail: Richmond National Cemetery, VA).	National Cemetery	Homer D. Hardamon
Leesburg (Balls Bluff National Cemetery, Route 7, 22075) (Mail: Culpeper National Cemetery, VA).	National Cemetery	James Wallace
Mechanicsville (Cold Harbor National Cemetery, Route 156 N., 23111) (Mail: Richmond National Cemetery, VA).	National Cemetery	Homer D. Hardamon
Richmond (1201 Broad Rock Rd., 23249)	Medical Center	James W. Dudley
Richmond (1701 Williamsburg Rd., 23231)	National Cemetery	Homer D. Hardamon
Richmond (Ft. Harrison National Cemetery, 8620 Varina Rd., 23231) (Mail: Richmond National Cemetery, VA).	National Cemetery	Homer D. Hardamon
Richmond (Glendale National Cemetery, 8301 Willis Church Rd., 23231) (Mail: Richmond National Cemetery, VA).	National Cemetery	Homer D. Hardamon
Roanoke (210 Franklin Rd. SW., 24011)	Regional Office	John W. Smith
Salem (24153)	Medical Center	Stephen Lemons
Sandston (Seven Pines National Cemetery, 400 E. Williamsburg Rd., 23150) (Mail: Richmond National Cemetery, VA).	National Cemetery	Homer D. Hardamon
Staunton (901 Richmond Ave., 24401) (Mail: Culpeper National Cemetery, VA).	National Cemetery	James Wallace
Triangle (Quantico National Cemetery, R No. 619, 18424 Joplin Rd., 22172).	National Cemetery	Patricia K. Novak
Winchester (401 National Ave., 22601) (Mail: Culpeper National Cemetery, VA).	National Cemetery	James Wallace
WASHINGTON:		
Kent (Takoma National Cemetery, 18600 SE. 240th St., 98042–4868).	National Cemetery	Sandra L. Noguez
Pugent Sound Health Care System (4435 Beacon Ave. S., Seattle, 98108).	Medical Center	Timothy Williams
Seattle (915 2d Ave., 98174)	Regional Office	Kristine A. Arnold
Spokane (N. 4815 Assembly St., 99205)	Medical Center	Joseph M. Manley
Walla Walla (77 Wainwright Dr., 99362)	Medical Center	(Vacancy)
WEST VIRGINIA:		
Beckley (200 Veterans Ave., 25801)	Medical Center	Gerard Husson
Clarksburg (26301)	Medical Center	Michael W. Neusch
Grafton (West Virginia National Cemetery, Rt. 2, Box 127, 26354).	National Cemetery	Deborah Poe
Grafton (431 Walnut St., 26354) (Mail: West Virginia National Cemetery, WV) (Grafton National Cemetery, WV).	National Cemetery	Deborah Poe
Huntington (1540 Spring Valley Dr., 25704)	Medical Center	David Pennington
Huntington (640 4th Ave., 25701)	Regional Office	Carl E. Lowe II
Martinsburg (25401)	Medical Center (medical and domiciliary).	George Moore, Jr.
WISCONSIN:		
Madison (William S. Middleton Memorial Veterans Hospital, 2500 Overlook Ter., 53705).	Medical Center	Nathan L. Geraths
Milwaukee (5000 W. National Ave., 53295–4000)	Medical Center (medical and domiciliary).	Glen Grippen
Milwaukee (5000 W. National Ave., Bldg. 6, 53295–4000).	Regional Office	Jon A. Baker
Milwaukee (Wood National Cemetery, 5000 W. National Ave., 53295–4000).	National Cemetery	Richard C. Anderson
Tomah (54660)	Medical Center	Stanley Q. Johnson
WYOMING:		
Cheyenne (2360 E. Pershing Blvd., 82001)	Medical Center	Richard Fry
Sheridan (82801)	Medical Center	Maureen Humphrys

Sources of Information

Audiovisuals Persons interested in the availability of VA video productions or exhibits for showing outside VA may write the Chief, Media Services Division (032B), Department of Veterans Affairs, 810 Vermont Avenue NW., Washington, DC 20420. Phone, 202–273–9781 or 9782.

Contracts Persons seeking to do business with the Department of Veterans Affairs may contact the Director, Acquisition Resources Service (95), 810 Vermont Avenue NW., Washington, DC 20420. Phone, 202–273–8815. A brochure entitled *Doing Business with the Department of Veterans Affairs* is available upon request. The Office of Acquisition and Materiel Management also distributes information regarding VA business opportunities through the Internet, at www.va.gov/oa&mm/index.htm.

Small Business Programs Persons seeking information on VA's small business programs may call 800–949–8387 (toll free) or 202–565–8124. The Office of Small and Disadvantaged Business Utilization website (Internet, www.va.gov/osdbu) contains a considerable amount of information about these programs.

Electronic Access Information concerning the Department of Veterans Affairs is available electronically through the Internet, at www.va.gov.

Employment The Department of Veterans Affairs employs physicians, dentists, podiatrists, optometrists, nurses, nurse anesthetists, physician assistants, expanded-function dental auxiliaries, registered respiratory therapists, certified respiratory technicians, licensed physical therapists, occupational therapists, pharmacists, and licensed practical or vocational nurses under VA's excepted merit system. This system does not require civil service eligibility. Other professional, technical, administrative, and clerical occupations exist in VA that do require civil service eligibility. Persons interested in employment should contact the Human Resources Management Office at their nearest VA facility. All qualified applicants will receive consideration for appointments without regard to race, religion, color, national origin, sex, political affiliation, or any nonmerit factor.

Freedom of Information Act Requests Inquiries should be directed to the Assistant Secretary for Information and Technology, Information Management Service (045A4), 810 Vermont Avenue NW., Washington, DC 20420. Phone, 202–273–8135.

Inspector General Inquiries and Hotline Publicly available documents and information on the VA Office of Inspector General are available electronically through the Internet, at www.va.gov/oig/homepage.htm. Complaints may be sent by mail to the VA Inspector General (53E), P.O. Box 50410, Washington, DC 20091–0410. Hotline phone, 800–488–8244. E-mail, vaoig.hotline@forum.va.gov.

Medical Center (Hospital) Design, Construction, and Related Services VA projects requiring services for design, construction, and other related services are advertised in the *Commerce Business Daily*. Architectural/engineering firms interested in designing VA medical center construction projects may write to the Director, Program Support Service (187B). Phone, 202–565–4181. Construction contractors should address their inquiries to the Chief, Office and Library Support Division (182C). Phone, 202–565–5171. Contact either office at the Department of Veterans Affairs Central Office, 810 Vermont Avenue NW., Washington, DC 20420; or write to the Chief, Acquisition and Materiel Management, at any VA medical center or regional office center (see listing in the preceding text).

News Media Representatives of the media outside Washington, DC, may contact VA through the nearest regional Office of Public Affairs:

Atlanta (404–347–3236)
Chicago (312–353–4076)
Dallas (214–767–9270)
Denver (303–914–5855)
Los Angeles (310–268–4207)
New York (212–807–3429)

National and Washington, DC, media may contact the Office of Public Affairs in the VA Central Office, 810 Vermont Avenue NW., Washington, DC 20420. Phone, 202–273–5700.

Publications The *Annual Report of the Secretary of Veterans Affairs* may be obtained (in single copies), without charge, from the Reports and Information Service (008C2), 810 Vermont Avenue NW., Washington, DC 20420.

The 1998 VA pamphlet *Federal Benefits for Veterans and Dependents* (80–98–1) is available for sale by the Superintendent of Documents, Government Printing Office, Washington, DC 20402.

The *Board of Veterans Appeals Index* (I–01–1), an index to appellate decisions, is available on microfiche in annual cumulation from July 1977 through December 1994. The quarterly indexes may be purchased for $7 and annual cumulative indexes for $22.50. Annual indexes and BVA decisions for 1992 and 1993 are also available on CD–ROM for $30. The VADEX/CITATOR of Appellate Research Materials is a complete printed quarterly looseleaf cumulation of research material which may be purchased for $175 with binder and for $160 without binder. The Vadex Infobase, a computer-searchable version of the VADEX, is also available on diskettes for $100 per copy. These publications may be obtained by contacting Promisel and Korn, Inc. Phone, 301–986–0650. Beginning in 1993, archived decisions of the Board of Veterans' Appeals are available on CD–ROM, which may be obtained from the Superintendent of Documents, Government Printing Office, Washington, DC 20402.

VA Pamphlet, *A Summary of Department of Veteran Affairs Benefits* (27–82–2), may be obtained, without charge, from any VA regional office.

Interments in VA National Cemeteries, VA NCA–IS–1, provides a list of national cemeteries and information on procedures and eligibility for burial. Copies may be obtained without charge from the National Cemetery Administration (402B2), 810 Vermont Avenue NW., Washington, DC 20420.

For further information, contact the Office of Public Affairs, Department of Veterans Affairs, 810 Vermont Avenue NW., Washington, DC 20420. Phone, 202–273–5700. Internet, www.va.gov.

Independent Establishments and Government Corporations

AFRICAN DEVELOPMENT FOUNDATION

1400 "I" Street NW., Washington, DC 20005
Phone, 202–673–3916. Internet, www.adf.gov.

Board of Directors:

Chairman	Ernest G. Green
Vice Chair	Willie Grace Campbell
Members of the Board	Marion Dawson-Carr, Henry McKoy, (3 vacancies)

Staff:

President	William R. Ford
Vice President	Nathaniel Fields
General Counsel	Doris Martin

[For the African Development Foundation statement of organization, see the *Code of Federal Regulations,* Title 22, Part 1501]

The African Development Foundation assists and supports indigenous, community-based self-help organizations in their efforts to solve their own development problems.

The African Development Foundation was established by the African Development Foundation Act (22 U.S.C. 290h) as a nonprofit Government corporation to support the self-help efforts of poor people in African countries. The Foundation became operational in 1984 and is governed by a seven-member Board of Directors, appointed by the President with the advice and consent of the Senate. By law, five Board members are from the private sector and two are from the Government.

The purposes of the Foundation are to:

—strengthen the bonds of friendship and understanding between the people of Africa and the United States;

—support self-help development activities at the local level designed to promote opportunities for community development;

—stimulate and promote effective and expanding participation of Africans in their development process; and

—encourage the establishment and growth of development institutions that are indigenous to particular countries in Africa and that can respond to the requirements of the poor in those countries.

To carry out its purposes, the Foundation makes grants, loans, and loan guarantees to African private groups, associations, or other entities engaged in peaceful activities that enable the people of Africa to develop more fully.

For further information, contact the Public Affairs Officer, African Development Foundation, 10th Floor, 1400 "I" Street NW., Washington, DC 20005. Phone, 202–673–3916. Fax, 202–673–3810. Internet, www.adf.gov.

CENTRAL INTELLIGENCE AGENCY

Washington, DC 20505
Phone, 703–482–1100. Internet, www.cia.gov.

Director of Central Intelligence	GEORGE J. TENET
Deputy Director of Central Intelligence	GEN. JOHN A. GORDON, USAF

[For the Central Intelligence Agency statement of organization, see the *Code of Federal Regulations,* Title 32, Part 1900]

The Central Intelligence Agency collects, evaluates, and disseminates vital information on political, military, economic, scientific, and other developments abroad needed to safeguard national security.

The Central Intelligence Agency was established under the National Security Council by the National Security Act of 1947, as amended (50 U.S.C. 401 *et seq.*). It now functions under that statute, Executive Order 12333 of December 4, 1981, and other laws, regulations, and directives.

The Director of Central Intelligence heads both the Intelligence Community and the Central Intelligence Agency and is the President's principal adviser on intelligence matters. The Director and Deputy Director of Central Intelligence are appointed by the President with the advice and consent of the Senate.

The Central Intelligence Agency, under the direction of the President or the National Security Council:

—advises the National Security Council in matters concerning such intelligence activities of the Government departments and agencies as relate to national security;

—makes recommendations to the National Security Council for the coordination of such intelligence activities of the departments and agencies of the Government as relate to the national security;

—correlates and evaluates intelligence relating to the national security and provides for the appropriate dissemination of such intelligence within the Government;

—collects, produces, and disseminates counterintelligence and foreign intelligence, including information not otherwise obtainable. The collection of counterintelligence or foreign intelligence within the United States shall be coordinated with the Federal Bureau of Investigation (FBI) as required by procedures agreed upon by the Director of Central Intelligence and the Attorney General;

—collects, produces, and disseminates intelligence on foreign aspects of narcotics production and trafficking;

—conducts counterintelligence activities outside the United States and, without assuming or performing any internal security functions, conducts counterintelligence activities within the United States in coordination with the FBI as required by procedures agreed upon by the Director of Central Intelligence and the Attorney General;

—coordinates counterintelligence activities and the collection of information not otherwise obtainable when conducted outside the United States by other departments and agencies;

—conducts special activities approved by the President. No agency, except the Central Intelligence Agency (or the Armed Forces of the United States in time of war declared by Congress or during any period covered by a report from the President to the Congress under the War Powers Resolution (50 U.S.C. 1541 *et seq.*)), may conduct any special activity unless the President determines that another agency is more likely to achieve a particular objective;

—carries out or contracts for research, development, and procurement of technical systems and devices relating to authorized functions;

—protects the security of its installations, activities, information, property, and employees by appropriate means, including such investigations of applicants, employees, contractors, and other persons with similar associations with the Agency, as are necessary;

—collects, produces, and disseminates military intelligence to military commands to enhance battlefield awareness;

—conducts such administrative and technical support activities within and outside the United States as are necessary to perform its functions, including procurement and essential cover and proprietary arrangements; and

—performs such other functions and duties relating to intelligence that affect the national security as the National Security Council may from time to time direct.

The Agency has no police, subpoena, or law enforcement powers or internal security functions.

For further information, contact the Central Intelligence Agency, Washington, DC 20505. Phone, 703–482–1100. Internet, www.cia.gov.

COMMODITY FUTURES TRADING COMMISSION

1155 Twenty-first Street NW., Washington, DC 20581
Phone, 202–418–5000. Internet, www.cftc.gov.

Chairman	WILLIAM J. RAINER
Commissioners	THOMAS J. ERICKSON, BARBARA P. HOLUM, JAMES E. NEWSOME, DAVID D. SPEARS
General Counsel	C. ROBERT PAUL
Executive Director	DONALD L. TENDICK, *Acting*

[For the Commodity Futures Trading Commission statement of organization, see the *Code of Federal Regulations,* Title 17, Part 140]

The mission of the Commodity Futures Trading Commission is to protect market users and the public from fraud, manipulation, and abusive practices related to the sale of commodity futures and options, and to foster open, competitive, and financially sound commodity futures and option markets.

The Commodity Futures Trading Commission (CFTC) , the Federal regulatory agency for futures trading, was established by the Commodity Futures Trading Commission Act of 1974 (7 U.S.C. 4a). The Commission began operation in April 1975, and its authority to regulate futures trading was renewed by Congress in 1978, 1982, 1986, 1992, and 1995.

The Commission consists of five Commissioners who are appointed by the President, with the advice and consent of the Senate. One Commissioner is designated by the President to serve as Chairperson. The Commissioners serve staggered 5-year terms, and by law no more than three Commissioners can belong to the same political party.

186-873 D-00--13

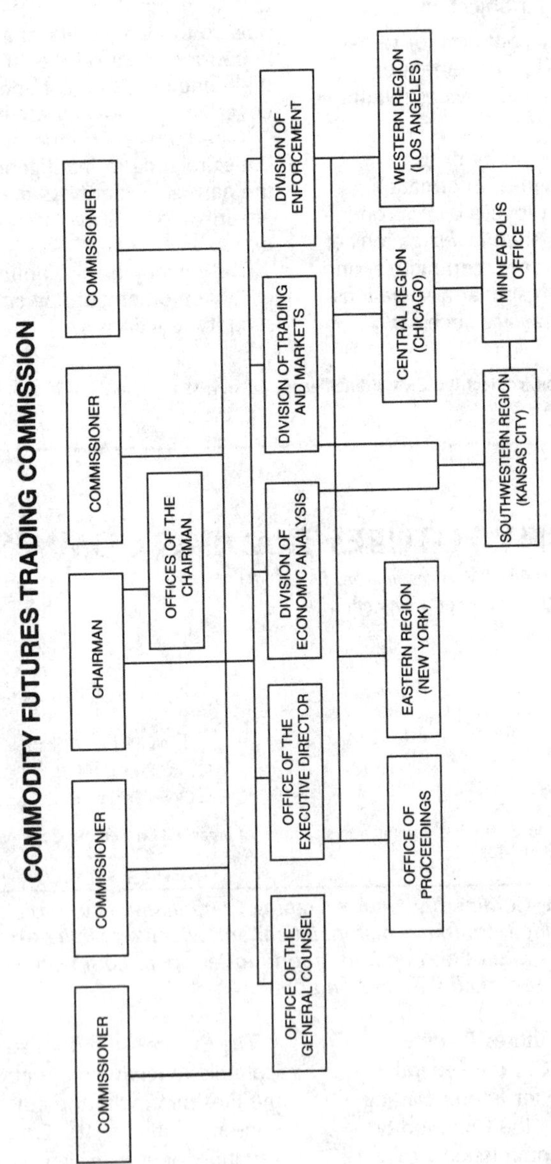
COMMODITY FUTURES TRADING COMMISSION
COMMISSIONER
COMMISSIONER
CHAIRMAN
COMMISSIONER
COMMISSIONER
OFFICES OF THE CHAIRMAN
OFFICE OF THE GENERAL COUNSEL
OFFICE OF THE EXECUTIVE DIRECTOR
DIVISION OF ECONOMIC ANALYSIS
DIVISION OF TRADING AND MARKETS
DIVISION OF ENFORCEMENT
OFFICE OF PROCEEDINGS
EASTERN REGION (NEW YORK)
SOUTHWESTERN REGION (KANSAS CITY)
CENTRAL REGION (CHICAGO)
MINNEAPOLIS OFFICE
WESTERN REGION (LOS ANGELES)

The Commission has five major operating components: the Divisions of Enforcement, Economic Analysis, and Trading and Markets, and the Offices of the Executive Director and the General Counsel.

Activities

The Commission regulates trading on the U.S. futures exchanges, which offer active futures and options contracts. It also regulates the activities of numerous commodity exchange members, public brokerage houses (futures commission merchants), Commission-registered futures industry salespeople (associated persons), commodity trading advisers, and commodity pool operators.

The Commission's regulatory and enforcement efforts are designed to ensure that the futures trading process is fair and that it protects both the rights of customers and the financial integrity of the marketplace. It oversees the rules under which an exchange operates and monitors exchange enforcement of those rules. It reviews the terms of proposed futures contracts, and registers companies and individuals who handle customer funds or give trading advice. The Commission also protects the public by enforcing rules that require that customer funds be kept in bank accounts separate from accounts maintained by firms for their own use, and that such customer accounts be marked to present market value at the close of trading each day.

Large regional offices are maintained in Chicago, IL, and New York, NY, where many of the Nation's futures exchanges are located. Smaller regional offices are located in Kansas City, MO, and Los Angeles, CA. A suboffice of the Kansas City regional office is located in Minneapolis, MN.

For further information, contact the Office of Public Affairs, Commodity Futures Trading Commission, 1155 Twenty-first Street NW., Washington, DC 20581. Phone, 202–418–5080. Internet, www.cftc.gov.

CONSUMER PRODUCT SAFETY COMMISSION

East-West Towers, 4330 East-West Highway, Bethesda, MD 20814
Phone, 301–504–0580. Internet, www.cpsc.gov.

Chairman	Ann Brown
Commissioners	Mary Sheila Gall, Thomas H. Moore, (2 vacancies)
General Counsel	Michael S. Solender
Director, Office of Congressional Relations	Robert J. Wager
Director, Office of the Secretary	Sadye E. Dunn
Freedom of Information Officer	Todd A. Stevenson
Director, Office of Equal Employment Opportunity and Minority Enterprise	Felipa C. Coleman
Executive Director	Pamela Gilbert
Deputy Executive Director	Thomas W. Murr, Jr.
Inspector General	Mary B. Wyles, *Acting*
Director, Office of Human Resources Management	M. Beverly St. Clair
Director, Office of Information Services	Douglas G. Noble
Director, Office of Planning and Evaluation	Nancy J. Scheers, *Acting*
Director, Office of Information and Public Affairs	Russell J. Rader
Director, Office of the Budget	Edward E. Quist
Associate Executive Director for Administration	Mauna V. Kammer

Assistant Executive Director for Compliance	ALAN H. SCHOEM
Associate Executive Director for Economic Analysis	WARREN J. PRUNELLA
Associate Executive Director for Engineering Sciences	ANDREW G. STADNIK
Associate Executive Director for Epidemiology	SUSAN AHMED
Associate Executive Director for Field Operations	PATRICK D. WEDDLE, *Acting*
Assistant Executive Director for Hazard Identification and Reduction	RONALD L. MEDFORD
Associate Executive Director for Health Sciences	MARY ANN DANELLO
Associate Executive Director for Laboratory Sciences	DAVID A. WALDEN, *Acting*
Associate Executive Director for Recalls and Compliance	MARC J. SCHOEM

[For the Consumer Product Safety Commission statement of organization, see the *Code of Federal Regulations,* Title 16, Part 1000]

The Consumer Product Safety Commission protects the public against unreasonable risks of injury from consumer products; assists consumers in evaluating the comparative safety of consumer products; develops uniform safety standards for consumer products and minimizes conflicting State and local regulations; and promotes research and investigation into the causes and prevention of product-related deaths, illnesses, and injuries.

The Consumer Product Safety Commission is an independent Federal regulatory agency established by the Consumer Product Safety Act (15 U.S.C. 2051 *et seq.*). The Commission consists of five Commissioners, appointed by the President with the advice and consent of the Senate, one of whom is appointed Chairman.

The Commission is responsible for implementing provisions of the Flammable Fabrics Act (15 U.S.C. 1191), the Poison Prevention Packaging Act of 1970 (15 U.S.C. 1471), the Federal Hazardous Substances Act (15 U.S.C. 1261), and the act of August 2, 1956 (15 U.S.C. 1211), which prohibits the transportation of refrigerators without door safety devices.

Activities

To help protect the public from unreasonable risks of injury associated with consumer products, the Commission:

—requires manufacturers to report defects in products that could create substantial hazards;

—requires, where appropriate, corrective action with respect to specific substantially hazardous consumer products already in commerce;

—collects information on consumer product-related injuries and maintains a comprehensive Injury Information Clearinghouse;

—conducts research on consumer product hazards;

—encourages and assists in the development of voluntary standards related to the safety of consumer products;

—establishes, where appropriate, mandatory consumer product standards;

—bans, where appropriate, hazardous consumer products; and

—conducts outreach programs for consumers, industry, and local governments.

Offices

The Commission's headquarters is located at East-West Towers, 4330 East-West Highway, Bethesda, MD 20814. Regional offices are located in Chicago, IL; New York, NY; and San Francisco,

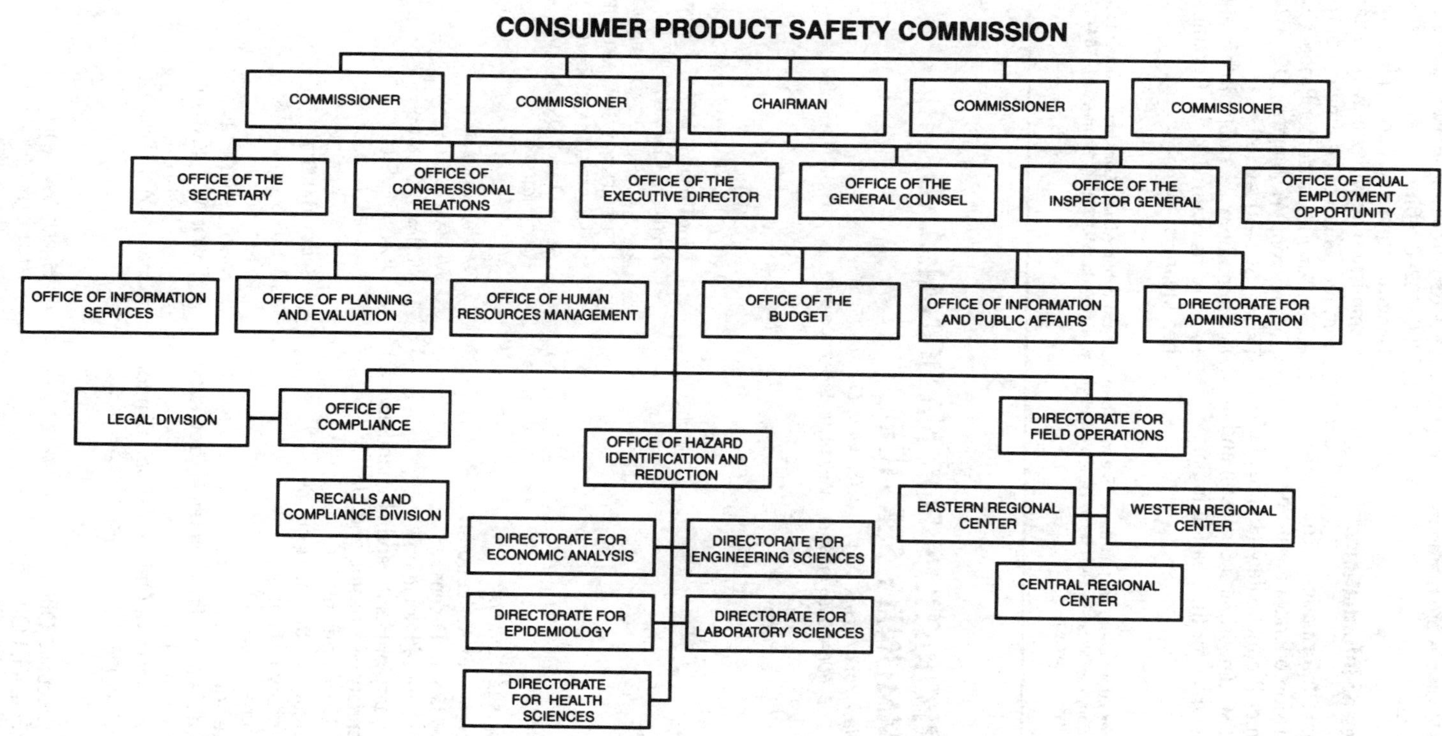

CONSUMER PRODUCT SAFETY COMMISSION
COMMISSIONER
COMMISSIONER
CHAIRMAN
COMMISSIONER
COMMISSIONER
OFFICE OF THE SECRETARY
OFFICE OF CONGRESSIONAL RELATIONS
OFFICE OF THE EXECUTIVE DIRECTOR
OFFICE OF THE GENERAL COUNSEL
OFFICE OF THE INSPECTOR GENERAL
OFFICE OF EQUAL EMPLOYMENT OPPORTUNITY
OFFICE OF INFORMATION SERVICES
OFFICE OF PLANNING AND EVALUATION
OFFICE OF HUMAN RESOURCES MANAGEMENT
OFFICE OF THE BUDGET
OFFICE OF INFORMATION AND PUBLIC AFFAIRS
DIRECTORATE FOR ADMINISTRATION
LEGAL DIVISION
OFFICE OF COMPLIANCE
RECALLS AND COMPLIANCE DIVISION
OFFICE OF HAZARD IDENTIFICATION AND REDUCTION
DIRECTORATE FOR ECONOMIC ANALYSIS
DIRECTORATE FOR ENGINEERING SCIENCES
DIRECTORATE FOR EPIDEMIOLOGY
DIRECTORATE FOR LABORATORY SCIENCES
DIRECTORATE FOR HEALTH SCIENCES
DIRECTORATE FOR FIELD OPERATIONS
EASTERN REGIONAL CENTER
WESTERN REGIONAL CENTER
CENTRAL REGIONAL CENTER

CA. Field offices are maintained in various cities.

Sources of Information

Consumer Information The Commission operates a toll-free Consumer Product Safety Hotline, 800–638–CPSC (English and Spanish); and a teletypewriter for the hearing-impaired, 800–638–8270 (or in Maryland only, 800–492–8140).

General Inquiries Information on Commission activities may be obtained from the Office of Information and Public Affairs, Consumer Product Safety Commission, Washington, DC 20207. Phone, 301–504–0580.

Reading Room A public information room is maintained at the Commission headquarters.

For further information, contact the Office of Information and Public Affairs, Consumer Product Safety Commission, East-West Towers, 4330 East-West Highway, Bethesda, MD 20814. Phone, 301–504–0580. Internet, www.cpsc.gov.

CORPORATION FOR NATIONAL AND COMMUNITY SERVICE

1201 New York Avenue NW., Washington, DC 20525
Phone, 202–606–5000. Internet, www.nationalservice.org.

Board of Directors:	
Chair	(VACANCY)
Members	AMY C. ACHOR, VICTOR ASHE, JUANITA SIMS DOTY, THOMAS EHRLICH, CHRISTOPHER C. GALLAGHER, DOROTHY JOHNSON, LESLIE LENKOWSKY, ARTHUR NAPARSTEK, MARC RACICOT, ALAN D. SOLOMONT, (4 VACANCIES)
Members (*ex officio*)	
(Secretary of Agriculture)	DAN GLICKMAN
(Secretary of Defense)	WILLIAM S. COHEN
(Secretary of Education)	RICHARD W. RILEY
(Secretary of Health and Human Services)	DONNA E. SHALALA
(Secretary of Housing and Urban Development)	ANDREW M. CUOMO
(Secretary of the Interior)	BRUCE BABBITT
(Secretary of Labor)	ALEXIS M. HERMAN
(Attorney General)	JANET RENO
(Director, Peace Corps)	MARK L. SCHEIDER
(Administrator, Environmental Protection Agency)	CAROL M. BROWNER
(Chief Executive Officer, Corporation for National and Community Service)	HARRIS WOFFORD
Staff:	
Chief Executive Officer	HARRIS WOFFORD
Chief Financial Officer	ANTHONY MUSICK
Chief Operating Officer	WENDY ZENKER

Chief of Staff to the CEO	JOHN S. GOMPERTS
Director, AmeriCorps	DEBORAH JOSPIN
Director, Congressional and Intergovernmental Affairs	MARK ISAAC
Director, Evaluation and Effective Practices	BILL BENTLEY
Director, Human Resources	PHYLLIS BEAULIEU
Director, Learn and Serve America	MARILYN W. SMITH
Director, National Senior Service Corps	THOMAS ENDRES
Director, Planning and Program Integration	GARY KOWALCZYK
Director, Public Affairs	TARA MURPHY
Director, Public Liaison	CHRISTINE BENERO
General Counsel	THOMASENIA DUNCAN
Inspector General	LUISE S. JORDAN

The Corporation for National and Community Service engages Americans of all backgrounds in community-based service that addresses the Nation's educational, public safety, environmental, and other human needs to achieve direct and demonstrable results. In so doing, the Corporation fosters civic responsibility, strengthens the ties that bind us together as a people, and provides educational opportunity for those who make a substantial service contribution.

The Corporation for National and Community Service oversees three major service initiatives: AmeriCorps, Learn and Serve America, and the National Senior Service Corps. The Corporation was established on October 1, 1993, by the National and Community Service Trust Act of 1993 (42 U.S.C. 12651 *et seq.*). In addition to creating several new service programs, the act consolidated the functions and activities of the former Commission on National and Community Service and the Federal agency ACTION.

The goal of the Corporation is to address the Nation's most critical problems in the areas of education, the environment, public safety, and other human needs, while fostering a service ethic in participants and beneficiaries.

The Corporation is a Federal corporation governed by a 15–member bipartisan Board of Directors, appointed by the President with the advice and consent of the Senate. The Secretaries of Agriculture, Defense, Education, Health and Human Services, Housing and Urban Development, Interior, and Labor; the Attorney General, the Environmental Protection Agency Administrator, the Peace Corps Director, and the Chief Executive Officer of the Corporation serve as *ex officio* members of the Board. The Board has responsibility for overall policy direction of the Corporation's activities and has the power to make all final grant decisions, approve the strategic plan and annual budget, and advise and make recommendations to the President and the Congress regarding changes in the national service laws.

AmeriCorps AmeriCorps, the domestic Peace Corps, engages more than 40,000 Americans in intensive results-oriented service. Most AmeriCorps members are selected by and serve with local and national organizations like Habitat for Humanity, the American Red Cross, Big Brothers/Big Sisters, and Boys and Girls Clubs. Others serve in AmeriCorps*VISTA (Volunteers in Service to America) and AmeriCorps*NCCC (the National Civilian Community Corps). After their term of service, AmeriCorps members receive education awards that help finance college or pay back student loans.

Many AmeriCorps grants are awarded through State commissions and other approved entities that submit State plans built on existing service initiatives. Public and nonprofit organizations can apply to the State commissions for subgrants, implement and operate service programs, and obtain education awards for eligible participants. National and multi-State nonprofit organizations,

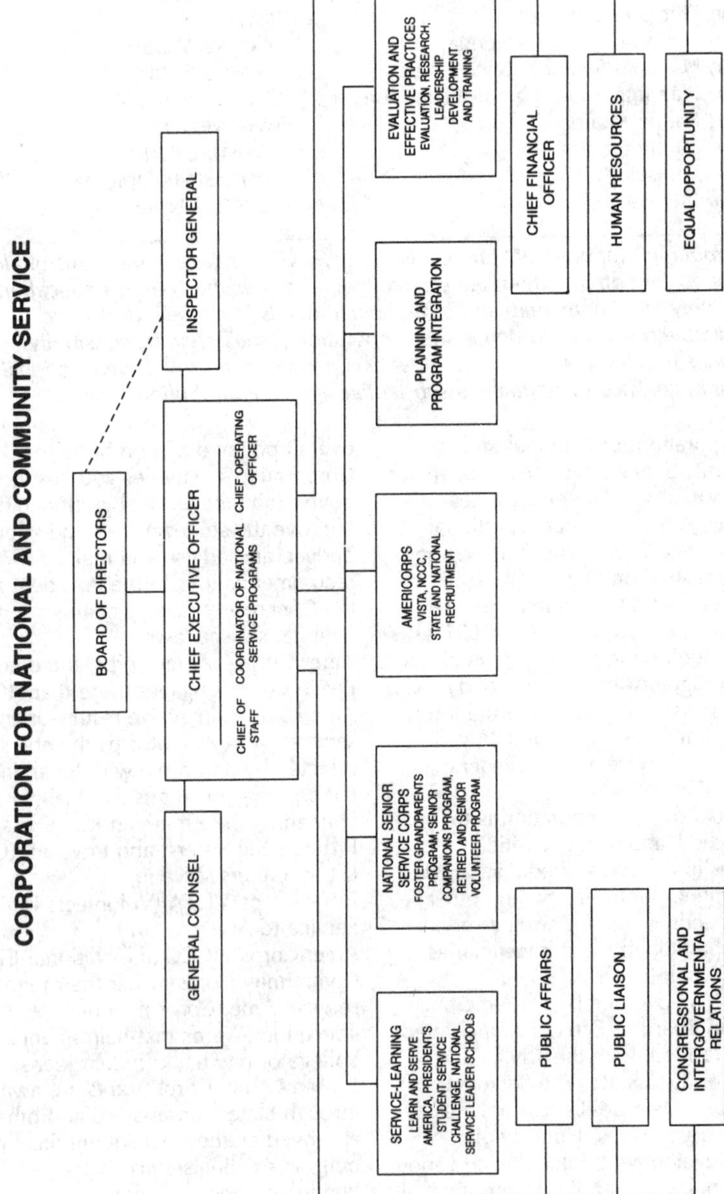
CORPORATION FOR NATIONAL AND COMMUNITY SERVICE
BOARD OF DIRECTORS
INSPECTOR GENERAL
CHIEF EXECUTIVE OFFICER
CHIEF OF STAFF
COORDINATOR OF NATIONAL SERVICE PROGRAMS
CHIEF OPERATING OFFICER
GENERAL COUNSEL
SERVICE-LEARNING LEARN AND SERVE AMERICA, PRESIDENT'S STUDENT SERVICE CHALLENGE, NATIONAL SERVICE LEADER SCHOOLS
NATIONAL SENIOR SERVICE CORPS FOSTER GRANDPARENTS PROGRAM, SENIOR COMPANIONS PROGRAM, RETIRED AND SENIOR VOLUNTEER PROGRAM
AMERICORPS VISTA, NCCC, STATE AND NATIONAL RECRUITMENT
PLANNING AND PROGRAM INTEGRATION
EVALUATION AND EFFECTIVE PRACTICES EVALUATION, RESEARCH, LEADERSHIP DEVELOPMENT AND TRAINING
PUBLIC AFFAIRS
PUBLIC LIAISON
CONGRESSIONAL AND INTERGOVERNMENTAL RELATIONS
CHIEF FINANCIAL OFFICER
HUMAN RESOURCES
EQUAL OPPORTUNITY

Indian tribes, and institutions of higher education can apply directly to the Corporation for AmeriCorps funding. In addition, organizations and public entities that manage their own nonfederally funded community service programs can apply directly to the Corporation for AmeriCorps education awards for their participants. All AmeriCorps grants require matching funds.

Learn and Serve America Learn and Serve America helps support nearly one million students from kindergarten through college who meet community needs while improving their academic skills and learning the habits of good citizenship. In addition to providing grants to schools and community organizations, the Corporation for National and Community Service also promotes student service through the President's student service challenge.

Grants are awarded through State educational agencies, State commissions, and directly by the Corporation. School-based programs receive grants through State educational agencies, while community-based programs apply for funding through the same State commissions that coordinate AmeriCorps grants. Higher education institutions apply directly to the Corporation for grants.

National Senior Service Corps Through the National Senior Service Corps (Senior Corps), nearly half a million Americans age 55 and older share their time and talents to help solve local problems. As foster grandparents, they serve one-on-one with young people with special needs; as senior companions, they help other seniors live independently in their homes; and as volunteers with the Retired and Senior Volunteers Program (RSVP), they help meet a wide range of community needs.

The Corporation's mission to develop and support an ethic of service in America involves initiatives, special demonstration projects, and other activities, in addition to the three major program areas. These include a disaster response initiative, the AmeriCorps Leaders Program, and short-term summer service initiatives. The Corporation also carries out an extensive training and technical assistance effort to support and assist State commissions and service programs. Through partnership with the private sector, other Federal agencies, and the Points of Light Foundation, the Corporation further advocates and advances service in America.

Sources of Information

Electronic Access Information regarding the Corporation's programs and activities is available on the Internet, at www.nationalservice.org.

General Information To obtain additional information regarding AmeriCorps, call 800–942–2677 (toll-free). For Senior Corps programs, call 800–424–8867 (toll-free).

Grants Notices of available funds are published in the *Federal Register* for most programs. State program offices and State commissions on national and community service are located in most States and are the best source of information on programs in specific States or communities.

Recruitment Persons interested in joining AmeriCorps should call 800–942–2677 (toll-free). To participate in other national service programs, contact State offices or State commissions on national and community service.

For further information, contact the Corporation for National and Community Service, 1201 New York Avenue NW., Washington, DC 20525. Phone, 202–606–5000. Internet, www.nationalservice.org.

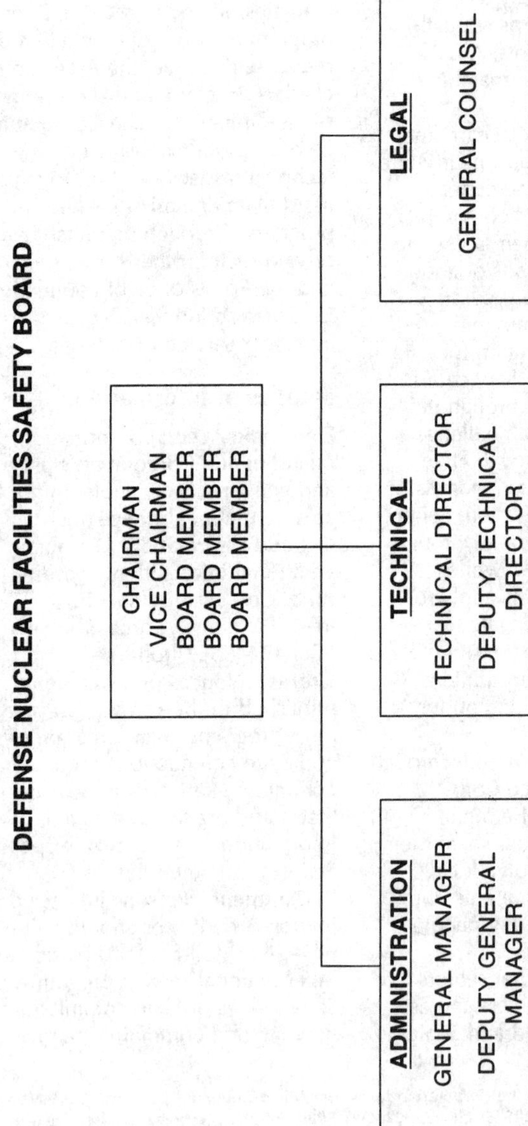
DEFENSE NUCLEAR FACILITIES SAFETY BOARD
CHAIRMAN
VICE CHAIRMAN
BOARD MEMBER
BOARD MEMBER
BOARD MEMBER
ADMINISTRATION
GENERAL MANAGER
DEPUTY GENERAL MANAGER
TECHNICAL
TECHNICAL DIRECTOR
DEPUTY TECHNICAL DIRECTOR
LEGAL
GENERAL COUNSEL

DEFENSE NUCLEAR FACILITIES SAFETY BOARD

Suite 700, 625 Indiana Avenue NW., Washington, DC 20004
Phone, 202–694–7000. Fax, 202–208–6518. Internet, www.dnfsb.gov.

Chairman	JOHN T. CONWAY
Vice Chairman	A.J. EGGENBERGER
Members	JOSEPH J. DINUNNO, JOHN E. MANSFIELD, JESSIE H. ROBERSON
General Counsel	RICHARD A. AZZARO
General Manager	KENNETH M. PUSATERI
Technical Director	J. KENT FORTENBERRY

The Defense Nuclear Facilities Safety Board reviews and evaluates the content and implementation of standards relating to the design, construction, operation, and decommissioning of defense nuclear facilities of the Department of Energy (DOE).

The Defense Nuclear Facilities Safety Board was established as an independent agency on September 29, 1988, by the Atomic Energy Act of 1954, as amended (42 U.S.C. 2286–2286i).

The Board is composed of five members appointed by the President with the advice and consent of the Senate. Members of the Board are appointed from among United States citizens who are respected experts in the field of nuclear safety.

Activities

The Defense Nuclear Facilities Safety Board reviews and evaluates the content and implementation of standards for defense nuclear facilities of DOE; investigates any event or practice at these facilities which may adversely affect public health and safety; and reviews and monitors the design, construction, and operation of facilities. The Board makes recommendations to the Secretary of Energy concerning DOE defense nuclear facilities to ensure adequate protection of public health and safety. In the event that any aspect of operations, practices, or occurrences reviewed by the Board is determined to present an imminent or severe threat to public health and safety, the Board transmits its recommendations directly to the President.

For further information, contact the Defense Nuclear Facilities Safety Board, Suite 700, 625 Indiana Avenue NW., Washington, DC 20004. Phone, 202–694–7000. Internet, www.dnfsb.gov.

ENVIRONMENTAL PROTECTION AGENCY

401 M Street SW., Washington, DC 20460
Phone, 888–372–8255 (toll-free). Internet, www.epa.gov.

Administrator	CAROL M. BROWNER
Deputy Administrator	W. MICHAEL MCCABE
Associate Administrator for Communications, Education, and Public Affairs	STEVE SNIDER

Associate Administrator for Congressional and Intergovernmental Relations	DIANE E. THOMPSON
Associate Administrator for Policy and Reinvention	RICK FARRELL
Chief Judge, Office of Administrative Law Judges	SUSAN L. BIRO
Director, Executive Secretariat	SANDRA L. HUDNALL
Director, Executive Support Office	DIANE N. BAZZLE
Director, Office of Children's Health Protection	E. RAMONA TROVATO
Director, Office of Civil Rights	ANNE E. GOODE
Director, Office of Cooperative Environmental Management	CLARENCE HARDY
Director, Office of Small and Disadvantaged Business Utilization	JEANETTE L. BROWN
Director, Regional Operations Staff	FRANCES T. GREENBERG, *Acting*
Director, Science Advisory Board	DONALD G. BARNES
Lead Environmental Appeals Judge, Environmental Appeals Board	RONALD L. MCCALLUM
Staff Offices:	
Assistant Administrator for Administration and Resources Management	ROMULO L. DIAZ, JR.
Assistant Administrator for Air and Radiation	ROBERT PERCIASEPE
Assistant Administrator for Enforcement and Compliance Assurance	STEVEN A. HERMAN
Assistant Administrator for Environmental Information	ALVIN M. PESACHOWITZ
Assistant Administrator for International Activities	WILLIAM A. NITZE
Assistant Administrator for Prevention, Pesticides, and Toxic Substances	(VACANCY)
Assistant Administrator for Research and Development	NORINE E. NOONAN
Assistant Administrator for Solid Waste and Emergency Response	TIMOTHY FIELDS, JR., *Acting*
Assistant Administrator for Water	JONATHON (CHUCK) C. FOX
Chief Financial Officer	MICHAEL W. S. RYAN
General Counsel	JONATHAN Z. CANNON
Inspector General	NIKKI L. TINSLEY

[For the Environmental Protection Agency statement of organization, see the *Code of Federal Regulations*, Title 40, Part 1]

The mission of the Environmental Protection Agency is to protect human health and to safeguard the natural environment—air, water, and land—upon which life depends to the fullest extent possible under the laws enacted by Congress.

The Environmental Protection Agency was established in the executive branch as an independent agency pursuant to Reorganization Plan No. 3 of 1970 (5 U.S.C. app.), effective December 2, 1970. It was created to permit coordinated and effective governmental action on behalf of the environment. The Agency is designed to serve as the public's advocate for a livable environment.

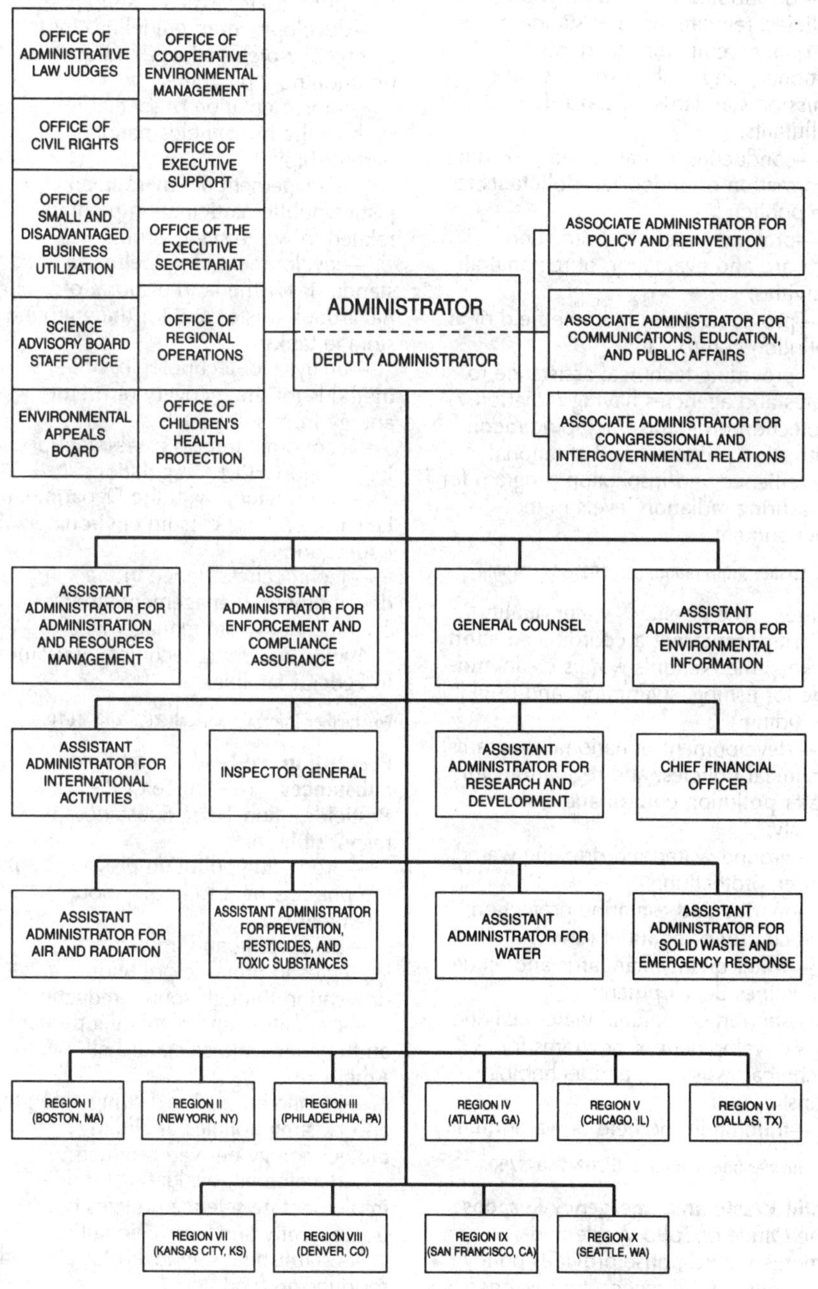
ENVIRONMENTAL PROTECTION AGENCY
OFFICE OF ADMINISTRATIVE LAW JUDGES
OFFICE OF COOPERATIVE ENVIRONMENTAL MANAGEMENT
OFFICE OF CIVIL RIGHTS
OFFICE OF EXECUTIVE SUPPORT
OFFICE OF SMALL AND DISADVANTAGED BUSINESS UTILIZATION
OFFICE OF THE EXECUTIVE SECRETARIAT
SCIENCE ADVISORY BOARD STAFF OFFICE
OFFICE OF REGIONAL OPERATIONS
ENVIRONMENTAL APPEALS BOARD
OFFICE OF CHILDREN'S HEALTH PROTECTION
ADMINISTRATOR
DEPUTY ADMINISTRATOR
ASSOCIATE ADMINISTRATOR FOR POLICY AND REINVENTION
ASSOCIATE ADMINISTRATOR FOR COMMUNICATIONS, EDUCATION, AND PUBLIC AFFAIRS
ASSOCIATE ADMINISTRATOR FOR CONGRESSIONAL AND INTERGOVERNMENTAL RELATIONS
ASSISTANT ADMINISTRATOR FOR ADMINISTRATION AND RESOURCES MANAGEMENT
ASSISTANT ADMINISTRATOR FOR ENFORCEMENT AND COMPLIANCE ASSURANCE
GENERAL COUNSEL
ASSISTANT ADMINISTRATOR FOR ENVIRONMENTAL INFORMATION
ASSISTANT ADMINISTRATOR FOR INTERNATIONAL ACTIVITIES
INSPECTOR GENERAL
ASSISTANT ADMINISTRATOR FOR RESEARCH AND DEVELOPMENT
CHIEF FINANCIAL OFFICER
ASSISTANT ADMINISTRATOR FOR AIR AND RADIATION
ASSISTANT ADMINISTRATOR FOR PREVENTION, PESTICIDES, AND TOXIC SUBSTANCES
ASSISTANT ADMINISTRATOR FOR WATER
ASSISTANT ADMINISTRATOR FOR SOLID WASTE AND EMERGENCY RESPONSE
REGION I (BOSTON, MA)
REGION II (NEW YORK, NY)
REGION III (PHILADELPHIA, PA)
REGION IV (ATLANTA, GA)
REGION V (CHICAGO, IL)
REGION VI (DALLAS, TX)
REGION VII (KANSAS CITY, KS)
REGION VIII (DENVER, CO)
REGION IX (SAN FRANCISCO, CA)
REGION X (SEATTLE, WA)

Activities

Air and Radiation The air activities of the Agency include:

—developing national programs, policies, regulations, and standards for air quality, emission standards for stationary and mobile sources, and emission standards for hazardous air pollutants;

—conducting research and providing information on indoor air pollutants to the public;

—providing technical direction, support, and evaluation of regional air activities;

—providing training in the field of air pollution control; and

—providing technical assistance to States and agencies having radiation protection programs, including radon mitigation programs and a national surveillance and inspection program for measuring radiation levels in the environment.

For further information, call 202–564–7400.

Water The Agency's water quality activities represent a coordinated effort to keep the Nation's waters clean and safe for fishing, swimming, and drinking, including:

—development of national programs, technical policies, and regulations for water pollution control and water supply;

—ground water and drinking water source protection;

—marine and estuarine protection;

—control of polluted runoff;

—water quality standards and effluent guidelines development;

—support of regional water activities;

—development of programs for technical assistance and technology transfer; and

—training in the field of water quality.

For further information, call 202–260–5700.

Solid Waste and Emergency Response The Office of Solid Waste and Emergency Response provides policy, guidance, and direction for the Agency's hazardous waste and emergency response programs, including:

—development of policies, standards, and regulations for hazardous waste treatment, storage, and disposal;

—national management of the Superfund toxic waste cleanup program;

—development of guidelines for the emergency preparedness and community right-to-know programs;

—implementation of special initiatives such as the brownfields national partnership;

—management of environmental justice/public participation programs related to waste siting issues;

—development of guidelines and standards for the land disposal of hazardous wastes and for underground storage tanks;

—analysis of technologies and methods for the recovery of useful energy from solid waste;

—economic impact assessment of RCRA and CERCLA regulations;

—coordination with the Department of Defense on base closure environmental issues; and

—technical assistance in the development, management, and operation of waste management activities, including technical assistance to Federal facilities.

For further information, call 202–260–4610.

Prevention, Pesticides, and Toxic Substances The Office of Prevention, Pesticides, and Toxic Substances is responsible for:

—promoting pollution prevention and the public's right to know about chemical risk;

—developing and implementing strategies to promote pollution prevention through source reduction;

—evaluating and regulating pesticides and chemicals to safeguard all Americans;

—identifying and reviewing emerging and existing policies, including biotechnology-derived products;

—developing, evaluating, and implementing science policies both domestically and internationally;

—establishing safe levels for pesticide residues on food;

—developing national strategies for control of toxic substances;

—developing criteria for assessing chemical substances, standards for test protocols for chemicals, rules and procedures for industry reporting, and scientific information for the regulation of substances that may be hazardous to people or the environment; and

—evaluating and assessing the impact of existing chemicals, new chemicals, and chemicals with new uses to determine the hazard and develop appropriate restrictions.

The Office also coordinates activities under its statutory responsibilities with other agencies for the assessment and control of toxic substances and pesticides.

For further information, call 202–260–2902.

Research and Development The Office of Research and Development (ORD) provides the scientific foundation for the Agency's environmental protection mission. ORD's chief role is to conduct and support high quality research targeted to understanding and resolving the Nation's most serious environmental threats. In addition, ORD develops methods and technologies to reduce exposures to pollution and prevent its creation. The Office is also a major player in sharing information on technological innovations to protect people and the environment. ORD prepares health and ecological risk assessments and makes recommendations for sound risk management strategies in order to assure that highest risk pollution problems receive optimum remediation. The Office manages a vital extramural grants program entitled Science To Achieve Results (STAR), which awards research grants to scientists in universities and students in environmental science. All ORD extramural and intramural research is carefully aligned to support Agency environmental goals and strategic priorities.

For further information, call 202–564–6620.

Regional Offices

The Agency's 10 regional offices represent its commitment to the development of strong local programs for pollution abatement. The Regional Administrators are responsible for accomplishing, within their regions, the national program objectives established by the Agency. They develop, propose, and implement an approved regional program for comprehensive and integrated environmental protection activities.

Regional Offices—Environmental Protection Agency

Region/Address/Areas Served	Administrator
Region I (John F. Kennedy Federal Bldg., 1 Congress St., Boston, MA 02114) (CT, MA, ME, NH, RI, VT).	Mindy S. Lubber, *Acting*
Region II (290 Broadway, New York, NY 10007) (NJ, NY, PR, VI)	Jeanne M. Fox
Region III (1650 Arch St., Philadelphia, PA 19103) (DC, DE, MD, PA, VA, WV)	Bradley M. Campbell
Region IV (61 Forsyth St. SW, Atlanta GA 30303) (AL, FL, GA, KY, MS, NC, SC, TN)	John H. Hankinson, Jr.
Region V (77 W. Jackson Blvd., Chicago, IL 60604) (IL, IN, MI, MN, OH, WI)	Francis X. Lyons
Region VI (1445 Ross Ave., Dallas, TX 75202) (AR, LA, NM, OK, TX)	Gregg A. Cooke
Region VII (901 N. 5th St., Kansas City, KS 66101) (IA, KS, MO, NE)	Dennis D. Grams
Region VIII (999 18th St., Denver, CO 80202) (CO, MT, ND, SD, UT, WY)	William P. Yellowtail, Jr.
Region IX (75 Hawthorne St., San Francisco, CA 94105) (AS, AZ, CA, GU, HI, NV)	Felicia A. Marcus
Region X (1200 6th Ave., Seattle, WA 98101) (AK, ID, OR, WA)	Charles C. Clarke

Sources of Information

Inquiries for information on the following subjects should be directed to the specified office of the Environmental Protection Agency, 1200 Pennsylvania Avenue NW., Washington, DC 20460.

Contracts and Procurement Office of Acquisition Management. Phone, 202–564–4310.

Employment Office of Human Resources and Organizational Services. Phone, 202–564–4606.

Freedom of Information Act Requests Freedom of Information Officer. Phone, 202–260–1050. E-mail, hq.foi@epamail.epa.gov.

Information Resources EPA Headquarters Information Resources Center. Phone, 202–260–5922.

Telephone Directory Available for sale by the Superintendent of Documents, Government Printing Office, Washington, DC 20402.

For further information, contact the Office of Communications, Education, and Media Relations, Environmental Protection Agency, 401 M Street SW., Washington, DC 20460. Phone, 202–564–9828. Internet, www.epa.gov.

EQUAL EMPLOYMENT OPPORTUNITY COMMISSION

1801 L Street NW., Washington, DC 20507
Phone, 202–663–4900. TTY, 202–663–4494. Internet, www.eeoc.gov.

Chairman	IDA L. CASTRO
Vice Chairman	PAUL M. IGASAKI
Commissioners	REGINALD E. JONES, PAUL STEVEN MILLER, (VACANCY)
Executive Officer	FRANCES M. HART
General Counsel	C. GREGORY STEWART
Inspector General	ALETHA L. BROWN
Director, Office of Communications and Legislative Affairs	WILLIAM J. WHITE, JR., *Acting*
Director, Office of Equal Opportunity	ROBBIE DIX III, *Acting*
Director, Office of Federal Operations	CARLTON M. HADDEN, *Acting*
Legal Counsel	ELLEN J. VARGYAS
Director, Office of Field Programs	ELIZABETH M. THORNTON
Director, Office of Financial and Resource Management	ALLAN M. FISHER
Director, Office of Human Resources	PATRICIA CORNWELL JOHNSON
Director, Office of Information Resources Management	SALLIE T. HSIEH
Director, Office of Research, Information, and Planning	DEIDRE FLIPPEN

The Equal Employment Opportunity Commission enforces laws which prohibit discrimination based on race, color, religion, sex, national origin, disability, or age in hiring, promoting, firing, setting wages, testing, training, apprenticeship, and all other terms and conditions of employment. The Commission conducts investigations of alleged discrimination; makes determinations based on gathered evidence; attempts conciliation when discrimination has taken place; files lawsuits; and conducts voluntary assistance programs for employers, unions, and community organizations. The Commission also has adjudicatory and oversight responsibility for all compliance and enforcement activities relating to equal employment opportunity among Federal employees and applicants, including discrimination against individuals with disabilities.

The Equal Employment Opportunity Commission (EEOC) was created by title VII of the Civil Rights Act of 1964 (42 U.S.C. 2000e–4), and became operational July 2, 1965. The Commission is comprised of five Commissioners appointed by the President, with the advice and consent of the Senate, for 5-year staggered terms. The President designates a Chairman and a Vice Chairman. The Commission

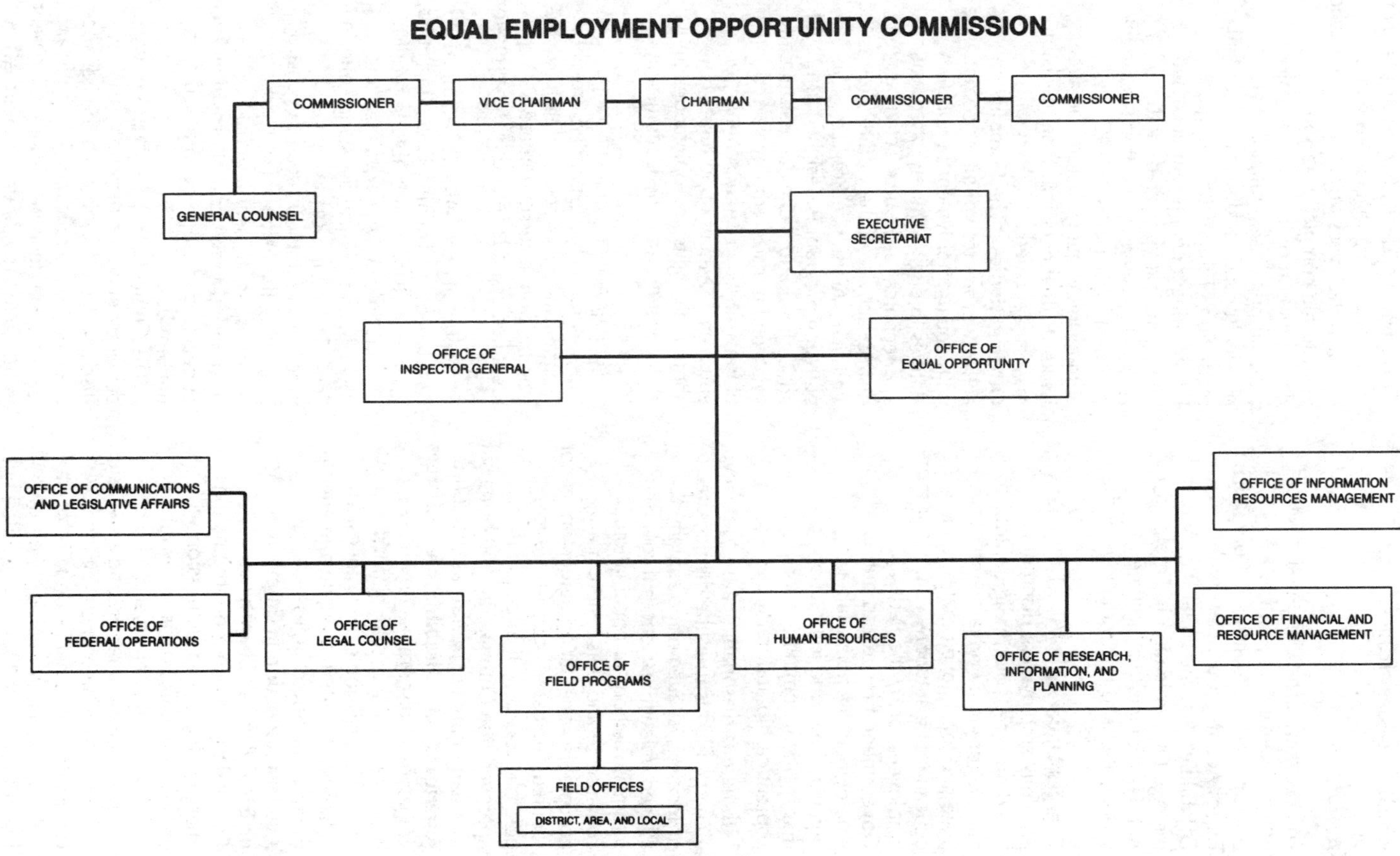
EQUAL EMPLOYMENT OPPORTUNITY COMMISSION
COMMISSIONER
VICE CHAIRMAN
CHAIRMAN
COMMISSIONER
COMMISSIONER
GENERAL COUNSEL
EXECUTIVE SECRETARIAT
OFFICE OF INSPECTOR GENERAL
OFFICE OF EQUAL OPPORTUNITY
OFFICE OF COMMUNICATIONS AND LEGISLATIVE AFFAIRS
OFFICE OF FEDERAL OPERATIONS
OFFICE OF LEGAL COUNSEL
OFFICE OF FIELD PROGRAMS
FIELD OFFICES
DISTRICT, AREA, AND LOCAL
OFFICE OF HUMAN RESOURCES
OFFICE OF RESEARCH, INFORMATION, AND PLANNING
OFFICE OF INFORMATION RESOURCES MANAGEMENT
OFFICE OF FINANCIAL AND RESOURCE MANAGEMENT

operates through 50 field offices, each of which processes charges.

Activities

Enforcement The Commission's field offices receive charges of job discrimination under title VII of the Civil Rights Act, the Americans with Disabilities Act, the Equal Pay Act, and the Age Discrimination in Employment Act. Field offices may initiate investigations to find violations of the acts.

Charges Under Title VII Title VII prohibits employment discrimination based on race, color, religion, sex, or national origin by private employers, State and local governments, and educational institutions with 15 or more employees, or by the Federal Government, private and public employment agencies, labor organizations, and joint labor-management committees for apprenticeship and training.

If there is reasonable cause to believe a charge filed is true, the district, area, or local office attempts to remedy the alleged unlawful practices through informal methods of conciliation, conference, and persuasion. If an acceptable conciliation agreement is not secured, the case is considered for possible litigation. If litigation is approved, the Commission will bring suit in an appropriate Federal district court.

Americans with Disabilities Act Charges Employment discrimination charges based on disability may be filed at any of the Commission's field offices. The Commission will investigate and attempt to conciliate the charges.

Age Discrimination in Employment Act or Equal Pay Act Charges and Complaints When a discrimination charge is filed, the Commission will attempt to eliminate the unlawful practice through informal methods of conciliation, conference, and persuasion. A lawsuit may be brought by the Commission if conciliation fails, or individuals may file suit on their own. A lawsuit under the EPA may be filed by the Commission or by the complainant.

Complaints Against the Federal Government The Commission's Federal sector processing regulations guide Federal employees or job applicants who want to file complaints of job discrimination based on race, color, national origin, sex, religion, age, or physical or mental disability. Informal mediation of the matter is required before filing a charge. An accepted complaint is investigated by the respondent agency, and there is a right to a hearing before an EEOC administrative judge before the agency issues its final decision. Final decisions may be appealed.

Other Activities The Commission actively promotes voluntary compliance with equal employment opportunity statutes through a variety of educational and technical assistance activities. A distinct activity of the Commission is the Voluntary Assistance Program. This outreach program is designed to provide educational and technical assistance to small and midsize employers and unions—through 1-day seminars on equal employment opportunity laws—about their rights and obligations under all the statutes that the Commission enforces.

Another activity initiated by the Commission is the Expanded Presence Program, which is designed to make the Commission accessible in areas identified as underserved by Commission offices.

Through its Educational Technical Assistance and Training Revolving Fund, the Commission is also able to provide its constituency with advanced and specialized technical assistance offerings. Fees charged for Revolving Fund products are not to exceed the cost of producing the materials or services provided, are to bear a direct relationship to the cost of providing such outreach, and are to be imposed on a uniform basis.

The Commission participates in the development of employment discrimination law through the issuance of guidelines, publication of significant Commission decisions, and involvement in litigation brought under the relevant statutes.

The Commission has direct liaison with Federal, State, and local governments, employers and union organizations, trade associations, civil rights organizations, and other agencies and organizations concerned with employment of minority group members and women.

The Commission develops and implements affirmative employment policies designed to enhance the occupational status of minorities, women, and persons with disabilities in the Federal Government.

The Commission also publishes data on the employment status of minorities and women. Through 6 employment surveys covering private employers, apprenticeship programs, labor unions, State and local governments, elementary and secondary schools, and colleges and universities, the Commission tabulates and stores data on the ethnic, racial, and sex composition of employees at all job levels within the reported groups.

Research information thus collected is shared with selected Federal agencies, and is made available, in appropriate form, for public use.

Field Offices—Equal Employment Opportunity Commission

(DO: District Office; AO: Area Office; LO: Local Office; FO: Field Office)

Office	Address/Telephone	Director
Albuquerque, NM (DO)	Suite 900, 505 Marquette NW., 87102. Ph., 505–248–5201. Fax, 505–248–5233. TTY, 505–248–5240.	Georgia Marchbanks
Atlanta, GA (DO)	Suite 4R30, 100 Alabama St. NW., 30303. Ph., 404–562–6930. Fax, 404–562–6909. TTY, 404–562–6801.	Bernice Williams-Kimbrough
Baltimore, MD (DO)	3d Fl., City Crescent Bldg., 10 S. Howard St., 21201. Ph., 410–962–3932. Fax, 410–962–2817. TTY, 410–962–6065.	Michael C. Fetzer, *Acting*
Birmingham, AL (DO)	Suite 101, 1900 3d Ave. N., 35203–2397. Ph., 205–731–0082. Fax, 205–731–2101. TTY, 205–731–0175.	Donald Burris
Boston, MA (AO)	Rm. 475, John F. Kennedy Fed. Bldg., 02203. Ph., 617–565–3190. Fax, 617–565–3196. TTY, 617–565–3204.	Robert L. Sanders
Buffalo, NY (LO)	Suite 350, 6 Fountain Plz., 14202. Ph., 716–551–4441. Fax, 716–551–4387. TTY, 716–551–5923.	Elizabeth Cadle
Charlotte, NC (DO)	Suite 400, 129 W. Trade St., 28202. Ph., 704–344–6682. Fax, 704–344–6734. TTY, 704–334–6684.	Marsha J. Drane
Chicago, IL (DO)	Suite 2800, 500 W. Madison St., 60661. Ph., 312–353–2713. Fax, 312–353–4041. TTY, 312–353–2421.	John P. Rowe
Cincinnati, OH (AO)	Suite 810, 525 Vine St., 45202–3122. Ph., 513–684–2851. Fax, 513–684–2361. TTY, 513–684–6698.	(Vacancy)
Cleveland, OH (DO)	Suite 850, 1660 W. 2d St., 44113–1454. Ph., 216–522–2001. Fax, 216–522–7395. TTY, 216–522–8441.	(Vacancy)
Dallas, TX (DO)	3d Fl., 207 S. Houston St., 75202–4726. Ph., 214–655–3355. Fax, 214–655–3443. TTY, 214–655–3363.	Thelma H. Taylor
Denver, CO (DO)	Suite 510, 303 E. 17th Ave., 80203. Ph., 303–866–1300. Fax, 303–866–1386. TTY, 303–866–1950.	Francisco J. Flores
Detroit, MI (DO)	Rm. 865, 477 Michigan Ave., 48226–9704. Ph., 313–226–4600. Fax, 313–226–2778. TTY, 313–226–7599.	James R. Neely, Jr.
El Paso, TX (AO)	Suite 100, Bldg. C, 4171 N. Mesa St., 79902. Ph., 915–534–6550. Fax, 915–534–6552. TTY, 915–534–6545.	Robert Calderon
Fresno, CA (LO)	Suite 103, 1265 W. Shaw Ave., 93711. Ph., 209–487–5793. Fax, 209–487–5053. TTY, 209–487–5837.	David Rodriguez
Greensboro, NC (LO)	801 Summit Ave., 27405–7813. Ph., 336–333–5174. Fax, 336–333–5051. TTY, 336–333–5542.	Patricia B. Fuller
Greenville, SC (LO)	Suite 530, 15 S. Main St., 29601. Ph., 864–241–4400. Fax, 864–241–4416. TTY, 864–241–4403.	Denise Anderson
Honolulu, HI (LO)	Rm. 7–127, 300 Ala Moana Blvd., 96850–0051. Ph., 808–541–3120. Fax, 808–541–3390. TTY, 808–541–3131.	Timothy A. Riera
Houston, TX (DO)	7th Fl., 1919 Smith St., 77002. Ph., 713–209–3320. Fax, 713–209–3381. TTY, 713–209–3439.	Harriet J. Ehrlich
Indianapolis, IN (DO)	Suite 1900, 101 W. Ohio St., 46204–4203. Ph., 317–226–7212. Fax, 317–226–7953, 317–226–5571. TTY, 317–226–5162.	Danny E. Harter
Jackson, MS (AO)	207 W. Amite St., 39201. Ph., 601–965–4537. Fax, 601–965–5272. TTY, 601–965–4915.	Benjamin Bradley
Kansas City, KS (AO)	Suite 905, 400 State Ave., 66101. Ph., 913–551–5655. Fax, 913–551–6956. TTY, 913–551–5657.	George Dixon
Little Rock, AR (AO)	Suite 625, 425 W. Capitol Ave., 72201. Ph., 501–324–5060. Fax, 501–324–5991. TTY, 501–324–5481.	Kay Klugh
Los Angeles, CA (DO)	4th Fl., 255 E. Temple St., 90012. Ph., 213–894–1000. Fax, 213–894–1118. TTY, 213–894–1121.	Thelma Taylor
Louisville, KY (AO)	Suite 268, 600 Dr. Martin Luther King Jr. Pl., 40202. Ph., 502–582–6082. Fax, 502–582–5895. TTY, 502–582–6285.	Marcia Hall Craig
Memphis, TN (DO)	Suite 621, 1407 Union Ave., 38104.	Walter S. Grabon

Field Offices—Equal Employment Opportunity Commission—Continued

(DO: District Office; AO: Area Office; LO: Local Office; FO: Field Office)

Office	Address/Telephone	Director
	Ph., 901–544–0115. Fax, 901–544–0111. TTY, 901–544–0112.	
Miami, FL (DO)	Suite 2700, 2 S. Biscayne Blvd., 33131. Ph., 305–536–4491. Fax, 305–536–4011. TTY, 305–536–5721.	Federico Costales
Milwaukee, WI (DO)	Suite 800, 310 W. Wisconsin Ave., 53203–2292. Ph., 414–297–1111. Fax, 414–297–4133. TTY, 414–297–1115.	Chester V. Bailey
Minneapolis, MN (AO)	Suite 430, 330 S. 2d Ave., 55401–2224. Ph., 612–335–4040. Fax, 612–335–4044. TTY, 612–335–4045.	Michael J. Bloyer
Nashville, TN (AO)	Suite 202, 50 Vantage Way, 37228–9940. Ph., 615–736–5820. Fax, 615–736–2107. TTY, 615–736–5870.	(Vacancy)
Newark, NJ (AO)	21st Fl., One Newark Ctr., 07102–5233. Ph., 973–645–6383. Fax, 973–645–4524. TTY, 973–645–3004.	Corrado Gigante
New Orleans, LA (DO)	Suite 600, 701 Loyola Ave., 70113–9936. Ph., 504–589–2329. Fax, 504–589–6861. TTY, 504–589–2958.	Patricia T. Bivins
New York, NY (DO)	18th Fl., 7 World Trade Ctr., 10048–1102. Ph., 212–748–8500. Fax, 212–748–8464. TTY, 212–748–8399.	Spencer H. Lewis, Jr.
Norfolk, VA (AO)	Suite 4300, 101 W. Main St., 23510. Ph., 757–441–3470. Fax, 757–441–6720. TTY, 757–441–3578.	Herbert Brown
Oakland, CA (LO)	Suite 1170–N, 1301 Clay St., 94612–5217. Ph., 510–637–3230. Fax, 510–637–3235. TTY, 510–637–3234.	Joyce A. Hendy
Oklahoma City, OK (AO)	Suite 1350, 210 Park Ave., 73102. Ph., 405–231–4911. Fax, 405–231–4140. TTY, 405–231–5745.	Alma Anderson
Philadelphia, PA (DO)	Suite 400, 21 S. 5th St., 19106–2515. Ph., 215–451–5800. Fax, 215–451–5804. TTY, 215–451–5814.	Marie M. Tomasso
Phoenix, AZ (DO)	Suite 690, 3300 N. Central Ave., 85012–2504. Ph., 602–640–5000. Fax, 602–640–5071. TTY, 602–640–5072.	Charles D. Burtner
Pittsburgh, PA (AO)	Suite 300, 1001 Liberty Ave., 15222–4187. Ph., 412–644–3444. Fax, 412–644–2664. TTY, 412–644–2720.	Eugene V. Nelson
Raleigh, NC (AO)	1309 Annapolis Dr., 27608–2129. Ph., 919–856–4064. Fax, 919–856–4151. TTY, 919–856–4296.	Richard E. Walz
Richmond, VA (AO)	Rm. 229, 3600 W. Broad St., 23230. Ph., 804–278–4651. Fax, 804–278–4660. TTY, 804–278–4654.	Gloria L. Underwood
San Antonio, TX (DO)	Suite 200, 5410 Fredericksburg Rd., 78229–3555. Ph., 210–281–7642. Fax, 210–229–4381. TTY, 210–229–4858.	Pedro Esquivel
San Diego, CA (AO)	Suite 1550, 401 B St., 92101. Ph., 619–557–7235. Fax, 619–557–7274. TTY, 619–557–7232.	Patrick Matarazzo
San Francisco, CA (DO)	Suite 500, 901 Market St., 94103. Ph., 415–356–5100. Fax, 415–356–5126. TTY, 415–356–5098.	Susan L. McDuffie
San Jose, CA (LO)	Suite 200, 96 N. 3d St., 95112. Ph., 408–291–7352. Fax, 408–291–4539. TTY, 408–291–7374.	(Vacancy)
Savannah, GA (LO)	Suite G, 410 Mall Blvd., 31406–4821. Ph., 912–652–4234. Fax, 912–652–4248. TTY, 912–652–4439.	Marvin C. Frazier
Seattle, WA (DO)	Suite 400, 909 First Ave., 98104–1061. Ph., 206–220–6883. Fax, 206–220–6911. TTY, 206–220–6882.	Jeanette M. Leino
St. Louis, MO (DO)	Rm. 8.100, 1222 Spruce St., 63103. Ph., 314–539–7800. Fax, 314–539–7894. TTY, 314–539–7803.	Lynn Bruner
Tampa, FL (AO)	Rm. 1020, 501 E. Polk St., 33602. Ph., 813–228–2310. Fax, 813–228–2841. TTY, 813–228–2003.	Manuel Zurita
Washington, DC (FO)	Suite 200, 1400 L St. NW., 20005. Ph., 202–275–7377. Fax, 202–275–6834. TTY, 202–275–7518.	Tulio Diaz, Jr.

Sources of Information

Electronic Access Information regarding the programs, publications, and activities of the Commission is available through the Internet, at www.eeoc.gov.

Employment The Commission selects its employees from various examinations and registers, including mid- and senior-level registers, secretarial, typing, and stenographic registers, and the Equal Opportunity Specialist register. Employment inquiries or applications for positions in the headquarters office should be directed to the Office of Human Resources, Equal Employment Opportunity Commission, 1801 L Street NW., Washington, DC 20507 (phone, 202–663–4306), or contact the appropriate district office for district office positions.

General Inquiries A nationwide toll-free telephone number links callers with the appropriate field office where charges may be filed. Phone, 800–669–4000. TTY, 800–669–6820.

Information About Survey Forms (EEO–1, 2, 3, 4, 5, and 6). Phone, 202–663–4958.

Media Inquiries Office of Communications and Legislative Affairs, 1801 L Street NW., Washington, DC 20507. Phone, 202–663–4900.
Publications Phone, 800–669–3362 (toll-free). TTY, 800–800–3302 (toll-free). Fax, 513–489–8692.
Reading Room EEOC Library, 1801 L Street NW., Washington, DC 20507. Phone, 202–663–4630.
Speakers Office of Communications and Legislative Affairs, 1801 L Street NW., Washington, DC 20507. Phone, 202–663–4900.

For further information, contact the Equal Employment Opportunity Commission, 1801 L Street NW., Washington, DC 20507. Phone, 202–663–4900. Internet, www.eeoc.gov.

EXPORT–IMPORT BANK OF THE UNITED STATES

811 Vermont Avenue NW., Washington, DC 20571
Phone, 800–565–EXIM. Internet, www.exim.gov.

President and Chairman	JAMES A. HARMON
First Vice President and Vice Chair and Chief Operating Officer	JACKIE M. CLEGG
Directors	DAN RENBERG, D. VANESSA WEAVER, (VACANCY)
Chief of Staff	(VACANCY)
Vice President and Counselor to the Chairman	CLYDE ROBINSON
Counselor to the Board	GLORIA B. CABE
Chief Financial Officer and Chief Information Officer	JAMES K. HESS
Director, Administrative Services	GEORGE SABO
Director, Equal Opportunity and Diversity Programs and Training	CYNTHIA B. WILSON
Director, Human Resources	DENNIS H. HEINS
Director, Trade Finance (Financial Institution Risk)	DEBORAH THOMPSON
Director, Trade Finance (Sovereign/Tied Aid)	LEROY M. LAROCHE
General Counsel	JOHN NIENUSS
Group Vice President, Resource Management	DELORES DE LA TORRE BARTNING
Group Manager, New and Small Business	WILLIAM W. REDWAY
Group Manager, Structured and Trade Finance	JEFFREY L. MILLER
Manager, Credit Administration	WAYNE L. GARDELIA
Vice President, Asset Management	CLEMENT K. MILLER
Vice President, Communications	MARSHA E. BERRY
Vice President, Congressional and External Affairs	SANDRA S. JACKSON
Vice President, Country Risk Analysis	PETER GOSNELL
Vice President, Engineering and Environment	JAMES A. MAHONEY, JR.
Vice President, Information Management	CANDELARIO TRUJILLO, JR.
Vice President, Insurance	PIPER STARR
Vice President, Policy	JAMES C. CRUSE
Vice President, Structured Finance	BARBARA O'BOYLE
Vice President, Transportation	ROBERT MORIN
Vice President, Trade Finance	KENNETH M. TINSLEY
Vice President, United States Division	SAM Z. ZYTCER

The Export-Import Bank of the United States helps the private sector to create and maintain U.S. jobs by financing exports of the Nation's goods and services. To accomplish this mission, the Bank offers a variety of loan, guarantee, and insurance programs to support transactions that would not be awarded to U.S. companies without the Bank's assistance.

The Export-Import Bank of the United States (Ex-Im Bank), established in 1934, operates as an independent agency of the U.S. Government under the authority of the Export-Import Bank Act of 1945, as amended (12 U.S.C. 635 *et seq.*). Its Board of Directors consists of a President and Chairman, a First Vice President and Vice Chairman, and three other Directors, all of whom are appointed by the President with the advice and consent of the Senate.

Ex-Im Bank's mission is to help American exporters meet government-supported financing competition from other countries, so that U.S. exports can compete for overseas business on the basis of price, performance, and service. The Bank also fills gaps in the availability of commercial financing for creditworthy export transactions.

Ex-Im Bank is required to find a reasonable assurance of repayment for each transaction it supports. Its legislation requires it to meet the financing terms of competitor export credit agencies, but not to compete with commercial lenders. Legislation restricts the Bank's operation in some countries and its support for military goods and services.

Activities

Ex-Im Bank is authorized to have outstanding at any one time loans, guarantees, and insurance in aggregate amount not in excess of $75 billion. It supports U.S. exporters through a range of diverse programs, which are offered under four broad categories of export financing:

—working capital guarantees, provided to lenders, so that they can provide creditworthy small- and medium-sized exporters with working capital they need to buy, build, or assemble products for export sale;

—export credit insurance which protects exporters and lenders against both the commercial and political risks of a foreign buyer defaulting on payment;

—loan guarantees which encourage sales to creditworthy foreign buyers by providing private sector lenders in medium- and long-term transactions with Ex-Im Bank guarantees against the political and commercial risks of nonpayment; and

—direct loans made to provide foreign buyers with competitive, fixed-rate medium- or long-term financing from Ex-Im Bank for their purchases from U.S. exporters.

Ex-Im Bank has initiated several new programs to broaden the range of customers and types of exporters it supports. It has also expanded its capabilities in the area of limited recourse project finance and has adopted a policy of matching foreign tied-aid credits to ensure that U.S. exporters do not lose sales in critical emerging markets. In order to make its programs more readily available, Ex-Im Bank works closely with many State and local governments in its City/State Partners Program.

Regional Offices

The Export-Import Bank operates six regional offices.

Regional and Satellite Offices—Export-Import Bank

Region	Address	Telephone	Fax
Regional Offices			
New York	Suite 635, 6 World Trade Ctr., New York, NY 10048	212–466–2950	212–466–2959
Miami	Suite 617, 5600 NW. 36th St., Miami, FL 33166	305–526–7425	305–526–7435
Chicago	Suite 2440, 55 W. Monroe St., Chicago, IL 60603	312–353–8081	312–353–8098

Regional and Satellite Offices—Export-Import Bank—Continued

Region	Address	Telephone	Fax
Houston	Suite 585, 1880 S. Dairy Ashford II, Houston, TX 77077	281–721–0465	281–679–0156
Los Angeles	Suite 1670, 1 World Trade Ctr., Long Beach, CA 90831	562–980–4580	562–980–4590
Mid Atlantic-DC	Room 911, 811 Vermont Ave. NW, Washington, DC 20571.	202–565–3940	202–565–3932
Satellite Offices			
San Jose, CA	Suite 1001, 101 Park Center Plz., San Jose, CA 95113	408–271–7300	408–271–7307
Orange County, CA	Suite 305, 3300 Irvine Ave., Newport Beach, CA 92660	949–660–1688	949–660–8039

For further information, contact the Export-Import Bank, Business Development Office, 811 Vermont Avenue NW., Washington, DC 20571. Phone, 202–565–3900 or 800–565–EXIM (toll-free). Internet, www.exim.gov.

FARM CREDIT ADMINISTRATION

1501 Farm Credit Drive, McLean, VA 22102–5090
Phone, 703–883–4000. Fax, 703–734–5784. Internet, www.fca.gov.

Farm Credit Administration Board:

Chairman and Chief Executive Officer	MICHAEL M. REYNA
Members of the Board	ANN JORGENSEN, (VACANCY)
Secretary to the Board	VIVIAN L. PORTIS
Staff:	
Director, Office of Congressional and Public Affairs	EILEEN M. MCMAHON
General Counsel	JEAN NOONAN
Associate General Counsels	KATHLEEN V. BUFFON, VICTOR A. COHEN
Inspector General	ELDON W. STOEHR
Director, Office of Examination and Chief Examiner	ROLAND E. SMITH
Director, Office of Policy and Analysis	THOMAS G. MCKENZIE
Director, Office of Secondary Market Oversight	CARL A. CLINEFELTER
Director, Office of Resources Management	DONALD P. CLARK

[For the Farm Credit Administration statement of organization, see the *Code of Federal Regulations,* Title 12, Parts 600 and 611]

The Farm Credit Administration is responsible for ensuring the safe and sound operation of the banks, associations, affiliated service organizations, and other entities that collectively comprise what is known as the Farm Credit System, and for protecting the interests of the public and those who borrow from Farm Credit institutions or invest in Farm Credit securities.

The Farm Credit Administration was established as an independent financial regulatory agency in the executive branch of the Federal Government by Executive Order 6084 of March 27, 1933. The Administration carries out its responsibilities by conducting examinations of the various Farm Credit lending institutions, which are Farm Credit Banks, the Agricultural Credit Bank, Federal Land Bank Associations, Production Credit Associations, Agricultural Credit Associations, and Federal Land Credit Associations. It also examines the service organizations owned by the Farm Credit lending institutions, as well as the National Consumer Cooperative Bank (also

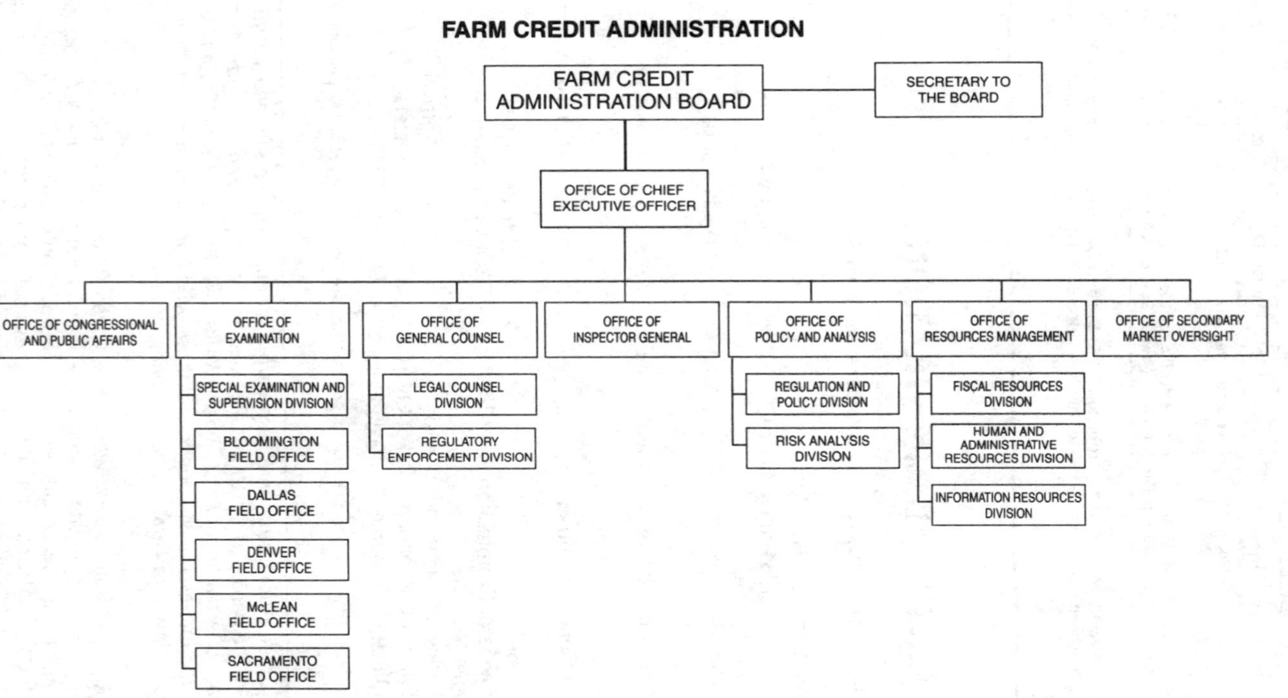
FARM CREDIT ADMINISTRATION
FARM CREDIT ADMINISTRATION BOARD
SECRETARY TO THE BOARD
OFFICE OF CHIEF EXECUTIVE OFFICER
OFFICE OF CONGRESSIONAL AND PUBLIC AFFAIRS
OFFICE OF EXAMINATION
SPECIAL EXAMINATION AND SUPERVISION DIVISION
BLOOMINGTON FIELD OFFICE
DALLAS FIELD OFFICE
DENVER FIELD OFFICE
McLEAN FIELD OFFICE
SACRAMENTO FIELD OFFICE
OFFICE OF GENERAL COUNSEL
LEGAL COUNSEL DIVISION
REGULATORY ENFORCEMENT DIVISION
OFFICE OF INSPECTOR GENERAL
OFFICE OF POLICY AND ANALYSIS
REGULATION AND POLICY DIVISION
RISK ANALYSIS DIVISION
OFFICE OF RESOURCES MANAGEMENT
FISCAL RESOURCES DIVISION
HUMAN AND ADMINISTRATIVE RESOURCES DIVISION
INFORMATION RESOURCES DIVISION
OFFICE OF SECONDARY MARKET OVERSIGHT

known as the National Cooperative Bank).

FCA policymaking is vested in the Farm Credit Administration Board, whose three full-time members are appointed to 6-year terms by the President, with the advice and consent of the Senate. One member of the Board is designated by the President as Chairman and serves as the Administration's chief executive officer. The Board is responsible for approving rules and regulations, providing for the examination and regulation of and reporting by Farm Credit institutions, and establishing the policies under which the Administration operates. Board meetings are regularly held on the second Thursday of the month and are subject to the Government in the Sunshine Act. Public announcements of these meetings are published in the *Federal Register*.

The lending institutions of the Farm Credit System were established to provide adequate and dependable credit and closely related services to farmers, ranchers, and producers or harvesters of aquatic products; persons engaged in providing on-the-farm services; rural homeowners; and associations of farmers, ranchers, and producers or harvesters of aquatic products, or federations of such associations that operate on a cooperative basis and are engaged in marketing, processing, supply, or business service functions for the benefit of their members. Initially capitalized by the United States Government, the Farm Credit lending institutions are organized as cooperatives and are completely owned by their borrowers. The loan funds provided to borrowers by these institutions are obtained primarily through the sale of securities to investors in the Nation's capital markets.

The Agricultural Credit Act of 1987, as amended (12 U.S.C. 2279aa-1), established the Federal Agricultural Mortgage Corporation (commonly known as "Farmer Mac"). The Corporation, designated as part of the Farm Credit System, is a federally chartered instrumentality of the United States and promotes the development of a secondary market for agricultural real estate and rural housing loans. Farmer Mac also provides guarantees for the timely payment of principal and interest on securities, representing interests in or obligations backed by pools of agricultural real estate loans. The Administration is responsible for the examination and regulation of Farmer Mac to ensure the safety and soundness of its operations.

The Administration manages regulations under which Farm Credit institutions operate. These regulations implement the Farm Credit Act of 1971, as amended, and have the force and effect of law. Similar to other Federal regulators of financial institutions, the Administration's authorities include the power to issue cease-and-desist orders, to levy civil monetary penalties, to remove officers and directors of Farm Credit institutions, and to establish financial and operating reporting requirements. Although it is prohibited from participation in routine management or operations of Farm Credit institutions, the Administration is authorized to become involved in these institutions' management and operations when the Farm Credit Act or its regulations have been violated, when taking an action to correct an unsafe or unsound practice, or when assuming a formal conservatorship over an institution.

The Administration does not operate on funds appropriated by Congress. Its income is derived from assessments collected from the institutions it regulates and examines. In addition to the headquarters office located in McLean, VA, the Administration maintains 4 field offices located in Aurora, CO; Bloomington, MN; Irving, TX; and Sacramento, CA.

Authority for the organization and activities of the institutions comprising the cooperative Farm Credit System and that operate under the regulation of the Farm Credit Administration may be found in the Farm Credit Act of 1971, as amended (12 U.S.C. 2001).

Sources of Information

Inquiries for information on the following subjects may be directed to the specified office, Farm Credit Administration, 1501 Farm Credit Drive, McLean, VA 22102–5090.

Contracts and Procurement Inquiries regarding the Administration's procurement and contracting activities should be directed in writing to Contracting and Procurement. Phone, 703–883–4145.

Employment Inquiries regarding employment with the Administration should be directed to the Human and Administrative Resources Division. Phone, 703–883–4135.

Freedom of Information Requests Requests for agency records must be submitted in writing, clearly identified with "FOIA Request" and addressed to the Office of General Counsel. Phone, 703–883–4020.

Publications Publications and information on the Farm Credit Administration may be obtained by writing the Office of Congressional and Public Affairs. Phone, 703–883–4056. Fax, 703–790–3260. E-mail, info-line@fca.gov.

For further information, contact the Office of Congressional and Public Affairs, Farm Credit Administration, 1501 Farm Credit Drive, McLean, VA 22102–5090. Phone, 703–883–4056. E-mail, info-line@fca.gov. Internet, www.fca.gov.

FEDERAL COMMUNICATIONS COMMISSION

445 Twelfth Street SW., Washington, DC 20554
Phone, 888–225–5322 (toll-free). TTY, 888–835–5322 (toll-free). Internet, www.fcc.gov.

Chairman	William E. Kennard
Commissioners	Harold Furchtgott-Roth, Susan Ness, Michael Powell, Gloria Tristani
Managing Director	Andrew S. Fishel
General Counsel	Christopher J. Wright
Inspector General	H. Walker Feaster III
Chief, Cable Services Bureau	Deborah Lathen
Chief, Common Carrier Bureau	Lawrence E. Strickling
Chief, Consumer Information Bureau	Lorraine C. Miller
Chief, Enforcement Bureau	David Solomon
Chief, International Bureau	Donald Abelson
Chief, Mass Media Bureau	Roy L. Stewart
Chief, Office of Administrative Law Judges	John M. Frysiak, *Acting*
Chief, Office of Engineering and Technology	Dale N. Hatfield
Chief, Office of Plans and Policy	Robert M. Pepper
Chief, Wireless Telecommunications Bureau	Thomas Sugrue
Director, Office of Communications Business Opportunities	Francisco Montero
Director, Office of Legislative and Intergovernmental Affairs	Sheryl J. Wilkerson
Director, Office of Media Relations	Joy Howell
Director, Office of Workplace Diversity	Jack W. Gravely

[For the Federal Communications Commission statement of organization, see the *Code of Federal Regulations,* Title 47, Part 0]

The Federal Communications Commission regulates interstate and foreign communications by radio, television, wire, satellite, and cable. It is responsible for the orderly development and operation of broadcast services and the provision of rapid, efficient nationwide and worldwide telephone and telegraph services at reasonable rates. Its responsibilities also include the use of communications for promoting safety of life and property and for strengthening the national defense.

The Federal Communications Commission (FCC) was created by the Communications Act of 1934 (47 U.S.C. 151 *et seq.*) to regulate interstate and foreign communications by wire and radio in the public interest. The scope of FCC regulation includes radio and television broadcasting; telephone, telegraph, and cable television operation; two-way radio and radio operators; and satellite communication.

The Commission is composed of five members, who are appointed by the President with the advice and consent of the Senate. One of the members is designated by the President as Chairman.

Activities

Cable Services Communications The Cable Services Bureau develops, recommends, and administers policies and programs for the regulation of cable television systems. The Bureau advises and recommends to the Commission, or acts for the Commission under delegated authority, in matters pertaining to the regulation and development of cable television. The Bureau is responsible for:

—investigating complaints and answering general inquiries from the public;

—planning and developing proposed rulemakings and conducting comprehensive studies and analyses (legal, social, and economic) of various petitions for policy or rule changes;

—processing applications for authorizations in the cable television relay service;

—participating in hearings before Administrative Law Judges and the Commission;

—conducting studies and compiling data relating to the cable industry for the Commission to develop and maintain an adequate regulatory program;

—collaborating and coordinating with State and local authorities in matters involving cable television systems; and

—advising and assisting the public, other Government agencies, and industry groups on cable television regulation and related matters.

For further information, contact the Cable Services Bureau. Phone, 202–418–7200 or 888–225–5322 (toll-free).

Common Carrier Communications The Common Carrier Bureau administers the regulatory program for interstate common carrier communications by telephone. Common carriers include companies, organizations, or individuals providing communications services to the public for hire, who must serve all who wish to use them at established rates.

For further information, contact the Common Carrier Bureau. Phone, 202–418–1500.

Consumer Information The Consumer Information Bureau is responsible for communicating information to the general public regarding the Commission's policies, programs, and activities. The Bureau develops, recommends, coordinates, and administers the Commission's consumer information program to enhance the public's understanding of and compliance with its regulatory requirements. The Bureau provides a single source for handling general inquiries and resolving individual consumer informal complaints for the Commission.

For further information, contact the Consumer Information Bureau. Phone, 888–CALL–FCC (toll-free).

Enforcement The Enforcement Bureau enforces the Communications Act and other communications statues, and the Commission's rules, orders, and authorizations. Much of the investigative work of the Commission is carried out by its field staff. The Bureau has 3 regional offices, 16 field offices, and resident agents in 9 additional cities. It also operates a nationwide fleet of mobile radio direction-finding vehicles for technical enforcement purposes. The field staff, in effect, are the Commission's

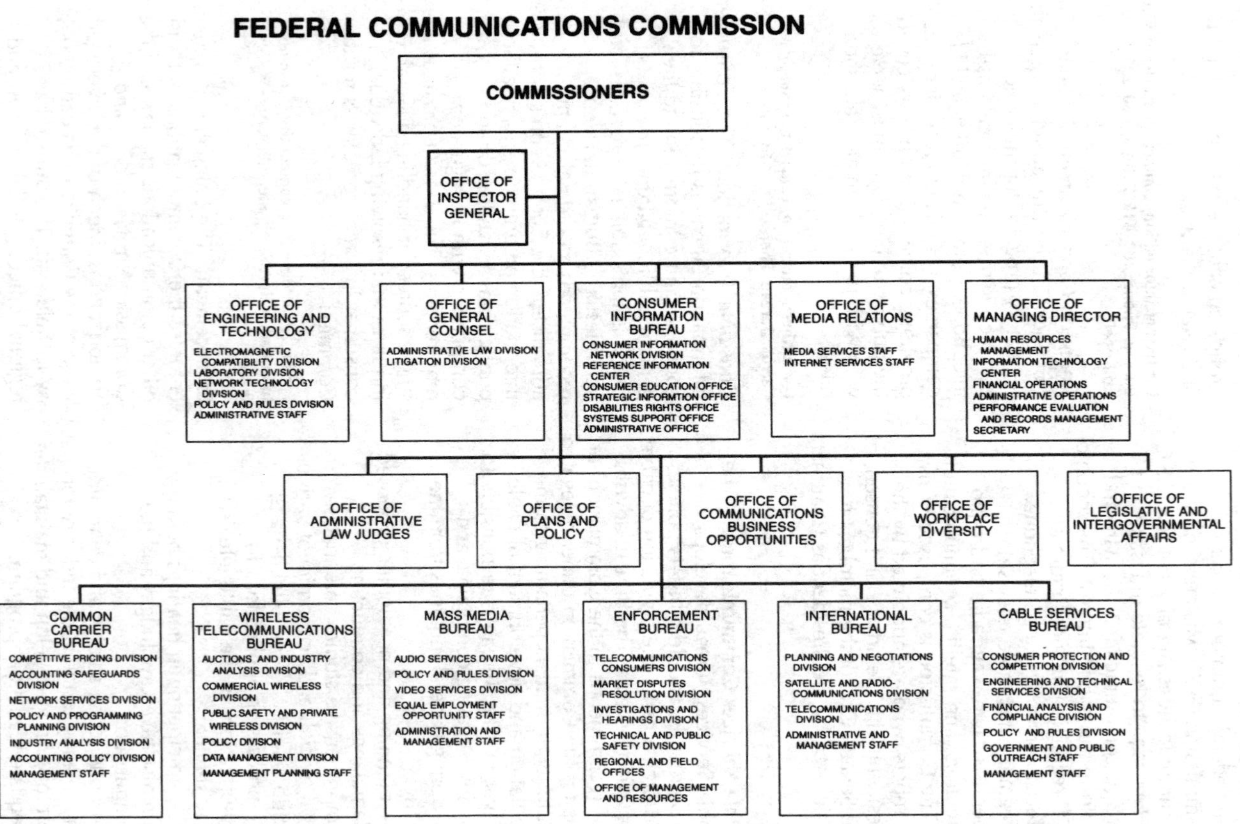
FEDERAL COMMUNICATIONS COMMISSION
COMMISSIONERS
OFFICE OF INSPECTOR GENERAL
OFFICE OF ENGINEERING AND TECHNOLOGY
ELECTROMAGNETIC COMPATIBILITY DIVISION
LABORATORY DIVISION
NETWORK TECHNOLOGY DIVISION
POLICY AND RULES DIVISION
ADMINISTRATIVE STAFF
OFFICE OF GENERAL COUNSEL
ADMINISTRATIVE LAW DIVISION
LITIGATION DIVISION
CONSUMER INFORMATION BUREAU
CONSUMER INFORMATION NETWORK DIVISION
REFERENCE INFORMATION CENTER
CONSUMER EDUCATION OFFICE
STRATEGIC INFORMTION OFFICE
DISABILITIES RIGHTS OFFICE
SYSTEMS SUPPORT OFFICE
ADMINISTRATIVE OFFICE
OFFICE OF MEDIA RELATIONS
MEDIA SERVICES STAFF
INTERNET SERVICES STAFF
OFFICE OF MANAGING DIRECTOR
HUMAN RESOURCES MANAGEMENT
INFORMATION TECHNOLOGY CENTER
FINANCIAL OPERATIONS
ADMINISTRATIVE OPERATIONS
PERFORMANCE EVALUATION AND RECORDS MANAGEMENT
SECRETARY
OFFICE OF ADMINISTRATIVE LAW JUDGES
OFFICE OF PLANS AND POLICY
OFFICE OF COMMUNICATIONS BUSINESS OPPORTUNITIES
OFFICE OF WORKPLACE DIVERSITY
OFFICE OF LEGISLATIVE AND INTERGOVERNMENTAL AFFAIRS
COMMON CARRIER BUREAU
COMPETITIVE PRICING DIVISION
ACCOUNTING SAFEGUARDS DIVISION
NETWORK SERVICES DIVISION
POLICY AND PROGRAMMING PLANNING DIVISION
INDUSTRY ANALYSIS DIVISION
ACCOUNTING POLICY DIVISION
MANAGEMENT STAFF
WIRELESS TELECOMMUNICATIONS BUREAU
AUCTIONS AND INDUSTRY ANALYSIS DIVISION
COMMERCIAL WIRELESS DIVISION
PUBLIC SAFETY AND PRIVATE WIRELESS DIVISION
POLICY DIVISION
DATA MANAGEMENT DIVISION
MANAGEMENT PLANNING STAFF
MASS MEDIA BUREAU
AUDIO SERVICES DIVISION
POLICY AND RULES DIVISION
VIDEO SERVICES DIVISION
EQUAL EMPLOYMENT OPPORTUNITY STAFF
ADMINISTRATION AND MANAGEMENT STAFF
ENFORCEMENT BUREAU
TELECOMMUNICATIONS CONSUMERS DIVISION
MARKET DISPUTES RESOLUTION DIVISION
INVESTIGATIONS AND HEARINGS DIVISION
TECHNICAL AND PUBLIC SAFETY DIVISION
REGIONAL AND FIELD OFFICES
OFFICE OF MANAGEMENT AND RESOURCES
INTERNATIONAL BUREAU
PLANNING AND NEGOTIATIONS DIVISION
SATELLITE AND RADIO-COMMUNICATIONS DIVISION
TELECOMMUNICATIONS DIVISION
ADMINISTRATIVE AND MANAGEMENT STAFF
CABLE SERVICES BUREAU
CONSUMER PROTECTION AND COMPETITION DIVISION
ENGINEERING AND TECHNICAL SERVICES DIVISION
FINANCIAL ANALYSIS AND COMPLIANCE DIVISION
POLICY AND RULES DIVISION
GOVERNMENT AND PUBLIC OUTREACH STAFF
MANAGEMENT STAFF

eyes and ears in detecting problems in the telecommunications environment and enforcing communications legislation and Commission rules.

For further information, contact the Enforcement Bureau. Phone, 888–225–5322 (toll-free).

Enforcement Bureau

Office	Address	Director
Regional Offices		
Kansas City, MO	2d Fl., 520 NE. Colbern Rd., Lee's Summit, 64086	Dennis P. Carlton
Park Ridge, IL	Rm. 306, 1550 Northwest Hwy., 60068–1460	Russell D. Monie
San Francisco, CA	Rm. 420, 3777 Depot Rd., Hayward, CA 94545–2756	Charles W. Craig
Field Offices		
Atlanta, GA	Rm. 320, 3575 Koger Blvd., Duluth 30136–4958	Fred L. Broce
Boston, MA	1 Batterymarch Pk., Quincy 02169–7495	Vincent F. Kajunski
Chicago, IL	Rm. 306, 1550 Northwest Hwy., Park Ridge 60068–1460	George M. Moffitt
Columbia, MD	9200 Farm House Ln., 21046	Charles C. Magin
Dallas, TX	Rm. 1170, 9330 LBJ Fwy., 75243–3429	James D. Wells
Denver, CO	Rm. 860, 165 S. Union Blvd., 80228–2213	Leo E. Cirbo
Detroit, MI	24897 Hathaway St., Farmington Hills 48335–1552	James A. Bridgewater
Kansas City, MO	2d Fl., 520 NE. Colbern Rd., Lee's Summit, 64086–4895	Robert C. McKinney
Los Angeles, CA	Rm. 660, 1800 Studebaker Rd., Cerritos 90703–3130	James R. Zoulek
New Orleans, LA	Rm. 460, 2424 Edenborn Ave., Metarie, 70001	James C. Hawkins
New York, NY	Rm. 1151, 201 Varick St., 10014–4870	Alexander J. Zimney
Philadelphia, PA	Rm. 404, 2300 E. Lincoln Hwy., Langhorne 19047–1859	John Rahtes
San Francisco, CA	Rm. 420, 3777 Depot Rd., Hayward 94545–2756	Thomas N. Van Stavern
San Diego, CA	Rm. 370, 4542 Ruffner St., 92111–2216	Jim Zoulek, *Acting*
Seattle, WA	Rm. 312, 11410 NE. 122d Way, Kirkland 98034–6927	Dennis Anderson
Tampa, FL	Rm. 1215, 2203 N. Lois Ave., 33607–2356	Ralph M. Barlow

International Bureau The International Bureau manages all FCC international telecommunications and satellite programs and policies, and represents the Commission at international conferences, meetings, and negotiations. The Bureau consists of three divisions: Telecommunications, Satellite and Radiocommunication, and Planning and Negotiations.

The Telecommunications Division develops and administers policy, rules, and procedures for the regulations of telecommunications facilities and services under section 214 of the Communications Act and Cable Landing License Act. In addition, the Division develops and administers regulatory assistance and training programs in conjunction with the administration's global information infrastructure (GII) initiative.

The Satellite and Radiocommunication Division develops and administers policy, rules, standards, and procedures for licensing and regulation of satellite and earth station facilities, both international and domestic, and oversight of Comsat as the U.S. Signatory to INTELSAT.

The Planning and Negotiations Division represents the Commission in negotiations of international agreements with Mexico, Canada, and other countries on the coordination and notification of domestic radio frequency assignments and resolution of international radio interference involving U.S. licensees. The Division processes license applications and conducts international coordination for high frequency (HF) international broadcast stations and acts on applications for delivery of broadcast programs to foreign stations.

For further information, contact the International Bureau. Phone, 202–418–0420, or 888–225–5322 (toll-free).

Mass Media The Mass Media Bureau administers the regulatory program for amplitude modulation (AM), frequency modulation (FM), television, low-power TV, translators, multipoint distribution service (MDS), instructional TV, and auxiliary services. The Bureau issues construction permits, operating licenses, and renewals or transfers of such broadcast licenses except for broadcast auxiliary services. It also oversees compliance by broadcasters with statutes and Commission policies.

For further information, contact the Mass Media Bureau. Phone, 202–418–2600.

Wireless Telecommunications The Wireless Telecommunications Bureau administers all domestic commercial and private wireless telecommunications programs and rules. The commercial wireless services include cellular, paging, personal communications, specialized mobile radio, air-ground, and basic exchange telecommunications services. The private wireless services generally serve the specialized internal communications needs of eligible users, and include the public safety, microwave, aviation, and marine services. Additionally, the Bureau serves as FCC's principal policy and administrative resource with regard to all spectrum auctions. It also implements the compulsory provisions of laws and treaties covering the use of radio for the safety of life and property at sea and in the air. The commercial and amateur radio operator programs are also administered by the Bureau.

For further information, contact the Wireless Telecommunications Bureau. Phone, 202–418–0600.

Sources of Information

Inquiries for information on the special subjects listed in the following paragraphs and those concerning licensing/grant requirements in the various services may be directed to the person or office specified or to the Chief of the Bureau or Office listed below as having responsibility for the service: Federal Communications Commission, 445 Twelfth Street SW., Washington, DC 20554.

Licensing/Grant Responsibility—Federal Communications Commission

Service	Bureau or Office
All broadcasting (except broadcast auxiliary services) and multipoint distribution services Cable TV relay services (CARS) Cable signal leakage Registration of cable systems	Mass Media Bureau Cable Services Bureau
Common carrier radio Emergency Alert System Amateur radio Auxiliary broadcast services Aviation radio Commercial radio operators Common carrier microwave services Interactive video and data services Land mobile radio Marine radio Private microwave radio	Common Carrier Bureau Enforcement Bureau Wireless Telecommunications Bureau
Direct broadcast satellites (DBS) Foreign carrier affiliation notification International accounting rate change applications International high frequency broadcast stations International public fixed radio communication applications Permit to deliver programs to foreign broadcast stations (Section 325–C applications) Requests for data network identification code (DNIC) assignment Requests for international signalling point code (ISPC) assignment Recognized private operating agencies Satellite Earth stations Satellite space stations (GSO) Satellite space stations (NGSO) Submarine cable landing license applications	International Bureau

Advisory Committee Management Direct inquiries to the Office of Performance Evaluation and Records Management. Phone, 202–418–0444.

Consumer Assistance Inquiries concerning general information on Commission operations and public participation in the decisionmaking process should be addressed to the Portals Consumer Center, Room CY–B523, 445 Twelfth Street SW., Washington, DC 20554. Phone, 888–225–5322 (toll-free). TTY, 888–835–5322.

Contracts and Procurement Direct inquiries to the Chief, Contracts and Purchasing Center. Phone, 202–418–0930.
Electronic Access Information regarding the Commission is also available electronically through the Internet, at www.fcc.gov.
Employment and Recruitment The Commission's programs require attorneys, electronics engineers, economists, accountants, administrative management and computer specialists, and clerical personnel. Requests for employment information should be directed to the Chief, Personnel Resources Service Center. Phone, 202–418–0130.
Equal Employment Practices by Industry Direct inquiries to the Portals Consumer Center. Phone, 888–225–5322 (toll-free).
Internal Equal Employment Practices Direct Inquiries to the Office of Workplace Diversity. Phone, 202–418–1799.
Ex-Parte Presentations Information concerning ex-parte presentations should be directed to the Commission's Office of General Counsel. Phone, 202–418–1720.
Fees Inquiries concerning the Commission's Fee Program should be addressed to the Portals Consumer Center, Room CY–B523, 445 Twelfth Street SW., Washington, DC 20554. Phone, 888–225–5322.
Freedom of Information Act Requests Requests should be directed to the Managing Director. Phone, 202–418–1919.
Information Available for Public Inspection At the Commission's headquarters office in Washington, DC, dockets concerning rulemaking and adjudicatory matters, copies of applications for licenses and grants, and reports required to be filed by licensees and cable system operators are maintained in the public reference rooms (some reports are by law held confidential). The Library has on file Commission rules and regulations (phone, 202–418–0450). General information is also available through the Commission's fax-on-demand (phone, 202–418–2830).

In addition to the information available at the Commission, each broadcasting station makes available for public reference certain information pertaining to the operation of the station, a current copy of the application filed for license, and nonconfidential reports filed with the Commission.
Publications The Office of Media Relations distributes publications, public notices, and press releases. Phone, 202–418–0500.

For further information, contact the Portals Consumer Center, Federal Communications Commission, 445 Twelfth Street SW., Washington, DC 20554. Phone, 888–522–5322. TTY, 888–835–5322. Internet, www.fcc.gov.

FEDERAL DEPOSIT INSURANCE CORPORATION

550 Seventeenth Street NW., Washington, DC 20429
Phone, 202–393–8400. Internet, www.fdic.gov.

Board of Directors:	
Chairman	DONNA TANOUE
Vice Chairman	ANDREW C. HOVE, JR.
Directors:	
(Comptroller of the Currency)	JOHN D. HAWKE, JR.
(Director, Office of Thrift Supervision)	ELLEN S. SEIDMAN
Appointive Director	(VACANCY)

Officials:

Deputy to the Chairman and Chief Operating Officer	JOHN F. BOVENZI
Deputy to the Chairman	JADINE NIELSEN
Deputy to the Chairman and Chief Financial Officer	MYRTA K. SALE
Chief of Staff, Office of the Chairman	MARK P. JACOBSEN
Deputy to the Vice Chairman	ROBERT W. RUSSELL
Deputy to the Director (Comptroller of the Currency)	THOMAS E. ZEMKE
Deputy to the Director (Office of Thrift Supervision)	WALTER B. MASON
Deputy to the Director (Appointive)	(VACANCY)
Chief Information Officer	DONALD C. DEMITROS
General Counsel	WILLIAM F. KROENER III
Director, Division of Administration	ARLEAS UPTON KEA
Director, Division of Compliance and Consumer Affairs	STEPHEN M. CROSS
Director, Division of Finance	FREDERICK S. SELBY
Director, Division of Information Resources Management	DONALD C. DEMITROS
Director, Division of Insurance	ARTHUR J. MURTON
Director, Division of Research and Statistics	WILLIAM R. WATSON
Director, Division of Resolutions and Receiverships	MITCHELL L. GLASSMAN
Director, Division of Supervision	JAMES L. SEXTON
Director, Office of Corporate Communications	PHIL BATTEY, *Acting*
Director, Office of Diversity and Economic Opportunity	D. MICHAEL COLLINS
Director, Office of Internal Control Management	VIJAY G. DESHPANDE
Director, Office of Legislative Affairs	ALICE C. GOODMAN
Director, Office of Ombudsman	RONALD F. BIEKER
Inspector General	GASTON L. GIANNI, JR.

The Federal Deposit Insurance Corporation promotes and preserves public confidence in U.S. financial institutions by insuring bank and thrift deposits up to the legal limit of $100,000; by periodically examining State-chartered banks that are not members of the Federal Reserve System for safety and soundness as well as compliance with consumer protection laws; and by liquidating assets of failed institutions to reimburse the insurance funds for the cost of failures.

The Federal Deposit Insurance Corporation (FDIC) was established under the Banking Act of 1933 in response to numerous bank failures during the Great Depression. FDIC began insuring banks on January 1, 1934. Congress has increased the limit on deposit insurance five times since 1934, the most current level being $100,000.

FDIC does not operate on funds appropriated by Congress. Its income is derived from insurance premiums on deposits held by insured banks and savings associations and from interest on the required investment of the premiums in U.S. Government securities. It also has authority to borrow from the Treasury up to $30 billion for insurance purposes.

Management of FDIC consists of a Board of Directors that includes the Chairman, Vice Chairman, and Appointive Director. The Comptroller of the Currency, whose office supervises national banks, and the Director of the

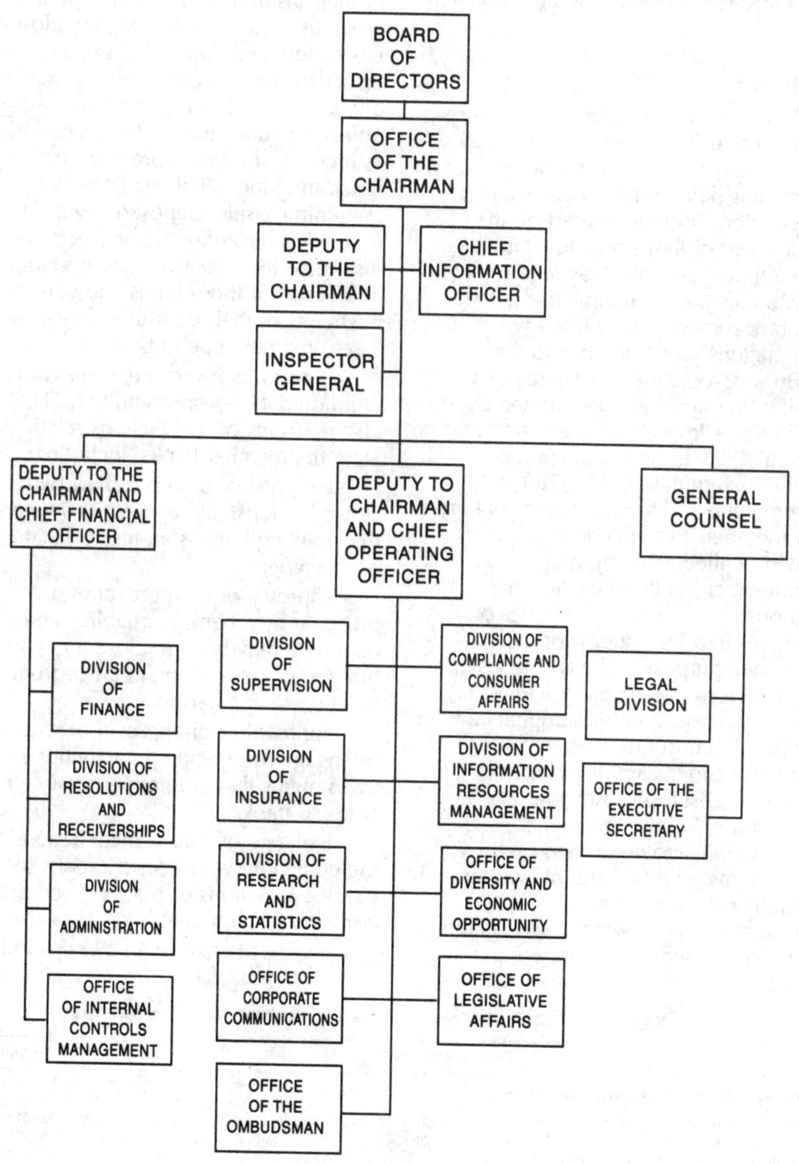
FEDERAL DEPOSIT INSURANCE CORPORATION
BOARD OF DIRECTORS
OFFICE OF THE CHAIRMAN
DEPUTY TO THE CHAIRMAN
CHIEF INFORMATION OFFICER
INSPECTOR GENERAL
DEPUTY TO THE CHAIRMAN AND CHIEF FINANCIAL OFFICER
DEPUTY TO CHAIRMAN AND CHIEF OPERATING OFFICER
GENERAL COUNSEL
DIVISION OF FINANCE
DIVISION OF RESOLUTIONS AND RECEIVERSHIPS
DIVISION OF ADMINISTRATION
OFFICE OF INTERNAL CONTROLS MANAGEMENT
DIVISION OF SUPERVISION
DIVISION OF COMPLIANCE AND CONSUMER AFFAIRS
DIVISION OF INSURANCE
DIVISION OF INFORMATION RESOURCES MANAGEMENT
DIVISION OF RESEARCH AND STATISTICS
OFFICE OF DIVERSITY AND ECONOMIC OPPORTUNITY
OFFICE OF CORPORATE COMMUNICATIONS
OFFICE OF LEGISLATIVE AFFAIRS
OFFICE OF THE OMBUDSMAN
LEGAL DIVISION
OFFICE OF THE EXECUTIVE SECRETARY

Office of Thrift Supervision, which supervises federally or State-chartered savings associations, are also members of the Board. All five Board members are appointed by the President and confirmed by the Senate, with no more than three being from the same political party.

Activities

FDIC insures about $2.9 trillion of U.S. bank and thrift deposits. The insurance funds are composed of insurance premiums paid by banks and savings associations and the interest on the investment of those premiums in U.S. Government securities, as required by law. Banks pay premiums to the Bank Insurance Fund (BIF), while savings associations pay premiums to the Savings Association Insurance Fund (SAIF). Premiums are determined by an institution's level of capitalization and potential risk to its insurance fund.

FDIC examines about 5,700 commercial and savings banks that are not members of the Federal Reserve System, called State-chartered nonmember banks. FDIC also has authority to examine other types of FDIC-insured institutions for deposit insurance purposes. The two types of examinations conducted are for safety and soundness, and for compliance with applicable consumer laws such as the Truth in Lending Act, the Home Mortgage Disclosure Act, and the Community Reinvestment Act. Examinations are performed on the institution's premises and off-site through computer data analysis.

A failed bank or savings association is generally closed by its chartering authority, and FDIC is named receiver. FDIC is required to resolve the closed institution in a manner that is least costly to FDIC. Ordinarily, FDIC attempts to locate a healthy institution to acquire the failed entity. If such an entity cannot be found, FDIC pays depositors the amount of their insured funds, usually by the next business day following the closing. Depositors with funds that exceed the insurance limit often receive an advance dividend, which is a portion of their uninsured funds that is determined by an estimate of the future proceeds from liquidating the failed institution's remaining assets. Depositors with funds in a failed institution that exceed the insurance limit receive a receivership certificate for those funds and partial payments of their uninsured funds as asset liquidation permits.

As part of its insurance, supervisory, and liquidation responsibilities, FDIC also performs other functions relating to State nonmember banks, including:

—approval or disapproval of mergers, consolidations, and acquisitions where the resulting bank is an insured State nonmember;

—approval or disapproval of a proposal by a bank to establish and operate a new branch, close an existing branch, or move its main office from one location to another;

—approval or disapproval of requests to engage as principal in activities and investments that are not permissible for a national bank;

—issuance of enforcement actions, including cease-and-desist orders, for specific violations or practices requiring corrective action; and

—review of changes in ownership or control of a bank.

Regional Offices—Federal Deposit Insurance Corporation

Region/Address	Telephone
Supervision/Compliance and Consumer Affairs.	
Atlanta, GA (Suite 1600, 1201 W. Peachtree St. NE., 30309)	404–817–1300
Boston, MA (15 Braintree Hill Office Park, Braintree, MA 02184)	781–794–5500
Chicago, IL (Suite 3600, 500 W. Monroe St., 60661)	312–382–7500
Dallas, TX (Suite 1900, 1910 Pacific Ave., 75201)	972–761–8475
Kansas City, MO (Suite 1200, 2345 Grand Ave., 64108)	816–234–8000
Memphis, TN (Suite 1900, 5100 Poplar Ave., 38137)	901–685–1603
New York, NY (20 Exchange Pl., 10005)	917–320–2500
San Francisco, CA (Suite 2300, 25 Ecker St., 94105)	415–546–0160
Resolutions and Receiverships.	

Regional Offices—Federal Deposit Insurance Corporation—Continued

Region/Address	Telephone
Southwest (1910 Pacific Ave., Dallas, TX 75201)	214–754–0098

Sources of Information

Consumer Information Information about deposit insurance and other consumer matters is available from the Division of Compliance and Consumer Affairs (DCA) at the same address or any regional office, or DCA's hotline, 800–934–3342. For a copy of a bank's quarterly Report of Condition, call 800–945–2186.

General Inquiries Written requests for general information may be directed to the Office of Corporate Communications, Federal Deposit Insurance Corporation, 550 Seventeenth Street NW., Washington, DC 20429.

Public Records Inquiries about the types of records available to the public, including records available under the Freedom of Information Act, should be directed to the Office of the Executive Secretary (phone, 202–898–7021) or any regional office.

Publications Publications, press releases, congressional testimony, directives to financial institutions, and other documents are available through the Public Information Center. Phone, 800–276–6003. E-mail, publicinfo@fdic.gov. Internet, www.fdic.gov.

For further information, contact the Corporate Communications Office, Federal Deposit Insurance Corporation, 550 Seventeenth Street NW., Washington, DC 20429. Phone, 202–898–6993. Internet, www.fdic.gov.

FEDERAL ELECTION COMMISSION

999 E Street NW., Washington, DC 20463
Phone, 202–694–1100 or 800–424–9530 (toll-free). Internet, www.fec.gov.

Chairman	DARRYL R. WOLD
Vice Chairman	DANNY L. MCDONALD
Commissioners	LEE ANN ELLIOTT, DAVID M. MASON, KARL J. SANDSTROM, SCOTT E. THOMAS
Staff Director	JAMES A. PEHRKON
General Counsel	LAWRENCE M. NOBLE
Inspector General	LYNNE A. MCFARLAND

The Federal Election Commission has exclusive jurisdiction in the administration and civil enforcement of laws regulating the acquisition and expenditure of campaign funds to ensure compliance by participants in the Federal election campaign process. Its chief mission is to provide public disclosure of campaign finance activities and effect voluntary compliance by providing the public with information on the laws and regulations concerning campaign finance.

The Federal Election Commission is an independent agency established by section 309 of the Federal Election Campaign Act of 1971, as amended (2 U.S.C. 437c). It is composed of six Commissioners appointed by the President with the advice and consent of the Senate. The act also provides for three statutory officers—the Staff Director, the General Counsel, and the

Inspector General—who are appointed by the Commission.

Activities

The Commission administers and enforces the Federal Election Campaign Act of 1971, as amended (2 U.S.C. 431 *et seq.*), and the Revenue Act, as amended (26 U.S.C. 1 *et seq.*). These laws provide for the public funding of Presidential elections, public disclosure of the financial activities of political committees involved in Federal elections, and limitations and prohibitions on contributions and expenditures made to influence Federal elections (Presidency, Senate, and House of Representatives).

Public Funding of Presidential Elections The Commission oversees the public financing of Presidential elections by certifying Federal payments to primary candidates, general election nominees, and national nominating conventions. It also audits recipients of Federal funds and may require repayments to the U.S. Treasury if a committee makes nonqualified campaign expenditures.

Disclosure The Commission ensures the public disclosure of the campaign finance activities reported by political committees supporting Federal candidates. Committee reports, filed regularly, disclose where campaign money comes from and how it is spent. The Commission places reports on the public record within 48 hours after they are received and computerizes the data contained in the reports.

Sources of Information

Clearinghouse on Election Administration The Clearinghouse compiles and disseminates election administration information related to Federal elections. It also conducts independent contract studies on the administration of elections. For further information, call 202–694–1095, or 800–424–9530 (toll-free).

Congressional Affairs Office This Office serves as primary liaison with Congress and executive branch agencies. The Office is responsible for keeping Members of Congress informed about Commission decisions and, in turn, for informing the Commission on legislative developments. For further information, call 202–694–1006, or 800–424–9530 (toll-free).

Employment Inquiries regarding employment opportunities should be directed to the Director, Personnel and Labor Management Relations. Phone, 202–694–1080, or 800–424–9530 (toll-free).

General Inquiries The Information Services Division provides information and assistance to Federal candidates, political committees, and the general public. This division answers questions on campaign finance laws, conducts workshops and seminars on the law, and provides publications and forms. For information or materials, call 202–694–1100, or 800–424–9530 (toll-free).

Media Inquiries The Press Office answers inquiries from print and broadcast media sources around the country, issues press releases on Commission actions and statistical data, responds to informational requests, and distributes other materials. All persons representing media should direct inquiries to the Press Office. Phone, 202–694–1220, or 800–424–9530 (toll-free).

Public Records The Office of Public Records, located at 999 E Street NW., Washington, DC, provides space for public inspection of all reports and statements relating to campaign finance since 1972. It is open weekdays from 9 a.m. to 5 p.m. and has extended hours during peak election periods. The public is invited to visit the Office or obtain information by calling 202–694–1120, or 800–424–9530 (toll-free).

Reading Room The library contains a collection of basic legal research resources, with emphasis on political campaign financing, corporate and labor political activity, and campaign finance reform. It is open to the public on weekdays between 9 a.m. and 5 p.m. For further information, call 202–694–1600, or 800–424–9530 (toll-free).

For further information, contact Information Services, Federal Election Commission, 999 E Street NW., Washington, DC 20463. Phone, 202–694–1100 or 800–424–9530 (toll-free). Internet, www.fec.gov.

FEDERAL EMERGENCY MANAGEMENT AGENCY

500 C Street SW., Washington, DC 20472
Phone, 202–646–4600. Internet, www.fema.gov.

Director	JAMES L. WITT
Deputy Director	ROBERT M. WALKER
Chief of Staff	JANE BULLOCK
General Counsel	ERNIE ABBOTT
Chief Financial Officer	GARY JOHNSON
Inspector General	GEORGE OPFER
Director, Office of Congressional and Legislative Affairs	RON GRIMES
Director, Office of Intergovernmental Affairs	MARTHA S. BRADDOCK
Director, Office of Public Affairs	MATTHEW FURMAN
Director, Office of Policy and Regional Operations	MICHELLE BURKETT
Associate Director, Response and Recovery Directorate	LACY E. SUITER
Associate Director, Information Technology Services Directorate	G. CLAY HOLLISTER
Associate Director, Mitigation Directorate	MICHAEL ARMSTRONG
Associate Director, Preparedness, Training, and Exercises Directorate	KAY GOSS
Associate Director, Operations Support Directorate	BRUCE CAMPBELL
Administrator, Federal Insurance Administration	JO ANN HOWARD
Administrator, United States Fire Administration	CARRYE BROWN

[For the Federal Emergency Management Agency statement of organization, see the *Code of Federal Regulations,* Title 44, Part 2]

The Federal Emergency Management Agency is the central agency within the Federal Government for emergency planning, preparedness, mitigation, response, and recovery. Working closely with State and local governments, the Agency funds emergency programs, offers technical guidance and training, and deploys Federal resources in times of catastrophic disaster. These coordinated activities ensure a broad-based program to protect life and property and provide recovery assistance after a disaster.

The Federal Emergency Management Agency (FEMA) was established by Executive Order 12127 of March 31, 1979, consolidating the Nation's emergency-related programs.

The Agency reports directly to the White House and manages the President's Disaster Relief Fund, the source of most Federal funding assistance after major disasters. Agency programs include response to and recovery from major natural disasters and human-caused emergencies, emergency management planning, flood-plain management, hazardous materials planning, dam safety, and multihazard

FEDERAL EMERGENCY MANAGEMENT AGENCY

OFFICE OF THE DIRECTOR
DIRECTOR
DEPUTY DIRECTOR
CHIEF OF STAFF

OFFICE OF INSPECTOR GENERAL

OFFICE OF CONGRESSIONAL AND LEGISLATIVE AFFAIRS
OFFICE OF PUBLIC AFFAIRS
OFFICE OF POLICY AND REGIONAL OPERATIONS
OFFICE OF NATIONAL SECURITY AFFAIRS
OFFICE OF INTERGOVERNMENTAL AFFAIRS

OFFICE OF HUMAN RESOURCES MANAGEMENT
OFFICE OF EQUAL RIGHTS
OFFICE OF FINANCIAL MANAGEMENT
OFFICE OF GENERAL COUNSEL

MITIGATION DIRECTORATE
- NATIONAL EARTHQUAKE PROGRAM OFFICE
- TECHNICAL SERVICES DIVISION
- PROGRAM ASSESSMENT AND OUTREACH DIVISION
- PROGRAM IMPLEMENTATION DIVISION

PREPAREDNESS, TRAINING, AND EXERCISES DIRECTORATE
- PARTNERSHIPS AND OUTREACH DIVISION
- TRAINING DIVISION
- MOUNT WEATHER MANAGEMENT DIVISION
- READINESS DIVISION
- CHEMICAL AND RADIOLOGICAL PREPAREDNESS DIVISION

RESPONSE AND RECOVERY DIRECTORATE
- OPERATIONS AND PLANNING DIVISION
- INFRASTRUCTURE DIVISION
- MOBILE OPERATIONS DIVISION
- HUMAN SERVICES DIVISION
- READINESS COORDINATION DIVISION

FEDERAL INSURANCE ADMINISTRATION
- FINANCIAL DIVISION
- OPERATIONS DIVISION
- CLAIMS AND UNDERWRITING DIVISION
- MARKETING DIVISION

UNITED STATES FIRE ADMINISTRATION
- MANAGEMENT OPERATIONS AND STUDENT SUPPORT DIVISION
- NATIONAL FIRE ACADEMY
- FIRE MANAGEMENT AND TECHNICAL PROGRAMS DIVISION

OPERATIONS SUPPORT DIRECTORATE
- OCCUPATIONAL SAFETY AND HEALTH PROGRAM OFFICE
- PROGRAM SERVICES DIVISION
- LOGISTICS DIVISION
- SECURITY DIVISION

INFORMATION TECHNOLOGY SERVICES DIRECTORATE
- MANAGEMENT DIVISION
- OPERATIONS DIVISION
- ENGINEERING DIVISION

REGIONAL OFFICES *REGIONS I–X*
- MITIGATION DIVISION
- PREPAREDNESS, TRAINING, AND EXERCISES DIVISION
- RESPONSE AND RECOVERY DIVISION
- OPERATIONS SUPPORT DIVISION

response planning. Other activities include off-site planning for emergencies at commercial nuclear power plants and the Army's chemical stockpile sites, emergency food and shelter funding for the homeless, plans to ensure the continuity of the Federal Government during national security emergencies, and Federal response to the consequences of major terrorist incidents.

The U.S. Fire Administration and its National Fire Academy are a part of FEMA, providing national leadership in fire safety and prevention. The U.S. Fire Administration has responsibility for all fire and emergency medical service programs and training activities. The Federal Insurance Administration is also a part of FEMA and manages the National Flood Insurance Program and crime insurance programs. The Emergency Management Institute at Emmitsburg, MD, offers centralized professional courses for the Nation's emergency managers.

Activities

Fire Prevention and Training This activity prepares Federal, State, and local officials, their staffs, emergency first responders, volunteer groups, and the public to meet the responsibilities of domestic emergencies through planning, mitigation, preparedness, response, and recovery. Educational programs are provided through the National Fire Academy at the National Emergency Training Center and through the field fire training delivery systems.

Mitigation Programs This activity provides for the development, coordination, and implementation of policies, plans, and programs to eliminate or reduce the long-term risk to life and property from natural hazards such as floods, earthquakes, hurricanes, and dam failures. A goal of this activity is to encourage and foster mitigation strategies at the State and local levels.

Preparedness, Training, and Exercises This activity provides policy guidance, financial and technical assistance, training, and exercise support required to establish or enhance all-hazard, risk-based emergency management capabilities of Federal, State, and local governments. In addition, this activity maintains a family protection program, utilizing private sector and volunteer organizations to encourage and assist families and neighborhoods to take actions to increase their emergency preparedness capabilities.

Response and Recovery This activity provides for the development and maintenance of an integrated operational capability to respond to and recover from the consequences of a disaster, regardless of its cause, in partnership with other Federal agencies, State and local governments, volunteer organizations, and the private sector.

Regional Offices Ten regional offices carry out FEMA's programs at the regional, State, and local levels. The regional offices are responsible for accomplishing the national program goals and objectives of the Agency and supporting development of national policy.

Regional Offices—Federal Emergency Management Agency

Region/Address	Telephone
Atlanta, GA (3003 Chamblee-Tucker Rd., 30341)	770–220–5200
Boston, MA (Rm. 442, J.W. McCormack Post Office & Courthouse Bldg., 02109–4595)	617–223–9540
Bothell, WA (130 228th St. SW., 98021–9796)	206–487–4765
Chicago, IL (4th Fl., 175 W. Jackson Blvd., 60604–2698)	312–408–5504
Denton, TX (800 N. Loop 288, 76201–3698)	817–898–5104
Denver, CO (Box 25267, Bldg. 710, Denver Federal Ctr., 80225–0267)	303–235–4812
Kansas City, MO (Suite 900, 2323 Grand Blvd., 64108–2670)	816–283–7061
New York, NY (Rm. 1337, 26 Federal Plz., 10278–0002)	212–225–7209
Philadelphia, PA (2d Fl., 105 S. 7th St., 19106–3316)	215–931–5608
San Francisco, CA (Bldg. 105, Presidio of San Francisco, 94129–1250)	415–923–7105

Sources of Information

Inquiries on the following subjects should be directed to the appropriate office of the Federal Emergency Management Agency, 500 C Street SW., Washington, DC 20472.

Acquisition Services: Office of Acquisition Management. Phone, 202–646–4168.

Employment: Office of Human Resources Management. Phone, 202–646–4040.

Freedom of Information Act requests: Office of General Counsel. Phone, 202–646–3840.

For further information, contact the Office of Public Affairs, Federal Emergency Management Agency, 500 C Street SW., Washington, DC 20472. Phone, 202–646–4600. Internet, www.fema.gov.

FEDERAL HOUSING FINANCE BOARD

1777 F Street NW., Washington, DC 20006
Phone, 202–408–2500. Internet, www.fhfb.gov.

Board of Directors:	
Chairman	BRUCE A. MORRISON
Members:	J. TIMOTHY O'NEILL, (2 VACANCIES)
(Secretary of Housing and Urban Development, *ex officio*)	ANDREW M. CUOMO
Housing and Urban Development Secretary's Designee to the Board	WILLIAM C. APGAR
Officials:	
Managing Director	WILLIAM W. GINSBERG
Director, Office of Communications	STEPHEN P. HUDAK
Director, Office of Information Management and Technology Support	HUNG PHAN
Director, Office of Policy, Research, and Analysis	JAMES L. BOTHWELL
Director, Office of Resource Management	BARBARA L. FISHER
Director, Office of Supervision	MITCHELL BERNS
General Counsel	DEBORAH F. SILBERMAN
Inspector General	EDWARD KELLEY

[For the Federal Housing Finance Board statement of organization, see the *Code of Federal Regulations,* Title 12, Part 900]

The Federal Housing Finance Board is responsible for the administration and enforcement of the Federal Home Loan Bank Act, as amended.

The Federal Housing Finance Board (Finance Board) was established by the Federal Home Loan Bank Act, as amended by the Financial Institutions Reform, Recovery, and Enforcement Act of 1989 (FIRREA) (12 U.S.C. 1421 *et seq.*), as an independent regulatory agency in the executive branch. The Finance Board succeeded the Federal Home Loan Bank Board for those functions transferred to it by FIRREA.

The Finance Board is managed by a five-member Board of Directors. Four members are appointed by the President with the advice and consent of the Senate for 7-year terms; one of the four is designated as Chairperson. The Secretary of the Department of Housing and Urban Development is the fifth member and serves in an *ex officio* capacity.

The Finance Board supervises the 12 Federal Home Loan Banks created in

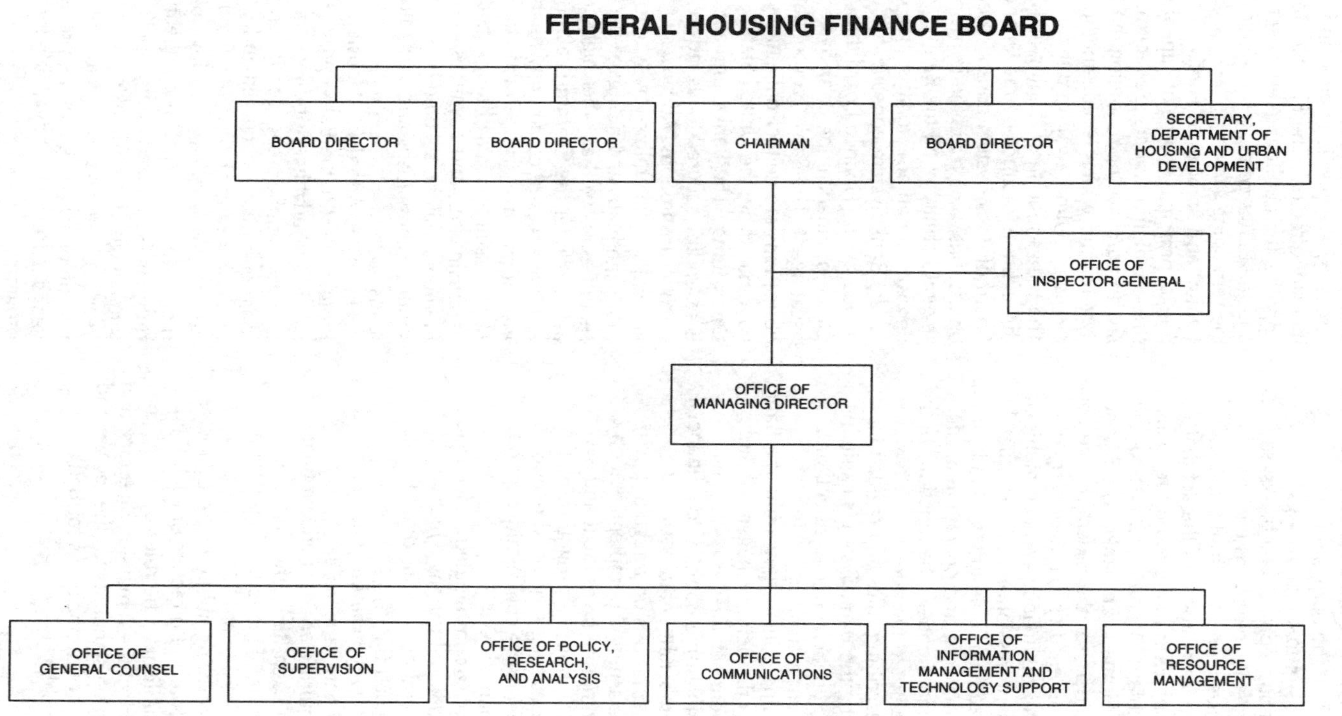
FEDERAL HOUSING FINANCE BOARD
BOARD DIRECTOR
BOARD DIRECTOR
CHAIRMAN
BOARD DIRECTOR
SECRETARY, DEPARTMENT OF HOUSING AND URBAN DEVELOPMENT
OFFICE OF INSPECTOR GENERAL
OFFICE OF MANAGING DIRECTOR
OFFICE OF GENERAL COUNSEL
OFFICE OF SUPERVISION
OFFICE OF POLICY, RESEARCH, AND ANALYSIS
OFFICE OF COMMUNICATIONS
OFFICE OF INFORMATION MANAGEMENT AND TECHNOLOGY SUPPORT
OFFICE OF RESOURCE MANAGEMENT

1932 by the Federal Home Loan Bank Act and issues regulations and orders for carrying out the purposes of the provisions of that act. Savings associations, commercial banks, savings banks, credit unions, insurance companies, and other institutions specified in section 4 of the act that make long-term home-mortgage loans are eligible to become members of the Federal Home Loan Banks. The Finance Board supervises the Federal Home Loan Banks and ensures that they carry out their housing finance and community investment mission, remain adequately capitalized and able to raise funds in the capital markets, and operate in a safe and sound manner. The functions of the Finance Board include:

—prescribing rules and regulations governing the Bank System's capital, lending, financial management, and investment activities;

—issuing policies governing the Bank System's financial management and investment activities;

—maintaining Bank System financial and membership databases and preparing reports on a regular basis;

—overseeing the implementation of the community investment and affordable housing programs;

—conducting a biennial review of each member's community support performance;

—issuing consolidated Federal Home Loan Bank obligations which are joint and several obligations of all Federal Home Loan Banks;

—annually examining each Federal Home Loan Bank;

—requiring an independent financial audit of each Bank, the Office of Finance, the Financing Corporation, and the Bank System;

—appointing public interest directors to the board of directors of each Bank and establishing the rules by which the Banks elect the remaining directors; and

—setting standards for the review and approval of applications for Bank membership.

Regional Banks

The System includes 12 regional Federal Home Loan Banks that are mixed-ownership Government corporations. Each Bank is managed by its board of directors, and public interest and industry directors. The Finance Board appoints the public interest directors, and the Banks conduct the election of the remaining directors.

Capital and Sources of Funds The Banks' principal source of capital is stock, which members are required by law to purchase upon joining the Bank System, and which is redeemed upon a member's withdrawal from the System. The Banks fund their lending activity through the issuance by the Finance Board of Bank System consolidated obligations, which are the joint and several liability of all the Banks. Member deposits are an additional source of funds. Bank System consolidated debt is issued by the Finance Board through the Office of Finance, the Bank System's fiscal agent. The Banks' consolidated obligations are neither obligations of, nor guaranteed by, the United States.

Operations The Banks' primary activity is extending secured loans (advances) to member institutions. Advances are generally collateralized by whole first mortgage loans and mortgage-backed securities, as well as other high-quality assets. Under the Gramm-Leach-Bliley Act, advances to community financial institutions may also be made to finance small businesses, small farms, and small agribusinesses, and advances to such members may be secured by secured small business loans and agricultural loans.

Under the Affordable Housing Program (AHP), the Banks provide subsidized advances or direct subsidies to Bank members engaged in lending for long-term owner-occupied and affordable rental housing targeted to households with very low, low, or moderate incomes. This competitive program is financed from a specified percentage of each Bank's previous year's net income. The greater of $100 million or 10 percent of the previous year's net income is available for the program.

Under the Community Investment Program (CIP), each Bank provides advances priced at the Bank's cost of consolidated obligations of comparable maturities plus reasonable administrative costs, to members engaged in community-oriented mortgage lending.

Financing Corporation

The Financing Corporation (FICO) was established by the Competitive Equality Banking Act of 1987 (12 U.S.C. 1441) with the sole purpose of issuing and servicing bonds, the proceeds of which were used to fund thrift resolutions. The Corporation has a three-member directorate, consisting of the Managing Director of the Office of Finance and two Federal Home Loan Bank presidents.

The Financing Corporation operates subject to the regulatory authority of the Federal Housing Finance Board.

Sources of Information

Requests for information relating to human resources and procurement should be sent to the Office of Resource Management, at the address listed below.

For further information, contact the Executive Secretariat, Federal Housing Finance Board, 1777 F Street NW., Washington, DC 20006. Phone, 202–408–2500. Fax, 202–408–2895. Internet, www.fhfb.gov.

FEDERAL LABOR RELATIONS AUTHORITY

607 Fourteenth Street NW., Washington, DC 20424–0001
Phone, 202–482–6560. Internet, www.flra.gov.

Chairman	DONALD S. WASSERMAN
Chief Counsel	ALICE BODLEY
Director of External Affairs	PATTY REILLY
Director of Case Management	PETER CONSTANTINE
Member	DALE CABANISS
Chief Counsel	KIRK UNDERWOOD
Member	PHYLLIS N. SEGAL
Chief Counsel	SUSAN D. MCCLUSKEY
Chief Administrative Law Judge	SAMUEL A. CHAITOVITZ
Solicitor	DAVID M. SMITH
Executive Director	SOLLY J. THOMAS, JR.
Assistant to the Executive Director	HAROLD D. KESSLER
Inspector General	FRANCINE C. EICHLER
General Counsel	JOSEPH SWERDZEWSKI
Deputy General Counsel	DAVID L. FEDER
Director of Operations and Resources Management	CLYDE B. BLANDFORD, JR.
Assistant General Counsel For Legal Services	STEVEN SVARTZ
Assistant General Counsel for Appeals	CAROL W. POPE
Director, Collaboration and Alternative Dispute Resolution Program	FERN FEIL KAUFMAN
Federal Service Impasses Panel	
Chair	BONNIE P. CASTREY
Members	STANLEY M. FISHER, EDWARD F. HARTFIELD, MARY E. JACKSTEIT, MARVIN E. JOHNSON, DAVID J. LELAND, JOHN G. WOFFORD
Executive Director	H. JOSEPH SCHIMANSKY
Foreign Service Labor Relations Board	

Chairman	Donald S. Wasserman
Members	Tia Schneider Denenberg, Richard I. Bloch
General Counsel	Joseph Swerdzewski

Foreign Service Impasse Disputes Panel

Chairperson	Thomas Colosi
Members	David Geiss, Allen L. Keiswetter, (2 vacancies)

The Federal Labor Relations Authority oversees the Federal service labor-management relations program. It administers the law that protects the right of employees of the Federal Government to organize, bargain collectively, and participate through labor organizations of their own choosing in decisions affecting them. The Authority also ensures compliance with the statutory rights and obligations of Federal employees and the labor organizations that represent them in their dealings with Federal agencies.

The Federal Labor Relations Authority was created as an independent establishment by Reorganization Plan No. 2 of 1978 (5 U.S.C. app.), effective January 1, 1979, pursuant to Executive Order 12107 of December 28, 1978, to consolidate the central policymaking functions in Federal labor-management relations. Its duties and authority are specified in title VII (Federal Service Labor-Management Relations) of the Civil Service Reform Act of 1978 (5 U.S.C. 7101–7135).

Activities

The Authority provides leadership in establishing policies and guidance relating to the Federal service labor-management relations program. In addition, it determines the appropriateness of bargaining units, supervises or conducts representation elections, and prescribes criteria and resolves issues relating to the granting of consultation rights to labor organizations with respect to internal agency policies and governmentwide rules and regulations. It also resolves negotiability disputes, unfair labor practice complaints, and exceptions to arbitration awards. The Chair of the Authority serves as the chief executive and administrative officer.

The General Counsel of the Authority investigates alleged unfair labor practices, files and prosecutes unfair labor practice complaints before the Authority, and exercises such other powers as the Authority may prescribe.

The Federal Service Impasses Panel, an entity within the Authority, is assigned the function of providing assistance in resolving negotiation impasses between agencies and unions. After investigating an impasse, the Panel can either recommend procedures to the parties for the resolution of the impasse or assist the parties in resolving the impasse through whatever methods and procedures, including factfinding and recommendations, it considers appropriate. If the parties do not arrive at a settlement after assistance by the Panel, the Panel may hold hearings and take whatever action is necessary to resolve the impasse.

The Foreign Service Labor Relations Board and the Foreign Service Impasse Disputes Panel administer provisions of chapter 2 of the Foreign Service Act of 1980 (22 U.S.C. 3921), concerning labor-management relations. This chapter establishes a statutory labor-management relations program for Foreign Service employees of the U.S. Government. Administrative and staff support is provided by the Federal Labor Relations Authority and the Federal Service Impasses Panel.

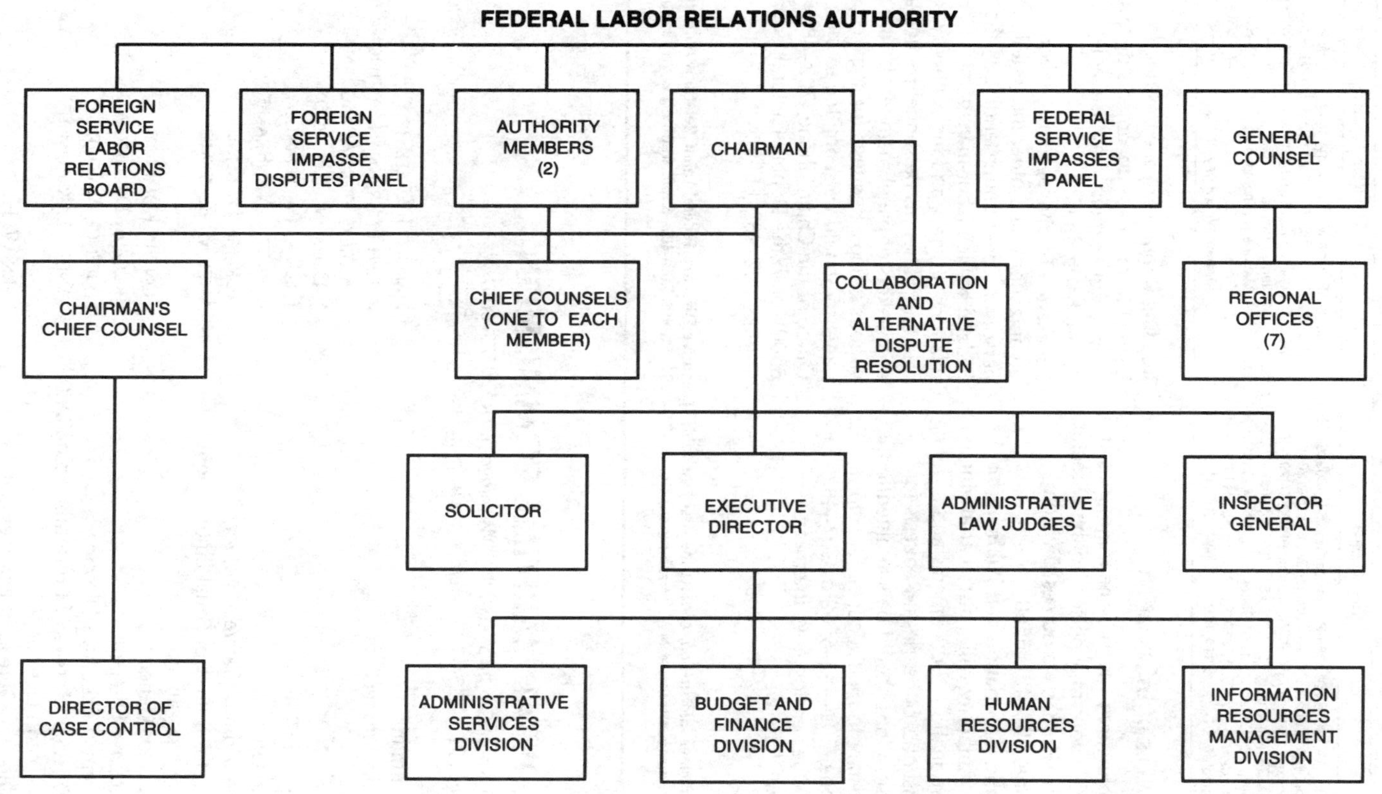
FEDERAL LABOR RELATIONS AUTHORITY
FOREIGN SERVICE LABOR RELATIONS BOARD
FOREIGN SERVICE IMPASSE DISPUTES PANEL
AUTHORITY MEMBERS (2)
CHAIRMAN
FEDERAL SERVICE IMPASSES PANEL
GENERAL COUNSEL
CHAIRMAN'S CHIEF COUNSEL
CHIEF COUNSELS (ONE TO EACH MEMBER)
COLLABORATION AND ALTERNATIVE DISPUTE RESOLUTION
REGIONAL OFFICES (7)
SOLICITOR
EXECUTIVE DIRECTOR
ADMINISTRATIVE LAW JUDGES
INSPECTOR GENERAL
DIRECTOR OF CASE CONTROL
ADMINISTRATIVE SERVICES DIVISION
BUDGET AND FINANCE DIVISION
HUMAN RESOURCES DIVISION
INFORMATION RESOURCES MANAGEMENT DIVISION

Regional Offices—Federal Labor Relations Authority

City/Address	Director	Telephone
Atlanta, GA (Suite 701, 285 Peachtree Ctr. Ave., 30303–1270)	Brenda M. Robinson	404–331–5212
Boston, MA (Suite 1500, 99 Summer St., 02110–1200)	Edward S. Davidson	617–424–5730
Chicago, IL (Suite 1150, 55 W. Monroe, 60603–9729)	William E. Washington	312–353–6306
Dallas, TX (Suite 926, 525 Griffin St., 75202–5903)	James Petrucci	214–767–4996
Denver, CO (Suite 100, 1244 Speer Blvd., 80204–3581)	Marjorie K. Thompson	303–844–5224
San Francisco, CA (Suite 220, 901 Market St., 94103–1791)	Gerald M. Cole	415–356–5000
Washington, DC (Suite 910, 800 K St. NW., 20001)	Michael W. Doheny	202–482–6700

Sources of Information

Employment Employment inquiries and applications may be sent to the Director of the Human Resources Division. Phone, 202–482–6660.

Public Information and Publications The Authority will assist in arranging reproduction of documents and ordering transcripts of hearings. Requests for publications should be submitted to the Assistant to the Executive Director. Phone, 202–482–6560 or 202–482–6690, extension 440. Internet, www.flra.gov.

Reading Room Anyone desiring to inspect formal case documents or read agency publications may use facilities of the Authority's offices.

Speakers To give agencies, labor organizations, and other interested persons a better understanding of the Federal service labor-management relations program and the Authority's role and duties, its personnel participate as speakers or panel members before various groups. Requests for speakers or panelists should be submitted to the Office of the Chair (phone, 202–482–6500); or to the Deputy General Counsel (phone, 202–482–6680).

For further information, contact the Assistant to the Executive Director, Federal Labor Relations Authority, 607 Fourteenth Street NW., Washington, DC 20424–0001. Phone, 202–482–6560. Internet, www.flra.gov.

FEDERAL MARITIME COMMISSION

800 North Capitol Street NW., Washington, DC 20573–0001
Phone, 202–523–5707. Internet, www.fmc.gov.

Chairman	HAROLD J. CREEL, JR.
Commissioners	JOSEPH E. BRENNAN, ANTHONY M. MERCK, JOHN A. MORAN, DELMOND J.H. WON
General Counsel	THOMAS PANEBIANCO
Secretary	BRYANT L. VANBRAKLE
Chief Administrative Law Judge	NORMAN D. KLINE
Director, Office of Equal Employment Opportunity	ALICE M. BLACKMON
Inspector General	TONY P. KOMINOTH
Executive Director	BRUCE A. DOMBROWSKI
Deputy Executive Director	FLORENCE A. CARR
Director, Bureau of Consumer Complaints and Licensing	SANDRA L. KUSUMOTO
Director, Bureau of Enforcement	VERN W. HILL
Director, Bureau of Trade Analysis	AUSTIN L. SCHMITT

The Federal Maritime Commission regulates the waterborne foreign commerce of the United States, ensures that U.S. international trade is open to all nations on fair and equitable terms, and protects against unauthorized, concerted activity in the waterborne commerce of the United States. This is accomplished through maintaining surveillance over steamship conferences and common carriers by water; reviewing agreements between persons subject to the Shipping Act of 1984; enforcing prohibitions against discriminatory acts and other prohibited practices of shippers, carriers, and other persons subject to the shipping statutes; and ensuring that adequate levels of financial responsibility are maintained for indemnification of passengers.

The Federal Maritime Commission was established by Reorganization Plan No. 7 of 1961 (5 U.S.C. app.), effective August 12, 1961. It is an independent agency that regulates shipping under the following statutes: the Shipping Act of 1984 (46 U.S.C. app. 1701–1720); the Merchant Marine Act, 1920 (46 U.S.C. app. 861 *et seq.*); the Foreign Shipping Practices Act of 1988 (46 U.S.C. app. 1710a); the Merchant Marine Act, 1936 (46 U.S.C. app. 1101 *et seq.*); and certain provisions of the act of November 6, 1966 (46 U.S.C. app. 817(d) and 817(e)).

Activities

Agreements The Commission reviews for legal sufficiency agreements filed under section 5 of the Shipping Act of 1984, including conference, interconference, and cooperative working agreements among common carriers, terminal operators, and other persons subject to the shipping statutes. It also monitors activities under all effective agreements for compliance with the provisions of law and its rules, orders, and regulations.

Tariffs The Commission monitors and prescribes requirements to ensure accessibility and accuracy of electronic tariff publications of common carriers engaged in the foreign commerce of the United States. Special permission applications may be submitted for relief from statutory and/or Commission tariff requirements.

Service Contracts The Commission receives and reviews filings of confidential service contracts between shippers and ocean common carriers. The Commission also monitors publication of certain essential terms of those service contracts.

Licenses The Commission issues licenses as ocean transportation intermediaries to those persons and entities who wish to carry out the business of providing freight forwarding services and non-vessel-operating common carrier services.

Passenger Indemnity The Commission administers the passenger indemnity provisions of the act of November 6, 1966, which require shipowners and operators to obtain certificates of financial responsibility to pay judgments for personal injury or death or to refund fares in the event of nonperformance of voyages.

Informal Complaints The Commission reviews alleged or suspected violations of the shipping statutes and rules and regulations of the Commission and may take administrative action to institute formal proceedings, to refer matters to other governmental agencies, or to bring about voluntary agreement between the parties.

Formal Adjudicatory Procedure The Commission conducts formal investigations and hearings on its own motion and adjudicates formal complaints in accordance with the Administrative Procedure Act (5 U.S.C. note prec. 551).

Rulemaking The Commission promulgates rules and regulations to interpret, enforce, and ensure compliance with shipping and related statutes by common carriers and other persons subject to the statutes.

Investigation and Financial and Economic Analyses The Commission prescribes and administers programs to

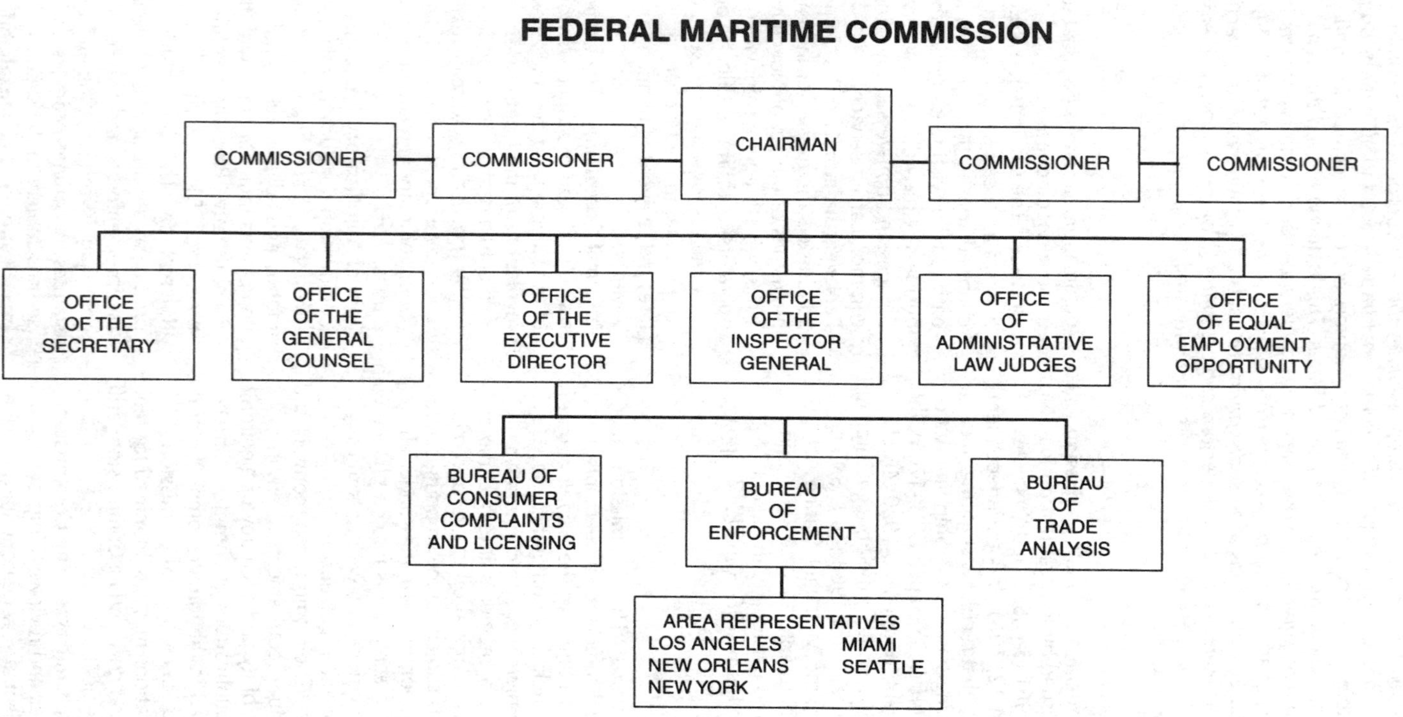
FEDERAL MARITIME COMMISSION
COMMISSIONER
COMMISSIONER
CHAIRMAN
COMMISSIONER
COMMISSIONER
OFFICE OF THE SECRETARY
OFFICE OF THE GENERAL COUNSEL
OFFICE OF THE EXECUTIVE DIRECTOR
OFFICE OF THE INSPECTOR GENERAL
OFFICE OF ADMINISTRATIVE LAW JUDGES
OFFICE OF EQUAL EMPLOYMENT OPPORTUNITY
BUREAU OF CONSUMER COMPLAINTS AND LICENSING
BUREAU OF ENFORCEMENT
BUREAU OF TRADE ANALYSIS
AREA REPRESENTATIVES
LOS ANGELES
NEW ORLEANS
NEW YORK
MIAMI
SEATTLE

ensure compliance with the provisions of the shipping statutes. These programs include the submission of information; field investigations of activities and practices of common carriers, conferences, terminal operators, freight forwarders, passenger vessel operations, and other persons subject to the shipping statutes; and rate analyses, studies, and economic reviews of current and prospective trade conditions, including the extent and nature of competition in various trade areas.

International Affairs The Commission conducts investigations of foreign governmental and foreign carrier practices that adversely affect the U.S. shipping trade and, in conjunction with the Department of State, conducts activities to effect the elimination of discriminatory practices on the part of foreign governments against United States-flag shipping and to achieve comity between the United States and its trading partners.

Area Representatives—Federal Maritime Commission

Area	Address/Phone	Representative
Los Angeles	Rm. 1018, 300 S. Ferry St., San Pedro, CA 90731. Phone, 310–514–4905. Fax, 310–514–3931. E-mail, oliverc@fmc.gov	Oliver E. Clark
Miami	Rm. 736, 909 SE. First Ave., Miami, FL 33131. Phone, 305–536–4316. Fax, 305–536–4317. E-mail, andrewm@fmc.gov	Andrew Margolis
New Orleans	Rm. 303, 423 Canal St., New Orleans, LA 70130. Phone, 504–589–6662. Fax, 504–589–6663. E-mail, alvink@fmc.gov	Alvin N. Kellogg
New York	P.O. Box 3461, New York, NY 10008. Phone, 212–637–2929. Fax, 212–637–2930. E-mail, emanuelm@fmc.gov	Emanuel J. Mingione
Seattle	Suite 100, 7 S. Nevada St., Seattle, WA 98134. Phone, 206–553–0221. Fax, 206–553–0222. E-mail, michaelm@fmc.gov	Michael A. Moneck

Sources of Information

Electronic Access Information about the Federal Maritime Commission is available in electronic form through the Internet, at www.fmc.gov.

Employment Employment inquiries may be directed to the Office of Human Resources, Federal Maritime Commission, 800 North Capitol Street NW., Washington, DC 20573–0001. Phone, 202–523–5773.

Informal Complaints Phone, 202–523–5807. E-mail, josephf@fmc.gov.

Publications The *Thirty-eighth Annual Report (1999)* is a recent publication of the Federal Maritime Commission.

For further information, contact the Office of the Secretary, Federal Maritime Commission, 800 North Capitol Street NW., Washington, DC 20573–0001. Phone, 202–523–5725. Fax, 202–523–0014. Internet, www.fmc.gov. E-mail, secretary@fmc.gov.

FEDERAL MEDIATION AND CONCILIATION SERVICE

2100 K Street NW., Washington, DC 20427
Phone, 202–606–8100. Internet, www.fmcs.gov.

Director	C. Richard Barnes
Deputy Director, Field Operations	George W. Buckingham, Jr., *Acting*
Deputy Director, National Office Operations	Vella M. Traynham

The Federal Mediation and Conciliation Service assists labor and management in resolving disputes in collective bargaining contract negotiation through voluntary mediation and arbitration services; provides training to unions and management in cooperative processes to improve long-term relationships under the Labor Management Cooperation Act of 1978, including Federal sector partnership training authorized by Executive Order 12871; provides alternative dispute resolution services and training to Government agencies, including the facilitation of regulatory negotiations under the Administrative Dispute Resolution Act and the Negotiated Rulemaking Act of 1996; and awards competitive grants to joint labor-management committees to encourage innovative approaches to cooperative efforts.

The Federal Mediation and Conciliation Service (FMCS) was created by the Labor Management Relations Act, 1947 (29 U.S.C. 172). The Director is appointed by the President with the advice and consent of the Senate.

Activities

The Federal Mediation and Conciliation Service helps prevent disruptions in the flow of interstate commerce caused by labor-management disputes by providing mediators to assist disputing parties in the resolution of their differences. Mediators have no law enforcement authority and rely wholly on persuasive techniques.

The Service offers its facilities in labor-management disputes to any industry affecting interstate commerce with employees represented by a union, either upon its own motion or at the request of one or more of the parties to the dispute, whenever in its judgment such dispute threatens to cause a substantial interruption of commerce. The Labor Management Relations Act requires that parties to a labor contract must file a dispute notice if agreement is not reached 30 days in advance of a contract termination or reopening date. The notice must be filed with the Service and the appropriate State or local mediation agency. The Service is required to avoid the mediation of disputes that would have only a minor effect on interstate commerce if State or other conciliation services are available to the parties.

For further information, contact one of the regional offices listed below.

Mediation Efforts of FMCS mediators are directed toward the establishment of sound and stable labor-management relations on a continuing basis, thereby helping to reduce the incidence of work stoppages. The mediator's basic function is to encourage and promote better day-to-day relations between labor and management, so that issues arising in negotiations may be faced as problems to be settled through mutual effort rather than issues in dispute.

For further information, contact the Office of Public Affairs. Phone, 202–606–8080.

Arbitration The Service, on the joint request of employers and unions, will also assist in the selection of arbitrators from a roster of private citizens who are qualified as neutrals to adjudicate matters in dispute.

For further information, contact the Office of Arbitration Services. Phone, 202–606–5111.

Regional Offices—Federal Mediation and Conciliation Service

Region/Address	Director	Telephone
Northeastern (16th Fl., 1 Newark Ctr., Newark, NJ 07102)	Kenneth C. Kowalski	973–645–2200
Southern (Suite 472, 401 W. Peachtree St. NW., Atlanta, GA 30308)	Fred W. Reebals	404–331–3995
Midwestern (Suite 120, 6161 Oak Tree Blvd., Independence, OH 44131)	John F. Buettner, *Acting*	216–522–4800
Upper Midwestern (Suite 3950, 1300 Godward St., Minneapolis, MN 55413)	Scot Beckenbaugh	612–370–3300
Western (Suite 1100, 2001 6th Ave., Seattle, WA 98121)	Douglas P. Hammond	206–553–5800

For further information, contact the Public Affairs Office, Federal Mediation and Conciliation Service, 2100 K Street NW., Washington, DC 20427. Phone, 202–606–8100. Internet, www.fmcs.gov.

FEDERAL MINE SAFETY AND HEALTH REVIEW COMMISSION

Suite 6000, 1730 K Street NW., Washington, DC 20006–3867
Phone, 202–653–5625. Internet, www.fmshrc.gov.

Chairman	MARY LU JORDAN
Commissioners	ROBERT H. BEATTY, JR., MARC L. MARKS, JAMES C. RILEY, THEODORE F. VERHEGGEN
Chief Administrative Law Judge	DAVID BARBOUR
General Counsel	NORMAN M. GLEICHMAN
Executive Director	RICHARD L. BAKER

The Federal Mine Safety and Health Review Commission ensures compliance with occupational safety and health standards in the Nation's surface and underground coal, metal, and nonmetal mines.

The Federal Mine Safety and Health Review Commission is an independent, quasi-judicial agency established by the Federal Mine Safety and Health Act of 1977 (30 U.S.C. 801 *et seq.*).

The Commission consists of five members who are appointed by the President with the advice and consent of the Senate and who serve staggered, 6-year terms. The Chairman is selected from among the Commissioners.

The Commission and its Office of Administrative Law Judges are charged with deciding cases brought pursuant to the act by the Mine Safety and Health Administration, mine operators, and miners or their representatives. These cases generally involve review of the Administration's enforcement actions including citations, mine closure orders, and proposals for civil penalties issued for violations of the act or the mandatory safety and health standards promulgated by the Secretary of Labor. The Commission also has jurisdiction over discrimination complaints filed by miners or their representatives in connection with their safety and health rights under the act, and over complaints for compensation filed on behalf of miners idled as a result of mine closure orders issued by the Administration.

Activities

Cases brought before the Commission are assigned to the Office of Administrative Law Judges, and hearings are conducted pursuant to the requirements of the Administrative Procedure Act (5 U.S.C. 554, 556) and the Commission's procedural rules (29 CFR Part 2700).

A judge's decision becomes a final but nonprecedential order of the Commission 40 days after issuance unless the Commission has directed the case for review in response to a petition or on its own motion. If a review is conducted, a decision of the Commission becomes final 30 days after issuance unless a party adversely affected seeks review in the U.S. Circuit Court of Appeals for the District of Columbia or the Circuit within which the mine subject to the litigation is located.

As far as practicable, hearings are held at locations convenient to the affected mines. The Office of Administrative Law Judges has two offices: the Falls Church Office, 2 Skyline, 5203 Leesburg Pike, Falls Church, VA 22041; and the Denver Office, Colonnade Center, Room 280, 1244 Speer Boulevard, Denver, CO 80204.

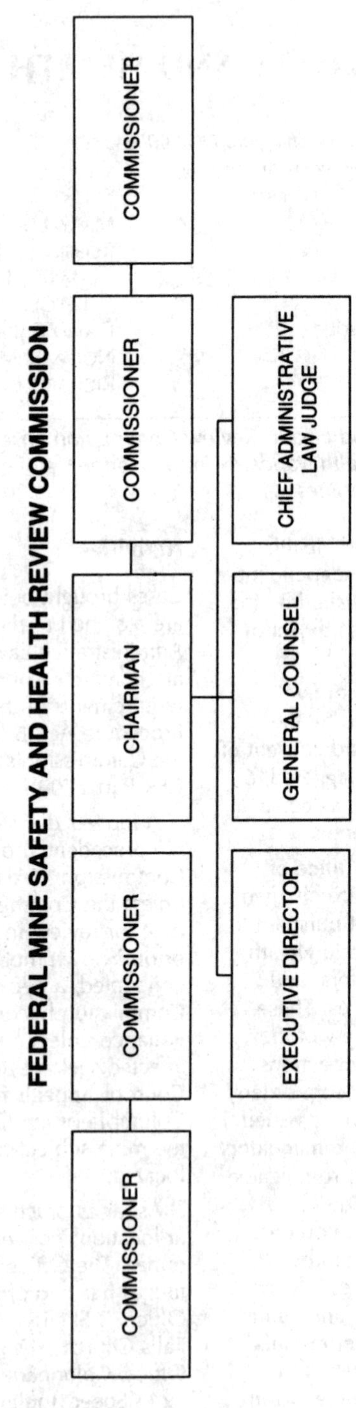
FEDERAL MINE SAFETY AND HEALTH REVIEW COMMISSION
COMMISSIONER
COMMISSIONER
CHAIRMAN
COMMISSIONER
COMMISSIONER
CHIEF ADMINISTRATIVE LAW JUDGE
GENERAL COUNSEL
EXECUTIVE DIRECTOR

Sources of Information

Commission decisions are published monthly and are available through the Superintendent of Documents, U.S. Government Printing Office, Washington, DC 20402. Requests for Commission records should be submitted in accordance with the Commission's Freedom of Information Act regulations. Other information, including Commission rules of procedure and brochures explaining the Commission's functions, is available from the Executive Director, Federal Mine Safety and Health Review Commission, Sixth Floor, 1730 K Street NW., Washington, DC 20006–3867. E-mail, info@fmshrc.gov.

For further information, contact the Executive Director, Federal Mine Safety and Health Review Commission, Suite 6000, 1730 K Street NW., Washington DC 20006–3867. Phone, 202–653–5625. Fax, 202–653–5030. Internet, www.fmshrc.gov. E-mail, info@fmshrc.gov.

FEDERAL RESERVE SYSTEM

Board of Governors of the Federal Reserve System
Twentieth Street and Constitution Avenue NW., Washington, DC 20551
Phone, 202–452–3000. Internet, www.federalreserve.gov.

Board of Governors

Chairman	ALAN GREENSPAN
Vice Chair	ROGER W. FERGUSON, JR.
Members	EDWARD M. GRAMLICH, EDWARD W. KELLEY, JR., LAURENCE H. MEYER, (2 VACANCIES)
Staff:	
Assistants to the Board	LYNN S. FOX, DONALD J. WINN
General Counsel	J. VIRGIL MATTINGLY, JR.
Secretary	JENNIFER J. JOHNSON
Director, Division of Banking Supervision and Regulation	RICHARD SPILLENKOTHEN
Director, Division of Consumer and Community Affairs	DOLORES S. SMITH
Director, Division of Federal Reserve Bank Operations and Payment Systems	LOUISE L. ROSEMAN
Director, Division of Information Resources Management	RICHARD C. STEVENS
Director, Division of International Finance	KAREN H. JOHNSON
Director, Management Division	STEPHEN R. MALPHRUS
Director, Division of Monetary Affairs	DONALD L. KOHN
Director, Division of Research and Statistics	MICHAEL J. PRELL
Director, Division of Support Services	ROBERT E. FRAZIER
Staff Director, Office of Staff Director for Management	STEPHEN R. MALPHRUS
Inspector General	BARRY R. SNYDER

Officers of the Federal Reserve Banks

Chairmen and Federal Reserve Agents:	
Atlanta, GA	JOHN F. WIELAND
Boston, MA	WILLIAM C. BRAINARD
Chicago, IL	LESTER H. MCKEEVER, JR.
Cleveland, OH	G. WATTS HUMPHREY, JR.

Dallas, TX	Roger R. Hemminghaus
Kansas City, MO	Jo Marie Dancik
Minneapolis, MN	David A. Koch
New York, NY	John C. Whitehead
Philadelphia, PA	Joan Carter
Richmond, VA	Claudine B. Malone
St. Louis, MO	Susan S. Elliott
San Francisco, CA	Gary G. Michael
Presidents:	
Atlanta, GA	Jack Guynn
Boston, MA	Cathy E. Minehan
Chicago, IL	Michael H. Moskow
Cleveland, OH	Jerry L. Jordan
Dallas, TX	Robert D. McTeer, Jr.
Kansas City, MO	Thomas M. Hoenig
Minneapolis, MN	Gary H. Stern
New York, NY	William J. McDonough
Philadelphia, PA	Edward G. Boehne
Richmond, VA	J. Alfred Broaddus, Jr.
St. Louis, MO	William Poole
San Francisco, CA	Robert T. Parry

Federal Open Market Committee

Chairman	Alan Greenspan
Vice Chairman	William J. McDonough
Members	J. Alfred Broaddus, Jr., Roger W. Ferguson, Jr., Edward M. Gramlich, Jack Guynn, Jerry L. Jordan, Edward W. Kelley, Jr., Laurence H. Meyer, Michael H. Moskow, Robert T. Parry, (2 vacancies)
Staff:	
Secretary and Economist	Donald L. Kohn
Assistant Secretaries	Lynn S. Fox, Gary P. Gillum
General Counsel	J. Virgil Mattingly, Jr.
Economists	Karen H. Johnson, Michael J. Prell
Co-Secretaries, Federal Advisory Council	James Annable, William J. Korsvik
Chairman, Consumer Advisory Council	Yvonne S. Sparks Strauther
President, Thrift Institutions Advisory Council	William A. Fitzgerald

The Federal Reserve System, the central bank of the United States, is charged with administering and formulating the Nation's credit and monetary policy. Through its supervisory and regulatory banking functions, the Federal Reserve maintains the safety and soundness of the Nation's economy, responding to the Nation's domestic and international financial needs and objectives.

The Federal Reserve System was established by the Federal Reserve Act (12 U.S.C. 221), approved December 23, 1913. The System serves as the Nation's central bank. As such, its major responsibility is in the execution of monetary policy. It also performs other functions, such as the transfer of funds, handling Government deposits and debt issues, supervising and regulating banks, and acting as lender of last resort.

It is the responsibility of the Federal Reserve System to contribute to the strength and vitality of the U.S. economy. By influencing the lending and investing activities of depository institutions and the cost and availability of money and credit, the Federal Reserve System helps promote the full use of human and capital resources, the growth of productivity, relatively stable prices, and equilibrium in the Nation's international balance of payments. Through its supervisory and regulatory banking functions, the Federal Reserve System helps maintain a commercial banking system that is responsive to the Nation's financial needs and objectives.

The System consists of the Board of Governors in Washington, DC; the 12 Federal Reserve Banks and their 25 branches and other facilities situated throughout the country; the Federal Open Market Committee; the Federal Advisory Council; the Consumer Advisory Council; the Thrift Institutions Advisory Council; and the Nation's financial institutions, including commercial banks, savings and loan associations, mutual savings banks, and credit unions.

Board of Governors

The Board is composed of seven members appointed by the President with the advice and consent of the Senate. The Chairman of the Board of Governors is a member of the National Advisory Council on International Monetary and Financial Policies. The Board determines general monetary, credit, and operating policies for the System as a whole and formulates the rules and regulations necessary to carry out the purposes of the Federal Reserve Act. The Board's principal duties consist of monitoring credit conditions; supervising the Federal Reserve Banks, member banks, and bank holding companies; and regulating the implementation of certain consumer credit protection laws.

Power To Influence Credit Conditions
The Board has the power, within statutory limitations, to fix the requirements concerning reserves to be maintained by depository institutions on transaction accounts or nonpersonal time deposits. The Board of Governors reviews and determines the discount rate charged by the Federal Reserve Banks. For the purpose of preventing excessive use of credit for the purchase or carrying of securities, the Board is authorized to regulate the amount of credit that may be initially extended and subsequently maintained on any security (with certain exceptions).

Supervision of Federal Reserve Banks
The Board is authorized to make examinations of the Federal Reserve Banks, to require statements and reports from such Banks, to supervise the issue and retirement of Federal Reserve notes, to require the establishment or discontinuance of branches of Reserve Banks, and to exercise supervision over all relationships and transactions of those Banks with foreign branches.

Supervision of Bank Holding Companies
The Federal Reserve has primary responsibility for supervising and regulating the activities of bank holding companies. The main objectives of this activity are to control the expansion of bank holding companies by avoiding the creation of monopoly or restraining trade in banking, and to limit the expansion of bank holding companies to those nonbanking activities that are closely related to banking, thus maintaining a separation between banking and commerce. A company that seeks to become a bank holding company must obtain the prior approval of the Federal Reserve. Any company that qualifies as a bank holding company must register with the Federal Reserve System and file reports with the System.

Supervision of Banking Organizations
The Federal Reserve is responsible for the supervision and regulation of domestic and international activities of U.S. banking organizations. It supervises State-chartered banks that are members of the System, all bank holding companies, and Edge Act and agreement corporations (corporations chartered to engage in international banking).

The Board has jurisdiction over the admission of State banks and trust companies to membership in the Federal Reserve System, the termination of membership of such banks, the establishment of branches by such banks, and the approval of bank mergers and consolidations where the resulting institution will be a State member bank. It receives copies of condition reports submitted to the Federal Reserve Banks. It has power to examine all member banks and the affiliates of member banks and to require condition reports from them. It has authority to require periodic and other public disclosure of information with respect to an equity security of a State member bank that is held by 500 or more persons. It establishes minimum standards with respect to installation, maintenance, and operation of security devices and procedures by State member banks. Also, it has authority to issue cease-and-desist orders in connection with violations of law or unsafe or unsound banking practices by State member banks and to remove directors or officers of such banks in certain circumstances, and it may suspend member banks from the use of the credit facilities of the Federal Reserve System for making undue use of bank credit for speculative purposes or for any other purpose inconsistent with the maintenance of sound credit conditions.

The Board may grant authority to member banks to establish branches in foreign countries or dependencies or insular possessions of the United States, to invest in the stocks of banks or corporations engaged in international or foreign banking, or to invest in foreign banks. It also charters, regulates, and supervises certain corporations that engage in foreign or international banking and financial activities.

The Board is authorized to issue general regulations permitting interlocking relationships in certain circumstances between member banks and organizations dealing in securities or between member banks and other banks.

Other Activities The Board reviewes other bank stock acquisitions, as listed below.

The Board prescribes regulations to ensure a meaningful disclosure by lenders of credit terms so that consumers will be able to compare more readily the various credit terms available and will be informed about rules governing credit cards, including their potential liability for unauthorized use.

The Board has authority to impose reserve requirements and interest rate ceilings on branches and agencies of foreign banks in the United States, to grant loans to them, to provide them access to Federal Reserve services, and to limit their interstate banking activities.

Federal Open Market Committee

The Federal Open Market Committee is comprised of the Board of Governors and five of the presidents of the Reserve Banks. The Chairman of the Board of Governors is traditionally the Chairman of the Committee. The president of the Federal Reserve Bank of New York serves as a permanent member of the Committee. Four of the twelve Reserve Bank presidents rotate annually as members of the Committee.

Open market operations of the Reserve Banks are conducted under regulations adopted by the Committee and pursuant to specific policy directives issued by the Committee, which meets in Washington at frequent intervals. Purchases and sales of securities in the open market are undertaken to supply bank reserves to support the credit and money needed for long-term economic growth, to offset cyclical economic swings, and to accommodate seasonal demands of businesses and consumers for money and credit. These operations are carried out principally in U.S. Government obligations, but they also include purchases and sales of Federal agency obligations. All operations are conducted in New York, where the primary markets for these securities are located; the Federal Reserve Bank of New York executes transactions for the Federal Reserve System Open Market Account in carrying out these operations.

Under the Committee's direction, the Federal Reserve Bank of New York also undertakes transactions in foreign currencies for the Federal Reserve System Open Market Account. The purposes of these operations include helping to safeguard the value of the dollar in international exchange markets and facilitating growth in international liquidity in accordance with the needs of an expanding world economy.

Federal Reserve Banks

The 12 Federal Reserve Banks are located in Atlanta, GA; Boston, MA; Chicago, IL; Cleveland, OH; Dallas, TX; Kansas City, MO; Minneapolis, MN; New York, NY; Philadelphia, PA; Richmond, VA; San Francisco, CA; and St. Louis, MO. Branch banks are located in Baltimore, MD; Birmingham, AL; Buffalo, NY; Charlotte, NC; Cincinnati, OH; Denver, CO; Detroit, MI; El Paso, TX; Helena, MT; Houston, TX; Jacksonville, FL; Little Rock, AR; Los Angeles, CA; Louisville, KY; Memphis, TN; Miami, FL; Nashville, TN; New Orleans, LA; Oklahoma City, OK; Omaha, NE; Pittsburgh, PA; Portland, OR; Salt Lake City, UT; San Antonio, TX; and Seattle, WA.

Reserves on Deposit The Reserve Banks receive and hold on deposit the reserve or clearing account deposits of depository institutions. These banks are permitted to count their vault cash as part of their required reserve.

Extensions of Credit The Federal Reserve is required to open its discount window to any depository institution that is subject to Federal Reserve reserve requirements on transaction accounts or nonpersonal time deposits. Discount window credit provides for Federal Reserve lending to eligible depository institutions under two basic programs. One is the adjustment credit program; the other supplies more extended credit for certain limited purposes.

Short-term adjustment credit is the primary type of Federal Reserve credit. It is available to help borrowers meet temporary requirements for funds. Borrowers are not permitted to use adjustment credit to take advantage of any spread between the discount rate and market rates.

Extended credit is provided through three programs designed to assist depository institutions in meeting longer term needs for funds. One provides seasonal credit—for periods running up to 9 months—to smaller depository institutions that lack access to market funds. A second program assists institutions that experience special difficulties arising from exceptional circumstances or practices involving only that institution. Finally, in cases where more general liquidity strains are affecting a broad range of depository institutions—such as those whose portfolios consist primarily of longer term assets—credit may be provided to address the problems of particular institutions being affected by the general situation.

Currency Issue The Reserve Banks issue Federal Reserve notes, which constitute the bulk of money in circulation. These notes are obligations of the United States and are a prior lien upon the assets of the issuing Federal Reserve Bank. They are issued against a pledge by the Reserve Bank with the Federal Reserve agent of collateral security including gold certificates, paper discounted or purchased by the Bank, and direct obligations of the United States.

Other Powers The Reserve Banks are empowered to act as clearinghouses and as collecting agents for depository institutions in the collection of checks and other instruments. They are also authorized to act as depositories and fiscal agents of the United States and to exercise other banking functions specified in the Federal Reserve Act. They perform a number of important functions in connection with the issue and redemption of United States Government securities.

Sources of Information

Employment Written inquiries regarding employment should be addressed to the Director, Division of Personnel, Board of Governors of the Federal Reserve System, Washington, DC 20551.

Procurement Firms seeking business with the Board should address their inquiries to the Director, Division of Support Services, Board of Governors of

the Federal Reserve System, Washington, DC 20551.
Publications Among the publications issued by the Board are *The Federal Reserve System—Purposes and Functions,* and a series of pamphlets including *Guide to Business Credit and the Equal Credit Opportunity Act; Consumer Handbook; Making Deposits: When Will Your Money Be Available;* and *When Your Home Is On the Line: What You Should Know About Home Equity Lines of Credit.* Copies of these pamphlets are available free of charge. Information regarding publications may be obtained in Room MP–510 (Martin Building) of the Board's headquarters. Phone, 202–452–3244.
Reading Room A reading room where persons may inspect records that are available to the public is located in Room B–1122 at the Board's headquarters, Twentieth Street and Constitution Avenue NW., Washington, DC. Information regarding the availability of records may be obtained by calling 202–452–3684.

For further information, contact the Office of Public Affairs, Board of Governors, Federal Reserve System, Washington, DC 20551. Phone, 202–452–3204 or 202–452–3215. Internet, www.federalreserve.gov.

FEDERAL RETIREMENT THRIFT INVESTMENT BOARD

1250 H Street NW., Washington, DC 20005
Phone, 202–942–1600. Fax, 202–942–1676. Internet, www.tsp.gov.

Chairman	JAMES H. ATKINS
Members	THOMAS A. FINK, SCOTT B. LUKINS, SHERYL R. MARSHALL, JEROME A. STRICKER
Officials:	
Executive Director	ROGER W. MEHLE
General Counsel	ELIZABETH S. WOODRUFF
Director of Accounting	DAVID L. BLACK
Director of Administration	STRAT D. VALAKIS
Director of Automated Systems	LAWRENCE E. STIFFLER
Director of Benefits and Investments	JAMES B. PETRICK
Director of Communications	VEDA R. CHARROW
Director of External Affairs	THOMAS J. TRABUCCO

The Federal Retirement Thrift Investment Board administers the Thrift Savings Plan, which provides Federal employees the opportunity to save for additional retirement security.

The Federal Retirement Thrift Investment Board was established as an independent agency by the Federal Employees' Retirement System Act of 1986 (5 U.S.C. 8472). The act vests responsibility for the agency in six named fiduciaries: the five Board members and the Executive Director. The five members of the Board, one of whom is designated as Chairman, are appointed by the President with the advice and consent of the Senate and serve on the Board on a part-time basis. The members appoint the Executive Director, who is responsible for the management of the agency and the Plan.

Activities

The Thrift Savings Plan is a tax-deferred, defined contribution plan that was established as one of the three parts of the Federal Employees' Retirement System. For employees covered under the System, savings accumulated through the Plan make an important addition to the retirement benefits provided by Social Security and the System's Basic Annuity. Civil Service Retirement System employees may also take advantage of the Plan to supplement their annuities.

The Board operates the Thrift Savings Plan and manages the investments of the Thrift Savings Fund solely for the benefit of participants and their beneficiaries. As part of these responsibilities, the Board maintains an account for each Plan participant, makes loans, purchases annuity contracts, and provides for the payment of benefits.

For further information, contact the Director of External Affairs, Federal Retirement Thrift Investment Board, 1250 H Street NW., Washington, DC 20005. Phone, 202-942-1640. Internet, www.tsp.gov.

FEDERAL TRADE COMMISSION

600 Pennsylvania Avenue NW., Washington, DC 20580
Phone, 202-326-2222. Internet, www.ftc.gov.

Chairman	ROBERT PITOFSKY
Executive Assistant	JAMES C. HAMILL
Commissioners	SHEILA F. ANTHONY, THOMAS B. LEARY, ORSON SWINDLE, MOZELLE W. THOMPSON
Executive Director	ROSEMARIE A. STRAIGHT
Deputy Executive Director	JUDITH BAILEY
Chief Information Officer	RICHARD G. TURNER
Chief Financial Officer	HENRY HOFFMAN
Director, Bureau of Competition	RICHARD G. PARKER
Senior Deputy Director	MOLLY S. BOAST
Deputy Director	WILLARD K. TOM
Director, Bureau of Consumer Protection	JODIE BERNSTEIN
Deputy Directors	LYDIA B. PARNES, TERESA MORAN SCHWARTZ
Director, Bureau of Economics	JEREMY I. BULOW
General Counsel	DEBRA A. VALENTINE
Deputy General Counsel	JOHN D. GRAUBERT
Director, Office of Congressional Relations	DAVID R. THOMAS
Director, Office of Public Affairs	(VACANCY)
Director, Office of Policy Planning	SUSAN S. DESANTI
Secretary of the Commission	DONALD S. CLARK
Chief Administrative Law Judge	JAMES P. TIMONY
Inspector General	FREDERICK J. ZIRKEL

[For the Federal Trade Commission statement of organization, see the *Code of Federal Regulations,* Title 16, Part 0]

The objective of the Federal Trade Commission is to maintain competitive enterprise as the keystone of the American economic system, and to prevent the free enterprise system from being fettered by monopoly or restraints on trade or corrupted by unfair or deceptive trade practices. The Commission is charged with keeping competition both free and fair.

The Federal Trade Commission was established in 1914 by the Federal Trade Commission Act (15 U.S.C. 41–58). The Commission is composed of five members appointed by the President, with the advice and consent of the Senate, for a term of 7 years. Not more than three of the Commissioners may be members of the same political party. One Commissioner is designated by the President as Chairman of the Commission and is responsible for its administrative management.

Activities

The Commission's principal functions are to:

—promote competition through the prevention of general trade restraints such as price-fixing agreements, boycotts, illegal combinations of competitors, and other unfair methods of competition;

—stop corporate mergers, acquisitions, or joint ventures that substantially lessen competition or tend to create a monopoly;

—prevent pricing discrimination, exclusive dealing, tying arrangements, and discrimination among competing customers by sellers;

—prevent interlocking directorates or officers' positions that may restrain competition;

—prevent the dissemination of false or deceptive advertisements of consumer products and services as well as other unfair or deceptive practices;

—promote electronic commerce by stopping fraud on the Internet and working with other domestic and foreign agencies to develop and promote policies to safeguard online privacy of personal information;

—stop various fraudulent telemarketing schemes and protect consumers from abusive and deceptive telephone tactics;

—ensure truthful labeling of textile, wool, and fur products;

—require creditors to disclose in writing certain cost information, such as the annual percentage rate, before consumers enter into credit transactions, as required by the Truth in Lending Act;

—protect consumers against circulation of inaccurate or obsolete credit reports and ensure that credit bureaus, consumer reporting agencies, credit grantors, and bill collectors exercise their responsibilities in a manner that is fair and equitable;

—educate consumers and businesses about their rights and responsibilities under FTC rules and regulations; and

—gather factual data concerning economic and business conditions and make it available to the Congress, the President, and the public.

Antitrust One of the two major missions of the Commission is to encourage competitive forces in the American economy. The Commission seeks to prevent unfair practices that undermine competition and attempts to prevent mergers of companies if the result may be to lessen competition. Under some circumstances, companies planning to merge must first give notice to the Commission and the Department of Justice's Antitrust Division and provide certain information concerning the operations of the companies involved.

The Commission also enforces the provisions of the Robinson-Patman Act, a part of the Clayton Act prohibiting companies from discriminating among other companies that are its customers in terms of price or other services provided.

Consumer Protection Consumer protection is the second of the two main missions of the Commission. The Commission works to:

—increase the usefulness of advertising by ensuring that it is truthful and not misleading;

—reduce instances of fraudulent, deceptive, or unfair marketing practices;

—prevent creditors from using unlawful practices when granting credit, maintaining credit information, collecting debts, and operating credit systems; and

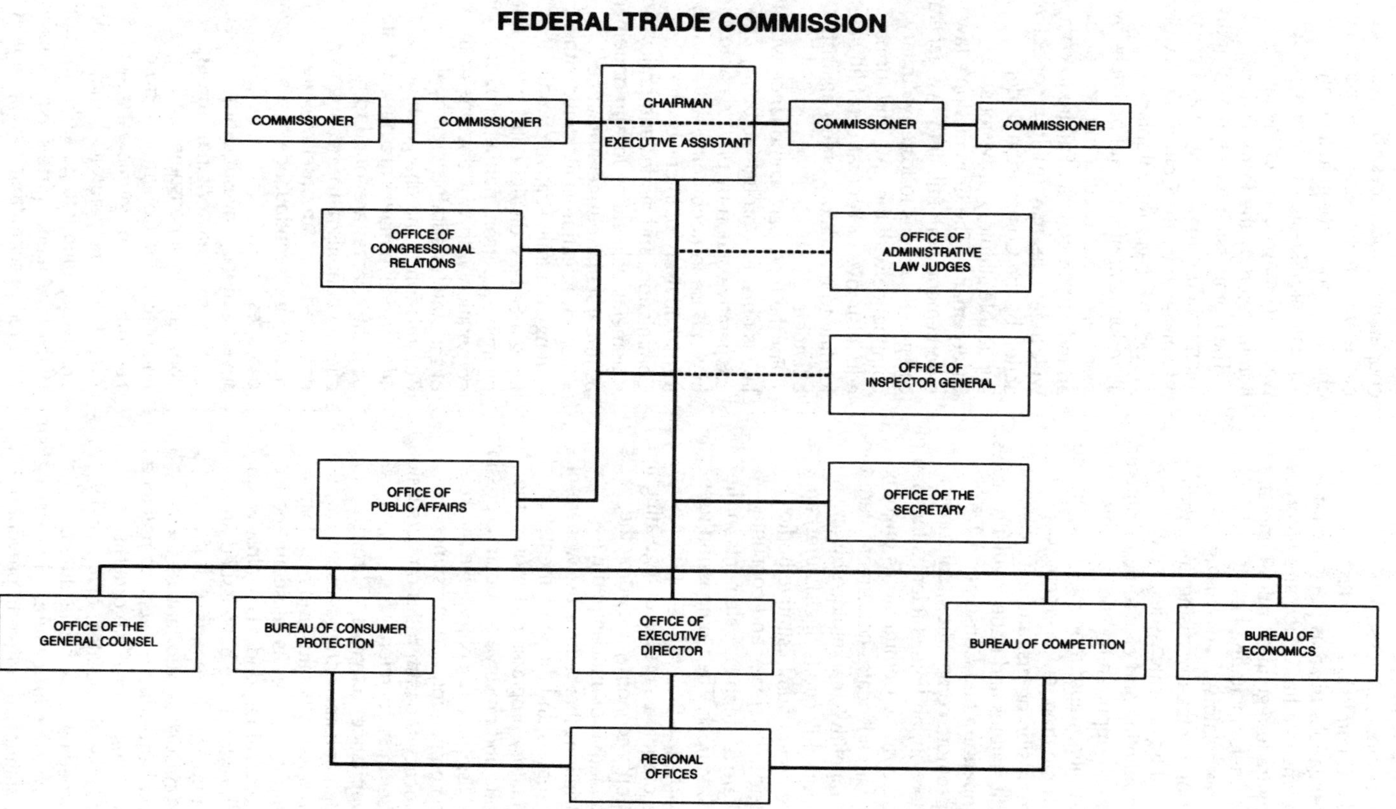
FEDERAL TRADE COMMISSION
COMMISSIONER
COMMISSIONER
CHAIRMAN
EXECUTIVE ASSISTANT
COMMISSIONER
COMMISSIONER
OFFICE OF CONGRESSIONAL RELATIONS
OFFICE OF ADMINISTRATIVE LAW JUDGES
OFFICE OF INSPECTOR GENERAL
OFFICE OF PUBLIC AFFAIRS
OFFICE OF THE SECRETARY
OFFICE OF THE GENERAL COUNSEL
BUREAU OF CONSUMER PROTECTION
OFFICE OF EXECUTIVE DIRECTOR
BUREAU OF COMPETITION
BUREAU OF ECONOMICS
REGIONAL OFFICES

—educate the public about Commission activities.

The Commission initiates investigations in areas of concern to consumers. It has issued and enforces many trade regulation rules important to consumers, including health and nutrition claims in advertising; environmental advertising and labeling; general advertising issues; health care, telemarketing and electronic commerce, business opportunity, and franchise and investment fraud; mortgage lending and discrimination; enforcement of Commission orders; and enforcement of credit statutes and trade regulation rules.

Competition and Consumer Advocacy To promote competition, consumer protection, and the efficient allocation of resources, the Commission's ongoing program advocates consumer interest in a competitive marketplace by encouraging courts, legislatures, and government administrative bodies to consider efficiency and consumer welfare as important elements in their deliberations. The Commission uses these opportunities to support procompetitive means of regulating the Nation's economy, including the elimination of anticompetitive restrictions that reduce the welfare of consumers and the implementation of regulatory programs that protect the public and preserve as much as possible the discipline of competitive markets. The competition and consumer advocacy program relies on persuasion rather than coercion.

Compliance Activities Through systematic and continuous review, the Commission obtains and maintains compliance with its cease-and-desist orders. All respondents against whom such orders have been issued are required to file reports with the Commission to substantiate their compliance. In the event compliance is not obtained, or if the order is subsequently violated, civil penalty proceedings may be instituted.

Cooperative Procedures In carrying out the statutory directive to prevent unfair methods of competition or unfair or deceptive practices, the Commission makes extensive use of voluntary and cooperative procedures. Through these procedures, business and industry may obtain authoritative guidance and a substantial measure of certainty as to what they may do under the laws administered by the Commission.

The Commission issues administrative interpretations in plain language of laws administered by the Commission. Guides provide the basis for voluntary abandonment of unlawful practices by members of a particular industry or by an industry in general. Failure to comply with the guides may result in corrective action by the Commission under applicable statutory provisions.

Enforcement The Commission's law enforcement work falls into two general categories: actions to foster voluntary compliance with the law, and formal administrative or Federal court litigation leading to mandatory orders against offenders.

For the most part, compliance with the law is obtained through voluntary and cooperative action by private companies in response to nonbinding staff advice, formal advisory opinions by the Commission, and guides and policy statements delineating legal requirements as to particular business practices.

Formal litigation is instituted either by issuing an administrative complaint or by filing a Federal district court complaint charging a person, partnership, or corporation with violating one or more of the statutes administered by the Commission. If the charges in an administrative matter are not contested or if the charges are found to be true after an administrative hearing in a contested case, an order may be issued requiring discontinuance of the unlawful practices.

Investigations Investigations by the Commission may originate through complaint by a consumer or a competitor, the Congress, or from Federal, State, or municipal agencies. Also, the Commission itself may initiate an investigation into possible violations of the laws it administers. No formality is required in submitting a complaint. A letter giving the facts in detail, accompanied by all supporting evidence in possession of the complaining party, is sufficient. It is the general policy of the Commission not to disclose the identity of any complainant, except as required by law or Commission rules.

Upon receipt of a complaint, various criteria are applied in determining whether the particular matter should be investigated.

An order issued after an administrative proceeding that requires the respondent to cease and desist or take other corrective action may be appealed. Appeals processes may go as far as the Supreme Court.

In addition to or in lieu of the administrative proceeding initiated by a formal complaint, the Commission may request that a U.S. district court issue a preliminary or permanent injunction to halt the use of allegedly unfair or deceptive practices, to prevent an anticompetitive merger or unfair methods of competition from taking place, or to prevent violations of any statute enforced by the Commission.

Reports The Commission prepares studies of conditions and problems affecting the marketplace. Such reports may be used to inform legislative proposals in response to requests of the Congress and statutory directions, or for the information and guidance of the Commission, the executive branch of the Government, and the public. Such reports have provided the basis for significant legislation and have also led to voluntary changes in the conduct of business, with resulting benefits to the public.

Regional Offices—Federal Trade Commission

Region	Address	Director
East Central (DC, DE, MD, MI, OH, PA, VA, WV)	Suite 200, 111 Superior Ave., Cleveland, OH 44114	John Mendenhall
Midwest (IA, IL, IN, KS, KY, MN, MO, ND, NE, SD, WI)	Suite 1860, 55 Monroe St., Chicago, IL 60603–5701	C. Steven Baker
Northeast (CT, MA, ME, NH, NJ, NY, RI, VT)	Suite 1300, 150 William St., New York, NY 10038	Barbara Anthony
Northwest (AK, ID, MT, OR, WA, WY)	Suite 2896, 915 2d Ave., Seattle, WA 98174	Charles A. Harwood
Southeast (AL, FL, GA, MS, NC, SC, TN)	Suite 5M35, 60 Forsyth St., SW., Atlanta, GA 30303	Andrea Foster
Southwest (AR, LA, NM, OK, TX)	Suite 2150, 1999 Bryan St., Dallas, TX 75201–0101	Thomas B. Carter
Western (AZ, CA, CO, HI, NV, UT)	Suite 700, 10877 Wilshire Blvd., Los Angeles, CA 90024	Jeffrey A. Klurfeld
	Suite 570, 901 Market St., San Francisco, CA 94103	

Sources of Information

Contracts and Procurement Persons seeking to do business with the Federal Trade Commission should contact the Assistant CFO for Acquisitions, Federal Trade Commission, Washington, DC 20580. Phone, 202–326–2258. Fax, 202–326–3529. Internet, www.ftc.gov/ftc/procurement/procure.htm.

Employment Civil service registers are used in filling positions for economists, accountants, investigators, and other professional, administrative, and clerical personnel. The Federal Trade Commission employs a sizable number of attorneys under the excepted appointment procedure. All employment inquiries should be directed to the Director of Human Resources Management, Federal Trade Commission, Washington, DC 20580. Phone, 202–326–2021. Fax, 202–326–2328.

General Inquiries Persons desiring information on consumer protection or restraint of trade questions, or to register a complaint, should contact the Federal Trade Commission (phone, 202–326–2222 or 877–382–4357 (toll free)) or the nearest regional office.

Publications Consumer and business education publications of the Commission are available through the Consumer Response Center, Federal Trade Commission, Washington, DC 20580. Phone, 202–382–4357 (FTC–HELP) or 877–382–4357 (toll free). TTY, 202–326–2502. Internet, www.ftc.gov.

For further information, contact the Office of Public Affairs, Federal Trade Commission, 600 Pennsylvania Avenue NW., Washington, DC 20580. Phone, 202–326–2180. Fax, 202–326–3676. Internet, www.ftc.gov.

GENERAL SERVICES ADMINISTRATION

Eighteenth and F Streets NW., Washington, DC 20405
Phone, 202–708–5082. Internet, www.gsa.gov.

Administrator of General Services	David J. Barram
Chairman, GSA Board of Contract Appeals	Stephen M. Daniels
Chief Knowledge Officer	Shereen Remez
Chief Operations Officer, Office Anywhere	Wanda Smith
Chief of Staff	Martha N. Johnson
Inspector General	William R. Barton
Deputy Administrator	Thurman M. Davis, Sr.
Associate Administrator for Child Care	Susan Clampitt
Associate Administrator for Civil Rights	(vacancy)
Associate Administrator for Communications	Beth Newburger
Associate Administrator for Congressional and Intergovernmental Affairs	William R. Ratchford
Associate Administrator for Enterprise Development	Jackie A. Robinson
Chief Information Officer	William Piatt
Chief Financial Officer	William B. Early, Jr.
Chief People Officer	Gail T. Lovelace
General Counsel	Stephenie Foster

FEDERAL SUPPLY SERVICE

Washington, DC 20406
Phone, 703–305–6667. Fax, 703–305–6577.

Commissioner	Frank P. Pugliese, Jr.
Deputy Commissioner	Donna D. Bennett
Chief of Staff	Barney Brasseux
Assistant Commissioner for Acquisition	William N. Gormley
Assistant Commissioner for Business Management and Marketing	Gary Feit
Assistant Commissioner for Contract Management	Patricia Mead
Assistant Commissioner for Distribution Management	John Roehmer
Assistant Commissioner for Transportation and Property Management	Allan Zaic
Assistant Commissioner for Vehicle Acquisition and Leasing Services	Lester Gray Jr.
Chief Information Officer	Edward O'Hare
Comptroller	Jon Jordan
Director of Transportation Audits	James F. Fitzgerald

FEDERAL TECHNOLOGY SERVICE

10304 Eaton Place, Fairfax, VA 22030
Phone, 703–306–6020

Commissioner	Sandra N. Bates
Deputy Commissioner	(vacancy)
Assistant Commissioner for Acquisition	C. Allen Olson
Assistant Commissioner for Information Security	Thomas R. Burke
Assistant Commissioner for Information Technology Integration	Charles Self
Assistant Commissioner for Regional Services	Margaret Binns
Assistant Commissioner for Service Delivery	Frank E. Lalley
Assistant Commissioner for Service Development	Bruce Brignull
Assistant Commissioner for Strategic Planning and Business Development	Abby Pirnie
Chief Financial Officer	Robert E. Suda

PUBLIC BUILDINGS SERVICE

Eighteenth and F Streets NW., Washington, DC 20405
Phone, 202–501–1100

Commissioner	Robert A. Peck
Chief of Staff	Kay McNew
Deputy Commissioner	Paul E. Chistolini
Assistant Commissioner for Business Performance	Paul Lynch
Assistant Commissioner for the Federal Protective Service	Clarence Edwards
Assistant Commissioner for Portfolio Management	Pamela Wessling
Assistant Commissioner for Property Disposal	Brian K. Polly
Chief Architect	Edward Feiner
Chief Financial Officer	Frederick T. Alt
Chief Information Officer	Albert Curley II

OFFICE OF GOVERNMENTWIDE POLICY

Eighteenth and F Streets NW., Washington, DC 20405
Phone, 202–501–8880

Associate Administrator for Governmentwide Policy	G. Martin Wagner
Chief of Staff	John G. Sindelar
Deputy Associate Administrator for Acquisition Policy	(vacancy)
Deputy Associate Administrator for Electronic Commerce	Mary J. Mitchell
Deputy Associate Administrator for Information Technology	Joan C. Steyaert

186-873 D-00--15

Deputy Associate Administrator for Intergovernmental Solutions	FRANCIS A. MCDONOUGH
Deputy Associate Administrator for Real Property	DAVID L. BIBB
Deputy Associate Administrator for Transportation and Personal Property	REBECCA R. RHODES

[For the General Services Administration statement of organization, see the *Code of Federal Regulations,* Title 41, Part 105–53]

The General Services Administration establishes policy for and provides economical and efficient management of Government property and records, including construction and operation of buildings; procurement and distribution of supplies; utilization and disposal of real and personal property; transportation, traffic, and communications management; and management of the governmentwide automatic data processing resources program.

The General Services Administration (GSA) was established by section 101 of the Federal Property and Administrative Services Act of 1949 (40 U.S.C. 751).

Contract Appeals The General Services Administration Board of Contract Appeals is responsible for resolving disputes arising out of contracts with the General Services Administration and other Government agencies. The Board is also empowered to hear and decide requests for review of transportation audit rate determinations; claims by Federal civilian employees regarding travel and relocation expenses; and claims for the proceeds of the sale of property of certain Federal civilian employees. In addition, the Board provides alternative dispute resolution services to executive agencies in both contract disputes which are the subject of a contracting officer's decision and other contract-related disputes. Although the Board is located within the agency, it functions as an independent tribunal.

For further information, contact the Board of Contract Appeals, General Services Administration, Washington, DC 20405. Phone, 202–501–0585.

Domestic Assistance Catalog The Federal Domestic Assistance Catalog Program collects and disseminates information on all federally operated domestic assistance programs such as grants, loans, and insurance. This information is published annually in the *Catalog of Federal Domestic Assistance.*

For further information, contact the Federal Domestic Assistance Catalog staff. Phone, 202–708–5126.

Governmentwide Policy The Office of Governmentwide Policy (OGP) collaborates with the Federal community to develop policies and guidelines, provide education and training, and identify best practices in the areas served by GSA's business lines: real property and personal property; travel and transportation; acquisition; information technology (IT) and electronic commerce; regulatory information; and use of Federal advisory committees.

The Office of Acquisition Policy provides resources to support the Federal acquisition system. The Office researches, develops, and publishes policy guidance, provides career development services for the Federal acquisition work force, and reports on more than 20 million contract actions annually. For further information, call 202–501–1043. For electronic access, contact www.arnet.gov.

The Office of Electronic Commerce develops electronic commerce policies for the Federal Government, including managing with the Department of Defense an electronic commerce program office which monitors and provides support for interagency efforts for electronic commerce across the

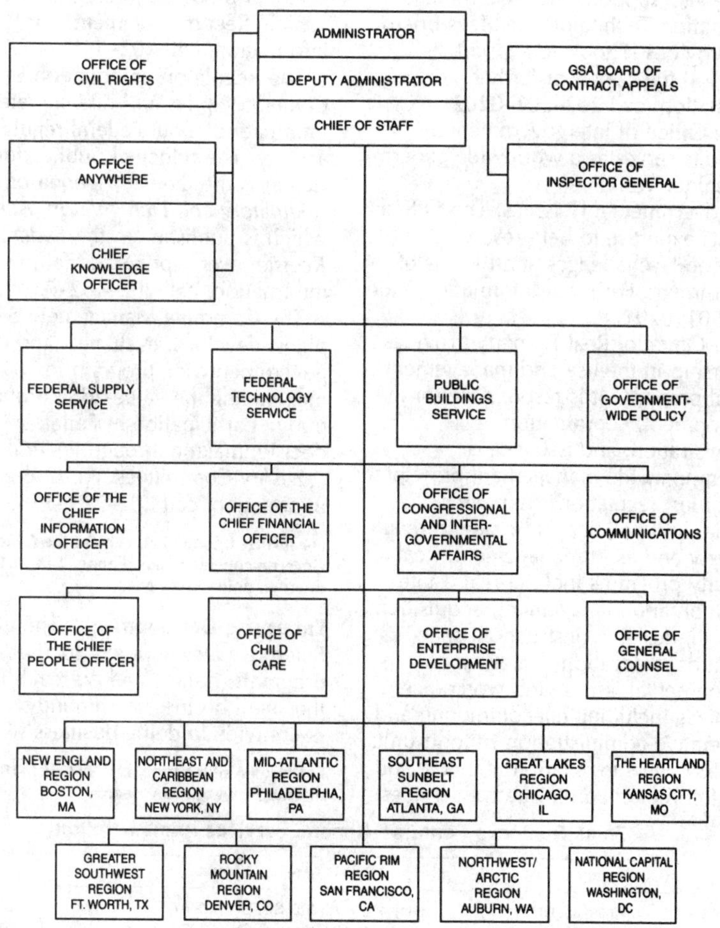
GENERAL SERVICES ADMINISTRATION
ADMINISTRATOR
DEPUTY ADMINISTRATOR
CHIEF OF STAFF
OFFICE OF CIVIL RIGHTS
OFFICE ANYWHERE
CHIEF KNOWLEDGE OFFICER
GSA BOARD OF CONTRACT APPEALS
OFFICE OF INSPECTOR GENERAL
FEDERAL SUPPLY SERVICE
FEDERAL TECHNOLOGY SERVICE
PUBLIC BUILDINGS SERVICE
OFFICE OF GOVERNMENT-WIDE POLICY
OFFICE OF THE CHIEF INFORMATION OFFICER
OFFICE OF THE CHIEF FINANCIAL OFFICER
OFFICE OF CONGRESSIONAL AND INTER-GOVERNMENTAL AFFAIRS
OFFICE OF COMMUNICATIONS
OFFICE OF THE CHIEF PEOPLE OFFICER
OFFICE OF CHILD CARE
OFFICE OF ENTERPRISE DEVELOPMENT
OFFICE OF GENERAL COUNSEL
NEW ENGLAND REGION BOSTON, MA
NORTHEAST AND CARIBBEAN REGION NEW YORK, NY
MID-ATLANTIC REGION PHILADELPHIA, PA
SOUTHEAST SUNBELT REGION ATLANTA, GA
GREAT LAKES REGION CHICAGO, IL
THE HEARTLAND REGION KANSAS CITY, MO
GREATER SOUTHWEST REGION FT. WORTH, TX
ROCKY MOUNTAIN REGION DENVER, CO
PACIFIC RIM REGION SAN FRANCISCO, CA
NORTHWEST/ ARCTIC REGION AUBURN, WA
NATIONAL CAPITAL REGION WASHINGTON, DC

Government and working with other agencies and with the private sector to develop and promote the use of standardized card technologies in order to advance a more streamlined electronic Government. For further information, call 202–501–1667.

The Office of Information Technology provides executive and interagency information technology (IT) support. The Office also supports the Government Information Technology Services Board and provides IT tools to support agencies' missions. For further information, call 202–501–0202.

The Office of Intergovernmental Solutions serves as a worldwide expert and unique resource on intergovernmental IT issues. The Office uses its expertise to help resolve common IT challenges at all levels of Government. For more information, call 202–501–0291.

The Office of Real Property provides leadership in the use and management of real property. It is responsible for the development, coordination, administration, and issuance of governmentwide management principles, guidelines, regulations, standards, criteria, and policies that relate to real property and asset management. Real property programs include real estate operation and management, acquisition, disposal, design, construction, space standards, delegations, safety and environmental issues, and workplace initiatives including telecommuting and cooperative administration support units, whereby agencies share in the cost and use of common administrative services. For further information, call 202–510–0856.

The Office of Transportation and Personal Property develops governmentwide policies for personal property utilization, donation, and sales, and participates in the development and evaluation of governmentwide issues, legislation, policies, and objectives related to travel, transportation, mail, personal property, aircraft, and the motor vehicle fleet management. For further information, call 202–501–1777.

The Regulatory Information Service Center compiles and disseminates information about Federal regulatory activity. The principal publication of the Center is the *Unified Agenda of Federal Regulatory and Deregulatory Actions,* which is published in the *Federal Register* every spring and fall. For further information, call 202–482–7345.

The Committe Management Secretariat plans, develops, evaluates, and directs a governmentwide program for maximizing the value-added role of public participation in Federal decisionmaking through Federal Advisory Committees. For further information, call 202–273–3565.

For further information, contact the Office of Governmentwide Policy. Phone, 202–501–8880. Internet, policyworks.gov.

Enterprise Development The Office of Enterprise Development focuses on programs, policy, and outreach to assist the small business community nationwide in doing business with GSA.

For further information, call 202–501–1021. Internet, www.gsa.gov/oed.

Small Business Centers—General Services Administration

Region	Address	Telephone
National Capital—Washington, DC	Rm. 1050, 7th & D Sts. SW., 20407	202–708–5804
New England—Boston, MA	Rm. 290, 10 Causeway St., 02222	617–565–8100
Northeast and Caribbean—New York, NY	Rm. 18–130, 26 Federal Plz., 10278	212–264–1234
Mid-Atlantic—Philadelphia, PA	Rm. 808, 100 Penn Sq. E., 19107–3396	215–656–5525
Southeast Sunbelt—Atlanta, GA	Rm. 2832, 401 W. Peachtree St. NW., 30303	404–331–5103
Great Lakes—Chicago, IL	Rm. 3714, 230 S. Dearborn St., 60604	312–353–5383
Heartland—Kansas City, MO	Rm. 1160, 1500 E. Bannister Rd., 64131	816–926–7203
Southwest—Fort Worth, TX	Rm. 11A09, 819 Taylor St., 76102	817–978–3284
Rocky Mountain—Denver, CO	Rm. 145, Denver Federal Ctr., 80225–0006	303–236–7408
Pacific Rim—San Francisco, CA	Rm. 405, 450 Golden Gate Ave., 94102	415–522–2700
Satellite office—Los Angeles, CA	Rm. 3259, 300 N. Los Angeles St., 90012	213–894–3210
Northwest/Arctic—Auburn, WA	400 15th St. SW., 98001	253–931–7956

Mobile Services Office Anywhere is responsible for developing a new product line for GSA offering mobile Federal workers cutting-edge products and services that cross GSA's Federal Supply Service, Federal Technology Service, and Public Buildings Service boundaries. It provides technical and procurement expertise and assistance to other Federal agencies in acquiring integrated service delivery, including portable computing devices, software, telecommunications, and other services to meet the critical needs of the mobile Federal worker. The Office develops and executes a marketing communications strategy to educate the Federal consumer about the use of mobile technology and its availability through GSA.

For further information, contact the Office Anywhere, General Services Administration, Eighteenth and F Streets NW., Washington, DC 20405. Phone, 202–208–7761.

Federal Technology Service

The Federal Technology Service (FTS) delivers reimbursable local and long-distance telecommunications, information technology (IT), and information security services to Federal agencies. Its mission is to provide IT solutions and network services to support its customers' missions worldwide through its business lines.

The network services business line enables FTS to provide its customers end-to-end telecommunications services. Included in this business line are the the FTS2001 contracts that provide world-class, worldwide long-distance telecommunications services including low-cost, state-of-the-art voice, data, and video telecommunications and the local telecommunications service that provides local voice and data telecommunications to Federal agencies nationwide

The IT solutions business line helps agencies acquire, manage, integrate, and use IT resources and protect the security of Federal information.

The smart card business line offers services to other Federal agencies including standardization of smart cards and building an open smart card system configuration consistent with industry standards.

The Federal Relay Service (TTY, 800–877–8339) ensures that all citizens—hearing individuals and individuals who are deaf, hard of hearing, or speech-disabled—have equal access to the Federal telecommunications system and enables Federal employees to conduct official duties and the general public to conduct business with the Federal Government and its agencies.

For further information, contact the Federal Technology Service. Phone, 703–306–6000.

Federal Supply Service

The Federal Supply Service (FSS) supports Federal agencies worldwide by providing them with supplies and services each year. By taking advantage of the Government's aggregate buying power, FSS achieves significant savings for both the customer and the taxpayer. Its programs are an important link in the Government's efforts to protect the environment and to give back to the community for the public benefit. FSS carries out its mission through the following four business lines:

—the supply and procurement business line operates a worldwide supply system to contract for and distribute personal property and services to Federal agencies. It offers convenience, quality, best value, and choice by making available a wide array of commercial products and services, from office equipment and supplies, paint, tools, IT equipment and software, and furniture, to contracts for services such as purchase cards, auditing and financial management, and airline travel.

—the vehicle acquisition and leasing services business line buys and leases new vehicles to provide Federal agencies with a modern fleet and timely replacement of vehicles, lower lease costs, professional maintenance management, and a selection of alternative-fuel vehicles. The GSA fleet is the largest alternative-fuel vehicle fleet in the Federal Government.

—the personal property business line helps to maximize the Government's investment in personal property as well as to serve the public benefit.

—the travel and transportation business line provides Federal agencies with easy access to commercial sources that can arrange employee travel or ship parcels, freight, and household goods.

For more information, contact the Federal Supply Service, Washington, DC 20406. Phone, 703–305–5600. Internet, www.fss.gsa.gov.

Public Buildings Service

The Public Buildings Service (PBS) provides work environments for over a million Federal employees nationwide. Since 1949, PBS has served as a builder, developer, lessor, and manager of federally owned and leased properties. It provides a full range of real estate services, property management, construction and repairs, security services, property disposal, and overall portfolio management.

For further information, contact the Office of the Commissioner, Public Buildings Service. Phone, 202–501–1100. Internet, www.pbs.gov/pbs.

Regional Offices—General Services Administration

Region	Address	Administrator
New England	Boston, MA (10 Causeway St., 02222)	Robert J. Dunfey, Jr.
Northeast and Caribbean	New York, NY (26 Federal Plz., 10278)	Thomas J. Ryan
Mid-Atlantic	Philadelphia, PA (100 Penn Sq. E., 19107–3396)	James A. Williams, *Acting*
Southeast Sunbelt	Atlanta, GA (Suite 2800, 401 W. Peachtree St. NW., 30365)	Carol A. Dortch
Great Lakes	Chicago, IL (230 S. Dearborn St., 60604)	William C. Burke
The Heartland	Kansas City, MO (1500 E. Bannister Rd., 64131)	Glen W. Overton
Greater Southwest	Fort Worth, TX (819 Taylor St., 76102)	John Pouland
Rocky Mountain	Denver, CO (Bldg. 41, Denver Federal Ctr., 80225–0006)	Susan B. Damour
Pacific Rim	San Francisco, CA (5th Fl., 450 Golden Gate Ave., 94102)	Kenn N. Kojima
Northwest/Arctic	Auburn, WA (GSA Ctr., 400 15th St. SW., 98002)	L. Jay Pearson
National Capital	Washington, DC (7th & D Sts. SW., 20407)	Nelson B. Alcalde

Sources of Information

Contracts Individuals seeking to do business with the General Services Administration may obtain detailed information from the Business Service Centers listed in the preceding text. Inquiries concerning programs to assist small business should be directed to one of the Business Service Centers.

Electronic Access Information about GSA is available electronically through the Internet, at www.gsa.gov.

Employment Inquiries and applications should be directed to the Human Resources Division (CPS), Office of Human Resources, General Services Administration, Washington, DC 20405. Phone, 202–501–0370.

Fraud and Waste Contact the Inspector General's Office. Phone, 202–501–1780, or 800–424–5210 (toll-free).

Freedom of Information and Privacy Act Requests Inquiries concerning policies pertaining to Freedom of Information Act and Privacy Act matters should be addressed to the GSA FOIA or Privacy Act Officer, General Services Administration, Room 7136, Washington, DC 20405. Phone, 202–501–2262 or 202–501–3415. Fax, 202–501–2727.

Property Disposal Inquiries about the redistribution or competitive sale of surplus real property should be directed to the Office of Property Disposal, Public Buildings Service, Eighteenth and F Streets NW., Washington, DC 20405. Phone, 202–501–0210.

Public and News Media Inquiries Inquiries from both the general public and news media should be directed to the Office of Communications, General Services Administration, Eighteenth and F Streets NW., Washington, DC 20405. Phone, 202–501–1231.

Publications Many publications are available at moderate prices through the bookstores of the Government Printing Office. Others may be obtained free or at production cost from a Small Business Center or the Federal Consumer Information Center (phone, 800–688–9889). The telephone numbers and addresses of the Government Printing Office bookstores are listed in local telephone directories. If a publication is not distributed by any of the stores, inquiries should be directed to the originating agency's service or office. The addresses for inquiries are:

Public Buildings Service (P), General Services Administration, Washington, DC 20405

Federal Supply Service (F), General Services Administration, Washington, DC 20406

Office of Finance (BC), General Services Administration, Washington, DC 20405

Federal Technology Service (T), General Services Administration, 10304 Eaton Place, Fairfax, VA 22030

For a free copy of the *U.S. Government TTY Directory*, contact the Federal Consumer Information Center, Department TTY, Pueblo, CO 81009. Phone, 888–878–3256. Internet, www.gsa.gov/frs. For a free copy of the quarterly *Consumer Information Catalog*, including information on food, nutrition, employment, Federal benefits, the environment, fraud, privacy and Internet issues, investing and credit, and education, write to the Federal Consumer Information Center, Pueblo, CO 81009. Phone, 800–688–9889. Internet, www.pueblo.gsa.gov.

For a free copy of the *Federal Relay Service Brochure*, contact the GSA Federal Telecommunications Service. Phone, 703–904–2848. TTY, 703–904–2440.

Small Business Activities Inquiries concerning programs to assist small businesses should be directed to one of the Small Business Centers listed in the preceding text.

Speakers Inquiries and requests for speakers should be directed to the Office of Communications (X), General Services Administration, Washington, DC 20405 (phone, 202–501–0705); or contact the nearest regional office.

For further information concerning the General Services Administration, contact the Office of Communications (X), General Services Administration, Washington, DC 20405. Phone, 202–501–0705. Internet, www.gsa.gov.

INTER–AMERICAN FOUNDATION

901 North Stuart Street, Arlington, VA 22203
Phone, 703–306–4301. Internet, www.iaf.gov.

Board of Directors:

Chair	KAY KELLEY ARNOLD, *Acting*
Vice Chair	(VACANCY)
Directors	NANCY P. DORN, PATRICIA HILL WILLIAMS, FRANK D. YTURRIA, (4 VACANCIES)

Staff:

President	ADOLFO A. FRANCO, *Acting*
Senior Vice President and General Counsel	(VACANCY)
Vice President for External Affairs	LINDA P. BORST
Vice President for Learning and Dissemination	ANNE B. TERNES
Vice President for Programs	DAVID VALENZUELA
Director for Financial Management and Systems	WINSOME WELLS

The Inter-American Foundation is an independent Federal agency that supports social and economic development in Latin America and the Caribbean. It makes grants primarily to private, indigenous organizations that carry out self-help projects benefiting poor people.

The Inter-American Foundation (IAF) was created in 1969 (22 U.S.C. 290f) as an experimental U.S. foreign assistance program. IAF works in Latin America and the Caribbean to promote equitable, participatory, and sustainable self-help development by awarding grants directly to local organizations throughout the region. It also enters into partnerships with public and private sector entities to scale up support and mobilize local, national, and international resources for grassroots development. From all of its innovative funding experiences, the Foundation extracts lessons learned and best practices to share with other donors and development practitioners throughout the hemisphere.

IAF is governed by a nine-person Board of Directors appointed by the President with the advice and consent of the Senate. Six members are drawn from the private sector and three from the Federal Government. The Board of Directors appoints the President of IAF.

For further information, contact the Office of the President, Inter-American Foundation, 901 North Stuart Street, Arlington, VA 22203. Phone, 703–306–4301. Internet, www.iaf.gov.

MERIT SYSTEMS PROTECTION BOARD

Fifth Floor, 1615 M Street NW., Washington, DC 20419
Phone, 202–653–7124. Internet, www.mspb.gov.

Chair	BETH S. SLAVET, *Acting*
Chief of Staff	TERRY VANN
Vice Chair	(VACANCY)
Member	SUSANNE T. MARSHALL
Office of the Chairman:	
Chief Administrative Law Judge	PAUL G. STREB
Director, Financial and Administrative Management	ROBERT W. LAWSHE
Director, Information Resources Management	BARBARA B. WADE
Director, Office of Appeals Counsel	STEPHEN E. ALPERN
Director, Office of Equal Employment Opportunity	JANICE E. PIRKLE
Director, Office of Policy and Evaluation	JOHN PALGUTA
Director, Office of Regional Operations	DARRELL L. NETHERTON
General Counsel	MARY L. JENNINGS

[For the Merit Systems Protection Board statement of organization, see the *Code of Federal Regulations,* Title 5, Part 1200]

The Merit Systems Protection Board protects the integrity of Federal merit systems and the rights of Federal employees working in the systems. In overseeing the personnel practices of the Federal Government, the Board conducts special studies of the merit systems, hears and decides charges of wrongdoing and employee appeals of adverse agency actions, and orders corrective and disciplinary actions when appropriate.

The Merit Systems Protection Board is a successor agency to the United States Civil Service Commission, established by act of January 16, 1883 (22 Stat. 403). Reorganization Plan No. 2 of 1978 (5 U.S.C. app.) redesignated part of the

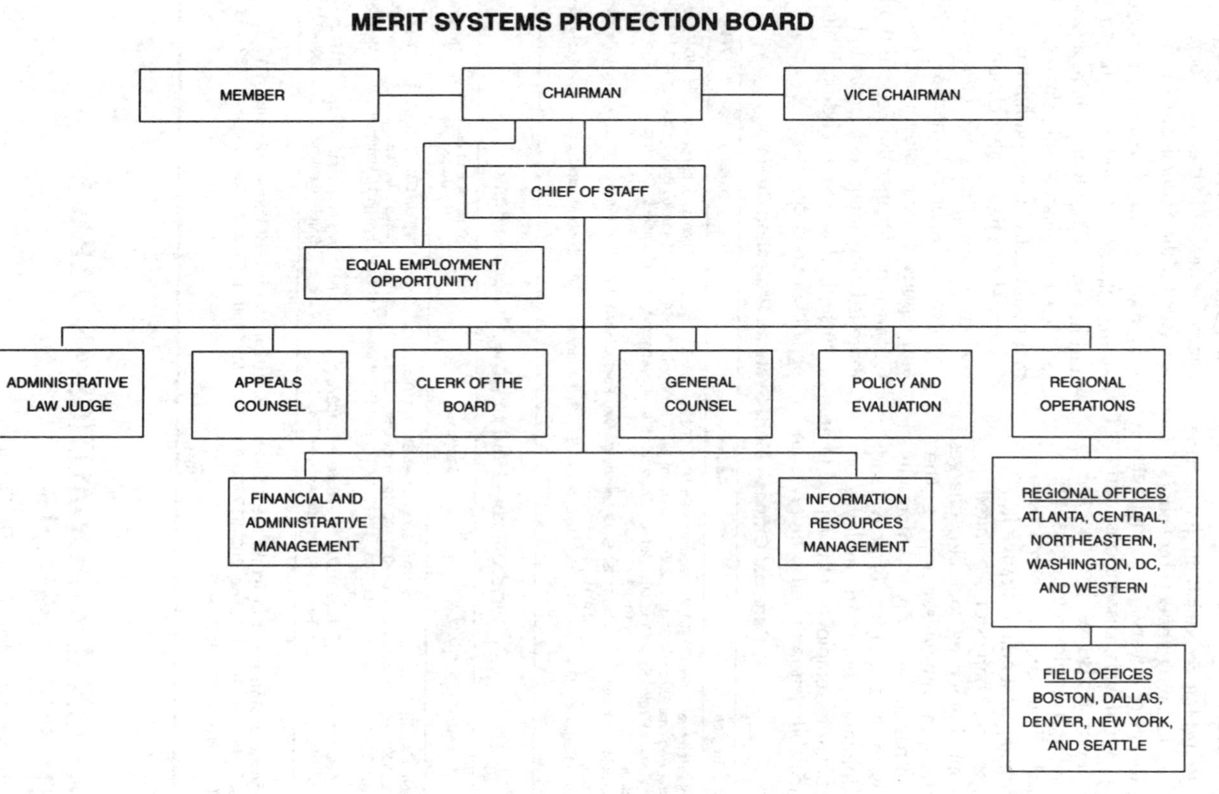
MERIT SYSTEMS PROTECTION BOARD
MEMBER
CHAIRMAN
VICE CHAIRMAN
CHIEF OF STAFF
EQUAL EMPLOYMENT OPPORTUNITY
ADMINISTRATIVE LAW JUDGE
APPEALS COUNSEL
CLERK OF THE BOARD
GENERAL COUNSEL
POLICY AND EVALUATION
REGIONAL OPERATIONS
FINANCIAL AND ADMINISTRATIVE MANAGEMENT
INFORMATION RESOURCES MANAGEMENT
REGIONAL OFFICES
ATLANTA, CENTRAL, NORTHEASTERN, WASHINGTON, DC, AND WESTERN
FIELD OFFICES
BOSTON, DALLAS, DENVER, NEW YORK, AND SEATTLE

Commission as the Merit Systems Protection Board.

Activities

The Board has responsibility for hearing and adjudicating appeals by Federal employees of adverse personnel actions, such as removals, suspensions, and demotions. It also resolves cases involving reemployment rights, the denial of periodic step increases in pay, actions against administrative law judges, and charges of prohibited personnel practices, including charges in connection with whistleblowing. The Board has the authority to enforce its decisions and to order corrective and disciplinary actions. An employee or applicant for employment involved in an appealable action that also involves an allegation of discrimination may ask the Equal Employment Opportunity Commission to review a Board decision. Final decisions and orders of the Board can be appealed to the U.S. Court of Appeals for the Federal Circuit.

The Board reviews regulations issued by the Office of Personnel Management and has the authority to require agencies to cease compliance with any regulation that could constitute a prohibited personnel practice. It also conducts special studies of the civil service and other executive branch merit systems and reports to the President and the Congress on whether the Federal work force is being adequately protected against political abuses and prohibited personnel practices.

Regional Offices—Merit Systems Protection Board

Region	Address	Director	Telephone
Atlanta Regional Office	401 W. Peachtree St. NW., 30308	Thomas J. Lanphear	404–730–2751
Central Regional Office	31st Fl., 230 S. Dearborn St., Chicago, IL 60604	Martin W. Baumgaertner	312–353–2923
Northeastern Regional Office.	Rm. 501, 2d & Chestnut Sts., Philadelphia, PA 19106.	Lonnie L. Crawford, Jr.	215–597–9960
Washington Regional Office.	Suite 1109, 5203 Leesburg Pike, Falls Church, VA 22041.	P.J. Winzer	703–756–6250
Western Regional Office	4th Fl., 250 Montgomery St., San Francisco, CA 94104.	Denis Marachi	415–705–2935

Field Offices—Merit Systems Protection Board

Region	Address	Chief Administrative Judge	Telephone
Boston, MA	Suite 1810, 99 Summer St., 02110	William Carroll	617–424–5700
Dallas, TX	Rm. 6F20, 1100 Commerce St., 75242	Sharon Jackson	214–767–0555
Denver, CO	Suite 100, 12567 W. Cedar Dr., Lakewood, CO 80228.	Joseph H. Hartman	303–969–5101
New York, NY	Rm. 3137A, 26 Federal Plz., 10278	Arthur Joseph	212–264–9372
Seattle, WA	Rm. 1840, 915 2d Ave., 98174	Carl Berkenwald	206–220–7975

For further information, contact the Merit Systems Protection Board, 1120 Vermont Avenue NW., Washington, DC 20419. Phone, 202–653–7200 or 800–209–8960. TDD, 202–653–8896. Fax, 202–653–7130. Internet, www.mspb.gov.

NATIONAL AERONAUTICS AND SPACE ADMINISTRATION

300 E Street SW., Washington, DC 20546
Phone, 202–358–0000. Internet, www.nasa.gov.

Administrator	DANIEL S. GOLDIN
Deputy Administrator	(VACANCY)
Associate Deputy Administrator	DANIEL R. MULVILLE

Chief Engineer	W. Brian Keegan
Chief Historian	Roger Launius
Chief Information Officer	Lee B. Holcomb
Chief Financial Officer	Arnold G. Holz
Deputy Chief Financial Officer	Kenneth J. Winter
Comptroller	Malcolm L. Peterson
Chief Scientist	Kathie L. Olsen
General Counsel	Edward A. Frankle
Deputy General Counsel	Robert M. Stephens
Staff Director, NASA Advisory Council	G. Michael Green
Director for Special Studies	Sylvia K. Kraemer
Associate Administrator for Aero-Space Technology	Samuel R. Venneri
Deputy Associate Administrator	(vacancy)
Deputy Associate Administrator (Space Transportation Technology)	Gary E. Payton
Associate Administrator for Earth Science	Ghassem R. Asrar
Deputy Associate Administrator	Michael L. Luther
Associate Administrator for Equal Opportunity Programs	George E. Reese
Deputy Associate Administrator	Oceola S. Hall
Associate Administrator for External Relations	John D. Shumacher
Deputy Associate Administrator	Lynn F.H. Cline
Deputy Associate Administrator (Space Flight)	Michael F. O'Brien
Associate Administrator for Headquarters Operations	Michael D. Christensen
Associate Administrator for Human Resources and Education	Vicki A. Novak
Associate Administrator for Legislative Affairs	Edward Heffernan
Deputy Associate Administrator	Mary D. Kerwin
Deputy Associate Administrator (Policy)	Phyllis A. Love
Associate Administrator for Life and Microgravity Sciences and Applications	Arnauld E. Nicogossian
Deputy Associate Administrator	Beth M. McCormick
Associate Administrator for Management Systems	Jeffrey E. Sutton
Deputy Associate Administrator	(vacancy)
Associate Administrator for Policy and Plans	Lori B. Garver
Associate Administrator for Procurement	Thomas S. Luedtke
Associate Administrator for Public Affairs	Peggy C. Wilhide
Deputy Associate Administrator	Paula M. Cleggett
Associate Administrator for Small and Disadvantaged Business Utilization	Ralph C. Thomas III
Associate Administrator for Space Flight	Joseph H. Rothenberg
Deputy Associate Administrator	William F. Readdy
Deputy Administrator for Interagency Enterprise	Albert DiMarcantonio
Deputy Associate Administrator (Business Management)	Michael J. Reilly
Deputy Associate Administrator (Enterprise Development)	Darrell R. Branscome
Deputy Associate Administrator (Space Communications)	Robert E. Spearing

Deputy Associate Administrator (Space Development)	W. Michael Hawes
Deputy Associate Administrator (Space Operations)	Norman B. Starkey
Associate Administrator for Space Science	Edward J. Weiler
Deputy Associate Administrator	Earle K. Huckins
Associate Administrator for Safety and Mission Assurance	Frederick D. Gregory
Deputy Associate Administrator	Michael A. Greenfield
Inspector General	Roberta L. Gross
Assistant Inspector General for Audits	Russell A. Rau
Assistant Inspector General for Investigations	Samuel A. Maxey
Assistant Inspector General for Inspections, Administrative Investigations, and Assessments	David M. Cushing

NASA Centers

Director, Ames Research Center	Henry McDonald
Director, Dryden Flight Research Center	Kevin L. Peterson
Director, John H. Glenn Research Center	Donald J. Campbell
Director, Goddard Space Flight Center	Alphonso V. Diaz
Director, Lyndon B. Johnson Space Center	George W.S. Abbey
Director, John F. Kennedy Space Center	Roy D. Bridges
Director, Langley Research Center	Jeremiah F. Creedon
Director, George C. Marshall Space Flight Center	Arthur G. Stephenson
Director, John C. Stennis Space Center	Roy S. Estess
Manager, NASA Management Office, Jet Propulsion Laboratory	Robert A. Parker

[For the National Aeronautics and Space Administration statement of organization, see the *Code of Federal Regulations,* Title 14, Part 1201]

The National Aeronautics and Space Administration conducts research for the solution of problems of flight within and outside the Earth's atmosphere and develops, constructs, tests, and operates aeronautical and space vehicles. It conducts activities required for the exploration of space with manned and unmanned vehicles and arranges for the most effective utilization of the scientific and engineering resources of the United States with other nations engaged in aeronautical and space activities for peaceful purposes.

The National Aeronautics and Space Administration was established by the National Aeronautics and Space Act of 1958, as amended (42 U.S.C. 2451 *et seq.*).

Activities

Aero-Space Technology The Office of Aero-Space Technology provides technology leadership and direction for programs that pioneer the identification, development, verification, and transfer of high-payoff aeronautics and space transportation technologies, and for facilitating the application and commercialization of these technologies. In addition, the Office is responsible for managing the Ames, Dryden Flight, Langley, and Glenn Research Centers.

For further information, call 202–358–2693.

Earth Science The Office of Earth Science manages NASA's Earth science enterprise. The goal of the Earth science enterprise is to understand the effects of natural and human-induced changes on the global environment. The unique vantage point of space provides information about Earth's land,

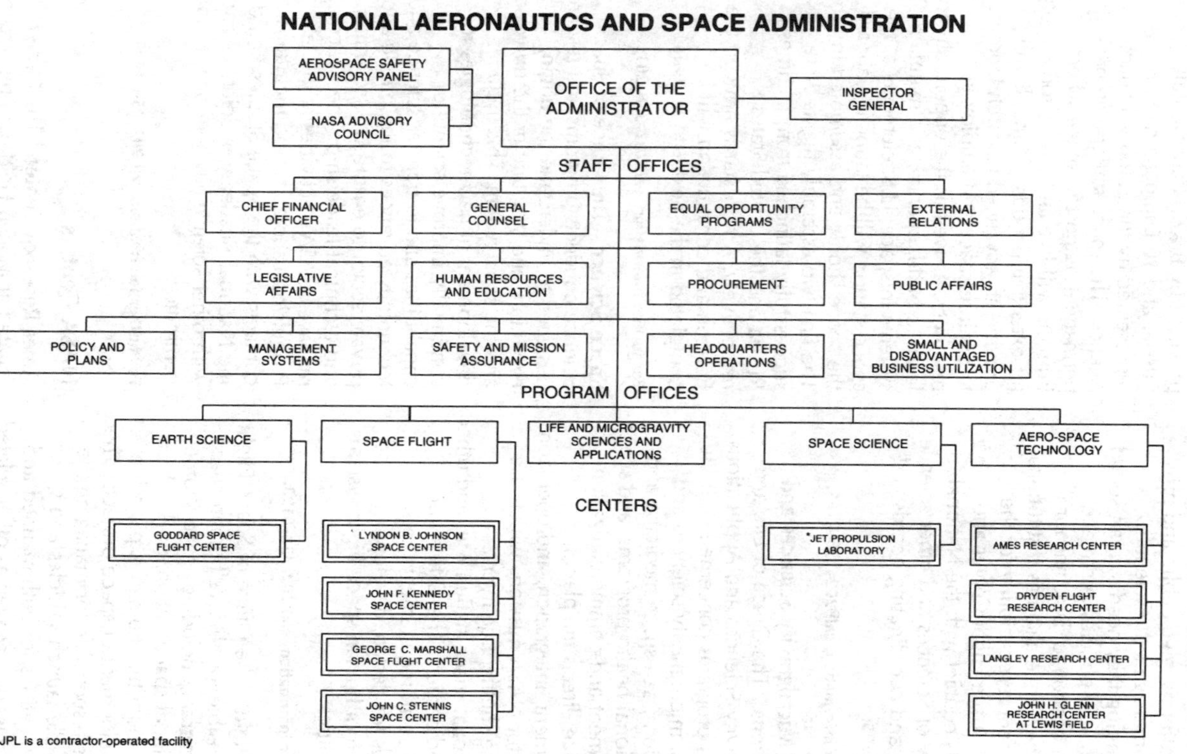
NATIONAL AERONAUTICS AND SPACE ADMINISTRATION
AEROSPACE SAFETY ADVISORY PANEL
NASA ADVISORY COUNCIL
OFFICE OF THE ADMINISTRATOR
INSPECTOR GENERAL
STAFF OFFICES
CHIEF FINANCIAL OFFICER
GENERAL COUNSEL
EQUAL OPPORTUNITY PROGRAMS
EXTERNAL RELATIONS
LEGISLATIVE AFFAIRS
HUMAN RESOURCES AND EDUCATION
PROCUREMENT
PUBLIC AFFAIRS
POLICY AND PLANS
MANAGEMENT SYSTEMS
SAFETY AND MISSION ASSURANCE
HEADQUARTERS OPERATIONS
SMALL AND DISADVANTAGED BUSINESS UTILIZATION
PROGRAM OFFICES
EARTH SCIENCE
SPACE FLIGHT
LIFE AND MICROGRAVITY SCIENCES AND APPLICATIONS
SPACE SCIENCE
AERO-SPACE TECHNOLOGY
CENTERS
GODDARD SPACE FLIGHT CENTER
LYNDON B. JOHNSON SPACE CENTER
JOHN F. KENNEDY SPACE CENTER
GEORGE C. MARSHALL SPACE FLIGHT CENTER
JOHN C. STENNIS SPACE CENTER
*JET PROPULSION LABORATORY
AMES RESEARCH CENTER
DRYDEN FLIGHT RESEARCH CENTER
LANGLEY RESEARCH CENTER
JOHN H. GLENN RESEARCH CENTER AT LEWIS FIELD
*JPL is a contractor-operated facility

atmosphere, ice, oceans, and life that could not be gathered in any other way. Data returned by satellites, expanded by data from aircraft, balloons, and ground-based platforms, give public and private resource managers the scientific understanding they need to craft sound environmental policies and make informed economic decisions for the future. The Office also has institutional management responsibility for the Goddard Space Flight Center and maintains contact with the National Academy of Sciences and other science advisory and coordinating boards and committees.

For further information, call 202–358–2165.

Life and Microgravity Sciences and Applications The Office of Life and Microgravity Sciences and Applications conducts programs concerned with life sciences, microgravity sciences and applications, aerospace medicine and occupational health programs, and space development and commercialization. The Office directs the planning, development, integration, and operations support for NASA missions which use the space shuttle, free flyers, international space station *Mir*, and other advanced carriers. The Office also establishes all requirements and standards for design, development, and operation of human space flight systems and facilities.

For further information, call 202–358–0123.

Space Flight The Office of Space Flight is responsible for NASA's human space flight program, including space shuttle, international space station, payload carrier, and future human exploration and development of space projects. The Office is responsible for managing the expendable launch vehicles and space communications for both manned and robotic missions, as well as other related space flight activities. It is also responsible for institutional management of the Kennedy Space Center, Marshall Space Flight Center, Johnson Space Flight Center, and the Stennis Space Center.

NASA is leading an international effort to build and deploy a permanently manned space station into Earth's orbit. Elements of the space station will be provided by Brazil, Canada, Italy, Japan, Russia, and 10 European nations represented by the European Space Agency. The space station will be a permanent outpost in space where humans will live and work productively for extended periods of time. It will provide an advanced research laboratory to explore space and employ its resources, as well as the opportunity to learn to build, operate, and maintain systems in space. U.S. elements of the space station will be launched aboard the space shuttle and assembled in orbit. The first two assembly flights were successfully launched from facilities in Russia and the United States respectively. A new star is now on the horizon and construction will be completed in the next 4 to 5 years.

For further information, call 202–358–2015.

Space Science The Office of Space Science conducts programs and research designed to understand the origin, evolution, and structure of the universe and the solar system. This includes the development of new technologies to continually improve scientific capabilities and to transfer science and technology advances to the public and private sector to ensure U.S. scientific and technical leadership. The Office also manages NASA's activities at the Jet Propulsion Laboratory and maintains contacts with the Space Studies Board of the National Academy of Sciences and with other science advisory boards and committees.

For further information, call 202–358–1409.

NASA Centers

Ames Research Center The Center, located at Moffett Field, CA, researches, develops, and transfers leading-edge aeronautical technologies through the unique utilization of computations, simulations, ground and flight experimentation, and information sciences. It provides answers to fundamental questions concerning the evolution of astronomical and planetary environments and of life, the adaptation of living systems to space, and the health of our planet. It designs, develops, and delivers integrated information systems technologies and applications, enabling revolutionary advances in aeronautics and space applications and processes, and it develops thermal protection systems for space flight.

Dryden Flight Research Center The Center, located at Edwards Air Force Base, CA, conducts aerospace flight research and aircraft operations in support of agency and national needs, assures preeminent flight research and atmospheric flight operations for science platform aircraft capability through effective management and maintenance of unique national expertise and facilities, and provides operational landing support for the space shuttle.

Glenn Research Center The John H. Glenn Research Center at Lewis Field, located in Cleveland, OH, provides leadership in aeropropulsion technology and is the center of excellence for turbomachinery. The Center also develops and transfers critical technologies, addressing national priorities through research, technology development, and systems development in aeronautics and space applications. Center specialities include commercial communications and enabling technologies. It also maintains a science research and technology development role in space power and onboard propulsion and microgravity fluid physics and combustion.

Goddard Space Flight Center The Center, which is located in Greenbelt, MD, conducts Earth science and applications programs and Earth-orbiting spacecraft and experiment development and flight operations. It develops and operates tracking and data acquisition systems and conducts supporting mission operations. It also develops and operates *Spacelab* payloads; space physics research programs; life science programs; information systems technology; sounding rockets and sounding rocket payloads; launch vehicles; balloons and balloon experiments; planetary science experiments; sensors for environmental monitoring and ocean dynamics; and manages the development of operational weather satellites for the National Oceanic and Atmospheric Administration.

Johnson Space Center The Lyndon B. Johnson Center, which is located in Houston, TX, is the NASA center of excellence for human operations in space. The Center strives to advance the national capability for human exploration and utilization of space by research, development, and operation of the space shuttle, the international space station (ISS), and other space systems and by developing and maintaining excellence in the fields of project management, space systems engineering, medical and life sciences, lunar and planetary geosciences, and crew and mission operations. It is also the lead center for several agencywide programs and initiatives, including the space shuttle and ISS program, space operations, extra-vehicular activity (EVA) projects, astromaterials sciences, biomedical research, advanced human support technology, and space medicine.

Kennedy Space Center The John F. Kennedy Center, which is located in Florida, manages space launches including the launching of astronaut crews, space station elements, and a wide variety of payloads. The Center is responsible for launch and payload processing systems and is home to the space shuttle fleet and the expendable launch vehicle program. It leads in the payload carriers and payload processing and support programs and supports the international space station program.

Langley Research Center The Center, located in Hampton, VA, is the NASA center of excellence for structures and materials. In cooperation with industry, other agencies, and academia, it develops airframe and synergistic spaceframe systems technologies to assure preeminence of the U.S. civil and military aeronautics and space industries. In conjunction with the Earth science community, the Center pioneers the scientific understanding of the Earth's atmospheric chemistry and radiation to preserve the environment.

Marshall Space Flight Center The George C. Marshall Center, located in Huntsville, AL, is responsible for transportation systems development, microgravity research, and optics manufacturing technology. It is the lead space propulsion center. The Center develops, integrates, and operates microgravity payloads, experiments, and research. In addition, it supports the Johnson Space Center in developing the international space station facilities. Other programs include microgravity research; space product development; the development of the X–33 reusable launch vehicle; the Chandra X–Ray Observatory Program; the Future-X (Pathfinders) Program, which provides demonstrations of experimental advanced flight technology; and the design, development, and integration of space transportation and propulsion systems including space shuttle propulsion improvements, reusable and expendable launch vehicles, and vehicles for orbital transfer and deep space missions.

Stennis Space Center The John C. Stennis Center, located near Bay St. Louis, MS, conducts rocket propulsion testing. The Center has a lead role in commercial remote sensing applications development; studies and researches Earth system sciences; and provides for technology transfers.

Government-Owned/Contractor-Operated Facility

Jet Propulsion Laboratory The Laboratory, which is operated under contract by the California Institute of Technology in Pasadena, CA, develops spacecraft and space sensors and conducts mission operations and ground-based research in support of solar system exploration, Earth science and applications, Earth and ocean dynamics, space physics and astronomy, and life science and information systems technology. It is also responsible for the operation of the Deep Space Network in support of NASA projects.

Sources of Information

Contracts and Small Business Activities Inquiries regarding contracting for small business opportunities with NASA should be directed to the Associate Administrator for Small and Disadvantaged Business Utilization, NASA Headquarters, 300 E Street SW., Washington, DC 20546. Phone, 202–358–2088.

Employment Direct all inquiries to the Personnel Director of the nearest NASA Center or, for the Washington, DC, metropolitan area, to the Chief, Headquarters Personnel Branch, NASA Headquarters, Washington, DC 20546. Phone, 202–358–1543.

OIG Hotline An individual may report crimes, fraud, waste, and abuse in NASA programs and operations by calling the OIG Hotline (phone, 800–424–9183); by writing to the NASA Inspector General, P.O. Box 23089, L'Enfant Plaza Station, Washington, DC 20026; or by sending an electronic message from the OIG's website (Internet, www.hq.nasa.gov/office/org/hq/hotline.html).

Publications, Speakers, Films, and Exhibit Services Several publications concerning these services can be obtained by contacting the Public Affairs Officer of the nearest NASA Center. Publications include *NASA Directory of Services for the Public, NASA Film List,* and *NASA Educational Publications List.* The Headquarters telephone directory and certain publications and picture sets are available for sale from the Superintendent of Documents, Government Printing Office, Washington, DC 20402. Telephone directories for NASA Centers are available only from the Centers. Publications and documents not available for sale from the Superintendent of Documents or the National Technical Information Service (Springfield, VA 22151) may be obtained from the NASA Center's Information Center in accordance with the NASA regulation concerning freedom of information.

Reading Room NASA Headquarters Information Center, Room 1H23, 300 E

Street SW., Washington, DC 20546.
Phone, 202–358–0000.

For further information, contact the Headquarters Information Center, National Aeronautics and Space Administration, Washington, DC 20546. Phone, 202–358–0000. Internet, www.nasa.gov.

NATIONAL ARCHIVES AND RECORDS ADMINISTRATION

8601 Adelphi Road, College Park, Maryland 20740–6001
Phone, 301–713–6800. Internet, www.nara.gov.

Archivist of the United States	JOHN W. CARLIN
Deputy Archivist of the United States	LEWIS J. BELLARDO
Assistant Archivist for Administrative Services	ADRIENNE C. THOMAS
Assistant Archivist for Human Resources and Information Services	L. REYNOLDS CAHOON
Assistant Archivist for Presidential Libraries	DAVID F. PETERSON
Assistant Archivist for Records Services—Washington, DC	MICHAEL J. KURTZ
Assistant Archivist for Regional Records Services	RICHARD L. CLAYPOOLE
Director of the Federal Register	RAYMOND A. MOSLEY
Director, Communications Staff	GERALD W. GEORGE
Director, Development Staff	NAOMI REVZIN
Director, Equal Employment Opportunity and Diversity Programs	(VACANCY)
Director, Information Security Oversight Office	STEVEN GARFINKEL
Director, Policy and Planning Staff	LORI A. LISOWSKI
Executive Director, National Historical Publications and Records Commission	ANN CLIFFORD NEWHALL
General Counsel	GARY M. STERN
Inspector General	PAUL BRACHFIELD

[For the National Archives and Records Administration statement of organization, see the *Federal Register* of June 25, 1985, 50 FR 26278]

The National Archives and Records Administration (NARA) ensures, for citizens and Federal officials, ready access to essential evidence that documents the rights of American citizens, the actions of Federal officials, and the national experience. It establishes policies and procedures for managing U.S. Government records and assists Federal agencies in documenting their activities, administering records management programs, scheduling records, and retiring noncurrent records. NARA accessions, arranges, describes, preserves, and provides access to the essential documentation of the three branches of Government; manages the Presidential Libraries system; and publishes the laws, regulations, and Presidential and other public documents. It also assists the Information Security Oversight Office, which manages Federal classification and declassification policies, and the National Historical Publications and Records Commission, which makes grants nationwide to help nonprofit organizations identify, preserve, and provide access to materials that document American history.

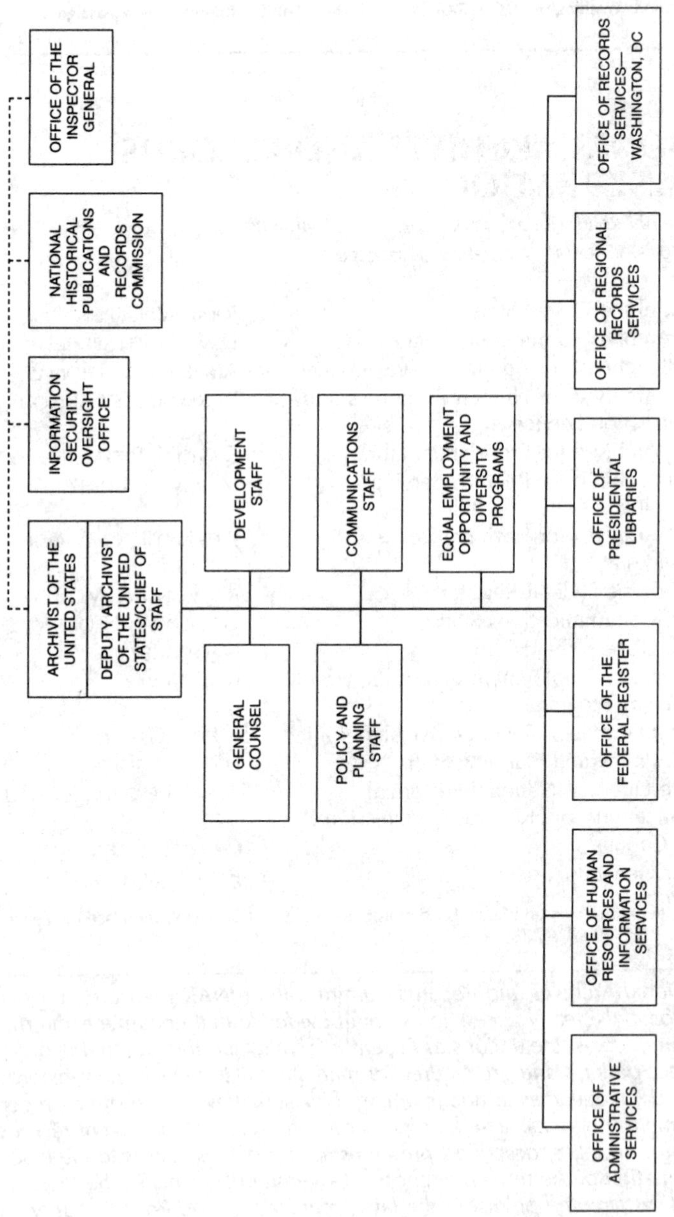
NATIONAL ARCHIVES AND RECORDS ADMINISTRATION
ARCHIVIST OF THE UNITED STATES
DEPUTY ARCHIVIST OF THE UNITED STATES/CHIEF OF STAFF
INFORMATION SECURITY OVERSIGHT OFFICE
NATIONAL HISTORICAL PUBLICATIONS AND RECORDS COMMISSION
OFFICE OF THE INSPECTOR GENERAL
DEVELOPMENT STAFF
GENERAL COUNSEL
COMMUNICATIONS STAFF
POLICY AND PLANNING STAFF
EQUAL EMPLOYMENT OPPORTUNITY AND DIVERSITY PROGRAMS
OFFICE OF ADMINISTRATIVE SERVICES
OFFICE OF HUMAN RESOURCES AND INFORMATION SERVICES
OFFICE OF THE FEDERAL REGISTER
OFFICE OF PRESIDENTIAL LIBRARIES
OFFICE OF REGIONAL RECORDS SERVICES
OFFICE OF RECORDS SERVICES—WASHINGTON, DC

The National Archives and Records Administration is the successor agency to the National Archives Establishment, which was created in 1934 and subsequently incorporated into the General Services Administration as the National Archives and Records Service in 1949. NARA was established as an independent agency in the executive branch of the Government by act of October 19, 1984 (44 U.S.C. 2101 *et seq.*), effective April 1, 1985.

Activities

Archival Program The National Archives and Records Administration maintains the historically valuable records of the U.S. Government dating from the Revolutionary War era to the recent past; arranges and preserves records and prepares finding aids to facilitate their use; makes records available for use in research rooms in its facilities; answers written and oral requests for information contained in its holdings; and, for a fee, provides copies of records. In addition, many important records are available on microfilm an on the NARA website, at www.nara.gov. Historically valuable records created in the Washington, DC, area and in the custody of NARA are maintained in NARA facilities in the Washington, DC, area. Historically valuable records that are primarily of regional or local interest and in the custody of NARA are maintained in the NARA regional records services facilities (see "Regional Records Services" below).

For further information concerning records in the custody of NARA, contact the Customer Services Division. Phone, 202–501–5400 or 301–713–6800.

Laws, Regulations, and Presidential Documents The agency prepares and publishes a wide variety of public documents. Upon issuance, acts of Congress are published immediately in slip law (pamphlet) form and then cumulated and published for each session of Congress in the *United States Statutes at Large*.

Each Federal workday, the *Federal Register* publishes (in both paper and electronic format) current Presidential proclamations and Executive orders, Federal agency regulations having general applicability and legal effect, proposed agency rules, and documents required by statute to be published. All Federal regulations in force are codified annually in the *Code of Federal Regulations*.

Presidential speeches, news conferences, messages, and other materials released by the White House Office of the Press Secretary are published each week in the *Weekly Compilation of Presidential Documents* (in both paper and electronic format) and annually in the *Public Papers of the Presidents*.

The *United States Government Manual*, published annually in both paper and electronic format, serves as the official handbook of the Federal Government, providing extensive information on agencies of the legislative, judicial, and executive branches.

For further information, contact Customer Service, Office of the Federal Register. Phone, 202–523–5227. TDD, 202–523–5229. Fax, 202–523–5216. E-mail, info@fedreg.nara.gov. Internet, www.nara.gov/fedreg.

Presidential Libraries Through the Presidential libraries, which are located at sites selected by the Presidents and built with private funds, NARA preserves and makes available the records and personal papers of a particular President's administration. In addition to providing reference services on Presidential documents, each library prepares documentary and descriptive publications and operates a museum to exhibit documents, historic objects, and other memorabilia of interest to the public.

The records of each President since Herbert Hoover are administered by NARA. While such records were once considered personal papers, all Presidential records created on or after January 20, 1981, are declared by law to be owned and controlled by the United States and are required to be transferred to NARA at the end of the administration, pursuant to the

Presidential Records Act of 1978 (44 U.S.C. 2201 *et seq.*).

For further information, contact the Office of Presidential Libraries. Phone, 301–713–6050.

Presidential Libraries—National Archives and Records Administration

Library	City/Address	Director	Telephone
Herbert Hoover Library	West Branch, IA 52358–0488	Timothy G. Walch	319–643–5301
Franklin D. Roosevelt Library	Hyde Park, NY 12538–1999	Cynthia M. Koch	914–229–8114
Harry S. Truman Library	Independence, MO 64050–1798	Larry J. Hackman	816–833–1400
Dwight D. Eisenhower Library	Abilene, KS 67410–2900	Daniel D. Holt	785–263–4751
John F. Kennedy Library	Boston, MA 02125–3398	Bradley S. Gerratt	617–929–4500
Lyndon B. Johnson Library	Austin, TX 78705–5702	Harry J. Middleton	512–916–5137
Nixon Presidential Materials Staff	College Park, MD 20740–6001	Karl Weissenbach, *Acting*	301–713–6950
Gerald R. Ford Library	Ann Arbor, MI 48109–2114	Richard Norton Smith	734–741–2218
Gerald R. Ford Museum	Grand Rapids, MI 49504–5353	Richard Norton Smith	616–451–9263
Jimmy Carter Library	Atlanta, GA 30307–1498	Jay E. Hakes	404–331–3942
Ronald Reagan Library	Simi Valley, CA 93065–0666	(Vacancy)	805–522–8444
George Bush Library	College Station, TX 77843	David E. Alsobrook	979–260–9554

Records Management To ensure proper documentation of the organization, policies, and activities of the Government, NARA develops standards and guidelines for the management and disposition of recorded information. It appraises Federal records and approves records disposition schedules. It also inspects agency records and records management practices, develops records management training programs, provides guidance and assistance on proper records management, and provides for storage of inactive records. For agencies headquartered in the Washington, DC, vicinity, these functions are assigned to the Office of Records Services. The Washington National Records Center, part of the Office of Records Services, also provides tailored workshops and reimbursable micrographic services. For records management services outside the Washington, DC, area, see "Regional Records Services" (above).

For further information, contact Modern Records Programs. Phone, 301–713–7100. For records center services in the Washington, DC, area, contact the Washington National Records Center. Phone, 301–457–7000.

Regional Records Services Outside the Washington, DC, area, NARA operates a system of nine regions comprised of individual regional records services facilities plus the National Personnel Records Center. Each of the nine regional administrators operates a program encompassing the full life cycle of records, including records management activities with records creators, disposal, archival accessioning, records processing, and access to records by the public. Historically valuable records that are primarily of regional or local interest are maintained in most of these facilities, which arrange and preserve the records and prepare finding aids to facilitate their use; make the records available for use in research rooms; answer written and oral requests for information contained in the holdings; and, for a fee, provide copies of the records. In addition, many important original records held in NARA facilities in the Washington, DC, area, are available in microform in most of these regional facilities.

The Office also operates Federal records centers for the storage and servicing of non-current and certain active records of Federal agencies. Services include reference including loan or return of records to the agency of origin; authenticated reproductions of documents; low-cost storage; and the disposal of records of transitory value or the transfer into archival custody of those records that have enduring value. Microfilming services are also available from some of the facilities. All records center services are offered to Federal agencies on a completely reimbursable basis.

In addition to archival holdings, the Office offers electronic records management assistance; records management staff training; advice on records creation, maintenance, storage, and disposition; and advice on vital records to Federal agencies.

For further information, contact the Office of Regional Records Services. Phone, 301–713–7200.

Regional Records Services Facilities—National Archives and Records Administration

(HQ: Headquarters facility; A: Facility holding archival records)

City	Address	Director	Telephone
Northeast Region (HQ)	380 Trapelo Rd., Waltham, MA 02154–6399	Diane LeBlanc	617–647–8745
Boston, MA (A)	380 Trapelo Rd., Waltham, 02154–6399		617–647–8104
Pittsfield, MA	100 Conte Dr., 01201–8230		413–445–6885
New York City, NY (A)	201 Varick St., 10014–4811		212–337–1300
Mid-Atlantic Region (HQ)	900 Market St., Philadelphia, PA 19107–4292	David Weber, *Acting*	215–671–9027
Center City Philadelphia, PA (A).	900 Market St., 19107–4292		215–597–3000
Northeast Philadelphia, PA	14700 Townsend Rd., 19154–1096		215–671–9027
Southeast Region (HQ)	1557 St. Joseph Ave., East Point, GA 30344–2593.	James McSweeney, *Acting*	404–763–7477
Great Lakes Region (HQ)	7358 S. Pulaski Rd., Chicago, IL 60629–5898	David E. Kuehl	773–581–7816
Chicago, IL (A)	7358 S. Pulaski Rd., 60629–5898		773–581–7816
Dayton, OH	3150 Springboro Rd., 45439–1883		513–225–2852
Central Plains Region (HQ) (A).	2312 E. Bannister Rd., Kansas City, MO 64131–3011.	R. Reed Whitaker	816–926–6920
Lee's Summit, MO	200 Space Ctr. Dr., 64064–1182		816–478–7089
Southwest Region (HQ) (A)	501 W. Felix St., Fort Worth, TX 76115–3405	Kent C. Carter	817–334–5515
Rocky Mountain Region (HQ) (A).	Bldg. 48, Denver Federal Ctr., Denver, CO 80225–0307.	Joel Barker, *Acting*	303–236–0801
Pacific Region (HQ)	1000 Commodore Dr., San Bruno, CA 94066	Sharon L. Roadway	415–876–9249
Laguna Niguel, CA (A)	1st Fl. E., 24000 Avila Rd., 92607–3497		714–360–2618
San Francisco, CA (A)	1000 Commodore Dr., San Bruno, 94066		415–876–9009
Pacific Alaska Region (HQ)	6125 Sand Point Way NE., Seattle, WA 98115–7999.	Steven M. Edwards	206–526–6501
Seattle, WA (A)	6125 Sand Point Way NE., 98115–7999		206–526–6501
Anchorage, AK (A)	654 W. 3d Ave., 99501–2145		907–271–2443
National Personnel Records Center (HQ).	9700 Page Ave., St. Louis, MO 63132	David L. Petree	314–538–4201

National Archives Trust Fund Board The National Archives Trust Fund Board receives funds from the sale of reproductions of historic documents and publications about the records, as well as from gifts and bequests. The Board invests these funds and uses income to support archival functions such as the preparation of publications that make information about historic records more widely available. Members of the Board are the Archivist of the United States, the Secretary of the Treasury, and the Chairman of the National Endowment for the Humanities.

For further information, contact the Secretary, National Archives Trust Fund Board. Phone, 301–713–6405.

National Historical Publications and Records Commission The Commission is the grant-making affiliate of the National Archives and Records Administration. Its mission is to promote the identification, preservation, and dissemination of essential historical documentation. Its grants help State and local archives, universities, historical societies, and other nonprofit organizations solve preservation problems dealing with electronic records, improve training and techniques, strengthen archival programs, preserve and process records collections, and provide access to them through the publication of finding aids and documentary editions of the papers of the Founding Era and other themes and historical figures in American history. The Commission works in partnership with a national network of State Historical Records Advisory Boards.

For further information, contact the National Historical Publications and Records Commission. Phone, 202–501–5600.

Sources of Information

Calendar of Events To be added to the mailing list for the monthly *National Archives Calendar of Events*, call 301–

713–7070. For a recorded announcement of events at the National Archives building and the National Archives at College Park, call 202–501–5000. The hearing impaired should call 202–501–5404 for events at the National Archives building and 301–713–7343 for events at the College Park building.

Congressional Affairs The Congressional Affairs staff maintains contact with and responds to inquiries from congressional offices. Phone, 301–713–7340. Fax, 301–713–7344.

Contracts Individuals seeking to do business with NARA may obtain detailed information from the Acquisitions Services Division, National Archives at College Park, 8601 Adelphi Road, College Park, MD 20740–6001. Phone, 301–713–6755. Fax, 301–713–6910.

Educational Opportunities The agency offers several courses on archival and records management principles and on using NARA resources for research. For information on specific topics, contact the public programs education staff at the telephone number listed.

"Going to the Source: An Introduction to Research in Archives." Phone, 202–501–6303.

"Introduction to Genealogy." Phone, 202–501–6694.

"Primarily Teaching." Phone, 202–501–6729. Internet, www.nara.gov/education.

For information about the "Modern Archives Institute," contact the Office of Staff Development Services, Room 1510, National Archives and Records Administration, 8601 Adelphi Road, College Park, MD 20740–6001. Phone 301–713–7390.

For information about records management workshops, contact the Life Cycle Management Division (phone, 301–713–6677), any regional records services facility, or the Office of Regional Records Services (phone, 301–713–7200).

For information about "The Federal Register: What It Is and How To Use It," call 202–523–4534.

For information about the "Institute for the Editing of Historical Documents" at the University of Wisconsin, Madison, or fellowships in documentary editing and archival administration contact NHPRC, National Archives and Records Administration, 700 Pennsylvania Avenue NW., Washington, DC 20408–0001. Phone, 202–501–5610.

Electronic Access Information about NARA and its holdings and publications is available electronically (Internet, www.nara.gov. E-mail, inquire@arch2.nara.gov).

Employment For job opportunities nationwide, contact the nearest NARA facility or the Human Resources Operations Branch, Room 2004, 9700 Page Avenue, St. Louis, MO 63132. Phone, 800–827–4898 (toll free). TDD, 314–538–4799. Internet, www.nara.gov.

Fax-on-Demand To use the fax-on-demand service, call 301–713–6905 from a fax machine handset and follow the voice instructions. One of the options that can be selected is a list of the available documents. There is no charge for using fax-on-demand, other than for any long distance telephone charges users may incur.

Freedom of Information Act/Privacy Act Requests Requests should be directed as follows:

For administrative records of the National Archives and Records Administration, contact the NARA Freedom of Information Act/Privacy Act Officer, General Counsel Staff, National Archives at College Park, 8601 Adelphi Road, College Park, MD 20740–6001. Phone, 301–713–6035. Fax, 301–713–6040.

For historically valuable records in the custody of the Office of Records Services, contact the Special Access/FOIA Staff, National Archives and Records Administration, 8601 Adelphi Road, College Park, MD 20740–6001. Phone, 301–713–6620.

For historically valuable records in the custody of a regional records services facility, contact the facility serving the appropriate region (see listing in the preceding text) or the Office of Regional Records Services (phone, 301–713–7200).

For historical records in the custody of a Presidential library, contact the library that has custody of the records (see listing in the preceding text).

For records in the physical custody of the Washington National Records Center or the records center operation in a regional records services facility, contact the Federal agency that transferred the records to the facility.

Museum Shops Publications, document facsimiles, and souvenirs are available for sale at the National Archives building, at each Presidential library, and at some regional records services facilities.

Public Affairs The Public Affairs staff maintains contact with and responds to inquiries from the media, issues press releases and other literature, and maintains contact with organizations representing the archival profession, scholarly organizations, and other groups served by NARA. Phone, 301–713–6000.

Public Programs Contact the Office of Public Programs (NWE), National Archives and Records Administration, Washington, DC 20408. Phone, 202–501–5210. Fax, 202–501–5239.

Publications Agency publications, including facsimiles of certain documents, finding aids to records, and *Prologue*, a scholarly journal published quarterly, are available from the Customer Service Center (NWCC1), NARA, Room 403, 700 Pennsylvania Avenue NW., Washington, DC 20408–0001. Phone, 800–234–8861 (toll free) or 202–501–5235. Fax, 202–501–7170.

Records management publications are available from the National Archives Customer Service Center (NWCC2), Room 1000, National Archives at College Park, 8601 Adelphi Road, College Park, MD 20740–6001. Phone, 800–234–8861. Fax, 301–713–6169. Internet, www.nara.gov/publications.

Information about laws, regulations, and Presidential documents is available from the Office of the Federal Register (NFS), NARA, Washington, DC 20408. Phone, 202–523–5227. Internet, www.nara.gov/fedreg.

Reference Services Records are available for research purposes in reading rooms at the National Archives building, 700 Pennsylvania Avenue NW., Washington, DC (phone, 202–501–5400); at the National Archives at College Park, 8601 Adelphi Road, College Park, MD (phone, 301–713–6800); and at each Presidential library and regional records services facility that holds archival records (see listings in the preceding text). Written requests for information may be sent to any of these units, or they may be addressed to the Customer Services Division, National Archives at College Park, Room 1000, 8601 Adelphi Road, College Park, MD 20740–6001. Phone, 301–713–6800. E-mail, inquire@arch2.nara.gov.

The Nixon Presidential Materials Staff is located in Room 1320 at the National Archives at College Park. Some Nixon materials are available for public inspection, but researchers are advised to contact the staff in advance to ascertain the availability of materials before visiting the facility. Phone, 301–713–6950.

The Public Inspection Desk of the Office of the Federal Register is open every Federal business day for public inspection of documents filed for publication in the next day's edition of the *Federal Register,* at Suite 700, 800 North Capitol Street NW., Washington, DC. Phone, 202–523–5240.

Speakers and Presentations Community and school outreach programs are presented upon request. Interested groups in the Washington, DC, area should call 202–501–5205. Groups outside the Washington, DC, area should contact the regional records services facility or Presidential library in their areas (see listings in the preceding text).

Education specialists present workshops at regional and national conferences of humanities professionals and as in-service training for teachers. For further information, contact the public programs education staff. Phone, 202–501–6729.

Teaching Materials Education specialists have developed low-cost documentary teaching materials for classroom use. Each kit deals with an historical event or theme and includes document facsimiles and teaching aids. For further information, contact the public programs education staff. Phone, 202–501–6729.

Tours Individuals or groups may request general or specialty tours behind the scenes at the National Archives building. Tours are given by reservation only, and individuals are requested to make reservations at least 3 weeks in advance. Tours are given at 10:15 a.m. and 1:15 p.m., Monday through Friday. Tours of the National Archives at College Park, MD, may also be arranged. For information and reservations, contact the Visitor and Volunteer Services between 9 a.m. and 4 p.m., Monday through Friday. Phone, 202–501–5205.

Volunteer Service Opportunities A wide variety of opportunities is available for volunteers. At the National Archives building and the National Archives at College Park, MD, volunteers conduct tours, provide information in the Exhibition Hall, work with staff archivists in processing historic documents, and serve as genealogical aides in the genealogical orientation room. For further information, call 202–501–5205. Similar opportunities exist in the Presidential libraries and at the regional records services facilities that house archival records. If outside the Washington, DC, area, contact the facility closest to you for further information on volunteer opportunities.

For further information, write or visit the National Archives and Records Administration, 700 Pennsylvania Avenue NW., Washington, DC 20408–0001. Phone, 202–501–5400. Internet, www.nara.gov. E-mail, inquire@arch2.nara.gov.

NATIONAL CAPITAL PLANNING COMMISSION

Suite 301, 801 Pennsylvania Avenue NW., Washington, DC 20576
Phone, 202–482–7200. Internet, www.ncpc.gov.

Chairman	HARVEY B. GANTT
Vice Chairman	PATRICIA ELWOOD
Members	ARRINGTON DIXON, ROBERT A. GAINES, MARGARET G. VANDERHYE
Ex Officio:	
(Secretary of the Interior)	BRUCE BABBITT
(Secretary of Defense)	WILLIAM S. COHEN
(Administrator of General Services)	DAVID J. BARRAM
(Chairman, Senate Committee on Governmental Affairs)	FRED THOMPSON
(Chairman, House Committee on Government Reform and Oversight)	DAN BURTON
(Mayor of the District of Columbia)	ANTHONY A. WILLIAMS
(Chairman, Council of the District of Columbia)	LINDA W. CROPP
Staff:	
Executive Director	REGINALD W. GRIFFITH
Assistant Executive Director (Management)	CONNIE M. HARSHAW
Assistant Executive Director (Programs)	WILLIAM R. LAWSON
Administrative Officer	TERESA M. JACKSON
Director, Office of Long-Range Planning	MELANIE WILSON
Director, Office of Plans Review	WILLIAM G. DOWD
Director, Technology Development and Applications Support	DERESENE WORSLEY
General Counsel	(VACANCY)

NATIONAL CAPITAL PLANNING COMMISSION

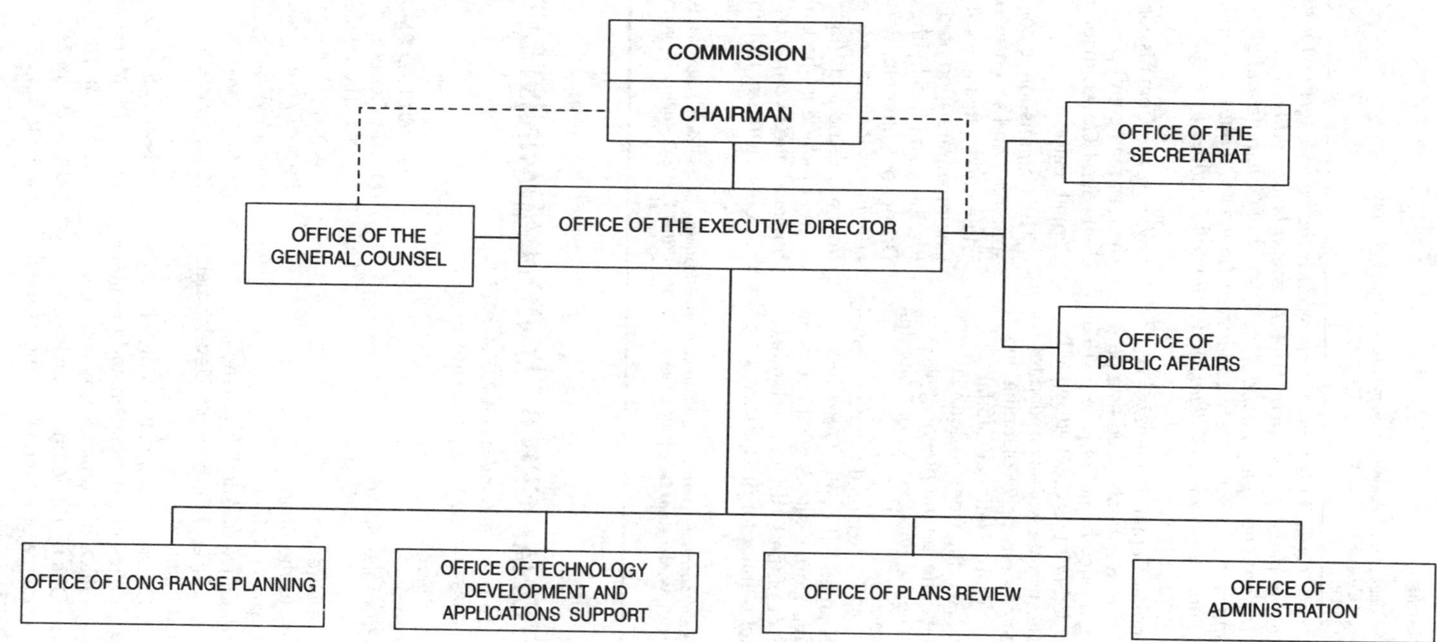

Public Affairs Officer	DENISE H. LIEBOWITZ
Secretariat	RAE N. ALLEN

[For the National Capital Planning Commission statement of organization, see the *Code of Federal Regulations,* Title 1, Part 456.2]

The National Capital Planning Commission is the central agency for conducting planning and development activities for Federal lands and facilities in the National Capital region. The region includes the District of Columbia and all land areas within the boundaries of Montgomery and Prince Georges Counties in Maryland and Fairfax, Loudoun, Prince William, and Arlington Counties in Virginia.

The National Capital Planning Commission was established as a park planning agency by act of June 6, 1924, as amended (40 U.S.C. 71 *et seq.*). Two years later its role was expanded to include comprehensive planning. In 1952, under the National Capital Planning Act, the Commission was designated the central planning agency for the Federal and District of Columbia governments.

In 1973, the National Capital Planning Act was amended by the District of Columbia Home Rule Act, which made the Mayor of the District of Columbia the chief planner for the District; however, the Commission continues to serve as the central planning agency for the Federal Government in the National Capital region.

The Commission is composed of five appointed and seven *ex officio* members. Three citizen members, including the Chairman, are appointed by the President and two by the mayor of the District of Columbia. Presidential appointees include one resident each from Maryland and Virginia and one from anywhere in the United States; however, the two mayoral appointees must be District of Columbia residents.

For further information, contact the National Capital Planning Commission, Suite 301, 801 Pennsylvania Avenue NW., Washington, DC 20576. Phone, 202–482–7200. Fax, 202–482–7272. Internet, www.ncpc.gov.

NATIONAL CREDIT UNION ADMINISTRATION

1775 Duke Street, Alexandria, VA 22314–3428
Phone, 703–518–6300. Internet, www.ncua.gov.

Chairman	NORMAN E. D'AMOURS
Members of the Board	DENNIS DOLLAR, YOLANDA TOWNSEND WHEAT
Executive Director	CAROLYN D. JORDAN
Secretary to the Board	BECKY BAKER
Chief Financial Officer	DENNIS WINANS
Director, Office of Administration	JAMES L. BAYLEN
Director, Office of Community Development Credit Unions	JOYCE JACKSON
Director, Office of Corporate Credit Unions	ROBERT F. SCHAFER
Director, Office of Examination and Insurance	DAVID M. MARQUIS
Director, Office of Human Resources	SHERRY TURPENOFF
Director, Office of Investment Services	EDWARD DUPCAK
Director, Office of Public and Congressional Affairs	ROBERT E. LOFTUS

Director, Office of Technology and Information Services — DOUG VERNER
Director, Office of Training and Development — ROBERT POMPA
General Counsel — ROBERT M. FENNER
Inspector General — H. FRANK THOMAS

[For the National Credit Union Administration statement of organization, see the *Code of Federal Regulations*, Title 12, Part 720]

The National Credit Union Administration Board is responsible for chartering, insuring, supervising, and examining Federal credit unions and administering the National Credit Union Share Insurance Fund. The Board also administers the Community Development Revolving Loan Fund and manages the Central Liquidity Facility, a mixed-ownership Government corporation whose purpose is to supply emergency loans to member credit unions.

The National Credit Union Administration was established by act of March 10, 1970 (12 U.S.C. 1752), and reorganized by act of November 10, 1978 (12 U.S.C. 226), as an independent agency in the executive branch of the Federal Government. It regulates and insures all Federal credit unions and insures State-chartered credit unions that apply and qualify for share insurance.

Activities

Chartering The Administration's Board grants Federal credit union charters to groups sharing a common bond of occupation or association, or groups within a well-defined neighborhood, community, or rural district. A preliminary investigation is made to determine if certain minimum standards are met before granting a Federal charter.

For further information, contact the appropriate regional office listed in the table below.

Examinations The Administration conducts annual examinations of Federal credit unions to determine their solvency and compliance with laws and regulations and to assist credit union management and operations.

For further information, contact the Director, Office of Examination and Insurance. Phone, 703–518–6360.

Share Insurance The act of October 19, 1970 (12 U.S.C. 1781 *et seq.*), provides for a program of share insurance. The insurance is mandatory for Federal credit unions and for State-chartered credit unions in many States and is optional for other State-chartered credit unions that meet Administration standards. Credit union members' accounts are insured up to $100,000. The National Credit Union Share Insurance Fund requires each insured credit union to place and maintain a 1 percent deposit of its insured savings with the Fund.

For further information, contact the Director, Office of Examination and Insurance. Phone, 703–518–6360.

Supervision Supervisory activities are carried out through annual examiner contacts and through periodic policy and regulatory releases from the Administration. The Administration also maintains a warning system designed to identify emerging problems as well as to monitor operations between examinations.

Regional Offices—National Credit Union Administration

Region	Address	Director	Telephone	Fax
Albany, NY—CT, MA, ME, NH, NY, RI, VT	9 Washington Sq., Washington Ave. Ext., 12205	Layne L. Bumgardner	518–862–7400	518–862–7420
Capital—DC, DE, MD, NJ, PA, VA, WV	Suite 4206, 1775 Duke St., Alexandria, VA 22314	Tawana James	703–519–4600	703–519–6674

Regional Offices—National Credit Union Administration—Continued

Region	Address	Director	Telephone	Fax
Atlanta, GA—AL, AR, FL, GA, KY, LA, MS, NC, PR, SC, TN, VI	Suite 1600, 7000 Central Pkwy., 30328	Alonzo A. Swann III	678–443–3000	678–443–3020
Chicago, IL—IL, IN, MI, MO, OH, WI	Suite 125, 4225 Naperville Rd., Lisle, 60532–3658	Melinda Love	630–955–4100	630–955–4120
Austin, TX—AZ, CO, IA, KS, MN, ND, NE, NM, OK, SD, TX, UT, WY	Suite 5200, 4807 Spicewood Springs Rd., 78759–8490	J. Leonard Skiles	512–342–5600	512–342–5620
Pacific—AK, AS, CA, GU, HI, ID, MT, NV, OR, WA	Suite 1350, 2300 Clayton Rd., Concord, CA 94520	Robert E. Blatner, Jr., *Acting*	925–363–6220	925–363–6220

Sources of Information

Consumer Complaints The Administration investigates the complaints of members who are unable to resolve problems with their Federal credit union when these problems relate to a possible violation of the Federal Credit Union Act or consumer protection regulations. Complaints should be sent directly to the appropriate regional office.

Employment Inquiries and applications for employment should be directed to the Office of Human Resources, National Credit Union Administration, 1775 Duke Street, Alexandria, VA 22314–3428.

Federally Insured Credit Unions A list of federally insured credit union names, addresses, asset levels, and number of members is available for review at NCUA's Alexandria and regional offices. Copies of the listing are available at a nominal fee from NCUA, Publications, 1775 Duke Street, Alexandria, VA 22314–3428. Phone, 703–518–6340.

Publications A listing and copies of NCUA publications are available from NCUA, Publications, 1775 Duke Street, Alexandria, VA 22314–3428. Phone, 703–518–6340. Publications are also available electronically through the Internet, at www.ncua.gov.

Starting a Federal Credit Union Groups interested in forming a Federal credit union may obtain free information by writing to the appropriate regional office.

For further information concerning the National Credit Union Administration, contact the Office of Public and Congressional Affairs, National Credit Union Administration, 1775 Duke Street, Alexandria, VA 22314–3428. Phone, 703–518–6330. Internet, www.ncua.gov.

NATIONAL FOUNDATION ON THE ARTS AND THE HUMANITIES

NATIONAL ENDOWMENT FOR THE ARTS

1100 Pennsylvania Avenue NW., Washington, DC 20506–0001
Phone, 202–682–5400

Chairman	WILLIAM J. (BILL) IVEY
Senior Deputy Chairman	SCOTT SHANKLIN-PETERSON
Deputy Chairman, Grants and Awards	KAREN CHRISTENSEN
Deputy Chairman, Guidelines, Panel, and Council Operations	A.B. SPELLMAN
Deputy Chairman, Management and Budget	LAWRENCE BADEN
Budget Officer	RON FINCMAN

Chief Information Officer	MIKE BURKE
Congressional and White House Liaison	DICK WOODRUFF
Contracts and Grants Officer	NICKI JACOBS
Coordinator, Leadership and Millennium	MICHAEL MCLAUGHLIN
Council Coordinator	MICHAEL FAUBION
Director, Administrative Services	MURRAY R. WELSH
Director, Civil Rights	ANGELIA RICHARDSON
Director, Information Management	ANDREA FOWLER
Director, Office of Human Resources	MAXINE JEFFERSON
Director, Office of Communications	CHERIE SIMON
Director, Policy Research and Analysis	(VACANCY)
Federal Partnership Director	ROSALIE KESSLER
Finance Officer	MARVIN MARKS
General Counsel	HOPE O'KEEFFE, *Acting*
Inspector General	ED JOHNS
Locals/ArtsREACH Director	PATRICE POWELL
State and Regional Director	ED DICKEY
Music/Opera Director	WAYNE BROWN
Presenting/Multidisciplinary Director	VANESSA WHANG
Dance Director	DOUG SONNTAG
Design Director	MARK ROBBINS
Arts Education Director	DOUG HERBERT
Folk/Traditional Arts Director	DAN SHEEHY
Literature Director	CLIFF BECKER
Media Arts Director	LAURA WELSH, *Acting*
Museum/Visual Arts Director	SARALYN REECE HARDY
Planning and Stabilization Director	LEE DENNISON
Theater/Musical Theater Director	GIGI BOLT

NATIONAL ENDOWMENT FOR THE HUMANITIES

1100 Pennsylvania Avenue NW., Washington, DC 20506
Phone, 202–606–8400. Internet, www.neh.gov.

Chairman	WILLIAM R. FERRIS
General Counsel	VIRGINIA CANTER
Inspector General	SHELDON BERNSTEIN
Deputy Chairman	JOHN W. ROBERTS
Accounting Officer	TONY BANKO
Administrative Services Officer	BARRY MAYNES
Chief Information Officer	BRETT BOBLEY
Director, Division of Education	CANDACE KATZ
Director, Division of Preservation and Access	GEORGE FARR
Director, Division of Public Programs	NANCY ROGERS
Director, Division of Research	JAMES HERBERT
Director, Federal/State Partnership	EDITH MANZA
Director, Office of Challenge Grants	STEPHEN M. ROSS
Director, Office of Human Resources	TIMOTHY G. CONNELLY
Director, Office of Strategic Planning	JEFFREY THOMAS
Equal Employment Officer	WILLIE MCGHEE
Grants Officer	DAVID WALLACE
Chief of Staff	ANN S. YOUNG ORR
Director, Enterprise Office	NANCY STURM
Director, Governmental Affairs	MICHAEL BAGLEY
Director, Office of Public Affairs	ROBERTA HEINE

INSTITUTE OF MUSEUM AND LIBRARY SERVICES

Room 510, 1100 Pennsylvania Avenue NW., Washington, DC 20506
Phone, 202–606–8536. Internet, www.imls.gov. E-mail, imlsinfo@imls.gov.

Director	BEVERLY SHEPPARD, *Acting*
Deputy Director for the Office of Library Services	ELIZABETH SYWETZ
Deputy Director for the Office of Museum Services	BEVERLY SHEPPARD
Director, Legislative and Public Affairs	MAMIE BITTNER
Director, Policy, Planning, and Budget	LINDA BELL
Director, Research and Technology	REBECCA DANVERS
Library Program Director	JOYCE RAY
Museum Program Director	MARY ESTELLE KENNELLY

[For the National Foundation on the Arts and the Humanities statement of organization, see the *Code of Federal Regulations,* Title 45, Part 1100]

The National Foundation on the Arts and the Humanities encourages and supports national progress in the humanities and the arts.

The National Foundation on the Arts and the Humanities was created as an independent agency by the National Foundation on the Arts and the Humanities Act of 1965 (20 U.S.C. 951). The Foundation consists of the National Endowment for the Arts, the National Endowment for the Humanities, the Federal Council on the Arts and the Humanities, and the Institute of Museum and Library Services. Each Endowment has its own Council, composed of the Endowment Chairman and 26 other members appointed by the President, which advises the Chairman with respect to policies, programs, and procedures, in addition to reviewing and making recommendations on applications for financial support.

The Federal Council on the Arts and the Humanities consists of 20 members, including the two Endowment Chairmen and the Director of the Institute of Museum and Library Services, and is designed to coordinate the activities of the two Endowments and related programs of other Federal agencies. Four members are excluded from the Federal Council when it is considering matters under the Arts and Artifacts Indemnity Act (20 U.S.C. 971).

National Endowment for the Arts

The National Endowment for the Arts, an investment in America's living cultural heritage, serves the public good by nurturing the expression of human creativity, supporting the cultivation of community spirit, and fostering the recognition and appreciation of the excellence and diversity of our Nation's artistic accomplishments.

The Arts Endowment serves as a catalyst to increase opportunities and resources for arts organizations, artists, and arts audiences. It promotes involvement in the arts by citizens, public and private nonprofit organizations, and States and local communities. The Endowment awards grants to nonprofit arts organizations in support of outstanding projects; honors artists of exceptional achievement; works to expand the Nation's artistic resources and promote preservation of the country's cultural heritage; and funds projects whose goal is to educate, formally or informally, both children and adults in the arts. The Endowment also disburses funds to State arts agencies and local and regional organizations in order to promote broad dissemination of the arts across America. Its grantmaking is conducted through the following funding categories: creation and presentation, education, access, heritage and preservation, planning and stabilization, and partnerships with State and regional arts agencies.

Sources of Information

Grants Persons interested in applying for a grant in the arts should contact the appropriate discipline Director at the National Endowment for the Arts. Phone, 202–682–5400.

Publications A report of the National Endowment for the Arts is issued annually and may be obtained, for a limited time, from the Public Information Office.

Information for prospective applicants may be obtained by requesting application guidelines from the Public Information Office.

For further information, contact the Public Information Office, National Endowment for the Arts, 1100 Pennsylvania Avenue NW., Washington, DC 20506–0001. Phone, 202–682–5400.

National Endowment for the Humanities

The National Endowment for the Humanities is an independent, grantmaking agency established by Congress in 1965 to support research, education, and public programs in the humanities.

According to the agency's authorizing legislation, the term "humanities" includes, but is not limited to, the study of the following: language, both modern and classical; linguistics; literature; history; jurisprudence; philosophy; archeology; comparative religion; ethics; the history, criticism, and theory of the arts; and those aspects of the social sciences that employ historical or philosophical approaches.

The Endowment makes grants to individuals, groups, or institutions—schools, colleges, universities, museums, public television stations, libraries, public agencies, and nonprofit private groups to increase understanding and appreciation of the humanities.

Challenge Grants Nonprofit institutions interested in developing new sources of long-term support for educational, scholarly, preservation, and public programs in the humanities may be assisted in these efforts by a challenge grant.

For further information, call 202–606–8309.

Education Through grants to educational institutions and fellowships to scholars and teachers, this division strengthens sustained thoughtful study of the humanities at all levels of education.

For further information, call 202–606–8376.

Federal/State Partnership Humanities committees in each of the 50 States, the Virgin Islands, Puerto Rico, the District of Columbia, the Northern Mariana Islands, American Samoa, and Guam receive grants from the Endowment, which they, in turn, grant to support humanities programs at the local level.

For further information, call 202–606–8254.

Preservation and Access This division supports projects that will create, preserve, and increase the availability of resources important for research, education, and public programming in the humanities.

For further information, call 202–606–8570.

Public Programs This division strives to fulfill the Endowment's mandate "to increase public understanding of the humanities" by supporting those institutions and organizations that develop and present humanities programming for general audiences.

For further information, call 202–606–8269.

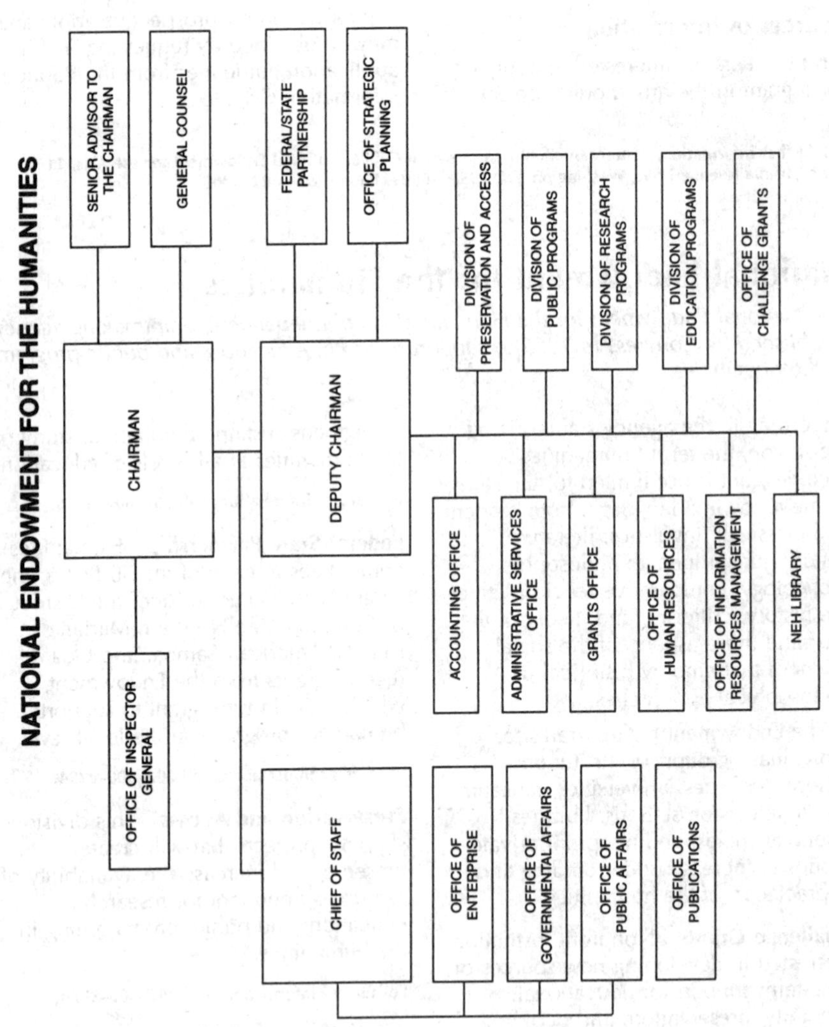
NATIONAL ENDOWMENT FOR THE HUMANITIES
SENIOR ADVISOR TO THE CHAIRMAN
GENERAL COUNSEL
CHAIRMAN
OFFICE OF INSPECTOR GENERAL
FEDERAL/STATE PARTNERSHIP
OFFICE OF STRATEGIC PLANNING
DEPUTY CHAIRMAN
CHIEF OF STAFF
DIVISION OF PRESERVATION AND ACCESS
DIVISION OF PUBLIC PROGRAMS
DIVISION OF RESEARCH PROGRAMS
DIVISION OF EDUCATION PROGRAMS
OFFICE OF CHALLENGE GRANTS
ACCOUNTING OFFICE
ADMINISTRATIVE SERVICES OFFICE
GRANTS OFFICE
OFFICE OF HUMAN RESOURCES
OFFICE OF INFORMATION RESOURCES MANAGEMENT
NEH LIBRARY
OFFICE OF ENTERPRISE
OFFICE OF GOVERNMENTAL AFFAIRS
OFFICE OF PUBLIC AFFAIRS
OFFICE OF PUBLICATIONS

Research This division promotes original research in the humanities by providing grants for significant research projects.

For further information, call 202–606–8200.

Sources of Information

Employment For employment information, contact the NEH Job Line. Phone, 202–606–8281.

Grants Those interested in applying for a grant in the humanities should request information, guidelines, and application forms from the Endowment's Office of Public Affairs, Room 401, 1100 Pennsylvania Avenue NW., Washington, DC 20506. Phone, 202–606–8400.

Publications The annual report and the *Overview of Endowment Programs* may be obtained from the Office of Public Affairs, National Endowment for the Humanities, Room 401, 1100 Pennsylvania Avenue NW., Washington, DC 20506. Phone, 202–606–8400.

The bimonthly review of issues in the humanities, entitled *Humanities,* is available by subscription ($22 domestic, $27.50 foreign) through the Superintendent of Documents, P.O. Box 371954, Pittsburgh, PA 15250–7954.

For further information, contact the Office of Public Affairs, National Endowment for the Humanities, Room 401, 1100 Pennsylvania Avenue NW., Washington, DC 20506. Phone, 202–606–8400. Internet, www.neh.gov. E-mail, info@neh.gov.

Institute of Museum and Library Services

The Institute of Museum and Library Services is an independent, grant-making agency that fosters leadership, innovation, and a lifetime of learning by supporting museums and libraries.

The Institute of Museum and Library Services was established within the National Foundation on the Arts and the Humanities by the Museum and Library Services Act of September 30, 1996 (110 Stat. 3009–293), which amended the Museum Services Act (20 U.S.C. 961 *et seq.*). The Institute combines administration of Federal museum programs formerly carried out by the Institute of Museum Services and Federal library programs formerly carried out by the Department of Education. The Institute's Director is appointed by the President with the advice and consent of the Senate and is authorized to make grants to museums and libraries. The Director receives policy advice on museum programs from the National Museum Services Board, which is comprised of 14 Presidentially appointed members and the Director.

In addition to providing distinct programs of support for museums and libraries, IMLS encourages collaboration between these community resources. The Institute's library programs help libraries use new technologies to identify, preserve, and share library and information resources across institutional, local, and State boundaries and to reach those for whom library use requires extra effort or special materials. Museum programs strengthen museum operations, improve care of collections, increase professional development opportunities, and enhance the community service role of museums.

IMLS awards grants to all types of museums and libraries. Eligible museums include art, history, general, children's, natural history, science and technology, as well as historic houses, zoos and aquariums, botanical gardens and arboretums, nature centers, and planetariums. Eligible libraries include public, school, academic, research, and special libraries. The Institute makes grants in 10 program categories.

States These grants improve electronic sharing of information and expand public access to an increasing wealth of information and services.

186-873 D-00--16

Native Americans This program provides small grants for core library operations of tribes and Alaska Native villages, technical assistance for these libraries, and enhancement grants to promote innovative practices in libraries serving Native Americans and Alaskan Native villages.
Native Hawaiians This program provides a single grant to an organization that primarily serves and represents Native Hawaiians.
National Leadership This program provides grants, contracts, and cooperative agreements to enhance the quality of library and museum services nationwide. The program supports model projects that can be widely replicated and encourages the use of promising practices in libraries and museums.
General Operating Support This program awards unrestricted grants to museums for ongoing institutional activities. General operating support, often cited as the most difficult type of money to raise, helps museums enhance their educational services, strengthen collections care, and raise funds from other sources.
Conservation Project Support This program awards matching grants to help museums identify conservation needs and priorities and perform activities to ensure the safekeeping of their collections.
Museum Assessment This program offers museums grants of technical assistance in the areas of institutional assessment, collections management assessment, and a public dimension assessment.
Conservation Assessment The program provides eligible museums with an alternative source of general conservation survey grants. For more information, contact the Conservation Assessment Program, Suite 566, 1730 K Street NW., Washington, DC 20006. Phone, 202–634–1422.
National Award for Museum Service This program recognizes outstanding museums that provide meaningful public service for their communities.

Sources of Information

Electronic Access Information about IMLS programs, application guidelines, and lists of grantees are available electronically. Internet, www.imls.gov. E-mail, imlsinfo@imls.gov.
Grants, Contracts, and Cooperative Agreements For information about applying for IMLS funding, contact the appropriate program office. Museums should contact the Office of Museum Services, Institute of Museum and Library Services, Room 609, 1100 Pennsylvania Avenue NW., Washington, DC 20506 (phone, 202–606–8539). Libraries should contact the Office of Library Services, Institute of Museum and Library Services, Room 802, 1100 Pennsylvania Avenue NW., Washington, DC 20506 (phone, 202–606–5227).

For further information, contact the Office of Legislative and Public Affairs, Institute of Museum and Library Services, Room 510, 1100 Pennsylvania Avenue NW., Washington, DC 20506. Phone, 202–606–8536. Internet, www.imls.gov. E-mail, imlsinfo@imls.gov.

NATIONAL LABOR RELATIONS BOARD

1099 Fourteenth Street NW., Washington, DC 20570
Phone, 202–273–1000. TDD, 202–273–4300. Internet, www.nlrb.gov.

Chairman	JOHN C. TRUESDALE
Members	J. ROBERT BRAME III, SARAH M. FOX, PETER J. HURTGEN, WILMA B. LIEBMAN
Chief Administrative Law Judge	ROBERT A. GIANNASI

Director, Division of Administration	GLORIA J. JOSEPH
Director, Division of Information	DAVID B. PARKER
Director, Equal Employment Opportunity	ROBERT J. POINDEXTER
Executive Secretary	JOHN J. TONER
General Counsel	FRED L. FEINSTEIN
Inspector General	AILEEN C. ARMSTRONG
Solicitor	JOHN E. HIGGINS, JR.

[For the National Labor Relations Board statement of organization, see the *Federal Register* of June 14, 1979, 44 FR 34215]

The National Labor Relations Board is vested with the power to prevent and remedy unfair labor practices committed by private sector employers and unions and to safeguard employees' rights to organize and determine whether to have unions as their bargaining representative.

The National Labor Relations Board (NLRB) is an independent agency created by the National Labor Relations Act of 1935 (Wagner Act) (29 U.S.C. 167).

The Board is authorized to designate appropriate units for collective bargaining and to conduct secret ballot elections to determine whether employees desire representation by a labor organization.

Activities

NLRB has two principal functions: preventing and remedying unfair labor practices by employers and labor organizations or their agents, and conducting secret ballot elections among employees in appropriate collective-bargaining units to determine whether or not they desire to be represented by a labor organization in bargaining with employers about their wages, hours, and working conditions. The agency also conducts secret ballot elections among employees who have been covered by a union-security agreement to determine whether or not they wish to revoke their union's authority to make such agreements. In jurisdictional disputes between two or more unions, the Board determines which competing group of workers is entitled to perform the work involved.

The regional directors and their staffs process representation, unfair labor practice, and jurisdictional dispute cases. They issue complaints in unfair labor practice cases; seek settlement of unfair labor practice charges; obtain compliance with Board orders and court judgments; and petition district courts for injunctions to prevent or remedy unfair labor practices. The regional directors direct hearings in representation cases; conduct elections pursuant to the agreement of the parties or the decision-making authority delegated to them by the Board or pursuant to Board directions; and issue certifications of representatives when unions win or certify the results when unions lose employee elections. They process petitions for bargaining unit clarification, for amendment of certification, and for rescission of a labor organization's authority to make a union-shop agreement. They also conduct national emergency employee referendums.

Administrative law judges conduct hearings in unfair labor practice cases, make findings of fact and conclusions of law, and recommend remedies for violations found. Their decisions can be appealed to the Board for a final agency determination. The Board's decisions are subject to review in the U.S. courts of appeals.

Field Offices—National Labor Relations Board
(HQ: Headquarters; RO: Resident office; SR: Subregion)

Office/Address	Director	Telephone	Fax
Region 1, 6th Fl., 10 Causeway St., Boston, MA 02222–1072	Rosemary Pye	617–565–6700	617–565–6725

Field Offices—National Labor Relations Board—Continued
(HQ: Headquarters; RO: Resident office; SR: Subregion)

Office/Address	Director	Telephone	Fax
Region 2, Rm. 3614, 26 Federal Plz., New York, NY 10278–0104.	Daniel Silverman	212–264–0300	212–264–8427
Region 3	Sandra Dunbar		
Rm. 901, 111 W. Huron St., Buffalo, NY 14202–2387 (HQ)		716–551–4931	716–551–4972
Rm. 342, Clinton Ave. at N. Pearl St., Albany, NY 12207–2350 (RO).	Jon Mackle	518–431–4155	518–431–4157
Region 4, 7th Fl., 615 Chestnut St., Philadelphia, PA 19106–4404.	Dorothy L. Moore-Duncan	215–597–7601	215–597–7658
Region 5	Louis J. D'Amico		
8th Fl., 103 S. Gay St., Baltimore, MD 21202–4026 (HQ)		410–962–2822	410–962–2198
Suite 5530, 1099 14th St., Washington, DC 20570–0001 (RO)	Karen V. Gearhard	202–208–3000	202–208–3013
Region 6, Rm. 1501, 1000 Liberty Ave., Pittsburgh, PA 15222–4173.	Gerald Kobell	412–395–4400	412–395–5986
Region 7	William C. Schaub, Jr.		
Rm. 300, 477 Michigan Ave., Detroit, MI 48226–2569 (HQ)		313–226–3200	313–226–2090
Rm. 330, 82 Ionia NW., Grand Rapids, MI 49503–3022 (RO)	Chet H. Byerly, Jr.	616–456–2679	616–456–2596
Region 8, Rm. 1695, 1240 E. 9th St., Cleveland, OH 44199–2086.	Frederick Calatrello	216–522–3715	216–522–2418
Region 9, Rm. 3003, 550 Main St., Cincinnati, OH 45202–3721	Richard L. Ahearn	513–684–3686	513–684–3946
Region 10	Martin M. Arlook		
Suite 1000, Harris Twr., 233 Peachtree St. NE., Atlanta, GA 30303 (HQ).		404–331–2896	404–331–2858
3d Fl., 1900 3d Ave. N., Birmingham, AL 35203–3502 (RO)	C. Douglas Marshall	205–731–1062	205–731–0955
Region 11, Suite 200, 4035 University Pkwy., Winston-Salem, NC 27106–3325.	Willie L. Clark, Jr.	336–631–5201	336–631–5210
Region 12	Rochelle Kentov		
Suite 530, 201 E. Kennedy Blvd., Tampa, FL 33602–5824 (HQ)		813–228–2641	813–228–2874
Rm. 214, 400 W. Bay St., Jacksonville, FL 32202–4412 (RO)	James L. McDonald	904–232–3768	904–232–3146
Rm. 1320, 51 SW. 1st Ave., Miami, FL 33130–1608 (RO)	Hector O. Nava	305–536–5391	305–536–5320
Region 13, Suite 800, 200 W. Adams St., Chicago, IL 60606–5208.	Elizabeth Kinney	312–353–7570	312–886–1341
Region 14, Rm. 8.302, 1222 Spruce St., St. Louis, MO 63103–2829.	Ralph R. Tremain	314–539–7770	314–539–7794
Region 15, Rm. 610, 1515 Poydras St., New Orleans, LA 70112–3723.	Curtis A. Wells	504–589–6361	504–589–4069
Region 16	(Vacancy)		
Rm. 8A24, 819 Taylor St., Fort Worth, TX 76102–6178 (HQ)		817–978–2921	817–978–2928
Suite 1545, 1919 Smith St., Houston, TX 77002–2649 (RO)	Ruth E. Small	713–209–4888	713–209–4890
Rm. 565, 615 E. Houston St., San Antonio, TX 78206–2040 (RO).	Ruben R. Armendariz	210–229–6140	210–472–6143
Region 17	F. Rozier Sharp		
Suite 100, 8600 Farley St., Overland Park, KS 66212–4677 (HQ)		913–967–3000	913–967–3010
Rm. 318, 224 S. Boulder Ave., Tulsa, OK 74103–4214 (RO)	Francis Molenda	918–581–7951	918–581–7970
Region 18	Ronald M. Sharp		
Suite 790, 330 S. 2d Ave., Minneapolis, MN 55401–2221 (HQ)		612–348–1757	612–348–1785
Rm. 439, 210 Walnut St., Des Moines, IA 50309–2116 (RO)	Morris E. Petersen	515–284–4391	515–284–4713
Region 19	Paul Eggert		
Rm. 2948, 915 2d Ave., Seattle, WA 98174–1078 (HQ)		206–220–6300	206–220–6305
No. 21, 222 W. 7th Ave., Anchorage, AK 99513–3546 (RO)	Minoru Hayashi	907–271–5015	907–271–3055
Suite 1920, 601 SW. 2d Ave., Portland, OR 97204 (SR 36)	Cathleen Shelton	503–326–3085	503–326–5387
Region 20	Robert H. Miller		
Suite 400, 901 Market St., San Francisco, CA 94103–1735 (HQ)		415–356–5130	415–356–5156
Rm. 7–245, 300 Ala Moana Blvd., Honolulu, HI 96850–4980 (SR 37).	Thomas W. Cestare	808–541–2814	808–541–2818
Region 21	Victoria E. Aguayo		
9th Fl., 888 S. Figueroa St., Los Angeles, CA 90017–5455 (HQ)		213–894–5200	213–894–2778
Suite 302, 555 W. Beech St., San Diego, CA 92101–2939 (RO)	Steven J. Sorensen	619–557–6184	619–557–6358
Region 22, Rm. 1600, 970 Broad St., Newark, NJ 07102–2570	Gary T. Kendellen	973–645–2100	973–645–3852
Region 24, Suite 1002, 525 F.D. Roosevelt Ave., Hato Rey, PR 00918–1720.	Mary Zelma Asseo	787–766–5347	787–766–5478
Region 25, Rm. 238, 575 N. Pennsylvania St., Indianapolis, IN 46204–1577.	Roberto G. Chavarry	317–226–7381	317–226–5103
Region 26	(Vacancy)		
Suite 800, 1407 Union Ave., Memphis, TN 38104–3627 (HQ)		901–544–0018	901–544–0008
Suite 375, 425 W. Capitol Ave., Little Rock, AR 72201–3489 (RO).	(Vacancy)	501–324–6311	501–324–5009
3d Fl., 801 Broadway, Nashville, TN 37203–3816 (RO)	Joseph H. Artilles	615–736–5921	615–736–7761
Region 27, 7th Fl. N. Twr., 600 17th St., Denver, CO 80202–5433.	B. Allan Benson	303–844–3551	303–844–6249
Region 28	Cornele A. Overstreet		
Suite 440, 234 N. Central Ave., Phoenix, AZ 85004–2212 (HQ)		602–379–3361	602–379–4982
Suite 1820, 505 Marquette Ave. NW., Albuquerque, NM 87102–2181 (RO).	(Vacancy)	505–248–5125	505–248–5134

Field Offices—National Labor Relations Board—Continued
(HQ: Headquarters; RO: Resident office; SR: Subregion)

Office/Address	Director	Telephone	Fax
Suite 400, 600 Las Vegas Blvd. S., Las Vegas, NV 89101–6637 (RO).	(Vacancy)	702–388–6416	702–388–6248
P.O. Box 23159, El Paso, TX 79923–3159 (RA)	Chris Lerma	915–565–2470	915–565–0847
Region 29, 10th Fl., Jay St. & Myrtle Ave., Brooklyn, NY 11201–4201.	Alvin P. Blyer	718–330–7713	718–330–7579
Region 30, Suite 700, 310 W. Wisconsin Ave., Milwaukee, WI 53203–2211.	Philip E. Bloedorn	414–297–3861	414–297–3880
Region 31, Suite 700, 11150 W. Olympic Blvd., Los Angeles, CA 90064–1824.	James J. McDermott	310–235–7352	310–235–7420
Region 32, Rm. 300N, 1301 Clay St., Oakland, CA 94612–5211	James S. Scott	510–637–3300	510–637–3315
Region 33, Suite 200, 300 Hamilton Blvd., Peoria, IL 61602–1246.	Glenn A. Zipp	309–671–7080	309–671–7095
Region 34, 21st Fl., 280 Trumbull St., Hartford, CT 06103–3503	Peter B. Hoffman	860–240–3522	860–240–3564

Sources of Information

Contracts Prospective suppliers of goods and services may inquire about agency procurement and contracting practices by writing to the Chief, Procurement and Facilities Branch, National Labor Relations Board, Washington, DC 20570. Phone, 202–273–4040.

Electronic Access Information about the Board's programs and activities is available through the Internet, at www.nlrb.gov.

Employment The Board appoints administrative law judges from a register established by the Office of Personnel Management. The agency hires attorneys, stenographers, and typists for all its offices; field examiners for its field offices; and administrative personnel for its Washington office. Inquiries regarding college and law school recruiting programs should be directed to the nearest regional office. Employment inquiries and applications may be sent to any regional office or the Washington personnel office.

Publications Anyone desiring to inspect formal case documents or read agency publications may use facilities of the Washington or field offices. The agency will assist in arranging reproduction of documents and order transcripts of hearings. The Board's offices offer free informational leaflets in limited quantities: *The National Labor Relations Board and YOU (Unfair Labor Practices)*, *The National Labor Relations Board and YOU (Representation Cases)*, *Your Government Conducts an Election for You on the Job*, and *The National Labor Relations Board—What It Is, What It Does*. The Superintendent of Documents, Government Printing Office, Washington, DC 20402, sells *A Guide to Basic Law and Procedures Under the NLRA*, the *Annual Report*, the *Classified Index of National Labor Relations Board Decisions and Related Court Decisions*, volumes of Board decisions, and a number of subscription services, including the *NLRB Casehandling Manual* (in three parts), the *Weekly Summary of NLRB Cases*, the *NLRB Election Report*, and *An Outline of Law and Procedure in Representation Cases*.

Speakers To give the public and persons appearing before the agency a better understanding of the National Labor Relations Act and the Board's policies, procedures, and services, Washington and regional office personnel participate as speakers or panel members before bar associations, labor, educational, civic, or management organizations, and other groups. Requests for speakers or panelists may be made to Washington officials or to the appropriate regional director.

For further information, contact the Information Division, National Labor Relations Board, 1099 Fourteenth Street NW., Washington, DC 20570. Phone, 202–273–1991. Internet, www.nlrb.gov.

NATIONAL MEDIATION BOARD

Suite 250 East, 1301 K Street NW., Washington, DC 20572
Phone, 202–692–5000. Internet, www.nmb.gov.

Chairman	ERNEST W. DUBESTER
Members	FRANCIS J. DUGGAN, MAGDALENA G. JACOBSEN
Chief of Staff	STEPHEN E. CRABLE
Senior Mediators	JOHN BAVIS, LARRY GIBBONS
General Counsel	RONALD M. ETTERS
Senior Hearing Officers	MARY JOHNSON, BENETTA MANSFIELD, SEAN ROGERS
Director of Public Affairs	JAMES E. ARMSHAW
Senior Research Analyst	DONALD L. WEST
Director of Arbitration Services	ROLAND WATKINS
Chief Financial Officer/Administration Officer	JUNE D.W. KING

The National Mediation Board assists in maintaining a free flow of commerce in the railroad and airline industries by resolving labor-management disputes that could disrupt travel or imperil the economy. The Board also handles railroad and airline employee representation disputes and provides administrative and financial support in adjusting grievances in the railroad industry.

The National Mediation Board was created on June 21, 1934, by an act amending the Railway Labor Act. (45 U.S.C. 151–158, 160–162, 1181–1188).

The Board's major responsibilities include preventing interruptions to interstate commerce in the airline and railroad industries; ensuring the right of employees to freely determine whether they wish to be represented for collective bargaining purposes; ensuring the independence of labor and management for self-organization to carry out the purposes of the Railway Labor Act; and providing for the prompt and orderly settlement of disputes in collective bargaining and over the interpretation of existing collective bargaining agreements.

Disputes arising out of grievances or interpretation or application of agreements concerning rates of pay, rules, or working conditions in the railroad industry are referable to the National Railroad Adjustment Board. This Board is divided into four divisions and consists of an equal number of representatives of the carriers and of national organizations of employees. In deadlocked cases the National Mediation Board is authorized to appoint a referee to sit with the members of the division for the purpose of making an award.

In the airline industry no national airline adjustment board has been established for settlement of grievances. Over the years the employee organizations and air carriers with established bargaining relationships have agreed to grievance procedures with final jurisdiction resting with a system board of adjustment. The Board is frequently called upon to name a neutral referee to serve on a system board when the parties are deadlocked and cannot agree on such an appointment themselves.

Activities

Alternative Dispute Resolution In addition to traditional mediation services, the Board provides alternative dispute resolution services. These services include premediation facilitation, training, and grievance mediation. The purpose of the program is to assist the parties in learning and applying more constructive, less confrontational methods for resolving their disputes and to resolve more of their own disputes without outside intervention.

Arbitration The Board provides grievance and interest arbitration for collective bargaining disputes. Grievance arbitration involves interpreting or applying an existing collective bargaining agreement. Interest arbitration is the process to establish terms of a new or modified collective bargaining agreement through arbitration instead of negotiation. Arbitration decisions are final and binding.

Mediation Disputes The National Mediation Board is charged with mediating disputes between carriers and labor organizations relating to initial contract negotiations or subsequent changes in rates of pay, rules, and working conditions. When the parties fail to reach accord in direct bargaining, either party may request the Board's services or the Board may on its own motion invoke its services. Thereafter, negotiations continue until the Board determines that its efforts to mediate have been unsuccessful, at which time it seeks to induce the parties to submit the dispute to arbitration. If either party refuses to arbitrate, the Board issues a notice stating that the parties have failed to resolve their dispute through mediation. This notice commences a 30-day cooling-off period after which self-help is normally available to either or both parties.

Employee Representation If a dispute arises among a carrier's employees as to who is to be the representative of such employees, it is the Board's duty to investigate such dispute and to determine by secret-ballot election or other appropriate means whether or not and to whom a representation certification should be issued. In the course of making this determination, the Board must determine the craft or class in which the employees seeking representation properly belong.

Presidential Emergency Boards The Board has the duty of notifying the President when the parties have failed to reach agreement through the Board's mediation efforts and that the labor dispute, in the judgment of the Board, threatens substantially to interrupt interstate commerce to a degree such as to deprive any section of the country of essential transportation service. In these cases, the President may, at his discretion, appoint an Emergency Board to investigate and report to him on the dispute. Self-help is barred for 60 days after appointment of the emergency board.

Sources of Information

Electronic Access Information pertaining to Board operations including weekly case activity reports, representation determinations, press releases, and a range of documents and forms is available on the Internet, at www.nmb.gov.

Publications The following documents are available for public distribution: *Determinations of the National Mediation Board* (26 volumes); *Interpretations Pursuant to Section 5, Second of the Act* (2 volumes); annual reports of the National Mediation Board including the report of the National Railroad Adjustment Board; *The Railway Labor Act at Fifty;* and *The National Mediation Board at Fifty—Its Impact on Railroad and Airline Labor Disputes.*

Reading Room Copies of collective-bargaining agreements between labor and management of various rail and air carriers are available for public inspection At the Board's headquarters in Washington, DC, by appointment, during office hours (1 to 4 p.m., Monday through Friday).

For further information, contact the Chief of Staff, National Mediation Board, Suite 250 East, 1301 K Street NW., Washington, DC 20572. Phone, 202–523–5920. Fax, 202–523–1494. Internet, www.nmb.gov.

NATIONAL RAILROAD PASSENGER CORPORATION (AMTRAK)

60 Massachusetts Avenue NE., Washington, DC 20002
Phone, 202–906–3000. Internet, www.amtrak.com.

Board of Directors:	
Chairman	TOMMY THOMPSON
Members	SYLVIA DE LEON, MICHAEL DUKAKIS, LINWOOD HOLTON, AMY ROSEN, JOHN ROBERT SMITH
Member *ex officio* (Secretary of Transportation)	RODNEY E. SLATER
Officers:	
President and Chief Executive Officer	GEORGE D. WARRINGTON
Chief Financial Officer	ARLENE FRINER
President, Amtrak Intercity	ED WALKER
President, Amtrak Northeast Corridor	E.S. BAGLEY, JR.
President, Amtrak West	GILBERT O. MALLERY
Executive Vice President	BARBARA RICHARDSON
Senior Vice President and General Counsel	JAMES LLOYD
Vice President and Counsel, Business Diversity and Strategic Initiatives	WANDA HIGHTOWER
Vice President, Freight Railroad Affairs	LEE BULLOCK
Vice President, Government Affairs	SANDRA J. BROWN
Vice President, High Speed Rail Development	DAVID J. CAROL
Vice President, Human Resources	LORRAINE A. GREEN
Vice President, Labor	JOSEPH M. BRESS
Vice President, Procurement	MICHAEL RIENZI
Vice President, Service Operations	ANNE W. HOEY

[For the National Railroad Passenger Corporation statement of organization, see the *Code of Federal Regulations*, Title 49, Part 700]

The National Railroad Passenger Corporation was established to develop the potential of modern rail service in meeting the Nation's intercity passenger transportation needs.

The National Railroad Passenger Corporation (Amtrak) was created by the Rail Passenger Service Act of 1970, as amended (49 U.S.C. 241), and was incorporated under the laws of the District of Columbia to provide a balanced national transportation system by developing, operating, and improving U.S. intercity rail passenger service.

Amtrak operates an average of 212 trains per day, serving over 540 station locations in 45 States, over a system of approximately 24,500 route miles. Of this route system, Amtrak owns less than 1,000 track miles in the Northeast Corridor (Washington-New York-Boston; New Haven-Springfield; Philadelphia-Harrisburg), and several other small track segments throughout the country.

Amtrak owns or leases its stations and owns its own repair and maintenance facilities. The Corporation employs a total work force of approximately 23,000 and provides all reservation, station, and on-board service staffs, as well as train and engine operating crews. Outside the Northeast Corridor, Amtrak has historically contracted with 14 privately owned railroads for the right to operate over their track and has compensated each railroad for its total package of services. Under contract, these railroads are responsible for the condition of the roadbed and for coordinating the flow of traffic.

In fiscal year 1999, Amtrak transported over 21 million people approximately 5.5 billion passenger miles. In addition, under contracts with several transit agencies, Amtrak carried over 48 million commuters.

Although Amtrak's basic route system was originally designated by the Secretary of Transportation in 1971, modifications have been made to the Amtrak system and to individual routes that have resulted in more efficient and cost-effective operations. Currently, in the face of ongoing budget constraints, new service will only be added if a State agrees to share any losses associated with the new service or if the new service demonstrates satisfactory market support.

Amtrak began operation in 1971 with an antiquated fleet of equipment inherited from private railroads; some cars were nearly 30 years old. Since then, the fleet has been modernized and new state-of-the-art single- and bi-level passenger cars and locomotives have been added.

Ridership is steadily rising, and Amtrak is finding it increasingly difficult to meet the demands of increased travel patterns with its limited passenger fleet. To ease these equipment constraints, the Corporation is working to identify innovative funding sources in order to acquire additional passenger cars and locomotives.

Although no rail passenger system in the world makes a profit, Amtrak has made significant progress in reducing its dependence on Federal support, while at the same time improving the quality of service. Every year Amtrak moves closer to increasing the ratio of its earned revenue to total costs, even though its Federal appropriations decrease. Amtrak's appropriation for the current fiscal year is approximately 50 percent below that for fiscal year 1978 (in constant dollars).

For further information, contact the Public Affairs Department, Amtrak, 60 Massachusetts Avenue NE., Washington, DC 20002. Phone, 202–906–3860. Internet, www.amtrak.com.

NATIONAL SCIENCE FOUNDATION

4201 Wilson Boulevard, Arlington, VA 22230
Phone, 703–306–1234. Internet, www.nsf.gov.

National Science Board

Chairman	EAMON M. KELLY
Vice Chairman	ANITA K. JONES
Members	JOHN A. ARMSTRONG, PAMELA A. FERGUSON, MARY K. GAILLARD, M.R.C. GREENWOOD, STANLEY V. JASKOLSKI, GEORGE M. LANGFORD, JOSEPH A. MILLER, JR., ROBERT C. RICHARDSON, MICHAEL G. ROSSMANN, VERA C. RUBIN, MAXINE L. SAVITZ, LUIS SEQUERIA, DANIEL SIMBERLOFF, BOB H. SUZUKI, RICHARD A. TAPIA, CHANG-LIN TIEN, (6 VACANCIES)
(*Ex officio*)	RITA R. COLWELL

Executive Officer	MARTA C. CEHELSKY
Inspector General	CHRISTINE C. BOESZ
Officials:	
Director	RITA R. COLWELL
Deputy Director	JOSEPH BORDOGNA
Assistant Director for Biological Sciences	MARY E. CLUTTER
Assistant Director for Computer and Information Science and Engineering	RUZENA BAJCSY
Assistant Director for Education and Human Resources	JUDITH S. SUNLEY, *Acting*
Assistant Director for Engineering	LOUIS MARTIN-VEGA, *Acting*
Assistant Director for Geosciences	MARGARET S. LEINEIN
Assistant Director for Mathematical and Physical Sciences	ROBERT A. EISENSTEIN
Assistant Director for Social, Behavioral, and Economic Sciences	NORMAN M. BRADBURN
Chief Financial Officer and Director, Office of Budget, Finance, and Award Management	THOMAS N. COOLEY, *Acting*
Director, Office of Integrative Activities	NATHANIEL G. PITTS
Director, Office of Legislative and Public Affairs	MICHAEL C. SIEVERTS, *Acting*
Director, Office of Polar Programs	KARL A. ERB
Director, Office of Information and Resource Management	LINDA P. MASSARO
General Counsel	LAWRENCE RUDOLPH

[For the National Science Foundation statement of organization, see the *Federal Register* of February 8, 1993, 58 FR 7587–7595; May 27, 1993, 58 FR 30819; May 2, 1994, 59 FR 22690; and Oct. 6, 1995, 60 FR 52431]

The National Science Foundation promotes the progress of science and engineering through the support of research and education programs. Its major emphasis is on high-quality, merit-selected research—the search for improved understanding of the fundamental laws of nature upon which our future well-being as a nation depends. Its educational programs are aimed at ensuring increased understanding of science and engineering at all educational levels, maintaining an adequate supply of scientists, engineers, and science educators to meet our country's needs.

The National Science Foundation is an independent agency created by the National Science Foundation Act of 1950, as amended (42 U.S.C. 1861–1875).

The purposes of the Foundation are: to increase the Nation's base of scientific and engineering knowledge and strengthen its ability to conduct research in all areas of science and engineering; to develop and help implement science and engineering education programs that can better prepare the Nation for meeting the challenges of the future; and to promote international cooperation through science and engineering. In its role as a leading Federal supporter of science and engineering, the agency also has an important role in national policy planning.

The Foundation consists of a National Science Board and a Director. The National Science Board is composed of 24 members and the Director *ex officio*. Members are appointed by the President with the advice and consent of the Senate, for 6-year terms, with one-third appointed every 2 years. They are selected because of their records of distinguished service in science, engineering, education, research management, or public affairs to be

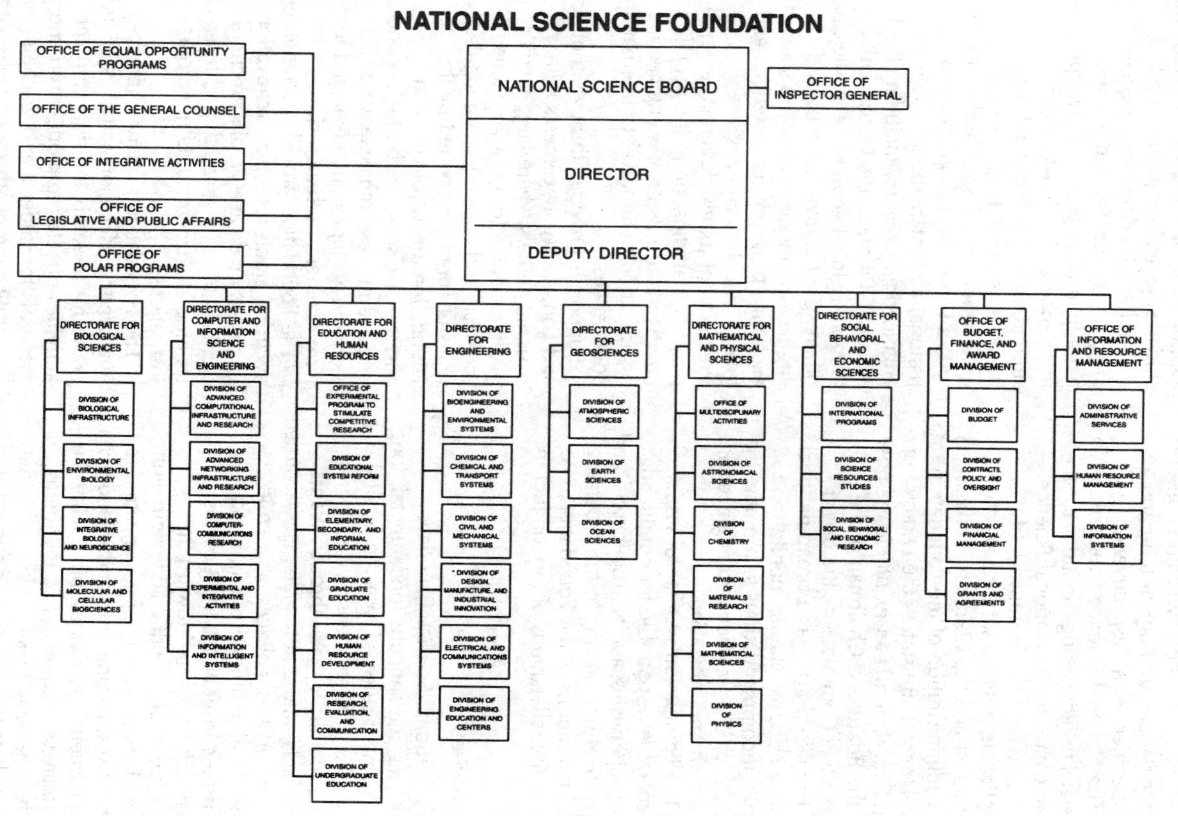
NATIONAL SCIENCE FOUNDATION
OFFICE OF EQUAL OPPORTUNITY PROGRAMS
OFFICE OF THE GENERAL COUNSEL
OFFICE OF INTEGRATIVE ACTIVITIES
OFFICE OF LEGISLATIVE AND PUBLIC AFFAIRS
OFFICE OF POLAR PROGRAMS
NATIONAL SCIENCE BOARD
DIRECTOR
DEPUTY DIRECTOR
OFFICE OF INSPECTOR GENERAL
DIRECTORATE FOR BIOLOGICAL SCIENCES
DIVISION OF BIOLOGICAL INFRASTRUCTURE
DIVISION OF ENVIRONMENTAL BIOLOGY
DIVISION OF INTEGRATIVE BIOLOGY AND NEUROSCIENCE
DIVISION OF MOLECULAR AND CELLULAR BIOSCIENCES
DIRECTORATE FOR COMPUTER AND INFORMATION SCIENCE AND ENGINEERING
DIVISION OF ADVANCED COMPUTATIONAL INFRASTRUCTURE AND RESEARCH
DIVISION OF ADVANCED NETWORKING INFRASTRUCTURE AND RESEARCH
DIVISION OF COMPUTER-COMMUNICATIONS RESEARCH
DIVISION OF EXPERIMENTAL AND INTEGRATIVE ACTIVITIES
DIVISION OF INFORMATION AND INTELLIGENT SYSTEMS
DIRECTORATE FOR EDUCATION AND HUMAN RESOURCES
OFFICE OF EXPERIMENTAL PROGRAM TO STIMULATE COMPETITIVE RESEARCH
DIVISION OF EDUCATIONAL SYSTEM REFORM
DIVISION OF ELEMENTARY, SECONDARY, AND INFORMAL EDUCATION
DIVISION OF GRADUATE EDUCATION
DIVISION OF HUMAN RESOURCE DEVELOPMENT
DIVISION OF RESEARCH, EVALUATION, AND COMMUNICATION
DIVISION OF UNDERGRADUATE EDUCATION
DIRECTORATE FOR ENGINEERING
DIVISION OF BIOENGINEERING AND ENVIRONMENTAL SYSTEMS
DIVISION OF CHEMICAL AND TRANSPORT SYSTEMS
DIVISION OF CIVIL AND MECHANICAL SYSTEMS
* DIVISION OF DESIGN, MANUFACTURE, AND INDUSTRIAL INNOVATION
DIVISION OF ELECTRICAL AND COMMUNICATIONS SYSTEMS
DIVISION OF ENGINEERING EDUCATION AND CENTERS
DIRECTORATE FOR GEOSCIENCES
DIVISION OF ATMOSPHERIC SCIENCES
DIVISION OF EARTH SCIENCES
DIVISION OF OCEAN SCIENCES
DIRECTORATE FOR MATHEMATICAL AND PHYSICAL SCIENCES
OFFICE OF MULTIDISCIPLINARY ACTIVITIES
DIVISION OF ASTRONOMICAL SCIENCES
DIVISION OF CHEMISTRY
DIVISION OF MATERIALS RESEARCH
DIVISION OF MATHEMATICAL SCIENCES
DIVISION OF PHYSICS
DIRECTORATE FOR SOCIAL, BEHAVIORAL, AND ECONOMIC SCIENCES
DIVISION OF INTERNATIONAL PROGRAMS
DIVISION OF SCIENCE RESOURCES STUDIES
DIVISION OF SOCIAL, BEHAVIORAL, AND ECONOMIC RESEARCH
OFFICE OF BUDGET, FINANCE, AND AWARD MANAGEMENT
DIVISION OF BUDGET
DIVISION OF CONTRACTS, POLICY, AND OVERSIGHT
DIVISION OF FINANCIAL MANAGEMENT
DIVISION OF GRANTS AND AGREEMENTS
OFFICE OF INFORMATION AND RESOURCE MANAGEMENT
DIVISION OF ADMINISTRATIVE SERVICES
DIVISION OF HUMAN RESOURCE MANAGEMENT
DIVISION OF INFORMATION SYSTEMS

broadly representative of the views of national science and engineering leadership. The Director and the Deputy Director are also appointed by the President, with the advice and consent of the Senate, to a 6-year term and an unspecified term, respectively.

The National Science Foundation Act assigns policymaking functions for the Foundation to the National Science Board, within the framework of applicable policies set forth by the President and the Congress, and assigns the administration of the Foundation to the Director. By statute the Director of the Foundation is an *ex officio* member of the Board and Chairman of the Executive Committee of the Board.

The Board also has a broad national policy responsibility to monitor and make recommendations to promote the health of U.S. science and engineering research and education.

The Foundation's Office of Inspector General is responsible for conducting and supervising audits, inspections, and investigations relating to the programs and operations of the Foundation, including allegations of misconduct in science.

Activities

The National Science Foundation initiates and supports fundamental, long-term, merit-selected research in all the scientific and engineering disciplines. This support is made through grants, contracts, and other agreements awarded to universities, colleges, academic consortia, and nonprofit and small business institutions. Most of this research is directed toward the resolution of scientific and engineering questions concerning fundamental life processes, natural laws and phenomena, fundamental processes influencing the human environment, and the forces affecting people as members of society as well as the behavior of society as a whole.

The Foundation encourages cooperative efforts by universities, industries, and government. It also promotes the application of research and development for better products and services that improve the quality of life and stimulate economic growth.

The Foundation promotes the development of research talent through support of undergraduate and graduate students, as well as postdoctoral researchers. It administers special programs to identify and encourage participation by groups underrepresented in science and technology and to strengthen research capability at smaller institutions, small businesses, undergraduate colleges, and universities.

The Foundation supports major national and international science and engineering activities, including the U.S. Antarctic Program, the Ocean Drilling Program, global geoscience studies, and others. Cooperative scientific and engineering research activities support exchange programs for American and foreign scientists and engineers, execution of jointly designed research projects, participation in the activities of international science and engineering organizations, and travel to international conferences.

Support is provided through contracts and cooperative agreements with national centers where large facilities are made available for use by qualified scientists and engineers. Among the types of centers supported by the Foundation are astronomy and atmospheric sciences, biological and engineering research, science and technology, supercomputers, and long-term ecological research sites.

The Foundation provides competitively awarded grants for repair, renovation, or, in exceptional cases, replacement of facilities used for research and research training at academic and nonprofit institutions.

The Foundation's science and engineering education activities include grants for research and development activities directed to model instructional materials for students and teachers and the application of advanced technologies to education. Grants also are available for teacher preparation and enhancement and informal science education activities. Funding is also provided for college science instrumentation, course and curriculum improvement, faculty and student activities, and minority resource centers. In addition, studies of the status of math, science, and engineering education are supported.

The National Science Board presents the Vannevar Bush Award annually to a person who, through public service activities in science and technology, has made an outstanding contribution toward the welfare of mankind and the Nation. It also presents the Public Service Award to an individual and to a company, corporation, or organization who, through contributions to public service in areas other than research, have increased the public understanding of science or engineering. The National Science Foundation annually presents the Alan T. Waterman Award to an outstanding young scientist or engineer for support of research and study. The Foundation also provides administrative support for the President's Committee on the National Medal of Science.

Information on these awards is available through the Internet, at www.nsf.gov/home/nsb/start.htm.

Sources of Information

Board and Committee Minutes Summary minutes of the open meetings of the Board may be obtained from the National Science Board Office. Phone, 703–306–2000. Information on NSB meetings, minutes, and reports is available through the Internet, at www.nsf.gov/home/nsb/start.htm. Summary minutes of the Foundation's advisory groups may be obtained from the contacts listed in the notice of meetings published in the *Federal Register.* General information about the Foundation's advisory groups may be obtained from the Division of Human Resource Management, Room 315, Arlington, VA 22230. Phone, 703–306–1181.

Contracts The Foundation publicizes contracting and subcontracting opportunities in the *Commerce Business Daily* and other appropriate publications. Organizations seeking to undertake contract work for the Foundation should contact either the Division of Contracts, Policy, and Oversight (phone, 703–306–1242) or the Division of Administrative Services (phone, 703–306–1122), National Science Foundation, Arlington, VA 22230.

Electronic Access Information regarding NSF programs and services is available through the Internet, at www.nsf.gov.

Employment Inquiries may be directed to the Division of Human Resource Management, National Science Foundation, Room 315, Arlington, VA 22230. Phone, 703–306–1182, or, for the hearing impaired (TDD), 703–306–0189. The Foundation's vacancy hotline numbers are 703–306–0080 or 800–628–1487. Internet, www.nsf.gov.

Fellowships Consult the *NSF Guide to Programs* and appropriate announcements and brochures for postdoctoral fellowship opportunities that may be available through some Foundation divisions. Beginning graduate and minority graduate students wishing to apply for fellowships should contact the Directorate for Education and Human Resources. Phone, 703–306–1694.

Freedom of Information Act Requests Requests for agency records should be submitted in accordance with the Foundation FOIA regulation at 45 CFR part 612. Such requests should be clearly identified with "FOIA REQUEST" and be addressed to the FOIA Officer, Office of General Counsel, National Science Foundation, Room 1265, Arlington, VA 22230. Phone, 703–306–1060. Fax, 703–306–0149. E-mail, foia@nsf.gov.

Grants Individuals or organizations who plan to submit grant proposals should refer to the *NSF Guide to Programs, Grant Proposal Guide* (NSF 00–2), and appropriate program brochures and announcements that may be obtained as indicated in the Publications section. Grant information is also available electronically through the Internet, at www.nsf.gov.

Office of Inspector General General inquiries may be directed to the Office of Inspector General, National Science

Foundation, Room 1135, Arlington, VA 22230. Phone, 703–306–2100.

Privacy Act Requests Requests for personal records should be submitted in accordance with the Foundation Privacy Act regulation at 45 CFR, part 613. Such requests should be clearly identified with "PRIVACY ACT REQUEST" and be addressed to the Privacy Act Officer, National Science Foundation, Room 1265, Arlington, VA 22230. Phone, 703–306–1060.

Publications The National Science Board assesses the status and health of science and its various disciplines, including such matters as human and material resources, in reports submitted to the President for submission to the Congress. The most recent report is *Science and Engineering Indicators, 1998* (NSB–98–1).

The National Science Foundation issues publications that announce and describe new programs, critical dates, and application procedures for competitions. Single copies of these publications can be ordered by writing to NSF Clearinghouse, P.O. Box 218, Jessup, MD 20794–0218. Phone, 301–947–2722. E-mail, pubinfo@nsf.gov. Internet, www.nsf.gov.

Other Foundation publications include: the *Grant Policy Manual* (NSF–95–26), which contains comprehensive statements of Foundation grant administration policy, procedures, and guidance; *Guide to Programs,* which summarizes information about support programs; the quarterly *Antarctic Journal of the United States* and its annual review issue; and the *NSF Annual Report.* These publications are available from the Superintendent of Documents, Government Printing Office, Washington, DC 20402. Internet, www.nsf.gov.

Reading Room A collection of Foundation policy documents and staff instructions, as well as current indexes, are available to the public for inspection and copying during regular business hours, 8:30 a.m. to 5 p.m., Monday through Friday, in the National Science Foundation Library, Room 225, Arlington, VA 22230. Phone, 703–306–0658.

Small Business Activities The Office of Small Business Research and Development provides information on opportunities for Foundation support to small businesses with strong research capabilities in science and technology. Phone, 703–306–1330. The Office of Small and Disadvantaged Business Utilization oversees agency compliance with the provisions of the Small Business Act and the Small Business Investment Act of 1958, as amended (15 U.S.C. 631, 661, 683). Phone, 703–306–1330.

For further information, contact the National Science Foundation Information Center, 4201 Wilson Boulevard, Second Floor, Arlington, VA 22230. Phone, 703–306–1234. TDD, 703–306–0900. E-mail, info@nsf.gov. Internet, www.nsf.gov.

NATIONAL TRANSPORTATION SAFETY BOARD

490 L'Enfant Plaza SW., Washington, DC 20594
Phone, 202–314–6000. Internet, www.ntsb.gov.

Chairman	JAMES E. HALL
Vice Chairman	(VACANCY)
Members	GEORGE W. BLACK, JR., CAROL J. CARMODY, JOHN J. GOGLIA, JOHN A. HAMMERSCHMIDT
Managing Director	DAN CAMPBELL
Deputy Managing Director	JANE MACKALL
Chief Financial Officer	CRAIG E. KELLER, SR.

Chief Administrative Law Judge	WILLIAM E. FOWLER, JR.
General Counsel	RONALD S. BATTOCCHI
Deputy General Counsel	DAVID BASS
Director, Office of Aviation Safety	BERNARD S. LOEB
Deputy Director for International Aviation Safety Affairs	RONALD SCHLEEDE
Deputy Director for Regional Technical/ Investigative Operations	GENE SUNDEEN
Deputy Director for Technical/Investigative Operations	JOHN CLARK
Director, Office of Government, Public, and Family Affairs	JAMIE FINCH
Deputy Director for Family Affairs	SHARON BRYSON
Deputy Director for Public Affairs	TED LOPATKIEWICZ
Director, Office of Highway Safety	JOSEPH E. OSTERMAN
Deputy Directory	CLAUDE HARRIS
Director, Office of Marine Safety	MARJORIE M. MURTAGH
Director, Office of Pipeline and Hazardous Materials Safety	ROBERT J. CHIPKEVICH
Director, Office of Railroad Safety	ROBERT C. LAUBY
Director, Office of Research and Engineering	VERNON ELLINGSTAD
Deputy Director	JEFFREY MARCUS
Director, Office of Safety Recommendations and Accomplishments	BARRY M. SWEEDLER
Deputy Director	RICHARD VAN WOERKOM

[For the National Transportation Safety Board statement of organization, see the *Code of Federal Regulations*, Title 49, Part 800]

The National Transportation Safety Board seeks to ensure that all types of transportation in the United States are conducted safely. The Board investigates accidents, conducts studies, and makes recommendations to Government agencies, the transportation industry, and others on safety measures and practices.

The National Transportation Safety Board (NTSB) was established in 1967 and made totally independent on April 1, 1975, by the Independent Safety Board Act of 1974 (49 U.S.C. 1111).

The Safety Board consists of five members appointed by the President with the advice and consent of the Senate for 5-year terms. The President designates two of these members as Chairman and Vice Chairman of the Board for 2-year terms. The designation of the Chairman is made with the advice and consent of the Senate.

Activities

Accident Investigation The Board is responsible for investigating, determining probable cause, making safety recommendations, and reporting the facts and circumstances of:

—U.S. civil aviation and certain public-use aircraft accidents;

—railroad accidents in which there is a fatality or substantial property damage, or that involve a passenger train;

—pipeline accidents in which there is a fatality, substantial property damage, or significant injury to the environment;

—highway accidents, including railroad grade-crossing accidents, that the Board selects in cooperation with the States;

—major marine casualties, and marine accidents involving a public vessel and a nonpublic vessel, in accordance with regulations prescribed jointly by the Board and the U.S. Coast Guard;

—certain accidents involving hazardous materials; and

—other transportation accidents that are catastrophic, involve problems of a recurring character, or otherwise should

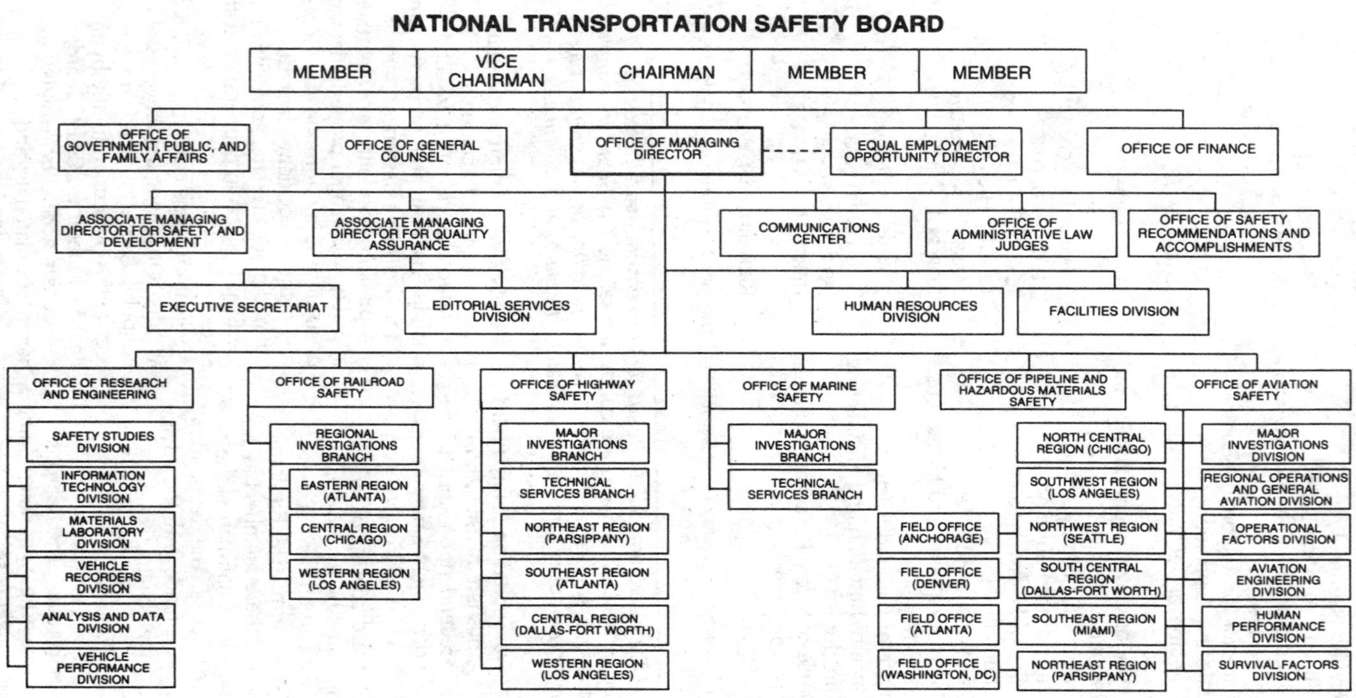
NATIONAL TRANSPORTATION SAFETY BOARD
MEMBER
VICE CHAIRMAN
CHAIRMAN
MEMBER
MEMBER
OFFICE OF GOVERNMENT, PUBLIC, AND FAMILY AFFAIRS
OFFICE OF GENERAL COUNSEL
OFFICE OF MANAGING DIRECTOR
EQUAL EMPLOYMENT OPPORTUNITY DIRECTOR
OFFICE OF FINANCE
ASSOCIATE MANAGING DIRECTOR FOR SAFETY AND DEVELOPMENT
ASSOCIATE MANAGING DIRECTOR FOR QUALITY ASSURANCE
COMMUNICATIONS CENTER
OFFICE OF ADMINISTRATIVE LAW JUDGES
OFFICE OF SAFETY RECOMMENDATIONS AND ACCOMPLISHMENTS
EXECUTIVE SECRETARIAT
EDITORIAL SERVICES DIVISION
HUMAN RESOURCES DIVISION
FACILITIES DIVISION
OFFICE OF RESEARCH AND ENGINEERING
SAFETY STUDIES DIVISION
INFORMATION TECHNOLOGY DIVISION
MATERIALS LABORATORY DIVISION
VEHICLE RECORDERS DIVISION
ANALYSIS AND DATA DIVISION
VEHICLE PERFORMANCE DIVISION
OFFICE OF RAILROAD SAFETY
REGIONAL INVESTIGATIONS BRANCH
EASTERN REGION (ATLANTA)
CENTRAL REGION (CHICAGO)
WESTERN REGION (LOS ANGELES)
OFFICE OF HIGHWAY SAFETY
MAJOR INVESTIGATIONS BRANCH
TECHNICAL SERVICES BRANCH
NORTHEAST REGION (PARSIPPANY)
SOUTHEAST REGION (ATLANTA)
CENTRAL REGION (DALLAS-FORT WORTH)
WESTERN REGION (LOS ANGELES)
OFFICE OF MARINE SAFETY
MAJOR INVESTIGATIONS BRANCH
TECHNICAL SERVICES BRANCH
OFFICE OF PIPELINE AND HAZARDOUS MATERIALS SAFETY
FIELD OFFICE (ANCHORAGE)
FIELD OFFICE (DENVER)
FIELD OFFICE (ATLANTA)
FIELD OFFICE (WASHINGTON, DC)
NORTH CENTRAL REGION (CHICAGO)
SOUTHWEST REGION (LOS ANGELES)
NORTHWEST REGION (SEATTLE)
SOUTH CENTRAL REGION (DALLAS-FORT WORTH)
SOUTHEAST REGION (MIAMI)
NORTHEAST REGION (PARSIPPANY)
OFFICE OF AVIATION SAFETY
MAJOR INVESTIGATIONS DIVISION
REGIONAL OPERATIONS AND GENERAL AVIATION DIVISION
OPERATIONAL FACTORS DIVISION
AVIATION ENGINEERING DIVISION
HUMAN PERFORMANCE DIVISION
SURVIVAL FACTORS DIVISION

be investigated in the judgment of the Board.

Safety Problem Identification In addition, the Board makes recommendations on matters pertaining to transportation safety and is a catalyst for transportation accident prevention by conducting safety studies and special investigations, assessing techniques of accident investigation and publishing recommended procedures for these investigations, establishing regulatory requirements for reporting accidents, evaluating the transportation safety consciousness and efficacy of other Government agencies in the prevention of accidents, evaluating the adequacy of safeguards and procedures concerning the transportation of hazardous materials and the performance of other Government agencies charged with ensuring the safe transportation of such materials, and reporting annually to the Congress on its activities.

Family Assistance for Aviation Disasters The Board coordinates the resources of the Federal Government and other organizations to support the efforts of local and State governments and airlines to meet the needs of aviation disaster victims and their families. NTSB assists in making Federal resources available to local authorities and airlines.

Certificate, Civil Penalty, or License Appeal The Board also reviews on appeal the suspension, amendment, modification, revocation, or denial of certain certificates, licenses, or assessments of civil penalties issued by the Secretary of Transportation and the decisions of the Commandant of the Coast Guard on appeals from the orders of any administrative law judge, revoking, suspending, or denying certain licenses, certificates, documents, or registers.

Regional/Field Offices—National Transportation Safety Board

(R: Regional Director; FC: Field Chief)

Region/Field Office	Address	Officer
AVIATION:		
North Central Region	31 W. 775 N. Ave., W. Chicago, IL 60185	Carl Dinwiddie (R)
South Central Region	Suite 150, 624 Six Flags Dr., Arlington, TX 76011	Tim Borson (R)
South Central Field	Suite 500, 4760 Oakland St., Denver, CO 80239	Norm Wiemeyer (FC)
Southwest Region	Suite 555, 1515 W. 190th St., Gardena, CA 90248	(Vacancy) (R)
Southeast Region	Suite B–103, 8405 NW. 53d St., Miami, FL 33166	Jorge Prellezo (R)
Southeast Field	Suite 3M25, 60 Forsyth St. SW., Atlanta, GA 30303	Preston Hicks (FC)
Northeast Region	Suite 203, 2001 Rte. 46, Parsippany, NJ 07054	Dennis Jones (R)
Northeast Field	490 L'Enfant Plz. SW., Washington, DC 20594	(Vacancy) (FC)
Northwest Region	Rm. 201, 19518 Pacific Hwy. S., Seattle, WA 98188	Keith McGuire (R)
Northwest Field	Box 11, Rm. 216, 222 W. 7th Ave., Anchorage, AK 99513	Jim LaBelle (FC)
RAILROAD:		
Central Region	31 W. 775 N. Ave., W. Chicago, IL 60185	(Vacancy) (R)
Western Region	Suite 555, 1515 W. 190th St., Gardena, CA 90248	Dave Watson (R)
Eastern Region	Suite 3M25, 60 Forsyth St. SW., Atlanta, GA 30303	(Vacancy) (R)
HIGHWAY:		
Central Region	Suite 150, 624 Six Flags Dr., Arlington, TX 76011	Kennith Rogers (R)
Western Region	Suite 555, 1515 W. 190th St., Gardena, CA 90248	Ronald Robinson (R)
Southeast Region	Suite 3M25, 60 Forsyth St. SW., Atlanta, GA 30303	Ken Suydam (R)
Northeast Region	Suite 203, 2001 Rte. 46, Parsippany, NJ 07054	Robert Accetta (R)

Sources of Information

Contracts and Procurement Inquiries regarding the Board's procurement and contracting activities should be addressed to the Contracting Officer, National Transportation Safety Board, Washington, DC 20594. Phone, 202–314–6220.

Electronic Access Agency information, including aircraft accident data, synopses of aircraft accidents, speeches and congressional testimony given by Board members and staff, press releases, job vacancy announcements, and notices of Board meetings, public hearings, and other agency events, is available in electronic form through the Internet, at www.ntsb.gov.

Employment Send applications for employment to the Human Resources

Division, National Transportation Safety Board, Washington, DC 20594. Phone, 202–314–6239.

Publications Publications are provided free of charge to the following categories of subscribers: Federal, State, or local transportation agencies; international transportation organizations or foreign governments; educational institutions or public libraries; nonprofit public safety organizations; and the news media. Persons in these categories who are interested in receiving copies of Board publications should contact the Public Inquiries Branch, National Transportation Safety Board, Washington, DC 20594. Phone, 202–314–6551. All other persons interested in receiving publications must purchase them from the National Technical Information Service, 5285 Port Royal Road, Springfield, VA 22161. Orders may be placed by telephone to the Subscription Unit at 703–487–4630, or the sales desk at 703–487–4768.

Reading Room The Board's Public Reference Room is available for record inspection or photocopying. It is located in Room 6500 at the Board's Washington, DC, headquarters and is open from 9 a.m. to 4 p.m. every business day. Requests for access to public records should be made in person at Room 6500, or by writing the Public Inquiries Branch, National Transportation Safety Board, Washington, DC 20594. Phone, 202–314–6551.

For further information, contact the Office of Public Affairs, National Transportation Safety Board, 490 L'Enfant Plaza SW., Washington, DC 20594. Phone, 202–314–6100. Fax, 202–314–6110. Internet, www.ntsb.gov.

NUCLEAR REGULATORY COMMISSION

Washington, DC 20555
Phone, 301–415–7000. Internet, www.nrc.gov.

Chairman	RICHARD A. MESERVE
Commissioners	GRETA JOY DICUS, NILS J. DIAZ, EDWARD MCGAFFIGAN, JR., JEFFREY S. MERRIFIELD
Chief Administrative Judge, Atomic Safety and Licensing Board Panel	G. PAUL BOLLWERK III
Director, Office of Commission Appellate Adjudication	JOHN F. CORDES
Director, Office of International Programs	JANICE DUNN LEE
General Counsel	KAREN D. CYR
Secretary of the Commission	ANNETTE VIETTI-COOK
Chairman, Advisory Committee on Medical Uses of Isotopes	MANUEL CERGUEIR
Chairman, Advisory Committee on Nuclear Waste	B. JOHN GARRICK
Chairman, Advisory Committee on Reactor Safeguards	DANA A. POWERS
Executive Director for Operations	WILLIAM D. TRAVERS
Deputy Executive Director for Materials, Research, and State Programs	CARL J. PAPERIELLO
Deputy Executive Director for Management Services	PATRICIA G. NORRY
Deputy Executive Director for Reactor Programs	FRANK J. MIRAGLIA, JR.
Chief Financial Officer	JESSIE L. FUNCHES

Chief Information Officer	STUART RELTER, *Acting*
Director, Office of Congressional Affairs	DENNIS K. RATHBUN
Director, Office of Public Affairs	WILLIAM M. BEECHER
Inspector General	HUBERT T. BELL, JR.

[For the Nuclear Regulatory Commission statement of organization, see the *Code of Federal Regulations,* Title 10, Part I]

The Nuclear Regulatory Commission licenses and regulates civilian use of nuclear energy to protect public health and safety and the environment. This is achieved by licensing persons and companies to build and operate nuclear reactors and other facilities and to own and use nuclear materials. The Commission makes rules and sets standards for these types of licenses. It also carefully inspects the activities of the persons and companies licensed to ensure that they do not violate the safety rules of the Commission.

The Nuclear Regulatory Commission (NRC) was established as an independent regulatory agency under the provisions of the Energy Reorganization Act of 1974 (42 U.S.C. 5801 *et seq.*) and Executive Order 11834 of January 15, 1975. All licensing and related regulatory functions formerly assigned to the Atomic Energy Commission were transferred to the Commission.

The Commission's major program components are the Office of Nuclear Reactor Regulation, the Office of Nuclear Material Safety and Safeguards, and the Office of Nuclear Regulatory Research. Headquarters offices are located in suburban Maryland, and there are four regional offices.

The Commission ensures that the civilian uses of nuclear materials and facilities are conducted in a manner consistent with the public health and safety, environmental quality, national security, and the antitrust laws. The major share of the Commission's effort is focused on regulating the use of nuclear energy to generate electric power.

Activities

The Nuclear Regulatory Commission is primarily responsible for:

—licensing the construction, operation, and closure of nuclear reactors and other nuclear facilities, such as nuclear fuel cycle facilities, low-level radioactive waste disposal sites under NRC jurisdiction, the geologic repository for high-level radioactive waste, and nonpower test and research reactors;

—licensing the possession, use, processing, handling, and export of nuclear material;

—licensing the operators of nuclear power and nonpower test and research reactors;

—inspecting licensed facilities and activities;

—conducting the U.S. Government research program on light-water reactor safety;

—developing and implementing rules and regulations that govern licensed nuclear activities;

—investigating nuclear incidents and allegations concerning any matter regulated by the NRC;

—maintaining the NRC Incident Response Program;

—collecting, analyzing, and disseminating information about the operational safety of commercial nuclear power reactors and certain nonreactor activities;

—and developing effective working relationships with the States regarding reactor operations and the regulation of nuclear material, including assurance that adequate regulatory programs are maintained by those States that exercise regulatory control over certain nuclear materials in the State.

Sources of Information

Contracts and Procurement Detailed information on how to do business with the Commission may be obtained by calling the Director, Division of Contracts and Property Management, at 301–415–7305. Information on programs

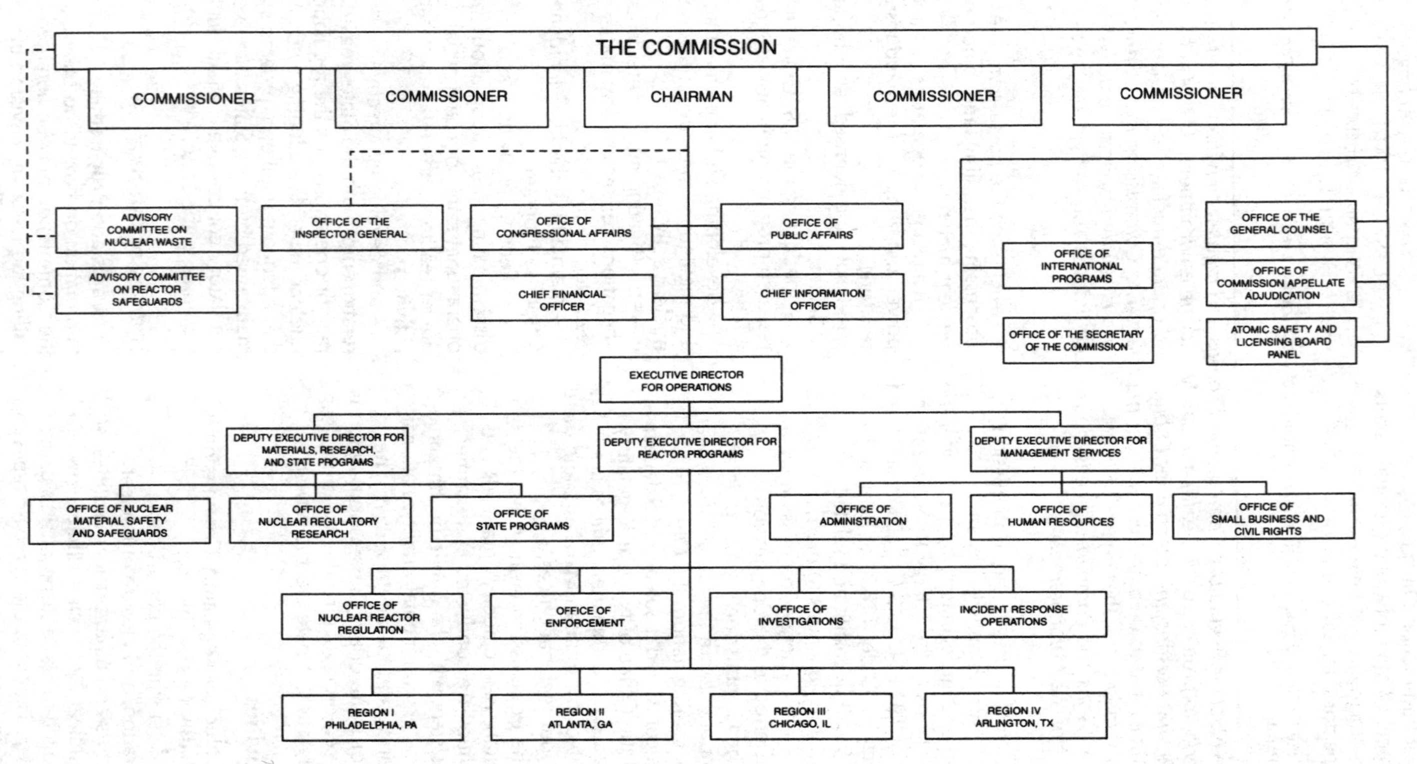
NUCLEAR REGULATORY COMMISSION
THE COMMISSION
COMMISSIONER
COMMISSIONER
CHAIRMAN
COMMISSIONER
COMMISSIONER
ADVISORY COMMITTEE ON NUCLEAR WASTE
ADVISORY COMMITTEE ON REACTOR SAFEGUARDS
OFFICE OF THE INSPECTOR GENERAL
OFFICE OF CONGRESSIONAL AFFAIRS
OFFICE OF PUBLIC AFFAIRS
CHIEF FINANCIAL OFFICER
CHIEF INFORMATION OFFICER
OFFICE OF INTERNATIONAL PROGRAMS
OFFICE OF THE SECRETARY OF THE COMMISSION
OFFICE OF THE GENERAL COUNSEL
OFFICE OF COMMISSION APPELLATE ADJUDICATION
ATOMIC SAFETY AND LICENSING BOARD PANEL
EXECUTIVE DIRECTOR FOR OPERATIONS
DEPUTY EXECUTIVE DIRECTOR FOR MATERIALS, RESEARCH, AND STATE PROGRAMS
DEPUTY EXECUTIVE DIRECTOR FOR REACTOR PROGRAMS
DEPUTY EXECUTIVE DIRECTOR FOR MANAGEMENT SERVICES
OFFICE OF NUCLEAR MATERIAL SAFETY AND SAFEGUARDS
OFFICE OF NUCLEAR REGULATORY RESEARCH
OFFICE OF STATE PROGRAMS
OFFICE OF ADMINISTRATION
OFFICE OF HUMAN RESOURCES
OFFICE OF SMALL BUSINESS AND CIVIL RIGHTS
OFFICE OF NUCLEAR REACTOR REGULATION
OFFICE OF ENFORCEMENT
OFFICE OF INVESTIGATIONS
INCIDENT RESPONSE OPERATIONS
REGION I PHILADELPHIA, PA
REGION II ATLANTA, GA
REGION III CHICAGO, IL
REGION IV ARLINGTON, TX

to assist small business is available from the Director, Office of Small Business and Civil Rights, Mail Stop T2F18, Nuclear Regulatory Commission, Washington, DC 20555–0001. Phone, 301–415–7380.

Employment The Commission's employment activities are exempt from civil service requirements and are conducted under an independent merit system. However, employees receive Federal employee benefits (retirement, group life insurance, and health benefits) on the same basis as other Federal employees.

Employment inquiries, applications, and requests from schools for participation in the recruitment program may be directed to the Director, Office of Human Resources, Mail Stop T3A2, Nuclear Regulatory Commission, Washington, DC 20555–0001. Phone, 301–415–7516.

Freedom of Information Act Requests Requests for copies of records should be directed to the Chief, FOIA/Privacy Act Officer, Mail Stop T6D8, Nuclear Regulatory Commission, Washington, DC 20555–0001. Phone, 301–415–7169.

Publications NRC publishes scientific, technical, and administrative information dealing with licensing and regulation of civilian nuclear facilities and materials, as well as periodic reports including the annual *Report to Congress on Abnormal Occurrences*, the annual *Accountability and Performance Report*, the quarterly *Licensee, Contractor, and Vendor Inspection Status Report*, and the *Nuclear Regulatory Commission Issuances*.

Some publications and documents, including the *Weekly Information Report*, are available on the Internet, at www.nrc.gov. The U.S. Government Printing Office and the National Technical Informations Service (NTIS) sell single copies of or subscriptions to NRC publications. To obtain prices and order NRC publications, contact the the Superintendent of Documents, GPO, P.O. Box 37082, Washington, DC 20013–7082 (phone, 202–512–1800; Internet, www.gpo.gov) or NTIS, Springfield, VA 22161–0002 (phone, 703–487–4650; Internet, ntis.gov/ordernow).

Active *Regulatory Guides* may be obtained without charge by faxed request to 301–415–5272 or by written request to the Nuclear Regulatory Commission, Washington, DC 20555, Attention: Publishing Services Branch. They may also be purchased, as they are issued, on standing orders from NTIS. These *Regulatory Guides* are published in 10 subject areas: power reactors, research and test reactors, fuels and materials facilities, environmental and siting, materials and plant protection, products, transportation, occupational health, antitrust and financial review, and general.

Draft Regulatory Guides are issued for public comment. These drafts may be downloaded from or commented on through the Internet, at www.nrc.gov. They may also be obtained, to the extent of supply, by faxed request to 301–415–5272 or by written request to the Nuclear Regulatory Commission, Washington, DC 20555, Attention: Publishing Services Branch.

Reading Rooms The Headquarters Public Document Room maintains an extensive collection of documents related to NRC licensing proceedings and other significant decisions and actions, and documents from the regulatory activities of the former Atomic Energy Commission. Persons interested in detailed, technical information about nuclear facilities and other licensees find this specialized research center to be a major resource. (Books, journals, trade publications, or documents on industry standards are not stocked in the Reading Room.) Located at 2120 L Street NW., Washington, DC, the Public Document Room is open Monday through Friday from 7:45 a.m. to 4:15 p.m., except on Federal holidays.

Documents from the collection may be reproduced, with some exceptions, on paper, microfiche, or diskette for a nominal fee. The Public Document Room also offers an order subscription service for selected serially published documents and reports. Certain items of immediate interest, such as press releases and meeting notices, are posted in the Reading Room. For additional information regarding the Public Document Room, contact the Nuclear Regulatory Commission, Public Document Room, Washington, DC 20555. Phone, 202–634–3273 (Washington, DC, area), or 800–397–4209 (toll-free). E-mail, pdr@nrc.gov. Fax, 202–634–3343.

The Commission also maintains approximately 86 local public document rooms around the country. The document rooms are located in libraries in cities and towns near commercially operated nuclear power reactors and certain nonpower reactor facilities. They contain detailed information specific to the nearby facilities, which are either licensed or under regulatory review. Power reactor and high-level radioactive waste local public document rooms also contain a microfiche file of all publicly available NRC documents issued since January 1981. A list of local public document rooms and information about the availability of documents at local public document rooms is available at the NRC Public Document Room at the address and telephone numbers above.

For further information, contact the Office of Public Affairs, Nuclear Regulatory Commission, Washington, DC 20555–0001. Phone, 301–415–8200. Internet, www.nrc.gov.

OCCUPATIONAL SAFETY AND HEALTH REVIEW COMMISSION

1120 Twentieth Street NW., Washington, DC 20036–3419
Phone, 202–606–5100. Internet, www.oshrc.gov.

Chairman	THOMASINA V. ROGERS
Commissioners	GARY L. VISSCHER, STUART E. WEISBERG
Executive Director	PATRICIA A. RANDLE
Chief Administrative Law Judge	IRVING SOMMER
General Counsel	EARL R. OHMAN, JR.
Executive Secretary	RAY H. DARLING, JR.
Public Information Officer	LINDA A. WHITSETT

The Occupational Safety and Health Review Commission works to ensure the timely and fair resolution of cases involving the alleged exposure of American workers to unsafe or unhealthy working conditions.

The Occupational Safety and Health Review Commission is an independent, quasi-judicial agency established by the Occupational Safety and Health Act of 1970 (29 U.S.C. 651–678).

The Commission is charged with ruling on cases forwarded to it by the Department of Labor when disagreements arise over the results of safety and health inspections performed by the Department's Occupational Safety and Health Administration. Employers have the right to dispute any alleged job safety or health violation found during the inspection by the Administration, the penalties it proposed, and the time given by the agency to correct any hazardous situation. Employees and representatives of employees may initiate a case by challenging the propriety of the time the Administration has allowed for correction of any violative condition.

The Occupational Safety and Health Act covers virtually every employer in the country. Enforced by the Secretary of Labor, the act is an effort to reduce the incidence of personal injuries, illness, and deaths among working men and

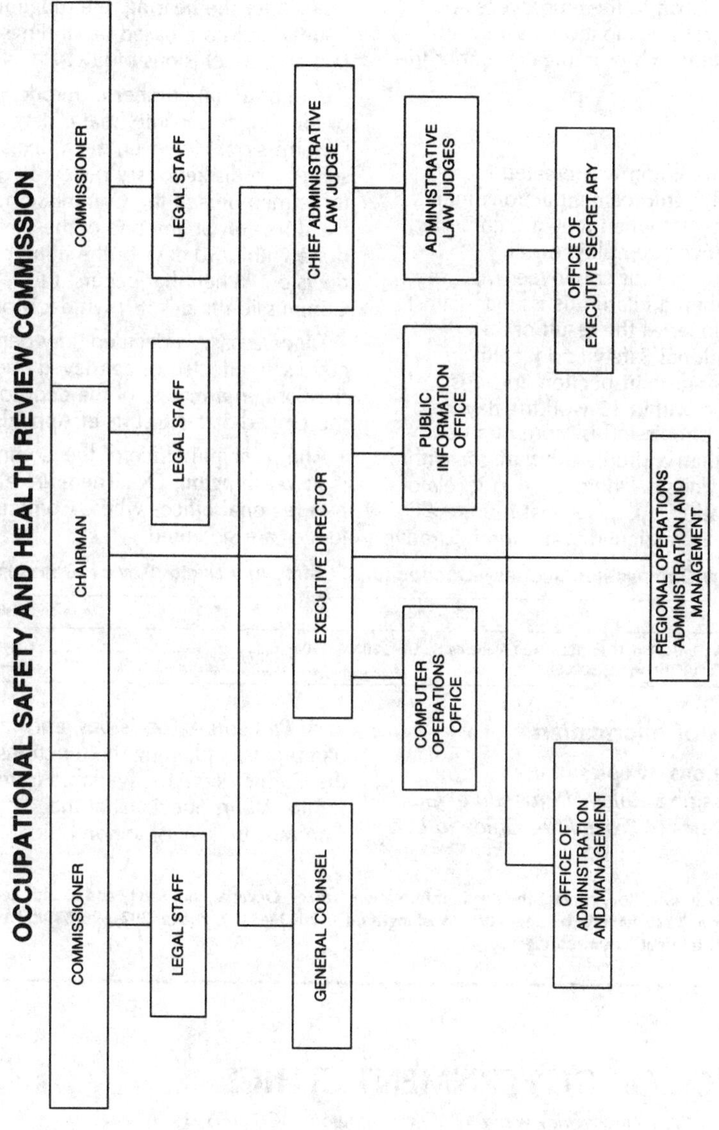
OCCUPATIONAL SAFETY AND HEALTH REVIEW COMMISSION
COMMISSIONER
CHAIRMAN
COMMISSIONER
LEGAL STAFF
LEGAL STAFF
LEGAL STAFF
GENERAL COUNSEL
EXECUTIVE DIRECTOR
CHIEF ADMINISTRATIVE LAW JUDGE
COMPUTER OPERATIONS OFFICE
PUBLIC INFORMATION OFFICE
ADMINISTRATIVE LAW JUDGES
OFFICE OF ADMINISTRATION AND MANAGEMENT
REGIONAL OPERATIONS ADMINISTRATION AND MANAGEMENT
OFFICE OF EXECUTIVE SECRETARY

women in the United States that result from their employment. It requires employers to furnish to each of their employees a working environment free from recognized hazards that are causing or likely to cause death or serious physical harm to the employees and to comply with occupational safety and health standards promulgated under the act.

Activities

The Commission was created to adjudicate enforcement actions initiated under the act when they are contested by employers, employees, or representatives of employees. A case arises when a citation is issued against an employer as the result of an Occupational Safety and Health Administration inspection and it is contested within 15 working days.

The Commission is more of a court system than a simple tribunal, for within the Commission there are two levels of adjudication. All cases that require a hearing are assigned to an administrative law judge, who decides the case. Ordinarily the hearing is held in the community where the alleged violation occurred or as close as possible. At the hearing, the Secretary of Labor will generally have the burden of proving the case. After the hearing, the judge must issue a decision, based on findings of fact and conclusions of law.

A substantial number of the decisions of the judges become final orders of the Commission. However, each decision is subject to discretionary review by the three members of the Commission upon the direction of any one of the three, if done within 30 days of the filing of the decision. When that occurs, the Commission issues its own decision.

Once a case is decided, any person adversely affected or aggrieved thereby may obtain a review of the decision in the United States Courts of Appeals.

The principal office of the Commission is in Washington, DC. There are also two regional offices where Commission judges are stationed.

Review Commission Judges—Occupational Safety and Health Review Commission

City/Address	Telephone
Atlanta, GA (Rm. 2R90, Bldg. 1924, 100 Alabama St. SW., 30303–3104)	404–562–1640
Denver, CO (1050 17th St., 80265)	303–844–2281

Sources of Information

Publications Copies of the Commission's *Rules of Procedure, Guide to the Rules of Procedure, Guide to E–Z Trial Procedures,* decisions, and pamphlets explaining the functions of the Commission are available from the Public Affairs Specialist at the Commission's Washington office.

For further information, contact the Public Information Officer, Occupational Safety and Health Review Commission, 1120 Twentieth Street NW., Washington, DC 20036–3419. Phone, 202–606–5398. Fax, 202–606–5050. Internet, www.oshrc.gov.

OFFICE OF GOVERNMENT ETHICS

Suite 500, 1201 New York Avenue NW., Washington, DC 20005–3917
Phone, 202–208–8000. Internet, www.usoge.gov.

Director	STEPHEN D. POTTS
Special Assistant to the Director	STUART C. GILMAN
Deputy Director	F. GARY DAVIS

Deputy Director for Government Relations and Special Projects	JANE S. LEY
General Counsel	MARILYN L. GLYNN
Deputy General Counsel	STUART D. RICK
Senior Associate Director for Agency Programs	JACK COVALESKI
Associate Director for Education	BARBARA A. MULLEN-ROTH
Associate Director for Administration	SEAN M. DONOHUE, *Acting*
Chief Information Officer	JAMES V. PARLE

[For the Office of Government Ethics statement of organization, see the *Code of Federal Regulations,* Title 5, Part 2600]

The Office of Government Ethics exercises leadership in the executive branch to prevent conflicts of interest on the part of Government employees and to resolve those conflicts of interest that do occur. In partnership with executive branch agencies and departments, the Office fosters high ethical standards for employees and strengthens the public's confidence that the Government's business is conducted with impartiality and integrity. The Office is the principal agency for administering the Ethics in Government Act for the executive branch.

The Office of Government Ethics is a separate executive agency established under the Ethics in Government Act of 1978, as amended (5 U.S.C. app. 401).

The Director of the Office is appointed by the President with the advice and consent of the Senate for a 5-year term, and is required to submit to Congress a biennial report concerning the implementation of the Director's functions and responsibilities.

Activities

The chief responsibilities of the Office are:

—developing, in consultation with the Attorney General and the Office of Personnel Management, rules and regulations to be promulgated by the President or the Director of the Office of Government Ethics pertaining to standards of ethical conduct of executive branch officials, public and confidential financial disclosure of executive branch officials, executive agency ethics training programs, and the identification and resolution of conflicts of interest;

—monitoring and investigating compliance with the executive branch financial disclosure requirements of the Ethics in Government Act of 1978, as amended;

—providing ethics program assistance and information to executive branch agencies through a desk officer system;

—conducting periodic reviews of the ethics programs of executive agencies;

—ordering corrective action on the part of agencies and employees that the Director of the Office deems necessary, including orders to establish or modify an agency's ethics program;

—providing guidance on and promoting understanding of ethical standards in executive agencies through an extensive program of Government ethics advice, education, and training;

—evaluating the effectiveness of the Ethics Act, the conflict of interest laws, and other related statutes; and

—recommending appropriate new legislation or amendments.

Sources of Information

Electronic Access Information regarding Office of Government Ethics services and programs is available in electronic format on the Internet, at www.usoge.gov.

Publications The Office of Government Ethics periodically updates its publication, *The Informal Advisory Letters and Memoranda and Formal Opinions of the United States Office of Government Ethics,* available from the Government Printing Office. In addition, the Office publishes a periodic newsletter on Government ethics and has available ethics publications, instructional videotapes, and a CD–ROM. Upon request, the Office also provides copies of executive branch public financial disclosure reports (SF 278's) in accordance with the Ethics Act and the Office's regulations.

For further information, contact the Office of Government Ethics, Suite 500, 1201 New York Avenue NW., Washington, DC 20005–3917. Phone, 202–208–8000. TDD, 202–208–8025. Fax, 202–208–8037. Internet, www.usoge.gov.

OFFICE OF PERSONNEL MANAGEMENT

1900 E Street NW., Washington, DC 20415–0001
Phone, 202–606–1800. Internet, www.opm.gov.

Director	Janice R. Lachance
Deputy Director	John U. Sepulveda
Associate Director, Employment Service	Carol J. Okin
Associate Director, Investigations Service	Richard A. Ferris
Associate Director, Office of Merit Systems Oversight and Effectiveness	(vacancy)
Associate Director, Retirement and Insurance Service	William E. Flynn III
Associate Director, Workforce Compensation and Performance Service	Henry Romero
Director, Office of Contracting and Administrative Services	Steve Van Rees
Director, Office of Executive and Management Development	Barbara Garvin-Kester
Director, Office of Executive Resources Management	K. Joyce Edwards
Director, Office of Human Resources and Equal Employment Opportunity	Kirke Harper
Director, Office of Workforce Relations	Steven R. Cohen
Chairman, Federal Prevailing Rate Advisory Committee	John F. Leyden
Chief Financial Officer	J. Gilbert Seaux
Chief Information Technology Officer	Janet L. Barnes
Director, Office of Congressional Relations	Cynthia Brock-Smith
Director, Office of Communications	Jon-Christopher Bua
General Counsel	Suzanne Seiden
Inspector General	Patrick E. McFarland

[For the Office of Personnel Management statement of organization, see the *Federal Register* of Jan. 5, 1979, 44 FR 1501]

The Office of Personnel Management (OPM) administers a merit system to ensure compliance with personnel laws and regulations and assists agencies in recruiting, examining, and promoting people on the basis of their knowledge and skills, regardless of their race, religion, sex, political influence, or other nonmerit factors. OPM's role is to provide guidance to agencies in operating human resources programs which effectively support their missions and to provide an array of personnel services to applicants and employees. OPM supports Government program managers in their human resources management responsibilities and provide benefits to employees, retired employees, and their survivors.

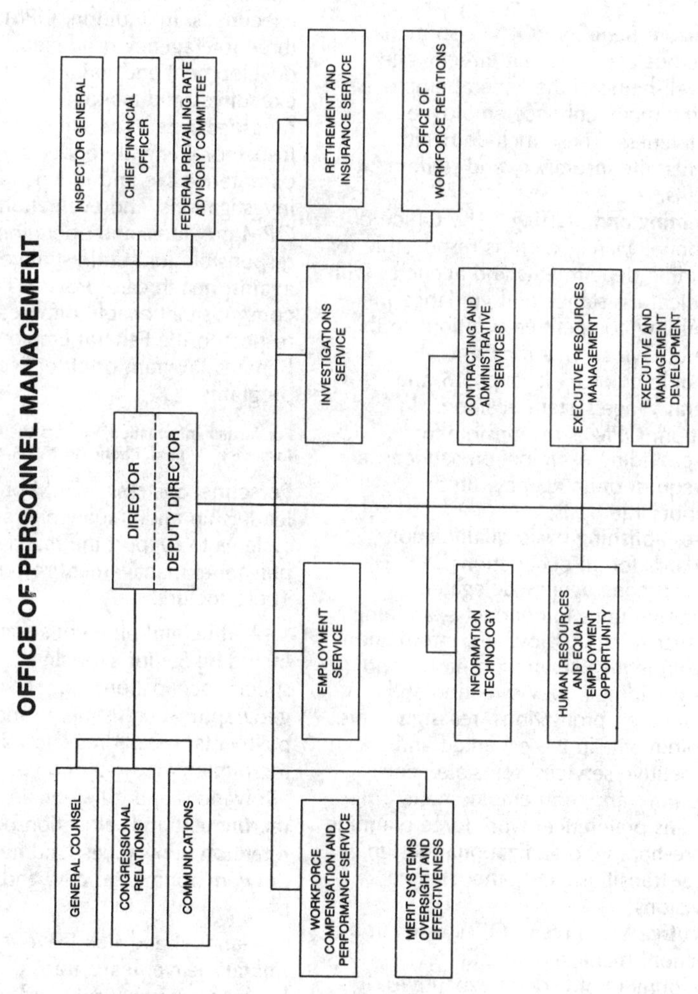
OFFICE OF PERSONNEL MANAGEMENT
DIRECTOR
DEPUTY DIRECTOR
INSPECTOR GENERAL
CHIEF FINANCIAL OFFICER
FEDERAL PREVAILING RATE ADVISORY COMMITTEE
GENERAL COUNSEL
CONGRESSIONAL RELATIONS
COMMUNICATIONS
WORKFORCE COMPENSATION AND PERFORMANCE SERVICE
EMPLOYMENT SERVICE
INVESTIGATIONS SERVICE
RETIREMENT AND INSURANCE SERVICE
MERIT SYSTEMS OVERSIGHT AND EFFECTIVENESS
OFFICE OF WORKFORCE RELATIONS
INFORMATION TECHNOLOGY
CONTRACTING AND ADMINISTRATIVE SERVICES
HUMAN RESOURCES AND EQUAL EMPLOYMENT OPPORTUNITY
EXECUTIVE RESOURCES MANAGEMENT
EXECUTIVE AND MANAGEMENT DEVELOPMENT

The Office of Personnel Management was created as an independent establishment by Reorganization Plan No. 2 of 1978 (5 U.S.C. app.), pursuant to Executive Order 12107 of December 28, 1978. Many of the functions of the former United States Civil Service Commission were transferred to OPM.

Activities

Employee Benefits OPM also manages numerous activities that directly affect the well-being of the Federal employee and indirectly enhance employee effectiveness. These include health benefits, life insurance, and retirement benefits.

Examining and Staffing The Office of Personnel Management is responsible for providing departments and agencies with technical assistance and guidance in examining competitive positions in the Federal civil service for General Schedule grades 1 through 15 and Federal Wage system positions. In addition, OPM is responsible for:

—providing examination services, at the request of an agency, on a reimbursable basis;

—establishing basic qualification standards for all occupations;

—certifying agency delegated examining units to conduct examining;

—providing employment information for competitive service positions; and

—providing policy direction and guidance on promotions, reassignments, appointments in the excepted and competitive services, reinstatements, temporary and term employment, veterans preference, work force planning and reshaping, organizational design, career transition, and other staffing provisions.

Executive Resources OPM leads in the selection, management, and development of Federal executives. It administers the Senior Executive Service program and other merit-based executive personnel systems that promote the development of a corporate perspective. OPM provides policy guidance, consulting services, and technical support in such areas as recruitment, selection, succession planning, mobility performance, awards, and removals. It reviews agency nominations for SES career appointments and administers the Qualifications Review Boards that certify candidates' executive qualifications. It manages SES, senior-level, and scientific and professional space allocations to agencies, administers the Presidential Rank Awards program, and conducts orientation sessions for newly appointed executives. In addition, OPM manages three interagency residential development and training centers for executives and managers.

Investigations The Office of the Inspector General conducts comprehensive and independent audits, investigations, and evaluations relating to OPM programs and operations. It is responsible for administrative actions against health care providers who commit sanctionable offenses with respect to the Federal Employees' Health Benefits Program or other Federal programs.

For further information, contact the Office of the Inspector General. Phone, 202–606–1200.

Personnel Systems OPM provides leadership and guidance to agencies on systems to support the manager's personnel management responsibilities. These include:

—white and blue collar pay systems, including Senior Executive Service and special occupational pay systems; geographical adjustments and locality payments; special rates to address recruitment and retention problems; allowances and differentials, including recruitment and relocation bonuses, retention allowances, and hazardous duty/environmental pay; and premium pay;

—annual and sick leave, court leave, military leave, leave transfer and leave bank programs, family and medical leave, excused absence, holidays, and scheduling of work—including flexible and compressed work schedules;

—performance management, covering appraisal systems, performance pay and awards, and incentive awards for suggestions, inventions, and special acts;

—classification policy and standards for agencies to determine the series and grades for Federal jobs;

—labor-management relations, including labor-management partnerships and consulting with unions on governmentwide issues;

—systems and techniques for resolving disputes with employees;

—quality of worklife initiatives, such as employee health and fitness, work and family, AIDS in the workplace, and employee assistance programs;

—training and employee development, including providing support to the Human Resources Development Council and the Government Performance and Results Act (GPRA) interest group;

—the Training Management Assistance program, to help agencies design and produce training systems and products, performance management systems, work force productivity systems, business process reengineering, compensation, and employee relations systems;

—information systems to support and improve Federal personnel management decisionmaking; and

—governmentwide instructions for personnel processing and recordkeeping, and for release of personnel data under the Freedom of Information Act and the Privacy Act.

OPM also provides administrative support to special advisory bodies, including the Federal Prevailing Rate Advisory Committee, the Federal Salary Council, and the National Partnership Council.

Oversight OPM assesses agencies' effectiveness in personnel management at the governmentwide, agency, and installation levels to gather information for policy development and program refinement, ensure compliance with personnel laws and regulations, enhance agency capability for human resources management accountability, and assist agencies in operating personnel programs which effectively support accomplishment of their primary missions consistent with merit system principles. OPM also works with other Federal agencies to explore potential improvements in personnel systems and better and simpler ways to manage Federal personnel.

Work Force Diversity OPM provides leadership, direction, and policy for governmentwide affirmative recruiting programs for women, minorities, individuals with disabilities, and veterans. It also provides leadership, guidance, and technical assistance to promote merit and equality in systemic work force recruitment, employment, training, and retention. In addition, OPM gathers, analyzes, and maintains statistical data on the diversity of the Federal work force, and prepares evaluation reports for Congress and others on individual agency and governmentwide progress toward full work force representation for all Americans in the Federal sector.

Other Personnel Programs OPM coordinates the temporary assignment of employees between Federal agencies and State, local, and Indian tribal governments; institutions of higher education; and other eligible organizations for up to 2 years, for work of mutual benefit to the participating organizations. It administers the Presidential Management Intern Program, which provides 2-year, excepted appointments with Federal agencies to recipients of graduate degrees in appropriate disciplines. In addition, the Office of Personnel Management administers the Federal Merit System Standards, which apply to certain grant-aided State and local programs.

Federal Executive Boards Federal Executive Boards (FEB's) were established by Presidential memorandum on November 13, 1961, to improve internal Federal management practices and to provide a central focus for Federal participation in civic affairs in major metropolitan centers of Federal activity. They carry out their functions under OPM supervision and control.

FEB's serve as a means for disseminating information within the Federal Government and for promoting discussion of Federal policies and activities of importance to all Federal executives in the field. Each Board is composed of heads of Federal field offices in the metropolitan area. A Chairman is elected annually from among the membership to provide overall leadership to the Board's operations. Committees and task forces carry out interagency projects consistent with the Board's missions.

Federal Executive Boards are located in 28 metropolitan areas that are important centers of Federal activity. These areas are: Albuquerque-Santa Fe, NM; Atlanta, GA; Baltimore, MD; Boston, MA; Buffalo, NY; Chicago, IL; Cincinnati, OH; Cleveland, OH; Dallas-Fort Worth, TX; Denver, CO; Detroit, MI; Honolulu, HI-Pacific; Houston, TX; Kansas City, MO; Los Angeles, CA; Miami, FL; New Orleans, LA; New York, NY; Newark, NJ; Oklahoma City, OK; Philadelphia, PA; Pittsburgh, PA; Portland, OR; St. Louis, MO; San Antonio, TX; San Francisco, CA; Seattle, WA; and the Twin Cities (Minneapolis-St. Paul, MN).

Federal Executive Associations, Councils, or Committees have been locally organized in over 100 other metropolitan areas to perform functions similar to the Federal Executive Boards but on a lesser scale of organization and activity.

For further information, contact the Assistant for Regional Operations, Office of Personnel Management, Room 5H22L, 1900 E Street NW., Washington, DC 20415–0001. Phone, 202–606–1001.

Sources of Information

Contracts For information, contact the Chief, Contracting Division, Office of Personnel Management, Washington, DC 20415–0001. Phone, 202–606–2240.

Employment Information about Federal employment and current job openings is available from USAJobs (phone, 912–757–3000; TTY, 912–744–2299; Internet, www.usajobs.opm.gov). USAJobs can also be accessed through touch-screen kiosks located at most OPM regional offices, in many Federal agency buildings, and at several colleges and universities. Contact information for your local OPM offices is available in the blue pages of the phone book, under U.S. Government, Office of Personnel Management.

For information about employment opportunities within the Office of Personnel Management, contact the Director for Human Resources. Phone, 202–606–2400.

Publications The Chief, Publications Services Division, can provide information about Federal personnel management publications. Phone, 202–606–1822.

For further information, contact the Office of Communications, Office of Personnel Management, 1900 E Street NW., Washington, DC 20415–0001. Phone, 202–606–1800. Internet, www.opm.gov.

OFFICE OF SPECIAL COUNSEL

Suite 300, 1730 M Street NW., Washington, DC 20036–4505
Phone, 800–872–9855. Fax, 202–653–5151. Internet, www.osc.gov.

Special Counsel	Elaine Kaplan
Deputy Special Counsel	Timothy Hannapel
Associate Special Counsel for Prosecution	William E. Reukauf
Associate Special Counsel for Investigation	Ruth Robinson Ertel
Associate Special Counsel for Planning and Advice	Erin McDonnell
Director, Congressional and Public Affairs	Jane McFarland

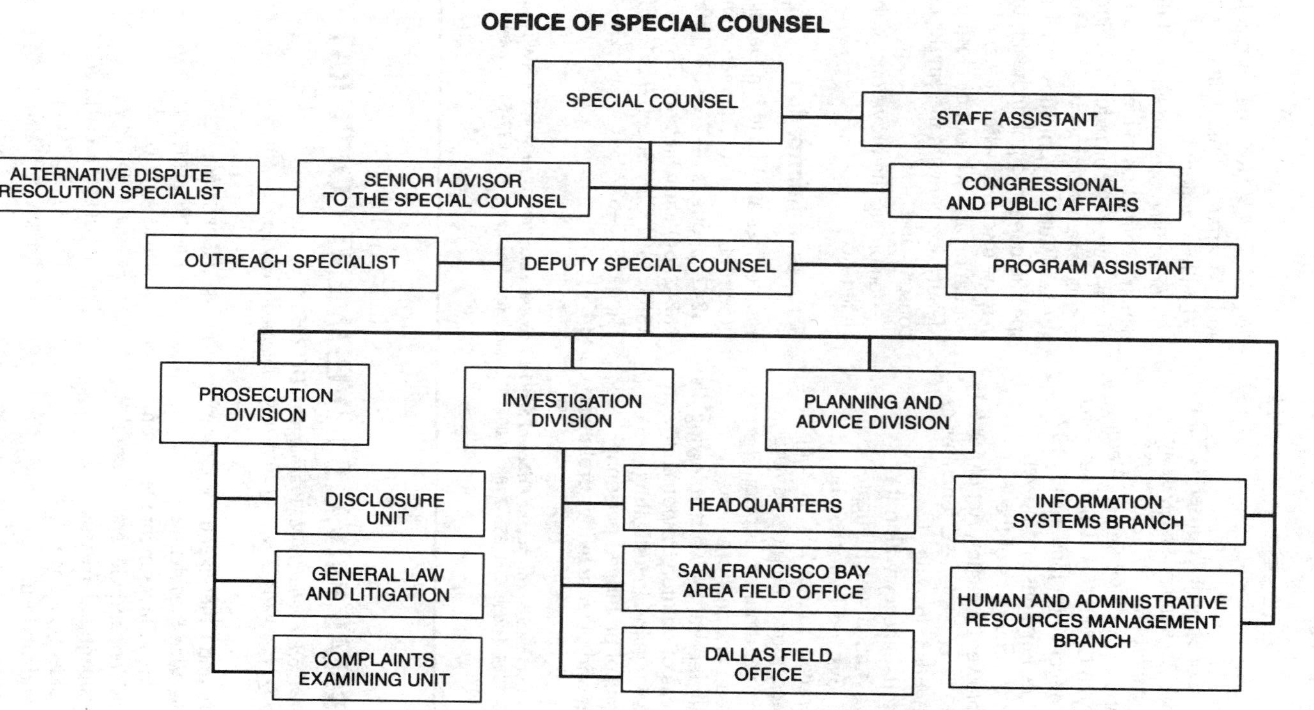
OFFICE OF SPECIAL COUNSEL
SPECIAL COUNSEL
STAFF ASSISTANT
ALTERNATIVE DISPUTE RESOLUTION SPECIALIST
SENIOR ADVISOR TO THE SPECIAL COUNSEL
CONGRESSIONAL AND PUBLIC AFFAIRS
OUTREACH SPECIALIST
DEPUTY SPECIAL COUNSEL
PROGRAM ASSISTANT
PROSECUTION DIVISION
INVESTIGATION DIVISION
PLANNING AND ADVICE DIVISION
DISCLOSURE UNIT
GENERAL LAW AND LITIGATION
COMPLAINTS EXAMINING UNIT
HEADQUARTERS
SAN FRANCISCO BAY AREA FIELD OFFICE
DALLAS FIELD OFFICE
INFORMATION SYSTEMS BRANCH
HUMAN AND ADMINISTRATIVE RESOURCES MANAGEMENT BRANCH

The Office of Special Counsel investigates allegations of certain activities prohibited by civil service laws, rules, or regulations and litigates before the Merit Systems Protection Board.

Activities

The Office of Special Counsel (OSC) was established on January 1, 1979, by Reorganization Plan No. 2 of 1978 (5 U.S.C. app.). The Civil Service Reform Act of 1978 (5 U.S.C. 1101 note), which became effective on January 11, 1979, enlarged its functions and powers. Pursuant to provisions of the Whistleblower Protection Act of 1989 (5 U.S.C. 1211 *et seq.*), OSC functions as an independent investigative and prosecutorial agency within the executive branch which litigates before the Merit Systems Protection Board.

The primary role of OSC is to protect employees, former employees, and applicants for employment from prohibited personnel practices, especially reprisal for whistleblowing. Its basic areas of statutory responsibility are:

—receiving and investigating allegations of prohibited personnel practices and other activities prohibited by civil service law, rule, or regulation and, if warranted, initiating corrective or disciplinary action;

—providing a secure channel through which information evidencing a violation of any law, rule, or regulation, gross mismanagement, gross waste of funds, abuse of authority, or substantial and specific danger to public health or safety may be disclosed without fear of retaliation and without disclosure of identity, except with the employee's consent; and

—enforcing the provisions of the Hatch Act.

Sources of Information

Field offices are located in Dallas, TX (Room 7C30, 1100 Commerce Street, 75242; phone, 214–767–8871; fax, 214–767–2764) and Oakland, CA (Suite 365S, 1301 Clay Street, 94612–5217; phone, 510–637–3460; fax, 510–637–3474).

For further information, contact the Office of Special Counsel, Suite 300, 1730 M Street NW., Washington, DC 20036–4505. Phone, 202–653–7188 or 800–872–9855 (toll-free). Fax, 202–653–5151. Internet, www.osc.gov.

OVERSEAS PRIVATE INVESTMENT CORPORATION

1100 New York Avenue NW., Washington, DC 20527

Phone, 202–336–8400. Fax, 202–408–9859. Internet, www.opic.gov.

President and Chief Executive Officer	George Muñoz
Executive Vice President	Kirk Robertson
Vice President, Investment Development	Mark van de Water
Vice President and General Counsel	Charles D. Toy
Vice President and Treasurer	Mildred O. Callear
Vice President, Finance	Robert B. Drumheller
Vice President, Insurance	Julie A. Martin

Vice President, Investment Funds	Jeffrey Griffin
Managing Director for Administration	Michael C. Cushing

[For the Overseas Private Investment Corporation statement of organization, see the *Code of Federal Regulations,* Title 22, Chapter VII]

The Overseas Private Investment Corporation is a self-sustaining Federal agency whose purpose is to promote economic growth in developing countries by encouraging U.S. private investment in those nations.

The Overseas Private Investment Corporation (OPIC) was established as an independent agency by the Foreign Affairs Reform and Restructuring Act of 1998 (112 Stat. 2681–790). OPIC assists American investors in four principal ways: financing of businesses through loans and loan guaranties; supporting private investment funds which provide equity for U.S. companies investing in projects overseas; insuring investments against a broad range of political risks; and engaging in outreach activities. All of these programs are designed to reduce the perceived stumbling blocks and risks associated with overseas investment.

Organized as a corporation and structured to be responsive to private business, OPIC is mandated to mobilize and facilitate the participation of U.S. private capital and skills in the economic and social development of developing countries and emerging economies. Currently, OPIC programs are available for new business enterprises or expansion in some 140 countries worldwide. The Corporation encourages American overseas private investment in sound business projects, thereby improving U.S. global competitiveness, creating American jobs, and increasing U.S. exports. The Corporation does not support projects that will result in the loss of domestic jobs or have a negative impact on the host country's environment or workers' rights.

The Corporation is governed by a 15-member Board of Directors, of whom 8 are appointed from the private sector and 7 from the Federal Government.

Activities

By reducing or eliminating certain perceived political risks for investors and providing financing and assistance not otherwise available, the Corporation helps to reduce the unusual risks and problems that can make investment opportunities in the developing areas less attractive than in advanced countries. At the same time, it reduces the need for government-to-government assistance by involving the U.S. private sector in establishing capital-generation and strengthening private-sector economies in developing countries.

The Corporation insures U.S. investors against the political risks of expropriation, inconvertibility of local currency earnings, and damage from war, revolution, insurrection, or civil strife. It also offers a special insurance policy to U.S. contractors and exporters against arbitrary drawings of letters of credit posted as bid, performance, or advance payment guaranties. Other special programs are offered for minerals exploration, oil and gas exploration, and development and leasing operations.

The Corporation offers U.S. lenders protection against both commercial and political risks by guaranteeing payment of principal and interest on loans (up to $200 million) made to eligible private enterprises.

Its Direct Investment loans, offered to small and medium-sized businesses, generally cover terms of from 5 to 15 years and usually range from $2 million to $30 million with interest rates depending on assessment of the commercial risks of the project financed.

Additionally, OPIC supports a family of privately managed direct investment funds in various regions and business sectors. Such funds currently operate in most countries in East Asia, sub-Saharan African, South America, Russia and other New Independent States, Poland and other countries in Central Europe, India, and Israel.

186-873 D-00--17

Programs are available only for a new facility, expansion or modernization of an existing plant, or technological or service products designed to generate investment that will produce significant new benefits for host countries.

Sources of Information

General Inquiries Inquiries should be directed to the Information Office, Overseas Private Investment Corporation, 1100 New York Avenue NW., Washington, DC 20527. Phone, 202–336–8799. E-mail, OPIC@opic.gov. Internet, www.opic.gov.

Publications OPIC programs are further detailed in the *Annual Report* and the *Program Summary*. These publications are available free of charge.

For further information, contact the Overseas Private Investment Corporation, 1100 New York Avenue NW., Washington, DC 20527. Phone, 202–336–8400. Fax, 202–408–9859. Internet, www.opic.gov.

PEACE CORPS

1111 Twentieth Street NW., Washington, DC 20526
Phone, 202–692–2000. Fax, 202–692–2231. Internet, www.peacecorps.gov.

Director	Mark L. Schneider
Deputy Director	Charles R. Baquet III
Chief of Staff	Thomas Tighe
General Counsel	Nancy Hendry
American Diversity Program Manager	Brenda Gooch
Inspector General	Charles Smith
Director for Office of Planning, Policy, and Analysis	(vacancy)
Director of Communications	Michael Chapman
Director of Press	(vacancy)
Director of Congressional Relations	Suzanne Palmieri
Director of Private Sector Cooperation and International Volunteerism	Victor Basile
Director of the Crisis Corps	Joan M. Timoney
Regional Director/Africa Operations	Earl Yates
Regional Director/Europe, Mediterranean, and Asia Operations	Ellen Paquette
Regional Director/Inter-American and the Pacific Operations	Patrick Fn'Piere
Director, Center for Field Assistance and Applied Research	Lani Havens
Chief Financial Officer	Lana Hurdle
Associate Director for Management	Douglas Greene
Associate Director for Volunteer Support	Mike Ward

Associate Director for Volunteer Recruitment and Selection — MONICA MILLS

[For the Peace Corps statement of organization, see the *Code of Federal Regulations,* Title 22, Part 302]

The Peace Corps' purpose is to promote world peace and friendship, to help other countries in meeting their needs for trained men and women, and to promote understanding between the American people and other peoples served by the Peace Corps. The Peace Corps Act emphasizes the Peace Corps commitment toward programming to meet the basic needs of those living in the countries where volunteers work.

The Peace Corps was established by the Peace Corps Act of 1961, as amended (22 U.S.C. 2501), and was made an independent agency by title VI of the International Security and Development Cooperation Act of 1981 (22 U.S.C. 2501–1).

The Peace Corps consists of a Washington, DC, headquarters; 11 area offices; and overseas operations in more than 80 countries.

Activities

To fulfill the Peace Corps mandate, men and women are trained for a 9- to 14-week period in the appropriate local language, the technical skills necessary for their particular job, and the cross-cultural skills needed to adjust to a society with traditions and attitudes different from their own. Volunteers serve for a period of 2 years, living among the people with whom they work. Volunteers are expected to become a part of the community through their voluntary service.

Thousands of volunteers serve throughout the world, working in six program areas: education, agriculture, health, small business development, urban development, and the environment. Community-level projects are designed to incorporate the skills of volunteers with the resources of host-country agencies and other international assistance organizations to help solve specific development problems, often in conjunction with private volunteer organizations.

In the United States, the Peace Corps is working to promote an understanding of people in other countries. Through its World Wise Schools Program, volunteers are matched with elementary and junior high schools in the United States to encourage an exchange of letters, pictures, music, and artifacts. Participating students increase their knowledge of geography, languages, and different cultures, while gaining an appreciation for volunteerism.

The Peace Corps offers other domestic programs involving former volunteers, universities, local public school systems, and private businesses and foundations in a partnership to help solve some of the United States most pressing domestic problems.

The Peace Corps Office of Private Sector Cooperation and International Volunteerism works with schools, civic groups, businesses, and neighborhood and youth organizations in the United States to facilitate their support of Peace Corps initiatives here and abroad.

Area Offices—Peace Corps

Office	Address	Telephone
Atlanta, GA (AL, FL, GA, MS, PR, SC, TN)	Suite 2R.70, 100 Alabama St., 30303	404–562–3456
Boston, MA (MA, ME, NH, RI, VT)	Rm. 450, 10 Causeway St., 02222	617–565–5555
Chicago, IL (IL, IN, KY, MI, MO, OH)	Suite 450, 55 W. Monroe St., 60603	312–353–4990
Dallas, TX (AR, LA, NM, OK, TX)	Rm. 527, 207 S. Houston, 75202	214–767–5435
Denver, CO (CO, KS, NE, UT, WY)	Suite 2205, 1999 Broadway, 80202	303–844–7020
Los Angeles, CA (AZ, southern CA)	Suite 8104, 11000 Wilshire Blvd., 90024	310–235–7444
Minneapolis, MS (IA, MN, ND, SD, WI)	Suite 420, 330 2d Ave. S., 55401	612–348–1480
New York, NY (CT, NJ, NY, PA)	Rm. 611, 6 World Trade Ctr., 10048	212–637–6498
San Francisco, CA (northern CA, HI, NV)	Suite 600, 333 Market St., 94105	415–977–8800
Seattle, WA (AK, ID, MT, OR, WA)	Rm. 1776, 2001 6th Ave., 98121	206–553–5490

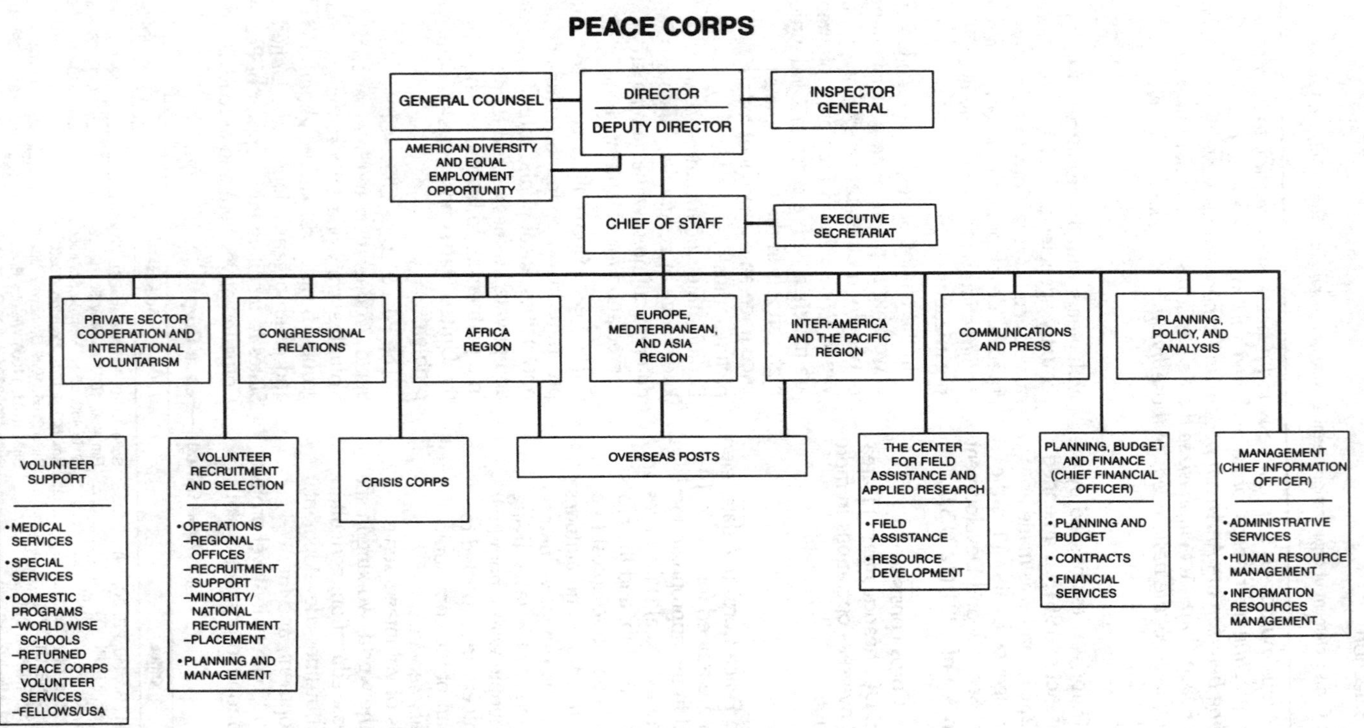
PEACE CORPS
GENERAL COUNSEL
DIRECTOR
DEPUTY DIRECTOR
INSPECTOR GENERAL
AMERICAN DIVERSITY AND EQUAL EMPLOYMENT OPPORTUNITY
CHIEF OF STAFF
EXECUTIVE SECRETARIAT
PRIVATE SECTOR COOPERATION AND INTERNATIONAL VOLUNTARISM
CONGRESSIONAL RELATIONS
AFRICA REGION
EUROPE, MEDITERRANEAN, AND ASIA REGION
INTER-AMERICA AND THE PACIFIC REGION
COMMUNICATIONS AND PRESS
PLANNING, POLICY, AND ANALYSIS
VOLUNTEER SUPPORT
•MEDICAL SERVICES
•SPECIAL SERVICES
•DOMESTIC PROGRAMS
–WORLD WISE SCHOOLS
–RETURNED PEACE CORPS VOLUNTEER SERVICES
–FELLOWS/USA
VOLUNTEER RECRUITMENT AND SELECTION
•OPERATIONS
–REGIONAL OFFICES
–RECRUITMENT SUPPORT
–MINORITY/NATIONAL RECRUITMENT
–PLACEMENT
•PLANNING AND MANAGEMENT
CRISIS CORPS
OVERSEAS POSTS
THE CENTER FOR FIELD ASSISTANCE AND APPLIED RESEARCH
•FIELD ASSISTANCE
•RESOURCE DEVELOPMENT
PLANNING, BUDGET AND FINANCE (CHIEF FINANCIAL OFFICER)
•PLANNING AND BUDGET
•CONTRACTS
•FINANCIAL SERVICES
MANAGEMENT (CHIEF INFORMATION OFFICER)
•ADMINISTRATIVE SERVICES
•HUMAN RESOURCE MANAGEMENT
•INFORMATION RESOURCES MANAGEMENT

Area Offices—Peace Corps

Office	Address	Telephone
Washington, DC (DC, DE, MD, NC, VA, WV)	Suite 250, 1525 Wilson Blvd., Arlington, VA 22209	703–235–9191

Sources of Information

Becoming a Peace Corps Volunteer Contact the nearest area office. Phone, 800–424–8580, extension 2293 (toll-free).

Employment Contact the Peace Corps, Office of Human Resource Management, Washington, DC 20526. Phone, 202–692–1200. For recorded employment opportunities, call 800–818–9579 (toll-free).

General Inquiries Information or assistance may be obtained by contacting the Peace Corps' Washington, DC, headquarters or any of its area offices. Frequently, information is available from local post offices.

For further information, contact the Press Office, Peace Corps, 1111 Twentieth Street NW., Washington, DC 20526. Phone, 202–692–2230 or 800–424–8580 (toll-free). Fax, 202–692–2231. Internet, www.peacecorps.gov.

PENSION BENEFIT GUARANTY CORPORATION

1200 K Street NW., Washington, DC 20005
Phone, 202–326–4000; 800–400–4272 (toll-free). Internet, www.pbgc.gov.

Board of Directors:	
Chairman (Secretary of Labor)	ALEXIS M. HERMAN
Members:	
(Secretary of the Treasury)	LAWRENCE H. SUMMERS
(Secretary of Commerce)	WILLIAM M. DALEY
Officials:	
Executive Director	DAVID M. STRAUSS
Chief Negotiator and Director, Corporate Finance and Negotiations Department	ANDREA E. SCHNEIDER
Deputy Executive Director and Chief Operating Officer	JOSEPH H. GRANT
General Counsel	JAMES J. KEIGHTLEY
Director, Corporate Policy and Research Department	STUART A. SIRKIN
Director, Insurance Operations Department	BENNIE L. HAGANS
Deputy Executive Director and Chief Financial Officer	N. ANTHONY CALHOUN
Director, Contracts and Controls Review Department	MARTY BOEHM
Director, Financial Operations Department	HAZEL BROADNAX
Director, Information Resources Management Department	CRIS BIRCH
Deputy Executive Director and Chief Management Officer	JOHN SEAL
Director, Budget Department	HENRY R. THOMPSON
Director, Facilities and Services Department	JANET A. SMITH
Director, Human Resources Department	SHARON BARBEE-FLETCHER
Director, Procurement Department	ROBERT W. HERTING

Director, Participant and Employer Appeals Department	HARRIET D. VERBURG
Director of Strategic Planning	KATHLEEN BLUNT
Assistant Executive Director for Legislative and Congressional Affairs	JUDY SCHUB
Senior Adviser	MONICA HEALY
Director, Communications and Public Affairs Department	JUDITH WELLES
Inspector General	WAYNE ROBERT POLL

The Pension Benefit Guaranty Corporation guarantees payment of nonforfeitable pension benefits in covered private-sector defined benefit pension plans.

The Pension Benefit Guaranty Corporation is a self-financing, wholly owned Government corporation subject to the Government Corporation Control Act (31 U.S.C. 9101–9109). The Corporation, established by Title IV of the Employee Retirement Income Security Act of 1974 (29 U.S.C. 1301–1461), is governed by a Board of Directors consisting of the Secretaries of Labor, Commerce, and the Treasury. The Secretary of Labor is Chairman of the Board. A seven-member Advisory Committee, composed of two labor, two business, and three public members appointed by the President, advises the agency on various matters.

Activities

Coverage The Corporation insures most private-sector defined benefit pension plans that provide a pension benefit based on factors such as age, years of service, and salary.

The Corporation administers two insurance programs separately covering single-employer and multiemployer plans. More than 42 million workers participate in approximately 44,000 covered plans.

Single-Employer Insurance Under the single-employer program, the Corporation guarantees payment of certain pension benefits if an insured plan terminates without sufficient assets to pay those benefits. However, the law limits the total monthly benefit that the agency may guarantee for one individual to $3,221.59 per month, at age 65, for a plan terminating during 2000, and sets other restrictions on PBGC's guarantee. The Corporation may also pay some benefits above the guaranteed amount depending on amounts recovered from employers.

A plan administrator may terminate a single-employer plan in a "standard" or "distress" termination if certain procedural and legal requirements are met. In either termination, the plan administrator must inform participants in writing at least 60 days prior to the date the administrator proposes to terminate the plan. Only a plan that has sufficient assets to pay all benefit liabilities may terminate in a standard termination. The Corporation also may institute termination proceedings in certain specified circumstances.

Multiemployer Insurance Under title IV, as originally enacted, the Corporation guaranteed nonforfeitable benefits for multiemployer plans in a similar fashion as for single-employer plans. However, the multiemployer program was revised in 1980 by the Multiemployer Pension Plan Amendments Act (29 U.S.C. 1001 note) which changed the insurable event from plan termination to plan insolvency. The Corporation now provides financial assistance to plans that are unable to pay nonforfeitable benefits. The plans are obligated to repay such assistance. The act also made employers withdrawing from a plan liable to the plan for a portion of its unfunded vested benefits.

Premium Collections All defined benefit pension plans insured by PBGC are required to pay premiums to the Corporation according to rates set by Congress. The annual premium per plan participant for multiemployer pension plans is $2.60 for plan years beginning

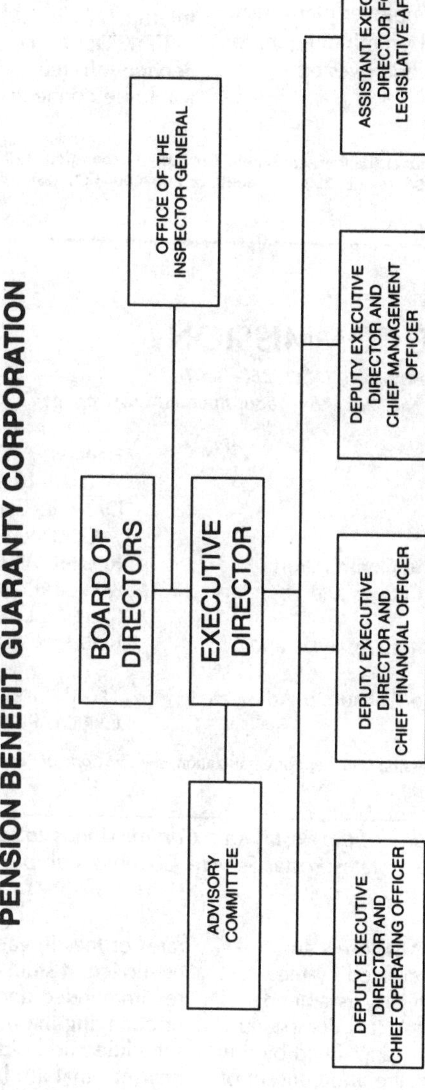
PENSION BENEFIT GUARANTY CORPORATION
BOARD OF DIRECTORS
EXECUTIVE DIRECTOR
OFFICE OF THE INSPECTOR GENERAL
ADVISORY COMMITTEE
DEPUTY EXECUTIVE DIRECTOR AND CHIEF OPERATING OFFICER
DEPUTY EXECUTIVE DIRECTOR AND CHIEF FINANCIAL OFFICER
DEPUTY EXECUTIVE DIRECTOR AND CHIEF MANAGEMENT OFFICER
ASSISTANT EXECUTIVE DIRECTOR FOR LEGISLATIVE AFFAIRS

after September 26, 1988. The basic premium for all single-employer plans is $19 per participant per year. Underfunded single-employer plans must also pay an additional premium equal to $9 per $1,000 of unfunded vested benefits.

Sources of Information

Access to the Pension Benefit Guaranty Corporation is available through the Internet, at www.pbgc.gov.

TTY/TDD users, call the Federal Relay Service toll-free at 800–877–8339 and ask to be connected to 202–326–4000.

For further information, contact the Pension Benefit Guaranty Corporation, 1200 K Street NW., Washington, DC 20005–4026. Phone, 202–326–4000, or 800–400–4272 (toll-free). Internet, www.pbgc.gov.

POSTAL RATE COMMISSION

1333 H Street NW., Washington, DC 20268–0001
Phone, 202–789–6800. Fax, 202–789–6886. Internet, www.prc.gov.

Chairman	EDWARD J. GLEIMAN
Vice Chairman	WILLIAM H. LEBLANC III
Commissioners	DANA B. COVINGTON, RUTH Y. GOLDWAY, GEORGE A. OMAS
Special Assistant to the Commission	ROBERT W. MITCHELL
Chief Administrative Officer and Secretary	MARGARET P. CRENSHAW
General Counsel	STEPHEN L. SHARFMAN
Director, Office of Rates, Analysis and Planning	ROBERT COHEN
Director, Office of the Consumer Advocate	TED P. GERARDEN
Personnel Officer	CYRIL J. PITTACK

[For the Postal Rate Commission statement of organization, see the *Code of Federal Regulations,* Title 39, Part 3002]

The major responsibility of the Postal Rate Commission is to submit recommended decisions to the United States Postal Service Governors on postage rates, fees, and mail classifications.

The Postal Rate Commission is an independent agency created by the Postal Reorganization Act, as amended (39 U.S.C. 3601–3604). It is composed of five Commissioners, appointed by the President with the advice and consent of the Senate, one of whom is designated as Chairman.

The Commission promulgates rules and regulations, establishes procedures, and takes other actions necessary to carry out its obligations. Acting upon requests from the U.S. Postal Service or on its own initiative, the Commission recommends and issues advisory opinions to the Board of Governors of the U.S. Postal Service on changes in rates or fees in each class of mail or type of service. It studies and submits recommended decisions on establishing or changing the mail classification schedule and holds on-the-record hearings that are lawfully required to attain sound and fair recommendations. It initiates studies on postal matters, such as cost theory and operations.

The Commission also receives, studies, conducts hearings, and issues recommended decisions and reports to the Postal Service on complaints received from interested persons relating to postage rates, postal classifications, and problems of national scope regarding postal services. It has appellate jurisdiction to review Postal Service determinations to close or consolidate small post offices. The Commission also prepares an annual report on international mail.

Sources of Information

Employment The Commission's programs require attorneys, economists, statisticians, accountants, industrial engineers, marketing specialists, and administrative and clerical personnel. Requests for employment information should be directed to the Personnel Officer.

Electronic Access Electronic access to current docketed case materials is available through the Internet, at www.prc.gov. Electronic mail can be sent to the Commission at prc-admin@prc.gov and prc-dockets@prc.gov.

Reading Room Facilities for inspection and copying of records, viewing automated daily lists of docketed materials, and accessing the Commission's Internet site are located at Suite 300, 1333 H Street, Washington, DC. The room is open from 8 a.m. to 4:30 p.m., Monday through Friday, except legal holidays.

Rules of Practice and Procedure The Postal Rate Commission's Rules of Practice and Procedure governing the conduct of proceedings before the Commission may be found in part 3001 of title 39 of the *Code of Federal Regulations.*

For further information, contact the Secretary, Postal Rate Commission, 1333 H Street NW., Washington, DC 20268–0001. Phone, 202–789–6840. Internet, www.prc.gov.

RAILROAD RETIREMENT BOARD

844 North Rush Street, Chicago, IL 60611–2092
Phone, 312–751–4776. Fax, 312–751–7154. Internet, www.rrb.gov.

Chair	CHERRYL T. THOMAS
Labor Member	V.M. SPEAKMAN, JR.
Management Member	JEROME F. KEVER
Inspector General	MARTIN J. DICKMAN
General Counsel	STEVEN A. BARTHOLOW
Director, Legislative Affairs	MARGARET A. STANLEY, *Acting*
Director, Hearings and Appeals	THOMAS W. SADLER
Secretary to the Board	BEATRICE E. EZERSKI
Chief Actuary	FRANK J. BUZZI
Chief Information Officer	ROBERT T. ROSE
Chief Financial Officer	KENNETH P. BOEHNE
Director, Fiscal Operations	PETER A. LARSON
Director, Programs	BOBBY V. FERGUSON
Director, Assessment and Training	CATHERINE A. LEYSER
Director, Field Service	MARTHA M. BARRINGER, *Acting*
Director, Operations	ROBERT J. DUDA
Director, Policy and Systems	RONALD RUSSO, *Acting*
Director, Resource Management Center	KEITH B. EARLY, *Acting*
Director, Administration	JOHN L. THORESDALE
Director of Equal Opportunity	CANDACE M. GABRIEL
Director, Personnel	CHARLENE T. KUKLA

Director, Public Affairs	WILLIAM G. POULOS
Director, Supply and Service	HENRY M. VALIULIS

[For the Railroad Retirement Board statement of organization, see the *Code of Federal Regulations,* Title 20, Part 200]

The Railroad Retirement Board administers comprehensive retirement-survivor and unemployment-sickness benefit programs for the Nation's railroad workers and their families.

The Railroad Retirement Board was originally established by the Railroad Retirement Act of 1934, as amended (45 U.S.C. 201–228z-1).

The Board derives statutory authority from the Railroad Retirement Act of 1974 (45 U.S.C. 231–231u) and the Railroad Unemployment Insurance Act (45 U.S.C. 351–369). It administers these acts and participates in the administration of the Social Security Act and the Health Insurance for the Aged Act insofar as they affect railroad retirement beneficiaries.

The Board is composed of three members appointed by the President with the advice and consent of the Senate—one upon recommendations of representatives of employees; one upon recommendations of carriers; and one, the Chair, as a public member.

Activities

The Railroad Retirement Act provides for the payment of annuities to individuals who have completed at least 10 years of creditable service and have ceased compensated service upon their attainment of specified ages, or at any age if permanently disabled for all employment. In some circumstances occupational disability annuities or supplemental annuities are provided for career employees.

A spouse's annuity is provided, under certain conditions, for the wife or husband of an employee annuitant. Divorced spouses may also qualify.

Survivor annuities are awarded to the qualified spouses, children, and parents of deceased career employees, and various lump-sum benefits are also available under certain conditions.

Benefits based upon qualifying railroad earnings in a preceding one-year period are provided under the Railroad Unemployment Insurance Act to individuals who are unemployed in a benefit year, but who are ready and willing to work, and to individuals who are unable to work because of sickness or injury.

The Board maintains, through its field offices, a placement service for unemployed railroad personnel.

Sources of Information

Benefit Inquiries The Board maintains direct contact with railroad employees and railroad retirement beneficiaries through its field offices located across the country. Field personnel explain benefit rights and responsibilities on an individual basis, assist employees applying for benefits, and answer questions related to the benefit programs.

To locate the nearest field office, individuals should check with their rail employer, local union official, local post office, or one of the regional offices listed below. Most offices are open to the public from 9 a.m. to 3:30 p.m., Monday through Friday. The Board also relies on railroad labor groups and employers for assistance in keeping railroad personnel informed about its benefit programs.

Regional Offices—Railroad Retirement Board

City	Address	Director	Telephone
Atlanta, GA	Rm. 1703, 401 W. Peachtree St., 30365–2550	Patricia Lawson	404–331–2691
Denver, CO	Suite 3300, 1999 Broadway, 80202–5737	Louis E. Austin	303–844–0800
Philadelphia, PA	Suite 304, 900 Market St., 19107–4228	Richard D. Baird	215–597–2646

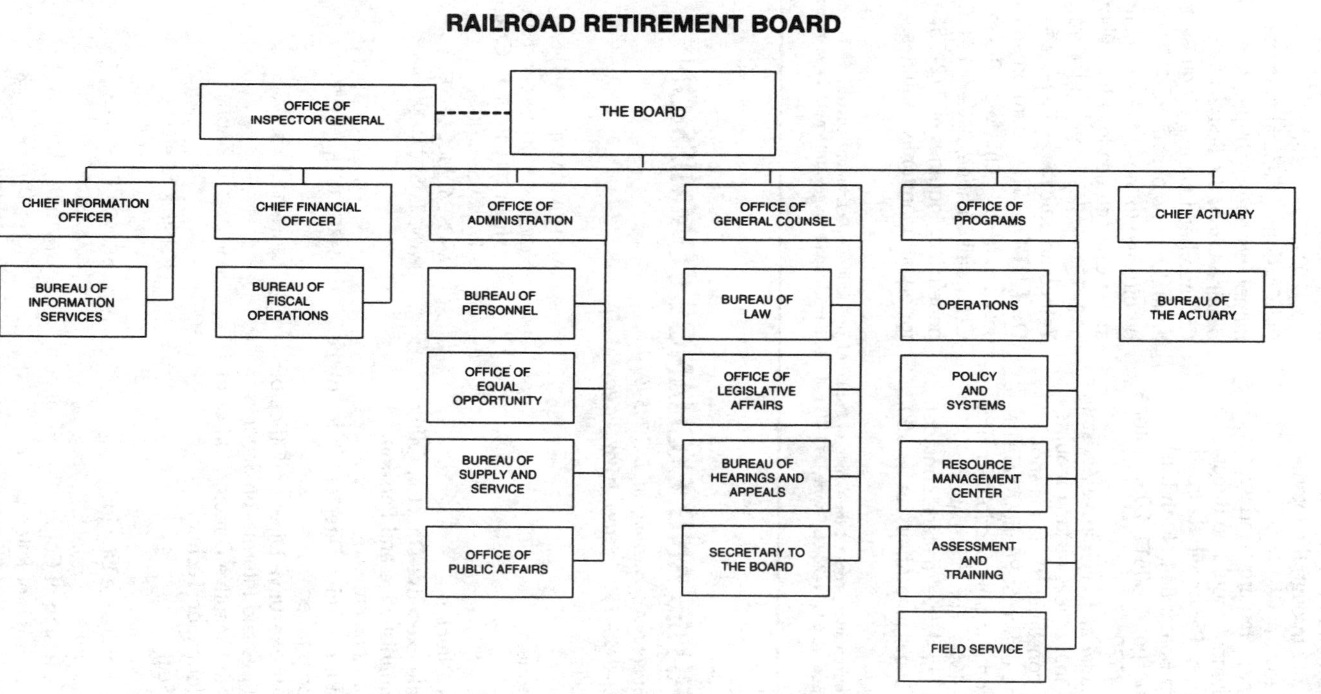
RAILROAD RETIREMENT BOARD
OFFICE OF INSPECTOR GENERAL
THE BOARD
CHIEF INFORMATION OFFICER
BUREAU OF INFORMATION SERVICES
CHIEF FINANCIAL OFFICER
BUREAU OF FISCAL OPERATIONS
OFFICE OF ADMINISTRATION
BUREAU OF PERSONNEL
OFFICE OF EQUAL OPPORTUNITY
BUREAU OF SUPPLY AND SERVICE
OFFICE OF PUBLIC AFFAIRS
OFFICE OF GENERAL COUNSEL
BUREAU OF LAW
OFFICE OF LEGISLATIVE AFFAIRS
BUREAU OF HEARINGS AND APPEALS
SECRETARY TO THE BOARD
OFFICE OF PROGRAMS
OPERATIONS
POLICY AND SYSTEMS
RESOURCE MANAGEMENT CENTER
ASSESSMENT AND TRAINING
FIELD SERVICE
CHIEF ACTUARY
BUREAU OF THE ACTUARY

Electronic Access Railroad Retirement Board information is available electronically through the Internet, at www.rrb.gov.

Employment Inquiries and applications for employment should be directed to the Bureau of Personnel, Railroad Retirement Board, 844 North Rush Street, Chicago, IL 60611–2092. Phone, 312–751–4570.

Congressional and Legislative Assistance Congressional offices making inquiries regarding constituents' claims should contact the Office of Public Affairs, Congressional Inquiry Section. Phone, 312–751–4974. For information regarding legislative matters, contact the Office of Legislative Affairs, Suite 500, 1310 G Street NW., Washington, DC 20005–3004. Phone, 202–272–7742. Fax, 202–272–7728.

Publications General information pamphlets on benefit programs may be obtained from the Board's field offices or Chicago headquarters. Requests for annual reports or statistical data should be directed to the Office of Public Affairs at the Chicago headquarters. Phone, 312–751–4776. E-mail, opa@rrb.gov.

Telecommunications Devices for the Deaf (TDD) The Board provides TDD services from 9 a.m. to 3:30 p.m. (CST/CDT) daily. Phone, 312–751–4701 for beneficiary inquiries or 312–751–4334 for equal opportunity inquiries.

For further information, contact the Office of Public Affairs, Railroad Retirement Board, 844 North Rush Street, Chicago, IL 60611–2092. Phone, 312–751–4776. E-mail, opa@rrb.gov. Internet, www.rrb.gov.

SECURITIES AND EXCHANGE COMMISSION

450 Fifth Street NW., Washington, DC 20549
Phone, 202–942–4150. Internet, www.sec.gov.

Chairman	Arthur Levitt
Commissioners	Norman S. Johnson, Isaac C. Hunt, Jr., Paul R. Carey, Laura S. Unger
Executive Director	James M. McConnell
Associate Executive Director, Office of Administrative and Personnel Management	Jayne L. Seidman
Associate Executive Director, Office of the Comptroller	Margaret J. Carpenter
Associate Executive Director, Office of Filings and Information Services	Kenneth A. Fogash
Associate Executive Director, Office of Information Technology	Michael E. Bartell
Chief of Staff	Jennifer Scardino
Chief Accountant	Lynn E. Turner
Chief Administrative Law Judge	Brenda P. Murray
Chief Economist	(vacancy)
Director, Division of Corporation Finance	David B. H. Martin
Director, Division of Enforcement	Richard H. Walker
Director, Division of Investment Management	Paul Roye
Director, Division of Market Regulation	Annette L. Nazareth
Director, Office of Compliance Inspections and Examinations	Lori A. Richards

Director, Office of Equal Employment Opportunity	DEBORAH K. BALDUCCHI
Director, Office of International Affairs	MARISA LAGO
Director, Office of Investor Education and Assistance	SUSAN F. WYDERKO
Director, Office of Legislative Affairs	TRACEY F. ARONSON
Director, Office of Municipal Securities	PAUL S. MACO
Director, Office of Public Affairs, Policy Evaluation, and Research	CHRISTOPHER ULLMAN
General Counsel	DAVID BECKER
Inspector General	WALTER STACHNIK
Secretary	JONATHAN G. KATZ

[For the Securities and Exchange Commission statement of organization, see the *Code of Federal Regulations*, Title 17, Part 200]

The Securities and Exchange Commission administers Federal securities laws that seek to provide protection for investors; to ensure that securities markets are fair and honest; and, when necessary, to provide the means to enforce securities laws through sanctions.

The Securities and Exchange Commission was created under authority of the Securities Exchange Act of 1934 (15 U.S.C. 78a-78jj) and was organized on July 2, 1934. The Commission serves as adviser to United States district courts in connection with reorganization proceedings for debtor corporations in which there is a substantial public interest. The Commission also has certain responsibilities under section 15 of the Bretton Woods Agreements Act of 1945 (22 U.S.C. 286k-1) and section 851(e) of the Internal Revenue Code of 1954 (26 U.S.C. 851(e)).

The Commission is vested with quasi-judicial functions. Persons aggrieved by its decisions in the exercise of those functions have a right of review by the United States courts of appeals.

Activities

Full and Fair Disclosure The Securities Act of 1933 (15 U.S.C. 77a) requires issuers of securities and their controlling persons making public offerings of securities in interstate commerce or through the mails to file with the Commission registration statements containing financial and other pertinent data about the issuer and the securities being offered. There are limited exemptions, such as government securities, nonpublic offerings, and intrastate offerings, as well as certain offerings not exceeding $1.5 million. The effectiveness of a registration statement may be refused or suspended after a public hearing if the statement contains material misstatements or omissions, thus barring sale of the securities until it is appropriately amended.

Regulation of Companies Controlling Utilities The Commission regulates the purchase and sale of securities and assets by companies in electric and gas utility holding company systems, their intrasystem transactions and service, and management arrangements. It limits holding companies to a single coordinated utility system and requires simplification of complex corporate and capital structures and elimination of unfair distribution of voting power among holders of system securities.

The purchase and sale of utility properties and other assets may not be made in contravention of rules, regulations, or orders of the Commission regarding the consideration to be received, maintenance of competitive conditions, fees and commissions, accounts, disclosure of interest, and similar matters. In passing upon proposals for reorganization, merger, or consolidation, the Commission must be satisfied that the objectives of the act generally are complied with and that the terms of the proposal are fair and

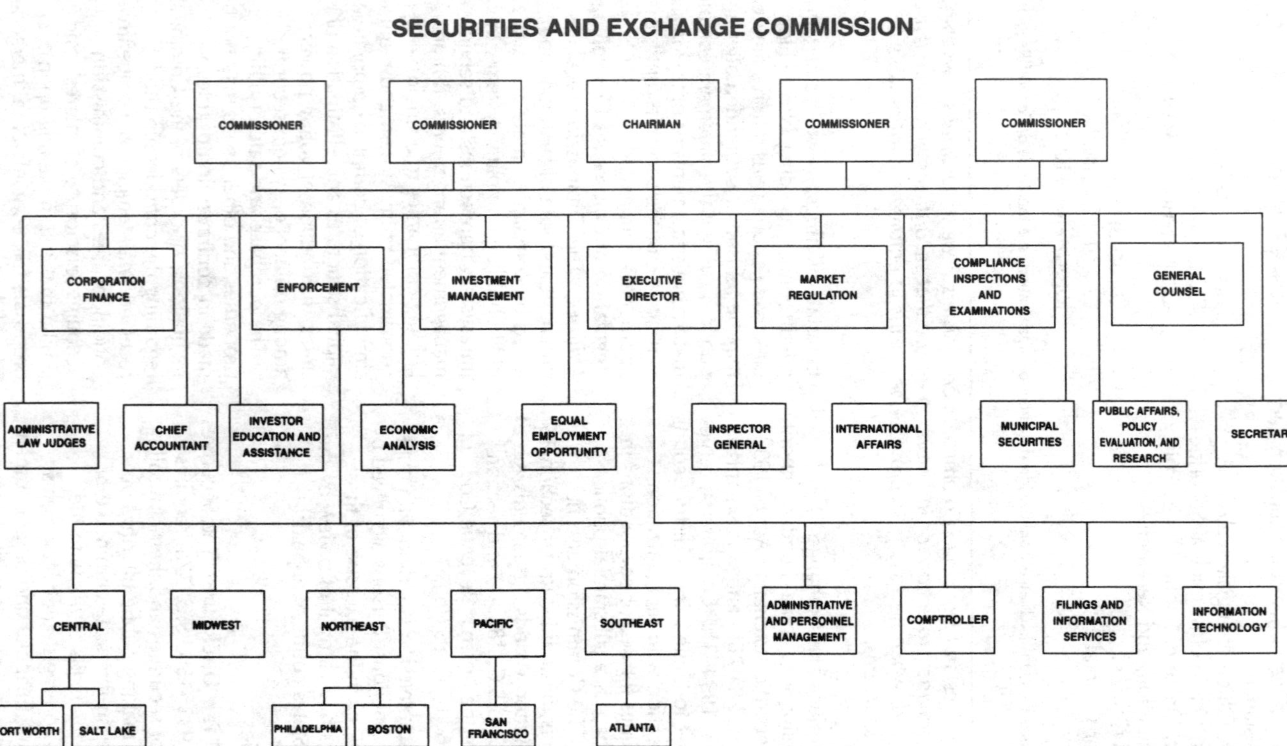
SECURITIES AND EXCHANGE COMMISSION
COMMISSIONER
COMMISSIONER
CHAIRMAN
COMMISSIONER
COMMISSIONER
CORPORATION FINANCE
ENFORCEMENT
INVESTMENT MANAGEMENT
EXECUTIVE DIRECTOR
MARKET REGULATION
COMPLIANCE INSPECTIONS AND EXAMINATIONS
GENERAL COUNSEL
ADMINISTRATIVE LAW JUDGES
CHIEF ACCOUNTANT
INVESTOR EDUCATION AND ASSISTANCE
ECONOMIC ANALYSIS
EQUAL EMPLOYMENT OPPORTUNITY
INSPECTOR GENERAL
INTERNATIONAL AFFAIRS
MUNICIPAL SECURITIES
PUBLIC AFFAIRS, POLICY EVALUATION, AND RESEARCH
SECRETARY
CENTRAL
MIDWEST
NORTHEAST
PACIFIC
SOUTHEAST
ADMINISTRATIVE AND PERSONNEL MANAGEMENT
COMPTROLLER
FILINGS AND INFORMATION SERVICES
INFORMATION TECHNOLOGY
FORT WORTH
SALT LAKE
PHILADELPHIA
BOSTON
SAN FRANCISCO
ATLANTA

equitable to all classes of securities holders affected.

Regulation of Investment Advisers Persons who, for compensation, engage in the business of advising others with respect to securities must register with the Commission. The Commission is authorized to define what practices are considered fraudulent or deceptive and to prescribe means to prevent those practices.

Regulation of Mutual Funds and Other Investment Companies The Commission registers investment companies and regulates their activities to protect investors. The regulation covers sales load, management contracts, composition of boards of directors, and capital structure. The Commission must also determine the fairness of various transactions of investment companies before these actually occur.

The Commission may institute court action to enjoin the consummation of mergers and other plans of reorganization of investment companies if such plans are unfair to securities holders. It also may impose sanctions by administrative proceedings against investment company management for violations of the act and other Federal securities laws and file court actions to enjoin acts and practices of management officials involving breaches of fiduciary duty and personal misconduct and to disqualify such officials from office.

Regulation of Securities Markets The Securities Exchange Act of 1934 assigns to the Commission broad regulatory responsibilities over the securities markets, the self-regulatory organizations within the securities industry, and persons conducting a business in securities. Persons who execute transactions in securities generally are required to register with the Commission as broker-dealers. Securities exchanges and certain clearing agencies are required to register with the Commission, and associations of brokers or dealers are permitted to register with the Commission. The act also provides for the establishment of the Municipal Securities Rulemaking Board to formulate rules for the municipal securities industry.

The Commission oversees the self-regulatory activities of the national securities exchanges and associations, registered clearing agencies, and the Municipal Securities Rulemaking Board. In addition, the Commission regulates industry professionals, such as securities brokers and dealers, certain municipal securities professionals, government securities brokers and dealers, and transfer agents.

Rehabilitation of Failing Corporations In cases of corporate reorganization proceedings administered in Federal courts, the Commission may participates as a statutory party. The principal functions of the Commission are to protect the interests of public investors involved in such cases through efforts to ensure their adequate representation, and to participate in legal and policy issues that are of concern to public investors generally.

Representation of Debt Securities Holders The Commission safeguards the interests of purchasers of publicly offered debt securities issued pursuant to trust indentures.

Enforcement Activities The Commission's enforcement activities are designed to secure compliance with the Federal securities laws administered by the Commission and the rules and regulations adopted thereunder. These activities include measures to:

—compel compliance with the disclosure requirements of the registration and other provisions of the relevant acts;

—prevent fraud and deception in the purchase and sale of securities;

—obtain court orders enjoining acts and practices that operate as a fraud upon investors or otherwise violate the laws;

—suspend or revoke the registrations of brokers, dealers, investment companies, and investment advisers who willfully engage in such acts and practices;

—suspend or bar from association persons associated with brokers, dealers, investment companies, and investment advisers who have violated any provision of the Federal securities laws; and

—prosecute persons who have engaged in fraudulent activities or other willful violations of those laws.

In addition, attorneys, accountants, and other professionals who violate the securities laws face possible loss of their privilege to practice before the Commission.

To this end, private investigations are conducted into complaints or other indications of securities violations. Evidence thus established of law violations is used in appropriate administrative proceedings to revoke registration or in actions instituted in Federal courts to restrain or enjoin such activities. Where the evidence tends to establish criminal fraud or other willful violation of the securities laws, the facts are referred to the Attorney General for criminal prosecution of the offenders. The Commission may assist in such prosecutions.

Regional/District Offices—Securities and Exchange Commission

(R: Regional Director; D: District Administrator)

Region/District	Address	Official	Telephone
Northeast			
New York, NY	Suite 1300, 7 World Trade Ctr., 10048	Carmen J. Lawrence (R)	212–748–8000
Boston, MA	Suite 600, 73 Tremont St., 02108–3912	Juan Marcel Marcelino (D)	617–424–5900
Philadelphia, PA	Suite 1120 E., 601 Walnut St., 19106–3322	Ronald C. Long (D)	215–597–3100
Southeast			
Miami, FL	Suite 200, 1401 Brickell Ave., 33131	Randall J. Fons (R)	305–536–4700
Atlanta, GA	Suite 1000, 3475 Lenox Rd. NE., 30326–1232	Richard P. Wessel (D)	404–842–7600
Midwest			
Chicago, IL	Suite 1400, 500 W. Madison St., 60661–2511	Mary Keefe (R)	312–353–7390
Central			
Denver, CO	Suite 4800, 1801 California St., 80202–2648	Daniel F. Shea (R)	303–844–1000
Fort Worth, TX	Suite 1900, 801 Cherry St., 76102	Harold F. Degenhardt (D)	817–978–3821
Salt Lake City, UT	Suite 500, 50 S. Main St., 84144–0402	Kenneth D. Israel, Jr. (D)	801–524–5796
Pacific			
Los Angeles, CA	Suite 1100, 5670 Wilshire Blvd., 90036–3648	Valerie Carponi (R)	323–965–3998
San Francisco, CA	Suite 1100, 44 Montgomery St., 94104	Helane Morrison (D)	415–705–2500

Sources of Information

Inquiries regarding the following matters should be directed to the appropriate office, Securities and Exchange Commission, 450 Fifth Street NW., Washington, DC 20549.

Contracts Inquires regarding SEC procurement and contracting activities should be directed to the Office of Administrative and Personnel Management. Phone, 202–942–4990.

Electronic Access Information on the Commission is available through the Internet, at www.sec.gov.

Employment With the exception of the attorney category, positions are in the competitive civil service, which means applicants must apply for consideration for a particular vacancy and go through competitive selection procedures. The Commission operates a college and law school recruitment program, including on-campus visitations for interview purposes. Inquiries should be directed to the Office of Administrative and Personnel Management. Phone, 202–942–4070. Fax, 703–256–2796 or 703–914–0556.

Investor Assistance and Complaints The Office of Investor Education and Assistance answers questions from investors, assists investors with specific problems regarding their relations with broker-dealers and companies, and advises the Commission and other offices and divisions regarding problems frequently encountered by investors and possible regulatory solutions to such problems. Phone, 202–942–7040. Consumer information line, 800–SEC–0330 (toll-free). Fax, 202–942–9634.

Complaints and inquiries may also directed to any regional or district office.

Publications Blank copies of SEC forms and other publications are available in the Publications Unit. Phone, 202–942–4040. *Official Summary*—A monthly summary of securities transactions and holdings of officers, directors, and principal stockholders ($47 per issue) is available through the Superintendent of Documents, Government Printing Office, Washington, DC 20402. Phone, 202–512–1800.

Reading Rooms The Commission maintains a public reference room (phone, 202–942–8090) in Washington, DC, where registration statements and other public documents filed with the Commission are available for public inspection. Much of this information is also available at the Northeast and Midwest regional offices. Copies of public material may be purchased from the Commission's contract copying service at prescribed rates. The Commission also maintains a library (phone, 202–942–7090; fax, 202–942–9629) where additional information may be obtained.

Small Business Activities Information on securities laws that pertain to small businesses in relation to securities offerings may be obtained from the Commission. Phone, 202–942–2950.

For further information, contact the Office of Public Affairs, Securities and Exchange Commission, 450 Fifth Street NW., Washington, DC 20549–0711. Phone, 202–942–0020. Fax, 202–942–9654. Internet, www.sec.gov.

SELECTIVE SERVICE SYSTEM

National Headquarters, Arlington, VA 22209–2425
Phone, 703–605–4000. Internet, www.sss.gov.

Director	GIL CORONADO
Deputy Director	WILLIE L. BLANDING, JR.
Chief of Staff	LT. COL. ROGELIO RODRIGUEZ, USAF
Counselor and General Counsel	(VACANCY)
Director for Information Management	NORMAN W. MILLER
Director for Operations	COL. JUSTO GONZALEZ, USA
Director for Public and Congressional Affairs	LEWIS C. BRODSKY
Director for Resource Management	D. FREIDA BROCKINGTON
Financial Manager	CARLO VERDINO
Inspector General	ALFRED RASCON

[For the Selective Service System statement of organization, see the *Code of Federal Regulations,* Title 32, Part 1605]

The mission of the Selective Service System is to provide untrained manpower to the Armed Forces in an emergency, and to operate an Alternative Service Program during a draft for men classified as conscientious objectors.

The Selective Service System was established by the Military Selective Service Act (50 U.S.C. app. 451–471a). The act requires the registration of male citizens of the United States and all other male persons who are in the United States and who are between the ages of 18 and 26. The act exempts members of the active Armed Forces and nonimmigrant aliens. Proclamation 4771 of July 20, 1980, requires male persons born on or after January 1, 1960, and who have attained age 18 but have not attained age 26 to register. Registration is

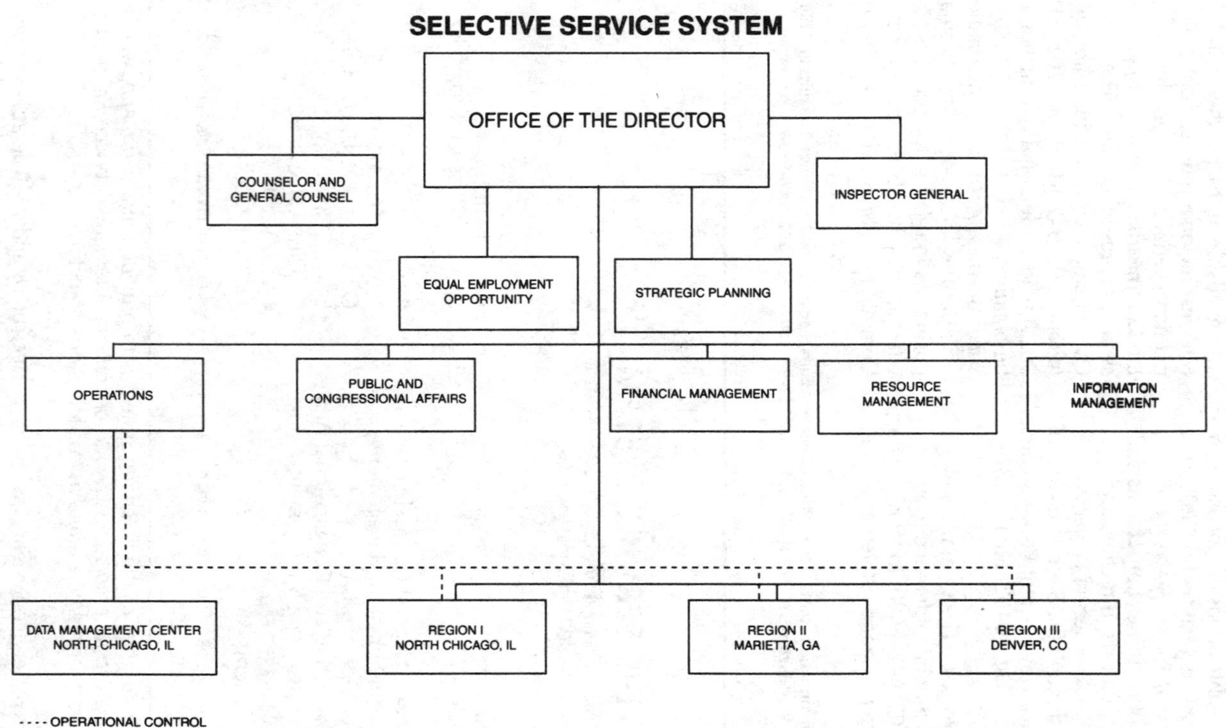
SELECTIVE SERVICE SYSTEM
OFFICE OF THE DIRECTOR
COUNSELOR AND GENERAL COUNSEL
INSPECTOR GENERAL
EQUAL EMPLOYMENT OPPORTUNITY
STRATEGIC PLANNING
OPERATIONS
PUBLIC AND CONGRESSIONAL AFFAIRS
FINANCIAL MANAGEMENT
RESOURCE MANAGEMENT
INFORMATION MANAGEMENT
DATA MANAGEMENT CENTER NORTH CHICAGO, IL
REGION I NORTH CHICAGO, IL
REGION II MARIETTA, GA
REGION III DENVER, CO
---- OPERATIONAL CONTROL

conducted at post offices within the United States and at U.S. Embassies and consulates outside the United States.

The act imposes liability for training and service in the Armed Forces upon registrants who are between the ages of 18 and 26, except those who are exempt or deferred. Persons who have been deferred remain liable for training and service until age 35. Aliens are not liable for training and service until they have remained in the United States for more than one year. Conscientious objectors who are found to be opposed to all service in the Armed Forces are required to perform civilian work in lieu of induction into the Armed Forces.

The authority to induct registrants, including doctors and allied medical specialists, expired July 1, 1973.

Regional Offices—Selective Service System

Region/Address	Director	Telephone
North Chicago, IL (Suite 276, 2834 Green Bay Rd., 60064–3038)	Lt. Col. Glen Ford, USA	847–688–7990
Marietta, GA (Suite 4, 805 Walker St., 30060–2731)	Col. Keith A. Scragg, USAF	770–590–6602
Denver, CO (Suite 1, 7245 E. Irvington Pl., 80220–6920)	Col. Lavoy M. Thiessen, USA	303–676–7809

Sources of Information

Employment Inquiries and applications should be directed to the Director, Selective Service System, Attn: RMH, Arlington, VA 22209–2425. Phone, 703–605–4056.

Procurement Inquiries should be directed to the Director, Selective Service System, Attn: RML, Arlington, VA 22209–2425. Phone, 703–605–4040.

Publications Selective Service Regulations appear in chapter XVI of title 32 of the *Code of Federal Regulations.*

Requirements of Law Persons desiring information concerning the requirements of the Military Selective Service Act should contact the National Headquarters of the Selective Service System. Phone, 703–605–4000.

For further information, contact the Office of Public and Congressional Affairs, Selective Service System, Arlington, VA 22209–2425. Phone, 703–605–4100. Internet, www.sss.gov.

SMALL BUSINESS ADMINISTRATION

409 Third Street SW., Washington, DC 20416
Phone, 202–205–6600. Fax, 202–205–7064. Internet, www.sba.gov.

Administrator	AIDA ALVAREZ
Deputy Administrator	FRED HOCHBERG
Chief Counsel for Advocacy	JERE W. GLOVER
Chief Financial Officer	JOE LODDO
Chief Operating Officer	KRIS MARCY
Chief of Staff	KRIS SWEDIN
Counselor to the Administrator	BETTY BACA
Director, Executive Secretariat	SUSAN WALTHALL
Director, External Affairs	(VACANCY)
General Counsel	MICHAEL SCHATTMAN
Inspector General	PHYLLIS FONG
Associate Administrator for Disaster Assistance	BERNARD KULIK
Associate Administrator for Communications and Public Liaison	(VACANCY)
Assistant Administrator for Congressional and Legislative Affairs	JANE MERKIN

Assistant Administrator for Equal Employment Opportunity and Civil Rights Compliance	ERLINE PATRICK
Associate Administrator for Field Operations	ROBERT BASKIN
Assistant Administrator for Hearings and Appeals	(VACANCY)
Associate Deputy Administrator for Capital Access	CHARLES TANSEY
Associate Administrator for Financial Assistance	JANE BUTLER
Assistant Administrator for International Trade	JAMES WILFONG
Associate Administrator for Investment	DON CHRISTENSEN
Associate Administrator for Surety Guarantees	ROBERT J. MOFFITT
Associate Deputy Administrator for Entrepreneurial Development	DARRYL DENNIS
Associate Administrator for Business Initiatives	MONIKA HARRISON
Assistant Administrator for Native American Affairs	LYDIA PICKFORD
Associate Administrator for Small Business Development Centers	JOHNNIE ALBERTSON
Assistant Administrator for Veterans Affairs	CLIFTON TOULSON, JR.
Assistant Administrator for Women's Business Ownership	SHERRYE HENRY
Associate Deputy Administrator for Government Contracting and Minority Enterprise Development	JAMES BALLENTINE
Associate Administrator for Government Contracting	BARRY MELTZ, *Acting*
Associate Administrator for Minority Enterprise Development	DELORICE FORD, *Acting*
Assistant Administrator for Size Standards	GARY M. JACKSON
Assistant Administrator for Technology	(VACANCY)
Associate Deputy Administrator for Management and Administration	ELIZABETH A. MONTOYA
Assistant Administrator for Administration	THOMAS DUMARESQ
Assistant Administrator for Human Resources	CAROLYN J. SMITH
Chief Information Officer	LAWRENCE BARRETT

[For the Small Business Administration statement of organization, see the *Code of Federal Regulations,* Title 13, Part 101]

The fundamental purposes of the Small Business Administration are to aid, counsel, assist, and protect the interests of small business; ensure that small business concerns receive a fair portion of Government purchases, contracts, and subcontracts, as well as of the sales of Government property; make loans to small business concerns, State and local development companies, and the victims of floods or other catastrophes, or of certain types of economic injury; and license, regulate, and make loans to small business investment companies.

The Small Business Administration (SBA) was created by the Small Business Act of 1953 and derives its present existence and authority from the Small Business Act (15 U.S.C. 631 *et seq.*) and the Small Business Investment Act of 1958 (15 U.S.C. 661).

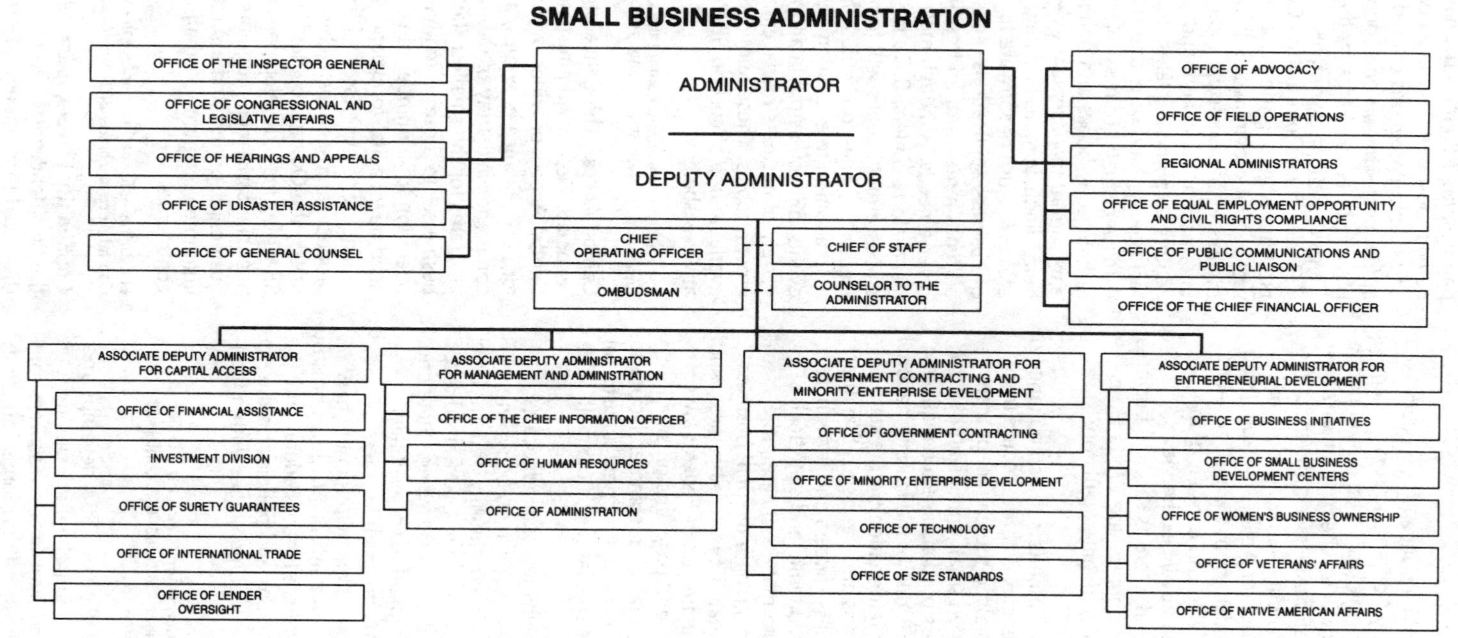
SMALL BUSINESS ADMINISTRATION
OFFICE OF THE INSPECTOR GENERAL
OFFICE OF CONGRESSIONAL AND LEGISLATIVE AFFAIRS
OFFICE OF HEARINGS AND APPEALS
OFFICE OF DISASTER ASSISTANCE
OFFICE OF GENERAL COUNSEL
ADMINISTRATOR
DEPUTY ADMINISTRATOR
CHIEF OPERATING OFFICER
OMBUDSMAN
CHIEF OF STAFF
COUNSELOR TO THE ADMINISTRATOR
OFFICE OF ADVOCACY
OFFICE OF FIELD OPERATIONS
REGIONAL ADMINISTRATORS
OFFICE OF EQUAL EMPLOYMENT OPPORTUNITY AND CIVIL RIGHTS COMPLIANCE
OFFICE OF PUBLIC COMMUNICATIONS AND PUBLIC LIAISON
OFFICE OF THE CHIEF FINANCIAL OFFICER
ASSOCIATE DEPUTY ADMINISTRATOR FOR CAPITAL ACCESS
OFFICE OF FINANCIAL ASSISTANCE
INVESTMENT DIVISION
OFFICE OF SURETY GUARANTEES
OFFICE OF INTERNATIONAL TRADE
OFFICE OF LENDER OVERSIGHT
ASSOCIATE DEPUTY ADMINISTRATOR FOR MANAGEMENT AND ADMINISTRATION
OFFICE OF THE CHIEF INFORMATION OFFICER
OFFICE OF HUMAN RESOURCES
OFFICE OF ADMINISTRATION
ASSOCIATE DEPUTY ADMINISTRATOR FOR GOVERNMENT CONTRACTING AND MINORITY ENTERPRISE DEVELOPMENT
OFFICE OF GOVERNMENT CONTRACTING
OFFICE OF MINORITY ENTERPRISE DEVELOPMENT
OFFICE OF TECHNOLOGY
OFFICE OF SIZE STANDARDS
ASSOCIATE DEPUTY ADMINISTRATOR FOR ENTREPRENEURIAL DEVELOPMENT
OFFICE OF BUSINESS INITIATIVES
OFFICE OF SMALL BUSINESS DEVELOPMENT CENTERS
OFFICE OF WOMEN'S BUSINESS OWNERSHIP
OFFICE OF VETERANS' AFFAIRS
OFFICE OF NATIVE AMERICAN AFFAIRS

Activities

Advocacy The Office of Advocacy is mandated by Congress to serve as an independent spokesperson within public policy councils for the more than 22.5 million small businesses throughout the country. The Office is headed by the Chief Counsel for Advocacy, appointed by the President from the private sector with the advice and consent of the Senate, who advances the views, concerns, and interests of small business before the Congress, the White House, and Federal and State regulatory agencies.

The Office monitors the compliance of Federal agencies with the requirement that they analyze the impact of their regulations on small entities and consider less burdensome alternatives. The Office is one of the leading national sources for information on the state of small business and the issues that affect small business success and growth. It conducts economic and statistical research into matters affecting the competitive strength of small business and jobs created by small business, and analyzes the impact of Federal laws, regulations, and programs on small businesses, making recommendations to policymakers for appropriate adjustments to meet the special needs of small business.

Additionally, regional advocates enhance communication between the small business community and the Chief Counsel. As the Chief Counsel's direct link to local business owners, State and local government agencies, State legislatures, and small business organizations, they help identify new issues and problems of small business by monitoring the effect of Federal and State regulations and policies on the local business communities within their regions.

For further information, contact the Office of Advocacy. Phone, 202–205–6533. Internet, www.sba.gov/advo.

Business Initiatives SBA develops and cosponsors counseling, education, training, and information resources for small businesses. It has forged ongoing partnerships with resource partners to deliver most of the business education and training programs offered annually at low cost. One-on-one counseling is provided free of charge by the Service Corps of Retired Executives.

The Business Information Center (BIC) program is among the most innovative methods of providing small business owners with a one-stop approach to information, education, and training. The centers combine the latest computer technology, hardware, and software, an extensive small business reference library of hard copy books and publications, and current management videotapes to help clients venture into new business areas. The use of software for a variety of business applications offers clients of all types a means of addressing their diverse needs. Although most BIC's are stand-alone centers, BIC's in empowerment zones will form the core element of one-stop capital shops.

In addition to education and training events, SBA offers publications on a variety of business management and growth topics. These publications are available free of cost on SBA's website, at www.sba.gov.

For further information, contact the Office of Business Initiatives. Phone, 202–205–6665.

Capital Access The Office of the Associate Deputy Administrator for Capital Access provides overall direction for SBA's finance programs, a comprehensive array of debt and equity programs for the smallest start-up businesses to those which have been in operation for a number of years and need new capital to expand. In addition to lending to businesses which sell their products and services within the United States, the Office provides direction for SBA's business development and financial assistance programs for small-business exporters and a surety bond guarantee program for small-business contractors.

For further information, contact the Office of Capital Access. Phone, 202–205–6657.

Community Development As part of the President's efforts to revitalize distressed inner cities and rural communities through Federal and local government cooperation, SBA initiated the one stop capital shop initiative in 1994. SBA makes a one stop capital shop available to each enterprise zone community to provide easy access to small business assistance in distressed, underserved communities. Each one stop capital shop has a BIC which offers extensive small business libraries and publications, as well as state-of-the-art computer resources, small business software, and Internet access. They offer extensive training services from local Small Business Development Centers, Service Corps of Retired Executives counseling, microenterprise loans, technical assistance, private sector lending partners, and government contracts assistance.

For further information, contact the Office of One Stop Capital Shop. Phone, 202–205–6706. Internet, www.sba.gov/onestop.

Disaster Assistance The Administration serves as the Federal disaster bank for nonfarm, private sector losses. It lends money to help the victims of floods, riots, or other catastrophes repair or replace most disaster-damaged property. Direct loans with subsidized interest rates are made to assist individuals, homeowners, businesses of all sizes and nonprofit organizations.

For further information, contact the Office of Disaster Assistance. Phone, 202–205–6734.

Financial Assistance SBA provides its guarantee to lending institutions and certified development companies which make loans to small-business concerns (including farms), which in turn, use the loans to provide working capital and help finance the acquisition of land and buildings; the construction, conversion, or expansion of facilities; and the purchase of machinery and equipment.

SBA provides revolving lines of credit and loan guarantees to finance commercial construction or building rehabilitation for sale. It makes loans to qualified employee trusts and may finance small firms that manufacture, sell, install, service, or develop specific energy measures, including engineering, architectural, consulting, or other professional services connected with eligible energy measures. SBA also makes loans for the installation of pollution control measures.

The Administration makes loans and grants to nonprofit organizations that act as intermediaries to provide technical and small-scale financial assistance to very small businesses under SBA's MicroLoan Program. The Administration also provides small-scale financial and technical assistance to very small businesses through loans and grants to nonprofit organizations that act as intermediaries.

For further information, contact the nearest Small Business Administration district office.

Government Contracting The Administration works closely with purchasing agencies of the Federal Government and with the Nation's major prime contractors in developing policies and procedures that will maximize practicable participation by small, small disadvantaged, historically underutilized, and women-owned small businesses in contracts awarded by the U.S. Government and subcontracts awarded by its large contractors. It sets aside or reserves applicable Government purchases for contracts competitively awarded to SBC's and provides an appeal procedure for a low-bidding small business whose ability to perform a contract is questioned by the contracting officer. SBA encourages subcontract opportunities for small businesses by maintaining close contact with large prime contractors and by referring qualified small businesses to them. It coordinates and manages setting of annual goals for contracts and subcontracts awarded to small businesses by Federal agencies.

The Administration maintains an Internet-based database (PRO–*Net*) that provides profiles of small businesses that can be readily accessed by Federal Government contracting officers, State and local governments, and other contractors seeking small business contractors, subcontractors, or partnerships for contracting opportunities. It cooperates with Government agencies in ensuring that small businesses have a fair opportunity to acquire new and surplus Government property, such as timber, royalty oil, strategic materials, and mineral leases, that is sold to the private sector.

For further information, contact the Office of Government Contracting. Phone, 202–205–6460.

International Trade The Office of International Trade provides export financing and export promotion services to small businesses. It administers the export working capital program, which provides short-term, transaction-specific financing for exporting, including pre-export financing of labor and materials, financing receivables generated from these sales, and standby letters of credit used as performance bonds or payment guarantees to foreign buyers.

The Office is a major participant in the U.S. Export Assistance Center (USEAC) initiative. The centers provide a single point of contact for all Federal export promotion and finance programs in the following cities: Atlanta, GA; Baltimore, MD; Boston, MA; Charlotte, NC; Chicago, IL; Cleveland, OH; Dallas, TX; Denver, CO; Detroit, MI; Long Beach, CA; Miami, FL; Minneapolis, MN; New Orleans, LA; New York, NY; Philadelphia, PA; Portland, OR; San Jose, CA; Seattle, WA; and St. Louis, MO.

The Office develops and recommends agency policy and procedures to effectively deliver the international trade program, provides tools for SBA's resource partners, and coordinates activities with agency resource partners and USEAC's to improve accessibility to its programs. The Office also coordinates with other Federal agencies, under the auspices of the Trade Promotion Coordinating Committee (TPCC), to ensure that trade promotion information and trade events are communicated to the small business community. The Office also works with agencies of the TPCC in coordinating and facilitating trade between the U.S. small business community and businesses and governments of other countries.

For further information, contact the Office of International Trade. Phone, 202–205–6720.

Investment The Administration licenses, regulates, and provides financial assistance to privately owned and managed small-business investment companies. The sole function of these investment companies is to provide venture capital in the form of equity financing, long-term loan funds, and management services to small-business concerns throughout the United States.

For further information, contact the Investment Division. Phone, 202–205–6510.

Minority Enterprise Development The Minority Enterprise Development Program is designed to promote and strengthen businesses owned by socially and economically disadvantaged persons. Program participants receive a wide variety of services from SBA including management and technical assistance, loans, and Federal contracts. Information regarding the program is provided by SBA district offices.

For further information, contact the Office of Minority Enterprise Development. Phone, 202–205–6412.

Native American Affairs The Office of Native American Affairs was established to assist and encourage the creation, development, and expansion of Native American-owned small businesses by developing and implementing initiatives designed to address those difficulties encountered by Native Americans in their quest to start, develop, and expand small businesses. In addition, in an effort to address the unique conditions encountered by reservation-based entrepreneurs, SBA has established the Tribal Business Information Centers (TBIC) pilot project. The project is a partnership arrangement between a tribe or tribal college and SBA.

TBIC's offer community access to business-related computer software technology, provide one-on-one business counseling, and hold business workshops on an ongoing basis. Additionally, all TBIC managers/ facilitators have received extensive training in all SBA entrepreneurial development programs, lending programs, and procurement programs. Currently there are 17 centers located in

Arizona, California, Minnesota, Montana, North Carolina, North Dakota, and South Dakota.

Besides administering the TBIC pilot project, the Office actively participates with other SBA program offices and other Federal agencies to ensure that Native American entrepreneurs are being actively encouraged to participate. Also, the Office maintains liaisons with tribal governments, business organizations, and Native American community organizations.

For further information, contact the Office of Native American Affairs. Phone, 202–205–7364.

Regulatory Fairness Program The Regulatory Fairness Program (RegFair) provides small businesses with a meaningful way to comment on the enforcement and compliance activities of the Federal agencies that regulate them. RegFair is headed by a national Ombudsman, who rates and evaluates efforts of Federal agencies to become more small-business friendly. Ten regional Regulatory Fairness Boards, comprised of 50 small business owners, support the Ombudsman by collecting information, making recommendations for agencies, and advising the Ombudsman on the regulatory climate faced by small businesses. Each board has five members who are small business owners, giving them an understanding of what small businesses face with Federal regulations. A small business can comment on Federal enforcement activities by contacting a Regulatory Fairness Board member, filing an agency appraisal form, or testifying at a RegFair public hearing.

For further information, contact the Office of the National Ombudsman. Phone, 312–353–0880, or 800–REG–FAIR (800–734–3247) (toll-free). Internet, www.sba.gov/regfair.

Small Business Development Centers Small Business Development Centers provide counseling and training to existing and prospective small business owners at approximately 1,000 locations around the country, operating in every State, Puerto Rico, the U.S. Virgin Islands, Guam, and American Samoa. The Small Business Development Center Program is a cooperative effort of the private sector, the educational community, and Federal, State, and local governments. It enhances economic development by providing small businesses with management and technical assistance.

The Office of Small Business Development Centers develops national policies and goals. It establishes standards for the selection and performance of Centers, monitors compliance with applicable Office of Management and Budget circulars and laws, and implements new approaches to improve operations of existing centers.

The Office is responsible for coordinating program efforts with other internal activities of SBA and with the activities of other Federal agencies. It maintains liaison with other Federal, State, and local agencies and private organizations whose activities relate to Small Business Development Centers, and it assesses how the program is affected by substantive developments and policies in other areas of the agency, in other government agencies, and in the private sector.

For further information, contact the Office of Small Business Development Centers. Phone, 202–205–6766.

Surety Bonds Through its Surety Bond Guarantee Program, SBA helps to make the contract bonding process accessible to small and emerging contractors who find bonding unavailable. It guarantees up to 90 percent of losses incurred under bid, payment, or performance bonds issued to small contractors on contracts valued up to $1.25 million.

For further information, contact the Office of Surety Guarantees. Phone, 202–205–6540.

Technology The Office of Technology has authority and responsibility for directing and monitoring the governmentwide activities of the Small Business Innovation Research Program (SBIR). In accordance with the Small Business Research and Development Enhancement Act of 1992, as amended (15 U.S.C. 631 note), the Office develops and issues policy directives for the general conduct of the programs within the Federal Government and maintains a source file and information program to provide each interested and qualified small business concern with information on opportunities to compete for SBIR program awards. The Office also coordinates with each participating Federal agency in developing a master release schedule of all program solicitations; publishes the *Presolicitation Announcement* quarterly, which contains pertinent facts on upcoming solicitations; and surveys and monitors program operations within the Federal Government and reports on the progress of the program each year to Congress.

The Office has four main objectives: to expand and improve SBIR; to increase private sector commercialization of technology developed through Federal research and development; to increase small business participation in Federal research and development; and to improve the dissemination of information concerning SBIR, particularly with regard to participation by women-owned small business concerns and by socially and economically disadvantaged small business concerns.

For further information, contact the Office of Technology. Phone, 202–205–6450.

Veterans Affairs The Office of Veterans' Affairs carries out the veterans affairs program to ensure that SBA gives special consideration in all its programs to veterans, their dependents, and survivors. The Office works with the Nation's 27 million veterans and the nearly 500,000 military personnel affected by downsizing, helping veterans who want to go into business.

The Office coordinates veteran training and counseling programs with other departments of SBA. It also measures veteran participation by monitoring loan, surety bond, procurement, and training activity within SBA. The Office maintains liaison with other veteran and veteran-related organizations to accomplish its goals.

For further information, contact the Office of Veterans Affairs. Phone, 202–205–6773.

Women's Business Ownership The Office of Women's Business Ownership (OWBO) provides assistance to the increasing number of current and potential women business owners and acts as their advocate in the public and private sectors. OWBO assists women in becoming full partners in economic development through technical, financial, and management information and training, business skills counseling, and research. Through a network of local SBA offices, OWBO offers a wide range of education and training services and resources.

SBA has established Women's Business Centers (WBC) to provide long-term training and counseling for women at every stage of their entrepreneurial career. There are currently WBC's in nearly every State, the District of Columbia, the Virgin Islands, and Puerto Rico. The centers offer assistance to current and potential women business owners, tailored to the particular needs of the community. The Online Women's Business Center, is an interactive, state-of-the-art website that offers virtually everything needed to start and build a successful business, including online training, mentoring, individual counseling, topic forums and newsgroups, market research, and information on all SBA programs and services, plus links to many other resources.

Women's business centers and SBA district offices, often in conjunction with the Service Corps of Retired Executives, provide mentoring for current and aspiring women business owners through the Women's Network for Entrepreneurial Training (WNET). There are now more than 165 WNET roundtable groups nationwide.

The Office of Government Contracting and OWBO have initiated a women's procurement pilot program to increase opportunities for women in the Federal market. SBA is developing formal partnerships with women's business organizations and other Federal agencies to help achieve the target goal. Efforts include trade fairs, marketing activities, publications, and use of the Administration's procurement network, PRO–*Net* (Internet, www.pro-net.sba.gov).

The Small Disadvantaged Business Program promotes equity in Federal contracting to small businesses owned and operated by those who are socially and economically disadvantaged, including women. Businesses that join the program are automatically listed in PRO–*Net.*

SBA has a number of loan programs to help women get the access to credit and capital they need. Among the most important for women are the Loan Prequalification Program, SBAExpress, and the MicroLoan Program. Through the Loan Prequalification Program, a woman entrepreneur gets help in packaging and marketing her loan. SBAExpress provides guaranties for loans of up to $150,000, including revolving lines of credit. The MiroLoan Program provides small loans through SBA-licensed intermediaries nationwide. Intermediaries also provide technical assistance.

For further information, contact the Office of Women's Business Ownership. Phone, 202–205–6673. Internet, www.sba.gov/womeninbusiness or www.onlinewbc.org. E-mail, owbo@sba.gov.

Field Operations The Office of Field Operations provides direction to SBA's 70 district and 10 regional offices, acting as the liaison between the district offices, the agency's program delivery system, and the headquarters' administrative and program offices.

For further information, contact the Office of Field Operations. Phone, 202–205–6808.

Field Offices—Small Business Administration

(RO: Regional Office; DO: District Office; BO: Branch Office; POD: Post of Duty)

Office	Address	Officer in Charge	Telephone
ATLANTA, GA (RO)	Suite 1800, 233 Peachtree St. NE. 30303	Billy Max Paul	404–331–0100
Atlanta, GA (DO)	6th Fl., 1720 Peachtree Rd. NW., 30309	Charles Anderson	404–331–0100
Birmingham, AL (DO)	Suite 200, 2121 8th Ave. N., 35203–2398	James C. Barksdale	205–731–1344
Charlotte, NC (DO)	Suite A2015, 200 N. College St., 28202–2173	Lee Corneliuson	704–344–6563
Columbia, SC (DO)	Rm. 358, 1835 Assembly St., 29201	Elliott Cooper	803–765–5339
Gulfport, MS (BO)	Suite 203, 2909 13th St., 39501	Charles Gillis	601–863–4449
Jackson, MS (DO)	Suite 400, 101 W. Capitol St., 39201	Janita Stewart	601–965–5371
Jacksonville, FL (DO)	Suite 100–B, 7825 Baymeadows Way, 32256–7504.	Wilfredo Gonzalez	904–443–1970
Louisville, KY (DO)	Rm. 188, 600 Dr. M.L. King, Jr. Pl., 40202	William Federhofer	502–582–5978
Miami, FL (DO)	7th Fl., 100 S. Biscayne Blvd., 33131	Gary Cook	305–536–5533
Nashville, TN (DO)	Suite 201, 50 Vantage Way, 37228–1500	Phil Mahoney	615–736–5850
BOSTON, MA (RO)	Suite 812, 10 Causeway St., 02222	Patrick McGowan	617–565–8415
Augusta, ME (DO)	Rm. 512, 40 Western Ave., 04330	Mary McAleney	207–622–8378
Boston, MA (DO)	Rm. 265, 10 Causeway St., 02222–1093	Elaine Guiney	617–565–5561
Concord, NH (DO)	Suite 202, 143 N. Main St., 03301	William K. Phillips	603–225–1400
Hartford, CT (DO)	2d Fl., 330 Main St., 06106	Marie Record	860–240–4700
Montpelier, VT (DO)	Rm. 205, 87 State St., 05602	Kenneth Silvia	802–828–4422
Providence, RI (DO)	5th Fl., 380 Westminster Mall, 02903	Mark Hayward, *Acting*	401–528–4561
Springfield, MA (BO)	Suite 410, 1441 Main St., 01103	Harold Webb	413–785–0484
CHICAGO, IL (RO)	Suite 1240, 500 W. Madison St., 60661	Barbara Notestein	312–353–0357
Chicago, IL (DO)	500 W. Madison St., 60661	Judith Roussel	312–353–5031
Cincinnati, OH (BO)	Suite 870, 525 Vine St., 45202	Ronald Carlson	513–684–2814
Cleveland, OH (DO)	Suite 630, 1111 Superior Ave., 44114–2507	Gilbert Goldberg	216–522–4180
Columbus, OH (DO)	Suite 1400, 2 Nationwide Plz., 43215–2592	Frank D. Ray	614–469–6860
Detroit, MI (DO)	Suite 515, 477 Michigan Ave., 48226	Eugene Cornelius	313–226–6075
Indianapolis, IN (DO)	Suite 100, 429 N. Pennsylvania Ave., 46204–1873.	Janice Wolfe	317–226–7272
Madison, WI (DO)	Suite 100, 740 Regent St., 53715	Eric Ness, *Acting*	608–264–5261
Milwaukee, WI (BO)	Suite 400, 310 W. Wisconsin Ave., 53203	Paul Roppuld, *Acting*	414–297–1178
Minneapolis, MN (DO)	Suite 610, 100 N. 6th St., 55403–1563	Nancy Gilbertson, *Acting*	612–370–2306
Springfield, IL (BO)	Suite 302, 511 W. Capitol Ave., 62704	Curtis Charter	217–492–4416
DALLAS, TX (RO)	Suite 108, 4300 Amon Carter Blvd., Ft. Worth, TX 76155.	Rueben Guerrero	817–684–5580
Albuquerque, NM (DO)	Suite 320, 625 Silver Ave. SW., 87102	Ed Cadena, *Acting*	505–346–6764
Corpus Christi, TX (BO)	Suite 101, 606 N. Carancahua, 78476	Jesse Sendejo	361–888–3331
El Paso, TX (DO)	Suite 320, 10737 Gateway W., 79935	Carlos Mendoza	915–633–7007
Fort Worth, TX (DO)	Suite 114, 4300 Amon Carter Blvd., 76155	Lavan Alexander	817–885–5500
Harlingen, TX (DO)	Rm. 500, 222 E. Van Buren St., 78550–6855	Sylvia Zamponi	956–427–8625
Houston, TX (DO)	Suite 550, 9301 Southwest Fwy., 77074–1591	Milton Wilson	713–773–6500
Little Rock, AR (DO)	Suite 100, 2120 Riverfront Dr., 72202	Joseph Foglia	501–324–5871
Lubbock, TX (DO)	Rm. 408, 1205 Texas Ave., 79401–2693	Tommy Dowell	806–472–7462
New Orleans, LA (DO)	Suite 2250, 365 Canal Pl., 70130	Randy Randolph	504–589–2744
Oklahoma City, OK (DO).	Suite 1300, 210 Park Ave., 73102	Ed Daum, *Acting*	405–231–5521
San Antonio, TX (DO)	5th Fl., 727 E. Durango Blvd., 78206	Rodney Martin	210–472–5904

Field Offices—Small Business Administration—Continued

(RO: Regional Office; DO: District Office; BO: Branch Office; POD: Post of Duty)

Office	Address	Officer in Charge	Telephone
DENVER, CO (RO)	Suite 400, 721 19th St., 80202–2599	Kathleen Piper	303–844–0500
Casper, WY (DO)	Rm. 4001, 100 E. B St., 82602–2839	Steve Despain	307–261–6500
Denver, CO (DO)	Suite 426, 721 19th St., 80202–2599	Patricia Barela Rivera	303–844–4028
Fargo, ND (DO)	Rm. 219, 657 2d Ave. N., 58108–3086	James L. Stai	701–239–5131
Helena, MT (DO)	Rm. 334, 301 S. Park, 59626	Jo Alice Mospan	406–441–1081
Salt Lake City, UT (DO)	Rm. 2237, 125 S. State St., 84138–1195	Stan Nakano	801–524–3200
Sioux Falls, SD (DO)	Suite 200, 110 S. Phillips Ave., 57104	Gene Van Arsdale	605–330–4231
KANSAS CITY, MO (RO)	Suite 307, 323 W. 8th St., 64105–1500	Brad Douglas, *Acting*	816–374–6380
Cedar Rapids, IA (DO)	Suite 200, 215 4th Ave. SE., 52401–1806	James Thomson	319–362–6405
Des Moines, IA (DO)	Rm. 749, 210 Walnut St., 50309–2186	Cheryl Eftink	515–284–4026
Kansas City, MO (DO)	Suite 501, 323 W. 8th St., 64105	Dorothy Kleeschulte	816–374–6708
Omaha, NE (DO)	11145 Mill Valley Rd., 68154	Glenn Davis	402–221–4691
Springfield, MO (BO)	Suite 110, 620 S. Glenstone St., 65802–3200	James R. Combs	417–864–7670
St. Louis, MO (DO)	Rm. 242, 815 Olive St., 63101	Robert L. Andrews	314–539–6600
Wichita, KS (DO)	Suite 2500, 271 W 3d St. N., 67202–1212	Elizabeth Auer	316–269–6566
NEW YORK, NY (RO)	Rm. 31–08, 26 Federal Plz., 10278	Tom Bettridge	212–264–1450
Buffalo, NY (DO)	Rm. 1311, 111 W. Huron St., 14202	Franklin J. Sciortino	716–551–4305
Elmira, NY (BO)	4th Fl., 333 E. Water St., 14901	James J. Cristofaro	607–734–1571
Hato Rey, PR (DO)	Suite 201, 252 Ponce de Leon Ave., 00918	Ivan Irizarry	787–766–5002
Melville, NY (BO)	Suite 207, 35 Pinelawn Rd., 11747	Burt Haggerty	516–454–0750
New York, NY (DO)	Rm. 3100, 26 Federal Plz., 10278	Aubrey A. Rogers	212–264–2454
Newark, NJ (DO)	15th Fl., 2 Gateway Ctr., 07102	Francisco Marrero	973–645–3580
Rochester, NY (BO)	Rm. 410, 100 State St., 14614	Peter Flihan	716–263–6700
St. Croix, VI (POD)	Suites 5 & 6, Sunny Isle Professional Bldg., Christiansted, VI 00820.	Carl Christensen	340–778–5380
St. Thomas, VI (POD)	3800 Crown Bay St., 00802	(Vacancy)	809–774–8530
Syracuse, NY (DO)	5th Fl., 401 S. Salina St., 13202	B.J. Paprocki	315–471–9393
PHILADELPHIA, PA (RO)	5th Fl., 900 Market St., 19107	Kerry Kirkland	215–580–2807
Baltimore, MD (DO)	Suite 6220, 10 S. Howard St., 21201–2525	Allan Stephenson	410–962–4392
Charleston, WV (BO)	Suite 412, 405 Capitol St., 25301	(Vacancy)	304–347–5220
Clarksburg, WV (DO)	320 W. Pike St., 26301	(Vacancy)	304–623–5631
Harrisburg, PA (BO)	Suite 107, 100 Chestnut St., 17101	(Vacancy)	717–782–3840
Philadelphia, PA (DO)	5th Fl., 900 Market St., 19107	Tom Tolan	215–580–2700
Pittsburgh, PA (DO)	Rm. 1128, 1000 Liberty Ave., 15222	Al Jones	412–395–6560
Richmond, VA (DO)	11th Fl., 400 N. 8th St., 23240	Charles J. Gaston	804–771–2400
Washington, DC (DO)	Suite 900, 1110 Vermont Ave. NW., 20005	Darryl Harriston	202–606–4000
Wilkes-Barre, PA (BO)	Suite 407, 7 N. Wilkes-Barre Blvd., 18702	(Vacancy)	570–826–6497
Wilmington, DE (BO)	1318 N. Market St., 19801–3011	Jayne Armstrong	302–571–5225
SAN FRANCISCO, CA (RO).	Suite 2200, 455 Market St., 94105	Viola Canales	415–744–2118
Aganá, GU (BO)	Suite 302, 400 Rt. 8, Mongmong, 96927	Kenneth Lujan	671–472–7277
Fresno, CA (DO)	Suite 200, 2719 N. Air Fresno Dr., 93727–1547	Antonio Valdez	559–487–5791
Glendale, CA (DO)	Suite 1200, 330 N. Brand Blvd., 91203–2304	Alberto Alvarado	818–552–3210
Honolulu, HI (DO)	Rm. 2–235, Box 50207, 300 Ala Moana Blvd., 96850–4981.	Andrew Poepoe	808–541–2990
Las Vegas, NV (DO)	Suite 100, 300 Las Vegas Blvd. South, 89101	John Scott	702–388–6611
Phoenix, AZ (DO)	Suite 800, 2828 N. Central Ave., 85004–1025	Bob Blaney	602–745–7200
Sacramento, CA (DO)	Rm. 215, 660 J St., 95814–2413	Jim O'Neal	916–498–6410
San Diego, CA (DO)	Suite 550, 550 W. C St., 92101	George P. Chandler, Jr.	619–557–7252
San Francisco, CA (DO)	6th Fl., 455 Market St., 94105	Mark Quinn	415–744–8474
Santa Ana, CA (DO)	Suite 700, 200 W. Santa Ana Blvd., 92701	Sandra Sutton	714–550–7420
SEATTLE, WA (RO)	Suite 1805, 1200 6th Ave., 98101–1128	Andrew Munro, *Acting*	206–553–5676
Anchorage, AK (DO)	Rm. A36, Box 67, 222 W. 8th Ave., 99513–7559	Frank Cox	907–271–4022
Boise, ID (DO)	Suite 290, 1020 Main St., 83702–5745	Thomas Bergdoll	208–334–1696
Portland, OR (DO)	Suite 1050, 1515 SW. 5th Ave., 97201–6695	Phil Gentry	503–326–5210
Seattle, WA (DO)	Suite 1700, 1200 6th Ave., 98101–1128	Robert P. Meredith	206–553–7040
Spokane, WA (DO)	Suite 200, 801 W. Riverside, 99201	Robert Wiebe	509–353–2808

Disaster Area Offices

Office	Address	Telephone
Atlanta, GA	Suite 300, 1 Baltimore Pl., 30308	404–347–3771
Fort Worth, TX	Suite 102, 4400 Amon Carter Blvd., 76155	817–885–7600
Niagara Falls, NY	3d Fl., 360 Rainbow Blvd. S., 14303	716–282–4612
Sacramento, CA	Suite 208, 1825 Bell St., 95825	916–566–7246

Regional Administrators

Region/Address	Administrator	Telephone
Atlanta, GA (Suite 496, 1720 Peachtree Rd. NW., 30309)	Billy M. Paul	404–347–4999

Regional Administrators—Continued

Region/Address	Administrator	Telephone
Boston, MA (Suite 812, 10 Causeway St., 02110)	Patrick K. McGowan	617–565–8415
Chicago, IL (Rm. 1975, 300 S. Riverside Plz., 60606–6611)	Peter Barca	312–353–0357
Denver, CO (Suite 400, 721 19th St., 80202–2599)	Thomas J. Redder	303–844–0500
Fort Worth, TX (Suite 108, 4300 Amon Carter Blvd., 76155)	James W. Breedlove	817–885–6581
Kansas City, MO (13th Fl., 911 Walnut St., 64106)	Bruce W. Kent	816–374–6380
New York, NY (Rm. 31–08, 26 Federal Plz., 10278)	Thomas M. Bettridge	212–264–1450
Philadelphia, PA (Suite 201, 475 Allendale Rd., King of Prussia, 19406	Susan M. McCann	610–962–3710
San Francisco, CA (20th Fl., 71 Stevenson St., 94105–2939)	Viola Canales	415–975–4804
Seattle, WA (S–1805, 1200 6th Ave., 98101–1128)	Gretchen Sorensen	206–553–0291

Sources of Information

Electronic Access Information on the Small Business Administration is available electronically by various means. Internet, www.sba.gov. FTP, ftp.sbaonline.sba.gov.

Access the U.S. Business Adviser through the Internet, at www.business.gov.

Access the Administration's electronic bulletin board by modem at 800–697–4636 (limited access), 900–463–4636 (full access), or 202–401–9600 (Washington, DC, metropolitan area).

General Information Contact the nearest Small Business Administration field office listed above, or call the SBA answer desk. Phone, 800–8–ASK–SBA. Fax, 202–205–7064. TDD, 704–344–6640.

Public Affairs For public inquiries and small-business advocacy affairs, contact the Office of Public Communications and Public Liaison, 409 Third Street SW., Washington, DC 20416. Phone, 202–205–6740. Internet, www.sba.gov.

Publications A free copy of *The Resource Directory for Small Business Management*, a listing of for-sale publications and videotapes, is available from any local SBA office or the SBA answer desk.

For further information, contact the Office of Public Communications and Public Liaison, Small Business Administration, 409 Third Street SW., Washington, DC 20416. Phone, 202–205–6740. Internet, www.sba.gov.

SOCIAL SECURITY ADMINISTRATION

6401 Security Boulevard, Baltimore, MD 21235
Phone, 410–965–1234. Internet, www.ssa.gov.

Commissioner of Social Security	Kenneth S. Apfel
Chief Actuary	Harry C. Ballantyne
General Counsel	Arthur J. Fried
Inspector General	James G. Huse, Jr.
Deputy Commissioner	William A. Halter
Executive Director to the Deputy Commissioner and Chief Information Officer	John R. Dyer
Chief of Staff	Brian D. Coyne
Deputy Commissioner for Communications	Joan E. Wainwright
Deputy Commissioner for Disability and Income Security Programs	Susan M. Daniels

Deputy Commissioner for Finance, Assessment, and Management and Chief Financial Officer	YVETTE S. JACKSON
Deputy Commissioner for Human Resources	PAUL D. BARNES
Deputy Commissioner for Legislation and Congressional Affairs	JUDY L. CHESSER
Deputy Commissioner for Operations	CAROLYN W. COLVIN
Deputy Commissioner for Policy	JANE L. ROSS
Deputy Commissioner for Systems	D. DEAN MESTERHARM

[For the Social Security Administration statement of organization, see the Code of Federal Regulations, Title 20, Part 422]

The Social Security Administration manages the Nation's social insurance program, consisting of retirement, survivors, and disability insurance programs, commonly known as Social Security. It also administers the Supplemental Security Income program for the aged, blind, and disabled. The Administration is responsible for studying the problems of poverty and economic insecurity among Americans and making recommendations on effective methods for solving these problems through social insurance. The Administration also assigns Social Security numbers to U.S. citizens and maintains earnings records for workers under their Social Security numbers.

The Social Security Administration (SSA) was established by Reorganization Plan No. 2 of 1946 (5 U.S.C. app.), effective July 16, 1946. It became an independent agency in the executive branch by the Social Security Independence and Program Improvements Act of 1994 (42 U.S.C. 901), effective March 31, 1995.

The Administration is headed by a Commissioner, appointed by the President with the advice and consent of the Senate.

In administering the programs necessary to carry out the agency's mission, by law the Commissioner is assisted by a Deputy Commissioner, who performs duties assigned or delegated by the Commissioner; a Chief Financial Officer; a General Counsel; a Chief Actuary; and an Inspector General.

Programs and Activities

Old-Age, Survivors, and Disability Insurance The agency administers these social insurance programs, which provide monthly benefits to retired and disabled workers, their spouses and children, and to survivors of insured workers. Financing is under a system of contributory social insurance, whereby employees, employers, and the self-employed pay contributions that are pooled in special trust funds. When earnings stop or are reduced because the worker retires, dies, or becomes disabled, monthly cash benefits are paid to partially replace the earnings the family has lost.

Supplemental Security Income The agency administers this needs-based program for the aged, blind, and disabled. A basic Federal monthly payment is financed out of general revenue, rather than a special trust fund. Some States, choosing to provide payments to supplement the benefits, have agreements with the Administration under which it administers the supplemental payments for those States.

Medicare While the administration of Medicare is the responsibility of the Health Care Financing Administration, Department of Health and Human Services, the Social Security Administration provides Medicare assistance to the public through SSA field offices and processing centers, and adjudicates requests for hearings and appeals of Medicare claims.

Black Lung By agreement with the Department of Labor, SSA is involved in certain aspects of the administration of the black lung benefits provisions of the Federal Coal Mine Health and Safety Act of 1969, as amended (30 U.S.C. 901).

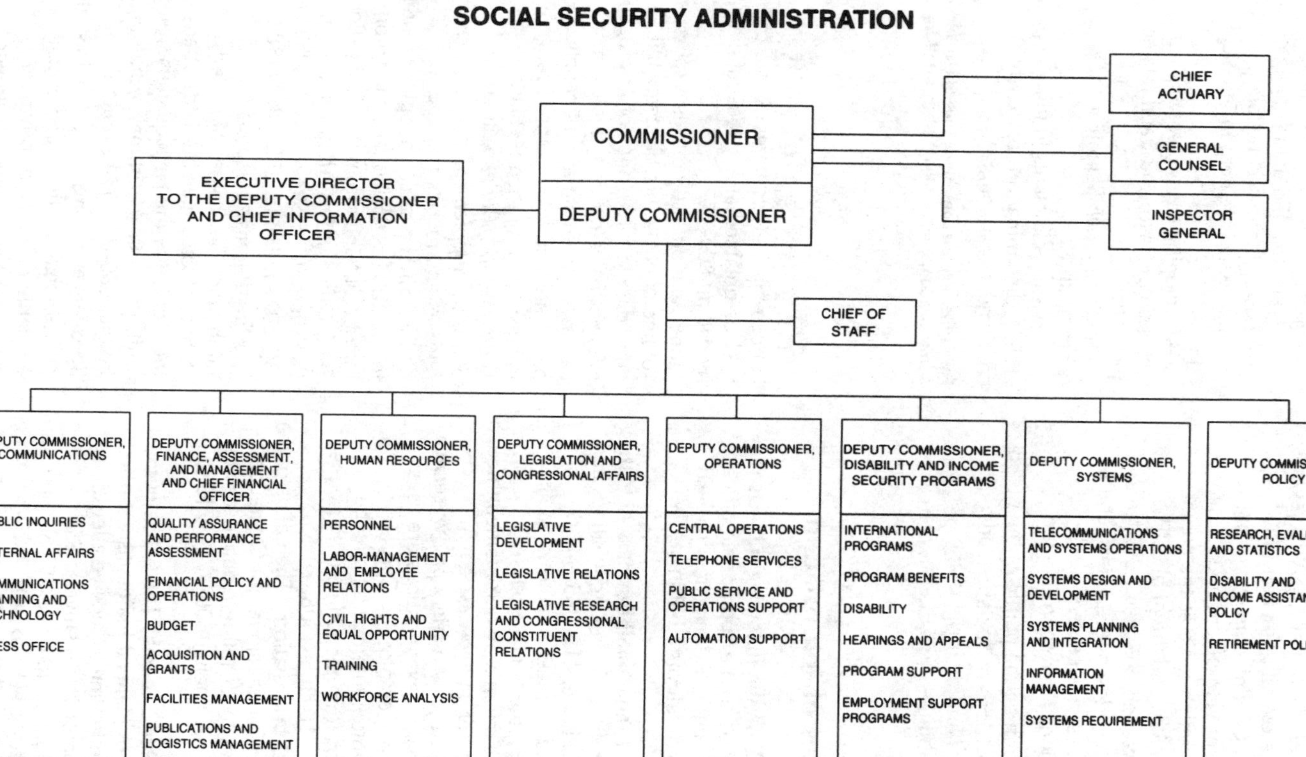
SOCIAL SECURITY ADMINISTRATION
COMMISSIONER
DEPUTY COMMISSIONER
EXECUTIVE DIRECTOR TO THE DEPUTY COMMISSIONER AND CHIEF INFORMATION OFFICER
CHIEF ACTUARY
GENERAL COUNSEL
INSPECTOR GENERAL
CHIEF OF STAFF
DEPUTY COMMISSIONER, COMMUNICATIONS
PUBLIC INQUIRIES
EXTERNAL AFFAIRS
COMMUNICATIONS PLANNING AND TECHNOLOGY
PRESS OFFICE
DEPUTY COMMISSIONER, FINANCE, ASSESSMENT, AND MANAGEMENT AND CHIEF FINANCIAL OFFICER
QUALITY ASSURANCE AND PERFORMANCE ASSESSMENT
FINANCIAL POLICY AND OPERATIONS
BUDGET
ACQUISITION AND GRANTS
FACILITIES MANAGEMENT
PUBLICATIONS AND LOGISTICS MANAGEMENT
DEPUTY COMMISSIONER, HUMAN RESOURCES
PERSONNEL
LABOR-MANAGEMENT AND EMPLOYEE RELATIONS
CIVIL RIGHTS AND EQUAL OPPORTUNITY
TRAINING
WORKFORCE ANALYSIS
DEPUTY COMMISSIONER, LEGISLATION AND CONGRESSIONAL AFFAIRS
LEGISLATIVE DEVELOPMENT
LEGISLATIVE RELATIONS
LEGISLATIVE RESEARCH AND CONGRESSIONAL CONSTITUENT RELATIONS
DEPUTY COMMISSIONER, OPERATIONS
CENTRAL OPERATIONS
TELEPHONE SERVICES
PUBLIC SERVICE AND OPERATIONS SUPPORT
AUTOMATION SUPPORT
DEPUTY COMMISSIONER, DISABILITY AND INCOME SECURITY PROGRAMS
INTERNATIONAL PROGRAMS
PROGRAM BENEFITS
DISABILITY
HEARINGS AND APPEALS
PROGRAM SUPPORT
EMPLOYMENT SUPPORT PROGRAMS
DEPUTY COMMISSIONER, SYSTEMS
TELECOMMUNICATIONS AND SYSTEMS OPERATIONS
SYSTEMS DESIGN AND DEVELOPMENT
SYSTEMS PLANNING AND INTEGRATION
INFORMATION MANAGEMENT
SYSTEMS REQUIREMENT
DEPUTY COMMISSIONER, POLICY
RESEARCH, EVALUATION, AND STATISTICS
DISABILITY AND INCOME ASSISTANCE POLICY
RETIREMENT POLICY

Regional Offices Social Security Administration operations are decentralized to provide services at the local level. Each of the SSA 10 regions, under the overall direction of its Regional Commissioner, contains a network of field offices and teleservice centers, which serve as the contact between SSA and the public. The Administration operates 1,292 field offices, 38 teleservice centers, and 6 program service centers. These installations are responsible for:

—informing the public of the purposes and provisions of Social Security programs and their rights and responsibilities;

—assisting with claims filed for retirement, survivors, disability, or health insurance benefits, black lung benefits, or Supplemental Security Income;

—developing and adjudicating claims;

—assisting certain beneficiaries in claiming reimbursement for medical expenses;

—developing cases involving earnings records, coverage, and fraud-related questions;

—making rehabilitation service referrals; and

—assisting claimants in filing appeals on SSA determinations of benefit entitlement or amount.

For further information, contact the Social Security Administration. Phone, 800–772–1213 (toll-free).

Sources of Information

Inquiries on the following subjects may be directed to the appropriate office, Social Security Administration, 6401 Security Boulevard, Baltimore, MD 21235.

Contracts and Small Business Activities Contact the Office of Acquisitions and Grants. Phone, 410–965–9457.

Electronic Access Information regarding the Social Security Administration may be obtained through the Internet, at www.ssa.gov.

Employment A variety of civil service registers and examinations are used in hiring new employees. Specific employment information may be obtained from the Office of Personnel. Phone, 410–965–4506.

General Information The Office of the Deputy Commissioner for Operations manages SSA's toll-free public service telephone. Phone, 800–772–1213 (toll-free).

Inspector General The Office of the Inspector General maintains a 24-hour toll-free hotline to receive allegations and complaints relative to SSA operations nationwide. Phone, 800–269–0271 (toll-free). Fax, 410–965–3011.

Publications The Office of the Deputy Commissioner for Communications publishes numerous pamphlets concerning SSA programs. Single copies may be obtained at any local office or by calling 800–772–1213. The Administration also collects a substantial volume of economic, demographic, and other data in furtherance of its program mission. Basic data on employment and earnings, beneficiaries and benefit payments, and other items of program interest are published regularly in the *Social Security Bulletin*, its *Annual Statistical Supplement*, and in special releases and reports that appear periodically on selected topics of interest to the public. Additional information may be obtained from the Publications Staff, Office of Research, Evaluation, and Statistics, 500 E Street SW., Washington, DC 20254. Phone, 202–282–7138.

Reading Rooms Requests for information, for copies of records, or to inspect records may be made at any local office or the Headquarters Contact Unit, Room G–44, Altmeyer Building. Phone, 800–772–1213 (toll-free).

Speakers and Films The Administration makes speakers, films, and exhibits available to public or private organizations, community groups, schools, etc., throughout the Nation. Requests for this service should be directed to the local Social Security Office.

For further information, contact the Office of Public Inquiries, Social Security Administration, 6401 Security Boulevard, Baltimore, MD 21235. Phone, 410–965–7700. Internet, www.ssa.gov.

TENNESSEE VALLEY AUTHORITY

400 West Summit Hill Drive, Knoxville, TN 37902
Phone, 865–632–2101. Internet, www.tva.gov.

One Massachusetts Avenue NW., Washington, DC 20444–0001
Phone, 202–898–2999

Chairman	CRAVEN CROWELL
Directors	SKILA HARRIS, GLENN L. MCCULLOUGH, JR.
Senior Vice President, Communications	STEVEN N. BENDER
President and Chief Operating Officer	OSWALD J. (IKE) ZERINGUE
Chief Nuclear Officer	JOHN A. SCALICE
Chief Financial Officer	DAVID N. SMITH
Chief Administrative Officer	NORMAN A. ZIGROSSI

The Tennessee Valley Authority conducts a unified program of resource development for the advancement of economic growth in the Tennessee Valley region. The Authority's program of activities includes flood control, navigation, electric power production, recreation improvement, and forestry and wildlife development.

The Tennessee Valley Authority (TVA) is a wholly owned Government corporation created by act of May 18, 1933 (16 U.S.C. 831–831dd). All functions of the Authority are vested in its three-member Board of Directors, the members of which are appointed by the President with the advice and consent of the Senate. The President designates one member as Chairman.

TVA's electric power program is financially self-supporting and operates as part of an independent system with TVA's system of dams on the Tennessee River and its larger tributaries. These dams provide flood regulation on the Tennessee and contribute to regulation of the lower Ohio and Mississippi Rivers. The system maintains a continuous 9-foot-draft navigation channel for the length of the 650-mile Tennessee River main stream, from Paducah, KY, to Knoxville, TN. The dams harness the power of the rivers to produce electricity. They also provide other benefits, notably outdoor recreation.

The Authority operates the river control system and provides assistance to State and local governments in reducing local flood problems. It also works with other agencies to encourage full and effective use of the navigable waterway by industry and commerce.

The Authority is the wholesale power supplier for 159 local municipal and cooperative electric systems serving customers in parts of 7 States. It supplies power to several Federal installations and 63 large companies whose power requirements are large or unusual. Power to meet these demands is supplied from dams, coal-fired powerplants, nuclear powerplants, combustion turbine installations, and a pumped-storage hydroelectric plant; U.S. Corps of Engineers dams in the Cumberland Valley; and Aluminum Company of America dams, whose operation is coordinated with TVA's system.

186-873 D-00--18

In economic and community development programs, TVA provides technical assistance in areas including industrial development, regional waste management, tourism promotion, community preparedness, and vanpool organization. It works with local communities and groups to develop maximum use of available area resources. Working with regional learning centers, businesses, and industries, the Authority has identified skills that are needed in the high-technology job market and has set up training centers.

At Muscle Shoals, AL, TVA operates a national laboratory for environmental research, focusing on the cleanup and protection of the Nation's land, air, and water resources. Projects include development of methods for reducing nonpoint source pollution from groundwater runoff, contaminated site remediation, bioenergy research, and industrial waste reduction. The work is centered on preventing and correcting environmental problems that are barriers to economic growth. TVA also operates the Public Power Institute, a research laboratory and a public-policy clearinghouse for energy and environmental issues.

In cooperation with other agencies, TVA conducts research and development programs in forestry, fish and game, watershed protection, health services related to its operations, and economic development of Tennessee Valley communities.

Sources of Information

Citizen Participation TVA Communications, ET 12A, 400 West Summit Hill Drive, Knoxville, TN 37902–1499. Phone, 865–632–2101.

Contracts Purchasing, WT 4D, 400 West Summit Hill Drive, Knoxville, TN 37902–1499. Phone, 865–632–4796. This office will direct inquiries to the appropriate procurement officer.

Economic Development 3E–NST, 565 Marriott Drive, Nashville, TN 37214. Phone, 615–882–2051.

Electric Power Supply and Rates ET 12A, 400 West Summit Hill Drive, Knoxville, TN 37902–1499. Phone 865–632–3108.

Employment Human Resources, ET 12A, 400 West Summit Hill Drive, Knoxville, TN 37902–1499. Phone, 865–632–3222. (Other personnel offices may be contacted at other major locations.)

Environmental and Energy Education BR 4F, 1101 Market Street, Chattanooga, TN 37402–2801. Phone, 865–751–4624.

Environmental Research Center TVA Reservation, P.O. Box 1010, Muscle Shoals, AL 35661–1010. Phone, 256–386–2026.

Environmental Quality Environmental Services, LP 5D, 1101 Market Street, Chattanooga, TN 37402–2801. Phone, 423–751–2293.

Land Management/Shoreline Permitting Land Management, FOR 3A, Forestry Building, Ridgeway Road, Norris, TN 37828. Phone, 865–632–1440.

Library Services Corporate Library, ET PC, 400 West Summit Hill Drive, Knoxville, TN 37902–1499. Phone, 865–632–3464. Chattanooga Office Complex, SP 1A, 1101 Market Street, Chattanooga, TN 37402–2801. Phone, 423–751–4913. Muscle Shoals, CTR 1A, P.O. Box 1010, Muscle Shoals, AL 35661–1010. Phone, 256–386–2417.

Maps Maps Information & Sales, HB 1A, 311 Broad Street, Chattanooga, TN 37402–2801. Phone, 423–751–6277.

Medical Services Health Services, EB 8A, 20 East Eleventh Street, Chattanooga, TN 37402–2801. Phone, 423–751–2091.

Publications TVA Communications, ET 6E, 400 West Summit Hill Drive, Knoxville, TN 37902–1499. Phone, 865–632–8039.

For further information, contact TVA Communications, 400 West Summit Hill Drive, Knoxville, TN 37902–1499. Phone, 865–632–8039; or TVA Washington Office, One Massachusetts Avenue NW., Washington, DC 20044. Phone, 202–898–2999. Internet, www.tva.gov.

TRADE AND DEVELOPMENT AGENCY

Suite 200, 1621 North Kent Street, Arlington, VA 22209–2131
Phone, 703–875–4357. Fax, 703–875–4009.
Internet, www.tda.gov. E-mail, info@tda.gov.

Director	J. JOSEPH GRANDMAISON
Deputy Director	BARBARA R. BRADFORD
General Counsel	LEOCADIA I. ZAK
Assistant Director for Management Operations	LARRY BEVAN
Director of Public Affairs and Marketing	JOHN F. LEYDEN, JR.
Congressional Liason	JULIE C. NORTON
Regional Directors:	
Africa and Middle East	HENRY D. STEINGASS
Central, Eastern, and Southern Europe	NED CABOT
New Independent States, Mongolia, and India	DANIEL D. STEIN
Asia and Pacific	GEOFFREY JACKSON
Latin America and Caribbean	ALBERT W. ANGULO
Economist/Evaluation Officer	DAVID DENNY
Financial Manager	NOREEN ST. LOUIS
Contracting Officer	DELLA GLENN
Administrative Officer	CAROLYN HUM
Grants Administrator	PATRICIA SMITH

The Trade and Development Agency's mission is to promote economic development in, and simultaneously export U.S. goods and services to, developing and middle-income nations in the following regions of the world: Africa/Middle East, Asia/Pacific, Central and Eastern Europe, Latin America and the Caribbean, and the New Independent States.

The Trade and Development Program was established on July 1, 1980, as a component organization of the International Development Cooperation Agency. Section 2204 of the Omnibus Trade and Competitiveness Act of 1988 (22 U.S.C. 2421) made it a separate component agency. The organization was renamed the Trade and Development Agency (TDA) and made an independent agency within the executive branch of the Federal Government on October 28, 1992, by the Jobs Through Exports Act of 1992 (22 U.S.C. 2421).

The Trade and Development Agency assists in the creation of jobs for Americans by helping U.S. companies pursue exports and other overseas business opportunities. It funds feasibility studies, orientation visits, training grants, business briefings, and various forms of technical assistance in support of specific projects, enabling American businesses to become involved in the planning of infrastructure and industrial projects in emerging markets. Working closely with a foreign nation sponsor, TDA makes its funds available on the condition that the foreign entity contract with a U.S. firm to perform the study. This affords American firms market entry, exposure, and information, thus helping them to establish a position in markets that are otherwise difficult to penetrate.

The Agency's focus is the planning phase of major infrastructure and industrial projects. It is involved in several sectors, including: agriculture, aviation, energy, environment, health care, manufacturing, mining and minerals development,

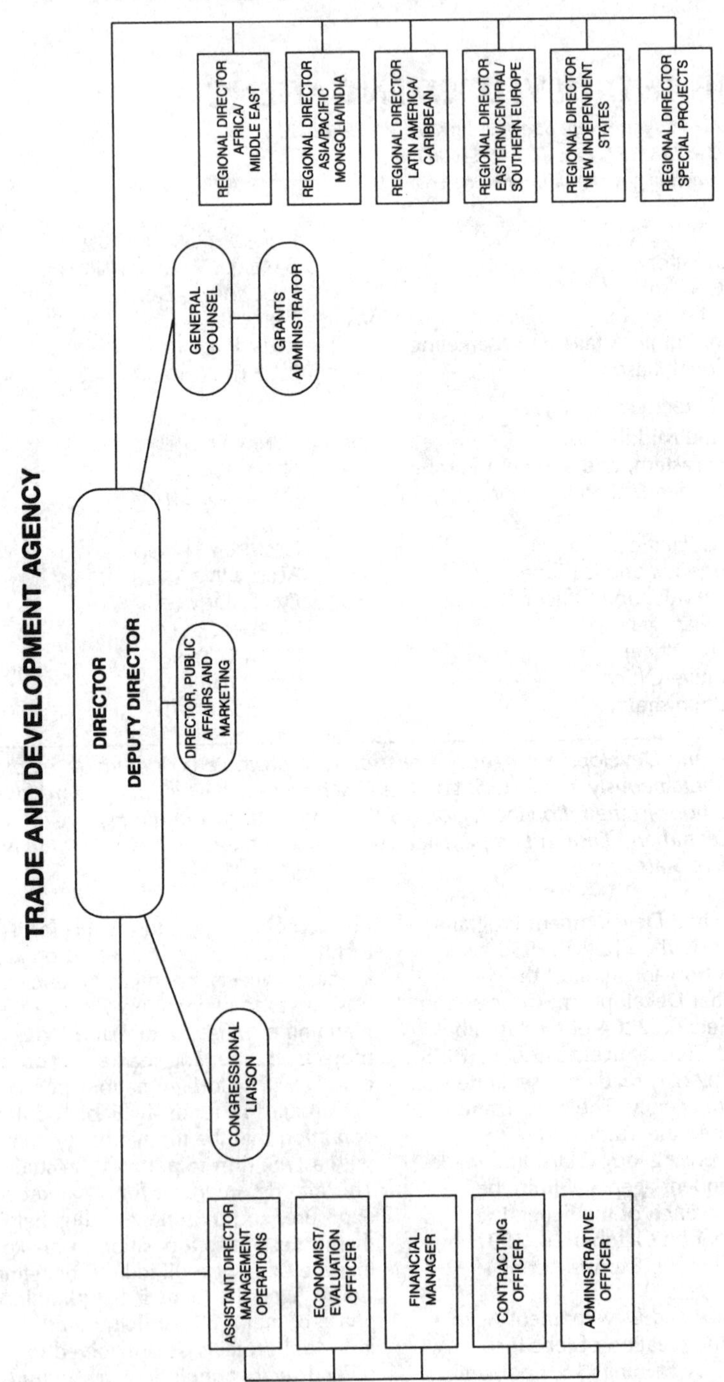
TRADE AND DEVELOPMENT AGENCY
DIRECTOR
DEPUTY DIRECTOR
CONGRESSIONAL LIAISON
DIRECTOR, PUBLIC AFFAIRS AND MARKETING
GENERAL COUNSEL
GRANTS ADMINISTRATOR
ASSISTANT DIRECTOR MANAGEMENT OPERATIONS
ECONOMIST/ EVALUATION OFFICER
FINANCIAL MANAGER
CONTRACTING OFFICER
ADMINISTRATIVE OFFICER
REGIONAL DIRECTOR AFRICA/ MIDDLE EAST
REGIONAL DIRECTOR ASIA/PACIFIC MONGOLIA/INDIA
REGIONAL DIRECTOR LATIN AMERICA/ CARIBBEAN
REGIONAL DIRECTOR EASTERN/CENTRAL/ SOUTHERN EUROPE
REGIONAL DIRECTOR NEW INDEPENDENT STATES
REGIONAL DIRECTOR SPECIAL PROJECTS

telecommunications, transportation, and water resources.

Activities

The Agency funds feasibility studies (or project plans) which evaluate the technical, economic, and financial aspects of a development project. These studies advise the host nation about the availability of U.S. goods and services and are required by financial institutions in assessing the creditworthiness of the undertaking. Funding activities are based upon an official request for assistance made by the sponsoring government or private sector organization of a developing or middle-income nation, and costs for a study typically are shared between TDA and the U.S. firm developing the project.

The Agency makes decisions on funding requests for feasibility studies based on the recommendations contained in the definitional mission or desk study report, the advice of the U.S. Embassy, and its internal analysis.

Sources of Information

Requests for proposals (RFP's) to conduct feasibility studies funded by TDA are listed in the *Commerce Business Daily.* Information on definitional mission opportunities can be obtained by calling TDA's DM Hotline at 703–875–7447. Small and minority U.S. firms that wish to be included in TDA's consultant database and considered for future solicitations should contact TDA's Contracts Office at 703–875–4357.

In an effort to provide timely information on Agency-supported projects, TDA publishes the *Pipeline* and a calendar of events which are available together on a paid subscription basis by calling 703–875–4246. They are also available through the Internet, at www.tda.gov. A quarterly publication, *TDA Update,* contains current items of interest on a variety of program activities. Region- or sector-specific fact sheets and case studies also are available. An annual report summarizes the Agency's activities.

Agency news, reports, and lists of upcoming orientation visits and business briefings are available through the Internet, at www.tda.gov.

Regional program inquiries should be directed to the assigned Country Manager. Phone, 703–875–4357. Fax, 703–875–4009. E-mail, info@tda.gov.

TDA's library maintains final reports on all TDA activities. These are available for public review Monday through Friday from 8:30 a.m. to 5:30 p.m. Copies of completed feasibility studies must be purchased through the Department of Commerce's National Technical Information Service (NTIS).

For further information, contact the Trade and Development Agency, Suite 200, 1621 North Kent Street, Arlington, VA. 22209–2131. Phone, 703–875–4357. Fax, 703–875–4009. E-mail, info@tda.gov. Internet, www.tda.gov.

UNITED STATES AGENCY FOR INTERNATIONAL DEVELOPMENT

1300 Pennsylvania Avenue NW., Washington, DC 20523–0001
Phone, 202–712–0000. Internet, www.info.usaid.gov.

Administrator	J. Brady Anderson
Deputy Administrator	Harriet C. Babbitt
Counselor	James H. Michel
Chief of Staff	B.A. Rudolph
Executive Secretary	Ryan Conroy

Assistant to the Administrator, Bureau for Policy and Program Coordination	THOMAS H. FOX
Director, Office of Small and Disadvantaged Business Utilization/Minority Resource Center	IVAN R. ASHLEY
Assistant Administrator for Africa	VIVIAN LOWERY DERRYCK
Assistant Administrator for Asia and the Near East	ROBERT RANDOLPH
Assistant Administrator for Europe and the New Independent States	DONALD L. PRESSLEY
Assistant Administrator for Global Programs, Field Support, and Research	BARBARA N. TURNER, *Acting*
Assistant Administrator for Humanitarian Response	HUGH PARMER
Assistant Administrator for Latin America and the Caribbean	CARL H. LEONARD, *Acting*
Assistant Administrator for Legislative and Public Affairs	JOSEPH R. CRAPA
Assistant Administrator for Management	RICHARD C. BROWN, *Acting*
Director, Office of Equal Opportunity Programs	JESSALYN L. PENDARVIS
Director, Office of Security	C. MICHAEL FLANNERY
General Counsel	SINGLETON B. MCALLISTER
Inspector General	EVERETT L. MOSLEY, *Acting*

[For the Agency for International Development statement of organization, see the *Federal Register* of Aug. 26, 1987, 52 FR 32174]

The U.S. Agency for International Development (USAID) administers U.S. foreign economic and humanitarian assistance programs worldwide in the developing world, Central and Eastern Europe, and the New Independent States of the former Soviet Union.

The United States Agency for International Development (USAID) was established as an independent agency by section 1413 of the Foreign Affairs Reform and Restructuring Act of 1998 (112 Stat. 2681–791) and serves as the focal point within the Government for economic matters affecting U.S. relations with developing countries. USAID administers international economic and humanitarian assistance programs. The Administrator is under the direct authority and foreign policy guidance of the Secretary of State.

Programs

The Agency meets its post-cold war era challenges by utilizing its strategy for achieving sustainable development in developing countries. It supports programs in four areas: population and health, broad-based economic growth, environment, and democracy. It also provides humanitarian assistance and aid to countries in crisis and transition.

Population and Health The Agency contributes to a cooperative global effort to stabilize world population growth and support women's reproductive rights. The types of population and health programs supported vary with the particular needs of individual countries and the kinds of approaches that local communities initiate and support. Most USAID resources are directed to the following areas: support for voluntary family planning systems, reproductive health care, needs of adolescents and young adults, infant and child health, and education for girls and women.

Economic Growth The Agency promotes broad-based economic growth by addressing the factors that enhance the capacity for growth and by working to remove the obstacles that stand in the way of individual opportunity. In this context, programs concentrate on

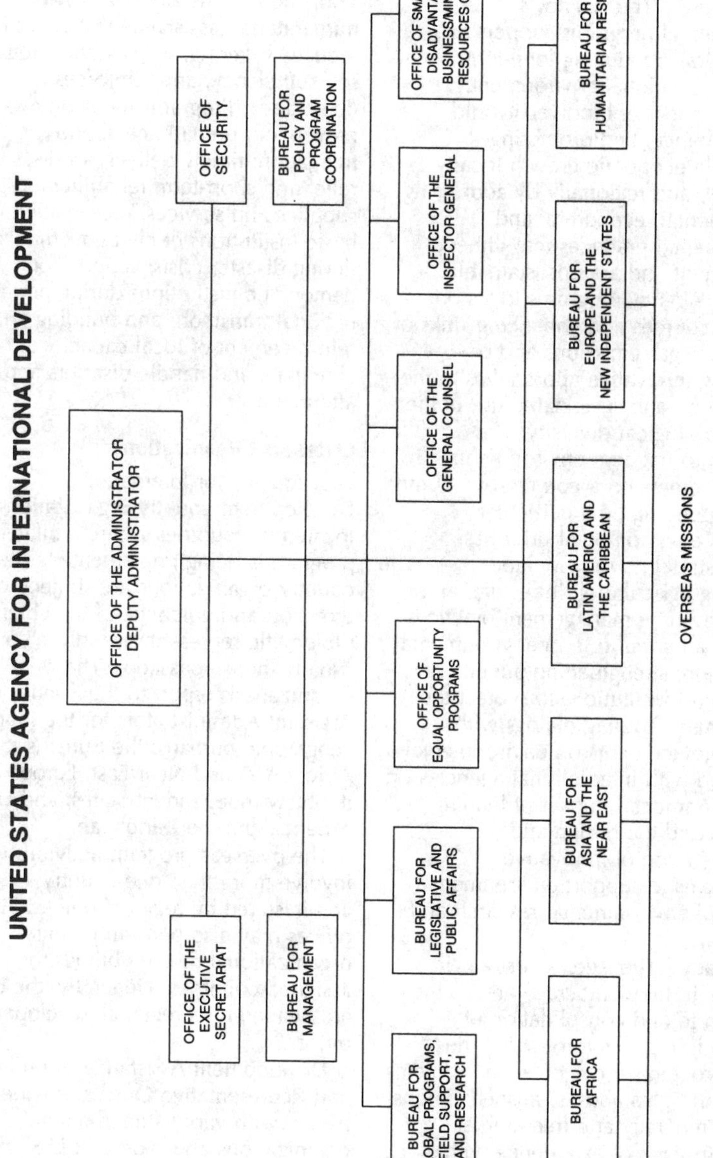
UNITED STATES AGENCY FOR INTERNATIONAL DEVELOPMENT
OFFICE OF THE ADMINISTRATOR
DEPUTY ADMINISTRATOR
OFFICE OF THE EXECUTIVE SECRETARIAT
OFFICE OF SECURITY
BUREAU FOR MANAGEMENT
BUREAU FOR POLICY AND PROGRAM COORDINATION
BUREAU FOR GLOBAL PROGRAMS, FIELD SUPPORT, AND RESEARCH
BUREAU FOR LEGISLATIVE AND PUBLIC AFFAIRS
OFFICE OF EQUAL OPPORTUNITY PROGRAMS
OFFICE OF THE GENERAL COUNSEL
OFFICE OF THE INSPECTOR GENERAL
OFFICE OF SMALL AND DISADVANTAGED BUSINESS/MINORITY RESOURCES CENTER
BUREAU FOR AFRICA
BUREAU FOR ASIA AND THE NEAR EAST
BUREAU FOR LATIN AMERICA AND THE CARIBBEAN
BUREAU FOR EUROPE AND THE NEW INDEPENDENT STATES
BUREAU FOR HUMANITARIAN RESPONSE
OVERSEAS MISSIONS

strengthening market economies, expanding economic opportunities for the less advantaged in developing countries, and building human skills and capacities to facilitate broad-based participation.

Environment The Agency's environmental programs support two strategic goals: reducing long-term threats to the global environment, particularly loss of biodiversity and climate change; and promoting sustainable economic growth locally, nationally, and regionally by addressing environmental, economic, and developmental practices that impede development and are unsustainable. Globally, Agency programs focus on reducing sources and enhancing sinks of greenhouse gas emissions and on promoting innovative approaches to the conservation and sustainable use of the planet's biological diversity. The approach to national environmental problems differs on a country-by-country basis, depending on a particular country's environmental priorities. Country strategies may include improving agricultural, industrial, and natural resource management practices that play a central role in environmental degradation; strengthening public policies and institutions to protect the environment; holding dialogs with country governments on environmental issues and with international agencies on the environmental impact of lending practices and the design and implementation of innovative mechanisms to support environmental work; and environmental research and education.

Democracy The Agency's strategic objective in the democracy area is the transition to and consolidation of democratic regimes throughout the world. Programs focus on such problems as: human rights abuses; misperceptions about democracy and free-market capitalism; lack of experience with democratic institutions; the absence or weakness of intermediary organizations; nonexistent, ineffectual, or undemocratic political parties; disenfranchisement of women, indigenous peoples, and minorities; failure to implement national charter documents; powerless or poorly defined democratic institutions; tainted elections; and the inability to resolve conflicts peacefully.

Humanitarian Assistance and Post-Crisis Transitions The Agency provides humanitarian assistance that saves lives, reduces suffering, helps victims return to self-sufficiency, and reinforces democracy. Programs focus on disaster prevention, preparedness, and mitigation; timely delivery of disaster relief and short-term rehabilitation supplies and services; preservation of basic institutions of civil governance during disaster crisis; support for democratic institutions during periods of national transition; and building and reinforcement of local capacity to anticipate and handle disasters and their aftermath.

Overseas Organizations

U.S. Agency for International Development country organizations are located in countries where a bilateral program is being implemented. The in-country organizations are subject to the direction and guidance of the chief U.S. diplomatic representative in the country, usually the Ambassador. The organizations report to the Agency's Assistant Administrators for the four geographic bureaus: the Bureau for Africa, Asia and Near East, Europe and the New Independent States, and Latin America and the Caribbean.

The overseas program activities that involve more than one country are administered by regional offices. These offices may also perform country organizational responsibilities for assigned countries. Generally, the offices are headed by a regional development officer.

Development Assistance Coordination and Representative Offices provide liaison with various international organizations and represent U.S. interests in development assistance matters. Such offices may be only partially staffed by Agency personnel and may be headed by employees of other U.S. Government agencies.

Country Organizations—U.S. Agency for International Development

Country	Officer in Charge [1]
Albania	Howard Sumka (MD)
Angola	Keith E. Simmons (MD)
Armenia	Dianne Tsitsos (MD)
Azerbaijan	William McKinney (DO)
Bangladesh	Gordon H. West (MD)
Belarus	Robert Simpson (DO)
Benin	Thomas E. Park (MD)
Bolivia	Liliana Ayalde (MD)
Bosnia	Edward Kadunc (MD)
Brazil	Janice Weber (MD)
Bulgaria	William Foerderer (MD)
Burundi	Donald R. MacKenzie, *Acting* (MD)
Cambodia	Willard J. Pearson, Jr. (MD)
Colombia	George Wachtenheim (MD)
Croatia	Charles R. Aaneson (MD)
Democratic Republic of the Congo.	Ronald Harvey (MD)
Dominican Republic	Leopoldo Garza, *Acting* (MD)
Ecuador	Hilda Arellano (MD)
Egypt	Richard M. Brown (MD)
El Salvador	Kenneth Ellis (MD)
Eritrea	William Garvelink (MD)
Ethiopia	Doug Sheldon (MD)
Georgia	Michael Farbman (MD)
Ghana	Frank J. Young (MD)
Guatemala	George Carner (MD)
Guinea	Harry Birnholz (MD)
Guinea-Bissau	Donald Clark, *Acting* (MD)
Guyana	Carol Becker (MD)
Haiti	Phyllis Dichter-Forbes (MD)
Honduras	Elena Brineman (MD)
India	Linda E. Morse (MD)
Indonesia	Desaix B. Meyers III (MD)
Israel	Larry Garber (MD)
Jamaica	Mosina Jordan (MD)
Jordan	Lewis W. Lucke (MD)
Kazakstan	Glenn Anders (MD)
Kenya	Jonathan Conly (MD)
REDSO in Kenya	Donald MacKenzie (MD)
Kosovo	Craig Buck (MD)
Kyrgyz Republic	Tracy Atwood (DO)
Lebanon	James Stephenson (MD)
Liberia	Rudolph Thomas (MD)
Lithuania	Christine Sheckler, *Acting* (MD)
Macedonia, FRY	Stephen Haynes (MD)
Madagascar	Karen M. Poe (MD)
Malawi	Kiertisak Toh (MD)
Mali	James Hradsky (MD)
Mexico	Paul White (MD)
Moldova	Tom Lofgren (DO)
Mongolia	Edward W. Birgells (MD)
Montenegro, FRY	Richard Hough (MD)
Morocco	James F. Bednar (MD)
Mozambique	Cynthia Rozell (MD)
Namibia	Carol Scherrer-Palma (MD)
Nepal	Joanne T. Hale (MD)
Nicaragua	Marilyn Zak (MD)
Nigeria	Thomas Hobgood (MD)
Panama	Lars Klassen (MD)
Paraguay	Wayne Tate (MD)
Peru	Thomas Geiger (MD)
Philippines	Patrick K. Buckles (MD)
Poland	Paula Goddard (MD)
Romania	Denny Robertson (MD)
Russia	Carol Peasley (MD)
Rwanda	George Lewis (MD)
Senegal	Donald Clark (MD)
Serbia, FRY	Richard Hough (MD)
Slovakia	Paula Goddard (MD)
South Africa	William S. Rhodes (MD)
Sri Lanka	Lisa Chiles (MD)
Tajikistan	Peter Downs (DO)
Tanzania	Lucretia Taylor (MD)
The Gambia	Donald Clark, *Acting* (MD)
Uganda	Dawn Liberi (MD)
Ukraine	Christopher Crowley (MD)
Uzbekistan	Theresa Ware (DO)
Zambia	Walter North (MD)
Zimbabwe	Rose Marie Depp (MD)

[1] MD: Mission Director; D: Director; OR: Office of the AID Representative; DO: Development Officer; RD: Regional Director; AAO: AID Affairs Officer for Section of Embassy; CO: Coordinator in Washington

International Organizations—U.S. Agency for International Development

(Selected Regional Organizations)

(A: Adviser; C: Counselor; D: Director; ED: Executive Director; MD: Mission Director; AID R: USAID Representative; RD: Regional Director)

Office	Officer in Charge
Regional Offices	
Regional Center for Southern Africa—Gaborone, Botswana	Edward Spriggs (RD)
Regional Economic Development Services Offices—Nairobi, Kenya	Donald R. MacKenzie (RD)
Regional Support Center—Budapest, Hungary	Patricia Lerner (RD)
International Organizations and USAID Contacts	
Office for Humanitarian Assistance, World Food Program Affairs—Rome, Italy	Douglas Sheldon (RD)
Office of the U.S. Representative to the Development Assistance Committee of the Organization for Economic Cooperation and Development—Paris, France.	Kelly Kammerer (AID R)
U.S. Mission to the European Office of the United Nations and Other International Organizations—Geneva, Switzerland.	Nance Kyloh (AID R)
AID Office for Development Cooperation—Tokyo, Japan	(Vacancy) (C)
Office of AID Coordination Representative—Brussels, Belgium	Kurt Fuller (C)

Sources of Information

General Inquiries Inquiries may be directed to the Bureau for Legislative and Public Affairs, USAID/LPA, Washington, DC 20523–0001. Phone, 202–712–4810. Fax, 202–216–3524.
Congressional Affairs Congressional inquiries may be directed to the Bureau for Legislative and Public Affairs, USAID/LPA, Washington, DC 20523–0001. Phone, 202–712–4810.
Contracting and Small Business Inquiries For information regarding contracting opportunities, contact the Office of Small and Disadvantaged Business Utilization, U.S. Agency for International Development, Washington, DC 20523–0001. Phone, 202–712–1500. Fax, 202–216–3056.
Employment For information regarding employment opportunities, contact the Workforce Planning, Recruitment, and Personnel Systems Division, Office of Human Resources, U.S. Agency for International Development, Washington, DC 20523–0001. Internet, www.info.usaid.gov.
General Inquiries General inquiries may be directed to the Bureau for Legislative and Public Affairs, USAID/LPA, Washington, DC 20523–0001. Phone, 202–712–4810. Fax, 202–216–3524.
News Media Inquiries from the media only should be directed to the Press Relations Division, Bureau for Legislative and Public Affairs, USAID/LPA, Washington, DC 20523–0001. Phone, 202–712–4320.

For further information, contact the United States Agency for International Development, 1300 Pennsylvania Avenue NW., Washington, DC 20523–0001. Phone, 202–712–0000. Internet, www.info.usaid.gov.

UNITED STATES COMMISSION ON CIVIL RIGHTS

624 Ninth Street NW., Washington, DC 20425
Phone, 202–376–8177. Internet, www.usccr.gov.

Chairperson	MARY FRANCES BERRY
Vice Chairman	CRUZ REYNOSO
Commissioners	CARL A. ANDERSON, CHRISTOPHER EDLEY, JR., YVONNE Y. LEE, ELSIE M. MEEKS, RUSSELL G. REDENBAUGH, VICTORIA WILSON
Staff Director	RUBY G. MOY
Deputy Staff Director	(VACANCY)
General Counsel	EDWARD A. HAILES, JR., *Acting*
Solicitor	EDWARD A. HAILES, JR., *Acting*
Assistant Staff Director for Civil Rights Evaluation	(VACANCY)
Assistant Staff Director for Congressional Affairs	(VACANCY)
Assistant Staff Director for Management	(VACANCY)
Chief, Civil Rights Evaluation	(VACANCY)

Chief, Public Affairs Unit	(VACANCY)
Chief, Regional Programs Coordination	CAROL-LEE HURLEY

[For the Commission on Civil Rights statement of organization, see the *Code of Federal Regulations,* Title 45, Part 701]

The Commission on Civil Rights collects and studies information on discrimination or denials of equal protection of the laws because of race, color, religion, sex, age, disability, national origin, or in the administration of justice in such areas as voting rights, enforcement of Federal civil rights laws, and equal opportunity in education, employment, and housing.

The Commission on Civil Rights was first created by the Civil Rights Act of 1957, as amended, and reestablished by the United States Commission on Civil Rights Act of 1983, as amended (42 U.S.C. 1975).

Activities

The Commission makes findings of fact but has no enforcement authority. Findings and recommendations are submitted to the President and Congress, and many of the Commission's recommendations have been enacted, either by statute, Executive order, or regulation. The Commission evaluates Federal laws and the effectiveness of Government equal opportunity programs. It also serves as a national clearinghouse for civil rights information.

Regional Programs The Commission maintains six regional divisions.

Regional Divisions

Region (Address/Telephone)	Director
Central (Suite 908, 400 State Ave., Kansas City, KS 66101–2406. Phone, 913–551–1400)	Melvin L. Jenkins
Eastern (Rm. 500, 624 9th St. NW., Washington, DC 20425. Phone, 202–376–7533)	Ki-Taek Chun
Midwestern (Suite 410, 55 W. Monroe St., Chicago, IL 60603. Phone, 312–353–8311)	Constance D. Davis
Rocky Mountain (Suite 710, 1700 Broadway, Denver, CO 80290. Phone, 303–866–1040)	John Foster Dulles
Southern (Suite 184OT, 61 Forsyth St. SW, Atlanta, GA 30303. Phone, 404–562–7000)	Bobby Doctor
Western (Rm. 810, 3660 Wilshire Blvd., Los Angeles, CA 90010. Phone, 213–894–3437)	Philip Montez

Sources of Information

Complaints Complaints alleging denials of civil rights may be reported to Complaints Referral, 624 Ninth Street NW., Washington, DC 20425. Phone, 202–376–8513 or 800–552–6843 (toll-free).

Employment Human Resources Office, Room 510, 624 Ninth Street NW., Washington, DC 20425. Phone, 202–376–8364.

Publications Commission publications are made available upon request from the Administrative Services and Clearinghouse Division, Room 550, 624 Ninth Street NW., Washington, DC 20425. Phone, 202–376–8105. A catalog of publications may be obtained from this office.

Reading Room The National Civil Rights Clearinghouse Library is located in Room 602, 624 Ninth Street NW., Washington, DC 20425. Phone, 202–376–8110.

For further information, contact the Public Affairs Unit, United States Commission on Civil Rights, Room 730, 624 Ninth Street NW., Washington, DC 20425. Phone, 202–376–8312. TTY, 202–376–8116. Internet, www.usccr.gov.

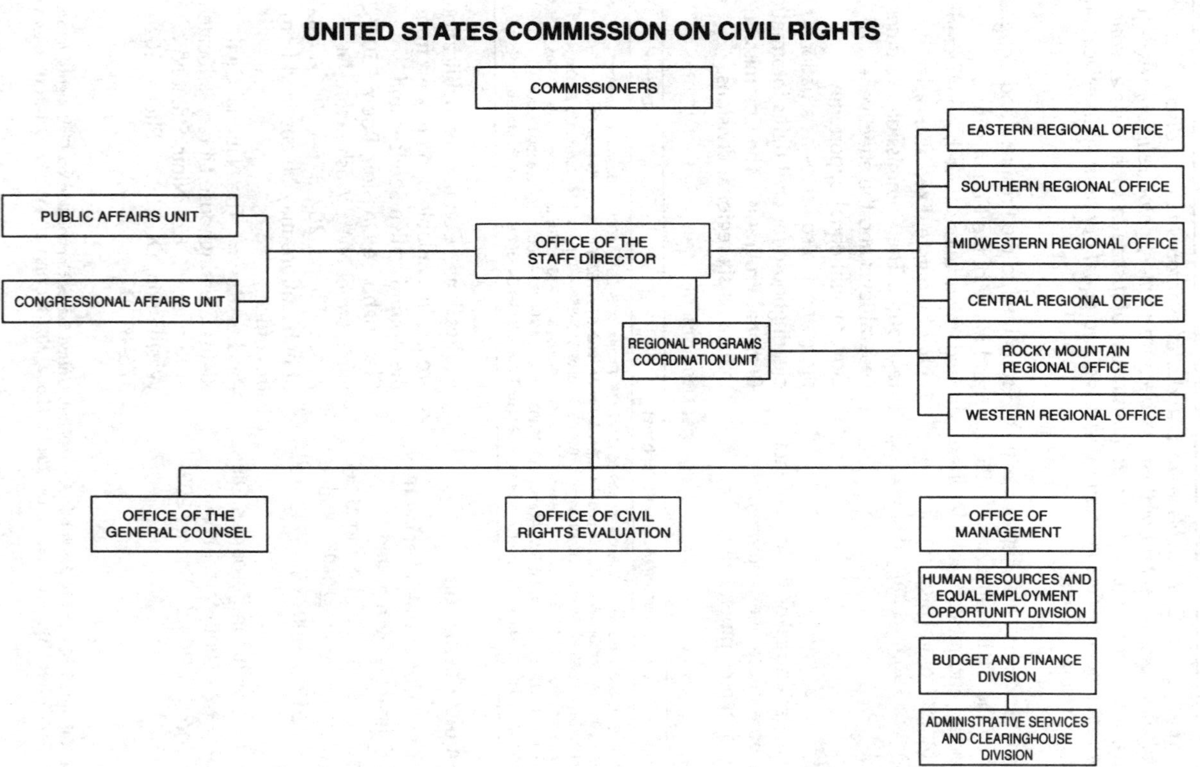
UNITED STATES COMMISSION ON CIVIL RIGHTS
COMMISSIONERS
PUBLIC AFFAIRS UNIT
CONGRESSIONAL AFFAIRS UNIT
OFFICE OF THE STAFF DIRECTOR
EASTERN REGIONAL OFFICE
SOUTHERN REGIONAL OFFICE
MIDWESTERN REGIONAL OFFICE
CENTRAL REGIONAL OFFICE
ROCKY MOUNTAIN REGIONAL OFFICE
WESTERN REGIONAL OFFICE
REGIONAL PROGRAMS COORDINATION UNIT
OFFICE OF THE GENERAL COUNSEL
OFFICE OF CIVIL RIGHTS EVALUATION
OFFICE OF MANAGEMENT
HUMAN RESOURCES AND EQUAL EMPLOYMENT OPPORTUNITY DIVISION
BUDGET AND FINANCE DIVISION
ADMINISTRATIVE SERVICES AND CLEARINGHOUSE DIVISION

UNITED STATES INTERNATIONAL TRADE COMMISSION

500 E Street SW., Washington, DC 20436
Phone, 202–205–2000. Internet, www.usitc.gov.

Chairman	LYNN M. BRAGG
Vice Chairman	MARCIA E. MILLER
Commissioners	JENNIFER A. HILLMAN, STEPHEN KOPLAN, THELMA J. ASKEY, DEANNA TANNER OKUN
Administrative Law Judges	SIDNEY HARRIS, PAUL J. LUCKERN, DEBRA MORRISS
Director, Office of Administration	STEPHEN MCLAUGHLIN
Director, Office of Economics	ROBERT B. KOOPMAN
Director, Office of External Relations	DANIEL F. LEAHY
Congressional Relations Officer	NANCY M. CARMAN
Public Affairs Officer	MARGARET M. O'LAUGHLIN
Trade Remedy Assistance Program Manager	JOHN J. GREER
Director, Office of Equal Employment Opportunity	JACQUELINE A. WATERS
Director, Office of Information Services	MARTIN SMITH
Director, Office of Industries	M. VERN SIMPSON, JR.
Division Chief, Agriculture and Forest Products	CATHY L. JABARA
Division Chief, Minerals, Metals, Machinery, and Miscellaneous Manufactures	LARRY L. BROOKHART
Division Chief, Energy, Chemicals, and Textiles	JOHN J. GERSIC
Division Chief, Electronics and Transportation	NORMAN MCLENNAN
Division Chief, Services and Investment	RICHARD W. BROWN
Director, Office of Investigations	LYNN FEATHERSTONE
Director, Office of Operations	ROBERT ROGOWSKY
Director, Office of Tariff Affairs and Trade Agreements	EUGENE A. ROSENGARDEN
Director, Office of Unfair Import Investigations	LYNN LEVINE
General Counsel	LYN M. SCHLITT
Inspector General	DEV JAGADESAN, *Acting*
Secretary	DONNA R. KOEHNKE

The United States International Trade Commission furnishes studies, reports, and recommendations involving international trade and tariffs to the President, the U.S. Trade Representative, and congressional committees. The Commission also conducts a variety of investigations pertaining to international trade relief.

The United States International Trade Commission is an independent agency created by act of September 8, 1916 (39 Stat. 795), and originally named the United States Tariff Commission. The name was changed to the United States International Trade Commission by section 171 of the Trade Act of 1974 (19 U.S.C. 2231).

Six Commissioners are appointed by the President with the advice and consent of the Senate for 9-year terms,

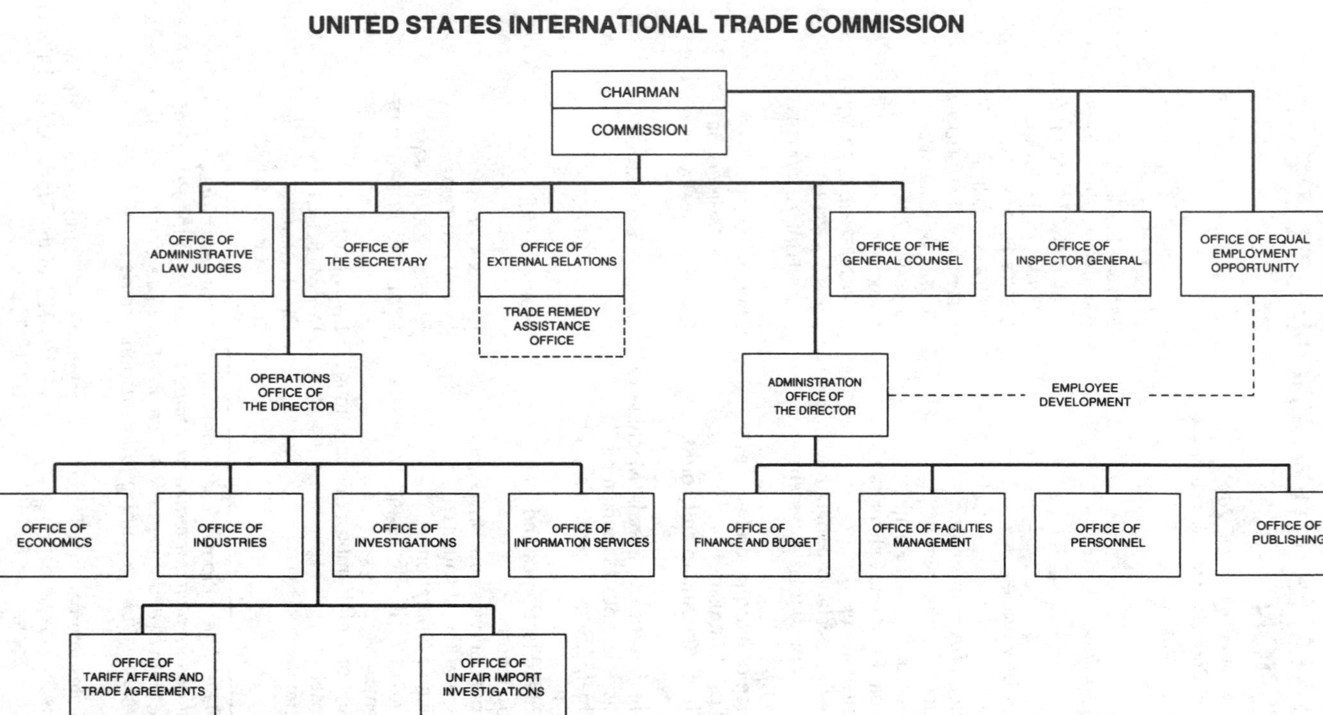
UNITED STATES INTERNATIONAL TRADE COMMISSION
CHAIRMAN
COMMISSION
OFFICE OF ADMINISTRATIVE LAW JUDGES
OFFICE OF THE SECRETARY
OFFICE OF EXTERNAL RELATIONS
TRADE REMEDY ASSISTANCE OFFICE
OFFICE OF THE GENERAL COUNSEL
OFFICE OF INSPECTOR GENERAL
OFFICE OF EQUAL EMPLOYMENT OPPORTUNITY
OPERATIONS OFFICE OF THE DIRECTOR
ADMINISTRATION OFFICE OF THE DIRECTOR
EMPLOYEE DEVELOPMENT
OFFICE OF ECONOMICS
OFFICE OF INDUSTRIES
OFFICE OF INVESTIGATIONS
OFFICE OF INFORMATION SERVICES
OFFICE OF FINANCE AND BUDGET
OFFICE OF FACILITIES MANAGEMENT
OFFICE OF PERSONNEL
OFFICE OF PUBLISHING
OFFICE OF TARIFF AFFAIRS AND TRADE AGREEMENTS
OFFICE OF UNFAIR IMPORT INVESTIGATIONS

unless appointed to fill an unexpired term. The Chairman and Vice Chairman are designated by the President for 2-year terms, and succeeding Chairmen may not be of the same political party. The Chairman generally is responsible for the administration of the Commission. Not more than three Commissioners may be members of the same political party (19 U.S.C. 1330).

Activities

The Commission performs a number of functions pursuant to the statutes referred to above. Under the Tariff Act of 1930, the Commission is given broad powers of investigation relating to the customs laws of the United States and foreign countries; the volume of importation in comparison with domestic production and consumption; the conditions, causes, and effects relating to competition of foreign industries with those of the United States; and all other factors affecting competition between articles of the United States and imported articles. The Commission is required to make available to the President and to the Committee on Ways and Means of the House of Representatives and to the Committee on Finance of the Senate, whenever requested, all information at its command and is directed to make such investigations and reports as may be requested by the President or by either of said committees or by either branch of the Congress.

In order to carry out these responsibilities, the Commission is required to engage in extensive research, conduct specialized studies, and maintain a high degree of expertise in all matters relating to the commercial and international trade policies of the United States.

Imported Articles Subsidized or Sold at Less Than Fair Value The Commission conducts preliminary-phase investigations to determine whether imports of foreign merchandise allegedly being subsidized or sold at less than fair value may pose a threat to an industry in the United States. If the Commission's determination is affirmative, and the Secretary of Commerce determines there is reason to believe or suspect such unfair practices are occurring, then the Commission conducts final-phase investigations to determine the potential threat to an industry because of such imports.

If the Secretary of Commerce determines to suspend an investigation upon acceptance of an agreement to terminate such imports, the Commission may conduct an investigation to determine whether the agreement completely eliminates the threat. The Commission also conducts investigations to determine whether revocation or modification of existing agreements due to changed circumstances would pose new threat.

Unfair Practices in Import Trade The Commission applies U.S. statutory and common law of unfair competition to the importation of products into the United States and their sale. If the Commission determines that there is a violation of law, it is to direct that the articles involved be excluded from entry into the United States, or it may issue cease-and-desist orders directing the person engaged in such violation to cease and desist from engaging in such unfair methods or acts.

Trade Negotiations The Commission advises the President as to the probable economic effect on the domestic industry and consumers of modification of duties and other barriers to trade that may be considered for inclusion in any proposed trade agreement with foreign countries.

Generalized System of Preferences The Commission advises the President with respect to every article that may be considered for preferential removal of the duty on imports from designated developing countries as to the probable economic effect the preferential removal of duty will have on the domestic industry and on consumers.

Industry Adjustment to Import Competition (Global Safeguard Actions) The Commission conducts investigations upon petition on behalf of an industry, a firm, a group of workers, or other entity representative of an industry to determine whether an article is being imported in such increased quantities as to pose a threat to the domestic industry producing an article like or directly competitive with the imported article. If the Commission's finding is affirmative, it recommends to the President the action that would address such a threat and be most effective in facilitating positive adjustment by the industry to import competition.

The Commission reports with respect to developments within an industry that has been granted import relief and advises the President of the probable economic effect of the reduction or elimination of the tariff increase that has been granted. The President may continue, modify, or terminate the import relief previously granted.

Imports From NAFTA Countries (Bilateral Safeguard Actions) The Commission conducts investigations to determine whether, as a result of the reduction or elimination of a duty provided for under the North American Free Trade Agreement (NAFTA), a Canadian article or a Mexican article, as the case may be, is being imported into the United States in such increased quantities and under such conditions so that imports of the article constitute a substantial cause of serious injury or (except in the case of a Canadian article) a threat of serious injury to the domestic industry producing an article that is like or directly competitive with the imported article. If the Commission's determination is in the affirmative, the Commission recommends to the President the relief which is necessary to prevent or remedy serious injury. Commission investigations under these provisions are similar procedurally to those conducted under the global safeguard action provisions.

Market Disruption From Communist Countries The Commission conducts investigations to determine whether increased imports of an article produced in a Communist country are causing market disruption in the United States. If the Commission's determination is in the affirmative, the President may take the same action as in the case of serious injury to an industry, except that the action would apply only to imports of the article from the Communist country. Commission investigations conducted under this provision are similar procedurally to those conducted under the global safeguard action provisions.

Import Interference With Agricultural Programs The Commission conducts investigations, at the direction of the President, to determine whether any articles are being or are practically certain to be imported into the United States under such conditions and in such quantities as to render or tend to render ineffective or to materially interfere with programs of the Department of Agriculture for agricultural commodities or products thereof, or to substantially reduce the amount of any product processed in the United States from such commodities or products, and makes findings and recommendations. The President may restrict the imports in question by imposition of either import fees or quotas. Such fees or quotas may be applied only against countries that are not members of the World Trade Organization.

Uniform Statistical Data The Commission, in cooperation with the Secretary of the Treasury and the Secretary of Commerce, establishes for statistical purposes an enumeration of articles imported into the United States and exported from the United States, and seeks to establish comparability of such statistics with statistical programs for domestic production.

Harmonized Tariff Schedule of the United States, Annotated The Commission issues a publication containing the U.S. tariff schedules and related matters and considers questions concerning the arrangement of such schedules and the classification of articles.

International Trade Studies The Commission conducts studies, investigations, and research projects on a broad range of topics relating to international trade, pursuant to requests of the President, the House Ways and Means Committee, the Senate Finance Committee, either branch of the

Congress, or on its own motion. Public reports of these studies, investigations, and research projects are issued in most cases.

The Commission also keeps informed of the operation and effect of provisions relating to duties or other import restrictions of the United States contained in various trade agreements. Occasionally the Commission is required by statute to perform specific trade-related studies.

Industry and Trade Summaries The Commission prepares and publishes a series of summaries of trade and tariff information. These summaries contain descriptions (in terms of the Harmonized Tariff Schedule of the United States) of the thousands of products imported into the United States, methods of production, and the extent and relative importance of U.S. consumption, production, and trade, together with certain basic factors affecting the competitive position and economic health of domestic industries.

Sources of Information

Inquiries should be directed to the specific organizational unit or to the Secretary, United States International Trade Commission, 500 E Street SW., Washington, DC 20436. Phone, 202–205–2000.

Contracts The Procurement Executive has responsibility for contract matters. Phone, 202–205–2722.

Electronic Access Commission publications, news releases, *Federal Register* notices, scheduling information, the Commission's interactive Trade and Tariff DataWeb, and general information about ITC are available for electronic access. Investigation-related public inspection files are available through the Electronic Document Imaging System (EDIS). Internet, www.usitc.gov.

Employment Information on employment can be obtained from the Director, Office of Personnel. The agency employs international economists, attorneys, accountants, commodity and industry specialists and analysts, and clerical and other support personnel. Phone, 202–205–2651.

Publications The Commission publishes results of investigations concerning various commodities and subjects. Other publications include *Industry and Trade Summaries,* an annual report to the Congress on the operation of the trade agreements program; and an annual report to the Congress of Commission activities. Specific information regarding these publications can be obtained from the Office of the Secretary.

Reading Rooms Reading rooms are open to the public in the Office of the Secretary and in the ITC National Library of International Trade and the ITC law library.

For further information, contact the Secretary, United States International Trade Commission, 500 E Street SW., Washington, DC 20436. Phone, 202–205–2000. Internet, www.usitc.gov.

UNITED STATES POSTAL SERVICE

475 L'Enfant Plaza SW., Washington, DC 20260–0010
Phone, 202–268–2000. Internet, www.usps.gov.

Board of Governors:

Chairman of the Board	EINAR V. DYHRKOPP
Vice Chairman of the Board	ROBERT F. RIDER
Secretary of the Board	THOMAS J. KOERBER
Inspector General	KARLA WOLFE CORCORAN

Governors	Ernesta Ballard, LeGree S. Daniels, Tirso del Junco, S. David Fineman, Ned R. McWherter, John F. Walsh, Sam Winters
Postmaster General and Chief Executive Officer	William J. Henderson
Deputy Postmaster General	John Nolan
Management:	
Postmaster General and Chief Executive Officer	William J. Henderson
President, Expedited/Package Services	John F. Kelly
Vice President, Strategic Planning	Robert A.F. Reisner
Deputy Postmaster General	John Nolan
Chief Postal Inspector	Kenneth C. Weaver
Executive Vice President and Chief Financial Officer	M. Richard Porras
Senior Vice President, Corporate/Business Development	(vacancy)
Senior Vice President, Government Relations and Public Policy	Deborah K. Willhite
Senior Vice President, Human Resources	Patrick R. Donahoe
Senior Vice President, Marketing, and Chief Marketing Officer	Allen Kane
Senior Vice President, Technology, and Chief Technology Officer	Peter A. Jacobson
Vice President and General Counsel	Mary Anne Gibbons
Executive Vice President and Chief Operating Officer	Clarence E. Lewis, Jr.
Senior Vice President, Operations	John E. Potter
Senior Vice President, Sales	Gail G. Sonnenberg
Area Operations:	
Vice President, Allegheny Area	(vacancy)
Vice President, Great Lakes Area	(vacancy)
Vice President, Mid-Atlantic Area	Henry A. Pankey
Vice President, Midwest Area	Suzanne Medvidovich
Vice President, New York Metro Area	David L. Solomon
Vice President, Northeast Area	Jon M. Steele
Vice President, Pacific Area	Jesse Durazo
Vice President, Southeast Area	Robert T. Davis
Vice President, Southwest Area	George L. Lopez
Vice President, Western Area	Craig G. Wade

[For the United States Postal Service statement of organization, see the *Code of Federal Regulations,* Title 39, Parts 221–226]

The United States Postal Service provides mail processing and delivery services to individuals and businesses within the United States. The Service is committed to serving customers through the development of efficient mail-handling systems and operates its own planning and engineering programs. It is also the responsibility of the Postal Service to protect the mails from loss or theft and to apprehend those who violate postal laws.

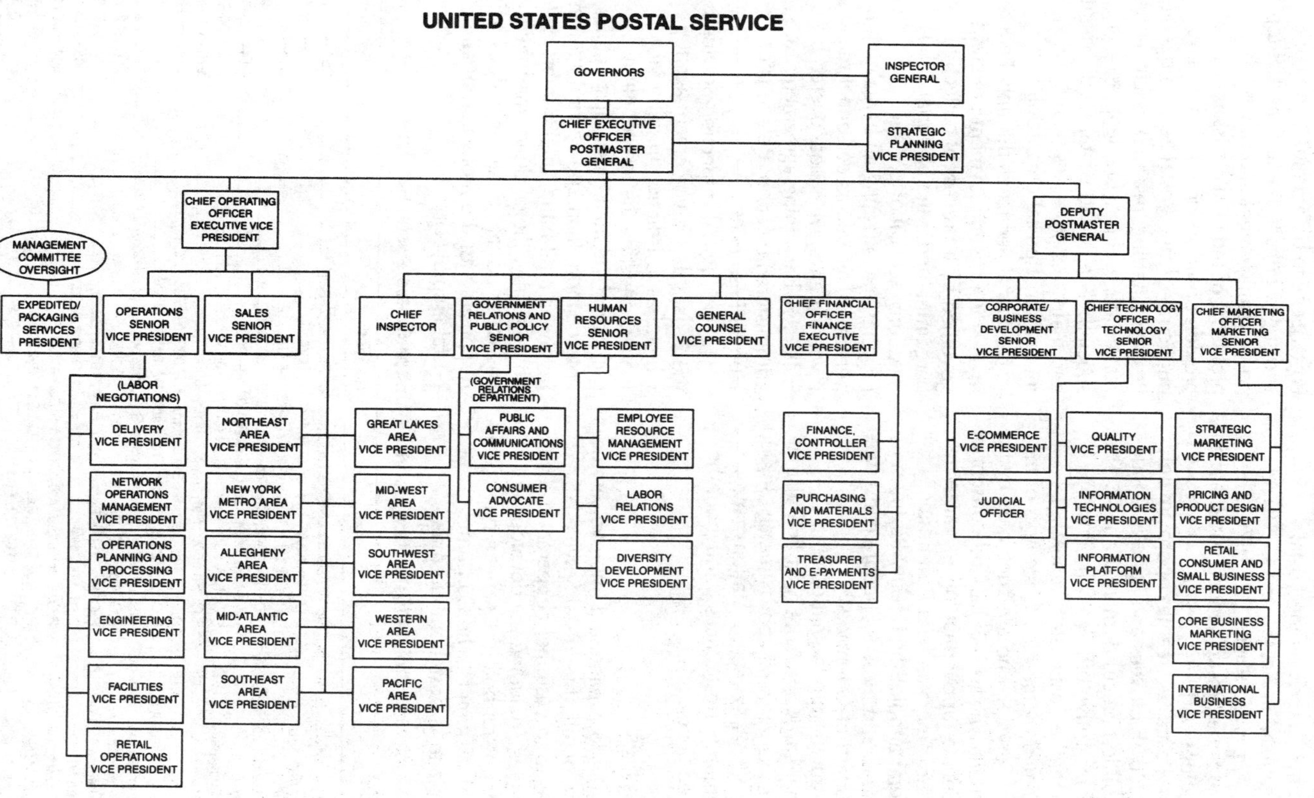
UNITED STATES POSTAL SERVICE
GOVERNORS
INSPECTOR GENERAL
CHIEF EXECUTIVE OFFICER POSTMASTER GENERAL
STRATEGIC PLANNING VICE PRESIDENT
MANAGEMENT COMMITTEE OVERSIGHT
CHIEF OPERATING OFFICER EXECUTIVE VICE PRESIDENT
DEPUTY POSTMASTER GENERAL
EXPEDITED/ PACKAGING SERVICES PRESIDENT
OPERATIONS SENIOR VICE PRESIDENT
SALES SENIOR VICE PRESIDENT
CHIEF INSPECTOR
GOVERNMENT RELATIONS AND PUBLIC POLICY SENIOR VICE PRESIDENT
HUMAN RESOURCES SENIOR VICE PRESIDENT
GENERAL COUNSEL VICE PRESIDENT
CHIEF FINANCIAL OFFICER FINANCE EXECUTIVE VICE PRESIDENT
CORPORATE/ BUSINESS DEVELOPMENT SENIOR VICE PRESIDENT
CHIEF TECHNOLOGY OFFICER TECHNOLOGY SENIOR VICE PRESIDENT
CHIEF MARKETING OFFICER MARKETING SENIOR VICE PRESIDENT
(LABOR NEGOTIATIONS)
DELIVERY VICE PRESIDENT
NETWORK OPERATIONS MANAGEMENT VICE PRESIDENT
OPERATIONS PLANNING AND PROCESSING VICE PRESIDENT
ENGINEERING VICE PRESIDENT
FACILITIES VICE PRESIDENT
RETAIL OPERATIONS VICE PRESIDENT
NORTHEAST AREA VICE PRESIDENT
NEW YORK METRO AREA VICE PRESIDENT
ALLEGHENY AREA VICE PRESIDENT
MID-ATLANTIC AREA VICE PRESIDENT
SOUTHEAST AREA VICE PRESIDENT
GREAT LAKES AREA VICE PRESIDENT
MID-WEST AREA VICE PRESIDENT
SOUTHWEST AREA VICE PRESIDENT
WESTERN AREA VICE PRESIDENT
PACIFIC AREA VICE PRESIDENT
(GOVERNMENT RELATIONS DEPARTMENT)
PUBLIC AFFAIRS AND COMMUNICATIONS VICE PRESIDENT
CONSUMER ADVOCATE VICE PRESIDENT
EMPLOYEE RESOURCE MANAGEMENT VICE PRESIDENT
LABOR RELATIONS VICE PRESIDENT
DIVERSITY DEVELOPMENT VICE PRESIDENT
FINANCE, CONTROLLER VICE PRESIDENT
PURCHASING AND MATERIALS VICE PRESIDENT
TREASURER AND E-PAYMENTS VICE PRESIDENT
E-COMMERCE VICE PRESIDENT
JUDICIAL OFFICER
QUALITY VICE PRESIDENT
INFORMATION TECHNOLOGIES VICE PRESIDENT
INFORMATION PLATFORM VICE PRESIDENT
STRATEGIC MARKETING VICE PRESIDENT
PRICING AND PRODUCT DESIGN VICE PRESIDENT
RETAIL CONSUMER AND SMALL BUSINESS VICE PRESIDENT
CORE BUSINESS MARKETING VICE PRESIDENT
INTERNATIONAL BUSINESS VICE PRESIDENT

The Postal Service was created as an independent establishment of the executive branch by the Postal Reorganization Act (39 U.S.C. 101 *et seq.*), approved August 12, 1970. The United States Postal Service commenced operations on July 1, 1971.

The Postal Service has approximately 798,000 employees and handles about 202 billion pieces of mail annually. The chief executive officer of the Postal Service, the Postmaster General, is appointed by the nine Governors of the Postal Service, who are appointed by the President with the advice and consent of the Senate for overlapping 9-year terms. The Governors and the Postmaster General appoint the Deputy Postmaster General, and these 11 people constitute the Board of Governors.

In addition to the national headquarters, there are area and district offices supervising approximately 38,000 post offices, branches, stations, and community post offices throughout the United States.

Activities

In order to expand and improve service to the public, the Postal Service is engaged in customer cooperation activities, including the development of programs for both the general public and major customers. The Consumer Advocate, a postal ombudsman, represents the interest of the individual mail customer in matters involving the Postal Service by bringing complaints and suggestions to the attention of top postal management and solving the problems of individual customers. To provide postal services responsive to public needs, the Postal Service operates its own planning, research, engineering, real estate, and procurement programs specially adapted to postal requirements, and maintains close ties with international postal organizations.

The Postal Service is the only Federal agency whose employment policies are governed by a process of collective bargaining under the National Labor Relations Act. Labor contract negotiations, affecting all bargaining unit personnel, as well as personnel matters involving employees not covered by collective bargaining agreements, are administered by Labor Relations or Human Resources.

The U.S. Postal Inspection Service is the Federal law enforcement agency which has jurisdiction in criminal matters affecting the integrity and security of the mail. Postal Inspectors enforce more than 200 Federal statutes involving mail fraud, mail bombs, child pornography, illegal drugs, mail theft, and other postal crimes, as well as being responsible for the protection of all postal employees.

Postal Inspection Service—United States Postal Service

Division	Address	Telephone
Florida	6th Fl., 3400 Lakeside Dr., Miramar, FL 33027–3242	954–436–7200
Gulf Coast	P.O. Box 1276, Houston, TX 77251–1276	713–238–4400
Michiana	P.O. Box 330119, Detroit, MI 48232–6119	313–226–8184
Mid-Atlantic	P.O. Box 3000, Charlotte, NC 28228–3000	704–329–9120
Midwest	1106 Walnut St., St. Louis, MO 63199–2201	314–539–9300
New York Metro	P.O. Box 555, New York, NY 10116–0555	212–330–3844
North Jersey/Caribbean	P.O. Box 509, Newark, NJ 07101–0509	973–693–5400
Northeast	7th Fl., 425 Summer St., Boston, MA 02210–1736	617–464–8000
Northern California	P.O. Box 882528, San Francisco, CA 94188–2528	415–778–5800
Northern Illinois	Rm. 50190, 433 W. Harrison St., Chicago, IL 60669–2201	312–983–7900
Northwest	P.O. Box 400, Seattle, WA 98111–4000	206–442–6300
Philadelphia Metro	P.O. Box 7500, Philadelphia, PA 19101–9000	215–895–8450
Rocky Mountain	Suite 900, 1745 Stout St., Denver, CO 80202–3034	303–313–5320
Southeast	P.O. Box 16489, Atlanta, GA 30321–0489	404–608–4500
Southern California	P.O. Box 2000, Pasadena, CA 91102–2000	626–405–1200
Southwest	P.O. Box 162929, Fort Worth, TX 76161–2929	817–317–3400
Washington Metro	P.O. Box 96096, Washington, DC 20066–6096	202–636–2300
Western Allegheny	Rm. 2101, 1001 California Ave., Pittsburgh, PA 15290–9000	412–359–7900

Sources of Information

Inquiries on the following information should be directed to the specified office, U.S. Postal Service, 475 L'Enfant Plaza SW., Washington, DC 20260.

Consumer Information For general information, call 800–275–8777 (800–ASK–USPS) 24 hours a day. Consumer Affairs Help Line, 202–268–2284. TDD, 202–268–2310. Express Mail Hotline, 800–222–1811. Fax, 202–268–2304. Information on past and present schemes used to defraud the public is available through Congressional and Public Affairs, Postal Inspection Service. Phone, 202–268–5400.

Contracts and Small Business Activities Contact Supplier Diversity. Phone, 202–268–4633.

Employment General information about jobs such as clerk, letter carrier, etc., including information about programs for veterans, may be obtained by contacting the nearest post office.

Individuals interested in working at the Postal Headquarters in Washington, DC, may obtain information by calling the U.S. Postal Service information hotline. Phone, 800–562–8777 (800–JOB–USPS).

Information about Postal Inspector employment may be obtained from the Office of Recruitment. Phone, 301–983–7400.

Inspector General The Office of Inspector General maintains a toll-free hotline as a means for individuals to report activities involving fraud, waste, or mismanagement. Phone, 888–USPS–OIG. Fax, 703–248–2259. Complaints may be sent by mail to the United States Postal Service, Office of Inspector General Hotline, 10th Floor, 1735 North Lynn Street, Arlington, VA 22209–2020. Publicly available documents and information on the Office of Inspector General and some Freedom of Information Act documents are available electronically through the Internet, at www.uspsoig.gov.

Philatelic Sales Contact the Philatelic Fulfillment Service Center, Kansas City, MO 64179–1009. Phone, 800–782–6724 (800–STAMP–24).

Publications Pamphlets on mailability, postage rates and fees, and many other topics may be obtained free of charge from the nearest post office.

Most postal regulations are contained in Postal Service manuals covering domestic mail, international mail, postal operations, administrative support, employee and labor relations, financial management, and procurement. These manuals and other publications including the *National Five-Digit ZIP Code and Post Office Directory* (Publication 65) may be purchased from the Superintendent of Documents, Government Printing Office, Washington, DC 20402–0001. The *National Five-Digit ZIP Code and Post Office Directory* is also available through local post offices.

Reading Rooms Located on 11th Floor North, Library. Phone, 202–268–2900.

For further information, contact the U.S. Postal Service, 475 L'Enfant Plaza SW., Washington, DC 20260. Phone, 202–268–2000. Internet, www.usps.gov.

Boards, Commissions, and Committees

Note: This is a listing of Federal boards, commissions, councils, etc., not listed elsewhere in the *Manual,* which were established by congressional or Presidential action, whose functions are not strictly limited to the internal operations of a parent department or agency and which are authorized to publish documents in the *Federal Register.* While the editors have attempted to compile a complete and accurate listing, suggestions for improving coverage of this guide are welcome. Please address your comments to the Office of the Federal Register, National Archives and Records Administration, Washington, DC 20408. Phone, 202–523–5230.

Federal advisory committees, as defined by the Federal Advisory Committee Act, as amended (5 U.S.C. app.), have not been included here. Information on Federal advisory committees may be obtained from the Committee Management Secretariat, General Services Administration, General Services Building (MC), Room G–230, Washington, DC 20405. Phone, 202–273–3556. Internet, www.policyworks.gov/FACA_Townhall.

Administrative Committee of the Federal Register

National Archives and Records Administration, Washington, DC 20408. Phone, 202–523–4534.

Advisory Council on Historic Preservation

Room 809, 1100 Pennsylvania Avenue NW., Washington, DC 20004. Phone, 202–606–8503. Internet, www.achp.gov.

American Battle Monuments Commission

Suite 500, 2300 Clarendon Boulevard, Court House Plaza Two, Arlington, VA 22201–3367. Phone, 703–696–6900. Internet, www.abmc.gov.

Appalachian Regional Commission

Suite 700, 1666 Connecticut Avenue NW., Washington, DC 20009–1068. Phone, 202–884–7799. Internet, www.arc.gov.

Architectural and Transportation Barriers Compliance Board [1]

Suite 1000, 1331 F Street NW., Washington, DC 20004–1111. Phone, 202–272–5434. Internet, www.access-board.gov.

Arctic Research Commission

Suite 630, 4350 North Fairfax Drive, Arlington, VA 22203. Phone, 703–525–0111. Internet, www.uaa.alaska.edu/enri/arc_web/archome.htm.

Arthritis and Musculoskeletal Interagency Coordinating Committee

National Institutes of Health/NIAMS, Building 31, Room 4C23, Bethesda, MD 20892–2350. Phone, 301–496–8271.

[1] Also known as the Access Board.

Barry M. Goldwater Scholarship and Excellence in Education Foundation

Suite 315, 6225 Brandon Avenue, Springfield, VA 22150–2519. Phone, 703–756–6012.

Chemical Safety and Hazard Investigation Board

Suite 400, 2175 K Street NW., Washington, DC 20037–1809. Phone, 202–261–7600. Internet, www.chemsafety.gov.

Citizens' Stamp Advisory Committee

United States Postal Service, Room 4474–E, 475 L'Enfant Plaza SW., Washington, DC 20260–2437. Phone, 202–268–6338.

Commission of Fine Arts

Suite 312, 441 F Street NW., Washington, DC 20001. Phone, 202–504–2200.

Committee on Foreign Investment in the United States

Department of the Treasury, Room 4201, 1440 New York Avenue NW., Washington, DC 20220. Phone, 202–622–1860.

Committee for the Implementation of Textile Agreements

Department of Commerce, Room 3001A, Fourteenth Street and Constitution Avenue NW., Washington, DC 20230. Phone, 202–482–3737.

Committee for Purchase From People Who Are Blind or Severely Disabled

Suite 310, 1215 Jefferson Davis Highway, Arlington, VA 22202–4302. Phone, 703–603–7740.

Coordinating Council on Juvenile Justice and Delinquency Prevention

Department of Justice, Office of Juvenile Justice and Delinquency Prevention, 810 Building, Seventh Street NW., Washington, DC 20531. Phone, 202–307–5911. Internet, www.ojjdps.ncjrs.org/council.

Delaware River Basin Commission

P.O. Box 7360, 25 State Police Drive, West Trenton, NJ 08628–0360. Phone, 609–883–9500. Internet, www.drbc.net.

Endangered Species Committee [1]

Department of the Interior, Room 4426, 1849 C Street NW., Washington, DC 20240. Phone, 202–208–4077.

Export Administration Review Board

Room 2639, Herbert C. Hoover Building, Fourteenth Street and Pennsylvania Avenue NW., Washington, DC 20230. Phone, 202–482–5863.

Federal Financial Institutions Examination Council

Suite 310, 2000 K Street NW., Washington, DC 20006. Phone, 202–872–7500. Internet, www.ffiec.gov.

Federal Financing Bank

South Court One, Main Treasury Building, 1500 Pennsylvania Avenue NW., Washington, DC 20220. Phone, 202–622–2470.

Federal Interagency Committee on Education

Department of Education, Federal Office Building 6, Room 5E200, 400 Independence Avenue SW., Washington, DC 20202–3572. Phone, 202–401–3673.

Federal Laboratory Consortium for Technology Transfer

Suite 800, 1850 M Street NW., Washington, DC 20036. Phone, 202–331–4220. Internet, www.fedlabs.gov.

Federal Library and Information Center Committee

Room 217, Second Street and Independence Avenue SE., Washington, DC 20541. Phone, 202–707–4800. Internet, lcweb.loc.gov/flicc/flchome.html.

---

[1] The Committee accepts applications for Endangered Species Act exemptions.

Harry S. Truman Scholarship Foundation

712 Jackson Place NW., Washington, DC 20006. Phone, 202–395–4831. Internet, www.truman.gov.

Illinois and Michigan Canal National Heritage Corridor Commission

15701 South Independence Boulevard, Lockport, IL 60441. Phone, 815–740–2047. Internet, www.nps.gov/ilmi/index.htm.

Indian Arts and Crafts Board

Department of the Interior, Room MS 4004–MIB, 1849 C Street NW., Washington, DC 20240. Phone, 202–208–3773.

Interagency Committee on Employment of People with Disabilities

Equal Employment Opportunity Commission, Federal Sector Programs, Room 5238, 1801 L Street NW., Washington, DC 20507. Phone, 202–663–4560. TDD, 202–663–4593.

Interagency Savings Bonds Committee

Office of the Committee Chair, Savings Bond Marketing Office, 999 E Street NW., Washington, DC 20226. Phone, 202–219–3914.

J. William Fulbright Foreign Scholarship Board

United States Information Agency, Room 247, 301 Fourth Street SW., Washington, DC 20547. Phone, 202–619–4290.

James Madison Memorial Fellowship Foundation

Suite 303, 2000 K Street NW., Washington, DC 20006–1809. Phone, 202–653–8700. Internet, www.jamesmadison.com.

Japan-United States Friendship Commission

Room 925, 1120 Vermont Avenue NW., Washington, DC 20005. Phone, 202–418–9800.

Joint Board for the Enrollment of Actuaries

1111 Constitution Avenue NW., Washington, DC 20224. Phone, 202–694–1891.

Marine Mammal Commission

Room 905, 4340 East-West Highway, Bethesda, MD 20814. Phone, 301–504–0087.

Medicare Payments Advisory Commission

Suite 800, 1730 K Street NW., Washington, DC 20006. Phone, 202–653–7220.

Migratory Bird Conservation Commission

Room 622, 4401 North Fairfax Drive, Arlington, VA 22203. Phone, 703–358–1716. Internet, realty.fws.gov/mbcc.html.

Mississippi River Commission

United States Army Corps of Engineers, Mississippi Valley Division, 1400 Walnut Street, P.O. Box 80, Vicksburg, MS 39181–0080. Phone, 601–634–5757. Internet, www.mvd.usace.army.mil.

Morris K. Udall Scholarship and Excellence in National Environmental Policy Foundation

Suite 3350, 110 South Church Avenue, Tucson, AZ 85701. Phone, 520–670–5299. Internet, www.udallfoundation.org.

National Commission on Libraries and Information Science

Suite 820, 1110 Vermont Avenue NW., Washington, DC 20005. Phone, 202–606–9200. Internet, www.nclis.gov.

National Council on Disability

Suite 1050, 1331 F Street NW., Washington, DC 20004. Phone, 202–272–2004. TDD, 202–272–2074. Internet, www.ncd.gov.

National Occupational Information Coordinating Committee

Suite 156, 2100 M Street NW., Washington, DC 20037. Phone, 202–653–5665. Internet, www.noicc.gov.

National Park Foundation
Suite 1102, 1101 Seventeenth Street NW., Washington, DC 20036–4704. Phone, 202–785–4500. Internet, www.nationalparks.org.

Navajo and Hopi Relocation Commission
Office of Navajo and Hopi Indian Relocation, P.O. Box KK, Flagstaff, AZ 86002. Phone, 520–779–2721.

Northwest Power Planning Council
Suite 1100, 851 Southwest Sixth Avenue, Portland, OR 97204–1348. Phone, 503–222–5161. Internet, www.nwppc.org.

Panama Canal Commission
Suite 1050, 1825 "I" Street NW., Washington, DC 20006–5402. Phone, 202–634–6441.

Permanent Committee for the Oliver Wendell Holmes Devise
Library of Congress, Manuscript Division, Washington, DC 20540–4680. Phone, 202–707–5383.

President's Committee on Employment of People With Disabilities
Suite 300, 1331 F Street NW., Washington, DC 20004–1107. Phone, 202–376–6200. TDD, 202–376–6205. Internet, www.pcepd.gov.

President's Council on Integrity and Efficiency
Office of Management and Budget, Room 6025, New Executive Office Building, Washington, DC 20503. Phone, 202–395–6911.

President's Foreign Intelligence Advisory Board
Room 340, Old Executive Office Building, Washington, DC 20502. Phone, 202–456–2352.

Presidio Trust
34 Graham Street, P.O. Box 29052, San Francisco, CA 94129–0052. Phone, 415–561–5300. Internet, www.presidiotrust.gov.

Social Security Advisory Board
Suite 625, 400 Virginia Avenue SW., Washington, DC 20024. Phone, 202–475–7700. Fax, 202–475–7715. Internet, www.ssab.gov.

Susquehanna River Basin Commission
1721 North Front Street, Harrisburg, PA 17102–2391. Phone, 717–238–0422. Internet, www.srbc.net.

Textile Trade Policy Group
Room 307, 600 Seventeenth Street NW., Washington, DC 20508. Phone, 202–395–3026.

Trade Policy Staff Committee
Office of Policy Coordination, Room 122, 600 Seventeenth Street NW., Washington, DC 20508. Phone, 202–395–3475.

United States Holocaust Memorial Museum
100 Raoul Wallenberg Place SW., Washington, DC 20024. Phone, 202–488–0400. Internet, www.ushmm.org.

United States Nuclear Waste Technical Review Board
Suite 1300, 2300 Clarendon Boulevard, Arlington, VA 22201. Phone, 703–235–4473. Internet, www.nwtrb.gov.

Veterans Day National Committee
Department of Veterans Affairs (80D), 810 Vermont Avenue NW., Washington, DC 20420. Phone, 202–273–5735.

White House Commission on Presidential Scholars
Department of Education, 400 Maryland Avenue SW., Washington, DC 20202–0498. Phone, 800–USA–LEARN.

QUASI–OFFICIAL AGENCIES

Note: This section contains organizations that are not Executive agencies under the definition in 5 U.S.C. 105 but that are required by statute to publish certain information on their programs and activities in the *Federal Register.*

LEGAL SERVICES CORPORATION

750 First Street NE., Washington, DC 20002–4250
Phone, 202–336–8800. Fax, 202–336–8959. Internet, www.lsc.gov.

President	JOHN MCKAY
Vice President for Administration	JAMES J. HOGAN
Comptroller/Treasurer	DAVID RICHARDSON
Director, Office of Administration and Human Resources	JOAN KENNEDY
Director, Office of Information Technology	LESLIE Q. RUSSELL
Vice President, Government Relations and Public Affairs	MAURICIO VIVERO
Vice President for Legal Affairs, General Counsel, and Corporate Secretary	VICTOR M. FORTUNO
Vice President for Programs	RANDI YOUELLS
Director, Office of Compliance and Enforcement	DANILO A. CARDONA
Director, Office of Information Management	(VACANCY)
Director, Office of Program Performance	MICHAEL GENZ
Inspector General	EDOUARD QUATREVAUX

[For the Legal Services Corporation statement of organization, see the *Code of Federal Regulations,* Title 45, Part 1601]

The Legal Services Corporation provides quality legal assistance for noncriminal proceedings to those who would otherwise be unable to afford such assistance.

The Legal Services Corporation is a private, nonprofit organization established by the Legal Services Corporation Act of 1974, as amended (42 U.S.C. 2996), to provide financial support for legal assistance in noncriminal proceedings to persons financially unable to afford legal services.

The Corporation is governed by an 11-member Board of Directors, appointed by the President with the advice and consent of the Senate. Each member serves for a term of 3 years, except that

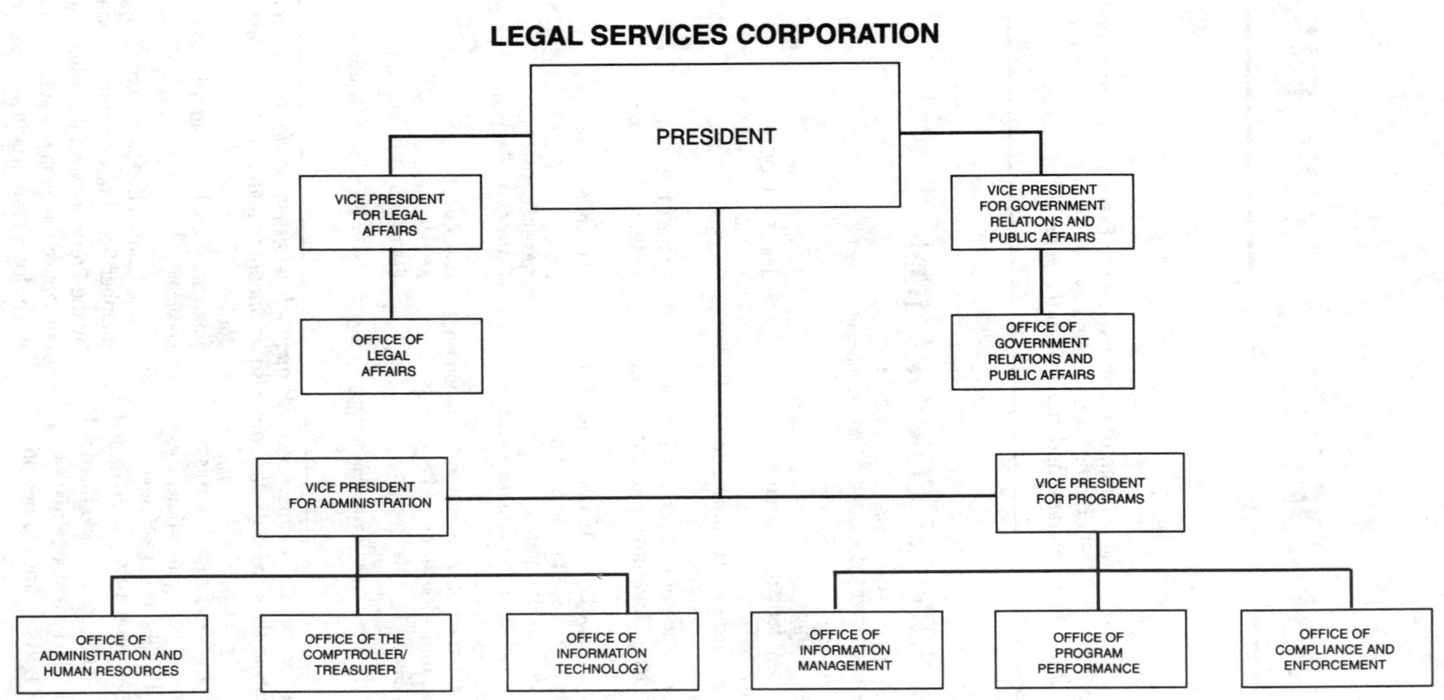
LEGAL SERVICES CORPORATION
PRESIDENT
VICE PRESIDENT FOR LEGAL AFFAIRS
OFFICE OF LEGAL AFFAIRS
VICE PRESIDENT FOR GOVERNMENT RELATIONS AND PUBLIC AFFAIRS
OFFICE OF GOVERNMENT RELATIONS AND PUBLIC AFFAIRS
VICE PRESIDENT FOR ADMINISTRATION
VICE PRESIDENT FOR PROGRAMS
OFFICE OF ADMINISTRATION AND HUMAN RESOURCES
OFFICE OF THE COMPTROLLER/ TREASURER
OFFICE OF INFORMATION TECHNOLOGY
OFFICE OF INFORMATION MANAGEMENT
OFFICE OF PROGRAM PERFORMANCE
OFFICE OF COMPLIANCE AND ENFORCEMENT

five of the members first appointed—as designated by the President at the time of appointment—serve 2-year terms. The President of the Corporation, appointed by the Board of Directors, is the chief executive officer of the Corporation and serves as an *ex officio* member of the Board of Directors.

The Corporation provides financial assistance to qualified programs furnishing legal assistance to eligible clients and makes grants to and contracts with individuals, firms, corporations, and organizations for the purpose of providing legal assistance to these clients.

The Corporation establishes maximum income levels for clients based on family size, urban and rural differences, and cost-of-living variations. Using these maximum income levels and other financial factors, the Corporation's recipient programs establish criteria to determine the eligibility of clients and priorities of service based on an appraisal of the legal needs of the eligible client community.

For further information, contact the Office of Communications, Legal Services Corporation, 750 First Street NE., Washington, DC 20002–4250. Phone, 202–336–8800. Fax, 202–336–8959. Internet, www.lsc.gov.

SMITHSONIAN INSTITUTION

1000 Jefferson Drive SW., Washington, DC 20560
Phone, 202–357–2700. Internet, www.si.edu.

Board of Regents:

The Chief Justice of the United States (*Chancellor*)	WILLIAM H. REHNQUIST
The Vice President of the United States	AL GORE
Members of the Senate	THAD COCHRAN, WILLIAM FRIST, DANIEL PATRICK MOYNIHAN
Members of the House of Representatives	SAMUEL JOHNSON, ROBERT MATSUI, RALPH REGULA
Citizen Members	HOWARD H. BAKER, JR., BARBER B. CONABLE, JR., ANNE D'HARNONCOURT, LOUIS V. GERSTNER, JR., HANNA HOLBORN GRAY, MANUEL L. IBAÑEZ, HOMER A. NEAL, FRANK A. SHRONTZ, WESLEY SAMUEL WILLIAMS, JR.

Officials:

The Secretary	LAWRENCE M. SMALL
The Inspector General	THOMAS D. BLAIR
Executive Director for Development	ROBERT V. HANLE
Director, Office of Policy and Analysis	CAROLE P. NEVES
Executive Assistant to the Secretary and Director, Smithsonian Institution Building and Arts and Industries Building	JAMES M. HOBBINS
Under Secretary for American Museums, Programs, and National Outreach	SHEILA BURKE

Counselor for Asian/Pacific-American Studies	Franklin Odo
Curator in Charge, Renwick Gallery	Kenneth R. Trapp
Director, Anacostia Museum and Center for African American History and Culture	Steven Newsome
Director, Archives of American Art	Richard Wattenmaker
Director, Arts and Industries Building	James M. Hobbins
Director, Center for Folklife and Cultural Heritage	Richard Kurin
Director, Cooper-Hewitt National Design Museum	(vacancy)
Director, National Air and Space Museum	Gen. John R. Dailey
Director, National Museum of American Art	Elizabeth Broun
Director, National Museum of American History	Spencer Crew
Director, National Museum of the American Indian	W. Richard West, Jr.
Director, National Portrait Gallery	(vacancy)
Director, National Postal Museum	James Bruns
Director, Office of Communications/Public Affairs	David J. Umansky
Director, Office of Exhibits Central	Michael Headley
Director, Office of Government Relations	(vacancy)
Director, Office of Special Events and Conference Services	Nicole L. Krakora
Director, Smithsonian Center for Education and Museum Studies	Ann Bay
Director, Smithsonian Center for Latino Initiatives	Refugio Rochin
Director, Smithsonian Institution Traveling Exhibition Service (SITES)	Anna R. Cohn
Director, Smithsonian's Affiliates Program	Michael Carrigan
Director, The Smithsonian Associates	Mara Mayor
Editor, Joseph Henry Papers Project	Marc Rothenberg
Under Secretary for Science	J. Dennis O'Connor
Director, Museum Support Center	(vacancy)
Director, National Museum of Natural History	Robert W. Fri
Director, National Science Resources Center	Douglas Lapp
Director, National Zoological Park	(vacancy)
Director, Office of Fellowships and Grants	Roberta Rubinoff
Director, Smithsonian Astrophysical Observatory	Irwin I. Shapiro
Director, Smithsonian Center for Materials Research and Education	Lambertus Van Zelst
Director, Smithsonian Environmental Research Center	Ross Simons
Director, Smithsonian Institution Press	Peter Cannell
Director, Smithsonian Marine Station	Mary Rice
Director, Smithsonian Tropical Research Institute	Ira Rubinoff

Under Secretary for Financial and Administrative Services	(VACANCY)
Chief, Information Technology Operations	GEORGE VAN DYKE
Chief, Information Technology Strategic Planning	JIM CONKLIN
Chief Financial Officer	RICK JOHNSON
Deputy Comptroller	BOB MILLS
Director, Office of Equal Employment and Minority Affairs	ERA MARSHALL
Director, Office of Human Resources	CAROLYN JONES
Director, Office of International Relations	FRANCINE BERKOWITZ
Director, Smithsonian Institution Archives	ETHEL W. HEDLIN
Director, Smithsonian Institution Libraries	NANCY E. GWINN
General Counsel	JOHN E. HUERTA
Ombudsman	CHANDRA HEILMAN
Senior Facilities Services Officer	RICHARD RICE
Director, International Art Museums Division	(VACANCY)
Director, Freer Gallery of Art and Arthur M. Sackler Gallery	MILO C. BEACH
Director, Hirshhorn Museum and Sculpture Garden	JAMES T. DEMETRION
Director, National Museum of African Art	ROSLYN A. WALKER
Chief Executive Officer of Smithsonian Business Ventures	GARY BEER
Director, Smithsonian Productions	PAUL JOHNSON
Editor, Smithsonian Magazine	DON MOSER
Publisher, Smithsonian Magazine	RONALD WALKER
Senior Business Officer	ROLAND BANSCHER, *Acting*

The John F. Kennedy Center for the Performing Arts [1]

Chairman	JAMES A. JOHNSON
President	LAWRENCE J. WILKER

National Gallery of Art [1]

President	ROBERT H. SMITH
Director	EARL A. POWELL III

Woodrow Wilson International Center for Scholars [1]

Director	LEE H. HAMILTON
Deputy Director	MICHAEL H. VAN DUSEN
Deputy Director for Planning and Management	DEAN W. ANDERSON
Chairman, Board of Trustees	JOSEPH A. CARI, JR.

More than 150 years old, the Smithsonian Institution is an independent trust instrumentality of the United States that fosters the increase and diffusion of knowledge. The world's largest museum complex, the Smithsonian includes 16 museums and galleries, the National Zoo, and research facilities in several States and the Republic of Panama. The Smithsonian holds more than 140 million artifacts and specimens in its trust for the American people. The Institution, a respected center for research, is dedicated to public education, national service, and scholarship in the arts, sciences, and history.

[1] Administered under a separate Board of Trustees.

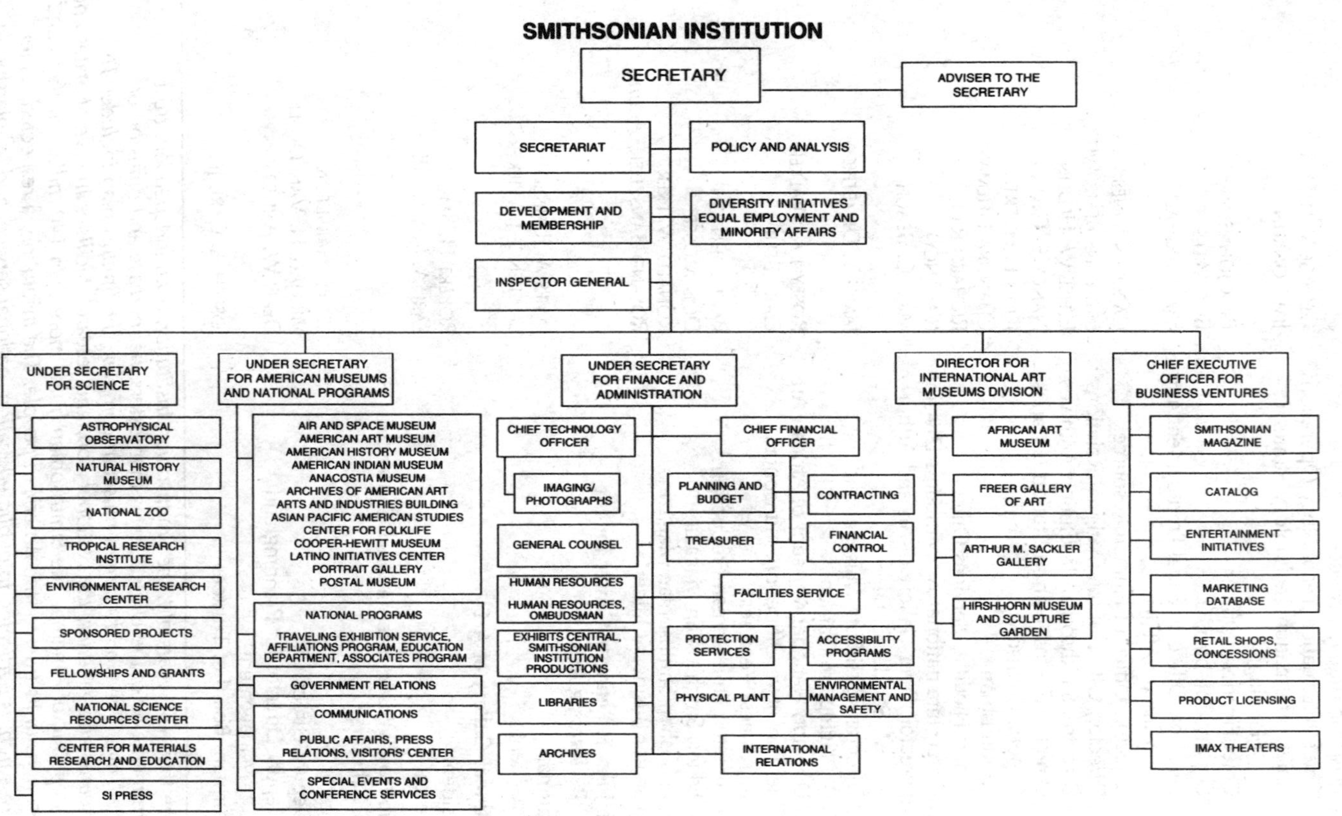
SMITHSONIAN INSTITUTION
SECRETARY
ADVISER TO THE SECRETARY
SECRETARIAT
POLICY AND ANALYSIS
DEVELOPMENT AND MEMBERSHIP
DIVERSITY INITIATIVES EQUAL EMPLOYMENT AND MINORITY AFFAIRS
INSPECTOR GENERAL
UNDER SECRETARY FOR SCIENCE
ASTROPHYSICAL OBSERVATORY
NATURAL HISTORY MUSEUM
NATIONAL ZOO
TROPICAL RESEARCH INSTITUTE
ENVIRONMENTAL RESEARCH CENTER
SPONSORED PROJECTS
FELLOWSHIPS AND GRANTS
NATIONAL SCIENCE RESOURCES CENTER
CENTER FOR MATERIALS RESEARCH AND EDUCATION
SI PRESS
UNDER SECRETARY FOR AMERICAN MUSEUMS AND NATIONAL PROGRAMS
AIR AND SPACE MUSEUM
AMERICAN ART MUSEUM
AMERICAN HISTORY MUSEUM
AMERICAN INDIAN MUSEUM
ANACOSTIA MUSEUM
ARCHIVES OF AMERICAN ART
ARTS AND INDUSTRIES BUILDING
ASIAN PACIFIC AMERICAN STUDIES
CENTER FOR FOLKLIFE
COOPER-HEWITT MUSEUM
LATINO INITIATIVES CENTER
PORTRAIT GALLERY
POSTAL MUSEUM
NATIONAL PROGRAMS
TRAVELING EXHIBITION SERVICE, AFFILIATIONS PROGRAM, EDUCATION DEPARTMENT, ASSOCIATES PROGRAM
GOVERNMENT RELATIONS
COMMUNICATIONS
PUBLIC AFFAIRS, PRESS RELATIONS, VISITORS' CENTER
SPECIAL EVENTS AND CONFERENCE SERVICES
UNDER SECRETARY FOR FINANCE AND ADMINISTRATION
CHIEF TECHNOLOGY OFFICER
IMAGING/ PHOTOGRAPHS
GENERAL COUNSEL
HUMAN RESOURCES
HUMAN RESOURCES, OMBUDSMAN
EXHIBITS CENTRAL, SMITHSONIAN INSTITUTION PRODUCTIONS
LIBRARIES
ARCHIVES
CHIEF FINANCIAL OFFICER
PLANNING AND BUDGET
CONTRACTING
TREASURER
FINANCIAL CONTROL
FACILITIES SERVICE
PROTECTION SERVICES
ACCESSIBILITY PROGRAMS
PHYSICAL PLANT
ENVIRONMENTAL MANAGEMENT AND SAFETY
INTERNATIONAL RELATIONS
DIRECTOR FOR INTERNATIONAL ART MUSEUMS DIVISION
AFRICAN ART MUSEUM
FREER GALLERY OF ART
ARTHUR M. SACKLER GALLERY
HIRSHHORN MUSEUM AND SCULPTURE GARDEN
CHIEF EXECUTIVE OFFICER FOR BUSINESS VENTURES
SMITHSONIAN MAGAZINE
CATALOG
ENTERTAINMENT INITIATIVES
MARKETING DATABASE
RETAIL SHOPS, CONCESSIONS
PRODUCT LICENSING
IMAX THEATERS

The Smithsonian Institution was created by an act of August 10, 1846 (20 U.S.C. 41 *et seq.*), to carry out the terms of the will of British scientist James Smithson (1765–1829), who in 1826 had bequeathed his entire estate to the United States "to found at Washington, under the name of the Smithsonian Institution, an establishment for the increase and diffusion of knowledge among men." On July 1, 1836, Congress accepted the legacy and pledged the faith of the United States to the charitable trust.

In September 1838, Smithson's legacy, which amounted to more than 100,000 gold sovereigns, was delivered to the mint at Philadelphia. Congress vested responsibility for administering the trust in the Secretary of the Smithsonian and the Smithsonian Board of Regents, composed of the Chief Justice, the Vice President, three Members of the Senate, three Members of the House of Representatives, and nine citizen members appointed by joint resolution of Congress. To carry out Smithson's mandate, the Institution:

—conducts scientific and scholarly research;

—publishes the results of studies, explorations, and investigations;

—preserves for study and reference more than 140 million artifacts, works of art, and scientific specimens;

—organizes exhibits representative of the arts, the sciences, and American history and culture;

—shares Smithsonian resources and collections with communities throughout the Nation; and

—engages in educational programming and national and international cooperative research.

Smithsonian activities are supported by its trust endowments and revenues; gifts, grants, and contracts; and funds appropriated to it by Congress. Admission to the museums in Washington, DC, is free.

Activities

Anacostia Museum and Center for African American History and Culture The Museum, located in the historic Fort Stanton neighborhood of southeast Washington, serves as a national resource for exhibitions, historical documentation, and interpretive and educational programs relating to African-American history and culture. The Museum is closed for renovation through spring 2001.

For further information, contact the Anacostia Museum, 1901 Fort Place SE., Washington, DC 20020. Phone, 202–357–2700.

Archives of American Art The Archives contains the Nation's largest collection of documentary materials reflecting the history of visual arts in the United States. On the subject of art in America, it is the largest archives in the world, holding more than 12 million documents. The Archives gathers, preserves, and microfilms the papers of artists, craftsmen, collectors, dealers, critics, and art societies. These papers include manuscripts, letters, diaries, notebooks, sketchbooks, business records, clippings, exhibition catalogs, transcripts of tape-recorded interviews, and photographs of artists and their work. The Archives are temporarily housed at 901 D Street NW., in Washington, DC.

For further information, contact the Archives of American Art, Smithsonian Institution, Washington, DC 20560. Phone, 202–314–3900.

Cooper-Hewitt National Design Museum The Museum is the only museum in the country devoted exclusively to historical and contemporary design. Collections include objects in such areas as applied arts and industrial design, drawings and prints, glass, metalwork, wallcoverings, and textiles. Changing exhibits and public programs seek to educate by exploring the role of design in daily life. The Museum is open daily except Mondays and holidays. An admission fee of $8 is charged.

For further information, contact Cooper-Hewitt National Design Museum, 2 East Ninety-First Street, New York, NY 10028. Phone, 212–860–6868.

Freer Gallery of Art The building, the original collection, and an endowment were the gift of Charles Lang Freer (1854–1919). The Gallery houses one of

186-873 D-00--19

the world's most renowned collections of Asian art, an important group of ancient Egyptian glass, early Christian manuscripts, and works by 19th and early 20th century American artists. The objects in the Asian collection represent the arts of East Asia, the Near East, and South and Southeast Asia, including paintings, manuscripts, scrolls, screens, ceramics, metalwork, glass, jade, lacquer, and sculpture. Members of the staff conduct research on objects in the collection and publish results in scholarly journals and books for general and scholarly audiences.

For further information, contact the Freer Gallery of Art, Jefferson Drive at Twelfth Street SW., Washington, DC 20560. Phone, 202–357–2700.

Hirshhorn Museum and Sculpture Garden From cubism to minimalism, the Museum houses major collections of modern and contemporary art. The nucleus of the collection is the gift and bequest of Joseph H. Hirshhorn (1899–1981). Supplementing the permanent collection are loan exhibitions. The Museum houses a collection research facility, a specialized art library, and a photographic archive, available for consultation by prior appointment. The outdoor sculpture garden is located nearby on the National Mall. There is an active program of public service and education, including docent tours, lectures on contemporary art and artists, and films of historic and artistic interest.

For further information, contact the Hirshhorn Museum and Sculpture Garden, Seventh Street and Independence Avenue SW., Washington, DC 20560. Phone, 202–357–2700.

National Air and Space Museum Created to memorialize the development and achievements of aviation and space flight, the Museum collects, displays, and preserves aeronautical and space flight artifacts of historical significance as well as documentary and artistic materials related to air and space. Among its artifacts are full-size planes, models, and instruments. Highlights of the collection include the Wright brothers' *Flyer,* Charles Lindbergh's *Spirit of St. Louis,* a Moon rock, and Apollo spacecraft. The exhibitions and study collections record human conquest of the air from its beginnings to recent achievements. The principal areas in which work is concentrated include flight craft of all types, space flight vehicles, and propulsion systems. Recent blockbuster exhibitions at this most popular museum have included "Star Wars: The Magic of Myth" and "Star Trek." The Museum's Langley Theater and the 70-foot domed Einstein Planetarium are popular attractions. The Steven F. Udvar-Hazy Center is being built at Washington Dulles International Airport and is scheduled to open in 2003, in time for the centennial of the Wright brothers' flight. Featured artifacts will include a space shuttle and the B–29 *Enola Gay.*

For further information, contact the National Air and Space Museum, Sixth Street and Independence Avenue SW., Washington, DC 20560. Phone, 202–357–2700.

National Museum of African Art This is the only art museum in the United States dedicated exclusively to portraying the creative visual traditions of Africa. Its research components, collection, exhibitions, and public programs establish the Museum as a primary source for the examination and discovery of the arts and culture of Africa. The collection includes works in wood, metal, fired clay, ivory, and fiber. The Eliot Elisofon Photographic Archives includes slides, photos, and film segments on Africa. There is also a specialized library.

For further information, contact the National Museum of African Art, 950 Independence Avenue SW., Washington, DC 20560. Phone, 202–357–2700.

National Museum of American Art The Museum's art collection spans centuries of American painting, sculpture, folk art, photography, and graphic art. Special exhibitions are presented each year. A major center for research in American art, the Museum has contributed to such resources as the Inventory of American Paintings Executed Before 1914; the Slide and Photographic Archives; the Smithsonian Art Index; and the Inventory of American Sculpture. The library, shared with the National Portrait Gallery, contains volumes on art, history, and biography, with special emphasis on the United States. The Old Patent Office Building, home to both the National Museum of American Art and the National Portarit Gallery also houses the Archives of American Art, with its vast holdings of documentary material on American art and artists. The building is currently closed for major renovation, during which time the museums are sponsoring traveling special exhibits around the country. Hundreds of images from the collection and extensive information on its collections, publications, and activities are available electronically (Internet, www.nmaa.si.edu). There is a research program for visiting scholars, and university interns are welcomed in many museum departments.

For further information, contact the National Museum of American Art, Eighth and G Streets NW., Washington, DC 20560. Phone, 202–357–2700.

Renwick Gallery The Gallery is dedicated to exhibiting crafts of all periods and to collecting 20th century American crafts. It offers changing exhibitions of American crafts and decorative arts, both historical and contemporary, and a rotating selection from its permanent collection. The Gallery's grand salon is elegantly furnished in the Victorian style of the 1860's and 1870's.

For further information, contact the Renwick Gallery, Seventeenth Street and Pennsylvania Avenue NW., Washington, DC 20560. Phone, 202–357–2700.

National Museum of American History In pursuit of its fundamental mission to inspire a broader understanding of the United States and its people, the Museum provides learning opportunities, stimulates the imagination of visitors, and presents challenging ideas about the Nation's past. The Museum's exhibits provide a unique view of the American experience. Emphasis is placed upon innovative individuals representing a wide range of cultures, who have shaped our heritage, and upon science and the remaking of our world through technology. Exhibits draw upon strong collections in the sciences and engineering, agriculture, manufacturing, transportation, political memorabilia, costumes, musical instruments, coins, Armed Forces history, photography, computers, ceramics, and glass. Classic cars, First Ladies' gowns, musical instruments, the Star-Spangled Banner flag, Whitney's cotton gin, Morse's telegraph, the John Bull locomotive, Dorothy's ruby slippers from "The Wizard of Oz," and other American icons are highlights of the collection.

For further information, contact the National Museum of American History, Fourteenth Street and Constitution Avenue NW., Washington, DC 20560. Phone, 202–357–2700.

National Museum of the American Indian The Museum was established in 1989, and the last of three locations is now being built. The collection of the Museum is comprised of the collection of the former Museum of the American Indian, Heye Foundation in New York City. It is an institution of living cultures dedicated to the collection, preservation, study, and exhibition of the life, languages, literature, history, and arts of the Native peoples of the Americas. Highlights include Northwest Coast carvings; dance masks; pottery and weaving from the Southwest; painted hides and garments from the North American Plains; goldwork of the Aztecs, Incas, and Maya; and Amazonian featherwork.

For further information, contact the National Museum of the American Indian, Suite 7102, 470 L'Enfant Plaza SW., Washington, DC 20560. Phone, 202–287–2523 or 202–357–2700.

National Museum of Natural History Dedicated to understanding the natural world and the place of humans in it, the Museum's permanent exhibits focus on human cultures, Earth sciences, biology, and anthropology, with the most popular displays featuring gemstones such as the Hope diamond, dinosaurs, marine ecosystems, birds, and mammals. To celebrate the millennial anniversary of the journey of Leif Ericson to America, the Museum mounted a special exhibition titled Vikings: The North Atlantic Saga. A new IMAX theater offers large-format nature films. The Museum's encyclopedic collections comprise more than 124 million specimens, making the Museum one of the world's foremost facilities for natural history research. Museum departments include anthropology, botany, paleobiology, entomology, vertebrate and invertebrate zoology, and mineral sciences. Doctorate-level staff researchers ensure the continued growth and value of the collection by conducting studies in the field and laboratory.

For further information, contact the National Museum of Natural History, Tenth Street and Constitution Avenue NW., Washington, DC 20560. Phone, 202–357–2700.

National Portrait Gallery The Gallery was established in 1962 for the exhibition and study of portraiture depicting men and women who have made significant contributions to the history, development, and culture of the United States. The Gallery contains nearly 18,000 works, including photographs and glass negatives. The first floor of the Gallery is devoted to changing exhibitions from the Gallery's collection of paintings, sculpture, prints, photographs, and drawings as well as to special portrait collections. On the second floor are featured the permanent collection of portraits of eminent Americans and the Hall of Presidents. The two-story American Victorian Renaissance Great Hall on the third floor of the gallery houses a Civil War exhibit, and is used for special events and public programs. A large library is shared with the National Museum of American Art and the Archives of American Art. The education department offers public programs; outreach programs for schools, senior adults, hospitals, and nursing homes; and walk-in and group tours. The Gallery is currently closed for renovation.

For further information, contact the National Portrait Gallery, Eighth and F Streets NW., Washington, DC 20560. Phone, 202–357–2700.

National Postal Museum The Museum houses the Nation's postal history and philatelic collection, the largest of its kind in the world, with more than 13 million objects. The Museum is devoted to the history of America's mail service, and major galleries include exhibits on mail service in colonial times and during the Civil War, the Pony Express, modern mail service, automation, mail transportation, and the art of letters, as well as displays of the Museum's priceless stamp collection. Highlights include three mail planes, a replica of a railway mail car, displays of historic letters, handcrafted mail boxes, and rare U.S. and foreign issue stamps and covers.

For further information, contact the National Postal Museum, 2 Massachusetts Avenue NE., Washington, DC 20560. Phone, 202–357–2700.

National Zoological Park The National Zoo encompasses 163 acres along Rock Creek Park in Northwest Washington, DC. Established in 1889, the Zoo is developing into a biopark with live animals, botanic gardens and aquaria, and artworks with animal themes. The collection today animals ranging in size and diversity from leaf-cutter ants to giraffes. The zoo's beloved giant pandas have recently died, but efforts are underway to bring a new pair of pandas to the Nation's Capital. Recent exhibits include "Amazonia," a simulated tropical rain forest; the "Pollinarium" exhibit; and the Reptile Discovery Center, featuring the world's largest lizards, Komodo dragons. Research on genetics, animal behavior, and reproductive studies has given the National Zoo a leadership role among the Nation's conservation institutions.

For further information, contact the National Zoo, 3000 Connecticut Avenue NW., Washington, DC 20008. Phone, 202–673–4717. E-mail, listserv@sivm.si.edu. Internet, www.si.edu/natzoo.

Center for Folklife and Cultural Heritage The Center is responsible for research, documentation, and presentation of grassroots cultural traditions. It maintains a documentary collection and produces Smithsonian Folkways Recordings, educational materials, documentary films, publications, and traveling exhibits, as well as the annual

Smithsonian Folklife Festival on the National Mall. Recent Folklife Festivals have featured a range of American music styles, a number of State tributes, and performers from around the world. Admission to the festival is free. The 2-week program includes Fourth of July activities on the National Mall.

For further information, contact the Center for Folklife and Cultural Heritage, Suite 2600, 955 L'Enfant Plaza SW., Washington, DC 20560. Phone, 202–357–2700.

International Center The International Center supports Smithsonian activities abroad and serves as liaison for the Smithsonian's international interests. The Smithsonian seeks to encourage a broadening of public understanding of the histories, cultures, and natural environments of regions throughout the world. The International Center provides a meeting place and an organizational channel to bring together the world's scholars, museum professionals, and the general public, to attend and participate in conferences, public forums, lectures, and workshops.

For further information, contact the Office of International Relations, MRC 705, 1100 Jefferson Drive SW., Washington, DC 20560. Phone, 202–357–1539.

Center for Museum Studies The Center is an outreach office of the Smithsonian that helps museums in the United States fulfill their public service mission. It conducts training programs for museum professionals on museum operational methods, management of collections, exhibitions techniques, and educational activities.

For further information, contact the Center for Museum Studies, 900 Jefferson Drive SW., Room 2235, MRC 427, Smithsonian Institution, Washington, DC 20560. Phone, 202–357–3101.

Arthur M. Sackler Gallery This Asian art museum opened in 1987 on the National Mall. Changing exhibitions drawn from major collections in the United States and abroad, as well as from the permanent holdings of the Sackler Gallery, are displayed in the distinctive below-ground museum. The Gallery's growing permanent collection is founded on a group of art objects from China, South and Southeast Asia, and the ancient Near East that was given to the Smithsonian by Arthur M. Sackler (1913–1987). The Museum's current collection features Persian manuscripts; Japanese paintings; ceramics, prints, and textiles; sculptures from India; and paintings and metalware from China, Korea, Japan, and Southeast Asia. The Sackler Gallery is connected by an underground exhibition space to the neighboring Freer Gallery.

For further information, contact the Arthur M. Sackler Gallery, 1050 Independence Avenue SW., Washington, DC 20560. Phone, 202–357–2700.

Smithsonian Institution Archives The Smithsonian Institution Archives acquires, preserves, and makes available for research the official records of the Smithsonian Institution and the papers of individuals and organizations associated with the Institution or with its work. These holdings document the growth of the Smithsonian and the development of American science, history, and art.

For further information, contact the Smithsonian Institution Archives, MRC 414, 900 Jefferson Drive SW., Washington, DC 20560. Phone, 202–357–1420. Fax, 202–357–2395.

Smithsonian Astrophysical Observatory The Smithsonian Astrophysical Observatory and the Harvard College Observatory have coordinated research activities under a single director in a cooperative venture, Harvard-Smithsonian Center for Astrophysics. The Center's research activities are organized in the following areas of study: atomic and molecular physics, radio and geoastronomy, high-energy astrophysics, optical and infrared astronomy, planetary sciences, solar and stellar physics, and theoretical astrophysics. Research results are published in the *Center Preprint Series* and other technical and nontechnical bulletins, and distributed to scientific and educational institutions around the world.

For more information, contact the Smithsonian Astrophysical Observatory, 60 Garden Street, Cambridge, MA 02138. Phone, 617–495–7461. Internet, cfa-www.harvard.edu.

Smithsonian Center for Materials Research and Education The Center researches preservation, conservation, and technical study and analysis of collection materials. Its researchers investigate the chemical and physical processes that are involved in the care of art, artifacts, and specimens, and attempt to formulate conditions and procedures for storage, exhibit, and stabilization that optimize the preservation of these objects. In interdisciplinary collaborations with archeologists, anthropologists, and art historians, natural and physical scientists study and analyze objects from the collections and related materials to expand knowledge and understanding of their historical and scientific context.

For further information, contact the Smithsonian Center for Materials Research and Education, Museum Support Center, Suitland, MD 20746. Phone, 301–238–3700.

Smithsonian Environmental Research Center (SERC) The Center measures physical, chemical, and biological interactions in the environment and determines how these interactions control biological responses. SERC is dedicated to increasing knowledge of the biological and physical processes that sustain life on Earth. The Center trains future generations of scientists to address ecological questions of the Nation and the globe.

For further information, contact the Smithsonian Environmental Research Center, 647 Contees Wharf Road, Edgewater, MD 21037. Phone, 410–798–4424. Internet, www.serc.si.edu.

Smithsonian Institution Libraries The libraries of the Smithsonian Institution include more than one million volumes (among them 40,000 rare books) with strengths in natural history, art, science, humanities, and museology. Many volumes are available through interlibrary loan.

For further information, contact the Smithsonian Institution Libraries, Tenth Street and Constitution Avenue NW., Washington, DC 20560. Phone, 202–357–2139. Internet, www.sil.si.edu. E-mail, libhelp@sil.si.edu.

Smithsonian Institution Traveling Exhibition Service (SITES) Since 1952, SITES has been committed to making Smithsonian exhibitions available to millions of people who cannot view them firsthand at the Smithsonian museums. Exhibitions on art, history, and science (including such exhibits as "Full Deck Art Quilts," "Red, Hot, and Blue: A Salute to American Musicals," and "Hubble Space Telescope") travel to more than 250 locations each year. SITES also offers exhibits in its International Gallery on the National Mall, in the S. Dillon Ripley Center (located at 1100 Jefferson Drive SW.)

For further information, contact the Smithsonian Institution Traveling Exhibition Service, MRC 706, Smithsonian Institution, Washington, DC 20560. Phone, 202–357–3168. Internet, www.si.edu/organiza/offices/sites.

Smithsonian Marine Station The research institute features a state-of-the-art laboratory where Station scientists catalog species and study marine plants and animals. Among the most important projects being pursued at the site is the search for possible causes of fish kills including *pfiesteria* and other organisms.

For further information, contact the Smithsonian Marine Station, 701 Seaway Drive, Fort Pierce, FL 34946. Phone, 561–465–6630.

Smithsonian Tropical Research Institute (STRI) The Institute is a research organization for advanced studies of tropical ecosystems. Headquartered in the Republic of Panama, STRI maintains extensive facilities in the Western Hemisphere tropics. It is the base of a corps of tropical researchers who study the evolution, behavior, ecology, and history of tropical species of systems ranging from coral reefs to rain forests. On December 31, 1999, as required by treaty, the Canal was transferred to Panama. The Government of Panama has stated that it wishes STRI to continue its activities on the isthmus beyond the year 2000.

For further information, contact the Smithsonian Tropical Research Institute, 900 Jefferson Drive SW., MRC 555, Washington, DC 20560. Phone, 202–786–2817. Fax, 202–786–2819. Phone (Panama), 011–507–62–6022. Internet, www.si.edu/stri. E-mail, visitors@tivoli.si.edu.

The John F. Kennedy Center for the Performing Arts The Center is the only official memorial in Washington, DC, to

President Kennedy. Since its opening in 1971, the Center has presented a year-round program of the finest in music, dance, and drama from the United States and abroad. The Kennedy Center box offices are open daily, and general information and tickets may be obtained by calling 202–467–4600 or 202–416–8524 (TDD). Full-time students, senior citizens over the age of 65, enlisted personnel of grade E–4 and below, fixed low-income groups, and the disabled may purchase tickets for most performances at a 50-percent discount through the Specially Priced Ticket Program. This program is designed to make the Center accessible to all, regardless of economic circumstance. Visitor services are provided by the Friends of the Kennedy Center volunteers. Tours are available free of charge between 10 a.m. and 5 p.m. on weekdays and between 10 a.m. and 1 p.m. on weekends. Free performances are given every day at 6 p.m. on the Millennium Stage in the Grand Foyer.

For further information, contact the Kennedy Center. Phone, 202–467–4600. Internet, www.kennedy-center.org.

National Gallery of Art The Gallery houses one of the finest collections in the world, illustrating Western man's achievements in painting, sculpture, and the graphic arts. The collections, beginning with the 13th century, are rich in European old master paintings and French, Spanish, Italian, American, and British 18th- and 19th-century paintings; sculpture from the late Middle Ages to the present; Renaissance medals and bronzes; Chinese porcelains; and about 90,000 works of graphic art from the 12th to the 20th centuries. The collections are acquired by private donation rather than by Government funds, which serve solely to operate and maintain the building and its collections. Graduate and postgraduate research is conducted under a fellowship program; programs for schoolchildren and the general public are conducted daily; and an extension service distributes loans of audiovisual materials, including films, slide lectures, and slide sets throughout the world. Publications, slides, and reproductions may be obtained through the Publications Service. The Micro Gallery is the most comprehensive interactive multimedia computer system in any American art museum. Thirteen computers enable visitors to see in magnified detail nearly every work of art on display in the permanent collection and provide access to information about artists, geographic areas, time periods, pronunciations (with sound), and more.

For further information, contact the National Gallery of Art. Phone, 202–737–4215. TTY, 202–842–6176. Internet, www.nga.gov.

Woodrow Wilson International Center for Scholars The Center is the Nation's official memorial to its 28th President. The Center's mandate is to integrate the world of learning with the world of public affairs. Through meetings and conferences, the Center brings scholars together with Members of Congress, Government officials, business leaders, and other policymakers. Through publication of books and the *Wilson Quarterly* and a nationally broadcast radio program, the results of the Center's research and meetings are made publicly available.

For further information, contact the Scholar Selection and Services Office, Woodrow Wilson Center, One Woodrow Wilson Plaza, 1300 Pennsylvania Avenue NW., Washington, DC 20004–3027. Phone, 202–691–4170. Fax, 202–691–4001. Internet, wwics.si.edu.

Sources of Information

Contracts and Small Business Activities Information may be obtained from the Director, Office of Contracting, Smithsonian Institution, Washington, DC 20560, regarding procurement of supplies; contracts for construction, services, etc.; and property management and utilization services for Smithsonian Institution organizations.

The following independent organizations should be contacted directly: John F. Kennedy Center for the Performing Arts, Washington, DC 20566; and National Gallery of Art, Sixth Street and Constitution Avenue NW., Washington, DC 20565. Phone, 202–842–6785. Fax, 202–289–3937.

Education and Research Write to the Directors of the following offices at the Smithsonian Institution, Washington, DC 20560: Office of Fellowships and Grants, Center for Folklife and Cultural Heritage, National Science Resources Center; and Smithsonian Center for Education and Museum Studies.

For information regarding Kennedy Center education programs, contact the John F. Kennedy Center for the Performing Arts, Washington, DC 20566 (phone, 202–416–8000).

For information about the National Gallery fellowship and education programs, contact the Center for Advanced Study in the Visual Arts, National Gallery of Art, Washington, DC 20565. Phone, 202–842–6480; or fax, 202–842–6733.

Electronic Access Information about the Smithsonian Institution is available electronically through the Internet, at www.si.edu. Websites with information about specific parts of the Smithsonian Insitution are listed bellow:

John F. Kennedy Center for the Performing Arts: www.kennedy-center.org.
National Gallery of Art: www.nga.gov.
Woodrow Wilson Center for International Scholars: wwics.si.edu.

Employment Employment information for the Smithsonian is available from the Office of Human Resources, Smithsonian Institution, Suite 2100, 955 L'Enfant Plaza SW., Washington, DC 20560. Phone, 202–287–3100. Recorded message, 202–287–3102.

Employment information for the following locations may be obtained by contacting the organizations directly as follows: Personnel Office, National Gallery of Art, Fourth Street and Constitution Avenue NW., Washington, DC 20565 (phone, 202–842–6298; or for the hearing impaired (TDD), 202–789–3021); and the John F. Kennedy Center for the Performing Arts, Human Resources Department, Washington, DC 20566 (phone, 202–416–8610).

Educational Resources The National Gallery of Art circulates films, slide programs, videos, teaching packets, and videodiscs to schools and civic organizations throughout the country. Contact the Department of Education Resources, National Gallery of Art, Washington, DC 20565. Phone, 202–842–6273. Please write to request a free catalog of programs.

Media Affairs Members of the press may contact the Smithsonian Office of Public Affairs, 1000 Jefferson Drive SW., Washington, DC 20560. Phone, 202–357–2627. Internet, newsdesk.si.edu.

Memberships For information about Smithsonian membership (Resident Program), write to The Smithsonian Associates, MRC 701, 1100 Jefferson Drive SW., Washington, DC 20560. Phone, 202–357–3030. For information about Smithsonian membership (National Program), call 202–357–4800. For information about the Contributing Membership, call 202–357–1699. For information about the Young Benefactors, call 202–357–1351.

The Circle of the National Gallery of Art is a membership program which provides support for special projects for which Federal funds are not available. For more information about membership in the Circle of the National Gallery of Art, please write to The Circle, National Gallery of Art, Washington, DC 20565. Phone, 202–842–6450.

Information about activities of the Friends of the National Zoo and their magazine, *The Zoogoer,* is available by writing to FONZ, National Zoological Park, Washington, DC 20008. Phone, 202–673–4950.

Information about the national and local activities of Friends of the Kennedy Center (including the bimonthly *Kennedy Center News* for members) is available at the information desks within the Center or by writing to Friends of the Kennedy Center, Washington, DC 20566.

Photographs Color and black-and-white photographs and slides are available to Government agencies, research and educational institutions, publishers, and the general public from the Smithsonian photographic archives. A searchable database of images is available through the Internet. Information, order forms, and price lists may be obtained from the Office of Imaging, Printing, and Photographic Services, MAH CB–054, Smithsonian Institution, Washington, DC 20560.

Internet, photos.si.edu. E-mail, psdmx@sivm.si.edu.

Publications To purchase the Smithsonian Institute's annual report, *Smithsonian Year,* call 202–357–2627. The Smithsonian Institution Press publishes a range of books and studies related to the sciences, technology, history, culture, air and space, and the arts. A book catalog is available from Publications Sales, Smithsonian Books or Smithsonian Institution University Press, 1111 North Capitol Street, Washington, DC 20002. Phone, 202–287–3738. To purchase a recording of the *Smithsonian Folkways Recordings,* call 800–410–9815. Internet, www.si.edu/folkways.

A free brochure providing a brief guide to the Smithsonian Institution is published in English and several foreign languages. For a copy, call Visitor Information, 202–357–2700, or pick up a copy at the information desks in the museums. A visitor's guide for individuals with disabilities is also available.

Smithsonian Institution Research Reports, containing news of current research projects in the arts, sciences, and history that are being conducted by Smithsonian staff, is produced by the Smithsonian Office of Public Affairs, Smithsonian Institution Building, 1000 Jefferson Drive SW., Washington, DC 20560. Phone, 202–357–2627.

To request a copy of *Smithsonian Runner,* a newsletter about Native American-related activities at the Smithsonian, contact the National Museum of the American Indian, Smithsonian Institution, Washington, DC 20560. Phone, 800–242–NMAI.

For the newsletter *Art to Zoo* for teachers of fourth through eighth graders, write to the Smithsonian Center for Education and Museum Studies, Room 1163, MRC 402, Arts and Industries Building, Washington, DC 20560. Phone, 202–357–2425.

The National Gallery shop makes available quality reproductions and publications about the Gallery's collections. To order, call 301–322–5900 or 800–697–9359. Selected items are also available for sale on the website at www.nga.gov. The Office of Press and Public Affairs offers a free bimonthly calendar of events, which can be ordered by calling 202–842–6662, or through E-mail at calendar@nga.gov. The calendar and *Brief Guide to the National Gallery of Art* are also available at art information desks throughout the Gallery or by calling Visitor Services at 202–842–6691.

Radio and Telephone *Dial-A-Museum,* 202–357–2020 provides a taped message with daily announcements on new exhibits and special events. *Smithsonian Skywatchers Report,* 202–357–2000 is a taped message with weekly announcements on stars, planets, and worldwide occurrences of short-lived natural phenomena. For a *Spanish Listing of Smithsonian Events,* call 202–633–9126.

A five-minute program, "This Week at the National Gallery," airs every Saturday at 1:24 p.m. on WGMS, Washington, and WBJC, Baltimore. It features a calendar of events and interviews with art experts, artists, and museum specialists about exhibitions, the permanent collection, and various Gallery activities. In addition, selections from Gallery concerts are broadcast at 9 p.m. on the second Sunday of each month on WGMS.

Speakers The Education Office of the National Gallery of Art provides gallery talks and lectures. For further information, contact the Education Office, National Gallery of Art, Fourth Street and Constitution Avenue NW., Washington, DC 20565. Phone, 202–842–6246.

Special Functions Inquiries regarding the use of Kennedy Center facilities for special functions may be directed to the Office of Special Events, John F. Kennedy Center for the Performing Arts, Washington, DC 20566. Phone, 202–416–8000.

Theater Operations Inquiries regarding the use of the Kennedy Center's theaters may be addressed to the Booking Coordinator, John F. Kennedy Center for the Performing Arts, Washington, DC 20566. Phone, 202–416–8000.

Tours For information about museum and gallery tours, contact the

Smithsonian Information Center, 1000 Jefferson Drive, SW., Washington, DC 20560. Phone, 202–357–2700. School groups are welcome. Special behind-the-scenes tours are offered through the various memberships.

Visitor Information The Smithsonian Information Center, located in the original Smithsonian building, commonly known as "The Castle," provides general orientation, through films, computer interactive programs, and visitor information specialists, to help members and the public learn about the national collections, museum events, exhibitions, and special programs. Write to the Smithsonian Information Center, 1000 Jefferson Drive SW., Washington, DC 20560. Phone, 202–357–2700. TTY, 202–357–1729.

The Visitor Services Office of the National Gallery of Art provides individual assistance to those with special needs, responds to written and telephone requests, and provides information to those planning to visit the Washington, DC, area. For more information, write to the National Gallery of Art, Office of Visitor Services, Washington, DC 20565. Phone, 202–842–6691.

Volunteer Service Opportunities The Smithsonian Institution welcomes volunteers and offers a variety of interesting service opportunities. For information, write to the Visitor Information and Associates' Reception Center, 1000 Jefferson Drive SW., Washington, DC 20560. Phone, 202–357–2700. TTY, 202–357–1729. For information about volunteering with the National Gallery of Art, write the Education Division, National Gallery of Art, Washington, DC 20565. Phone, 202–842–6246. TDD, 202–842–6176. For library volunteering inquiries, call 202–842–6510. For information about volunteer opportunities at the Kennedy Center, write to Friends of the Kennedy Center, Washington, DC 20566. Phone, 202–416–8000.

For further information, contact the Smithsonian Information Center, 1000 Jefferson Drive SW., Washington, DC 20560. Phone, 202–357–2700. TDD, 202–357–1729. Internet, www.si.edu.

STATE JUSTICE INSTITUTE

Suite 600, 1650 King Street, Alexandria, VA 22314
Phone, 703–684–6100. Internet, www.statejustice.org.

Board of Directors:

Chairman	ROBERT A. MILLER
Vice Chairman	JOSEPH F. BACA
Secretary	SANDRA A. O'CONNOR
Executive Committee Member	TERRENCE B. ADAMSON
Members	ROBERT N. BALDWIN, CARLOS R. GARZA, SOPHIA H. HALL, TOMMY JEWELL, ARTHUR MCGIVERIN, KEITH MCNAMARA, FLORENCE R. MURRAY

Officers:

Executive Director	DAVID I. TEVELIN
Deputy Director	KATHY SCHWARTZ

The State Justice Institute was established to award grants to improve judicial administration in the State courts of the United States.

The State Justice Institute was created by the State Justice Institute Act of 1984 (42 U.S.C. 10701) as a private, nonprofit corporation to further the development and improvement of judicial administration in the State courts.

The Institute is supervised by a Board of Directors consisting of 11 members appointed by the President with the advice and consent of the Senate. The Board is statutorily composed of six judges, a State court administrator, and four members of the public, of whom no more than two can be of the same political party.

The goals of the Institute are to:

—direct a national program of assistance to ensure that all U.S. citizens have ready access to a fair and effective judicial system;

—foster coordination and cooperation with the Federal Judiciary;

—serve as a clearinghouse and information center for the dissemination of information regarding State judicial systems; and

—encourage education for judges and support personnel of State court systems.

To accomplish these broad objectives, the Institute is authorized to provide funds, through grants, cooperative agreements, and contracts, to State courts and organizations that can assist in the achievement of improving judicial administration of the State courts.

Sources of Information

Inquiries concerning the following programs and activities should be directed to the specified office of the State Justice Institute, Suite 600, 1650 King Street, Alexandria, VA 22314. Phone, 703–684–6100.

Grants—Chief, Program Division.

Publications, consumer information, speakers, Privacy Act/Freedom of Information Act requests—Executive Assistant, Office of the Executive Director.

Employment/personnel—Personnel Specialist.

Information regarding the programs and services of the State Justice Institute is also available through the Internet, at www.statejustice.org.

For further information, contact the State Justice Institute, Suite 600, 1650 King Street, Alexandria, VA 22314. Phone, 703–684–6100. Internet, www.statejustice.org.

UNITED STATES INSTITUTE OF PEACE

Suite 200, 1200 Seventeenth Street NW., Washington, DC 20037–3011
Phone, 202–457–1700. Fax, 202–429–6063. Internet, www.usip.org.

Board of Directors:

Public Members:

Chairman	CHESTER A. CROCKER
Vice Chairman	MAX M. KAMPELMAN
Members	DENNIS L. BARK, STEPHEN J. HADLEY, THEODORE M. HESBURGH, ZALMAY KHALILZAD, SEYMOUR MARTIN LIPSET, W. SCOTT THOMPSON, ALLEN WEINSTEIN, HARRIET ZIMMERMAN, (2 VACANCIES)

Ex officio:

Assistant Secretary of State for Intelligence and Research	J. STAPLETON ROY
Vice President, National Defense University	DANIEL H. SIMPSON

Under Secretary of Defense for Policy	WALTER B. SLOCOMBE
President, U.S. Institute of Peace	RICHARD H. SOLOMON
Officials:	
President	RICHARD H. SOLOMON
Executive Vice President	HARRIET HENTGES
Vice President	CHARLES E. NELSON
Director, Education	PAMELA AALL
Director, Training	GEORGE WARD
Director, Research and Studies	PATRICK CRONIN
Director, Grants Program	(VACANCY)
Director, Jennings Randolph Fellowship Program for International Peace	JOSEPH L. KLAITS
Director, Jeannette Rankin Library Program	MARGARITA STUDEMEISTER
Director, Administration	BERNICE J. CARNEY
Director, Office of Communications	SHERYL BROWN
Director, Rule of Law Initiative	NEIL J. KRITZ
Senior Scholar for Religion, Ethics, and Human Rights	DAVID R. SMOCK

The United States Institute of Peace was established to promote research, policy analysis, education, and training on international peace and conflict resolution.

The United States Institute of Peace is an independent Federal institution created and funded by Congress to develop and disseminate knowledge about international peace and conflict resolution. The Institute addresses this mandate in three principal ways:

—by expanding basic and applied knowledge about the origins, nature, and processes of peace and war, encompassing the widest spectrum of approaches and insights;

—by disseminating this knowledge to officials, policymakers, diplomats, and others engaged in efforts to promote international peace; and

—by supporting education and training programs and providing information for secondary and university-level teachers and students and the general public.

The Institute's primary activities are grantmaking, fellowships, in-house research projects, public education and outreach activities, publications, and library services.

The Grants Program provides financial support for research, information services, education, and training. Eligible grantees include nonprofit organizations; official public institutions, such as public schools, colleges, universities, libraries, and State and local agencies; and individuals.

The Jennings Randolph Program for International Peace provides fellowships to scholars, doctoral candidates, practitioners, and other professionals to undertake research and other appropriate forms of work on issues of international peace and the management of international conflicts. The Research and Studies Program conducts conferences, seminars, and study groups on issues of short- and long-term significance.

The Jeannette Rankin Library Program has four main components: a specialized research library; a network with and support for other libraries, both private and public; an oral history resource; and bibliographic as well as other databases.

The Office of Communications fulfills requests for speakers and media services, answers general inquiries, and conducts outreach programs in Washington, DC, and elsewhere. Institute-directed activities under the Education and Training Program include educational video programs, teacher training projects, and a National Peace Essay Contest for high school students. Institute publications include the *Biennial Report to Congress and the President;* a newsletter, *Peace Watch;* periodic papers on selected topics, *Peaceworks;*

and monographs, books, and *Special Reports* generated from Institute-sponsored projects.

Sources of Information

Electronic access to the Institute is available through the Internet, at www.usip.org.

For further information, contact the Office of Communications, United States Institute of Peace, Suite 200, 1200 Seventeenth Street NW., Washington, DC 20036–3011. Phone, 202–457–1700. Internet, www.usip.org.

SELECTED MULTILATERAL ORGANIZATIONS

MULTILATERAL INTERNATIONAL ORGANIZATIONS IN WHICH THE UNITED STATES PARTICIPATES

Explanatory note: The United States participates in the organizations named below in accordance with the provisions of treaties, other international agreements, congressional legislation, or executive arrangements. In some cases, no financial contribution is involved.

Various commissions, councils, or committees subsidiary to the organizations listed here are not named separately on this list. These include the international bodies for narcotics control, which are subsidiary to the United Nations.

I. United Nations, Specialized Agencies, and International Atomic Energy Agency

Food and Agricultural Organization
International Atomic Energy Agency
International Civil Aviation Organization
International Labor Organization
International Maritime Organization
International Telecommunication Union
United Nations
Universal Postal Union
World Health Organization
World Intellectual Property Organization
World Meteorological Organization

II. Peacekeeping

United Nations Disengagement Observer Force (Golan Heights)
United Nations Force in Cyprus
United Nations Interim Force in Lebanon
United Nations Iraq-Kuwait Observer Mission
United Nations Military Observer Group in India and Pakistan
United Nations Mission in Bosnia-Herzegovina
United Nations Mission in the Democratic Republic of Congo
United Nations Mission in Kosovo
United Nations Mission in Sierra Leone
United Nations Mission of Observers in Tajikistan
United Nations Mission to Prevlaka
United Nations Mission for the Referendum in Western Sahara
United Nations Observer Mission in Angola
United Nations Observer Mission in Georgia
United Nations Transitional Administration in East Timor
United Nations Truce Supervision Organization (Middle East)

III. Inter-American Organizations

Inter-American Indian Institute
Inter-American Institute for Cooperation on Agriculture
Inter-American Tropical Tuna Commission
Organization of American States
Pan American Health Organization (PAHO)
Pan American Institute of Geography and History
Postal Union of the Americas and Spain and Portugal

IV. Regional Organizations

Asia-Pacific Economic Cooperation

Colombo Plan for Cooperative Economic and Social Development in Asia and the Pacific
North Atlantic Assembly
North Atlantic Treaty Organization
Organization for Economic Cooperation and Development (OECD)
South Pacific Commission

V. Other International Organizations

Bureau of International Expositions
Commission for the Conservation of Antarctic Marine Living Resources
Customs Cooperation Council (CCC)
Fund for the Protection of the World Cultural and Natural Heritage
Hague Conference on Private International Law
International Agency for Research on Cancer
International Bureau of the Permanent Court of Arbitration
International Bureau for the Publication of Customs Tariffs
International Bureau of Weights and Measures
International Center for the Study of the Preservation and the Restoration of Cultural Property (ICCROM)
International Commission for the Conservation of Atlantic Tunas
International Copper Study Group
International Cotton Advisory Committee
International Council for the Exploration of the Seas (ICES)
International Council of Scientific Unions and Its Associated Unions (20)
International Criminal Police Organization (INTERPOL)
International Hydrographic Organization
International Institute for Cotton
International Institute for the Unification of Private Law
International Lead and Zinc Study Group
International Natural Rubber Organization
International North Pacific Fisheries Commission
International Office of Epizootics
International Office of Vine and Wine
International Organization for Legal Metrology
International Rubber Study Group
International Seed Testing Association
International Tropical Timber Organization
International Union for the Conservation of Nature and Natural Resources (IUNC)
International Union for the Protection of New Varieties of Plants (UPOV)
International Whaling Commission
International Wheat Council
Interparliamentary Union
North Atlantic Ice Patrol
North Atlantic Salmon Conservation Organization
Organization for the Prevention of Chemical Weapons
Permanent International Association of Navigation Congresses
Permanent International Association of Road Congresses
United Nations Compensation Commission
World Trade Organization (WTO)/ General Agreement on Tariffs and Trade (GATT)

VI. Special Voluntary Programs

Colombo Plan Drug Advisory Program
Consultative Group on International Agricultural Research
Convention on International Trade in Endangered Species of Wild Fauna and Flora (CITES)
International Atomic Energy Agency Technical Assistance and Cooperation Fund
International Atomic Energy Agency Voluntary Programs
International Civil Aviation Organization (ICAO) Aviation Security Fund
International Contributions for Scientific, Educational, and Cultural Activities
International Fund for Agricultural Development (IFAD)
International Organization for Migration (IOM)
Korean Peninsula Energy Development Organization
Montreal Protocol Multilateral Fund
Organization of American States Fund for Strengthening Democracy
Organization of American States Special Cultural Fund
Organization of American States Special Development Assistance Fund
Organization of American States Special Multilateral Fund (Education and Science)

Organization of American States Special Projects Fund (Mar del Plata)
Pan American Health Organization Special Health Promotion Funds
United Nations Afghanistan Emergency Trust Fund
United Nations Center for Human Settlements (Habitat) (UNCHS)
United Nations Children's Fund (UNICEF)
United Nations Development Fund for Women (UNIFEM)
United Nations Development Program (UNDP)
United Nations Environment Program (UNEP)
United Nations/Food and Agricultural Organization World Food Program (WFP)
United Nations Fund for Drug Abuse Control (UNFDAC)
United Nations High Commissioner for Refugees Program (UNHCR)
United Nations Population Fund
United Nations Relief and Works Agency (UNRWA)
United Nations Volunteers (UNV)
World Health Organization Special Programs
World Meteorological Organization Special Fund for Climate Activities
World Meteorological Organization Voluntary Cooperation Program

African Development Bank

Headquarters: 01 B.P. 1387, Abidjan 01, Côte d'Ivoire. Internet, www.afdb.org

President: Omar Kabbaj

The African Development Bank (AFDB) was established in 1963 and, by charter amendment, opened its membership to non-African countries in 1982. Its mandate is to contribute to the economic development and social progress of its regional members. Bank members total 77, including 53 African countries and 24 nonregional countries. With the September 1999 ratification of the agreement on the fifth general capital increase, Bank ownership is 60 percent African and 40 percent nonregional.

The African Development Fund (AFDF), the concessional lending affiliate, was established in 1973 to complement AFDB operations by providing concessional financing for high-priority development projects in the poorest African countries. The Fund's membership consists of 25 nonregional member countries and AFDB, which represents its African members and is allocated half of the votes.

Asian Development Bank

Headquarters: 6 ADB Avenue, Mandaluyong City, 0401 Metro Manila, Philippines. Phone, 632–632–4444. Fax, 632–636–2444. Internet, www.adb.org.

President: Tadao Chino

The Asian Development Bank commenced operations on December 19, 1966. It now has 57 member countries—41 from Asia and 16 from outside the region.

The purpose of the Bank is to foster sustainable economic development, poverty alleviation, and cooperation among its developing member countries in the Asia/Pacific region.

For further information, contact the Asian Development Bank, P.O. Box 789, 0980 Manila, Philippines. E-mail, adbhq@mail.asiandevbank.org. Internet, www.adb.org.

Inter-American Defense Board

2600 Sixteenth Street NW., Washington, DC 20441. Phone, 202–939–6600. Internet, www.jid.org. E-mail, iadb@jid.org.

Chairman: Maj. Gen. John C. Thompson, USA

The Inter-American Defense Board is the oldest permanently constituted, international military organization in the world. It was founded by Resolution XXXIX of the Meeting of Foreign Ministers at Rio de Janeiro in January 1942. Senior army, navy, and air force officers from 25 member nations staff the various agencies of the Board. Its four major agencies are: the Council of Delegates, the decisionmaking body; the International Staff; the Inter-American Defense College; and the Secretariat, which provides administrative and logistical support.

The Board studies and recommends to member governments measures necessary for close military collaboration in preparation for the collective self-defense of the American Continents. It also acts as a technical military adviser for the Organization of American States, and is involved in projects such as disaster relief planning and demining programs in Central America.

The College prepares senior military officers and civilian functionaries for positions in their respective governments.

Inter-American Development Bank

Headquarters: 1300 New York Avenue NW., Washington, DC 20577. Phone, 202–623–1000. Internet, www.iadb.org.

President: Enrique V. Iglesias

The Inter-American Development Bank (IDB) was established in 1959 to help accelerate economic and social development in Latin America and the Caribbean. It is based in Washington, DC.

The Bank has 28 member countries in the Western Hemisphere and 18 outside of the region.

Inter-American Investment Corporation

Headquarters: 1300 New York Avenue NW., Washington, DC 20577. Phone, 202–623–3900

Chairman of Board of Directors: Enrique V. Iglesias
General Manager: Jacques Rogozinski

The Inter-American Investment Corporation (IIC), an affiliate of the Inter-American Development Bank, was established in 1984 to promote the economic development of its Latin American and Caribbean members by financing small and medium-size private enterprises. IIC makes direct loans and equity investments and grants lines of credit to local financial intermediaries. It is based in Washington, DC.

IIC has 37 member countries, of which 27 are in the Western Hemisphere, including the United States, and 10 are outside the region.

International Bank for Reconstruction and Development

Headquarters: 1818 H Street NW., Washington, DC 20433. Phone, 202–477–1234

President: James D. Wolfensohn

The International Bank for Reconstruction and Development (IBRD), also known as the World Bank, officially came into existence on December 27, 1945.

The Bank's purpose is to promote economic, social, and environmental progress in developing nations by reducing poverty so that their people may live better and fuller lives. The Bank lends funds at market-determined interest rates, provides advice, and serves as a catalyst to stimulate outside investments. Its resources come primarily from funds raised in the world capital markets, its retained earnings, and repayments on its loans.

International Development Association The International Development Association (IDA) came into existence on September 24, 1960, as an affiliate of IBRD. The Association's resources consist of subscriptions and supplementary resources in the form of general replenishments, mostly from its more industrialized and developed members; special contributions by its richer members; repayments on earlier credits; and transfers from IBRD's net earnings.

The Association promotes economic development, reduces poverty, and raises the standard of living in the least developed areas of the world. It does this by financing their developmental requirements on concessionary terms, which are more flexible and bear less heavily on the balance of payments than those of conventional loans, thereby furthering the objectives of IBRD and supplementing its activities.

International Finance Corporation

Headquarters: 1850 "I" Street NW., Washington, DC 20433. Phone, 202–477–1234. Internet, www.ifc.org.

President: James D. Wolfensohn

Executive Vice President: Peter Woicke

The International Finance Corporation (IFC), an affiliate of the World Bank, was established in July 1956, to promote productive private enterprise in developing member countries.

The Corporation pursues its objective principally through direct debt and equity investments in projects that establish new businesses or expand, modify, or diversify existing businesses. It also encourages cofinancing by other investors and lenders. For every dollar of financing approved by IFC for its own account, other investors and lenders provide almost six dollars.

Additionally, advisory services and technical assistance are provided by IFC to developing member countries in areas such as capital market development, privatization, corporate restructuring, and foreign investment.

International Monetary Fund

700 Nineteenth Street NW., Washington, DC 20431. Phone, 202–623–7000. Internet, www.imf.org.

Managing Director and Chairman of the Executive Board: Horst Koehler

The Final Act of the United Nations Monetary and Financial Conference, signed at Bretton Woods, NH, on July 22, 1944, set forth the original Articles of Agreement of the International Monetary Fund (IMF). The Agreement became effective on December 27, 1945, when the President, authorized by the Bretton Woods Agreements Act (22 U.S.C. 286) accepted membership for the United States in IMF, the Agreement having thus been accepted by countries whose combined financial commitments (quotas) equaled approximately 80 percent of IMF's total commitments. The inaugural meeting of the Board of Governors was held in March 1946, and the first meeting of the Executive Directors was held May 6, 1946.

On May 31, 1968, the Board of Governors approved an amendment to the Articles of Agreement for the establishment of a facility based on Special Drawing Rights (SDR) in IMF and for modification of certain IMF rules and practices. The amendment became effective on July 28, 1969, and the Special Drawing Account became operative on August 6, 1969. United States acceptance of the amendment and participation in the Special Drawing Account were authorized by the Special Drawing Rights Act (22 U.S.C. 286 *et seq.*).

On April 30, 1976, the Board of Governors approved a second amendment to the Articles of Agreement, which entered into force on April 1, 1978. This amendment gave members the right to adopt exchange arrangements of their choice while placing certain obligations on them regarding their exchange rate policies, over which IMF was to exercise firm surveillance. The official price of gold was abolished and the SDR account was promoted as the principal reserve asset of the international monetary system. United States acceptance of this amendment was authorized by the Bretton Woods Agreements Act Amendments (22 U.S.C. 286e–5).

On June 28, 1990, the Board of Governors approved a third amendment to the Articles of Agreement, which became effective on November 11, 1992. Under this amendment, a member's voting rights and certain related rights may be suspended by a 70-percent majority of the executive board if the member, having been declared ineligible to use the general resources of the Fund, persists in its failure to fulfill any of its obligations under the Articles.

As of December 31, 1999, IMF had 182 member countries. Total quotas were SDR 212 billion (equivalent to approximately $284 billion).

The purposes of IMF are to promote international monetary cooperation through a permanent forum for consultation and collaboration on international monetary problems; to facilitate the expansion and balanced growth of international trade; to promote exchange rate stability; to assist in the establishment of an open multilateral system of payments for current transactions between members; and to give confidence to members by making

IMF resources temporarily available to them under adequate safeguards.

In accordance with these purposes, IMF seeks to help its members correct the imbalances in their international balances of payments. It periodically examines the economic developments and policies of its member countries and offers policy advice. IMF also provides financial assistance to aid its members in handling balance-of-payment difficulties through a variety of financial facilities designed to address specific problems. These lending mechanisms include stand-by and extended arrangements, as well as separate facilities which provide compensatory and contingency financing to countries suffering temporary declines in their export earnings, and a concessional (low-interest rate) financial facility to support structural adjustment programs in the poorest countries and to provide emergency financial assistance to countries experiencing financial crises. IMF also provides technical assistance and training to its members.

For further information, contact the Chief, Editorial Division, External Relations Department, International Monetary Fund, 700 Nineteenth Street NW., Washington, DC 20431. Phone, 202–623–7364. Internet, www.imf.org.

International Organization for Migration

Headquarters: 17 Route des Morillons, Grand-Saconnex, Geneva. Mailing address, P.O. Box 71, CH–1211, Geneva 19, Switzerland. Phone, 011–41–22–717–9111. Fax, 011–41–22–798–6150. Internet, www.iom.int.

Director General: Brunson McKinley (United States)

Deputy Director General: Ndioro Ndiaye (Senegal)

Washington Office: Suite 700, 1752 N Street NW., Washington, DC 20036. Phone, 202–862–1826. Fax, 202–862–1879. E-mail, srowashington@iom.int

Regional Representative: William Hyde (United States)

New York Office: Suite 1610, 122 E. 42d Street, New York, NY 10168. Phone, 212–681–7000. Fax, 212–867–5887. E-mail, newyork@iom.int

Chief of Mission: Andrew Bruce (New Zealand)

Permanent United Nations Observer: Robert G. Paiva (United States)

The International Organization for Migration (IOM), formerly the Intergovernmental Committee for Migration, was created in 1951 at an international migration conference in Brussels sponsored by the United States and Belgium. It was formed outside the United Nations system in order to provide assistance, including health screening and transportation, to refugees as well as to persons not under the protection of the U.N. High Commissioner for Refugees, and to be concerned with international migration issues in general such as the links between migration and development.

As a technical, nonpolitical organization committed to the statement that humane and orderly migration benefits migrants and society, IOM has four strategic objectives:

—to cooperate with its partners in the international community to assist in meeting the operational challenges of migration;

—to advance understanding of migration issues;

—to encourage social and economic development through migration; and

—to work toward effective respect of the human dignity and well-being of migrants.

The Organization plans and carries out refugee migration schemes, programs for returning migrants, and emergency relief activities at the request of its member states and in cooperation with other international organizations, especially U.N. agencies. In addition, it publishes surveys and sponsors conferences on migration trends and issues.

In the United States, IOM carries out certain activities for the U.S. Refugee Admissions Program, facilitates sponsor prepayment for other U.S.-bound immigrants, and operates a limited number of return migration programs. In addition to Washington, DC, and New York, IOM has offices in Chicago, Los Angeles, Miami, and San Francisco.

The Organization comprises 118 states (71 members and 47 observers). They meet once a year in Geneva as the Council, to consider global migration issues and the Organization's work, direction, and budget. Mandatory assessed contributions from member states finance IOM's administrative budget, whereas its operational budget is funded through voluntary contributions. Member states elect the Director General and the Deputy Director General, whose regular terms are 5 years. Several international governmental and nongovernmental organizations are invited to observe and address the IOM Council.

The Organization has observer status at U.N. agencies, the Organization of American States, and other organizations.

Multilateral Investment Guarantee Agency

Headquarters: 1818 H Street NW., Washington, DC 20433. Phone, 202–477–1234. Internet, www.miga.org.

President: James D. Wolfensohn
Executive Vice President: Moromichi Ikawa

The Multilateral Investment Guarantee Agency (MIGA), an affiliate of the World Bank, was formally constituted in April 1988.

Its basic purpose is to facilitate the flow of foreign private investment for productive purposes to developing member countries by offering long-term political risk insurance in the areas of expropriation, currency transfer, and war and civil disturbance; and by providing advisory and consultative services. The Agency cooperates with national investment insurance schemes, such as OPIC, and with private insurers.

Organization of American States

General Secretariat: 1889 F Street NW., Washington, DC 20006. Phone, 202–458–3000. Fax, 202–458–3967. Internet, www.oas.org.

Secretary General: César Gaviria
Assistant Secretary General: Christopher Thomas
Executive Secretary for Integral Development: Leonel Zuñiga, *Acting*
Assistant Secretary for Management: James Harding
Assistant Secretary for Legal Affairs: Enrique Lagos

The Organization of American States (OAS) is a regional, intergovernmental organization whose primary purposes are to strengthen the peace and security of the continent; to promote and consolidate representative democracy, with due respect for the principle of nonintervention; to prevent possible causes of difficulties and to conciliate disputes that may arise among the member states; to provide for common action by those states in the event of aggression; to seek the solution of political, juridical, and economic problems that may arise among them; to promote, by cooperative action, their economic, social, and cultural development; and to achieve an effective limitation of conventional weapons that will make it possible to devote the largest amount of resources to the economic and social development of the member states.

With roots dating from 1890, the first OAS Charter was signed in 1948. Three subsequent protocols of amendment, Buenos Aires 1967, Cartagena de Indias 1985, and Washington 1992, gave it its present form. The Protocol of Washington, which entered into force on September 25, 1997, incorporated provisions for the protection of democratically constituted governments and will include among the essential purposes of the Organization the eradication of extreme poverty, which constitutes an obstacle to the full democratic development of the peoples of the hemisphere. A fourth protocol of amendment, the Protocol of Managua 1993, which entered into force on January 29, 1996, established the Inter–American Council for Integral Development (CIDI), which replaces the Inter–American Councils for Economic and Social Affairs and Education, Science and Culture.

The Organization's member states are Argentina, Antigua and Barbuda,

Commonwealth of the Bahamas, Barbados, Belize, Bolivia, Brazil, Canada, Chile, Colombia, Costa Rica, Cuba, Commonwealth of Dominica, Dominican Republic, Ecuador, El Salvador, Grenada, Guatemala, Guyana, Haiti, Honduras, Jamaica, Mexico, Nicaragua, Panama, Paraguay, Peru, St. Kitts and Nevis, St. Lucia, St. Vincent and the Grenadines, Suriname, Trinidad and Tobago, the United States of America, Uruguay, and Venezuela. The present Government of Cuba is excluded from participation by a decision of the Eighth Meeting of Consultation of Ministers of Foreign Affairs in 1962. In addition to the Holy See and the European Union, 44 non-American countries are permanent observers.

The principal organs of the OAS are:

—the General Assembly, which is normally composed of the foreign ministers of the member states and meets at least once a year to decide the general action and policy of the Organization;

—the Meeting of Consultation of Ministers of Foreign Affairs, which meets on call to consider urgent matters of common interest or threats to the peace and security of the hemisphere;

—the Permanent Council, which meets twice a month at OAS headquarters;

—the Inter-American Council for Integral Development;

—the Inter-American Juridical Committee;

—the Inter-American Commission on Human Rights; and

—the General Secretariat, which is the central and permanent organ, headquartered in Washington, DC.

The Organization has six specialized organizations that handle technical matters of common interest to the American States. It also holds specialized conferences on specific technical matters.

For further information, contact the Director, Department of Public Information, Organization of American States, Seventeenth Street and Constitution Avenue NW., Washington, DC 20006. Phone, 202–458–3760. Fax, 202–458–6421. Internet, www.oas.org.

United Nations

United Nations, New York, NY 10017. Phone, 212–963–1234. Internet, www.un.org.
Secretary-General: Kofi A. Annan

United Nations Office at Geneva: Palais des Nations, 1211 Geneva 10, Switzerland
Director-General: Vladimir Petrovsky

United Nations Office at Vienna: Vienna International Centre, P.O. Box 500, A–1400, Vienna, Austria
Director-General: Pino Arlacchi

Washington, DC, Office: U.N. Information Centre, Suite 400, 1775 K Street NW., Washington, DC 20006. Phone, 202–331–8670. Fax, 202–331–9191
Director: Catherine O'Neill

The United Nations is an international organization that was set up in accordance with the Charter [1] drafted by governments represented at the Conference on International Organization meeting at San Francisco. The Charter was signed on June 26, 1945, and came into force on October 24, 1945, when the required number of ratifications and accessions had been made by the signatories. Amendments increasing membership of the Security Council and the Economic and Social Council came into effect on August 31, 1965.

The United Nations now consists of 188 member states, of which 51 are founding members.

The purposes of the United Nations set out in the Charter are: to maintain international peace and security; to develop friendly relations among nations; to achieve international cooperation in solving international problems of an economic, social, cultural, or humanitarian character and in promoting respect for human rights; and to be a center for harmonizing the

[1] Charter of the United Nations, together with the Statute of the International Court of Justice (Department of State Publication No. 2353, International Organization and Conference Series III, 21), June 26, 1945. Available for sale from the Superintendent of Documents, Government Printing Office, Washington, DC 20402. Phone, 202–512–1800.

actions of nations in the attainment of these common ends.

The principal organs of the United Nations are:

General Assembly All states that are members of the United Nations are members of the General Assembly. Its functions are to consider and discuss any matter within the scope of the Charter of the United Nations and to make recommendations to the members of the United Nations and other organs. It approves the budget of the organization, the expenses of which are borne by the members as apportioned by the General Assembly.

The General Assembly may call the attention of the Security Council to situations likely to endanger international peace and security, may initiate studies, and may receive and consider reports from other organs of the United Nations. Under the "Uniting for Peace" resolution adopted by the General Assembly in November 1950, if the Security Council fails to act on an apparent threat to or breach of the peace or act of aggression because of lack of unanimity of its five permanent members, the Assembly itself may take up the matter within 24 hours—in emergency special session—and recommend collective measures, including, in case of a breach of the peace or act of aggression, use of armed force when necessary to maintain or restore international peace and security.

The General Assembly normally meets in regular annual session in September. It also has met in special sessions and emergency special sessions.

Security Council The Security Council consists of 15 members, of which 5—the People's Republic of China, France, Russia, the United Kingdom, and the United States of America—are permanent members and are elected each year. The 10 nonpermanent members are elected for 2-year terms by the General Assembly. The primary responsibility of the Security Council is to act on behalf of the members of the United Nations in maintenance of international peace and security. Measures that may be employed by the Security Council are outlined in the Charter.

The Security Council, together with the General Assembly, also elects the judges of the International Court of Justice and makes a recommendation to the General Assembly on the appointment of the Secretary-General of the organization.

The Security Council first met in London on January 17, 1946, and is so organized as to be able to function continuously.

Economic and Social Council This organ is responsible, under the authority of the General Assembly, for the economic and social programs of the United Nations. Its functions include making or initiating studies, reports, and recommendations on international economic, social, cultural, educational, health, and related matters; promoting respect for and observance of human rights and fundamental freedoms for all; calling international conferences and preparing draft conventions for submission to the General Assembly on matters within its competence; negotiating agreements with the specialized agencies and defining their relationship with the United Nations; coordinating the activities of the specialized agencies; and consulting with nongovernmental organizations concerned with matters within its competence. The Council consists of 54 members of the United Nations elected by the General Assembly for 3-year terms; 18 are elected each year.

The Council usually holds two regular sessions a year. It has also held a number of special sessions.

Trusteeship Council The Trusteeship Council was initially established to consist of any member states that administered trust territories, permanent members of the Security Council that did not administer trust territories, and enough other nonadministering countries elected by the General Assembly for 3-year terms to ensure that membership would be equally divided between administering and nonadministering members. Under authority of the General Assembly, the Council considered reports from members administering trust territories, examined petitions from trust territory inhabitants, and provided for periodic inspection visits to trust territories.

With the independence of Palau, the last remaining U.N. trust territory, the Trusteeship Council formally suspended operations after nearly half a century. The council will henceforth meet only on an extraordinary basis, as the need may arise.

International Court of Justice The International Court of Justice is the principal judicial organ of the United Nations. It has its seat at The Hague, The Netherlands. All members of the United Nations are *ipso facto* parties to the Statute of the Court. Nonmembers of the United Nations may become parties to the Statute of the Court on conditions prescribed by the General Assembly on the recommendation of the Security Council.

The jurisdiction of the Court comprises all cases that the parties refer to it and all matters specially provided for in the Charter of the United Nations or in treaties and conventions in force.

The Court consists of 15 judges known as "members" of the Court. They are elected for 9-year terms by the General Assembly and the Security Council, voting independently, and may be reelected.

Secretariat The Secretariat consists of a Secretary-General and "such staff as the Organization may require." The Secretary-General, who is appointed by the General Assembly on the recommendation of the Security Council, is the chief administrative officer of the United Nations. He acts in that capacity for the General Assembly, the Security Council, the Economic and Social Council, and the Trusteeship Council. Under the Charter, the Secretary-General "may bring to the attention of the Security Council any matter that in his opinion may threaten the maintenance of international peace and security."

SELECTED BILATERAL ORGANIZATIONS

International Boundary Commission, United States and Canada

United States Section: Suite 100, 1250 Twenty-third Street NW., Washington, DC 20440. Phone, 202–736–9100.

Canadian Section: Room 555, 615 Booth Street, Ottawa, ON K1A 0E9. Phone, 613–995–4951.

International Boundary and Water Commission, United States and Mexico

United States Section: Suite C–310, 4171 North Mesa Street, El Paso, TX 79902. Phone, 915–832–4100. Internet, www.ibwc.state.gov.

Mexican Section: No. 2180, Avenida Universidad, Ciudad Juárez, Chihuahua, Mexico 32310; or P.O. Box 10525, El Paso, TX 79995. Phone, 011–52–161–37363.

International Joint Commission—United States and Canada

United States Section: Suite 100, 1250 Twenty-third Street NW., Washington, DC 20440. Phone, 202–736–9000. Fax, 202–736–9015. Internet, www.ijc.org.

Canadian Section: 100 Metcalfe Street, Ottawa, ON K1P 5M1. Phone, 613–995–2984. Fax, 613–993–5583.

Regional Office: 100 Ouellette Avenue, Windsor, ON N9A 6T3; or P.O. Box 32869, Detroit MI 48232. Phone, 519–257–6700 or 313–226–2170. Fax, 519–257–6740.

Joint Mexican-United States Defense Commission

United States Section: 5134 Joint Staff, Room 2D959, Pentagon, Washington, DC 20318–5134. Phone, 703–695–8164.

Mexican Section: 1911 Pennsylvania Avenue NW., Mexican Embassy, Sixth Floor, Washington, DC 20006. Phone, 202–728–1748.

Permanent Joint Board on Defense—United States and Canada

United States Section: Suite 511, 1111 Jefferson Davis Highway, Arlington, VA 22202. Phone, 703–604–0488. Fax, 703–604–0486.

Canadian Section: National Defense Headquarters, 125 Sussex Drive, Ottawa, ON K1A 0K2. Phone, 613–992–5457.

Appendices

APPENDIX A: Commonly Used Abbreviations and Acronyms

AARCC Alternative Agricultural Research and Commercialization Corporation
ABMC American Battle Monuments Commission
ACF Administration for Children and Families
ACYF Administration on Children, Youth, and Families
ADA Americans with Disabilities Act of 1990
ADB Asian Development Bank
ADD Administration on Developmental Disabilities
AFAA Air Force Audit Agency
AFDB African Development Bank
AFDC Aid to Families with Dependent Children
AFDF African Development Fund
AFSC Armed Forces Staff College
AGRICOLA Agricultural Online Access
AHCPR Agency for Health Care Policy and Research
AmeriCorps NCCC AmeriCorps*National Civilian Community Corps
AMS Agricultural Marketing Service
Amtrak National Railroad Passenger Corporation
ANA Administration for Native Americans
AOA Administration on Aging
APHIS Animal and Plant Health Inspection Service
ARC Appalachian Regional Commission
ARS Agricultural Research Service
ATF Bureau of Alcohol, Tobacco, and Firearms
ATSDR Agency for Toxic Substances and Disease Registry
BEA Bureau of Economic Analysis
BIA Bureau of Indian Affairs
BIC Business Information Center (SBA)
BJA Bureau of Justice Assistance
BJS Bureau of Justice Statistics
BLM Bureau of Land Management
BLS Bureau of Labor Statistics
BTS Bureau of Transportation Statistics
BVA Board of Veterans' Appeals
C^3I Command, Control, Communications, and Intelligence
C^4 Command, Control, Communications, and Computers
C^4I Command, Control, Communications, Computers, and Intelligence
CBO Congressional Budget Office
CCC Commodity Credit Corporation
CDBG Community Development Block Grant

CDC Centers for Disease Control and Prevention
CEA Council of Economic Advisers
CEOS Child Exploitation and Obscenity Section (Justice)
CEQ Council on Environmental Quality
CFA Commission of Fine Arts
CFR *Code of Federal Regulations*
CFTC Commodity Futures Trading Commission
CIA Central Intelligence Agency
CITES Convention on International Trade in Endangered Species of Wild Fauna and Flora
CNO Chief of Naval Operations
COPS Office of Community Oriented Policing Services (Justice)
CPSC Consumer Product Safety Commission
CRS Congressional Research Service
CSAP Center for Substance Abuse Prevention
CSAT Center for Substance Abuse Treatment
CSB Chemical Safety and Hazard Investigation Board
CSE Office of Child Support Enforcement
CSREES Cooperative State Research, Education, and Extension Service
CSS Central Security Service
DA Department of the Army
DARPA Defense Advanced Research Projects Agency
DCAA Defense Contract Audit Agency
DCMC Defense Contract Management Command
DEA Drug Enforcement Administration
DIA Defense Intelligence Agency
DISA Defense Information Systems Agency
DLA Defense Logistics Agency
DLSA Defense Legal Services Agency
DOC Department of Commerce
DOD Department of Defense
DOE Department of Energy
DOL Department of Labor
DOT Department of Transportation
DSCA Defense Security Cooperation Agency
DSS Defense Security Service
DTRA Defense Threat Reduction Agency
EDA Economic Development Administration
EEOC Equal Employment Opportunity Commission
EO Executive order
EOUSA Executive Office for United States Attorneys
EPA Environmental Protection Agency
ERS Economic Research Service
Ex-Im Bank Export-Import Bank of the United States
FAA Federal Aviation Administration
Fannie Mae Federal National Mortgage Association
Farmer Mac Federal Agricultural Mortgage Corporation
FAS Foreign Agricultural Service
FBI Federal Bureau of Investigation
FCC Federal Communications Commission
FDA Food and Drug Administration
FDIC Federal Deposit Insurance Corporation
FEB's Federal Executive Boards
FEC Federal Election Commission
FEMA Federal Emergency Management Agency
FERC Federal Energy Regulatory Commission
FFB Federal Financing Bank
FHA Federal Housing Administration
FHWA Federal Highway Administration
FIA Federal Insurance Administration
FICO Financing Corporation

FLRA Federal Labor Relations Authority
FMC Federal Maritime Commission
FMCS Federal Mediation and Conciliation Service
FMS Financial Management Service
FNCS Food, Nutrition, and Consumer Services
FNMA Federal National Mortgage Association
FNS Food and Nutrition Service
FOIA Freedom of Information Act
FR *Federal Register*
FRS Federal Reserve System
FSA Farm Service Agency
FSIS Food Safety and Inspection Service
FSS Federal Supply Service
FTC Federal Trade Commission
FWS Fish and Wildlife Service
GAO General Accounting Office
GATT General Agreement on Tariffs and Trade
Ginnie Mae Government National Mortgage Association
GIPSA Grain Inspection, Packers, and Stockyards Administration
GNMA Government National Mortgage Association
GPO Government Printing Office
GSA General Services Administration
HCFA Health Care Financing Administration
HHS Department of Health and Human Services
HRSA Health Resources and Services Administration
HUD Department of Housing and Urban Development
HUMINT Defense Human Intelligence Service
IAF Inter-American Foundation
IBRD International Bank for Reconstruction and Development
IDB Inter-American Development Bank
IFC International Finance Corporation
IHA's Indian Housing Authorities
IHS Indian Health Service
ILAB Bureau of International Labor Affairs
ILO International Labor Organization
IMF International Monetary Fund
IMLS Institute of Museum and Library Services
INS Immigration and Naturalization Service
INTERPOL International Criminal Police Organization
IOM International Organization for Migration
IRMC Information Resources Management College
IRS Internal Revenue Service
ISOO Information Security Oversight Office
ITA International Trade Administration
JAG Judge Advocate General
JCS Joint Chiefs of Staff
LMI Office of One-Stop/Labor Market Information (Labor)
MA Maritime Administration
MASINT Central Measurement and Signals Intelligence Office
MBDA Minority Business Development Agency
MIGA Multilateral Investment Guarantee Agency
MMS Minerals Management Service
MSHA Mine Safety and Health Administration
MSPB Merit Systems Protection Board
NARA National Archives and Records Administration
NASA National Aeronautics and Space Administration
NASS National Agricultural Statistics Service
NATO North Atlantic Treaty Organization
NCA National Cemetery Administration
NCPC National Capital Planning Commission

NCRR	National Center for Research Resources
NCUA	National Credit Union Administration
NEA	National Endowment for the Arts
NEH	National Endowment for the Humanities
NHI	National Highway Institute
NHPRC	National Historical Publications and Records Commission
NHTSA	National Highway Traffic Safety Administration
NIH	National Institutes of Health
NIJ	National Institute of Justice
NIMA	National Imagery and Mapping Agency
NIMH	National Institute of Mental Health
NIST	National Institute of Standards and Technology
NLM	National Library of Medicine
NLRB	National Labor Relations Board
NOAA	National Oceanic and Atmospheric Administration
NPS	National Park Service
NRC	Nuclear Regulatory Commission
NRCS	Natural Resources Conservation Service
NSA	National Security Agency
NSC	National Security Council
NSF	National Science Foundation
NTIA	National Telecommunications and Information Administration
NTID	National Technical Institute for the Deaf
NTIS	National Technical Information Service (Commerce)
NTSB	National Transportation Safety Board
OAS	Organization of American States
OCS	Officer Candidate School
OECD	Organization for Economic Cooperation and Development
OGE	Office of Government Ethics
OMB	Office of Management and Budget
OPIC	Overseas Private Investment Corporation
OPM	Office of Personnel Management
ORR	Office of Refugee Resettlement
OSC	Office of Special Counsel
OSDBU	Office of Small and Disadvantaged Business Utilization (Commerce)
OSHA	Occupational Safety and Health Administration
OSHRC	Occupational Safety and Health Review Commission
OSM	Office of Surface Mining Reclamation and Enforcement
OTS	Office of Thrift Supervision
OWBO	Office of Women's Business Ownership
PBGC	Pension Benefit Guaranty Corporation
PBS	Public Buildings Service
PHA's	Public Housing Agencies
PHS	Public Health Service
POW/MP	Prisoner of War/Missing Personnel
PRC	Postal Rate Commission
PSC	Program Support Center (Health and Human Services)
PTO	Patent and Trademark Office
PWBA	Pension and Welfare Benefits Administration
RHS	Rural Housing Service
RICO	Racketeer Influenced and Corrupt Organizations
RIT	Rochester Institute of Technology
RMA	Risk Management Agency (Agriculture)
ROTC	Reserve Officer Training Corps
RRB	Railroad Retirement Board
RSPA	Research and Special Programs Administration (Transportation)

RTB Rural Telephone Bank
RUS Rural Utilities Service
SAIF Savings Association Insurance Fund
SAMHSA Substance Abuse and Mental Health Services Administration
SBA Small Business Administration
SEC Securities and Exchange Commission
SITES Smithsonian Institution Traveling Exhibition Service
SSA Social Security Administration
SSI Supplemental Security Income Program
SSS Selective Service System
START Strategic Arms Reduction Treaty
Stat. United States Statutes at Large
TASC Transportation Administrative Service Center
TDA Trade and Development Agency
TPCC Trade Promotion Coordinating Committee
TVA Tennessee Valley Authority
U.N. United Nations[1]
UNESCO United Nations Educational, Scientific and Cultural Organization
UNHCR United Nations High Commissioner for Refugees Program

[1] Acronyms for other U.N. agencies can be found under *Selected Multilateral Organizations* in the preceding text.

UNICEF United Nations Children's Fund (formerly United Nations International Children's Emergency Fund)
UNICOR Federal Prison Industries, Inc.
USA United States Army
USAF United States Air Force
USAID United States Agency for International Development
U.S.C. United States Code
USCG United States Coast Guard
USDA United States Department of Agriculture
USFA United States Fire Administration
USGS United States Geological Survey
USITC United States International Trade Commission
USMC United States Marine Corps
USN United States Navy
VA Department of Veterans Affairs
VISTA Volunteers in Service to America
VOA Voice of America
WHO World Health Organization
WIC Special supplemental food program for Women, Infants, and Children
WNET Women's Network for Entrepreneurial Training (SBA)
WTO World Trade Organization
YCC Youth Conservation Corps

APPENDIX B: Federal Executive Agencies Terminated, Transferred, or Changed in Name Subsequent to March 4, 1933

NOTE: Italicized terms indicate obsolete agencies, organizations, and entities. In most instances, explanatory remarks are written at those terms elsewhere in this appendix. Dates prior to March 4, 1933, are included to provide additional information about the agencies.

This appendix is indexed in a format considered to be useful to the reader. Entries are carried at the most significant term in their titles, or when there is more than one significant term, the entry is carried at the first significant term. Thus, **Bureau of the Budget** is found at **Budget, Bureau of the,** and **Annual Assay Commission** is found at **Assay Commission, Annual.** Reader comments on the format are encouraged and should be sent to the address shown on page iv of the *Manual.*

ACTION Established by Reorg. Plan No. 1 of 1971 (5 U.S.C. app.), effective July 1, 1971. Reorganized by act of Oct. 1, 1973 (87 Stat. 405). Functions relating to SCORE and ACT programs transferred to Small Business Administration by EO 11871 of July 18, 1975 (40 FR 30915). Functions exercised by the Director of ACTION prior to Mar. 31, 1995, transferred to the Corporation for National and Community Service (107 Stat. 888 and Proclamation 6662 of Apr. 4, 1994 (57 FR 16507)).

Acts of Congress *See* **State, Department of**

Administrative Conference of the United States Established by act of Aug. 30, 1964 (78 Stat. 615). Terminated by act of Nov. 19, 1995 (109 Stat. 480).

Advanced Research Projects Agency *See* Defense Advanced Research Projects Agency

Advisory Board, Commission, Committee. *See other part of title*

Aeronautical Board Organized in 1916 by agreement of *War* and Navy Secretaries. Placed under supervision of President by military order of July 5, 1939. Dissolved by Secretary of Defense letter of July 27, 1948, and functions transferred to *Munitions Board* and *Research and Development Board.* Military order of July 5, 1939, revoked by military order of Oct. 18, 1948.

Aeronautics, Bureau of Established in the Department of the Navy by act of July 12, 1921 (42 Stat. 140). Abolished by act of Aug. 18, 1959 (73 Stat. 395) and functions transferred to *Bureau of Naval Weapons.*

Aeronautics, National Advisory Committee for Established by act of Mar. 3, 1915 (38 Stat. 930). Terminated by act of July 29, 1958 (72 Stat. 432), and functions transferred to National Aeronautics and Space Administration, established by same act.

Aeronautics Administration, Civil *See* **Aeronautics Authority, Civil**

Aeronautics Authority, Civil Established under act of June 23, 1938 (52 Stat. 973). Renamed *Civil Aeronautics Board* and Administrator transferred to the Department of Commerce by Reorg. Plan Nos. III and IV of 1940, effective June 30, 1940. Office of Administrator designated *Civil Aeronautics Administration* by Department Order 52 of Aug. 29, 1940. *Administration* transferred to *Federal Aviation Agency* by act of Aug. 23, 1958 (72 Stat. 810). Functions of *Board* under act of Aug. 23, 1958 (72 Stat. 775), transferred to National Transportation Safety Board by act of Oct. 15, 1966 (80 Stat. 931). Functions of *Board* terminated or transferred—effective in part Dec. 31, 1981; in part Jan. 1, 1983; and in part Jan. 1, 1985—by act of Aug. 23, 1958 (92 Stat. 1744). Most remaining functions transferred to Secretary of Transportation, remainder to U.S. Postal Service. Termination of *Board* finalized by act of Oct. 4, 1984 (98 Stat. 1703).

Aeronautics Board, Civil *See* **Aeronautics Authority, Civil**

Aeronautics Branch Established in the Department of Commerce to carry out provisions of act of May 20, 1926 (44 Stat. 568). Renamed *Bureau of Air Commerce* by Secretary's administrative order of July 1, 1934. Personnel and property transferred to *Civil Aeronautics Authority* by EO 7959 of Aug. 22, 1938.

Aeronautics and Space Council, National Established by act of July 29, 1958 (72 Stat. 427). Abolished by Reorg. Plan No. 1 of 1973, effective June 30, 1973.

Aging, Administration on Established by *Secretary of Health, Education, and Welfare* on Oct. 1, 1965, to carry out provisions of act of July 14, 1965 (79 Stat. 218). Reassigned to *Social and Rehabilitation Service* by Department reorganization of Aug. 15,

186-873 D-00--20

1967. Transferred to Office of Assistant Secretary for Human Development by Secretary's order of June 15, 1973. Transferred to the Office of the Secretary of Health and Human Services by Secretary's reorganization notice dated Apr. 15, 1991.

Aging, Federal Council on Established by Presidential memorandum of Apr. 2, 1956. Reconstituted at Federal level by Presidential letter of Mar. 7, 1959, to *Secretary of Health, Education, and Welfare.* Abolished by EO 11022 of May 15, 1962, which established *President's Council on Aging.*

Aging, Office of Established by *Secretary of Health, Education, and Welfare* June 2, 1955, as *Special Staff on Aging.* Terminated Sept. 30, 1965, and functions assumed by Administration on Aging.

Aging, President's Council on Established by EO 11022 of May 14, 1962. Terminated by EO 11022, which was revoked by EO 12379 of Aug. 17, 1982.

Agricultural Adjustment Administration Established by act of May 12, 1933 (48 Stat. 31). Consolidated into *Agricultural Conservation and Adjustment Administration* as *Agricultural Adjustment Agency,* Department of Agriculture, by EO 9069 of Feb. 23, 1942. Grouped with other agencies to form *Food Production Administration* by EO 9280 of Dec. 5, 1942. Transferred to *War Food Administration* by EO 9322 of Mar. 26, 1943. Administration terminated by EO 9577 of June 29, 1945, and functions transferred to Secretary of Agriculture. Transfer made permanent by Reorg. Plan No. 3 of 1946, effective July 16, 1946. Functions of *Agricultural Adjustment Agency* consolidated with *Production and Marketing Administration* by Secretary's Memorandum 1118 of Aug. 18, 1945.

Agricultural Adjustment Agency *See* **Agricultural Adjustment Administration**

Agricultural Advisory Commission, National Established by EO 10472 of July 20, 1953. Terminated Feb. 4, 1965, on resignation of members.

Agricultural Chemistry and Engineering, Bureau of *See* **Agricultural Engineering, Bureau of**

Agricultural Conservation and Adjustment Administration Established by EO 9069 of Feb. 23, 1942, consolidating *Agricultural Adjustment Agency, Sugar Agency, Federal Crop Insurance Corporation,* and *Soil Conservation Service.* Consolidated into *Food Production Administration* by EO 9280 of Dec. 5, 1942.

Agricultural Conservation Program Service Established by Secretary of Agriculture Jan. 21, 1953, from part of *Production and Marketing Administration.* Merged with *Commodity Stabilization Service* by Secretary's Memorandum 1446, supp. 2, of Apr. 19, 1961.

Agricultural Developmental Service, International Established by Secretary of Agriculture memorandum of July 12, 1963. Functions and delegations of authority transferred to Foreign Agricultural Service by Secretary's memorandum of Mar. 28, 1969. Functions transferred by Secretary to *Foreign Economic Development Service* Nov. 8, 1969.

Agricultural Economics, Bureau of Established by act of May 11, 1931 (42 Stat. 532). Functions transferred to other units of the Department of Agriculture, including *Consumer and Marketing Service* and Agricultural Research Service, under Secretary's Memorandum 1320, supp. 4, of Nov. 2, 1953.

Agricultural Engineering, Bureau of Established by act of Feb. 23, 1931 (46 Stat. 1266). Merged with *Bureau of Chemistry and Soils* by Secretarial order of Oct. 16, 1938, to form *Bureau of Agricultural Chemistry and Engineering.*

Agricultural and Industrial Chemistry, Bureau of *Bureau of Chemistry* and *Bureau of Soils,* created in 1901, combined into *Bureau of Chemistry and Soils* by act of Jan. 18, 1927 (44 Stat. 976). Soils units transferred to other agencies of the Department of Agriculture and remaining units of *Bureau of Chemistry and Soils* and *Bureau of Agricultural Engineering* consolidated with *Bureau of Agricultural Chemistry and Engineering* by Secretary's order of Oct. 16, 1938. In February 1943 agricultural engineering research made part of *Bureau of Plant Industry, Soils, and Agricultural Engineering,* and organization for continuing agricultural chemistry research relating to crop utilization named *Bureau of Agricultural and Industrial Chemistry,* in accordance with *Research Administration* Memorandum 5 issued pursuant to EO 9069 of Feb. 23, 1942, and in conformity with Secretary's Memorandums 960 and 986. Functions transferred to *Agricultural Research Service* under Secretary's Memorandum 1320, supp. 4, of Nov. 2, 1953.

Agricultural Library, National Established by Secretary of Agriculture Memorandum 1496 of Mar. 23, 1962. Consolidated into *Science and Education Administration* by Secretary's order of Jan. 24, 1978. Reestablished as National Agricultural Library by Secretary's order of June 16, 1981. Became part of Agricultural Research Service in 1994 under Department of Agriculture reorganization.

Agricultural Marketing Administration Established by EO 9069 of Feb. 23, 1942, consolidating *Surplus Marketing Administration, Agricultural Marketing Service,* and *Commodity Exchange Administration. Division of Consumers' Counsel* transferred to *Administration* by Secretary's memorandum of Feb. 28, 1942. Consolidated into *Food Distribution Administration* in the Department of Agriculture by EO 9280 of Dec. 5, 1942.

Agricultural Marketing Service Established by the Secretary of Agriculture pursuant to act of June 30, 1939 (53 Stat. 939). Merged into *Agricultural Marketing Administration* by EO 9069 of Feb. 23, 1942. Renamed *Consumer and Marketing Service* by Secretary's Memorandum 1567, supp. 1, of Feb. 8, 1965. Reestablished as Agricultural Marketing Service by the Secretary of Agriculture on Apr. 2, 1972, under authority of Reorg. Plan No. 2 of 1953 (67 Stat. 633).

Agricultural Relations, Office of Foreign *See* **Agricultural Service, Foreign**

Agricultural Research Administration Established by EO 9069 of Feb. 23, 1942. Superseded by Agricultural Research Service.

Agricultural Research Service Established by Secretary of Agriculture Memorandum 1320, supp. 4, of Nov. 2, 1953. Consolidated into *Science and Education Administration* by Secretary's order of Jan. 24, 1978. Reestablished as Agricultural Research Service by Secretarial order of June 16, 1981.

Agricultural Service, Foreign Established by act of June 5, 1930 (46 Stat. 497). Economic research and agricultural attaché activities administered by *Foreign Agricultural Service Division, Bureau of Agricultural Economics,* until June 29, 1939. Transferred by Reorg. Plan No. II of 1939, effective July 1, 1939, from the Department of Agriculture to the Department of State. Economic research functions of *Division* transferred to *Office of Foreign Agricultural Relations* June 30, 1939. Functions of *Office* transferred to Foreign Agricultural Service Mar. 10, 1953. Agricultural attachés placed in the Department of Agriculture by act of Aug. 28, 1954 (68 Stat. 908).

Agricultural Stabilization and Conservation Service Established June 5, 1961, by the Secretary of Agriculture under authority of revised statutes (5 U.S.C. 301) and Reorg. Plan No. 2 of 1953 (5 U.S.C. app.). Abolished and functions assumed by the *Farm Service Agency* by Secretary's Memorandum 1010–1 dated Oct. 20, 1994 (59 FR 60297, 60299).

Agricultural Statistics Division Transferred to *Bureau of Agricultural Economics* by EO 9069 of Feb. 23, 1942.

Agriculture, Division of *See* **Farm Products, Division of**

Air Commerce, Bureau of *See* **Aeronautics Branch**

Air Coordinating Committee Established Mar. 27, 1945, by interdepartmental memorandum; formally established by EO 9781 of Sept. 19, 1946. Terminated by EO 10883 of Aug. 11, 1960, and functions transferred for liquidation to *Federal Aviation Agency.*

Air Force Management Engineering Agency Established in 1975 in Air Force as separate operating unit. Made subordinate unit of Air Force Military Personnel Center (formerly Air Force Manpower and Personnel Center) in 1978. Reestablished as separate operating unit of Air Force, effective Mar. 1, 1985, by Secretarial order.

Air Force Manpower and Personnel Center Certain functions transferred on activation of Air Force Management Engineering Agency, which was made separate operating unit from Air Force Manpower and Personnel Center (later Air Force Military Personnel Center) in April 1985 by general order of Chief of Staff.

Air Force Medical Service Center Renamed Air Force Office of Medical Support by Program Action Directive 85–1 of Mar. 6, 1985, approved by Air Force Vice Chief of Staff.

Air Mail, Bureau of Established in Interstate Commerce Commission to carry out provisions of act of June 12, 1934 (48 Stat. 933). Personnel and property transferred to *Civil Aeronautics Authority* by EO 7959 of Aug. 22, 1938.

Air Patrol, Civil Established in *Civilian Defense Office* by Administrative Order 9 of Dec. 8, 1941. Transferred to *Department of War* as auxiliary of Army Air Forces by EO 9339 of Apr. 29, 1943. Transferred to the Department of the Air Force by Secretary of Defense order of May 21, 1948. Established as civilian auxiliary of U.S. Air Force by act of May 26, 1948 (62 Stat. 274).

Air Safety Board Established by act of June 23, 1938 (52 Stat. 973). Functions transferred to *Civil Aeronautics Board* by Reorg. Plan No. IV of 1940, effective June 30, 1940.

Airways Modernization Board Established by act of Aug. 14, 1957 (71 Stat. 349). Transferred to *Federal Aviation Agency* by EO 10786 of Nov. 1, 1958.

Alaska, Board of Road Commissioners for Established in *Department of War* by act of Jan. 27, 1905 (33 Stat. 616). Functions transferred to the Department of Interior by act of June 30, 1932 (47 Stat. 446), and delegated to *Alaska Road Commission.* Functions transferred to the Department of Commerce by act of June 29, 1956 (70 Stat. 377), and terminated by act of June 25, 1959 (73 Stat. 145).

Alaska, Federal Field Committee for Development Planning in Established by EO 11182 of Oct. 2, 1964. Abolished by EO 11608 of July 19, 1971.

Alaska, Federal Reconstruction and Development Planning Commission for Established by EO 11150 of Apr. 2, 1964. Abolished by EO 11182 of Oct. 2, 1964, which established *President's Review Committee for Development Planning in Alaska* and *Federal Field Committee for Development Planning in Alaska.*

Alaska, President's Review Committee for Development Planning in Established by EO 11182 of Oct. 2, 1964. Superseded by *Federal Advisory Council on Regional Economic Development* established by EO 11386 of Dec. 28, 1967. EO 11386 revoked by EO 12553 of Feb. 25, 1986.

Alaska Communication System Operational responsibility vested in Secretary of the Army by act of May 26, 1900 (31 Stat. 206). Transferred to Secretary of the Air Force by Secretary of Defense reorganization order of May 24, 1962.

Alaska Engineering Commission *See* **Alaska Railroad**

Alaska Game Commission Established by act of Jan. 13, 1925 (43 Stat. 740). Expired Dec. 31, 1959, pursuant to act of July 7, 1958 (72 Stat. 339).

Alaska International Rail and Highway Commission Established by act of Aug. 1, 1956 (70 Stat. 888). Terminated June 30, 1961, under terms of act.

Alaska Power Administration Established by the Secretary of the Interior in 1967. Transferred to the

Department of Energy by act of Aug. 4, 1977 (91 Stat. 578).

Alaska Railroad Built pursuant to act of Mar. 12, 1914 (38 Stat. 305), which created *Alaska Engineering Commission.* Placed under the Secretary of the Interior by EO 2129 of Jan. 26, 1915, and renamed Alaska Railroad by EO 3861 of June 8, 1923. Authority to regulate tariffs granted to Interstate Commerce Commission by EO 11107 of Apr. 25, 1963. Authority to operate Railroad transferred to the Secretary of Transportation by act of Oct. 15, 1966 (80 Stat. 941), effective Apr. 1, 1967. Railroad purchased by State of Alaska, effective Jan. 5, 1985.

Alaska Road Commission *See* **Alaska, Board of Road Commissioners for**

Alcohol, Bureau of Industrial Established by act of May 27, 1930 (46 Stat. 427). Consolidated into *Bureau of Internal Revenue* by EO 6166 of June 10, 1933. Consolidation deferred until May 11, 1934, by EO 6639 of Mar. 10, 1934. Order also transferred to Internal Revenue Commissioner certain functions imposed on Attorney General by act of May 27, 1930, with relation to enforcement of criminal laws concerning intoxicating liquors remaining in effect after repeal of 18th amendment; personnel of, and appropriations for, *Bureau of Industrial Alcohol;* and necessary personnel and appropriations of *Bureau of Prohibition,* Department of Justice.

Alcohol, Drug Abuse, and Mental Health Administration Established by the *Secretary of Health, Education, and Welfare* by act of May 21, 1972 (88 Stat. 134). Redesignated as an agency of the Public Health Service from the *National Institute of Mental Health* Sept. 25, 1973, by the Secretary of Health, Education, and Welfare. Functions transferred to the Department of Health and Human Services by act of Oct. 17, 1979 (93 Stat. 695). Established as an agency of the Public Health Service by act of Oct. 27, 1986 (100 Stat. 3207–106). Renamed Substance Abuse and Mental Health Services Administration by act of July 10, 1992 (106 Stat. 325).

Alcohol Abuse and Alcoholism, National Institute on Established within the National Institute of Mental Health, *Department of Health, Education, and Welfare* by act of Dec. 31, 1970 (84 Stat. 1848). Removed from within the National Institute of Mental Health and made an entity within the Alcohol, Drug Abuse, and Mental Health Administration by act of May 14, 1974 (88 Stat. 1356). Functions transferred to the Department of Health and Human Services by act of Oct. 17, 1979 (93 Stat. 695). (*See also* act of Oct. 27, 1986; 100 Stat. 3207–106.) Abolished by act of July 10, 1992 (106 Stat. 331). Reestablished by act of July 10, 1992 (106 Stat. 359).

Alcohol Administration, Federal *See* **Alcohol Control Administration, Federal**

Alcohol Control Administration, Federal Established by EO 6474 of Dec. 4, 1933. Abolished Sept. 24, 1935, on induction into office of Administrator, *Federal Alcohol Administration,* as provided in act of Aug. 29, 1935 (49 Stat. 977). Abolished by Reorg. Plan No. III of 1940, effective June 30, 1940, and functions consolidated with activities of Internal Revenue Service.

Alexander Hamilton Bicentennial Commission Established by act of Aug. 20, 1954 (68 Stat. 746). Terminated Apr. 30, 1958.

Alien Property Custodian Appointed by President Oct. 22, 1917, under authority of act of Oct. 6, 1917 (40 Stat. 415). Office transferred to *Alien Property Division,* Department of Justice, by EO 6694 of May 1, 1934. Powers vested in President by act delegated to Attorney General by EO 8136 of May 15, 1939. Authority vested in Attorney General by EO's 6694 and 8136 transferred by EO 9142 of Apr. 21, 1942, to *Office of Alien Property Custodian, Office for Emergency Management,* as provided for by EO 9095 of Mar. 11, 1942.

American Republics, Office for Coordination of Commercial and Cultural Relations between the Established by *Council of National Defense* order approved by President Aug. 16, 1940. Succeeded by *Office of the Coordinator of Inter-American Affairs, Office for Emergency Management,* established by EO 8840 of July 30, 1941. Renamed *Office of Inter-American Affairs* by EO 9532 of Mar. 23, 1945. Information functions transferred to the Department of State by EO 9608 of Aug. 31, 1945. Terminated by EO 9710 of Apr. 10, 1946, and functions transferred to the Department of State, functioning as *Institute of Inter-American Affairs.* Transferred to *Foreign Operations Administration* by Reorg. Plan No. 7, effective Aug. 1, 1953.

American Revolution Bicentennial Administration *See* **American Revolution Bicentennial Commission**

American Revolution Bicentennial Commission Established by act of July 4, 1966 (80 Stat. 259). *American Revolution Bicentennial Administration* established by act of Dec. 11, 1973 (87 Stat. 697), to replace *Commission. Administration* terminated June 30, 1977, pursuant to terms of act. Certain continuing functions transferred to the Secretary of the Interior by EO 12001 of June 29, 1977.

Anacostia Neighborhood Museum Renamed Anacostia Museum by Smithsonian Institution announcement of Apr. 3, 1987.

Animal Industry, Bureau of Established in the Department of Agriculture by act of May 29, 1884 (23 Stat. 31). Functions transferred to Agricultural Research Service by Secretary's Memorandum 1320, supp. 4, of Nov. 2, 1953.

Apprenticeship, Federal Committee on Previously known as *Federal Committee on Apprentice Training,* established by EO 6750–C of June 27, 1934. Functioned as part of *Division of Labor Standards,* Department of Labor, pursuant to act of Aug. 16, 1937 (50 Stat. 664). Transferred to *Office of Administrator, Federal Security Agency,* by EO 9139 of Apr. 18, 1942. Transferred to *Bureau of Training, War Manpower Commission,* by EO 9247 of Sept. 17, 1942. Returned to the Department of Labor by EO 9617 of Sept. 19, 1945.

Archive of Folksong Renamed Archive of Folk Culture by administrative order of Deputy Librarian of Congress, effective Sept. 21, 1981.

Archives Council, National Established by act of June 19, 1934 (48 Stat. 1122). Transferred to General Services Administration by act of June 30, 1949 (63 Stat. 378). Terminated on establishment of Federal Records Council by act of Sept. 5, 1950 (64 Stat. 583).

Archives Establishment, National *Office of Archivist of the U.S.* and *National Archives* created by act of June 19, 1934 (48 Stat. 1122). Transferred to General Services Administration by act of June 30, 1949 (63 Stat. 381), and incorporated as *National Archives and Records Service* by order of General Services Administrator, together with functions of *Division of the Federal Register, National Archives Council, National Historical Publications Commission,* National Archives Trust Fund Board, *Trustees of the Franklin D. Roosevelt Library,* and Administrative Committee of the Federal Register. Transferred from General Services Administration to National Archives and Records Administration by act of Oct. 19, 1984 (98 Stat. 2283), along with certain functions of Administrator of General Services transferred to Archivist of the United States, effective Apr. 1, 1985.

Archives and Records Service, National *See* **Archives Establishment, National**

Archives Trust Fund Board, National *See* **Archives Establishment, National**

Area Redevelopment Administration Established May 8, 1961, by the Secretary of Commerce pursuant to act of May 1, 1961 (75 Stat. 47) and Reorg. Plan No. 5 of 1950, effective May 24, 1950. Terminated Aug. 31, 1965, by act of June 30, 1965 (79 Stat. 195). Functions transferred to Economic Development Administration in the Department of Commerce by Department Order 4–A, effective Sept. 1, 1965.

Arlington Memorial Amphitheater Commission Established by act of Mar. 4, 1921 (41 Stat. 1440). Abolished by act of Sept. 2, 1960 (74 Stat. 739), and functions transferred to the Secretary of Defense.

Arlington Memorial Bridge Commission Established by act of Mar. 4, 1913 (37 Stat. 885; D.C. Code (1951 ed.) 8–158). Abolished by EO 6166 of June 10, 1933, and functions transferred to *Office of National Parks, Buildings, and Reservations.*

Armed Forces Medical Library Founded in 1836 as *Library of the Surgeon General's Office,* U.S. Army. Later known as *Army Medical Library,* then *Armed Forces Medical Library* in 1952. Personnel and property transferred to National Library of Medicine established in Public Health Service by act of Aug. 3, 1956 (70 Stat. 960).

Armed Forces Museum Advisory Board, National Established by act of Aug. 30, 1961 (75 Stat. 414). Functions discontinued due to lack of funding.

Armed Services Renegotiation Board Established by Secretary of Defense directive of July 19, 1948. Abolished by Secretary's letter of Jan. 18, 1952, and functions transferred to *Renegotiation Board.*

Arms Control and Disarmament Agency, U.S. Established by act of Sept. 26, 1961 (75 Stat. 631). Abolished by act of Oct. 21, 1998 (112 Stat. 2681–767) and functions transferred to the Secretary of State.

Army Communications Command, U.S. Renamed U.S. Army Information Systems Command by Department General Order No. 26 of July 25, 1984.

Army Materiel Development and Readiness Command, U.S. Renamed U.S. Army Materiel Command by Department General Order No. 28 of Aug. 15, 1984.

Army and Navy, Joint Board Placed under direction of President by military order of July 5, 1939. Abolished Sept. 1, 1947, by joint letter of Aug. 20, 1947, to President from Secretaries of *War* and Navy.

Army and Navy Staff College Established Apr. 23, 1943, and operated under Joint Chiefs of Staff. Redesignated the National War College, effective July 1, 1946.

Army Specialist Corps Established in *Department of War* by EO 9078 of Feb. 26, 1942. Abolished by the *Secretary of War* Oct. 31, 1942, and functions merged into central *Officer Procurement Service.*

Arthritis, Diabetes, and Digestive and Kidney Diseases, National Institute of *See* **Arthritis, Metabolism, and Digestive Diseases, National Institute of**

Arthritis, Metabolism, and Digestive Diseases, National Institute of Renamed *National Institute of Arthritis, Diabetes, and Digestive and Kidney Diseases* by Secretary's order of June 15, 1981, pursuant to act of Dec. 19, 1980 (94 Stat. 3184). Renamed National Institute of Diabetes and Digestive and Kidney Diseases and National Institute of Arthritis and Musculoskeletal and Skin Diseases by act of Nov. 20, 1985 (99 Stat. 820).

Arts, Advisory Committee on the Established under authority of act of Sept. 20, 1961 (75 Stat. 527). Terminated July 1973 by act of Oct. 6, 1972. Formally abolished by Reorg. Plan No. 2 of 1977, effective Apr. 1, 1978.

Arts, National Council on the Established in Executive Office of the President by act of Sept. 3, 1964 (78 Stat. 905). Transferred to National Foundation on the Arts and the Humanities by act of Sept. 29, 1965 (79 Stat. 845).

Assay Commission, Annual Established initially by act of Apr. 2, 1792 (1 Stat. 250) and by act of Feb. 12, 1873 (Revised Statute sec. 3647; 17 Stat. 432). Terminated and functions transferred to the Secretary of the Treasury by act of Mar. 14, 1980 (94 Stat. 98).

Assistance, Bureau of Public Renamed *Bureau of Family Services* by order of the *Secretary of Health, Education, and Welfare,* effective Jan. 1, 1962. Functions redelegated to *Social and Rehabilitation*

Service by Secretary's reorganization of Aug. 15, 1967.

Assistance Coordinating Committee, Adjustment Established by act of Jan. 3, 1975 (88 Stat. 2040). Inactive since 1981.

Assistance Payments Administration Established by *Secretary of Health, Education, and Welfare* reorganization of Aug. 15, 1967. Transferred by *Secretary's* reorganization of Mar. 8, 1977 (42 FR 13262), from *Social and Rehabilitation Service* to Social Security Administration.

Athletics, Interagency Committee on International Established by EO 11117 of Aug. 13, 1963. Terminated by EO 11515 of Mar. 13, 1970.

Atlantic-Pacific Interoceanic Canal Study Commission Established by act of Sept. 22, 1964 (78 Stat. 990). Terminated Dec. 1, 1970, pursuant to terms of act.

Atomic Energy Commission Established by act of Aug. 1, 1946 (60 Stat. 755). Abolished by act of Oct. 11, 1974 (88 Stat. 1237) and functions transferred to *Energy Research and Development Administration* and Nuclear Regulatory Commission.

Aviation, Interdepartmental Committee on Civil International Established by Presidential letter of June 20, 1935. Terminated on organization of *Civil Aeronautics Authority.*

Aviation Agency, Federal Established by act of Aug. 23, 1958 (72 Stat. 731). Transferred to Secretary of Transportation by act of Oct. 15, 1966 (80 Stat. 931). *Agency* reestablished as Federal Aviation Administration by act of Jan 12, 1983 (96 Stat. 2416).

Aviation Commission, Federal Established by act of June 12, 1934 (48 Stat. 938). Terminated Feb. 1, 1935, under provisions of act.

Beltsville Research Center Established to operate with other agencies of the Department of Agriculture under *Agricultural Research Administration.* Consolidated into *Agricultural Research Administration,* the Department of Agriculture, by EO 9069 of Feb. 23, 1942.

Biological Service, National Established in the the Department of the Interior in 1995 by Secretarial order. Transferred to U.S. Geological Survey as new Biological Resources Division by Secretarial Order No. 3202, Sept. 30, 1996.

Biological Survey, Bureau of Established by Secretary's order July 1, 1885, as part of *Division of Entomology,* Department of Agriculture. Made separate bureau by act of Apr. 23, 1904 (33 Stat. 276). Transferred to the Department of the Interior by Reorg. Plan No. II of 1939, effective July 1, 1939. Consolidated with *Bureau of Fisheries* into *Fish and Wildlife Service* by Reorg. Plan No. III of 1940, effective June 30, 1940.

Biological Survey, National Established in the the Department of the Interior by Secretarial Order 3173 of Sept. 29, 1993. Renamed *National Biological Service* by Secretarial order in 1995.

Blind, Inc., American Printing House for the Established in 1858 as privately owned institution in Louisville, KY. Functions of the Secretary of the Treasury, except that relating to perpetual trust funds, transferred to *Federal Security Agency* by Reorg. Plan No. II of 1939, effective July 1, 1939. Functions performed by *Department of Health, Education, and Welfare* transferred to the Department of Education.

Blind-made Products, Committee on Purchases of Established by act of June 25, 1938 (52 Stat. 1196). Renamed *Committee for Purchase of Products and Services of the Blind and Other Severely Handicapped* by act of June 23, 1971 (85 Stat. 77). Renamed *Committee for Purchase from the Blind and Other Severely Handicapped* by act of July 25, 1974 (88 Stat. 392). Renamed Committee for Purchase From People Who Are Blind or Severely Disabled by act of Oct. 29, 1992 (106 Stat. 4486).

Blind and Other Severely Handicapped, Committee for Purchase of Products and Services of the *See* **Blind-made Products, Committee on Purchases of**

Board. *See other part of title*

Bond and Spirits Division Established as *Taxes and Penalties Unit,* as announced by Assistant to Attorney General in departmental circular of May 25, 1934, pursuant to EO 6639 of May 10, 1934. Abolished by administrative order of October 1942, and functions transferred to Tax, Claims, and Criminal Divisions, Department of Justice.

Bonneville Power Administration Established by the Secretary of the Interior pursuant to act of Aug. 20, 1937 (50 Stat. 731). Transferred to the Department of Energy by act of Aug. 4, 1977 (91 Stat. 578).

Boston National Historic Sites Commission Established by joint resolution of June 16, 1955 (69 Stat. 137). Terminated June 16, 1960, by act of Feb. 19, 1957 (71 Stat. 4).

Brazil-U.S. Defense Commission, Joint Established in May 1942 by agreement between the U.S. and Brazil. Terminated in September 1977 at direction of Brazilian Government.

Broadcast Bureau Merged with *Cable Television Bureau* to form Mass Media Bureau by Federal Communications Commission order, effective Nov. 30, 1982.

Broadcast Intelligence Service, Foreign *See* **Broadcast Monitoring Service, Foreign**

Broadcast Monitoring Service, Foreign Established in Federal Communications Commission by Presidential directive of Feb. 26, 1941. Renamed *Foreign Broadcast Intelligence Service* by FCC order of July 28, 1942. Transferred to *Department of War* by Secretarial order of Dec. 30, 1945. Act of May 3, 1945 (59 Stat. 110), provided for liquidation 60 days after Japanese armistice. Transferred to *Central Intelligence Group* Aug. 5, 1946, and renamed *Foreign Broadcast Information Service.*

Budget, Bureau of the Established by act of June 10, 1921 (42 Stat. 20), in the Department of the

Treasury under immediate direction of President. Transferred to Executive Office of the President by Reorg. Plan No. I of 1939, effective July 1, 1939. Reorganized by Reorg. Plan No. 2 of 1970, effective July 1, 1970, and renamed Office of Management and Budget.

Buildings Administration, Public Established as part of *Federal Works Agency* by Reorg. Plan No. I of 1939, effective July 1, 1939. Abolished by act of June 30, 1949 (63 Stat. 380), and functions transferred to General Services Administration.

Buildings Branch, Public Organized in *Procurement Division,* established in the Department of the Treasury by EO 6166 of June 10, 1933. Consolidated with *Branch of Buildings Management,* National Park Service, to form *Public Buildings Administration, Federal Works Agency,* under Reorg. Plan No. I of 1939, effective July 1, 1939.

Buildings Commission, Public Established by act of July 1, 1916 (39 Stat. 328). Abolished by EO 6166 of June 10, 1933, and functions transferred to *Office of National Parks, Buildings, and Reservations,* Department of the Interior. Functions transferred to *Public Buildings Administration, Federal Works Agency,* under Reorg. Plan No. I of 1939, effective July 1, 1939.

Buildings Management, Branch of Functions of National Park Service (except those relating to monuments and memorials) consolidated with *Public Buildings Branch, Procurement Division,* Department of the Treasury, to form *Public Buildings Administration, Federal Works Agency,* in accordance with Reorg. Plan No. I of 1939, effective July 1, 1939.

Buildings and Public Parks of the National Capital, Office of Public Established by act of Feb. 26, 1925 (43 Stat. 983), by consolidation of *Office of Public Buildings and Grounds* under Chief of Engineers, U.S. Army, and *Office of Superintendent of State, War, and Navy Department Buildings.* Abolished by EO 6166 of June 10, 1933, and functions transferred to *Office of National Parks, Buildings, and Reservations,* Department of the Interior.

Bureau. *See other part of title*

Business, Cabinet Committee on Small Established by Presidential letter of May 31, 1956. Dissolved January 1961.

Business Administration, Domestic and International *See* **Business and Defense Services Administration**

Business and Defense Services Administration Established by the Secretary of Commerce Oct. 1, 1953, and operated under Department Organization Order 40–1. Abolished by Department Organization Order 40–1A of Sept. 15, 1970, and functions transferred to *Bureau of Domestic Commerce.* Functions transferred to *Domestic and International Business Administration,* effective Nov. 17, 1972. *Administration* terminated by Secretary's order of Dec. 4, 1977, and functions assumed by *Industry and Trade Administration.*

Business Economics, Office of Established by the Secretary of Commerce Jan. 17, 1946. Renamed *Office of Economic Analysis* Dec. 1, 1953. Transferred to the *Administration of Social and Economic Statistics* along with Bureau of the Census and renamed Bureau of Economic Analysis on Jan. 1, 1972.

Business Operations, Bureau of International Established by the Secretary of Commerce Aug. 8, 1961, by Departmental Orders 173 and 174. Abolished by Departmental Order 182 of Feb. 1, 1963, which established *Bureau of International Commerce.* Functions transferred to *Domestic and International Business Administration,* effective Nov. 17, 1972.

Cable Television Bureau Merged with *Broadcast Bureau* by Federal Communications Commission order to form Mass Media Bureau, effective Nov. 30, 1982.

California Debris Commission Established by act of Mar. 1, 1893 (27 Stat. 507). Abolished by act of Nov. 17, 1986 (100 Stat. 4229), and functions transferred to the Secretary of the Interior.

Canal Zone Government Established by act of Aug. 24, 1912 (37 Stat. 561). Abolished by act of Sept. 27, 1979 (93 Stat. 454).

Capital Housing Authority, National Established by act of June 12, 1934 (48 Stat. 930). Made agency of District of Columbia government by act of Dec. 24, 1973 (87 Stat. 779), effective July 1, 1974.

Capital Park Commission, National Established by act of June 6, 1924 (43 Stat. 463). *National Capital Park and Planning Commission* named successor by act of Apr. 30, 1926 (44 Stat. 374). Functions transferred to National Capital Planning Commission by act of July 19, 1952 (66 Stat. 781).

Capital Park and Planning Commission, National *See* **Capital Park Commission, National**

Capital Regional Planning Council, National Established by act of July 19, 1952 (66 Stat. 785). Terminated by Reorg. Plan No. 5 of 1966, effective Sept. 8, 1966.

Capital Transportation Agency, National Established by act of July 14, 1960 (74 Stat 537). Authorized to establish rapid rail transit system by act of Sept. 8, 1965 (79 Stat. 663). Functions transferred to Washington Metropolitan Area Transit Authority by EO 11373 of Sept. 20, 1967.

Career Executive Board Established by EO 10758 of Mar. 4, 1958. Terminated July 1, 1959, and EO 10758 revoked by EO 10859 of Feb. 5, 1960.

Caribbean Organization Act of June 30, 1961 (75 Stat. 194), provided for acceptance by President of Agreement for the Establishment of the Caribbean Organization, signed at Washington, June 21, 1960. Article III of Agreement provided for termination of *Caribbean Commission,* authorized by Agreement signed Oct. 30, 1946, on first meeting of Caribbean Council, governing body of *Organization.* Terminated, effective Dec. 31, 1965, by resolution adopted by Council.

Cemeteries and Memorials in Europe, National Supervision transferred from *Department of War* to American Battle Monuments Commission by EO 6614 of Feb. 26, 1934, which transfer was deferred to May 21, 1934, by EO 6690 of Apr. 25, 1934.

Cemeteries and Parks, National *Department of War* functions regarding National Cemeteries and Parks located in continental U.S. transferred to *Office of National Parks, Buildings, and Reservations,* Department of the Interior, by EO 6166 of June 10, 1933.

Cemetery System, National Established in the *Veterans' Administration* by act of June 18, 1973 (87 Stat. 75). Redesignated as the National Cemetery Administration by act of Nov. 11, 1998 (112 Stat. 3337).

Censorship, Office of Established by EO 8985 of Dec. 19, 1941. Terminated by EO 9631 of Sept. 28, 1945.

Censorship Policy Board Established by EO 8985 of Dec. 19, 1941. Terminated by EO 9631 of Sept. 28, 1945.

Census, Bureau of the *See* **Census Office**

Census Office Established temporarily within the the Department of the Interior in accordance with act of Mar. 3, 1899. Established as a permanent office by act of Mar. 6, 1902. Transferred from the Department of the Interior to *Department of Commerce and Labor* by act of Feb. 14, 1903. Remained in the Department of Commerce under provisions of Reorganization Plan No. 5 of May 24, 1950, effective May 24, 1950.

Center. *See other part of title*

Central. *See other part of title*

Chemistry and Soils, Bureau of *See* **Agricultural and Industrial Chemistry, Bureau of**

Chesapeake Bay Center for Environmental Studies Established in 1965 in Annapolis, MD, as part of Smithsonian Institution by Secretarial order. Merged with *Radiation Biology Laboratory* by Secretarial Order July 1, 1983, to form Smithsonian Environmental Research Center.

Child Development, Office of *See* **Children's Bureau**

Children's Bureau Established by act of Apr. 9, 1912 (37 Stat. 79). Placed in the Department of Labor by act of Mar. 4, 1913 (37 Stat. 737). Transferred, with exception of child labor functions, to *Social Security Administration, Federal Security Agency,* by Reorg. Plan No. 2 of 1946, effective July 16, 1946. Continued under *Administration* when *Agency* functions assumed by the *Department of Health, Education, and Welfare.* Reassigned to *Welfare Administration* by Department reorganization of Jan. 28, 1963. Reassigned to *Social and Rehabilitation Service* by Department reorganization of Aug. 15, 1967. Reassigned to *Office of Child Development* by Department reorganization order of Sept. 17, 1969.

China, U.S. Court for Established by act of June 30, 1906 (34 Stat. 814). Transferred to the Department of Justice by EO 6166 of June 10, 1933, effective Mar. 2, 1934. Act of June 30, 1906, repealed effective Sept. 1, 1948 (62 Stat. 992).

Christopher Columbus Quincentenary Jubilee Commission Established by act of Aug. 7, 1984 (98 Stat. 1257). Terminated pursuant to terms of act.

Civil defense. *See* **Defense**

Civil Rights, Commission on Established by act of Sept. 9, 1957 (71 Stat. 634). Terminated in 1983 and reestablished by act of Nov. 30, 1983 (97 Stat. 1301). Renamed United States Commission on Civil Rights by act of Nov. 2, 1994 (108 Stat. 4683).

Civil Service Commission, U.S. Established by act of Jan. 16, 1883 (22 Stat. 403). Redesignated as Merit Systems Protection Board and functions transferred to Board and Office of Personnel Management by Reorg. Plan No. 2 of 1978, effective Jan. 1, 1979.

Civil War Centennial Commission Established by act of Sept. 7, 1957 (71 Stat. 626). Terminated May 1, 1966, pursuant to terms of act.

Civilian Conservation Corps Established by act of June 28, 1937 (50 Stat. 319). Made part of *Federal Security Agency* by Reorg. Plan No. I of 1939, effective July 1, 1939. Liquidation provided for by act of July 2, 1942 (56 Stat. 569), not later than June 30, 1943.

Civilian Health and Medical Program of the United States, Office of Established as field activity in the Department of Defense in 1974. Functions consolidated into the TRICARE Management Activity in November 1997 by Defense Reform Initiative.

Civilian Production Administration Established by EO 9638 of Oct. 4, 1945. Consolidated with other agencies to form *Office of Temporary Controls, Office for Emergency Management,* by EO 9809 of Dec. 12, 1946.

Civilian Service Awards Board, Distinguished Established by EO 10717 of June 27, 1957. Terminated by EO 12014 of Oct. 19, 1977, and functions transferred to *U.S. Civil Service Commission.*

Claims, U.S. Court of Established Feb. 25, 1855 (10 Stat. 612). Abolished by act of Apr. 2, 1982 (96 Stat. 26) and trial jurisdiction transferred to *U.S. Claims Court* and appellate functions merged with those of *U.S. Court of Customs and Patent Appeals* to form U.S. Court of Appeals for the Federal Circuit. *U.S. Claims Court* renamed U.S. Court of Federal Claims by act of Oct. 29, 1992 (106 Stat. 4516).

Claims Commission of the United States, International Established in the Department of State by act of Mar. 10, 1950 (64 Stat. 12). Abolished by Reorg. Plan No. 1 of 1954, effective July 1, 1954, and functions transferred to Foreign Claims Settlement Commission of the United States.

Claims Settlement Commission of the United States, Foreign Established by Reorg. Plan No. 1 of 1954, effective July 1, 1954. Transferred to the Department of Justice by act of Mar. 14, 1980 (94 Stat. 96).

Clark Sesquicentennial Commission, George Rogers Established by Public Resolution 51 (45 Stat. 723). Expenditures ordered administered by the Department of the Interior by EO 6166 of June 10, 1933.

Classification Review Committee, Interagency Established by EO 11652 of Mar. 8, 1972. Abolished by EO 12065 of June 28, 1978.

Clemency Board, Presidential Established in Executive Office of the President by EO 11803 of Sept. 16, 1974. Final recommendations submitted to President Sept. 15, 1975, and *Board* terminated by EO 11878 of Sept. 10, 1975.

Coal Commission, National Bituminous Established under authority of act of Aug. 30, 1935 (49 Stat. 992). Abolished by Reorg. Plan No. II of 1939, effective July 1, 1939, and functions transferred to *Bituminous Coal Division,* Department of the Interior.

Coal Consumers' Counsel, Office of the Bituminous Established by act of Apr. 11, 1941 (55 Stat. 134), renewing provisions of act of Apr. 23, 1937 (50 Stat. 72) for 2 years to continue functions of *Consumers' Counsel Division,* Department of the Interior. Functions continued by acts of Apr. 24, 1943 (57 Stat. 68), and May 21, 1943 (57 Stat. 82). Terminated Aug. 24, 1943.

Coal Division, Bituminous Established July 1, 1939, by Secretary of the Interior Order 1394 of June 16, 1939, as amended by Order 1399, of July 5, 1939, pursuant to act of Apr. 3, 1939 (53 Stat. 562) and Reorg. Plan No. II of 1939, effective July 1, 1939. Administered functions vested in *National Bituminous Coal Commission* by act of Apr. 23, 1937 (50 Stat. 72). Act extended to Aug. 24, 1943, on which date it expired.

Coal Labor Board, Bituminous Established by act of July 12, 1921 (42 Stat. 140). Abolished as result of U.S. Supreme Court decision, May 18, 1936, in case of *Carter* v. *Carter Coal Company et al.*

Coal Mine Safety Board of Review, Federal Established by act of July 16, 1952 (66 Stat. 697). Inactive after Mar. 30, 1970, pursuant to act of Dec. 30, 1969 (83 Stat. 803).

Coal Mines Administration Established by the Secretary of the Interior July 1, 1943. Abolished by Secretary's Order 1977 of Aug. 16, 1944, as amended by Order 1982 of Aug. 31, 1944, and functions assumed by *Solid Fuels Administration for War. Administration* reestablished in the Department of the Interior by EO 9728 of May 21, 1946. Terminated June 30, 1947, by act of Mar. 27, 1942 (56 Stat. 176).

Coal Research, Office of Established in the Department of the Interior by act of July 7, 1960 (74 Stat. 336). Functions transferred to *Energy Research and Development Administration* by act of Oct. 11, 1974 (88 Stat. 1237).

Coast and Geodetic Survey *See* **Coast Survey**

Coast Guard, U.S. Transferred from the Department of the Treasury to the Department of the Navy by EO 8929 of Nov. 1, 1941. Returned to the Department of the Treasury by EO 9666 of Dec. 28, 1945. Transferred to the Department of Transportation by act of Oct. 15, 1966 (80 Stat. 931).

Coast Survey Established by act of Feb. 10, 1807 (2 Stat. 413). Redesignated as *Coast and Geodetic Survey* by act of June 20, 1878 (20 Stat. 206). Transferred to *Environmental Science Services Administration* by Reorg. Plan No. 2 of 1965, effective July 13, 1965.

Codification Board Established by act of June 19, 1937 (50 Stat. 304). Abolished by Reorg. Plan No. II of 1939, effective July 1, 1939, and functions transferred to *Division of the Federal Register.*

Coinage, Joint Commission on the Established by act of July 23, 1965 (79 Stat. 258). Expired Jan. 4, 1975, pursuant to act of Oct. 6, 1972 (88 Stat. 776).

Collection of Fine Arts, National Established within Smithsonian Institution by act of Mar. 24, 1937 (50 Stat. 51). Renamed National Museum of American Art in Smithsonian Institution by act of Oct. 13, 1980 (94 Stat. 1884).

Columbia Institution for the Instruction of the Deaf and Dumb, and the Blind Established by act of Feb. 16, 1857 (11 Stat. 161). Renamed *Columbia Institution for the Instruction of the Deaf and Dumb* by act of Feb. 23, 1865 (13 Stat. 436). Renamed *Columbia Institution for the Deaf* by act of Mar. 4, 1911 (36 Stat. 1422). Renamed *Gallaudet College* by act of June 18, 1954 (68 Stat. 265). Functions of the *Department of Health, Education, and Welfare* transferred to the Department of Education by act of Oct. 17, 1979 (93 Stat. 695). Renamed Gallaudet University by act of Aug. 4, 1986 (100 Stat. 781).

Commander in Chief, U.S. Fleet, and Chief of Naval Operations Duties of two positions prescribed by EO 8984 of Dec. 18, 1941. Combined under one officer by EO 9096 of Mar. 12, 1942.

Commerce, Bureau of Domestic *See* **Business and Defense Services Administration**

Commerce, Bureau of Foreign Established by the Secretary of Commerce Oct. 12, 1953, by Reorg. Plan No. 5 of 1950, effective May 24, 1950. Abolished by department order of Aug. 7, 1961, and functions vested in *Bureau of International Programs* and *Bureau of International Business Operations.*

Commerce, Bureau of Foreign and Domestic Established by act of Aug. 23, 1912 (37 Stat. 407). Functions reassigned to other offices of the Department of Commerce due to internal reorganizations.

Commerce, Bureau of International *See* **Business Operations, Bureau of International**

Commerce Service, Foreign Established in *Bureau of Foreign and Domestic Commerce,* Department of Commerce, by act of Mar. 3, 1927 (44 Stat. 1394). Transferred to the Department of State as part of

Foreign Service by Reorg. Plan No. II of 1939, effective July 1, 1939.

Commercial Company, U.S. Established Mar. 27, 1942, as subsidiary of *Reconstruction Finance Corporation.* Transferred to *Office of Economic Warfare* by EO 9361 of July 15, 1943. *Office* consolidated into *Foreign Economic Administration* by EO 9380 of Sept. 25, 1943. Functions returned to *Corporation* by EO 9630 of Sept. 27, 1945, until June 30, 1948.

Commercial Policy, Executive Committee on Established by Presidential letter of Nov. 11, 1933, to Secretary of State. Abolished by EO 9461 of Aug. 7, 1944.

Commercial Standards Division Transferred with *Division of Simplified Trade Practice* from *National Bureau of Standards* to the Secretary of Commerce by Reorg. Plan No. 3 of 1946, effective July 16, 1946, to permit reassignment to *Office of Domestic Commerce.* Functions transferred to *National Bureau of Standards* by the Department of Commerce Order 90, June 7, 1963, pursuant to Reorg. Plan No. 5 of 1950, effective May 24, 1950.

Commission. *See other part of title*

Committee. *See also other part of title*

Committee Management Secretariat Established in the Office of Management and Budget Jan. 5, 1973, by act of Oct. 6, 1972 (86 Stat. 772). Functions transferred to General Services Administrator by Reorg. Plan No. 1 of 1977, effective Apr. 1, 1978. Reassigned to the *National Archives and Records Service* by GSA order of Feb. 22, 1979. Transferred in Archives to Office of the Federal Register by GSA order of Oct. 14, 1980. Transferred to Office of the Archivist of the United States by GSA order of Sept. 24, 1982. Reassigned to Office of Program Initiatives, GSA, by GSA order of May 18, 1984. Transferred to Office of Management Services, GSA, by GSA order of Apr. 7, 1986.

Commodities Corporation, Federal Surplus *See* **Relief Corporation, Federal Surplus**

Commodity Credit Corporation Organized by EO 6340 of Oct. 16, 1933, and managed in close affiliation with *Reconstruction Finance Corporation.* Transferred to the Department of Agriculture by Reorg. Plan No. I of 1939, effective July 1, 1939.

Commodity Exchange Administration *See* **Grain Futures Administration**

Commodity Exchange Authority *See* **Grain Futures Administration**

Commodity Exchange Commission Established by act of Sept. 21, 1922 (42 Stat. 998). Functions transferred to Commodity Futures Trading Commission by act of Oct. 23, 1974 (88 Stat. 1414).

Commodity Stabilization Service Established in the Department of Agriculture Nov. 2, 1953, by Secretary's Memorandum 1320, supp. 4. Renamed Agricultural Stabilization and Conservation Service by Secretary's Memorandum 1458 of June 14, 1961, effective June 5, 1961.

Communication Agency, International *See Information Agency, U.S.*

Communications Program, Joint Tactical Combined with *Joint Interoperability of the Tactical Command and Control Systems Programs* to form Joint Tactical Command, Control, and Communications Agency in July 1984, pursuant to DOD Directive 5154.28.

Community Development Corporation Established in the Department of Housing and Urban Development by act of Dec. 31, 1970 (84 Stat. 1791). Renamed *New Community Development Corporation* by act of Aug. 22, 1974 (88 Stat. 725). Abolished Nov. 30, 1983, by act of Nov. 30, 1983 (97 Stat. 1238), and functions transferred to Assistant Secretary for Community Planning and Development, Department of Housing and Urban Development.

Community Development Corporation, New *See* **Community Development Corporation**

Community Facilities, Bureau of Established in 1945 by *Federal Works Administrator.* Transferred by act of June 30, 1949 (63 Stat. 380), to General Services Administration, functioning as *Community Facilities Service.* Certain functions transferred to various agencies, including the Department of the Interior, *Housing and Home Finance Agency,* and *Federal Security Agency* by Reorg. Plans Nos. 15, 16, and 17 of 1950, effective May 24, 1950.

Community Facilities Administration Established in *Housing and Home Finance Agency* by Administrator's Organizational Order 1 of Dec. 23, 1954. Terminated by act of Sept. 9, 1965 (79 Stat. 667), and functions transferred to the Department of Housing and Urban Development.

Community Organization, Committee on Established in *Office of Defense Health and Welfare Services* Sept. 10, 1941. Functions transferred to *Federal Security Agency* by EO 9338 of Apr. 29, 1943.

Community Relations Service Established in the Department of Commerce by act of July 2, 1964 (78 Stat. 241). Transferred to the Department of Justice by Reorg. Plan No. 1 of 1966, effective Apr. 22, 1966.

Community Service, Commission on National and Established by act of Nov. 16, 1990 (104 Stat. 3168). Abolished by act of Sept. 21, 1993, and functions vested in the Board of Directors or the Executive Director prior to Oct. 1, 1993, transferred to the Corporation for National and Community Service (107 Stat. 873, 888).

Community Services Administration Established by act of Jan. 4, 1975 (88 Stat. 2291) as successor to *Office of Economic Opportunity.* Abolished as independent agency through repeal of act of Aug. 20, 1964 (except titles VIII and X of such act) by act of Aug. 13, 1981 (95 Stat. 519).

Community Services Administration Functions concerning Legal Services Program transferred to Legal Services Corporation by act of July 25, 1974 (88 Stat. 389). Renamed *Public Services*

Administration by *Health, Education, and Welfare* departmental notice of Nov. 3, 1976. Transferred to *Office of Human Development* by Secretary's reorganization of Mar. 8, 1977 (42 FR 13262).

Community War Services Established in *Office of the Administrator* under EO 9338 of Apr. 29, 1943, and *Federal Security Agency* order. Terminated Dec. 31, 1946, by act of July 26, 1946 (60 Stat. 695).

Conciliation Service, U.S. Established by act of Mar. 4, 1913 (37 Stat. 738). Functions transferred to Federal Mediation and Conciliation Service, established by act of June 23, 1947 (61 Stat. 153).

Conference on Security and Cooperation in Europe Renamed Organization for Security and Cooperation in Europe by EO 13029, Dec. 3, 1996 (61 FR 64591).

Consolidated Farm Service Agency Established by act of Oct. 13, 1994 (108 Stat. 3214). Renamed Farm Service Agency (61 FR 1109), effective Jan. 16, 1996.

Constitution, Commission on the Bicentennial of the United States Established by act of Sept. 29, 1983, as amended (97 Stat. 722). Terminated by act of Dec. 3, 1991 (105 Stat. 1232).

Constitution, transfer of functions *See* **Statutes at Large and other matters**

Construction, Collective Bargaining Committee in Established by EO 11849 of Apr. 1, 1975. Inactive since Jan. 7, 1976. Formally abolished by EO 12110 of Dec. 28, 1978.

Construction, Equipment and Repairs, Bureau of Established in the Department of the Navy by act of Aug. 31, 1842 (5 Stat. 579). Abolished by act of July 5, 1862 (12 Stat. 510), and functions distributed among *Bureau of Equipment and Recruiting, Bureau of Construction and Repair,* and *Bureau of Steam Engineering.*

Construction Branch Established in the Department of the Treasury in 1853 and designated *Bureau of Construction* under control of *Office of Supervising Architect* by Sept. 30, 1855. *Office* incorporated into *Public Buildings Branch, Procurement Division,* by EO 6166 of June 10, 1933. Transferred to *Federal Works Agency* by Reorg. Plan No. I of 1939, effective July 1, 1939, when *Public Buildings Branch* of *Procurement Division, Bureau of Buildings Management,* National Park Service, Department of the Interior—so far as latter concerned with operation of public buildings for other departments or agencies—and *U.S. Housing Corporation* consolidated with *Public Buildings Administration, Federal Works Agency.*

Construction Industry Stabilization Committee Established by EO 11588 of Mar. 29, 1971. Abolished by EO 11788 of June 18, 1974.

Construction and Repair, Bureau of Established by act of July 5, 1862 (12 Stat. 510), replacing *Bureau of Construction, Equipment and Repairs.* Abolished by act of June 20, 1940 (54 Stat. 492), and functions transferred to *Bureau of Ships.*

Consumer Advisory Council Established by EO 11136 of Jan. 3, 1964. *Office of Consumer Affairs* established in Executive Office of the President by EO 11583 of Feb. 24, 1971, and Council reestablished in *Office.*

Consumer Affairs, Office of Established by EO 11583 of Feb. 24, 1971. Transferred to the *Department of Health, Education, and Welfare* by EO 11702 of Jan. 25, 1973.

Consumer Affairs Staff, National Business Council for Established in the Department of Commerce by departmental organization order of Dec. 16, 1971. Terminated by departmental order of Dec. 6, 1973, due to lack of funding.

Consumer agencies Consumer agencies of *National Emergency Council* and *National Recovery Administration* reorganized and functions transferred, together with those of *Consumers' Advisory Board, NRA,* and *Cabinet Committee on Price Policy,* to *Consumers' Division, NRA,* by EO 7120 of July 30, 1935. *Division* transferred to the Department of Labor by EO 7252 of Dec. 21, 1935. Transferred to *Division of Consumers' Counsel, Agricultural Adjustment Administration,* Department of Agriculture, by Secretary of Labor letter of Aug. 30, 1938, to the Secretary of Agriculture. Continued as *Consumer Standards Project* until June 30, 1941. Research on consumer standards continued by *Consumer Standards Section, Consumers' Counsel Division,* transferred to *Agricultural Marketing Administration* by administrative order of Feb. 28, 1942. Other project activities discontinued.

Consumer Cooperative Bank, National Established by act of Aug. 20, 1978 (92 Stat. 499). Removed from mixed-ownership, Government corporation status by acts of Sept. 13, 1982 (96 Stat. 1062) and Jan. 12, 1983 (96 Stat. 2478).

Consumer Interests, President's Committee on Established by EO 11136 of Jan. 3, 1964. Abolished by EO 11583 of Feb. 24, 1971.

Consumer and Marketing Service Established by the Secretary of Agriculture Feb. 2, 1965. Renamed Agricultural Marketing Service Apr. 2, 1972, by Secretary's order and certain functions transferred to Animal and Plant Health Inspection Service.

Consumers' Counsel Established in *National Bituminous Coal Commission* by act of Aug. 30, 1935 (49 Stat. 993). Office abolished by Reorg. Plan No. II of 1939, effective July 1, 1939, and functions transferred to Office of Solicitor, Department of the Interior, to function as *Consumers' Counsel Division* under direction of the Secretary of the Interior. Functions transferred to *Office of the Bituminous Coal Consumers' Counsel* June 1941 by act of Apr. 11, 1941 (55 Stat. 134).

Consumers' Counsel Division *See* **Consumers' Counsel**

Consumers' Counsel, Division of Established by act of May 12, 1933 (48 Stat. 31). Transferred by order of the Secretary of Agriculture from *Agricultural Adjustment Administration* to supervision of *Director of Marketing,* effective Feb. 1, 1940. Transferred to

Agricultural Marketing Administration by administrative order of Feb. 28, 1942.

Consumers' Problems, Adviser on *See* **Consumer agencies**

Contract Committee Government *See* **Contract Compliance, Committee on Government**

Contract Compliance, Committee on Government Established by EO 10308 of Dec. 3, 1951. Abolished by EO 10479 of Aug. 13, 1953, which established successor *Government Contract Committee.* Abolished by EO 10925 of Mar. 6, 1961, and records and property transferred to *President's Committee on Equal Employment Opportunity.*

Contract Settlement, Office of Established by act of July 1, 1944 (58 Stat. 651). Transferred to *Office of War Mobilization and Reconversion* by act of Oct. 3, 1944 (58 Stat. 785). Terminated by EO 9809 of Dec. 12, 1946, and Reorg. Plan No. 1 of 1947, effective July 1, 1947, and functions transferred to the Department of the Treasury. Functions transferred to General Services Administration by act of June 30, 1949 (63 Stat. 380).

Contract Settlement Advisory Board Established by act of July 1, 1944 (58 Stat. 651). Transferred to the Department of the Treasury by EO 9809 of Dec. 12, 1946, and by Reorg. Plan No. 1 of 1947, effective July 1, 1947. Transferred to General Services Administration by act of June 30, 1949 (63 Stat. 380) and established as *Contract Review Board.* Renamed Board of Contract Appeals in 1961 by Administrator's order. Board established as independent entity within General Services Administration Feb. 27, 1979, pursuant to act of Nov. 1, 1978 (92 Stat. 2383).

Contract Settlement Appeal Board, Office of Established by act of July 1, 1944 (58 Stat. 651). Transferred to the Department of the Treasury by EO 9809 of Dec. 12, 1946, and by Reorg. Plan No. 1 of 1947, effective July 1, 1947. Functions transferred to General Services Administration by act of June 30, 1949 (63 Stat. 380). Abolished by act of July 14, 1952 (66 Stat. 627).

Contract Termination Board, Joint Established Nov. 12, 1943, by *Director of War Mobilization.* Functions assumed by *Office of Contract Settlement.*

Contracts Division, Public Established in the Department of Labor to administer act of June 30, 1936 (49 Stat. 2036). Consolidated with Wage and Hour Division by Secretarial order of Aug. 21, 1942. Absorbed by Wage and Hour Division by Secretarial order of May 1971.

Cooperation Administration, International Established by Department of State Delegation of Authority 85 of June 30, 1955, pursuant to EO 10610 of May 9, 1955. Abolished by act of Sept. 4, 1961 (75 Stat. 446), and functions redelegated to Agency for International Development pursuant to Presidential letter of Sept. 30, 1961, and EO 10973 of Nov. 3, 1961.

Cooperative State Research Service Established in the Department of Agriculture. Incorporated into Cooperative State, Research, Education, and Extension Service under Department of Agriculture reorganization in 1995.

Coordinating Service, Federal *Office of Chief Coordinator* created by Executive order promulgated in *Bureau of the Budget* Circular 15, July 27, 1921, and duties enlarged by other *Bureau* circulars. Abolished by EO 6166 of June 10, 1933. Contract form, Federal traffic, and surplus property functions transferred to *Procurement Division* by order of the Secretary of the Treasury, approved by President Oct. 9, 1933, issued pursuant to EO's 6166 of June 10, 1933, and 6224 of July 27, 1933.

Copyright Royalty Tribunal Established as an independent entity within the legislative branch by act of Oct. 19, 1976 (90 Stat. 2594). Abolished by act of Dec. 17, 1993 (107 Stat. 2304), and functions transferred to copyright arbitration royalty panels.

Copyrighted Works, National Commission on New Technological Uses of Established by act of Dec. 31, 1974 (88 Stat. 1873). Terminated Sept. 29, 1978, pursuant to terms of act.

Corporate Payments Abroad, Task Force on Questionable Established by Presidential memorandum of Mar. 31, 1976. Terminated Dec. 31, 1976, pursuant to terms of memorandum.

Corporation, Federal Facilities Established in the Department of the Treasury by EO 10539 of June 22, 1954. Placed under supervision of Director appointed by General Services Administrator by EO 10720 of July 11, 1957. Dissolved by act of Aug. 30, 1961 (75 Stat. 418), and functions transferred to Administrator of General Services.

Corregidor-Bataan Memorial Commission Established by act of Aug. 5, 1953 (67 Stat. 366). Terminated May 6, 1967, by act of Dec. 23, 1963 (77 Stat. 477).

Cost Accounting Standards Board Established by act of Aug. 15, 1970 (84 Stat. 796). Terminated Sept. 30, 1980, due to lack of funding. Reestablished by act of Nov. 17, 1988 (102 Stat. 4059).

Cost of Living Council Established by EO 11615 of Aug. 15, 1971. Abolished by EO 11788 of June 18, 1974.

Cotton Stabilization Corporation Organized June 1930 under laws of Delaware by *Federal Farm Board* pursuant to act of June 15, 1929 (46 Stat. 11). Certificate of dissolution filed with Corporation Commission of Delaware Dec. 27, 1934.

Council. *See other part of title*

Counter-. *See other part of title*

Courts Under act of Aug. 7, 1939 (53 Stat. 1223), and revised June 25, 1948 (62 Stat. 913), to provide for administration of U.S. courts, administrative jurisdiction over all continental and territorial courts transferred to Administrative Office of the U.S. Courts, including U.S. courts of appeals and district courts, District Court for the Territory of Alaska, U.S. District Court for the District of the Canal Zone, District Court of Guam, District Court of the Virgin

Islands, Court of Claims, Court of Customs and Patent Appeals, and Customs Courts.

Credit Unions, Bureau of Federal *See* **Credit Union System, Federal**

Credit Union System, Federal Established by act of June 26, 1934 (48 Stat. 1216), to be administered by *Farm Credit Administration.* Transferred to Federal Deposit Insurance Corporation by EO 9148 of Apr. 27, 1942, and Reorg. Plan No. 1 of 1947, effective July 1, 1947. Functions transferred to *Bureau of Federal Credit Unions, Federal Security Agency,* established by act of June 29, 1948 (62 Stat. 1091). Functions transferred to the *Department of Health, Education, and Welfare* by Reorg. Plan No. 1 of 1953, effective Apr. 11, 1953. Functions transferred to National Credit Union Administration by act of Mar. 10, 1970 (84 Stat. 49).

Crime, National Council on Organized Established by EO 11534 of June 4, 1970. Terminated by EO 12110 of Dec. 28, 1978.

Critical Materials Council, National Established within Executive Office of the President by act of July 31, 1984 (98 Stat. 1250). *Office* abolished in September 1993 due to lack of funding and functions transferred to the Office of Science and Technology Policy.

Crop Production Loan Office Authorized by Presidential letters of July 26, 1918, and July 26, 1919, to the Secretary of Agriculture. Further authorized by act of Mar. 3, 1921 (41 Stat. 1347). Transferred to Farm Credit Administration by EO 6084 of Mar. 27, 1933.

Cultural Center, National Established in Smithsonian Institution by act of Sept. 2, 1958 (72 Stat. 1698). Renamed John F. Kennedy Center for the Performing Arts by act of Jan. 23, 1964 (78 Stat. 4).

Customs, Bureau of Functions relating to award of numbers to undocumented vessels, vested in *Collectors of Customs,* transferred to Commandant of Coast Guard by EO 9083 of Feb. 27, 1942. Transfer made permanent by Reorg. Plan No. 3 of 1946, effective July 16, 1946. Redesignated U.S. Customs Service by the Department of the Treasury Order 165–23 of Apr. 4, 1973.

Customs Court, U.S. Formerly established as Board of General Appraisers by act of June 10, 1890 (26 Stat. 136). Renamed *U.S. Customs Court* by act of May 26, 1926 (44 Stat. 669). Renamed U.S. Court of International Trade by act of Oct. 10, 1980 (94 Stat. 1727).

Customs and Patent Appeals, U.S. Court of Established by act of Mar. 2, 1929 (45 Stat. 1475). Abolished by act of Apr. 2, 1982 (96 Stat. 28) and functions merged with appellate functions of *U.S. Court of Claims* to form U.S. Court of Appeals for the Federal Circuit.

Dairy Industry, Bureau of *Bureau of Dairying* established in the Department of Agriculture by act of May 29, 1924 (43 Stat. 243). *Bureau of Dairy Industry* designation first appeared in act of May 11, 1926 (44 Stat. 499). Functions transferred to Agricultural Research Service by Secretary's Memorandum 1320, supp. 4, of Nov. 2, 1953.

Defense, Advisory Commission to the Council of National *See* **Defense, Council of National**

Defense, Council of National Established by act of Aug. 29, 1916 (39 Stat. 649). *Advisory Commission*—composed of Advisers on Industrial Production, Industrial Materials, Employment, Farm Products, Price Stabilization, Transportation, and Consumer Protection—established by *Council* pursuant to act and approved by President May 29, 1940. *Commission* decentralized by merging divisions with newly created national defense units. Agencies evolved from *Commission,* except *Office of Agricultural War Relations* and *Office of Price Administration,* made units of *Office for Emergency Management. Council* inactive.

Defense, Office of Civilian Established in *Office for Emergency Management* by EO 8757 of May 20, 1941. Terminated by EO 9562 of June 4, 1945.

Defense Administration, Federal Civil Established in *Office for Emergency Management* by EO 10186 of Dec. 1, 1950; subsequently established as independent agency by act of Jan. 12, 1951 (64 Stat. 1245). Functions transferred to *Office of Defense and Civilian Mobilization* by Reorg. Plan No. 1 of 1958, effective July 1, 1958.

Defense Advanced Research Projects Agency Established as a separate agency of the Department of Defense by DOD Directive 5105.41 dated July 25, 1978. Renamed *Advanced Research Projects Agency* by order of the Secretary of Defense dated July 13, 1993. Reestablished by P.L. 104–106, Feb. 10, 1996 (110 Stat. 406).

Defense Advisory Council, Civil Established by act of Jan. 12, 1951 (64 Stat. 1245). Transferred to *Office of Defense and Civilian Mobilization* by Reorg. Plan No. 1 of 1958, effective July 1, 1958.

Defense Aid Reports, Division of Established in *Office for Emergency Management* by EO 8751 of May 2, 1941. Abolished by EO 8926 of Oct. 28, 1941, which created *Office of Lend-Lease Administration.*

Defense Air Transportation Administration Established Nov. 12, 1951, by Department of Commerce Order 137. Abolished by Amendment 3 of Sept. 13, 1962, to Department Order 128 (revised) and functions transferred to *Office of the Under Secretary of Commerce for Transportation.*

Defense Atomic Support Agency Renamed *Defense Nuclear Agency* by General Order No. 1 of July 1, 1971.

Defense Audiovisual Agency Established by DOD Directive 5040.1 of June 12, 1979. Abolished by Secretary's memorandum of Apr. 19, 1985, and functions assigned to the military departments.

Defense Audit Service Established by DOD Directive of Oct. 14, 1976. Abolished by Deputy Secretary's memorandum of Nov. 2, 1982, and functions transferred to Office of the Inspector General.

Defense Civil Preparedness Agency Functions transferred from the Department of Defense to the Federal Emergency Management Agency by EO 12148 of July 20, 1979.

Defense and Civilian Mobilization Board Established by EO 10773 of July 1, 1938. Redesignated *Civil and Defense Mobilization Board* by act of Aug. 26, 1958 (72 Stat. 861). Abolished by *Office of Emergency Preparedness* Circular 1200.1 of Oct. 31, 1962.

Defense Communications Agency Established by direction of the Secretary of Defense on May 12, 1960. Renamed Defense Information Systems Agency by DOD Directive 5105.19 dated June 25, 1991.

Defense Communications Board Established by EO 8546 of Sept. 24, 1940. Renamed *Board of War Communications* by EO 9183 of June 15, 1942. Abolished by EO 9831 of Feb. 24, 1947, and property transferred to Federal Communications Commission.

Defense Coordinating Board, Civil Established by EO 10611 of May 11, 1955. EO 10611 revoked by EO 10773 of July 1, 1958.

Defense Electric Power Administration Established by Order 2605 of Dec. 4, 1950 of the Secretary of the Interior. Abolished June 30, 1953, by Secretary's Order 2721 of May 7, 1953. Reestablished by Departmental Manual Release No. 253 of Aug. 6, 1959. Terminated by Departmental Manual Release No. 1050 of Jan. 10, 1977.

Defense Fisheries Administration Established by Order 2605 of Dec. 4, 1950 of the Secretary of the Interior. Abolished June 30, 1953, by Secretary's Order 2722 of May 13, 1953.

Defense Health and Welfare Services, Office of Established by EO 8890 of Sept. 3, 1941. Terminated by EO 9338 of Apr. 29, 1943, and functions transferred to *Federal Security Agency*.

Defense Homes Corporation Incorporated pursuant to President's letter to the Secretary of the Treasury of Oct. 18, 1940. Transferred to *Federal Public Housing Authority* by EO 9070 of Feb. 24, 1942.

Defense Housing Coordinator Office established July 21, 1940, by *Advisory Commission to Council of National Defense*. Functions transferred to *Division of Defense Housing Coordination, Office for Emergency Management*, by EO 8632 of Jan. 11, 1941.

Defense Housing Division, Mutual Ownership Established by Administrator of *Federal Works Agency* under provisions of act of June 28, 1941 (55 Stat. 361). Functions transferred to *Federal Public Housing Authority, National Housing Agency*, by EO 9070 of Feb. 24, 1942.

Defense Investigative Service Established by the Secretary of Defense Jan. 1, 1972. Renamed Defense Security Service in November 1997 by Defense Reform Initiative.

Defense Manpower Administration Established by the Secretary of Labor by General Order 48, pursuant to EO 10161 of Sept. 9, 1950, and Reorg. Plan No. 6 of 1950, effective May 24, 1950. General Order 48 revoked by General Order 63 of Aug. 25, 1953, which established *Office of Manpower Administration* in Department.

Defense Mapping Agency Established as a the Department of Defense agency in 1972. Functions transferred to the National Imagery and Mapping Agency by P.L. 104–201, Sept. 23, 1996 (110 Stat. 2677).

Defense Materials Procurement Agency Established by EO 10281 of Aug. 28, 1951. Abolished by EO 10480 of Aug. 14, 1953, and functions transferred to General Services Administration.

Defense Materials Service *See* **Emergency Procurement Service**

Defense Mediation Board, National Established by EO 8716 of Mar. 19, 1941. Terminated on creation of *National War Labor Board, Office for Emergency Management* by EO 9017 of Jan. 12, 1942. Transferred to the Department of Labor by EO 9617 of Sept. 19, 1945. *Board* terminated by EO 9672 of Dec. 31, 1945, which established *National Wage Stabilization Board* in the Department of Labor. Terminated by EO 9809 of Dec. 12, 1946, and functions transferred to the Secretary of Labor and the Department of the Treasury, effective Feb. 24, 1947.

Defense Medical Programs Activity Functions consolidated into the TRICARE Management Activity in November 1997 by Defense Reform Initiative.

Defense Minerals Administration Established by Order 2605 of Dec. 4, 1950 of the Secretary of the Interior. Functions assigned to *Defense Materials Procurement Agency*. Functions of exploration for critical and strategic minerals redelegated to the Secretary of the Interior and administered by *Defense Minerals Exploration Administration* by Secretary's Order 2726 of June 30, 1953. Termination of program announced by Secretary June 6, 1958. Certain activities continued in *Office of Minerals Exploration*, Department of the Interior.

Defense Minerals Exploration Administration *See* **Defense Minerals Administration**

Defense Mobilization, Office of Established in Executive Office of the President by EO 10193 of Dec. 16, 1950. Superseded by *Office of Defense Mobilization* established by Reorg. Plan No. 3 of 1953, effective June 12, 1953, which assumed functions of former *Office, National Security Resources Board*, and critical materials stockpiling functions of Army, Navy, Air Force, and Interior Secretaries and of *Army and Navy Munitions Board*. Consolidated with *Federal Civil Defense Administration* into *Office of Defense and Civilian Mobilization* by Reorg. Plan No. 1 of 1958, effective July 1, 1958, and offices of Director and Deputy Director terminated.

Defense Mobilization Board Established by EO 10200 of Jan. 3, 1951, and restated in EO 10480 of

Aug. 14, 1953. Terminated by EO 10773 of July 1, 1958.

Defense Nuclear Agency Established in 1971. Renamed *Defense Special Weapons Agency* by DOD Directive 5105.31 of June 14, 1995.

Defense Plant Corporation Established by act of June 25, 1940 (54 Stat. 572). Transferred from *Federal Loan Agency* to the Department of Commerce by EO 9071 of Feb. 24, 1942. Returned to *Federal Loan Agency* pursuant to act of Feb. 24, 1945 (59 Stat. 5). Dissolved by act of June 30, 1945 (59 Stat. 310), and functions transferred to *Reconstruction Finance Corporation.*

Defense Plants Administration, Small Established by act of July 31, 1951 (65 Stat. 131). Terminated July 31, 1953, by act of June 30, 1953 (67 Stat. 131). Functions relating to liquidation transferred to Small Business Administration by EO 10504 of Dec. 1, 1953.

Defense Production Administration Established by EO 10200 of Jan. 3, 1951. Terminated by EO 10433 of Feb. 4, 1953, and functions transferred to *Office of Defense Mobilization.*

Defense Property Disposal Service Renamed Defense Reutilization and Marketing Service by Defense Logistics Agency General Order 10–85, effective July 1, 1985.

Defense Prisoner of War/Missing in Action Office Established by DOD Directive 5110.10, July 16, 1993. Renamed Defense Prisoner of War/Missing Personnel Office by Secretary of Defense memorandum of May 30, 1996.

Defense Public Works Division Established in *Public Works Administration.* Transferred to *Office of Federal Works Administrator* by administrative order of July 16, 1941. Abolished by administrative order of Mar. 6, 1942, and functions transferred to *Office of Chief Engineer, Federal Works Agency.*

Defense Purchases, Office for the Coordination of National Established by order of *Council of National Defense,* approved June 27, 1940. Order revoked Jan. 7, 1941, and records transferred to Executive Office of the President.

Defense Research Committee, National Established June 27, 1940, by order of *Council of National Defense.* Abolished by order of *Council* June 28, 1941, and reestablished in *Office of Scientific Research and Development* by EO 8807 of June 28, 1941. *Office* terminated by EO 9913 of Dec. 26, 1947, and property and records transferred to *National Military Establishment.*

Defense Resources Committee Established by Administrative Order 1496 of June 15, 1940. Replaced by *War Resources Council* by Administrative Order 1636 of Jan. 14, 1942. Inactive.

Defense Security Assistance Agency Established on Sept. 1, 1971. Renamed the Defense Security Cooperation Agency by DOD Directive 5105.38.

Defense Solid Fuels Administration Established by Order 2605 of Dec. 4, 1950 of the Secretary of the Interior. Abolished June 29, 1954, by Secretary's Order 2764.

Defense Special Weapons Agency Established by General Order No. 1 of July 1, 1971. Functions transferred to the Defense Threat Reduction Agency by DOD Directive 5105.62 of Sept. 30, 1998.

Defense Stockpile Manager, National Established by act of Nov. 14, 1986 (100 Stat. 4067). Functions transferred from the Administrator of General Services to the Secretary of Defense by EO 12626 of Feb. 25, 1988.

Defense Supplies Corporation Established under act of June 25, 1940 (54 Stat. 572). Transferred from *Federal Loan Agency* to the Department of Commerce by EO 9071 of Feb. 24, 1942. Returned to *Federal Loan Agency* by act of Feb. 24, 1945 (59 Stat. 5). Dissolved by act of June 30, 1945 (59 Stat. 310), and functions transferred to *Reconstruction Finance Corporation.*

Defense Supply Agency Renamed Defense Logistics Agency by DOD Directive 5105.22 of Jan. 22, 1977.

Defense Supply Management Agency Established in the Department of Defense by act of July 1, 1952 (66 Stat. 318). Abolished by Reorg. Plan No. 6 of 1953, effective June 30, 1953, and functions transferred to the Secretary of Defense.

Defense Technology Security Administration Established on May 10, 1985. Functions transferred to the Defense Threat Reduction Agency by DOD Directive 5105.62 of Sept. 30, 1998.

Defense Transport Administration Established Oct. 4, 1950, by order of Commissioner of *Interstate Commerce Commission* in charge of *Bureau of Service,* pursuant to EO 10161 of Sept. 9, 1950. Terminated by DTA Commissioner's order, effective July 1, 1955, and functions transferred to *Bureau of Safety and Service, Interstate Commerce Commission.*

Defense Transportation, Office of Established in *Office for Emergency Management* by EO 8989 of Dec. 18, 1941. Terminated by EO 10065 of July 6, 1949.

Director. *See other part of title*

Disarmament Administration, U.S. Established in the Department of State. Functions transferred to *U.S. Arms Control and Disarmament Agency* by act of Sept. 26, 1961 (75 Stat. 638).

Disarmament Problems, President's Special Committee on Established by President Aug. 5, 1955. Dissolved in February 1958.

Disaster Assistance Administration, Federal Functions transferred from the Department of Housing and Urban Development to the Federal Emergency Management Agency by EO 12148 of July 20, 1979.

Disaster Loan Corporation Grouped with other agencies to form *Federal Loan Agency* by Reorg.

Plan No. I of 1939, effective July 1, 1939. Transferred to the Department of Commerce by EO 9071 of Feb. 24, 1942. Returned to *Federal Loan Agency* by act of Feb. 24, 1945 (59 Stat. 5). Dissolved by act of June 30, 1945 (59 Stat. 310), and functions transferred to *Reconstruction Finance Corporation.*

Disease Control, Center for Established within the Public Health Service by the *Secretary of Health, Education, and Welfare* on July 1, 1973. Renamed *Centers for Disease Control* by Health and Human Services Secretary's notice of Oct. 1, 1980 (45 FR 67772). Renamed Centers for Disease Control and Prevention by act of Oct. 27, 1992 (106 Stat. 3504).

Displaced Persons Commission Established by act of June 25, 1948 (62 Stat. 1009). Terminated Aug. 31, 1952, pursuant to terms of act.

District of Columbia Established by acts of July 16, 1790 (1 Stat. 130), and Mar. 3, 1791. *Corporations of Washington and Georgetown* and *levy court of Washington County* abolished in favor of territorial form of government in 1871. Permanent commission government established July 1, 1878. District Government created as municipal corporation by act of June 11, 1878 (20 Stat. 102). Treated as branch of U.S. Government by various statutory enactments of Congress. District Government altered by Reorg. Plan No. 3 of 1967, effective Nov. 3, 1967. Charter for local government in District of Columbia provided by act of Dec. 24, 1973 (87 Stat. 774).

District of Columbia, Highway Commission of the Established by act of Mar. 2, 1893 (27 Stat 532). *National Capital Park and Planning Commission* named successor by act of Apr. 30, 1926 (44 Stat. 374). Functions transferred to National Capital Planning Commission by act of July 19, 1952 (66 Stat. 781).

District of Columbia, Reform-School of the Established by act of May 3, 1876 (19 Stat. 49). Renamed *National Training School for Boys* by act of May 27, 1908 (35 Stat. 380). Transferred to the Department of Justice by Reorg. Plan No. II of 1939, effective July 1, 1939, to be administered by Director of Bureau of Prisons.

District of Columbia Auditorium Commission Established by act of July 1, 1955 (69 Stat. 243). Final report submitted to Congress Jan. 31, 1957, pursuant to act of Apr. 27, 1956 (70 Stat. 115).

District of Columbia Redevelopment Land Agency Established by act of Aug. 2, 1946 (60 Stat. 790). Agency established as instrumentality of District Government by act of Dec. 24, 1973 (87 Stat. 774), effective July 1, 1974.

District of Columbia-Virginia Boundary Commission Established by act of Mar. 21, 1934 (48 Stat. 453). Terminated Dec. 1, 1935, to which date it had been extended by Public Resolution 9 (49 Stat. 67).

Division. *See other part of title*

Domestic Council Established in Executive Office of the President by Reorg. Plan No. 2 of 1970, effective July 1, 1970. Abolished by Reorg. Plan No. 1 of 1977, effective Mar. 26, 1978, and functions transferred to President and staff designated as *Domestic Policy Staff.* Pursuant to EO 12045 of Mar. 27, 1978, *Staff* assisted President in performance of transferred functions. Renamed Office of Policy Development in 1981. Abolished in February 1992 by President's reorganizational statement, effective May 1992.

Domestic Policy Staff *See* **Domestic Council**

Dominican Customs Receivership Transferred from *Division of Territories and Island Possessions,* Department of the Interior, to the Department of State by Reorg. Plan No. IV of 1940, effective June 30, 1940.

Drug Abuse, National Institute on Established within the National Institute of Mental Health, *Department of Health, Education, and Welfare* by act of Mar. 21, 1972 (86 Stat. 85). Removed from within the National Institute of Mental Health and made an entity within the Alcohol, Drug Abuse, and Mental Health Administration by act of May 14, 1974 (88 Stat. 136). Functions transferred to the Department of Health and Human Services by act of Oct. 17, 1979 (93 Stat. 695). (*See also* act of Oct. 27, 1986; 100 Stat. 3207–106.) Abolished by act of July 10, 1992 (106 Stat. 331). Reestablished by act of July 10, 1992 (106 Stat. 361).

Drug Abuse, President's Advisory Commission on Narcotic and Established by EO 11076 of Jan. 15, 1963. Terminated November 1963 under terms of order.

Drug Abuse Control, Bureau of Established in Food and Drug Administration, Department of Health and Human Services, to carry out functions of act of July 15, 1965 (79 Stat. 226). Functions transferred to *Bureau of Narcotics and Dangerous Drugs,* Department of Justice, by Reorg. Plan No. 1 of 1968, effective Apr. 8, 1968. Abolished by Reorg. Plan No. 2 of 1973, effective July 1, 1973, and functions transferred to Drug Enforcement Administration.

Drug Abuse Law Enforcement, Office of Established by EO 11641 of Jan. 28, 1972. Terminated by EO 11727 of July 6, 1973, and functions transferred to Drug Enforcement Administration.

Drug Abuse Policy, Office of Established in Executive Office of the President by act of Mar. 19, 1976 (90 Stat. 242). Abolished by Reorg. Plan No. 1 of 1977, effective Mar. 26, 1978, and functions transferred to President.

Drug Abuse Prevention, Special Action Office for Established by EO 11599 of June 17, 1971, and act of Mar. 21, 1972 (86 Stat. 65). Terminated June 30, 1975, pursuant to terms of act.

Drug Abuse Prevention, Treatment, and Rehabilitation, Cabinet Committee on Established Apr. 27, 1976, by Presidential announcement. Terminated by Presidential memorandum of Mar. 14, 1977.

Drug Law Enforcement, Cabinet Committee for Established Apr. 27, 1976, pursuant to Presidential message to Congress of Apr. 27, 1976. Abolished by Presidential memorandum of Mar. 14, 1977.

Drugs, Bureau of Narcotics and Dangerous *See* **Drug Abuse Control, Bureau of**

Drugs and Biologics, National Center for Renamed *Center for Drugs and Biologics* by Food and Drug Administration notice of Mar. 9, 1984 (49 FR 10166). Reestablished as Center for Drug Evaluation and Research and Center for Biologics Evaluation and Research by Secretary's notice of Oct. 6, 1987 (52 FR 38275).

Drunk Driving, Presidential Commission on Established by EO 12358 of Apr. 14, 1982. Terminated Dec. 31, 1983, by EO 12415 of Apr. 5, 1983.

Dryden Research Center, Hugh L. Formerly separate field installation of National Aeronautics and Space Administration. Made component of Ames Research Center by NASA Management Instruction 1107.5A of Sept. 3, 1981.

Economic Administration, Foreign Established in *Office for Emergency Management* by EO 9380 of Sept. 25, 1943. Functions of *Office of Lend-Lease Administration, Office of Foreign Relief and Rehabilitation Operations, Office of Economic Warfare* (together with *U.S. Commercial Company, Rubber Development Corporation, Petroleum Reserves Corporation,* and *Export-Import Bank of Washington* and functions transferred thereto by EO 9361 of July 15, 1943), and foreign economic operations of *Office of Foreign Economic Coordination* transferred to *Administration.* Foreign procurement activities of *War Food Administration* and Commodity Credit Corporation transferred by EO 9385 of Oct. 6, 1943. Terminated by EO 9630 of Sept. 27, 1945, and functions redistributed to the Departments of State, Commerce, and Agriculture and the *Reconstruction Finance Corporation.*

Economic Analysis, Office of *See* **Business Economics, Office of**

Economic Cooperation Administration Established by act of Apr. 3, 1948 (62 Stat. 138). Abolished by act of Oct. 10, 1951 (65 Stat. 373), and functions transferred to *Mutual Security Agency* pursuant to EO 10300 of Nov. 1, 1951.

Economic Coordination, Office of Foreign *See* **Board of Economic Operations**

Economic Defense Board Established by EO 8839 of July 30, 1941. Renamed *Board of Economic Warfare* by EO 8982 of Dec. 17, 1941. *Board* terminated by EO 9361 of July 15, 1943, and *Office of Economic Warfare* established in *Office for Emergency Management. Office of Economic Warfare* consolidated with *Foreign Economic Administration* by EO 9380 of Sept. 25, 1943.

Economic Development, Office of Regional Established by the Secretary of Commerce Jan. 6, 1966, pursuant to act of Aug. 26, 1965 (79 Stat. 552). Abolished by Department Order 5A, Dec. 22, 1966, and functions vested in Economic Development Administration.

Economic Development Service, Foreign Established by order of the Secretary of Agriculture Nov. 8, 1969. Abolished by order of Secretary Feb. 6, 1972, and functions transferred to Economic Research Service.

Economic Growth and Stability, Advisory Board on Established by Presidential letter to Congress of June 1, 1953. Superseded by *National Advisory Board on Economic Policy* by Presidential direction Mar. 12, 1961. *Cabinet Committee on Economic Growth* established by President Aug. 21, 1962, to succeed *Board.*

Economic Management Support Center Established by Secretary of Agriculture Memorandum 1836 of Jan. 9, 1974. Consolidated with other Department units into *Economics, Statistics, and Cooperatives Service* by Secretary's Memorandum 1927, effective Dec. 23, 1977.

Economic Operations, Board of Established by Department of State order of Oct. 7, 1941. Abolished by departmental order of June 24, 1943, and functions transferred to *Office of Foreign Economic Coordination* established by same order. *Office* abolished by departmental order of Nov. 6, 1943, pursuant to EO 9380 of Sept. 25, 1943.

Economic Opportunity, Office of Established in Executive Office of the President by act of Aug. 20, 1964 (78 Stat. 508). All OEO programs except three transferred by administrative action to the Departments of *Health, Education, and Welfare,* Labor, and Housing and Urban Development July 6, 1973. Community Action, Economic Development, and Legal Services Programs transferred to *Community Services Administration* by act of Jan. 4, 1975 (88 Stat. 2310).

Economic Policy, Council on Established by Presidential memorandum of Feb. 2, 1973. Functions absorbed by *Economic Policy Board* Sept. 30, 1974.

Economic Policy, Council on Foreign Established Dec. 22, 1954, by Presidential letter of Dec. 11, 1954. Abolished by President Mar. 12, 1961, and functions transferred to Secretary of State.

Economic Policy, Council on International Established in Executive Office of the President by Presidential memorandum of January 1971. Reestablished by act of Aug. 29, 1972 (86 Stat. 646). Terminated Sept. 30, 1977, on expiration of statutory authority.

Economic Policy, National Advisory Board on *See* **Economic Growth and Stability, Advisory Board on**

Economic Policy Board, President's Established by EO 11808 of Sept. 30, 1974. Terminated by EO 11975 of Mar. 7, 1977.

Economic Research Service Established by Secretary of Agriculture Memorandum 1446, supp. 1, of Apr. 3, 1961. Consolidated with other Department of Agriculture units into *Economics, Statistics, and Cooperatives Service* by Secretary's Memorandum 1927, effective Dec. 23, 1977. Redesignated as Economic Research Service by Secretarial order of Oct. 1, 1981.

Economic Security, Advisory Council on Established by EO 6757 of June 29, 1934. Terminated on approval of act of Aug. 14, 1935 (49 Stat. 620) Aug. 14, 1935.

Economic Security, Committee on Established by EO 6757 of June 29, 1934. Terminated as formal agency in April 1936, as provided in act, but continued informally for some time thereafter.

Economic Stabilization, Office of Established in *Office for Emergency Management* by EO 9250 of Oct. 3, 1942. Terminated by EO 9620 of Sept. 20, 1945, and functions transferred to *Office of War Mobilization and Reconversion.* Reestablished in *Office for Emergency Management* by EO 9699 of Feb. 21, 1946. Transferred by EO 9762 of July 25, 1946, to *Office of War Mobilization and Reconversion.* Consolidated with other agencies to form *Office of Temporary Controls* by EO 9809 of Dec. 12, 1946.

Economic Stabilization Agency Established by EO 10161 of Sept. 9, 1950, and EO 10276 of July 31, 1951. Terminated, except for liquidation purposes, by EO 10434 of Feb. 6, 1953. Liquidation completed Oct. 31, 1953, pursuant to EO 10480 of Aug. 14, 1953.

Economic Stabilization Board Established by EO 9250 of Oct. 3, 1942. Transferred to *Office of War Mobilization and Reconversion* by EO 9620 of Sept. 20, 1945. Returned to *Office of Economic Stabilization* on reestablishment by EO 9699 of Feb. 21, 1946. *Board* returned to *Office of War Mobilization and Reconversion* by EO 9762 of July 25, 1946. Functions terminated by EO 9809 of Dec. 12, 1946.

Economic Warfare, Board of *See* **Economic Defense Board**

Economic Warfare, Office of *See* **Economic Defense Board**

Economics, Bureau of Industrial Established by the Secretary of Commerce Jan. 2, 1980, in conjunction with Reorg. Plan No. 3 of 1979, effective Oct. 1, 1980, and operated under Department Organization Order 35–5B. Abolished at bureau level by Secretarial order, effective Jan. 22, 1984 (49 FR 4538). Industry-related functions realigned and transferred from Under Secretary for Economic Affairs to Under Secretary for International Trade. Under Secretary for Economic Affairs retained units to support domestic macroeconomic policy functions.

Economics, Statistics, and Cooperatives Service Renamed *Economics and Statistics Service* by Secretary of Agriculture Memorandum 2025 of Sept. 17, 1980. Redesignated as Economic Research Service and *Statistical Reporting Service* by Secretarial order of Oct. 1, 1981.

Economy Board, Joint Placed under direction of President by military order of July 5, 1939. Abolished Sept. 1, 1947, by joint letter of Aug. 20, 1947, from Secretaries of *War* and Navy to President.

Education, Federal Board for Vocational Established by act of Feb. 23, 1917 (39 Stat. 929). Functions transferred to the Department of the Interior by EO 6166 of June 10, 1933. Functions assigned to *Commissioner of Education* Oct. 10, 1933. *Office of Education* transferred from the Department of the Interior to the *Federal Security Agency* by Reorg. Plan No. I of 1939, effective July 1, 1939. *Board* abolished by Reorg. Plan No. 2 of 1946, effective July 16, 1946.

Education, National Institute of Established by act of June 23, 1972 (86 Stat. 327). Transferred to Office of Educational Research and Improvement, Department of Education, by act of Oct. 17, 1979 (93 Stat. 678), effective May 4, 1980.

Education, Office of Established as independent agency by act of Mar. 2, 1867 (14 Stat. 434). Transferred to the Department of the Interior by act of July 20, 1868 (15 Stat. 106). Transferred to *Federal Security Agency* by Reorg. Plan No. I of 1939, effective July 1, 1939. Functions of *Federal Security Administrator* administered by *Office of Education* relating to student loans and defense-related education transferred to *War Manpower Commission* by EO 9247 of Sept. 17, 1942.

Education, Office of Bilingual Abolished by act of Oct. 17, 1979 (93 Stat. 675), and functions transferred to Office of Bilingual Education and Minority Languages Affairs, Department of Education.

Education Beyond the High School, President's Committee on Established by act of July 26, 1956 (70 Stat. 676). Terminated Dec. 31, 1957. Certain activities continued by *Bureau of Higher Education, Office of Education.*

Education Division Established in the *Department of Health, Education, and Welfare* by act of June 23, 1972 (86 Stat. 327). Functions transferred to the Department of Education by act of Oct. 17, 1979 (93 Stat. 677).

Education Statistics, National Center for Established in the Office of the Assistant Secretary, Department of Health and Human Services, by act of Aug. 21, 1974 (88 Stat. 556). Transferred to the Office of Educational Research and Improvement, Department of Education, by act of Oct. 17, 1979 (93 Stat. 678), effective May 4, 1980. Renamed *Center for Education Statistics* by act of Oct. 17, 1986 (100 Stat. 1579). Renamed National Center for Education Statistics by act of Apr. 28, 1988 (102 Stat. 331).

Educational and Cultural Affairs, Bureau of Established by Secretary of State in 1960. Terminated by Reorg. Plan No. 2 of 1977, effective July 1, 1978, and functions transferred to *International Communication Agency,* effective Apr. 1, 1978.

Educational and Cultural Affairs, Interagency Council on International Established Jan. 20, 1964, by Foreign Affairs Manual Circular, under authority of act of Sept. 21, 1961 (75 Stat. 527). Terminated Oct. 1973 following creation of Subcommittee on

International Exchanges by National Security Council directive.

Educational Exchange, U.S. Advisory Commission on Established by act of Jan. 27, 1948 (62 Stat. 10). Abolished by act of Sept. 21, 1961 (75 Stat. 538), and superseded by U.S. Advisory Commission on International Educational and Cultural Affairs.

Efficiency, Bureau of Organized under act of Feb. 28, 1916 (39 Stat. 15). Abolished by act of Mar. 3, 1933 (47 Stat. 1519), and records transferred to *Bureau of the Budget.*

Elderly, Committee on Mental Health and Illness of the Established by act of July 29, 1975 (89 Stat. 347). Terminated Sept. 30, 1977.

Electoral votes for President and Vice President, transfer of functions *See* **State, Department of**

Electric Home and Farm Authority Incorporated Aug. 1, 1935, under laws of District of Columbia. Designated as U.S. agency by EO 7139 of Aug. 12, 1935. Continued by act of June 10, 1941 (55 Stat. 248). Grouped with other agencies in *Federal Loan Agency* by Reorg. Plan. No. I of 1939, effective July 1, 1939. Functions transferred to the Department of Commerce by EO 9071 of Feb. 24, 1942. Terminated by EO 9256 of Oct. 13, 1942.

Electric Home and Farm Authority, Inc. Organized Jan. 17, 1934, under laws of State of Delaware by EO 6514 of Dec. 19, 1933. Dissolved Aug. 1, 1935, and succeeded by *Electric Home and Farm Authority.*

Emergency Administration of Public Works, Federal Established by act of June 16, 1933 (48 Stat. 200). Operation continued by subsequent legislation, including act of June 21, 1938 (52 Stat. 816). Consolidated with *Federal Works Agency* as *Public Works Administration* by Reorg. Plan No. I of 1939, effective July 1, 1939. Functions transferred to *Office of Federal Works Administrator* by EO 9357 of June 30, 1943.

Emergency Conservation Work Established by EO 6101 of Apr. 5, 1933. Succeeded by *Civilian Conservation Corps.*

Emergency Council, National Established by EO 6433–A of Nov. 17, 1933. Consolidated with *Executive Council* by EO 6889–A of Oct. 29, 1934. Abolished by Reorg. Plan No. II of 1939, effective July 1, 1939, and functions (except those relating to *Radio Division* and *Film Service*) transferred to Executive Office of the President.

Emergency Council, Office of Economic Adviser to National Established by EO 6240 of Aug. 3, 1933, in connection with *Executive Council,* which later consolidated with *National Emergency Council.* Records and property used in preparation of statistical and economic summaries transferred to *Central Statistical Board* by EO 7003 of Apr. 8, 1935.

Emergency Management, Office for Established in Executive Office of the President by administrative order of May 25, 1940, in accordance with EO 8248 of Sept. 8, 1939. Inactive.

Emergency Mobilization Preparedness Board Established Dec. 17, 1981, by the President. Abolished by Presidential directive of Sept. 16, 1985.

Emergency Planning, Office of Established as successor to *Office of Civil and Defense Mobilization* by act of Sept. 22, 1961 (75 Stat. 630). Renamed *Office of Emergency Preparedness* by act of Oct. 21, 1968 (82 Stat. 1194). Terminated by Reorg. Plan No. 2 of 1973, effective July 1, 1973, and functions transferred to the the Departments of the Treasury and Housing and Urban Development and the General Services Administration.

Emergency Preparedness, Office of *See* **Emergency Planning, Office of**

Emergency Procurement Service Established Sept. 1, 1950, by Administrator of General Services. Renamed *Defense Materials Service* Sept. 7, 1956. Functions transferred to *Property Management and Disposal Service* July 29, 1966. *Service* abolished July 1, 1973, and functions transferred to Federal Supply Service, Public Buildings Service, and Federal Property Resources Service.

Emergency Relief Administration, Federal Established by act of May 12, 1933 (48 Stat. 55). Expired June 30, 1938, having been liquidated by *Works Progress Administrator* pursuant to act of May 28, 1937 (50 Stat. 352).

Employee-Management Relations Program, President's Committee on the Implementation of the Federal Established by EO 10988 of Jan. 17, 1962. Terminated upon submission of report to President June 21, 1963.

Employees' Compensation, Bureau of Transferred from *Federal Security Agency* to the Department of Labor by Reorg. Plan No. 19 of 1950, effective May 24, 1950. Functions absorbed by Employment Standards Administration Mar. 13, 1972.

Employees' Compensation Appeals Board Transferred from *Federal Security Agency* to the Department of Labor by Reorg. Plan No. 19 of 1950, effective May 24, 1950.

Employees' Compensation Commission, U.S. Established by act of Sept. 7, 1916 (39 Stat. 742). Abolished by Reorg. Plan No. 2 of 1946, effective July 16, 1946, and functions transferred to *Federal Security Administrator.*

Employment Board, Fair Established by *U.S. Civil Service Commission* pursuant to EO 9980 of July 26, 1948. Abolished by EO 10590 of Jan. 18, 1955.

Employment of the Physically Handicapped, President's Committee on Established by EO 10640 of Oct. 10, 1955, continuing *Committee* established by act of July 11, 1949 (63 Stat. 409). Superseded by President's Committee on Employment of the Handicapped established by EO 10994 of Feb. 14, 1962.

Employment Policy, President's Committee on Government Established by EO 10590 of Jan. 18, 1955. Abolished by EO 10925 of Mar. 6, 1961, and functions transferred to *President's Committee on Equal Employment Opportunity.*

Employment Practice, Committee on Fair Established in *Office of Production Management* by EO 8802 of June 25, 1941. Transferred to *War Manpower Commission* by Presidential letter effective July 30, 1942. Committee terminated on establishment of *Committee on Fair Employment Practice, Office for Emergency Management,* by EO 9346 of May 27, 1943. Terminated June 30, 1946, by act of July 17, 1945 (59 Stat. 743).

Employment Security, Bureau of Transferred from *Federal Security Agency* to the Department of Labor by Reorg. Plan No. 2 of 1949, effective Aug. 20, 1949. Abolished by order of Mar. 14, 1969 of the Secretary of Labor, and functions transferred to *Manpower Administration.*

Employment Service, U.S. Established in the Department of Labor in 1918 by departmental order. Abolished by act of June 6, 1933 (48 Stat. 113), and created as bureau with same name. Functions consolidated with unemployment compensation functions of *Social Security Board, Bureau of Employment Security,* and transferred to *Federal Security Agency* by Reorg. Plan No. I of 1939, effective July 1, 1939. *Service* transferred to *Bureau of Placement, War Manpower Commission,* by EO 9247 of Sept. 17, 1942. Returned to the Department of Labor by EO 9617 of Sept. 19, 1945. Transferred to *Federal Security Agency* by act of June 16, 1948 (62 Stat. 443), to function as part of *Bureau of Employment Security,* Social Security Administration. *Bureau,* including *U.S. Employment Service,* transferred to the Department of Labor by Reorg. Plan No. 2 of 1949, effective Aug. 20, 1949. Abolished by reorganization of *Manpower Administration,* effective Mar. 17, 1969, and functions assigned to *U.S. Training and Employment Service.*

Employment Stabilization Board, Federal Established by act of Feb. 10, 1931 (46 Stat. 1085). Abolished by EO 6166 of June 10, 1933. Abolition deferred by EO 6623 of Mar. 1, 1934, until functions of *Board* transferred to *Federal Employment Stabilization Office,* established in the Department of Commerce by same order. *Office* abolished by Reorg. Plan No. I of 1939, effective July 1, 1939, and functions transferred from the Department of Commerce to *National Resources Planning Board,* Executive Office of the President.

Employment Stabilization Office, Federal. *See* **Employment Stabilization Board, Federal**

Employment and Training, Office of Comprehensive Established in the Department of Labor. Terminated due to expiration of authority for appropriations after fiscal year 1982. Replaced by *Office of Employment and Training Programs.*

Employment and Training Programs, Office of Renamed Office of Job Training Programs by Employment and Training Administration reorganization in the Department of Labor, effective June 1984.

Endangered Species Scientific Authority Established by EO 11911 of Apr. 13, 1976. Terminated by act of Dec. 28, 1979 (93 Stat. 1228), and functions transferred to the Secretary of the Interior.

Energy Administration, Federal Established by act of May 7, 1974 (88 Stat. 96). Assigned additional responsibilities by acts of June 22, 1974 (88 Stat. 246), Dec. 22, 1975 (89 Stat. 871), and Aug. 14, 1976 (90 Stat. 1125). Terminated by act of Aug. 4, 1977 (91 Stat. 577), and functions transferred to the Department of Energy.

Energy Conservation, Office of Established by Interior Secretarial Order 2953 May 7, 1973. Functions transferred to *Federal Energy Administration* by act of May 7, 1974 (88 Stat. 100).

Energy Data and Analysis, Office of Established by Interior Secretarial Order 2953 of May 7, 1973. Functions transferred to *Federal Energy Administration* by act of May 7, 1974 (88 Stat. 100).

Energy Policy Office Established in Executive Office of the President by EO 11726 of June 29, 1973. Abolished by EO 11775 of Mar. 26, 1974.

Energy Programs, Office of Established by Department of Commerce Organization Order 25–7A, effective Sept. 24, 1975. Terminated by act of Aug. 4, 1977 (91 Stat. 581), and functions transferred to the Department of Energy.

Energy Research and Development Administration Established by act of Oct. 11, 1974 (88 Stat. 1234). Assigned responsibilities by acts of Sept. 3, 1974 (88 Stat. 1069, 1079), Oct. 26, 1974 (88 Stat. 1431), and Dec. 31, 1974 (88 Stat. 1887). Terminated by act of Aug. 4, 1977 (91 Stat. 577), and functions transferred to the Department of Energy.

Energy Resources Council Established in Executive Office of the President by act of Oct. 11, 1974 (88 Stat. 1233). Establishing authority repealed by act of Aug. 4, 1977 (91 Stat. 608), and *Council* terminated.

Energy Supplies and Resources Policy, Presidential Advisory Committee on Established July 30, 1954, by President. Abolished Mar. 12, 1961, by President and functions transferred to the Secretary of the Interior.

Enforcement Commission, National Established by General Order 18 of *Economic Stabilization Administrator,* effective July 30, 1952. Functions transferred to Director, *Office of Defense Mobilization,* and Attorney General by EO 10494 of Oct. 14, 1953.

Engineering, Bureau of *See* **Steam Engineering, Bureau of**

Entomology, Bureau of *See* **Entomology and Plant Quarantine, Bureau of**

Entomology and Plant Quarantine, Bureau of *Bureau of Entomology* and *Bureau of Plant Quarantine* created by acts of Apr. 23, 1904 (33 Stat. 276), and July 7, 1932 (47 Stat. 640), respectively. Consolidated with disease control and eradication functions of *Bureau of Plant Industry* into

Bureau of Entomology and Plant Quarantine by act of Mar. 23, 1934 (48 Stat. 467). Functions transferred to Agricultural Research Service by Secretary's Memorandum 1320, supp. 4, of Nov. 2, 1953.

Environment, Cabinet Committee on the *See* **Environmental Quality Council**

Environmental Financing Authority Established by act of Oct. 18, 1972 (86 Stat. 899). Expired June 30, 1975, pursuant to terms of act.

Environmental Quality Council Established by EO 11472 of May 29, 1969. Renamed *Cabinet Committee on the Environment* by EO 11514 of Mar. 5, 1970. EO 11514 terminated by EO 11541 of July 1, 1970.

Environmental Science Services Administration Established in the Department of Commerce by Reorg. Plan No. 2 of 1965, effective July 13, 1965, by consolidating *Weather Bureau* and *Coast and Geodetic Survey.* Abolished by Reorg. Plan No. 4 of 1970, effective Oct. 3, 1970, and functions transferred to National Oceanic and Atmospheric Administration.

Equal Employment Opportunity, President's Committee on Established by EO 10925 of Mar. 6, 1961. Abolished by EO 11246 of Sept. 24, 1965, and functions transferred to the Department of Labor and *U.S. Civil Service Commission.*

Equal Opportunity, President's Council on Established by EO 11197 of Feb. 5, 1965. Abolished by EO 11247 of Sept. 24, 1965, and functions transferred to the Department of Justice.

Equipment, Bureau of Established as *Bureau of Equipment and Recruiting* by act of July 5, 1862 (12 Stat. 510), replacing *Bureau of Construction, Equipment and Repairs.* Designated as *Bureau of Equipment* in annual appropriation acts commencing with fiscal year 1892 (26 Stat. 192) after cognizance over enlisted personnel matters transferred, effective July 1, 1889, to *Bureau of Navigation.* Functions distributed among bureaus and offices in the Department of the Navy by act of June 24, 1910 (61 Stat. 613). Abolished by act of June 30, 1914 (38 Stat. 408).

Ethics, Office of Government Established in the Office of Personnel Management by act of Oct. 26, 1978 (92 Stat. 1862). Became a separate executive agency status by act of Nov. 3, 1988 (102 Stat. 3031).

European Migration, Intergovernmental Committee for Renamed Intergovernmental Committee for Migration by Resolution 624, passed by Intergovernmental Committee for European Migration Council, effective Nov. 11, 1980.

Evacuation, Joint Committee on *See* **Health and Welfare Aspects of Evacuation of Civilians, Joint Committee on**

Exchange Service, International Established in 1849 in Smithsonian Institution. Renamed Office of Publications Exchange by Secretary's internal directive of Jan. 11, 1985.

Executive Branch of the Government, Commission on Organization of the Established by act of July 7, 1947 (61 Stat. 246). Terminated June 12, 1949, pursuant to terms of act. Second *Commission on Organization of the Executive Branch of the Government* established by act of July 10, 1953 (67 Stat. 142). Terminated June 30, 1955, pursuant to terms of act.

Executive Council Established by EO 6202–A of July 11, 1933. Consolidated with *National Emergency Council* by EO 6889–A of Oct. 29, 1934.

Executive Exchange, President's Commission on *See* **Personnel Interchange, President's Commission on**

Executive orders *See* **State, Department of**

Executive Organization, President's Advisory Council on Established by President Apr. 5, 1969. Terminated May 7, 1971.

Executives, Active Corps of Established in ACTION by act of Oct. 1, 1973 (87 Stat. 404). Transferred to Small Business Administration by EO 11871 of July 18, 1975.

Export Control, Administrator of Functions delegated to Administrator by Proc. 2413 of July 2, 1940, transferred to *Office of Export Control, Economic Defense Board,* by EO 8900 of Sept. 15, 1941. Renamed *Board of Economic Warfare* by EO 8982 of Dec. 17, 1941. *Board* terminated by EO 9361 of July 15, 1943.

Export Control, Office of *See* **Export Control, Administrator of**

Export-Import Bank of Washington Organization of District of Columbia banking corporation directed by EO 6581 of Feb. 2, 1934. Certificate of incorporation filed Feb. 12, 1934. Grouped with other agencies to form *Federal Loan Agency* by Reorg. Plan No. I of 1939, effective July 1, 1939. Transferred to the Department of Commerce by EO 9071 of Feb. 24, 1942. Functions transferred to *Office of Economic Warfare* by EO 9361 of July 15, 1943. Established as permanent independent agency by act of July 31, 1945 (59 Stat. 526). Renamed Export-Import Bank of the U.S. by act of Mar. 13, 1968 (82 Stat. 47).

Export-Import Bank of Washington, DC, Second Authorized by EO 6638 of Mar. 9, 1934. Abolished by EO 7365 of May 7, 1936, and records transferred to *Export-Import Bank of Washington,* effective June 30, 1936.

Export Marketing Service Established by the Secretary of Agriculture Mar. 28, 1969. Merged with Foreign Agricultural Service by Secretary's memorandum of Dec. 7, 1973, effective Feb. 3, 1974.

Exports and Requirements, Division of Established in *Office of Foreign Economic Coordination* by the Department of State order of Feb. 1, 1943. Abolished by departmental order of Nov. 6, 1943, pursuant to EO 9380 of Sept. 25, 1943.

Extension Service Established by act of May 14, 1914 (38 Stat. 372). Consolidated into *Science and Education Administration* by Secretary's order of Jan. 24, 1978. Reestablished as *Extension Service* by Secretarial order of June 16, 1981. Became part of Cooperative State, Research, Education, and Extension Service under Department of Agriculture's reorganization in 1995.

Facts and Figures, Office of Established in *Office for Emergency Management* by EO 8922 of Oct. 24, 1941. Consolidated with *Office of War Information* in *Office for Emergency Management* by EO 9182 of June 13, 1942.

Family Security Committee Established in *Office of Defense Health and Welfare Services* Feb. 12, 1941, by administrative order. Terminated Dec. 17, 1942.

Family Services, Bureau of *See* **Assistance, Bureau of Public**

Family Support Administration Established on Apr. 4, 1986, in the Department of Health and Human Services under authority of section 6 of Reorganization Plan No. 1 of 1953, effective Apr. 11, 1953 (*see also* 51 FR 11641). Merged into Administration for Children and Families by Secretary's reorganization notice dated Apr. 15, 1991.

Farm Board, Federal Established by act of June 15, 1929 (46 Stat. 11). Renamed Farm Credit Administration and certain functions abolished by EO 6084 of Mar. 27, 1933. Administration placed under the Department of Agriculture by Reorg. Plan No. I of 1939, effective July 1, 1939. Made independent agency in the executive branch of the Government, to be housed in the Department of Agriculture, by act of Aug. 6, 1953 (67 Stat. 390). Removed from the Department of Agriculture by act of Dec. 10, 1971 (85 Stat. 617).

Farm Credit Administration *See* **Farm Board, Federal**

Farm Loan Board, Federal Established in the Department of the Treasury to administer act of July 17, 1916 (39 Stat. 360). Offices of appointed members of *Board,* except member designated as *Farm Loan Commissioner,* abolished by EO 6084 of Mar. 27, 1933, and *Board* functions transferred to *Farm Loan Commissioner,* subject to jurisdiction and control of Farm Credit Administration. Title changed to *Land Bank Commissioner* by act of June 16, 1933. Abolished by act of Aug. 6, 1953 (67 Stat. 393).

Farm Loan Bureau, Federal Established in the Department of the Treasury under supervision of *Federal Farm Loan Board* and charged with execution of act of July 17, 1916 (39 Stat. 360). Transferred to *Farm Credit Administration* by EO 6084 of Mar. 27, 1933.

Farm Loan Commissioner *See* **Farm Loan Board, Federal**

Farm Mortgage Corporation, Federal Established by act of Jan. 31, 1934 (48 Stat. 344). Transferred to the Department of Agriculture by Reorg. Plan No. I of 1939, effective July 1, 1939, to operate under supervision of Farm Credit Administration. Abolished by act of Oct. 4, 1961 (75 Stat. 773).

Farm Products, Division of (Also known as *Division of Agriculture*) Established by *Advisory Commission to Council of National Defense* pursuant to act of Aug. 29, 1916 (39 Stat. 649). *Office of Agricultural Defense Relations* (later known as *Office for Agricultural War Relations*) established in the Department of Agriculture by Presidential letter of May 5, 1941, which transferred to the Secretary of Agriculture functions previously assigned to *Division of Agriculture.* Functions concerned with food production transferred to *Food Production Administration* and functions concerned with food distribution transferred to *Food Distribution Administration* by EO 9280 of Dec. 5, 1942.

Farm Security Administration *See* **Resettlement Administration**

Farm Service Agency Established by Secretary's Memorandum 1010–1 dated Oct. 20, 1994, under authority of the act of Oct. 13, 1994 (7 U.S.C. 6901), and assumed certain functions of the *Agricultural Stabilization and Conservation Service,* the *Farmers' Home Administration,* and the *Federal Crop Insurance Corporation.* Renamed *Consolidated Farm Service Agency* by Acting Administrator on Dec. 19, 1994.

Farmer Cooperative Service Established by Secretary of Agriculture Memorandum 1320, supp. 4, of Dec. 4, 1953. Consolidated with other Department of Agriculture units into *Economics, Statistics, and Cooperatives Service* by Secretary's Memorandum 1927, effective Dec. 23, 1977.

Farmers' Home Administration. *See* **Resettlement Administration**

Federal. *See also other part of title*

Federal Advisory Council Established in *Federal Security Agency* by act of June 6, 1933 (48 Stat. 116). Transferred to the Department of Labor by Reorg. Plan No. 2 of 1949, effective Aug. 20, 1949.

Federal Crop Insurance Corporation Established by act of Feb. 16, 1938. Consolidated with the *Agricultural Stabilization and Conservation Service* and *Farmers' Home Administration* in 1995 to form the *Farm Service Agency* pursuant to act of Oct. 13, 1994 (108 Stat. 3178).

Federal Grain Inspection Service Established in the Department of Agriculture by act of Oct. 21, 1976 (90 Stat. 2868). Abolished by Secretary's Memorandum 1010–1 dated Oct. 20, 1994, and program authority and functions transferred to the Grain Inspection, Packers and Stockyards Administration.

Federal Register, Administrative Committee of the *See* **Archives Establishment, National**

Federal Register, Division of the Established by act of July 26, 1935 (49 Stat. 500). Transferred to General Services Administration as part of *National Archives and Records Service* by act of June 30, 1949 (63 Stat. 381). Renamed Office of the Federal

Register by order of General Services Administrator, Feb. 6, 1959. Transferred to National Archives and Records Administration by act of Oct. 19, 1984 (98 Stat. 2283).

Federal Register, Office of the *See* **Federal Register, Division of the**

Federal Reserve Board Renamed Board of Governors of the Federal Reserve System, and Governor and Vice Governor designated as Chairman and Vice Chairman, respectively, of Board by act of Aug. 23, 1935 (49 Stat. 704).

Field Services, Office of Established by the Secretary of Commerce Feb. 1, 1963, by Department Organization Order 40–3. Terminated by Department Organization Order 40–1A of Sept. 15, 1970, and functions transferred to *Bureau of Domestic Commerce.*

Filipino Rehabilitation Commission Established by act of June 29, 1944 (58 Stat. 626). Inactive pursuant to terms of act.

Film Service, U.S. Established by *National Emergency Council* in September 1938. Transferred to *Office of Education, Federal Security Agency,* by Reorg. Plan No. II of 1939, effective July 1, 1939. Terminated June 30, 1940.

Films, Coordinator of Government Director of *Office of Government Reports* designated *Coordinator of Government Films* by Presidential letter of Dec. 18, 1941. Functions transferred to *Office of War Information* by EO 9182 of June 13, 1942.

Financial Operations, Bureau of Government Renamed Financial Management Service by Order 145–21 of the Secretary of the Treasury, effective Oct. 10, 1984.

Fire Administration, U.S. *See* **Fire Prevention and Control Administration, National**

Fire Council, Federal Established by EO 7397 of June 20, 1936. Transferred July 1, 1939, to *Federal Works Agency* by EO 8194 of July 6, 1939, with functions under direction of *Federal Works Administrator.* Transferred with *Federal Works Agency* to General Services Administration by act of June 30, 1949 (63 Stat. 380). Transferred to the Department of Commerce by EO 11654 of Mar. 13, 1972.

Fire Prevention and Control, National Academy for Established in the Department of Commerce by act of Oct. 29, 1974 (88 Stat. 1537). Transferred to Federal Emergency Management Agency by Reorg. Plan No. 3 of 1978, effective Apr. 1, 1979.

Fire Prevention and Control Administration, National Renamed U.S. Fire Administration by act of Oct. 5, 1978 (92 Stat. 932). Transferred to Federal Emergency Management Agency by Reorg. Plan No. 3 of 1978, effective Apr. 1, 1979.

Fish Commission, U.S. *Commissioner of Fish and Fisheries* established as head of *U.S. Fish Commission* by joint resolution of Feb. 9, 1871 (16 Stat. 594). *Commission* established as *Bureau of Fisheries* in *Department of Commerce and Labor* by act of Feb. 14, 1903 (32 Stat. 827). Department of Labor created by act of Mar. 4, 1913 (37 Stat. 736), and *Bureau* remained in the Department of Commerce. Transferred to the Department of the Interior by Reorg. Plan No. II of 1939, effective July 1, 1939. Consolidated with *Bureau of Biological Survey* into *Fish and Wildlife Service* by Reorg. Plan No. III of 1940, effective June 30, 1940.

Fish and Wildlife Service Established by Reorg. Plan No. III of 1940, effective June 30, 1940, consolidating *Bureau of Fisheries* and *Bureau of Biological Survey.* Succeeded by U.S. Fish and Wildlife Service.

Fisheries, Bureau of *See* **Fish Commission, U.S.**

Fisheries, Bureau of Commercial Organized in 1959 under U.S. Fish and Wildlife Service, the Department of the Interior. Abolished by Reorg. Plan No. 4 of 1970, effective Oct. 3, 1970, and functions transferred to National Oceanic and Atmospheric Administration.

Fishery Coordination, Office of Established in the Department of the Interior by EO 9204 of July 21, 1942. Terminated by EO 9649 of Oct. 29, 1945.

Flood Indemnity Administration, Federal Established in *Housing and Home Finance Agency* by Administrator's Organizational Order 1, effective Sept. 28, 1956, redesignated as Administrator's Organizational Order 2 on Dec. 7, 1956, pursuant to act of Aug. 7, 1956 (70 Stat. 1078). Abolished by Administrator's Organizational Order 3, effective July 1, 1957, due to lack of funding.

Food, Cost of Living Council Committee on Established by EO 11695 of Jan. 11, 1973. Abolished by EO 11788 of June 18, 1974.

Food, Drug, and Insecticide Administration Established by act of Jan. 18, 1927 (44 Stat. 1002). Renamed Food and Drug Administration by act of May 27, 1930 (46 Stat. 422). Transferred from the Department of Agriculture to *Federal Security Agency* by Reorg. Plan No. IV of 1940, effective June 30, 1940. Transferred to *Department of Health, Education, and Welfare* by Reorg. Plan No. 1 of 1953, effective Apr. 11, 1953.

Food Distribution Administration Established in the Department of Agriculture by EO 9280 of Dec. 5, 1942, consolidating *Agricultural Marketing Administration, Sugar Agency,* distribution functions of *Office for Agricultural War Relations,* regulatory work of *Bureau of Animal Industry,* and food units of *War Production Board.* Consolidated with other agencies by EO 9322 of Mar. 26, 1943, to form *Administration of Food Production and Distribution.*

Food and Drug Administration *See* **Food, Drug, and Insecticide Administration**

Food Industry Advisory Committee Established by EO 11627 of Oct. 15, 1971. Abolished by EO 11781 of May 1, 1974.

Food and Nutrition Service Established Aug. 8, 1969, by Secretary of Agriculture under authority of 5 U.S.C. 301 and Reorg. Plan No. 2 of 1953 (5

U.S.C. app.). Abolished by Secretary's Memorandum 1010–1 dated Oct. 20, 1994. Functions assumed by Food and Consumer Service.

Food Production Administration Established in the Department of Agriculture by EO 9280 of Dec. 5, 1942, which consolidated *Agricultural Adjustment Agency,* Farm Credit Administration, *Farm Security Administration,* Federal Crop Insurance Corporation, Soil Conservation Service, and food production activities of *War Production Board, Office of Agricultural War Relations,* and *Division of Farm Management and Costs, Bureau of Agricultural Economics.* Consolidated with other agencies by EO 9322 of Mar. 26, 1943, to form *Administration of Food Production and Distribution.*

Food Production and Distribution, Administration of Established by consolidation of *Food Production Administration, Food Distribution Administration,* Commodity Credit Corporation, and Extension Service, Department of Agriculture, by EO 9322 of Mar. 26, 1943, under direction of Administrator, directly responsible to President. Renamed *War Food Administration* by EO 9334 of Apr. 19, 1943. Terminated by EO 9577 of June 29, 1945, and functions transferred to the Secretary of Agriculture. Transfer made permanent by Reorg. Plan No. 3 of 1946, effective July 16, 1946.

Food Safety and Quality Service Renamed Food Safety and Inspection Service by Agriculture Secretary's memorandum of June 19, 1981.

Foods, Bureau of Renamed Center for Food Safety and Applied Nutrition by Food and Drug Administration notice of Mar. 9, 1984 (49 FR 10166).

Foreign. *See also other part of title*

Foreign Aid, Advisory Committee on Voluntary Established by President May 14, 1946. Transferred from the Department of State to the Director of the *Mutual Security Agency,* and later to Director of the *Foreign Operations Administration,* by Presidential letter of June 1, 1953.

Foreign Operations Administration Established by Reorg. Plan No. 7 of 1953, effective Aug. 1, 1953, and functions transferred from *Office of Director of Mutual Security, Mutual Security Agency, Technical Cooperation Administration, Institute of Inter-American Affairs.* Abolished by EO 10610 of May 9, 1955, and functions and offices transferred to the Departments of State and Defense.

Foreign Scholarships, Board of Renamed J. William Fulbright Foreign Scholarship Board by act of Feb. 16, 1990 (104 Stat. 49).

Forest Reservation Commission, National Established by act of Mar. 1, 1911 (36 Stat. 962). Terminated by act of Oct. 22, 1976 (90 Stat. 2961), and functions transferred to the Secretary of Agriculture.

Forests, Director of Established by Administrative Order 1283 of May 18, 1938. Made part of *Office of Land Utilization,* Department of the Interior, by Administrative Order 1466 of Apr. 15, 1940.

Freedmen's Hospital Established by act of Mar. 3, 1871 (16 Stat. 506; T. 32 of D.C. Code). Transferred from the Department of the Interior to *Federal Security Agency* by Reorg. Plan No. IV of 1940, effective June 30, 1940.

Fuel Yards Established by act of July 1, 1918 (40 Stat. 672). Transferred from *Bureau of Mines,* Department of Commerce, to *Procurement Division,* Department of the Treasury, by EO 6166 of June 10, 1933, effective Mar. 2, 1934.

Fuels Coordinator for War, Office of Solid *See* **Fuels Administration for War, Solid**

Fuels Corporation, U.S. Synthetic Established by act of June 30, 1980 (94 Stat. 636). Terminated Apr. 18, 1986, by act of Dec. 19, 1985 (99 Stat. 1249), and functions transferred to the Secretary of the Treasury.

Fund-Raising Within the Federal Service, President's Committee on Established by EO 10728 of Sept. 6, 1957. Abolished by EO 10927 of Mar. 18, 1961, and functions transferred to *U.S. Civil Service Commission.*

Gallaudet College *See* **Columbia Institution for the Instruction of the Deaf and Dumb, and the Blind**

General Programs, Office of Renamed Office of Public Programs by the Chairman, National Endowment for the Humanities, in January 1991.

Geographic Board, U.S. Established by EO 27–A of Sept. 4, 1890. Abolished by EO 6680 of Apr. 17, 1935, and duties transferred to *U.S. Board on Geographical Names,* Department of the Interior, effective June 17, 1934. *Board* abolished by act of July 25, 1947 (61 Stat. 457), and duties assumed by *Board on Geographic Names.*

Geographical Names, U.S. Board on *See* **Geographic Board, U.S.**

Geography, Office of Function of standardizing foreign place names placed in the Department of the Interior conjointly with the *Board on Geographic Names* by act of July 25, 1947 (61 Stat. 456). Functions transferred to the Department of Defense by memorandum of understanding by the Departments of the Interior and Defense and the *Bureau of the Budget* Mar. 9, 1968.

Geological Survey Established in the the Department of the Interior by act of Mar. 3, 1879 (20 Stat. 394). Renamed United States Geological Survey by acts of Nov. 13, 1991 (105 Stat. 1000) and May 18, 1992 (106 Stat. 172).

Germany, Mixed Claims Commission, U.S. and Established by agreement of Aug. 10, 1922, between U.S. and Germany. Duties extended by agreement of Dec. 31, 1928. Time limit for filing claims expired June 30, 1928. All claims disposed of by Oct. 30, 1939. Terminated June 30, 1941.

Goethals Memorial Commission Established by act of Aug. 4, 1935 (49 Stat. 743). Placed under jurisdiction of *Department of War* by EO 8191 of July 5, 1939.

Government. *See other part of title*

Grain Futures Administration Established in the Department of Agriculture under provisions of act of Sept. 21, 1922 (42 Stat. 998). Superseded by *Commodity Exchange Administration* by order of Secretary, effective July 1, 1936. Consolidated with other agencies into *Commodity Exchange Branch, Agricultural Marketing Administration,* by EO 9069 of Feb. 23, 1942. Functions transferred to the Secretary of Agriculture by EO 9577 of June 29, 1945. Transfer made permanent by Reorg. Plan No. 3 of 1946, effective July 16, 1946. Functions transferred to *Commodity Exchange Authority* by Secretary's Memorandum 1185 of Jan. 21, 1947. Functions transferred to Commodity Futures Trading Commission by act of Oct. 23, 1974 (88 Stat. 1414).

Grain Stabilization Corporation Organized as Delaware corporation to operate in connection with *Federal Farm Board* pursuant to act of June 15, 1929 (46 Stat. 11). Terminated by filing of certificate of dissolution with Corporation Commission of State of Delaware Dec. 14, 1935.

Grants and Program Systems, Office of Abolished and functions transferred to Cooperative State Research Service, Department of Agriculture, by Secretarial Memorandum 1020–26 of July 1, 1986.

Grazing Service Consolidated with *General Land Office* into Bureau of Land Management, Department of the Interior, by Reorg. Plan No. 3 of 1946, effective July 16, 1946.

Great Lakes Basin Commission Established by EO 11345 of Apr. 20, 1967. Terminated by EO 12319 of Sept. 9, 1981.

Great Lakes Pilotage Administration Established in the Department of Commerce to administer act of June 30, 1960 (74 Stat. 259). Administration of act transferred to the Secretary of Transportation by act of Oct. 15, 1966 (80 Stat. 931).

Handicapped, National Center on Education Media and Materials for the Established by agreement between the *Secretary of Health, Education, and Welfare* and Ohio State University, pursuant to acts of Aug. 20, 1969 (83 Stat. 102) and Apr. 13, 1970 (84 Stat. 187). Authorization deleted by act of Nov. 29, 1975 (89 Stat. 795), and the Secretary was authorized to enter into agreements with non-Federal organizations to establish and operate centers for handicapped.

Handicapped, National Council on the Established in the *Department of Health, Education, and Welfare* by act of Nov. 6, 1978 (92 Stat. 2977). Transferred to the Department of Education by act of Oct. 17, 1979 (93 Stat. 677). Reorganized as independent agency by act of Feb. 22, 1984 (98 Stat. 26).

Handicapped Employees, Interagency Committee on Alternately renamed Interagency Committee on Employment of People with Disabilities by EO 12704 of Feb. 26, 1990.

Handicapped Individuals, White House Conference on Established by act of Dec. 7, 1974 (88 Stat. 1617). Terminated Dec. 30, 1977, pursuant to terms of act.

Handicapped Research, National Institute of Renamed National Institute on Disability and Rehabilitation Research by act of Oct. 21, 1986 (100 Stat. 1820).

Health, Cost of Living Council Committee on Established by EO 11695 of Jan. 11, 1973. Abolished by EO 11788 of June 18, 1974.

Health, Education, and Welfare, Department of Established by Reorganization Plan No. 1 of 1953 (5 U.S.C. app.), effective Apr. 11, 1953. Renamed Department of Health and Human Services by act of Oct. 17, 1979 (93 Stat. 695).

Health, Welfare, and Related Defense Activities, Office of the Coordinator of *Federal Security Administrator* designated as Coordinator of health, welfare, and related fields of activity affecting national defense, including aspects of education under *Federal Security Agency,* by *Council of National Defense,* with approval of President, Nov. 28, 1940. Office of Coordinator superseded by *Office of Defense Health and Welfare Services,* established in *Office for Emergency Services* by EO 8890 of Sept. 3, 1941.

Health Care Technology, National Council on Established by act of July 1, 1944, as amended (92 Stat. 3447). Renamed *Council on Health Care Technology* by act of Oct. 30, 1984 (98 Stat. 2820). Name lowercased by act of Oct. 7, 1985 (99 Stat. 493). Terminated by act of Dec. 19, 1989 (103 Stat. 2205).

Health Facilities, Financing, Compliance, and Conversion, Bureau of Renamed Bureau of Health Facilities by Department of Health and Human Services Secretarial order of Mar. 12, 1980 (45 FR 17207).

Health Industry Advisory Committee Established by EO 11695 of Jan. 11, 1973. Abolished by EO 11781 of May 1, 1974.

Health Manpower, Bureau of Renamed Bureau of Health Professions by Department of Health and Human Services Secretarial order of Mar. 12, 1980 (45 FR 17207).

Health and Medical Committee Established by *Council of National Defense* order of Sept. 19, 1940. Transferred to *Federal Security Agency* by *Council* order approved by President Nov. 28, 1940. Reestablished in *Office of Defense Health and Welfare Services, Office for Emergency Management,* by EO 8890 of Sept. 3, 1941. *Committee* transferred to *Federal Security Agency* by EO 9338 of Apr. 29, 1943.

Health Resources Administration Established in Public Health Service. Abolished by Department of Health and Human Services Secretarial reorganization of Aug. 20, 1982 (47 FR 38409), and functions transferred to Health Resources and Services Administration.

Health Service, Public Originated by act of July 16, 1798 (1 Stat. 605). Transferred from the Department of the Treasury to the *Federal Security Agency* by Reorg. Plan No. I of 1939, effective July 1, 1939.

Health Services Administration Established in Public Health Service. Abolished by Department of Health and Human Services Secretarial reorganization of Aug. 20, 1982 (47 FR 38409), and functions transferred to Health Resources and Services Administration.

Health Services Industry, Committee on the Established by EO 11627 of Oct. 15, 1971. Abolished by EO 11695 of Jan. 11, 1973.

Health Services and Mental Health Administration Established in Public Health Service Apr. 1, 1968. Abolished by *Department of Health, Education, and Welfare* reorganization order and functions transferred to *Centers for Disease Control, Health Resources Administration,* and *Health Services Administration,* effective July 1, 1973.

Health Services Research, National Center for Established by act of July 23, 1974 (88 Stat. 363). Transferred from *Health Resources Administration* to Office of the Assistant Secretary for Health by *Department of Health, Education, and Welfare* reorganization, effective Dec. 2, 1977. Renamed *National Center for Health Services Research and Health Care Technology Assessment* by Secretary's order, pursuant to act of Oct. 30, 1984 (98 Stat. 2817). Terminated by act of Dec. 19, 1989 (103 Stat. 2205).

Health Statistics, National Center for Established by act of July 23, 1974 (88 Stat. 363). Transferred from *Health Resources Administration* to Office of the Assistant Secretary for Health by the *Department of Health, Education, and Welfare* reorganization, effective Dec. 2, 1977. Transferred to *Centers for Disease Control* by Secretary's notice of Apr. 2, 1987 (52 FR 13318).

Health and Welfare Activities, Interdepartmental Committee to Coordinate Appointed by President Aug. 15, 1935, and reestablished by EO 7481 of Oct. 27, 1936. Terminated in 1939.

Health and Welfare Aspects of Evacuation of Civilians, Joint Committee on Established August 1941 as joint committee of *Office of Defense Health and Welfare Services* and *Office of Civilian Defense.* Reorganized in June 1942 and renamed *Joint Committee on Evacuation. Office of Defense Health and Welfare Services* abolished by EO 9388 of Apr. 29, 1943, and functions transferred to *Federal Security Agency. Committee* terminated.

Heart and Lung Institute, National Renamed National Heart, Lung, and Blood Institute by act of Apr. 22, 1976 (90 Stat. 402).

Heritage Conservation and Recreation Service Established by the Secretary of the Interior Jan. 25, 1978. Abolished by Secretarial Order 3060 of Feb. 19, 1981, and functions transferred to National Park Service.

Highway Safety Agency, National Established in the Department of Commerce by act of Sept. 9, 1966 (80 Stat. 731). Functions transferred to the Department of Transportation by act of Oct. 15, 1966 (80 Stat. 931). Functions transferred to *National Highway Safety Bureau* by EO 11357 of June 6, 1967. *Bureau* renamed National Highway Traffic Safety Administration by act of Dec. 31, 1970 (84 Stat. 1739).

Highway Safety Bureau, National *See* **Highway Safety Agency, National**

Home Economics, Bureau of Human Nutrition and *See* **Home Economics, Office of**

Home Economics, Office of Renamed *Bureau of Home Economics* by Secretary's Memorandum 436, effective July 1, 1923, pursuant to act of Feb. 26, 1923 (42 Stat. 1289). Redesignated *Bureau of Human Nutrition and Home Economics* February 1943 in accordance with *Research Administration* Memorandum 5 issued pursuant to EO 9069 of Feb. 23, 1942, and in conformity with Secretary's Memorandums 960 and 986. Functions transferred to Agricultural Research Service by Secretary's Memorandum 1320, supp. 4, of Nov. 2, 1953.

Home Loan Bank Administration, Federal *See* **Home Loan Bank Board, Federal**

Home Loan Bank Board *See* **Home Loan Bank Board, Federal**

Home Loan Bank Board, Federal Established by acts of July 22, 1932 (47 Stat. 725), June 13, 1933 (48 Stat. 128), and June 27, 1934 (48 Stat. 1246). Grouped with other agencies to form *Federal Loan Agency* by Reorg. Plan No. I of 1939, effective July 1, 1939. Functions transferred to *Federal Home Loan Bank Administration, National Housing Agency,* by EO 9070 of Feb. 24, 1942. Abolished by Reorg. Plan No. 3, effective July 27, 1947, and functions transferred to *Home Loan Bank Board, Housing and Home Finance Agency.* Renamed *Federal Home Loan Bank Board* and made independent agency by act of Aug. 11, 1955 (69 Stat. 640). Abolished by act of Aug. 9, 1989 (103 Stat. 354, 415), and functions transferred to Office of Thrift Supervision, Resolution Trust Corporation, Federal Deposit Insurance Corporation, and Federal Housing Finance Board.

Home Loan Bank System, Federal Grouped with other agencies to form *Federal Loan Agency* by Reorg. Plan No. I of 1939, effective July 1, 1939. Functions transferred to *Federal Home Loan Bank Administration, National Housing Agency,* by EO 9070 of Feb. 24, 1942. Transferred to *Housing and Home Finance Agency* by Reorg. Plan No. 3 of 1947, effective July 27, 1947.

Home Mortgage Credit Extension Committee, National Voluntary Established by act of Aug. 2, 1954 (68 Stat 638). Terminated Oct. 1, 1965, pursuant to terms of act.

Home Owners' Loan Corporation Established by act of June 13, 1933 (48 Stat. 128), under supervision of *Federal Home Loan Bank Board.* Grouped with other agencies to form *Federal Loan Agency* by Reorg. Plan No. I of 1939, effective July 1, 1939. Transferred to *Federal Home Loan Bank Administration, National Housing Agency,* by EO 9070 of Feb. 24, 1942. Board of Directors abolished by Reorg. Plan No. 3 of 1947, effective July 27, 1947, and functions transferred, for liquidation of assets, to *Home Loan Bank Board, Housing and Home Finance Agency.* Terminated by order of *Secretary of the Home Loan Bank Board,* effective

Feb. 3, 1954, pursuant to act of June 30, 1953 (67 Stat. 121).

Homesteads, Division of Subsistence Established by act of June 16, 1933 (48 Stat. 205). Secretary of the Interior authorized to administer section 208 of act by EO 6209 of July 21, 1933. *Federal Subsistence Homesteads Corporation* created by Secretary's order of Dec. 2, 1933, and organization incorporated under laws of Delaware. Transferred to *Resettlement Administration* by EO 7041 of May 15, 1935.

Homesteads Corporation, Federal Subsistence *See* **Homesteads, Division of Subsistence**

Hospitalization, Board of Federal Organized Nov. 1, 1921. Designated as advisory agency to *Bureau of the Budget* May 7, 1943. Terminated June 30, 1948, by Director's letter of May 28, 1948.

Housing, President's Committee on Equal Opportunity in Established by EO 11063 of Nov. 20, 1962. Inactive as of June 30, 1968.

Housing Administration, Federal Established by act of June 27, 1934 (48 Stat. 1246). Grouped with other agencies to form *Federal Loan Agency* by Reorg. Plan No. I of 1939, effective July 1, 1939. Functions transferred to *Federal Housing Administration, National Housing Agency,* by EO 9070 of Feb. 24, 1942. Transferred to *Housing and Home Finance Agency* by Reorg. Plan No. 3, effective July 27, 1947. Functions transferred to the Department of Housing and Urban Development by act of Sept. 9, 1965 (79 Stat. 667).

Housing Administration, Public Established as constituent agency of *Housing and Home Finance Agency* by Reorg. Plan No. 3 of 1947, effective July 27, 1947. Functions transferred to the Department of Housing and Urban Development by act of Sept. 9, 1965 (79 Stat. 667).

Housing Agency, National Established by EO 9070 of Feb. 24, 1942, to consolidate housing functions relating to *Federal Home Loan Bank Board, Federal Home Loan Bank System, Federal Savings and Loan Insurance Corporation, Home Owners' Loan Corporation, U.S. Housing Corporation, Federal Housing Administration, U.S. Housing Authority, Defense Homes Corporation, Division of Defense Housing Coordination, Central Housing Committee, Farm Security Administration* with respect to nonfarm housing, *Public Buildings Administration, Division of Defense Housing, Mutual Ownership Defense Housing Division, Office of Administrator of Federal Works Agency,* and the Departments of *War* and the Navy with respect to housing located off military installations. Agency dissolved on creation of *Housing and Home Finance Agency* by Reorg. Plan No. 3 of 1947, effective July 27, 1947.

Housing Authority, Federal Public Established by EO 9070 of Feb. 24, 1942. Public housing functions of *Federal Works Agency, the Departments of War* and the Navy (except housing located on military installations), and *Farm Security Administration* (nonfarm housing) transferred to *Authority,* and *Defense Homes Corporation* administered by the Commissioner of the *Authority'.* Functions transferred to *Public Housing Administration, Housing and Home Finance Agency,* by Reorg. Plan No. 3 of 1947, effective July 27, 1947.

Housing Authority, U.S. Established in the Department of the Interior by act of Sept. 1, 1937 (50 Stat. 888). Transferred to *Federal Works Agency* by Reorg. Plan No. I of 1939, effective July 1, 1939. Transferred to *Federal Public Housing Authority, National Housing Agency,* by EO 9070 of Feb. 24, 1942. Office of Administrator abolished by Reorg. Plan No. 3 of 1947, effective July 27, 1947, and functions transferred to *Public Housing Administration, Housing and Home Finance Agency.*

Housing Corporation, U.S. Incorporated July 10, 1918, under laws of New York. Transferred from the Department of Labor to the Department of the Treasury by EO 7641 of June 22, 1937. Transferred from the Department of the Treasury to the *Public Buildings Administration, Federal Works Agency,* by EO 8186 of June 29, 1939. Functions transferred for liquidation to *Federal Home Loan Bank Administration, National Housing Agency,* by EO 9070 of Feb. 24, 1942. Terminated Sept. 8, 1952, by the *Secretary of the Home Loan Bank Board.*

Housing Council, National Established in *Housing and Home Finance Agency* by Reorg. Plan No. 3 of 1947, effective July 27, 1947. Terminated by Reorg. Plan No. 4 of 1965, effective July 27, 1965, and functions transferred to President.

Housing Division Established in *Public Works Administration* by act of June 16, 1933 (48 Stat. 195). Functions transferred to *U.S. Housing Authority* by EO 7732 of Oct. 27, 1937.

Housing Expediter, Office of the Established in *Office of War Mobilization and Reconversion* by Presidential letter of Dec. 12, 1945, to *Housing Expediter.* Functions of *Housing Expediter* defined by EO 9686 of Jan. 26, 1946. *Housing Expediter* confirmed in position of *National Housing Administrator* Feb. 6, 1946. *Office of the Housing Expediter* established by act of May 22, 1946 (60 Stat. 208). Functions of *Office* and *National Housing Administrator* segregated by EO 9820 of Jan. 11, 1947. Housing functions of *Civilian Production Administration* transferred to *Office* by EO 9836 of Mar. 22, 1947, effective Apr. 1, 1947. Rent control functions of *Office of Temporary Controls* transferred to *Office* by EO 9841 of Apr. 23, 1947. *Office* terminated by EO 10276 of July 31, 1951, and functions transferred to *Economic Stabilization Agency.*

Housing and Home Finance Agency Established by Reorg. Plan No. 3 of 1947, effective July 27, 1947. Terminated by act of Sept. 9, 1965 (79 Stat. 667), and functions transferred to the Department of Housing and Urban Development.

Howard University Established by act of Mar. 2, 1867 (14 Stat. 438). Functions of the Department of the Interior transferred to *Federal Security Agency* by Reorg. Plan No. IV of 1940, effective June 30, 1940. Functions of the *Department of Health, Education, and Welfare* transferred to the Department of Education by act of Oct. 17, 1979 (93 Stat. 678).

Human Development, Office of Established in *Department of Health, Education, and Welfare.* Renamed Office of Human Development Services and component units transferred to or reorganized under new administrations in Office by Secretary's reorganization order of July 26, 1977. Merged into the Administration for Children and Families by Secretary of Health and Human Services reorganization notice dated Apr. 15, 1991.

Human Development Services, Office of *See* **Human Development, Office of**

Hydrographic Office Jurisdiction transferred from *Bureau of Navigation* to Chief of Naval Operations by EO 9126 of Apr. 8, 1942, and by Reorg. Plan No. 3 of 1946, effective July 16, 1946. Renamed U.S. Naval Oceanographic Office by act of July 10, 1962 (76 Stat. 154).

Imagery Office, Central Established as a Department of Defense agency on May 6, 1992. Functions transferred to National Imagery and Mapping Agency by P.L. 104–201, Sept. 23, 1996 (110 Stat. 2677).

Immigration, Bureau of Established as branch of the Department of the Treasury by act of Mar. 3, 1891 (26 Stat. 1085). Transferred to *Department of Commerce and Labor* by act of Feb. 14, 1903 (34 Stat. 596). Made *Bureau of Immigration and Naturalization* by act of June 29, 1906 (37 Stat. 736). Made separate division after the Department of Labor created by act of Mar. 4, 1913 (37 Stat. 736). Consolidated into Immigration and Naturalization Service, Department of Labor, by EO 6166 of June 10, 1933. Transferred to the Department of Justice by Reorg. Plan No. V of 1940, effective June 14, 1940.

Immigration, Commissioners of Offices of commissioners of immigration of the several ports created by act of Aug. 18, 1894 (28 Stat. 391). Abolished by Reorg. Plan No. III of 1940, effective June 30, 1940, and functions transferred to *Bureau of Immigration and Naturalization,* Department of Labor.

Immigration and Naturalization, Bureau of *See* **Immigration, Bureau of**

Immigration and Naturalization, District Commissioner of Created by act of Aug. 18, 1894 (28 Stat. 391). Abolished by Reorg. Plan No. III of 1940, effective June 30, 1940. Functions administered by the Commissioner of Immigration and Naturalization, Department of Justice, through district immigration and naturalization directors.

Immigration and Naturalization Service *See* **Immigration, Bureau of**

Import Programs, Office of Established by the Secretary of Commerce Feb. 14, 1971. Functions transferred to *Domestic and International Business Administration,* effective Nov. 17, 1972.

Indian Claims Commission Established by act of Aug. 13, 1946 (60 Stat. 1049). Terminated by act of Oct. 8, 1976 (90 Stat. 1990), and pending cases transferred to *U.S. Court of Claims* Sept. 30, 1978.

Indian Commissioners, Board of Established by section 2039, Revised Statutes. Abolished by EO 6145 of May 25, 1933.

Indian Medical Facilities Functions transferred from the Department of the Interior to the *Department of Health, Education, and Welfare,* to be administered by the Surgeon General of Public Health Service, by act of Aug. 5, 1954 (68 Stat. 674).

Indian Opportunity, National Council on Established by EO 11399 of Mar. 6, 1968. Terminated Nov. 26, 1974, by act of Nov. 26, 1969 (83 Stat. 220).

Indian Policy Review Commission, American Established by act of Jan. 2, 1975 (88 Stat. 1910). Terminated June 30, 1977, pursuant to terms of act.

Industrial Analysis, Committee of Established by EO 7323 of Mar. 21, 1936. Terminated Feb. 17, 1937.

Industrial Cooperation, Coordinator for Established by EO 7193 of Sept. 26, 1935. Continued by EO 7324 of Mar. 30, 1936. Terminated June 30, 1937.

Industrial Emergency Committee Established by EO 6770 of June 30, 1934. Consolidated with *National Emergency Council* by EO 6889–A of Oct. 29, 1934.

Industrial Pollution Control Council Staff, National Established by Department of Commerce Organization Order 35–3 of June 17, 1970. *Staff* abolished by departmental organization order of Sept. 10, 1973. Council inactive.

Industrial Recovery Board, National Established by EO 6859 of Sept. 27, 1934. Terminated by EO 7075 of June 15, 1935.

Industrial Recovery Board, Special Established by EO 6173 of June 16, 1933. Functions absorbed by *National Emergency Council* under terms of EO 6513 of Dec. 18, 1933.

Industrial Relations, Office of Activated in the Department of the Navy Sept. 14, 1945. Superseded June 22, 1966, by creation of *Office of Civilian Manpower Management.*

Industry and Trade Administration *See* **Business and Defense Services Administration**

Information, Committee for Reciprocity Established by EO 6750 of June 27, 1934; reestablished by EO 10004 of Oct. 5, 1948, which revoked EO 6750. Superseded by EO 10082 of Oct. 5, 1949; abolished by EO 11075 of Jan. 15, 1963, which revoked EO 10082.

Information, Coordinator of Established by Presidential order of July 11, 1941. Functions exclusive of foreign information activities transferred by military order of June 13, 1942, to jurisdiction of Joint Chiefs of Staff, *War Department,* as *Office of Strategic Services.* Foreign information functions transferred to *Office of War Information* by EO 9182 of June 13, 1942.

Information, Division of Established pursuant to Presidential letter of Feb. 28, 1941, to *Liaison Officer, Office of Emergency Management.* Abolished by EO 9182 of June 13, 1942. Functions relating to public information on war effort transferred and consolidated with *Office of War Information,* and publication services relating to specific agencies of OEM transferred to those agencies.

Information, Office of Coordinator of Transferred, exclusive of foreign information activities, to *Office of War Information* by EO 9182 of June 13, 1942. Designated *Office of Strategic Services* and transferred to jurisdiction of Joint Chiefs of Staff by military order of June 13, 1942. Terminated by EO 9621 of Sept. 20, 1945, and functions distributed to the Departments of State and *War.*

Information Administration, International Transferred from the Department of State to the *U.S. Information Agency* by Reorg. Plan No. 8 of 1953, effective Aug. 1, 1953.

Information Agency, U.S. Established by Reorg. Plan No. 8 of 1953, effective Aug. 1, 1953. Abolished by Reorg. Plan No. 2 of 1977, effective Apr. 1, 1978; replaced by and functions transferred to *International Communication Agency.* Redesignated *U.S. Information Agency* by act of Aug. 24, 1982 (96 Stat. 291). Abolished by act of Oct. 21, 1998 (112 Stat. 2681–761), and functions transferred to the Department of State, effective Oct. 1, 1999.

Information and Public Affairs, Office of Merged with *Office of Intergovernmental Affairs* to form Office of Public and Intergovernmental Affairs by Order 1–85 of June 5, 1985 of the Secretary of Labor.

Information Resources Management, Office of *See* **Telecommunications Service, Automated Data**

Information Resources Management Service Established in the General Services Administration. Renamed Information Technology Service in 1995.

Information Security Committee, Interagency Established by EO 12065 of June 28, 1978. Abolished by EO 12356 of Apr. 2, 1982.

Information Security Oversight Office Established in General Services Administration by EO 12065 of June 28, 1978. EO 12065 revoked by EO 12356 of Apr. 2, 1982, which provided for continuation of Office.

Information Service, Government *See* **Information Service, U.S.**

Information Service, Interim International Established in the Department of State by EO 9608 of Aug. 31, 1945. Abolished Dec. 31, 1945, pursuant to terms of order.

Information Service, U.S. Established in March 1934 as division of *National Emergency Council.* Transferred to *Office of Government Reports* by Reorg. Plan No. II of 1939, effective July 1, 1939. Consolidated, along with other functions of *Office,* into *Division of Public Inquiries, Bureau of Special Services, Office of War Information,* by EO 9182 of June 13, 1942. *Bureau of Special Services* renamed *Government Information Service* and transferred to *Bureau of the Budget* by EO 9608 of Aug. 31, 1945. *Service* transferred to *Office of Government Reports* by EO 9809 of Dec. 12, 1946.

Information Technology Service Established in General Services Administration. Abolished by General Services Administrative Order No. 5440.492, Aug. 21, 1996, and functions transferred to Federal Telecommunications Service.

Insane, Government Hospital for the Established by act of Mar. 3, 1855 (10 Stat. 682). Renamed Saint Elizabeth's Hospital by act of July 1, 1916 (39 Stat. 309). Transferred from the Department of the Interior to *Federal Security Agency* by Reorg. Plan No. IV of 1940, effective June 30, 1940. Transferred to *Department of Health, Education, and Welfare* by Reorg. Plan No. 1 of 1953, effective Apr. 11, 1953. Functions redelegated to National Institute of Mental Health by Secretary's reorganization order of Aug. 9, 1967. Property and administration transferred to District of Columbia Government by act of Nov. 8, 1984 (98 Stat. 3369).

Installations, Director of Established in the Department of Defense by act of July 14, 1952 (66 Stat. 625). Abolished by Reorg. Plan No. 6 of 1953, effective June 30, 1953, and functions transferred to the Secretary of Defense.

Insular Affairs, Bureau of Transferred from *Department of War* to *Division of Territories and Island Possessions,* the Department of the Interior, by Reorg. Plan No. II of 1939, effective July 1, 1939.

Insurance Administrator, Federal Established by act of Aug. 1, 1968 (82 Stat. 567). Functions transferred to Federal Emergency Management Agency by Reorg. Plan No. 3 of 1978, effective Apr. 1, 1979.

Integrity and Efficiency, President's Council on Established by EO 12301 of Mar. 26, 1981 (46 FR 19211). Abolished and reestablished by EO 12625 of Jan 27, 1988 (53 FR 2812). Abolished and reestablished by EO 12805 of May 11, 1992 (57 FR 20627).

Intelligence Activities, President's Board of Consultants on Foreign Established by EO 10656 of Feb. 6, 1956. EO 10656 revoked by EO 10938 of May 4, 1961, and *Board* terminated. Functions transferred to President's Foreign Intelligence Advisory Board.

Intelligence Advisory Board, President's Foreign Established by EO 11460 of Mar. 20, 1969. Abolished by EO 11984 of May 4, 1977. Reestablished by EO 12331 of Oct. 20, 1981.

Intelligence Authority, National Established by Presidential directive of Jan. 22, 1946. Terminated on creation of Central Intelligence Agency under National Security Council by act of July 26, 1947 (61 Stat. 497).

Intelligence Group, Central Terminated on creation of Central Intelligence Agency by act of July 26, 1947 (61 Stat. 497).

Inter-American Affairs, Institute of *See* **American Republics, Office for Coordination of Commercial and Cultural Relations between the**

Inter-American Affairs, Office of *See* **American Republics, Office for Coordination of Commercial and Cultural Relations between the**

Inter-American Affairs, Office of the Coordinator of *See* **American Republics, Office for Coordination of Commercial and Cultural Relations between the**

Interagency. *See other part of title*

Interdepartmental. *See also other part of title*

Interdepartmental Advisory Council Established January 1941 to advise *Coordinator of Health, Welfare, and Related Defense Activities.* Terminated on creation of *Office of Defense Health and Welfare Service* Sept. 3, 1941.

Interest and Dividends, Committee on Established by EO 11695 of Jan. 11, 1973. Abolished by EO 11781 of May 1, 1974.

Intergovernmental Affairs, Office of Merged with *Office of Information and Public Affairs* to form Office of Public and Intergovernmental Affairs by Order 1–85 of June 5, 1985 of the Secretary of Labor.

Intergovernmental Relations, Advisory Commission on Established by act of Sept. 24, 1959 (73 Stat. 703). Terminated pursuant to act of Nov. 19, 1995 (109 Stat. 480). Continued in existence by P.L. 104–328, Oct. 19, 1996 (110 Stat. 4004).

Intergovernmental Relations, Commission on Established by act of July 10, 1953 (67 Stat. 145). Final report submitted to Congress by June 30, 1955, pursuant to act of Feb. 7, 1955 (69 Stat. 7).

Intergovernmental Relations, Office of Established by EO 11455 of Feb. 14, 1969. Functions transferred to *Domestic Council* by EO 11690 of Dec. 14, 1972.

Interim Compliance Panel Established by Dec. 30, 1969 (83 Stat. 774). Terminated June 30, 1976, pursuant to terms of act.

Internal Revenue Service Functions relating to alcohol, tobacco, firearms, and explosives transferred to Bureau of Alcohol, Tobacco, and Firearms by Department of Treasury order of July 1, 1972.

Internal Security Division Established July 9, 1945, by transfer of functions from Criminal Division. Abolished Mar. 22, 1973, and functions transferred to Criminal Division, Department of Justice.

International. *See also other part of title*

International Activities, Office of Renamed *Office of Service and Protocol* by Secretary of the Smithsonian Institution internal directive of Jan. 11, 1985.

International Development, Agency for Transferred from the Department of State to *U.S. International Development Cooperation Agency* by Reorg. Plan No. 2 of 1979, effective Oct. 1, 1979. Continued as agency within *IDCA* by IDCA Delegation of Authority No. 1 of Oct. 1, 1979. By act of Oct. 21, 1998 (112 Stat. 2681–790), became independent agency.

International Development Cooperation Agency, U.S. Established by Reorg. Plan No. 2 of 1979, effective Oct. 1, 1979. Abolished by act of Oct. 21, 1998 (112 Stat. 2681–790) and functions transferred to the Department of State, U.S. Agency for International Development, and Overseas Private Investment Corporation.

Interstate Commerce Commission Created by act of Feb. 4, 1887 (24 Stat. 379). Certain functions as cited in act of Oct. 15, 1966 (80 Stat. 931) transferred to the Secretary of Commerce. Functions relating to railroad and pipeline safety transferred to Federal Railroad Administrator and motor carrier safety to Federal Highway Administrator by act. Abolished by act of Dec. 29, 1995 (109 Stat. 932) and many functions transferred to the newly created Surface Transportation Board within the Department of Transportation.

Investigation, Bureau of Established by act of May 22, 1908 (35 Stat. 235). Functions consolidated with investigative functions of *Bureau of Prohibition, Division of Investigation,* Department of Justice, by EO 6166 of June 10, 1933, effective Mar. 2, 1934.

Investigation, Division of Designated as Federal Bureau of Investigation in the Department of Justice by act of Mar. 22, 1935 (49 Stat. 77).

Investigation and Research, Board of Established by act of Sept. 18, 1940 (54 Stat. 952). Extended to Sept. 18, 1944, by Proc. 2559 of June 26, 1942.

Investigations, Division of Established by administrative order of Apr. 27, 1933. Abolished Jan. 17, 1942, by administrative order and functions transferred to *Branch of Field Examination, General Land Office,* Department of the Interior.

Investments, Office of Foreign Direct Established in the Department of Commerce Jan. 2, 1968, by Departmental Organization Order 25–3 to carry out provisions of EO 11387 of Jan. 1, 1968. Controls on foreign investments terminated Jan. 29, 1974.

Jamestown-Williamsburg-Yorktown National Celebration Commission Established by act of Aug. 13, 1953 (67 Stat. 576). Terminated upon submission of final report to Congress Mar. 1, 1958.

Joint. *See also other part of title*

Joint Resolutions of Congress *See* **State, Department of**

Judicial Procedure, Commission on International Rules of Established by act of Sept. 2, 1958 (72 Stat. 1743). Terminated Dec. 31, 1966, by act of Aug. 30, 1964 (78 Stat. 700).

Justice Assistance, Research, and Statistics, Office of Established in the Department of Justice by act of Dec. 27, 1979 (93 Stat. 1201). Abolished by act of Oct. 12, 1984 (98 Stat. 2091).

Kennedy, Commission To Report Upon the Assassination of President John F. Established by EO 11130 of Nov. 29, 1963. Report submitted Sept. 24, 1964, and *Commission* discharged by Presidential letter of same date.

Labor, President's Committee on Migratory Appointed by Presidential letter of Aug. 26, 1954. Formally established by EO 10894 of Nov. 15, 1960. Terminated Jan. 6, 1964, by the Secretary of Labor in letter to members, with approval of President.

Labor and Commerce, Department of Established by act of Feb. 14, 1903 (32 Stat. 825). Reorganized into separate Departments of Labor and Commerce by act of Mar. 4, 1913 (37 Stat. 736).

Labor Department, Solicitor for Transferred from the Department of Justice to the Department of Labor by EO 6166 of June 10, 1933.

Labor-Management Advisory Committee Established by EO 11695 of Jan. 11, 1973. Abolished by EO 11788 of June 18, 1974.

Labor-Management Policy, President's Advisory Committee on Established by EO 10918 of Feb. 16, 1961. Abolished by EO 11710 of Apr. 4, 1973.

Labor-Management Relations Services, Office of Established by Order 3–84 of May 3, 1984 of the Secretary of Labor. Renamed Bureau of Labor-Management Relations and Cooperative Programs by Secretarial Order 7–84 of Sept. 20, 1984 (49 FR 38374).

Labor-Management Services Administration *Office of Pension and Welfare Benefit Programs* transferred from *Administration* and constituted as separate unit by Order 1–84 of Jan. 20, 1984 of the Secretary of Labor (49 FR 4269). Remaining labor-management relations functions reassigned by Secretarial Order 3–84 of May 3, 1984.

Labor Organization, International Established in 1919 by Treaty of Versailles with U.S. joining in 1934. U.S. membership terminated Nov. 1, 1977, at President's direction.

Labor Relations Council, Federal Established by EO 11491 of Oct. 29, 1969. Abolished by Reorg. Plan No. 2 of 1978, effective Jan. 1, 1979, and functions transferred to Federal Labor Relations Authority.

Labor Standards, Apprenticeship Section, Division of Transferred to *Federal Security Agency* by EO 9139 of Apr. 18, 1942, functioning as *Apprentice Training Service*. Transferred to *War Manpower Commission* by EO 9247 of Sept. 17, 1942, functioning in *Bureau of Training*. Returned to the Department of Labor by EO 9617 of Sept. 19, 1945.

Labor Standards, Bureau of Established by Labor departmental order in 1934. Functions absorbed by Occupational Safety and Health Administration in May 1971.

Land Bank Commissioner *See* **Farm Loan Board, Federal**

Land Law Review Commission, Public Established by act of Sept. 19, 1964 (78 Stat. 982). Terminated Dec. 31, 1970, pursuant to terms of act.

Land Office, General Consolidated with *Grazing Service* into Bureau of Land Management, Department of the Interior, by Reorg. Plan No. 3 of 1946, effective July 16, 1946.

Land Office, Office of Recorder of the General Created in the Department of the Interior by act of July 4, 1836 (5 Stat. 111). Abolished by Reorg. Plan No. III of 1940, effective June 30, 1940, and functions transferred to *General Land Office*.

Land Policy Section Established in 1934 as part of *Program Planning Division, Agricultural Adjustment Administration*. Personnel taken over by *Resettlement Administration* in 1935.

Land Problems, Committee on National Established by EO 6693 of Apr. 28, 1934. Abolished by EO 6777 of June 30, 1934.

Land Program, Director of Basis of program found in act of June 16, 1933 (48 Stat. 200). *Special Board of Public Works* established by EO 6174 of June 16, 1933. Land Program established by *Board* by resolution passed Dec. 28, 1933, and amended July 18, 1934. *Federal Emergency Relief Administration* designated to administer program Feb. 28, 1934. Land Program transferred to *Resettlement Administration* by EO 7028 of Apr. 30, 1935. Functions of *Administration* transferred to the Secretary of Agriculture by EO 7530 of Dec. 31, 1936. Land conservation and land-utilization programs administered by *Administration* transferred to *Bureau of Agricultural Economics* by Secretary's Memorandum 733. Administration of land programs placed under Soil Conservation Service by Secretary's Memorandum 785 of Oct. 6, 1938.

Land Use Coordination, Office of Established by Secretary of Agriculture Memorandum 725 of July 12, 1937. Abolished Jan. 1, 1944, by General Departmental Circular 21 and functions administered by *Land Use Coordinator*.

Land Use and Water Planning, Office of Established in the Department of the Interior by Secretarial Order No. 2953 of May 7, 1973. Abolished by Secretarial Order No. 2988 of Mar. 11, 1976.

Law Enforcement Assistance Administration Established by act of June 19, 1968 (82 Stat. 197). Operations closed out by the Department of Justice due to lack of appropriations and remaining functions transferred to *Office of Justice Assistance, Research, and Statistics*.

Law Enforcement Training Center, Consolidated Federal Renamed Federal Law Enforcement Training Center by Amendment No. 1 of Aug. 14, 1975, to Department of the Treasury Order 217 (Revision 1).

Legislative Affairs, Office of Renamed Office of Intergovernmental and Legislative Affairs Feb. 24, 1984, by Attorney General's Order 1054–84 (49 FR 10177).

Lend-Lease Administration, Office of Established by EO 8926 of Oct. 28, 1941, to replace *Division of Defense Aid Reports*. Consolidated with *Foreign Economic Administration* by EO 9380 of Sept. 25, 1943.

Lewis and Clark Trail Commission Established by act of Oct. 6, 1964 (78 Stat. 1005). Terminated October 1969 by terms of act.

Lighthouses, Bureau of Established in the Department of Commerce by act of Aug. 7, 1789 (1 Stat. 53). Consolidated with U.S. Coast Guard by Reorg. Plan No. II of 1939, effective July 1, 1939.

Lincoln Sesquicentennial Commission Established by joint resolution of Sept. 2, 1957 (71 Stat. 587). Terminated Mar. 1, 1960, pursuant to terms of joint resolution.

Liquidation, Director of Established in *Office for Emergency Management* by EO 9674 of Jan. 4, 1946. Terminated by EO 9744 of June 27, 1946.

Liquidation Advisory Committee Established by EO 9674 of Jan. 4, 1946. Terminated by EO 9744 of June 27, 1946.

Loan Agency, Federal Established by Reorg. Plan No. I of 1939, effective July 1, 1939, by consolidating *Reconstruction Finance Corporation*—including subordinate units of *RFC Mortgage Company, Disaster Loan Corporation, Federal National Mortgage Association, Defense Plant Corporation, Defense Homes Corporation, Defense Supplies Corporation, Rubber Reserve Company, Metals Reserve Company,* and *War Insurance Corporation* (later known as *War Damage Corporation*)—with *Federal Home Loan Bank Board, Home Owners' Loan Corporation, Federal Savings and Loan Insurance Corporation, Federal Housing Administration, Electric Home and Farm Authority,* and *Export-Import Bank of Washington. Federal Home Loan Bank Board, Federal Savings and Loan Insurance Corporation, Home Owners' Loan Corporation, Federal Housing Administration,* and *Defense Homes Corporation* transferred to *National Housing Agency* by EO 9070 of Feb. 24, 1942. *Reconstruction Finance Corporation* and its units (except *Defense Homes Corporation*), *Electric Home and Farm Authority,* and *Export-Import Bank of Washington* transferred to the Department of Commerce by EO 9071 of Feb. 24, 1942. *RFC* and units returned to *Federal Loan Agency* by act of Feb. 24, 1945 (59 Stat. 5). *Agency* abolished by act of June 30, 1947 (61 Stat. 202), and all property and records transferred to *Reconstruction Finance Corporation.*

Loan Fund, Development Established in *International Cooperation Administration* by act of Aug. 14, 1957 (71 Stat. 355). Created as independent corporate agency by act of June 30, 1958 (72 Stat. 261). Abolished by act of Sept. 4, 1961 (75 Stat. 445), and functions redelegated to Agency for International Development.

Loan Policy Board Established by act of July 18, 1958 (72 Stat. 385). Abolished by Reorg. Plan No. 4 of 1965, effective July 27, 1965, and functions transferred to Small Business Administration.

Longshoremen's Labor Board, National Established in the Department of Labor by EO 6748 of June 26, 1934. Terminated by Proc. 2120 of Mar. 11, 1935.

Low-Emission Vehicle Certification Board Established by act of Dec. 31, 1970 (84 Stat. 1701). Terminated by act of Mar. 14, 1980 (94 Stat. 98).

Lowell Historic Canal District Commission Established by act of Jan. 4, 1975 (88 Stat. 2330). Expired January 1977 pursuant to terms of act.

Loyalty Review Board Established Nov. 10, 1947, by *U.S. Civil Service Commission,* pursuant to EO 9835 of Mar. 21, 1947. Abolished by EO 10450 of Apr. 27, 1953.

Management Improvement, Advisory Committee on Established by EO 10072 of July 29, 1949. Abolished by EO 10917 of Feb. 10, 1961, and functions transferred to *Bureau of the Budget.*

Management Improvement, President's Advisory Council on Established by EO 11509 of Feb. 11, 1970. Inactive as of June 30, 1973.

Manpower, President's Committee on Established by EO 11152 of Apr. 15, 1964. Terminated by EO 11515 of Mar. 13, 1970.

Manpower Administration Renamed Employment and Training Administration by Order 14–75 of Nov. 12, 1975 of the Secretary of Labor.

Manpower Management, Office of Civilian Renamed Office of Civilian Personnel by Notice 5430 of Oct. 1, 1976 of the Secretary of the Navy.

Marine Affairs, Office of Established by the Secretary of the Interior Apr. 30, 1970, to replace *Office of Marine Resources,* created by Secretary Oct. 22, 1968. Abolished by Secretary Dec. 4, 1970.

Marine Corps Memorial Commission, U.S. Established by act of Aug. 24, 1947 (61 Stat. 724). Terminated by act of Mar. 14, 1980 (94 Stat. 98).

Marine Inspection and Navigation, Bureau of *See* **Navigation and Steamboat Inspection, Bureau of**

Marine Resources and Engineering Development, National Council on Established in Executive Office of the President by act of June 17, 1966 (80 Stat. 203). Terminated Apr. 30, 1971, due to lack of funding.

Maritime Administration Established in the Department of Commerce by Reorg. Plan No. 21 of 1950, effective May 24, 1950. Transferred to the Department of Transportation by act of Aug. 6, 1981 (95 Stat. 151).

Maritime Advisory Committee Established by EO 11156 of June 17, 1964. Terminated by EO 11427 of Sept. 4, 1968.

Maritime Board, Federal *See* **Maritime Commission, U.S.**

Maritime Commission, U.S. Established by act of June 29, 1936 (49 Stat. 1985), as successor agency to *U.S. Shipping Board* and *U.S. Shipping Board Merchant Fleet Corporation.* Training functions transferred to Commandant of Coast Guard by EO 9083 of Feb. 27, 1942. Functions further transferred to *War Shipping Administration* by EO 9198 of July 11, 1942. Abolished by Reorg. Plan No. 21 of 1950, effective May 24, 1950, which established *Federal Maritime Board* and *Maritime Administration* as successor agencies. *Board* abolished, regulatory functions transferred to Federal Maritime Commission, and functions relating to subsidization of merchant marine transferred to the Secretary of Commerce by Reorg. Plan No. 7 of 1961, effective Aug. 12, 1961.

Maritime Labor Board Authorized by act of June 23, 1938 (52 Stat. 968). Mediatory duties abolished by act of June 23, 1941 (55 Stat. 259); title expired June 22, 1942.

Marketing Administration, Surplus Established by Reorg. Plan No. III of 1940, effective June 30, 1940, consolidating functions vested in *Federal Surplus Commodities Corporation* and *Division of Marketing and Marketing Agreements, Agricultural Adjustment Administration*. Consolidated with other agencies into *Agricultural Marketing Administration* by EO 9069 of Feb. 23, 1942.

Marketing and Marketing Agreements, Division of Established in the Department of Agriculture by act of June 3, 1937 (50 Stat. 246). Consolidated with *Federal Surplus Commodities Corporation* into *Surplus Marketing Administration* by Reorg. Plan No. III of 1940, effective June 30, 1940.

Mediation, U.S. Board of Established by act of May 20, 1926 (44 Stat. 577). Abolished by act of June 21, 1934 (48 Stat. 1193), and superseded by National Mediation Board, July 21, 1934.

Medical Information Systems Program Office, Tri-Service Renamed Defense Medical Systems Support Center by memorandum of the Assistant Secretary of Defense (Health Affairs) May 3, 1985.

Medical Services Administration Established by the *Secretary of Health, Education, and Welfare* reorganization of Aug. 15, 1967. Transferred from *Social and Rehabilitation Service* to Health Care Financing Administration by Secretary's reorganization of Mar. 8, 1977 (42 FR 13262).

Medicine and Surgery, Department of Established in the *Veterans Administration* by act of Sept. 2, 1958 (72 Stat. 1243). Renamed *Veterans Health Services and Research Administration* in the the Department of Veterans Affairs by act of Oct. 25, 1988 (102 Stat. 2640). Renamed Veterans Health Administration by act of May 7, 1991 (105 Stat. 187).

Memorial Commission, National Established by Public Resolution 107 of Mar. 4, 1929 (45 Stat. 1699). Terminated by EO 6166 of June 10, 1933, and functions transferred to *Office of National Parks, Buildings, and Reservations,* Department of the Interior.

Mental Health, National Institute of Established by act of July 3, 1946 (60 Stat. 425). Made entity within the Alcohol, Drug Abuse, and Mental Health Administration by act of May 14, 1974 (88 Stat. 135). Functions transferred to the Department of Health and Human Services by act of Oct. 17, 1979 (93 Stat. 695). (*See also* act of Oct. 27, 1986; 100 Stat. 3207–106.) Abolished by act of July 10, 1992 (106 Stat. 331). Reestablished by act of July 10, 1992 (106 Stat. 364).

Metals Reserve Company Established June 28, 1940, by act of Jan. 22, 1932 (47 Stat. 5). Transferred from *Federal Loan Agency* to the Department of Commerce by EO 9071 of Feb. 24, 1942. Returned to *Federal Loan Agency* by act of Feb. 24, 1945 (59 Stat. 5). Dissolved by act of June 30, 1945 (59 Stat. 310), and functions transferred to *Reconstruction Finance Corporation.*

Metric Board, U.S. Established by act of Dec. 23, 1975 (89 Stat. 1007). Terminated Oct. 1, 1982, due to lack of funding.

Mexican-American Affairs, Interagency Committee on Established by Presidential memorandum of June 9, 1967. Renamed *Cabinet Committee on Opportunities for Spanish-Speaking People* by act of Dec. 30, 1969 (83 Stat. 838). Terminated Dec. 30, 1974, pursuant to terms of act.

Mexican Claims Commission, American Established by act of Dec. 18, 1942 (56 Stat. 1058). Terminated Apr. 4, 1947, by act of Apr. 3, 1945 (59 Stat. 59).

Mexican Claims Commission, Special Established by act of Apr. 10, 1935 (49 Stat. 149). Terminated by EO 7909 of June 15, 1938.

Mexico Commission for Border Development and Friendship, U.S.- Established through exchange of notes of Nov. 30 and Dec. 3, 1966, between U.S. and Mexico. Terminated Nov. 5, 1969.

Micronesian Claims Commission Established by act of July 1, 1971 (85 Stat. 92). Terminated Aug. 3, 1976, pursuant to terms of act.

Migration, Intergovernmental Committee for European Renamed Intergovernmental Committee for Migration by Resolution 624, passed by *Intergovernmental Committee for European Migration Council,* effective Nov. 11, 1980.

Migration, International Committee for Created in 1951. Renamed International Organization for Migration pursuant to article 29, paragraph 2, of the ICM constitution, effective Nov. 14, 1989.

Migratory Bird Conservation Commission Chairmanship transferred from the Secretary of Agriculture to the Secretary of the Interior by Reorg. Plan No. II of 1939, effective July 1, 1939.

Military Air Transport Service Renamed *Military Airlift Command* in U.S. Air Force by HQ MATS/MAC Special Order G–164 of Jan. 1, 1966.

Military Airlift Command Inactivated June 1, 1992.

Military Appeals, United States Court of Established under Article I of the Constitution of the United States pursuant to act of May 5, 1950, as amended. Renamed United States Court of Appeals for the Armed Forces by act of Oct. 5, 1994 (108 Stat. 2831).

186-873 D-00--21

Military Establishment, National Established as executive department of the Government by act of July 26, 1947 (61 Stat. 495). Designated Department of Defense by act of Aug. 10, 1949 (63 Stat. 579).

Military Purchases, Interdepartmental Committee for Coordination of Foreign and Domestic Informal liaison committee created on Presidential notification of Dec. 6, 1939, to the Secretaries of the Treasury and *War* and the Acting Secretary of the Navy. Committee dissolved in accordance with Presidential letter to the Secretary of the Treasury Apr. 14, 1941, following approval of act of Mar. 11, 1941 (55 Stat. 31).

Military Renegotiation Policy and Review Board Established by directive of the Secretary of Defense July 19, 1948. Abolished by Secretary's letter of Jan. 18, 1952, which transferred functions to *Renegotiation Board.*

Military Sea Transportation Service Renamed Military Sealift Command in U.S. Navy by COMSC notice of Aug. 1, 1970.

Militia Bureau Established in 1908 as *Division of Militia Affairs, Office of the Secretary of War.* Superseded in 1933 by National Guard Bureau.

Mine Health and Safety Academy, National Transferred from the Department of the Interior to the Department of Labor by act of July 25, 1979 (93 Stat. 111).

Minerals Exploration, Office of Established by act of Aug. 21, 1958 (72 Stat. 700). Functions transferred to *Geological Survey* by Order 2886 of Feb. 26, 1965 of the Secretary of the Interior.

Minerals Mobilization, Office of Established by the Secretary of the Interior pursuant to act of Sept. 8, 1950 (64 Stat. 798) and EO 10574 of Nov. 5, 1954, and by order of *Office of Defense Mobilization.* Succeeded by *Office of Minerals and Solid Fuels* Nov. 2, 1962. *Office of Minerals Policy Development* combined with *Office of Research and Development* in the Department of the Interior May 21, 1976, under authority of Reorg. Plan No. 3 of 1950, to form *Office of Minerals Policy and Research Analysis.* Abolished Sept. 30, 1981, by Secretarial Order 3070 and functions transferred to Bureau of Mines.

Minerals Policy and Research Analysis, Office of *See* **Minerals Mobilization, Office of**

Minerals and Solid Fuels, Office of Established by the Secretary of the Interior Oct. 26, 1962. Abolished and functions assigned to Deputy Assistant Secretary—Minerals and Energy Policy, Office of the Assistant Secretary—Mineral Resources, effective Oct. 22, 1971.

Mines, Bureau of Established in the Department of the Interior by act of May 16, 1910 (36 Stat. 369). Transferred to the Department of Commerce by EO 4239 of June 4, 1925. Transferred to the Department of the Interior by EO 6611 of Feb. 22, 1934. Renamed United States Bureau of Mines by act of May 18, 1992 (106 Stat. 172). Terminated pursuant to P.L. 104–99, Jan. 26, 1996 (110 Stat. 32). Certain functions transferred to Secretary of Energy by P.L. 104–134, Apr. 26, 1996 (110 Stat. 1321–167).

Mining Enforcement and Safety Administration Established by Order 2953 of May 7, 1973 of the Secretary of the Interior. Terminated by departmental directive Mar. 9, 1978, and functions transferred to Mine Safety and Health Administration, Department of Labor, established by act of Nov. 9, 1977 (91 Stat. 1319).

Minority Business Enterprise, Office of Renamed Minority Business Development Agency by Commerce Secretarial Order DOO–254A of Nov. 1, 1979.

Mint, Bureau of the Renamed U.S. Mint by Treasury Secretarial order of Jan. 9, 1984 (49 FR 5020).

Missile Sites Labor Commission Established by EO 10946 of May 26, 1961. Abolished by EO 11374 of Oct. 11, 1967, and functions transferred to Federal Mediation and Conciliation Service.

Missouri Basin Survey Commission Established by EO 10318 of Jan. 3, 1952. Final report of *Commission* submitted to President Jan. 12, 1953, pursuant to EO 10329 of Feb. 25, 1952.

Missouri River Basin Commission Established by EO 11658 of Mar. 22, 1972. Terminated by EO 12319 of Sept. 9, 1981.

Mobilization, Office of Civil and Defense *See* **Mobilization, Office of Defense and Civilian**

Mobilization, Office of Defense and Civilian Established by Reorg. Plan No. 1 of 1958, effective July 1, 1958. Redesignated as *Office of Civil and Defense Mobilization* by act of Aug. 26, 1958 (72 Stat. 861), consolidating functions of *Office of Defense Mobilization* and *Federal Civil Defense Administration.* Civil defense functions transferred to the Secretary of Defense by EO 10952 of July 20, 1961, and remaining organization redesignated *Office of Emergency Planning* by act of Sept. 22, 1961 (75 Stat. 630).

Mobilization Policy, National Advisory Board on Established by EO 10224 of Mar. 15, 1951. EO 10224 revoked by EO 10773 of July 1, 1958.

Monetary and Financial Problems, National Advisory Council on International Established by act of July 31, 1945 (59 Stat. 512). Abolished by Reorg. Plan No. 4 of 1965, effective July 27, 1965, and functions transferred to President. Functions assumed by National Advisory Council on International Monetary and Financial Policies, established by EO 11269 of Feb. 14, 1966.

Monument Commission, National Established by act of Aug. 31, 1954 (68 Stat. 1029). Final report submitted in 1957, and audit of business completed September 1964.

Monuments in War Areas, American Commission for the Protection and Salvage of Artistic and Historic Established by President June 23, 1943; announced by Secretary of State Aug. 20, 1943.

Activities assumed by the Department of State Aug. 16, 1946.

Mortgage Association, Federal National Chartered Feb. 10, 1938, by act of June 27, 1934 (48 Stat. 1246). Grouped with other agencies to form *Federal Loan Agency* by Reorg. Plan No. I of 1939, effective July 1, 1939. Transferred to the Department of Commerce by EO 9071 of Feb. 24, 1942. Returned to *Federal Loan Agency* by act of Feb. 24, 1945 (59 Stat. 5). Transferred to *Housing and Home Finance Agency* by Reorg. Plan No. 22 of 1950, effective July 10, 1950. Rechartered by act of Aug. 2, 1954 (68 Stat. 590) and made constituent agency of *Housing and Home Finance Agency*. Transferred with functions of *Housing and Home Finance Agency* to the Department of Housing and Urban Development by act of Sept. 9, 1965 (79 Stat. 667). Made Government-sponsored, private corporation by act of Aug. 1, 1968 (82 Stat. 536).

Motor Carrier Claims Commission Established by act of July 2, 1948 (62 Stat. 1222). Terminated Dec. 31, 1952, by acts of July 11, 1951 (65 Stat. 116), and Mar. 14, 1952 (66 Stat. 25).

Mount Rushmore National Memorial Commission Established by act of Feb. 25, 1929 (45 Stat. 1300). Expenditures ordered administered by the Department of the Interior by EO 6166 of June 10, 1933. Transferred to National Park Service, Department of the Interior, by Reorg. Plan No. II of 1939, effective July 1, 1939.

Munitions Board Established in the Department of Defense by act of July 26, 1947 (61 Stat. 499). Abolished by Reorg. Plan No. 6 of 1953, effective June 30, 1953, and functions vested in the Secretary of Defense.

Munitions Board, Joint Army and Navy Organized in 1922. Placed under direction of President by military order of July 5, 1939. Reconstituted Aug. 18, 1945, by order approved by President. Terminated on establishment of *Munitions Board* by act of July 26, 1947 (61 Stat. 505).

Museum of History and Technology, National Renamed National Museum of American History in Smithsonian Institution by act of Oct. 13, 1980 (94 Stat. 1884).

Museum Services, Institute of Established by act of June 23, 1972 (86 Stat. 327). Transferred to Office of Educational Research and Improvement, Department of Education, by act of Oct. 17, 1979 (93 Stat. 678), effective May 4, 1980. Transferred to National Foundation on the Arts and the Humanities by act of Dec. 23, 1981 (95 Stat. 1414). Functions transferred to the Institute of Museum and Library Services by P.L. 104–208, Sept. 30, 1996 (110 Stat. 3009–307).

Narcotics, Bureau of Established in the Department of the Treasury by act of June 14, 1930 (46 Stat. 585). Abolished by Reorg. Plan No. 1 of 1968, effective Apr. 8, 1968, and functions transferred to *Bureau of Narcotics and Dangerous Drugs*, Department of Justice.

Narcotics, President's Council on Counter- Renamed President's Drug Policy Council by EO 13023, Nov. 6, 1996 (61 FR 57767).

Narcotics Control, Cabinet Committee on International Established by Presidential memorandum of Aug. 17, 1971. Terminated by Presidential memorandum of Mar. 14, 1977.

National. *See other part of title*

Naval Material, Office of Established by act of Mar. 5, 1948 (62 Stat. 68). Abolished by the Department of Defense reorg. order of Mar. 9, 1966, and functions transferred to the Secretary of the Navy (31 FR 7188).

Naval Material Command *See* **Naval Material Support Establishment**

Naval Material Support Establishment Established by Department of the Navy General Order 5 of July 1, 1963 (28 FR 7037). Replaced by *Naval Material Command* pursuant to General Order 5 of Apr. 29, 1966 (31 FR 7188). Functions realigned to form Office of Naval Acquisition Support, and termination of *Command* effective May 6, 1985.

Naval Observatory Jurisdiction transferred from *Bureau of Navigation* to Chief of Naval Operations by EO 9126 of Apr. 8, 1942, and by Reorg. Plan No. 3 of 1946, effective July 16, 1946.

Naval Oceanography Command Renamed Naval Meteorology and Oceanography Command in 1995.

Naval Petroleum and Oil Shale Reserves, Office of Established by the Secretary of the Navy, as required by law (70A Stat. 457). Jurisdiction transferred to the Department of Energy by act of Aug. 4, 1977 (91 Stat. 581).

Naval Weapons, Bureau of Established by act of Aug. 18, 1959 (73 Stat. 395), to replace *Bureau of Ordnance and Aeronautics*. Abolished by Department of Defense reorg. order of Mar. 9, 1966, and functions transferred to the Secretary of the Navy (31 FR 7188), effective May 1, 1966.

Navigation, Bureau of Created by act of July 5, 1884 (23 Stat. 118), as special service under the Department of the Treasury. Transferred to the *Department of Commerce and Labor* by act of Feb. 4, 1903 (32 Stat. 825). Consolidated with *Bureau of Navigation and Steamboat Inspection* by act of June 30, 1932 (47 Stat. 415).

Navigation, Bureau of Renamed Bureau of Naval Personnel by act of May 13, 1942 (56 Stat. 276).

Navigation and Steamboat Inspection, Bureau of Renamed *Bureau of Marine Inspection and Navigation* by act of May 27, 1936 (49 Stat. 1380). Functions transferred to *Bureau of Customs*, Department of the Treasury, and U.S. Coast Guard by EO 9083 of Feb. 28, 1942. Transfer made permanent and *Bureau* abolished by Reorg. Plan. No. 3 of 1946, effective July 16, 1946.

Navy Commissioners, Board of Established by act of Feb. 7, 1815 (3 Stat. 202). Abolished by act of Aug. 31, 1842 (5 Stat. 579).

Navy, Department of Defense housing functions transferred to *Federal Public Housing Authority, National Housing Agency,* by EO 9070 of Feb. 24, 1942.

Neighborhoods, National Commission on Established by act of Apr. 30, 1977 (91 Stat. 56). Terminated May 4, 1979, pursuant to terms of act.

Neighborhoods, Voluntary Associations and Consumer Protection, Office of Abolished and certain functions transferred to Office of the Assistant Secretary for Housing—Federal Housing Commissioner and Office of the Assistant Secretary for Community Planning and Development. Primary enabling legislation, act of Oct. 31, 1978 (92 Stat. 2119), repealed by act of Aug. 13, 1981 (95 Stat. 398). Abolishment of *Office* and transfer of functions carried out by Housing and Urban Development Secretarial order.

New England River Basins Commission Established by EO 11371 of Sept. 6, 1967. Terminated by EO 12319 of Sept. 9, 1981.

Nicaro Project Responsibility for management of Nicaro nickel producing facilities in Oriente Province, Cuba, transferred from *Office of Special Assistant to the Administrator (Nicaro Project)* to *Defense Materials Service* by General Services Administrator, effective July 7, 1959. Facilities expropriated by Cuban Government and nationalized Oct. 26, 1960.

Northern Mariana Islands Commission on Federal Laws Created by joint resolution of Mar. 24, 1976 (90 Stat. 263). Terminated upon submission of final report in August 1985.

Nursing Research, National Center for Renamed National Institute of Nursing Research by act of June 10, 1993 (107 Stat. 178).

Nutrition Division Functions transferred from *Department of Health, Education, and Welfare* to the Department of Agriculture by EO 9310 of Mar. 3, 1943.

Ocean Mining Administration Established by Interior Secretarial Order 2971 of Feb. 24, 1975. Abolished by Department Manual Release 2273 of June 13, 1980.

Oceanography, Interagency Committee on Established by *Federal Council for Science and Technology* pursuant to EO 10807 of Mar. 13, 1959. Absorbed by *National Council on Marine Resources and Engineering Development* pursuant to Vice Presidential letter of July 21, 1967.

Office. *See also other part of title*

Office Space, President's Advisory Commission on Presidential Established by act of Aug. 3, 1956 (70 Stat. 979). Terminated June 30, 1957, by act of Jan. 25, 1957 (71 Stat. 4).

Official Register Function of preparing *Official Register* vested in Director of the Census by act of Mar. 3, 1925 (43 Stat. 1105). Function transferred to *U.S. Civil Service Commission* by EO 6166 of June 10, 1933. Yearly compilation and publication required by act of Aug. 28, 1935 (49 Stat. 956). Act repealed by act of July 12, 1960 (74 Stat. 427), and last *Register* published in 1959.

Ohio River Basin Commission Established by EO 11578 of Jan. 13, 1971. Terminated by EO 12319 of Sept. 9, 1981.

Oil and Gas, Office of Established by the Secretary of the Interior May 6, 1946, in response to Presidential letter of May 3, 1946. Transferred to *Federal Energy Administration* by act of May 7, 1974 (88 Stat. 100).

Oil Import Administration Established in the Department of the Interior by Proc. 3279 of Mar. 10, 1959. Merged into *Office of Oil and Gas* Oct. 22, 1971.

Oil Import Appeals Board Established by the Secretary of Commerce Mar. 13, 1959, and made part of Office of Hearings and Appeals Dec. 23, 1971.

On-Site Inspection Agency Established on Jan. 26, 1988. Functions transferred to the Defense Threat Reduction Agency by DOD Directive 5105.62 of Sept. 30, 1998.

Operations Advisory Group Established by EO 11905 of Feb. 18, 1976. Abolished by Presidential Directive No. 2 of Jan. 20, 1977.

Operations Coordinating Board Established by EO 10483 of Sept. 2, 1953, which was superseded by EO 10700 of Feb. 25, 1957. EO 10700 revoked by EO 10920 of Feb. 18, 1961, and *Board* terminated.

Ordnance, Bureau of *See* **Ordnance and Hydrography, Bureau of**

Ordnance and Hydrography, Bureau of Established in the Department of the Navy by act of Aug. 31, 1842 (5 Stat. 579). Replaced under act of July 5, 1862 (12 Stat. 510), by *Bureau of Ordnance* and *Bureau of Navigation.* Abolished by act of Aug. 18, 1959 (73 Stat. 395), and functions transferred to *Bureau of Naval Weapons.*

Organization, President's Advisory Committee on Government Established by EO 10432 of Jan. 24, 1953. Abolished by EO 10917 of Feb. 10, 1961, and functions transferred to *Bureau of the Budget* for termination.

Organizations Staff, International Functions merged with Foreign Agricultural Service by memorandum of Dec. 7, 1973 of , effective Feb. 3, 1974.

Overseas Private Investment Corporation Transferred as separate agency to *U.S. International Development Cooperation Agency* by Reorg. Plan No. 2 of 1979, effective Oct. 1, 1979. Became an independent agency following the abolition of *IDCA* by act of Oct. 21, 1998 (112 Stat. 2681–790).

Oversight Board (for the Resolution Trust Corporation) Established by act of Aug. 9, 1989 (103 Stat. 363). Renamed *Thrift Depositor Protection Oversight Board* by act of Dec. 12, 1991 (105 Stat. 1767). Abolished by act of July 29, 1998 (112 Stat.

908). Authority and duties transferred to the Secretary of the Treasury.

Pacific Northwest River Basins Commission Established by EO 11331 of Mar. 6, 1967. Terminated by EO 12319 of Sept. 9, 1981.

Packers and Stockyards Administration Established by Memorandum 1613, supp. 1, of May 8, 1967 of the Secretary of Agriculture. Certain functions consolidated into Agricultural Marketing Service by Secretary's Memorandum 1927 of Jan. 15, 1978. Remaining functions incorporated into the Grain Inspection, Packers and Stockyards Administration by Secretary's Memorandum 1010–1 dated Oct. 20, 1994.

Panama Canal Operation of piers at Atlantic and Pacific terminals transferred to *Panama Railroad Company* by EO 7021 of Apr. 19, 1935. Panama Canal reestablished as *Canal Zone Government* by act of Sept. 26, 1950 (64 Stat. 1038).

Panama Canal Commission Established by act of Oct. 1, 1979, as amended (22 U.S.C. 3611). U.S. responsibility terminated by stipulation of the Panama Canal Treaty of 1977, which transferred responsibility for the Panama Canal to the Republic of Panama, effective Dec. 31, 1999.

Panama Canal Company Established by act of June 29, 1948 (62 Stat. 1076). Abolished and superseded by *Panama Canal Commission* (93 Stat. 454).

Panama Railroad Company Incorporated Apr. 7, 1849, by New York State Legislature. Operated under private control until 1881, when original *French Canal Company* acquired most of its stock. *Company* and its successor, *New Panama Canal Company,* operated railroad as common carrier and also as adjunct in attempts to construct canal. In 1904 their shares of stock in *Panama Railroad Company* passed to ownership of U.S. as part of assets of *New Panama Canal Company* purchased under act of June 28, 1902 (34 Stat. 481). Remaining shares purchased from private owners in 1905. *Panama Railroad Company* reincorporated by act of June 29, 1948 (62 Stat. 1075) pursuant to requirements of act of Dec. 6, 1945 (59 Stat. 597). Reestablished as *Panama Canal Company* by act of Sept. 26, 1950 (64 Stat. 1038). The Secretary of the Army was directed to discontinue commercial operations of *Company* by Presidential letter of Mar. 29, 1961.

Paperwork, Commission on Federal Established by act of Dec. 27, 1974 (88 Stat. 1789). Terminated January 1978 pursuant to terms of act.

Park Service, National Functions in District of Columbia relating to space assignment, site selection for public buildings, and determination of priority in construction transferred to *Public Buildings Administration, Federal Works Agency,* under Reorg. Plan No. I of 1939, effective July 1, 1939.

Park Trust Fund Board, National Established by act of July 10, 1935 (49 Stat. 477). Terminated by act of Dec. 18, 1967 (81 Stat. 656), and functions transferred to National Park Foundation.

Parks, Buildings, and Reservations, Office of National Established in the Department of the Interior by EO 6166 of June 10, 1933. Renamed National Park Service by act of Mar. 2, 1934 (48 Stat. 362).

Parole, Board of Established by act of June 25, 1948 (62 Stat. 854). Abolished by act of Mar. 15, 1976 (90 Stat. 219), and functions transferred to U.S. Parole Commission.

Patent Office Provisions of first patent act administered by the Department of State, with authority for granting patents vested in board comprising Secretaries of State and *War* and Attorney General. Board abolished, authority transferred to Secretary of State, and registration system established by act of Feb. 21, 1793 (1 Stat. 318). *Office* made bureau in the Department of State in October 1802, headed by *Superintendent of Patents. Office* reorganized in 1836 by act of June 4, 1836 (5 Stat. 117) under *Commissioner of Patents. Office* transferred to the Department of the Interior in 1849. *Office* transferred to the Department of Commerce by EO 4175 of Mar. 17, 1925.

Patents Board, Government Established by EO 10096 of Jan. 23, 1950. Abolished by EO 10930 of Mar. 24, 1961, and functions transferred to the Secretary of Commerce.

Pay Board Established by EO 11627 of Oct. 15, 1971. Abolished by EO 11695 of Jan. 11, 1973.

Peace Corps Established in the Department of State by EO 10924 of Mar. 1, 1961, and continued by act of Sept. 22, 1961 (75 Stat. 612), and EO 11041 of Aug. 6, 1962. Functions transferred to ACTION by Reorg. Plan No. 1 of 1971, effective July 1, 1971. Made independent agency in executive branch by act of Dec. 29, 1981 (95 Stat. 1540).

Pennsylvania Avenue, Temporary Commission on Established by EO 11210 of Mar. 25, 1956. Inactive as of Nov. 15, 1969, due to lack of funding.

Pennsylvania Avenue Development Corporation Established by act of Oct. 27, 1972 (86 Stat. 1266). Terminated pursuant to P.L. 104–99, Jan. 26, 1996 (110 Stat. 32) and P.L. 104–134, Apr. 26, 1996 (110 Stat. 1321–198). Functions transferred to General Services Administration, National Capital Planning Commission, and National Park Service (61 FR 11308), effective Apr. 1, 1996.

Pension and Welfare Benefit Programs, Office of *See* **Labor-Management Services Administration**

Pensions, Commissioner of Provided for by act of Mar. 2, 1833 (4 Stat. 668). Continued by act of Mar. 3, 1835 (4 Stat. 779), and other acts as *Office of the Commissioner of Pensions.* Transferred to the Department of the Interior as bureau by act of Mar. 3, 1849 (9 Stat. 395). Consolidated with other bureaus and agencies into *Veterans Administration* by EO 5398 of July 21, 1930.

Pensions, Office of the Commissioner of *See* **Pensions, Commissioner of**

Perry's Victory Memorial Commission Created by act of Mar. 3, 1919 (40 Stat. 1322). Administration of Memorial transferred to National Park Service by act of June 2, 1936 (49 Stat. 1393). *Commission* terminated by terms of act and membership reconstituted as advisory board to the Secretary of Interior.

Personal Property, Office of *See* **Supply Service, Federal**

Personnel, National Roster of Scientific and Specialized Established by *National Resources Planning Board* pursuant to Presidential letter of June 18, 1940, to the Secretary of the Treasury. After Aug. 15, 1940, administered jointly by *Board* and *U.S. Civil Service Commission.* Transferred to *War Manpower Commission* by EO 9139 of Apr. 18, 1942. Transferred to the Department of Labor by EO 9617 of Sept. 19, 1945. Transferred with *Bureau of Employment Security* to *Federal Security Agency* by act of June 16, 1948 (62 Stat. 443). Transferred to the Department of Labor by Reorg. Plan No. 2 of 1949, effective Aug. 20, 1949, and became inactive. Roster functions transferred to National Science Foundation by act of May 10, 1950 (64 Stat. 154). Reactivated in 1950 as *National Scientific Register* by *Office of Education, Federal Security Agency,* through *National Security Resources Board* grant of funds, and continued by National Science Foundation funds until December 1952, when *Register* integrated into Foundation's National Register of Scientific and Technical Personnel project in Division of Scientific Personnel and Education.

Personnel Administration, Council of Established by EO 7916 of June 24, 1938, effective Feb. 1, 1939. Made unit in *U.S. Civil Service Commission* by EO 8467 of July 1, 1940. Renamed *Federal Personnel Council* by EO 9830 of Feb. 24, 1947. Abolished by act of July 31, 1953 (67 Stat. 300), and personnel and records transferred to *Office of Executive Director, U.S. Civil Service Commission.*

Personnel Council, Federal *See* **Personnel Administration, Council of**

Personnel Interchange, President's Commission on Established by EO 11451 of Jan. 19, 1969. Continued by EO 12136 of May 15, 1979, and renamed *President's Commission on Executive Exchange.* Continued by EO 12493 of Dec. 5, 1984. Abolished by EO 12760 of May 2, 1991.

Personnel Management, Liaison Office for Established by EO 8248 of Sept. 8, 1939. Abolished by EO 10452 of May 1, 1953, and functions transferred to *U.S. Civil Service Commission.*

Petroleum Administration for Defense Established under act of Sept. 8, 1950 (64 Stat. 798) by Order 2591 of Oct. 3, 1950 of the Secretary of the Interior, pursuant to EO 10161 of Sept. 9, 1950. Continued by Secretary's Order 2614 of Jan. 25, 1951, pursuant to EO 10200 of Jan. 3, 1951, and PAD Delegation 1 of Jan. 24, 1951. Abolished by Secretary's Order 2755 of Apr. 23, 1954.

Petroleum Administration for War *See* **Petroleum Coordinator for War, Office of**

Petroleum Administrative Board Established Sept. 11, 1933, by the Secretary of the Interior. Terminated Mar. 31, 1936, by EO 7076 of June 15, 1935. The Secretary of the Interior was authorized to execute functions vested in President by act of Feb. 22, 1935 (49 Stat. 30) by EO 7756 of Dec. 1, 1937. Secretary also authorized to establish *Petroleum Conservation Division* to assist in administering act. Records of *Petroleum Administrative Board* and *Petroleum Labor Policy Board* housed with *Petroleum Conservation Division, Office of Oil and Gas,* acting as custodian for the Secretary of the Interior.

Petroleum Coordinator for War, Office of Secretary of the Interior designated *Petroleum Coordinator for National Defense* pursuant to Presidential letter of May 28, 1941, and approved *Petroleum Coordinator for War* pursuant to Presidential letter of Apr. 20, 1942. *Office* abolished by EO 9276 of Dec. 2, 1942, and functions transferred to *Petroleum Administration for War,* established by same EO. *Administration* terminated by EO 9718 of May 3, 1946.

Petroleum Labor Policy Board Established by the Secretary of the Interior, as *Administrator of Code of Fair Competition for Petroleum Industry,* on recommendation of Planning and Coordination Committee Oct. 10, 1933. Reorganized by Secretary Dec. 19, 1933, and reorganization confirmed by order of Mar. 8, 1935. Terminated Mar. 31, 1936, when *Petroleum Administrative Board* abolished by EO 7076 of June 15, 1935.

Petroleum Reserves Corporation Established June 30, 1943, by *Reconstruction Finance Corporation.* Transferred to *Office of Economic Warfare* by EO 9360 of July 15, 1943. *Office* consolidated into *Foreign Economic Administration* by EO 9380 of Sept. 25, 1943. Functions transferred to *Reconstruction Finance Corporation* by EO 9630 of Sept. 27, 1945. *RFC's* charter amended Nov. 9, 1945, to change name to *War Assets Corporation. Corporation* designated by *Surplus Property Administrator* as disposal agency for all types of property for which *Reconstruction Finance Corporation* formerly disposal agency. Domestic surplus property functions of *Corporation* transferred to *War Assets Administration* by EO 9689 of Jan. 31, 1946. *Reconstruction Finance Corporation Board of Directors* ordered by President to dissolve *War Assets Corporation* as soon after Mar. 25, 1946, as practicable.

Philippine Alien Property Administration Established in *Office for Emergency Management* by EO 9789 of Oct. 14, 1946. Abolished by EO 10254 of June 15, 1951, and functions transferred to the Department of Justice.

Philippine War Damage Commission Established by act of Apr. 30, 1946 (60 Stat. 128). Terminated Mar. 31, 1951, by act of Sept. 6, 1950 (64 Stat. 712).

Photographic Interpretation Center, National Functions transferred to the National Imagery and Mapping Agency by P.L. 104–201, Sept. 23, 1996 (110 Stat. 2677).

Physical Fitness, Committee on Established in *Office of Federal Security Administrator* by EO 9338 of Apr. 29, 1943. Terminated June 30, 1945.

Physical Fitness, President's Council on *See* **Youth Fitness, President's Council on**

Physician Payment Review Commission Established by act of Apr. 7, 1986 (100 Stat. 190). Terminated by act of Aug. 5, 1997 (111 Stat. 354). Assets, staff, and continuing responsibility for reports transferred to the Medicare Payment Advisory Commission.

Planning Board, National Established by *Administrator of Public Works* July 30, 1933. Terminated by EO 6777 of June 30, 1934.

Plant Industry, Bureau of Established by act of Mar. 2, 1902 (31 Stat. 922). Soil fertility and soil microbiology work of *Bureau of Chemistry and Soils* transferred to *Bureau* by act of May 17, 1935. Soil chemistry and physics and soil survey work of *Bureau of Chemistry and Soils* transferred to *Bureau* by Secretary's Memorandum 784 of Oct. 6, 1938. In February 1943 engineering research of *Bureau of Agricultural Chemistry and Engineering* transferred to *Bureau of Plant Industry, Soils, and Agricultural Engineering* by Research Administration Memorandum 5 issued pursuant to EO 9069 of Feb. 23, 1942, and in conformity with Secretary's Memorandums 960 and 986. Functions transferred to Agricultural Research Service by Secretary's Memorandum 1320, supp. 4, of Nov. 2, 1953.

Plant Industry, Soils, and Agricultural Engineering, Bureau of *See* **Plant Industry, Bureau of**

Plant Quarantine, Bureau of *See* **Entomology and Plant Quarantine, Bureau of**

Policy Development, Office of *See* **Domestic Council**

Post Office, Department of *See* **Postal Service**

Postal Savings System Established by act of June 25, 1910 (36 Stat. 814). System closed by act of Mar. 28, 1966 (80 Stat. 92).

Postal Service Created July 26, 1775, by Continental Congress. Temporarily established by Congress by act of Sept. 22, 1789 (1 Stat. 70), and continued by subsequent acts. *Department of Post Office* made executive department under act of June 8, 1872 (17 Stat. 283). Offices of First, Second, Third, and Fourth Assistant Postmasters General abolished and Deputy Postmaster General and four Assistant Postmasters General established by Reorg. Plan No. 3 of 1949, effective Aug. 20, 1949. Reorganized as U.S. Postal Service in executive branch by act of Aug. 12, 1970 (84 Stat. 719), effective July 1, 1971.

Power Commission, Federal Established by act of June 10, 1920 (41 Stat. 1063). Terminated by act of Aug. 4, 1977 (91 Stat. 578), and functions transferred to the Department of Energy.

Preparedness, Office of Renamed *Federal Preparedness Agency* by General Services Administrator's order of June 26, 1975.

Preparedness Agency, Federal Functions transferred from General Services Administration to Federal Emergency Management Agency by EO 12148 of July 20, 1979.

Presidential. *See other part of title*

President's. *See other part of title*

Press Intelligence, Division of Established in August 1933. Made division of *National Emergency Council* July 10, 1935. Continued in *Office of Government Reports* by Reorg. Plan No. II of 1939, effective July 1, 1939. Transferred to *Office of War Information* by EO 9182 of June 13, 1942, functioning in *Bureau of Special Services. Office* abolished by EO 9608 of Aug. 31, 1945, and *Bureau* transferred to *Bureau of the Budget.* Upon reestablishment of *Office of Government Reports,* by EO 9809 of Dec. 12, 1946, *Division of Press Intelligence* made unit of *Office.*

Price Administration, Office of Established by EO 8734 of Apr. 11, 1941, combining *Price Division* and *Consumer Division* of *National Defense Advisory Commission.* Renamed *Office of Price Administration* by EO 8875 of Aug. 28, 1941, which transferred *Civilian Allocation Division* to *Office of Production Management.* Consolidated with other agencies into *Office of Temporary Controls* by EO 9809 of Dec. 12, 1946, except *Financial Reporting Division,* transferred to Federal Trade Commission.

Price Commission Established by EO 11627 of Oct. 15, 1971. Abolished by EO 11695 of Jan. 11, 1973.

Price Decontrol Board Established by act of July 25, 1946 (60 Stat. 669). Effective period of act of Jan. 30, 1942 (56 Stat. 23), extended to June 30, 1947, by joint resolution of June 25, 1946 (60 Stat. 664).

Price Stability for Economic Growth, Cabinet Committee on Established by Presidential letter of Jan. 28, 1959. Abolished by Presidential direction Mar. 12, 1961.

Price Stabilization, Office of Established by General Order 2 of *Economic Stabilization Administrator* Jan. 24, 1951. *Director of Price Stabilization* provided for in EO 10161 of Sept. 9, 1950. Terminated Apr. 30, 1953, by EO 10434 of Feb. 6, 1953, and provisions of acts of June 30, 1952 (66 Stat. 296) and June 30, 1953 (67 Stat. 131).

Prices and Costs, Committee on Government Activities Affecting Established by EO 10802 of Jan. 23, 1959. Abolished by EO 10928 of Mar. 23, 1961.

Priorities Board Established by order of *Council of National Defense,* approved Oct. 18, 1940, and by EO 8572 of Oct. 21, 1940. EO 8572 revoked by EO 8629 of Jan. 7, 1941.

Prison Industries, Inc., Federal Established by EO 6917 of Dec. 11, 1934. Transferred to the Department of Justice by Reorg. Plan No. II of 1939, effective July 1, 1939.

Prison Industries Reorganization Administration Functioned from Sept. 26, 1935, to Sept. 30, 1940, under authority of act of Apr. 8, 1935 (49 Stat. 115), and of EO's 7194 of Sept. 26, 1935, 7202 of Sept. 28, 1935, and 7649 of June 29, 1937. Terminated due to lack of funding.

Private Sector Programs, Office of Functions transferred to the Office of Citizen Exchanges within the Bureau of Educational and Cultural Affairs, USIA, by act of Feb. 16, 1990 (104 Stat. 56).

Processing tax *Agricultural Adjustment Administration's* function of collecting taxes declared unconstitutional by U.S. Supreme Court Jan. 6, 1936. Functions under acts of June 28, 1934 (48 Stat. 1275), Apr. 21, 1934 (48 Stat. 598), and Aug. 24, 1935 (49 Stat. 750) discontinued by repeal of these laws by act of Feb. 10, 1936 (49 Stat. 1106).

Processing Tax Board of Review Established in the Department of the Treasury by act of June 22, (49 Stat. 1652). Abolished by act of Oct. 21, 1942 (56 Stat. 967).

Proclamations *See* **State, Department of**

Procurement, Commission on Government Established by act of Nov. 26, 1969 (83 Stat. 269). Terminated Apr. 30, 1973, due to expiration of statutory authority.

Procurement and Assignment Service Established by President Oct. 30, 1941. Transferred from *Office of Defense Health and Welfare Services* to *War Manpower Commission* by EO 9139 of Apr. 18, 1942. Transferred to *Federal Security Agency* by EO 9617 of Sept. 19, 1945, which terminated *Commission.*

Procurement Division Established in the Department of the Treasury by EO 6166 of June 10, 1933. Renamed *Bureau of Federal Supply* by Department of the Treasury Order 73 of Nov. 19, 1946, effective Jan. 1, 1947. Transferred to General Services Administration as Federal Supply Service by act of June 30, 1949 (63 Stat. 380).

Procurement Policy, Office of Federal Established within Office of Management and Budget by act of Aug. 30, 1974 (88 Stat. 97). Abolished due to lack of funding and functions transferred to Office of Management and Budget by act of Oct 28, 1993 (107 Stat. 1236).

Product Standards Policy, Office of Formerly separate operating unit under Assistant Secretary for Productivity, Technology, and Innovation, Department of Commerce. Transferred to *National Bureau of Standards* by departmental reorganization order, effective Apr. 27, 1982.

Production Areas, Committee for Congested Established in Executive Office of the President by EO 9327 of Apr. 7, 1943. Terminated Dec. 31, 1944, by act of June 28, 1944 (58 Stat. 535).

Production Authority, National Established in the Department of Commerce Sept. 11, 1950, by EO's 10161 of Sept. 9, 1950, 10193 of Dec. 16, 1950, and 10200 of Jan. 3, 1951. Abolished by order of Oct. 1, 1953 of the Secretary of Commerce, and functions merged into *Business and Defense Services Administration.*

Production Management, Office of Established in *Office for Emergency Management* by EO 8629 of Jan. 7, 1941. Abolished by EO 9040 of Jan. 24, 1942, and personnel and property transferred to *War Production Board.*

Production and Marketing Administration Established by Secretary of Agriculture Memorandum 1118 of Aug. 18, 1945. Functions transferred under Department reorganization by Secretary's Memorandum 1320, supp. 4, of Nov. 2, 1953.

Productivity Council, National Established by EO 12089 of Oct. 23, 1978. EO 12089 revoked by EO 12379 of Aug. 17, 1982.

Programs, Bureau of International Established by the Secretary of Commerce Aug. 8, 1961, by Departmental Orders 173 and 174. Abolished by Departmental Order 182 of Feb. 1, 1963, which established *Bureau of International Commerce.* Functions transferred to *Domestic and International Business Administration,* effective Nov. 17, 1972.

Programs, Office of Public Established in the National Archives and Records Administration. Reorganized by Archivist under Notice 96–260, Sept. 23, 1996, effective Jan. 6, 1997. Functions restructured and transferred to Office of Records Services—Washington, DC.

Prohibition, Bureau of Established by act of May 27, 1930 (46 Stat. 427). Investigative functions consolidated with functions of *Bureau of Investigation* into *Division of Investigation,* Department of Justice. by EO 6166 of June 10, 1933, which set as effective date Mar. 2, 1934, or such later date as fixed by President. All other functions performed by *Bureau of Prohibition* ordered transferred to such division in the Department of Justice as deemed desirable by Attorney General.

Property, Office of Surplus Established in *Procurement Division,* Department of the Treasury, by EO 9425 of Feb. 19, 1944, and act of Oct. 3, 1944 (58 Stat. 765), under general direction of *Surplus Property Board* established by same legislation. Transferred to the Department of Commerce by EO 9541 of Apr. 19, 1945. Terminated by EO 9643 of Oct. 19, 1945, and activities and personnel transferred to *Reconstruction Finance Corporation.*

Property Administration, Surplus *See* **War Property Administration, Surplus**

Property Board, Surplus *See* **War Property Administration, Surplus**

Property Council, Federal Established by EO 11724 of June 25, 1973, and reconstituted by EO 11954 of Jan. 7, 1977. Terminated by EO 12030 of Dec. 15, 1977.

Property Management and Disposal Service *See* **Emergency Procurement Service**

Property Office, Surplus Established in *Division of Territories and Island Possessions,* Department of the Interior, under Regulation 1 of *Surplus Property Board,* Apr. 2, 1945. Transferred to *War Assets Administration* by EO 9828 of Feb. 21, 1947.

Property Review Board Established by EO 12348 of Feb. 25, 1982. EO 12348 revoked by EO 12512 of Apr. 29, 1985.

Prospective Payment Assessment Commission Established by act of Apr. 20, 1983 (97 Stat. 159). Terminated by act of Aug. 5, 1997 (111 Stat. 354). Assets, staff, and continuing responsibility for reports transferred to the Medicare Payment Advisory Commission.

Provisions and Clothing, Bureau of Established by acts of Aug. 31, 1842 (5 Stat. 579), and July 5, 1862 (12 Stat. 510). Designated *Bureau of Supplies and Accounts* by act of July 19, 1892 (27 Stat. 243). Abolished by Department of Defense reorg. order of Mar. 9, 1966, and functions transferred to the Secretary of the Navy (31 FR 7188).

Public. *See other part of title*

Publications Commission, National Historical Established by act of Oct. 22, 1968 (82 Stat. 1293). Renamed National Historical Publications and Records Commission by act of Dec. 22, 1974 (88 Stat. 1734).

Puerto Rican Hurricane Relief Commission Established by act of Dec. 21, 1928 (45 Stat. 1067). No loans made after June 30, 1934, and *Commission* abolished June 3, 1935, by Public Resolution 22 (49 Stat. 320). Functions transferred to *Division of Territories and Island Possessions,* Department of the Interior. After June 30, 1946, collection work performed in *Puerto Rico Reconstruction Administration.* Following termination of *Administration,* remaining collection functions transferred to the Secretary of Agriculture by act of July 11, 1956 (70 Stat. 525).

Puerto Rico, U.S.-Puerto Rico Commission on the Status of Established by act of Feb. 20, 1964 (78 Stat. 17). Terminated by terms of act.

Puerto Rico Reconstruction Administration Established in the Department of the Interior by EO 7057 of May 28, 1935. Terminated Feb. 15, 1955, by act of Aug. 15, 1953 (67 Stat. 584).

Radiation Biology Laboratory *See* **Radiation and Organisms, Division of**

Radiation Council, Federal Established by EO 10831 of Aug. 14, 1959, and act of Sept. 23, 1959 (73 Stat. 688). Abolished by Reorg. Plan No. 3 of 1970, effective Dec. 2, 1970, and functions transferred to Environmental Protection Agency.

Radiation and Organisms, Division of Established by Secretarial order of May 1, 1929, as part of Smithsonian Astrophysical Observatory. Renamed *Radiation Biology Laboratory* by Secretarial order of Feb. 16, 1965. Merged with *Chesapeake Center for Environmental Studies* by Secretarial order of July 1, 1983, to form Smithsonian Environmental Research Center.

Radio Commission, Federal Established by act of Feb. 23, 1927 (44 Stat. 1162). Abolished by act of June 19, 1934 (48 Stat. 1102), and functions transferred to Federal Communications Commission.

Radio Division Established by *National Emergency Council* July 1, 1938. Transferred to *Office of Education, Federal Security Agency,* by Reorg. Plan No. II of 1939, effective July 1, 1939. Terminated June 30, 1940, by terms of act of June 30, 1939 (53 Stat. 927).

Radio Propagation Laboratory, Central Transferred from *National Bureau of Standards* to *Environmental Science Services Administration* by the Department of Commerce Order 2–A, effective July 13, 1965.

Radiological Health, National Center for Devices and Renamed Center for Devices and Radiological Health by Food and Drug Administration notice of Mar. 9, 1984 (49 FR 10166).

Rail Public Counsel, Office of Established by act of Feb. 5, 1976 (90 Stat. 51). Terminated Dec. 1, 1979, due to lack of funding.

Railroad Administration, U.S. *See* **Railroads, Director General of**

Railroad and Airline Wage Board Established by *Economic Stabilization Administrator's* General Order 7 of Sept. 27, 1951, pursuant to act of Sept. 8, 1950 (64 Stat. 816). Terminated Apr. 30, 1953, by EO 10434 of Feb. 6, 1953, and acts of June 30, 1952 (66 Stat. 296), and June 30, 1953 (67 Stat. 131).

Railroads, Director General of Established under authority of act of Aug. 29, 1916 (39 Stat. 645). Organization of *U.S. Railroad Administration* announced Feb. 9, 1918. Office abolished by Reorg. Plan No. II of 1939, effective July 1, 1939, and functions transferred to the Secretary of the Treasury.

Railway Association, U.S. Established by act of Jan. 2, 1974 (87 Stat. 985). Terminated Apr. 1, 1987, by act of Oct. 21, 1986 (100 Stat. 1906).

Railway Labor Panel, National Established by EO 9172 of May 22, 1942. EO 9172 revoked by EO 9883 of Aug. 11, 1947.

Real Estate Board, Federal Established by EO 8034 of Jan. 14, 1939. Abolished by EO 10287 of Sept. 6, 1951.

Reclamation, Bureau of *See* **Reclamation Service**

Reclamation Service Established July 1902 in *Geological Survey* by the Secretary of the Interior, pursuant to act of June 17, 1902 (32 Stat. 388). Separated from Survey in 1907 and renamed *Bureau of Reclamation* June 1923. Power marketing functions transferred to the Department of Energy by act of Aug. 4, 1977 (91 Stat. 578). *Bureau* renamed *Water and Power Resources Service* by Secretarial Order 3042 of Nov. 6, 1979. Renamed Bureau of Reclamation by Secretarial Order 3064 of May 18, 1981.

Reconciliation Service Established by Director of Selective Service pursuant to EO 11804 of Sept. 16, 1974. Program terminated Apr. 2, 1980.

Reconstruction Finance Corporation Established Feb. 2, 1932, by act of Jan. 22, 1932 (47 Stat. 5). Grouped with other agencies to form *Federal Loan Agency* by Reorg. Plan No. I of 1939, effective July 1, 1939. Transferred to the Department of Commerce by EO 9071 of Feb. 24, 1942. Returned to *Federal Loan Agency* by act of Feb. 24, 1945 (59 Stat. 5). *Agency* abolished by act of June 30, 1947 (61 Stat. 202), and functions assumed by *Corporation.* Functions relating to financing houses or site improvements, authorized by act of Aug. 10, 1948 (61 Stat. 1275), transferred to *Housing and Home Finance Agency* by Reorg. Plan No. 23 of 1950, effective July 10, 1950. *Corporation* Board of Directors, established by act of Jan. 22, 1932 (47 Stat. 5), abolished by Reorg. Plan No. 1 of 1951, effective May 1, 1951, and functions transferred to Administrator and *Loan Policy Board* established by same plan, effective Apr. 30, 1951. Act of July 30, 1953 (67 Stat. 230), provided for *RFC* succession until June 30, 1954, and for termination of its lending powers Sept. 28, 1953. Certain functions assigned to appropriate agencies for liquidation by Reorg. Plan No. 2 of 1954, effective July 1, 1954. *Corporation* abolished by Reorg. Plan No. 1 of 1957, effective June 30, 1957, and functions transferred to *Housing and Home Finance Agency,* General Services Administration, Small Business Administration, and the Department of the Treasury.

Records Administration, Office of Established in the National Archives and Records Administration. Reorganized by Archivist under Notice 96–260, Sept. 23, 1996, effective Jan. 6, 1997. Functions restructured and transferred to Office of Records Services—Washington, DC.

Records Centers, Office of Federal Established in the National Archives and Records Administration. Reorganized by Archivist under Notice 96–260, Sept. 23, 1996, effective Jan. 6, 1997. Functions restructured and transferred to Office of Regional Records Services.

Records and Information Management, Office of Functions transferred from *National Archives and Records Service* to *Automated Data and Telecommunications Service* by General Services Administrator's decision, effective Jan. 10, 1982, regionally and Apr. 1, 1982, in Washington, DC.

Recovery Administration, Advisory Council, National Established by EO 7075 of June 15, 1935. Transferred to the Department of Commerce by EO 7252 of Dec. 21, 1935, and functions ordered terminated not later than Apr. 1, 1936, by same order. *Committee of Industrial Analysis* created by EO 7323 of Mar. 21, 1936, to complete work of *Council.*

Recovery Administration, National Established by President pursuant to act of June 16, 1933 (48 Stat. 194). Provisions of title I of act repealed by Public Resolution 26 of June 14, 1935 (49 Stat. 375), and extension of *Administration* in skeletonized form authorized until Apr. 1, 1936. *Office of Administrator, National Recovery Administration,* created by EO 7075 of June 15, 1935. *Administration* terminated by EO 7252 of Dec. 21, 1935, which transferred *Division of Review, Division of Business Corporation,* and *Advisory Council* to the Department of Commerce for termination of functions by Apr. 1, 1936. *Consumers' Division* transferred to the Department of Labor by same order.

Recovery Review Board, National Established by EO 6632 of Mar. 7, 1934. Abolished by EO 6771 of June 30, 1934.

Recreation, Bureau of Outdoor Established in the Department of the Interior by act of May 28, 1963 (77 Stat. 49). Terminated by Secretary's order of Jan. 25, 1978, and functions assumed by *Heritage Conservation and Recreation Service.*

Recreation and Natural Beauty, Citizens' Advisory Committee on Established by EO 11278 of May 4, 1966. Terminated by EO 11472 of May 29, 1969.

Recreation and Natural Beauty, President's Council on Established by EO 11278 of May 4, 1966. Terminated by EO 11472 of May 29, 1969.

Recreation Resources Review Commission, Outdoor Established by act of June 28, 1958 (72 Stat. 238). Final report submitted to President January 1962 and terminated Sept. 1, 1962.

Regional Action Planning Commissions Authorized by act of Aug. 26, 1965 (79 Stat. 552). Federal role abolished through repeal by act of Aug. 13, 1981 (95 Stat. 766). At time of repeal, eight commissions—Coastal Plains, Four Corners, New England, Old West Ozarks, Pacific Northwest, Southwest Border, Southwest Border Region, and Upper Great Lakes—affected.

Regional Archives, Office of Special and Established in the National Archives and Records Administration. Reorganized by Archivist under Notice 96–260, Sept. 23, 1996, effective Jan. 6, 1997. Functions restructured and transferred between Office of Records Services—Washington, DC and Office of Regional Records Services.

Regional Councils, Federal Established by EO 12314 of July 22, 1981. Abolished by EO 12407 of Feb. 22, 1983.

Regional Operations, Executive Director of Established in Food and Drug Administration by order of May 20, 1971 of the *Secretary of Health, Education, and Welfare.* Merged into Office of Regulatory Affairs by order of Nov. 5, 1984 of the Secretary of Health and Human Services.

Regulatory Council, U.S. Disbanded by Vice Presidential memorandum of Mar. 25, 1981. Certain functions continued in Regulatory Information Service Center.

Regulatory Relief, Presidential Task Force on Establishment announced in President's remarks Jan. 22, 1981. Disbanded and functions transferred to Office of Management and Budget in August 1983.

Rehabilitation Services Administration Functions transferred from *Department of Health, Education, and Welfare* to Office of Special Education and Rehabilitative Services, Department of Education, by act of Oct. 17, 1979 (93 Stat. 678), effective May 4, 1980.

Relief Corporation, Federal Surplus Organized under powers granted to President by act of June 16, 1933 (48 Stat. 195). Charter granted by State of Delaware Oct. 4, 1933, and amended Nov. 18, 1935, changing name to *Federal Surplus Commodities Corporation* and naming the Secretary of Agriculture, *Administrator of Agricultural Adjustment Administration,* and *Governor of Farm Credit Administration* as Board of Directors. Continued as agency under the Secretary of Agriculture by acts of June 28, 1937 (50 Stat. 323) and Feb. 16, 1938 (52 Stat. 38). Consolidated with *Division of Marketing and Marketing Agreements* into *Surplus Marketing Administration* by Reorg. Plan No. III of 1940, effective June 30, 1940. Merged into *Agricultural Marketing Administration* by EO 9069 of Feb. 23, 1942.

Relief and Rehabilitation Operations, Office of Foreign Established in the Department of State as announced by White House Nov. 21, 1942. Consolidated with *Foreign Economic Administration* by EO 9380 of Sept. 25, 1943.

Renegotiation Board Established by act of Mar. 23, 1951 (65 Stat. 7). Terminated Mar. 31, 1979, by act of Oct. 10, 1978 (92 Stat. 1043).

Rent Advisory Board Established by EO 11632 of Nov. 22, 1971. Abolished by EO 11695 of Jan. 11, 1973.

Rent Stabilization, Office of Established by General Order 9 of *Economic Stabilization Administrator* July 31, 1951, pursuant to act of June 30, 1947 (61 Stat. 193), and EO' s 10161 of Sept. 9, 1950, and 10276 of July 31, 1951. Abolished by EO 10475 of July 31, 1953, and functions transferred to *Office of Defense Mobilization. Office of Research and Development* combined with *Office of Minerals Policy Development* in the Department of the Interior May 21, 1976, under authority of Reorg. Plan No. 3 of 1950, effective May 24, 1950, to form *Office of Minerals Policy and Research Analysis.* Abolished Sept. 30, 1981, by Secretarial Order 3070 and functions transferred to *Bureau of Mines.*

Reports, Office of Government Established July 1, 1939, to perform functions of *National Emergency Council* abolished by Reorg. Plan No. II of 1939, effective July 1, 1939. Established as administrative unit of Executive Office of the President by EO 8248 of Sept. 8, 1939. Consolidated with *Office of War Information, Office for Emergency Management,* by EO 9182 of June 13, 1942. Reestablished in Executive Office of the President by EO 9809 of Dec. 12, 1946, which transferred to it functions of *Media Programming Division* and *Motion Picture Division, Office of War Mobilization and Reconversion,* and functions transferred from *Bureau of Special Services, Office of War Information,* to *Bureau of the Budget* by EO 9608 of Aug. 31, 1945. Subsequent to enactment of act of July 30, 1947 (61 Stat. 588), functions of *Office* restricted to advertising and motion picture liaison and operation of library. Terminated June 30, 1948.

Research, Office of University Transferred from *Office of Program Management and Administration,* Research and Special Programs Administration, to Office of Economics, Office of the Assistant Secretary for Policy and International Affairs, under authority of the Department of Transportation appropriation request for FY 1985, effective Oct. 1, 1984.

Research and Development Board Established in the Department of Defense by act of July 26, 1947 (61 Stat. 499). Abolished by Reorg. Plan No. 6 of 1953, effective June 30, 1953, and functions vested in the Secretary of Defense.

Research and Development Board, Joint Established June 6, 1946, by charter of Secretaries of *War* and Navy. Terminated on creation of *Research and Development Board* by act of July 26, 1947 (61 Stat. 506).

Research and Intelligence Service, Interim Established in the Department of State by EO 9621 of Sept. 20, 1945. Abolished Dec. 31, 1945, pursuant to terms of order.

Research Resources, Division of Established in National Institutes of Health, Department of Health and Human Services. Renamed National Center for Research Resources by Secretarial notice of Feb. 23, 1990 (55 FR 6455) and act of June 10, 1993 (107 Stat. 178).

Research Service, Cooperative State Established by Secretary of Agriculture Memorandum 1462, supp. 1, of Aug. 31, 1961. Consolidated into *Science and Education Administration* by Secretary's order of Jan. 24, 1978. Reestablished as Cooperative State Research Service by Secretarial order of June 16, 1981.

Research and Service Division, Cooperative Functions transferred to the Secretary of Agriculture in *Farmer Cooperative Service* by act of Aug. 6, 1953 (67 Stat. 390).

Resettlement Administration Established by EO 7027 of Apr. 30, 1935. Functions transferred to the Department of Agriculture by EO 7530 of Dec. 31, 1936. Renamed *Farm Security Administration* by Secretary's Memorandum 732 of Sept. 1, 1937. Abolished by act of Aug. 14, 1946 (60 Stat. 1062) and functions incorporated into the *Farmers' Home Administration,* effective Jan. 1, 1947. *Farmers' Home Administration* abolished, effective Dec. 27, 1994, under authority of Secretary's Memorandum 1010–1 dated Oct. 20, 1994 (59 FR 66441). Functions assumed by the *Consolidated Farm Service Agency* and the *Rural Housing and Community Development Service.*

Resolution Trust Corporation Established by act of Aug. 9, 1989 (103 Stat. 369). Board of Directors of the Corporation abolished by act of Dec. 12, 1991 (105 Stat. 1769). Corporation functions terminated pursuant to act of Dec. 17, 1993 (107 Stat. 2369).

Resources Board and Advisory Committee, National Established by EO 6777 of June 30, 1934. Abolished by EO 7065 of June 7, 1935, and functions transferred to *National Resources Committee.*

Resources Committee, National Established by EO 7065 of June 7, 1935. Abolished by Reorg. Plan No. I of 1939, effective July 1, 1939, and functions transferred to *National Resources Planning Board* in Executive Office of the President. *Board* terminated by act of June 26, 1943 (57 Stat. 169).

Resources Planning Board, National *See* **Resources Committee, National**

Retired Executives, Service Corps of Established in ACTION by act of Oct. 1, 1973 (87 Stat. 404). Transferred to Small Business Administration by EO 11871 of July 18, 1975.

Retraining and Reemployment Administration Established by EO 9427 of Feb. 24, 1944, and act of Oct. 3, 1944 (58 Stat. 788). Transferred from *Office of War Mobilization and Reconversion* to the Department of Labor by EO 9617 of Sept. 19, 1945. Terminated pursuant to terms of act.

Revenue Sharing, Office of Established by the Secretary of the Treasury to administer programs authorized by acts of Oct. 20, 1972 (86 Stat. 919), and July 22, 1976 (90 Stat. 999). Transferred from the Office of the Secretary to Assistant Secretary (Domestic Finance) by Department of the Treasury Order 242, rev. 1, of May 17, 1976.

Review, Division of Established in *National Recovery Administration* by EO 7075 of June 15, 1935. Transferred to the Department of Commerce by EO 7252 of Dec. 21, 1935, and functions terminated Apr. 1, 1936. *Committee of Industrial Analysis* created by EO 7323 of Mar. 21, 1936, to complete work of *Division*.

RFC Mortgage Company Organized under laws of Maryland Mar. 14, 1935, pursuant to act of Jan. 22, 1932 (47 Stat. 5). Grouped with other agencies to form *Federal Loan Agency* by Reorg. Plan No. I of 1939, effective July 1, 1939. Transferred to the Department of Commerce by EO 9071 of Feb. 24, 1942. Returned to *Federal Loan Agency* by act of Feb. 24, 1945 (59 Stat. 5). Assets and liabilities transferred to *Reconstruction Finance Corporation* by act of June 30, 1947 (61 Stat. 207).

River Basins, Neches, Trinity, Brazos, Colorado, Guadalupe, San Antonio, Nueces, and San Jacinto, and Intervening Areas, U.S. Study Commission on Established by act of Aug. 28, 1958 (72 Stat. 1058). Terminated June 30, 1962.

River Basins, Savannah, Altamaha, Saint Marys, Apalachicola-Chattahoochee, and Perdido-Escambia, and Intervening Areas, U.S. Study Commission on Established by act of Aug. 28, 1958 (72 Stat. 1090). Terminated Dec. 23, 1962.

Road Inquiry, Office of Established by the Secretary of Agriculture under authority of act of Aug. 8, 1894 (28 Stat. 264). Federal aid for highways to be administered by the Secretary of Agriculture through *Office of Public Roads and Rural Engineering* authorized by act of July 11, 1916 (39 Stat. 355), known as *Bureau of Public Roads* after July 1918. Transferred to *Federal Works Agency* by Reorg. Plan No. I of 1939, effective July 1, 1939, and renamed *Public Roads Administration*. Transferred to General Services Administration as *Bureau of Public Roads* by act of June 30, 1949 (63 Stat. 380). Transferred to the Department of Commerce by Reorg. Plan No. 7 of 1949, effective Aug. 20, 1949. Transferred to the Secretary of Transportation by act of Oct. 15, 1966 (80 Stat. 931), and functions assigned to Federal Highway Administration.

Roads, Bureau of Public *See* **Road Inquiry, Office of**

Roads Administration, Public *See* **Road Inquiry, Office of**

Roads and Rural Engineering, Office of Public *See* **Road Inquiry, Office of**

Rock Creek and Potomac Parkway Commission Established by act of Mar. 14, 1913 (37 Stat. 885). Abolished by EO 6166 of June 10, 1933, and functions transferred to *Office of National Parks, Buildings, and Reservations*, Department of the Interior.

Roosevelt Centennial Commission, Theodore Established by joint resolution of July 28, 1955 (69 Stat. 383). Terminated Oct. 27, 1959, pursuant to terms of act.

Roosevelt Library, Franklin D. Functions assigned to National Park Service by Reorg. Plan No. 3 of 1946, effective July 16, 1946, transferred to General Services Administration by Reorg. Plan No. 1 of 1963, effective July 27, 1963.

Roosevelt Library, Trustees of the Franklin D. Established by joint resolution of July 18, 1939 (53 Stat. 1063). Transferred to General Services Administration by act of June 30, 1949 (63 Stat. 381). Abolished by act of Mar. 5, 1958 (72 Stat. 34), and Library operated by *National Archives and Records Service*, General Services Administration.

Roosevelt Memorial Commission, Franklin Delano Established by joint resolution of Aug. 11, 1955 (69 Stat. 694). Terminated by act of Nov. 14, 1997 (111 Stat. 1601).

Rubber Development Corporation Establishment announced Feb. 20, 1943, by the Secretary of Commerce. Organized under laws of Delaware as subsidiary of *Reconstruction Finance Corporation*. Assumed all activities of *Rubber Reserve Company* relating to development of foreign rubber sources and procurement of rubber therefrom. Functions transferred to *Office of Economic Warfare* by EO 9361 of July 15, 1943. *Office* consolidated into *Foreign Economic Administration* by EO 9380 of Sept. 25, 1943. *Office* returned to *Reconstruction Finance Corporation* by EO 9630 of Sept. 27, 1945. Certificate of incorporation expired June 30, 1947.

Rubber Producing Facilities Disposal Commission Established by act of Aug. 7, 1953 (67 Stat. 408). Functions transferred to *Federal Facilities Corporation* by EO 10678 of Sept. 20, 1956.

Rubber Reserve Company Established June 28, 1940, under act of Jan. 22, 1932 (47 Stat. 5). Transferred from *Federal Loan Agency* to the Department of Commerce by EO 9071 of Feb. 24, 1942. Returned to *Federal Loan Agency* by act of Feb. 24, 1945 (59 Stat. 5). Dissolved by act of June 30, 1945 (59 Stat. 310), and functions transferred to *Reconstruction Finance Corporation*.

Rural Areas Development, Office of Established by Secretary of Agriculture memorandum in 1961 (revised Sept. 21, 1962). Renamed *Rural Community Development Service* by Secretary's Memorandum 1570 of Feb. 24, 1965.

Rural Business and Cooperative Development Service Established within the Department of Agriculture by Secretary's Memorandum 1020–34 dated Dec. 31, 1991. Renamed Rural Business-Cooperative Service (61 FR 2899), effective Jan. 30, 1996.

Rural Community Development Service Established by Secretary of Agriculture Memorandum 1570 of Feb. 25, 1965, to supersede *Office of Rural Areas Development.* Abolished Feb. 2, 1970, by Secretary's Memorandum 1670 of Jan. 30, 1970, and functions transferred to other agencies in the Department of Agriculture.

Rural Development Administration Established within the Department of Agriculture by Secretary's Memorandum 1020–34 dated Dec. 31, 1991. Abolished Dec. 27, 1994 (59 FR 66441) under authority of Secretary's Memorandum 1010–1 dated Oct. 20, 1994. Functions assumed by the Rural Business and Cooperative Development Service.

Rural Development Committee *See* **Rural Development Program, Committee for**

Rural Development Policy, Office of Established initially as *Office of Rural Development Policy Management and Coordination,* Farmers Home Administration, by Secretary of Agriculture Memorandum 1020–3 of Oct. 26, 1981. Abolished in 1986 due to lack of funding.

Rural Development Program, Committee for Established by EO 10847 of Oct. 12, 1959. Abolished by EO 11122 of Oct. 16, 1963, which established *Rural Development Committee. Committee* superseded by EO 11307 of Sept. 30, 1966, and functions assumed by the Secretary of Agriculture.

Rural Development Service Established by Agriculture Secretarial order in 1973. Functions transferred to *Office of Rural Development Coordination and Planning, Farmers Home Administration,* by Secretarial order in 1978.

Rural Electrification Administration Established by EO 7037 of May 11, 1935. Functions transferred by EO 7458 of Sept. 26, 1936, to *Rural Electrification Administration* established by act of May 20, 1936 (49 Stat. 1363). Transferred to the Department of Agriculture by Reorg. Plan No. II of 1939, effective July 1, 1939. Abolished by Secretary's Memorandum 1010–1 dated Oct. 20, 1994, and functions assumed by Rural Utilities Service.

Rural Housing and Community Development Service Established by act of Oct. 13, 1994 (108 Stat. 3219). Renamed Rural Housing Service (61 FR 2899), effective Jan. 30, 1996.

Rural Rehabilitation Division Established April 1934 by act of May 12, 1933 (48 Stat. 55). Functions transferred to *Resettlement Administration* by *Federal Emergency Relief Administrator's* order of June 19, 1935.

Saint Elizabeth's Hospital *See* **Insane, Government Hospital for the**

Saint Lawrence Seaway Development Corporation Established by act of May 13, 1954 (68 Stat. 92). Secretary of Commerce given direction of general policies of *Corporation* by EO 10771 of June 20, 1958. Transferred to the Department of Transportation by act of Oct. 15, 1966 (80 Stat. 931).

Salary Stabilization, Office of *See* **Salary Stabilization Board**

Salary Stabilization Board Established May 10, 1951, by *Economic Stabilization Administrator's* General Order 8. Stabilization program administered by *Office of Salary Stabilization.* Terminated Apr. 30, 1953, by EO 10434 of Feb. 6, 1953, and acts of June 30, 1952 (66 Stat. 296), and June 30, 1953 (67 Stat. 131).

Sales Manager, Office of the General Established by the Secretary of Agriculture Feb. 29, 1976. Consolidated with Foreign Agricultural Service by Secretary's Memorandum 2001 of Nov. 29, 1979.

Savings Bonds, Interdepartmental Committee for the Voluntary Payroll Savings Plan for the Purchase of U.S. Established by EO 11532 of June 2, 1970. Superseded by EO 11981 of Mar. 29, 1977, which established Interagency Committee for the Purchase of U.S. Savings Bonds.

Savings and Loan Advisory Council, Federal Established by act of Oct. 6, 1972 (86 Stat. 770). Continued by act of Dec. 26, 1974 (88 Stat. 1739). Terminated by act of Aug. 9, 1989 (103 Stat. 422).

Savings and Loan Insurance Corporation, Federal Established by act of June 27, 1934 (48 Stat. 1246). Grouped with other agencies to form *Federal Loan Agency* by Reorg. Plan No. I of 1939, effective July 1, 1939. Transferred to *Federal Home Loan Bank Administration, National Housing Agency,* by EO 9070 of Feb. 24, 1942. Board of Trustees abolished by Reorg. Plan No. 3 of 1947, effective July 27, 1947, and functions transferred to *Home Loan Bank Board.* Abolished by act of Aug. 9, 1989 (103 Stat. 354).

Savings Bonds Division, United States Established by Departmental Order 62 of Dec. 26, 1945, as successor to the War and Finance Division, War Savings Staff, and Defense Savings Staff. Functions transferred to Bureau of Public Debt by Departmental Order 101–05 of May 11, 1994, and *Division* renamed Savings Bond Marketing Office.

Science, Engineering, and Technology, Federal Coordinating Council for Established by act of May 11, 1976 (90 Stat. 471). Abolished by Reorg. Plan No. 1 of 1977, effective Feb. 26, 1978, and functions transferred to President. Functions redelegated to Director of the Office of Science and Technology Policy and Federal Coordinating Council for Science, Engineering, and Technology, established by EO 12039 of Feb. 24, 1978.

Science, Engineering, and Technology Panel, Intergovernmental Established by act of May 11, 1976 (90 Stat. 465). Abolished by Reorg. Plan No. 1 of 1977, effective Feb. 26, 1978, and functions transferred to President. Functions redelegated to Director of Office of Science and Technology Policy by EO 12039 of Feb. 24, 1978, which established Intergovernmental Science, Engineering, and Technology Advisory Panel.

Science Advisory Committee, President's Established by President Apr. 20, 1951, and reconstituted Nov. 22, 1957. Terminated with *Office of Science and Technology,* effective July 1, 1973.

Science Exhibit-Century 21 Exposition, U.S. Established Jan. 20, 1960, by Department of Commerce Order 167. Abolished by revocation of order on June 5, 1963.

Science and Technology, Federal Council for *See* **Scientific Research and Development, Interdepartmental Committee on**

Science and Technology, Office of Established by Reorg. Plan No. 2 of 1962, effective June 8, 1962. *Office* abolished by Reorg. Plan No. 1 of 1973, effective June 30, 1973, and functions transferred to National Science Foundation.

Science and Technology, President's Committee on Established by act of May 11, 1976 (90 Stat. 468). Abolished by Reorg. Plan No. 1 of 1977, effective Feb. 26, 1978, and functions transferred to President.

Scientific and Policy Advisory Committee Established by act of Sept. 26, 1961 (75 Stat. 631). Terminated Apr. 30, 1996 under terms of act.

Scientific Research and Development, Interdepartmental Committee on Established by EO 9912 of Dec. 24, 1947. EO 9912 revoked by EO 10807 of Mar. 13, 1959, which established *Federal Council for Science and Technology.* Abolished by act of May 11, 1976 (90 Stat. 472).

Scientific Research and Development, Office of Established in *Office for Emergency Management* by EO 8807 of June 28, 1941. Terminated by EO 9913 of Dec. 26, 1947, and property transferred to *National Military Establishment* for liquidation.

Scientists and Engineers, National Committee for the Development of Established by President Apr. 3, 1956. Renamed *President's Committee on Scientists and Engineers* May 7, 1957. Final report submitted Dec. 17, 1958, and expired Dec. 31, 1958.

Scientists and Engineers, President's Committee on *See* **Scientists and Engineers, National Committee for the Development of**

Screw Thread Commission, National Established by act of July 18, 1918 (40 Stat. 912). Terminated by EO 6166 of June 10, 1933, and records transferred to the Department of Commerce, effective Mar. 2, 1934. Informal Interdepartmental Screw Thread Committee established on Sept. 14, 1939, consisting of representatives of the Departments of *War,* the Navy, and Commerce.

Security, Commission on Government Established by act of Aug. 9, 1955 (69 Stat. 595). Terminated Sept. 22, 1957, pursuant to terms of act.

Security, Office of the Director for Mutual *See* **Security Agency, Mutual**

Security Agency, Federal Established by Reorg. Plan No. I of 1939, effective July 1, 1939, grouping under one administration *Office of Education, Public Health Service, Social Security Board, U.S. Employment Service, Civilian Conservation Corps,* and *National Youth Administration.* Abolished by Reorg. Plan No. 1 of 1953, effective Apr. 11, 1953, and functions and units transferred to *Department of Health, Education, and Welfare.*

Security Agency, Mutual Established and continued by acts of Oct. 10, 1951 (65 Stat. 373) and June 20, 1952 (66 Stat. 141). *Agency* and *Office of Director for Mutual Security* abolished by Reorg. Plan No. 7 of 1953, effective Aug. 1, 1953, and functions transferred to *Foreign Operations Administration,* established by same plan.

Security and Individual Rights, President's Commission on Internal Established by EO 10207 of Jan. 23, 1951. Terminated by EO 10305 of Nov. 14, 1951.

Security Resources Board, National Established by act of July 26, 1947 (61 Stat. 499). Transferred to Executive Office of the President by Reorg. Plan No. 4 of 1949, effective Aug. 20, 1949. Functions of *Board* transferred to Chairman and *Board* made advisory to him by Reorg. Plan No. 25 of 1950, effective July 10, 1950. Functions delegated by Executive order transferred to *Office of Defense Mobilization* by EO 10438 of Mar. 13, 1953. *Board* abolished by Reorg. Plan No. 3 of 1953, effective June 12, 1953, and remaining functions transferred to *Office of Defense Mobilization.*

Security Training Commission, National Established by act of June 19, 1951 (65 Stat. 75). Expired June 30, 1957, pursuant to Presidential letter of Mar. 25, 1957.

Seed Loan Office Authorized by Presidential letters of July 26, 1918, and July 26, 1919, to the Secretary of Agriculture. Further authorized by act of Mar. 3, 1921 (41 Stat. 1347). Office transferred to Farm Credit Administration by EO 6084 of Mar. 27, 1933.

Selective Service Appeal Board, National Established by EO 9988 of Aug. 20, 1948. Inactive as of Apr. 11, 1975.

Selective Service Records, Office of *See* **Selective Service System**

Selective Service System Established by act of Sept. 16, 1940 (54 Stat. 885). Placed under jurisdiction of *War Manpower Commission* by EO 9279 of Dec. 5, 1942, and designated *Bureau of Selective Service.* Designated Selective Service System, separate agency, by EO 9410 of Dec. 23, 1943. Transferred for liquidation to *Office of Selective Service Records* established by act of Mar. 31, 1947 (61 Stat. 31). Transferred to Selective Service System by act of June 24, 1948 (62 Stat. 604).

Self-Help Development and Technical Development, Office of Established in *National Consumer Cooperative Bank* by act of Aug. 20, 1978 (92 Stat. 499). Abolished by act of Aug. 13, 1981 (95 Stat. 437), and assets transferred to Consumer Cooperative Development Corporation, Department of Commerce, Dec. 30, 1982.

Services, Bureau of Special *See* **Office of War Information**

Services, Division of Central Administrative Established by *Liaison Officer for Emergency Management* pursuant to Presidential letter of Feb. 28, 1941. Terminated by EO 9471 of Aug. 25, 1944, and functions discontinued or transferred to constituent agencies of *Office for Emergency Management* and other agencies.

Shipbuilding Stabilization Committee Originally organized by *National Defense Advisory Commission* in 1940. Established August 1942 by *War Production Board.* Transferred to the Department of Labor from *Civilian Production Administration,* successor agency to *Board,* by EO 9656 of Nov. 15, 1945. Terminated June 30, 1947.

Shipping Board, U.S. Established by act of Sept. 7, 1916 (39 Stat. 729). Abolished by EO 6166 of June 10, 1933, and functions, including those with respect to *U.S. Shipping Board Merchant Fleet Corporation,* transferred to *U.S. Shipping Board Bureau,* Department of Commerce, effective Mar. 2, 1934. Separation of employees deferred until Sept. 30, 1933, by EO 6245 of Aug. 9, 1933. Functions assumed by *U.S. Maritime Commission* Oct. 26, 1936, pursuant to act of June 29, 1936 (49 Stat. 1985).

Shipping Board Bureau, U.S. *See* **Shipping Board, U.S.**

Shipping Board Emergency Fleet Corporation, U.S. Established Apr. 16, 1917, under authority of act of Sept. 7, 1916 (39 Stat. 729). Renamed *U.S. Shipping Board Merchant Fleet Corporation* by act of Feb. 11, 1927 (44 Stat. 1083). Terminated Oct. 26, 1936, under provisions of act of June 29, 1936 (49 Stat. 1985), and functions transferred to *U.S. Maritime Commission.*

Shipping Board Merchant Fleet Corporation, U.S. *See* **Shipping Board Emergency Fleet Corporation, U.S.**

Ships, Bureau of Established by act of June 20, 1940 (54 Stat. 493), to replace *Bureau of Engineering* and *Bureau of Construction and Repair.* Abolished by Department of Defense reorg. order of Mar. 9, 1966, and functions transferred to the Secretary of the Navy (31 FR 7188).

Simpson Historical Research Center, Albert F. Renamed Headquarters USAF Historical Research Center by special order of Dec. 16, 1983 of the Secretary of Defense.

Smithsonian Symposia and Seminars, Office of Renamed Office of Interdisciplinary Studies by Smithsonian Institution announcement of Mar. 16, 1987.

Social Development Institute, Inter-American Established by act of Dec. 30, 1969 (83 Stat. 821). Renamed Inter-American Foundation by act of Feb. 7, 1972 (86 Stat. 34).

Social Protection, Committee on Established in *Office of Defense Health and Welfare Services* by administrative order June 14, 1941. Functions transferred to *Federal Security Agency* by EO 9338 of Apr. 29, 1943.

Social and Rehabilitation Service Established by the *Secretary of Health, Education, and Welfare* reorganization of Aug. 15, 1967. Abolished by Secretary's reorganization of Mar. 8, 1977 (42 FR 13262), and constituent units—*Medical Services Administration, Assistance Payments Administration, Office of Child Support Enforcement, and Public Services Administration*—transferred.

Social Security Administration *See* **Social Security Board**

Social Security Board Established by act of Aug. 14, 1935 (49 Stat. 620). Incorporated into *Federal Security Agency* by Reorg. Plan No. I of 1939, effective July 1, 1939. *Social Security Board* abolished and Social Security Administration established by Reorg. Plan No. 2 of 1946 (5 U.S.C. app.), effective July 16, 1946, and functions of the *Board* transferred to *Federal Security Administrator.* Social Security Administration transferred from the *Federal Security Agency* by Reorganization Plan No. 1 of 1953 (5 U.S.C. app.), effective Apr. 11, 1953, to the *Department of Health, Education, and Welfare.* Social Security Administration became an independent agency in the executive branch by act of Aug. 15, 1994 (108 Stat. 1464), effective Mar. 31, 1995.

Soil Conservation Service *See* **Soil Erosion Service**

Soil Erosion Service Established in the Department of the Interior following allotment made Aug. 25, 1933. Transferred to the Department of Agriculture by Secretary of Interior administrative order of Mar. 25, 1935. Made *Soil Conservation Service* by order of the Secretary of Agriculture, Apr. 27, 1935, pursuant to provisions of act of Apr. 27, 1935 (49 Stat. 163). Certain functions of *Soil Conservation Service* under jurisdiction of the Department of the Interior transferred from the Department of Agriculture to the Department of the Interior by Reorg. Plan No. IV of 1940, effective June 30, 1940. *Soil Conservation Service* abolished by act of Oct. 13, 1994 (108 Stat. 3225) and functions assumed by the Natural Resources Conservation Service.

Soils, Bureau of *See* **Agricultural and Industrial Chemistry, Bureau of** and **Plant Industry, Bureau of**

Solicitor General, Office of Assistant Established in the Department of Justice by act of June 16, 1933 (48 Stat. 307). Terminated by Reorg. Plan No. 2 of 1950, effective May 24, 1950.

Southeastern Power Administration Established by the Secretary of the Interior in 1943 to carry out functions under act of Dec. 22, 1944 (58 Stat. 890). Transferred to the Department of Energy by act of Aug. 4, 1977 (91 Stat. 578).

Southwestern Power Administration Established by the Secretary of the Interior in 1943 to carry out functions under act of Dec. 22, 1944 (58 Stat. 890). Transferred to the Department of Energy by act of Aug. 4, 1977 (91 Stat. 578).

Space Access and Technology, Office of Established in the National Aeronautics and Space Administration. Abolished by Administrator's order of Feb. 24, 1997.

Space Communications, Office of Established in the National Aeronautics and Space Administration. Abolished by Administrator's order of Feb. 24, 1997.

Space Science, Office of *See* **Space and Terrestrial Applications, Office of**

Space Science Board Renamed Space Studies Board by authority of the National Research Council, National Academy of Sciences, effective May 8, 1989.

Space Station, Office of Established in the National Aeronautics and Space Administration. Abolished in 1990 and remaining functions transferred to the Office of Space Flight.

Space Technology Laboratories, National Renamed John C. Stennis Space Center by EO 12641 of May 20, 1988.

Space and Terrestrial Applications, Office of Combined with *Office of Space Science* to form Office of Space Science and Applications by National Aeronautics and Space Administrator's announcement of Sept. 29, 1981.

Space Tracking and Data Systems, Office of Renamed Office of Space Operations by National Aeronautics and Space Administrator's announcement of Jan. 9, 1987.

Space Transportation Operations, Office of Combined with *Office of Space Transportation Systems* to form Office of Space Transportation Systems, National Aeronautics and Space Administration, effective July 1982.

Space Transportation Systems, Office of *See* **Space Transportation Operations, Office of**

Spanish-Speaking People, Cabinet Committee on Opportunities for *See* **Mexican-American Affairs, Interagency Committee on**

Special. *See other part of title*

Specifications Board, Federal Established by *Bureau of the Budget* Circular 42 of Oct. 10, 1921. Transferred from *Federal Coordinating Service* to *Procurement Division* by order of Oct. 9, 1933 of the Secretary of the Treasury. *Board* superseded by *Federal Specifications Executive Committee,* set up by *Director of Procurement* under Circular Letter 106 of July 16, 1935.

Sport Fisheries and Wildlife, Bureau of Established in the Department of the Interior by act of Aug. 8, 1956 (70 Stat. 1119). *Bureau* replaced by U.S. Fish and Wildlife Service pursuant to act of Apr. 22, 1974 (88 Stat. 92).

Standards, National Bureau of *See* **Weights and Measures, Office of Standard**

State, Department of Duty of Secretary of State of procuring copies of all statutes of the States, as provided for in act of Sept. 28, 1789 (R.S. 206), abolished by Reorg. Plan No. 20 of 1950, effective May 24, 1950. Functions of numbering, editing, and distributing proclamations and Executive orders transferred from the Department of State to the *Division of the Federal Register, National Archives,* by EO 7298 of Feb. 18, 1936. Duty of Secretary of State of publishing Executive proclamations and treaties in newspapers in District of Columbia, provided for in act of July 31, 1876 (19 Stat. 105), abolished by Reorg. Plan No. 20 of 1950, effective May 24, 1950. Functions concerning publication of U.S. Statutes at Large, acts and joint resolutions in pamphlet form known as slip laws, and amendments to the Constitution; electoral votes for President and Vice President; and Territorial papers transferred from the Department of State to the Administrator of the General Services Administration by Reorg. Plan No. 20 of 1950. (*See also* **Archives Establishment, National**)

State and Local Cooperation, Division of Established by *Advisory Commission to Council of National Defense* Aug. 5, 1940. Transferred to *Office of Civilian Defense.*

State and Local Government Cooperation, Committee on Established by EO 11627 of Oct 15, 1971. Abolished by EO 11695 of Jan. 11, 1973.

State Technical Services, Office of Established by the Secretary of Commerce Nov. 19, 1965, pursuant to act of Sept. 14, 1965 (79 Stat. 697). Abolished by Secretary, effective June 30, 1970.

Statistical Board, Central Organized Aug. 9, 1933, by EO 6225 of July 27, 1933. Transferred to *Bureau of the Budget* by Reorg. Plan No. I of 1939, effective July 1, 1939. Expired July 25, 1940, and functions taken over by *Division of Statistical Standards, Bureau of the Budget.*

Statistical Committee, Central Established by act of July 25, 1935 (49 Stat. 498). Abolished by Reorg. Plan No. I of 1939, effective July 1, 1939, and functions transferred to *Bureau of the Budget.*

Statistical Policy Coordination Committee Established by EO 12013 of Oct. 7, 1977. Abolished by EO 12318 of Aug. 21, 1981.

Statistical Reporting Service Established by Memorandum 1446, supp. 1, part 3, of 1961 of the Secretary of Agriculture. Consolidated with other departmental units into *Economics, Statistics, and Cooperatives Service* by Secretary's Memorandum 1927, effective Dec. 23, 1977. Redesignated as *Statistical Reporting Service* by Secretary's order of Oct. 1, 1981. Renamed National Agricultural Statistics Service.

Statistics Administration, Social and Economic Established Jan. 1, 1972, by the Secretary of Commerce. Terminated by Department of Commerce Organization Order 10–2, effective Aug. 4, 1975 (40 FR 42765). Bureau of Economic Analysis and Bureau of the Census restored as primary operating units of the Department of Commerce by Organization Orders 35–1A and 2A, effective Aug. 4, 1975.

Statutes at Large *See* **State, Department of**

Statutes of the States *See* **State, Department of**

Steam Engineering, Bureau of Established in the Department of the Navy by act of July 5, 1862 (12 Stat. 510). Redesignated as *Bureau of Engineering* by act of June 4, 1920 (41 Stat. 828). Abolished by act of June 20, 1940 (54 Stat. 492), and functions transferred to *Bureau of Ships.*

Steamboat Inspection Service President authorized to appoint *Service* by act of June 28, 1838 (5 Stat. 252). Secretary of Treasury authorized to establish boards of local inspectors at enumerated ports throughout the U.S. by act of Feb. 28, 1871 (16 Stat. 440). Authority to appoint boards of local inspectors delegated to *Secretary of Commerce and Labor* by act of Mar. 4, 1905 (33 Stat. 1026). Consolidated with *Bureau of Navigation and Steamboat Inspection* by act of June 30, 1932 (47 Stat. 415).

Stock Catalog Board, Federal Standard Originated by act of Mar. 2, 1929 (45 Stat. 1461). Transferred from *Federal Coordinating Service* to *Procurement Division* by order of Oct. 9, 1933 of the Secretary of the Treasury.

Strategic Defense Initiative Organization Established in 1986 as a separate agency of the Department of Defense. Renamed Ballistic Missile Defense Organization by Deputy Secretary's memorandum in May 1993.

Strategic Services, Office of *See* **Information, Office of Coordinator of**

Subversive Activities Control Board Established by act of Sept. 23, 1950 (64 Stat. 987). Terminated June 30, 1973, due to lack of funding.

Sugar Division Created by act of May 12, 1933 (48 Stat. 31), authorized by act of Sept. 1, 1937 (50 Stat. 903). Taken from *Agricultural Adjustment Administration* and made independent division of the Department of Agriculture by Secretary's Memorandum 783, effective Oct. 16, 1938. Placed under *Agricultural Conservation and Adjustment Administration* by EO 9069 of Feb. 23, 1942, functioning as *Sugar Agency.* Functions transferred to *Food Distribution Administration* by EO 9280 of Dec. 5, 1942.

Sugar Rationing Administration Established by Memorandum 1190 of Mar. 31, 1947, of the Secretary of Agriculture under authority of act of Mar. 31, 1947 (61 Stat. 35). Terminated Mar. 31, 1948, on expiration of authority.

Supplies and Accounts, Bureau of *See* **Provisions and Clothing, Bureau of**

Supplies and Shortages, National Commission on Established by act of Sept. 30, 1974 (88 Stat. 1168). Terminated Mar. 31, 1977, pursuant to terms of act.

Supply, Bureau of Federal *See* **Procurement Division**

Supply, Office of Renamed Office of Procurement and Property by Smithsonian Institution announcement of Nov. 4, 1986.

Supply Committee, General Established by act of June 17, 1910 (36 Stat. 531). Abolished by EO 6166 of June 10, 1933, effective Mar. 2, 1934, and functions transferred to *Procurement Division,* the Department of the Treasury.

Supply Priorities and Allocations Board Established in *Office for Emergency Management* by EO 8875 of Aug. 28, 1941. Abolished by EO 9024 of Jan. 16, 1942, and functions transferred to *War Production Board.*

Supply Service, Federal Renamed *Office of Personal Property* by General Services Administration order, effective Sept. 28, 1982; later renamed *Office of Federal Supply and Services* by GSA order of Jan. 22, 1983; then redesignated Federal Supply Service.

Surveys and Maps, Federal Board of *See* **Surveys and Maps of the Federal Government, Board of**

Surveys and Maps of the Federal Government, Board of Established by EO 3206 of Dec. 30, 1919. Renamed *Federal Board of Surveys and Maps* by EO 7262 of Jan. 4, 1936. Abolished by EO 9094 of Mar. 10, 1942, and functions transferred to Director, *Bureau of the Budget.*

Space System Development, Office of Established in the National Aeronautics and Space Administration. Renamed Office of Space Access and Technology in 1995.

Tariff Commission, U.S. Established by act of Sept. 8, 1916 (39 Stat. 795). Renamed U.S. International Trade Commission by act of Jan. 3, 1975 (88 Stat. 2009).

Tax Appeals, Board of Established as an independent agency within the executive branch by act of June 2, 1924 (43 Stat. 336). Continued by acts of Feb. 26, 1926 (44 Stat. 105) and Feb. 10, 1939 (53 Stat. 158). Renamed *Tax Court of the United States* by act of Aug. 16, 1954 (68A Stat. 879). Renamed United States Tax Court by act of Dec. 30, 1969 (83 Stat. 730).

Technical Cooperation Administration Transferred from the Department of State to *Mutual Security Agency* by EO 10458 of June 1, 1953. Transferred to *Foreign Operations Administration* by Reorg. Plan No. 7 of 1953, effective Aug. 1, 1953.

Technical Services, Office of Designated unit of Office of the Secretary of Commerce by Department Order 179, July 23, 1962. Functions transferred to *National Bureau of Standards* by Order 90 of Jan. 30, 1964.

Technology Assessment, Office of Created by act of Oct. 13, 1972 (86 Stat. 797). Office inactive as of Sept. 30, 1995.

Technology, Automation, and Economic Progress, National Commission on Established by act of Aug. 19, 1964 (78 Stat. 463). Terminated January 1966 pursuant to terms of act.

Telecommunications Adviser to the President Established in Executive Office of the President by EO 10297 of Oct. 9, 1951. EO 10297 revoked by EO 10460 of June 16, 1953, and functions transferred to Director of *Office of Defense Mobilization.*

Telecommunications Management, Director of Established in *Office of Emergency Planning* by EO 10995 of Feb. 16, 1962. Assignment of radio frequencies delegated to Government agencies and foreign diplomatic establishments by EO 11084 of Feb. 16, 1963. Abolished by Reorg. Plan No. 1 of 1970, effective Apr. 20, 1970.

Telecommunications Policy, Office of Established in Executive Office of the President by Reorg. Plan No. 1 of 1970, effective Apr. 20, 1970. Abolished by Reorg. Plan No. 1 of 1977, effective Mar. 26, 1978, and certain functions transferred to President with all other functions transferred to the Department of Commerce.

Telecommunications Service, Automated Data Renamed *Office of Information Resources Management* by General Services Administration order of Aug. 17, 1982. Later renamed Information Resources Management Service.

Temporary Controls, Office of Established in *Office for Emergency Management* by EO 9809 of Dec. 12, 1946, consolidating *Office of War Mobilization and Reconversion, Office of Economic Stabilization, Office of Price Administration,* and *Civilian Production Administration.* Functions with respect to Veterans' Emergency Housing Program transferred to *Housing Expediter* by EO 9836 of Mar. 22, 1947. Functions with respect to distribution and price of sugar products transferred to the Secretary of Agriculture by act of Mar. 31, 1947 (61 Stat. 36). Office terminated by EO 9841 of Apr. 23, 1947, and remaining functions redistributed.

Temporary Emergency Court of Appeals Established by act of Dec. 22, 1971 (85 Stat. 749). Abolished by act of Oct. 29, 1992, effective Apr. 30, 1993 (106 Stat. 4507). Court's jurisdiction and pending cases transferred to the United States Court of Appeals for the Federal Circuit.

Territorial Affairs, Office of Established by Interior Secretarial Order 2951 of Feb. 6, 1973. Abolished by Departmental Manual Release 2270 of June 6, 1980, and functions transferred to Office of Assistant Secretary for Territorial and International Affairs.

Territorial papers *See* **State, Department of**

Territories, Office of Established by the Secretary of the Interior July 28, 1950. Functions reassigned to *Deputy Assistant Secretary for Territorial Affairs* in *Office of the Assistant Secretary—Public Land Management,* Department of the Interior, by Secretarial Order 2942, effective July 1, 1971.

Terrorism, Cabinet Committee To Combat Established by Presidential memorandum of Sept. 25, 1972. Terminated by National Security Council memorandum of Sept. 16, 1977.

Textile Industry, Board of Inquiry for the Cotton Established by EO 6840 of Sept. 5, 1934. Abolished by EO 6858 of Sept. 26, 1934.

Textile National Industrial Relations Board Established by administrative order of June 28, 1934. Abolished by EO 6858 of Sept. 26, 1934, which created *Textile Labor Relations Board* in connection with the Department of Labor. *Board* terminated July 1, 1937, and functions absorbed by *U.S. Conciliation Service,* Department of Labor.

Textile National Industrial Relations Board, Cotton Established by original Code of Fair Competition for the Cotton Textile Industry, as amended July 10, 1934. Abolished by EO 6858 of Sept. 26, 1934.

Textile Work Assignment Board, Cotton Amendments to Code of Fair Competition for Cotton Textile Industry approved by EO 6876 of Oct. 16, 1934, and *Cotton Textile Work Assignment Board* appointed by *Textile Labor Relations Board. Board* expired June 15, 1935.

Textile Work Assignment Board, Silk Appointed by *Textile Labor Relations Board* following President's approval of amendments to Code of Fair Competition for Silk Textile Industry by EO 6875 of Oct. 16, 1934. Terminated June 15, 1935.

Textile Work Assignment Board, Wool Established by EO 6877 of Oct. 16, 1934. Terminated June 15, 1935.

Textiles, Office of Established by the Secretary of Commerce Feb. 14, 1971. Functions transferred to *Domestic and International Business Administration,* effective Nov. 17, 1972.

Thrift Depositor Protection Oversight Board. *See* **Oversight Board (of the Resolution Trust Corporation).**

Trade, Special Adviser to the President on Foreign Established by EO 6651 of Mar. 23, 1934. Terminated on expiration of *National Recovery Administration.*

Trade Administration, International *See* **Business and Defense Services Administration**

Trade Agreements, Interdepartmental Committee on Established by Secretary of State in 1934 and reestablished by EO 9832 of Feb. 25, 1947. Abolished by EO 11075 of Jan. 15, 1963.

Trade and Development Program Established by act of Sept. 4, 1961, as amended (88 Stat. 1804). Designated separate entity within the *U.S. International Development Cooperation Agency* by act of Sept. 4, 1961, as amended (102 Stat. 1329). Renamed Trade and Development Agency by act of Oct. 28, 1992 (106 Stat. 3657).

Trade Expansion Act Advisory Committee Established by EO 11075 of Jan. 15, 1963. Abolished by EO 11846 of Mar. 27, 1975, and records transferred to Trade Policy Committee established by same EO.

Trade Negotiations, Office of the Special Representative for Renamed Office of the U.S. Trade Representative by EO 12188 of Jan. 4, 1980.

Trade Policy Committee Established by EO 10741 of Nov. 25, 1957. Abolished by EO 11075 of Jan. 15, 1963.

Traffic Safety, President's Committee for Established by Presidential letter of Apr. 14, 1954. Continued by EO 10858 of Jan. 13, 1960. Abolished by EO 11382 of Nov. 28, 1967.

Traffic Safety Agency, National Established in the Department of Commerce by act of Sept. 9, 1966 (80 Stat. 718). Activity transferred to the Department of Transportation by act of Oct. 15, 1966 (80 Stat. 931). Responsibility placed in *National Highway Safety Bureau* by EO 11357 of June 6, 1967.

Training and Employment Service, U.S. Established in *Manpower Administration,* Department of Labor, Mar. 17, 1969. Abolished by Secretary's letter of Dec. 6, 1971, and functions assigned to *Office of Employment Development Programs* and *U.S. Employment Service.*

Training School for Boys, National *See* **District of Columbia, Reform-School of the**

Transportation, Federal Coordinator of Established by act of June 16, 1933 (48 Stat. 211). Expired June 16, 1936, under provisions of Public Resolution 27 (49 Stat. 376).

Transportation, Office of Established in the Department of Agriculture by Secretary's Memorandum 1966 dated Dec. 12, 1978. Abolished by Secretary's Memorandum 1030–25 dated Dec. 28, 1990.

Transportation and Communications Service Established by General Services Administrator Oct. 19, 1961. Abolished by Administrator's order, effective July 15, 1972. Motor equipment, transportation, and public utilities responsibilities assigned to Federal Supply Service; telecommunications function assigned to *Automated Data Telecommunications Service.*

Transportation and Public Utilities Service Abolished by General Services Administration order of Aug. 17, 1982. Functions transferred to various GSA organizations.

Transportation Safety Board, National Established in the Department of Transportation by act of Oct. 15, 1966 (80 Stat. 935). Abolished by act of Jan. 3, 1975 (88 Stat. 2156), which established independent National Transportation Safety Board.

Travel Service, U.S. Replaced by *U.S. Travel and Tourism Administration,* Department of Commerce, pursuant to act of Oct. 16, 1981 (95 Stat. 1014).

Travel and Tourism Administration, U.S. Established by act of Oct. 16, 1981 (95 Stat. 1014). Abolished by P.L. 104–288, Oct. 11, 1996 (110 Stat. 3407).

Travel and Tourism Advisory Board Established by act of Oct. 16, 1981 (95 Stat. 1017). Abolished by P.L. 104–288, Oct. 11, 1996 (110 Stat. 3407).

Treasury, Office of the Assistant Secretary of the—Electronics and Information Technology Established by Secretary's Order 114–1 of Mar. 14, 1983. Abolished by Secretary's Order 114–3 of May 17, 1985, and functions transferred to Office of the Assistant Secretary for Management. Certain provisions effective Aug. 31, 1985 (50 FR 23573).

Treasury, Solicitor of the Position established when certain functions of *Solicitor of the Treasury* transferred to the Department of Justice by EO 6166 of June 10, 1933. *Solicitor of the Treasury* transferred from the Department of Justice to the Department of the Treasury by same order. *Office of Solicitor of the Treasury* abolished by act of May 10, 1934 (48 Stat. 758), and functions transferred to General Counsel, the Department of the Treasury.

Treasury Secretary, Assistant Office abolished by Reorg. Plan No. III of 1940, effective June 30, 1940, and functions transferred to Fiscal Assistant Secretary, Department of the Treasury.

Treaties *See* **State, Department of**

Typhus Commission, U.S. of America Established in *Department of War* by EO 9285 of Dec. 24, 1942. Abolished June 30, 1946, by EO 9680 of Jan. 17, 1946.

U.S. *See other part of title*

Uniformed Services University of the Health Sciences, School of Medicine of the Renamed F. Edward Hébert School of Medicine by act of Sept. 24, 1983 (97 Stat. 704).

United Nations Educational, Scientific and Cultural Organization U.S. membership in UNESCO authorized by act of July 30, 1946 (60 Stat. 712). Announcement of U.S. intention to withdraw made Dec. 28, 1983, in accordance with UNESCO constitution. Official U.S. withdrawal effective Dec. 31, 1984, by Secretary of State's letter of Dec. 19, 1984. U.S. maintains status as observer mission in UNESCO.

United States Court of Military Appeals Established under Article I of the Constitution of the United States pursuant to act of May 5, 1950, as amended (10 U.S.C. 867). Renamed United States Court of Appeals for the Armed Forces by act of Oct. 5, 1995 (108 Stat. 2831).

Upper Mississippi River Basin Commission Established by EO 11659 of Mar. 22, 1972. Terminated by EO 12319 of Sept. 9, 1981.

Urban Affairs, Council for Established in Executive Office of the President by EO 11452 of Jan. 23, 1969. Terminated by EO 11541 of July 1, 1970.

Urban Mass Transportation Administration Functions regarding urban mass transportation established in the Department of Housing and Urban Development by act of July 9, 1964 (78 Stat. 302). Most functions transferred to the Department of Transportation by Reorg. Plan No. 2 of 1968, effective June 30, 1968 (82 Stat. 1369), and joint responsibility assigned to the Departments of Transportation and Housing and Urban Development for functions relating to research, technical studies, and training. Transportation and Housing and Urban Development Under Secretaries agreed in November 1969 that the Department of

Transportation should be focal point for urban mass transportation grant administration; at which time functions transferred to the Department of Transportation. Renamed Federal Transit Administration by act of Dec. 18, 1991 (105 Stat. 2088).

Urban Renewal Administration Established in *Housing and Home Finance Agency* by Administrator's Organizational Order 1 of Dec. 23, 1954. Functions transferred to the Department of Housing and Urban Development by act of Sept. 9, 1965 (78 Stat. 667), and *Administration* terminated.

Utilization and Disposal Service Established July 1, 1961, by Administrator of General Services and assigned functions of Federal Supply Service and Public Buildings Service. Functions transferred to *Property Management and Disposal Service* July 29, 1966.

Veterans Administration Legal work in defense of suits against the U.S. arising under act of June 7, 1924 (43 Stat. 607), transferred to the Department of Justice by EO 6166 of June 10, 1933. Transfer deferred to Sept. 10, 1933, by EO 6222 of July 27, 1933. Established as an independent agency under the President by Executive Order 5398 of July 21, 1930, in accordance with the act of July 3, 1930 (46 Stat. 1016) and the act of Sept. 2, 1958 (72 Stat. 1114). Made an executive department in the executive branch and redesignated the Department of Veterans Affairs by act of Oct. 25, 1988 (102 Stat. 2635).

Veterans Appeals, U.S. Court of Established by act of Nov. 18, 1988 (102 Stat. 4113). Renamed U.S. Court of Appeals for Veterans Claims by act of Nov. 11, 1998 (112 Stat. 3341).

Veterans Education Appeals Board *See* **Veterans Tuition Appeals Board**

Veterans Employment Service Renamed Veterans' Employment and Training Service by Order 4–83 of Mar. 24, 1983 of the Secretary of Labor (48 FR 14092).

Veterans Health Administration *See* **Medicine and Surgery, Department of**

Veterans Health Services and Research Administration *See* **Medicine and Surgery, Department of**

Veterans Placement Service Board Established by act of June 22, 1944 (58 Stat. 293). Abolished by Reorg. Plan No. 2 of 1949, effective Aug. 20, 1949, and functions transferred to the Secretary of Labor.

Veterans Tuition Appeals Board Established by act of Aug. 24, 1949 (63 Stat. 654). Functions assumed by *Veterans Education Appeals Board* established by act of July 13, 1950 (64 Stat. 336). *Board* terminated by act of Aug. 28, 1957 (71 Stat. 474).

Veterinary Medicine, Bureau of Established in Food and Drug Administration, *Department of Health, Education, and Welfare.* Renamed Center for Veterinary Medicine by FDA notice of Mar. 9, 1984 (49 FR 10166).

Virgin Islands Public works programs under act of Dec. 20, 1944 (58 Stat. 827), transferred from General Services Administrator to the Secretary of the Interior by Reorg. Plan No. 15 of 1950, effective May 24, 1950.

Virgin Islands Company Established in 1934. Reincorporated as Government corporation by act of June 30, 1949 (63 Stat. 350). Program terminated June 30, 1965, and *Corporation* dissolved July 1, 1966.

Virgin Islands Corporation *See* **Virgin Islands Company**

Visitor Facilities Advisory Commission, National Established by act of Mar. 12, 1968 (82 Stat. 45). Expired Jan. 5, 1975, pursuant to act of Oct. 6, 1972 (86 Stat. 776).

Vocational Rehabilitation, Office of Established to administer provisions of act of July 6, 1943 (57 Stat. 374). Other duties delegated by acts of Aug. 3, 1954 (68 Stat. 652), Nov. 8, 1965 (79 Stat. 1282), July 12, 1960 (74 Stat. 364), and July 10, 1954 (68 Stat. 454). Redesignated *Vocational Rehabilitation Administration* Jan. 28, 1963. Made component of newly created *Social and Rehabilitation Service* as *Rehabilitation Services Administration* by *Department of Health, Education, and Welfare* reorganization of Aug. 15, 1967.

Vocational Rehabilitation Administration *See* **Vocational Rehabilitation, Office of**

Voluntary Citizen Participation, State Office of Renamed State Office of Volunteerism in ACTION by notice of Apr. 18, 1986 (51 FR 13265), effective May 18, 1986.

Volunteer Service, International, Secretariat for Established in 1962 by International Conference on Middle Level Manpower called by President. Terminated Mar. 31, 1976, due to insufficient funding.

Volunteers in Service to America Established by act of Nov. 8, 1966 (80 Stat. 1472). *Service* administered by *Office of Economic Opportunity* and functions transferred to ACTION by Reorg. Plan No. 1 of 1971, effective July 1, 1971.

Wage Adjustment Board Established May 29, 1942, by the Secretary of Labor at Presidential direction of May 14, 1942, to accomplish purpose of act of Mar. 3, 1931 (46 Stat. 1494), as amended by acts of Aug. 30, 1935 (49 Stat. 1011), and Jan. 30, 1942 (56 Stat. 23). Disbanded on termination of *National Wage Stabilization Board.*

Wage and Price Stability, Council on Established in Executive Office of the President by act of Aug. 24, 1974 (88 Stat. 750). Abolished by EO 12288 of Jan. 29, 1981. Funding ceased beyond June 5, 1981, by act of June 5, 1981 (95 Stat. 74), and authorization for appropriations repealed by act of Aug. 13, 1981 (95 Stat. 432).

Wage and Price Stability Program *See* **Wage and Price Stability, Council on**

Wage Stabilization Board Established by EO 10161 of Sept. 9, 1950. Reconstituted by EO 10377 of July 25, 1952. Terminated Apr. 30, 1953, by EO 10434 of Feb. 6, 1953, and acts of June 30, 1952 (66 Stat. 296), and June 30, 1953 (67 Stat. 131).

Wage Stabilization Board, National *See* **Defense Mediation Board, National**

Wallops Flight Center, Wallops Island, VA Formerly separate field installation of National Aeronautics and Space Administration. Made component of Goddard Space Flight Center by NASA Management Instruction 1107.10A of Sept. 3, 1981.

War, Solid Fuels Administration for Established in the Department of the Interior by EO 9332 of Apr. 19, 1943. Absorbed *Office of Solid Fuels Coordinator for War* (originally established as *Office of Solid Fuels Coordinator for National Defense*) pursuant to Presidential letter of Nov. 5, 1941; later changed by Presidential letter of May 25, 1942. Terminated by EO 9847 of May 6, 1947.

War Assets Administration Established in *Office for Emergency Management* by EO 9689 of Jan. 31, 1946. Functions transferred to *Surplus Property Administration* by Reorg. Plan No. 1 of 1947, effective July 1, 1947, and agency renamed *War Assets Administration.* Abolished by act of June 30, 1949 (63 Stat. 738), and functions transferred for liquidation to General Services Administration.

War Assets Corporation *See* **Petroleum Reserves Corporation**

War Claims Commission Established by act of July 3, 1948 (62 Stat. 1240). Abolished by Reorg. Plan No. 1 of 1954, effective July 1, 1954, and functions transferred to Foreign Claims Settlement Commission of the U.S.

War Commodities Division Established in *Office of Foreign Economic Coordination* by Department of State Order of Aug. 27, 1943. *Office* abolished by departmental order of Nov. 6, 1943, pursuant to EO 9380 of Sept. 25, 1943, which established *Foreign Economic Administration* in *Office for Emergency Management.*

War Communications, Board of *See* **Defense Communications Board**

War Contracts Price Adjustment Board Established by act of Feb. 25, 1944 (58 Stat. 85). Abolished by act of Mar. 23, 1951 (65 Stat. 7), and functions transferred to *Renegotiation Board,* established by same act, and General Services Administrator.

War Damage Corporation *See* **War Insurance Corporation**

War, Department of Established by act of Aug. 7, 1789 (1 Stat. 49), succeeding similar department established prior to adoption of the Constitution. Three military departments—Army; Navy, including naval aviation and U.S. Marine Corps; and Air Force—reorganized under *National Military Establishment* by act of July 26, 1947 (61 Stat. 495).

War Finance Corporation Established by act of Apr. 5, 1918 (40 Stat. 506). Functions and obligations transferred by Reorg. Plan No. II of 1939, effective July 1, 1939, to the Secretary of the Treasury for liquidation not later than Dec. 31, 1939.

War Food Administration *See* **Food Production and Distribution, Administration of**

War Information, Office of Established in *Office of Emergency Management* by EO 9182 of June 13, 1942, consolidating *Office of Facts and Figures; Office of Government Reports; Division of Information, Office for Emergency Management;* and *Foreign Information Service—Outpost, Publications, and Pictorial Branches, Coordinator of Information.* Abolished by EO 9608 of Aug. 31, 1945. *Bureau of Special Services* and functions with respect to review of publications of Federal agencies transferred to *Bureau of the Budget.* Foreign information activities transferred to the Department of State.

War Insurance Corporation Established Dec. 13, 1941, by act of June 10, 1941 (55 Stat. 249). Charter filed Mar. 31, 1942. Renamed *War Damage Corporation* by act of Mar. 27, 1942 (56 Stat. 175). Transferred from *Federal Loan Agency* to the Department of Commerce by EO 9071 of Feb. 24, 1942. Returned to *Federal Loan Agency* by act of Feb. 24, 1945 (59 Stat. 5). *Agency* abolished by act of June 30, 1947 (61 Stat. 202), and functions assumed by *Reconstruction Finance Corporation.* Powers of *War Damage Corporation,* except for purposes of liquidation, terminated as of Jan. 22, 1947.

War Labor Board, National *See* **Defense Mediation Board, National**

War Manpower Commission Established in *Office for Emergency Management* by EO 9139 of Apr. 18, 1942. Terminated by EO 9617 of Sept. 19, 1945, and functions, except *Procurement and Assignment Service,* transferred to the Department of Labor.

War Mobilization, Office of Established by EO 9347 of May 27, 1943. Transferred to *Office of War Mobilization and Reconversion* by EO 9488 of Oct. 3, 1944.

War Mobilization and Reconversion, Office of Established by act of Oct. 3, 1944 (58 Stat. 785). Consolidated with other agencies by EO 9809 of Dec. 12, 1946, to form *Office of Temporary Controls. Media Programming Division* and *Motion Picture Division* transferred to *Office of Government Reports,* reestablished by same order. Certain other functions transferred to President and the Secretary of Commerce.

War Mobilization and Reconversion Advisory Board, Office of Established by act of Oct. 3, 1944 (58 Stat. 788). Transferred to *Office of Temporary Controls* by EO 9809 of Dec. 12, 1946.

War Plants Corporation, Smaller Established by act of June 11, 1942 (56 Stat. 351). Functions transferred by EO 9665 of Dec. 27, 1945, to *Reconstruction Finance Corporation* and the Department of Commerce. Abolished by act of June 30, 1947 (61 Stat. 202), and functions transferred for liquidation to

General Services Administration by Reorg. Plan No. 1 of 1957, effective July 1, 1957.

War and Post War Adjustment Policies, Advisory Unit on Established in *Office of War Mobilization* by Presidential direction Nov. 6, 1943. Report submitted Feb. 15, 1944, and Unit Director and Assistant Director submitted letter to Director of *War Mobilization* ending their work May 12, 1944.

War Production Board Established in *Office for Emergency Management* by EO 9024 of Jan. 16, 1942. *Board* terminated and successor agency, *Civilian Production Administration,* established by EO 9638 of Oct. 4, 1945.

War Property Administration, Surplus Established in *Office of War Mobilization* by EO 9425 of Feb. 19, 1944. Terminated on establishment of *Surplus Property Board* by act of Oct. 3, 1944 (58 Stat. 768). *Surplus Property Administration* established in *Office of War Mobilization and Reconversion* by act of Sept. 18, 1945 (59 Stat. 533), and *Board* abolished. Domestic functions of *Administration* merged into *War Assets Corporation, Reconstruction Finance Corporation,* by EO 9689 of Jan. 31, 1946. Foreign functions transferred to the Department of State by same order. Transfers made permanent by Reorg. Plan No. 1 of 1947, effective July 1, 1947.

War Refugee Board Established in Executive Office of the President by EO 9417 of Jan. 22, 1944. Terminated by EO 9614 of Sept. 14, 1945.

War Relations, Agricultural, Office for *See* **Farm Products, Division of**

War Relief Agencies, President's Committee on Established by Presidential letter of Mar. 13, 1941. *President's War Relief Control Board* established by EO 9205 of July 25, 1942, to succeed *Committee. Board* terminated by EO 9723 of May 14, 1946, and functions transferred to the Department of State.

War Relief Control Board, President's *See* **President's Committee on War Relief Agencies**

War Relocation Authority Established in *Office for Emergency Management* by EO 9102 of Mar. 18, 1942. Transferred to the Department of the Interior by EO 9423 of Feb. 16, 1944. Terminated by EO 9742 of June 25, 1946.

War Resources Board Established in August 1939 as advisory committee to work with *Joint Army and Navy Munitions Board.* Terminated by President Nov. 24, 1939.

War Resources Council *See* **Defense Resources Committee**

War Shipping Administration Established in *Office for Emergency Management* by EO 9054 Feb. 7, 1942. Terminated by act of July 8, 1946 (60 Stat. 501), and functions transferred to *U.S. Maritime Commission,* effective Sept. 1, 1946.

Water, Office of Saline Established to perform functions vested in the Secretary of the Interior by act of July 29, 1971 (85 Stat. 159). Merged with *Office of Water Resources Research* to form *Office of Water Research and Technology* by Secretary's Order 2966 of July 26, 1974.

Water Commission, National Established by act of Sept. 26, 1968 (82 Stat. 868). Terminated Sept. 25, 1973, pursuant to terms of act.

Water Policy, Office of Established by Department of the Interior Manual Release 2374 of Dec. 29, 1981, under authority of Assistant Secretary. Abolished by Secretarial Order No. 3096 of Oct. 19, 1983, and functions transferred to *Geological Survey* and *Office of Policy Analysis.*

Water Pollution Control Administration, Federal Established under the *Secretary of Health, Education, and Welfare* by act of Oct. 2, 1965 (79 Stat. 903). Transferred to the Department of the Interior by Reorg. Plan No. 2 of 1966, effective May 10, 1966. Renamed *Federal Water Quality Administration* by act of Apr. 3, 1970. Abolished by Reorg. Plan No. 3 of 1970, effective Dec. 2, 1970, and functions transferred to Environmental Protection Agency.

Water and Power Resources Service Renamed Bureau of Reclamation May 18, 1981, by Interior Secretarial Order 3064.

Water Quality Administration, Federal *See* **Water Pollution Control Administration, Federal**

Water Research and Technology, Office of Established by Interior Secretarial Order 2966 of July 26, 1974. Abolished by Secretarial order of Aug. 25, 1982, and functions transferred to Bureau of Reclamation, Geological Survey, and *Office of Water Policy.*

Water Resources Council Established by act of July 22, 1965 (89 Stat 575). Inactive as of Oct. 1, 1982.

Water Resources Research, Office of Established to perform functions vested in the Secretary of the Interior by act of July 17, 1964 (78 Stat. 329). Merged with *Office of Saline Water* to form *Office of Water Research and Technology* by Secretary's Order 2966 of July 26, 1974.

Watergate Special Prosecution Force Established by Attorney General order, effective May 25, 1973. Terminated by Attorney General order, effective June 20, 1977.

Waterways Corporation, Inland Incorporated under act of June 3, 1924 (43 Stat. 360). Transferred from the *Department of War* to the Department of Commerce by Reorg. Plan No. II of 1939, effective July 1, 1939. *Corporation* sold to *Federal Waterways Corporation* under contract of July 24, 1953. Renamed *Federal Barge Lines, Inc.* Liquidated by act of July 19, 1963 (77 Stat. 81).

Weather Bureau Established in the Department of Agriculture by act of Oct. 1, 1890 (26 Stat. 653). Transferred to the Department of Commerce by Reorg. Plan No. IV of 1940, effective June 30, 1940. Functions transferred to *Environmental Science Services Administration* by Reorg. Plan No. 2 of 1965, effective July 13, 1965.

Weather Control, Advisory Committee on Established by act of Aug. 13, 1953 (67 Stat. 559).

Act of Aug. 28, 1957 (71 Stat. 426), provided for termination by Dec. 31, 1957.

Weights and Measures, Office of Standard Renamed *National Bureau of Standards* by act of Mar. 3, 1901 (31 Stat. 1449). *Bureau* transferred from the Department of the Treasury to the *Department of Commerce and Labor* by act of Feb. 14, 1903 (32 Stat. 825). *Bureau* established within the Department of Commerce by act of Mar. 4, 1913 (37 Stat. 736). Renamed National Institute of Standards and Technology by act of Aug. 23, 1988 (102 Stat. 1827).

Welfare Administration Established by the *Secretary of Health, Education, and Welfare* reorganization of Jan. 28, 1963. Components consisted of *Bureau of Family Services, Children's Bureau, Office of Juvenile Delinquency and Youth Development,* and *Cuban Refugee Staff.* These functions reassigned to *Social and Rehabilitation Service* by Department reorganization of Aug. 15, 1967.

Wilson Memorial Commission, Woodrow Established by act of Oct. 4, 1961 (75 Stat. 783). Terminated on submittal of final report to President and Congress Sept. 29, 1966.

Women, Interdepartmental Committee on the Status of Established by EO 11126 of Nov. 1, 1963. Terminated by EO 12050 of Apr. 4, 1978.

Women, President's Commission on the Status of Established by EO 10980 of Dec. 14, 1961. Submitted final report to President Oct. 11, 1963.

Women's Army Auxiliary Corps Established by act of May 14, 1942 (56 Stat. 278). Repealed in part and superseded by act of July 1, 1943 (57 Stat. 371), which established *Women's Army Corps. Corps* abolished by the Secretary of Defense Apr. 24, 1978, pursuant to provisions of 10 U.S.C. 125A.

Women's Business Enterprise Division Renamed *Office of Women's Business Enterprise* by Small Business Administrator's reorganization, effective Aug. 19, 1981. Renamed Office of Women's Business Ownership Aug. 19, 1982.

Women's Reserve Established in U.S. Coast Guard by act of Nov. 23, 1942 (56 Stat. 1020).

Women's Year, 1975, National Commission on the Observance of International Established by EO 11832 of Jan. 9, 1975. Continued by act of Dec. 23, 1975 (89 Stat. 1003). Terminated Mar. 31, 1978, pursuant to terms of act.

Wood Utilization, National Committee on Established by Presidential direction in 1925. Abolished by EO 6179–B of June 16, 1933.

Work Projects Administration *See* **Works Progress Administration**

Work-Training Programs, Bureau of Abolished by reorganization of *Manpower Administration* and functions assigned to *U.S. Training and Employment Service,* effective Mar. 17, 1969.

Working Life, Productivity and Quality of, National Center for Established by act of Nov. 28, 1975 (89 Stat. 935). Authorized appropriations expired Sept. 30, 1978, and functions assumed by *National Productivity Council.*

Works, Advisory Committee on Federal Public Established by President Oct. 5, 1955. Abolished by President Mar. 12, 1961, and functions assigned to *Bureau of the Budget.*

Works Administration, Federal Civil Established by EO 6420–B of Nov. 9, 1933. Function of employment expired March 1934. Function of settling claims continued under *Works Progress Administration.*

Works Administration, Public *See* **Emergency Administration of Public Works, Federal**

Works Agency, Federal Established by Reorg. Plan No. I of 1939, effective July 1, 1939. Functions relating to defense housing transferred to *Federal Public Housing Authority, National Housing Agency,* by EO 9070 of Feb. 24, 1942. Abolished by act of June 30, 1949 (63 Stat. 380), and functions transferred to General Services Administration.

Works Emergency Housing Corporation, Public Established by EO 6470 of Nov. 29, 1933. Incorporated under laws of State of Delaware. Abolished and liquidated as of Aug. 14, 1935, by filing of certificate of surrender of corporate rights.

Works Emergency Leasing Corporation, Public Incorporated Jan. 3, 1934, under laws of Delaware by direction of Administrator of Public Works. Terminated with filed certificate of dissolution with secretary of state of Delaware Jan. 2, 1935.

Works Progress Administration Established by EO 7034 of May 6, 1935, and continued by subsequent yearly emergency relief appropriation acts. Renamed *Work Projects Administration* by Reorg. Plan No. I of 1939, effective July 1, 1939, which provided for consolidation of *Works Progress Administration* into *Federal Works Agency.* Transferred by President to *Federal Works Administrator* Dec. 4, 1942.

Works, Special Board of Public *See* **Land Program, Director of**

Yards and Docks, Bureau of Established by acts of Aug. 31, 1842 (5 Stat. 579), and July 5, 1862 (12 Stat. 510). Abolished by Department of Defense reorg. order of Mar. 9, 1966, and functions transferred to the Secretary of the Navy (31 FR 7188).

Youth Administration, National Established in *Works Progress Administration* by EO 7086 of June 26, 1935. Transferred to *Federal Security Agency* by Reorg. Plan No. I of 1939, effective July 1, 1939. Transferred to *Bureau of Training, War Manpower Commission,* by EO 9247 of Sept. 17, 1942. Terminated by act of July 12, 1943 (57 Stat. 539).

Youth Crime, President's Committee on Juvenile Delinquency and Established by EO 10940 of May 11, 1961. Terminated by EO 11529 of Apr. 24, 1970.

Youth Fitness, President's Council on Established by EO 10673 of July 16, 1956. Renamed *President's*

Council on Physical Fitness by EO 11074 of Jan. 8, 1963. Renamed President's Council on Physical Fitness and Sports by EO 11398 of Mar. 4, 1968.

Youth Opportunity, President's Council on Established by EO 11330 of Mar. 5, 1967. Inactive as of June 30, 1971; EO 11330 revoked by EO 12379 of Aug. 17, 1982.

Youth Programs, Office of Established in the Department of the Interior by Secretarial Order No. 2985 of Jan. 7, 1965. Functions moved to Office of Historically Black College and University Programs and Job Corps, Office of the Secretary, by Departmental Manual Release 2788 of Mar. 22, 1988.

APPENDIX C: Agencies Appearing in the Code of Federal Regulations

NOTE: This section contains an alphabetical listing of agencies appearing in the *Code of Federal Regulations* (CFR). The listing was revised as of April 1, 2000.

Agency	CFR Title, Subtitle or Chapter
Administrative Committee of the Federal Register	1, I
Advanced Research Projects Agency	32, I
Advisory Commission on Intergovernmental Relations	5, VII
Advisory Council on Historic Preservation	36, VIII
African Development Foundation	22, XV
Federal Acquisition Regulation	48, 57
Agency for International Development, United States	22, II
Federal Acquisition Regulation	48, 7
Agricultural Marketing Service	7, I, IX, X, XI
Agricultural Research Service	7, V
Agriculture Department	5, LXXIII
Agricultural Marketing Service	7, I, IX, X, XI
Agricultural Research Service	7, V
Animal and Plant Health Inspection Service	7, III; 9, I
Chief Financial Officer, Office of	7, XXX
Commodity Credit Corporation	7, XIV
Cooperative State Research, Education, and Extension Service	7, XXXIV
Economic Research Service	7, XXXVII
Energy, Office of	7, XXIX
Environmental Quality, Office of	7, XXXI
Farm Service Agency	7, VII, XVIII
Federal Acquisition Regulation	48, 4
Federal Crop Insurance Corporation	7, IV
Food and Nutrition Service	7, II
Food Safety and Inspection Service	9, III
Foreign Agricultural Service	7, XV
Forest Service	36, II
Grain Inspection, Packers and Stockyards Administration	7, VIII; 9, II
Information Resources Management, Office of	7, XXVII
Inspector General, Office of	7, XXVI
National Agricultural Library	7, XLI
National Agricultural Statistics Service	7, XXXVI
Natural Resources Conservation Service	7, VI
Operations, Office of	7, XXVIII
Procurement and Property Management, Office of	7, XXXII
Rural Business-Cooperative Service	7, XVIII, XLII
Rural Development Administration	7, XLII
Rural Housing Service	7, XVIII, XXXV
Rural Telephone Bank	7, XVI
Rural Utilities Service	7, XVII, XVIII, XLII
Secretary of Agriculture, Office of	7, Subtitle A
Transportation, Office of	7, XXXIII
World Agricultural Outlook Board	7, XXXVIII
Air Force Department	32, VII
Federal Acquisition Regulation Supplement	48, 53
Alcohol, Tobacco and Firearms, Bureau of	27, I
AMTRAK	49, VII
American Battle Monuments Commission	36, IV
American Indians, Office of the Special Trustee	25, VII
Animal and Plant Health Inspection Service	7, III; 9, I

Agency	CFR Title, Subtitle or Chapter
Appalachian Regional Commission	5, IX
Architectural and Transportation Barriers Compliance Board	36, XI
Arctic Research Commission	45, XXIII
Armed Forces Retirement Home	5, XI
Army Department	32, V
Engineers, Corps of	33, II; 36, III
Federal Acquisition Regulation	48, 51
Assassination Records Review Board	36, XIV
Benefits Review Board	20, VII
Bilingual Education and Minority Languages Affairs, Office of	34, V
Blind or Severely Disabled, Committee for Purchase From People Who Are	41, 51
Board for International Broadcasting	22, XIII
Broadcasting Board of Governors	22, V
Federal Acquisition Regulation	48, 19
Census Bureau	15, I
Central Intelligence Agency	32, XIX
Chief Financial Officer, Office of	7, XXX
Child Support Enforcement, Office of	45, III
Children and Families, Administration for	45, II, III, IV, X
Civil Rights, Commission on	45, VII
Civil Rights, Office for	34, I
Coast Guard	33, I; 46, I; 49, IV
Coast Guard (Great Lakes Pilotage)	46, III
Commerce Department	44, IV
Census Bureau	15, I
Economic Affairs, Under Secretary	37, V
Economic Analysis, Bureau of	15, VIII
Economic Development Administration	13, III
Emergency Management and Assistance	44, IV
Export Administration, Bureau of	15, VII
Federal Acquisition Regulation	48, 13
Fishery Conservation and Management	50, VI
Foreign-Trade Zones Board	15, IV
International Trade Administration	15, III; 19, III
National Institute of Standards and Technology	15, II
National Marine Fisheries Service	50, II, IV, VI
National Oceanic and Atmospheric Administration	15, IX; 50, II, III, IV, VI
National Telecommunications and Information Administration	15, XXIII; 47, III
National Weather Service	15, IX
Patent and Trademark Office	37, I
Productivity, Technology and Innovation, Assistant Secretary for	37, IV
Secretary of Commerce, Office of	15, Subtitle A
Technology, Under Secretary for	37, V
Technology Administration	15, XI
Technology Policy, Assistant Secretary for	37, IV
Commercial Space Transportation	14, III
Commodity Credit Corporation	7, XIV
Commodity Futures Trading Commission	5, XLI; 17, I
Community Planning and Development, Office of Assistant Secretary for	24, V, VI
Community Services, Office of	45, X
Comptroller of the Currency	12, I
Construction Industry Collective Bargaining Commission	29, IX
Consumer Product Safety Commission	5, LXXI; 16, II
Cooperative State Research, Education, and Extension Service	7, XXXIV
Copyright Office	37, II
Corporation for National and Community Service	45, XII, XXV
Cost Accounting Standards Board	48, 99
Council on Environmental Quality	40, V
Customs Service, United States	19, I
Defense Contract Audit Agency	32, I
Defense Department	5, XXVI; 32, Subtitle A; 40, VII
Advanced Research Projects Agency	32, I

Agency	CFR Title, Subtitle or Chapter
Air Force Department	32, VII
Army Department	32, V; 33, II; 36, III, 48, 51
Defense Intelligence Agency	32, I
Defense Logistics Agency	32, I, XII; 48, 54
Engineers, Corps of	33, II; 36, III
Federal Acquisition Regulation	48, 2
National Imagery and Mapping Agency	32, I
Navy Department	32, VI; 48, 52
Secretary of Defense, Office of	32, I
Defense Contract Audit Agency	32, I
Defense Intelligence Agency	32, I
Defense Logistics Agency	32, XII; 48, 54
Defense Nuclear Facilities Safety Board	10, XVII
Delaware River Basin Commission	18, III
Drug Enforcement Administration	21, II
East-West Foreign Trade Board	15, XIII
Economic Affairs, Under Secretary	37, V
Economic Analysis, Bureau of	15, VIII
Economic Development Administration	13, III
Economic Research Service	7, XXXVII
Education, Department of	5, LIII
Bilingual Education and Minority Languages Affairs, Office of	34, V
Civil Rights, Office for	34, I
Educational Research and Improvement, Office of	34, VII
Elementary and Secondary Education, Office of	34, II
Federal Acquisition Regulation	48, 34
Postsecondary Education, Office of	34, VI
Secretary of Education, Office of	34, Subtitle A
Special Education and Rehabilitative Services, Office of	34, III
Vocational and Adult Education, Office of	34, IV
Educational Research and Improvement, Office of	34, VII
Elementary and Secondary Education, Office of	34, II
Emergency Oil and Gas Guaranteed Loan Board	13, V
Emergency Steel Guarantee Loan Board	13, IV
Employees' Compensation Appeals Board	20, IV
Employees Loyalty Board	5, V
Employment and Training Administration	20, V
Employment Standards Administration	20, VI
Endangered Species Committee	50, IV
Energy, Department of	5, XXIII; 10, II, III, X
Federal Acquisition Regulation	48, 9
Federal Energy Regulatory Commission	5, XXIV; 18, I
Property Management Regulations	41, 109
Energy, Office of	7, XXIX
Engineers, Corps of	33, II; 36, III
Engraving and Printing, Bureau of	31, VI
Environmental Protection Agency	5, LIV; 40, I, VII
Federal Acquisition Regulation	48, 15
Property Management Regulations	41, 115
Environmental Quality, Office of	7, XXXI
Equal Employment Opportunity Commission	5, LXII; 29, XIV
Equal Opportunity, Office of Assistant Secretary for	24, I
Executive Office of the President	3, I
Administration, Office of	5, XV
Environmental Quality, Council on	40, V
Management and Budget, Office of	25, III, LXXVII; 48, 99
National Drug Control Policy, Office of	21, III
National Security Council	32, XXI; 47, 2
Presidential Documents	3
Science and Technology Policy, Office of	32, XXIV; 47, II
Trade Representative, Office of the United States	15, XX
Export Administration, Bureau of	15, VII
Export-Import Bank of the United States	5, LII; 12, IV
Family Assistance, Office of	45, II
Farm Credit Administration	5, XXXI; 12, VI

Agency	CFR Title, Subtitle or Chapter
Farm Credit System Insurance Corporation	5, XXX; 12, XIV
Farm Service Agency	7, VII, XVIII
Federal Acquisition Regulation	48, 1
Federal Aviation Administration	14, I
Commercial Space Transportation	14, III
Federal Claims Collection Standards	4, II
Federal Communications Commission	5, XXIX; 47, I
Federal Contract Compliance Programs, Office of	41, 60
Federal Crop Insurance Corporation	7, IV
Federal Deposit Insurance Corporation	5, XXII; 12, III
Federal Election Commission	11, I
Federal Emergency Management Agency	44, I
Federal Acquisition Regulation	48, 44
Federal Employees Group Life Insurance Federal Acquisition Regulation	48, 21
Federal Employees Health Benefits Acquisition Regulation	48, 16
Federal Energy Regulatory Commission	5, XXIV; 18, I
Federal Financial Institutions Examination Council	12, XI
Federal Financing Bank	12, VIII
Federal Highway Administration	23, I, II
Federal Home Loan Mortgage Corporation	1, IV
Federal Housing Enterprise Oversight Office	12, XVII
Federal Housing Finance Board	12, IX
Federal Labor Relations Authority, and General Counsel of the Federal Labor Relations Authority	5, XIV; 22, XIV
Federal Law Enforcement Training Center	31, VII
Federal Management Regulation	41, 102
Federal Maritime Commission	46, IV
Federal Mediation and Conciliation Service	29, XII
Federal Mine Safety and Health Review Commission	5, LXXIV; 29, XXVII
Federal Motor Carrier Safety Administration	49, III
Federal Prison Industries, Inc.	28, III
Federal Procurement Policy Office	48, 99
Federal Property Management Regulations	41, 101
Federal Property Management Regulations System	41, 101, 102, 105
Federal Railroad Administration	49, II
Federal Register, Administrative Committee of	1, I
Federal Register, Office of	1, II
Federal Reserve System	12, II
Board of Governors	5, LVIII
Federal Retirement Thrift Investment Board	5, VI, LXXVI
Federal Service Impasses Panel	5, XIV
Federal Trade Commission	5, XLVII; 16, I
Federal Transit Administration	49, VI
Federal Travel Regulation System	41, Subtitle F
Fine Arts, Commission on	45, XXI
Fiscal Service	31, II
Fish and Wildlife Service, United States	50, I, IV
Fishery Conservation and Management	50, VI
Food and Drug Administration	21, I
Food and Nutrition Service	7, II
Food Safety and Inspection Service	9, III
Foreign Agricultural Service	7, XV
Foreign Assets Control, Office of	31, V
Foreign Claims Settlement Commission of the United States	45, V
Foreign Service Grievance Board	22, IX
Foreign Service Impasse Disputes Panel	22, XIV
Foreign Service Labor Relations Board	22, XIV
Foreign-Trade Zones Board	15, IV
Forest Service	36, II
General Accounting Office	4, I, II
General Services Administration	5, LVII
Contract Appeals, Board of	48, 61
Federal Acquisition Regulation	48, 5
Federal Property Management Regulations System	41, 101, 102, 105
Federal Travel Regulation System	41, Subtitle F
General	41, 300

Agency	CFR Title, Subtitle or Chapter
Payment From a Non-Federal Source for Travel Expenses	41, 304
Payment of Expenses Connected With the Death of Certain Employees	41, 303
Relocation Allowances	41, 302
Temporary Duty (TDY) Travel Allowances	41, 301
Geological Survey	30, IV
Government Ethics, Office of	5, XVI
Government National Mortgage Association	24, III
Grain Inspection, Packers and Stockyards Administration	7, VIII; 9, II
Harry S. Truman Scholarship Foundation	45, XVIII
Health and Human Services, Department of	5, XLV; 45, Subtitle A
Child Support Enforcement, Office of	45, III
Children and Families, Administration for	45, II, III, IV, X
Community Services, Office of	45, X
Family Assistance, Office of	45, II
Federal Acquisition Regulation	48, 3
Food and Drug Administration	21, I
Health Care Financing Administration	42, IV
Human Development Services, Office of	45, XIII
Indian Health Service	25, V
Inspector General (Health Care), Office of	42, V
Public Health Service	42, I
Refugee Resettlement, Office of	45, IV
Health Care Financing Administration	42, IV
Housing and Urban Development, Department of	5, LXV; 24, Subtitle B
Community Planning and Development, Office of Assistant Secretary for	24, V, VI
Equal Opportunity, Office of Assistant Secretary for	24, I
Federal Acquisition Regulation	48, 24
Federal Housing Enterprise Oversight, Office of	12, XVII
Government National Mortgage Association	24, III
Housing—Federal Housing Commissioner, Office of Assistant Secretary for	24, II, VIII, X, XX
Inspector General, Office of	24, XII
Multifamily Housing Assistance Restructuring, Office of	24, IV
Public and Indian Housing, Office of Assistant Secretary for	24, IX
Secretary, Office of	24, Subtitle A, VII
Housing—Federal Housing Commissioner, Office of Assistant Secretary for	24, II, VIII, X, XX
Human Development Services, Office of	45, XIII
Immigration and Naturalization Service	8, I
Independent Counsel, Office of	28, VII
Indian Affairs, Bureau of	25, I, V
Indian Affairs, Office of the Assistant Secretary	25, VI
Indian Arts and Crafts Board	25, II
Indian Health Service	25, V
Information Resources Management, Office of	7, XXVII
Information Security Oversight Office, National Archives and Records Administration	32, XX
Inspector General	
Agriculture Department	7, XXVI
Health and Human Services Department	42, V
Housing and Urban Development Department	24, XII
Institute of Peace, United States	22, XVII
Inter-American Foundation	5, LXIII; 22, X
Intergovernmental Relations, Advisory Commission on	5, VII
Interior Department	
American Indians, Office of the Special Trustee	25, VII
Endangered Species Committee	50, IV
Federal Acquisition Regulation	48, 14
Federal Property Management Regulations System	41, 114
Fish and Wildlife Service, United States	50, I, IV
Geological Survey	30, IV
Indian Affairs, Bureau of	25, I, V
Indian Affairs, Office of the Assistant Secretary	25, VI
Indian Arts and Crafts Board	25, II
Land Management, Bureau of	43, II

Agency	CFR Title, Subtitle or Chapter
Minerals Management Service	30, II
Mines, Bureau of	30, VI
National Indian Gaming Commission	25, III
National Park Service	36, I
Reclamation, Bureau of	43, I
Secretary of the Interior, Office of	43, Subtitle A
Surface Mining and Reclamation Appeals, Board of	30, III
Surface Mining Reclamation and Enforcement, Office of	30, VII
Internal Revenue Service	26, I
International Boundary and Water Commission, United States and Mexico, United States Section	22, XI
International Development, United States Agency for	22, II
Federal Acquisition Regulation	48, 7
International Development Cooperation Agency, United States	22, XII
International Fishing and Related Activities	50, III
International Investment, Office of	31, VIII
International Joint Commission, United States and Canada	22, IV
International Organizations Employees Loyalty Board	5, V
International Trade Administration	15, III; 19, III
International Trade Commission, United States	19, II
Interstate Commerce Commission	5, XL
James Madison Memorial Fellowship Foundation	45, XXIV
Japan–United States Friendship Commission	22, XVI
Joint Board for the Enrollment of Actuaries	20, VIII
Justice Department	5, XXVIII; 28, I
Drug Enforcement Administration	21, II
Federal Acquisition Regulation	48, 28
Federal Claims Collection Standards	4, II
Federal Prison Industries, Inc.	28, III
Foreign Claims Settlement Commission of the United States	45, V
Immigration and Naturalization Service	8, I
Offices of Independent Counsel	28, VI
Prisons, Bureau of	28, V
Property Management Regulations	41, 128
Labor Department	5, XLII
Benefits Review Board	20, VII
Employees' Compensation Appeals Board	20, IV
Employment and Training Administration	20, V
Employment Standards Administration	20, VI
Federal Acquisition Regulation	48, 29
Federal Contract Compliance Programs, Office of	41, 60
Federal Procurement Regulations System	41, 50
Labor-Management Standards, Office of	29, II, IV
Mine Safety and Health Administration	30, I
Occupational Safety and Health Administration	29, XVII
Pension and Welfare Benefits Administration	29, XXV
Public Contracts	41, 50
Secretary of Labor, Office of	29, Subtitle A
Veterans' Employment and Training, Office of the Assistant Secretary for	41, 61; 20, IX
Wage and Hour Division	29, V
Workers' Compensation Programs, Office of	20, I
Labor-Management Standards, Office of	29, II, IV
Land Management, Bureau of	43, II
Legal Services Corporation	45, XVI
Library of Congress	36, VII
Copyright Office	37, II
Management and Budget, Office of	5, III, LXXVII; 48, 99
Marine Mammal Commission	50, V
Maritime Administration	46, II
Merit Systems Protection Board	5, II
Micronesian Status Negotiations, Office for	32, XXVII
Mine Safety and Health Administration	30, I
Minerals Management Service	30, II
Mines, Bureau of	30, VI
Minority Business Development Agency	15, XIV
Miscellaneous Agencies	1, IV

Agency	CFR Title, Subtitle or Chapter
Monetary Offices	31, I
Multifamily Housing Assistance Restructuring, Office of	24, IV
National Aeronautics and Space Administration	5, LIX; 14, V
Federal Acquisition Regulation	48, 18
National Agricultural Library	7, XLI
National Agricultural Statistics Service	7, XXXVI
National and Community Service, Corporation for	45, XII, XXV
National Archives and Records Administration	5, LXVI; 36, XII
Information Security Oversight Office	32, XX
National Bureau of Standards	15, II
National Capital Planning Commission	1, IV
National Commission for Employment Policy	1, IV
National Commission on Libraries and Information Science	45, XVII
National Council on Disability	34, XII
National Counterintelligence Center	32, XVIII
National Credit Union Administration	12, VII
National Drug Control Policy, Office of	21, III
National Foundation on the Arts and the Humanities	45, XI
National Highway Traffic Safety Administration	23, II, III; 49, V
National Imagery and Mapping Agency	32, I
National Indian Gaming Commission	25, III
National Institute for Literacy	34, XI
National Institute of Standards and Technology	15, II
National Labor Relations Board	5, LXI; 29, I
National Marine Fisheries Service	50, II, IV, VI
National Mediation Board	29, X
National Oceanic and Atmospheric Administration	15, IX; 50, II, III, IV, VI
National Park Service	36, I
National Railroad Adjustment Board	29, III
National Railroad Passenger Corporation (AMTRAK)	49, VII
National Science Foundation	5, XLIII; 45, VI
Federal Acquisition Regulation	48, 25
National Security Council	32, XXI
National Security Council and Office of Science and Technology Policy	47, II
National Telecommunications and Information Administration	15, XXIII; 47, III
National Transportation Safety Board	49, VIII
National Weather Service	15, IX
Natural Resources Conservation Service	7, VI
Navajo and Hopi Indian Relocation, Office of	25, IV
Navy Department	32, VI
Federal Acquisition Regulation	48, 52
Neighborhood Reinvestment Corporation	24, XXV
Northeast Dairy Compact Commission	7, XIII
Nuclear Regulatory Commission	5, XLVIII; 10, I
Federal Acquisition Regulation	48, 20
Occupational Safety and Health Administration	29, XVII
Occupational Safety and Health Review Commission	29, XX
Offices of Independent Counsel	28, VI
Oklahoma City National Memorial Trust	36, XV
Operations Office	7, XXVIII
Overseas Private Investment Corporation	5, XXXIII; 22, VII
Panama Canal Commission	48, 35
Panama Canal Regulations	35, I
Patent and Trademark Office	37, I
Payment From a Non-Federal Source for Travel Expenses	41, 304
Payment of Expenses Connected With the Death of Certain Employees	41, 303
Peace Corps	22, III
Pennsylvania Avenue Development Corporation	36, IX
Pension and Welfare Benefits Administration	29, XXV
Pension Benefit Guaranty Corporation	29, XL
Personnel Management, Office of	5, I, XXXV; 45, VIII
Federal Acquisition Regulation	48, 17
Federal Employees Group Life Insurance Federal Acquisition Regulation	48, 21
Federal Employees Health Benefits Acquisition Regulation	48, 16

Agency	CFR Title, Subtitle or Chapter
Postal Rate Commission	5, XLVI; 39, III
Postal Service, United States	5, LX; 39, I
Postsecondary Education, Office of	34, VI
President's Commission on White House Fellowships	1, IV
Presidential Commission on the Assignment of Women in the Armed Forces	32, XXIX
Presidential Documents	3
Presidio Trust	36, X
Prisons, Bureau of	28, V
Procurement and Property Management, Office of	7, XXXII
Productivity, Technology and Innovation, Assistant Secretary	37, IV
Public Contracts, Department of Labor	41, 50
Public and Indian Housing, Office of Assistant Secretary for	24, IX
Public Health Service	42, I
Railroad Retirement Board	20, II
Reclamation, Bureau of	43, I
Refugee Resettlement, Office of	45, IV
Regional Action Planning Commissions	13, V
Relocation Allowances	41, 302
Research and Special Programs Administration	49, I
Rural Business-Cooperative Service	7, XVIII, XLII
Rural Development Administration	7, XLII
Rural Housing Service	7, XVIII, XXXV
Rural Telephone Bank	7, XVI
Rural Utilities Service	7, XVII, XVIII, XLII
Saint Lawrence Seaway Development Corporation	33, IV
Science and Technology Policy, Office of	32, XXIV
Science and Technology Policy, Office of, and National Security Council	47, II
Secret Service	31, IV
Securities and Exchange Commission	17, II
Selective Service System	32, XVI
Small Business Administration	13, I
Smithsonian Institution	36, V
Social Security Administration	20, III; 48, 23
Soldiers' and Airmen's Home, United States	5, XI
Special Counsel, Office of	5, VIII
Special Education and Rehabilitative Services, Office of	34, III
State Department	22, I
Federal Acquisition Regulation	48, 6
Surface Mining and Reclamation Appeals, Board of	30, III
Surface Mining Reclamation and Enforcement, Office of	30, VII
Surface Transportation Board	49, X
Susquehanna River Basin Commission	18, VIII
Technology Administration	15, XI
Technology Policy, Assistant Secretary for	37, IV
Technology, Under Secretary for	37, V
Tennessee Valley Authority	5, LXIX; 18, XIII
Thrift Supervision Office, Department of the Treasury	12, V
Trade Representative, United States, Office of	15, XX
Transportation, Department of	5, L
Coast Guard	33, I; 46, I; 49, IV
Coast Guard (Great Lakes Pilotage)	46, III
Commercial Space Transportation	14, III
Contract Appeals, Board of	48, 63
Emergency Management and Assistance	44, IV
Federal Acquisition Regulation	48, 12
Federal Aviation Administration	14, I
Federal Highway Administration	23, I, II
Federal Motor Carrier Safety Administration	49, III
Federal Railroad Administration	49, II
Federal Transit Administration	49, VI
Maritime Administration	46, II
National Highway Traffic Safety Administration	23, II, III; 49, V
Research and Special Programs Administration	49, I
Saint Lawrence Seaway Development Corporation	33, IV
Secretary of Transportation, Office of	14, II; 49, Subtitle A

Agency	CFR Title, Subtitle or Chapter
Surface Transportation Board	49, X
Transportation Statistics Bureau	49, XI
Transportation, Office of	7, XXXIII
Transportation Statistics Brureau	49, XI
Travel Allowances, Temporary Duty (TDY)	41, 301
Treasury Department	5, XXI; 12, XV; 17, IV
Alcohol, Tobacco and Firearms, Bureau of	27, I
Community Development Financial Institutions Fund	12, XVIII
Comptroller of the Currency	12, I
Customs Service, United States	19, I
Engraving and Printing, Bureau of	31, VI
Federal Acquisition Regulation	48, 10
Federal Law Enforcement Training Center	31, VII
Fiscal Service	31, II
Foreign Assets Control, Office of	31, V
Internal Revenue Service	26, I
International Investment, Office of	31, VIII
Monetary Offices	31, I
Secret Service	31, IV
Secretary of the Treasury, Office of	31, Subtitle A
Thrift Supervision, Office of	12, V
Truman, Harry S. Scholarship Foundation	45, XVIII
United States and Canada, International Joint Commission	22, IV
United States and Mexico, International Boundary and Water Commission, United States Section	22, XI
Utah Reclamation Mitigation and Conservation Commission	43, III
Veterans Affairs Department	38, I
Federal Acquisition Regulation	48, 8
Veterans' Employment and Training, Office of the Assistant Secretary for	41, 61; 20, IX
Vice President of the United States, Office of	32, XXVIII
Vocational and Adult Education, Office of	34, IV
Wage and Hour Division	29, V
Water Resources Council	18, VI
Workers' Compensation Programs, Office of	20, I
World Agricultural Outlook Board	7, XXXVIII

186-873 D-00--22

NAME INDEX

NOTE: Separate listings of Senators and Representatives can be found beginning on pages 32 and 34, respectively. Any other references to said persons can be found in this index.

A

B

C

D

H

I

J

K

L

M

Q

R

S

T

U

V

W

Y

Z

AGENCY/SUBJECT INDEX

NOTE: This index does not include material appearing in Appendices A–C.

D

E

RECENT CHANGES

Personnel actions brought to the attention of *Manual* editors June 2–July 31, 2000

Page	Position	Action
Court of Appeals for the Federal Circuit		
72	U.S. Circuit Judge for the Ninth Circuit	Johnnie B. Rawlinson, confirmed July 21.
Agriculture Department		
108	Administrator, Rural Utilities Service	Chris McLean confirmed June 7.
Commerce Department		
133	Secretary of Commerce	Norman Y. Mineta, confirmed July 20, vice William M. Daley.
Defense Department		
157	General Counsel	Douglas A. Dworkin confirmed June 9.
Energy Department		
214	Under Secretary for Nuclear Security and Administrator for Nuclear Security	Gen. John A. Gordon, USAF, confirmed June 14.
214	Director of Science	Mildred Spiewak Dresselhaus, confirmed July 26.
State Department		
303	U.S. Ambassador to Argentina	James Donald Walsh confirmed June 9.
303	U.S. Ambassador to Australia	Edward William Gnehm confirmed June 9.
303	U.S. Ambassador to Bolivia	V. Manuel Rocha confirmed June 9.
303	U.S. Ambassador to Colombia	Anne Woods Patterson confirmed June 9.
303	U.S. Ambassador to El Salvador	Rose M. Likins confirmed June 9.
303	U.S. Ambassador to Kyrgyzstan	Martin O'Keefe confirmed June 9.
303	U.S. Ambassador to Lithuania	John F. Tefft confirmed June 9.
303	U.S. Ambassador to Mongolia	John R. Dinger confirmed June 9.
304	U.S. Ambassador to Papua New Guinea	Susan S. Jacobs confirmed June 9.
304	U.S. Ambassador to Paraguay	David N. Greenlee confirmed June 9.
304	U.S. Ambassador to the Solomon Islands	Susan S. Jacobs confirmed June 9.
304	U.S. Ambassador to Suriname	Daniel A. Johnson confirmed June 9.
304	U.S. Ambassador to Turkey	Robert Pearson confirmed June 9.
304	U.S. Ambassador to Vanuatu	Susan S. Jacobs confirmed June 9.
304	U.S. Ambassador to Venezuela	Donna Jean Hrinak confirmed June 9.
Veterans Affairs Department		
360	Secretary of Veterans Affairs	Togo D. West, Jr., resigned July 25.

ISBN 0-16-050292-6
90000
9 780160 502927